# The University of Oklahoma

*The original building of the University of Oklahoma in Norman, 1893*

# The University of Oklahoma
# A History

~

## Volume 1
## 1890–1917

### David W. Levy

Foreword by David L. Boren

University of Oklahoma Press : Norman

## Other Books by David W. Levy

(ed. with Melvin I. Urofsky) *The Letters of Louis D. Brandeis*. 5 vols. (Albany, 1971, 1972, 1973, 1975, 1978)

*Herbert Croly of the New Republic: The Life and Thought of an American Progressive* (Princeton, 1985)

(ed. with Melvin I. Urofsky) *"Half Brother, Half Son": The Letters of Louis D. Brandeis to Felix Frankfurter* (Norman, 1991)

*The Debate over Vietnam* (Baltimore, 1991; 2nd ed., 1995)

(ed. with Russell D. Buhite) *FDR's Fireside Chats* (Norman, 1992; New York, 1993)

(ed. with Melvin I. Urofsky) *The Family Letters of Louis D. Brandeis* (Norman, 2002)

Library of Congress Cataloging-in-Publication Data

Levy, David W., 1937–
   The University of Oklahoma: a history / David W. Levy; foreword by David L. Boren.
      p. cm.
   Includes bibliographical references and index.
   Contents: v. 1 1890–1917
   ISBN 978-0-8061-3703-2 (cloth) — ISBN 978-0-8061-3976-0 (paper)
      1. University of Oklahoma—History. I. Title.

LD4323.L48 2005
378.766'37—dc22

2005046920

The paper in this book meets the guidelines for permanence and durability of the Committee on Production Guidelines for Book Longevity of the Council on Library Resources, Inc. ∞

2   3   4   5   6   7   8   9   10

*To all the members of the University community*
*past, present, and future*
*students, staff, faculty, and administrators*

I looked off to the southwest where our university was to be located. There was not a tree or shrub in sight. All I could see was the monotonous stillness of prairie grass. . . . Behind me was a crude little town of 1,500 people and before me was a stretch of prairie on which my helpers and I were to build an institution of culture.

*David Ross Boyd*

# Contents

List of Illustrations . . . . . . . . . . . . . . . . . . . . . . . . . . . . . . . . . . . . . . . . . . . . . . . . . ix

Foreword, by David L. Boren . . . . . . . . . . . . . . . . . . . . . . . . . . . . . . . . . . . . . . xiii

Preface . . . . . . . . . . . . . . . . . . . . . . . . . . . . . . . . . . . . . . . . . . . . . . . . . . . . . . . . xvii

Acknowledgments . . . . . . . . . . . . . . . . . . . . . . . . . . . . . . . . . . . . . . . . . . . . . . . xxi

I. A University Is Located in Norman, Oklahoma . . . . . . . . . . . . . . . . . . . . . 3

II. Preparing the Ground . . . . . . . . . . . . . . . . . . . . . . . . . . . . . . . . . . . . . . . . 24

III. Attracting Students and Building a Faculty, 1892–1902 . . . . . . . . . . . . . . . . . 48

IV. Mastering a Thousand Details, 1892–1902 . . . . . . . . . . . . . . . . . . . . . . . . . 76

V. Rising Out of the Ashes, 1903–1907 . . . . . . . . . . . . . . . . . . . . . . . . . . . . . 117

VI. The University Besieged, 1907–1908 . . . . . . . . . . . . . . . . . . . . . . . . . . . . . 150

VII. "Corpses Strewed about the Campus," 1908 . . . . . . . . . . . . . . . . . . . . . . . . 175

VIII. The Evans Years: Some Achievements and More "Corpses," 1908–1911 . . . . 200

IX. New Leader, New Programs, New Faces, 1912–1917 . . . . . . . . . . . . . . . . . . 234

Epilogue . . . . . . . . . . . . . . . . . . . . . . . . . . . . . . . . . . . . . . . . . . . . . . . . . . . . . . 272

Works Cited . . . . . . . . . . . . . . . . . . . . . . . . . . . . . . . . . . . . . . . . . . . . . . . . . . 285

Index . . . . . . . . . . . . . . . . . . . . . . . . . . . . . . . . . . . . . . . . . . . . . . . . . . . . . . . 301

# Illustrations

Delbert LaSalle Larsh . . . . . . . . . . . . . . . . . . . . . . . . . . . . . . . . . . . . . . . 14

Charles T. Gorton . . . . . . . . . . . . . . . . . . . . . . . . . . . . . . . . . . . . . . . . . . 22

The University's original building . . . . . . . . . . . . . . . . . . . . . . . . . . . . . . 27

David Ross Boyd in 1893 . . . . . . . . . . . . . . . . . . . . . . . . . . . . . . . . . . . . . 36

Edwin C. DeBarr . . . . . . . . . . . . . . . . . . . . . . . . . . . . . . . . . . . . . . . . . . . 41

Professors Rice, Boyd, Amos, and DeBarr in the early 1930s . . . . . . . . . . . . 42

The first students, of 1892–93 . . . . . . . . . . . . . . . . . . . . . . . . . . . . . . . . . 46

Joseph Francis Paxton . . . . . . . . . . . . . . . . . . . . . . . . . . . . . . . . . . . . . . . 56

James Shannon Buchanan . . . . . . . . . . . . . . . . . . . . . . . . . . . . . . . . . . . . 57

Grace A. King . . . . . . . . . . . . . . . . . . . . . . . . . . . . . . . . . . . . . . . . . . . . . 59

Vernon Louis Parrington . . . . . . . . . . . . . . . . . . . . . . . . . . . . . . . . . . . . . 60

Albert Heald Van Vleet . . . . . . . . . . . . . . . . . . . . . . . . . . . . . . . . . . . . . . 64

Charles Newton Gould . . . . . . . . . . . . . . . . . . . . . . . . . . . . . . . . . . . . . . 67

Roy Gittinger . . . . . . . . . . . . . . . . . . . . . . . . . . . . . . . . . . . . . . . . . . . . . 70

Jesse Lee Rader . . . . . . . . . . . . . . . . . . . . . . . . . . . . . . . . . . . . . . . . . . . . 73

President Boyd at work . . . . . . . . . . . . . . . . . . . . . . . . . . . . . . . . . . . . . . . 76

President Boyd's original home . . . . . . . . . . . . . . . . . . . . . . . . . . . . . . . . . 82

Another view of Boyd's first home, circa 1899 . . . . . . . . . . . . . . . . . . . . . . 82

The University Building, circa 1900 . . . . . . . . . . . . . . . . . . . . . . . . . . . . . 95

University Boulevard, circa 1903 . . . . . . . . . . . . . . . . . . . . . . . . . . . . . . . 96

Students assembled for chapel services, 1901 . . . . . . . . . . . . . . . . . . . . . . . 105

Women exercising . . . . . . . . . . . . . . . . . . . . . . . . . . . . . . . . . . . 106

The football team of 1899 . . . . . . . . . . . . . . . . . . . . . . . . . . . . . 110

Zetalethean Literary Society, 1909 . . . . . . . . . . . . . . . . . . . . . . . 111

Masthead of the *University Umpire* . . . . . . . . . . . . . . . . . . . . . . . 113

Aftermath of the 1903 fire . . . . . . . . . . . . . . . . . . . . . . . . . . . . . 119

The new Administration Building . . . . . . . . . . . . . . . . . . . . . . . . 126

The wood-frame gymnasium . . . . . . . . . . . . . . . . . . . . . . . . . . . 128

Science Hall . . . . . . . . . . . . . . . . . . . . . . . . . . . . . . . . . . . . . . . 129

The Carnegie Library . . . . . . . . . . . . . . . . . . . . . . . . . . . . . . . . . 130

Fredrik Gustav Holmberg with the University orchestra . . . . . . . . . . 134

James Huston Felgar . . . . . . . . . . . . . . . . . . . . . . . . . . . . . . . . . 137

Samuel Watson Reaves . . . . . . . . . . . . . . . . . . . . . . . . . . . . . . . 137

Jerome Dowd . . . . . . . . . . . . . . . . . . . . . . . . . . . . . . . . . . . . . . 138

Guy Yandall Williams . . . . . . . . . . . . . . . . . . . . . . . . . . . . . . . . 139

Coach Benjamin Gilbert Owen . . . . . . . . . . . . . . . . . . . . . . . . . . 142

Boyd Field . . . . . . . . . . . . . . . . . . . . . . . . . . . . . . . . . . . . . . . . 144

Kappa Alpha fraternity in 1906 . . . . . . . . . . . . . . . . . . . . . . . . . . 147

The second Administration Building ablaze . . . . . . . . . . . . . . . . . . 158

Ernest Taylor Bynum . . . . . . . . . . . . . . . . . . . . . . . . . . . . . . . . 165

The Reverend Nathaniel Linebaugh . . . . . . . . . . . . . . . . . . . . . . . 166

President Arthur Grant Evans . . . . . . . . . . . . . . . . . . . . . . . . . . . 174

Lyman Abbott . . . . . . . . . . . . . . . . . . . . . . . . . . . . . . . . . . . . . 187

Lee Cruce . . . . . . . . . . . . . . . . . . . . . . . . . . . . . . . . . . . . . . . . 187

Theodore Hampton Brewer . . . . . . . . . . . . . . . . . . . . . . . . . . . . 191

C. Lucile Dora . . . . . . . . . . . . . . . . . . . . . . . . . . . . . . . . . . . . . 194

David Ross Boyd in 1908 . . . . . . . . . . . . . . . . . . . . . . . . . . . . . . 196

The new administration building under construction, 1910 . . . . . . . . 211

Administration Hall completed . . . . . . . . . . . . . . . . . . . . . . . . . . . 212

Julien Charles Monnet . . . . . . . . . . . . . . . . . . . . . . . . . . . . . . . 220

John Begg Cheadle . . . . . . . . . . . . . . . . . . . . . . . . . . . . . . . . . . 222

Roy Temple House . . . . . . . . . . . . . . . . . . . . . . . . . . . . . . . . . . 230

John Alley . . . . . . . . . . . . . . . . . . . . . . . . . . . . . . . . . . . . . . . 231

Edmund P. Duval . . . . . . . . . . . . . . . . . . . . . . . . . . . . . . . . . . 232

President Stratton Duluth Brooks . . . . . . . . . . . . . . . . . . . . . . . . . 239

The inauguration of President Brooks, 1912 . . . . . . . . . . . . . . . . . . . 241

Errett Rains Newby. . . . . . . . . . . . . . . . . . . . . . . . . . . . . . . . . . 242

Emil R. Kraettli . . . . . . . . . . . . . . . . . . . . . . . . . . . . . . . . . . . . 244

George E. Wadsack. . . . . . . . . . . . . . . . . . . . . . . . . . . . . . . . . . . 246

Warren Waverly Phelan . . . . . . . . . . . . . . . . . . . . . . . . . . . . . . . . 248

H. H. Herbert . . . . . . . . . . . . . . . . . . . . . . . . . . . . . . . . . . . . . 250

Arthur Barto Adams . . . . . . . . . . . . . . . . . . . . . . . . . . . . . . . . . 252

LeRoy Long . . . . . . . . . . . . . . . . . . . . . . . . . . . . . . . . . . . . . . 257

Oscar Brousse Jacobson and the Kiowa Five, in 1929 . . . . . . . . . . . . . . 262

Edgar Meacham . . . . . . . . . . . . . . . . . . . . . . . . . . . . . . . . . . . . 263

Patricio Gimeno . . . . . . . . . . . . . . . . . . . . . . . . . . . . . . . . . . . . 265

Gayfree Ellison . . . . . . . . . . . . . . . . . . . . . . . . . . . . . . . . . . . . 266

Victor E. Monnett . . . . . . . . . . . . . . . . . . . . . . . . . . . . . . . . . . . 266

Edward Everett Dale . . . . . . . . . . . . . . . . . . . . . . . . . . . . . . . . . 269

Walter S. Campbell ("Stanley Vestal") . . . . . . . . . . . . . . . . . . . . . . . 271

Boyd House in 1917 . . . . . . . . . . . . . . . . . . . . . . . . . . . . . . . . . 273

DeBarr Hall . . . . . . . . . . . . . . . . . . . . . . . . . . . . . . . . . . . . . . 274

Monnet Hall . . . . . . . . . . . . . . . . . . . . . . . . . . . . . . . . . . . . . . 275

All photographs are courtesy Western History Collections,
University of Oklahoma Libraries.

# Foreword

DAVID L. BOREN

This beautifully and powerfully written book by David Levy is far more than just a history of the earliest years of the University of Oklahoma. It is, to a great degree, a story of how the frontier experience helped shape the American character and continues to influence our national self-image.

The strength of a nation can be measured by its belief in its future. Generations of Americans have worked to build a better and fuller life for those who would follow them. Their perseverance has been exceptional because they had complete faith that the dream could come true. From the beginning of the eighteenth century through the conclusion of the twentieth, their faith has largely found justification. This unbroken belief in our future merits careful examination as we enter the twenty-first century.

Throughout his history of the building of the University of Oklahoma, Levy captures the "daring courage" of those who confronted the raw and often harsh land. He chronicles their "determined ambition" to transform it and to build new lives for themselves and their families. He focuses upon their understanding that access to advanced education was crucial to the opportunities that they wanted to give to their children.

No one captures the perseverance and determination of the American pioneer more dramatically than the University's first president, David Ross Boyd. As he described his reaction to his first sight of the treeless, desolate prairie where he was to build a university, he said that he felt no discouragement and saw only possibilities.

Boyd recruited the first students from farm communities where skeptical parents were reluctant to give up the labor their children contributed to the family enterprise. He enlightened the entire territory about the importance of higher education. He helped students understand that in being able to attend the University, they had been given a precious gift. He selected and recruited incredibly talented teachers to join him in what was, realistically, an adventure of uncertain outcome. He created a physical and cultural environment that encouraged academic excellence.

When the trees he had planted to transform the prairie into a campus died, Boyd planted more. When the fire destroyed the first main building, he did not allow himself time to mourn its loss. Instead, he made certain that makeshift quarters were ready so that not a single day of class was missed. In short, he never gave up. He never stopped seeing and believing in the possibilities.

This book is also about the importance of institutions. There was an understanding among the pioneers that their values and good works would not survive beyond their own life spans unless they established institutions to preserve them.

Fortunately, they understood that a university was one of the most important institutions that they should establish. More intellectual vitality and creative energy are unleashed by a university than by any other institution in our society. It is a place where the generations come together and the experience of the faculty meets the idealism and challenging questions of the student. For the university to be strong, both the faculty and the students must bring their own commitment to the process.

The first faculty and those who later joined it were strongly committed to their academic disciplines and to their students. As one of Vernon Parrington's students wrote of Parrington's classes in literature: "We went into this man's room and for an hour at least we lived in a different world. . . . We lost ourselves in the love of David Copperfield for his Dora. . . . We listened to the majestic roll of Milton. . . . [S]omehow, in Professor Parrington's room we forgot the dry sun and the never-ending wind, and the painful and pressing problem of how to make a living, and while we were there, we lived."

To build a great university, the students must also have an understanding of the importance of their role. They too must regard themselves as builders of the university instead of passive recipients of what is handed out to them by faculty, staff, and administrators. Levy writes eloquently of the consciousness of students that they were helping to build the University.

Tracing their views through the student newspaper, he writes admiringly of the students of that day: "They were so determinedly optimistic, so wonderfully confident of the futures that awaited them. They were full of fun and innocent mischief. . . . They understood, somehow, that college was a privilege and an opportunity and that they should not waste the chance. . . . They were making a culture. And the culture they were making was joyful yet purposeful, respectful of their elders yet brash and sassy. . . . They kept a sharp and suspicious eye on the practices of older and more prestigious colleges, but they were also proud as punch about what was being created on the Oklahoma frontier."

Institutions, especially universities, are clearly at the core of our continuity as a people. What is also clear from Levy's volume is that institutions are extremely fragile. They do not survive and flourish without wise and strong leadership.

David Ross Boyd was an exceptional leader. He was a visionary and a conceptual thinker who had a firm grasp of his goals and was constantly measuring his progress toward them. He had the ability to communicate that vision to others and to give to faculty, staff, students, and citizens a sense of common ownership of the institution.

He not only was focused on the big picture but realized as well that excellence would not be achieved without attention to the details. He had an uncanny ability to spot talent and was personally secure enough to surround himself with extremely talented faculty members and administrators. He was gifted in human relations and in the diplomatic and political arts. Along with all of these qualities he had boundless energy and a willingness to commit it unselfishly to the good of the institution. A university is one of the most diverse and complex of all institutions, and it is a demanding mistress of its leaders. Boyd understood it, loved it, and gave himself totally to it. Few leaders could have accomplished as much as he in such a brief time.

The shocking removal of this great leader and the period that followed should cause us never to forget the fragility of institutions. They can decline and indeed disappear with even greater speed than they are built. Human institutions must be carefully tended without interruption by every succeeding generation. Universities are no exception.

Much of what Boyd and the outstanding faculty, staff, students, and generous citizens had built together over sixteen years was almost destroyed in four short years. Fortunately an able leader of a different kind, Stratton Brooks, arrived in 1912 to reverse the decline. After Boyd's departure, there was a vacuum of strong leadership at the top. Others, including regents, moved to use the institution to further their own personal, partisan, and sectarian purposes. Academic excellence was supplanted by political loyalties and family friendships in the selection of the faculty.

Levy offers us the unspoken lesson that institutions are no stronger than those who lead them and the love and loyalty of those who protect and support them. If they are to last, institutions must be generously served and not selfishly used.

As this country enters the twenty-first century and ponders the strength of the institutions that have sustained it, this insightful history of the University of Oklahoma should prove instructive.

There could be no more appropriate author of this history than David Levy, a distinguished scholar and teacher in the field of American intellectual history who has unselfishly invested his life in his students at the University of Oklahoma.

# Preface

This project had its origin almost fifteen years ago, when the University of Oklahoma was deciding how to mark the momentous occasion of its centennial. One of the committees considering that question determined that a scholarly history of the institution would be appropriate. I need hardly say that being selected to prepare that history was a high honor and, I have always felt, a very large responsibility. Almost as soon as I entered seriously upon the task, several aspects of the project became apparent. First, to present the University's history in a fitting way would require tackling it in segments–this volume covers the first of the three segments I have in mind. Second, there was a huge body of source material with which I had to become acquainted—more material, in fact, than the most assiduous scholar could hope to master in a lifetime. But above all, I came quickly to the conviction that the story these materials told was a thoroughly fascinating one, filled with both dramatic human interest and genuine historic importance. A story, in short, well worth telling.

But in writing the history of an institution as multifaceted and complex as the University of Oklahoma, a historian must face certain challenging problems. For one thing, institutions, if they are successful, tend to become larger, ever more complicated and diverse, less easy to know and encompass and explain in detail. When the first fifty-seven students appeared in Norman in September 1892, there were four teachers, and they taught their young charges on the second floor of a rented building in downtown Norman. By the time the story told in this volume ends, there were thousands of students, spread over two campuses, taught in numerous buildings by a faculty that numbered more than 150. The University had created dozens of degree programs and had divided itself into colleges, schools, and departments. To deal with this steady growth in complexity and diversity, the historian must always be prepared to step back a little, view things from a further distance, a greater height, and make more rigorous (and painful) choices about what to highlight and whom to leave out.

Another challenge arises because of the two sorts of readers a work such as this is likely to attract. I realize that some will pick up this book hurriedly to check a fact or two—to learn when a particular building was built or a particular professor was hired or a particular program was started. Others may wish to read the work straight through from cover to cover. Both of these purposes seem to me perfectly appropriate; but the first group will want "the facts" and plenty of them; the second will be hoping for an interesting tale. Fulfilling both sets of expectations, pleasing both sorts of readers simultaneously is not always a simple task and sometimes, I fear, not an entirely possible one.

A third difficulty involves the effort to tie together the various aspects of the story so that it will not appear that the University's many facets evolved independently, with no relation to one another. This means attempting to integrate what was occurring on the Norman campus with what was happening at the School of Medicine in Oklahoma City. It also means trying to show how territorial and state politics affected the University's operations and how the institution's development proceeded hand in hand with the growth of the town of Norman. What were the connections between the University's administration and the culture of the student body, between the Physics Department and the football team, between the training of engineers and the teaching of Spanish?

One way that I have tried to integrate the varied elements of the University's early history is to tie as many aspects of it as possible to two overriding themes that run through the entire period. The first is the inspiring tale of pioneering, the typically American impulse—so characteristic of the country's westward movement into new settlements—to improvise, invent, and build for the future. Much in the University's beginning years can be accounted for, at least in part, by that intoxicating motive. The second theme that runs through the school's history during this time is the danger of political and sectarian interference with the institution. Again and again, as readers will see, powerful outside forces attempted to work their wills on the independence of the University, and almost always those attempts involved tragic and unjust consequences. But choosing these two unifying themes presents its own problems, its own nagging questions. The pioneering spirit and outside interference may explain a good deal about the first quarter-century of the University's career, but they cannot explain it all. Should other unifying strands have been emphasized? Were other themes more important, more revealing?

Finally, there has been the problem of defining my own attitude toward the enterprise. This is a problem, of course, that every historian faces no matter what the subject of his or her work. In this case, however, the difficulty might be accentuated by the fact that I have spent more than half of my life teaching at the University of Oklahoma and that I feel a considerable affection for the institution, for my colleagues, coworkers, and students; these are feelings that pull in the direction of rendering one sort of account. At the same time, I am wedded to the professional historian's commitment to disinterested impartiality and the exercise of detached judgment (insofar as those ideals are *ever* attainable by mortals); and that commitment sometimes pulls in a different direction. I have tried to navigate these hazardous waters carefully, praising the institution when I thought it lived up to its ideals and was worthy of praise, and criticizing when it appeared to fall short of its best motives, when it was less than it might have been.

In the end, however, the difficulties of telling the story have been dwarfed for me—and

I hope for readers as well—by the story itself. The founding and earliest development of the University of Oklahoma is a tale of high purposes, purposes that called forth admirable traits: significant self-sacrifice and dedication, faith in the value of learning, the courage and tenacity to overcome tremendous obstacles, confidence in the future, a laudable sense of the needs of the community. If there was pettiness and intolerance, there was also vision and openness and heroic effort. The work of these pioneering men and women lives on. They made their own monument, and they have lessons to teach us all.

# Acknowledgments

I have accumulated a multitude of debts in connection with this project, and it is a genuine pleasure to acknowledge some of them here. I am grateful, first of all, to the committee chaired by Professor Ronald Peters of the Political Science Department, for initially determining that the University should have a new scholarly history and for then giving me the privilege of writing it. Joan Wadlow, who was provost at the time, concluded arrangements, gave me a guarantee of absolute authorial freedom, and provided me with salaries for three summers of research and writing. Other officials of the University have been uniformly cooperative and helpful, but I want to mention the current provost, Nancy Mergler, for granting me access to the personnel folders of deceased members of the faculty and for other courtesies.

I owe a great deal to the many others who have written about the history of the University of Oklahoma, and I have tried to indicate, in footnotes and bibliography, my enormous debt to those who have preceded me. But I must especially acknowledge the splendid scholarship of Roy Gittinger, Dorothy Gittinger Wardner, Mark R. Everett, Harold Keith, George Lynn Cross, Charles Long, Carolyn Hart, and Daniel Wren (who, in addition to writing an excellent history of the College of Business Administration, carefully reviewed my manuscript and offered valuable suggestions). Herbert R. Hengst, emeritus professor of education, has performed a notable service in collecting dozens of oral histories from members of the University community. I have had steady resort to Carol Burr, editor of the *Sooner Magazine*; she has been both a skilled editor of a series of historical articles I have written for that publication and a storehouse of information about the University's history. Anyone who works on the history of the institution in the future will owe a great deal to Ginger Murray, Jana Moring, and Sarah Robbins for their painstaking work in indexing and making accessible the contents of the *Sooner Magazine* since its first issue in 1928.

Donald DeWitt, the curator of the Western History Collections (WHC), generously provided me with a place to work in Monnet Hall that was convenient to the University Archives; he has been a perfect host over the years. I owe a considerable debt to John Lovett, the assistant curator and librarian of the WHC. He has been a fount of knowledge about the history of the University, the undisputed authority on the photographic record of the institution, and a consistently helpful, patient, and friendly guide to the WHC's resources. Many other staff members at Monnet Hall have helped this enterprise along the way; unfortunately they are too numerous to mention individually, but I must certainly single out Kristina Southwell, Bradford Koplowitz, and Josh Clough. The WHC has proved to be a wonderfully pleasant place to do scholarly work.

Since the day they first arrived on the campus, President David L. Boren and Molly Shi Boren have evinced an enthusiastic regard for the University's history. They have been consistently encouraging and interested as the work progressed. I am particularly grateful to President Boren for his willingness to write the foreword to this volume. He also made a generous grant to the University of Oklahoma Press to help defray the work's production costs so that the price of this book might be kept as low as possible.

A number of friends were kind enough to read the manuscript in part or in its entirety. I am especially pleased that George Lynn Cross was able to read and comment on the first few chapters and that Paul F. Sharp, an expert on the general history of higher education in the United States, was willing to read all of it. J. R. Morris, who served the institution with distinction for many years and who knows much about its past, also read the manuscript and offered valuable observations. Among colleagues and friends whose comments were both helpful and encouraging were Penny Hopkins, W. R. Johnson, Tom Love, Andy Magid, Melissa Stockdale, Kenneth Taylor, Rick Tepker, Alan Velie, Thurman White, and Leon Zelby. William Savage, with his deep knowledge of Oklahoma history and his infallible eye for infelicities and errors, gave the manuscript a thorough review. I would never dream that any manuscript of mine was fully ready for publication until it had passed under the expert scrutiny of my longtime colleague and friend Robert Shalhope; in this case, as in many others, he made dozens of thoughtful suggestions that have found their way into the final version of the book.

David B. Potts, an authority on the history of American higher education and the author of an outstanding history of Wesleyan University, read the manuscript with meticulous care and graciously spent two or three hours on the telephone with me, making numerous substantive and stylistic suggestions and corrections.

The staff at the University of Oklahoma Press have been everything that any author could hope. Both John Drayton, the director, and Charles Rankin, the associate director, have been unfailingly helpful, sympathetic, and patient; I owe much to both of them for their kindness along the way. The same is certainly true of Alice Stanton, the managing editor, who has moved this book (and its author) through the complex procedure with steady good sense and professional skill of a high order. I would like to think that all three have become friends as well as coworkers. There is no page of this volume that has not been made clearer and more correct by the conscientious and sharp-eyed copyediting of Kathy Burford Lewis.

It is not easy to put into words what I owe to my wife, Lynne Hunt Levy, or to my children, Beth and Benjamin. I can only hope that they have at least a dim understanding of how much their support and love has meant to me, of how much their presence is reflected in this book and in everything else I do, and of how deeply I realize the immeasurable extent of my debt to them.

DAVID W. LEVY

*Norman, Oklahoma*

# The University of Oklahoma

CHAPTER I

# A University Is Located
# in Norman, Oklahoma

To modern eyes, the most remarkable feature of the earliest photographs of the University of Oklahoma is undoubtedly the stark loneliness, the sheer barren emptiness of the surrounding landscape. The human figures seem dwarfed by the enormous sky stretching toward the horizon, by the flat plain stretching unbroken as far into the distance as the eye can see. The first buildings look as if they had somehow been dropped into position from above and as if they do not quite belong where they had landed. Those old pictures give a sense of the extent to which the institution was imposed upon the land, set down willfully by men and women who were determined to make a school and would not easily be deterred. It is true, of course, that *every* institution is imposed upon some landscape by willful people. But in this instance the imposition, so striking and obvious in those old pictures, seems somehow more dramatic and decisive than is usually the case. This was because of the suddenness of the intrusion and the primitive conditions under which it occurred. In older, more settled places colleges grew gradually out of the soil. They were physical responses to felt needs, slowly drawn into existence by surrounding communities. Their buildings had originally been constructed for other purposes: former churches, stately homes, or private academies now appropriated to accommodate the needs of higher education. They were, in short, transformed and modified by long experience. The great exception was America's first institution of higher learning, Harvard College. But even the Puritans who settled Boston in 1630 waited six years before starting their college. The eager pioneers who invaded Oklahoma—and who started a university even before the Territory could boast of having produced any high-school graduates—were not so patient.

What follows in these pages is the story of how these pioneers performed the breathtaking feat of building an institution of higher education in that stark and barren wilderness: what moved them to try it, how well in some respects and how poorly in others they succeeded in realizing their hopes and ambitions, and what this product of their willfulness and impatience meant to them and to their children . . . and to all of those who were to follow.

~

IN THE BEGINNING there was only the open and empty land. The place where the campus now stands occupies a transitional zone between two distinctive kinds of landscape. A few miles to the east lay the infamous Cross Timbers, a north-south strip of thick blackjack and post oaks, growing so close together, with branches so low to the ground and intertwined, that the early travelers found it almost impossible to traverse. "I shall not easily forget the mortal toil, and the vexations of flesh and spirit, that we underwent occasionally, in our wanderings through the Cross Timbers," recalled the famous writer Washington Irving, who toured the area in 1832. "It was like struggling through forests of cast iron."[1] At one point in their journey, Irving and his companions were a few miles east of the future site of the Health Sciences Center in what is today Oklahoma City. He again mentions the Cross Timbers: "[A]nd a cheerless prospect it was; hill beyond hill, forest beyond forest, all of one sad russet hue." But suddenly, "to the left, the eye stretched beyond this rugged wilderness of hills, and ravines, and ragged forests, to a prairie about ten miles off, extending in a clear blue line along the horizon. It was like looking from among rocks and breakers upon a distant tract of tranquil ocean."[2]

A few days later, near what is today east Norman, Irving came upon a more congenial setting:

> After proceeding about two hours in a southerly direction, we emerged toward midday from the dreary belt of the Cross Timber, and to our infinite delight beheld "the great Prairie" stretching to the right and left before us. We could distinctly trace the meandering course of the main Canadian [River], and various smaller streams, by the strips of green forest that bordered them. The landscape was vast and beautiful. There is always an expansion of feeling in looking upon these boundless and fertile wastes; but I was doubly conscious of it after emerging from our "close dungeon of innumerous boughs."[3]

Stretching westward from the Cross Timbers was the start of the great prairies: endless reaches of land, mostly flat, covered with grama and buffalo grass; here and there a gently rolling hill rose easily off the plain, lending interest to the otherwise level topography. The only trees to be seen were along the river and creek bottoms—cottonwoods and elms, oaks, hackberries, and pecans.[4] The high grass blowing in the wind was so often compared to the gently flowing sea (Irving's phrase "a distant tract of tranquil ocean" was typical) that the sea became the chief metaphor for that landscape. It is not surprising that the big wagons that eventually carried settlers westward were called "schooners."

The place where the town of Norman would someday be built, therefore, lay a little to

---

1. Washington Irving, *A Tour on the Prairies*, 125.

2. Ibid., 151.

3. Ibid., 171. Irving quotes from John Milton's poem "Comus" (1634), line 349.

4. Frank E. Studnicka, "Some Aspects of the Norman Area Landscape, 1832–1889," in John W. Morris MSS Box 19, Folder 5.

the west of the boundary between the tortuous woodlands and the vast prairie grasslands. Numerous creeks and springs provided a goodly supply of water that the first government surveyor described in his report of 1873 as being "clean and pure."[5] Attracted by the abundant prairie grass, antelope, wild horses, prairie dogs, and deer abounded. Raccoons, quail, ducks, and prairie chickens also occupied the grasslands, and wild turkeys could be found nearer the wooded areas to the east. But it was the buffalo that dominated for most of the nineteenth century. Irving gave a vivid description of a buffalo hunt near what is today the town of Moore.[6] Two years later, north of the present town of Purcell, General Henry Leavenworth's expedition reported seeing "an abundance of buffalo" with "immense herds in every direction";[7] and the celebrated artist George Catlin, a member of that expedition, recorded with his artist's eye that the plains were "literally speckled with buffalo."[8] By the mid-1870s, however, the wanton slaughter of these animals had decimated the herds and practically removed them from the area.[9] The early travelers mention wolves and cougars that preyed upon the grass-eaters. They also mention the blowflies, ticks, and fierce mosquitoes that preyed upon them.

The buffalo herds and other game also sustained tribes of American Indians. Although they probably never occupied the area around Norman for long periods at a time, bands of Osages and Comanches, of Kiowas and Pawnees, regularly crisscrossed the region, hunting and raiding and skirmishing among themselves.[10] The lands they roamed became part of the Louisiana Purchase of 1803, and the future state of Oklahoma became the place to which land-hungry eastern whites, aided by their government in Washington, exiled the Five Civilized Tribes before the Civil War. In exchange for their lands in the Southeast, they were awarded tribal holdings in what became known as the "Indian Territory."[11] The land where the University of Oklahoma now stands was originally assigned to the Creeks by treaties of 1832 and 1833. The Seminoles were soon united to the Creeks in a joint-ownership arrangement that lasted until an agreement of August 1856 separated the two tribes and gave the land in question to the Seminoles. Pressured by the federal government, which unfairly accused the tribes of fighting for the Confederacy, the Seminoles and other tribes ceded territory to the United States in 1866. In the case of the Seminole lands, including the future site of the University, the tribe received fifteen cents per acre.

5. Dave Loftin, "The Geography of Cleveland County, 1873: A Reconstruction," 13, in John W. Morris MSS, Box 14, Folder 14.

6. Irving, *A Tour on the Prairies*, chap. 29.

7. Quoted in John Womack, *Norman: An Early History, 1820–1900*, 5.

8. George Catlin, *North American Indians, Being Letters and Notes on Their Manners, Customs, and Conditions, Written during Eight Years' Travel amongst the Wildest Tribes of Indians in North America*, 2:51.

9. Frank Gilbert Roe, *The North American Buffalo: A Critical Study of the Species in Its Wild State*, chap. 15. See also William T. Hornaday, "The Extermination of the American Bison, with a Sketch of Its Discovery and Life History," in *Smithsonian Report, 1887*, 2:367–548.

10. Muriel Wright, *A Guide to the Indian Tribes of Oklahoma*, 5–9; Rennard Strickland, *The Indians in Oklahoma*, chap. 1.

11. See Grant Foreman, *Indian Removal: The Emigration of the Five Civilized Tribes of Indians*; and Foreman, *The Five Civilized Tribes*.

In addition to the requirements for abolishing slavery in Indian Territory, the treaties of 1866 contained two provisions heavy with implications for the future: first, carved out of the cessions was a large area of "unassigned lands" near the center of the present state of Oklahoma (close to 2 million acres); and second, the tribes were pressured into permitting the eventual construction of railroads through their lands.[12]

From time to time before the 1880s white Americans had evinced an interest in the area. During the 1830s and 1840s, a series of exploratory expeditions passed through what would someday be Cleveland County. Beginning with Major Stephen H. Long, in 1820, famous explorers and military men arrived in the neighborhood and registered their impressions in official reports, private diaries, or reminiscences. After the visit of Irving and his entourage in 1832 came the Leavenworth expedition of 1834, which included (in addition to the artist Catlin) illustrious members such as Stephen Kearney, Jefferson Davis, and a scout named Jesse Chisholm. In May 1839 a party led by Josiah Gregg, the great pioneer of the Santa Fe trail, passed through the future townsite of Norman. Four years later, in July 1843, Daniel Boone's youngest son, Nathan (who had been with Leavenworth and Catlin in 1834), spent one night near what is today Rock Creek Road and 48th Street N.E. and another on the spot now occupied by the Odd Fellows cemetery.[13]

Eventually two trails came through the area. One of them ran east-west and crossed the present county three miles north of the site of the future town of Lexington; it was used by travelers leaving Fort Smith, Arkansas, to head for California. The other was a cattle trail running north-south. The ranching industry grew rapidly in the Chickasaw Nation (just across the Canadian River to the south) and even farther south, in Texas. The cattle had to be driven north through Indian Territory in order to reach the railhead in Kansas. Most came up along the Chisholm trail, about thirty-five miles to the west, but the Arbuckle trail, a feeder into the Chisholm, passed just east of the future site of the University, crossing what would be Lindsey Street between 12th and 24th Avenue S.E.[14]

There were those in the federal government who harbored a hope that the unassigned lands, which were originally intended to serve as a place to relocate other Indian tribes, might instead be given to whites. Toward this end, a federal survey of the empty land, dividing it into townships and sections, was undertaken in the early 1870s. The head of the surveying project hired a twenty-three-year-old Kentucky surveyor to superintend part of the larger enterprise. The young surveyor's name was Abner Ernest Norman. One of Norman's crews—probably operating without Norman himself—pitched its camp about half

12. The definitive study is still Roy Gittinger, *The Formation of the State of Oklahoma (1803–1906)*; for the Civil War experience, see chaps. 4–6. Also helpful is John W. Morris, Charles R. Goins, and Edwin C. McReynolds, *Historical Atlas of Oklahoma*, maps 23, 26, and 33.

13. The early explorations are expertly traced by the premier local historian of Norman and Cleveland County; see Womack, *Norman: An Early History*, 1–8.

14. Grant Foreman, "Early Trails through Oklahoma," *Chronicles of Oklahoma* 3 (1925): 99–119; and Foreman, "Survey of a Wagon Road from Fort Smith to the Colorado River," *Chronicles of Oklahoma* 12 (1934): 74–96. See also Womack, *Norman: An Early History*, 9–14; and Morris et al., *Historical Atlas of Oklahoma*, map 46.

a mile south of the present corner of Classen and Lindsey Streets, and the men, perhaps jokingly, carved a sign on an elm tree saying "Norman's Camp" in honor of their absent boss. Once the surveying was completed in late 1873, Norman returned to Kentucky, got married, farmed for a while, and then went into the lumber business in Louisville. He died in March 1922, never having visited the town that was eventually to bear his name.[15]

In early August 1886, thirteen years after the government survey, the Atchison, Topeka & Santa Fe Railroad began work on a rail line that was to stretch southward from Arkansas City, Kansas, down the center of the unassigned lands and into Texas. By the end of September the construction teams had completed a bridge over the Arkansas River, and more than 5,000 workers joined in pushing the enterprise into the present state of Oklahoma. Through the empty land the railroad came, with track being laid at a rate of more than two miles a day. By the end of 1886 there were stations at Willow Springs and Ponca City, and the rails extended more than forty miles down from Arkansas City. By mid-March 1887 more than a hundred miles of track were open, past Perry and Guthrie and almost to the present site of Edmond; a few weeks later the road had reached what was called Oklahoma Station; and on April 15 it passed within two blocks of old Norman's Camp. Eleven days later it stopped at what is now Purcell, where it joined with a line that had been building northward from Gainesville, Texas. The headline in the *Arkansas City Weekly Republican-Traveler* proclaimed: "United! Kansas and Texas. By the Strong Bands of Steel . . . Arkansas City and Galveston Shake Hands across the Great Indian Territory." On June 13, shortly after noon, the first passenger train passed Norman's Camp, heading north to Kansas. From the start, the implications of this development were crystal clear— even in the East. As soon as permission to build the road was given, the *Boston Transcript* predicted (correctly) that "this will inevitably open up the long coveted Oklahoma land to settlement by whites."[16]

~

THE BOSTON NEWSPAPER was quite right to call the unassigned lands of Oklahoma "long coveted." Almost since the day the lands had been designated as unassigned in 1866, ambitious whites had hungered for the chance to occupy them. Employing both legal and illegal means, these land-seeking white agrarians schemed and clamored for two decades to invade the territory that had been set aside for American Indians.[17] Despite the opposi-

15. Womack, *Norman: An Early History*, 11–13; Ed Montgomery, "Setting the Facts Straight on Abner Norman," *Norman Transcript*, July 28, 2003, A2. Writers who claim that Norman was a surveyor for the Santa Fe railroad are in error on this point.

16. Both quotations are cited in Stan Hoig, "The Rail Line That Opened the Unassigned Lands," in Donovan L. Hofsommer, ed., *Railroads in Oklahoma*, 23, 29. See also Womack, *Norman: An Early History*, 17–19; Preston George and Sylvan R. Wood, "The Railroads of Oklahoma," in *Railroads of Oklahoma, June 6, 1870–July 1, 1974*, 7–25; and Alpheus C. Bray, "A Story of the Building of the Railroads in the State of Oklahoma," 58–62.

17. Carl Coke Rister, *Land Hunger: David L. Payne and the Oklahoma Boomers*; Stan Hoig, *David L. Payne: The Oklahoma Boomer*.

tion of the Indians and their philanthropic friends in the East, opposition from ranchers who wanted cheap grazing land, and objections from some within the federal government itself, the insistent pioneers were not to be denied. In March 1889 President Benjamin Harrison acceded to the relentless pressure. He proclaimed that on April 22 the unas-signed lands, already known as Oklahoma Territory, would be thrown open for settlement by whites. Thousands of hopeful men and women began to gather on the Territory's north-ern and southern boundaries, where they waited impatiently for the great race to begin.

The land run of April 22, 1889—depicted so often and so graphically by reporters, historians, novelists, painters, and film makers—was one of those symbolic and defining moments in the chronicle of America's westward expansion.[18] Few episodes displayed as dramatically those features of the pioneering spirit that were admirable alongside those that were unworthy and reprehensible. On the one side, there was the bold individualism and sturdy independence, the daring courage and determined ambition to improve one's prospects, that explained so much about the development of the American character. On the other side, the men and women who lined up in April 1889 to make the run into Oklahoma were driven by a frantic desire for land that, in many cases, blinded them to the needs and rights of others—whether Native Americans or steely-eyed competitors who were lining up beside them waiting for the gun to go off. Their individualism could easily slip into a grasping and grotesque materialism and an indifference to the require-ments of the communities they were about to form. They could be callous to the weak and brutal toward those who were different; some of them, no doubt, were impatient of rules and prone to violence. If they were wonderfully democratic and stunningly practical and refreshingly informal, they could also be uncultured, narrow-minded, heedless of social responsibilities, wasteful of resources such as the land, and ready to move on once the resources were gone. They tended to be more interested in immediate exploitation than in long-term investment. It should go without saying that both the admirable and the less admirable aspects of the pioneering spirit would make themselves felt when the time came to build a university.

In any case, between 50,000 and 60,000 Americans waited nervously for the signal and cursed the unscrupulous "Sooners" who, despite the efforts of the army and the marshals to keep them out, had sneaked across the lines early in order to scout out the choicest claims. The more law-abiding (or timid) who entered Oklahoma Territory from the south collected at Purcell, directly across the South Canadian River in the Chickasaw Nation. Purcell had been a quiet town of around three hundred, founded two years earlier as a divi-sion point on the Santa Fe; four days before the run, however, a *New York Times* reporter observed that there were "at least five persons to every bed in town and more arriving every hour."[19] Those waiting to invade from the north gathered in the towns of southern

18. Stan Hoig, *The Oklahoma Land Rush of 1889*. Hoig's bibliography constitutes a useful survey of literature on the land run.

19. Quoted in John Womack, "Countdown to the Run," *Cleveland County Reporter*, April 17, 1980, 4b.

Kansas, especially in Arkansas City, whose railroad connection provided the best route into the heart of the still vacant land. On April 19 they were permitted to cross the boundary into Indian Territory, pass through the sixty-mile-wide Cherokee Outlet, and line up on the northern border of Oklahoma Territory. When the signal finally came at noon on April 22, the throng of humanity charged across the lines to stake their claims. On horseback, by wagon, on special Santa Fe trains that chugged southward and northward into the unassigned lands, the eager competitors scrambled for their town lots and their 160-acre farms.

Back in July 1887 the Santa Fe had sent W. E. Thomas to live in a boxcar on a siding fifteen miles north of Purcell in order to operate a telegraph station there. He called the place "Norman" because of the old sign that had been carved nearby. Soon a section house was erected for Thomas on the west side of the track, where it passed the present Duffy Street; he lived there for eighteen lonely months and left before the excitement of April 1889. In September 1888 Lem Hefley and his large family took over the section house, feeding and boarding the crews that worked up and down the track. Less than a week before the run, Andrew Kingkade was appointed as the Santa Fe's agent in Norman. He and his wife and son moved into a cottage that was built in the railroad's right-of-way.[20] On the day before the land run, therefore, Norman, Oklahoma, consisted of the section house occupied by the Hefleys and the Kingkade cottage next door. The only legal residents of the future town—indeed of the whole county—were the members of these two families.[21]

Many years later, one of the Hefley daughters described the scene she had observed as a young woman of fifteen. "All of our family were out in the yard," she recalled. Their house was on the west side of the tracks, so they gathered out back and strained their eyes toward the southeast, toward Purcell, from whence they expected the first of the racers to arrive. But then came a surprise: "We heard them coming up in back of us and turned to see them. The horses and carriages came first, and then the wagons and men on foot. They came from every direction. We didn't know where they were coming from. I heard my parents say later that these were the sooners, camping out on the streams. They had been there three or four days and no one knew it." Soon the place was filled with confusion, with "more noise and excitement than you can imagine." And then the train from Purcell appeared on the horizon: it was required to proceed at roughly the same pace as those coming by horseback or wagon in order to give all the competitors a fair chance for the best claims.

> I saw the train come in, with twenty-two cars on it. It was spectacular. The engine just barely pulled it. Men were all over it, on top, hanging out the windows and doors and

20. Bonnie Speer, *Cleveland County: Pride of the Promised Land, an Illustrated History,* chap. 2; Womack, *Norman: An Early History,* 20. Both books reprint a photograph of the Hefleys' section house. See also Nellie Hefley Lyle, "The Hefleys: Early-Day Cleveland County Family," in Nadine Runyon, ed., *Pioneers of Cleveland County, 1889–1907,* 89–95.

21. Womack reports that on April 20 the cavalry arrested and removed seventeen Sooners hiding in dugouts near the Santa Fe station. He also notes that reliable witnesses spotted "a few unauthorized persons" hanging around the railroad tracks on the morning of April 22 (*Norman: An Early History,* 42).

on the steps, holding to anything they could. Anyone could get on the train, so long as he could hold onto it. . . . This train made such an impression on me as a child, just running so slowly, puff, puff, puff. . . . Men would drop off at intervals and start running out into the country. They knew a townsite would be started and a lot got off to get a claim in the townsite.[22]

By nightfall, Norman was the fourth largest town in Oklahoma Territory, with a population of at least 150.[23] Among that number were two men who had come from Purcell on that first puffing train: Del Larsh and Tom Waggoner. And more than anyone else, they deserve the credit for establishing the University of Oklahoma in the new town of Norman.

~

DELBERT LASALLE LARSH was born in March 1863 into a family of pioneers who had moved west from Ohio, to Illinois (where Del had been born), to Pawnee County, Kansas. The young man learned to operate a telegraph and got a job first at Great Bend, Kansas, and then at Dodge City. The telegraph work at Dodge City was not enough to occupy him fully, so he took a second job as assistant to the Santa Fe freight agent. He rose rapidly in the Santa Fe organization, soon managing the freight office at Dodge City and then taking jobs in Abbeyville and Rush Center, Kansas. In 1887, with the completion of the Santa Fe track across the unassigned lands, Larsh became the first agent at Purcell, Indian Territory. Still only in his mid-twenties, he was a man of enormous ambition and, as it turned out, enormous entrepreneurial energy.[24] When President Harrison made his announcement on March 23, 1889, authorizing the opening of Oklahoma Territory a month later, young Del Larsh sprang into action.

He called a meeting. One of those in attendance at the Santa Fe office in Purcell was his assistant, Thomas R. Waggoner, the chief clerk and cashier at the train station. Others who came to Larsh's meeting that day included John Helvie, a locomotive engineer for the Santa Fe; Albert Rennie, a lawyer from nearby Whitebead; Ed Ingle, editor of the *Purcell Register*; and two Purcell businessmen (a father and his son), Tyler and George Blake, whom Larsh had known back in Kansas. Finally, Larsh invited two cattlemen who ranched in the Chickasaw Nation, just across the Canadian River from the Norman station: nobody knew the uninhabited target area any better than Pryor Adkins and Charles T. Gorton. The purpose of the meeting at Del Larsh's Santa Fe office was to plan the seizure of the 320-acre townsite at Norman and to consider attorney Rennie's plat for the place once it

22. Quoted in Speer, *Cleveland County*, 16–17.

23. Estimates of the population on "the first day" vary, with Stan Hoig and others estimating "some 500 persons" (*The Oklahoma Land Rush*, 172). The figure of 150 is from Pendleton Woods, "The Oklahoma City Metropolitan Area," in John W. Morris, ed., *Cities of Oklahoma*, 143. At the census of 1890, Norman had a population of 787. By mid-1891 the *Norman Transcript* (May 30, 1891) claimed a population of 1,500.

24. Georgetta Larsh Starzer and Nadine Runyan, "D. L. Larsh and Family," in Runyan, *Pioneers of Cleveland County, 1889–1907*, 110–13.

could be legally claimed on the afternoon of April 22 by members of the group.[25]

Because Santa Fe employees were prohibited from participating in the land run, both Larsh and Waggoner resigned from the railroad company. On the morning of the great day, members of Larsh's group got places on that crowded northbound train that young Nellie Hefley was shortly to see puffing toward the Norman station. They had no doubt benefited from the contacts of Helvie, Larsh, and Waggoner among the railroad workers. But when they leaped off the train at Norman, they were in for a surprise. Some Santa Fe surveyors were already there and had already laid out a townsite for the 320 acres in question, even staking out Main Street. What might have been a tense confrontation ended peacefully when the railroad surveyors, recognizing Larsh and Waggoner, handed over their plan, packed up their gear, and left the field to the Purcell entrepreneurs. Larsh put Rennie's plat into his pocket and went about his business.[26] The business of Larsh and the others in the group during those first frantic hours and days was twofold: laying claim to choice town lots and neighboring quarter sections for themselves and organizing the new town of Norman, Oklahoma Territory.[27]

The rancher Pryor Adkins was the most mature member of the Larsh group. He had been an officer in the Confederate army and had lived across the river from Norman station since 1886. For the first two weeks after the land run, he seems to have served as a kind of unofficial mayor.[28] On May 4 Adkins called a mass meeting, which was dominated by the Larsh group: Tom Waggoner was elected provisional mayor; three of the four councilmen were Adkins, Del Larsh, and Santa Fe agent Andrew Kingkade. Young George Blake (whose father, according to legend, had ridden up from Purcell on the cowcatcher of the packed train and who staked his claim on the spot where the present county courthouse stands) was named to the particularly important post of city clerk, where he would supervise the registration of claims. At another election in November 1889, the voters once again chose Waggoner to be mayor.[29]

25. Womack, *Norman: An Early History*, 25–27.

26. Ibid., 24–34; Speer, *Cleveland County*, 14–17. See also the fine account in John Alley, *City Beginnings in Oklahoma Territory*, 73–77. Naturally, the Santa Fe surveyors laid out their streets so that they would cross the railroad track at right angles. Unfortunately, the track through Norman ran not due north but north-northwest. Later additions to the original townsite were laid off according to the cardinal points of the compass. This accounts for the otherwise mystifying curves in the streets heading between Main Street and the campus. As Alley put it in 1939 (*City Beginnings*, 77), "And so today when a motorist approaches Norman from the north on United States Highway 77 [Porter-Classen Street] and makes a right turn into Main Street [no longer possible because that street is now one-way in the wrong direction], he probably thinks he is driving west, when actually he is driving southwest. When he turns left off Main Street at the west edge of the business district and starts toward the state university he seems to be driving south, when as a matter of fact he is driving southeast."

27. Their claims in and around town are detailed in Womack, *Norman: An Early History*, 28–34.

28. Jean Holland, "C. D. Adkins, 1868–1947," in Nadine Runyan, ed., *Pioneers of Cleveland County, 1889–1907*, 1–2. C. D. Adkins was the son of Pryor Adkins.

29. These primitive governmental arrangements were all extralegal. From April 22, 1889, until May 2, 1890, no law authorized city governments in Oklahoma Territory. After May 2 city government was authorized by the Organic Act that brought the Oklahoma Territory into official existence or by the territorial legislature authorized by that act (Alley, *City Beginnings in Oklahoma Territory*, viii).

From the very start, the Santa Fe tracks divided the town of Norman into an east side and a west side, a division that soon became bitter because it was fortified by political and economic rivalries as well. The town was settled by men and women who had come both from Texas to the south and from Kansas to the north; although there were doubtless some exceptions, the Kansans were usually Republicans and the Texans, Democrats. Roy Gittinger, the first historian of the University and a very keen observer, arrived in Norman around the turn of the century. He reported that the people on the east side tended to be southern Democrats, while those on the west side came from both the North and the South.[30] Luckily, there happens to be a convenient way to assess the relative strength of the two factions. On August 5, 1890, the citizens of what had hitherto been known only as "County Three" of Oklahoma Territory got to vote on a permanent name for their new county. The Republicans hoped to call it Lincoln County; the Democrats wanted to name it in honor of Grover Cleveland, who was between his two separated terms as president. When the votes were tallied, the Democrat-favored "Cleveland" had won over the Republican-favored "Lincoln" by better than two to one (829 to 405).[31]

In the meantime, however, Benjamin Harrison, the Indiana Republican who was currently president of the United States, had named an Indiana Republican friend of his to be the first territorial governor of Oklahoma. During the Civil War, George Washington Steele had risen from private to lieutenant-colonel by successfully waging war against southern Democrats. He had been a loyal Republican congressman from Indiana from 1881 to 1889, until Democrats defeated him. Out of a job, he was appointed on May 15, 1890, two weeks after the Organic Act had established government in Oklahoma Territory. A week later, on May 23, he arrived in Guthrie, where he took two adjoining rooms at a hotel—one room for an office, the other divided by a curtain into a reception area and the governor's bedroom.[32] One of his first tasks was to arrange for the selection of the territorial legislative assembly; on July 8 he announced that the counties would choose their representatives four weeks later, on August 5.

In the same election in which they voted to name their county after the Democrat Grover Cleveland, the voters of County Three also chose Democrats for every position in both branches of the territorial legislature. Two Democrats from the town of Norman appeared at the McKennon opera house in Guthrie on August 27 to take part in the opening session: former mayor Tom Waggoner and Mort L. Bixler, the owner and publisher of the *Norman Advance*, the town's first newspaper. Like most of the other delegates from the

30. Roy Gittinger, "The University Reorganizations of 1908 and 1911," in George Lynn Cross President Emeritus MSS, Box 14, 3–4.

31. Womack, *Norman: An Early History*, 79. Farther to the north of Cleveland County, where Kansas Republicans dominated, the counties were eventually named for such renowned Republicans as Abraham Lincoln, Ulysses S. Grant, James G. Blaine, James Garfield, Union general and Illinois senator John Logan, and John W. Noble, Harrison's secretary of the interior at the time of the land run.

32. Thomas Arthur Hazell, "George Washington Steele," in LeRoy Fischer, ed., *Territorial Governors of Oklahoma*, 9–22; see also "Oklahoma's Territorial Governors," *Sturm's Oklahoma Magazine* 5 (January 1908): 61–66.

other six counties in Oklahoma Territory, they had come to Guthrie not so much for the purpose of making wise laws as for the purpose of dividing up whatever plums the territorial government had at its disposal. As it happened, the staunch Democrat representatives from Norman, who faced the staunch Republican governor from Indiana, had a very specific plum in mind.

~

IT IS NOT CLEAR exactly when Del Larsh and Tom Waggoner first conceived the notion of locating the Territory's university in the town of Norman. It might even have been as early as the meeting in Larsh's Purcell office in late March or early April 1889. Even though Larsh was a Republican from Kansas and Waggoner a Democrat from Tennessee and Texas, the two men were extremely close friends and partners. They opened a furniture store together immediately after the land run and claimed adjoining quarter sections of land just south and west of the townsite area. From the start they probably realized that making Norman the territorial capital was not possible. In the first place, publicity before the run made it perfectly clear that Guthrie and Oklahoma City would attract more settlers than any other locations in Oklahoma Territory; in the second place, unlike those two towns, Norman was too far from the center of the new Territory to make a convincing case for serving as the site for the capital. No doubt Larsh and Waggoner regarded the relatively modest idea of getting the University for Norman as being more practical and attainable than going for the capital. But once having decided on the particular prize they wanted, they were ready to pursue it with a remarkable combination of single-minded determination and—considering that they were amateurs—impressive political dexterity. They also had an adroit and intelligent ally in Mort Bixler.

The territorial legislature consisted of a twenty-six-member House of Representatives and a thirteen-member Council (eventually called the Senate). Republicans claimed majorities in both chambers. In the House there were fourteen Republicans and twelve Democrats and Populists; in the Council there were seven Republicans and six Democrats and Populists. But when it came to dividing up spoils, partisan loyalties took second place to local interests. The main prize, of course, was the location of the capital. The leading contenders were, as expected, Guthrie (named as temporary capital in the Organic Act) and Oklahoma City, with Kingfisher being an unlikely third possibility. In addition, there were other potentially lucrative institutions that the legislature planned to distribute through the seven counties: a state university; an agricultural and mechanical college; at least one normal college for the training of teachers; a penitentiary; a reform school; an insane asylum; homes for the deaf, dumb, and blind; and "a school for the imbecile."[33] Two decades later, one member of the first territorial legislature recalled the scramble for the booty:

33. W. H. Merten, "Oklahoma Territory's First Legislature," *Sturm's Oklahoma Magazine* 5 (January 1908): 36–41. Merten was a member of the first House, representing Logan County.

When a bill came up involving the location of the capital or other public institution, the decks were instantly cleared for action, galleries and lobbies being quickly filled by interested adherents of the various localities proposed, and the battle was on in earnest, lasting often far into the night, and sometimes longer, both sides contesting fiercely every inch of ground by every conceivable form of parliamentary practice known to the contestants; and it may be truthfully said that for resourcefulness and ability to bring into play at critical moments all the fine and confusing points of parliamentary tactics, the first assembly stands among its successors without a peer.[34]

*Delbert LaSalle Larsh, pioneering Norman settler and a moving spirit in locating the University there*

In such a setting, of course, the premium was placed on coalition building, and the Cleveland County delegates quickly attached themselves to a powerful grouping of county interests that commanded narrow majorities in both branches. This coalition committed itself to placing the capital in Oklahoma City (Oklahoma County), the state university in Norman (Cleveland County), the agricultural and mechanical (A & M) college in Stillwater (Payne County), and the normal school in Edmond (Oklahoma County). The Speaker of the House was to be A. N. Daniels, a Populist from Canadian County. Minor plums were also to go to the towns of Guthrie, Mulhall, Kingfisher, El Reno, and Hennessey.[35] The ambitious Norman representatives understood that the outcome was to be determined in three places: the Council, the House of Representatives, and the office of Governor Steele.

The first decision that the Norman delegates had to make was whether to try to get the university for Norman by means of an omnibus bill that would locate all the Territory's institutions at one time. Tom Waggoner decided against that tactic, probably because Governor Steele made it clear early that he wanted no part in the fight between Oklahoma City and Guthrie and that he would probably veto any bill that attempted to fix the capital permanently.

On October 30, two months into the four-month session, Mort Bixler introduced Council Bill No. 56. Bixler was a Democrat (although his father was the Republican treasurer of Oklahoma County). The year before, he had moved from Oklahoma City, where

34. Ibid., 38.

35. For the perspective of an Oklahoma City Democrat participant in the first territorial legislature, see Dan W. Peery, "The Struggle for the Removal of the Territorial Capital," *Chronicles of Oklahoma* 2 (1924): 319–24. See also Dorothy Gittinger Wardner, "The Territorial University of Oklahoma," 6–14. It is a particular pleasure to acknowledge this excellent master's thesis. Wardner, the daughter of OU historian Roy Gittinger, performed an important service in preserving this period of the University's history so thoroughly and accurately. I have relied on her pioneering work in many places.

he had been assistant editor of the *Oklahoma City Daily Times*, to Norman, where he took over the *Norman Advance*. He still had friends, relatives, and connections in Oklahoma City, and it was natural that he would want to cooperate with the coalition that hoped to place the capital there. At the same time, however, he wanted very much to see the university landed for Norman. A representative from Oklahoma City remembered Mort Bixler as being "bright, educated and versatile. . . . It was largely through his skill and sagacity that the Council was organized and lined up to locate the capital at Oklahoma City and the University at Norman."[36] Bixler called his bill "an act to locate and establish the University of Oklahoma at Norman," and it was drawn with provisions that were the most favorable and least restrictive to the town.

Two weeks later the bill emerged from the appropriate Council committee with some significant changes—including the omission of the words "at Norman" from the bill's title. The biggest substantive change was a response to views that Governor Steele had expressed back in mid-September. Because there were only so many institutional prizes to bestow, the governor told the legislature in his message of September 17: "I would earnestly impress upon you the importance of so legislating as to invite competition for locating them." Steele had in mind asking the counties getting the benefits to make substantial contributions, "which may not only go far in the direction of relieving the Territory of expense, but will especially relieve counties receiving no direct benefit."[37] When the bill came out of the Council's committee, therefore, it stipulated (in an addition to Bixler's original Section 1) that Norman could get its wish, provided that Cleveland County present the Territory with a $5,000 bond and donate forty acres of land within a half-mile of downtown Norman for the establishment of the University. The committee also added two new sections giving the University's Board of Regents the powers to receive gifts and to draw warrants on University funds.[38] With these changes in place, Bixler's bill passed the territorial Council by a unanimous vote on November 18.

Tom Waggoner took over the management of the measure in the House of Representatives when it arrived from the Council. The same observer who described Mort Bixler as "bright, educated, and versatile" left behind a much less favorable assessment of Waggoner. "He was a shrewd scheming business man, and politics was also business with him," wrote Waggoner's fellow Democrat Dan Peery, of Oklahoma City.

> He had no altruistic thought in his mind and when he was planning to locate the University at Norman, he was figuring how much it would be worth to Tom Wagoner [*sic*]. . . . He was a subtle organizer and I think he did more to fuse and bring together the many discordant elements of the House that made up the organization that located the University at his town and voted the capital to Oklahoma City than any other man, and he did it all for Tom Wagoner.[39]

36. Dan W. Peery, "The First Two Years," *Chronicles of Oklahoma* 7 (1929): 442.

37. *Journal of the First Session of the Legislative Assembly of Oklahoma Territory*, 127–28.

38. *Statutes of Oklahoma, 1890*, 1196–1200.

39. Peery, "The First Two Years," 443. Waggoner was chosen to be Speaker of the House in the second territorial

The House's committee voted four to one on November 26 to recommend passage of the Council's bill establishing the University of Oklahoma at Norman.

Unfortunately, when the measure got to the House floor on December 11, it ran into some trouble. Waggoner succeeded in having the bill voted on one section at a time. He was able to fend off an amendment (to Section 2) that would have reduced the governor to being merely a nonvoting, *ex officio* member of the Regents instead of a full voting member. But he was not able to forestall the imposition of a heavy new burden on his town and county. The House substituted a new Section 16 that required Cleveland County to "provide, by sale of bonds, or otherwise, the sum of ten thousand dollars, which sum shall be placed in the hands of the Territorial treasurer, to be by him held for the use of the board of regents for the purpose of erecting the buildings and procuring the apparatus necessary to put the Territorial University in operation."[40] The House also added to Section 17 a line stipulating that, if Cleveland County did not meet the conditions within a year, the whole law was to be considered null and void. As with the amendment in the Council requiring the donation of land, this addition requiring the raising of $10,000 reflected the influence of Governor Steele and his conviction that towns ought to bid for territorial institutions by contributing to defray the expenses connected with them.

Back to the Council came the amended bill. Bixler quickly moved that the House amendments be accepted. This time there was some opposition and a little parliamentary maneuvering. Part of the opposition apparently came from those who had no objection to locating the University in Norman but who did not wish to impose the additional burden on the people of Cleveland County. Proponents of the amended bill also claimed to be against the bond requirement, but they argued that Governor Steele would never sign the measure without the $10,000 stipulation in it. Finally, the Council embodied the House's changes in a new bill (Council Bill No. 114, entitled "An act to cure certain defects in Council Bill No. 56") and passed it. The next day the House also passed Council Bill No. 114. The governor approved on December 19, 1890, and the business was finished.

As it was finally passed and signed by the governor, "AN ACT to locate and establish the University of Oklahoma" consisted of eighteen brief paragraphs.[41] A large part of the measure was devoted to defining the duties and responsibilities of a six-member Board of Regents. Five of them were to be appointed by the governor, with the governor being the sixth. Serving four-year terms, the members of the Board were granted "all the powers necessary or convenient to accomplish the objects and perform the duties prescribed by law, and shall have the custody of the books, records, buildings and all other property of the university." The law also required that "no instruction either sectarian in religion

---

legislature. Apparently something of an opportunist drifter, Waggoner soon headed to California, where—according to Delbert Larsh's interview with Dorothy Gittinger Wardner—he died in 1896. Larsh stayed in town and lived to be eighty, dying in October 1943; see "Pioneer Sooner Dies," *Sooner Magazine* 16 (January 1944): 22.

40. *Statutes of Oklahoma, 1890,* 1199.

41. *Statutes of Oklahoma, 1893,* 1164–69.

or partisan in politics shall ever be allowed in any department of the University, and no sectarian or partisan test shall ever be allowed or exercised in the appointment of regents, or in the election of professors or other officers of the University, or in the admission of students thereto, or for any purpose whatever." In addition, it stipulated that the school "be open to female as well as male students" and that no tuition was to be charged to any student who had lived in the Territory for one year.

The lawmakers also attempted (in Section 9) to define the new institution's purpose: "The object of the University of Oklahoma shall be to provide the means of acquiring a thorough knowledge of the various branches of learning connected with scientific, indus-trial and professional pursuits, in the instruction and training of persons in the theory and art of teaching, and also instruction in the fundamental laws of the United States and of this Territory, in what regards the rights and duties of citizens."[42] Thus three central goals were uppermost in the minds of the lawmakers who founded the University: preparation for scientific, industrial, and professional careers; the training of teachers for the Territory; and the inculcation of good citizenship. They were nothing if they were not practical men. No doubt some of them would have been mystified by those purposes of higher education that had no immediate payoff: the pursuit of knowledge for its own sake; the consideration of philosophic, aesthetic, and moral questions that had little relation to either vocation or citizenship; the appreciation of art, music, and literature; the quest for new knowledge in the sciences, social sciences, and humanities.

Nevertheless, the legislators and people of Oklahoma had, quite unconsciously, taken their place in the furtherance of the nation's greatest contribution to the history of higher education. Both in the frank practicality of their pedagogical aims and in the democratic spirit in which they hoped to make a college education available to a broad range of citizens—irrespective of religion, politics, or gender (but remembering that they were not able to be similarly inclusive when it came to the sensitive matter of race)—Oklahomans were following long-established American patterns. Like the people and the legislators who founded public universities in the other states, the people and the legislators of Okla-homa had agreed to create a citizen-supported university for the twin purposes of helping individuals to reach their best potential and helping the community to improve the pros-perity and quality of its collective life.[43]

As might have been expected, the new law was greeted with appropriate enthusiasm back in Norman. The *Norman Transcript*, owned and edited by Ed Ingle, a man who had been part of the founding of the town from the first meeting in Del Larsh's office, was euphoric. "That Norman will be the educational center of the Territory is now an assured

42. Ibid. This section of the law was reprinted at the beginning of each early issue of the University of Oklahoma *Catalogue*.

43. For the context of state-supported higher education in the United States, see John S. Brubacher and Willis Rudy, *Higher Education in Transition: A History of American Colleges and Universities*, chap. 8; Norman Foerster, *The American State University*; and Allan Nevins, *The State University and Democracy*.

fact. Truly the people of Norman and Cleveland county are to be congratulated. . . . Let the good work of still further improving Norman go on. The future greatness of the city is assured if everyone will do a share in the further advancement."[44]

~

THE FIRST TASK, OF COURSE, was to raise the money that the territorial legislature had demanded.[45] The $5,000 bond, mandated by Section 1 of the law, had to be given to the Territory within thirty days in order to assure a deed to the forty acres required for the campus. That bond was quickly issued by the city. Much more problematic was the $10,000 that the legislature had stipulated for the purpose of constructing a building to house the new university. All the voters of the county, not just those who lived in the town of Norman, were to participate in deciding whether or not to issue these bonds; if issued, the bonds would have to be sold and the hard cash handed over to the territorial treasurer. Although Cleveland County was given a year to perform this task, a careful strategy had to be developed first to get the bond issue passed by the voters and then to get the bonds actually sold for the required cash.

On March 5, 1891, the county commissioners were scheduled to discuss the submission of the bond issue to the voters. Realizing, however, that the action would be premature and that a deliberate campaign would have to be planned if the project were to succeed, they decided to postpone the matter. The detailed planning was undertaken by the Norman Board of Trade. The most powerful businessmen in town gathered on April 6 to consider how to put the bonds over.[46] One week later, believing that they were now ready to move, the county commissioners met and fixed the big election for May 19. This gave promoters of the University a little more than a month to work.[47] A furious campaign of boosterism ensued, led by the business leaders of Norman and enthusiastically promoted by the town's two newspapers. The specific appeals made to the local farmers, who were the preponderant majority of the electorate, reveal a great deal about the spirit and the motives behind the founding of the University of Oklahoma.

From the very beginning the farmers were instructed on the enticing economic advantages of locating a university in the neighborhood. A week after the legislature passed the bill, the *Norman Transcript* sounded the note that would prevail through the whole campaign: "No farmer who has the good of the people and the progress of the country at heart, will refuse to vote the bonds necessary to secure the University here. It means

44. *Norman Transcript*, December 27, 1890.

45. For detailed accounts of the campaign to raise the money, see Wardner, "Territorial University," 18–22; and Womack, *Norman: An Early History*, 120–22.

46. The names of those attending are given in Womack, *Norman: An Early History*, 121.

47. By law the bonds were to be payable in twenty years, they could not pay more than 5 percent, and they could not be sold at a discount. The interest was to be paid by a tax of not more than one mill on each dollar's valuation of all personal and real property and the principal, paid by a similar levy at the end of the first ten years. Womack, *Norman: An Early History*, 121; Wardner, "Territorial University," 18–19.

dollars instead of cents in their pockets in future."[48] Two weeks later, the *Transcript* urged: "Talk up the University matter and convince that doubting neighbor of yours that it will pay every resident of the county to assist in meeting the obligations."[49] Nor was the paper particularly subtle in offering the farmers a rationale for voting yes: "It will increase the value of every foot of real estate in Southern Oklahoma."[50]

As the election approached, the campaign became more intense. Two weeks before the fateful day, the *Transcript* elaborated the chief argument:

> The farmer who is talking and working against the voting of the University bonds for this county, is talking and working against his own interests and the prosperity and future welfare of this county. . . . The location of the institution in our midst will mean the creating of markets for every product that can be raised and who then will be bene-fitted more than the farming community? . . . Another point worthy of consideration is the fact that with the University located here will come an increase in population, for people from not only this county but the surrounding Indian counties too, will be here to give their children the benefits of a finished education. All this would bring money here and every dollar brought in would be disposed of in ways that would result in the farmer getting a good share of it. Probably not less than $50,000 would be annually expended and where that amount of ready cash is spent how can it fail to be advanta-geous to the farmers?[51]

A thousand copies of the last *Transcript* issue before the election were distributed free across the county. In case anyone had hitherto missed the point, the *Transcript* spelled it out one more desperate time: "Every Cleveland county farmer who votes in favor of the university can make several hundred dollars by going home from the polls and pushing up the figures on his farm. He can rest assured that the value of every foot of real estate in this county will be enhanced by the location of the institution here."[52] On the night before the vote, members of the Norman Board of Trade gathered again. They divided themselves into "precinct committees" to ensure that voters known to be favorable to the bonds would be certain to vote.[53]

The question was approved by a substantial majority. The voters of Moore, the town north of Norman, voted decisively against the bonds, 174 to 29; Noble and Lexington, to the south of the proposed site of the University, were both narrowly in favor of issuing the bonds. Noble voters cast 107 ballots for the proposition and 103 against; Lexington's vote was 85 to 67 in favor. It was the town of Norman itself that passed the question. The final

48. *Norman Transcript*, December 27, 1890.

49. *Norman Transcript*, January 10, 1891.

50. *Norman Transcript*, January 17, 1891.

51. *Norman Transcript*, May 9, 1891.

52. *Norman Transcript*, May 16, 1891. No copies of the town's other newspaper, the *Norman Advance*, survive. But it may be assumed that the paper owned and published by Mort Bixler, the man who introduced the Council bill that would locate the University in his town, would also be enthusiastic in support of the project.

53. Wardner, "Territorial University," 20–21.

tally indicated that the campaign had succeeded, at least in Norman, beyond what might have been hoped. Norman's four precincts reported a total vote of 539 for the bonds and only 20 against. The vote for the entire county was 804 in favor and 463 against.[54]

Now that the bond issue had been approved by the voters, the task was to dispose of the twenty $500 bonds so that the needed $10,000 could be turned over to the territorial treasurer before the year's time was up on December 19, 1891. This would prove to be a very tricky business. As in the case of every new settlement, money in Norman was scarce; and whatever sums were available for investment were capable of drawing interest at a rate of around 12 to 14 percent.[55] The law, however, required the bonds to be sold at only 5 percent. They also had to be sold at par value—that is, they could not be discounted to be disposed of at a price fixed by the market, which would have been considerably lower than the face value. Indeed, the highest bid for the bonds was only for 72 percent of their face value, making it necessary to come up with an additional $2,800 somehow and to make it appear as if the purchasers had paid the full price. To make matters even more complicated, the law prohibited the county from expending public money to make up the deficit between the face and the market value of the bonds.

Into this breach jumped the Norman Board of Trade. For strategic reasons, it was deemed advisable to have a Republican as head of the Board of Trade, to deal more effectively with the Republican authorities in Guthrie. In April 1891, however, a Democrat had been elected to this position. This problem was quickly settled in July with the amicable resignation of the Democrat and the selection in his place of the town's leading Republican, Delbert Larsh. He and other members of the Board of Trade plunged energetically into the effort to make up the deficit. By soliciting around a hundred citizens, they raised the needed $2,800. The most generous contributor to the deficit fund, giving triple the amount of the second largest donation, was none other than Del Larsh. The county commissioners then "hired" a bond "agent" who generously donated his commission to the deficit fund. By a not very subtle laundering process, the agent turned over to the county commissioners the required sum of $10,000. The commissioners delivered the money to the territorial treasurer on December 14, 1891, five days before the deadline.[56]

---

54. *Norman Transcript*, May 23, 1891. See also Womack, *Norman: An Early History*, 121; and Wardner, "Territorial University," 21–22.

55. The figure is the recollection of Delbert Larsh, given in an interview of August 12, 1938, to Dorothy Wardner; see "Territorial University," 25–26. John Womack (*Norman: An Early History*, 121) estimates that the going interest rate was about 10 percent.

56. This complex story is well told in Womack, *Norman: An Early History*, 121–22; Wardner, "Territorial University," 26–27; and "How Norman Got the University: An Interview with Charles H. Bessent," *Sooner Magazine* 1 (February 1929): 157–58. The bonds were bought by the Wallace brothers, two Oklahoma City bankers ($8,000), the president of the Santa Fe Railroad ($1,000), and A. D. Acers, manager of Norman's Carey Lumber Company ($1,000). The donors to the $2,800 deficit fund are listed in Womack, *Norman: An Early History*, 126–27.

~

GOVERNOR STEELE DID NOT WAIT until Cleveland County came up with the actual money. Two weeks after the May 19 election approving the bond issue, he announced
the appointment of the University of Oklahoma's first Board of Regents. The five appointees came from five of the seven Oklahoma counties; only the sparsely settled Beaver
County and Cleveland County itself were without representatives on the Board. Two of
the five had served in the first territorial legislature, and a third was to serve in the second.
With Governor Steele as the sixth member, the Republicans outnumbered the Democrats
by four to two.[57] At their first meeting, on June 30, the members demonstrated their keen
awareness of the political situation. They chose as president of the first Board John Morgan Canon, an orthodox Kansas Republican, a former member of that state's legislature,
and a man who spent his life seeking new business and political opportunities. He had
come from Kansas in the land run of 1889 and staked a claim in Kingfisher County. After
a few days there he was convinced that better prospects awaited him in the town of Frisco,
in Canadian County; there he occupied various appointed and elected offices before coming to the new university's Board of Regents.[58] The Board chose as its secretary Leander G.
Pitman, a popular Democratic lawyer from Oklahoma City who would later enjoy a long
judicial career.[59]

During the summer of 1891, while the businessmen of Norman were scurrying about
to raise the needed $10,000, the Board of Regents over which John M. Canon presided
set about to discharge the critical responsibility of locating the University's campus. The
legislature had stipulated the donation of forty acres, it will be recalled; but other than
specifying that the donation be within half a mile of the townsite, it did not define where
those forty acres should be. Assuming that the county could come up with the money by
December 19, where (near the town of Norman) should the school be put? That question
exploded in the middle of a raging controversy between those who lived to the east and
those who lived to the west of the Santa Fe tracks. The battle flared up anew each time it
was necessary to establish a public facility—a park, a city or county office building, the fire
station, the county courthouse. Now the biggest plum of all was coming up for disposition.
As might have been expected, the feelings engendered were intense and bitter. Probably
half a dozen potential sites were offered for consideration, but by the time the Regents had
to choose (at a meeting held in Oklahoma City in July) only two possibilities were actually
in contention. The east side's choice was northeast of Main Street, north of the present

57. The first Board of Regents consisted of John M. Canon (sometimes spelled Cannon), a Republican from Canadian
County; L. G. Pitman, a Democrat from Oklahoma County; Edward G. Tritt, a Republican from Kingfisher County;
Andrew F. Pentecost, a Republican from Logan County; and Albert Taggart, a Democrat from Payne County. Taggart
quickly resigned and was replaced by John R. Clarke, another Payne County Democrat.

58. *Portrait and Biographical Record of Oklahoma, Commemorating the Achievements of Citizens Who Have Contributed to
the Progress of Oklahoma and the Development of Its Resources,* 84.

59. See the charming sketch of Pitman in Peery, "The First Two Years," 437.

*Charles T. Gorton, who laid claim
to the land where the University
of Oklahoma now stands*

Griffin Memorial Hospital.[60]

The location preferred by the west side, the location that was actually chosen by the Regents, had an especially interesting history. The proposed forty acres lay in a quarter section south and a little west of the townsite. That quarter section had been claimed by Charles T. Gorton, the Chickasaw Nation rancher who lived right across the Canadian River and who had been enlisted as part of the Larsh group along with his neighbor and friend Pryor Adkins. There has been some speculation that Charley Gorton was a "Sooner," who had sneaked across the river early to stake out the claim.[61] In any case, Gorton filed his claim two days after the land run. But whether it had been claimed legally or not, the land was turned over to his father-in-law, Seth Moore, in June or July 1890.[62] Moore, who came from Kansas to take possession, had to live on the claim for one year in order to get title to it. On July 7, 1891, he got his title; on July 8 he and his wife deeded the forty acres to the Oklahoma territorial government for the purposes of building the University of Oklahoma. The forty acres consisted of prairie land in the shape of a square, each side a quarter of a mile long; it is the place that is bordered today by Boyd Street on the north and Brooks Street on the south, by Elm on the west and Asp on the east. Moore received $1,000 for the land.[63]

Thus the Republican Board of Regents chose to locate the school on the west side, where so many of the most prominent and influential of the town's Republicans lived and had invested. The disgruntled east-side partisans, most of them southerners and Democrats, were angry. Some of them charged the Regents with taking bribes, and the allegation appeared in an Oklahoma City newspaper.[64] No wrongdoing or corruption was ever proved

60. Wardner ("Territorial University," 24) gives the site's legal description as the northeast forty of the northwest quarter, section 29, township 9, range 2 west.

61. Harold Keith, in *Oklahoma Kickoff: An Informal History of the First Twenty-five Years of Football at the University of Oklahoma and of the Amusing Hardships That Attended Its Pioneering*, 4, is unequivocal in his allegation: "A sure enough Sooner staked his claim on the land that is now the university site. His name was Charley Gorton and he slipped through the lines and settled the land before the bugles ever blew on the day of the opening in '89." Keith also quotes the town marshal, Ben Clay, as saying that "they ruined the best farm in the country when they located the university there."

62. John Womack's account (*Norman: An Early History*, 43–44) is authoritative on the history of this quarter section. He quotes Gorton's daughter as saying that her parents gave title to her grandfather as a hedge against the financial risks that her father was taking in the cattle business. Perhaps it should also be noted that the town of Moore did not take its name from Seth Moore, but from a Santa Fe conductor named Al Moore. See George H. Shirk, *Oklahoma Place Names*, 163.

63. Womack, *Norman: An Early History*, 122. Wardner, basing her opinion on an interview with Delbert Larsh almost forty years after the fact, thinks that Moore was paid "$1500 or $1800 for the property" ("Territorial University," 24–25).

64. Wardner, "Territorial University," 25.

or admitted in this regard, and it is likely that the matter had been settled by the informal friendships and tacit political understandings between the majority on the Board and the west-siders who had so much to gain. Two of those west-siders were Tom Waggoner and Del Larsh. It just so happened that they owned adjoining quarter sections that lay between the southern boundary of the townsite and the northern boundary of the forty acres where the University was to be built. One of the two men donated a narrow strip on the east end of his property, and the other donated a narrow strip on the west end of his. These two adjoining strips combined to make a public access (actually little more than a broad path) between the ragtag town of about twelve hundred souls and the flat and empty field, where, they believed, a worthy institution of higher education would someday stand.

It is a touching measure of their brave self-confidence and their remarkable capacity to dream large dreams that the citizens of Norman decided to give this path the imposing name of "University Boulevard."

CHAPTER II

# Preparing the Ground

Four tasks had to be completed before the vacant prairie half a mile south of the Norman townsite could be transformed into an institution of higher learning, ready to receive and instruct the youth of Oklahoma. To begin with, there had to be a place to house the instruction; the broad and dusty path, boldly called University Boulevard, actually had to lead to . . . *something*. And second, the institution had to be staffed by those qualified not only to school the young but also to manage the countless details that went into such an enterprise—details that were especially daunting in this case because there were as yet no established routines. Who among all of those ambitious and well-meaning territorial legislators, Norman businessmen, and Regents had the faintest idea of what it really meant to start, equip, and run a university? Third, some serious thought had to be given to what precisely was to be taught, what courses and programs and degrees were to be offered. Finally, if there was to be a school, there had to be some pupils: word of the new opportunity available in Norman had to be broadcast, and a student body somehow had to be recruited. None of these tasks was going to be particularly easy.

~

THE PEOPLE OF NORMAN harbored two great hopes about the building that was destined to house their university. First, they wanted the structure to be appropriately grand—a suitable monument to the high purposes and noble aspirations of the town that was already calling itself "the Athens of Oklahoma." Second, it would be very nice if the construction of this proud monument could throw a little honest work and profit in the community's direction. The University's Board of Regents, which would make the decisions, was in entire agreement with the first desire; its members, none of whom came from Cleveland County, were less deeply committed to the second.

The funds to erect the building were to come partly from the $10,000 deposited with the territorial treasurer in December 1891 and partly from a half-mill levy established by the legislature for support of the University.[1] That fund had accumulated more than

1. *Statutes of Oklahoma, 1890*, 1079. For a thorough discussion of all aspects of the construction of the first building, see

$3,400 by the end of 1891, and there was every prospect that at least $5,000 more would flow in during 1892. Probably at their meeting in Guthrie in December 1891, the Regents decided to issue a call for architectural plans for the building.[2] Perhaps it is not particularly surprising that this Board—firmly Republican and with strong Kansas ties—should brush aside proposals from architects in Texas and Guthrie and accept the one from H. M. Hadley of Topeka. After a bidding process, the award for constructing the building went to the architect's Topeka neighbor, builder C. H. Colcraft.

Architect Hadley's plans were grand indeed.[3] When it was eventually completed, the edifice was to boast a basement and three stories, with twenty-two rooms to accommodate all the academic and administrative functions of the University. The stories were to be connected by broad, winding stairways with elegant banisters; and the floors were to be made of three-inch pine boards. (After the building was finished, a writer for the *Kansas City Times* reported that "the doors and doorways are simply trophies of the cabinet-maker's art.")[4] The basement was to house four large furnaces to supply heat to the rooms above. Partly as a precaution against unpredictable Oklahoma storms, the building's walls were to be two feet thick. The base was to be first-class white stone topped with pressed red brick; there would be striking arches of various shapes and sizes, white trim masonry, towers and turrets and dormers. A recent student of the building calls it "an awkward attempt at monumentality, clearly influenced by the Romanesque Revival style of H. H. Richardson."[5]

An unseemly struggle immediately erupted over who would supply the stone. Cleveland County businessmen naturally hoped to get the contract for themselves, but it became painfully clear that the rock produced in the area was inferior. Once again, the Norman Board of Trade sprang into action. In order to convince the Regents that, by George, there was plenty of first-rate building material available in the neighborhood of Norman, some of the town's businessmen traveled to Guthrie in May 1892. They brought along some samples to show the Regents. The chair of the Board of Regents, J. M. Canon, judged that the stone from the quarries around the town of Frisco, in Canadian County, was far superior. By a remarkable coincidence, Canon came from Frisco. The quarrel became even nastier when the rival newspapers got involved. "In their eagerness to get a little extra work at home the Norman people may do something that will be a permanent injury to the coming state of Oklahoma," charged the *Canadian County Courier*. Nonsense, replied the *Transcript*: "The people of Norman would be the last to insist upon Cleveland County

Wardner, "Territorial University," 28–32.

2. No Regents' minutes survive for the first two years of the University's history.

3. The best discussion is in Carolyn S. Sorrels, "Eight Early Buildings on the Norman Campus of the University of Oklahoma," 4–9.

4. These details are from a *Kansas City Times* story reprinted by the *Norman Transcript*, August 25, 1893.

5. Sorrels, "Eight Early Buildings," 8. See also Montgomery Schuyler, "The Romanesque Revival in America," *Architectural Record* 1 (October 1891): 151–98; and Paul Clifford Lawson with Susan M. Brown, eds., *The Spirit of H. H. Richardson on the Midland Prairies*. For a general look at college building in this period, see Charles Z. Klauder and Herbert C. Wise, *College Architecture in America*; and Paul Venable Turner, *Campus: An American Planning Tradition*.

stone merely for the expenditure that would be made here knowing the material to be poor. . . . We claim the rock is as good as any that has ever been used in the territory."[6] The Regents had the Cleveland County stone tested in three different laboratories, and it failed to pass. In July the Regents went to the same place for the stone that they had gone to for the architectural plans and the construction company; they gave the contract to a quarry in Cottonwood Falls, Kansas.

The Regents apparently believed that they had the power to spend money for the building in anticipation of funds from the Territory's mill levy. They projected a building that would cost around $26,000 and contracted for supplies and labor far beyond the funds they had in hand.[7] By the end of April 1892 the builders had excavated the basement, giving rise to the hope that the building might be ready for the official opening of the University in September. Before long, however, construction slowed. By the end of October the stone base was completed, the steps and the lathing were done, the steeple was constructed and needed only to be roofed, and the plasterers were ready to start. But if there were hopes that things would be ready in time for the start of the second semester in January, they were dashed by the new territorial governor, Abraham Seay.[8] He questioned the authority of the Regents to spend money that they did not yet have (they had already issued $17,000 in warrants); and the Regents decided in December to halt the practice, thereby slowing construction to a crawl and ending the possibility that any of the first year's instruction could take place in the magnificent building.

On the other hand, Governor Seay was enthusiastic about trees. He organized the Territory's first Arbor Day for mid-March 1892; unfortunately, a blizzard caused a three-week postponement. In any case, those who were building the University in Norman recognized the need for trees and other landscaping. Regent Andrew Pentecost came down from Logan County to tend to the beautification of the area around the construction site, and dozens of trees were planted. The job of laying out the campus area and fashioning a wide road around the grounds went to Seth Moore, who had originally owned the acreage and still owned the land bordering it, and to Tom Waggoner, the man who had done so much to bring the University to Norman in the first place and who owned the land just north of the campus.[9]

The University building was finally finished in mid-August 1893, in time for the opening of the second year of instruction. Predictably, the *Norman Transcript* was enthralled

6. Quoted in Wardner, "Territorial University," 31. For a rather defensive analysis and vindication of the native product, see Clarence Dunn Storm, "The Building Stones of the State of Oklahoma."

7. But then a decision to appease Cleveland County interests by topping the stone base with pressed brick instead of making a building entirely of stone added $1,900 to construction costs. The final cost of the building was $32,000. See Wardner, "Territorial University," 40–41, 46.

8. Governor Steele resigned effective November 8, 1891. President Harrison appointed in his place another veteran of the Union army and a staunch Republican who had been serving as an associate justice of the Territory's Supreme Court. See Harry E. Henslick, "Abraham Jefferson Seay, Governor of Oklahoma Territory, 1892–1893," in LeRoy H. Fischer, ed., *Territorial Governors of Oklahoma*, 28–45.

9. Wardner, "Territorial University," 29–30.

*"Ugly in its lines and with a wart atop—a sort of misshapen cross between a cupola and a dome":*
*Vernon Parrington's description of the University's first building*

with it: "Both the interior and the exterior of the Oklahoma University building is not alone a picture of beauty, and symmetry, but a model of art, an encomium upon the architect and a living panegyric upon the skill of the contractor."[10] Four years later, on September 8, 1897, a twenty-six-year-old English professor named Vernon Parrington arrived in Norman to take up his new teaching duties. It had been a hot and dusty summer, Parrington recalled a few years later.

> I had never been in Oklahoma, and as I got off the train, that September day, what lay before one was disheartening. . . . My mind was busy with the weather, the ugliness of the raw little town, the barrenness of the streets and yards. As I came on to the campus I stopped—this was the University! The word had always meant—well, something very different to me. A single small red brick building—ugly in its lines and with a wart atop—a sort of misshapen cross between a cupola and a dome—stood in a grove of tiny elms. Across the front and especially about the door, some ivy had made a fine growth and was the one restful thing that met my eyes.[11]

10. *Norman Transcript*, August 18, 1893.

11. Vernon L. Parrington, "Early Days," in *Mistletoe*, 1905, 82. See also H. Lark Hall, *V. L. Parrington: Through the Avenue of Art*, 81.

Once the building was begun, the Board of Regents turned to the task of finding a proper president to lead the institution. Several things about the outcome of their search were crystal clear from the outset. That the president would be a man and not a woman was every bit as certain as that he would be white, not African American or Indian. It was nearly as predictable, moreover, that the Regents would insist upon two other requirements. The new president would almost certainly be a Republican and would almost certainly be brought from Kansas. Given the constraints under which they were operating, the Regents made a very fortunate choice. Indeed, it is hard to see how they could have chosen any better.

~

DAVID ROSS BOYD was born in rural Coshocton County, Ohio, on July 31, 1853.[12] His father, James Boyd, had been born near Antietam Creek, Pennsylvania, in 1820, while the Boyds were traveling from Pennsylvania to Ohio. Eventually James bought a 256-acre farm in Coshocton County and became a justice of the peace. When he was thirty-two he married Mary Ann Ross, a twenty-three-year-old woman from the next county. Thirteen months later, their first child, David Ross Boyd, was born. The couple had four more children, all boys, before Mary Ann Boyd died twelve years after her marriage. James Boyd soon married again and produced another four children, not counting the stepdaughter that his second wife (the widow of a fallen Union officer) brought into the marriage. Thus David was the eldest of ten children, eight of them boys.

From his parents the youngster received some legacies that lasted him the rest of his life. Both his mother and father were deeply religious; James in particular inherited from his own Scottish parents an uncompromising devotion to the sternest tenets of the Presbyterian Church. Part of that religious faith was an insistent and proud commitment to a very rigorous code of morality derived from a midwestern, rural, Protestant reading of Scripture. It placed a heavy emphasis on "duty" and social responsibility and celebrated the old virtues of hard work, conscience, honesty, and iron self-discipline. To people like the Boyds, life was a serious business. They tended to frown on mere frivolity and to look askance at those who wasted their time. A lively and playful sense of humor was not their strongest suit. In addition to an abiding faith in God and unquestioning allegiance to a life of strict moral behavior, the Boyds also instilled in their son an endless capacity for

12. The best source for his early life is Edward Everett Dale, "David Ross Boyd: Pioneer Educator," *Chronicles of Oklahoma* 42 (1964): 2–35. Dale's account is derived, in part, from interviews during a month-long visit with Boyd and his wife in California in 1936. Professor Dale's copious notes from those interviews are preserved in the Edward Everett Dale MSS, Box 212. See also Dale's brief article "David Ross Boyd, 1853–1936," *Sooner Magazine* 9 (January 1937): 80ff.; George Milburn, "Planting a University: First Varsity President Recounts How He Did It," *Sooner Magazine* 1 (November 1928): 39–41; John Terry, "Coshocton County Native Was Founder of the University of Oklahoma," *Coshocton County (Ohio) Tribune*, October 15, 1972; and S. E. Henry, "Religious Development of David Ross Boyd," an unpublished forty-one-page typescript written in 1941 by a friend and former minister of Boyd, found in the David Ross Boyd MSS, Box 1, Folder 4. Robert Stephen Morrissey, "David Ross Boyd and the University of Oklahoma: An Analysis of the Educational Contributions of the First President," contains much useful information based on the author's meticulous examination of the Boyd papers.

hard work and a devotion to education. James Boyd had tried his hand at teaching; Mary Ann Ross had been a teacher before she met him; and all ten of the Boyd children were destined to teach school at one time or another.

The things that the aged David Ross Boyd was to remember from his youth reflected exactly these characteristics of his family. He recalled, for example, his father's abolitionism, including his activities on "the underground railroad," hiding escaping slaves in the attic and driving them by night (sometimes with young David along for the ride) to the next stop on their flight to Canada.[13] Boyd also claimed until the end of his life to have vivid memories of the presidential campaign of 1860, culminating in the election of Abraham Lincoln. He certainly remembered the day in 1861 that Lincoln's train stopped in town on its way to Washington, D.C., and how his father lifted him to the platform, and how the president-elect said, "God bless you, my boy." It was little wonder that Boyd would be a proud Republican for the rest of his life.

Far more complicated and troubling than the political part of his upbringing was the religious part. Since both of his parents were such devout Christians, religious observance was part of the daily routine. Mrs. Boyd was always eager to line up her boys for visiting ministers and have them recite from the Children's Catechism or the Shorter Catechism. There were many such opportunities, moreover, because the local Presbyterian church was too small to afford a regular preacher, and James Boyd was generous in providing hospitality to the visiting ministers. The congregation was also (despite miscalling itself Amity Church) terribly riven by deep and bitter sectarian controversies. Years later, David Ross Boyd described the Amity congregation to his Norman, Oklahoma, minister, the Reverend S. E. Henry, who in turn gave a harsh account of it. "The men of that day of Scotch and Scotch-Irish descent were strong men, men with iron in their blood, individualistic in their thinking, narrow and intolerant, many of them, in their attitude toward the opinions of others."[14] In the end, David's father told his sons that the congregation was so torn by doctrinal bickering that he could not in good conscience ask his boys to become members. Nevertheless, Boyd always recalled how his mother took him by the hand as he was about to leave for his very first day of public school and knelt with him in prayer, begging God's blessings upon this and all future endeavors.[15]

It was his mother who taught David to read, so that on that first day of school he was well ahead of his classmates and began to work on the second McGuffey Reader rather

---

13. After the Civil War many midwesterners claimed that they had taken part in the heroic work of the underground railroad—more than ever did so in actuality. Historian Larry Gara writes: "Although the underground railroad was a reality, much of the material relating to it belongs in the realm of folklore rather than history" (*The Liberty Line: The Legend of the Underground Railroad*, 2). Nevertheless, Coshocton, Ohio, was the scene of considerable underground railroad activity, and Boyd's recollections of the episodes are so vivid and detailed that there is some reason to credit his stories. Dale, "David Ross Boyd: Pioneer Educator," 2–3.

14. Henry, "Religious Development of David Ross Boyd," 3–4.

15. Boyd shared this memory with both S. E. Henry ("Religious Development of David Ross Boyd," 3) and E. E. Dale ("David Ross Boyd: Pioneer Educator," 4).

than the first. His mother also apparently instilled in him a desire eventually to go to college—a desire that remained strong in him despite his mother's death when he was only eleven. He progressed through a series of country schools and during the summers took private instruction in Latin from the local Methodist minister. When he was sixteen he enrolled for a short time in a curious experiment in higher education called "One Study University" in Scio, Ohio; students there studied only one subject at a time and, when sufficient mastery was shown, moved to another.[16] Young Boyd started with geology but quickly gave up on the institution and came back to the farm. At seventeen he began his teaching career by getting a teaching certificate and a position in a small school in the northwest corner of the county. Boyd quickly abandoned another abortive attempt at higher education (this one at the Normal University in Lebanon, Ohio), complaining of low standards. This time he was determined to save some money and enter a real college. He had his eye on a new institution, about forty-five miles up the road from Coshocton, calling itself Wooster University.

Another year of teaching school at forty dollars a month resulted in accumulated savings (at the end of the term in the spring of 1873) of around $150. Boyd's father then made him an offer: he could not give him money for college, but he would give him the free use of forty acres of the farm. David was to work the land, sell the crop, and keep the money. He could also live at home without paying rent. The land was rich, having been used to pasture sheep. The neighbors pitched in to help the boy get rid of some stumps. He planted corn, worked hard, emerged with $700, and in September 1873, at the age of twenty, headed to Wooster.[17]

Wooster University (later to be called Wooster College) had graduated its first class only two years before and was still feeling its way when Boyd arrived. It is hard to gauge how many of the young man's observations of a university getting started, practically from scratch, would later be useful to him or what lessons he learned from observing Wooster's pioneering president, Archibald Taylor, that would help him as he began to carry out his own pioneering duties in Oklahoma Territory two decades later.[18] Wooster was founded by ambitious Presbyterians who hoped to make a "western Princeton." President Taylor and many of his faculty were Princeton graduates, and together they were determined to achieve the high purpose promised in Wooster's charter: "the promotion of sound learning and education under religious influences."[19] But the sort of Presbyterianism that Boyd found at Wooster was far different from the kind he had seen at the Amity Church of Coshocton. According to the man who was to be his minister in Norman, "When David Ross Boyd entered Wooster College his religious views were very immature, and, such as they were, very conservative." He had grown up among strict Presbyterians who believed

16. Morrissey, "David Ross Boyd," 153–55.

17. Dale, "David Ross Boyd: Pioneer Educator," 5–6.

18. For some interesting speculation, see Morrissey, "David Ross Boyd," 160–84.

19. Quoted in ibid., 160.

in "the verbal inspiration and absolute inerrancy of the Bible. Sovereignty was the chief characteristic of the God whom they worshiped. It was a stern, intolerant type of religion they stood for." But at Wooster the young man found "a broader, more liberal, a more wholesome interpretation of the Christian faith." Boyd joined the Wooster church and took over one of the Sunday school classes.[20]

David Ross Boyd had come to study at a religious college in the midst of the most serious intellectual crisis that religion was to face during the nineteenth century. In the popular shorthand of the time, the dispute was thought of as being a monumental struggle between "religion" and "science." The simple orthodoxy represented by the Amity Church of Coshocton found itself belabored on all sides by new intellectual challenges. German scholars who subjected biblical texts to the searching philological scrutiny that became known as "higher criticism" seemed to be calling into question the scientific reliability of literal interpretations of the Bible. The rising popularity of a field of study called "comparative religion" tended to blur the lines between Christian belief and practice and those of other faiths. Most upsetting of all, Charles Darwin's theory of evolution seemed to be hurling enormous challenges to the traditional biblical versions of creation, human nature, and sin. Darwin's *Origin of Species* had been published when Boyd was six years old; *The Descent of Man* appeared when he was seventeen.[21] Virtually every Protestant denomination felt the force of these scientific assaults on traditional beliefs, and virtually every religious man or woman who had pretensions to the intellectual life had to come to some conclusions about the new questions. One of these was certainly the sober twenty-one-year-old student at Wooster.

The reconciliation between religion and science became Boyd's chief intellectual task while at college. His Christian faith was so strong, so firmly planted during his youth and so sympathetically reinforced at college, that he left Wooster as devout and unshaken as when he had entered. As the Reverend Henry, his future Norman minister, put it, "he retained all that was vital in the old faith. . . . His faith in God and in the Christian tradition had been strengthened rather than weakened as a result of the conflict which had been raging about him." At the same time, however, Boyd "saw the need of a mediator between the old faith and the new science." He "accepted the new light of science which had dawned upon the earth in his day"; he concluded that there could be no real contradiction between true Christian faith, on the one side, and Darwinian evolution and the teachings of higher criticism, on the other. Truth was single, after all, and without contradiction; it did not matter whether that truth was revealed through Scripture or science: it all emanated from God.[22] In all probability, Boyd's synthesis of religion and science owed much to the extremely influential teachings of James McCosh, the president of Princeton and the

20. Henry, "Religious Development of David Ross Boyd," 5.

21. For an intelligent analysis of this crisis in American Protestant thought, see Ferenc Morton Szasz, *The Divided Mind of Protestant America, 1880–1930*.

22. Henry, "Religious Development of David Ross Boyd," 18.

chief intellectual force within American Presbyterianism, whose work along these lines was well known at Wooster.[23]

The Reverend Henry reveals how this combination of respect for both science and religion made itself felt in practice, in his somewhat flowery description of the way in which David Ross Boyd taught his Bible classes, from college days forward through the rest of his life:

> In his teaching of the Bible . . . he was considerate of the older generation who held very tenaciously to the older interpretations. He sought not to wound or alienate any sensitive soul whose loyalty to and reverence for the older views led them to be suspicious of the new. . . . [On the other hand], cautiously, but openly he let the new light illumine the old truth until the doubts and suspicions of those holding the older, more conservative views, disappeared in a glad new certainty.[24]

At Wooster, one of Boyd's classmates was Ella Alexander, who (as Ella Alexander Boole) was later to make a small reputation as an ardent reformer in various causes. Her father was president of the Board of Trustees of the school system at Van Wert, in west-central Ohio. She mentioned to him the bright and serious young man at Wooster, who had already accumulated considerable teaching experience; and upon his graduation in 1878, Boyd was hired as principal of the Van Wert high school. After one year in that capacity, he replaced the Van Wert school superintendent and continued in those duties from 1878 to 1888. In 1882 Boyd married Jennie Thompson, who came from his old hometown and whom he had been seeing steadily for at least five years.[25] Within a short time the couple produced their only child, a daughter named Alice.

After ten years in Van Wert, however, Boyd grew restless. He had always harbored a vague desire to study law; he probably felt that Van Wert was a dead end; and he no doubt wished for more money. When a Van Wert friend suggested that the two go into the real-estate business out west, Boyd resigned his position; he and his wife packed up and started toward Salt Lake City.[26] On the way, the Boyds stopped to visit Jennie's sister in Winfield, Kansas, a town that was to have a curious and persistent place in the early history of the University of Oklahoma. Leaving his wife in Kansas, Boyd continued to Utah, where he made a quick $4,000 selling options, learned enough of the real-estate business to understand that it was not for him, and returned to his wife and daughter in Winfield. As it happened, Arkansas City, Kansas, a dozen miles due south of Winfield, was looking for a school superintendent. It also happened that one of Arkansas City's leading real-estate

---

23. The Reverend Henry ascribes the formative influence to Henry Drummond, a very popular Scottish evangelist and theological writer whose mediation between religion and evolution convinced many conservative Christians to make an accommodation with Darwinism. But this is almost certainly an error on Henry's part. Drummond was unknown when Boyd went to Wooster, his first book not appearing until 1883. For McCosh, see J. David Hoeveler, Jr., *James McCosh and the Scottish Intellectual Tradition: From Glasgow to Princeton*, 202–11.

24. Henry, "Religious Development of David Ross Boyd," 22.

25. Jennie Thompson Boyd to Edward E. Dale [November 1936], in the Edward Everett Dale MSS, Box 212, Folder 2.

26. Dale, "David Ross Boyd: Pioneer Educator," 7–8.

men had come from Van Wert and recalled Boyd's work as superintendent there. Boyd accepted the job at $1,500 a year, returned to Van Wert to sell his old house, moved to his new town for the opening of the 1888–89 school year, and became an elder in the local Presbyterian church.

"We had never seen Arkansas City, much less heard of it," Mrs. Boyd remembered ten years later. "But upon coming there we found a town of ten thousand people; a restless, transient, nomad population waiting for the opening of [Oklahoma Territory]. . . . [W]hile living one year in a home we had fifteen different neighbors on either side of us."[27] The town had no high-school building, and Boyd's first task was to supervise the construction of one. But by the start of spring 1889 Oklahoma land fever was in the air:

> [P]eople were gathering in crowds, coming in boomer wagons from every direction and by the first of April and before anyone realized it our town had doubled in population—a new town had sprung up in the park. . . . In the town proper we no longer used the sidewalks but on account of the crowd were content to walk in the middle of the streets or anywhere to get room. . . . [Y]ou would be accosted many times with the questions, "Can't I sleep in your barn or on your porch; we have no place to stay?" Arkansas City was not prepared for such a crowd and they could not ship in sufficient supplies fast enough.[28]

At this point, David Ross Boyd got a stunning idea: nothing less than organizing a series of Works Progress Administration projects forty-five years before Franklin Roosevelt and the New Deal. He persuaded the town to hire the transients for $1.50 a day. Although the newcomers had little money, many of them had mules or horses. Boyd supervised them in a multitude of projects: they built and graded roads for the little country town; they made parks and planted trees that Boyd procured from a nursery in Winfield; they drained and filled ditches. Each day Boyd started them on their work at seven in the morning before going off to his superintendent's duties. Not only did desperately poor men get to earn some money, but as the spring progressed, Arkansas City began to take on the shape of a real town.[29]

The day that the home-seekers crossed the Kansas border and moved south sixty miles through the Cherokee Outlet to await the beginning of the land run was a happy one for both the town and the Boyds. "So tired was I of the crowds," recalled Jennie Boyd, "that when my neighbors invited me to ride with them down to the Kansas line I said 'No, I don't care enough about it to waken Alice and take her out on such a frosty morning.' I did not realize that I was missing the wonderful sight of seeing 3,000 wagons pass a certain point."[30] Many of those wagons, of course, were carrying into Oklahoma Territory fami-

27. Jennie Thompson Boyd, " 'In the Lineup'—A Bit of History," *March Quarterly* (1897): 1. A copy of this three-page typescript of Mrs. Boyd's reminiscence can be found in Vertical File: "University Statistics, circa 1892–93."

28. Ibid.

29. Dale, "David Ross Boyd: Pioneer Educator," 5. For some random aspects of the city's history, see Mrs. Bennett Rinehart, *Blaze Marks on the Border: The Story of Arkansas City, Kansas, Founded 1870–1871.*

30. Boyd, " 'In the Lineup'—A Bit of History."

lies that had some reason to admire and be grateful to her husband, the energetic school superintendent.

One elderly gentleman had a particular reason for gratitude. Boyd was on the county board of education and one of a three-person committee that passed on applicants for teaching certificates. The man, a Civil War veteran, had a chance to teach in a small school but needed his certificate. He had not studied for a long while, he confessed, and thought he did not have much chance to pass the exam. Boyd encouraged him to try it anyway. When the exams were graded, the county superintendent said that in her opinion the candidate had failed. Boyd and the other member of the committee, however, passed the man; Boyd brought him home to dinner that evening. It turned out to be one of those good deeds that before long was to bear quite unpredictable consequences.

Although it appears that the Boyds were content in Arkansas City and that they would have been satisfied to stay there for the indefinite future, Boyd's reputation was on the rise in Kansas. R. W. Stevenson, the superintendent of the Wichita system, was ready to retire and wanted Boyd to replace him in that leading Kansas city; Stevenson had known the younger man back in Ohio when Stevenson was superintendent at Columbus and Boyd was at Van Wert. In addition, the chancellor of the University of Kansas, Francis H. Snow, tried to persuade Boyd to enter politics and become a candidate for state superintendent.[31] He was not yet forty years old, and things were looking bright for him in Kansas. But another, entirely unexpected opportunity was about to surface.

～

THAT OPPORTUNITY OCCURRED because the contract to construct the University of Oklahoma's building did not include provisions for a heating system. The contractor was merely to make the chimneys, and the Regents would install a proper system later. Boyd had selected an advanced and popular modern heating system, manufactured by the Isaac D. Smead Co., for the high-school building that he was erecting in Arkansas City at the same time that the future Oklahomans were camping in the parks and clogging the sidewalks.[32] Now, in the spring of 1892, two members of the University's Board of Regents climbed aboard the Santa Fe and traveled up to Arkansas City to take a look at the high school's heating plant. One of the Regents was A. F. Pentecost. And although at first Boyd did not recognize him in his prosperous new clothes, Regent Pentecost was none other than the nervous Civil War veteran who had been given a teaching certificate by Boyd

31. Dale, "David Ross Boyd: Pioneer Educator," 10.

32. According to John M. Weidman, "A History of the University of Oklahoma," 12, "The most popular type of heating for buildings at the time was that manufactured by the Smead company. It provided for a then new system of fresh air and forcing of the air into the rooms, in such a way as to provide universally healthful heat throughout the building." Boyd himself, forty years later, wrote: "By 1891, Arkansas City had erected a fine high school building, one of the finest at that time in the State of Kansas. We had installed a new heating system called the Isaac D. Smead heating and ventilating system; at that time it was the only possible system to be used where there was no sewerage system." David Ross Boyd to Roscoe Cate, November 22, 1932, in David Ross Boyd MSS, Box 2, Folder 1. This important letter is reprinted in full in Morrissey, "David Ross Boyd," 260–63.

and a dinner by Mrs. Boyd three or four years before.

It was not unusual for visitors to come to inspect the Smead heating system: Boyd called it "almost a daily occurrence." Boyd (who remembered "being surprised at the idea of wanting a university in a place as primitive as I knew [Oklahoma] must be") welcomed the two men. Before they left his office to examine the miraculous furnace, however, they asked if they might speak to him later. Boyd told them that after school he had a teachers' meeting. They said they would wait; and when he returned to his office late that afternoon, he found them there. They asked him a few questions about the heating system. "I was getting ready to go as it was late." They said they were looking for a president to lead the new university and wondered if Boyd had any ideas. The superintendent said that he would think it over and write to them soon. Regent Pentecost suggested that Boyd try to make two suggestions: an older man of experience and "a younger person who has already accomplished some success." A few days later, Boyd offered two names, both of them Ohio friends of his. For the older man he suggested Stevenson, the former Columbus educator who was now hoping that Boyd would replace him as superintendent at Wichita. For the younger, Boyd proposed John W. Knott of Tiffin, Ohio, an old college friend from Wooster.[33]

What occurred next has a ring of the improbable about it, but it is Boyd's own version of the story. Boyd was a director of the Winfield Chautauqua. School being over in Arkansas City, he was sent south during the first week of June 1892 in order to drum up attendance from Guthrie and Oklahoma City. On the train between the two towns, Boyd recalled, he accidentally met the agent for the Smead Company, who was going to Oklahoma City to meet with the University Regents that evening. The agent asked Boyd to come along to the meeting and offer the Board a testimonial to his heating system, which Boyd agreed to do. At the Grand Hotel the agent introduced him to Regent Canon and got permission for Boyd to speak to the Board about his school's heating plant. Boyd spent the afternoon "looking after people that I wanted to attend the Chautauqua at Winfield." Returning to the hotel, he was introduced to the other Regents but thought that the two who had come to Arkansas City a few weeks before "looked a little surprised" to see him there.

> Later, when the Board convened, they left the agents and me in an outside room, separated by sliding doors from the room in which the session was held. I could hear the usual order of business—reading minutes, reports of standing committees, etc. Finally, I could plainly hear the president of the Board ask if the special committee on selecting of the president was ready to report. I immediately became very much interested, wondering if by chance either of my friends, Stevenson or Knott, had been selected. Mr. Pentecost said "Yes, Mr. President, we are ready to report. We went to Arkansas City on a certain date and spent a night and a whole day making investigations. We were very favorably impressed with what we learned. . . . We are, therefore, ready to report recommending the election of Prof. David R. Boyd, Supt. of Schools of Arkansas City, Kansas to be the first president of the University of Oklahoma."

33. Boyd to Roscoe Cate, November 22, 1932, Boyd MSS, Box 2, Folder 1.

*David Ross Boyd in 1893*

Boyd was then ushered into the meeting. "Of course, I was surprised, not to say astounded. I told them that I had not thought of such a thing, that I would have to take it under advisement, that I was then considering an offer to go to Wichita as Supt. of Schools." The Regents scheduled a meeting for two weeks later, when they would learn Boyd's decision.[34]

Although the candidate probably consulted many of his friends, he remembered the advice of two men as being especially important. One was Henry E. Asp, an attorney friend from Winfield who had moved to Guthrie and was soon to play such a major part in the development of the University that one of the main streets leading to the campus would be named for him.[35] The other was Professor James Hulme Canfield of the University of Kansas (today remembered principally as the father of the noted writer Dorothy Canfield Fisher), with whom he discussed the Oklahoma offer at the Winfield Chautauqua. Both of these advisors urged Boyd to take the job, pointing out the rare opportunity to shape at its birth a major institution of higher learning in the United States. Asp emphasized Oklahoma's potential, and Canfield stressed the qualifications and experience that Boyd could bring to the task: "[H]e flattered me and I think much overestimated his conception of my personal fitness for the work." Two weeks later, on July 6, Boyd accepted the offer. He was to be given $2,400 a year. The superintendency at Wichita was paying $3,000.[36]

And so David Ross Boyd came to Norman, Oklahoma, for the first time in his life, on Saturday, August 6, 1892. "I looked off to the southwest where our university was to be

34. Two days later, the offer came to Boyd in writing. L. G. Pitman to David Ross Boyd, June 17, 1892, David Ross Boyd MSS, Box 1, Folder 2.

35. On Asp, see Roy Gittinger, *The University of Oklahoma: A History of Fifty Years, 1892–1942,* 54.

36. The foregoing account of Boyd's hiring is drawn from his letter to Roscoe Cate, November 22, 1932. We may dismiss as apocryphal the absurd version that first appeared in 1957 (see the *Daily Oklahoman,* September 15, 1957). By that account, Boyd was supposed to have told a young reporter for the *Daily Oklahoman,* while visiting Norman back in 1925, that he had originally come to Oklahoma to sell school supplies: "peddling chalk, erasers, desks and miscellaneous items to school houses in south Kansas and in the Territory of Oklahoma." Hoping to get a big order, he attended the Regents' meeting and "went into his sales pitch." When they asked him some questions about how *he* would organize their new school, he gave his opinions, interspersing them with plugs for his wares ("'by the way,' the always-in-there-pitching salesman said, 'you'll need books, tablets, and . . . oh yes, blackboards too'"). Impressed by his answers, they offered him the presidency on the spot and he accepted. This ridiculous story would probably never have been printed if the young reporter of 1925 had not been Fayette Copeland, later a distinguished professor of journalism at the University and a leading figure among Oklahoma newsmen. The story is demolished by Morrissey, "David Ross Boyd," 191–99, who thinks that Boyd, in a playful mood, might have strung along the green reporter as a joke, never thinking the story would ever get printed. I find Morrissey's analysis and discussion of this matter entirely persuasive.

located," he remembered a quarter-century later. "There was not a tree or shrub in sight. All I could see was the monotonous stillness of prairie grass. . . . Behind me was a crude little town of 1,500 people and before me was a stretch of prairie on which my helpers and I were to build an institution of culture. Discouraged? Not a bit. The sight was a challenge."[37] He made his way to the Agnes Hotel, on the south side of the 100 block of West Main Street, where he booked a room. The earliest official correspondence of the University of Oklahoma listed that hotel as a return address. But Mrs. Boyd and Alice were to arrive in three weeks, and Boyd rented rooms on West Gray, where the family stayed until Christmas. Then they moved to the home of Charlie Dibble and his mother, where they boarded until the house they were building on University Boulevard was completed.[38]

Almost the very first thing that Boyd did upon his arrival in Norman was to stroll over to the First Presbyterian Church on East Gray Street and Crawford Avenue. The building had been finished and dedicated only a week before, and there were wood shavings still on the floor. Boyd found a broom and swept the place out in preparation for next day's Sabbath service. "I recall I rendered that service as my first contribution to the work of the church."[39] On October 8 he and his wife were enrolled as members of the church; and on the same day Boyd was appointed clerk of the session and delegate to the meeting of the Presbytery in El Reno later in the month. At that time he also began his long service as a ruling elder of the congregation.[40]

The man who came to Norman on that hot Saturday and who promptly walked over to sweep out the Presbyterian church was not especially typical of the people among whom he had come to live. He was a staunch Republican in a town that had just voted two to one to reject Abraham Lincoln's name and take Grover Cleveland's for their county. He was a northerner in a place settled mostly by southerners. His abolitionist upbringing had given him much different views about African Americans than those of his neighbors. He was better educated, by far, than those among whom he was about to cast his lot. In religion, his openness to the new scientific dispensations made him more liberal than most of them. "Although President Boyd became very popular with the people of Norman," Edward Everett Dale wrote more than seventy years later, "there is evidence that for the first year or so at least a few persons were a bit suspicious of this Kansas Yankee."[41]

David Ross Boyd was not a very complicated person. By no stretch of the imagina-

---

37. David Ross Boyd, "My Days as First University President: Told by Dr. David Ross Boyd to Dr. Roy Hadsell, '04, and Betty Kirk, '29," part 1, *Sooner Magazine* 2 (October 1929), 24–25.

38. This house is not to be confused with the home that the Boyds later built on the corner of University Boulevard and the present Boyd Street. That house, now known as Boyd House, was to serve as the home for many of the University's presidents. The Boyds' first home was built a few lots farther north on University Boulevard, across the street and a little south of the present McFarlin Methodist Church at 526 University Boulevard. The family moved into it in March 1893.

39. Quoted in John B. Thompson, *First Presbyterian Church, Norman, Oklahoma: Golden Anniversary, 1891–1941*, 12. See also Henry, "Religious Development of David Ross Boyd," 32.

40. Thompson, *First Presbyterian Church*, 6, 12–13.

41. Dale, "David Ross Boyd: Pioneer Educator," 17.

tion was he much of an intellectual. His strengths were not in subtle reasoning or mental dexterity. He was never a gifted scholar or a brilliant conversationalist or a flashing wit.[42] His ideas were not original. His imagination was not prone to wild and daring flights. But he was not without important strengths. Early in his life he had wedded himself to a few basic principles; and because he followed those principles without distraction or deviation, they gave his life clear direction and purpose. To some modern sophisticates these guiding articles of faith may seem like mere platitudes; but they were not platitudes to him. He believed that humans served God primarily through doing their duty. He believed that this duty required hard, concentrated, and energetic labor performed daily. He believed that such work forged character and that character made for leadership. He believed in tolerance—both for new ideas and for those persons who did not always see things his way. His tolerance, however, never led to the slightest weakening of a set of rigidly held moral truths. Boyd had a very firm sense of what was right and what was wrong. He believed that education was the chief implement that society possessed for the inculcation of this moral sense and that inculcating it was the educator's chief task. He believed that an upright and disciplined life was the first goal of true education, and his own life was an inspiring example of stern and stoic self-discipline. He was intensely practical; no detail was so small, so insignificant or trivial, that it failed to command his complete attention. Throughout his long and active life, few, if any, had any reason to doubt his absolute integrity.

It was this peculiar combination of high principle and attention to detail, this special blending of inflexible moral purpose in the name of duty with an uncanny sense of what was actually possible in the everyday world, that made David Ross Boyd so fortunate a choice for the position he now moved to fill.

~

THERE WAS PLENTY for him to do. The Regents had declared on July 2, two weeks after offering him the presidency and four days before he accepted it, that school would be open for registration on the first Monday in September and that classes would start on September 15. Boyd moved to Norman on August 6. This gave him a scant five weeks to get things ready, and there were a hundred things to do. He flew into his work with a furious energy. He must have felt that the various facets of the task were bombarding him with staggering force, that each problem was automatically an emergency. Using a cramped hotel room as an office, with almost no help from anyone else, he had to do everything at once.

Half a mile from the town, the University's building stood starkly in the August sun, not even half finished. Obviously, the new president had to find a place to hold classes. There were not many buildings in Norman in the summer of 1892 that could accommodate even a small college. Fortunately for Boyd, two Norman businessmen—P. L. Welch,

---

42. I disagree a little here with Morrissey, who attempts (not very successfully I think) to make a case for what he calls Boyd's "Humoristic Philosophy." For his view, see "David Ross Boyd," 215–21.

a broker, and Pryor Adkins, the rancher from across the river who had joined Del Larsh's scheme to enter Norman on the day of the land run—had erected a two-story building on the south side of Main Street, a block and a half west of the railroad tracks. They named it the Adkins-Welch building; but because it was constructed of Cleveland County rock, it was usually called the Rock Building. The owners had hoped to use the building to lure county government, which had established itself on the east side of the tracks at Main and Peters, over to the west side. They offered the county a year's free rent if the county commissioners would take the building and agree to a $500 rental starting in 1892; the commissioners decided to stay on the east side and rejected the offer. The owners then rented the space through the spring of 1892 for the instruction of Norman schoolchildren, one of several buildings in town where such instruction took place. Boyd inspected the building and rented the second floor, three large rooms, for $20 a month. Still optimistic about the prospects for a speedy completion of the University's own building down on the campus, Boyd rented the Rock Building only through the end of December 1892. On January 1, 1893, the county, now persuaded by the owners' promise to add an additional building for county purposes next door, was scheduled to take over the property.[43]

But a building would be of no use without teachers. The first person Boyd chose was William N. Rice, a teacher of languages, particularly Greek and Latin; the Regents announced his appointment on July 9.[44] Rice's career paralleled Boyd's own to a remarkable degree. Like Boyd, Rice was an Ohio farm boy who decided to become a teacher. He too taught in the Ohio public schools before going to college. He graduated from Ohio Wesleyan in Delaware, Ohio, in 1880, two years after Boyd had graduated from Wooster, about seventy miles to the east. Rice taught Greek and Latin at Richmond College in Richmond, Ohio, for two years and then stayed on to serve as Richmond's superintendent of schools. Like Boyd, Rice gave up his superintendency to move to Kansas. He taught for four years in the public schools there and then for three more at the Southwest Kansas College in Winfield. It was probably there that he encountered Boyd, who lived in Winfield briefly before moving the dozen miles south to Arkansas City.[45]

For someone to teach the science courses at the University, Boyd wrote to the Albert Teachers' Agency in Chicago, an employment bureau where those seeking teaching jobs and those seeking teachers were put in contact. Boyd had frequent resort to this agency during his years as president. In this case, C. J. Albert suggested a thirty-three-year-old who was to become an extremely important and occasionally extremely controversial figure in the history of the University of Oklahoma. Edwin C. DeBarr was a short and stocky man, packing almost 200 pounds onto his five-foot-six frame. He was also a man of an almost Jeffersonian range of interests. His first love was chemistry. But he also read litera-

43. Womack, *Norman: An Early History*, 98, 110, 125; Wardner, "Territorial University," 36–37.

44. Wardner, "Territorial University," 34.

45. *Norman Transcript*, September 15, 1892, 1.

ture in French and German, loved music and poetry, and was an accomplished surveyor, naturalist, pharmacist, and physicist.

DeBarr had been born in Michigan in January 1859 and educated in the public school system. Like Boyd and Rice, he had accumulated extensive experience as a teacher, principal, and superintendent, much of it before receiving his college degree. He had taught for eight years in Michigan elementary schools and for another five in high school. He graduated from Michigan's Normal School in Ypsilanti in 1886 and from the school that later became Michigan State University in Lansing in 1890. At the start of 1892 he was finishing work on another bachelor's degree, this one in pharmacy, at the University of Michigan in Ann Arbor.[46] On March 19 DeBarr was offered the chance to teach chemistry at nearby Albion College through the end of the semester. He left his mother, his invalid wife, Hattie, and their infant daughter, Helen, to take up his duties at Albion in the first week of April. The Sunday before leaving, he recorded in his diary: "Take Hattie and baby for a drive. This is baby's first drive. I shall miss Hattie & baby so much when I go to Albion." After a week by himself, he wrote: "I wish that I could see Hattie & baby to-night"; and two days later: "It is a very lonesome day, and I wish that I could be at home to-day."[47] When his duties at Albion were finally done, he quickly returned to the family at Ann Arbor and by August had received several offers through the Albert Agency. He chose the one from Boyd because he thought the Oklahoma climate would be best for his sickly wife.

On August 29 DeBarr began his arduous western trek alone. He told his diary: "Start for Norman, Ok. T[erritor]y. from Battle Creek where I leave Hattie & baby Helen, the most precious things to me in the world. Reach Chicago at 9 P.M." After spending the night and most of the next day there, he noted: "[A]t 6 P.M. I start from Chicago. All the time I think of my darlings in Mich." The next day: "Arrive in Kansas City too late for my train but take the 2nd section of the 10.45 A.M. train. Arrive at Florence to take the special train from Arkansas City to Norman." On the following day he recorded: "Reach Norman at 3 A.M. but get no bed till 4 A.M. I sleep till 8.30 A.M. Meet Pres. Boyd at 9 A.M. and take dinner with him after going to the University grounds. Prof. Rice comes on P.M. train. Meet the Regents." After working to get ready for his courses and ordering books for the library, it was his first Saturday in Oklahoma: "My first letter from Hattie comes. I wish it were she." On his first Sunday he went to President Boyd's church (where he, like Boyd, soon became a ruling elder);[48] and that afternoon: "Pres. Boyd, Prof. Rice & I take a 3 mi. walk towards the Canadian River."[49] Early the following week, DeBarr and Rice

---

46. Ibid. DeBarr's education, personal characteristics, and career are recounted on an application form in his own handwriting, Edwin DeBarr MSS, Box 1, Folder 8. Wardner gives additional information that she gleaned from an interview with DeBarr in 1938, in "Territorial University," 34–35.

47. Edwin DeBarr, "Diary," March 19, April 3, 8, and 10, 1892. The "Diary" is in the DeBarr MSS, Box 4.

48. Thompson, *First Presbyterian Church,* 6.

49. DeBarr, "Diary," August 29–31 and September 1–4, 1892.

*Edwin C. DeBarr*

found themselves a place to room together and a place to board. The tables and chairs arrived for the college, and DeBarr pitched in to set them up. Inevitably, perhaps, one of the greatest and most persistent difficulties that the University had to face entered into his consciousness: "I feel somewhat blue over the finances, but will not let Hattie know it. I wish I could see her & baby Helen."[50] He went about his work, getting ready for the students who would arrive in less than a week.

Boyd, Rice, and DeBarr were all midwestern Republicans. The Democratic minority on the Board of Regents insisted that the fourth member of the new faculty be a southern Democrat; and Leander Pitman, the secretary of the Board and one of its two Democrats, thought he knew just the right man. French Stanton Evans Amos (named after an uncle) was born on New Year's Day, 1871, seven miles south of the Mason-Dixon line in Marion County, West Virginia, the son of a Confederate veteran. The family moved to south Texas when French was eleven. When he was only seventeen, he was awarded a bachelor's degree from Centenary College, a short-lived Methodist school in Lampasas. The president of the college persuaded the youngster to stay on as an instructor. Four years later Centenary gave him a master's degree.

In the meantime, French Amos's father and an uncle participated in the Oklahoma land run of April 1889. After staking claims of their own and buying the claims of others, they ended with a good-sized farm in what is today Nichols Hills in northern Oklahoma City. One of the neighbors was Regent Pitman, who became a good friend of French Amos's father. Pitman suggested that French Amos apply for work at Norman; and although he was only twenty-one and likely to be younger than most of the students, Boyd hired him to teach English, history, and civics.[51]

Perhaps the most noteworthy fact about the University of Oklahoma's first faculty was its youthfulness. Boyd, the eldest of the four, had just turned thirty-nine. Rice and De-Barr were in their mid-thirties; Amos was still four months away from his twenty-second

50. Ibid., September 6, 1892.

51. Amos never disguised the politics behind his appointment. See French S. E. Amos, "Early Days in the University of Oklahoma," in Vertical File: "History of O.U. (1890–1908)," 14. Near the end of his life, he recounted the story of his hiring in much the same way; see Frank L. Dennis, "The Professor Graduates," *Daily Oklahoman*, June 19, 1938, D1.

*Professors William Rice,
David Ross Boyd, French Amos,
and Edwin DeBarr, reunited forty years
after the University's founding*

birthday. Moreover, only young Amos had advanced beyond the bachelor's degree. All four had earned their degrees at tiny, relatively new colleges; only DeBarr, at Lansing and Ann Arbor, had gotten a taste of the life of a modern, large, and well-equipped university. Except for Amos, the great bulk of their educational experience had been at the high-school level or below. Three of the four had been school superintendents or principals. The Regents, having hired Boyd at $2,400, paid Rice and DeBarr $1,500 each, and Amos $900.[52]

By the time Edwin DeBarr climbed wearily off the train at 3 A.M. on the first day of September 1892, discovered that his luggage had been lost, made his way through the darkness to the hotel, "and there had a fine breakfast" before finding a place to grab his four hours of sleep,[53] Boyd and Amos were already in town. Rice came later that day. The four men (along with Mrs. Boyd and daughter Alice, who just arrived from Arkansas City) met together for the first time over dinner at the home of L. J. Edwards, near the present Acers and N.E. 12th Streets. After dinner the four men walked through the dusty streets to the Rock Building, climbed the steps to the second floor, and surveyed the scene. With four teachers and only three rooms, it was obvious that two classes would have to meet in the same place. The first real "faculty meeting" took place in Boyd's rooms,

52. Gittinger, *University of Oklahoma,* 9. The faculty was paid in "warrants," which local merchants discounted slightly; therefore, their actual pay was somewhat less than their contracts stipulated.

53. Edwin DeBarr, interview with Lida White, Norman, March 1935, in Lida White MSS, Box 9.

at what is now 303 W. Gray Street. It began with the sharing of what DeBarr called "the biggest watermelon I had ever seen." Boyd had bought it from a passing farmer.[54]

The watermelon gathering was followed by a series of daylong meetings in Boyd's rooms. The students were to arrive in a little more than a week, and there were many things to arrange. One of them was the matter of what precisely the students should be taught once they got to Norman.

~

THE CURRICULUM HURRIEDLY ESTABLISHED by the four young faculty members in early September 1892 was influenced by a pair of important but embarrassingly contradictory considerations. In the first place, the territorial legislature had written a very ambitious plan of instruction into the original law of December 1890. To realize its lofty purposes, the University of Oklahoma, according to the lawmakers, should consist of a department of arts, a department of letters, and a department devoted to the training of teachers. In addition, the Board of Regents was authorized "to establish such professional and other colleges or departments when in their judgment they may be deemed necessary and proper."[55] The legislature blithely went on to specify what should be taught in each of the divisions: "The college department of arts shall embrace courses of instruction in mathematical, physical, and natural sciences, with their application to the industrial arts, such as agriculture, mechanics, engineering, mining and metallurgy, manufactures, architecture and commerce."[56] The legislators in Guthrie were less clear about the second college or department: letters. They wrote that it should include "such branches . . . as shall be necessary to proper fitness of the pupils in the scientific and practical courses for their chosen pursuits and in military tactics." Perhaps realizing that they had not drawn a very sharp distinction between these two divisions of the University and that they had also left out some traditional subjects, they stated later in the law: "The college of letters shall be co-existent with the college of arts, and shall embrace a liberal course of instruction in language, literature and philosophy." That the normal college or department would concern itself with "the theory and art of teaching . . . in the common schools" seemed evident enough.

It must have been painfully obvious to the four faculty members that, no matter how

54. Accounts of these days in early September 1892 vary and contradict one another, although the details are not terribly important. Compare the stories given in Womack, *Norman: An Early History,* 126; Wardner, "Territorial University," 37; Gittinger, *University of Oklahoma,* 12; DeBarr, interview with Lida White; and Dennis, "The Professor Graduates."

55. *Statutes of Oklahoma, 1893,* 1166–67.

56. Ibid. The inclusion in the legislation of agriculture, mining, and metallurgy is something of a puzzle, particularly in view of the fact that the territorial legislature had created a separate agricultural and mechanical college at Stillwater. Dorothy Gittinger Wardner and her father, Roy Gittinger, however, seem to have discovered an entirely plausible solution to the mystery. They suggest that the Oklahoma lawmakers simply used the legislation establishing the University of Nebraska as a model, despite the fact that Nebraska was a land-grant college (requiring instruction in agriculture and the mechanic arts in order to receive funds under the Morrill Act of 1862) and the University of Oklahoma was not. See Wardner, "Territorial University," 14–15; and Gittinger, *University of Oklahoma,* 5.

the jumbled directive from the legislature was to be interpreted, its dictates were far beyond their abilities to fulfill. Four men, however gifted and energetic, could scarcely be expected to operate three colleges. In addition, a second consideration tempered the legislature's ambitious scheme as the men sitting in David Ross Boyd's rooms on Gray Street pondered over the curriculum. The four professors surely must have understood with excruciating clarity exactly what sort of students would be coming to the University. After all, many settlements in Oklahoma Territory still had no high school in the fall of 1892. Only a little over three years after the land run, moreover, no high school in the Territory had existed long enough to have seen any young man or woman through to graduation.[57] Some of the students who would be coming to Norman might have had no formal schooling at the secondary level at all. At the very least, their training would probably have suffered from serious interruptions incurred during the processes of migration and resettlement.

It was perfectly plain to the first faculty, therefore, that the University of Oklahoma, like many other American universities and colleges, would have to start a "Preparatory Department" to train prospective students up to the point where they were ready to embark upon actual college work. The curriculum that they devised encompassed the basic subjects that could be found in most well-equipped high schools in settled regions of the country and was designed so that a student entering with minimal training and starting from scratch could be ready to begin actual college work in three years. In mathematics, for example, such a student would study basic arithmetic during the first year, algebra the second, and geometry the third. In natural science, the beginning student would study "the human body" during the second semester of the first year and move to geography and botany in the second year and to physics in the third. Similar progressions were outlined for English and Latin.[58] The arriving students were to have an interview with President Boyd and then be placed into the various sequences at levels appropriate to their previous training.

In addition to the coursework to be offered through the Preparatory Department at the high-school level, the faculty shamelessly announced a preposterous list of classes in the "Collegiate Department." These four men proposed four programs of study: classical, philosophical, scientific, and English. The first *Catalogue* bravely listed no fewer than ten courses in mathematics, eight in chemistry, six in physics, and four each in physiology, zoology, and botany. Work was also "offered" in German, Greek, French, and Latin, in psychology and geology and astronomy, in the philosophy of history and the history of philosophy, in both English and American literature, in political economy and civic law. If, by some miracle, real college students had appeared in September 1892 and by some

57. For a good survey, see E. Sherman Nunn, "A History of Education in Oklahoma Territory"; also see R. R. Tompkins, "The Development of Secondary Education in Oklahoma," chap. 3. A sense of the primitive conditions of early Oklahoma education can be derived from Frank A. Balyeat, "Rural Schoolhouses in Early Oklahoma," *Chronicles of Oklahoma* 22 (1944): 315–23.

58. *University of Oklahoma Catalogue, 1892–93,* 7–11.

catastrophic bad luck had demanded instruction in each of the courses mentioned in the University's official *Catalogue*, Professor Edwin DeBarr would have been responsible for about thirty different courses, not counting the four years of German that he might also be assigned or his high-school teaching in the Preparatory Department. None of the four professors in Norman was qualified to offer the ambitious courses being promised by the *Catalogue* in English and American literature. We may feel certain that it was only the knowledge that few, if any, college-level students would actually enroll that led them to propose the impossible curriculum that they so boldly announced.

~

THE TASK OF RECRUITING STUDENTS absorbed David Ross Boyd from the first and would require enormous energy from him throughout his years as president of the University of Oklahoma. From the first week after his arrival in Norman, Boyd began flooding territorial newspapers with advertisements for the new school. Since French Amos was the first employee to reach Norman, Boyd (who was still living at the Agnes Hotel) enlisted him to help write a four-page brochure. Amos recalled the sweltering August work in Boyd's room ("sans desk, sans electric fans, sans . . . almost everything") and how Sam Crawford set the type by hand and Ed Ingle ran it off on the *Norman Transcript*'s press.[59] The brochure was mailed to anyone who expressed the smallest interest in the University and to those throughout the Territory in a position to influence young people to enroll. Soon Boyd would be crisscrossing the prairie by horse and buggy, speaking in small towns, patiently and endlessly explaining to the youth of Oklahoma that they would find a warm welcome at the new school at Norman.

The message of Boyd's recruitment publicity, as might be expected, was that the University would accept any serious young man or woman who was "willing to work." The president took special pains to emphasize that the instruction to be offered in Norman would not be too difficult: "Knowing well that the disadvantages incident to the settlement of a new country have debarred many from the privileges of school for some time," he assured them, "the university has established a general PREPARATORY COURSE of three years, which is designed to give about such training as would be received in a well conducted high school." And if Boyd was careful to stress the accessibility of the instruction, he also knew how important it was to reassure Oklahomans, both students and parents, about the expenses involved. By decree of the legislature, tuition was to be free, and "the cost of living is as low in Norman as in any place in the Territory." In one advertisement that tried to recruit students for the University's second year, President Boyd practically begged: "It is hoped that no one will conclude that he is too poor or too old to take a course of study until after he has gone over the matter in correspondence with the president, or some member of the faculty."[60]

59. Amos, "Early Days in the University of Oklahoma," 3.

60. *Norman Transcript*, April 22, 1893 (Special Fourth Anniversary Issue), 12. The first *Catalogue* gives the estimate of

*The first students, of 1892–93, posing in the Rock Building on Main Street*

A note in the *Norman Transcript* indicates the lengths to which Boyd was willing to go: "Our people have responded nobly to the call for accommodations for boarding students here but there is still a demand for more facilities," wrote editor Ingle. "Everyone who can take care of students should promptly report to Prof. Boyd, who is anxious to make arrangements for the accommodations of all who may come."[61] The feverish attempt to bring students to Norman—even to the extent of operating a housing bureau out of the president's office—of course reflects Boyd's determination to make the place succeed. But it also shows something about his educational philosophy and his democratic instincts. "From the very beginning," French Amos believed, "it was the idea of the university fixed by Doctor Boyd . . . that every applicant for advanced education should have the opportunity to obtain one, no matter what his financial status."[62]

At last the day came. Early on the morning of September 15, 1892, fifty-seven young men and women appeared at the entrance to the Rock Building on Main Street. Someone opened the front door. They climbed nervously to the second floor, where President Boyd and the faculty were waiting. Eighteen years later, Professor William Rice recalled the scene:

> Up the steps of the old stone building come the University students to enroll. All are very quiet, some painfully bashful, and not a few extremely awkward. Most of them are the unspoiled products of pioneer life, without pretension and without conventionalism. But, best of all, they are in dead earnest and feel they are facing a great opportunity. After a short conference with President Boyd, in which they make known

---

"from $10 to $13 per month" for room and board and promises: "Clubs will be organized at which the expense will be very much reduced," 23.

61. *Norman Transcript*, September 9, 1892, 1.

62. Dennis, "The Professor Graduates."

their attainments and deficiencies, he gives them a tentative list of subjects which it is presumed they will be able to pursue successfully.[63]

Each student then met the appropriate teacher, enrolled in a suitable class, and received the first assignment. Academic work at the University of Oklahoma had begun.

63. William N. Rice, "The University in the Old Stone Building," *Sooner Yearbook, 1911,* 15–17. According to legend, probably passed on orally, the first student to register was Marion Donehew of Norman, later of Pauls Valley. His name is sometimes spelled "Donahew." Not much is known of him, but the often-reproduced photograph of him as a mature man, holding school books, a pencil, and a satchel, was obviously staged long after 1892. A group picture of the original student body shows him as a youngster.

CHAPTER III

# Attracting Students and Building a Faculty, 1892–1902

Although only fifty-seven students appeared on that first September morning in 1892, additional students kept coming. By the end of the academic year, in June 1893, the new university boasted an enrollment of 119.[1] As it happened, not a single one was ready for college-level work. President David Ross Boyd placed all of them in the Preparatory Department. No fewer than 82 of the 119 reported themselves as being from Norman, but it is difficult to know how many were actually from town and how many had come from other places but now listed themselves as residents. A dozen students arrived from the neighboring towns of Moore, Tecumseh, and Lexington; and another eleven came from Oklahoma City or from Britton, a small town that would later be incorporated into Oklahoma City. Four students in the first class came from the nearby Indian Territory communities of Alex and Purcell. With one exception, the other ten were from scattered Oklahoma towns, none of which contributed more than a single student. The exception was O. M. Ball, who came from Charlottesville, Virginia.

No doubt the most remarkable fact about the University's pioneer class related to gender. At the precise moment when the United States commissioner of education was observing that "collegiate education is still principally confined to men,"[2] exactly half of the entering class at the University of Oklahoma was female.[3] This was a quite remarkable statistic. In the nation as a whole in 1892, only 32 percent of American college students were women; but that number included many who were studying in all-female colleges.[4]

1. A list of their names appears in the *University of Oklahoma Catalogue, 1892–1893*, 26–28, and is conveniently reproduced in Gittinger, *University of Oklahoma*, 178–81.

2. *Annual Report of the United States Commissioner of Education, 1892–1893*, 17.

3. There were sixty women and fifty-nine men (*Catalogue, 1892–93*, 28).

4. Of 72,460 college students in 1892, 49,100 (67.8%) were male; 23,360 (32.2%) were female (*Annual Report of the United States Commissioner of Education, 1892–1893*, 18). An excellent older study is Mabel Newcomer, *A Century of Higher Education for American Women*; see also the able modern discussions: Barbara Miller Solomon, *In the Company of Educated Women: A History of Women and Higher Education in America*; and Lynn D. Gordon, *Gender and Higher Education in the Progressive Era*.

If one confined the count to public institutions of higher education, it emerged that males accounted for 81 percent and females 19 percent of the student population.[5] Thus if the fledgling University of Oklahoma did not enroll the largest percentage of women students in the entire country, it was certainly among the two or three public institutions with the highest record in this regard.

Two reasons help to account for the University's extremely high percentage of women students. First, women seeking higher education in public institutions was a much more common phenomenon in the western states than in the nation as a whole. Among college students in the West, 31.3 percent were women. Oklahoma, therefore, was located in the region where female entrance into public colleges and universities was the most usual.[6] Second, while it is true that women constituted less than one-fifth of the students in public higher education, it is also true that young women greatly outnumbered young men in public high schools in America. In fact, 59.4 percent of all public high school students were female.[7] Thus the impressive percentage of women in Norman might be another indication that, when it opened, the University of Oklahoma was more like a good-quality high school than an actual college.

Another feature of the entering class was less satisfying. Although more than 18,000 African Americans lived in Indian Territory in 1890 and around 3,000 more in Oklahoma Territory (numbers that combined to make up almost 4 percent of the population),[8] not a single African American attempted to enroll in the new university. In 1900, when African Americans in the two territories numbered 55,684 (7 percent of the population),[9] the school had still never admitted a single African American man or woman. It would fail to do so for another half-century. In view of the racial attitudes in both of the territories, this outcome was not entirely surprising.

Black children were carefully segregated in the public education systems of the Five Tribes except in the case of the Seminoles.[10] In Oklahoma Territory between 1891 and 1897 each county could decide for itself whether to practice racial segregation in its lower schools, but the law was silent about the three colleges that the territorial legislature had created in 1891. Theoretically, therefore, it was possible until 1897 for an African Ameri-

5. *Annual Report of the United States Commissioner of Education, 1892–1893*, 18.

6. Ibid. The commissioner stated: "In fact the number of female students in public universities and colleges is insignificant in all except the North Central and Western States."

7. Ibid., 15. The commissioner attributed this imbalance to the fact that many young men sought work after elementary school and many others entered vocational training programs. Interestingly, *private* high schools, many of which served as college-preparatory institutions, had 55 percent male students.

8. Estimates of Oklahoma's African American population vary; see Arthur L. Tolson, *The Black Oklahomans: A History, 1541–1972*, 53–55. I am relying on the government's figures as reported in U.S. Bureau of the Census, *Negro Population, 1790–1915*, 786–87.

9. U.S. Bureau of the Census, *Negro Population, 1790–1915*, 786.

10. Ollie Everett Hatcher, "The Development of Legal Controls in Racial Segregation in the Public Schools of Oklahoma, 1865–1952." For the racial situation in Oklahoma Territory educational institutions, see Frank A. Balyeat, "Segregation in the Public Schools of Oklahoma Territory," *Chronicles of Oklahoma* 39 (1961): 180–92.

can man or woman to apply for admission to the University of Oklahoma. As far as can be determined, none did.[11] In 1897 the territorial legislature responded to the Supreme Court's "separate but equal" ruling in the landmark case of *Plessy v. Ferguson*,[12] by abolishing the county-option system in favor of required territory-wide segregation of African Americans in education and by establishing the Colored Agricultural and Normal University of Oklahoma, at Langston.[13]

There is evidence that the question of admitting African American students to the University received considerable attention in Norman before the law of 1897 made it illegal. Among the four members of the first faculty, one was a strident racist. Despite coming from Michigan and being a Republican, Edwin DeBarr admitted to an irrational fear of black people.[14] Opposing the racist views of DeBarr was William N. Rice, a Republican from Ohio and Kansas, who approved of mixed-race schools. David Ross Boyd, the son of the Ohio abolitionist and underground railroad conductor, also favored integration. Evidently there were some spirited discussions of the issue during the first year of the University's existence. But it must be remembered that those discussions took place in an all-white town that had been settled largely by southern Democrats who were extremely hostile to any gesture in the direction of "race mixing."

One curious incident illustrates these feelings. Among the wave of black migrants into Kansas during the 1870s and 1880s was the family of Alexander Work.[15] The family settled near Arkansas City; and a son, Monroe Work (having postponed his education for family and financial reasons until he was twenty-three), enrolled at the Arkansas City high school while Boyd was superintendent. Work grew discouraged and went to tell Boyd that he was leaving school. But Boyd, recognizing that Work was a young man of extraordinary intelligence and scholarly potential, persuaded him to stay. He also loaned him a hundred dollars so that he could finish school. When graduation day arrived, Superintendent Boyd loaned Work his own wedding suit to wear to the commencement ceremony. One morning shortly after Boyd moved to Norman to open the University of Oklahoma, Monroe Work appeared in town to repay Boyd's hundred dollars. Not realizing that Boyd was in Guthrie or that Mrs. Boyd was away from home, Work began wandering around the dusty town inquiring after President Boyd's whereabouts.

11. Hatcher, "The Development of Legal Controls," chap. 3. See also John T. Hubbell, "Racial Desegregation at the University of Oklahoma, 1946–1950," chap. 1.

12. 163 U.S. 537 (1896).

13. Zella Black Patterson, *Langston University: A History*, chap. 2.

14. In March 1935 DeBarr spoke frankly of his personal attitude with an interviewer who summarized his remarks: "The ground DeBarr took was this: He being from Michigan was unused to negroes. He said the first one he ever saw scared him into convulsions." Apparently, as a small child, DeBarr was sitting on a fence when a rail broke. "Uncle Dorsey caught me and I had convulsions. It took a year to pacify me. When I see a negro I still think of it." DeBarr also recalled: "A negro in Michigan gave me more trouble than all the other pupils put together." See Lida White, interview with Edwin DeBarr, March 1935, 2, in Lida White MSS, Box 9. Ms. White was a longtime Norman teacher who embarked on a series of interviews under the auspices of the federal WPA program during the 1930s.

15. On the general phenomenon, see Nell Irvin Painter, *Exodusters: Black Migration to Kansas after Reconstruction*.

Instantly, the rumor that a black man had come to enroll at the University of Oklahoma swept through Norman. Professor Rice said that he did not see why not—the laws of the Territory, after all, did not prohibit it. An excited crowd of townspeople, however, did not see things in quite the same way; by nightfall some of them had burned Boyd in effigy. In the meantime, Work had boarded the train and headed for Boyd's hotel in Guthrie. Of course he was not allowed to register in the hotel because of his race, but the two had breakfast together. Work repaid Boyd the money and offered interest, which Boyd refused to take. While chatting over their meal, Work indicated that he was eager to continue his education but did not see how he could afford to do it, given his financial circumstances. Boyd immediately telegraphed his friend William Rainey Harper, president of the University of Chicago, asking if some job could be found for this extremely gifted and ambitious young man. Harper telegraphed back that he had such a job. Boyd handed Work back the hundred dollars, and the young man went to Chicago, where he eventually earned a Ph.D.[16] After Boyd returned to town and heard what had happened when it was thought that an African American wanted to enter the University, he undoubtedly realized that, whatever his private views, it might be unwise to press them at the moment.[17] As DeBarr recalled it forty-five years later, "The populace of Oklahoma were, for the most part, averse to mixed schools. Rice, being from Kansas, approved them. Boyd believed in them too, at first, then backed out."[18]

Despite the rigid exclusion of one segment of Oklahoma's population, the University experienced gratifying growth over the next decade. In part this increase was the natural result of the astounding increase in the population of the two territories: between 1890 and 1900 that population more than tripled, skyrocketing from 258,000 to 790,000.[19] In part the surge in the number of students coming to Norman was attributable to the restoration of national prosperity after the catastrophic depression of the mid-1890s. By late in the decade it seemed apparent that good times were back, and farm families that had once been unable to send a promising son or daughter to college could now afford to do it. Finally, in August 1899 the Regents took an early step toward the eventual union of the two territories: upon the motion of Governor Cassius M. Barnes, they directed the University to admit applicants from Indian Territory on the same (tuition-free) basis as applicants from Oklahoma Territory. In a move that revealed starkly the marked difference between

16. By the time of his death in 1945, Monroe N. Work was known as one of the leading scholars of the black experience in the United States. For his remarkable story, see Linda O. McMurry, *Recorder of the Black Experience: A Biography of Monroe Nathan Work*. Work is best known for his massive book *A Bibliography of the Negro in Africa and America*.

17. The Monroe Work incident is told in E. E. Dale, "David Ross Boyd," in the Edward Everett Dale MSS, Box 212, Folder 7, 28; and in White's interview with DeBarr, 2. A published version is Dale, "David Ross Boyd: Pioneer Educator," 17. In 1903 Boyd tried to get Monroe Work appointed as president of Langston University. See Morrissey, "David Ross Boyd and the University of Oklahoma," 202–205.

18. White, interview with DeBarr, 2.

19. Morris, Goins, and McReynolds, *Historical Atlas of Oklahoma*, No. 75.

popular attitudes toward Native Americans and those toward African Americans, the University invited the citizens of Indian Territory "to avail themselves of this splendid opportunity to give their youth the benefits and advantages of a first class education."[20] The citizens of Indian Territory responded with alacrity: during the academic year 1898–99, only six students had come from there; by 1900–1901 that number was up to twenty; and by 1903–1904 it stood at fifty-six.[21] All these factors meant that by the close of the academic year 1901–1902 the student body had tripled in size to 359 students.

As noteworthy as the growth in numbers, moreover, was the fact that within ten years the University was drawing its students from a much wider area. By the end of the first decade, the percentage of students listing Norman as their hometown dropped from 70 to around 45. Whereas in 1892 only fifteen towns in Oklahoma Territory had sent a student to study in Norman, ten years later students arrived from sixty-five Oklahoma towns. A dozen students came from four other states. Ten years after the school had opened, the Preparatory Department was still accounting for around 60 percent of the University's enrollment. But eighty-seven students were now enrolled in the College of Arts and Sciences, twenty-two in Pharmacy, and thirty-eight in Fine Arts (two-thirds of those studying piano); another thirty-two were in the Business School. Three students were doing postgraduate work in various fields. The admirable percentage of women students dipped slightly from 50 to 41 percent, although it was already possible to discern some subtle patterns. Women still made up 40 percent of the Preparatory Department. But they were only 13 percent of the pharmacy/medicine program and only 28 percent of the business students. However, 89 percent of those studying the genteel pursuits of voice or piano were women.[22]

Even though a college education was still the privilege of a very narrow segment of the nation's population, the years between 1890 and 1900 were ones of healthy growth in American colleges and universities generally, especially considering the devastating national depression. In 1890 there were roughly 157,000 college students in the United States, only 1.8 percent of the population between the ages of eighteen and twenty-four. By 1900 there were 238,000 college students or 2.3 percent of the college-age population. Thus, in tripling the student body during its first decade, the University of Oklahoma grew at a much faster rate than the national average.[23] The expansion of the University of Oklahoma's student population was roughly comparable to that being experienced by both the University of Texas and the University of Kansas, however, and also roughly

20. Regents' "Minutes," August 1, 1899. The greater tolerance for Indians than for blacks was characteristic of white racial thought nationally. As the historian Brian W. Dippie put it, "it was the Indian who was invited to join in the affairs of the nation, even to intermarry with the white race, while the black was consistently shunned" (*The Vanishing American: White Attitudes and U.S. Indian Policy*, 253).

21. See the *University Catalogues* for 1898–99, 1900–1901, and 1903–1904.

22. These figures may be distilled from the listing of the student body in *University Catalogue, 1902–1903*, 93–105.

23. U.S. Bureau of the Census, *Historical Statistics of the United States, from Colonial Times to 1970*, 383.

comparable to the increase in the population of the two territories.[24]

Obviously, this rapid growth was to require substantial adjustments during the University's first decade. From 1892 to 1902 the University of Oklahoma, despite the depression and despite the continuing pressure of political interference from the territorial capital in Guthrie, managed to accomplish a good deal toward becoming a respectable institution of higher education. And nowhere were the dramatic differences between 1892 and 1902 more obvious or important than in the growth of the University's faculty, a growth not only in sheer numbers but in genuine quality as well.

~

TWO MEMBERS OF THE ORIGINAL FACULTY left Norman almost at once, but it would be hard to argue that their departures constituted serious losses for the University. In both cases President Boyd was able to replace them with men who were abler and whose long tenure at the University of Oklahoma was to provide a beneficial continuity to instruction. William Rice, the first to go, was a victim of politics. In March 1893 Grover Cleveland became president of the United States, the only Democrat in the White House during the whole territorial history of Oklahoma. He naturally appointed the only Democrat to serve as a governor of Oklahoma Territory, William C. Renfrow, a Norman banker and businessman.[25] Renfrow's elevation may have had something to do with the fact that it was he, back in 1890, who had first proposed that the county in which he lived be named for the very man who now appointed him governor. Renfrow had been born in North Carolina, had fought for the Confederacy, and had come to Norman from Arkansas. He could hardly have been expected to keep Rice, a Republican and a man who had no particular objection to admitting African Americans to the University located in the governor's all-white hometown. Rice left at the end of the 1892–93 academic year. The real question is why Renfrow did not also remove DeBarr and Boyd. The former case might be accounted for by DeBarr's essentially Democratic position on the race issue. In the latter case, Renfrow was undoubtedly motivated by admiration for Boyd's guidance of the University and by a genuine friendship that had developed over the previous year—the two men got along famously. And besides, Professor DeBarr, President Boyd, and Governor Renfrow all worshiped side by side every Sunday at Norman's First Presbyterian Church.[26]

French Amos, of course, was in no political danger from the presence of a fellow Democrat in Guthrie. He stayed at the University through its second and then through its third

---

24. Texas, for example, increased its student body between 1892–93 and 1902–1903 from 353 to 1,086. See H. Y. Benedict, *A Source Book Relating to the History of the University of Texas*, 806. For Kansas's enrollment during this period, see Clifford S. Griffin, *The University of Kansas: A History*, 116, 242.

25. James F. Morgan, "William Cary Renfrow, Governor of Oklahoma Territory, 1893–1897," in LeRoy H. Fischer, ed., *Territorial Governors of Oklahoma*, 46–65.

26. That he could be a hard-headed and ruthless partisan politician is shown by the fact that Governor Renfrow quickly appointed Democrats to the presidencies of all the other state colleges. See Gittinger, "University Reorganizations of 1908 and 1911," 2–3.

year, leaving in the spring of 1895. Amos's most notable achievement as a faculty member came in December 1894, when he organized one of his history classes to form the Oklahoma Historical Society. Under Amos's urging, Boyd applied for a charter from the territorial legislature, which was granted in January 1895. The collection made by Amos and his students was combined with a much larger one begun two years earlier in Kingfisher by the Oklahoma Press Association. This depository for official territorial publications, many early newspapers, and other documents was housed in a room in the University building in Norman; it might have remained a part of the University had Amos stayed on the faculty.[27] But French Amos was a restless spirit. He left the University, still a young man, to take over a small Cherokee school in Vinita. When that failed, he became a newspaperman, a political insider in Democrat circles, and a personal secretary to Governor Lee Cruce from 1910 to 1913. After serving as Vinita's city manager, he returned to Norman in 1925 to teach government and stayed until his retirement in 1938.[28]

The responsibility for replacing Rice and Amos, and for all other replacements and additions to the faculty, fell entirely on President Boyd. He might ask others for suggestions and opinions, but in the end he was the one who selected the members of the faculty.[29] As has been noted, he regularly used the C. J. Albert Teachers' Agency in Chicago, the employment agency that had sent Edwin DeBarr to the University. Boyd called upon Albert often during his presidency, sometimes going to Chicago to interview candidates, sometimes just trusting Albert's choices. "I am needed here," he wrote Albert in June 1903, "so I am expecting to employ persons you recommend and am depending on your judgment."[30] Albert mainly placed high-school not college teachers, however, and Boyd hoped to keep the relationship a secret. In 1904 he wrote a sharp note to Albert: "[I]t will be a great disadvantage to us to have any information given out that would let it become known that any member of our faculty was employed through a teachers agency. . . . I fear it would result harmfully to the University and to those members of the faculty. I trust you have not given any publicity to these transactions of ours."[31]

Boyd had two essential criteria in mind as he chose his faculty. In the first place, it was important to him that they come from the most prestigious institutions of higher education. "The thing to be considered here," he confided to Albert, "is the lack of confidence there is in the instruction in so young an institution. We have to overcome this difficulty and when we can place before the public in our catalog the names of men trained in insti-

---

27. Emil L. Fraker, *Oklahoma Historical Society: Semi-Centennial of Oklahoma Issue;* and Fred S. Standley, "The Oklahoma Historical Society, 1893–1943," chap. 2. In January 1902 the materials in Norman were removed to the Carnegie Library in Oklahoma City and in December 1917 to the State Capitol Building. The collection was then housed in a special building on the Capitol grounds, which was opened in November 1930. If the collection had remained at the University, of course, it would probably have been completely destroyed by the fire in January 1903.

28. Dennis, "The Professor Graduates," D1.

29. For Boyd's methods in choosing faculty members, see Morrissey, "David Ross Boyd," 62–68.

30. David Ross Boyd to C. J. Albert, June 9, 1903, David Ross Boyd Presidential MSS, Box 1, Folder 4.

31. Cited in Morrissey, "David Ross Boyd," 67, as David Ross Boyd to C. J. Alberts [sic], January 18, 1904.

tutions of national reputation it is of great value to us."[32] Boyd's second requirement was that his professors be devoted to teaching. Many years later he reminisced about how he picked the faculty: "I received many applications to teach. These I first answered asking them what their motives were in coming here. Too often the reply was that the applicant wanted to do research work or to write. These I didn't even consider. What I wanted was teachers, men and women who would be willing to devote all of their energies to developing the fiercely earnest young students who had enrolled."[33]

~

AFTER REPLACING WILLIAM RICE with James Anderson, a Ph.D. graduate of Johns Hopkins who remained for only two years, Boyd settled upon Joseph Francis Paxton, who had earned an M.A. from Harvard. Paxton fulfilled both of Boyd's expectations. Not only had he come from the most prestigious school in the United States, but his entire professional life was devoted to his work in the classroom. Affable, gregarious, and serene (at least one of his colleagues thought him "lazy"[34]), Paxton was capable of stirring himself on behalf of the library and, occasionally, on behalf of his own modest salary. But his real passions were Latin and Greek, and he shared them with two generations of Oklahoma undergraduates until he died in June 1939.[35] During the academic year 1900–1901, when Paxton took a leave of absence, Boyd hired James W. Sturgis, a steady and congenial Latinist who had earned an M.A. from the University of Michigan. The twenty-nine-year-old Sturgis was able to stay on even after Paxton's return, and he remained for his whole career. When he retired in 1943 at seventy-two, he was the longest-serving professor at the University.[36]

To replace French Amos, Boyd chose a man who was to develop into one of the most important figures in the early history of the University of Oklahoma. James Shannon Buchanan was born in Franklin, Tennessee, in 1864 to a planter family that had deep roots in Tennessee history. At the time of his birth, his eighteen-year-old brother John was off fighting for the Confederacy. Young James graduated from Cumberland University in Lebanon, Tennessee, in 1885 and became principal of a small rural school in a place called Cornersville. Meanwhile, his brother John, the Confederate veteran, was a rising star in Tennessee politics. The rural Democrats nominated him as their candidate for governor in 1891; riding on a tide of southern populism, he swamped both the Republican and the Prohibitionist, garnering 57 percent of the vote.[37] John Buchanan rose to power

32. Cited in Morrissey, "David Ross Boyd," 64, as David Ross Boyd to C. J. Alberts [sic], June 17, 1903.

33. Boyd, "My Days as First University President," *Sooner Magazine* 2 (January 1930): 133.

34. Vernon L. Parrington to Julia Parrington, quoted in Hall, *V. L. Parrington*, 148.

35. See Paxton's obituary in *Oklahoma Daily*, June 13, 1939.

36. Sturgis earned a Ph.D. from Michigan in 1910. See his obituary in *Sooner Magazine* 20 (April 1948): 21.

37. On John Price Buchanan (1847–1930), see Robert Sobel, ed., *Biographical Directory of the Governors of the United States, 1789–1978*, 3:1490.

*Joseph Francis Paxton*

by repeating the slogans of that ancient but abiding hero of Tennessee Democrats Andrew Jackson; and like Jackson himself, Buchanan believed that winners were entitled to distribute the spoils. Suddenly the governor's little brother, the twenty-seven-year-old principal at Cornersville, found himself the assistant state superintendent of schools. He moved to Nashville with his brother, did a little lecturing at Watkins Institute, and learned a lot about practical politics. He rose with his brother and fell with him. When John failed to handle a series of riots by miners and convicts, he was defeated in 1893. His brother James left political office but stayed in Nashville to do some graduate work in history at Vanderbilt University. At the end of the year, the unmarried Buchanan decided to try his chances in the West. He took a job teaching history at the Central Normal School in Edmond, Oklahoma. One year later, in the fall of 1895, he came to Norman to take over French Amos's job.[38] He once told a friend in the English Department that he arrived thinking he would stay a year or two "for the experience."[39] James S. Buchanan was to remain connected with the University of Oklahoma until the day he died, thirty-five years later.

Whether Buchanan, the southern Democrat, was hired under pressure from Governor Renfrow and the new Democratic Regents or whether Boyd made the decision on his own (perhaps aiming to please the governor and the Regents) is unclear. In any case, Buchanan came from Edmond to Norman to teach American history. He did so with considerable verve. His lectures were largely the traditional straight political history, and his idol, naturally, was Andrew Jackson of Tennessee.[40] Indeed, Buchanan had a lifelong fascination with Jackson, and the scant research he did was devoted to that heroic figure. The new history professor was extraordinarily popular. At Buchanan's funeral in 1930, President William Bennett Bizzell acknowledged Buchanan's preeminence in that respect:

> I think all of his associates, who are assembled here today, will concede that he was the most popular man among us. Students everywhere affectionately called him "Uncle Buck." Into this phrase they reflected their affection and their admiration for the man who had guided their intellectual lives during their college days or who had counseled

38. On James S. Buchanan, see the various reminiscences and addresses in William Bennett Bizzell et al., *An Appreciation of James Shannon Buchanan by William Bennett Bizzell and Others;* see also "James Shannon Buchanan," *Chronicles of Oklahoma* 8 (1930): 353–54.

39. Theodore H. Brewer, " 'Uncle Buck' as I Knew Him," in Bizzell et al., *An Appreciation of James Shannon Buchanan*, 19.

40. Buchanan's lecture notes survive in the James Shannon Buchanan Collection, Western History Collections, University of Oklahoma, Box 1, Folders 1–11.

*James Shannon Buchanan*

with them from time to time about their problems and their aspirations. Doctor Buchanan was one of the kindest men I ever knew.[41]

"No one would call him particularly brilliant," admitted one close friend;[42] and another agreed that "he was not an original thinker, and perhaps not a great scholar in the technical sense of the word."[43] But his stature in the community never rested on brilliance or scholarship. It rested on steady common sense, a genuine interest in students and colleagues, a reputation for integrity and generosity, a certain talent for public speaking, an instinctive political sense, and, above all, an enormous capacity for friendship. Everywhere he went, Buchanan made friends. "One of his outstanding qualities was that of friendship," remembered a colleague in the sciences. "Everybody liked Professor Buchanan. I presume he never had an enemy."[44] "Without conscious striving after popularity," remarked another from the English Department, "he was probably the most popular man in both town and gown circles in the city of Norman."[45] There was something about his easy informality, his conversational wit, and the absence of affectation that won people over. He was elected to the Norman City Council, and everyone in town that mattered liked and admired him. He served as a delegate to Oklahoma's Constitutional Convention in 1906 and for the rest of his life was a valued member of that close-knit brotherhood of the men who had crafted the state's fundamental law. In 1909 he was appointed the first dean of the College of Arts and Sciences. And at a time of special crisis in the mid-1920s—with his innumerable friends in high places, his thirty years' worth of affectionate and loyal former students scattered around the state, and his political savvy—he was the logical choice to step into the presidency of the University.

~

BESIDES APPOINTING PAXTON in classics and Buchanan in history, President Boyd made two more important additions to the arts and humanities side of the University. The first, Grace Adaline King, was quite remarkable: she was named to head the University's

41. William Bennett Bizzell, "A Friendly Tribute," in Bizzell et al., *An Appreciation of James Shannon Buchanan*, 10–11. The story of his nickname, Uncle Buck, can be found in Charles N. Gould, "Buchanan, the Man," in ibid., 16.

42. Gould, "Buchanan, the Man," 15–16.

43. Brewer, " 'Uncle Buck' as I Knew Him," 23.

44. Gould, "Buchanan, the Man," 16.

45. Brewer, " 'Uncle Buck' as I Knew Him," 23.

Music School at the astonishing age of eighteen.[46] When one of Boyd's Emporia connections called his attention to the vivacious young graduate of the Emporia State Teacher's College, the president, hinting at the possibility of a permanent position on the faculty, invited her to come to Norman to give a concert. Her touching renditions of "When the Heart Is Young" and "Goodbye, Sweet Day" won over any doubters; and the Regents quickly offered her a contract. She got her mother's permission, came to Norman in the fall of 1896, and proceeded to captivate the community with her enthusiasm, endless energy, and bubbling, simplistic optimism. "It is simpler to smile than to frown," this youngster blithely told the students, most of whom had seen at least as much of life as she had. "It is sweeter to sing than to weep. We will go through life with a bright song on our lips and melody in our hearts and the resulting harmony will be the glorious music of a noble life."[47] She herself had the voice of an angel and no thought of conserving it: scarcely a program at the University or in Norman failed to feature a few numbers from "Miss Grace." She provided noontime music for the students who wanted to dance; she started the glee club and toured with it all over Oklahoma as an effective advertisement for the University; she apparently had no difficulty controlling students twice her size and ten years older than herself. She became a favorite of Boyd, who brought her out to perform whenever he wanted to impress important guests (including legislators). In 1901, however, Grace King won the heart of no less a personage than the handsome widower James Maguire, a local hardware dealer and a prominent figure in the early history of the University who was at the time of his infatuation chair of the University's Board of Regents. The two married and moved to Lawton.[48]

Grace King performed numerous services for the University, but none, perhaps, was more momentous than her recommendation of another potential faculty member to President Boyd. Vernon Louis Parrington, the second of Boyd's noteworthy appointments in the arts and humanities, was also from Emporia. He was the son of an undistinguished family that had moved from Illinois to Kansas when he was six. Parrington attended the College of Emporia, a new Presbyterian school; but, always intellectually ambitious, he gained admission to Harvard in his junior year and graduated with a B.A. degree in 1893. The president back at Emporia College invited him to join the faculty (at $500 a year), and in July 1893 he returned to his hometown and his old college to teach English and

---

46. King's age upon coming to the University is given as sixteen in Charles F. Long and Carolyn G. Hart, *The Sooner Story: Ninety Years at the University of Oklahoma, 1890–1980,* 13, accepting an account in an interview in the *Sooner State Press* (date unknown) found in her Personnel File in the Provost's Office. This seems to be an exaggeration of her youthfulness, however, as she was born on April 6, 1878, which made her a little more than eighteen in the fall of 1896.

47. Grace A. King, "Unwritten Music," *University Umpire* 1 (October 15, 1897): 2–3.

48. Grace Maguire Personnel File, Office of the Provost. In the early 1930s, with her husband in poor health and struggling economically in the Great Depression, Grace King Maguire returned to the University and, starting in 1935, worked in various capacities in the library until her death on February 3, 1951. See Marilyn Davis Ingler, " 'Miss Grace' Put Life into O.U.," *Sooner Magazine* 20 (February 1948): 9; and a reminiscence of her in *Sooner Magazine* 3 (Spring 1984): 32.

*Grace A. King*

French.[49] At twenty-two, Vern Parrington was already quite exceptional. Handsome and ruggedly athletic, he was an impressive combination of high intelligence, enormous social charm, thoughtful introspection and self-analysis, and a voracious appetite for learning. He was a hero of the town's athletic teams, the winner of local oratorical contests, the amusing life of many an Emporia young people's party, a serious diarist bent on exploring his own character and defining, in very ambitious terms, his own future. Parrington asked himself big questions about religion, vocation, and literature. If Grace King did not have a crush on him, she was probably one of the few Emporia girls her age who did not.

King had been at the University of Oklahoma only since the start of the 1896 school year; but when she learned in the summer of 1897 that Boyd might be looking for someone to build an English department, she boldly recommended the bright and promising young teacher from back home in Emporia. Acting upon her suggestion, President Boyd telegraphed Parrington in late July 1897. He would be passing through Emporia on the Santa Fe, he said, and would welcome the opportunity for a few words at the train station. At the appointed hour, Vern Parrington hopped on his bicycle and pedaled to the station. He and Boyd introduced themselves and were engrossed in conversation about the new university at Norman when it was time for Boyd's train to pull away. In a flash Parrington flung his bike onto the train, continued his talk with Boyd until the next station, and then pedaled himself back home.[50] In early August an offer came from Boyd: for $1,000 a year Parrington was hired to organize the study of English at the University of Oklahoma. News of his leaving hit hard at the College of Emporia, and the student newspaper offered a sad and affectionate farewell:

> In every department of College work he was a master. In social life his genial humor and sterling manhood won him a large circle of sincere friends. In the classroom his quiet dignity and brilliant mind held the undivided attention of his students and stimulated them to realize the possibilities of the powers that lay in them. On the athletic field he was conscientious and painstaking, and in match games the life and mainstay of the team. . . . [W]hile new duties and responsibilities demand his time and ability, we would wish to have him remember us.[51]

49. Much has been written about Parrington, but it is all eclipsed by Hall's full biography, *V. L. Parrington*. See also her article "V. L. Parrington's Oklahoma Years, 1897–1908: 'Few Highlights and Much Monotone'?" *Pacific Northwest Quarterly* 72 (1981): 22–28.

50. The story of Parrington, Boyd, and the bicycle surfaced at Grace King Maguire's death; see *Norman Transcript*, February 8, 1951, 1.

51. Quoted in Hall, *V. L. Parrington*, 79.

Over the next eleven years there were to be many young Oklahomans who would concur heartily with the views of the student editor from Emporia.

*Vernon Louis Parrington*

As we have seen, young Parrington, who climbed down from the train on an exceptionally hot September 8, 1897, was not much impressed with "the ugliness of the raw little town" or, when he walked down to it, the University's single building, "ugly in its lines and with a wart atop." He ventured inside to inspect. "The first person whom I met was a boyish looking fellow who told me . . . he was part freshman and part secretary to the president.[52] He showed me around. It didn't take long." When they got to the "library," Parrington was stunned: "The room was fair-sized and pleasant, only where were the books? . . . There were perhaps three or four hundred books, all told, but of those that could be used for the work in English, there were not fifty."[53]

But if Parrington was discouraged, he did not show it for long. From the day of his arrival, he threw himself into the work of the University with energy and enthusiasm. On October 15, five weeks after his coming, the first issue of the *University Umpire*, the first student periodical, appeared. Vernon Parrington was the advisor to the students on the editorial board; he himself edited the paper for a year and a half and then served as an advisory editor. He immediately took over the arduous task of preparing the annual University *Catalogue*. He coached and played first base for the University's baseball team, helped to introduce football to the school, coached the team to a record of nine wins, two losses, and a tie during his first year, and chaired the faculty Athletic Committee; he worked out with the athletes almost every day. After gaining twelve pounds eating hotel food, he (like several other members of the faculty) started taking his meals with Mrs. Louise Williams, a charming and well-educated woman who had a sick husband and two daughters. A few years later, he moved into a room at the Williams house; he married Julia, his landlady's elder daughter, when he was thirty and she was eighteen.[54]

In the entire history of the University, it is not likely that any other professor who served for so short a period wielded a greater or a more lasting influence. And in the end

52. This line in Parrington's reminiscence is a bit of an inside joke, a kind of literary "wink" at a good friend. The unnamed youngster who showed him around was George Bucklin; by the time Parrington wrote these words, he and Bucklin were colleagues and very close friends.

53. Parrington, "Early Days," 82; see also Hall, *V. L. Parrington*, 81.

54. Hall, *V. L. Parrington*, chap. 4; see also the warmly appreciative essay by Sardis Roy Hadsell, "Parrington in Oklahoma," an undated typescript in the Hadsell MSS.

it was not Parrington's athletic or editorial work but his brilliant teaching that made the greatest impact. The most interesting experiment in the teaching of college English at the end of the nineteenth century was being undertaken by Professor Barrett Wendell at Harvard. Boyd, many years later, remembered: "I wanted to install the 'Harvard English' so reputed at that time and developed by Barrett Wendell, and by the merest accident fell onto Vernon L. Parrington through Mrs. [Grace King] McGuire [*sic*]."[55] For the sake of bringing "Harvard English" to the University, Boyd was willing to overlook the fact that Parrington's highest earned degree was (and would always be) the B.A.[56] Before Parrington came to Norman, English composition had been taught to the largely Preparatory Department students by people with other specialties, including the historian Buchanan. With his arrival, everything changed.

Like his teacher Professor Wendell, Parrington required his composition students to write short daily themes. Every Monday each of them wrote an outline for a longer paper to be turned in the following Monday. One of his students recalled that "we wrote many short themes on the blackboard, and Professor Parrington would proceed to tear them to pieces, ridicule our mistakes, glow with enthusiasm at our successes, pick out the misplaced commas, question our hand writing, and magnify our misspelled words. How we loved it, even when he reduced us to tears, or made us angry, for we felt that Parrington was interested in us, and we knew that he hated shoddy English. . . . Among students, he made disciples."[57] "His English was sweet upon the tongue. He charmed us, even when he was wrong." The first fifteen minutes he devoted to a review of the previous class. "He would polish his eye glasses, with a clean handkerchief, hold them up to the light, and say, 'Is that clear, Miss Barnett?' . . . That searching analysis at the beginning of the hour made us squirm, if we had not reviewed the notes, if we had not understood their import. Then for forty-five minutes he would advance the subject."[58] Gradually, Parrington's composition duties in the Preparatory Department were parceled out to advanced undergraduate tutors, and he was freed from teaching languages (although he always taught some French). As these changes came, he developed eleven courses in literature, ranging from "Chaucer" and "Shakespeare" to "Modern English Prose." Toward the end of his career at Norman he regularly introduced a little American literature (the field in which he was later to win lasting fame), but for the most part he concentrated on English writers.[59]

Both before he came to Norman and after he left, political questions played an important part in Parrington's intellectual development. When he returned from Harvard to

55. Quoted in Hadsell, "Parrington in Oklahoma," 1. For Professor Wendell's methods while Parrington took courses under him, see his *English Composition*; and Hall, *V. L. Parrington*, 24–28, 37–41.

56. In 1895 the College of Emporia awarded their young English professor an M.A. degree "in course," which Hall describes (*V. L. Parrington*, 65) as being given "without completing a prescribed curriculum but honoring personal study."

57. Hadsell, "Parrington in Oklahoma," 2, 4.

58. Ibid., 5.

59. Hall, *V. L. Parrington*, chaps. 4, 6; Hadsell, "Parrington in Oklahoma," 20, gives a list of the courses that Parrington introduced while at Oklahoma.

Kansas and saw firsthand the suffering of Kansas farmers in the depression of the 1890s, he left his family's staunch Republicanism and joined hands with the Populists. He voted for William Jennings Bryan in November 1896 and even ran unsuccessfully for the Emporia school board on the Populist ticket four months before coming to Oklahoma. In Norman he seems to have been absorbed by philosophic, religious, and aesthetic matters but was probably well on his way to that strident Jeffersonian liberalism, that faith in the common people, and that distrust of business and finance that were to characterize his mature political views and lend the distinctive coloration to his later writings. In any case, he tended to keep his political views to himself. Parrington was anything but radical in his cultural standards or his personal style. "He has been called a Jeffersonian democrat," wrote a former student who was eventually to follow him as a professor in the English Department. "He seems to have sympathy with the common man. Yet like Jefferson, he was an aristocrat. In his dress, deportment, talk, tastes, interests he was an aristocrat. . . . I can see him now, in salt and pepper suit, his hair parted in the middle, a black silk cord attached to his spectacles, over his ear, busy in the library."[60]

Perhaps his favorite student at the University was another future member of the department that he was creating, his hand-picked successor, Adelaide Loomis. When word came of his unexpected death in 1929, at the age of only fifty-eight, she found it difficult to write about him for the *Sooner Magazine*. "How can I tell you all it meant to us to have him for a teacher?" she asked. They had been students from small Oklahoma towns and from "little frame houses that braced themselves in such shallow toe-holds against the prairie winds." Every morning in chapel someone reminded them that their parents were making sacrifices to send them to college. They worried about money and about jobs. "Then we went into this man's room and for an hour at least we lived in a different world. . . . We could take our eyes off the windy horizon. We could follow the grim and watery struggle between Grendel and Beowulf, or laugh at the table manners of Chaucer's dainty prioress. . . . We shed a bitter tear when fate had played its game out with Tess. We lost ourselves in the love of David Copperfield for his Dora. . . . We listened to the majestic roll of Milton." Loomis knew that there were other fine teachers when she was a student in Norman. "But somehow in Professor Parrington's room we forgot the dry sun and the never-ending wind, and the painful and pressing problem of how to make a living, and while we were there, we lived."[61] Another former undergraduate, who was to become a colleague in the University's History Department, put it more succinctly: "Parrington's students, including the writer, thought that he was the best English teacher in the world."[62]

60. Hadsell, "Parrington in Oklahoma," 6, 10.

61. Adelaide Loomis Parker, "Vernon Louis Parrington: An Appreciation," *Sooner Magazine* 2 (October 1929): 20.

62. Gittinger, "Reorganizations of 1908 and 1911," 30.

~

PRESIDENT BOYD WAS TOO CLOSE an observer of both modern culture and modern higher education to believe that the University could ignore mathematics and the sciences. He had himself been profoundly touched and thoroughly stimulated by his own teachers' attempts to explain the latest scientific advances and by their efforts (and his own) to reconcile these scientific findings with the traditional religious teachings of his youth. During the first three years, Edwin DeBarr (with some help from Boyd, who occasionally taught a little basic algebra) had carried this side of the curriculum by himself. But between 1895 and 1902 Boyd moved decisively to strengthen the University's instruction in mathematics and science.

In September 1895 the University began a Department of Mathematics. To organize it, Boyd chose Frederick Stanton Elder, another member of the faculty with a connection to Southwest Kansas College in Winfield, where Boyd had lived briefly before moving the dozen miles south to Arkansas City and where he and Mrs. Boyd still had relatives and friends. Elder studied at Southwest during the late 1880s (when William Rice was there teaching Greek and Latin) but elected to finish his B.A. at Princeton. He then took a position at Parsons College in Iowa and began graduate work at the University of Chicago. Two years later, he arrived in Norman as an instructor; and three years after that he was promoted to professor. By the time Elder left the University of Oklahoma in 1905, he and a young instructor, Frank E. Knowles, were offering two basic courses in the Preparatory Department (solid geometry and algebraic theory) and eleven courses, through advanced calculus and projective geometry, for college students.[63]

Boyd's appointment of Albert Heald Van Vleet as professor of biology in 1898 lifted the University of Oklahoma to a new level of prestige and sophistication. With DeBarr in the physical sciences and Elder taking charge of mathematics, Boyd decided that the next step should be in the natural sciences: botany, zoology, physiology, anatomy, and geology. After estimating the expenses needed for equipment in these fields, Boyd concluded that the University could afford to spend only $1,200 on a teacher; and he wrote to universities around the country that gave graduate instruction in those studies. During the first week of July 1898, the National Education Association met in Washington, D.C., and Boyd attended as head of the Oklahoma branch. One night Albert Van Vleet appeared at the door of his hotel room. He had come to ask about the job and about Oklahoma. Boyd's visitor was a few weeks short of thirty-seven; he had studied in his native Iowa and in Nebraska and earned a bachelor's degree at the University of Wisconsin. Van Vleet then went to Europe and earned a doctorate from the University of Leipzig. When he came to Boyd's hotel room, he was enrolled in postgraduate study at the Johns Hopkins University in Baltimore.

Boyd saw at once that this man would be a very notable catch for the University of

63. *University Catalogue, 1905–1906*, 5, 72–75.

Oklahoma and proceeded to describe the school as persua-
sively as possible. It is a measure of how much he wanted
Van Vleet that Boyd, who normally disdained the
research interests of prospective faculty members
(if such interests did not almost automatically
disqualify a candidate in his eyes), on this occasion emphasized the research opportunities of the
position. "I told him as clearly as I could of the
situation, of the needs of the institution, and of
my faith and confidence in its growth and development, and I called attention to the opportunity
for original investigation and research. The flora
and fauna of Oklahoma had not at that time been
studied except in the most desultory way; the mineral,
geological, and geographical resources were practically unknown," the eager president explained. Boyd
also spoke of the high quality of the student body:
their modest economic circumstances, their genuine
desire to learn, the complete absence of discipline

*Albert Heald Van Vleet*

problems. Van Vleet was impressed and agreed to come for the salary of $1,200. "By this
transaction," Boyd later proudly asserted, "the university secured a teacher who was little
short of a genius."[64]

Albert Van Vleet was to bring to the University not merely a doctorate but also a taste
for serious scholarship, scientific investigation, and publication.[65] By March 1899, seven
months after his arrival, he and Boyd had persuaded the territorial legislature to create
(with an appropriation of $200) a "natural history and geological survey," with the profes-
sor of natural sciences and geology at the University of Oklahoma as its head. Thereafter,
Van Vleet made numerous trips, especially during the summers, crisscrossing the state.
He devised a topographical map and made large collections of native animals and of native rocks and minerals. He was an avid photographer and compiled a large collection of
Oklahoma natural settings and geological features. Above all, Van Vleet collected botanical specimens; for of all his diverse interests in the natural world, botany was his greatest
passion. The courses he devised and taught spanned the whole spectrum of the natural
sciences, and he set forth the curriculum that evolved into pre-medicine. His teaching
was characterized by modesty, good humor, and tolerance for the poorly prepared students

64. Boyd recalled the Washington interview during a memorial address for Van Vleet, delivered in Norman on
November 20, 1925. See Boyd, "Address of Dr. David Ross Boyd," in *In Memory of Albert Heald Van Vleet*, 13–14.

65. Van Vleet was not the first holder of a Ph.D. to come to the University of Oklahoma, as is sometimes claimed.
James N. Anderson, the Latin professor who stayed in Norman for only two years (1894–96), had earned a Ph.D. from
Johns Hopkins University.

who found their way to the University in the early days. "He was extremely patient and considerate," recalled a former student who eventually became a chemistry professor at the University. "No student was ever so dull but that he was treated in the most kindly manner. . . . As a student and later as a faculty member, I never heard Dr. Van Vleet make a flippant or sarcastic reply to a seeker after information, no matter how inane or foolish the question might be."[66] In addition to this modesty, good nature, and gentle tolerance the University received another benefit from Van Vleet: when the time came to divide the natural sciences into separate departments of zoology, geology, and botany, "he might have fought to be the director of a large general department of biology; instead he permitted his work to be divided, promoted his instructors, and kept what was left."[67]

Van Vleet's pioneering journeys across Oklahoma accorded well with his love of the outdoors, his addiction to camping and hunting, and his love of the athletic life. These traits drew him close to Parrington (who once told one of his English classes that "the trouble with Hamlet was that he needed to camp out"[68]); despite a general disagreement on almost every political question, the two men became the closest of friends. Van Vleet performed the same service for track and field that Parrington performed for football and baseball. He trained the pole vaulters, the runners, the high jumpers; but he always insisted that students get off the team if their schoolwork was suffering. For nearly three decades he officiated at every Annual Field and Track Meet. "We rode together, tramped together, slept together, did the camp chores together, got wet and cold and tired together," wrote Parrington, "yet in all the intimacy of such experiences, with the ragged nerves that sometimes come from such experiences, I found him always the same equable, generous, kindly nature that I had come to expect him to be. There was no smallness or meanness in him. His wit was as genial at the end of a hard day as at the beginning. . . . The zest of a boy was in him, and the self control of a man."[69]

The joining of the biological sciences with geology under Van Vleet was, of course, not an entirely smooth marriage. Whether geology is a natural or a physical science is open to question because it shares the characteristics of both. By 1900, with the growing interest in the potential profitability of Oklahoma's natural resources, it became apparent that geology ought to have a position of its own at the University of Oklahoma. To direct the study of geology President Boyd once again chose with singular wisdom and again chose a man whose life story significantly paralleled his own. Charles Newton Gould, like Boyd, was born in Ohio into a country family that also claimed to have played a role in the underground railroad before the Civil War. Raised on "pure and unadulterated Republicanism" and educated through the eighth grade in Ohio country schools, Charlie Gould was eighteen when he and his family moved to Kansas and took up residence in a dugout on

66. Guy Y. Williams, "An Appreciation of Dr. Albert Heald Van Vleet," in *In Memory of Albert Heald Van Vleet*, 27.

67. Sardis Roy Hadsell, "Dean of the Graduate School," in *In Memory of Albert Heald Van Vleet*, 25.

68. Hadsell, "Parrington in Oklahoma," 8.

69. Vernon L. Parrington, "Albert Heald Van Vleet as I Knew Him," in *In Memory of Albert Heald Van Vleet*, 21–22.

a rented farm in the spring of 1887.[70] A year later David and Jennie Boyd were to take up their own duties at Arkansas City.

Two years after his move, Gould attended a teacher-training institute in Kingman, Kansas. On a sweltering August night he heard a lecture entitled "The Geological Story of Kansas." It enthralled and transformed him. "I hung entranced on every word," he remembered almost sixty years later. "I felt the spinal shiver which betokens the last word in emotional appeal. This was my conversion. Up to that time, I do not believe that I had heard the word geology spoken. . . . This lecture changed the entire current of my life. At that time I did not know what a geologist did, but I then and there resolved that whatever things a geologist did, those things must I do."[71] He taught in small Kansas schools until 1892, finally earning enough money to enroll in college. He attended Southwest Kansas College in Winfield but dropped out regularly to pick up some money as a teacher or principal, until he earned his B.A. in 1899. Then it was off to the University of Nebraska to work on his M.A.

Two of Gould's closest friends at Southwest were to be important a year later in bringing Charlie to the University of Oklahoma: Sardis Roy Hadsell and George Bucklin. Hadsell had already tramped around the countryside with Gould in a covered wagon searching for fossils. George Bucklin had grown up in Kingman and was a boyhood friend of Gould's. Young Bucklin had moved to Winfield (as had the Gould family) in order to take advantage of the college there. He roomed with Charlie Gould's mother, a woman who had labored side by side with his own mother back in the Kingman Women's Christian Temperance Union. When Charlie headed off to Nebraska to do graduate work, George came to Norman, where he became both a student and the trusted secretary to President Boyd. Thus when Gould was finishing his M.A. and looking around for a permanent job, it happened that he had some well-placed friends in Norman.

As soon as Boyd's secretary learned that the president was thinking about establishing a geology department, he mentioned his friend Gould as a promising candidate. Boyd instructed Bucklin to write to him, and during Christmas vacation in 1899 Gould came down from Lincoln to talk to Boyd and Van Vleet. It was arranged that Gould would join Van Vleet's field camp in the summer of 1900 (without pay, but Roy Hadsell had volunteered to come along and do the cooking) and in September begin to organize the study of geology at the University of Oklahoma. He would be paid the extraordinarily meager sum of $400 for his first year.[72] Gould found conditions at the University inauspicious: "There

70. Charles N. Gould, *Covered Wagon Geologist*, chaps. 1–2. See also Ronald L. Clifton, *Memorial to Charles Newton Gould*, 165–74.

71. Gould, *Covered Wagon Geologist*, 3–4.

72. Ibid., 73–75, 101. For charming descriptions of the collecting expedition in the summer of 1900, see "Across Oklahoma by Covered Wagon," in ibid., chap. 4; and Ed Mills, "Genesis in Geology: Dr. C. N. Gould Tells of Establishing That Department Here," *Sooner Magazine* 1 (January 1929): 120–24. See also Charles N. Gould, "Beginning of the Geological Work in Oklahoma," *Chronicles of Oklahoma* 10 (1932): 196–203.

*Charles Newton Gould*

was absolutely no equipment for carrying on the work of the department; no classrooms, no laboratories, no collections, no library, nothing but a young chap just out of college, turned loose on his own resources and permitted to sink or swim." There was not even an office. So Gould moved a desk into Van Vleet's office and set to work.[73] Only ten students enrolled in the two geology classes that he taught in the fall of 1900. But it was never a question of "sinking" for Charles Gould. By the time he closed his illustrious career, he was one of the best-known geologists in the United States, the teacher of a generation of distinguished geologists and the founder of perhaps the best-known school of its kind in the nation. By one compilation he produced 260 papers, 572 reports on oil properties, and 251 studies for the National Park Service.[74] A significant part of Oklahoma's oil industry was to owe its origins to the work of this scientist.

~

THE QUALITY OF THE FACULTY he hired indicates that one of President Boyd's greatest gifts was his ability to recognize talent. That gift was not only exercised in selecting shrewdly from among the dossiers that came to him from the Albert Teachers' Agency, nor by detecting special qualities in youngsters who angelically rendered sentimental ballads or charmed him by throwing a bicycle onto the train and riding with him to the next station or came tapping on his hotel room door late at night. President Boyd also had an uncanny knack for looking into his own student body and picking out of it students of unusual intelligence and promise. He had the magical ability to persuade such students to stay in Norman and to join their fortunes, at least for a while, with the institution he was trying to build. During the first decade of his administration, he exercised this gift with important results four times.

The two boyhood friends from Winfield, Kansas, who helped to lure their schoolmate Charlie Gould to Norman have already been mentioned. George Augustus Bucklin left Southwest Kansas College in 1895 and read law for a couple of years before arriving in Norman in the fall of 1897. He was a few weeks shy of twenty-two, handsome, athletic, and gregarious. Boyd immediately hired him to work in his own office as his only secretary. Thus Bucklin had been on the campus less than a month himself when he encountered

73. Gould, *Covered Wagon Geologist*, 101–102.

74. B. W. Beebe, "Introduction," to ibid., vii. See also "Dr. Charles Gould Dies," *Sooner Magazine* 21 (August 1949): 16.

Vernon Parrington, just off the train and wandering through the building, and offered to show him around. By the time he was a sophomore, he was also the University's registrar. When he graduated in 1903, Boyd granted him an informal leave of absence for a year, and Bucklin went to Yale and earned a master's degree. He returned to Oklahoma with a bride and was named professor and head of the new Department of Sociology and Economics. Unfortunately for the University, he left teaching in 1906 (only thirty years old) and embarked upon a distinguished career in the foreign service.[75]

The third member of the group from Winfield was Sardis Roy Hadsell. He was just finishing his freshman year at Southwest Kansas when he was persuaded to come along as the cook on the expedition that included his friends Gould and Bucklin. Instead of returning to Winfield at the end of the summer, he stayed in Norman and enrolled at the University in the fall of 1900. Bucklin got him a stenographer's job in the president's office, and he quickly came to Boyd's attention. From 1901 until 1904, while he was himself an undergraduate, he also taught English in the Preparatory Department and continued his duties as stenographer to the president. He fell quite under the spell of Vernon Parrington; when he wrote of Parrington many years later that "among students, he made disciples,"[76] he probably had himself in mind. During his senior year, with Bucklin off at Yale, Hadsell stepped into the position of University registrar. Upon his graduation Boyd appointed him to the Department of English. Three years later he earned a master's degree from Harvard and twenty years after that a Ph.D. from the University of Chicago. He taught at the University of Oklahoma until his retirement in 1941.[77] Roy Hadsell was also something of a camera enthusiast, and a substantial part of the photographic record of the early history of the University was his work.

Another young man of extraordinary ability plucked from the University's student body by the alert president also had a connection to Southwest Kansas University in Winfield. Again, like Boyd himself, Lawrence Wooster Cole had come from Ohio and had taught school and been a principal even before finishing college. He left Winfield to finish his undergraduate career at Norman. Perhaps because of the similarities in their careers, Lawrence Cole was a special favorite of Boyd's; the two former Ohioans had known one another back in Kansas high-school circles. When Cole graduated in June 1899, at the age of twenty-nine, Boyd prevailed upon him to organize the University's first twenty-one graduates into an Alumni Association and to serve as its first president.[78] While still an undergraduate at the University of Oklahoma, Cole was also the principal of the

75. Before his retirement George Bucklin served in Germany, Mexico, Guatemala, Canada, and New Zealand; during World War I he was the American consul at Bordeaux.

76. Hadsell, "Parrington in Oklahoma," 2.

77. Gittinger, *University of Oklahoma*, 44; Ed Mills, "Three Decades with the University: Adventure Called Doctor Hadsell, Learning Claimed Him," *Sooner Magazine* 1 (February 1929): 154ff. See also the review of his career at his death: *Sooner Magazine* 15 (September 1942): 21.

78. For a list of early graduates through 1901, see Gittinger, *University of Oklahoma*, 182–83.

El Reno High School and the superintendent of El Reno schools.[79] Now that Cole had his B.A., Boyd took advantage of Cole's considerable administrative experience and named him principal of the University's Preparatory Department. He was a logical choice for the Norman school board and was elected to it from 1901 to 1907. Cole also taught classes in education and psychology and established the Psychology Department at the University. The same year that Bucklin went to Yale for his M.A., Cole temporarily relinquished his teaching, administrative, and school-board duties and went to Harvard for his; there he studied with William James, the celebrated psychologist and philosopher. Like Bucklin, he returned to Norman, where he taught psychology for another four years.[80]

But Boyd's most notable and illustrious selection from his own student body was undoubtedly young Roy Gittinger. Upon the occasion of Gittinger's retirement (a half-century after Boyd had hired him) another president of the University sent him a personal letter. George Lynn Cross, the eighth president under whom Gittinger had worked, wrote in the spring of 1950: "In my opinion, you have made a greater contribution to the University of Oklahoma than any other person in the entire history of the institution. No one else has served the University for as long a period of time. No one else has served the institution in such a versatile manner. And no one's services have been of better quality than your own."[81] If President Cross's remarks were magnified to fit the occasion and to bring pleasure to Gittinger, the exaggeration was only a slight one.

Roy Gittinger was born in a small Iowa town called Melrose and spent a year at nearby Simpson College in Indianola. In March 1900 he married; and he and his new wife, Frances, appeared in Norman in June. He was twenty-one years old. Soon he was tutoring history and civics in the Preparatory Department. When Cole vacated the principalship of that department, Gittinger took it over. In addition to all his other duties over the years— registrar, dean of undergraduates, dean of the graduate school, dean of admissions, dean of administration, editor of the University catalogue for a quarter-century—Gittinger taught in the History Department. He loved equally the histories of England and the United States. Most of his teaching was in English history (since for much of Gittinger's early career James Buchanan covered the American history courses); most of his research and writing was in American history. After 1904 he spent his summers at the University of Chicago and finally finished his M.A. there in 1907. The University granted him a leave of absence to complete his doctorate at the University of California in 1917. His disserta-

79. Wardner, "Territorial University," 98.

80. *Who Was Who in America* (Chicago: Marquis, 1966), 2:122; Gittinger, *The University of Oklahoma*, 28, 31. Upon leaving Norman in 1908, Lawrence Cole (after one year at Wellesley College) taught psychology and education at the University of Colorado from 1910 until his retirement in 1938, when he became a state regent. Cole died in March 1946. His career is reviewed in "First Alumni President Dies," *Sooner Magazine* 18 (May 1946): 24.

81. George Lynn Cross to Roy Gittinger, May 20, 1950, in Roy Gittinger's Personnel File, Office of the Provost. See also Cross's published remarks about Gittinger in *Professors, Presidents, and Politicians: Civil Rights and the University of Oklahoma, 1890–1968*, xvi–xvii.

tion, *The Formation of the State of Oklahoma*, was published by
the University of California Press and remains one of the
chief landmarks of prestatehood Oklahoma history.

As the years passed, Roy Gittinger became the
guardian of academic standards at the University of
Oklahoma. As teacher and dean, he enforced his
stern principles and regulations on students and
colleagues alike, insisting on serious scholarship
and the rigorous fulfillment of duties, courtesies,
and traditions. He worked tirelessly with the state
high schools and community colleges in an effort to
elevate standards. Gittinger could be cranky about
colleagues who missed class too often or permitted
smoking in the University buildings or were late with
their grades.[82] For years he was the official disciplinarian of the student body, listened to many sad stories
from students, and gave much fatherly advice. After the
University became so large that social pressure no longer could be relied upon to ensure proper decorum and
responsible behavior, it fell to Dean Gittinger to devise
the rules for hours and dating and dances.

*Roy Gittinger*

Roy Gittinger's greatest gift, however, was his legendary memory. He could recall with
perfect clarity the details of events that had occurred a third- or half-century earlier; he
never forgot a name. George Cross alleged that prior to the expansion of the University
in the 1930s "there wasn't a student whose name Dr. Gittinger didn't know."[83] Gittinger
was appointed David Ross Boyd Professor of History in 1946 and was the first person ever
to hold the title of Regents' Professor. His long career in Norman, his varied experience
at the institution, his historian's training and scholarly habits, and his fabulous memory
made him the perfect choice to write *The University of Oklahoma: A History of Fifty Years,
1892–1942* (1942), the indispensable starting point for every subsequent work on the history of the University of Oklahoma.

~

AS A YOUNGSTER IN DEXTER, KANSAS, Nahum E. Butcher attended a high school
where Lawrence W. Cole happened to be the principal. When Cole moved from Dexter to
Southwest Kansas College, Butcher went with him, completing his high-school prepara-

---

82. See, for example, a series of letters written in mid-March 1921 to President Stratton Brooks, in Gittinger's
Personnel File, Office of the Provost.

83. George Lynn Cross, "The President of O.U. Speaks," transcript of undated radio broadcast [ca. 1945–46], Station
WNAD, Norman, in Roy Gittinger Personnel File, Office of the Provost. Gittinger's career is reviewed in "No Other Like

tion in Winfield. He took his first year of Latin there with William N. Rice, who was soon to become one of the original members of the University of Oklahoma faculty. It was probably through Rice that Butcher and Cole learned about the new university being opened in Oklahoma Territory under the direction of Superintendent David Ross Boyd of nearby Arkansas City. Butcher had never met Boyd, but Cole knew and liked him; and the two friends from Winfield decided to transfer to Norman at the beginning of the 1893 school year. Butcher paused to participate in the run into the Cherokee Strip on September 15 and then had to return his horse to Kansas, so Cole was the first to arrive. Years later Butcher recalled his arrival in Norman and the momentous occurrence in connection with it:

> [B]y the time I got my grip packed and went over to the Redrock to catch the Santa Fe train to Norman, it was the 20th or the 21st or the 22nd, maybe, of September. Anyway, I landed in Norman at midnight and stopped at the Agnes Hotel and in the morning I got up and hunted up Mr. Cole. He took me into the President's office. Dr. Boyd, himself, enrolled me and looked over my grades and qualifications, and he said "Well, I'm going to enter you in the college department." I didn't know when he said that, that I was the first one to enter that department, but later on I found out that when he printed the first catalogue, my name was in the college department all by itself, and the rest of the students were in the preparatory school department.[84]

Nahum Butcher was not only the first student in the University's history to gain admission into actual college-level work: he was also the University's very first librarian.

In the same way that he recruited promising faculty members from among his small student body, President Boyd also recruited librarians. Indeed, the library (such as it was) was to be the province of University of Oklahoma students until 1951. In the earliest years, being the librarian was not an especially arduous task. The books were originally housed in a twenty-by-thirty-foot room on the east wing of the second floor of the University's only building. This room was the "library" that so stunned and dismayed Vernon Parrington in 1897 ("the room was fair-sized and pleasant, only where were the books?").[85] During the 1893–94 academic year, the Regents authorized President Boyd to spend thirty dollars on improvements for the library room.[86] And at the start of the next year, he hired Nahum Butcher at ten dollars a month to be the librarian. Butcher held that position for two years, from the fall of 1894 until the spring of 1896. In the first year, Boyd allowed his young librarian to spend $500 on books. There were already some volumes there, Butcher later remembered, "very few of which would apply to education purposes in a university because they were given to us by ministers over the state and other people who had libraries they

---

Him," *Sooner Magazine* 30 (October 1957): 18–19.

84. "Interview of Mr. N. E. Butcher by Dr. F. A. Balyeat" (1957), Nahum Ellsworth Butcher MSS. Butcher was to serve as superintendent of the Norman public schools and president of the Oklahoma Educational Association. For his subsequent career, see *Sooner Magazine* 30 (January 1958): 24.

85. Parrington, "Early Days," 82.

86. Wardner, "Territorial University," 70–71.

wanted to give away and they gave them to us." Butcher received requests from the faculty for particular books and tried, as long as the money lasted, to act upon them.[87]

By the time Butcher relinquished his position, Boyd felt ready to use the library as one of the chief attractions of the University in his quest for new students. In advertisements he wrote in the fall of 1895, he boasted that "the library will be in charge of a competent librarian, and the books will be so indexed and catalogued, as to make the resources of the library available to students. The reading room will be open at all hours of the day, where in addition to the newspapers of the Territory and the leading papers from all parts of the United State[s], will be found a full list of the leading magazines for the use of the students."[88] The "competent librarian" he chose to replace Butcher was Maude DeCou, an undergraduate who had already served as a school superintendent at Ponca City. She was paid $200 a year and was the first to attempt to index and catalogue the collection. After two years on the job, DeCou left Norman, without a degree, to assume the principalship of the Newkirk High School.[89] She was replaced by Maud Rule, another student, who managed the library for four years. She hired as her assistant Milton Jay Ferguson, who graduated in 1901. After a year at Melvil Dewey's famous library school in Albany, New York, Ferguson returned to campus in June 1902 and became the first full-time librarian of the University.[90] Just as it seemed that the library was fated to be the responsibility of able but highly transient students and former students, Ferguson chose an assistant librarian who changed everything.

Jesse Lee Rader was born in Prairie Home, Missouri, in April 1883. When he was eleven his family moved to Newkirk. His high-school principal was none other than Maude DeCou, former University librarian. Perhaps it was DeCou herself, some years later, who invited David Ross Boyd to Newkirk to give his recruitment talk on the importance of education. Rader, who never forgot that evening, left home, moved to Norman, and entered the Preparatory Department in 1902. Two years later he was ready for college work. Milton Ferguson asked him if he would like to work as his assistant in the library. Rader realized that he could not manage school, play on the football team, and undertake the library job all at once and that he had to choose between football and the library. He thought about it a while and—in a decision crucial to the history of the University—opted for the library. By the time Ferguson left in January 1907, the twenty-four-year-old Rader knew as much about the library as anyone and ran the place as a student for six months after Ferguson's departure. In June 1908 he received his bachelor's degree and was given the title of assistant librarian for the 1908–1909 academic year. Jesse Lee Rader became the librarian at the University of Oklahoma in 1909 and remained in that position until 1951—an

87. "Interview of Mr. N. E. Butcher," 4.

88. *Norman Transcript*, August 30 or September 6, 1895.

89. Wardner, "Territorial University," 71.

90. Gittinger, *University of Oklahoma*, 41.

extraordinary record of service to the institution.[91]

Meanwhile, the library's collection was growing at a steady and healthy rate. By the end of the first decade of the University's existence, the library boasted 4,023 accessioned and around 4,500 unaccessioned volumes. In addition, the library had become an official U.S. government depository and contained another 9,000 pamphlets, monographs, and government reports. The University's *Catalogue* for 1902–1903 also claimed that the library contained runs of most of the Territory newspapers and that it subscribed to forty popular and scholarly periodicals. Still located on the east wing of the University's building, it had expanded to include a stack room, a small librarian's office, another small room to work on the cataloguing, and a reading room for use of the students every weekday from 7:45 A.M. to 5 P.M. and every Saturday morning.[92]

*Jesse Lee Rader*

BY THE END OF HIS FIRST DECADE as president of the University, therefore, David Ross Boyd had gathered together a very respectable faculty—a far better faculty, in fact, than might reasonably have been predicted ten years before. The *Catalogue* for the 1902–1903 academic year listed fifteen full-time professors and instructors, including the president himself; also listed were a librarian (Milton Ferguson) and seven tutors and assistants. Among the fifteen regular professors, there were some who were, by any standard, either excellent acquisitions for the University or young men of considerable promise. Vernon Parrington, Albert Van Vleet, and Charles N. Gould could no doubt have secured respectable positions at many more prestigious and longer-established colleges. Two young men on the faculty in 1902, both recent graduates of the University of Oklahoma, showed unusual potential: Lawrence Cole and Roy Gittinger. Edwin DeBarr, James Buchanan, Frederick Elder, and Joseph Paxton also made substantial contributions, each in his own way, to the instructional program of the University. The institution employed in 1902 two undergraduates—George Bucklin and Roy Hadsell—who were soon to take their places as valuable teachers. Roy Gittinger, still tutoring in the Preparatory Department, was about to assume his important and lasting place on the faculty as well.

91. *Who Was Who in America* (Chicago: Marquis, 1981), 7:468. See "An Unforgettable Link," *Sooner Magazine* 24 (August–September 1951): 14; and his front-page obituary, *Norman Transcript*, June 4, 1973.

92. Gittinger, *University of Oklahoma*, 41, 61–62; *University Catalogue, 1902–1903*, 17–19.

But the faculty that David Ross Boyd had drawn together during his first decade in office also suffered from some weaknesses. The most obvious, of course, was the absence of women. With the marriage and departure of Grace King the year before, the faculty was entirely male. Of the seven who were listed as tutors and assistants, only two were women; one taught voice and women's physical culture, and the other gave instruction in piano.[93] Besides the lack of women teachers among the professors and instructors, only two of the fifteen (DeBarr and Van Vleet) had earned Ph.D. degrees, although some of the others would continue their studies while teaching and eventually receive doctorates.

In addition, the faculty of the University of Oklahoma suffered from two other deficiencies, which were someday to prove to be important and explosive ones. As far as religion was concerned, the faculty, not surprisingly, consisted entirely of Protestants; but they were Protestants of a particular kind. The members of the faculty were overwhelmingly Presbyterians and might be seen on Sunday mornings worshiping beside President Boyd at the church on Gray and Crawford Streets. Those who were not Presbyterians were members of the Methodist Episcopal (the Northern Methodist) or the Disciples of Christ churches, and one was an Episcopalian. But the portentous thing was that not a single member of the faculty was a Southern Baptist and not one was a member of the Southern Methodist Church, despite the fact that those two denominations were by far the largest in the state of Oklahoma.[94]

The faculty members hired by President Boyd not only failed to share the theological preferences of most Oklahomans but also did not share most Oklahomans' political allegiances. The members of the faculty were overwhelmingly northern Republicans. By 1904 there were twenty-one teachers of various ranks at the University. Eight had come from Kansas; another eight were from other northern states; and three were (more or less) native Oklahomans. These, of course, tended to be Republicans. Only two professors were from the South. James Buchanan was from Tennessee, and Joseph Paxton came from Missouri. Both of them (naturally) had been hired during that brief four-year period, 1893 to 1897, when the Democrat Grover Cleveland was in the White House and the Democrat territorial governor, William C. Renfrow, appointed a Democrat-controlled Board of Regents for the University.[95] But this largely Republican faculty was surrounded by a citizenry that was staunchly Democratic. In every single statewide election between 1907, when

93. *University Catalogue, 1902–1903*, 5–7.

94. According to a religious census conducted in 1906, there were a total of 4,497 congregations in the "Twin Territories." Of that number, fully 856 were Southern Baptist (with around 50,000 adherents) and 683 were Southern Methodist (with around 45,000). The denominations to which the University's faculty belonged were much less formidable. The Presbyterian Church, excluding the essentially southern Cumberland branch, claimed only 179 churches in the two territories (about 9,700 adherents); the Methodist Episcopal Church (the Northern Methodists), 479 churches (23,300 adherents); and the Disciples or Christians (together with the Churches of Christ) 481 churches (around 32,300 adherents). No other white Protestant denomination, except the Cumberland Presbyterians, numbered more than 100 congregations; and none claimed more than 5,000 members.

95. Gittinger, "University Reorganizations of 1908 and 1911," 6.

Oklahoma first became a state, and 1963, its citizens never once elected anyone who was not a Democrat.[96]

Like other Americans, Oklahomans took their religion and their politics very seriously; and the failure of the University to hire Baptists, Southern Methodists, southerners, and Democrats irritated many of them. For the moment there was not much they could do about it. But if the time ever came when it might be possible to redress these insults, there would be no shortage of citizens who would be ready to act on their feelings.

96. *Oklahoma Almanac, 1995–1996* (Oklahoma City: Oklahoma Department of Libraries, 1996), tables showing "Elective State Officers since Statehood," 548–52.

# CHAPTER IV

# Mastering a Thousand Details, 1892–1902

On the evening of December 28, 1871, James A. Garfield, then an Ohio congressman but destined nine years later to become president of the United States, addressed a group of graduates from his old school. The New York City alumni of Williams College had gathered at the fashionable Delmonico's Restaurant for a night of fine dining and cigars, reminiscence, and speeches. When it was Garfield's turn, he chose to honor Wil-liams's legendary teacher and retiring president, Mark Hopkins. "The ideal college," Garfield declared, "is Mark Hopkins on one end of a log and a student on the other." That re-mark has been quoted so often, historian Frederick Rudolph writes, that "no one can properly address himself to the question of higher education in the United States without pay-ing homage in some way to the aphorism of the log and to Mark Hopkins."[1]

*President Boyd at work*

The belief that a perfectly satisfactory college might consist entirely of gifted professors at one end of a log and eager students at the other, and the clear implication that every-thing else was somehow superfluous and a waste of effort and resources, has always had its adherents—mostly among professors. And if good teachers and willing students were *all*

1. Frederick Rudolph, *Mark Hopkins and the Log: Williams College, 1836–1872*, vi, 225–28.

that was needed, David Ross Boyd had admirably fulfilled his duties during the first decade of the University of Oklahoma's existence. By the end of the tenth academic year more than 350 students were studying at Norman. They were being taught by almost two dozen faculty members and assistants.[2] If none of those teachers had yet earned the reputation of a Mark Hopkins, they were nonetheless dedicated, hardworking, and competent—and some of them much more than that.

But universities have never consisted only of teachers, students, and logs. Boyd knew very well that the University had other needs and that these also required careful thought and hard work. Boyd and the University had somehow to find resources, provide space, set standards, create procedures, and expand educational programs during the school's opening decade. And no one understood better than the students that college life consisted of more than classroom lessons, no matter how gifted their instructors. They set about also during the first ten years of the University's life to create an energetic, robust, and healthy student culture.

~

FIRST THERE WAS THE MATTER OF MONEY. Throughout the entire history of the University getting enough funds to conduct day-to-day operations, if not at every single moment uppermost in the minds of those responsible, was always at least very close to being uppermost. The University of Oklahoma, of course, shared this obsessive worry about funding with virtually every other institution of higher learning, public or private, in the United States.

At the start finances were extremely precarious. Not counting the $10,000 that Cleveland County had deposited in Guthrie for the construction of the University building, the institution's resources consisted of the proceeds from a one-half mill levy provided by the legislature and to be divided among the schools at Stillwater, Edmond, and Norman.[3] The University received $3,439 from this source in 1891 (a year in which there were few expenses because there were still no teachers or students) and $5,742 in 1892.[4] The legislature had prohibited the school from charging tuition to the citizens of Oklahoma Territory; and in February 1893 Boyd reported that the University had acquired only a scant $75 in nonresident tuition.[5] Meanwhile, expenses began to mount: salaries, the building, printing, furniture, advertising, insurance, the heating system, coal, travel expenses of the Regents.[6] Even after December 1892, with work on the building held practically at a

2. The *University Catalogue, 1902–1903* lists fifteen faculty members, with two vacancies to be filled, and seven tutors and assistants, with one vacancy to be filled.

3. *Statutes of Oklahoma, 1890,* 1079; *Statutes of Oklahoma, 1893,* 1047.

4. The figures were reported to the House, which investigated finances at the University after the Regents had spent money in anticipation of currently available tax proceeds. See *Journal of the House Proceedings of the Second Legislative Assembly of the Territory of Oklahoma,* 346. Because of a typographical error, Wardner, "Territorial University of Oklahoma," 28, gives a wrong figure for the 1892 receipts.

5. *Journal of the House Proceedings,* 339. According to Boyd, nonresident tuition was $20 per year, $10 per semester.

standstill until more funds became available, the University was in dire financial trouble. On March 1, 1893, a legislative investigating committee concluded that, once all the 1892 taxes were collected, the University would have at its disposal $19,182 (including the $10,000 from the sale of those Cleveland County bonds); it had by that date issued warrants worth $32,370. In other words, midway into its second semester of operation, the University was $13,188 in the red.[7]

Two results ensued immediately from this shocking discovery. On March 16 the legislature authorized $48,000 in bonds, from which the University was to receive $18,000; by the end of the month construction on the building resumed.[8] And even though the Democratic legislature investigating the Republican Regents deadlocked,[9] all the Regents decided to resign. They did so quickly and for a good reason. The Democrats had taken over in Washington: Grover Cleveland was inaugurated the same week that the legislature was reviewing University finances and would surely appoint some Democrat to be the territorial governor. It was best to act fast so that the Republican governor, Abraham Seay, got to make the new appointments in late April and to attend their first meeting on May 6.[10] Cleveland's gubernatorial appointee, Norman banker William C. Renfrow, was inaugurated on May 10.

The political crisis passed predictably enough, but the financial one remained. Neither the hard fact nor its underlying cause was difficult to understand. The legislature, hoping to placate the citizenry by a generous distribution of public institutions, had decided to create three colleges and to divide the tax receipts among them. It had simply established more than it could possibly support adequately. This would not be the last time. To make things immeasurably worse, moreover, the three schools were in the midst of their very first year when the entire nation was hit by the most devastating economic crisis in the history of the United States to that point. The depression of the mid-1890s inevitably meant scarce money, severe unemployment, lowered incomes, and reduced tax receipts as more and more Oklahomans were forced to default.[11]

This desperate situation provoked Boyd and others concerned about financing higher education to a bold stratagem. Ever since the Land Ordinance of 1785, they knew, public education at the *lower* levels had been funded in part by grants of land from the federal government. Before a territory was officially opened for settlement, it was surveyed and

6. The first 133 expenditures by the Regents, from January 18 to December 7, 1892, are itemized in *Journal of the House Proceedings*, 335–37.

7. Ibid., 334.

8. Gittinger, *University of Oklahoma*, 14–15.

9. The legislature investigated both the practice of financing in anticipation of receipts and the persistent charge that some Regents were improperly influenced to locate the University on the west side of Norman; see Wardner, "Territorial University," 42–43.

10. This new Board kept official "Minutes," and our collection of Regents' "Minutes" begins with their first meeting on May 6, 1893.

11. See Charles Hoffman, *The Depression of the Nineties: An Economic History;* and Gerald T. White, *The United States and the Problem of Recovery after 1893.*

divided into six-by-six-mile squares called townships. Townships were then divided into thirty-six numbered sections, each one square mile in area. Originally one of those sections was reserved for the public school system; in 1850 the law was changed to set aside two sections in each township (numbered 16 and 36) for school purposes.[12] This practice applied in Oklahoma Territory to the lands ceded by Indian tribes and opened to settlement.[13] At the beginning of 1893, Boyd—together with his friend Henry Asp and others—attempted to expand the traditional scheme to include higher-education funding.

Their campaign began in January. Boyd was active and influential in the Territorial Educational Association, which met in Kingfisher that month. The association passed a resolution calling attention to Oklahoma's special handicaps and needs and urging "upon our delegate in congress and all other friends there" the necessity of securing "as liberal grants of land as possible for . . . the endowment of the Agricultural College, Normal School and University already established."[14] A bill opening the Cherokee Outlet (more than 6 million acres) was pending in Congress. Boyd and the others assumed (correctly) that the customary provision of Sections 16 and 36 would be made for the common schools. But he wanted to persuade Congress to set aside one section in each township for higher-education purposes and (after the traumatic experience in financing the University building) another section for the financing of public buildings. He proposed that Section 13 be devoted to the former purpose and Section 33 to the latter.

Boyd and Asp, probably thinking that they would fare better with a Republican administration, appeared in Washington, D.C., during the last hours of Benjamin Harrison's term. They attempted to convince the Republican-controlled Senate Committee on Territories to write into the Cherokee Outlet law a provision for reserving the two additional sections. Opposition, partly from Kansas Republicans, eager to preserve as much of the public domain as possible for potential homesteaders, spelled defeat in the committee. The committee's chair, however, Senator Orville Platt, a powerful Republican from Connecticut, liked the idea and devised a scheme to accomplish it. Platt himself wrote an amendment to the Cherokee bill that empowered the president, after reserving in his proclamation the usual two sections for the common schools, also to reserve "such other lands" as he might deem advisable. That amendment—which historian Edward Everett Dale has called "the joker in the bill"—got by the committee and was signed into law by Harrison on the last day of his administration, March 3, 1893.[15]

At the first meeting of the new Regents, on May 6, Boyd explained his plan and what had been done thus far. The Regents granted him permission to go to Washington to

12. Paul Wallace Gates, *History of Public Land Law Development*, chap. 4.

13. R. E. Wood, "History of Oklahoma's School Endowment," *Chronicles of Oklahoma* 13 (1935): 381–90. At statehood, the federal government gave $5 million to the state, in lieu of Sections 16 and 36 in the Indian Territory part of the new state.

14. Quoted in Wardner, "Territorial University," 51.

15. Wood, "History of Oklahoma School Endowment," 382; Dale, "David Ross Boyd: Pioneer Educator," 18–19.

urge the new president, Grover Cleveland, actually to include the two additional sections when he issued his proclamation. Before Boyd left, Governor Renfrow called together all the Regents of the Territory's three colleges for a meeting in his office, where they agreed on the strategy of sending Boyd as their representative.[16] It seems likely that Boyd, the Republican, carried with him a letter of introduction from his friend and fellow Normanite Governor Renfrow, the Democrat. And it probably did not hurt that Renfrow had been the very man who had first proposed the name "Cleveland" for the county in which the University now proudly resided.

Until the end of his life Boyd could still recall the scene in the office of the secretary of the interior, Hoke Smith. It was mid-June, but Smith's office was still filled with hopeful Democrats looking for government jobs. Boyd explained to the receptionist that he already had a job and was not seeking another but merely wanted to take up some business with the secretary. He sat down to wait. At the end of the day, Smith shouted to the receptionist "to bring that fellow who doesn't want an office."[17] Boyd found a sympathetic listener. Hoke Smith's father had been the president of a small college and a professor at the University of North Carolina; Secretary Smith had himself served on the Atlanta School Board and was keenly interested in public education. Smith listened closely to his visitor and then said, "If we do this, nobody must know about it until the President's proclamation has been issued. Otherwise, there will be enormous pressure put upon him not to do it."[18] The next day, Smith arranged for Boyd to meet with President Cleveland.

"When I went in to see the president he was standing behind a chair, had it balanced on one leg, and was twisting it around all the time I was talking with him. He listened to my suggestion. . . . When I had finished he told me to write up the provisions as I had suggested them to him and gave me a note to Hoke Smith saying that he approved of this move. When the proclamation for the opening of the [Cherokee] strip was read by the president it included this clause, just as I had framed it."[19] Two months later, on August 19, Cleveland's proclamation opening the Cherokee Outlet reserved Section 13 for the three universities and Section 33 for public buildings.[20] Even more important, the practice of reserving those two sections was continued in future openings of Indian lands, including the huge Kiowa-Comanche-Wichita-Caddo lands distributed by lottery in August 1901. By 1897 the University was getting around $7,500 from Section 13 funds—about half the institution's total budget. And once oil and gas were found under some of the reserved

16. Regents' "Minutes," May 6, 1893; Wardner, "Territorial University," 52.

17. Boyd, "My Days as First University President," part 5, *Sooner Magazine* 2 (March 1930): 205. See also Dale, "David Ross Boyd: Pioneer Educator," 18.

18. Dale, "David Ross Boyd: Pioneer Educator," 19.

19. Boyd, "My Days as First University President," part 5, 205.

20. James D. Richardson, ed., *The Messages and Papers of the Presidents, 1789–1897,* 414. These reservations were made subject to the approval of Congress, which was given on May 4, 1894 (28 *U.S. Statutes at Large,* 71); Wood, "History of Oklahoma's School Endowment," 383.

lands, the money flowing into Oklahoma's higher education system became significant.[21] President Boyd's diplomatic mission to Washington did not solve his school's budgetary problems, of course; nothing would ever do that. But it made a good deal of difference to the infant enterprise.

$\sim$

IF MONEY WAS ONE LARGE CONCERN, space was another. There was a campus to plan and build and expand. The forty acres chosen by the Regents for the site of the University were in the middle of a wheat field. The earliest students and faculty therefore had to find lodging downtown and make their way to the campus on foot or by bicycle. Some followed the path made by thirsty cowboys who crossed from dry Indian Territory at Adkins Ford (where the bridge on the modern interstate highway now spans the river) and headed northeast to visit the numerous saloons of early Norman.[22] That route was soon replaced by one where students walked westward toward University Boulevard and then turned left toward the campus.[23] As early as September 1892 the town discussed the construction of an oak-board sidewalk along the west side of University Boulevard, from the intersection of Apache Street down to the entrance to the campus, and then angling off southwest to the new building.[24] In December an ordinance was passed,[25] but there was no rush to complete the project, since classes would not actually be held on the forty acres for another nine months. Although the wood sidewalk was the most convenient route to the campus, it had its own problems. The summer heat caused the nails to draw out of the boards, and they continually snagged the women's long skirts; men were hired regularly to pound the nails back into place. Weeds were always encroaching on the walkway and had to be trimmed. Rabbits found shady homes under the boards; but after an enterprising student introduced a bullsnake to solve the rabbit problem, a bullsnake problem suddenly erupted. Once, for example, Grace King was badly frightened by one of them as she walked down the sidewalk. The boulevard itself was divided into two sections by a row of little trees planted down the middle; the western half (next to the sidewalk) was for wagons and buggies, the eastern half for bicycles.[26]

21. Wardner, "Territorial University," 53–54; Dale, "David Ross Boyd: Pioneer Educator," 19. For the total amounts of money contributed to the school system through June 1935, see Wood, "History of Oklahoma's School Endowment," 388–90.

22. For the extent of liquor selling in Norman, see John Womack, *The Wet Years in Cleveland County, Oklahoma, 1889–1907: A Self-Imposed Investigation*, 15–18. A bill presented in the territorial legislature in 1895 would have prohibited liquor sales within a five-mile radius of the University of Oklahoma, but the bill was defeated.

23. Actually, as we have seen, students walking down Main or parallel streets toward University Boulevard were headed in a southwesterly direction. When they turned left to reach the campus, they were walking southeasterly before the Boulevard curved to due south at the corner where the McFarlin Methodist Church now stands.

24. The University building was erected just southwest of the present-day Holmberg Hall, between that building and the present Chemistry Building.

25. Wardner, "Territorial University," 55.

26. There are many descriptions of University Boulevard in the 1890s. See for example, Grace E. Ray, "Sooner Mishaps

*President Boyd's original home, with the plank sidewalk along University Boulevard*

*Another view of Boyd's first home and the plank walk, circa 1899*

By the end of the first decade, the lone building that was the students' destination had settled into a fixed familiarity. The basement was divided between the two scientists: the biology and anatomy laboratories of Van Vleet occupied the east wing; the pharmacy and chemistry labs of DeBarr, the west. Between them was the janitor's room. The first floor consisted of classrooms, offices, and a gymnasium that the *Catalogue* described as "a commodious room on the ground floor with a floor space of 24 × 77 feet. . . . fitted with the best of the more essential pieces of apparatus, together with a full outfit of dumb bells and wands for class drill in calisthenics and light gymnastics."[27] By 1902 there were bathroom facilities and a shower connected to the gym. The combination chapel and auditorium took up the west wing of the second floor; the east wing was shared by President Boyd, the registrar, and the small library. The top floor was given over to various activities, including those run by the students.

By 1900 it was perfectly clear that the University would soon require more land. In their *Biennial Report* (1900–1902) the Regents requested permission to purchase fifty acres north and east of the original forty. They emphasized the need for a water supply and sewer drainage, as well as expansion; and they pointed out that the experience of other universities showed the wisdom of buying additional land *before* it rose in value and the price became burdensome. The legislature declined to authorize the purchase.[28] In September 1901, however, the legislature did permit the Regents to buy twenty acres, provided that the town of Norman donated the purchase price. The law also permitted them to institute condemnation proceedings if a satisfactory arrangement could not be negotiated with the owner. The Regents chose the twenty acres lying directly east of the campus, between the present Asp and Jenkins Avenues. That land was owned by the same Charley Gorton who had joined Del Larsh and the others to lay claim to large sections in and around Norman back in April 1889; Gorton's personal claim contained the school's original forty acres. After resorting to condemnation proceedings, the Regents paid $5,088 for the property.[29] This twenty-acre parcel was to be the last land added to the campus until 1914.[30]

~

ENROLLMENT AT THE UNIVERSITY, hampered by the calamitous depression of the mid-1890s, remained fairly static. During the first year, as we have seen, 119 students appeared in Norman; four years later, in the academic year 1896–97, the number of students

of Twenty Years Ago," *University of Oklahoma Magazine* (February 1920): 9; Boyd, "My Days as First University President," part 3, *Sooner Magazine* 2 (December 1929): 95.

27. *University Catalogue, 1901–1902*, 10–11.

28. Judy Day, "University of Oklahoma Land Acquisition, 1891–1976," in Vertical File: "Land Acquisition," 4–5. She cites *The Biennial Report of the Board of Regents to the Governor, 1900–1902* (Norman: University of Oklahoma, 1902), 15–16. I am glad to acknowledge here the special benefit I received from Day's excellent paper.

29. Day, "University of Oklahoma Land Acquisition," 4–5. Gorton's home was on the corner of Jenkins and Boyd.

30. In February 1907, after another mission to Washington (where he had two interviews with President Theodore

had risen only to 161. But the return of prosperity sent the enrollment rocketing: 359 students came in 1897–98, more than double the preceding year. Faced with the happy prospect of increasing numbers, President Boyd recognized that he would have to devise and put into place more systematic ways of conducting the University's business. Not even he, with all his relentless energy and passion for detail, could be expected to superintend every facet of each student's program from his desk on the second floor of the University building. The problem became increasingly obvious as smaller percentages of the student body enrolled in the Preparatory Department, and ever greater numbers arrived ready for collegiate work, including work in a major field.[31]

By 1900 there were three ways to be admitted to collegiate-level work in the College of Arts and Sciences. Those who had graduated from the University's own Preparatory Department were deemed ready for college work and accepted on that basis alone. Those applicants who had not gone through the Preparatory Department were required to pass examinations in history and civics, English, mathematics, elementary science, and Latin. The work on which the exams were to be based was described in the *Catalogue*. In math, for example, the prospective student could expect questions over material through solid geometry; in Latin, not only grammar was tested, but also reading from Caesar, Cicero, and Virgil. In English, the test covered grammar, composition ("the candidate will be examined upon his ability to paragraph and to write good English") and familiarity with certain British and American classics. Finally, by 1900 the University was ready to acknowledge that some Oklahoma high schools had progressed to the point where work completed there was of sufficient rigor to permit admission without the entrance examination. The *Catalogue* listed four high schools that were "accredited in full for two years," two more that were accredited for one year, and twenty-two others whose work was "accredited in part" for purposes of admission to the University of Oklahoma.[32]

Classes generally began on a Wednesday or Thursday in mid-September; the first days of that week were devoted to registering students. Two days of vacation were given for Thanksgiving and around two weeks for Christmas. Students returned to campus soon after New Year's Day to finish the first semester and take final exams. There was no break between the first semester and the second, which began in early February. Holidays commemorated Washington's birthday and Decoration Day; and the second semester ended in early June, followed directly by commencement ceremonies.

In 1900 a new system of advising relieved President Boyd of that crushing burden. A Committee of Freshman Studies was to oversee the coursework of students during their

---

Roosevelt), Boyd secured the donation of the school section west of Norman to the University. The *Norman Transcript* (January 31 and February 21, 1907) estimated the value of the 640 acres at $50,000.

31. Until the 1896–97 academic year, all but about ten students at the University were in the Preparatory Department. In that year, twenty-one students were doing collegiate-level work. These are the figures thereafter: 1897–98, 50; 1898–99, 49; 1899–1900, 64; 1900–1901, 155; 1901–1902, 137; 1902–1903, 216; 1903–1904, 249; 1904–1905, 290.

32. The details are spelled out in the *University Catalogue, 1900–1901* (20–23), and in the annual catalogues thereafter.

first two years. The first appointees to this committee were Parrington and Paxton, with Van Vleet as chair. No student could take a class unless the choice had been approved by the committee. When students became juniors, they "pass[ed] from the control of the Committee of Freshman Studies to that of the professor under whom their major work is to be done; and all plans for work thereafter must be approved by the advising professor."[33] Once the student's list of courses was approved, he or she went to the Registrar and received for each class a card that was handed to the teacher on the first day of instruction. The average student enrolled for fifteen hours per semester. Those wishing to take less than thirteen or more than eighteen hours had to secure the permission of the Committee of Freshman Studies. There were about equal numbers of three- and four-hour courses offered each semester. Students were solemnly warned that an hour of credit normally required two additional hours each week for study, additional reading, or other preparation outside the classroom.[34]

At the semester's end the student received a grade. Until 1903 the University used a six-point grade scale: A (excellent); B (good); C (fair); D (poor); E (conditional); and F (failure). The conditional grade of E permitted the student to make up deficiencies; but if that was not accomplished within a year, the E became an F. After discussion among the faculty in 1903, the University moved to a five-point scale; the grade of E was dropped, and a D became the conditional grade. Grades were sent home to parents or guardians, together with a report of "any delinquencies of conduct." By 1900 it was also necessary to establish some policy on absences. Two kinds of absences were sanctioned: "permitted" and "excused." The former indicated a leave of absence from the University and was granted by President Boyd; the latter denoted an absence "for sickness or for some other cause in every way out of the ordinary," and it also could only be granted by President Boyd. Unexcused absences were another matter. If students cut more times than there were credit hours in the course, they had to present themselves to the instructor and submit to a "preliminary examination" before being admitted to the regular exam. Absences in excess of these limits deprived students of "the privilege of continuing" in the class without special permission of the faculty.[35]

By the end of the 1890s it was obvious that some system of record keeping was needed. The practices at other universities were studied; and President Boyd sent young George Bucklin, his student registrar, to the state universities in Kansas and Missouri to see how they did it. The method instituted in the 1900–1901 academic year used a complicated series of cards. At the time of their initial enrollment, students filled out one side of an "Information Card," giving name, birthdate, parents' names, and address. On the back of

---

For the national context of college admissions policy, see Harold Wechsler, *The Qualified Student: A History of Selective College Admission in America,* especially the "Preface" and chap. 1.

33. *University Catalogue, 1901–1902,* 29.

34. Ibid., 19–21; see also Wardner, "Territorial University," 90–91.

35. *University Catalogue, 1901–1902,* 21–22.

that card was recorded the semesters in which the student enrolled. Then an "Enrollment Card" was filled out, indicating the classes that the student was to take. The final grades were recorded, each semester, on a "Permanent Record Card."[36]

~

JUST AS THE INCREASE IN THE STUDENT BODY demanded new procedures, it also required new programs. By the close of the institution's first decade, students in the college could choose from a variety of major fields. In the sciences, they might major in chemistry, geology, physics, or mathematics; in the humanities, they could choose philosophy, history, Greek, Latin, German, French, or English; and in the social sciences, psychology, political science, or economics. In addition to these standard majors within the college, however, the University also established three new technical schools. Each of these pioneering programs was to prove extremely important in the development of the University of Oklahoma.

The study of pharmacy, the first strictly professional program begun by the University, had a unique and important place in the institution's early history. The *Catalogue* for 1893 explained: "The University this year responds to a demand made by those in the drug and prescription business for a department that will fit young men and women for the very responsible position of preparing and compounding medicines." The pharmacy program was under the direction of Edwin DeBarr, who held a bachelor of pharmacy degree from the University of Michigan. DeBarr, in fact, probably had a hand in stimulating the "demand" from the Territory's pharmacists, for he had been active in the Oklahoma Pharmaceutical Association since his arrival in Norman and served as secretary of the organization from 1893 to 1900.[37] He wrote back home to Michigan to the Parke-Davis Company, which donated fifty dollars' worth of supplies, and the program was underway. Seven students enrolled in each of the first two years; and by 1897–98 that number had more than doubled.[38] The first two students to earn collegiate degrees at the University of Oklahoma (Lemuel Dorrance of Lexington and Marshall A. Tucker of Norman) earned them in pharmaceutical chemistry in 1896.[39] In these early years, graduates from the pharmacy program accounted for an astounding percentage of the University's degree recipients. During the

36. "New System of Enrollment," *University Umpire*, February 15, 1901, 14–15; Wardner, "Territorial University," 92–93.

37. William G. Bray, "The History of Pharmacy in Oklahoma," 26.

38. Wardner, "Territorial University," 63–64.

39. Both of the first two graduates had interesting lives. Lem Dorrance gave up pharmacy and sought his fortune in Costa Rica, where he started a chocolate plantation, worked as a chemist for a gold-mining company, and went into the mahogany-exporting business in Nicaragua. He died of sunstroke in Central America around 1920. The pharmacy museum at the present College of Pharmacy in Oklahoma City is named in his honor. Marshall Tucker moved to Michigan and was attached to the famous Kellogg Sanitarium at Battle Creek. In 1902 he returned to Oklahoma and opened the first pharmacy in Lawton. From 1914 until his death in 1939, he was an Oklahoma City pharmacist and drugstore owner. Leo Glenn Tate, *Centennial: A History of the University of Oklahoma College of Pharmacy, 1893–1933*, 9–11.

territorial period, the University granted exactly two hundred degrees; eighty-six of them were in pharmaceutical chemistry.[40]

Pharmacy and chemistry, the two disciplines headed by DeBarr, used one large lecture room, a dispensing room, and a laboratory that had work-table space for about forty students. The pharmacy program won immediate credibility: in 1895, a year before there were any actual graduates, a delegation from the Territorial Pharmaceutical Board inspected the facilities (no doubt being ushered around by their secretary, Professor DeBarr) and agreed to accept any future graduates automatically as registered pharmacists without making them pass an examination.[41] In 1901 a weighing room and thirty chemical balances were added; and during the next year the entire chemistry-pharmacy operation was moved to the west end of the basement, where it expanded its facilities.[42] In 1899 the Department of Pharmacy became the School of Pharmacy; and the School of Pharmacy became the College of Pharmacy half a century later, in 1950.

Professor DeBarr was also intimately involved in a second professional program opened by the University. The great technological advances of the late nineteenth century created the need for engineers. The University's response to this need was not nearly as prompt as to the demand for pharmacists.[43] Nevertheless, students could soon cobble together a program of coursework that constituted suitable preparation for an engineering career. At first these courses were the physics and chemistry offerings of DeBarr. After the arrival of Frederick Stanton Elder, the mathematics professor from Princeton, in September 1895, other courses suitable for engineering ("Analytics of Three Dimensions and Surfaces," "Trigonometry and Surveying") made their way into the *Catalogue*. By 1903 Elder was offering courses in "Graphics" and by 1904 in "Strength of Materials." When Charles N. Gould, the geologist, joined the faculty in 1900, he added work in prospecting, mining, quarrying, and assaying—with special attention given to products found in Oklahoma. In the *Catalogue* for 1901–1902 the new heading "Engineering Courses" summarized the situation:

> Full courses are not as yet offered nor degrees granted along the lines of civil, mechanical, mining, or sanitary engineering. Nevertheless by a proper choice of courses already scheduled here in the subjects of mathematics, surveying, graphics, chemistry, geology, mineralogy, German and French, students may find full equivalents for courses as provided in the first two years at the best scientific and technical schools of the east.

40. Gittinger, *The University of Oklahoma*, 187.

41. This was the same arrangement as for graduates of other accredited pharmacy programs across the nation. The examination was principally for those who had "apprenticed" in drugstores around the state. In the spring of 1899 the territorial legislature required the Pharmacy Board automatically to register graduates from the Norman program. Tate, *Centennial*, 14.

42. Bray, "History of Pharmacy in Oklahoma," 39–40.

43. Tom Love, "History of the University of Oklahoma College of Engineering"; see especially chap. 1: "The Beginning, 1892–1908."

There can be little doubt that the flurry of engineering-related activity after 1900 was provoked by President Boyd's fear of what was going on in Stillwater.[44] The Oklahoma Agricultural and Mechanical College had a natural claim to engineering instruction; and although there was some tension between the "agricultural" and "mechanical" halves of that school's mission in the 1890s, Oklahoma A & M had made an impressive start by 1898. That year President George Morrow established an engineering subdivision, and a dozen men began the program in the new mechanical arts shop. Very quickly the Stillwater program began to produce large numbers of graduates.[45] The A & M Regents authorized the construction of an engineering building in 1902 and then expanded it four years later. At this early stage, Boyd was cognizant of developments in Stillwater and determined not to surrender engineering education to the University's rival to the north. His anxiety was reflected in the hammering together of a rudimentary engineering program at Norman. But the showdown would not come until 1904, when each school marshaled all the political influence it could command.

Education in medicine was a third technical and professional undertaking during the University's opening years, but here too the effort was embryonic and primitive.[46] Strictly speaking, medical education began in 1898, with the arrival of Albert Van Vleet and the establishment of the Department of Biology. Before Van Vleet, there had been courses in chemistry, physics, and pharmacy; and while these were doubtless valuable, they in no sense constituted a systematic or coherent program leading to the practice of medicine. With the arrival of Van Vleet, the University felt able to announce two programs in medical education. Students could now complete a four-year course majoring in biology, under essentially the same format that led to other bachelor of science degrees at the University. In addition to their scientific course work, students choosing this path were exposed to foreign language, history, astronomy, and more than thirty hours of electives that did not have to be taken in science.[47] For those students in a hurry, however, the University also announced a two-year course. It was "independent of the College of Arts and is offered to meet the needs of those who desire to devote their entire time to strictly professional studies."[48] This streamlined path attempted to duplicate the first two years' work of "the best medical schools" and led to a "certificate of standing," which, it was hoped, would get students admitted directly into the advanced clinical work of regular medical schools. The

---

44. Philip Reed Rulon, *Oklahoma State University, since 1890*, 90–91.

45. By 1912, 122 people had earned degrees in architectural, civil, electrical, and mechanical engineering fields. Between 1898 and 1914, enrollments increased more than twelvefold in the Stillwater engineering program. Ibid., 90.

46. The indispensable source remains Mark R. Everett, *Medical Education in Oklahoma: The University of Oklahoma School of Medicine and Medical Center, 1900–1931*. See also Elroy L. Rice and George Lynn Cross, *A History of the Department of Botany and Microbiology at the University of Oklahoma: The First Hundred Years*, chap. 2; A. C. Scott, "The University of Oklahoma School of Medicine," in George Lynn Cross, President Emeritus MSS, Box 6, Folder: "University of Oklahoma"; and Wardner, "Territorial University," 78–81.

47. *University Catalogue, 1898–99*, 19.

48. *University Catalogue, 1900–1901*, 36–37.

"Pre-Medical Course" (encompassing both the two-year and the four-year plans) included from the start extensive coursework in the relevant fields. Seventy-nine hours (twenty-six courses) were offered, including histology, anatomy, physiology, embryology, urinary analysis, materia medica (the study of drugs and other substances used in medicine), toxicology, and, of course, pharmacy. In 1899 the territorial legislature contributed to the effort by permitting the University to use unclaimed human bodies for dissection.[49]

By 1900, despite the fact that only eight students had enrolled in the medical course, the enthusiasm was growing. A small wooden one-story building (twenty-five by seventy-five feet) was built that year for work in anatomy, the facilities that DeBarr and Van Vleet needed were expanded in the University building's basement (at the expense of Professor Buchanan's history courses), and the Regents allocated $450 for biological apparatus.[50]

One of the first two graduates from the College of Arts and Sciences (i.e., not from the pharmacy program) was Roy Philson Stoops. He received his degree in 1898 and proceeded to the University of Illinois to study medicine. Forty years later he wrote a letter to the dean of the University of Oklahoma Medical School, recounting a revealing episode in the early history of medical education at the school:

> President Boyd had considerable difficulty in finding a man to head the department [of medicine]. I received a letter from him stating his difficulty and asking me to see what I could do in Chicago. I was only a third year medical student, so I called upon Dr. William A. Evans in Pathology at the University of Illinois. Dr. Evans recommended three physicians. President Boyd corresponded with all three, and finally wrote me that the men would not come for $1,000 a year, and that he had secured the services of Dr. L. N. Upjohn, a graduate of Ann Arbor, Michigan.[51]

The "official" beginning of the Medical School may in fact be dated to 1900, with the arrival of Dr. Lawrence Northcote Upjohn. He was twenty-seven years old and had just earned his M.D. degree from Michigan. He came from a family of physicians; and his father and an uncle founded the famous Upjohn drug company in Kalamazoo. In conjunction with Upjohn's hiring, the University proudly announced its "preclinical medical school" and added a Department of Pathology. The first head of the School of Medicine lasted only until 1904; he resigned to join the family's drug firm and became its president in 1930. But he left behind the rudiments of a full-fledged program in medicine. His successor in the position was none other than Dr. Roy Stoops. He had come back to Norman the year before as an instructor in physiology at $500 a year; he and his physician wife supplemented their income with their private practice in offices behind the First National Bank building in downtown Norman.[52]

---

49. Wardner, "Territorial University," 79–80; *University Catalogue, 1900–1901*, 37.

50. Wardner, "Territorial University," 80–81.

51. Roy P. Stoops to Robert U. Patterson, January 18, 1939, quoted in Everett, *Medical Education in Oklahoma*, 8–9.

52. Everett, *Medical Education in Oklahoma*, 9–11; Scott, "The University of Oklahoma School of Medicine," 2.

Meanwhile, the physicians of Oklahoma City were eager to have a full medical school in their own municipality. By 1903 they felt confident enough to ask for a meeting with University officials. Boyd sent Upjohn to hear their plan for starting a medical school with the full clinical component. Upjohn reported negatively to Boyd, and the president told the doctors that the University would not at that time establish a four-year medical school. The doctors turned immediately to the authorities of Epworth College, a new Methodist school that was to open its doors in September 1904. Officials at this school, which was destined to become Oklahoma City University, were less hesitant than Boyd. From the very beginning Epworth embarked upon a full program in medical education, its faculty being composed entirely of practicing city physicians. By 1910 Epworth's Medical College had forty-seven students and sixteen graduates.[53] And by that time the rivalry was serious, President Boyd was gone, and all parties were eager for some diplomatic solution to the problem of having one medical enterprise in Norman and the other in Oklahoma City.

In addition to the three technical programs in pharmacy, engineering, and medicine, the University boasted a fourth course of study outside of the College of Arts and Sciences. Almost from the start, the University offered work in music: voice, piano, and string instruments. Boyd hired a series of instructors (eighteen between 1893 and 1907) to teach these fields, but none of them lasted very long. Grace King, who served from 1896 until her marriage in 1901, had the longest tenure. These teachers (exactly half of them women) were supported not by state appropriations but by fees from students enrolled with them for training. A disproportionate number of the Fine Arts students were women. In 1903 the School of Fine Arts enrolled seventy-six students. Sixty-five of them were women.[54] The study of music attracted women students for obvious reasons. At a time when most professions were regarded as male preserves and effectively closed to women, music was still regarded as a sign of feminine accomplishment and gentility. For many parents of women, no doubt, studying music was a way for their daughters to partake of the advantages of college education (including the social and matrimonial advantages) while still adhering to the traditional requirements of stereotypical femininity. In addition, this was still the day when husbands whose "cultured" wives could comfort them after a trying day at the office, playing softly at the piano and singing to them sweetly, were thought to be particularly fortunate. For women who were destined to remain unmarried, the ability to give lessons in small Oklahoma towns might be their only way to sustain themselves economically.

53. For the account of an important participant in the story of Epworth and early medical training in Oklahoma City, see H. Coulter Todd, "History of Medical Education in Oklahoma from 1904 to 1910," *University of Oklahoma Bulletin*, n.s. 402 (1928): 1–30. Dr. Todd had been one of those who negotiated with Upjohn in 1903 about the creation of a four-year University program in Oklahoma City. See also Gaston Litton, *History of Oklahoma at the Golden Anniversary of Statehood*, 2:403–404; and Paul W. Milhouse, *Oklahoma City University: A Miracle at 23rd and Blackwelder*, chap. 4. For a list of Epworth's graduates in medicine, see Gittinger, *University of Oklahoma*, 200–201.

54. *University Catalogue, 1903–1904*, 119–21.

At the start of the 1903–1904 academic year, after a decade of educational work, the University of Oklahoma enrolled 465 students. More than half of them (259: 56 percent) were still enrolled in the Preparatory Department. The College of Arts and Sciences had 123 students (about 26.5 percent) who were pursuing various majors; 2 of them were listed as graduate students and another 8 as working in the Medical Course. The School of Pharmacy had 19 students (4 percent) and the School of Fine Arts, 76 (16 percent). Another 39 students were pursuing work in business, which was not yet a formal program.

~

WHAT WOULD NEW STUDENTS ARRIVING at the turn of the century have seen as they strode down the oak sidewalk toward the campus? Charles Gould came to Norman to teach geology in June 1900. He remembered that the University consisted of one three-story building. There were no houses built on the east side of University Boulevard and only four along the west side of the street between Main and the campus. "Everything between [University] Boulevard and the section line, now Jenkins Street, was a wheat field. Asp and DeBarr avenues had not yet been laid out. . . . The elm and locust trees on campus were little higher than a man's head."[55] Those trees, diminutive as they were, represented the efforts of several people; the first attempts to beautify the campus, it will be recalled, were made as early as the spring of 1892 in response to Governor Seay's proclamation of an Oklahoma "Arbor Day."

In large measure, however, the trees that were planted on the campus were the work—almost the obsession—of President Boyd. There are so many myths connected to the story of Boyd and his trees that it is difficult to know which ones are true. The survival of so many stories, however, indicates that landscaping the town and the campus was profoundly important to Boyd, at the heart of his vision of the future. One persistent story, very widely repeated in early accounts of the University, is that Boyd bought out a Perry nursery (or in some versions a Winfield, Kansas, nursery and in others a Wisconsin nursery) with his own money and not only planted the trees on the campus himself and personally watered them during their first year but also donated many of them to residents of Norman who would plant and care for them. According to the legend, he gave the trees free of charge if they lived for at least a year; but if they died, the recipient was required to pay. Another story is that some cranky townspeople complained about taxpayer money being wasted on trees, but they were effectively silenced when it was revealed that Boyd had paid for them himself. Still another story has Boyd personally maintaining a nursery behind the University Building (or, in other renditions, southwest of that building and, in still others, behind the place where Evans Hall now stands) and selling trees both for their natural beauty and as a way to make some money for the school; but in some versions, Boyd distributed these seedlings free of charge.

---

55. Gould is quoted in Day, "University of Oklahoma Land Acquisition," 4.

Four decades later, Boyd shared a memory with an ornithologist, Margaret Morse Nice. "When we set out the first trees (in 1893), there were no woodpeckers to get the insect enemies and they could hardly survive the borers," Boyd recalled. "Finally I thought of the plan to haul a number of large dead trunks of cottonwood trees—beginning to decay and full of insects, and I 'planted' them in different locations. It was not long till the wood-peckers and other birds discovered them and they soon dug into the old trunks of trees and found food and made cavities for nests and inside of a year several nested; they soon settled the borers and other insect enemies." But even this direct testimony from Boyd differs in various narrations.[56] According to one tale, Boyd got history professor and city councilman James Buchanan to push through a Norman ordinance prohibiting the killing of these insect-eating woodpeckers; this feat of lawmaking, moreover, was accomplished against the influence of the owner of the local telephone company (in other tellings, the local electric light magnate), who thought that woodpeckers were bad for his poles and who paid a bounty to boys who would kill them.[57]

There is doubtless a good deal of truth behind these old stories. Even in Arkansas City, Superintendent Boyd emphasized tree-planting and the building of parks as part of his pro-gram for putting to work those awaiting the opening of Oklahoma Territory. It was, more-over, precisely the "treelessness" of the landscape that Boyd most readily recalled when he reminisced about his arrival in Norman. Dozens of his surviving letters are concerned with trees.[58] "I find almost as much pleasure in observing the development of a tree as in enjoying it after it is grown," he wrote to John Blakeny, the state senator from Shawnee in 1903.[59] And yet, even when full credit is given to Boyd's undoubted devotion to trees, beautification, and landscaping, there is certainly some wild exaggeration involved. In a speech to the Faculty Forum in March 1929, for example, J. J. Burke, a newspaperman who had come to Oklahoma City in the land run, recalled the old days:

56. Margaret Morse Nice, "A List of the Birds of the Campus of the University of Oklahoma," *Publications of the University of Oklahoma Biological Survey* 2 (1930): 195–96. For the variations, see Blake Gumprecht, "Trees for a Prairie Town: Early Tree Planting in Norman, Oklahoma," 17. I have relied heavily on Gumprecht's meticulous research, and uncited facts in this section are drawn from his work. His original seminar paper can be found in Vertical File: "Tree Planting." A modified version of his original seminar paper was published as "Transforming the Prairie: Early Tree Planting in an Oklahoma Town," *Historical Geography* 29 (2001): 116–34.

57. On Boyd and his trees, see (in addition to Gumprecht, "Trees for a Prairie Town") George Milburn, "Planting a University: First Varsity President Recounts How He Did It," *Sooner Magazine* 1 (November 1928): 39–41; Boyd, "My Days as First University President," part 3, 94; Long and Hart, *The Sooner Story*, 11–13; Gittinger, *University of Oklahoma*, 20–21; Errett Rains Newby, "Notes on Incidents at the University of Oklahoma," in Vertical File: "History of O.U. (Newby)," 20; Wardner, "Territorial University," 57; Dale, "David Ross Boyd, 1853–1936," 80, 92; Morrissey, "David Ross Boyd," 207–10.

58. Morrissey, "David Ross Boyd," 208, writes that "during the sixteen years of his presidency at the University of Oklahoma he wrote hundreds of letters in which he mentioned, ordered, or praised trees." See also Gumprecht, "Trees for a Prairie Town," 21. In 1931 a *Daily Oklahoman* reporter wrote that "while on his last visit to the University of Oklahoma, Doctor Boyd manifested almost as much interest in the campus trees as he did in the buildings. He had caused the trees to be planted as the 40 acres on which the University was built was beyond the timber belt. He personally assisted in planting many of the trees." See Alan Rucker, "The Daddy of O.U.," *Daily Oklahoman*, February 8, 1931, D6.

59. Cited by Morrissey, "David Ross Boyd," 208, as Boyd to Blakeny, April 10, 1903.

At that time West Norman was an almost treeless raw prairie, and now—just look at it! Is there a prettier little city in any part of the West?—and a whole lot of that prettiness is due to the continual and everlasting propaganda of Dr. Boyd in those early days. He was as one "crying in the wilderness; 'Plant Trees! Plant Trees!! Plant Trees!!!' " Why, one of his neighbors told me many years ago that he . . . was so everlastingly at him with his "Plant Trees!! Plant Trees!!" that to get rid of him he had to plant trees, and then became so interested in seeing the darn things grow that he became almost as pestiferous to his friends in telling them about it as Dr. Boyd had been to him.[60]

But it is quite unfair to the other early settlers in Norman to portray President Boyd as one "crying in the wilderness," a "pestiferous" lone crusader for trees, preaching their benefits and beauties to an indifferent frontier community. The passion for planting trees was widespread among pioneers who came to the plains from the forested eastern United States; they were men and women whose idea of a home was closely bound up with the presence of trees.[61] Before Boyd ever arrived in Norman, two nurseries were doing business in town, and many trees had already been planted. The editor of the *Norman Transcript*, Ed Ingle, was an especially persistent evangelist for the planting of trees; and nearly every early issue of his paper urged citizens to "plant a tree if possible."[62] Before Boyd came to Norman, moreover, a citizens' committee discussed planting trees on the University's grounds, and another committee gave attention to planting trees along University Boulevard. "Trees will be badly needed," the editor of the *Transcript* noted in March 1892, months before Boyd first stepped off the train and began to organize the University. "Everybody interested in this great institution is invited and urged to bring trees to the ground next week for planting."[63]

Moreover, if Boyd did spend his own money on trees, he urged the use of public money as well: on November 22, 1892, for example, the Board of Regents spent $70.00 to purchase a thousand shade trees.[64] And if Boyd gave trees away to the citizens of the town (a story for which there is no evidence in the newspapers), he also sold them from a private nursery; beginning in 1896, he ran weekly ads in the *Transcript* advertising shade trees "for sale cheap."[65] Boyd also sold trees to the Normal School in Edmond, to the Southwestern Normal in Weatherford, and to the college for African Americans at Langston. In April

60. J. J. Burke, "Why the University Is Located Where It Is: Address before Faculty Forum, March 27, 1929," in Charles N. Gould MSS, Box 34, Folder 4.

61. On the general phenomenon, see Wilmon H. Droze, *Trees, Prairies and People: A History of Tree Planting on the Great Plains*; Roger Welsch, *Of Trees and Dreams: The Fiction, Fact and Folklore of Tree Planting on the Northern Plains*; David M. Emmons, *Garden in the Grasslands*; and Edward Everett Dale, "Wood and Water: Twin Problems of the Prairie Plains," *Nebraska History* 29 (1948): 87–104. I am indebted to Gumprecht, "Trees for a Prairie Town," for these citations.

62. Gumprecht, "Trees for a Prairie Town," 5–10, gives an exhaustive account of the many pre-Boyd tree planting efforts in Norman. The *Norman Transcript* reported on April 18, 1890, two years before Boyd's arrival, that in response to the first Arbor Day "thousands of trees" had been planted in town.

63. *Norman Transcript*, March 19, 1892. See Gumprecht, "Trees for a Prairie Town," 7.

64. *Journal of the House Proceedings, 1893*, 336.

65. Gumprecht, "Trees for a Prairie Town," 16.

1903 he estimated that he had sold at least 15,000 trees that spring and said that he could have sold many more if he had them.[66]

Even though the record casts doubt on some aspects of the mythology of Boyd and the trees, he still deserves enormous credit for his efforts. When, in the spring of 1893, the trees that the Regents had purchased the previous fall finally arrived (from the same Winfield, Kansas, nursery that Boyd had patronized when he was organizing public beautification in Arkansas City), he helped to plant them on the campus and along University Boulevard. For months he watered them himself with water bought for fifteen cents a barrel (Norman did not build its first water system until 1894). When a drought killed many of them two years later, he doggedly replanted. By Christmas 1893 the *Transcript* claimed that President Boyd had planted around 10,000 trees. But that claim may be doubted: it would have required Boyd to plant more than twenty trees every single day for the sixteen months since arriving in Norman. Shortly thereafter he began two large nurseries. One of them was near his new home on University Boulevard. There he planted thousands of shade and fruit trees that he had purchased, apparently with his own money, from a nursery in Washington. Elm trees predominated in Boyd's nursery, and Elm Street took its name from these early efforts. Boyd's second nursery was located on five acres across the street on the campus, south of the University's building and west of where Bizzell Memorial Library now stands. From these two sources, Boyd supplied the campus and the town. By 1898 the *Kansas City Star* was able to tell its readers that "[t]he most marked change has taken place at the territorial university of Norman. President D. R. Boyd is an enthusiast of tree culture and has transformed the campus from a treeless waste into a magnificent grove of elms, maples, ash and other trees."[67]

According to one tale about President Boyd and the trees (a tale that first appeared in 1929), a season of drought had struck Oklahoma one summer in the 1890s; no year is given, but it was probably 1895. When President Boyd left town "in early July" for an educational conference in Denver, his saplings had not yet sprouted leaves. But while he was gone, a heavy rain fell; and when he returned and got off the train in Norman, he saw "in the August moonlight" his beloved saplings heavy with foliage. It was, he said, the happiest sight of his life.[68] The story has such metaphorical and symbolic power—Boyd as the "planter" and "cultivator" not only of delicate young trees, rich with the promise of growth and fruition, but of a delicate and promising young university as well—that one very much hopes it is true.

---

66. Ibid., 21.

67. Quoted in the *Norman Transcript*, June 17, 1898.

68. The story first appears in Boyd, "My Days as First University President," part 3, 95, which is based on an extended interview with Boyd by Roy Hadsell and an undergraduate working for the *Sooner Magazine*, Betty Kirk; it is repeated in Long and Hart, *The Sooner Story*, 11. Interestingly, the episode is not mentioned in an interview of 1928 given by Boyd to another undergraduate, George Milburn, in the *Sooner Magazine*: "Planting a University." This omission is curious, because Milburn's story emphasizes Boyd's tree-planting work.

*The University building, surrounded by President Boyd's trees, circa 1900*

~

GETTING MONEY, ACQUIRING LAND, landscaping the campus, establishing administrative procedures, expanding and establishing programs, and recruiting students might have been the major problems facing President Boyd and the University during the 1890s, but they were hardly the only ones. Another troubling factor was competition. The University of Oklahoma was not the only institution of higher education in the neighborhood, and each competitor drew off potential students. Some of the rivals were quickly and easily disposed of. In January 1891 Aaron McDaniel began offering classes in penmanship and bookkeeping in Norman. He found the response encouraging enough to start the Norman Business College in June 1892; both Tom Waggoner and Mort Bixler were trustees.[69] Other competitors were the short-lived Noble Academy to the south;[70] and, more formidably, Epworth College (forerunner of Oklahoma City University), which opened in September 1904, to the north.[71]

69. Womack, *Norman: An Early History*, 114–15.

70. Ibid., 117.

71. Milhouse, *Oklahoma City University*, chaps. 3 and 4.

*Trees sheltering the walk along the west side of University Boulevard, circa 1903*

Then came a shock from Washington, D.C. On February 7, 1894, Representative Walter Hayes of Iowa introduced into Congress a bill that would have placed "the University of Oklahoma" near Kildare, a few miles north of Ponca City in the newly opened Cherokee Outlet. An identical bill was offered in the Senate by Eppa Hunton of Virginia.[72] Either unaware of the existence of the school at Norman or indifferent to it, the Congress sent the proposal to the House Committee on Public Lands for a recommendation. Both the commissioner of the Land Office, S. W. Lamoreaux, and secretary of the interior Hoke Smith informed the committee in March that they knew no reason why Congress could not enact the measure if it chose to do so. Nevertheless, on August 7 the committee reported negatively on the idea, and the proposal was tabled. One suspects that sometime between March and August of 1894 the Oklahoma delegate, Dennis Flynn, had quietly informed the members that there already was a University of Oklahoma, that it had been in existence for more than two years, and that it was located in Norman.[73]

72. House Bill 5652 (introduced on February 7) and Senate Bill 1642 (introduced on February 16) would have set aside Sec. 13 of township 27, north of range 2 east, for the "University of Oklahoma." See *Congressional Record*, 53rd Congress, 2nd Sess. (1894), vol. 26, part 2: 2015 and part 3: 2246.

73. *Reports of Committees of the House of Representatives for the Second Session of the Fifty-third Congress, 1893–94*, Report #1320, 583–94. Wardner, "Territorial University," 55, speculates that the negative report of the committee was also occasioned by the fact that Congress had gotten around to approving President Cleveland's August 1893 reservations for the Cherokee Outlet and that the proposed section, being a Section 13, was covered, thus removing the land from congressional disposition.

But the most troubling competitor, as far as David Ross Boyd was concerned, was located right on the opposite side of town. The Southern Methodists, in cooperation with town leaders, had previously established their own school. It predated the University by two full years and enrolled around 130 students when it opened on September 18, 1890. For its first three years it met in rooms at and adjacent to the Southern Methodist church at Crawford and Tonhawa Streets. It charged a tuition of $3 per month and prided itself on its strict moral atmosphere and "kind but firm" discipline. After three years of arduous fundraising, the college moved to its new quarters at the eastern end of Main Street, where the Central State Griffin Memorial Hospital now stands. The land and the building (ninety by forty feet and three stories tall) had been provided by the town. In honor of its commanding position atop a low rise overlooking the town of Norman to the west, the name High Gate College was chosen. After its move from the church to east Norman, the school restricted its enrollment to young women; but prospective students were given an unusually frank and solemn warning by school officials: "Young ladies desiring to have a good time will not find this institution to their liking." Among other regulations imposed by the stern Southern Methodists was a rule permitting the inspection of the letters the women wrote and an absolute prohibition against their attendance at "places of amusement."[74] Even before the full effects of the crushing economic depression of the 1890s, High Gate was in trouble. Changing leadership, sinking enrollments, a cooling interest on the part of Norman civic leaders, and, above all, the rise of the tuition-free University about two miles away all contributed to the school's difficulties.

Despite the college's problems, High Gate's presence still worried Boyd. In the first place, every young woman enrolled there meant that in the midst of the depression there was one less potential student for the University of Oklahoma. Worse, Boyd could imagine an even more harrowing nightmare. What if High Gate proved to be just the beginning? What if a series of small denominational colleges eventually surrounded his new university, seducing away students and diverting the affections and loyalties of various religionists to themselves and away from the state institution? It was a disturbing vision, and Boyd must have given considerable thought to combating the possibility. The answer was to come from an unlikely source.

At Christmas time, 1893, Bishop John H. Vincent of the Methodist Episcopal Church (the northern Methodists) presided over the Second Session of the Oklahoma Annual Conference in Guthrie.[75] There he made a proposal destined to be known as "the Vincent plan." If the town of Norman would donate five acres of land, the northern Methodists would build a dormitory costing not less than $5,000 for Methodist students of the Uni-

74. Oscar A. Kinchen, "Oklahoma's First College, Old High Gate at Norman," *Chronicles of Oklahoma* 14 (1936): 312–23; quotations on 317. Other accounts of this school closely follow Kinchen's excellent article. See Womack, *Norman: An Early History*, 115–20; Wardner, "Territorial University," 58–62; Gittinger, *University of Oklahoma*, 22; Morrissey, "David Ross Boyd," 117–20.

75. H. E. Brill, comp., *Story of the Methodist Episcopal Church in Oklahoma*, 33.

versity of Oklahoma. The students and their parents would be assured of a moral atmosphere, Bible study, and a chapel for daily and Sunday services. The dormitory would be "an annex to the University, but under the control of the Church, where students could be as well cared for as in a denominational school."[76] A Norman banker who had attended the Guthrie meeting reported Vincent's idea to Boyd, who saw immediately that such a scheme, particularly if followed by other denominations, would obviate the need for rival denominational colleges. Together with Professor Rice and two prominent businessmen, he rushed up to Guthrie to talk to Vincent about his plan and to invite him to Norman. On January 9, 1894, Bishop Vincent arrived and received treatment normally reserved for heads of state. A welcoming committee escorted him from the train station to the Victoria Hotel, where he dined with Norman leaders. He had the honor of giving the very first lecture at the new University chapel; and his talk, "Tom and His Teachers," was heard by an overflow crowd of appreciative townspeople. He met with fellow ministers and a committee of the most important Norman businessmen.[77] The townspeople could smell the prospect of vast new building activity if the other denominations followed the northern Methodists' lead. A five-acre donation at the northeast corner of Boyd and University (where Whitehand Hall now stands) was agreed upon; and more than eighty Normanites quickly oversubscribed the $1,200 fund to purchase the land. It was also hinted that similar arrangements could be made for any other denomination that wished to build a dormitory near the campus.[78]

It is difficult to say whether Vincent's proposal involved an element of interdenominational competition against the southern Methodists, who owned High Gate College. It is certainly true that rivalry between the northern and southern Methodist branches was particularly lively in border states. Oklahoma, with some of its migrants coming from the South and others from the North, was the scene of some especially intense struggle.[79] In any case, the Vincent plan probably was the final blow for High Gate. On October 27 Bishop R. K. Hargrove of the Methodist Episcopal Church, South, arrived in town for what amounted to a formal surrender. He was also accorded respectful treatment by Boyd and the University community and by the ministers and leaders of Norman. He was escorted from the train to a tour of the campus and "gave his approval to that institution." What else transpired between Boyd and Bishop Hargrove is unknown, but in November the women of High Gate began to transfer to the University of Oklahoma; and by Christmas the building was dark, vacant, and abandoned. The beleaguered president of the beleaguered college was rewarded for his trials with the plum of a choice church in Purcell;

76. Quoted in Kinchen, "Oklahoma's First College," 318.

77. *Norman Transcript*, January 12, 1894.

78. Wardner, "Territorial University," 59–60.

79. For the competition between the Methodist denominations in the state, see Leland Clegg and William B. Oden, *Oklahoma Methodism in the Twentieth Century*, chaps. 2–5. The denominations within Methodism were not finally united until 1939.

and on April 12, 1895, the building was purchased by the Oklahoma Sanitarium Company. On July 27, after a large expansion and remodeling project had been completed, the newspaper reported that "a car load of insane people" had arrived at their new home.[80]

Nothing ever came of the Vincent plan. Nor did anything come of a similar proposal that Boyd engineered with the Presbyterians. In early November 1894 the Presbyterian Synod selected a group of trustees to erect a dormitory for around fifty Presbyterian students at the University. The Presbyterians received the same terms as the northern Methodists: the people of Norman would donate the land, and the denomination would raise the money for construction of the building. Boyd persuaded his own church to contribute $500 toward the effort. Early University catalogues confidently announced the imminent opening of the two dormitories.[81] But by 1897–98 the hope was abandoned. The intention had been defeated by the difficulty of raising money during the depression. In November 1899 the trustees for Vincent Hall admitted defeat and gave any unclaimed donations to the Norman Public Library.[82] By that time, of course, the Vincent plan had served one of its major purposes as far as David Ross Boyd was concerned; it had helped to defeat the worrisome prospect of competition from a multitude of small denominational colleges. Boyd was not the sort of fellow to gloat or to boast of his victories in public. But in mid-December 1894 he made an uncharacteristically bold statement to a newspaper reporter: "As is usual in new settlements, the different churches tried to start schools. The first was the Methodist Church, South. Bishop Vincent and myself stopped their attempts, and we substituted a novel plan for theirs. We succeeded in getting them to adopt it."[83]

~

THE WILLINGNESS OF THE YOUNG LADIES from the Southern Methodist school at High Gate to escape the iron confines of such strict discipline and flee to the more relaxed atmosphere of the state University at the other end of town indicates something important about the students in Norman. They were not averse to having a good time. The amusements in which they indulged and the society that they created among themselves may seem innocent and a little frivolous to modern observers. But it was, in general, enthusiastic and wholesome and joyful. It was also what the students remembered most readily and most vividly about the glad days that they had spent at college.

The town of Norman was completely isolated except for the railroad. Although the trains did heavy service (even before settlement in 1889 the Santa Fe was running eight trains north and south through Norman each day), the town was an island surrounded by a sea of prairie grass. Here and there a few old trails—mere paths through the grass, follow-

80. Both quotations cited in Kinchen, "Oklahoma's First College," 321, 323.

81. See catalogues for 1894–95, 1895–96, and 1896–97.

82. Wardner, "Territorial University," 60–61.

83. Cited in Kinchen, "Oklahoma's First College," 322, as *State Democrat*, December 12, 1894.

ing the easiest way—crisscrossed the land; but soon farmers built their fences across even these. The government made little provision for road construction: except for a few postal roads, significant road building in the region had to wait until World War I. To whatever extent the early citizens of Norman were concerned about transportation, they worried about streets *within* the town and (for purposes of limited trade in the neighborhood) about bridges and ferries over the Canadian River.[84]

New students who did not live in town arrived at school by arduous journeys. Carleton Ross Hume, son of a government doctor at the Kiowa and Comanche agency in Anadarko, entered the University in 1894. Almost forty-five years later, he could still recall his trip to Norman. "I left Anadarko on Sunday afternoon by buggy, caught the midnight Rock Island train from Chickasha to El Reno; then took the morning train on the Choctaw (now Rock Island) to Oklahoma City, there changed to the Santa Fe afternoon train, and reached Norman, Monday Sept. 8th, about 2:00 P.M."[85] Hume's odyssey (twenty-four hours to travel about fifty-five miles) was typical.

Once they got off the train, students had to find places to live in town. Norman's isolation made commuting even short distances impossible. Naturally, the arrival late every summer of hundreds of residence-seeking students opened an enormous economic opportunity to townspeople willing to house and feed them. "The people in Norman take a special interest in making the students at home and their stay pleasant," the *Norman Transcript* boasted in 1897. "Private homes and well furnished rooms are open to them at reasonable terms, and the two hundred students now in attendance find desirable places to board and room with very little difficulty."[86] Students sometimes got a different impression. Ross Hume remembered that, when he arrived, "rooming and boarding places were very scarce." He found a place to stay, but he boarded "near the Santa Fe depot, almost a mile from my room, and with hardly any sidewalks it was very inconvenient. . . . The out of town students did not receive much welcome into the community, and my first social function was about six weeks later, and I had many homesick days."[87]

The early catalogues emphasized the inexpensiveness of a college education in Norman:

> Board, including furnished rooms, can be had at from $2.50 to $3.00 per week. Clubs have been organized which bring the expenses of board much lower. . . . Unfurnished rooms and rooms for self boarding may be had at very reasonable rates. When students can do so it is a very good plan to rent a small house of say two to four rooms, furnish them and board in one of the clubs. The whole expense for the year for a student may

84. See the excellent account in Speer, *Cleveland County,* chap. 5.

85. Carleton Ross Hume, "The Beginning of Some Oklahoma University Traditions: A Story of Student Life in Oklahoma University in the Last Decade of the Nineteenth Century" (a 20-page typescript, 1940), in Vertical File: "Traditions of O.U.," 6–7.

86. *Norman Transcript,* October 22, 1897, 1.

87. Hume, "Beginning of Some Oklahoma University Traditions," 7–8.

with reasonable economy be made to range between $140 to $190 per year. Inquiry should be made of the President.[88]

The catalogues also offered prospective students detailed estimates of the costs of attending the University of Oklahoma. According to the version of 1901–1902, for example, students could expect to pay:

| | |
|---|---|
| Board per week | $2.00 |
| Room rent per week | .75 |
| Laundry per week | .25 |
| Athletics, etc., per week | .10 |
| Entertainments, per week | .25 |
| All other, per week | .25 |
| **Total** | **$3.60** |
| For nineteen weeks | $68.40 |
| Books per semester | 6.00 |
| Tuition per semester | 3.00 |
| Laboratory fees per semester | 3.00 |
| **Total for semester** | **$80.40** |

Another example provided by the same *Catalogue* added up to only $71.15 for the semester.

The Oklahoma youth who came to Norman to study were probably not, in general, from among the very poorest families in the territories. Nonetheless, the typical student of the 1890s was far from affluent and had to give careful attention to finances. An exchange of letters in May 1904 between President Boyd and a young man named W. H. Barnes, from Kiowa in Indian Territory, was typical. In his crude and unlettered but nonetheless appealing way, young Barnes wrote to Boyd:

> Dear Sir: I received your Catalogue, and am very well pleased with your school. I paid more attention to the school of Pharmacy as that is the kind I desire to attend. Maby I am asking to much favor from you, but hope you will pardon me if so. I would like very much to attend your school, but the fact of it is, I have a very small amount of money, and I am compelled to go to some school where I can work mornings and evenings for my board and room.
>
> If it isent asking to much of you, please try to find me a place where I can earn my board at odd times. I would not ask this of you if I could do any other wise, but I am a young man trying to make something of myself, and do not want to ask my folks for any help if I can git out of it. . . . Please let me hear from you real soon, and let me know what to build hopes on.

This was precisely the sort of student that David Ross Boyd wanted to attract to Norman.

---

88. This wording, from *University Catalogue, 1894–1895,* 31, varied only slightly over the years. By the 1901 *Catalogue,* estimates of boarding had risen to "from $2.50 to $3.50 per week" and yearly expense "from $140 to $250 a year."

He lost no time in answering.

> My dear friend: I am very glad to note the contents of your letter. . . . We have about sixty out of four hundred and fifty students who are paying their expenses in whole or in part, but I find that a great deal depends on the individual and the conditions are about the same as for securing other work. Those who are intelligent, energetic and capable of doing work efficiently after a little time find places that are quite a little help to them. We have students here who have worked their way through school who have more when they come out than when they began. I suggest that you start with enough money to go one semester as by that time you would become acquainted with conditions and people here. . . . It would be impossible for me not knowing you and not knowing just what you can do to find a place for you, but if you are competent and determined and can come on your own resources for a time, it is almost certain you could find work to pay expenses. I want to say that there is no more heroic spectacle than to see a young man put his shoulder with heroism to the conditions that surround him and push himself up through them to success. Your letter indicates that you are that kind of a young man and I fully expect to see you here fully determined to push your way through.[89]

Forty years later, French Amos remembered the University's first students: "There were no silk hose in those days, no flappers, no jellies," he wrote. "Life in the Oklahoma of 1892 was too strenuous for that. These were sons and daughters of pioneers, mostly poor folk who were having the hardest kind of struggle to keep the wolf from the door. Most of the students came from farms or from small towns."[90]

Boyd was deeply concerned about maintaining a proper religious and moral atmosphere on the campus. The young women fleeing from the severe restrictions of High Gate were not exactly plunging themselves into Sodom and Gomorrah. In part, no doubt, Boyd understood the disastrous consequences for the future of his institution if the God-fearing people of Oklahoma ever got the idea that Norman was a place for loose living and lax morals. But in addition to his political sense of the need to maintain a reputation for propriety, Boyd himself also was a sincere believer in the value of religion as a mainstay and support in the conduct of a worthy and successful life. It was the quiet assumption of his own Ohio upbringing, his own collegiate experience, and he saw no reason to question the central place of religious teaching. There is not much evidence, however, that the sort of religious training the University promoted was deeply theological or evangelical. It was practical rather than theoretical, moral rather than abstract. It aimed principally at encouraging good behavior, ethical principle, consistent devotion throughout life to duty, character, honor, kindness to those less fortunate, love of all humanity, truthfulness. The religious teachings found at the University also contained a strain of muscular, strenuous,

89. W. H. Barnes, Kiowa, I.T., to David Ross Boyd, May 11, 1904; and Boyd to Barnes, May 13, 1904, in David Ross Boyd Presidential MSS, Box 1, Folder 20.

90. Amos, "Early Days in the University of Oklahoma" (typescript) in Vertical File: "History of O.U. (1890–1907)," 2–3.

determinedly energetic living. Students were instructed that genuinely religious men and women avoided sloth and lives of lazy pleasure; they were told to labor diligently and patiently, to do their best always, to find even in hardship the inspiration and strength to strive and work and succeed.

Each year the University inquired into the religious affiliations of its students, and we have a good picture of the student body's patterns of religious practice. In 1900–1901, to take a typical year, of the 361 students who answered the question about their church preference, 29 said they had no preference. The overwhelming majority of the others were northern or southern Methodists, Baptists, Christians (Disciples), or Presbyterians. Of the 332 revealing their affiliations, no fewer than 301 belonged to one of those five denominations. There were, in addition, 11 Roman Catholics and a single Jew. The remaining 19 students represented twelve other denominations.[91] Not counting the African American denominations in the Oklahoma and Indian Territories, the religious composition of the student body reflected fairly accurately the religious affiliations in the surrounding region.[92]

One of the main ways in which Boyd tried to maintain the proper atmosphere on campus was by holding daily chapel services. The services were part of the regular instruction at the University of Oklahoma from the very beginning, even during that first year in the Rock Building,[93] until about 1912. Classes began at 8 o'clock and lasted for fifty minutes. After two of them, at 9:40, the students gathered in the chapel for brief exercises that lasted about fifteen minutes. When they were completed, students marched off to their 10 o'clock classes. The students were not required to attend, but most of them did. President Boyd expected the faculty to appear, and they always occupied the last two rows in the rear of the auditorium at the speaker's right. The speaker was usually the president; but when he was out of town, Professor DeBarr (who always led the singing) took over. Other faculty members pitched in from time to time, and visiting dignitaries and ministers were occasionally invited to conduct the services.[94] A student who arrived in 1904 recalled the nature of Boyd's little sermons: "He would give us concise preachments about how to conduct ourselves so that we could have lives that would be worthwhile and would earn us the respect of those who knew us. I remember one of those talks quite well. He said: 'You are here to learn how to conduct yourselves and how to make a living. It is not necessary that you make a living but it is necessary that you make a life.' He always held before us moral

---

91. The results of the 1900–1901 survey were printed in the *University Catalogue, 1901–1902*, 18. The five leading denominations among the students were Methodist Episcopal (northern Methodist) (75); Baptist (61); Christian (Disciples of Christ) (58); Methodist Episcopal South (56); and Presbyterian (40).

92. For Oklahoma (including Indian Territory) religious affiliation statistics, see U.S. Bureau of the Census, *Religious Bodies: 1906*, 252–55.

93. For a description of the earliest chapel services in the Rock Building, see Rice, "The University in the Old Stone Building," 16.

94. Roy Gittinger, "Milestones" (radio broadcast of 1949), Roy Gittinger MSS, Box 5, Folder 4.

precepts."[95] In addition to the daily chapel services, there were other ways of accentuating moral and religious propriety at the University. The local churches welcomed students of their denominations with various receptions. In 1896–97 the Young Men's Christian Association (YMCA) organized a branch near the campus and held weekly devotional meetings that were popular and well attended. The YMCA became an important center of University life at the turn of the century, and by 1907 fully one-half of the males on the campus were members.[96]

President Boyd himself led a determined campaign against the consumption of alcohol. According to one story, he enlisted a local saloon owner to persuade the others in town to refuse to sell liquor to minors.[97] Boyd was perfectly capable of writing to a student's father that "before he was here two weeks, I learned that he had been drinking, and in fact had become drunk."[98] Once Boyd and his wife were walking to church when they spotted two students busily sweeping out McCarty's Saloon. The president suspected that they were performing this task to pay off a debt to the saloonkeeper. It happened that one of the students, Walter Ferguson, was the son of the territorial governor in Guthrie and the other, Deak Parker, was the brother-in-law of Professor James W. Sturgis, who taught Latin and Greek. Boyd wondered for a few days about what to do about it, but the boys appeared in his office and confessed the whole sordid tale in "so frank and manly" a way that he decided to do nothing.[99] In 1898 the new student paper the *Umpire* summed it up approvingly: "Disorder certainly has a poor chance to creep into the school while it is under his masterly supervision."[100]

~

IF BOYD PLACED A HIGH VALUE on moral behavior, he also greatly valued physical fitness. Even before the opening of the gymnasium on the ground floor of the University building during the 1901–1902 school year, the University rented a place in downtown Norman where students could exercise. It was open from 3:00 in the afternoon until 9:00 at night, and two afternoons each week were given over to women students. When "Physical Culture," as it was called, moved to the campus, Boyd hired a former Olympian, D. C. Hall of Brown University, to supervise the program for men and Kate McBride to do the same

95. Errett R. Newby, untitled typescript of reminiscences written in 1973, in Vertical File: "History of O.U. (1890–1908)," 2. Newby's assertion, written almost seventy years later, that attendance was "required" seems to be an error, but it may indicate the extent to which students assumed that they were expected to attend.

96. Wardner, "Territorial University," 72. See also Paul McClung, "The 'Y' Means Success at O.U.," *Sooner Magazine* 20 (May 1948): 16. The campus Young Women's Christian Association (YWCA) was organized by University women at the start of the 1902 academic year. For brief sketches of each institution's early history, see *Mistletoe, 1905,* 62–63.

97. Long and Hart, *The Sooner Story,* 8–9.

98. David Ross Boyd to J. Bitner (Cushing), April 20, 1905, David Ross Boyd Presidential MSS, Box 2, Folder 8.

99. The tale is told by Boyd in a long unpublished series of interviews of 1936 with Edward Everett Dale. Edward Everett Dale MSS, Box 212, Folder 7, 53–54.

100. *University Umpire,* February 15, 1898, 9.

*Students assembled for chapel services, 1901*

for women; the pair married in 1905 and worked together at the University until 1906. Every Preparatory Department student was required to do gymnasium work from early September through the end of March; other students below the rank of senior did not have to start their workouts until November 1. Each student was required to undergo a medical examination prior to starting the exercise programs so that "physical defects may be noted and suitable exercises for their correction advised."[101] Boyd was proud of the good results of the physical culture program. In June 1903 he boasted to one correspondent: "This year we did not have a single case of illness among students who took the drill."[102]

It was only a series of short steps from gymnasium-centered physical fitness to organized college athletics. The first of these steps was the informal and recreational participation in various sports, and tennis was probably the first such pastime to emerge. The game had considerable popularity at the end of the nineteenth century, and there were some enthusiasts among the first faculty and students. Edwin DeBarr was one of these and possibly the one who laid out the first makeshift court. Track sports began after the arrival of Albert Van Vleet in 1898. By 1900 some students were getting together to train, and they began to agitate for a meet. The first track meet was a local affair held near the juncture of

101. *University Catalogue, 1901–1902,* 11.
102. Cited in Wardner, "Territorial University," 82–83.

*Women exercising*

Apache Street and University Boulevard; it lasted all day and included races, high jumping, pole vaulting, and other events. After a second meet in 1901, the University fielded a
team for the intercollegiate contests in Guthrie. In the spring of 1902 the sport had won
enough acceptance and popularity to be moved south to the campus itself, and the events
took place on the drive in front of the University building. The longer races went up University Boulevard. Baseball had only a few devotees during the 1890s, and it was not until
1905 that a creditable team could be fielded.[103] Basketball made an early appearance on
the campus in 1900, but there was no school team in that sport until 1906.[104]

It was, of course, football that captured most student enthusiasm. Almost from the very
beginning, it became the most glamorous and discussed activity on the campus. Although
scarcely recognizable as the game being played today, football was already fairly well developed by the time it arrived in Norman. It had grown gradually out of a combination
of rugby, soccer, and the often brutal ritual of class fights on many American campuses.
Many historians fix the first collegiate contest in November 1869, between Rutgers and
Princeton; but because of the steady evolution of the rules of the game, it is impossible to
say with precision when it started.[105] Designed originally for privileged young aristocrats at
elite eastern colleges, intimately associated with post–Civil War ideals of manliness, valor,
discipline, and teamwork, the sport spread like wildfire westward across the continent and
downward through the economic class structure of America. By the time the University
of Oklahoma was founded, football was a permanent fixture on college campuses across
the nation.

103. *Mistletoe, 1905*, 54–58.

104. Keith, *Oklahoma Kickoff*, 50–51.

105. In the Rutgers-Princeton game of 1869, for example, there were twenty-five players on a side, a touchdown
counted only four points, and it was illegal to throw the ball forward. For a comprehensive review of the development
of the game to 1890, see David M. Nelson, *The Anatomy of a Game: Football, the Rules and the Men Who Made the Game*,
21–78 and appendix 1 ("Rule Changes by Year").

Because of the University's later prominence in the sport, its very earliest appearance in Norman has been invested by devotees with a kind of legendary significance, roughly analogous to the "creation myths" piously repeated in various world religions. Edwin DeBarr, who had played the game at Michigan, apparently organized some male students to purchase a football—a genuine, roundish, Spaulding "pigskin." He and the others kicked it around the campus in the afternoons.[106] DeBarr may also have had a hand in measuring out the first football field; he certainly laid out the first baseball diamond. As early as the end of 1893, the *Norman Transcript* reported that two football teams had been organized at the University; only a year later, the paper declared that down on the campus "football is all the rage."[107] But the credit for introducing football as a University team sport does not go to Professor DeBarr but to an enterprising undergraduate named John A. Harts. In September 1895 he arrived at the University (like so much else) from Winfield, Kansas, where he had played football. One day, while sitting in Bud Risinger's barbershop on the north side of Main Street, Harts spoke the immortal words: "Let's get up a football team." And, behold, it was done!

That first primitive team—coached, captained, and doctored by young Harts—included the barber Risinger and Fred Perry, who drove the town's street-sprinkling wagon. On a field laid out north-south to the northwest of the present location of Holmberg Hall, it played its only game of 1895, a contest against a more experienced team made up of Oklahoma City high schoolers, town toughs, and a few college students from the Methodist Epworth College. Unfortunately, young Harts was recovering from an ankle injury and had to watch from the sidelines as the University lost 34 to 0. Thus in its first "season" the University of Oklahoma football team went scoreless; indeed, it never even achieved a first down. "Shortly afterward," Harold Keith has written, "Jack Harts left school to prospect for gold in the Arctic, never dreaming that he had started at Norman an autumnal mania that would fetch crowds . . . back to the campus . . . , help fuse the alumni into an intimate and permanent union, become the torment of the university's presidents and the hobby of its Boards of Regents."[108]

After an uneventful and uncoached year (consisting of two victories against the Norman High School), a new epoch in Oklahoma football was introduced in the fall of 1897, with the arrival of Vernon Parrington. The handsome and energetic young English professor had played at Emporia and had been a member of the scrub team at Harvard. After President Boyd placed him in charge of athletics at the University, Parrington poured himself into the effort—entirely without extra pay. Not only did he coach and train and manage the football team, but he wrote up accounts of the games for the campus biweekly

---

106. Keith, *Oklahoma Kickoff*, 6–7; see also J. Brent Clark, *Sooner Century: 100 Glorious Years of Oklahoma Football*, chap. 1.

107. *Norman Transcript*, December 1, 1893, and November 30, 1894, quoted in Keith, *Oklahoma Kickoff*, 7.

108. Keith, *Oklahoma Kickoff*, 12; see also Clark, *Sooner Century*, 27–29.

paper (which he had started himself and which he edited and advised in its earliest years). After coaching the team to nine victories, two defeats, and a tie, Parrington laid down his coaching duties in 1901 in order to concentrate on his teaching. The game still had a charming aura of amateurism and innocence: the coach played when required, and so did local farm boys who had no connection to the University; the players had to provide their own uniforms, and there was only one helmet on the entire team; sometimes the grass had to be burned off the field before the game.

Nevertheless, the foundations for the future of the sport at Oklahoma had been established; even the zealous lingo that was destined to characterize generations of ardent Sooner fans was present from the start in all its avid and unembarrassed bravado. "Our foot ball team is very anxious to kill off two or three good teams this fall," boasted the *University Umpire* at the opening of the 1897 season. "We have a wedge that would go through a brick wall. A snow plow, with a locomotive behind it is no comparison. They move like a cyclone and leave destruction in their path."[109] The game soon commanded passionate interest across the campus. After a contest against the Oklahoma City football club, the *Umpire* reported that "the attendance was between four and five hundred; the gate receipts were $102.00 and the expenses about $29.00. . . . Nobody enjoyed the game more than the members of the faculty. They were out in force."[110] Games against other colleges (including the University of Texas after 1900) were scheduled; and the players practiced with grim determination, certain that they represented the honor and the glory and the reputation of their school.

There were also, from the very beginning, football heroes who strode the campus with a special air and were important topics of conversation. The first of these idols was Columbus ("Lum") C. Roberts, who had delayed his education for five years in order to "prove up" his farm, which he then mortgaged so he could come to school. C. C. Roberts was the same age as Coach Parrington, and he combined with his undoubted prowess on the field so likeable and dignified and gentlemanly a presence that he was elected captain of the team for four consecutive years—an honor no one else was ever to share.[111] There was his cousin Fred Roberts, a fabled runner; Clyde Boggle, who arose at 4 A.M. to milk his cows before school and football practice; and the Merkle brothers, Joe and Fred, bone-crushing linemen. They did not know it, of course, but they and a handful of others stood at the head of a long line of Oklahoma football sensations that over the years would dazzle and thrill and be worshiped and remembered fondly.

By 1900 nothing in the collective life of the campus could rival the hold of football over the imagination and enthusiasm of the student body—with one possible exception. Participation in oratorical contests was originally justified in terms of self-improvement:

109. *University Umpire,* October 15, 1897, 15.

110. *University Umpire,* December 1, 1897, 7.

111. C. C. Roberts was later to marry the University's librarian, Maud Rule.

"There is hardly any better way for a young man or young woman in college to develop his or her thinking powers than to put a few weeks hard labor upon writing an oration," urged the *Umpire* in 1897.[112] Other reasons for learning and practicing the art of formal speaking existed: the attainment of poise, the better use of language, cultivation of social skills that would be useful in business and club life, and, for male students, the preparation for a career in public life, including politics. But if the vogue of oratory began in self-betterment, the oratorical contest soon became an important focus of school spirit and pride.

"Our third annual oratorical contest was held in the chapel on Wednesday evening," the *Umpire* reported in December 1897. "The house was crowded to its utmost capacity. . . . As to the winner [Jesse Hefley], he is one in whom the school has unbounded confidence, and feels sure that he will gain the victory at Guthrie on the night of the 31st. The association is making arrangements for a special [railroad] car for our delegation and a rousing college time is expected."[113] Two weeks later, under the glorious headline "The Victory Is Ours," the *Umpire* reported the Guthrie oratorical contest. "It was a gala day all round. Large delegations from the four college towns and friends of these from all parts of the Territory came flocking in on every train until by evening Guthrie was one mass of people with horns tooting, bands playing, and colors flying, with the crimson and cream very much in evidence. . . . By half past seven the opera house was packed and crowds were being turned away." A blow-by-blow account of the orations followed; the *Umpire* even reprinted the judges' scorecards for each speaker![114]

Indeed, it was the combination of the first football game and the first oratorical contest, in the fall of 1895, that occasioned the creation of a set of "school colors" and an official "school yell." The colors of crimson and cream were selected by a faculty committee headed by May Overstreet, an instructor in English and at the time the only woman member of the staff. The chosen colors were presented to the entire student body "and secured the most enthusiastic approval. . . . Immediately pennants, banners, badges and decorations of every description appeared on the streets, in the windows, at chapel, in class rooms, and all public places. The merchants could not supply the demand."[115] The school yell was first adapted from the yell of the Sigma Nu fraternity at Southwestern College in Winfield. Sophomore Carleton Ross Hume remembered "attending an oratorical contest in Guthrie, and spending some three hours giving [the yell]." After another adaptation, its final form was honed into perfection as "Hi rickety whoop te-do; Boomer, Sooner, Okla. U."[116] Thus did football and oratory share the spotlight in the 1890s, and thus did they join in calling into being the venerable tokens of school spirit.

112. *University Umpire*, October 15, 1897, 8.

113. *University Umpire*, Christmas 1897, 8.

114. *University Umpire*, January 15, 1898, 9. For another description of a raucous oratorical contest, see *University Umpire*, May 15, 1900, 4.

115. See the account by May Overstreet in "The Origin of the University Yell and Colors," in *Sooner Yearbook, 1916*, 326.

116. The exact wording and origin of the official yell soon became, astonishingly, the subject of a spirited debate, with

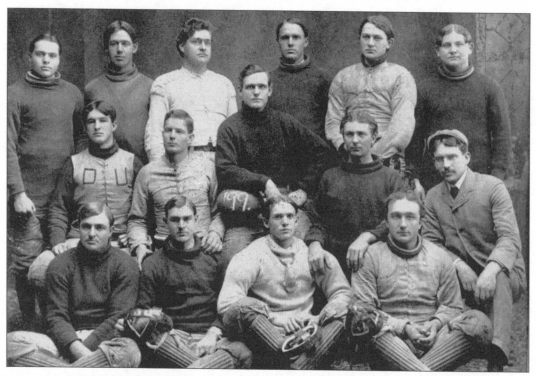

*The football team of 1899. Top row, left to right: Dan Short, Fred Merkle, John Hefley, Delbert Jenkins, Ray Smith, Bob Wingate. Middle row: Jay Ferguson, Clyde Bogle, Captain C. C. "Lum" Roberts, Jap Clapham, Coach Vernon L. Parrington. Bottom row: Joe Merkle, Harvey Short, Oscar Johnston, Fred Roberts. Not pictured: Tom Tribbey.*

Related to the vogue of oratory in the 1890s was the campus "literary society." The first such society was called the Pierian, organized almost the moment the University moved out of the Rock Building and onto the campus in the fall of 1893. In fact, the first, proud "entertainment" in the new University building was presented by the Pierian right before Christmas. The chapel could not hold the audience, and many were turned away. The program featured music, a formal debate over whether wealth was detrimental to morals, some recitations, and a declamation.[117] After the Pierian's success, other literary societies were founded in quick order: the Philomathean (1895), the Lyceum (1896), the Senate (1897), the Forum (1898), the Websterian (1903), the Zetalethean (1904). Each had a specialty: the Pierian took only the best; the Senate was composed of "the less experienced"; the Lyceum was affiliated with a national organization; the Forum included women for a while

---

competing versions in circulation. The definitive account seems to be that of Hume, himself a central figure in the whole episode; see *Sooner Yearbook, 1916*, 326–27. For an alternative version, however, see Wardner, "Territorial University," 73, n. 94.

117. For a fulsome description of the entire evening, see *Norman Transcript*, December 29, 1893. "This entertainment will go down in University history as one of the brilliant affairs of the University and we feel safe in saying that every one who attended feels proud of the fact that they were present."

*The women of the Zetalethean Literary Society, 1909*

before excluding them in 1900; the Websterian was for Preparatory boys who had ambition; the Zetalethean was for women.[118] Like the Oratorical Society, the literary societies were expected to train students in a kind of practical culture. The participants learned to write a constitution for their organization; became adepts at Robert's rules of order; studied how to conduct a meeting, speak extemporaneously, debate topics of current interest, gain polish and self-confidence. They also undertook what the first *Mistletoe* yearbook (1905) called "general literary work."[119]

~

THE CHIEF VEHICLE FOR STUDENT "literary work," however, was to be the *University Umpire*, the first student publication at the University of Oklahoma. Its creation was due to the fortuitous coming together of a group of ambitious and literarily inclined students and their energetic new professor of English, Vernon Parrington. The professor first appeared in August 1897; the first appearance of the periodical was in mid-October. Among the students heading the enterprise were the campus stars whose names were known to everyone: Nahum Butcher, Maud Rule, Ross Hume, C. C. Roberts, George Bucklin. The periodical came out every two weeks and, to the great credit of these students and their dozens of successors over the years, rarely missed an issue.[120] Their feat was all the more remarkable considering that no journalism department (almost a prerequisite at many other colleges for a successful student publication) was to materialize for another sixteen years. Parrington contributed regularly to the periodical, took over as editor from November 1898 until January 1900, and then served as advisory editor until 1902. The paper sold for

118. *University Catalogue, 1894–95*, 33; *Mistletoe, 1905*, 38–45.

119. *Mistletoe, 1905*, 40.

120. Harold Donald Arnold, "A Descriptive Analysis of Selected Publications of the University of Oklahoma—Academic, Alumni, Student, and of Allied Organizations," 87–95, 110–14. See also Sardis Roy Hadsell, "The Umpire Story," in *Mistletoe, 1905*, 76–78.

a nickel, and yearly subscriptions cost seventy-five cents. Both students and members of the faculty wrote pieces to fill up the paper; and each issue came with substantial advertising from local businesses and "exchanges" from other college newspapers and magazines.

From the beginning, the *University Umpire* was a curious combination of earnest moral uplift, college humor, campus gossip, and official announcements. The moral preachments came in about equal parts from faculty members exhorting their charges and students exhorting each other. The tone of these inspirational moral essays was invariably upbeat, optimistic, serious. They beseeched the young to approach life with purpose, will, good faith, and stamina: "Let us remember," wrote Professor Paxton in one early issue, "that even in the midst of untoward environments our characters need not be besmirched if we are determined to keep them clean."[121] Grace King warned the students against surrendering in the battles of life: "Dear boys and girls what ever else you do, *never give up*. Although earth itself seems slipping from you, never once give up the battle. You haven't time to look back, for you must follow the star. Cross that word *discouragement* out of your vocabulary or else never learn its definition."[122] The *Umpire* also featured healthy doses of patriotism, respectful references to religious faith, pleas for good manners, constant reminders of the opportunities students enjoyed at college, and constant admonitions to hone the skills of writing, reading, and speaking. Each issue contained at least one of these tracts. They paraded under such uplifting titles as "What Should a College Training Do?"; "The Social Hero of Today"; "Our National Destiny"; and "Nature Poetry of the Bible."[123] No doubt many of the student contributions were hand-selected for publication by Parrington from among the essays his classes were assigned.

The humor sprinkled through each issue of the *Umpire* varied in quality. The jokes were often reprinted from other places, and many seem quaint and tame and unamusing today:

> First Stranger: "I say, that's my umbrella you have."
>
> Second Stranger: "I don't doubt it, sir, I don't doubt it; I bought it at the pawnbroker's."

Some of the humor flirts tentatively with sexual innuendo, but the flirtation never gets very far:

> "I went in for amateur photography during my vacation," said the summer man. "There was no end of girls for subjects."
>
> "But how did you make out among the girls?"
>
> "Oh, I got lots of negatives."[124]

---

121. *University Umpire*, November 15, 1897, 3.

122. Grace A. King, " 'Hitch Your Wagon to a Star,' " *University Umpire*, March 1, 1898, 1.

123. These particular examples were all chosen from issues published during 1900: March 15, April 2, May 15, and November 15.

124. Both of these examples were drawn from the *University Umpire* issue of October 15, 1897, 6.

# THE UMPIRE

### UNIVERSITY OF OKLAHOMA

| Vol. I. | Norman, Oklahoma, Tuesday, Nov. 20, 1906 | No. 21 |
|---|---|---|

### RHODES SCHOLARSHIP.

#### Regulations Governing the Granting of the Cecil Rhodes Scholarship.

The following regulations for the granting of the Rhodes Scholarships were received from the trustees of Mr. Rhodes' will. The summary of these regulations is as follows:

The next qualifying examinations for scholars in the United States under the Rhodes bequest will be held about the middle of January, 1907; the selection of scholars will be completed before the end of March, and the elected scholars will begin residence at Oxford in October of that year.

The examinations will be held in each State and Territory to which the scholarships are assigned, at centers to be fixed by the local committee of selection. This committee will appoint suitable persons to supervise the examinations, and will arrange for its impartial conduct. It should be clearly understood that this examination is not competitive, but simply qualifying, and is merely intended to give assurance that every elected scholar measures up to the standard of the first examination (Responsions), which the University demands of all candidates for the B. A. degree. The Rhodes scholars will be selected from candidates who have successfully passed the qualifying examination. One

tory either in the same year or in successive years.

For the Responsions Examination of 1907, candidates will be examined in the following subjects:

1. Arithmetic—the whole.
2. Either the Elements of Algebra or the Elements of Geometry.
3. Greek and Latin Grammar.
4. Translation from English into Latin.
5. One Greek and one Latin book.

As soon as the report of the examiners has been received, the chairman of the Committee of Selection in each State will be furnished with a list of the candidates who have passed and are therefore eligible for selection. The Committee of Selection will then proceed to choose the scholar for the year.

In accordance with the wish of Mr. Rhodes, the trustees desire that "in the election of a student to a scholarship, regard shall be had to (1) his literary and scholastic attainments, (2) his fondness for and success in manly out-door sports, such as cricket, football and the like, (3) his qualities of manhood, truth, courage, devotion to duty, sympathy for and protection of the weak, kindliness, unselfishness and fellowship, and (4) his exhibition during school-days of moral force of character, and of instincts to lead and to take an interest in his schoolmates." Mr. Rhodes suggested that (2) and (3) should be decided in any school or college by the votes of fellow-stu-

### SCRUBS SCORE ON VARSITY

#### Game Between Scrubs and Varsity Results in Score of Twenty-Six to Twelve.

The match game, played Saturday between the second team and Varsity resulted in a score of 26 to 12 in favor of the 'Varsity. After Tuesday of last week, each team practiced separately until Saturday, when they played a regular game.

The scrubs sprung a surprise on the first team by making two touchdowns and goals, one touchdown being made by a line buck and the other around end. Taylor, who played fullback for the scrubs, plunged straight into the line, soon after the game began, and, finding the first team bunched closely, dodged around with Regner in the interference, and ran about 20 yards for a touchdown. The other touchdown was made by Ratliffe, right half back, who got an open field around end and ran 35 yards for touchdown. Severin caught him from behind just as he crossed the line but too late to save the score.

The 'Varsity made five touchdowns but were able to kick but one goal. All of the new formations were used, and the forward pass worked for good gains almost every time.

Only one half, of forty minutes, was played, darkness preventing the usual time of halves to be observed.

O. Bodine, 158, left guard; Cassity, 140, right tackle; L. Bodine, 170, left tackle; Bailey, 120, right end; Williams, 125, left end; Hardy, 125, quarter back; Capshaw, 120, right half Morter, 140, left half; Roberts, 140, full back.

Officials: Referee, Bennie Owens. Umpire, Monette. Head linesman, Truesdell. Time of halves, 25 minutes.

#### Basket Ball Suits Here.

The suits for the basket ball team have come, and the team was out in them for the first time, Saturday. They are very neat looking suits, composed of white trousers, and red jerseys and stockings, each with one wide white stripe.

The following men are wearing the suits, as members of the first team: Carey, Buchanan, Davis, Morris, Bridgewater, Thompson, and Hughes. Morris and Thompson play a swift game at guards. Carey is an experienced player and plays a fast, heady game at forward. Bridgewater and Hughes also play well at forward. Hughes is especially sure at goal throwing. With regular practice between now and the beginning of the season, this team will be in good condition to play fast and successful ball.

There are several men on the football team who expect to try for basket ball, and these, with the men who

*The* University Umpire, *the first student publication at the University*

Nor were the students incapable, now and then, of smuggling in a little political sexism under the cover of "humor":

> The student who, in addition to wearing his hair parted in the middle and delicate rings upon his fingers, carries a large handsome ladies [sic] breast pin, pinned upon his coat, is we presume a type of the coming man who will care for the little ones while the new woman sits in Congress.[125]

There were also occasional little forays into black humor:

> Little Willie had a mirror
> And he licked the back all off,
> Thinking in his childish error
> It would cure the whooping cough

125. Ibid., 12.

> At the funeral Willie's mother
> Smartly said to Mrs. Brown
> "It was a chilly day for Willie
> When the mercury went down."[126]

When they targeted local topics, however, the students were sometimes capable of genuine cleverness—as in one sly reference to the librarian, Maud Rule: "Although there is always perfect order and deportment in the library, still it is not a paradox to say that Mis(s) Rule reigns."[127]

One of the most remarkable and interesting characteristics of the paper—particularly in view of the proclivities of later generations of students—is the tone of unfailing respect toward both the president and the Regents of the University. There were frequent summaries of Boyd's chapel talks, always complimentary: "President Boyd illustrated his remarks by reading some brief sketches from the life of Washington. His whole talk was full of interest and was appreciated by the students."[128] Even on occasions when the president was forced to warn and discipline, the editors of the *Umpire* understood completely: "President Boyd's kind reproof of some of the practices of the students, and some little misdemeanors, demonstrates his executive ability on overseeing the school. All his advice has been heeded and his requests respected."[129] His actions to build up the University—dealing with the legislature, making countless recruiting trips throughout the two territories, purchasing equipment or books, greeting distinguished visitors, expanding the faculty and the curriculum—were meticulously reported and consistently praised. The praise and respect extended to the Regents as well: "The regents of the U are very attentive to the needs of the school," the editors observed in their first issue. "The chapel is being supplied with elegant opera chairs. A great number of new song books has just been procured for use in the morning devotional exercises. Necessary books are purchased for the library whenever occasion demands them."[130] And a few months later: "Our president and Board of Regents are ever solicitous for the welfare and enjoyment of the students."[131] Many future presidents and future Boards of Regents no doubt would have welcomed some of those kindly sentiments.

The majority of the students who paid their nickel for the *Umpire*, however, probably did so for two additional services that the paper performed. In the first place, it quickly became the chief means for informing the University community of what was happening on the campus. The paper covered sporting events, summarized the words of visiting lecturers

126. *University Umpire*, March 1, 1898, 5.

127. *University Umpire*, February 1, 1898, 9.

128. *University Umpire*, March 1, 1898, 7.

129. *University Umpire*, February 1, 1898, 9.

130. *University Umpire*, October 15, 1897.

131. *University Umpire*, January 15, 1898.

and preachers, and announced academic calendars and changes in the regulations. The doings of the glee club and the mandolin club and the literary societies were duly noted. The Santa Fe published its schedule, and campus businesses made known their wares and their prices. One merchant informed the students that they could purchase ink for three cents, four pens or four colored crayons for a penny; another declared that the new spring hats were now available; others offered to cut hair or provide jewelry or sell bicycles or chocolates or fine shoes.

A second important reason to buy the *University Umpire* was to keep up on the gossip.

> Mr. Boory has recovered from the typhoid fever, but he will not be in school again. He is going to teach.

> Charley Fisher was married in December.

> Mrs. Gittinger who intended to enter school again will possibly not be able to do so. She is quite sick.

> Frances and Bess Quarles of Lawton visited Norman friends and the University last week. The girls were students here last year.

> Crow, Sherwin and Professor Gould geologized during holiday. Professor Parrington, Dr. Van Vleet, Mr. Bunker and the Hefley boys were hunting.

> On New Year's morning Miss Elma Britt was married to Mr. Frank Briggs. Miss Britt was in school at the beginning of this year. Mr. Briggs is one of the Pharmacy graduates.[132]

It is from the gossip that one gets a sense of the tenor of student life. Who was spotted strolling hand-in-hand with whom in the moonlight? What happened at the picnic down by the river? Who made up the cast for the production of Gilbert and Sullivan's *H.M.S. Pinafore*, and what new numbers would Miss King be singing at her upcoming recital?

The students' youthful vigor, their seriousness of purpose, the infectious high spirits and ambition, both for themselves and for the University of Oklahoma, all shine through the pages of the *Umpire*. They were so determinedly optimistic, so wonderfully confident of the futures that awaited them. They were full of fun and innocent mischief and awkward sexuality and cleverness. They understood, somehow, that college was a privilege and an opportunity and that they should not waste the chance. They kept telling each other that they were almost adults. It is difficult not to be captivated (and envious) of their energy, their buoyant enthusiasm, their happiness. They were making a culture. And the culture they were making was joyful yet purposeful, respectful of their elders yet brash and sassy, sarcastic yet strangely sentimental. They kept a sharp and suspicious eye on the practices of older and more prestigious colleges, but they were also as proud as punch about what was being created out on the Oklahoma frontier.

132. All these examples were taken from *University Umpire*, January 15, 1901, 12–14.

~

WE DO NOT KNOW PRECISELY how David Ross Boyd spent the afternoon and evening on Tuesday, January 6, 1903. The University's official Christmas vacation had ended the day before, the students had returned, and school had started smoothly again. Professor DeBarr led the chapel service that morning. Final exams for the first semester were still three weeks away. As the day grew late, the students filed out of the building after their last classes. One by one, members of the faculty—their teaching done for the day—locked their offices and went home in the disappearing light of the late afternoon. No doubt President Boyd shut his own office and headed up University Boulevard to putter around his house before dinner. Perhaps he did a little work on the trees at his nursery.

We cannot know what he was thinking that evening. It is unlikely that he indulged himself in a meditation on what he had accomplished during these last ten years. But it would be pleasant to hope that sometime during that fateful evening he thought a little about the growth and development of the University that he, more than any other person, had guided and supervised: the expansion of the student body, faculty, and programs; the grappling with finances and land and potential competitors; the establishment of procedures and standards; the mastery of the thousand details of administrative duty; the hundreds of trips to high schools and churches of both Oklahoma and Indian Territory; the hundreds of hours of counseling students, watching them arrive in Norman and embark on their studies and, with their companions, make a happy and wholesome way of life. It would be pleasant to think that Boyd felt some of the satisfaction that he *deserved* to feel that night as he turned down the lights and went off to bed. Unfortunately, he was not destined to sleep through the whole night.

# CHAPTER V

# Rising Out of the Ashes, 1903–1907

The night watchman spotted the flames shortly after 11 o'clock.[1] He noticed them issuing from the southeast basement, the room where Professor Gould taught and kept his geological collections. The watchman shouted the alarm. The fire bell, located on the north side of Main Street adjoining the train station, roused the sleeping town; and within minutes almost the entire citizenry had gathered at the site. The Norman fire department proved useless: the campus lay outside the town limits, and the longest hose was too short to reach the nearest hydrant. Bystanders grabbed some buckets and, using the vat at the south corner of the building, began "a heroic effort" to save the building. Suddenly, however, the situation worsened: the flames burst up through the basement. The hardwood floors had recently been oiled, and now they burned ferociously. All hope for saving the structure evaporated. The urgent task now became to rescue what could be saved.

George Bucklin, one of the first to arrive on the scene, and Walker Field, a freshman from Guthrie and the business manager of the *Umpire*, found a ladder, propped it on the front steps, and climbed into President Boyd's office. They snatched up whatever they could: the records of students' grades and credits, insurance documents, the voucher book, even a few of the president's private papers. Meanwhile, Tom Tribbey, a medical student from Moral, Oklahoma, rounded up some others and headed for the chemistry lab. The fire had started in the eastern part of the basement, but chemistry was in the western part, so there were some brief moments of opportunity. The students ran out of Professor DeBarr's laboratory carrying whole drawers of valuable chemicals and equipment; thirteen of the balances were saved as well as some smaller apparatus. According to the *Umpire*, Charles Kirk, an Oklahoma City junior, "did some nervy work" in getting three precious microscopes out of Professor Van Vleet's biology lab. A couple of students ran a ladder through the window of Professor Buchanan's lecture room and somehow were able to slide his desk

---

1. The principal accounts of the fire, all anonymous, appeared in the *Daily Oklahoman*, January 7, 1903, *Norman Transcript*, January 8, 1903, and *University Umpire*, January 15, 1903, 8–9. The *Transcript* version fixes the discovery of the fire at "about 11:30" and the *Daily Oklahoman* "at midnight." For the early history of fires and firefighting in Norman, see Womack, *Norman: An Early History*, 101–104.

down to safety, along with his maps and a few books. Some hides and stuffed animals were carried out through the door behind the front steps that led down to the basement.[2] President Boyd himself tried to enter the building through the back door, but the smoke was so intense that he fell to the floor and—revived by the better air there—made his escape; he complained of sore lungs for several weeks.[3]

And then (in a description so elegant that one strongly suspects it must have come from the pen of Professor Parrington) "just at midnight the dome quivered, groaned with breaking timber, turned gracefully over and with point down, crashed through the chapel into the first floor and basement." It was all over. "Everything possible had been done, so all stood back, watched the floors fall and listened to the explosions in the glowing mass of debris where was once the chemical laboratory."[4] Through the long, cold January night, a handful of students maintained a somber watch until sunrise over the small pile of rescued things. The sight that greeted the throng of students and townspeople the next morning was macabre. Most of the stone and brick walls still remained, blackened and hollow, but the windows now looked "like the eyeless sockets of a grinning skull."[5] Smoke still rose from the smoldering ruins, and the four stark brick chimneys stood like four ghostly sentries standing guard over the devastation.

If some items had been saved, many, many more were lost. Everything that had been on the third floor was gone. Everything that had been in the chapel was gone. Every book that had been in the library was gone. The only volumes *not* destroyed were those few that happened to be checked out to students; around twelve thousand books and five thousand pamphlets went up in flames. The herbarium (which contained more than ten thousand specimens), the collection of 150 birds, and Gould's geological collections were all destroyed. Some of the losses were personal and agonizing: the works of English literature that Parrington had labored so hard to gather, to say nothing of his lecture notes; the books and art that Professor Paxton had collected in Europe; Gould's field notes and his private library; Professor Van Vleet's microscope slides. When it came to assessing the losses in terms of cash, the picture was grim. The building was valued at $40,000; the library at $25,000; the furniture at another $5,000. Perhaps $1,000 worth of chemicals and apparatus had been saved from DeBarr's laboratory, but around $5,000 worth had been lost. In all, the authorities figured the damages at $84,000. The University had $35,000 in insurance.[6]

David Ross Boyd, "with his calm and undisturbed manner,"[7] took charge. It is impossible not to admire his dignity and courage under the pressure of this catastrophe. Ap-

---

2. *University Umpire*, January 15, 1903, 8–9.

3. Wardner, "Territorial University," 113.

4. *University Umpire*, January 15, 1903, 8–9.

5. Ibid., 7.

6. Ibid., 12; *Norman Transcript*, January 22, 1903, 1.

7. *Daily Oklahoman*, January 7, 1903, 1.

*Aftermath of the 1903 fire*

parently he never considered for a moment the option of not pressing forward with the work of the University. Instead he announced that the faculty would meet at nine o'clock the very next morning to consider what had to be done and that there would be a mass meeting in a local church at two in the afternoon. At the meeting, Boyd "spoke briefly of the misfortune that had befallen us" and praised the students for their efforts at the fire, singling out Bucklin and Kirby Prickett, the janitor, who had risked their lives.[8] He then called upon the students to be loyal in the difficult days ahead. According to the *Umpire*, "[T]hough we were in a church building the 'yell' went up. We had heard it given defiantly in the morning [*sic*], and, after the day was won, triumphantly, but that day it touched a deeper chord of patriotism than it ever had before."[9]

The arrangements for the three remaining weeks of the semester, Boyd announced, would be simple enough. The old Rock Building, where instruction at the University of Oklahoma had begun more than a decade before, would be pressed into service again. The University had been using it lately for a gymnasium and music studios, but now five of its

8. Kirby Prickett was a particular favorite of President Boyd's and a popular figure among the early students, who might recall him "with a smudgy face, a wrench in hand, always busy." His quarters in the basement were directly under Boyd's office, two floors above, and connected by a speaking tube so that Boyd could always communicate directly with his janitor and handyman. See Sardis Roy Hadsell's warmly appreciative memorial, "Kirby Prickett," *Sooner Magazine* 8 (November 1935): 36. Prickett died on August 5, 1935.

9. *University Umpire*, January 15, 1903, 7.

rooms would house classes. Boyd's own office and two recitation rooms would be moved to the Arline Home, a privately owned dormitory on the corner of Main and Asp Avenue, designed to accommodate eighty or a hundred women students.[10] What was left of the library would also be housed there, as would the music studios that had to be moved from the Rock Building to make room for classes. The newly constructed First Baptist Church, in close proximity to the Rock Building, would be utilized for both classes and chapel services.[11] The town of Norman offered the Commercial Club room, and other churches promised space if needed.[12] Some classes would be held in the residences of faculty members. Evidently, Boyd had found both the time and the presence of mind on that first day, "while the smoke was yet hovering over the blackened ruins,"[13] to place orders for books, chemicals, and apparatus. All in all, it was a stunning achievement. Within twenty-four hours of the fire, the University's functions, all housed within a two-block area of downtown Norman, were again in operation. A church bell in front of the Rock Building "was ringing the class hours and class work was going on."[14]

Telegrams and letters poured in from all over the Territory and the nation, expressing sympathy and grief at the loss. None was more touching than the letter from William Jennings Bryan. The twice-defeated Democratic presidential candidate from Nebraska had given the last public address in the destroyed building. He was in Enid when he heard the news of the tragedy and immediately wrote to Charles Kirk, the Oklahoma City junior who had done such "nervy work" the night of the fire and who was the president of the University's Oratorical Association: "Thinking that your Association might have lost by the fire and remembering its very courteous treatment of me, I beg to enclose a check for $25.00." If the Oratorical Association did not need the money, Bryan suggested, it should be turned over to President Boyd. Bryan's letter was read in chapel, at the Baptist church, and "was followed by prolonged applause and yells." That afternoon, the Oratorical Association voted to follow Boyd's suggestion that the money be sent to the library to purchase a complete set of Thomas Brackett Reed's *Modern Eloquence* and that the set of books be known as "the Bryan Donation."[15] Other expressions of sympathy and sorrow arrived. "All my college life is in some way associated with the old building and by its burning so many

---

10. The Arline Home for Young Women was the first women's residence. It advertised "home cooking, home comfort and home restrictions." It also boasted basketball and tennis courts. Room and board averaged $4.00 per week. See Edith Walker, "This Is College," *Sooner Magazine* 15 (October 1942): 16.

11. Wardner, "Territorial University," 120.

12. *Daily Oklahoman*, January 8, 1903, 1.

13. Ibid.

14. Cited by Wardner, "Territorial University," 120, as *People's Voice*, January 16, 1903.

15. *Norman Transcript*, January 15, 1903; *University Umpire*, February 1, 1903, 12. *Modern Eloquence* was a multivolume set of inspiring examples of recent public speaking by leading Americans. It was compiled by former Speaker of the House Thomas Brackett Reed (himself a famous orator) and others. The University Library presently owns several sets of *Modern Eloquence* dating from this period. On the basis of her interview with librarian Jesse Rader in June 1939, Dorothy Wardner concluded that, at that time, "only volume two of this set is now available in the library. The others have been lost or worn out." Wardner, "Territorial University," 121n.

bright memories have been destroyed," one anonymous alumnus sadly recalled. "And strange as it may seem, one of the first things that came to my mind when I heard of the fire was the old ivy on the front of the building. I always thought that was one of the prettiest and most attractive things about the place. Then the recitation rooms, the apparatus I used, the office, the chapel and the library, all these things gone seem to me like the loss of so many friends." But the writer concluded his letter with the sentiment that seemed from the very day of the fire itself to characterize everyone concerned: "But it happened and it can't be helped," he wrote, "so let us look to the future."[16]

On Saturday, January 10, the Regents briefly toured the ruins and then met in Boyd's office at the Arline Home, where the president told them the extent of the losses. The *Transcript* reported that "the board expressed its hearty commendation" of Boyd's efforts and approved his plans for continuing instruction.[17] That same afternoon the Regents ordered the quick construction of two frame buildings. One of them was to be twenty-four by eighty-six feet and would house the sciences; the second, twenty-six by forty-six feet, was for medicine and pharmacy. The contractor F. W. Flood (for whom Flood Street was later named) promised to have the two side-by-side buildings up and ready within ten days. He also promised to build them in such a way "as to make them convenient for permanent buildings at any time in the future."[18]

The students and faculty, meanwhile, took the disaster in stride. Perhaps drawing their cue from the resiliency of President Boyd, they too were resilient. Everyone knew of the spunky remark of Frederick Elder, the professor of mathematics, who said that all *he* would need to continue his work was a box of chalk and a couple of yards of blackboard.[19] Even in the very first issue of the *Umpire* after the fire, the destruction of the University's building had to share space with an ecstatic and affectionate account of the marriage of Professor Joseph Paxton to Fantine Samuels, who had graduated from the University in 1901. The writer, Sardis Roy Hadsell, apologized that he had to reconstruct the details of the nuptials from memory because the wedding invitation had burned in the fire. He gave his report the significant title "Our Wedding." "Now laugh because we claim it," he declared. "If we have not a right to do so, we do not know who has. It was our senior bachelor and our first girl graduate; isn't that claim enough?"[20] Elsewhere in the issue, a waggish and (appropriately) anonymous editor, almost certainly male, gave vent to what he no doubt

16. *University Umpire*, February 1, 1903, 12.

17. *Norman Transcript*, January 15, 1903, 1; but there is no mention in the official "Minutes" (January 10, 1903) of the Board commending Boyd.

18. Regents' "Minutes," January 10, 1903, 1. Frank W. Flood was a Norman builder-contractor and sometime business partner of Boyd. He was the University's superintendent of buildings and probably built Boyd House, the home of most of the University's presidents. For his career, see Jane Frost Teague and Thomas G. Teague, *The Flood Family History* (no pagination).

19. *University Umpire*, January 15, 1903, 16; Walker, "This Is College," 16–17.

20. Sardis Roy Hadsell, "Our Wedding," *University Umpire*, January 15, 1903, 13. Samuels was the first woman to receive a B.A. at the University; other women had earlier received degrees in pharmacy.

thought was high humor: "This should encourage the young women who are now undergraduates to finish the course, for are there not yet one, two, three, four marriageable
young professors?"[21]

And if, within a week of the fire, the faculty and students were going about their business as usual, they were also willing to attempt a few lame jokes about the whole affair.
"Yes, Prof. Parrington's lectures burned," one witticism went. "Those extra loud reports
were his jokes cracking." Or "Who saved the barrel of alcohol? Dick Broadus, unfortunately it was only part full." Or "Fire drove the students to the Baptist church." Or "Dr.
DeBarr at the fire[:] 'There, enough laughing gas is generating to last the students the
remainder of the year.' "[22] It would not be difficult, of course, to find more adroit examples
of college hilarity. These, however, coming as they did literally out of the ashes, are notable for their phoenix-like buoyancy, for the optimism and adaptability and youthful
confidence they reveal.

The resolute attitudes of Boyd, his faculty, the students, the University's Regents, and
the citizens of Norman were certainly the chief source of hopefulness in the days immediately after the fire. But there was one other bright spot in the disaster, and it was an
important one. The University was on the verge of bringing to completion what was to
have been a second and quite magnificent new building.

～

THE CAMPAIGN FOR A NEW BUILDING had been long and arduous. Even before
the fire the rapid growth of the student body, especially after the return of good economic times in the late 1890s, made the need for more space undeniable. The Regents—
encouraged by the fact that the legislature had given both Oklahoma A & M in Stillwater
and the Normal College in Edmond new buildings in 1899—opened their campaign for
a building appropriation at the start of the 1900 academic year.[23] Their plan, no doubt
devised by President Boyd, was ambitious. The existing building would be converted to
the sole use of chemistry, pharmacy, medicine, and biology. If a second building could be
constructed, it would "contain suites of rooms for the departments of Latin and Greek,
English and other modern languages, mathematics, history and civics, economics, civil
engineering and architecture, and administration offices; a large fireproof vault; rooms for
a library and the department of physics; four literary society halls; a small auditorium, seating 500; a large auditorium, seating 1000; cloak rooms and lavatories."[24]

President Boyd's old friend Henry Asp, the chief Oklahoma attorney for the Atchison, Topeka & Santa Fe Railroad and, at the moment, the president of the Board of

21. *University Umpire*, January 15, 1903, 7.

22. All the jokes are in ibid., 16.

23. For the details of the effort, see Wardner, "Territorial University," 106–16.

24. Cited by Wardner, "Territorial University," 107, as *Report of Board of Regents, 1899–1900*, 2.

Regents, appeared at the legislature in late January 1901 to plead for a new building. He told the education committees of both houses that the University desperately required $100,000. The much-needed new building could be constructed for around $75,000, he thought; adding $14,000 for heating it and $6,000 for a gymnasium building would leave enough money to remodel the existing building for the sciences. The sum could be had, Asp pointed out, by appropriating a one-mill levy on the assessed valuations of taxable property for 1901 and 1902. He may have tried to create the impression that the student population had doubled in the last year and that it would probably double again in the coming year—sliding quickly over the fact that he was talking only about the *college*-level students and not the student population as a whole. He then compared the expenditures of a dozen other states for college buildings to Oklahoma's and found the discrepancies alarming.[25] Regent Asp summed up his case before the lawmakers: "The University since its organization has been starved; it has been compelled to struggle along and practice the most rigid economy."[26] Identical bills embodying the University's request were introduced in both houses of the legislature.

In the process of working its way toward passage, the original proposal was reduced to 0.7 mill for the two years and to a sum not to exceed $90,000.[27] On February 26 the bill passed the House (having previously passed the Council), and the *Norman Transcript* went berserk:

$90,000!

The House Passes Uni-

versity Appropriation

Measure

Up to Governor

No Doubt of His Action—A

Righteous Measure—Big

Thing for Town and

Institution—Jol-

lifications

Nor did the *Transcript* attempt to disguise the reasons for its euphoria: "This appropriation is the biggest thing that has come down the pike for Norman for some time. It means a steady increase in its population, an increased demand for property, a building boom in every part of the city and an increased value."[28] Naturally, David Ross Boyd was in Guth-

25. *Norman Transcript*, February 7, 1901, 5. Asp alleged that Oklahoma spent five cents per capita on university buildings, while Arkansas spent sixteen, California fifty, Illinois thirty, Kansas thirty-eight, Missouri twenty, Nebraska thirty-five, and so on. Asp's numbers were questionable. First, he did not figure monies spent for buildings in Edmond or Stillwater. Second, he calculated the University's building at only $19,000; but when it burned two years later, the loss was fixed at almost double that amount.

26. Ibid.

27. The *Norman Transcript* reprinted the final version of the bill, March 7, 1901, 1.

28. *Norman Transcript*, February 28, 1901, 1. The same notes were struck in the next issue, March 7, 1901, 1. The

rie on Tuesday for the big vote. That night, weary but satisfied, he returned to Norman and "was met at the train by the students, who gave him a royal welcome. They turned themselves loose and the college yell was very much in evidence." For good measure, the students decided to give themselves a holiday the next day![29]

One aspect of the debate in the legislature is worth noting. D. H. Van Kirk, one of the two dissenters in the lower house, explained his negative vote by referring to Norman's attitude toward African Americans: "I am in favor of education," Van Kirk told his colleagues. "I want to see a great university in Oklahoma, but I do not want it located and fostered in a community where any person is deprived of any right guaranteed by the constitution to every American citizen. For this reason I vote 'No'!"[30] The *Transcript* leapt to the town's defense. "The hardest thing the advocates of the University ran up against in the Oklahoma legislature," the paper admitted, "was the reputation Norman enjoys (?) [sic] of being a negro-hating community." The editor found it "surprising" that the town suffered so much antagonism because of "her position on this question." He did not claim that the charges against Norman were false, only that "the reports . . . have greatly exaggerated the feeling said to be entertained by the people of Norman against the negro." Nonetheless, he conceded, "it must be confessed the town has given ample room for her enemies to base charges against her in this particular." About the best the editor could do was to point out that "the enemies of education, enemies of law and order, enemies of the University were the aggressors in every attack on negroes that has occurred in Norman." "The most that can be charged against the better element" was that they remained "quiescent in the matter: that, while condemning the assaults utterly, they did not rise in their might and put stops to the outrages."[31]

But despite some reservations about Norman's race attitudes, the legislative hurdle had been passed, and events moved quickly.[32] The Regents appointed Arthur J. Williams of Oklahoma City as both architect and superintendent of construction, and by October his plans for the new building were on display. When an initial set of bids was deemed too high in December, the architect and the Regents simply chopped off plans for the building's west wing, decided not to fireproof the building, and tried again. This time a Nebraska firm won the contract for $68,040. The basement was dug in May and June 1902, and work was started on the structure itself. The University's original building was now being called Science Hall and was being modified for its new function. The inevitable

---

*Transcript* pointed out that this investment would end forever any foolish talk about moving the University of Oklahoma to another city. "Norman and Cleveland county are certainly much to be congratulated. This is the 'Athens of Oklahoma' in truth and in fact."

29. *Norman Transcript*, February 28, 1901, 1.

30. *Journal of House Proceedings of the Sixth Legislative Assembly* . . . *(January 8, 1901–March 8, 1901)*, 303.

31. *Norman Transcript*, March 14, 1901, 5.

32. For an exhaustive account of the details of the new building's construction, see Wardner, "Territorial University," 112–17.

delays, meanwhile, prevented the contractor from realizing his promised completion date of December 31, 1902. Six days later, of course, Science Hall burned to the ground. News stories of the fire all carried the optimistic promise that the new building would be ready for the start of the second semester on February 2. As usual, however, the optimism was unwarranted; it was not ready until March 16.

The new building was called University Hall. It bore no resemblance to the original Romanesque structure with its twenty-two rooms. This one was built in an imposing Renaissance style and was much larger than the first: it contained around eighty rooms and was fully 240 feet long and 120 feet deep.[33] The new building was located to the south and east of the original.[34] It was particularly notable for three of its features. First, the entrance was grandiose; a flight of steps forty feet wide led past four enormous Ionic columns on heavy pedestals to the front doors. Second, above the main entrance, supported by the four columns, was an entablature that bore a terra-cotta version of the University seal. Finally, there was the great dome: a fifty-foot square at its base, it changed as it rose, becoming first octagonal and then spherical. The space below the dome was open down to the basement, and places were set aside for statuary on the two landings below. The top of the dome was planned to afford a splendid view of the city of Norman. When the building finally opened, however, the view was marred by the depressing remains of the first building, not yet completely torn down, standing black and skeletal among Boyd's trees and dominating the immediate foreground to the northwest.[35] Some thoughtful soul had remembered to plant ivy from around the first building at the base of the second. The decision to eliminate the west wing on economic grounds gave the building a slightly lopsided appearance, but the air was filled with optimism that some future appropriation might someday enable the University to realize the original plan for the building.

In the meantime, it seemed entirely appropriate to open the stately edifice with a grand celebration. On the morning of March 16 the faculty and students assembled downtown at the Baptist church. Shortly after 9 o'clock, the students were arranged by classes, and "with flags floating to the breeze and amidst the college yell the parade left the church, and marched through the streets toward their college grounds."[36] The classes of the Preparatory Department led the way, with the youngest first. These were followed by college classes and finally by the faculty. As the parade approached the new building, the students formed a double file. The faculty passed between them and into the building, then the seniors and juniors, and down through the ranks, so that those who had led the procession were the last to enter the hall. They filed down to the chapel in the basement. "By this time the

33. For a technical description, see Sorrels, "Eight Early Buildings," chap. 3.

34. University Hall was built on the exact site where Evans Hall now stands, at the deepest point of what would someday be the Parrington (or North) Oval.

35. *University Umpire, Commencement Number,* 1903, 38.

36. *Norman Transcript,* March 19, 1903, 1. For an eyewitness account of the pageantry, see Gittinger, *University of Oklahoma,* 38.

*The University's lopsided new Administration Building*

visitors and the friends of the school had begun to arrive and by the time President Boyd called the meeting to order at 10 o'clock every seat was taken and before the exercises were over every foot of standing room was taken."

After some music, Boyd offered a few words. He was followed to the podium by representatives from each class. "Much feeling was shown by all of the speakers and the sentiments spoken were heartily endorsed by the students with cheers and class yells." Professor Buchanan (who "has long had the name of being equal to any emergency") was chosen to speak for the faculty and, as far as the *Transcript* reporter was concerned, "he certainly covered himself all over with glory." The students responded (naturally) "by making the chapel and even the halls ring with the old college yell of Hi! Rickety! Whoop Te Do. Boomer Sooner, Okla. U." Then President Boyd closed his short speech of thanks to all with the glad announcement that there would be no school for the rest of the day. "The students immediately organized picnic parties and spent the afternoon in having a good time and as soon in the evening as it grew dark a bonfire was started on the college campus and all the boys turned out in a gang and made the night hideous till way after midnight with their songs and yells."[37]

37. *Norman Transcript,* March 19, 1903, 1.

~

ALTHOUGH THE CONSTRUCTION OF UNIVERSITY HALL was well under way—
indeed, nearing completion—at the time of the January 6, 1903, fire, the fire led directly
to a major building boom during the remainder of that year. During the summer, the city
of Norman finally tore up the boardwalk leading to the campus and replaced it with a cement sidewalk. "The enraged girl with the torn skirt may bid farewell forever to the nails
which had bobbed up so incessantly," wrote one newspaperman.[38] The sidewalk was also
good news for the many bicycle riders of the period, and they entered into a wary competition with strollers enjoying the leafy shade provided by Boyd's trees, now tall enough
to arch the walk. During the same summer of 1903, moreover, electricity finally came to
the campus, as the University was connected to the city's light plant.[39] In addition to the
modern new sidewalk and the miracle of electric power, 1903 also saw the construction or
the beginnings of no fewer than six additional buildings.

Two of these were the quick, flimsy, and cheap frame buildings constructed as a temporary home for the sciences immediately after the fire. They were located directly to the
west of University Hall and separated from each other by about fifty feet. Between the
frame buildings and University Hall was the small new heating and lighting power house
made out of brick and lent a certain prominence by the smoke stack and water tower,
each rising above it sixty feet into the sky. The fourth new building was the gymnasium,
obtained as part of the $90,000 appropriation that had made University Hall possible. The
gym was constructed of wood and placed east and a little north of University Hall.[40] The
cost-conscious Regents saw to it that the foundations of both the gymnasium and the two
frame science buildings were constructed of stone carried over from the black hulk of the
burned old building.[41] The final two buildings, begun in 1903, were substantial, invaluable, and permanent additions to the Norman campus.

Boyd and the Regents had early decided to apply the insurance money from the original building ($35,000) to the construction of a Science Hall. Plans were approved at the
April 1903 Regents' meeting, and construction began in August. The building (125 by 60
feet) was finished during the summer of 1904 and ready to occupy at the opening of the
academic year. Science Hall had a basement and two floors. DeBarr's chemistry and pharmacy operation took over the basement; Van Vleet's work in biology and medicine got the
first floor; and Gould's geological collections and laboratory occupied most of the second.
Also on the second floor was a substantial (32 by 54 feet) Museum of Natural History,
specializing in zoological, botanical, and geological materials.[42] A recent student of the
building's architecture detects the "unmistakable" influence of the great American archi-

38. Quoted in Gittinger, *University of Oklahoma*, 43.

39. Wardner, "Territorial University," 128.

40. Gittinger, *University of Oklahoma*, 41–43; *University Umpire, Commencement Number, 1903*, 38.

41. Wardner, "Territorial University," 128.

42. For a thorough description of each of the laboratories in Science Hall, see *University Catalogue*, 1905, 14–22.

*The wood-frame gymnasium*

tect Frank Lloyd Wright. She mentions, in particular, "the organic simplicity of Wright's Prairie style" and its characteristic "low-pitched roof and unembellished skyline."[43]

While Boyd and the Regents were occupied with the new Science Hall, Boyd was embarked on a building project of his own. He had entered into correspondence with the famous American industrialist and philanthropist Andrew Carnegie, who ultimately was to fund nearly 1,700 libraries across the country.[44] Until 1903, however, none of his libraries had been constructed at a college or university. Boyd believed that Carnegie had been ready to fund a library at the University of Missouri, but that project was lost in the fury of Missouri politics.[45] Whether Boyd began his own campaign before the fire of January 1903

43. Sorrels, "Eight Early Buildings," 22. Sorrels is critical of "the awkward pedimented entrance" that was placed halfway between the first and second floors. She also criticizes "the unadorned rectangular windows of the north and south wings," which seem almost to be "punched out of the thin fabric of the wall with a cookie cutter." "None of this," she writes, "creates a feeling of continuity or even appropriateness. Too much activity in too little space generates an uneasy, crowded feeling."

44. Theodore Jones, *Carnegie Libraries across America: A Public Legacy*. For the Oklahoma story, see Tanya D. Finchum and G. Allen Finchum, "Celebrating the Library Spirit: A Look at the Carnegie Libraries in Oklahoma," *Chronicles of Oklahoma* 79 (2002): 454–75. Unaccountably, the Finchums seem unaware of the Carnegie library on the Norman campus.

45. Boyd thought that William Stone, campaigning to be Missouri's senator in 1902, expressed himself in public as decidedly opposed to taking Carnegie money, arguing that the proud state of Missouri would equip and maintain its own university free from corporate, sectarian, or other influences. Officials at the University of Missouri then reluctantly declined the Carnegie offer of $50,000. See Morrissey, "David Ross Boyd," 126.

*Science Hall*

is unclear.[46] But after at least eight letters to New York, he at last received the response from Carnegie's private secretary that he was hoping for: "Mr. Carnegie is very glad to share in the work of re-construction of the University which was burned, to the extent of providing a Library Building to cost Thirty Thousand Dollars, if the authorities will pledge that it shall be maintained at a cost of not less than Three Thousand Dollars a year."[47] On April 11, the same day that they approved plans for the new Science Hall, the Regents accepted Carnegie's offer. The contract for constructing the library was awarded (after a first round of bids was rejected for being too high) in September; the building was ready for use in January 1905. Although Boyd wrote to the librarian at Carnegie's Pittsburgh library for architectural advice,[48] and although many Carnegie libraries share a sort of family resemblance, the philanthropist did not require a particular architectural design but left the choice of style to local communities.[49] The new campus library sported a monumental entrance, atop two flights of steps and framed by large square columns, leading to "another essentially Prairie style building."[50] For the time being, of course, the building was more

46. For a thorough account, see ibid., 125–29.

47. James Bertram to David Ross Boyd, February 20, 1903, David Ross Boyd Presidential MSS, Box 3, Folder 5A.

48. David Ross Boyd to Mr. Anderson, April 13, 1903, in ibid.

49. See the discussion of "The Architecture of Carnegie Libraries," in Jones, *Carnegie Libraries,* 53–82.

50. Sorrels, "Eight Early Buildings," 27–28. Sorrels believes that the Carnegie building is the better of the two

*The Library, a gift of philanthropist Andrew Carnegie*

than was needed to house the University's meager library holdings—the fire had seen to that. During the first few years, therefore, the basement of the Carnegie building served as the women's gymnasium.[51] No account seems to have survived that records what it was like to have some students studying quietly upstairs while the women were exercising to music in the basement below.

Whether the new Science Hall and the new Carnegie library building were more notable architecturally for their differences or their similarities is open to dispute. But with the first placed to the northwest of University Hall facing east and the second placed to the northeast facing west, the two were fated, after January 1905, to stare amicably across the grass at each other down through the years.

~

IN COMMON WITH OTHER HUMAN BEINGS, university presidents are not given the power to look into the future. They cannot know what the faculty they have assembled (or inherited) will be like five or ten years down the road, because professors retire or die

---

buildings: "The horizontal lines are more stressed than in Old Science Hall, and the building seems more comfortable on its site and with itself."

51. Gittinger writes: "The university catalog published in the spring of 1905 announced with pride that women now had a separate gymnasium. Until this time men and women had used the same gymnasium, but on different days. The author of the catalog stated gravely that 'the work is carried on for the most part in classes accompanied by music,' and further, that 'women's gymnasium suits require four yards of dark blue serge or flannel. They consist of two pieces, a blouse and bloomers' " (*University of Oklahoma*, 44).

or are lured to other schools. If, however, David Ross Boyd had somehow been given the ability in 1903 to peer into the future of the University, he would have had the satisfaction of seeing how the faculty that he had selected was to lay the groundwork for pedagogy at the University of Oklahoma for decades to come. In field after field, Boyd's appointments decisively shaped the future. Edwin DeBarr in chemistry and pharmacy, Albert Van Vleet in biology, Charles Gould in geology, James Buchanan and Roy Gittinger in history, Joseph Paxton and James Sturgis in classics, Roy Hadsell in English, and Jesse Rader in the library would all continue at the University of Oklahoma into the 1920s, most of them into the 1930s, and some beyond. In at least three cases, however, Boyd would no doubt have been disappointed by a glimpse into the future. He probably hoped that Vernon Parrington's influence in English would be long lasting and that he had established a firm foundation for the social sciences in George Bucklin and Lawrence W. Cole, both of them his protégés and both graduates of the University of Oklahoma. All three were young men in 1903 and had years of service ahead of them. Unfortunately for Boyd's hopes, Bucklin left academic life for the diplomatic service. A more violent and abrupt fate awaited Parrington and Cole—and Boyd himself.

Even without the power to peer into the future, Boyd must have been troubled, as he looked over his faculty, by the absence of stability in several of the disciplines: his teachers coming and going with annoying and demoralizing frequency, the lack of continuity (let alone steady development), the feeling of always seeming to have to start all over again. Boyd probably felt with particular force the need for greater constancy in these areas, and between the end of the 1902–1903 academic year and 1908 he moved decisively and effectively to strengthen some crucially important parts of the University's program. Thus, accompanying the significant changes in the physical appearance of the campus after 1903 were some extremely significant additions in personnel.

Among the most important for the future of the University was the earnest young man who arrived in the late summer of 1903. On the morning of September 1, his first morning in town, Fredrik Gustav Holmberg deposited his trunk in his room at the Grand Hotel and headed east down Main Street toward the state mental hospital. He carried his violin under his arm, and from a distance the hospital building and grounds seemed to be the only thing in sight that looked anything like a college. "I didn't think that the people looked much like a school crowd. I saw no one who had the earmarks of a college professor, nor did I notice anyone who looked like a student. Having almost arrived at the buildings, I asked a man if this were the University of Oklahoma. He immediately answered, 'Hell, no! This is the bug house!' "[52]

Holmberg had been born in West Gotland, Sweden, in August 1872. When he was fifteen, his prosperous father (a lumber merchant) lost his business; and the youngster was

---

52. Mary Kimbrough, "Dean Holmberg," *Sooner Magazine* 7 (January 1935): 80–81; David W. Levy, " 'I Had a Certain Pioneer Spirit So I Stayed': Fredrik Holmberg Comes to Oklahoma," *Sooner Magazine* 19 (1998): 25–29.

cast adrift. After a few years working around Scandinavia as a mechanic, he made his way to America and to the Swedish-American settlement at Lindsborg, Kansas. He worked in the wheat fields in order to pay his way through Lindsborg's Bethany College and began his music-teaching career there. In the musical town of Lindsborg, Holmberg developed his views about the importance of shared culture, especially music, for the formation of a community. He attributed the town's high moral standards, for example, to its love of music and thought that every town in America should hire a "music supervisor," whose salary would be more than paid for by the elevation of morality and the results of awakened civic pride. Holmberg was very careful, naturally, to distinguish wholesome classical and genuine folk music from such pernicious "disease music" as ragtime.[53]

Holmberg was later to claim that, although he was happy at Bethany College, he saw little hope for advancement there and decided to move on. In fact, another professor's return made it impossible for the little college to keep him. Bethany's president, Carl Swensson, wrote a strong letter of recommendation to President Boyd: "When our regular man returned from Europe we could not use both and so we had to let Prof. Holmberg go. He is good on the violin, as an orchestra conductor, Harmony, Musical History, Piano tuning &c. Why not use him as your musical director."[54] Thus Holmberg was looking for work during the academic year 1902–1903. He made the discovery that there was actually a university in Oklahoma in a somewhat unusual way: "Sometime late in the year of 1902 or early in the year 1903 when I was teaching at Bethany College, Lindsborg, Kansas, I happened to look over the football schedule of that college for the following year and found that the team would play the University of Oklahoma in the fall of 1903." Holmberg quickly wrote to the president of that University ("no one seemed to know his name"), and Boyd promptly hired the thirty-year-old Holmberg at $600 a year.

After someone informed him that the genuine campus was a mile and a half southwest of the mental hospital, Holmberg "walked in the heat and dust from the hospital grounds to what was called the University. My spirits were rather dampened . . . when I approached the place and found that there was only one building in the whole university and that only one wing had been finished in that." The discouraged Holmberg decided to locate the president, confess that he had made a terrible mistake, pick up his still-packed trunk at the Grand Hotel, and head back to Kansas. Fortunately for the University, "Dr. Boyd, who . . . had a way of making things seem better, of giving one an optimistic outlook, changed my mind. . . . [A]nd too, I had a certain pioneer spirit so I stayed."[55]

Holmberg had been hired to teach violin and harmony, but he took it upon himself to bring musical culture not only to the school but to the whole state of Oklahoma. With his mild manner, his unfailing courtesy, his charming Swedish accent, he plunged into

53. See the undated newspaper account of his speech to the Sorosis club in the Fredrik Holmberg MSS, Folder 2.

54. Carl Swennson to David Ross Boyd, June 22, 1903, in Fredrik Holmberg's Personnel File, Provost's Office.

55. Holmberg's autobiographical notes "For the Sooner Magazine," probably written in 1934, in ibid.

the work. Within six weeks Holmberg had organized a glee club for men, another one for women, a mixed oratorio chorus, a band, and an orchestra. Not since the days of Grace King had there been such musical energy on the campus. "[T]he door for a missionary was wide open," he once reminisced, "and it was merely a question of taking advantage of this situation. I soon found that one could start anything in Oklahoma and there would be no particular opposition towards it."[56] Among the other things Holmberg began were state-wide contests—apparently the first to be held anywhere in the United States—in voice, piano, violin, choruses, bands, and orchestras. He organized and conducted the Oklahoma City Symphony Orchestra in the early 1920s and continued to lead it for many years.[57] Holmberg was willing to undertake the symphony duties (weekly rehearsals and seven concerts a year), he said, because "I feel that I am really helping to 'spread the gospel of good music' by conducting this organization. I also feel that this Orchestra is doing much to put the State of Oklahoma on the 'cultural map.' " He was quick to insist that this additional burden "will not hamper my work at the University. In fact, I endeavor to make up for the time spent on the Orchestra by working in my office at nights."[58] In making this critical appointment in 1903, President Boyd assured consistency, high quality, and steady growth in music and the fine arts for the next third of a century. Fredrik Holmberg was to guide the fine arts at the University of Oklahoma until his death on New Year's Day, 1936.[59]

If the acquisition of Holmberg was to bring a certain stability to the fine arts at the University, the effort to do the same for engineering was more complicated. This was because for a long time it was not clear if engineering should be taught at all. True, the original "Act to Locate and Establish the University of Oklahoma" seemed to sanction the teaching of engineering at Norman.[60] But the agricultural and mechanical college at Stillwater could also press a strong claim to oversee engineering instruction in Oklahoma. We have seen how Boyd watched warily as Oklahoma A & M developed its engineering program by dramatic increases in students, faculty, and facilities and how Boyd responded by blending various courses offered by DeBarr in chemistry and physics, Elder in mathematics, and Gould in geology, hoping that students in Norman could prepare themselves as fledgling engineers. In 1900–1901 Elder introduced a course (Math 7 and 8) entitled

56. Ibid.

57. J. Roberta Wood, "The Oklahoma City Symphony Orchestra," *Harlow's Weekly* 23 (October 18, 1924): 9. The symphony was organized in 1922, but Holmberg judged that it was not ready to give its first public concert until October 27, 1924.

58. Fredrik Holmberg to William Bennett Bizzell, December 14, 1925, Holmberg MSS, Folder 2.

59. David W. Levy, " 'An Imperishable Part of Our Traditions': Fredrik Holmberg Departs," *Sooner Magazine* 19 (1999): 25–29.

60. The act read: "The college department of arts shall embrace courses of instruction in mathematics, physical and natural sciences with their application to the industrial arts, such as agriculture, mechanics, engineering, mining and metallurgy, manufacturing, architecture." In addition that act gave the Regents the power "to establish such professional or other colleges or departments when in their judgment they may deem it proper" (*Statutes of Oklahoma, 1893*, 1166–67).

*Fredrik Gustav Holmberg with the University orchestra, circa 1904*

"Mechanics of Engineering."[61]

In midsummer of 1904 rumors of an attempt to remove the study of engineering to Oklahoma A & M suddenly erupted. Boyd suspected that the moving spirit behind this diabolical scheme was none other than Joseph B. Thoburn, the secretary of the Territorial Board of Agriculture.[62] Boyd attributed an anonymous editorial in the *Oklahoma Farmer*, offering precisely that suggestion, to Thoburn. Boyd (uncharacteristically) exploded. He wrote a remarkable and wildly angry letter to his old friend and advisor Henry Asp. Boyd suggested that Asp should "intimate to Mr. Thoburn" that if he were really on the look-out for examples of unnecessary expense and duplication of effort in Oklahoma Territory, "there are a great many people of the belief that the Secretary of the Territorial Board of Agriculture is an unnecessary position." Boyd thought it would be nice if people like Thoburn could "perceive clearly the limitations that surround the[ir] position; and then to have such a sense of propriety and such a capacity to tend to their own business, that they would always be within these limitations." Boyd was very nearly out of control. Thoburn had personal interests before the legislature, he ranted on to Asp, and "I think you could have it intimated to him that it will not help his purposes for him to be assaulting the

61. Love, "History of the University of Oklahoma College of Engineering," especially chap. 1: "The Beginning, 1892–1908." See also Joseph Kornfeld, "Engineering History," *Sooner Magazine* 1 (1928–29): 176; and J. H. Felgar, "A History of the College of Engineering," *Sooner Magazine* 12 (August 1940): 27ff.

62. Thoburn was soon to become Oklahoma's prolific and path-breaking historian. For a full account of his life and work, see Muriel H. Wright, "Pioneer Historian and Archeologist of the State of Oklahoma," *Chronicles of Oklahoma* 24 (1946–47): 396–414; and Paul F. Lambert, *Joseph B. Thoburn, Pioneer Historian and Archaeologist*.

University." As far as Boyd could see, Thoburn was motivated by "a vicious animus" and was "starting a campaign . . . against the University."[63]

The examples of Michigan, Indiana, Iowa, Kansas, Colorado, and Texas, Boyd insisted, ought to be worth more than Thoburn's view about the dangers and waste of duplication. After all, Boyd pointed out, "some of the best engineering schools of the country are in the Universities of the states named above." He claimed that his school's work in "Hydraulic, Sanitary, Electrical, Mechanical, Civil, Mining, and numerous other departments of engineering" was covered, "including the preparatory work," in six or seven years, while "the A. & M., preparatory and all, does not cover more than four or five years and is called only a 'Mechanical Department.' " Once he got going, Boyd found it hard to stop. As far as the University of Oklahoma straying from its main business was concerned, how about Stillwater? "[I]t could be appropriately pointed out that the output of the A. & M. College does not . . . produce educated farmers. I have noticed that the A. & M. College, for a number of years back, has called attention, with a great deal of apparent pride, to what its graduates are doing along lines for which it was never intended the A. & M. College should prepare them." Suddenly Boyd seemed to catch hold of himself; he thought he had better explain his rampage to Asp: "This letter accomplishes two purposes," he told his confidant. "First, it gives me an opportunity to let off steam to a confidential friend who will sympathize with me in my emotions as well as in my ideas. But, second, especially to have you know the situation that you may be able to do whatever comes your way to promote the general welfare."[64]

Asp tried to cool Boyd down by suggesting a face-to-face chat at his Guthrie office; and Boyd, who was going to Perry for a speech anyway, agreed. It seems probable that the two men decided that the best strategy was to emphasize that the engineering work in Norman cost almost nothing, since the classes were all being offered in other departments already. But when the president got back to his office, he found a letter waiting for him from Governor Ferguson, suggesting a meeting to talk the issue over. Once again Boyd was troubled. He sent the governor's letter to Asp and reviewed the strategy: "I think I can see him and arrange to have matters go on just as we had planned for this year as the work we are planning does not involve any expense not provided for within the limits of the Equipment fund." But Boyd was still plenty angry: "It appears to me that the A. & M. people are proposing to cut us out of this work and we want to rally the friends of the University and see that she is not allowed to displace us in this way."[65]

---

63. David Ross Boyd to Henry E. Asp, July 18, 1904, in David Ross Boyd Presidential MSS, Box 1, Folder 16.

64. Ibid. For a calmer argument, see Boyd's letter to Regent Harry Gilstrap, August 6, 1904, quoted at length in Wardner, "Territorial University," 162. In his letter to Gilstrap, Boyd makes a more openly economic argument: "You can see if we had no Mining School before the bill becomes a law, we would not get our half of the appropriation." Boyd refers to a pending federal law that was to provide $25,000 to each state and territory to maintain a mining school; in states with both an A. & M. and a regular university, the appropriation was to be divided.

65. David Ross Boyd to Henry E. Asp, 1 August 1904, in ibid. Governor Ferguson's letter, July 25, 1904, is quoted fully in Wardner, "Territorial University," 161.

It was in this precarious context that Boyd hoped to establish engineering on firm ground. His first step was to unveil in the *Catalogue* for 1904–1905 a new School of Applied Science and, as its head, Charles Curtis Major, a professor of physics and electricity who had earned a degree in mechanical engineering from Cornell and had taught briefly at the University of California. The School of Applied Science was to be divided into three departments (mechanical, electrical, and civil engineering); mechanical engineering claimed nine students, but the other two departments were still purely fictitious, marks of Boyd's ambitious plans rather than indications of the University's actual capability at this stage.[66] Unfortunately, Boyd's hopes for establishing the engineering curriculum under Major's direction suffered a setback when Major left for a position at Ohio State after only one year. He was replaced by Cyril Methodius Jansky, who had earned his degrees at Valparaiso and the University of Michigan. Jansky had been a school superintendent in the Michigan system for seven years; but after finishing his degree at Ann Arbor, he moved to the Bureau of Standards in Washington, D.C. Boyd brought him to Norman in 1905 to replace Major in physics and electrical engineering. Like Major, however, Jansky did not stay very long; by the fall of 1908 he too was gone.

The problem of establishing stability in the engineering field was finally solved for Boyd with the acquisition of James Huston Felgar, who arrived one year after Jansky but who remained in Norman until his death in July 1946. Felgar taught in the secondary schools of Newton, Kansas, for five years then earned a bachelor's degree from the University of Kansas in 1901 and a degree in mechanical engineering from the Armour Institute (later known as the Illinois Institute of Technology). After the thirty-year-old Felgar taught for a semester in Stillwater, Boyd brought him to Norman to add his mechanical specialty to Jansky's electrical.[67] When Jansky left in 1908, Boyd named the affable and efficient Felgar to head the School of Applied Science. James Felgar was hardworking, deeply interested in students, and a tireless counselor of them, devoted entirely to engineering education and the professionalization of the engineer's calling. When the generations of his students later unveiled a portrait of him to commemorate his forty years at the University of Oklahoma, one of them stated the obvious: "[H]e can truly be called the father of engineering in Oklahoma."[68]

Because mathematics underpins so much of engineering, the loss of Professor Frederick Elder at the close of the 1904–1905 school year spelled trouble for both engineering and the traditional arts and sciences curricula. Once again, however, Boyd was able to locate and entice to Oklahoma a superb replacement who was to make important contributions

66. Gittinger, *University of Oklahoma*, 47; for Charles C. Major, see *University Catalogue, 1904–1905*, 6–7.

67. Boyd attempted to fill out the third specialty, civil engineering, with George A. Hool from MIT in 1907, but Hool only lasted until 1909.

68. James H. Felgar Personnel File, Office of the Provost. The speech of Loyal B. Holland, May 7, 1946, can be found in that folder. In addition to fortifying the faculty, Boyd also tried to establish the University's claim by purchasing large quantities of equipment for the forge, foundry, woodworking, and machine shop. This machinery was in place and ready by the opening of the 1906 school year; see Felgar, "History of the College of Engineering," 27.

*James Huston Felgar*

*Samuel Watson Reaves*

to the University. Samuel Watson Reaves was a southerner, a Democrat, and a Baptist—all rarities on the faculty. Born in South Carolina and educated at the Citadel, the University of North Carolina, and Cornell, he came to replace Elder in the fall of 1905. The charming, courteous, easygoing Reaves was popular with students and faculty colleagues alike. "In the thirty years I have been a college president," said William Bennett Bizzell, "I have never been more happily associated with any man than with you. Your integrity, your loyalty, and your devotion to duty have been a constant source of satisfaction to me." The sentiment was echoed by George Lynn Cross, another University president under whom Reaves served: "Few men have left or will leave their marks on universities as you have left yours on the University of Oklahoma."[69]

At the same time that Holmberg, Felgar, and Reaves were beginning to provide consistency and orderly development to fine arts, engineering, and mathematics, Jerome Dowd was able to offer some of the same benefits to the social sciences. Dowd, like Reaves, was a southerner. Born in North Carolina in March 1864, while the Civil War still raged, Dowd earned a master's degree from Trinity College (later to become Duke University) in 1896. He taught there and at the University of Wisconsin before coming to Norman in the autumn of 1907 to teach sociology. Simultaneous with his arrival at the University of Oklahoma was the publication of the first volume of his survey *The Negro Races*. The

69. Both Bizzell's and Cross's remarks are in a radio "salute" to Reaves, broadcast on March 10, 1947, copy in Reaves's Personnel File, Provost's Office.

book examined all aspects of life among three groups of Africans; the second volume, written in Oklahoma, continued the study. It was not until 1926 that Dowd tackled *The Negro in American Life*. His ambitious plan at the outset of his career was nothing less than to produce a series of volumes that would constitute "a sociological study of mankind from the standpoint of race,"[70] but he was unable to complete the task. Dowd also wrote numerous articles on various sociological subjects and half a dozen other books. He soon became known, by colleagues and students alike, for his rare combination of self-deprecating and good-natured humor and his scholarly diligence and national reputation. He was greatly interested in the development of the social sciences at the University of Oklahoma and can be credited as the founder, over the

*Jerome Dowd*

years, of the Departments of Sociology, Anthropology, and Economics. Dowd also played a part in starting the School of Journalism, the College of Business Administration, and the School of Social Work. He stayed at the University until his retirement at the age of eighty-one but was a lively and popular figure on the campus until his death in August 1952.[71]

One more faculty member hired during this period deserves to be mentioned. Although he cannot be credited with establishing a particular discipline, Guy Yandell Williams was to become an almost legendary figure at the University. A good part of his mystique derived from the way he had spent his youth. He was born near Gainesville, Texas, in September 1881 but moved with his family to the Cherokee Strip near Enid when his father became a frontier peace officer. As a teenager, Guy Williams worked as a guard at his father's jail, a cowhand on neighboring ranches, and a ditch-digger in the city of Enid. There he met a retired acrobat and promptly concluded that the circus life was to be the life for him. He built a little gym and trained himself to be a professional acrobat, earning $10 a night after a day of ditch-digging. Then one day he was browsing through some of his father's medical books and became entranced by the chemical formulae he encountered. In the fall of 1902, at the age of twenty-one, Williams arrived in Norman to study chemistry with

---

70. Jerome Dowd, *The Negro Races: A Sociological Study*. The first volume was published by Macmillan in 1907; the second by the Neale Publishing Co. in 1914. The American installment was Dowd, *The Negro in American Life*.

71. George Lynn Cross, "President Cross Salutes . . . ," *Sooner Magazine* 19 (May 1947): 21–22.

*Chemistry professor Guy Yandall Williams in later years (but still doing his stuff)*

Professor DeBarr.[72]

Upon his graduation in 1906, Boyd and DeBarr immediately hired Williams to teach chemistry. He earned a master's degree from Oklahoma in 1910, a second M.A. from the University of Chicago in 1911, and a Ph.D. from the University of Illinois in 1913. For forty-six years "Guy Y" was a fixture on the campus, a lively and popular teacher. Well into his sixties, Williams astounded students by now and then springing agilely into a handstand; presumably to demonstrate chemical "equilibrium," he would occasionally place one hand on the corner of his desk and lift his body until it was exactly parallel to the floor. He was known sometimes to enter his classroom through the transom. The students greatly admired these antics for some reason, and his classes were always among the most popular of the Chemistry Department's offerings. Guy Williams was spirited and opinionated; he could be stubborn and abrasive and sharply cantankerous. "No one ever doubted where you stood on an issue," one friend politely remarked upon Williams's retirement in 1952.[73] He did little original research; but alongside DeBarr and for three decades after DeBarr's departure, he was to provide continuity and a certain stability ("equilibrium"?) in the field of chemistry.

Thus, between 1903 and 1908, Boyd added to the faculty a group of men (Holmberg, Felgar, Reaves, Dowd, and Williams) who were in Norman to stay. Alongside his most important appointments of the 1890s (Buchanan, Gittinger, Paxton, Sturgis, DeBarr, Van

72. See Williams's obituary, *Daily Oklahoman*, February 1, 1968; and George Lynn Cross, "President Cross Salutes . . . ," *Sooner Magazine* 19 (April 1947): 10.

73. Emil R. Kraettli to Guy Y. Williams, June 2, 1952, in Williams's Personnel File, Office of the Provost.

Vleet, Gould, Hadsell, and Rader), they were to determine the future direction of serious study at the University of Oklahoma at least through the 1930s.

~

IN ADDITION TO BOYD'S BRILLIANT CHOICES on the academic side of the University, he made another acquisition that was probably more important to most Oklahomans and to most students than any mere professor, no matter how dedicated, learned, engaging, or quaintly acrobatic. It is not too much to say that the early history of athletics at the University of Oklahoma may appropriately be divided into two parts: before and after the arrival of a new football coach, Benjamin Gilbert Owen.

In 1901 Vernon Parrington gave up coaching, after four years, in order to concentrate on his teaching, writing, and other duties. President Boyd praised the retiring coach at a chapel service, and with good reason: the teams that the English professor coached won nine games, lost two, and tied one, giving him a stunning "lifetime" winning percentage of better than 81 percent.[74] One of the heroes of early Norman football, Fred Roberts, was induced to take over as coach (and player). He quit after a year to work on his farm, but he was always ready to jump into his buggy and appear at some big game when the varsity really needed the services of a great halfback. In the middle of the 1902 season a tough Texan named Mark McMahon, only twenty-four years old, agreed to coach for $250. He stayed for two years, long enough to introduce the nine-game season as well as the tricky wing-shift play and to earn enough to pay off his law-school debts. McMahon was replaced by an even younger man, twenty-two-year-old Fred Ewing. The new coach, although he had been an illustrious football player at Knox College, was the first of the school's five coaches to refrain from playing himself and the first to insist that all the players were to be actual students at the University. After a mediocre year, Ewing headed off to medical school at the University of Chicago. Thus, at the end of the 1904 season, the University of Oklahoma was once again in search of a football coach. Whoever got the job would be the sixth occupant since that historic September day in 1895 when Jack Harts first made his bold and fateful suggestion at Bud Risinger's barbershop.[75]

The final game of that 1904 season had been played against the "Terrible Swedes" of Bethany College, Lindsborg, Kansas. That game was not Oklahoma's first encounter with the Swedes. The year before the team had played Bethany on Thanksgiving Day in Oklahoma City. This was the game that caught the attention of Bethany's young violin teacher, Fredrik Holmberg, and provoked him to apply for a teaching position in Norman. On that occasion the Bethany team—accompanied by two hundred rooters who bewildered the Oklahomans by shouting their cheers entirely in Swedish—narrowly defeated the University's squad by 12 to 10. At the return match in 1904, Bethany crushed the

---

74. Keith, *Oklahoma Kickoff*, 53. Parrington retained his unpaid duties as athletic director.

75. For the story of early University of Oklahoma football, see ibid., 1–102; and Clark, *Sooner Century*, chap. 1.

Oklahomans, 36 to 9. As Harold Keith put it: "The Swedes seemed to achieve the sublimity of their wrath in the first half which they led, 24 to 4. In no department of play was the [Oklahoma] varsity as good as the [Bethany] visitors. The university band ceased playing and the varsity cheering had died away in the stands."[76] In both of the games against Bethany College the Oklahomans were impressed by more than the Swedes' prowess. In sharp contrast to many of the University's other opponents, the Bethany players were unfailingly courteous, gentlemanly, almost bashful. They also played the cleanest football imaginable: they rarely incurred a penalty, never kneed or slugged or deliberately roughed an opponent. They were also noted for their superb conditioning, their tactical innovations, their blinding speed, their rapid-fire play-calling. Some of these traits could be attributed to the serious religious atmosphere of Lindsborg; some, however, were attributable to the Terrible Swedes' brilliant young coach.

Bennie Owen had been born in Chicago in 1874. The family moved to St. Louis when he was twelve, and Bennie divided his time between school, hanging around the wharves along the Mississippi, and following the St. Louis Browns baseball team. After he finished high school, his family moved to a wheat farm near Arkansas City, Kansas. They arrived in 1891, a year before the Boyds left town for the new university in Oklahoma Territory. Although he had always been fascinated by sports, particularly baseball, the young man set his sights on a medical career and apprenticed himself to a local doctor for three years. Meanwhile, football came to Arkansas City; and Bennie Owen discovered that, although he weighed less than 130 pounds, he had a certain knack for the game. In 1897 he enrolled at the University of Kansas to pursue his medical studies. But Kansas had a football team, Owen liked to play, and soon he was the quarterback. Owen learned football at Kansas under two excellent but contrasting coaches. Wylie Woodruff, who came to Kansas at the same time as Owen, specialized in tough, hard-hitting brutality (his motto was "hurdle the wounded, step on the dead"). Fielding Yost, who took over the Kansas team in 1899, believed in innovation, speed, and cunning. With Yost as coach and Owen at quarterback the Kansas team went undefeated in 1899. Becoming a doctor was looking less and less attractive.[77]

Owen thought things over during an adventurous trip with two classmates to the Paris Exposition and then accepted his first coaching job, at Washburn College, Topeka, in 1900. After a year at Washburn, his old Kansas mentor Coach Yost, now at the University of Michigan, asked him to become his assistant. The Michigan team, under Yost and Owen, was one of the strongest in the country: in its undefeated season, the team scored 550 points and was never scored against. Then Owen decided to strike out on his

76. Keith, *Oklahoma Kickoff*, 100. The games against Bethany are colorfully described by Keith at 84–86 and 100–101.

77. The best account of Owen's early life is Keith, *Oklahoma Kickoff*, chap. 10; for a helpful brief summary, see Clark, *Sooner Century*, 44–46. For a summary of his illustrious record as a coach, see Harold Keith, "Soonerland's Undefeated Elevens," *Sooner Magazine* 1 (November 1928): 56–57; see also Charles Long, "Gee Cly, Youse Guys," *Sooner Magazine* 36 (November 1963): 13–17.

own and accepted the offer from President Swensson at Bethany College. He arrived in the summer of 1902 and stayed in Lindsborg for three years. In that period Coach Owen's teams won 91 percent of their games and, in the process, built a reputation for innovation, physical conditioning, sportsmanship, and integrity.

One of the greatest mysteries in the story of Oklahoma football is why Bennie Owen decided to come to coach in Norman. Parrington, as head of the Athletic Association, could offer him only $900 for a three-month football season; there was no guarantee of a second year. At Bethany, Owen was being employed for the full academic year as coach and chemistry teacher. Moreover, the financial arrangement at Oklahoma was precarious. Money was still owed to the two previous coaches, McMahon and Ewing, and the Athletic Association was more than $700 in debt. If this did not suffice to discourage Owen from taking up Parrington's offer, Pittsburgh University was also anxious to obtain Owen's services and had invited him to visit the campus. Pitt had already lured five of Owen's Terrible Swedes to play there. And yet, despite the financial uncertainty and the competing offer at Pitt, Owen agreed to come to the University of Oklahoma. Perhaps it was the same pioneering spirit that had brought his colleague Holmberg from Lindsborg to Norman two years before.

*The legendary Coach
Benjamin Gilbert "Bennie" Owen*

The arrival of Bennie Owen set off a firestorm of enthusiasm. Although the team was mediocre by Bethany standards, it managed to win its first game against the Normal in Edmond by 28 to 0. The second was scheduled against the rough Haskell Indians, a team that had beaten Kansas four years running and had come to town fresh from a 17 to 0 defeat of Texas. The Haskell game was one of those legendary contests that old-timers were to recall for decades.[78] It was punctuated by unusually foul play and, to Coach Owen's horror, numerous fistfights among the participants. After a heroic effort, Oklahoma emerged victorious by 18 to 12. Guy Y. Williams recalled rushing around after the game, taking clubs and sticks out of the hands of students and Norman citizens who were intent on murdering

78. The Haskell-Oklahoma game is fulsomely described in Keith, *Oklahoma Kickoff*, 125–29.

the Haskell team! That night, according to the *Umpire*, the University "felt the greatest throb of enthusiasm that she ever knew. She had a celebration that made the foundations of the old main hall tremble with feeling." Roy Hadsell, mimicking the meter of Henry Wadsworth Longfellow's "Hiawatha," rubbed it in on the *Umpire's* first pages:

> When the game was done and over
> And the score stood twelve to eighteen,
> Twelve to eighteen in our favor,
> Said the captain of the Haskells,
> He the chief of all the redmen,
> To his team of profs. and tutors,
> To his braves and tomahawkers,
> To his braves of many nations,
> Braves of many tribes and countries,
> Spoke to them and spoke in thuswise:
> "Is there not some back road from here,
> Some dark trail not often traveled,
> So the crowd, there, can not see us,
> Can not see us and laugh at us
> And the score they made against us?"[79]

Before the season, President Boyd had (foolishly) offered to buy the team a big dinner ("a royal spread") if they beat any two of their three most formidable opponents: Haskell, Kansas, and Texas. After the Haskell game, the team telegraphed the final score to Boyd, who was in Champaign, Illinois. The telegram ended: "Ready for supper."[80]

That fall the University laid out Boyd Field, the home of football, track, and baseball for the next nineteen years. It was located just west of the present fieldhouse; its northern half took up the ground where the University of Oklahoma Press operated for many years. That autumn Arthur Alden, a student of history and physiology and the son of a Norman jeweler, appropriated the tune of Yale's "Boola, Boola" and put new words to it, starting with "Boomer, Sooner." A year later a similar appropriation from North Carolina's "I'm a Tarheel Born" was made, and the University's fight song came into existence.[81]

The football craze that swept over Oklahoma at the turn of the century was, of course, a nationwide phenomenon. For some reason, the marriage of higher education and the sport of football (presided over by the nation's newspapers) carried everything before it.[82] The remarkable appeal of college football had something to do with the juxtaposition of violence and rules, something to do with social Darwinism and ideals of manhood and

79. *University Umpire*, November 1, 1905, 8, 6.

80. Keith, *Oklahoma Kickoff*, 121–29; quotations on 129. Later Oklahoma was to beat Texas, 2 to 0. The team was walloped by Kansas, 34 to 0.

81. Ibid., 123–25.

82. For a prosaic year-by-year look at the phenomenon, see Tom Perrin, *Football: A College History*, chap. 2, "The Turning Point: 1900–1909." More imaginative and perceptive is Ronald A. Smith, *Sports and Freedom: The Rise of Big-Time College Athletics*.

*Boyd Field, with the second Administration Building, Science Hall, and gymnasium in the background*

beliefs about power. Several historians think it had something to do with the deep anxieties of elite Americans about immigration, the challenge of "inferior races," the alleged softness and effeminacy of the nation's upper and middle classes that troubled many social observers during these years.[83] Over the course of the twentieth century a very few American colleges and universities proved capable of loosening the bonds between football and their institutions; a few found other sports, principally basketball, a suitable substitute; and some others banned the game entirely. This was not to occur at the University of Oklahoma. For a few more years, perhaps, the oratorical contest continued to exercise its attraction and maintain its excitement for some students. But the handwriting was already on the wall. With the heartening success of Bennie Owen's teams year after year, football was rapidly outdistancing every rival on campus.

~

IN ADDITION TO FOOTBALL GAMES and oratorical contests, there were numerous other ways for students to edify and amuse themselves outside of the classroom. Indeed,

83. For an intelligent and stimulating analysis, as well as a close study of how newspapers portrayed and nurtured college football at the turn of the century, see Michael Oriard, *Reading Football: How the Popular Press Created an American Spectacle*.

coming to Norman from an Oklahoma village or small town—to say nothing of arriving fresh from an isolated farm—must have been an intoxicating experience for hundreds of these youngsters, almost like coming into a new and slightly bewildering world. There were so many enticing possibilities, so many opportunities to practice some already acquired skill or to learn a new one, so many chances to mingle with other bright and energetic and ambitious young people. For the musical, there was the Glee Club or the band or the orchestra or the Ladies Quartette or the Mandolin Club. The YMCA and the YWCA were available for those who wished to socialize in a properly religious atmosphere. Those hoping to try their literary talents could turn to the *Umpire* or the *Mistletoe*, the new yearbook published by juniors. For those of an intellectual bent there were the seven literary societies and the Oratorical Association. Athletics were everywhere—not only the University's teams in football and baseball but less august games between the University's classes as well as track and field and basketball games for both men and women and tennis on the four courts just south of the men's gymnasium.

If all those extracurricular possibilities were not enough, another innovation heavy with implications for the future also appeared during these years. By 1904 there were four Greek letter societies on the campus, two for women (Eta Beta Pi and Zeta Zeta Zeta) and two for men (Gamma Phi and Omega Psi). These were rather informal and nonresidential associations, little more than clubs, groups of friends who occasionally invited others to join them. There was some casual talk among the women of someday applying for affiliation with a national sorority. But it was one of the fraternities, Omega Psi, that carried within itself, for good or ill, the seeds of the future. The group consisted of some of the most talented, handsome, and well-liked young men on the campus. The ringleaders were Walter Scott Ferguson, the popular and gregarious son of the territorial governor, and George Bertrand ("Deak") Parker, another gifted and popular student; this was the very pair that Boyd suspected of drinking to excess at McCarty's Saloon when he and his wife spotted them sweeping the place out.[84] Other members of Omega Psi (which according to legend was merely the Greek equivalent of "O.S.," for Oklahoma Sooners) were well-known baseball and football players. The boys improvised an insignia: a white collar button worn on the lapel.[85]

Two Norman businessmen, co-owners of the electric light and power plant, had come up from the University of Texas. They had been members of Kappa Alpha, a fraternity steadfastly devoted to "southern culture and ideals" whose hero was Robert E. Lee. They

84. Both of these young men went on to distinguished careers. Walter Ferguson (1886–1936) was a journalist until becoming a prominent Oklahoma banker, businessman, and political insider. George B. Parker (1886–1949) remained a journalist and rose to become editor-in-chief of the Scripps-Howard newspaper chain. He won the Pulitzer Prize for his editorials in 1936. Parker was the first alumnus invited to give a commencement address at the University, and he began his speech with an amusing quotation from his old friend Walter Ferguson. See David Ross Boyd MSS, Box 1, Folder 10, for a copy of the speech. Parker's nickname is sometimes given as "Deak" and sometimes as "Deke."

85. R. Vincent Lackey, *Our First Fifty Years: A Short History of the Kappa Alpha Order in Oklahoma*, 10–11.

observed the lads of Omega Psi and decided that they were promising raw material for an Oklahoma chapter of their beloved fraternity. The boys were willing; and on November 17, 1905, the solemn installation ceremony took place in the town's Masonic hall. It was followed by a night of oysters and revelry that began in Norman, moved to Oklahoma City, and lasted until 4 A.M. The boys moved into a house on College and set about planning the three dances and two smokers for the year. They attended oratorical contests and football games as a group (half the football players were Kappa Alphas). The idea of Greek letter societies caught on quickly; in the 1906–1907 school year another national fraternity was chartered (Kappa Sigma), and a third was petitioning for inclusion in Sigma Alpha Epsilon.[86] By 1910 the Norman campus had five fraternities and three sororities; by 1920 the numbers were eleven and ten.[87] From the beginning, these nationally affiliated Greek letter societies—residential, self-selecting, and exclusive—determined much of the tone of social life at the University of Oklahoma.

~

IN THE SECOND WEEK OF MARCH 1904 President Boyd gave one of his classes a revealing homework assignment. He asked his students to turn in papers listing the reasons why a young person should choose to come to the University of Oklahoma. Forty-one students presented their lists, and most of them were able to give ten or fifteen justifications for attending the University. For some reason Boyd chose to save these papers, and they provide an invaluable insight into why students came to Norman at the turn of the century and what they found most appealing once they arrived.[88]

Virtually all of the students mentioned prominently—often as the first or second of their reasons—the fact that the University of Oklahoma was free ("Why should a student go to another college and pay tuition when his father is paying taxes to support this one?" asked a student named J. L. Lysinger). Many of them also noted that the cost of living in Norman was low, that residents of the town were friendly and helpful, and that employment opportunities were abundant. A surprising number of the papers also extolled the wholesome climate of the town, its clean and abundant water and fresh air ("the pure and bracing atmosphere is very healthful," observed Jesse Best). The warmest praise, however, was for the community's moral and religious tone: The town of Norman, wrote Guy Baker, "is comparatively free from vice. It has a church for almost every Christian denomination." Many others praised the churches of Norman and their welcoming attitude toward the students. An astonishing number of the students singled out the moral and religious work of the YMCA and the YWCA for special praise.

86. Ibid., 11–12.

87. See the *Sooner* yearbooks for those years.

88. The folder containing the students' papers somehow survived the fire of December 1907 and can be found as Vertical File: "University of Ok. Essays." See also David W. Levy, "Why Did You Come to the University," *Sooner Magazine* 25 (Fall 2004): 15–19.

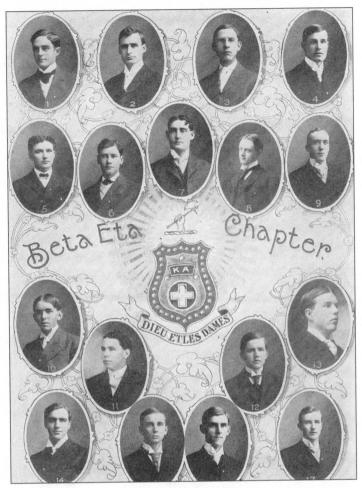

*The men of Kappa Alpha, the University's first fraternity, in 1906, including Walter Ferguson (1), George "Deak" Parker (3), and future oilman and philanthropist Everette Lee DeGolyer (12)*

Boyd's students also unanimously praised the faculty for their learning, their attention to them as individuals, and their energy: "The faculty is composed of progressive, ambitious and patriotic young men who are otherwise well qualified," declared George Smith. The students also applauded the wide variety of courses and the buildings and other facilities; the library (which was under construction at the time but due to open soon) and the gymnasium were singled out by nearly every student for special acclaim. Student activities—especially the oratorical society and the literary societies—were also often cited as attractive features of life at the University. Naturally, the athletic teams were a particular source of satisfaction (even though this was still six months before the arrival of Bennie Owen): "The University has the best athletes of any school in Oklahoma and has made World Reckords," wrote one student. The students' responses also indicate an interesting mixture of pride in the quality of the institution and a sober realization that the University was not in the front rank of American institutions of higher education: on the one hand, many students pointed out (proudly) that the school was easily the finest in the Territory and even, they claimed, among the finest in the West; on the other hand, they also wrote (proudly) that the faculty in Norman came from "the greatest universities" in the United States and that academic work completed in Norman was accepted even by "the finest colleges" in the country.

The students had nothing but praise for their fellow students: their upright characters, their seriousness of purpose, their friendliness and helpfulness to newcomers. J. L. Lysinger wrote a particularly thoughtful response:

> The student is not surrounded by the temptations usually to be found in college life. The student body is homogeneous and therefore the student is not thrown in contact with a class of people whom he feels to be superior to him and in trying to keep up with whose fastidious society he is tempted to spend more money than he can afford to spend. . . . The student body is made up of congenial democratic young people culled from such a class of people as can be found only in Oklahoma. The new student is taken in charge by the older students and immediately made to feel at home.

They were not unaware of the personal, vocational, and professional opportunities that the University opened to them ("A person must have mental training if they expect to be more than one of the crowd that stand on the street corners," wrote J. C. Port); but a very strong note that emerged from the students' responses was that they were mingling with tomorrow's leaders. As Tom F. Carey put it: "One meets and associates with the men who are to do the most in moulding Oklahoma's future. The men Oklahomans will have to deal most with in the future." Alfred Cheney thought that "you will here meet the 'to come' of the Territory. The student of today will be the leading citizens of tomorrow." There is much talk in these student papers about Oklahoma's glorious future and much unabashed patriotism for the soon-to-be state and its chief university. "The university is a great blessing to the student in many ways," wrote John M. Dye (who addressed his paper to "Professor Boid"), and "one of the greatest is to make usefull sittisons of our great common-wealth."

Perhaps President Boyd took special satisfaction from Reason No. 8, given by Beulah Long: a student should come to Norman, she wrote, "because we owe something to the world in return for our living, and should fit ourselves for becoming great scientists and leaders in noble works. The training for all this can best be gained in the University of Okla."

~

ON DECEMBER 16, 1903, a few weeks before giving his class that homework assignment, President Boyd wrote a letter to his friend and protégé Lawrence W. Cole. The president had first encountered young Cole in 1889 back in Winfield, Kansas, where Boyd was helping to instruct at a summer institute for hopeful beginning teachers; he took a fatherly interest in Cole and brought him to Norman as a student and then kept him on as a teacher of psychology. During the 1903–1904 school year, Cole was away at Harvard working on his master's degree. Boyd reviewed developments on the campus and proudly wrote: "[W]e can really begin to feel that we are a university."[89]

89. Quoted in Morrissey, "David Ross Boyd," 46. For Cole's first encounter with Boyd, see Cole to David Ross Boyd, July 26, 1933, David Ross Boyd MSS, Box 1, Folder 10.

It was, by nearly any standard, a gross overestimate on Boyd's part. The fire had destroyed the original building, including the University's library, only eleven months before. When Boyd wrote to Cole, the campus consisted of a single building and two makeshift frame structures built in the wake of the fire. The University was still teaching many more students in the Preparatory Department than in all the other branches of the enterprise combined. Fewer than 470 students had been registered at the end of the previous academic year.[90] There were nineteen professors and five instructors on the campus, and the football team was being coached by someone working to pay off his law-school loans. It was, in short, a long way from being a real institution of higher education, despite the bravado of Boyd's letter to Cole.

A scant four years later, however, Boyd's claim to Cole would have been much more credible. By the start of the 1907–1908 academic year, the institution looked a lot more like a real university. The faculty had grown to twenty-two professors and fourteen instructors, and important additions had been made in fine arts, engineering, and the social sciences. The campus now had seven buildings and a growing library. The Preparatory Department was shrinking, both in absolute numbers and as a percentage of the student body.[91] And whether one approved of every aspect of extracurricular life or not, the students coming to Norman in September 1907 had spread before them a banquet of possibilities in an increasingly important athletic program, in a growing range of social activities, and in an embryonic system of residential Greek sororities and fraternities. In its faculty, its physical facilities, and its student life, the institution had come a long way since that terrifying night in January 1903 when the night watchman noticed the ominous glow coming from the basement of Science Hall.

One significant measure of how far the University had come and how firmly its roots had been planted by 1907 was that it was able to survive, largely intact, the catastrophic events that lay just ahead.

90. *Catalogue, 1903–1904*, 130. There were 465 students enrolled as of May 11, 1903, and 249 were in the Preparatory Department.

91. As of March 1907 enrollment in the Preparatory Department had dropped to 229, while total enrollment had reached 623; *Catalogue, 1906–1907*, 174.

# CHAPTER VI

# The University Besieged, 1907–1908

The academic year 1907–1908 was easily the most dramatic and eventful in the life of the University of Oklahoma up to that point—indeed, it could register a plausible claim for being the most dramatic and eventful year in the entire history of the institution. In some ways, those months mark the close of the first phase of the University's life, the territorial period of planting and pioneering. When the next academic year began in September 1908, of course, much remained the same—in personnel, in curriculum, in procedures, in problems. But much had suddenly become vastly different as well.

The school term that started in September 1907 began amid encouraging signs of continuing growth and progress. The University enrolled 790 students, a substantial and gratifying increase of 167 over the 1906–1907 total. There was also evidence in the enrollment figures of the institution's growing reputation: of Oklahoma's seventy-five counties, sixty-six now had representatives in the student body. In addition to the Oklahomans, the University also enrolled young men and women from fourteen other states, including seven from Texas and fourteen from Missouri.[1]

Affairs seemed so promising that President Boyd asked Roy Gittinger to begin planning for the University's first summer school since 1899, an eight-week session to start immediately after the June 1908 commencement.[2] Optimism was in the air. "The outlook for a successfully [sic] year in everything at Okla. U. this year is most flattering," crowed the *Umpire* in September 1907. "The enrollment is better by over a hundred that [sic] last year and there seems to be more spirit in everything than ever before." By June 1908, a scant ten months later, not many people on the campus were talking with quite so much confidence.[3]

---

1. Gittinger, *University of Oklahoma*, 55–56. See also *University Catalogue, 1908*, 169–91.

2. The University's first summer school had been in 1898, and it was repeated in 1899. Expenses and lack of interest caused the University to abandon summer schools until 1908; see Wardner, "Territorial University," 153–54. The session in 1908 was to be the first in the eight-week (half-semester) format that became common afterward.

3. *University Umpire*, September 13, 1907, 2.

~

OVER THE LIVELY BUSTLE OF THE UNIVERSITY during the autumn months of 1907 hung the shadow of the thrilling events that were about to transform the "twin territories" into the new state of Oklahoma. From the very formation of Oklahoma Territory onward, settlers had been agitating for incorporation into the United States of America. It had always been understood that a state, or perhaps two states, would eventually be formed out of Indian Territory in the east and Oklahoma Territory to the west. Now at last matters were rushing to a climax.[4]

The last of several attempts to form a separate state (Sequoyah) out of Indian Territory, which was overwhelmingly Democratic in its partisan loyalties, was probably doomed during the first months of 1906 by the reluctance of the Republican administration and the Republican Congress in Washington, D.C., to admit another staunchly Democratic state. Instead, Congress approved and President Theodore Roosevelt signed the Oklahoma Enabling Act in June, paving the way for the combination of the two territories into a single state.[5] Politically, Oklahoma Territory was far more evenly divided between the parties, with Republicans dominant in the north and Democrats in the south; the Republicans probably enjoyed a slim majority in Oklahoma Territory as a whole (in seven consecutive elections the citizens of the Territory had sent a Republican to Washington as their delegate to the Congress).[6]

The Enabling Act mandated a constitutional convention to consist of 112 delegates.[7] The elections for the convention were held on November 6, 1906, and they ended in a tremendous sweep for the Democrats. They had expected to win, but the extent of their victory surprised even them: of the 112 delegates, 99 were Democrats, 12 were Republicans, and 1 former Democrat won as an Independent. The solidly Republican *Norman Transcript* growled sarcastically, "Why Not Make It Unanimous?"[8] The rout was far out of proportion to the actual political makeup of the two territories, and a reasonable explanation is that voters were rebelling against the years of Republican rule imposed from the Republican White House through the appointed Republican governors and administered by Republican judges, land office bureaucrats, federal marshals, Indian agents, University

4. For helpful discussions of events leading to Oklahoma statehood, see Gittinger, *Formation of the State of Oklahoma*, 196–214; Joseph B. Thoburn and Muriel H. Wright, *Oklahoma: A History of the State and Its People*, 2:627–39; and Litton, *History of Oklahoma*, 1:474–504. For a judicious attempt to place the story of Oklahoma statehood into a national, progressive-era perspective, see Danney Goble, *Progressive Oklahoma: The Making of a New Kind of State*.

5. 34 *U.S. Statutes*, 267. The most thorough discussion of the legislative history of the Enabling Act is in Gittinger, *Formation of Oklahoma*, 210–12.

6. Goble, *Progressive Oklahoma*, 94–95; part of the Republican ascendancy can be accounted for by the divisions between Democrats and Populists during some of this period.

7. Fifty-five from Indian Territory; fifty-five from Oklahoma Territory; and two from the Osage Nation, which had not yet been incorporated into the Oklahoma Territory's county system.

8. Cited in Goble, *Progressive Oklahoma*, 201, as *Norman Transcript*, November 8, 1906. For an analysis of those elected to the convention, see Lewis E. Solomon, "The Personnel of the Oklahoma Constitutional Convention of 1906–1907."

Regents, and other officials. To many southern Democrats, it must have seemed a bit like the hated Reconstruction days of carpetbagging, especially when the Republican officials arrived from other states, having been handed soft jobs on the basis of a personal friendship with some congressman or president. One historian goes so far as to suggest that "had there been a Democratic national administration at Washington for eight years, or even for four years, immediately preceding the passage of the Enabling Act, the settlers of the twin territories might have viewed matters very differently."[9]

Whatever the explanation, however, the Democrats' landslide must have caused considerable anxiety at the University of Oklahoma, which, as we have seen, was largely Republican from President Boyd down through the great majority of the faculty. Part of the nervousness no doubt had to do with the policies that Democrats might incorporate into the new constitution, but part of it certainly was caused by what the Democrats' triumph augured for the University's future in Oklahoma politics. The vote revealed a considerable resentment toward outside appointees, Republicans, and carpetbaggers. David Ross Boyd, after all, was a Republican appointee from the outside; so were many members of his faculty.

On November 20, 1906, two weeks after their election, the delegates gathered in Guthrie to frame the fundamental law of Oklahoma. Boyd probably hoped that the interests of the University during the proceedings would be protected by special friends of the institution who were at the convention. One of the delegates was twenty-six-year-old Carlton Weaver of Ada (Indian Territory). Weaver was a student at the University, but he was a Democrat and very young.[10] Two of the other delegates were more experienced and influential and likely to be more reliable. History professor James S. Buchanan had been elected from Norman, where he also served on the city council. "Uncle Buck" had been a highly regarded member of the faculty since 1895, popular on and off the campus. But he was also a southerner and a Democrat, an admirer of Andrew Jackson and the brother of a former Confederate officer and governor of Tennessee. Boyd was shrewd enough to understand that in a crunch Buchanan would be torn between his unquestioned loyalty to the University and his easygoing affability and natural desire to get along with his fellow delegates. Still, it was good that he would be present in Guthrie.

Boyd probably placed heaviest reliance, however, on another delegate. Henry Asp, his longtime confidant and advisor, was one of the few self-confessed Republicans at the Guthrie convention and the acknowledged leader of the small Republican band. He was one of the men Boyd had consulted when trying to decide whether or not to come to Oklahoma,

9. Litton, *History of Oklahoma*, 1:500. Litton points out that "the policy of the [Democratic] Cleveland administration [1893–97], in regard to territorial appointments, had not been materially different from those of the three Republican presidents who were last to hold office preceding the passage of the Enabling Act. The memory of man is short, as the Republicans discovered in 1906." Litton may have meant the *two* Republican presidents to hold office (McKinley, 1897–1901; and Roosevelt, 1901–1909).

10. Solomon, "Personnel of the Oklahoma Constitutional Convention," 40; Goble, *Progressive Oklahoma*, 203.

he had served as a chair of the Board of Regents. His devotion to the University of Oklahoma and to its president was beyond questioning. As the chief attorney for the Atchison, Topeka & Santa Fe, he was also one of the most powerful men in Oklahoma. A classic description of him was left by the famous reformer Kate Barnard: "For twenty years," she wrote, "Henry Asp ruled the State of Oklahoma[,] buying, cajoling, needling, coercing every successive territorial legislature. . . . Kindly, determined, master executive, resourceful to the nth degree, with a fund of wit, humor, and satire to penetrate, amuse, coax, wheedle, coerce, or buy—with a pocketful of railroad passes. . . . he was able to manipulate a majority in every succeeding legislature during territorial days."[11] Boyd had every reason to be hopeful because of the presence of Asp at the constitutional convention.

Unfortunately, Henry Asp was quickly neutralized in the deliberations. He had been off in Washington, working his special magic, while the Enabling Act was being drafted; and he was given credit back home for the provision ensuring that Guthrie, his hometown, would continue to be the state capital at least until 1913. The voters of District Twenty-five rewarded his efforts by choosing him as their delegate to the constitutional convention. But, as historians Joseph B. Thoburn and Muriel H. Wright note, "Mr. Asp was the attorney of the Atchison, Topeka & Santa Fe Railway Company for Oklahoma and this fact entirely overshadowed the personal element which had led to his nomination in the first place. Far and near, over both territories, the nomination of Henry E. Asp was heralded as an evidence of affinity or collusion between the Republican party and the railroads for control of the Constitutional Convention."[12] A Democrat from Purcell confessed that he owed his own slim victory to his skill at "picturing Henry Asp as a monster, eighteen feet high, his arms nine feet long, and his eyes like the headlight of a Santa Fe locomotive."[13] It suddenly appeared most unlikely that Asp had the power to represent or defend the college in Norman effectively.

The convention met from November 20, 1906, to April 22, 1907, and again for a week in July to make some final modifications. It produced the longest and most progressive state constitution in America. The document's 346 sections were so solicitous of farmers, workers, children, and the poor and so suspicious of monopolies, corporations, and government that progressive reformers from all across the nation lined up to sing its praises. The Boston editor of one liberal magazine, the *Arena*, thought that Oklahoma's proposed constitution guaranteed that "no privileged class or law-defying corporations or set of capitalists could levy extortion on a helpless people or unite to plunder the wealth creators at will."[14] The territorial governor announced that the document was to be presented to the people for their decision, and he fixed September 17 for the momentous election. On that

11. The description from Barnard's "Memoirs" is quoted in Goble, *Progressive Oklahoma*, 109.

12. Thoburn and Wright, *Oklahoma: A History*, 2:632.

13. Cited by Goble, *Progressive Oklahoma*, 195, as *Norman Transcript*, February 28, 1907.

14. For this and other progressive praise of the Oklahoma constitution, see ibid., 226–27.

same day, the governor announced, the voters were to select the first set of state officials. Naturally, the Democrats urged a vote for the proposed constitution and for their party's candidates; the Republicans said they were for statehood, but they vigorously condemned the document that the Guthrie convention had produced and urged a vote against it.

Meanwhile, the atmosphere in Norman was growing increasingly apprehensive. Roy Gittinger recalled that, despite the outward signs of growth and progress, "the school year 1907–08 opened with a feeling of unrest on the campus. . . . Rumors were already current that considerable reorganization, not only of the university faculty but of the university itself, might be expected under the new state government."[15] Classes began on Tuesday, September 10. When President Boyd made his annual opening address to the University community at 10 A.M. on the morning of Thursday, September 12, the election was five days away. "We are beginning our sixteenth year," he said. "In a few days we will pass from territoryhood into the sisterhood of states that form this great nation. That very fact, I believe, causes a welling up of emotion in every one of us; that we are now to step up on the plane of a really fully equipped citizenship of these great United States."[16] He spoke extemporaneously, avoided talking about the constitution or the coming vote, but tried to define a mission for the University to which all sides could subscribe. "This institution has been established by the state. The whole reason for maintaining it is that it may furnish and equip leaders and citizens for its own maintenance and support." Above all Boyd tried in his little talk to position the University above religious and partisan bickering, insisting that it not become a political football, no matter how the vote turned out. The University, he told the assembly, "has not been organized for any sect, any club, denomination or any party I hope, but it has been organized that the state itself might use the latent power and energy that is born into its population."[17]

It was a noble try and a sincere one, but the president was whistling in the dark, and he probably knew it. On September 17 the people of the twin territories went to the polls. They overwhelmingly approved the proposed constitution (180,333 to 73,059) and swept the Democrats into state, county, and municipal office. The Democratic candidate for governor, Charles N. Haskell, received 137,579 votes; his opponent, the Republican territorial governor Frank Frantz, got 110,283.[18] The Democrats had been excluded from power for a long time. Perhaps it was too much to hope that—on the basis of some noble and admirable self-restraint—they would now refrain from exercising it in their own partisan interest.

15. Gittinger, *University of Oklahoma*, 54.

16. *University Umpire*, September 27, 1907, 1.

17. Ibid.

18. Thoburn and Wright, *Oklahoma: A History*, 2:637–38; Litton, *History of Oklahoma*, 1:504.

~

IT IS DIFFICULT TO ASSESS THE ATTITUDE of the students toward these exciting political developments. No doubt there were many student opinions on Oklahoma's new constitution, the Democratic sweep, and the prospects for their school under an unfamiliar state government. The prevailing student attitude to be gleaned from reading the *Umpire* during these weeks is a stolid and happy indifference. The student newspaper seemed blithely unconcerned about events in Oklahoma and entirely absorbed by the parties and dances of the fraternities and sororities, the doings of the literary and oratorical societies, the Sooners' prospects for the next big game. (Some of the enormous attention to football that fall was certainly occasioned by the shocking news of the tragic hunting accident on October 16 that cost Coach Bennie Owen his right arm.)[19]

Nevertheless, the *Umpire* contains some indications of political interest and, just as important, of social attitudes among at least some of the students. The Democrat Club organized itself again in late October, but its main business was to create a committee to petition for a student holiday on the sacred day when statehood was to be officially declared (November 16).[20] Plans were made to send a student delegation to the festivities in Guthrie on that day. Although there were originally predictions of four hundred students heading to the capital,[21] only about one hundred actually made the trip. When President Roosevelt duly announced in Washington that "Oklahoma is a state," the glad news was telegraphed on an open line to Guthrie, and the cannon gave a seventeen-volley salute. And when the wild celebrations erupted as Charles Haskell was solemnly sworn in as the state's first governor, the University band and the University orchestra and the shouting students were prominently in evidence.[22]

But there were also indications, unfortunately, of a growing breach between the University's students and the common people of the state. The latter were coming increasingly to regard the former as privileged, spoiled, and leisured—bent on frivolous amusements, college tomfoolery . . . perhaps worse! The students, meanwhile, were quite capable of portraying everyday citizens as benighted, primitive, ignorant, and comical. If it had ever been the case, as the University community (and especially the faculty) liked to believe and regularly asserted, that the students were just plain Oklahoma offspring, the children of poor and unpretentious farmers, that perception was beginning to evaporate. There were certainly such students in Norman in 1907, and probably more of them than in most other American colleges and universities. But evidence of a widening and troubling divide

19. See the series of stories on Owen's recovery in the *Umpire* starting with October 18, 1907, 1. For the details of the accident, see Keith, *Oklahoma Kickoff*, 148–50.

20. *University Umpire*, November 1, 1907, 2.

21. *University Umpire*, November 15, 1907, 1.

22. For the day itself, see Litton, *History of Oklahoma*, 1:506–509; for the students' part, see *University Umpire*, November 19, 1907, 1. The band marched in the big parade, and the orchestra played at the governor's reception that evening.

between the students and the citizenry, a feeling of growing suspicion (if not yet of frank and open contempt), was beginning to appear.

In the *Umpire* for November 15, 1907, the very week that statehood was declared and ordinary Oklahomans shot off their six-shooters and celebrated, some of the views of the Norman students surfaced, and their attitudes could scarcely be considered democratic or egalitarian. Apparently President Boyd had received some letters complaining about the atmosphere at the college, "stating that, from all the writers could gather from the college publication, there was little going on at the University at the present time except football games and social stunts." The president called the editor to his office and "kindly admonished that such an impression should not be allowed to get out among the good people of Oklahoma." The editor was not, perhaps, as conciliatory as the discreet Boyd probably had hoped: "The trouble lies in the ignorance of the people themselves," the young editor declared. "They write in that they are taxpayers and that they do not want to help support an institution that spends yearly some great sum of money on a football team, etc." To the writer, "the thing resolves itself down to the fact that the people of the state who want most to run the University and The Umpire are the ones who know least about colleges or how they should be run." And then came a passage that must have made Boyd wince (on both diplomatic and grammatical grounds): "The students here are doing their best to shake the dust from his coat tails and brush the cobwebs out of his ears, and if his ma and pa at Neckeyoke Crossing will just let this beloved alone the transformation bids fair to take place."[23]

Not quite content with the assault on the ignorant and meddling taxpayer, the same issue of the *Umpire* offered a gratuitous observation about the folks back home: "If you are ever in doubt as to whether a college education is doing you good or not just stop and look back to where your old high school chums are still running in the same old rut they were in when you knew them last. Still loafing on the same corners and on Saturdays making fifty cents working in the same old grocery store."[24] These scornful views, of course, did not represent the full range of student opinion. Surely numerous students did not share (or at least would never have openly expressed) these feelings of superiority over the citizens whose taxes were making possible their bright opportunities.[25] Nor was this disdain for the folks back home exclusive to college students in Oklahoma. The idea of the smart and alert and witty and fashionable college insiders beleaguered by unschooled and backward average Americans was already well fixed in American college culture by 1907. The feelings of separateness, of superiority, of being misunderstood and underappreciated, would

23. "Editorial: The People v. Student Activities," *University Umpire*, November 15, 1907, 1. The editor also pointed out that "the great educational work of the University goes on silently and efficiently" and does not necessarily make the paper and that no taxpayer funds went to support the football team anyway.

24. Ibid., 3.

25. In the next issue of the *Umpire* (November 19, 2), however, the editor remarked that a number of students had come forward to say that the editorial had expressed their sentiments exactly.

grow steadily, reaching their most pronounced expressions during the 1920s. Then they would be somewhat mitigated by the hardships of the Great Depression and especially by the flooding of colleges and universities with veterans returning from World War II.[26]

Nevertheless, although there were many on the campus who did not share the view and many non-Oklahoma collegians who did, it was genuinely unfortunate that this mutual suspicion between those at the University and those outside should have surfaced at this particular time in the history of Oklahoma. It was, after all, an exceptionally sensitive moment of transition, of the transfer of power. The University was nervously treading an unknown path, and it was going to need all the friends it could muster in the new state.

~

ALL OF THESE CONCERNS WERE BRIEFLY FORGOTTEN on Friday, December 20, 1907, when the University suffered its second devastating fire in less than five years.[27] By mid-afternoon of that gray and chilly afternoon the campus was almost completely deserted. The Christmas vacation had officially started three hours earlier, at 12:30, and most of the students had already gone. A handful were milling around downtown, waiting at the Santa Fe station for the northbound train that would take them home too. On the empty campus, the library in the Carnegie building was securely locked up for the break; Science Hall, across the oval, was empty. Three men were painting the roof of the main building.[28] Because of the chill, a gasoline stove was placed in the dome to heat a pot of linseed oil. The stove exploded shortly after 3 p.m., and the painters saw smoke pouring from one of the dome windows. The dome itself was immediately engulfed in flame, and the freshly oiled banisters, floors, and woodwork went up like candles. The workers ran to save themselves: the only way down from the roof was through the burning dome. They shouted the alarm, and the fire bell downtown aroused the citizenry. By this time the students waiting at the railroad station had seen the smoke and came running back to the campus; some were carrying their suitcases.

The painters and some of the students dragged out pieces of hose and linked them together. But when the hose was attached to the street tap, it "sprang numerous liberal

26. "In the absence of a system of hereditary ranks and titles, without a tradition of honors conferred by a monarch, and with no well-known status ladder even of high-class regiments to confer various degrees of cachet," wrote the critic Paul Fussell in 1982, "Americans have had to depend for their mechanism of snobbery far more than other peoples on their college and university hierarchy." The remark is cited in the excellent study by David O. Levine, *The American College and the Culture of Aspiration, 1915–1940*, 7. For a helpful survey, see Helen Lefkowitz Horowitz, *Campus Life: Undergraduate Culture from the End of the Eighteenth Century to the Present*.

27. The principal accounts of the second fire are in the *Daily Oklahoman*, December 21, 1907, 1, 3; the *Norman Transcript*, December 26, 1907, 1; and the *University Umpire*, January 7, 1908. For a lively secondary account, see Long and Hart, *The Sooner Story*, 23–24.

28. Long and Hart, *The Sooner Story*, 23, write that the workmen were "tarring the roof"; but the contemporary accounts all say that they were painting it. The *Norman Transcript* story gives the names of "three students . . . [who] were painting the roof of the building." The *Umpire* version speaks of "two men and a boy" who were "busily engaged in painting the roof of the building." The *Daily Oklahoman*, however, insists that "J. Lewis, a painter, and three students . . . were painting the roof of the building when the fire started. They had finished painting the dome."

*The University's second Administration Building ablaze, December 20, 1907*

leaks"; and the pressure "was insufficient to throw the water to the dome." No one could locate a ladder tall enough to let the men carry the hose up to the roof, and the idea of dragging the hose up the steps and through the front door was abandoned when "falling brands which began to tumble down the rotunda forced failure on the attempt to meet the fire from the inside." Then "in the midst of all this the Norman fire department came clanging and clattering down the [University] boulevard, with its accompanyment [*sic*] of old buggies and wagons overloaded with excited men. At the side raced bicycles, saddle horses, and small boys, all panting and pointing toward the University with each fresh leap of the flames." The fire department quickly proved itself inept. The firemen attached their hose to the hydrant in front of President Boyd's house on the boulevard and sped the hose cart down the oval to the building. When the power was turned on, a trickle of water "about sufficient to put out the fire in a kitchen stove flowed feebly from the end of the hose." The water "came pattering back on the grass."[29]

By this time it was quite hopeless. The center of the building, under the stately dome, burned first. The west wing, which had never been finished, was the next to go (ironically, the University harbored high hopes that the new legislature was ready at last to appro-

29. These quotations are all from the *University Umpire* account.

priate funds for its completion during the present session). Finally, the flames spread to the east wing, where the president's office was located. Unable to save the building, the bystanders directed their frantic efforts toward two purposes. First, they managed to rescue a good bit of equipment through various doors and smashed windows. Desks, pianos, type-writers, bookcases, rugs, furniture, and scientific instruments were carried to safety. Some things—such as the static electricity machines in the physics laboratory—were shattered as students hurled them from the windows.[30] Second, and more importantly, by what the *Norman Transcript* called "heroic work," they were able to prevent the flames from spread-ing to either the Carnegie building or Science Hall—despite the brisk southeast breeze that put the latter building in particular danger.[31] The fire had broken out about 3:15; by 5:00 the building lay in smouldering ruins.

Those inclined to look on the bright side quickly pointed out that things were really not so bad. Two students had been slightly injured (one by a chair thrown from a second floor window, the other by shattering glass that cut his hand), but thankfully no one had been seriously hurt. The most valuable papers of the institution were locked in a fireproof vault; and although the vault was buried under tons of rubble, the contents emerged un-scathed.[32] As far as insurance was concerned, the University was in fairly good shape. None other than Delbert Larsh, who by this time must have regarded the school as a kind of godchild, had seen to that. Larsh, a Republican, had been a Regent from 1901 to 1907 and secretary of the Board for much of that time. Although no longer a Regent, he still managed the University's business affairs; and he had insured the building for its maxi-mum. This required special dexterity on his part: no fewer than sixteen insurance policies were held on the building, and the cautious Larsh had wisely insisted that a gasoline line permit be part of every one of them. In the end, the fire loss was fixed at around $85,000, and the insurance policies covered $67,500 of it.[33]

Because the fire occurred during a vacation, moreover, Boyd and the others had plenty of time to make alternative arrangements—a luxury they did not have in the case of the 1903 fire. The president could quite confidently assert that "classes will not lose one day as a result of the fire"; and when the students returned to school on January 6, they found things crowded but functioning satisfactorily. The women's gymnasium in the basement of the library was converted to four sizable classrooms; the adjoining locker room became five partitioned rooms and was turned over to the School of Music. Across the way, in Science Hall, other changes had been made during the students' absence. The small audi-torium was divided into two classrooms for the social sciences; the museum's exhibits were

30. Long and Hart, *The Sooner Story*, 43.

31. *Norman Transcript*, December 26, 1907, 3.

32. *University Umpire*, January 14, 1908, 3.

33. For retrospective admiration of Larsh, see Gittinger, *University of Oklahoma*, 54–55; for contemporary praise of him, see "D. L. Larsh's Good Work," *Norman Transcript*, December 26, 1907, 3. The details of insurance coverage can be found in ibid. and in the *Daily Oklahoman*, December 21, 1907, 3.

consolidated to make additional space; and some classes were taught up in the attic. "By this arrangement and by managing so as to utilize all the rooms continually throughout the day," the *Umpire* told the returning students, "space has been made for every class and with little inconvenience school is going on absolutely uninterrupted."[34] Not everyone was quite so sanguine. One student reminisced about "how crude things were"; and Professor Buchanan thought "we should have been arrested for holding classes in that attic [in Science Hall]. It was poorly lighted and ventilated, and there was no fire escape leading from it."[35]

Comparisons with the 1903 fire were inevitable, and everyone agreed that this fire was not as serious as the first had been. The principal reason, of course, was that then the fire had taken the University's only building. "In those days," said the *Umpire*, "the grief was much deeper than it is today. . . . We should be thankful that our loss is the one which at this time could be best sustained. It is the one which will be easiest made up." The writer's message to the returning students was that they should be of good cheer: "When we feel that we are unfortunate we should look back to the time five years ago and hope that this conflagration may be as great a blessing in disguise to the University as was the first fire." After all, that single lost building was replaced by seven (including two substantial ones, the Carnegie library and Science Hall). If that pattern should hold, the writer mused, "in five more years Oklahoma University would have fourteen buildings. Let us hope."[36]

The most interesting and by far the most revealing response to the fire, however, came from the *Norman Transcript*, a journal that carried on its banner the slogan "A Live Republican Newspaper" and that wore its partisan heart on its sleeve. The editor knew that among the other rumors flying around with the November arrival of statehood and the Democrats was the town's very worst nightmare: that the new authorities in Guthrie were hoping and scheming to move the University out of Norman—probably to somewhere in the former Indian Territory. The hopes of the town, and especially of its business leaders, rested on the presence and continued growth of the school. And now along comes this fire, destroying the largest building on the campus. Would the politicians in the capital seize upon this tragedy and steal away the town's central institution? In that frame of mind, the paper covered the story of the fire. The strategy it chose was to minimize the disaster, to appear entirely unconcerned, to emphasize the investment that the people of Oklahoma had already sunk in Norman, and, above all, to imply that it would be exceedingly silly and shortsighted (not to say wicked) even to *dream* of moving the University. These fears imparted to the *Transcript*'s "news story" on the fire a tone that is half comical, half pathetic:

---

34. *University Umpire*, January 7, 1908, 1.

35. Both quotations are in Long and Hart, *The Sooner Story*, 23–24.

36. *University Umpire*, January 7, 1908, 3. By a strange coincidence, the students had returned to Norman on the five-year anniversary of the first fire.

It was a great misfortune, but out of the evil good will surely come. The building will be replaced, greater and grander and better than ever, and the force and strength and good-will of the whole state will be back of it. This is no time for pessimism concerning the future of the State University of Oklahoma. What was destroyed by the fire was really a small part of the State's holdings here. The elegant Science Hall with its thousands upon thousands of dollars worth of appliances, the Carnegie Library building with its magnificent library, the fine gymnasium buildings, the beautiful and spacious campus and grounds upon which twenty years of hard labor have been expended, the very valuable section of land . . . all remain. And the insurance carried on the building will almost rebuild the new building . . . so that the splendid work and progress and influence of the institution will not be retarded.[37]

The *Transcript* was profoundly aware, of course, that the brand-new (Democratic) Board of Regents appointed by Governor Haskell was to have its first meeting in Guthrie the next day. On Saturday the Regents would be coming to Norman to inspect the damage. Perhaps a little flattery would not hurt: "Hon. Lee Cruce will be president of the board and it is very probable Gov. Haskell will turn all matters over to him. He is a warm friend of the University and emphatically denounces any talk of removal or of retarding the work of the institution in any manner. He and Gov. Haskell and the board are our friends and undoubtedly will at once order work commenced on rebuilding." Or let's hope so![38]

The *Transcript*'s nervous report of the fire shows very clearly the fears that surrounded the University with the coming of statehood, the sense that the institution was in grave danger, the worry that power now resided in the hands of those who were not its friends. The next six months were to show that these fears had not been unduly exaggerated. The attack on the University that was about to unfold is an enormously complicated story, involving a host of hidden relationships, private motives, secret loyalties, and petty ambitions.[39] It arose chiefly from two separate but related aspects of the culture of Oklahoma. Both of these elements carried enormous influence, strength, and emotional intensity, and

37. *Norman Transcript,* December 26, 1907, 1. The paper failed to explain how "hard labor" on the University grounds could have begun two years before the land run and four years before the territorial legislature placed the institution in Norman!

38. Ibid.

39. My attempt to unravel this story relies very heavily on an unpublished account by Roy Gittinger, and it is a special pleasure to acknowledge here the exceptional quality of Gittinger's reminiscence. His manuscript derives its usefulness from a unique combination of perceptive analysis and his uncanny memory for the events that he witnessed. When writing the semiofficial *The University of Oklahoma: A History of Fifty Years, 1892–1942,* Professor Gittinger, regrettably, chose to pass over the events of 1908 entirely without description or comment. Not a single sentence indicates that David Ross Boyd was fired. But hidden away in his confidential files, Gittinger had a remarkable fifty-page manuscript that he entitled "The University Reorganizations of 1908 and 1911." When he died in 1957, his widow, following her husband's instructions, presented the typescript to President George Lynn Cross, who relied on it heavily (as I do here) for the appropriate sections in his own book, *Professors, Presidents, and Politicians: Civil Rights and the University of Oklahoma, 1890–1968.* Dr. Cross tells how he received the Gittinger manuscript (xvi–xvii). Those interested in reading it in the original will find it in the George Lynn Cross President Emeritus MSS, Box 14. Readers of my account may assume that any uncited statements derive from Gittinger's "University Reorganizations."

their eventual coming together practically ensured the success of the devastating assault on the University of Oklahoma. One of those features of Oklahoma's life was partisan politics; the other was religion. Both parts of the tale have roots in events that took place long before the winter and spring of 1908. Let us begin with the part played by the religious tensions and rivalries in Norman, Oklahoma.

∽

UNTIL THE END OF HIS LIFE, Roy Gittinger remembered what happened when he and his wife walked back home after attending a lecture late one afternoon in March 1908. The lecturer was Lyman Abbott, one of the best-known religious thinkers in the United States. Abbott had taken over the Plymouth Congregational Church in Brooklyn, New York, from the illustrious preacher Henry Ward Beecher. He was an eloquent speaker and a prolific writer. In addition to his ministerial duties, Abbott was also the editor of the *Outlook,* one of the most important and widely read magazines in the country and reputed to be the mouthpiece of Abbott's close friend President Theodore Roosevelt. He was also a theological liberal, who had long since made his peace with Charles Darwin and who had written one book called *The Evolution of Christianity* (1892) and another called *The Theology of an Evolutionist* (1897).[40] Somehow Boyd and Abbott had become acquainted; and when Abbott indicated that he would like to visit Oklahoma and see a brand-new state in the making, Boyd invited him to Norman. A collection was taken up on campus and in town to pay the expenses for bringing him. Arrangements were completed in November 1907,[41] and the great minister's highly anticipated talks were scheduled for the week of March 4.

During the question period after one of his lectures, someone in the audience asked Abbott what he thought about the story of the virgin birth of Christ. As Roy Gittinger recalled it, "his answer was orthodox but included the statement that after all belief in the Virgin Birth was not of supreme importance and that many who were good and useful Christians doubted it." Afterward, six of Abbott's hearers found themselves walking together toward their homes in the neighborhood of the campus: the Gittingers, engineering professor Cyril Methodius Jansky and his wife, and Mr. and Mrs. John Hardie, two ardent members of the Southern Methodist Church, not connected with the University. It appeared to Gittinger that Mrs. Hardie was "very much upset," and she kept denouncing "Abbott's terrible statement." Professor Jansky stepped in and "sought to placate her." He pointed out that some very good men and women did not accept the story of the virgin birth and mentioned the revered American philosopher and essayist Ralph Waldo Emerson as one of them. "This remark served to excite Mrs. Hardie even more. She became hysterical and said that Abbott was an infidel and that Jansky must be an infidel to defend

40. For Abbott's life, see Ira V. Brown, *Lyman Abbott, Christian Evolutionist: A Study in Religious Liberalism.*

41. The *Umpire* announced his coming in the November 26, 1907, issue.

Abbott, in fact that the University was a nest of infidels, or it would not have brought an infidel to the campus to lecture on religion."[42]

The story indicates a good deal about the religious makeup of Norman and the tensions between some denominations and the University. At the close of the 1903–1904 academic year (as we have seen), the faculty, including President Boyd, was made up mostly of Presbyterians. Other professors were members of the Methodist Episcopal Church (so-called northern Methodists) and the Christian Church (Disciples of Christ); one was "nominally an Episcopalian."[43] The important thing was that in June 1904 not a single member of the faculty attended either the Southern Methodist or the Baptist church, despite the fact that these two denominations were by far the largest in Norman and in the "twin territories." Boyd was not a fool. He noted the religious imbalance and knew that there had been considerable grumbling about "the University crowd" among the Baptists and especially among the Southern Methodists in town. In the summer of 1904, therefore, the president moved to defuse the situation with a new appointment to the faculty. His choice was a fateful one.

Ernest Taylor Bynum arrived in August 1904 to teach German and French. He had been teaching in Pennsylvania; but he was, importantly, both a southerner (from North Carolina) and a Southern Methodist; he had also taught at the University of Arkansas for a while. Gittinger believed that Boyd knew in advance that Ernest Bynum could be troublesome; authorities at Arkansas had warned Boyd that Bynum was asked to leave Fayetteville because of his constant criticism of the university administration there. Boyd was undeterred and hired Bynum anyway.[44] It must be remembered that Gittinger came to detest Bynum and that his judgments about him must be weighed carefully. But he insists that

> President Boyd soon had reason to regret his selection, as Bynum at once began to criticize the University. He could find many things on the campus that in his opinion could be bettered. Bynum was a good speaker and a good mixer, and he made friends both in Norman and over the Territory. His complaints about the University were vigorous, especially his condemnation of the morals of students and faculty. He could claim to speak as an insider. Dancing, playing cards, and smoking cigarettes were condemned, and above all the lack of supervision of the outside activities of young women students.[45]

42. Gittinger, "Reorganizations of 1908 and 1911," 13.

43. Ibid., 6. The nominal Episcopalian was Vernon Parrington.

44. Gittinger ("Reorganizations of 1908 and 1911," 6) reports that Boyd said that Bynum's disagreement with the Arkansas administration might actually be a recommendation for him; Gittinger gave the remark as evidence "to show Boyd's prejudice [against the South], sometimes expressed indiscreetly, a prejudice that did not help him in his relations with many of the residents of east Norman [where southern Democrats were preponderant]."

45. Gittinger, "Reorganizations of 1908 and 1911," 6–7.

Apparently an unmarried young woman, "a voice student, the daughter of a prominent citizen of the Territory," gave birth to a child in her room near the campus; and "another young woman was said to have disappeared from classes just then because of her desire to avoid the notoriety of a similar happening." Bynum claimed to know of a third case.

Another clash between Boyd and Bynum occurred over the coming to the campus of the first fraternity, Kappa Alpha, in 1905. As we have seen, the fraternity was strongly southern in its loyalties, symbols, and ideals. At the outset, President Boyd opposed the establishment of a Kappa Alpha chapter at the University "on the ground that Oklahoma's fraternities should be national and not sectional." Bynum quickly leapt to the defense of the fraternity, and in the process he helped to spread the view that Boyd was "bigoted in his dislike of the South and of all things Southern," a charge that may not have been entirely inaccurate. In any case, partly because of Bynum's allegations, the squabble over the fraternity had the effect of confirming to some of the Southern Methodists that David Ross Boyd was intolerant of their section and of everything it stood for.[46]

After more than a year of Ernest Bynum's constant public criticism of the University, "President Boyd felt that he had no recourse but to ask for Bynum's resignation. Accordingly, Bynum was a member of the faculty for only two years, from 1904 to 1906."[47] Naturally, his denunciation of Boyd and the University, followed by his dismissal, further embittered Southern Methodists in town. Boyd, who had hired Samuel W. Reaves, a South Carolina Baptist, to teach mathematics in 1905, replaced Bynum with a young man named George D. Davidson, another southerner and a Southern Methodist. "Both the President and the faculty," Gittinger recalled, "sought to play up Davidson as more than able to take Bynum's place." Boyd tried again, but unsuccessfully, to mollify Southern Methodist suspicions and animosities in 1907 by hiring the social scientist Jerome Dowd, another southerner and a member of the denomination. Meanwhile, Ernest Bynum went to teach at Epworth University in Oklahoma City, a Methodist school run jointly by southern and northern members of the faith. Boyd had not heard the last of Ernest Taylor Bynum.

At the same time that Boyd was scrambling to hire professors who might help to quiet the criticism from Southern Methodists and Baptists, developments within the Southern Methodist Church in Oklahoma were about to place another powerful opponent of Boyd into a position of power. The former minister of Norman's Southern Methodist church was, according to Gittinger, "a kindly, likeable man" named W. D. Matthews.[48] The affable Matthews tried to get along with everyone; he had two daughters enrolled at the University and was a frequent leader of the chapel services at the school. But in 1901 it was suddenly announced that Matthews was to trade churches with the Reverend Nathaniel

46. Ibid., 15–16.

47. Ibid., 7.

48. Ibid. Gittinger said of the Reverend Matthews: "[H]e seems to have served for a time in the Confederate army. He assumed the pose of a Confederate Veteran and always wore gray."

Lee Linebaugh, the minister at Paul's Valley. Matthews was to
leave his family in Norman (so that his girls could continue
school) to take a position that paid about the same. Why
would he do such a thing? Roy Gittinger believed he
knew: "The only answer to this is a supposition that a
number of the Norman congregation were dissatisfied
with their pastor. . . . The probable reason for the dissatisfaction was that a part of the Southern Methodists
thought Matthews to be too friendly with the 'University crowd.' "[49]

The new minister, Nathaniel Linebaugh, was to be
nothing but trouble for Boyd. Gittinger described him as
"young, able, and ambitious." He was only in Norman for
a short period, because he became ill early in his ministry
and had to leave church work for a time. But he had seen
enough to form "a poor impression of the University."
According to Gittinger, "Linebaugh and his church were          *Ernest Taylor Bynum*
displeased that no member of the faculty at that time at-
tended their services." Moreover, Boyd never went to see Linebaugh and never asked him
to lead a chapel service at the University. Linebaugh felt slighted in every way, and "he
left Norman in a bitter frame of mind, antagonistic to the University and especially to
President Boyd." Gittinger solemnly asserted, moreover, that "Linebaugh made a statement to this effect early in 1908 in the writer's presence to explain his determination to
oust Boyd."[50] Eventually, Linebaugh recovered his health and resumed his labors in the
denomination; by 1907 he was the pastor at McAlester and an increasingly influential figure in the Church's Oklahoma Conference. In that same year, the young minister worked
hard for the election of Charles Haskell, both in the Democratic primary and in the general election, as the new state's first governor. He had been drawn to Haskell because of
the candidate's uncompromising position in favor of the prohibition of alcohol. Once he
was elected, Governor Haskell rewarded Linebaugh for his help by appointing him to the
University of Oklahoma Board of Regents.

Roy Gittinger, who came to despise Linebaugh as much as he despised Ernest Bynum,
thought that Linebaugh "decided that he was now in a position to do something about the
University. He persuaded himself that the University needed to be made over completely.
Both because of his bias and because of prodding from members of the local Southern
Methodist congregation he set to work to reorganize the faculty, both head and members,
and especially to replace Boyd with Bynum who was now a candidate for the University

49. Ibid., 8–9.
50. Ibid., 9.

*The Reverend Nathaniel Linebaugh*

presidency."[51] At this point there is outside confirmation of Gittinger's allegations. The *Norman Transcript,* a month after Haskell's inauguration, revealed the plot. Under the headline "E. T. Bynum for President," the newspaper reported that "there is a persistent rumor that President Boyd is to be deposed as President of the University and Prof. E. T. Bynum, formerly connected with the University and now vice chancellor of Epworth University, named in his stead." The *Transcript* claimed that Bynum was a friend of the Democratic candidate for the presidency of the United States, William Jennings Bryan, and that Bryan was expected to intercede with Governor Haskell on Bynum's behalf.[52]

Many years later, when Roy Gittinger sat down to write his reminiscence, he reluctantly concluded that he had to tell a story that involved himself. "It seems necessary here to tell as briefly as possible of a part in all this that the writer played. I should like to omit this part of the story, as it is, to say the least, unpleasant, indeed humiliating to me." But Gittinger's personal tale reveals much about the atmosphere at the University at the end of 1907 and the beginning of 1908. In December things could not have looked much worse. Bynum, with the support of Linebaugh, "was working quietly but with seeming success, to oust Boyd and secure the position for himself." Then on December 20 the University's main building burned to the ground. Rumors were rampant of the new governor's desire to move the institution to the eastern part of the state. In this setting, shortly after Christmas, Boyd asked Gittinger and the University's registrar (soon to be English professor), Roy Hadsell, to represent the school at the Oklahoma Teachers' Association meeting in Muskogee. The pair had to change trains in Oklahoma City and, while they were waiting, decided to take in the musical comedy *The Pink Lady,* playing at the Overholser Opera House. They got there late and sat near the back of the auditorium.

During the intermission, a former student named Ralph ("Inky") Campbell slipped into an empty seat behind them.

51. Ibid., 10. Gittinger suggests another reason for Linebaugh's resolve. The minister wanted to be elected bishop at the next General Conference of the Church. "It was openly asserted by some at the time," wrote Gittinger, that the new Regent "was trying to use the choice of new members of the university faculty to strengthen his candidacy." The strategy backfired, and the notoriety surrounding his part in the coming University shakeup resulted in his being defeated at the General Conference by a three-to-one majority.

52. *Norman Transcript,* December 21, 1907, 1.

Young Campbell at once began to talk to us and professed great sympathy for the University and its faculty under the circumstances. He spoke of the recent disastrous fire and the possible shake up of the faculty and the University administration. In the conversation he mentioned Bynum's campaign to supplant Boyd. Neither Mr. Hadsell nor I had very much to say and I should have kept out of the conversation entirely, but for some reason I made an extravagant statement.

That very morning, before leaving Norman, Gittinger had chatted with his friend (and Boyd's) John Taylor, who "casually remarked that Bynum was a worse danger to the University than even the fire and that he would rather see all the buildings burn than to see Bynum president." Gittinger, without revealing Taylor's name, reported the remark in an attempt to show young Campbell "the opposition of many Norman people to Bynum's candidacy." The show resumed, and "Inky" disappeared. But he took the story to the *Daily Oklahoman* (which refused to have anything to do with it) and then to a new paper, the *Oklahoma City News*, which, according to Gittinger, was "anxious to print sensational matter."

Campbell and the editor of the *News* then took a few small liberties with their account. In the first place, they made it seem as though Gittinger had granted Campbell a formal interview; and, in the second, Taylor's statement, which "I had so unwisely quoted," was attributed to Gittinger himself. The episode had several dramatic results. The least important was that Campbell "was criticized so severely that he left the State in a short time." Much more noteworthy was that Bynum's campaign for the presidency was badly hurt. He "was naturally horrified," Gittinger reported, "and rushed into print . . . answering me with statements as extravagant as the one [erroneously] attributed to me." The furor greatly damaged Bynum's effort to replace Boyd. The incident had made public Bynum's campaign; and "Boyd's friends and Bynum's enemies" leaped eagerly into the fight. They revealed, published, and distributed "the whole story of Bynum's career, his ambitions, and his series of attacks on the University." They also told the story of Bynum's "difficulties" at the University of Arkansas.

"It goes without saying," Gittinger lamented, "that my reputation suffered" because of the sensational publicity. Roy Hadsell, who was not mentioned in the *News* story, nevertheless "loyally came to my support"; he confirmed both that Gittinger had never given a formal interview and that the extreme remark about the burning down of the University's other buildings was not Gittinger's own. "[A]nd some people believed me." Since Gittinger could not deny that he was "bitterly opposed to Bynum," he was roundly condemned by Bynum's friends; but "even those who did not like Bynum felt that I was indiscreet in my conversation and lacking in judgment to talk to a reporter as I did. It was useless to explain that I did not know that Campbell was supposed to be a reporter. My friends tried to stand by me." (Perhaps Gittinger was exaggerating his disgrace and the damage to his reputation: in February the county Democratic convention sent him to the state convention as its delegate, and in April he was convincingly reelected to the Norman City Council by a vote of 130 to 80, "rather a large vote for the time.")[53] Whatever the impact on Gittinger's reputation in town, the episode exposes some of the harrowing tensions in Norman during the winter and spring of 1908.

The most bizarre and in many ways the most revealing moment in the Southern Methodist attack on Boyd and the University faculty involved a notorious letter. Dated April 28, 1908, it was written by the pastor of the Southern Methodist church in Norman, the Reverend R. E. L. Morgan, and sent to Nathaniel Linebaugh, his fellow-minister and now a University Regent. Linebaugh was in Norman investigating the faculty as a member of a three-man Regents' committee (whose work is examined below). Regent Linebaugh carelessly left behind the letter from Morgan in his room at the Arline Hotel. The maid picked it up and gave it to a Dr. Stockwell, a physician who lived at the hotel; Stockwell promptly turned the letter over to the newspapers. This explosive letter played so crucial part in future developments that it is necessary to quote it at length:

> Dear Brother Linebaugh:
>
> In answer to yours of the 21st. will say that I just returned here yesterday afternoon, found things at the farm in splendid condition.
>
> The following are the names of University Professors who dance, play cards and who are immoral in their lives. J. F. Paxton, V. L. Parrington, L. W. Cole, H. D. Guelich, W. R. Humphreys, [E.] M. Williams, [G. A.] Hool, Miss Berenice Rice and Miss Ruby Givens. C. M. Jansky is an infidel, so I hear, and Roy Gittinger is the man that said that he would rather see all the buildings at the University burn than to see Bynum elected President. I suppose you know Guelich and his wife, they lead all the dancing crowd, their influence is very bad. There are a number that I have been unable to find out about. A number of those who dance are also immoral and cigarette fiends. If I can find out anything further I will let you know.
>
> Now there are some good men in the faculty. Frank E. Knowles is a good man, he is a member of the Christian Church and I am informed is a Christian gentleman. S. W. Reaves is the Superintendent of the Baptist Sunday School, is well qualified for the position he holds. I had a talk with him this morning, and I don't think you would make a mistake in retaining him in his present position. Fredrik Holmberg is one of the best qualified men in the University, and I would like to see you oust Guelich and if possible put Holmberg in his place.
>
> Holmberg was a leader in our choir for a long time, so I am informed. Miss Nellie Goodrich is the assistant in music. She is one of the finest Christian girls I ever met, is a member of our Church and was our organist. I do not know what she will apply for but I wish you would use your influence to get her just as high up as possible. She is well qualified and I would like to see her get the place of Miss Rice at least.
>
> I have asked Prof. Weaver, principal of the Temple School, to write you, if there is a chance to get him in do so, he is a strong Southern Methodist, and would be a great help to us here. Miss Elizabeth Gray asked me to write you. I guess you know her. She

---

53. Gittinger gives the story of his part in events in "Reorganizations of 1908 and 1911," 10–13; all the quotations are from those pages.

lived at Temple for quite a while, is a member of the Cumberlands, and is a deserving girl. She is an A.B. from the Lebanon, Tenn., Female College.

Do your best to get as many strong Southern Methodists in the faculty as possible. . . .

With best wishes, as ever. Your friend

R. E. L. Morgan

I have been informed that DeBarr is skeptical.[54]

Naturally, the Morgan letter provoked a firestorm of accusations, denials, and outrage from all sides. A full month before the letter, the *Norman Transcript* had lamented "what seems like a concerted effort . . . to besmirch and defame the fair name of our city and institution. . . . an evident intention to give a black-eye, if possible, to our city and the University." The *Transcript* considered it to be the work of liars: "There is not a more peaceable, home-loving, church-going Christian community in the State than that of Norman, including the faculty of the University and the student body."[55] After printing the Morgan letter, the *Transcript* was beside itself. These teachers have been here for a long time, the editor declared, "and this is the first time, in our knowledge, that even a whisper has been made against their characters as honest, upright, christian, God-fearing men. And not a word, either, can, we believe, be truthfully said against the virtue, purity and modesty of the ladies mentioned in the letter."[56]

Nevertheless, the Morgan letter and the reaction to it show how high religious and sectarian emotions had become by May 1908 and how deeply affected was the atmosphere in town and on the campus. But the letter reveals one other important thing: the writer does not bother to attack President David Ross Boyd. No need. By May he was clearly on his way out.

~

THE POLITICAL MOTIVES, while no less intense than the sectarian ones, are easier to understand because they are so transparently uncomplicated. It was the old story of Democrats against Republicans. The bitter division, fueled by Civil War and Reconstruction animosities between southern Democrats and northern Republicans, had echoes throughout Oklahoma. In the town of Norman, Democrats dominated east of the Santa Fe tracks, while Republicans generally lived, among other Democrats, west of them. The town's major newspaper was firmly Republican. In the former Oklahoma Territory, the Democrats, coming in from Texas and Arkansas, dominated the southern counties; and

54. The letter was reprinted in whole by the *Norman Transcript*, May 21, 1908; it is reprinted in Cross, *Professors, Presidents, and Politicians*, 21–22; and quoted at length in Long and Hart, *The Sooner Story*, 26. Lyman Abbott's *Outlook* gave the letter wide national exposure in the issue of September 5, 1908. Both Long and Hart and the *Outlook* reprint the letter, but without disclosing the names of those the Reverend Morgan accused of being immoral.

55. *Norman Transcript*, March 26, 1908, 1.

56. *Norman Transcript*, May 21, 1908, 1.

the Republicans, coming down from Kansas, controlled the northern ones. In the Territory as a whole, as we have seen, the Republicans enjoyed a slim majority. That majority, however, was more than offset by the solidly Democratic former Indian Territory. Now the new state administration was firmly in the hands of the Democrats and their newly chosen governor, Charles N. Haskell.

Haskell immediately dismissed the University's old six-member Board of Regents and replaced them with a new eight-member Board, and the fate of President David Ross Boyd was, for all practical purposes, sealed. After sixteen years of watching Oklahoma politics, Boyd must have understood from the beginning how the game was played and how slim his chances for retention were. From territorial days onward, Republican governors had appointed Republicans to desirable offices, and Democrats had appointed Democrats. Before statehood this had almost always meant Republicans like Boyd. In 1893, when Democrat Grover Cleveland returned to the White House, all the Republican college presidents were summarily fired by his appointee, Governor William C. Renfrow. Boyd alone was spared because of the lucky accident that Renfrow was a Norman banker who knew and admired him. When the Republican William McKinley took over the presidency in 1897, all the Democrats were promptly fired and replaced by Republicans; naturally, Boyd was allowed to retain his place. At the beginning of 1907 the territorial governor, all five territorial judges, and all six college presidents were Republicans who had come to Oklahoma from Kansas.[57] Now with Haskell in office and a new set of Regents, the question was not whether Boyd was to be fired but rather who was to replace him.[58]

Ernest Bynum's campaign for the presidency had faltered badly by March 1908. Partly this was due to the bad publicity he had been garnering lately and a distaste, in certain influential circles, for his methods. But perhaps the main reason for Haskell's turning away from Bynum was the advice of a man who had become a close friend and politically astute advisor. This man was Arthur Grant Evans, and for the next few years he was to play an extremely important part in the history of the University of Oklahoma.[59]

Arthur Evans came from a deeply religious background. He was born in Madras, India, on September 9, 1858, the son of two English missionaries. His parents were very earnest Presbyterians, laboring to propagate their faith in that distant British colony. They were also adherents of a curious educational system that had its birth in India, was attempted in

---

57. Gittinger, "Reorganizations of 1908 and 1911," 2–3.

58. Ironically, Gittinger reported (ibid., 14), Haskell probably admired Boyd; both men had come to Oklahoma from Ohio. "[A]lthough [Haskell] liked Boyd personally and perhaps would have preferred his retention he was too canny to say it, lest he himself might be accused of being Anti-Southern because of his support of Boyd. Such an accusation would have been fatal to the political aspirations of an Oklahoma Democrat recently arrived from Ohio."

59. Biographical sources for Arthur Grant Evans are slim. Brief summaries of his life can be found in *The National Cyclopedia of American Biography* (New York: J. T. White and Co., 1943), 27:331; *Who Was Who in America* (Chicago: A. N. Marquis Co., 1943), 1:376; and Guy W. Logsdon, *The University of Tulsa*, 60. See also Frank A. Balyeat, "Arthur Grant Evans," *Chronicles of Oklahoma* 38 (1960–61): 245–52; Roy Temple House, "New Oklahoma School Presidents," *Sturm's Oklahoma Magazine* 7 (December 1908): 38–41; and Luthera Mills, "Second Varsity President Dies," *Sooner Magazine* 1 (January 1929): 107–108.

England, and played a role in the training of young Arthur. In the late eighteenth century an army chaplain named Bell, assigned the task of providing education for British orphans in India, had devised a scheme of "monitors," where one trained teacher was to instruct a handful of the brightest students who would, in turn, fan out to teach groups of around ten ordinary pupils. In this way, it was supposed, a single trained teacher could bring knowledge to hundreds of students in settings where instructors were scarce and funds were limited. An enterprising English Quaker, Joseph Lancaster, introduced this method in the poor districts of south London. The Evans family returned to England while Arthur was still an infant; and when he was old enough, he was sent to a Lancastrian school and served as a monitor. His postsecondary education was in a Lancastrian college, picturesquely named the Borough Road College of London. That institution awarded him a bachelor's degree in 1879. Upon his graduation he served for five years as the principal of public schools in Northampton, England.

In 1883 Arthur and his sister Carrie decided to cross the Atlantic and settle in North America. Carrie soon returned home to England; but her brother, after teaching briefly in a private school in Canada, came south to the United States. In the summer of 1884 he was teaching school in Nashville. A group of Cherokee teachers, led by the Cherokee leader and future Oklahoma senator Robert L. Owen,[60] came to town on their way to a Chautauqua; and Evans helped to entertain them. Owen apparently liked what he saw in the twenty-six-year-old Evans, and the Englishman was hired as an assistant principal of the Cherokee Male Seminary in Tahlequah. Evans continued his nomadic life from 1885 until 1898. In 1887 he was ordained a Presbyterian minister. He worked for five years as a missionary to the Cherokees; served as a pastor in southwestern Kansas and then in Pendleton, Oregon; headed a school in Salida, Colorado; and took a congregation in Leadville. In 1891 Evans married Katherine Robb, the daughter of an influential Muskogee family;[61] and in the late 1890s the couple returned to Muskogee, Indian Territory.

The Presbyterians, under the leadership of Alice Robertson (a highly regarded missionary to the Creeks), had organized a school in Muskogee for Indian young women in 1884. Soon young men were also enrolling. In 1894 the school, still under the control of the Presbyterian Board of Home Missions, became known as Henry Kendall College.[62] Arthur Evans joined the faculty in 1898. The college's president resigned at the end of that academic year, and Evans was named to succeed him. From 1899 until 1908 Evans led the school. In 1907 he supervised its move to Tulsa (it would be renamed the University of Tulsa in 1920). Evans's administration of the college was not without controversy. According to Guy Logsdon, the historian of the University of Tulsa, the first two presidents of

60. On Owen's career, see Wyatt W. Belcher, "Political Leadership of Robert L. Owen," *Chronicles of Oklahoma* 31 (1953–54): 361–71.

61. Katherine's elder sister Jennie was the first Anglo-American child born in Muskogee; see D. C. Gideon, *Indian Territory: Descriptive, Biographical and Genealogical . . .* , 388–89.

62. For the early history of the institution, see Logsdon, *University of Tulsa,* chaps. 1–2.

the school "were devoted to Indian education." But "the white leaders in both Muskogee and Tulsa were more interested in the advancements of whites than in Indian education; they used Indians for white advantage (behavior which certainly was not unique to them). Evans aligned himself with those leaders."[63] Evans's own explanation, offered almost thirty years later, was that he could see that "white pressure was going to force the end of the Indian dream of keeping their own territory, and it seemed to me imperative that the children should learn to understand one another."[64]

Meanwhile, Evans—who had taken up American citizenship during his Muskogee years and was now going by the name A. Grant Evans—was becoming more and more keenly involved with the political, social, and religious life of Indian Territory. He had a charming English accent and a solid reputation for being cultured, literate, intelligent, pious, and upright. The Presbyterians elected him moderator of the Indian Territory Synod and sent him as their delegate to the general assembly in 1895 and again in 1904; in that same year, he went to the Pan-Presbyterian council in Liverpool. He was also an avid Mason and high in the ranks of that organization.[65] It was inevitable that Evans, the president of the local college, and Charles Haskell, the railroad builder and entrepreneur who arrived in Muskogee in 1901, would quickly be thrown together. They were easily the two most prominent citizens in town and soon became warm friends and political allies. The Reverend Evans, like the Southern Methodist Reverend Linebaugh, was won over to Haskell by his firm position in favor of the strict prohibition of alcohol. Evans went to Washington to argue before a House Committee on behalf of combining the twin territories into a single state, but he also took a leading role, at the side of Haskell, when the Sequoyah Convention met in 1905 to agitate for a separate Indian state.[66] And when Haskell ran for the governorship, he had no more loyal supporter than the president of Henry Kendall College.

Roy Gittinger believed that Evans urged Governor Haskell to retain David Ross Boyd, "both as good educational policy and as good politics."[67] Boyd himself thought that Evans was two-faced: Boyd "honestly believed that Evans, while posing as Boyd's friend, had been pulling wires secretly to bring about his own selection [as president of the University]."[68] In any case, Charles Haskell soon made it clear that his choice for the presidency of the University of Oklahoma was none other than A. Grant Evans, his townsman, friend, and political ally. Haskell undoubtedly regarded this as a shrewd political move. It would

63. Ibid., 60.

64. Evans to F. A. Balyeat, May 22, 1926, reprinted in *Chronicles of Oklahoma* 37 (1959): 241.

65. Gideon, *Indian Territory*, 389.

66. Evans played an important role in designing an official seal for the proposed state of Sequoyah, and that design was eventually adapted to make the state of Oklahoma's seal. Thoburn and Wright, *Oklahoma: A History*, 2:639; and Balyeat, "Arthur Grant Evans," 248.

67. Gittinger, "Reorganizations of 1908 and 1911," 14.

68. Ibid., 17.

please the people of the former Indian Territory, who wanted, finally, a genuine stake in the state university; it would please Boyd's foes; it would gratify the Democrats. The Reverend Evans, a minister with a spotless reputation, was certainly able to pass the "morality" test; and as the president of another college in the state he appeared to have the necessary educational credentials. Haskell might even have hoped that some of Boyd's friends would approve of his selection because, as a public supporter of Boyd, Evans seemed to be one of their number.[69]

There was a small detour on the way toward making Evans president. The governor asked the State Board of Education to fire Boyd and name Evans. The Board consisted of the governor, the superintendent of public instruction, and other elected officials. Its powers were largely undefined, but Haskell persuaded the state's attorney general to render an opinion that the Board of Education could choose the University's president. In late March the Board announced that it had considered two candidates, Ernest Bynum and A. Grant Evans, and had chosen Evans. On March 24 the *Umpire* blandly made the announcement, managing to get the new president's name wrong: "E. Grant Evans Elected President."[70] But the new Board of Regents, led by Lee Cruce, went to court—not to save Boyd or to prevent Evans from becoming president but to protect the prerogatives of the Regents. Three weeks later the Oklahoma Supreme Court ruled that the State Board of Education had exceeded its powers and that the Regents were responsible for hiring and firing presidents.[71] With the jurisdictional matter having been settled, the Board of Regents was more than ready to endorse Governor Haskell's choice of Evans.[72]

One morning that spring Professor Joseph Paxton happened to be conducting chapel exercises on the top floor of the Carnegie building. He looked up and recognized Evans entering quietly at the back of the room. Paxton promptly motioned the newcomer to the front of the auditorium and introduced him to the assembled students. Then he invited the students to file forward, introduce themselves, and greet their new leader.[73]

So much for the matter of the University's presidency. Next came the faculty.

---

69. Ibid. There were several other applicants for the presidency of the University of Oklahoma besides Bynum and Evans. Their letters of application and numerous letters of support for individual candidates can be found in the Charles N. Haskell MSS, RG 8-A-4, Box 3, Folders 7 and 8.

70. *University Umpire*, March 24, 1908. Surprisingly, through all of these turbulent months the *Umpire* made almost no comment, editorial or otherwise, on the dramatic events that were reshaping the school. See also the disgruntled account of Boyd's being replaced published in the *Norman Transcript*, March 26, 1908, 1.

71. *University Umpire*, April 14, 1908, 1; *Norman Transcript*, April 16, 1908, 1.

72. Gittinger, "Reorganizations of 1908 and 1911," 16; *University Umpire*, April 14, 1908.

73. Mills, "Second Varsity President Dies," 107.

*Arthur Grant Evans, second president of the University*

CHAPTER VII

# "Corpses Strewed about the Campus," 1908

In one of their first meetings, Governor Haskell's new University Regents, acting as though there had been no institutional history before their own arrival on the scene, blithely declared that all faculty positions at the University of Oklahoma were to be considered "open" as of the end of the 1907–1908 school year. The Board invited those members of the faculty wishing to do so to apply for their old jobs and named a three-man committee to go to Norman to interview those professors who hoped to be retained. One member of that committee was the Reverend Nathaniel Linebaugh (it was while staying overnight in Norman in connection with this duty that Linebaugh carelessly left behind that controversial letter from his friend and fellow Southern Methodist minister R. E. L. Morgan).

A second member of the committee was Lee Cruce, already a leading Democratic politician. Born in Kentucky during the Civil War, Cruce came to Ardmore, Indian Territory, as a young lawyer in 1891, promptly married into a prominent Chickasaw family, and became a banker. He was soon deeply involved in politics; and in 1907 he mounted an impressive challenge to Charles Haskell in the Democratic gubernatorial primary. Upon losing, he unhesitatingly threw his support behind his rival. Haskell rewarded Cruce's loyalty by making him the president of the Board of Regents.[1] The third member of the interviewing committee was Regent C. J. Pratt, an Oklahoma City lawyer. Pratt was one of the two Republicans on the Board, but he was an old Kentucky friend of Cruce's and was appointed a Regent at Cruce's urging. Roy Gittinger reports that this committee "was at once dubbed 'the smelling committee' that is, the committee to smell out how much of [Ernest T.] Bynum's and Linebaugh's charges were true."[2]

On the afternoon of Tuesday, May 12, 1908, therefore, the members of the faculty of the University of Oklahoma paraded before the committee to plead for their jobs. Git-

1. Bobby Dean Smith, "Lee Cruce, 1911–1915," in LeRoy H. Fischer, ed., *Oklahoma's Governors, 1907–1929: Turbulent Politics*, 47–65.

2. Gittinger, "University Reorganizations of 1908 and 1911," 17.

tinger, who was one of the petitioners, reported that "Cruce, Linebaugh, and Pratt listened to the applicants with courtesy." The interviews were brief, and some of the nervous professors were assured on the spot that "the committee were entirely satisfied with them and with their work."[3] After dinner that evening, the committee members held a public hearing in downtown Norman. They bade citizens of the town who had anything they wished to say to appear before them and frankly speak their minds. A few people came, and they apparently warmly praised the University and the faculty. But at one point in the process Linebaugh asked that a member of Norman's Southern Methodist church come to relate the views of the congregation. That church, of course, was the center of what Gittinger called the "smouldering indignation" against Boyd and the University.[4] And Linebaugh asked particularly for John Hardie, the cashier of the Cleveland County National Bank, a devoted Southern Methodist, and the husband of the indignant woman who thought the University was a den of infidels for having invited the infidel Lyman Abbott to the campus two months before. Although he was an Iowa Republican, Hardie "hated playing cards, dancing, and liberal views of any kind."[5]

John Hardie's testimony was what might have been expected. He verbally assaulted those whom Linebaugh wanted to replace with good Southern Methodists. Professor Jansky was obviously an infidel—or why else would he have attempted to defend Lyman Abbott? Vernon Parrington was not a good Christian and was a bad influence on the students, and the same was true of Lawrence W. Cole, Boyd's disciple who taught psychology and education. Roy Gittinger was too active in politics.[6] Other members of the faculty were criticized; some received faint praise. The room was filled with townspeople, who naturally spread the word of Hardie's testimony; and both the campus and the town "rang with angry replies." Gittinger (who could manifest a wry sense of humor) wrote that the next morning "Parrington and I went at once to Hardie's bank, asked to see the cashier, gravely drew out the money on deposit belonging to the [University's] Athletic Association, and ostentatiously carried it across the street to the First National Bank."[7]

Meanwhile, E. D. Cameron, the state superintendent of public instruction and also a minister, took the occasion of a speech to the Logan County High School to attack an

3. Ibid.

4. Gittinger recalled (ibid., 18–19) how George Miller (for whom Miller Avenue in the Classen-Miller neighborhood was later named) stopped him in the post office and "upbraided me for opposing Bynum." Miller was a very active member of the Southern Methodist church in Norman. "The Northern Presbyterians, he said, had run the University long enough. It was now the turn of the Southern Methodists." See also Mary Emelyn Miller Bagby, "The History of the George W. Miller Family," in Runyon, *Pioneers of Cleveland County,* 130–34.

5. The Hardie family had another grudge against the University. John's son Ralph, who had come to town in 1902, was principal of Norman High School and later the town's school superintendent. He regarded the University's Preparatory Department as an unfair competitor of the high school. It was, he believed, the bastion of the west-siders and a refuge for any student disgruntled with Norman High.

6. Gittinger could not resist pointing out that while he himself had just won reelection to the City Council, Hardie had been defeated in the same election and in the same ward as a candidate for the school board. For Gittinger's summary of the Hardie testimony, see "Reorganizations of 1908 and 1911," 20.

7. Ibid.

unnamed Norman professor who did not believe the first chapters of the Book of Genesis. "If that man knows more than Moses," Superintendent Cameron solemnly declared, "he knows too much to teach school in Oklahoma." The *Norman Transcript* (which spent much of the spring of 1908 in a high state of outrage) summed it all up: "In addition to the inquisition now being held as to the personal habits of professors in the statee [*sic*] university, including their views on dancing, card playing and smoking, it is also possible that there may be an inquiry into whether their theological views are wholly orthodox."[8]

~

THE HEARINGS OF MAY 12, the subsequent publication of the Morgan letter, and the general atmosphere of hostility, suspicion, and panic sent individual members of the faculty scrambling to see what could be done to save their jobs. Three women were mentioned in the Morgan letter. Bernice Rice and Ruby Givens were listed as being among those "who dance, play cards and who are immoral in their lives." Morgan called Nellie Goodrich, in contrast, "one of the finest Christian girls I ever met." She was, after all, "a member of our Church and was our organist." Her pastor had urged Regent Linebaugh to "use your influence to get her just as high up as possible. She is well qualified and I would like to see her get the place of Miss Rice at least." Allegations of personal immorality were serious enough when they were applied to men; when leveled against women they were devastating. In an age of rigid female subordination and stern ideals of purity and spotless virtue, the slightest hint of irregular behavior was more than sufficient to ruin a woman's reputation forever. The publication of Morgan's letter constituted, in two of the women's cases, a good bit more than a slight hint. What happened to these three women?

Ruby Givens's father was a banker from Mountain View. A few days after Morgan's letter appeared in the press, he—together with his lawyer and a small number of Norman friends—came to see the minister. They demanded proof of the allegations or a retraction. Morgan decided to retract his charges; but Givens went on to say that if his daughter was not reappointed to her position, Morgan could expect to hear more. Morgan quickly hired Ben F. Williams, Jr., a member of his congregation and a man whom Gittinger called "the shrewdest lawyer in Norman." At the moment of truth on June 23 the Regents, at Linebaugh and Morgan's recommendation, voted to reappoint both Ruby Givens and Bernice Rice, who had been denounced along with her. Rice chose to decline reappointment and went to teach at the Normal School in Emporia, Kansas. Givens (who was not technically a faculty member but a senior music student who taught piano to beginners) stayed on for a year. The third woman, Nellie Goodrich, who had received such warm praise from her minister, remained at the University until June 1910, when she resigned to marry one of the institution's most distinguished graduates, Everette Lee DeGolyer.[9]

8. *Norman Transcript*, May 21, 1908, 2.

9. Gittinger, "Reorganizations of 1908 and 1911," 23.

Two members of the Mathematics Department—Frank Knowles and Samuel Reaves—had been singled out for praise in the Morgan letter. At the time, they shared their bizarre stories with Roy Gittinger. Knowles was an Iowan who had taught at the University for five years. He had heard a rumor that Regent Linebaugh had a candidate in mind for his position, and the professor went to see John Hardie, a fellow Iowa Republican; Knowles was also a depositor in Hardie's bank. Hardie sent the fearful Knowles to see Linebaugh's close friend (and Hardie's own minister) the Reverend Morgan. The interview with Morgan went so well that Knowles suggested to the head of his department, Professor Reaves, that he might also want to talk to Morgan. Reaves's interview also went nicely;[10] and perhaps it was Morgan who advised him to go and see Regent Pratt, one of the three members of the "smelling committee." In Gittinger's words, "Pratt was obviously happy to see Reaves, greeting him with a couplet from an old hymn: 'While the lamp holds out to burn, the vilest sinner may return.' Pratt indicated that other applicants had been visiting him."[11] Pratt's visitors included both those, like Reaves, who wanted to keep their jobs and those who were eager to be appointed to the vacancies that were clearly in prospect. In any case, as the words of praise in Morgan's letter reveal, Knowles and Reaves were now safe.

The three-man committee, it turned out, was not unanimous about whom to retain and whom to dismiss. Despite the denunciations of John Hardie and the desires of Regent Linebaugh to place Southern Methodists on the faculty, Lee Cruce and his friend C. J. Pratt agreed to few changes. Cruce later confided to Gittinger that "nearly all" of those hoping for reappointment had the approval of two of the three committee members; and Cruce was confident that the full Board of Regents would accept the majority report by himself and Regent Pratt. Cruce and Pratt, according to rumor, had assented only to two firings. An instructor in pathology and bacteriology, Edward Marsh Williams, "had been the subject a year before of considerable gossip, which," according to the tactful Gittinger, "unfortunately seemed to have a basis of truth." And (of all people!) George Davidson, the Southern Methodist whom Boyd had hired to replace the trouble-maker Bynum, was not to be retained. "Davidson had a bad reputation locally because he had set his mattress on fire while smoking a cigarette in bed, and had nearly burned down the house in which he roomed." Morgan had neither praised nor condemned Davidson in his letter, because "Davidson was a member of his flock and he did not wish to criticise him, but under the circumstances he felt that he could not recommend him."[12]

But then a disastrous falling-out apparently occurred in the three-man committee. According to the rumors, Linebaugh would agree to the mild majority report of Cruce and

10. It may be recalled that in his notorious letter to Regent Linebaugh, the Reverend Morgan wrote of Reaves: "I had a talk with him this morning, and I don't think you would make a mistake in retaining him in his present position." This would fix the date of the Reaves interview as April 28, two weeks before the Norman hearings of May 12.

11. Gittinger, "Reorganizations of 1908 and 1911," 22–23.

12. Ibid., 24.

Pratt if those two would agree to fire two men that Linebaugh was particularly eager to oust: they were Lawrence Cole and Vernon Parrington. Lee Cruce would not go along, and two momentous things then quickly occurred. Linebaugh drew up a much more extensive list of those to be fired; and a few days before the crucial Regents' meeting of June 23, "to Cruce's disgust," he won Regent Pratt over to his side. Lee Cruce was now the minority. Gittinger admitted that he could only speculate about Pratt's defection, but he guessed that "presumably Linebaugh persuaded him that Governor Haskell was in favor of Linebaugh's report and might revamp the board if his wishes should be ignored." In any case, Pratt himself had only two demands: he wanted to gratify Roy Hadsell's wish that he be moved from registrar to an associate professorship in English; and he wanted to retain Henry Higgins Lane, a professor of zoology who had come in 1906. How did these two lucky men earn Pratt's support? Hadsell's father-in-law (a former postmaster in Norman) had, like Pratt, come from Kentucky; and Henry Lane's father happened to be the minister of Pratt's church in Oklahoma City. But Pratt need not have worried. Hadsell and Lane were safely on the retention lists of Cruce and Linebaugh too.[13]

The Board of Regents met in Oklahoma City on June 23. Seven voting members were present.[14] Four votes would decide. Two Regents voted with Linebaugh and Pratt; and, according to Gittinger, neither was an entirely disinterested party. Regent J. Matt Gordon (Weatherford) admitted that his only concern was that his old schoolmate Monroe Allen Floyd take over the Preparatory Department from Roy Gittinger, who was (prematurely as it turned out) presumed to be doomed because of the Inky Campbell incident back in December. Regent J. P. Hickam (Perkins) was apparently involved with some of the smaller textbook companies and believed that President Boyd and Lawrence Cole were tools of the powerful American Book Company, the outfit that sold most of the books used in Oklahoma schools. (Candidate Haskell had denounced the "book trust" during his campaign for governor.) Hickam was willing to vote for the Linebaugh-Pratt report in order to fire Cole. Thus four Regents (Linebaugh, Pratt, Gordon, and Hickam) voted for the Linebaugh firings; two others—William E. Rowsey (Muskogee), the secretary of the Board, and Flowers Nelson (Tulsa)—voted with Lee Cruce. No one on the Board of Regents was willing to vote against Governor Haskell's recommendation that David Ross Boyd be replaced by the governor's friend A. Grant Evans.[15]

13. Ibid., 24–25.

14. One position on the ten-person board remained vacant. One Regent (A. J. Rittenhouse) was ill. Governor Haskell was an *ex officio* member of the Board. According to Gittinger, he did not attend the meeting; but according to the *Norman Transcript* (June 26, 1908, 1), "Gov. C. N. Haskell was present and took part in the deliberations." Lee Cruce's account is probably the most accurate. In a letter to Lyman Abbott, Cruce wrote: "The Governor was present during the selection of President Evans, the head of one department, and a music teacher. The selection of the remainder of the Faculty was made in his absence, and by seven members of the Board." Cruce's letter is published in the *Outlook* 90 (October 3, 1908): 249–51. Unfortunately, the official minutes of this Regents' meeting are lost.

15. Gittinger, "Reorganizations of 1908 and 1911," 24–25.

As a result of the Regents' meeting of June 23, 1908, twenty-four members of the old faculty were retained.[16] Despite Morgan's allegations that DeBarr was "skeptical" and that Professors Paxton (Latin) and George A. Hool (Engineering) were among the card-playing, dancing, and smoking group, all three were rehired. Others who were important in the life of the University were also kept: Van Vleet (Botany), Buchanan (History), Dowd (Economics), Sturgis (Latin), Williams (Chemistry), Owen (Athletics), Gould (Geology), and Felgar (Engineering). Hadsell had his wish granted and was moved from registrar to the English Department; Holmberg was promoted, as Morgan's letter had urged. Knowles took Hadsell's place as registrar. A handful of those who were reappointed chose to resign for better jobs. Charles N. Gould had been appointed Oklahoma's first state geologist and was relieved of his teaching duties, but he remained head of the Geology Department.[17]

In addition to Boyd, ten members of the faculty and three other employees were fired (one of whom was later rehired). The *Norman Transcript* made no attempt to disguise its contempt and outrage: "The Board of Regents of the State University met in Oklahoma City on Tuesday. . . . The meat axe was at once put in operation, and when it ceased the 'corpses' . . . were strewed about the campus."[18] The three nonfaculty members who were dismissed were Frank Flood and Kirby Prickett, the University's carpenter and head janitor (both of whom had achieved a kind of legendary status on the campus among students and the faculty), and Thomas Carey, the University's treasurer. All three "were disappointed but not greatly surprised to be replaced by Linebaugh's candidates."

Among the faculty "corpses" some were certainly to be expected. Morgan had written to Linebaugh: "I suppose you know Guelich and his wife, they lead all the dancing crowd, their influence is very bad." Henry David Guelich had come to teach music in 1903; his wife, Mary Louise, taught drama. They were both fired and went to the Kansas State Normal School in Emporia (taking the maligned Bernice Rice with them). Cyril Methodius Jansky (the infidel) was fired in June but in July was asked to stay on as an assistant to his replacement; he was glad to go instead to the University of Wisconsin, where he had a long career. Davidson (the bed-burner) and Williams (about whom damaging gossip had circulated) had no support on the Board of Regents and were both dismissed. It is not clear whether two others (Roy Philson Stoops in anatomy and Clara Miller in physical education) had formally applied for retention, but their fates were sealed by the fact that Linebaugh had in mind replacements for both of them.[19]

---

16. Ibid., 27; and *Norman Transcript*, June 26, 1908, 1.

17. For full details, see Gittinger, "Reorganizations of 1908 and 1911," 27–28. On Gould, see his autobiography, *Covered Wagon Geologist*, 148.

18. *Norman Transcript*, June 26, 1908, 1.

19. Gittinger, "Reorganizations of 1908 and 1911," 28–29.

~

THREE OF THE FACULTY "CORPSES" (one of whom was resurrected) deserve special attention. In view of his later eminence as a Pulitzer Prize–winning analyst of American thought, the firing of Vernon Parrington has been regarded as one of the most shocking and ignorant injustices in the history of American higher education. The judgment of the great American historian Richard Hofstadter in this regard is not untypical. "At the end of his long spell of generous service," Hofstadter wrote sixty years after the event, "Parrington lost his job in what must surely be one of the most scandalous episodes in American academic history."[20] Parrington's popularity on the campus had continued unbroken; it was obvious that his students worshipped him. Gittinger, who had been a student in his classroom, said that Parrington's students including himself "thought that he was the best English teacher in the world." Parrington's second daughter had been born in April, and he had completed an elegant new home that he had designed after the pattern of an English cottage and had helped to build with his own hands. Suddenly he discovered that he was obliged to fight to keep his job—and he fought hard.

Letters began coming in to the Board of Regents on Parrington's behalf. They included one from "the sage of Emporia," the well-known journalist William Allen White. Parrington's banker wrote; even Lee Cruce sent a letter to his fellow Regents. On June 14, ten days before the axe fell, Parrington wrote a letter of his own to Regent Rowsey, the secretary of the Board, replying to the allegations that he was immoral: "My life may not be as Cotton Mather said of an old Puritan divine 'A trembling walk with God'—that high faith seems not to be given to men of our generation—but it is I believe, a serious attempt to find out what is sane and just and honorable and to make them prevail. . . . I know how to teach my subject better than any other man in the southwest. That may not seem modest, but it is a fact." Two days later, the embattled English professor wrote directly to Nathaniel Linebaugh, and there were tinges of anger and resentment in his eloquent confession of faith:

> No one holds the profession of the teacher in higher respect than I. If I did not have a high opinion of the profession I should not be a teacher. You may be sure it is not the pay: I could make more money laying brick and I should not be a victim of the meddling tongues and busy-bodies in that case. . . . If I believe[d] that my influence were bad or if indeed I were not certain that my influence is strongly and positively for good I should not have [been] teaching all these years. I look upon my work very much I suspect as you look upon yours—as missionary work. Officially I am a teacher of English literature, but in reality my business in life is to wage war on the crude and selfish materialism that is biting so deeply into our national life and character, and I do it by teaching whomever I can lay hands on that the worship of materialism can never make a people either noble or great, but that if we hope to become men we had better study to learn what things produce manhood.

20. Richard Hofstadter, *The Progressive Historians: Turner, Beard, and Parrington.* See also Hall, *V. L. Parrington,* 146–54.

Parrington responded directly to the charge by Linebaugh's friend, Morgan, that he was not a moral man. "Whatever gifts are mine are devoted to teaching the need of a high civic and personal morality: and I mean by morality that integrity of purpose that keeps one upright and just and honorable, and that endeavors to enlarge the realm of sanity and justice and honor in this world."[21]

Neither the testimony of others nor his own words could save Vernon Louis Parrington. His former student and then colleague Roy Gittinger believed that he was fired for three reasons. First, he was from Kansas; and even the fact that he was "a partisan Democrat" did not help him. Second, "he was not popular with Norman people . . . he was considered snobbish." Because of these attitudes toward Parrington, Gittinger remembered that "unpleasant stories were reported about his private life." He was nominally an Episcopalian but rarely attended church. And then there was the business of dancing, card playing, and smoking.[22] His disciple Roy Hadsell said: "I never heard of Parrington dancing or playing cards."[23] He "did smoke cigarettes. . . . He was therefore considered by some as a bad example for youth." Hadsell reported a story about Parrington's appearance before the three-man "smelling committee" that had come to Norman to ferret out sin:

> When Parrington was called in the board asked him if he smoked. He replied, according to the story, "Yes, but not on the street, or about my class room." A little later Professor [Joseph F.] Paxton was called in. "Do you smoke?" they asked him. "Yes, but I don't go behind the barn to do it, I smoke in the open when I feel like it." The room was blue with cigar smoke at the time, for the Regents were smoking.[24]

If smoking was a crime, there were other members of the faculty besides Paxton who indulged in it and who were not dismissed. In the end, Gittinger's third reason for the Regents' termination of Parrington seems to have been decisive: "[T]he important reason for his dismissal was that Linebaugh had a candidate for his position."[25]

The second most prominent and respected member of the faculty to be fired was Lawrence Wooster Cole, who taught courses in psychology, philosophy, and education. Like Parrington and Boyd, Cole was a Kansan. According to Gittinger, he "was not as popular on the campus as Parrington, but he was better known over the State, especially by public-school men, and he was not unpopular in Norman." As we have seen, Cole was elected regularly to the Norman school board. Gittinger acquits him of all charges of immorality: "Cole like Parrington was too busy to dance or play cards at the time, and, contrary to the

---

21. Both letters are quoted in Hall, *V. L. Parrington*, 148–49.

22. Gittinger, "Reorganizations of 1908 and 1911," 30.

23. Gittinger (ibid.) agrees: "He was too wrapped up in his work to have time for either dancing or card playing."

24. Hadsell, "Parrington in Oklahoma," 12. Hadsell (6) confirms that Parrington appeared "snobbish." "He has been called a Jeffersonian democrat. He seems to have sympathy with the common man. Yet like Jefferson, he was an aristocrat. In his dress, deportment, talk, tastes, interests he was an aristocrat. He could never have been elected to an office in Norman. . . . He was not well known, not well understood on 'main street.'"

25. Gittinger, "Reorganizations of 1908 and 1911," 30.

statement of Regent Linebaugh, Pastor Morgan, and Brother Hardie, he did not smoke at all. In fact Cole was about as strait-laced as either of his accusers."[26] Cole was fired for two reasons. His connection with the American Book Company angered Regent Hickam. And, once again, Regent Linebaugh had somebody else in mind for the job.

Somehow rumors began to spread a month after the firings that the Regents just might reconsider the dismissal of Lawrence Cole. Former students wrote emotional letters straight to the governor, asking that Cole be kept. "The case for his discharge was the charge of immoral conduct," wrote one alumnus. "While a student in the University I was in close contact with Professor Cole and knew him both in the class room and as a man. I have always considered him one of the most moral men that I have ever met with." The writer then commented on the man that the Regents had chosen to replace Cole: "His successor, I am told, is a man who has never taken special work in Psychology and has never taught it. His only qualification, I am informed, is that he is a good strong South Methodist." Another student wrote Governor Haskell that "in the recent changes in the University faculty there were many surprises to those of us who have spent years there and who know the men personally. Many men who to us alumni were regarded as the best qualified men in every sense for the places have gone, but perhaps no surprise was so great as that of Mr. Lawrence W. Cole from the chair of Psychology."[27] It was all in vain. The Regents had never considered reinstating Cole, and he headed off to teach for a year at Wellesley, earn a Ph.D. from Harvard, and then enjoy a long and notable career at the University of Colorado.

The faculty member who miraculously returned from the dead was Roy Gittinger. The *Norman Transcript* had listed his name (albeit spelled incorrectly as "Gettinger") as among those whose bodies "were strewed about the campus."[28] After all, he had been (falsely) quoted in both the *News* and the Morgan letter as one who preferred that the University go down in flames rather than having the Southern Methodist Ernest Bynum as its president. But it will be remembered that President Boyd, at the start of school in September 1907, had asked Gittinger to organize a summer-school session. It turned out that 122 students enrolled.[29] Thus Evans, who came into the presidency officially on July 1, was in daily contact with Gittinger, the school's director, for six weeks. "We did not discuss the possibility of my reappointment to the faculty," Gittinger maintained; but others took up his case during the summer. Frank Alexander, Gittinger's Presbyterian pastor, went to see his fellow Presbyterian minister Grant Evans on his parishioner's behalf. Professor Buchanan, another active member of the Norman Presbyterian church, indicated that

26. Ibid., 31.

27. Both letters, and others in support of Cole, are in the Charles N. Haskell MSS RG 8-A-4, Box 3, Folder 11.

28. *Norman Transcript*, June 26, 1908.

29. Gittinger wrote ("Reorganizations of 1908 and 1911," 28): "This was the first University summer session planned as a regular half-semester, and, so far as I know, the first in the United States so organized."

room could be found in the History Department for Gittinger.[30] "Evans on the last day of the summer school, August 7, recommended my reelection at a meeting of the board held in his office," Gittinger recalled. Regent Gordon (whose one demand in all of this was that his old friend Monroe Floyd be given Gittinger's job as director of the Preparatory Department) was not present at the meeting "and ostensibly on that account Linebaugh objected; but, as no other member of the Board joined him, he somewhat grudgingly withdrew his objection." Thus on the very afternoon when his connection with the University was to have ended, Roy Gittinger rejoined the faculty. It was a fortunate day for the University of Oklahoma; Gittinger was to render exceptional service in the classroom, in the administration, and as a historian of the institution for more than four decades after the harrowing events of 1908. His terse remark concerning his own rescue says much, not only about his own fate, but about the fates of his less fortunate colleagues: "One might note the church influence in this."[31]

~

IF THE REGENTS HAD HOPED to keep their actions during the spring and summer of 1908 hidden from derogatory national attention, President Boyd's New York friend Lyman Abbott disappointed them. The editor of the influential *Outlook* magazine published a string of withering articles and editorials that brought the Oklahoma outrages to public attention from coast to coast. Abbott opened fire only a few weeks after returning from his stay with the Boyds while giving his lectures at the University. The occasion was the firing of Boyd by the State Board of Education (later to be reversed by the Oklahoma Supreme Court). Under the title "A Serious Educational Blunder," the *Outlook* made its opinion crystal clear: "[T]he State Board of Education has disregarded all the experience of older communities, as well as fundamental educational and political principles, by interjecting partisan politics into the educational administration of the State." Abbott reviewed Boyd's admirable record in building a campus and a faculty who, Abbott asserted, "in their several departments, measure well up in ability to the younger men of older universities." The editor charged that, although Boyd enjoyed "the cordial support of his faculty and of the students," the politicians "removed him in order to put a Democrat in his place." Lamenting the decision to dismiss someone "who has done so large a work for the State and done it so well," the editorial ended with an observation that could hardly have pleased the men who fired Boyd: "Infantile communities have to have their mumps and measles, and we may hope that when the Board of Education of the State of Oklahoma is older it will be wiser."[32]

At the end of the summer the *Outlook* struck again. By then the Regents had fired not

30. For James Buchanan's prominence in the church, see Thompson, *First Presbyterian Church*, 6, 18, and 21–22.

31. Gittinger, "Reorganizations of 1908 and 1911," 28.

32. "A Serious Educational Blunder," *Outlook* 88 (April 11, 1908): 809–10.

only Boyd but "with him more than a third of the Faculty. . . . Even so humble servitors of the University as the night watchman, the carpenter, and the head janitor were not exempt from the general decapitation." Abbott claimed that on July 28 he had written to Governor Haskell, asking for his side of the story; but "to this request we have had no reply." The editor was certain that "the removal could not be an endeavor to secure superior scholarship" and devastatingly compared those who were fired with those who replaced them, starting at the top by contrasting Boyd with Evans and moving down through the fired faculty and their inferior replacements: "we have not learned that any one of the new appointees had collegiate advantages equal to those of the men whom they supplanted." The *Outlook* discreetly gave no names other than those of the outgoing and incoming presidents, because "we wish our readers to consider the principles, not the persons, involved." But it was worth noting that some of those fired "have already been called to other institutions of learning at increased salary."[33]

Abbott's article brushed aside the allegations that those removed were political activists ("President Boyd, although a Republican, never belonged to any political organization, [and] never attended a political convention in the State even as a spectator"). Equally untenable was the charge that they were "carpetbaggers" (after all, every non-Indian in the former Oklahoma Territory older than nineteen was a carpetbagger, and "some of the men removed have been citizens of Oklahoma three or four times as long as its present Governor"). If those charges against the fired faculty were untrue, what might be the real reason for their dismissals? At this point the editorialist reprinted in full (with all the names omitted) Morgan's letter to Regent Linebaugh, repeating, in case careless readers missed it the first time, the line: "Do your best to get as many strong Southern Methodists on the faculty as possible."[34]

Governor Haskell lashed out against Abbott in a speech in Guthrie. He charged that the editor of the *Outlook* "is living on past greatness, but in present demented condition" and that he was "easily misled by false statements." He also suggested that Abbott write to Lee Cruce, president of the Regents, for an explanation of the official side of the story. Abbott did just that. And Cruce dutifully composed a long letter as a spirited defense of the Regents' actions, pointing out that "since my vote was cast for the retention of practically all of the men removed, it cannot be said that I am prejudiced against them." The firings, Cruce argued, were neither political nor sectarian. After all, two members of the Board of Regents were Republicans, and they both voted to dismiss Boyd; the Board was

33. "Shall the People Rule—in Oklahoma?" *Outlook* 90 (September 5, 1908): 15–18; quotation on 16.

34. Lyman Abbott had a second motive in launching this attack. The election of 1908 was two months away, and it pitted William Jennings Bryan, the Democrat, against William Howard Taft, the hand-picked successor of Abbott's friend Theodore Roosevelt. The editorial stressed Governor Haskell's ties to Bryan: Haskell "was one of Mr. Bryan's right-hand men in the Democratic Convention and, at Mr. Bryan's instance, has been made treasurer of the Democratic National Committee." Voters should ask themselves, Abbott maintained, whether they wanted this unprincipled political and sectarian corruption applied to the various departments of the federal government, for surely that would be a possibility if Bryan won the election.

also religiously diverse (two Southern Methodists, two Presbyterians, a Baptist, a member of the Disciples of Christ, and one Regent whose affiliation Cruce did not know). "I mention the politics and religion of these gentlemen to show how unwarrantable are your charges."[35] Cruce praised Boyd's work generously;[36] but he contended that statehood had changed things by uniting Indian Territory, with its large population of American Indians, to Oklahoma Territory:

> The Board of Regents thought it was their duty to try to interest this Indian citizenship in the University. Mr. Evans had spent many years as President of a Presbyterian school in the Indian Territory, and possibly no man in the State has a stronger hold upon, and a more helpful influence with, the Indians of the State than he. With all, he is a splendid scholar, a man of great and tried executive ability, and under his guardianship the University will continue the wonderful growth it has hitherto enjoyed. Thus it came to pass that Dr. Boyd was supplanted by Dr. Evans.

And if politics had nothing to do with the switch (since both Republicans on the board voted for it), neither did religion (after all, both Boyd and Evans were devout Presbyterians). Cruce went on to praise the credentials of the new faculty appointed by the board and to insist that, contrary to the *Outlook*'s allegation that a third of the University's teachers had been fired, "less than one-fifth of the Faculty was removed."

Cruce closed his defense of the Regents' actions with an attack on Abbott and the *Outlook*. Declaring that "your editorial is the first serious criticism that has been aimed at the University" and complaining that the magazine's words had been "extensively copied and commented upon throughout the State," Cruce charged that "acting upon wrong information, you have done our University a great wrong. You have injured the young State of Oklahoma." It was obvious to Cruce that Abbott had been misled and "imposed upon." But that did not change the fact that "the people look to you as a teacher whose integrity is manifest, and [that] you owe it to them to teach them correctly." Although Abbott had done Oklahoma an "irreparable" wrong, Regent Cruce claimed to still retain "an abiding faith in your fairness and honesty." Thus, Cruce concluded, "I confidently expect to read from your pen an article that will, as far as possible, correct the wrong impression that your editorial has created."[37]

Lyman Abbott did not quite see it that way. To Governor Haskell's ill-tempered accusation that Abbott was "demented," the editor maintained that "no answer is required." But if an answer had been needed, it would have been enough to quote from Lee Cruce's letter a few of the words of praise that the president of the Board of Regents had bestowed

---

35. For Cruce's letter, see "Shall the People Rule—in Oklahoma?: Reply from the Board of Regents," *Outlook* 90 (October 3, 1908): 249–51.

36. "Dr. Boyd has served the University faithfully and efficiently. He has successfully encountered many difficulties, and under his guiding counsel the University has grown steadily and rapidly, until it ranks with the best State universities of the Nation" (ibid., 249–50).

37. Ibid., 251.

*Lyman Abbott, editor of the* Outlook

*Lee Cruce, University Regent, defender of the firings of 1908, and future governor of Oklahoma*

on the magazine.[38] And regarding Cruce's more measured statements, defending the Regents and their motives, Abbott saw little reason to take them seriously. "Mr. Cruce's letter denies some statements in The Outlook's editorial and modifies some others"; but Abbott insisted that "our statements were based on authentic and authoritative information." If the details were important to "the main issue," he suggested, "we might call in question the accuracy of some of his statements, might comment upon the inadequacy of others, and might add some information respecting the personal relationship of some of the new appointments to members of the Board to whose influence they owed their appointment." There was no need for any of that, Abbott contended, because "the general issue is not affected by these questions of details." Even assuming the absolute accuracy of Cruce's statements, Abbott saw no reason to change his view that an enormous injustice had occurred.

After all, *everyone* praised the achievements of David Ross Boyd. Nevertheless he was to be replaced by a man whose principal claim, according to Regent Cruce, his defender, was that "possibly no man in the State has a stronger hold upon and a more helpful influence with the Indians of the State than he." Abbott responded with undisguised fury: "If

38. Cruce had written that the *Outlook* was so extensively read that it exerted a "wonderful influence." "The world is your field of action," he told Abbott. "Your Outlook is read wherever good literature is sought" (ibid.).

this is not political influence, we do not know what is. There is no suggestion of any failure in the administration of Dr. Boyd, or any lack of ability in him to continue his confessedly admirable administration":

> Mr. Evans led the movement to make Indian Territory a separate State. It was this fact that gave him his "hold" upon the Indians. To appoint him President of the State University will give to the authorities of the State something of his "hold" on the Indian population. This is not the way to administer a great university. Its President should be appointed because of his ability to administer its affairs, not to give a "hold" to any one on a special section of the State or a special class of the population.

Abbott pointed out, correctly, that in Lee Cruce's letter "no reason for the discharge of this one-third or one-fifth of the faculty is even hinted at." In the last analysis, the factual details are trivial when compared to the central and irrefutable point: "The one essential fact that appears in this whole miserable business is that the President and a large proportion of the faculty have been summarily removed from office, and that there is no pretense that any question of their scholarly attainments or their competence to teach was involved in the removal. To the charge [by the *Outlook*] that the reasons for the removal were political, ecclesiastical, and personal favoritism, only one answer is possible. That answer is a clear statement of some other reason and no other reason is even suggested."[39]

Lyman Abbott was an experienced polemicist—hardened in theological and political battles for decades. He closed his assault on Cruce and the Regents with an eloquence that is worth quoting at length:

> Mr. Cruce is mistaken in thinking that "your editorial is the first serious criticism that has been aimed at the University." . . . [T]he report of the action of the Board of Regents has aroused in academic circles a deep feeling of indignation. If Mr. Cruce could see some of the letters which have come to The Outlook . . . he would certainly not think that our editorial is the only serious criticism. Wherever disinterested men are to be found who desire to see the educational institutions of the country conducted solely in the interest of the youth who are being educated in them; wherever there is a sense of fair play and even-handed justice, this summary removal of a university president in order to substitute one who has a "hold" on a large body of voters, and this summary removal, without cause, of faithful, efficient, competent teachers, whose successful work has attested their ability, will arouse something more than "serious criticism." It will arouse hot and righteous indignation.
>
> We are glad to be assured that our editorial has been extensively copied and commented upon throughout the State. We are glad to be assured that The Outlook has a "wonderful influence" in the State. And we hope that both Mr. Cruce's letter and this editorial may be equally widely copied and commented upon, and that our influence may have some effect in calling to account the men who have inflicted this great in-

---

39. Abbott's reply to Cruce is in "Do the People Rule—in Oklahoma?" *Outlook* 90 (September 5, 1908): 242–44. The reply *precedes* the Cruce letter: the former is an editorial printed on the first pages of the issue, and the latter is published in the magazine's "Correspondence" section near the end of the issue.

justice on the faculty of its State University, and this great wrong upon the people, for whose benefits that University was organized and should be maintained.[40]

Roy Gittinger did not accuse President Boyd of having supplied Lyman Abbott with the ammunition for his furious attack on the governor and his Regents; but it seems likely that, in fact, Abbott's information came from the ousted president. (Other informants might possibly have known, for example, that Boyd "never belonged to any political organization, [and] never attended a political convention in the State even as a specta-tor," but Boyd must at least be considered a prime suspect.) Of course, he had very strong and understandable motives for lashing out at the men who had treated him so shabbily. Nonetheless, Gittinger, whose first loyalty was always to the University of Oklahoma and its reputation, expresses a mild irritation with Boyd for dragging the *Outlook* into the whole sordid episode: "From one point of view the worst feature of Abbott's visit . . . was that he became interested in President Boyd's retention. Perhaps Boyd had hoped for this, and after the drastic changes in faculty and administration were announced three months later, Abbott's magazine published all the unpleasant details, and what might have passed over with little attention except locally all at once became a national scandal."[41]

~

LEE CRUCE'S LETTER TO THE *OUTLOOK* conveniently neglected to mention that Haskell's choice to be the new president of the University of Oklahoma just happened to be the governor's personal friend, trusted political associate, and townsman; and some readers might have felt that Cruce's argument was not entirely unsound. There was a certain plau-sibility in the suggestion that citizens of the former Indian Territory had to be shown that the University of Oklahoma belonged to them too and that choosing a president in whom they had confidence was not an unreasonable thing to do. But Lyman Abbott was assuredly correct in charging that no proper justification was offered by Cruce or anyone else for the wholesale firing of the faculty. Abbott concluded that it was precisely this part of the story that exposed the true motives of the new authorities in Oklahoma, motives grounded in politics, religion, and patronage. Who were the men and women that the Regents chose to replace those they had dismissed and on what basis were they selected?

One indication of the kind of appeals that were made on behalf of hopeful new ap-plicants can be found in a letter that Bill Cross, Oklahoma's new secretary of state, sent to the Board of Regents on the day before the Regents met to fire some and hire others. Cross's recommendation of Bess Gano shows how a politically astute state official believed the Regents might be persuaded. "Miss Gano is a granddaughter of General Gano of Texas, who so valiantly fought for the Southern Confederacy during the war of the 60s," Cross

---

40. Ibid. Abbott was not yet finished with this issue. See the editorial "Haskellism in Oklahoma University," *Outlook* 90 (October 17, 1908): 325–26.

41. Gittinger, "Reorganizations of 1908 and 1911," 14.

told the Regents. "She and all her people are Democrats of the Rock Ribbed Type, tried and true, and I have known this young lady for a number of years, and know her to be competent and well qualified to assume this position. . . . Miss Gano is also the grand-daughter of Hon. T. J. Lowe, the Secretary of the Territory, under President Cleveland."[42] As it happened, Cross's advocacy of Gano failed. Linebaugh and his fellow Regents had their own favorites in mind.

Regent Linebaugh's most notable victory was to place on the University's faculty three members of the Brewer family. The patriarch of that family was Theodore Frelinghuysen Brewer, one of the most prominent Southern Methodist ministers of the Indian Territory and a close personal friend of Linebaugh.[43] Brewer was willing to come to Norman, but he wished to bring along his brother's widow and her two children, his nephew and niece. The Regents appointed Virginia, the niece, to be instructor in piano. The nephew, Theo-dore Hampton Brewer, was given Vernon Parrington's place in the English Department. In fact, Linebaugh's desire to hire young Brewer may have been the principal reason for his determination to remove Parrington. The patriarch himself was to be the professor of sec-ondary education. He was in his sixties when he was hired and was not expected to teach. His job was to travel around the state and "inspect" Oklahoma high schools (although Gittinger mentions these school "visits," he insists that "they can hardly be called inspec-tions"). Drawing upon his undoubted popularity, wide acquaintanceship, and charm, the Reverend Brewer probably played a part in encouraging high-school students from eastern Oklahoma to attend the University in Norman. Virginia Brewer remained on the faculty for two years and then left to get married; she was promptly replaced by her cousin Bess, the patriarch's own daughter, until, three years later, Bess Brewer also chose to marry.[44]

The nephew, however, was another story. Theodore Hampton Brewer had earned a bachelor's degree (1896) and a master's degree (1907) from Vanderbilt. He taught a little and then worked extensively in journalism. He was witty and a good mixer and gained a reputation as a clever and engaging toastmaster. He had taken no part, of course, in the machinations that had led to his coming to the University; as Gittinger put it, "he knew only that he had been invited to apply for a position in English as there was to be a vacan-cy." During his first years, he must have labored in Parrington's shadow and in various ways must have been made to feel it, but he persisted and slowly and quietly won the affection of his colleagues.[45] The other members of the Brewer family soon departed, but Theodore

---

42. Bill Cross to Board of Regents, June 22, 1908, copy in the Charles N. Haskell MSS, RG 8-A-4, Box 3, Folder 6.

43. Gittinger ("Reorganizations of 1908 and 1911," 32) called Brewer "perhaps the leading minister of the Southern Methodist Church in the old Indian Territory." For an account of his career, see Clegg and Oden, *Oklahoma Methodism in the Twentieth Century*, 93–95. The church's Indian conference was later named the Brewer Indian Mission in his honor.

44. Gittinger, "Reorganizations of 1908 and 1911," 32–33.

45. At Brewer's death, Parrington's disciple Sardis Roy Hadsell wrote of his colleague of thirty-two years: "His department ran without friction. He was fair and kindly as an administrator. He never knowingly injured anyone. His word was good" ("Scholar and Teacher," *Sooner Magazine* 13 [November 1940]: 28–29). Hadsell's article is the best summary of Brewer's career and character.

*Theodore Hampton Brewer*

Hampton Brewer taught English until his death in 1940. Drawing on his own early newspaper and magazine experience, he also began the University's formal instruction in journalism, teaching the first class in that subject in 1911 (within the English Department) and serving as director of a new School of Journalism from 1913 until 1917.

Two other Linebaugh appointments quickly proved themselves incompetent and had to be asked to resign. Lawrence Cole's successor was a Linebaugh protégé named Mortimer Stanfield Gardner. He also studied at Vanderbilt but left without finishing his B.A. He probably served as a minister to several small Southern Methodist churches in Texas and also did some public school teaching there. When he was about forty, in June 1908 (a month before being hired to head the Psychology Department in Norman), he completed the requirements for his bachelor's degree at the University of Texas. According to Gittinger, "Gardner came to the University of Oklahoma with a great show of confidence, but soon realized dimly his lack of preparation and his unfitness for college teaching. . . . All in all, his efforts were pitiful. The other new members of the faculty shunned him. The new president tried to support him, but he soon gave up." One of Gardner's first responsibilities was to present to a faculty meeting his overall plan for instruction in psychology. He suggested some general classes and also some classes for advanced undergraduates and even for graduate students; for each of his proposed courses, however, he listed the same textbook: William James's famous *Briefer Course in Psychology*. "The faculty listened to him in astonished silence. President Evans who was the presiding officer said quietly that it would be better for Gardner's new program to go over until the next meeting." Somehow Gardner managed to get through the year, and somehow he was hired again for a second year; but in 1910 he complied with a request for his resignation.[46]

To replace Jansky in physics and engineering, Linebaugh picked another Southern Methodist minister, George Childs Jones. He had earned a master's degree from Vanderbilt in 1879 and also did work at the University of Chicago and in Berlin. Jones had been president of the Arkadelphia (Arkansas) Methodist College for ten years (1894–1904) and then moved to teach chemistry and physics at Epworth in Oklahoma City. But he quickly resigned from Epworth to head a private Methodist school in the city, the Oklahoma College for Young Ladies. Gittinger believed that Jones had hoped to become the University's president (and that he even claimed that he might have been but did not want the job of

46. Gittinger, "Reorganizations of 1908 and 1911," 33–34.

"cleaning up the mess on the campus"). Jones was probably capable of handling the basic courses in physics, but the higher-level work in that discipline and in engineering was beyond him. Moreover, he wanted to retain his position at the College for Young Ladies and, for that purpose, to live in Oklahoma City. He therefore tried to rehire the infidel Jansky to teach; Jansky accepted briefly but elected to go to the University of Wisconsin instead. Jones was determined to live in Oklahoma City and run his private school, so he found someone to replace Jansky. But every day Jones got on the train, came to Norman to teach the elementary classes, and promptly returned home. After a year of this, he too was asked to resign.[47]

The Regents placed the School of Medicine under the direction of Charles Sharp Bobo; he replaced Roy Philson Stoops, who had been one of the University's first two graduates. Bobo had graduated from the Louisville Medical College in 1881, set up a medical practice in Norman, and joined the Southern Methodist congregation. He had been a lecturer at the University since 1906. Bobo was to be assisted by another new appointee, Walter L. Capshaw, another Norman physician and member of the Norman Southern Methodist church. A position in mathematics went to Edmund Pendleton Randolph Duval, a teacher at the University of Wisconsin with degrees from Texas and Harvard. How did Duval happen to end up at the University of Oklahoma? His brothers-in-law, it turned out, were leading members of the Southern Methodist church in Tulsa. The man backed by Regent Gordon for Gittinger's old job as head of the Preparatory Department, Monroe A. Floyd, was duly hired in that position.[48] Linebaugh also chose a handful of women to join the faculty, but only one of them stayed for any length of time. The fired campus employees (Frank Flood, Tom Carey, and Kirby Prickett) Linebaugh replaced with choices of his own; this he did without consulting with President Evans.[49]

Back in January 1908 (six months before the axe fell), the University's librarian, Milton J. Ferguson, left his position to go to the state library in Sacramento, California. As we have seen, Boyd named young Jesse Rader (a senior at the University and Ferguson's assistant) to replace him for the rest of the year. In mid-June, with everything still up in the air, Rader sent a long, sincere, and dignified letter to Governor Haskell, pleading for the position on the grounds of his dedication to the University and his familiarity with the library's collection—familiarity, he pointed out, that no outsider could match.[50] The Regents chose to pass over Rader and to name John Sherwood McLucas, a man with more impressive credentials than Rader could boast: McLucas had a master's degree from

47. Ibid., 34–35.

48. Gittinger (ibid., 36) wrote a balanced characterization of his replacement: "Floyd had three bachelor's degrees, two from the University of Missouri, dating from 1895 to 1905. He had been a high-school teacher for three years, and . . . he was in 1908 principal of a large elementary school in Oklahoma City. Floyd, an able and well-meaning man, was not especially fitted to be a college teacher, but he remained at the University of Oklahoma for twelve years."

49. Ibid., 31–32.

50. Jesse L. Rader to Governor Charles N. Haskell, June 13, 1908, Haskell MSS, Box 3, Folder 6.

Harvard (1899) and a good deal of library experience. He perhaps had another advantage over Rader: he was courting and would soon wed the niece of Theodore Frelinghuysen Brewer, the young woman Linebaugh had placed as a piano instructor. McLucas had the good sense to retain Rader as his assistant; and when he left for the University of Colorado after only a year in Norman, Rader became the University's librarian, a job he held until his retirement in 1953.[51]

The one woman who stayed was C. Lucile Dora, who soon became one of the great campus "characters" in the history of the institution. There was always some mystery about her early life—for example, no one ever found out what the "C." in her name stood for. She also affected the pronunciation of her last name, enunciating it as though it were "Doray"; one old friend remarked that her father would turn over in his grave if he knew how his daughter was pronouncing the family name. It is fairly certain that she was born in southern Illinois, but the date of her birth is hotly disputed.[52] Gittinger says that "she had a degree from Christian College conferred in 1898, but she never told where this Christian College was located." He adds that "she had a master's degree from Hellmuth College conferred in 1901. She gave out that Hellmuth College was in London. Since Oklahomans really knew of only one London they assumed that Hellmuth College was in England, but ultimately it came out that the London of Hellmuth College was in Ontario."[53] But Dora's department chair, many years later, claimed to have evidence that Hellmuth never offered the master's degree and may have already been out of existence by 1901. He also alleged that she falsified the title of a degree she earned at a provincial French university.[54]

In any case, in 1907–1908 Dora was teaching high-school French in Oklahoma City. She was somehow able to ingratiate herself with Regents Cruce and Pratt, and her hiring was the work of these two rather than of Regent Linebaugh. The rumors about the scandalous behavior of certain young women at the University had received such wide notice that the position of a "dean of women" was a certainty, and Lucile Dora persuaded Cruce and Pratt that she could do the job. "She soon had them both actively on her side with the other members of the board not disposed to object to her." Gittinger suspected that she might not even have wanted a teaching position. But it was necessary to replace George Davidson, the man who had himself replaced Ernest Bynum and then proceeded almost to burn down his rooming house with a cigarette. Consequently, at the fateful Regents' meeting of June 23, Lucile Dora was made both dean of women and professor of Romance languages.[55]

51. Gittinger, "Reorganizations of 1908 and 1911," 36.

52. For many years Dora claimed to have been born in March 1881, but there is convincing evidence that she was older than she said. See Roy Temple House to William Bennett Bizzell, April 27, 1940, in Lucille Dora's Personnel File, Office of the Provost. See also Emil Kraettli to United States Census Bureau, January 8, 1940, in ibid. There is an entire folder in the Kraettli MSS (Box 1, Folder 2) devoted to solving the mystery of Professor Dora's birthdate.

53. Gittinger, "Reorganizations of 1908 and 1911," 37.

54. Roy Temple House to William Bennett Bizzell, April 27, 1940, Lucille Dora Personnel File.

55. Gittinger, "Reorganizations of 1908 and 1911," 37. Gittinger also alleges that "she did not know a great deal of

She did not last long as dean. At a meeting in Chicago
in 1910, she boasted about how she had tamed the
young women at the University of Oklahoma and
apparently mentioned by name the daughter of
an important Oklahoma City family as one of her
problems. Word of this indiscretion sped home.
President Evans asked for her resignation as dean,
and for the next thirty-five years Lucile Dora was
merely a professor of French. Gittinger reported:

C. *Lucile Dora*

> During her long stay at the University she de-
> veloped a number of idiosyncrasies that made her
> something of a joke, albeit a pleasant one. She
> always carried a green parasol, which became her
> symbol just as an umbrella later became that of
> [English prime minister Neville] Chamberlain. She
> designed for herself an academic costume, a yellow
> outfit all her own, which attracted a great deal of attention at Commencement time.
> Her real eccentricity, however, was her practice of taking on her plate all she could at a
> dinner, whether at a fraternity house or at a University affair, eating what she wanted,
> folding what was left in a napkin, placing it in her handbag, and carrying it home to
> be eaten later. In spite of her oddities, she had many fiercely loyal friends, both on and
> off the campus.[56]

Thus the group of those who replaced the fired professors in 1908 was a mixed one.
Most of them were ephemeral figures at the University and were soon gone. The two
ministers who were brought in to head the Physics and Psychology Departments were unequal to the task (Gittinger calls them "misfits"). Theodore Brewer in English and Lucile
Dora in French taught at the University for many years and rendered satisfactory service.
The other newcomers, in general, were probably at least adequate to their responsibilities.
Whether they were the equals of those they replaced is an open question. Certainly none
of them was as able as Vernon Parrington or Lawrence Cole, and none of them made careers even roughly comparable. To some extent, moreover, they all bore the stigma of having received their jobs on the basis of factors that had little to do with academic criteria or
standards. They arrived at the University on the basis of their political loyalties, religious
affiliations, and personal connections. No matter how long they remained or how valuable
their contributions, the questionable way in which they came into their positions hung
like a shadow over their careers at the University of Oklahoma.

---

French and she had no knowledge of other Romance languages. She spent the summer of 1908 with a French-Canadian
family to secure a speaking knowledge of French."

56. Ibid., 37–38. For a more laudatory view of Dora, see E.[laine] L.[earcy], "Everyone's French Teacher," *Sooner
Magazine* 17 (December 1944): 3–4. In 1950 Lucile Dora's former students and other admirers commissioned a portrait of
her to hang in the University's library; see "Possessed of a Grand Manner," *Sooner Magazine* 22 (July 1950): 7.

~

ON THE NIGHT HE WAS FIRED, David Ross Boyd caught the train from Oklahoma City and returned home. He was, the *Norman Transcript* reported, "the recipient of many warm expressions of good will and good wishes." Naturally, the *Transcript* reporter asked him for a statement. His own fate he accepted—as might have been expected from him, at least in public—with entire self-control and a calm and philosophic dignity. After all, for weeks he had suspected that this was coming, and he had ample time to prepare himself. But his statement also reveals deep feelings about the fates of the men and women he had hired. "I was not surprised to learn that the Board of Regents had elected my successor," he said, "but I felt that when the administration had displaced me with a new man that they would feel satisfied with that and would leave the faculty without much change. I feel more disappointed at the extensive changes in the faculty than I do for myself."[57] He dutifully acknowledged the right of the Regents to name the University's president and added: "My heart has been very close to the results of my sixteen years' labor here and I think it is rather natural that I should very much desire to see what has been done for the University continue to grow and develop. I therefore want to do everything I can to assist my successor, Rev. A. Grant Evans, in every way that I properly can. . . . I shall always retain a deep interest in the University and shall always rejoice and hope for its growth and development." He hoped, he said, that "our whole community will reserve criticism of the new administration and give it cordial support and help."[58]

A curious final incident between Boyd and the Board of Regents occurred almost a full year after his dismissal. At their meeting on April 3, 1909, the Regents, without consulting the faculty, voted to bestow honorary degrees upon three men: President Evans, Regent Linebaugh, and the former president, David Ross Boyd. Linebaugh and Evans took the honor; Boyd (who *had* accepted an honorary degree from his alma mater, Wooster) spurned it. The gist of his letter to the secretary of the Board was entered into the minutes of its next meeting: "A letter from Dr Boyd to Mr Rowsey stated that while he thanked the Board for intended honor in offering LL.D degree, he had always opposed honorary degrees except in unusual circumstances and declined the honor."[59] Gittinger wrote: "The degrees conferred on Evans and Linebaugh must have given them little comfort as the action was practically *sub rosa*, and the degree[s] conferred without public ceremony."[60]

57. *Norman Transcript*, June 26, 1908, 1.

58. Ibid.

59. For the award of the degree, see Regents' "Minutes," April 2–3, 1909, 5. For Boyd's refusal, see ibid., June 9, 1909, 12. One honorary degree had been given previously, on June 9, 1899, to John I. Dille, a former Regent who was leaving the state. It would be more than three-quarters of a century before the University gave another (Gittinger, "Reorganizations of 1908 and 1911," 40–41). We may dismiss the mythical tale, sometimes repeated (see, for example, Dave R. McKown, *The Dean: The Life of Julien C. Monnet*, 146, quoting "a newspaper") that "when the honorary degree was offered Dr. Boyd, a deep pink emerged from his collar suffusing his ears in dark red. Then, with grave dignity but with polite firmness, he rose to decline the offer." A year after his dismissal, of course, Boyd was not in the room when the Regents voted him the degree.

60. Gittinger, "University Reorganizations of 1908 and 1911," 41. In actuality, the Regents voted that the degrees were

*David Ross Boyd in 1908*

The former president's main business for the rest of the summer of 1908 was to attempt, through letters and direct personal appeals, to find positions for his fired colleagues. He had been one of the organizers of the Association of State University Presidents and knew many other presidents well. He wrote a letter to each member of the association, detailing the occurrences at the University and reviewing the credentials and abilities of the members of the faculty who had been dismissed. To his daughter Alice, he wrote: "[W]hile I was in Chicago I prevailed on Pres. Thos. F. Kane of the University of Washington, who is east looking for instructors, to stop here next week and see if he could not take on some of our fellows. I think he will take at least three."[61] Partly as a result of Boyd's efforts and partly, no doubt, on the strength of their own merits, every fired member of the faculty who wanted work was employed at another college or university by September.[62]

For a while, the former president's own fate was uncertain. He had told the reporter on that fateful June evening that he hoped "to take some time to rest and look after my personal business affairs . . . I expect to continue as a citizen of Norman."[63] But Boyd was only fifty-five years old in the summer of 1908 and probably eager for some new work. It was perhaps fitting that the Presbyterian affiliation that he had so loyally maintained should now come riding to his rescue. Back in the old days in Van Wert, Ohio, Boyd had greeted and helped a fresh new Presbyterian minister named Edgar Work, and the two men became good friends. Boyd went on to Kansas and then Oklahoma; Work ended up in New York City, where he led a large congregation and served on the Presbyterian Board of Home Missions. One branch of the Home Missions was the Women's Board. When Work learned that Boyd was looking for a job, he recommended him for the position of superintendent of education, a position that entailed establishing, visiting, and improving

to be bestowed at the June commencement exercises two months later. But the *Norman Transcript's* two rather detailed accounts of those exercises make no mention of honorary degrees conferred upon Linebaugh and Evans.

61. David Ross Boyd to Alice Boyd, July 13, 1908, David Ross Boyd Presidential MSS, Box 38, Folder 20. His prediction was correct. The University of Washington hired Vernon Parrington, George Davidson, and David C. Hall, the professor of physical training (who was not fired, but resigned).

62. Dale, "David Ross Boyd: Pioneer Educator," 26–27. Not all of them wanted to resume teaching immediately.

63. *Norman Transcript,* June 26, 1908, 1.

Presbyterian schools, especially among American Indians, the Mexican Americans of the Southwest, Utah Mormons, and mountaineers in the remote regions of Appalachia. Boyd was offered the job and accepted it immediately; his salary was to be $2,000.[64] He moved to New York City and took up the work from his Fifth Avenue office. Mrs. Boyd and Alice remained in Norman for a year and then joined him. For the next four years Boyd was on the road almost constantly; he claimed to have traveled 25,000 miles in the first year alone, visiting established Presbyterian schools, creating many new ones, and doing what amounted to missionary work in some of the most isolated regions of the United States.[65]

In connection with these efforts, Boyd spent a good deal of time among the Navajos in New Mexico. He was introduced to some of the most prominent citizens of Albuquerque by Alonzo McMillan, an old student of Boyd's from the days when he had been superintendent at Van Wert and now a wealthy lawyer in the city. When the president of the University of New Mexico resigned in 1912, the Regents asked Boyd to interview for the job. He liked his work with the Presbyterian Mission but was tired of the travel and the long separations from his wife and daughter. He also preferred the West to New York City. The Regents offered him the position, and David Ross Boyd became president of the University of New Mexico in September 1912.

The school was small and poor.[66] Although it was already twenty-five years old, it had only about two hundred students; and only seventy-eight of these were doing actual college work. The school had a little more than a dozen faculty members, buildings in serious disrepair, and a campus that consisted of a mere twenty acres. Even the University's title to the land was in question, given the complexity and confusion of the early Spanish grants. In short, there was plenty to do, and Boyd was in his element. The family returned to Norman to pack up their furniture and rent a railroad car to carry it to Albuquerque. Boyd's house was rented, unfurnished, to the new University president, Stratton D. Brooks. In many ways Boyd's work in New Mexico duplicated what he had tried to do in Oklahoma. He started a "push class"; he became a member of the State Board of Education and worked hard to improve secondary education in New Mexico (which had become a state in 1912, the same year that Boyd took over the University); he started a geological survey like the one he had helped begin in Oklahoma. He proposed a building program, but the University of New Mexico could never afford it during his years there; so he concentrated on repairing the existing buildings. He persuaded the Regents to purchase an additional 230 acres. Naturally, he attended to the business of landscaping and tree-planting.[67] Boyd was careful to do one other thing: he looked up his old Oklahoma janitor and friend Kirby Prickett and brought him to New Mexico as superintendent of buildings and grounds.[68]

64. David Ross Boyd to Alice Boyd, July 13, 1908, David Ross Boyd Presidential MSS, Box 38, Folder 20.

65. Dale, "David Ross Boyd: Pioneer Educator," 27–30.

66. Dorothy Hughes, *Pueblo on the Mesa: The First Fifty Years at the University of New Mexico*.

67. Ibid., 43–45; Dale, "David Ross Boyd: Pioneer Educator," 30–33.

68. Hadsell, "Kirby Prickett," 36. Prickett stayed in New Mexico until the outbreak of World War I, when he went into

In 1919 Boyd decided to resign from the University of New Mexico's presidency. The decision was not prompted by any difficulties at Albuquerque, but by a range of other factors. He was now sixty-six. He had far-flung real-estate and other interests that required his attention (among other holdings, he owned 640 acres near Norman and 250 acres in McClain County; he was also one of the organizers of the People's Finance and Thrift Co. in Oklahoma City). The Boyds retained their home in Albuquerque until 1921. Then they followed their daughter, Alice, to Glendale, California, where she had found a job in the city library. The Boyds lived quietly in Glendale for the rest of their lives, but Boyd made numerous trips to Norman during his retirement. He came back partly to look after his business interests, partly to visit old colleagues and acquaintances, partly just to walk on the campus and see how his trees were doing. He struck up warm personal friendships with his successors; and in 1930 one of them, William Bennett Bizzell, arranged for the Regents to grant him the title of "President Emeritus." David Ross Boyd died in Glendale on November 17, 1936.[69]

By that time, of course, there was general recognition of what Boyd had accomplished while he was at the University of Oklahoma. The historian Edward Everett Dale reported that even Governor Haskell "said later that he deeply regretted his action and that this was perhaps the greatest mistake of his administration."[70] George ("Deak") Parker, that illustrious and popular undergraduate of 1904–1908, went on, after graduation, to a distinguished career in journalism; he won the Pulitzer Prize in 1936 for his editorials. It was fitting, therefore, that in 1933 he should be the very first alumnus invited to give the commencement address. He chose to begin by recalling the man who had been president while he was a student. He remarked that he was sorry that Boyd had not made it back to Norman for the day's celebration: "I should love to recall with him some of the differences we used to have over certain matters of discipline and conduct," he joked. But Parker also knew how to be serious:

> That I should pay tribute to the founder should be only natural in view of the fact that he was in charge during my college days. But that I could find words adequate to such a tribute is impossible. I can only do my best. . . . In a very peculiar sense David R. Boyd had made the University of Oklahoma. It would not be too much of an exaggeration to say that he had made it with his bare hands. . . . Every faculty member, every course in the curriculum, every student, every custom, every stick and stone in the campus, was there because of him. Such driving energy, such abundant vitality, such singleness of purpose, such executive genius, are rare in this planet. Dr. Boyd was the University, and the University was Dr. Boyd.[71]

---

public service and then retired to California.

69. Dale, "David Ross Boyd: Pioneer Educator," 33–34.

70. Ibid., 27.

71. A copy of George Parker's commencement address may be found in the David Ross Boyd MSS, Box 1, Folder 9.

A few weeks before his death, Boyd received a letter from William Bennett Bizzell. It was a tribute from the fifth president of the University of Oklahoma to the first and must have moved the eighty-three-year-old Boyd deeply:

> As your humble successor, I want you to know that I am not unmindful of the great traditions you left behind you at the end of your brilliant administration of the affairs of the University. The foundations you laid and the scholastic ideals you disseminated are still being fostered and cherished by the small group of colleagues who worked with you in the early days and by all of us who have inherited the sound policies you promulgated as president of the University. It shall be my earnest desire for such time as I may serve as president of the University to keep alive in the consciousness of students, faculty members, and the citizenship generally the debt we owe to you for laying a good foundation and launching the institution on its great career.[72]

Those tributes from Parker and Bizzell were delivered a quarter-century after the dramatic events of 1908, and much history was to unfold in the interim. In the meantime, a new administration arrived and with it a greatly changed faculty. It would be a mistake to believe that the troubles were now over or that the new state's political leaders had finished their meddling with the University of Oklahoma.

72. William Bennett Bizzell to David Ross Boyd, September 24, 1936, David Ross Boyd MSS, Box 1, Folder 8.

CHAPTER VIII

# The Evans Years: Some Achievements and More "Corpses," 1908–1911

The city of Norman prospered alongside the University, and by the time President Evans and the new faculty arrived to take up their duties, it was a vastly different place than David Ross Boyd had found when he stepped down from the train sixteen years before. There were probably around 3,500 citizens in Norman as the 1908–1909 school year began.[1] Like countless other American cities and towns, Norman was riding the nationwide wave of economic good times. Naturally, it was still a town of new arrivals: John Millar, the mayor in 1908, had only been in residence for four years. His political prominence was no doubt due to his contagious optimism about the town's future. He and the boosters in the Norman Commercial Club, described as "one of the livest organizations of the kind in the new state,"[2] were determined to pave the way for "progress," which to them meant more population, more business, more prosperity. The city felt itself to be on the move.

By the fall of 1908 there were eighty businesses in town,[3] including three newspapers.[4] The town's four banks carried on a lively competition, particularly after the National Bank of Norman announced (two years after its establishment in 1904) that it would pay actual interest on deposits (4 percent); the other banks, of course, scrambled to do the same. Mayor Millar was adamant about improving the city's infrastructure. In February he

1. Population estimates are unreliable. It is not always clear whether the figures include University students or inmates in the state mental hospital. At statehood the official figure was 3,040 (not counting students); but Hunter James, "Norman, Home of State University," 22–30, estimates the population at around 4,500, a number that seems possible only if the University students are included. A brochure entitled "Norman, Oklahoma," published by the Norman Development Co. (no date, but internal evidence indicates that it was published in late 1907) estimates the town's population at 4,200. On May 18, 1911, the *Norman Transcript* reported a figure of 3,724 from the U.S. Census (not counting students).

2. James, "Norman, Home of State University," 26.

3. Ibid. But the booster brochure "Norman, Oklahoma" (44) claims "more than one hundred business houses, all prosperous and contented." It also asserts that "there has not been a [business] failure in the town in the past two years."

4. James, "Norman, Home of State University," 22. They were the *Norman Transcript*, the *Democratic Topic*, and the *People's Voice*. For the earliest history of Norman newspapers, see Womack, *Norman: An Early History*, 58–62.

managed to get a large majority of the voters to approve an $80,000 bond issue to extend the waterworks and install a modern sewer system. Twelve miles of sanitary sewers and five new miles of water mains were under construction as A. Grant Evans came to town. (When the project was completed, one observer noted, "Norman will be one of the best watered and sewered cities in the state, which should add materially to its already very healthy atmosphere."[5]) City engineers outlined plans for paving another five miles of the city's street system.[6] Sidewalks were another large concern. Norman boasted about fourteen miles of "first-class brick and cement sidewalks," but the Post Office could not start free home delivery until more were built and the houses were numbered, which would require a few more years to accomplish.[7]

The largest businesses in town reflected Norman's chief economic preoccupation: the collection, processing, and distribution of the agricultural produce of the surrounding countryside. In the year from July 1906 to July 1907, the town shipped out 217 railroad cars of corn, 54 of wheat and oats, 68 of hogs, 64 of flour and other milled goods, and more than 100 cars of cottonseed meal and cottonseed oil.[8] The town had two grain elevators and a flour mill, a cotton gin, and the cottonseed-oil plant of the Norman Cotton Oil Company. There was talk of establishing a creamery that would process not only dairy products but truck commodities as well. It took six blacksmith shops to meet the needs of Norman residents and neighboring farmers. But there were also indications of a lessening dependence on agriculture and a branching out into consumer services. The town had three hotels, a laundry, an ice plant, and a real restaurant called the English Kitchen, established in 1902. In March 1908 three picture shows suddenly appeared in town, and the thrills of the silent screen began offering stiff competition to John Franing's 850-seat Seawell Opera House, which had been entertaining townspeople since the glittering evening in November 1902 when the Gordon-Shay Grand Opera Company opened the house with a rousing production of *Il Trovatore*.

The town also supported three lumberyards to supply the burgeoning home-building industry. Authors of the University's *Bulletin* were at pains to point out what a pleasant residential setting Norman had become: "Although, like other towns of Oklahoma, it was hastily built, the larger number of the first buildings have been torn down, and much of the crudity that inevitably attaches to a newly settled country has disappeared. Already it is one of the most home-like and attractive places of the state and is fast becoming a substantial town worthy of being the seat of the university of a great state."[9] The State Investment Company, capitalized at $25,000, was doing a brisk business in real-estate de-

---

5. James, "Norman, Home of State University," 22.

6. John Womack, ed., *The Annals of Cleveland County Oklahoma, 1889–1959*, 30; see also Speer, *Cleveland County*, 103.

7. James, "Norman, Home of State University," 22; Speer, *Cleveland County*, 103.

8. "Norman, Oklahoma," 44. The brochure, quoting "the railway agent," lists for the year sixteen carloads of apples, fifty-one of cattle, and nineteen of potatoes. It also claims the shipment of 14,000 bales of cotton.

9. *University Catalogue, 1908*, 21.

velopment, and Peters Avenue, north of Main Street, was emerging as the "silk stocking" neighborhood.

Norman had a high school and two common schools, and it was a point of pride that all three buildings were brick. The voters easily approved a $40,000 bond issue in December to improve them and six months later added another $10,000 for good measure. The schools served 1,400 students. At the start of the 1909 school year, the common schools' names were changed from East Side and West Side to Jefferson and Washington. A Roman Catholic and ten Protestant churches catered to the city's spiritual requirements. Norman "boasts of having a greater percentage of its population affiliated with its churches than any city in the state and especially is the morality of the city equal to or superior to any in the state, just the kind of a city that should be the home of the State University of Oklahoma and the home of those with families to rear."[10] The town's chief jewel and most jealously guarded possession, of course, was the University.

～

AT THE CLOSE OF THE SCHOOL YEAR, June 11, 1908, the University claimed 743 students. In contrast to the first days of the University, when women accounted for half of the student body, they now comprised less than a third (499 men and 244 women). The Preparatory Department still numbered 251 students, around 34 percent of the whole. The remaining students were predominantly enrolled in the School of Fine Arts (203), the College of Arts and Sciences (194), the School of Applied Science (53), and Pharmacy (51). There were only three graduate students on the campus.[11] Compared to other state universities in the region, Oklahoma was among the smallest in the number of its students: Texas (with 2,462), Kansas (2,250), Arkansas (1,800), Missouri (2,536), Iowa (2,315), Iowa State (2,383), and Nebraska (3,237) were way ahead. It must be remembered, however, that all of these schools had been in business much longer than the University of Oklahoma. Among the state universities that were roughly as old (institutions that were themselves frontier outposts of frontier states), the University of Oklahoma compared favorably: Arizona (with 237 students), Idaho (400), Montana (177), Nevada (276), New Mexico (158), and Wyoming (243) lagged well behind.[12]

What might a new student, strolling down University Boulevard to the campus in

10. The quotation is from James, "Norman, Home of State University," 26. The details of Norman's business, educational, and religious institutions can be found in ibid.; Speer, *Cleveland County*, 103; Womack, *Annals of Cleveland County*, 30–32. There are numerous photographs in the brochure "Norman, Oklahoma."

11. These figures come from a report given to President Evans by Frank E. Knowles, registrar (undated, but probably October 1909), A. Grant Evans Presidential MSS, Box 11, Folder 8. The discrepancy in numbers is caused by some students being "double-counted."

12. These figures, some of which are approximate, can be found in "Statistics Regarding State Universities," compiled by the National Association of State Universities; the report compares enrollment and many other aspects (capital investment, numbers of faculty, volumes in the library, student-teacher ratio, etc.) of forty-eight state universities for both 1906–1907 and 1907–1908 . A copy can be found in Evans Presidential MSS, Box 11, Folder 9.

September 1908, have seen? The school's grounds consisted of sixty acres.[13] The trees that President Boyd had planted, mostly elm and ash, had grown admirably; and the *University Catalogue* bragged that they "were now of a size to make the campus with its approach [down University Boulevard], one of the most attractive spots in Oklahoma." The student could have counted eight buildings on the campus, but only two of them were respectable brick edifices.

The other six were frame structures that had been thrown up in the aftermath of the fire of 1903 or built between then and the autumn of 1908. The gymnasium, on the east side of the campus, consisted of a large exercise floor (3,200 square feet), six smaller rooms, a shower, and a locker room that could handle five hundred students. During the 1908–1909 academic year, it was to be expanded (from 5,500 to 10,000 square feet). On the west side still stood the two frame buildings hastily erected in 1903 to house the engineering laboratories and shops. The anatomical laboratory, just to the west of the engineering buildings, consisted of a dissecting room, a class room, and a small library; farther to the west was a tiny building used for taxidermy and preparing museum materials. Finally, there was the heating plant that provided steam heat to all the other buildings.

The freshman's eye would naturally have been drawn to the two substantial structures facing each other across the grass. On the west side, a little to the north of the engineering and anatomical buildings, stood Science Hall. Since its opening in September 1904, the basement had been dedicated to chemistry and pharmacy, the first floor to the biological sciences, and the second floor to geology and the small museum. But, as we have seen, the fire the preceding December required crowding new classrooms, other departments, and the University's administrative offices into the structure. On the campus's east side, opposite Science Hall, stood the gray brick Carnegie Library, which had opened in January 1905. As school ended in May 1908, the library boasted a collection of 11,910 books.[14] It too had been affected by the fire, the principal change being the conversion into classrooms of the women's gymnasium that had once occupied the basement.

Perhaps the most notable feature of the landscape, however, was the glaring gap where University Hall had once proudly presided over the deepest point of the campus, between and a little to the south of the two brick structures. The charred rubble could still be seen, a depressing reminder of the University's second great fire. In addition to all of its other results, that fire, by necessity, caused some serious thought to be given to the shape and architectural appearance of the campus. And ironically, the most concerted, dedicated, and creative thought about the ultimate look of the University of Oklahoma was undertaken by two men who, quite mistakenly, thought that their own future careers would be spent there: Vernon Parrington and David Ross Boyd.

---

13. The federal government had also bestowed on the University the full Section 36 (640 acres) of the township. This section was about a mile west of the campus and was valued at around $40,000. The University planned to sell off the land to buy additional acreage adjoining the campus. *University Catalogue, 1908,* 22.

14. *University Umpire,* May 26, 1908, 1.

Parrington had a deep and passionate interest in architecture and landscaping; and at this period of his life he studied these subjects almost as assiduously as he studied literature.[15] Indeed, immediately after the first fire of 1903, he sat down and sketched a plan for the future layout of the campus.[16] The second fire of 1907 set Parrington to work again. This time the product was an impressive twenty-four-page letter to the Regents dated April 25, 1908, bearing the title "On Recent Developments in American College Architecture." He came right to the point:

> Gentlemen:
>
> The late burning of University Hall has brought before the Regents for solution a problem of first importance in its bearing upon the architectural development of our University. Not only must University Hall be rebuilt, but other halls must follow shortly, so that within the next ten years the physical appearance of the University will be fixed in its main features. . . . I have taken the liberty, therefore, to put into convenient form certain facts that I have gathered during the past few years bearing upon the subject of recent developments in college architecture in the United States.[17]

There were two pressing problems, Parrington told the Regents: "1. The preparation of a campus plan according to which the different buildings may be grouped effectively. 2. The selection of a style according to which the several buildings shall be designed."

Parrington then presented the results of his intensive study of the campus plans of twenty-five other universities.[18] As far as the first large question—campus layout—was concerned, Parrington contrasted two principal forms: some universities were planned around an open court surrounded on three sides by widely spaced buildings, walkways, and extensive landscaping; others were developed around closed quadrangles. Parrington made a strong plea for the quadrangles: four-sided groupings of buildings by function, compactly designed, with the quadrangles carefully placed in relation to one another. He suggested that the Regents stretch their imaginations to envision a campus that would someday accommodate 5,000 students and be divided into nine building-groups (Science, Fine Arts, Arts and Sciences, Law, Medicine, and so on).[19] He pointed to the recent move toward the quadrangle system at Stanford, the University of Chicago, Washington University in

15. Some of that passion could be seen in Parrington's meticulous and detailed work in building his own home in Norman. See Hall, *V. L. Parrington*, 123–24.

16. Parrington's 1903 sketch of the future campus is reproduced in University of Oklahoma Center of Urban and Regional Studies, *The University of Oklahoma and Environs: The Physical Development Plan for the University of Oklahoma, 1965–1985*, 12; and also in Sorrels, "Eight Early Buildings," 48. It suggested extending University Boulevard south past Boyd Street to what is today Felgar Street. The boulevard would then divide and rejoin, forming an oval, with the main building centered at the foot of the grass oval (which was done). It also envisioned a drive circling the campus (made by extending Asp Avenue southward and looping it westward behind the main building). Parrington's plan for this part of the campus makes it especially fitting that today the area is named the Parrington Oval.

17. Parrington's long letter to the Regents can be found in Vertical File: "Architecture of O.U." It is reprinted as "Appendix F" in Sorrels, "Eight Early Buildings," 109–32.

18. Parrington (ibid.) lists them on page 3 of his letter. Two-thirds of them were state schools.

19. Ibid., 8.

St. Louis, and numerous other institutions of higher education. To Parrington, making a university on the old-fashioned basis of widely scattered buildings was "clearly an archaism," the work of an architect "who is either not familiar with the best practice of the day or who is primarily a landscape gardener trained in developing city parks."[20]

When it came to the second decision that the Regents had to face—determining the artistic style of campus buildings—Parrington was no less outspoken. Until recently, he complained, few college administrators had given much thought to collegiate architecture: "Each building as it was provided for was left to the taste or fancy of the architect, who in most cases had no clear notions of what would adapt itself to collegiate needs or would be in keeping with university traditions." The sad result of this practice was that "the grounds of well nigh every one of our older universities are covered with a clutter of buildings in no order, most of which not only have no architectural distinction but too often are an offense to good taste."[21] Just as Parrington contrasted two forms of campus layout (the "open court" and the "quadrangle") and made a strong case for the latter, he contrasted two styles of campus architecture: the "classical" and the "gothic." He told the Regents that "between these two . . . our choice must be made."[22] After systematically reviewing the advantages and disadvantages of each of the forms, he made a strong plea for the gothic: it had long academic traditions, flexibility, economic practicality (no need for useless pillars, domes, and other costly appendages), and it had been endorsed by the most advanced college planners and architects in America. In addition, it lent itself most readily to the quadrangle form of campus planning.[23]

Because he felt matters of taste and beauty so fiercely (in both literature and architecture), Parrington could not close his letter to the Regents without adding a few additional thoughts. They were typical of Parrington in their passion and eloquence:

> Personally I feel that we talk too much about a big university and too little about a beautiful university. To prefer the utilitarian and to assume that the utilitarian must necessarily be ugly, and conversely that the beautiful is useless and therefore effeminate, is one of our national heresies. Nevertheless so strong is this belief that even the gentle art of scholarship is in danger of becoming ugly and material and the home in which this scholarship must live is fast becoming a combination of barrack and factory. . . . If we hope to educate cultivated men and women we shall do well to surround them with those things which will inspire a wish for culture. I hold that it is a social crime, graver still because committed against youth, for any state to educate its young men and women amidst surroundings that are ugly, or shoddy, or pretentious. If there is any spot that should be made homely and honest and beautiful, it is a school, and it is

---

20. Ibid., 5.

21. Ibid., 10.

22. For Parrington, "classical" ranged "from pure neo-classic to Italian, French or English Renaissance" and "gothic" meant "some form of the collegiate gothic—ranging from mediaeval to Jacobean." Ibid., 18–19.

23. Parrington (ibid.) argued that if the Regents wished to emulate any single University's architecture, they would be well advised to study the work done at Washington University in St. Louis.

a short sighted view, that only the American people are guilty of, that looks wholly at the utilitarian side and deliberately chooses the ugly and the shoddy. . . . For my part I feel this contrast keenly and it is with the earnest hope that the Board of Regents will recognize the imperative need of giving to our university a fitting architectural dress, that shall be at once homely, honest and beautiful, that I have put together this hasty report.

> Respectfully submitted,
> V. L. Parrington
> Professor of English Literature[24]

Of course, by the time it was necessary to act on these recommendations, the foolish men to whom they were addressed had chosen to fire the brilliant man who made them.

If Parrington's suggestions for the future of the campus were based (fittingly for him) on philosophic and aesthetic considerations, the suggestions of President Boyd (fittingly for him) were based on practical experience and direct observation. The Regents appointed a three-man committee (Rowsey, Linebaugh, and Hickam) to make a tour of college and university campuses for the purpose of studying their architecture and talking to their architects. Linebaugh and Hickam backed out, and the Regents authorized President Boyd, who still imagined that he had a future at the University, to accompany the Board's secretary, W. E. Rowsey. On May 9 Boyd and Rowsey embarked on their extensive trip to the north and east to examine the buildings at twelve colleges and universities. Their travels took them from Minnesota, Wisconsin, and Chicago to New York, Pennsylvania, and Virginia. A month after Parrington's letter to the Regents, the two returned to Norman and reported their findings to the Board.[25] Three weeks later, of course, Boyd was looking for other work.

Coming to some decisions about these various proposals and observations suddenly gained urgency when, in late May 1908 (during the very week when Boyd and Rowsey returned from their tour), the state legislature passed a very handsome appropriation of $132,500. This sum was to be added to the insurance money of $67,500 to erect a new building to be valued at $200,000. The citizens of Norman were deliriously happy, not only because the huge new construction project would add to the town's bustling prosperity but also because the appropriation was an absolutely conclusive pledge on the part of the state that the University of Oklahoma would remain in Norman forever. Indeed, the new money rather quickly led the *Transcript* to forget about the injustice being done to Boyd and the other members of the faculty.[26]

24. Ibid., 23–24. A month later, on May 29, 1908, the *Umpire* printed a harsh denunciation of the destroyed University Hall and a plea for a better result in the new building that was to replace it. The article bears the influence of Professor Parrington ("Let us have something that age will beautify and not cripple. Let us have a building made from honest material, honestly put together"), but it was probably written by a student.

25. *University Umpire*, May 29, 1908, 1. Part of the Boyd-Rowsey report, including a list of the places they visited, can be found in the A. Grant Evans Presidential MSS, Box 11, Folder 8.

26. *Norman Transcript*, May 28, 1908.

~

INTO THIS BUSILY GROWING TOWN, onto this busily growing campus, came Arthur Grant Evans. He took over his new responsibilities on July 1, 1908, and held his office until May 22, 1911, five weeks less than three full years. The most astute short summary of him and his brief administration was left by Roy Gittinger, the young man whose job Evans had saved on the last day of summer school in 1908. "He was," Gittinger judged, "a kindly, earnest, and religious man. He was not fitted to be a University president, and he perhaps realized this. . . . All in all, the three years that President Evans spent in Norman were not very happy ones for him."[27]

Evans was primarily a man of the cloth, and he possessed in abundance those qualities that made for a successful ministry: gentleness, a concern for individuals, generosity of spirit, and humility. As soon as he left Norman in 1911, he returned gladly to the church, first as a missionary to the Indians for five years and then as pastor to a Presbyterian church in Santa Barbara, California, until his death in 1928. All university presidents must give deference to their Boards of Regents: it is the price paid for holding onto the position. Some presidents, however, find ways to assert varying measures of independence and leadership. Evans gave the impression of being little more than a conduit for the wishes and commands of the Board of Regents. In part this was due to the unusually overbearing nature of this particular group of Regents; they had made it abundantly clear from the moment Governor Haskell appointed them that they were in charge. Both the "corpses" of the fallen strewn about the campus and the flood of newcomers appointed to their positions without the slightest pretense of consultation with the new president were convincing evidence that the relationship between the Regents and the president had changed and that these Regents meant business. However, Evans's deference was also in part the product of his peculiar character.

On one point the desires of the Regents and the president were in perfect accord. Both were deeply anxious about the moral tone of the campus, among the students and the faculty alike. The Regents manifested their determination to safeguard the morals of the women at the University by their creation of the post of dean of women and their appointment of Lucile Dora to fill it. At their meeting of April 3, 1909, they turned their attention to the morals of the faculty. Proclaiming that the University "should be conducted in a way that the humblest citizen cannot justly criticize it or any member of the faculty," the Regents passed an extraordinary resolution: "Whereas, a goodly number of our citizens very seriously object to members of the faculty engaging in the public and indiscriminate dance and card parties; Therefore, be it resolved by the Board of Regents . . . that we request the members of the faculty of this University to refrain from these amusements during their connection with this University." Evans was directed by the Regents to send

27. Gittinger, "University Reorganizations of 1908 and 1911," 26–27.

a copy of the resolution to every faculty member; but in his accompanying letter he could not resist a few moralistic words of his own:

> May I add the expression of my own conviction that we cannot arrive at a satisfactory status in matters of this kind by merely avoiding conformity to the least intellectual and elevating amusements common in Society, but that it is one of the most important as well as delicate duties coming to us as members of the faculty of the University to help, by example and advice, in the development of forms of amusement which shall be really recreative and at the same time elevating both morally and intellectually.[28]

At some point in his presidency, Arthur Grant Evans penned a quite remarkable poem, which may give some insight into his personal perception of life as the chief executive of the University of Oklahoma:

> When labor's grim, relentless grip
> > Makes muscles ache and nerves recoil
> Lord! help us sing with quivering lip
> > "Thank God for toil! Thank God for toil!"

> When in the age-long strife with wrong
> > We stagger, bruised by brutal blows,
> Lord! help us raise our battle song
> > "Thank God for foes! Thank God for foes!"

> When health gives way to suffering
> > That chills the heart and numbs the brain
> Lord! help our trembling voices sing
> > "Thank God for pain! Thank God for pain!"

> When every path of memory
> > Some grave of dear dead joys must cross
> Lord! help our breaking hearts to cry
> > "Thank God for loss! Thank God for loss!"

> Let us but know we work Thy will
> > Through toil and strife, through pain and loss,
> Then shall we shout in triumph still
> > "Praise for the Cross! Praise for the Cross!"[29]

---

28. Regents' "Minutes," April 2–3, 1909, 3–4. Copies of the resolution can be found in the Evans Presidential MSS, Box 11, Folder 12; and in the James Shannon Buchanan MSS, Box 1, Folder 11. See also David W. Levy, "Combating the Image of 'Godlessness' in 1909," *Sooner Magazine* 16 (Spring 1996): 28–30.

29. The poem is undated but typed on University stationery sometime during the Evans administration (he is listed as president on the letterhead). It can be found in Arthur Grant Evans III, "Arthur Grant Evans, 1858–1928," a scrapbook made by a grandson and found in "Unprocessed Papers: Newspaper Clippings & Certificates," in the A. Grant Evans Presidential MSS, Box 1, Folder 1 (no pagination).

One hopes that this poem about how faithful Christians must thank God for the toil, enmity, pain, and loss that He sends their way gave its author some comfort as he endured his three years in Norman, years that were (as Roy Gittinger observed) "not very happy ones for him."

And yet, despite the heavy cost to him personally and the considerable restrictions on his freedom of action imposed by the Board of Regents, Evans's years as head of the University of Oklahoma deserve to be remembered for four substantial achievements.

~

THE ACCOMPLISHMENT that bears Evans's personal stamp most fully was the construction of the new building. From start to finish, President Evans was intimately involved in every detail of the process. At the beginning, the plan was not only to replace the burned University Hall but (as Parrington would have hoped) to consider as well the long-range architectural future of the campus. The architects were to be the firm of Shepley, Rutan & Coolidge, which was winning national renown for exciting work at the University of Chicago.[30] The whole autumn of 1908 was taken up by the preliminary arrangements. On October 31 Evans reported to Lee Cruce, president of the Board, that "we had a visit the first of this week from two members of the firm. . . . They went over the grounds here and think they have sufficient knowledge on them to prepare for submission to the Regents a general plan for the layout of the grounds as well as a sketch plan for the next building."[31] By December 5 the architects were ready to report their recommendations. In a long letter to Rowsey, secretary of the Board, they offered two plans for the campus layout, neither of which bore much relationship to the ultimate development of the north oval.

The architects also had some thoughts about how the buildings should look: "We have given the question of style considerable thought and believe . . . the Classic style is best suited, it being our idea to use a combination of brick and stone with the Classic somewhat Colonial in feeling. If Collegiate Gothic were to be followed, the general grouping arrangement of the buildings would necessarily be modified considerably, as such a style to be most successful, would require the buildings in each group to be closed or joined together, forming what would be termed a closed quadrangle." But a quadrangle would mean making four buildings at once, which was probably not within the range of the University's finances; and "this would mean the various buildings constructed from time to time with unfinished ends."[32]

Originally the new building was to house what Evans, somewhat vaguely, termed "the civic work of the University," which probably meant the traditional social sciences. The

30. The firm also had to its credit the layout of Stanford University and the Boston medical school buildings of Harvard University.

31. A. Grant Evans to Lee Cruce, October 31, 1908, Evans Presidential MSS, Box 1, Folder 2.

32. For the architects' initial recommendations about both layout and style, see William J. Clark to W. E. Rowsey, December 5, 1908, in ibid. William Jerome Clark was the architect assigned by the firm to the Oklahoma project.

institution's administrative offices would be placed there only temporarily, Evans hoped, and a building devoted entirely to administration would soon be erected closer to Boyd Street and the entrance to the campus.[33] Evans thought that the new building should be built on the site where the charred ruins of the old building still lay. But the Regents and some members of the legislature were apparently trying (unsuccessfully) to persuade Andrew Carnegie to donate a new and bigger central library; and Evans believed that perhaps *that* structure should dominate the foot of the oval. In that case, he suggested that the new building be placed at the very head of the oval, the entrance to the campus, with an open archway through its central tower leading to "the main plaza of the campus."[34] Back and forth went the negotiations. On December 9 Evans gently tried to break the news to the architects that, contrary to their recommendation, the Regents were leaning toward the gothic and away from the classic colonial. They were eager to see the plans for the new building, the president wrote, "but express very strongly the hope that you would let them see what your idea of the building will be in both the style which you suggest and something of the collegiate gothic."[35] Perhaps part of the letter that Vernon Parrington had written to them eighteen months earlier had stuck in the Regents' minds. In mid-December a contract was given to Shepley, Rutan & Coolidge, but the design of the building was still undecided. Finally, in February 1909, the wisdom of Solomon prevailed: the campus was to be laid out in the classic style of widely spaced individual buildings (no quadrangles), but the buildings were to be gothic.

President Evans threw himself into the most minute details of the new building. He visited Chicago to consult with the architects. He advised on electrical connections to Norman's power plant ("alternating current, single phase, 60 cycle, 104 volt, two wire system," he noted) and on plumbing ("one pipe separate water return into receiver pump . . . automatic air vents"). He helped to decide where the telephones should be located and how the furniture should look. He thought that the museum and the art gallery planned for the third floor should be switched and the gallery placed at the east end: "This would give for the art gallery much better light during the greater part of the day." He believed that for each of the classrooms on the first and second floors "there should be at least one wall covered with black boarding . . . and of course so arranged that the students facing it will have the light behind them and, if possible, on their left hand." The president had a suggestion for every floor, for every room, for every decorative feature of the exterior.[36] It was almost as if Evans knew from the outset that the building was eventually going to bear

33. Evans makes this clear in his speech at the laying of the cornerstone on November 16, 1909, almost a year after the contract had been negotiated. For his remarks on that occasion, see the Evans Presidential MSS, Box 11, Folder 12. By December 1909, however, the building was being called Administration Hall.

34. A. Grant Evans to William J. Clark, November 6, 1908, in ibid.

35. A. Grant Evans to William J. Clark, December 9, 1908, in ibid.

36. Evans's extensive correspondence about the building can be found in the Evans Presidential MSS, Box 1, Folders 2–8.

*The new administration building under construction, 1910*

his name. What he probably did not guess, however, was that before the edifice was ready for use he would be out doing missionary work among the Indians.

Actual work on the building was started on September 6, 1909, and the cornerstone was laid, with proper speeches and ceremonies, on November 16—a date chosen because it marked the second anniversary of statehood. In the end the building was to be an imposing and impressive achievement. By virtue of both its placement at the foot of the oval and its stately appearance it quickly became the chief architectural signature and landmark of the campus. Facing north, it consisted of a basement and three stories, with a four-story entry tower at its center.[37] On each side of the tower were four bays and, at either end, a gable featuring ornate perpendicular windows. There were niches for statuary,[38] interlocking semicircular arches, and friezes; and centered on the frieze above the entranceway was a square bearing the seal of the state of Oklahoma (which Evans himself had played an important part in designing). The corners of the tower were turrets, embellished with gargoyles. The window design on the facade was repeated at the buildings east and west sides. In the words of one commentator, the building "seems to be an eclectic collection of stylistic elements ranging from the Early English of the Norman period through the Jacobean period."[39] When the contractor decided to raise the building three feet above ground level—effectively making the structure appear as a "visual stop" to the campus as one approached down University Boulevard—a terrace was constructed. Although it was a bald attempt to save a little money, there is a certain poignancy in the fact that this terrace was constructed of long white stones salvaged from the ruins of the destroyed building that had once occupied the very spot.[40]

37. For a technical description of the building, see Sorrels, "Eight Early Buildings," 65–68.

38. These niches remained empty for more than ninety years, until statues of presidents of the University were placed in them in the fall of 2001, at the direction of President David L. Boren.

39. Sorrels, "Eight Early Buildings," 68. The derisive term "Cherokee gothic," often applied to this and other buildings on the campus, is ascribed to the great American architect Frank Lloyd Wright, who visited the campus in the 1950s. Wright, of course, had little tolerance for historical architecture of any sort.

40. Ibid. Carolyn Sorrels gleaned this piece of information from a conversation with longtime secretary to the Board of Regents Barbara Tuttle. Some brick recovered from the burned building was also used in the interior of Evans Hall (see Evans to William J. Clark, May 2, 1909, Evans Presidential MSS, Box 1, Folder 4).

*Administration Hall completed*

THE SECOND DEVELOPMENT OF THE EVANS YEARS was an extensive (and per-haps overdue) administrative reorganization of the University's offerings. That process took place on several fronts. In the first place, it was high time to phase out the Preparatory Department. It had certainly served its purpose since 1892, when there were as yet no high schools in Oklahoma Territory that were able to provide students with a four-year education. But now there were fully seventy high schools recognized by the University as adequately preparing students for college work.[41] President Evans therefore recom-mended to the Regents that the first year of the Preparatory Department be discontinued after the end of the 1908–1909 school year and that the entire department be disbanded in June 1910.[42]

Just as important as the discontinuation of the Preparatory Department was President Evans's decision to reorganize the University's colleges and schools. In President Boyd's

41. These "affiliated" high schools are listed in the *University Catalogue, 1911,* 64.

42. Evans, "Report of the President of the University to the Regents, December 15, 1909," in Evans Presidential MSS, Box 11, Folder 8. The closing of the Preparatory Department helps to account for what appear to be stagnant enrollment figures. The number of students actually declined in the first year of Evans's administration, from 790 to 696. But the figure of 692 for the next year (1909–10) hides the fact that the first year of the Preparatory Department, usually accounting for around a hundred new students, was gone. Thus although total enrollment remained virtually the same, the figure indicates a rapidly increasing college-level enrollment.

last year, there had been one "college" (Arts and Sciences) and five "schools" (Applied Science, Pharmacy, Medicine, Mines, and Fine Arts). By the time Evans had completed his rearrangement, the University of Oklahoma was to consist of (1) a Graduate School; (2) a College of Arts and Sciences, including a brand new "School of Teaching"; (3) a School of Fine Arts; (4) a School of Medicine; (5) a School of Pharmacy; and (6) a College of Engineering that consisted of schools of Chemical, Civil, Electrical, and Mechanical Engineering and a School of Mining Geology.[43]

These administrative bodies needed deans, a position hitherto unknown at the University of Oklahoma.[44] In the spring of 1909 the University suddenly acquired a full complement of them. The choice for dean of the Graduate School narrowed between two men, Albert Van Vleet and Edwin DeBarr. The appointment finally went to Van Vleet; but to soothe any ill feelings, Professor DeBarr (now the longest-serving professor at the institution) was named to the honorary title of vice president of the University. The College of Arts and Sciences, which, except for the addition of the School of Teaching, remained largely the same,[45] was to be headed by the popular history teacher James Shannon Buchanan. The other deans were the logical choices: James H. Felgar was to be the dean of engineering; Fredrik Holmberg, the head of the School of Fine Arts for the past year, was now its dean; Charles S. Bobo was the new dean of medicine; and Professor Homer C. Washburn, whom Boyd had made head of pharmacy in 1904, now assumed the deanship of that school.[46]

Along with the other administrative changes (and even before some of them were in place), President Evans announced the creation of a new entity to be called the Senate, which was to take the place of the general faculty. Its first meeting occurred on April 19, 1909. The Senate was to consist of the president and vice president, the various deans, and representatives of eight subject-matter groups within the College of Arts and Sciences.[47] The body was to discuss and make recommendations on matters that affected the entire University or that touched more than one of the colleges or schools.

These changes were long lasting and important. The Senate retained its exalted position until it was replaced by a Faculty Senate in a dramatic, almost revolutionary change more than three decades later. Naturally, there would be additions to and further rearrangements among the schools and colleges in the years ahead, as new fields emerged and were institutionalized into new academic units. But it would be hard to overestimate

43. For the administrative arrangement in Boyd's last year, see *University Catalogue, 1908*, 18–19; for Evans's scheme, see *University Catalogue, 1911–1912*, 18–19.

44. An exception was the appointment of Roy Philson Stoops (the "head" of the School of Medicine) to "acting dean" in 1907, to conform to the requirements of the Association of American Medical Colleges. See the clear discussion in Everett, *Medical Education in Oklahoma*, 15–16.

45. For the new School of Teaching, see Evans, "Report, 1909."

46. Gittinger, *University of Oklahoma*, 59. For the career of Homer Washburn, who remained in his position until 1912, see Tate, *Centennial*, 18–19.

47. Gittinger, *University of Oklahoma*, 60.

the effects of the continuity provided by the long-serving deans that Evans appointed: Van Vleet, Buchanan, Holmberg, and Felgar would control the policies and programs of their administrative units for many years beyond 1909.

Just as important as the administrative juggling carried out by President Evans and the Regents were developments in two professional disciplines of enormous importance to the future of the University. These years saw both a significant change in the teaching of medicine and the inauguration of serious study in the field of law.

~

THE THIRD CRUCIAL DEVELOPMENT during the presidency of Evans was the establishment of the medical school in Oklahoma City. We have seen how medical education at the University began with Van Vleet's creation of the Department of Biology in 1898 and how the institution developed both a four-year bachelor of science program and a two-year, strictly professional course (both of which were designed to prepare students to enter first-class medical schools anywhere in the nation). We have also seen how two heads of the University's premedical course, Lawrence N. Upjohn (1900–1904) and Roy Philson Stoops (1904–1908), resisted the wishes of Oklahoma City physicians for a four-year medical school located in their city and how they were supported by President Boyd. Although there were ten faculty members and fifteen students in the School of Medicine by the time Boyd left office, medical education in the state of Oklahoma was centered not at the University in Norman but in the Epworth Medical College. That school had been started in 1904, had already produced more than a dozen physicians by 1910, and had a current enrollment of nearly fifty students.[48] The situation in Norman was summarized in the Regents' report to Governor Haskell in the fall of 1908: "We are able to insure students that they will be received into any of the medical schools of the Association of American Medical Colleges so as to carry on their work from the point to which we take them here. We must, however, look forward to the time before long when the state of Oklahoma shall offer its own people the opportunity for a complete and thorough medical training."[49]

The way was made easier by some obvious weaknesses in the medical education being provided by Epworth. The entire faculty there consisted of Oklahoma City physicians, none of whom was actually paid for teaching. The "teaching hospital" being used had thirty or forty beds, and the school's laboratory facilities were meager and disorganized. The American Medical Association's Council on Medical Education had rated Epworth as "unacceptable" since 1907, and Epworth retained that damaging rating until it finally shut down. Finally, the opportunity for the University of Oklahoma to open a medical school in Oklahoma City was measurably aided by the findings of the famous "Flexner Report."[50]

48. Everett, *Medical Education in Oklahoma*, chaps. 1 and 2.

49. Quoted in ibid., 31.

50. Named for its author, Abraham Flexner, the historic *Medical Education in the United States and Canada* was commissioned by the Carnegie Foundation and published in 1910.

That respected and influential survey of American medical education criticized Epworth sharply and then went on to say that "it would be advisable for the State University of Oklahoma to engage in clinical work in Oklahoma City. Oklahoma may from Norman govern a medical school in Oklahoma City." The historian of the University's medical school, Mark R. Everett, has written that Flexner's findings "exerted a profound influence upon medical education throughout the country. In Oklahoma the *Flexner Report* marked the end of the ten-year span of attempts by physicians to establish proprietary schools of medicine in the state."[51]

In early 1910, all signs being favorable, negotiations were undertaken between the doctors and stockholders of the Epworth College of Medicine and the Regents of the University of Oklahoma. On March 8 the president of Epworth's Board of Directors came to the Regents' meeting to discuss the situation.[52] Evans informed the Board that "overtures have been made during . . . the last few weeks by the Epworth College of Medicine for us to arrange some method by which we could take over their work, receiving such first and second year students as they can send to us here, and making provision for the work of the third and fourth years in Oklahoma City where they can have the hospital and clinical advantages necessary for this work."[53] The Epworth students promptly took to the streets of Oklahoma City, "armed with megaphones, bedecked with ribbons, flying pennants, and a complement of yells guaranteed to raise the dead." They were eager "to express their hearty endorsement of the proposed plan to amalgamate the medical schools of Epworth and Oklahoma University into one strong institution. . . . After completely subduing the business districts, the celebrating students boarded street cars and went for the conquest of the residence portions of the city fastening their banners to the backs of cars, and hanging from the windows."[54]

At their next meeting, after listening to the recommendation of a committee, the Regents authorized the deal. The minutes of that meeting list more than forty members of a medical faculty, the majority of them being private Oklahoma City physicians who agreed to participate in the arrangement.[55] The University would continue to offer the first two years of medical training on the Norman campus, and students would take the last two years of clinical preparation in Oklahoma City under the auspices of the University of Oklahoma. On May 5, 1910, the Epworth College of Medicine closed its doors forever.[56] During the summer, the new dean, Charles Bobo, moved his office from Norman to the Oklahoma City facilities at Northwest 10th and Lee Streets. And on August 28

51. Everett, *Medical Education in Oklahoma*, 43.

52. Regents' "Minutes," March 8, 1910.

53. Quoted in Everett, *Medical Education in Oklahoma*, 45–46.

54. Cited by Everett in ibid., 48, as *Daily Oklahoman*, March 9, 1910.

55. Regents' "Minutes," April 13, 1910.

56. Everett, *Medical Education in Oklahoma*, 42–43, 49.

President Evans dedicated the building with an appropriate address. More than sixty students enrolled during the first year. Thus began an illustrious new chapter in the University's history.

∽

ALTHOUGH THE CHANGES IN MEDICAL EDUCATION at the University were momentous, they had, after all, evolved out of a history of instruction in that realm that stretched back over more than a decade. This was not the case for the study of law. The creation of that field—the fourth great development during the brief time when Evans was president—took place with almost no preparation. As in the case of the introduction of medicine into the curriculum (and of pharmacy before that), however, the University introduced legal studies in response to strong pressure from the state's professional practitioners. Oklahoma's lawyers, like those in every part of the country, were eager to formalize and specialize professional training, award proper credentials, and discourage the entrance into their guild of untrained and inferior attorneys.[57]

On April 3, 1909, a full year before the medical merger with Epworth, the Board of Regents responded to the pressure and authorized the creation of the School of Law, promising to begin instruction in that field in September. The work of preparing the ground was to be assigned to a brand new dean; and a two-man committee of the Board of Regents was assigned the task of finding the right man. That committee (composed of Regent Lee Cruce and Regent J. D. Lydick, a Shawnee attorney) amicably invited a three-man committee of the Oklahoma Bar Association to participate in the search process. Given the pressing needs he saw all around him, President Evans probably secretly opposed the creation of a law school; at best he was lukewarm to the whole notion. But his views were brushed aside, and he was quite effectively marginalized in the search for a dean. Indifferent to the views of the president, the search committee sent notices of the opening in Oklahoma; and one of them came to the attention of the legendary dean of the Harvard Law School, James Barr Ames. Dean Ames wasted no time in recommending for the position a very unusual recent graduate of the Harvard Law School who was completing his first year as a law professor at George Washington University in Washington, D.C.

On August 6 Lee Cruce wrote a letter to the professor: "I have been appointed chairman of a committee to select a dean for the Law School of the University of Oklahoma. This school is just being organized and has neither a dean nor a faculty. We are anxious to secure the very best man possible, and you have been highly recommended." Cruce explained that the Regents had set aside $7,000 for the first year and that the new dean would get "no less than $3,500" of it, with the rest going for "the teaching force." He

57. This was a pattern that characterized many of the professions during this period. On the general phenomenon and its relation to colleges and universities, see Burton J. Bledstein, *The Culture of Professionalism: The Middle Class and the Development of Higher Education in America.*

pointed out that young men were already bombarding the University with their applications to enter the program in September (only five weeks away!). "The field for a good law school is exceptional," Cruce declared, "and the time ripe for the establishment of a first class school. . . . If interested, please reply by return mail, saying you can come for a personal interview and see for yourself the opportunity we offer."[58]

When Julien Charles Monnet opened that letter, he was forty years old and could already look back on a rather curious and interesting career.[59] He was born in 1868 in a small town in southeastern Iowa, the son of French immigrants. Possessed from his earliest days by a passion for study, he worked his way through the University of Iowa, developing even as an undergraduate considerable skill in public speaking, an enthusiasm for local Republican politics, and a love of amateur tennis—a sport he played at championship levels for many years. Out of necessity Monnet learned rigorous frugality; even with several campus jobs, he had to drop out of school after his sophomore year to earn enough money to continue. And out of fervent intellectual curiosity he developed considerable powers of scholarly self-discipline. Even before completing his B.A. requirements, Monnet entered Iowa's School of Law, graduating in June 1893. Within a month he was practicing in Bathgate, a remote town in the new state of North Dakota; within a year he had married a college sweetheart and was well on the way to a life as a highly successful lawyer. A reputation for integrity and shrewdness, together with some astute investments in North Dakota real estate, earned him a more than comfortable livelihood.

After nearly a dozen years of practice, however, Julien Monnet grew discontented and restless. This was due in part to the nearly unbearable climate in North Dakota. It also resulted in part from a series of health problems exacerbated, he believed, by the long hours and constant stress of being a horse-and-buggy lawyer. But mostly, it appears, Monnet's uneasiness sprang from growing doubts about whether he was using his abilities in the best possible way—doubts about whether continuing to devote himself to the steady accumulation of ever more money was, in the end, going to constitute a satisfying and worthy life. He poured out his dissatisfaction to a Congregational minister back in Iowa. Although his own letter has been lost, the minister's reply indicates the crisis that Monnet was going through. "I received your poignant letter two weeks ago," the minister answered. "In general, your question is: How can I make my life more fruitful? How can I utilize my talents for the greater good?" After tentatively suggesting that Monnet use his abilities and his money "in the missionary field," his counselor offered a second suggestion. "[T]here are colleges and universities crying for just such talent as you possess in abundance. Why not

58. Lee Cruce to Julien C. Monnet, August 6, 1909, quoted in McKown, *The Dean*, 128.

59. The story of Monnet's life is engagingly and affectionately told by McKown in ibid. Uncited material in the following paragraphs is derived from that source. McKown was the son-in-law of Julien Monnet. See also Howard Cotner, "Substantial Growth of O.U. Law School Outmatched Only by Its National Standing," *Sooner Magazine* 19 (January 1947): 12–13, 28; and "President Cross Salutes . . . ," *Sooner Magazine* 19 (June 1947): 8.

teach? Financially, you are independent and can easily afford to accept the small salaries commonly paid professors."[60]

In the spring of 1904 Julien Monnet left behind both North Dakota and the daily grind of the law office. He returned to Iowa with his growing family (he and his wife had three children by this time) and enrolled again at the University of Iowa. He finished his M.A. degree in a year, and then in the autumn of 1905, nearly thirty-seven years of age, he entered the Harvard Law School. He had come with the intention of preparing himself to teach law. The other students, noting his nearly total baldness and his family, called him "Pop." Monnet had teaching offers at the end of his second year in Cambridge but decided to stay for the full three years. He made an impressive record at Harvard, was an editor of the *Harvard Law Review*, and graduated in the spring of 1908 near the top of his class. He took a job at George Washington; and after he indicated that he would be willing to stay there for a second year, the letter arrived from Regent Cruce.

Until the end of his life, Monnet swore that it was 114 degrees on August 17, 1909, the day he came to look over the ground in Norman prior to his interview in Oklahoma City the next day. He checked into the Agnes Hotel (which he thereafter referred to as the Agony Hotel), inspected the town and the campus, with the rubble of the burned building still dominating the landscape, and wrote his wife: "There is not enough money in the whole state to induce me to accept a position in Oklahoma!"[61] It was still sweltering when he returned to his second-floor hotel room with its single small window and its creaking fan. The next day he appeared for his interview before the Regents and the representatives of the Oklahoma Bar Association; President Evans was also in the room. The group looked over the wiry, diminutive candidate (five foot seven inches tall and 175 pounds in a tennis-champion's body), listened as he answered their questions, and decided they wanted him. They turned on their charm, bragged about the prospects of the state and the University and the law school, and acceded to his three principal demands. Like every other academic in the country, Monnet knew about the political slaughter that had occurred at the University of Oklahoma the year before; and he wanted assurances of complete political independence, including a pledge of noninterference in the hiring of professors. He also told the Regents that he would require a three-month vacation every summer. Finally, he insisted that his salary be fixed at $4,000. Despite the fact that this was equal to the salaries of both President Evans and Governor Haskell, the Regents agreed.[62] The salary might have been the beginning of the friction between Evans and Monnet, but there would soon be other causes as well.[63]

60. Quoted in McKown, *The Dean*, 102.

61. For Monnet's arrival in Norman, see ibid., 3–8. McKown, citing "inexplicable failure of the mails," reports that the letter to Monnet's wife never actually arrived. It is possible, of course, that no such letter was written and that Monnet made up the story later to indicate how unimpressed he was by his first sight of Oklahoma and its university.

62. Ibid., 129.

63. Gittinger, "University Reorganizations of 1908 and 1911," 42.

In any case, after brief consultation with friends and relatives, Monnet, on August 26, agreed to take the job. The president at George Washington University wrote: "I have your letter of resignation which is accepted with sincere regret. However, I congratulate you upon your appointment as dean at Oklahoma. It is a splendid opportunity for you."[64] Leaving his wife behind to pack up and ship the household goods, Julien Charles Monnet arrived in Norman on September 1, 1909, and rented a house on Asp Avenue, about four blocks from the campus. Although the *Umpire* misspelled the new dean's name, it was properly keen about the development: "The law school is now a reality," the paper announced, and "the Board of Regents has been extremely fortunate in securing J. C. Monnett. . . . Dr. Monnett is a native Iowan, a thorough-going westerner, a tennis champion, and is enthusiastic about prospects for a new law school. . . . Welcome, Dr. Monnett."[65] The dean had fifteen full days to make ready the "splendid opportunity" that awaited him.

He had some thorny problems to solve during those two weeks. The first was where to locate the school, and he began by firmly rejecting two obvious possible sites. Oklahoma City lawyers were eager, even insistent, that it be put in their city. They pointed out that the state capital would inevitably be moved there (as indeed it was in 1910) and that its presence would open valuable opportunities, experiences, and associations for fledgling law students. Others advised Monnet to rent a building in downtown Norman, at least for the time being, and to start the law school there. Monnet, however, was certain that the law school belonged in the midst of the campus and that the benefits to be derived from contact with other students, other faculty members, and other disciplines were invaluable and easily outweighed the disadvantages of cramped quarters. He prevailed, and the school opened on the third floor of Science Hall. Charles Gould readily agreed to condense the museum's holdings in order to make some room, and the new dean's desk was placed between two cabinets filled with mineral specimens.[66] A second decision to be made involved curriculum and staff. Probably while still negotiating with the Regents, Monnet had won agreement to his proposal: during the first year, only first-year instruction would be offered; during the second year, second-year courses would be added; and not until the third year would the full program be available. To teach these courses, Monnet proposed that one assistant be hired immediately, that a second be hired for the second year, and that two more professors be added during the third year, making a staff of five by the time the school was ready to offer its entire three-year program.[67]

Selecting that first assistant proved to be an epic struggle that would have been trying even if it did not have to be accomplished in two weeks. The saga also reveals a good deal about what academic life at the University of Oklahoma was like with a weak president

64. Charles W. Needham to Monnet, August 30, 1909, quoted in McKown, *The Dean*, 129–30.

65. *University Umpire*, September 17, 1909, 1.

66. McKown, *The Dean*, 162–64. After a year in the Science Hall, the School of Law was moved across the grass to the basement of the Carnegie Building.

67. Ibid., 162.

and a Board of Regents that was whimsical, domineering, and highly politicized. Monnet's first choice for an associate, a classmate from Harvard, declined the offer. The dean's second choice was approved by Regents Cruce and Lydick (all of Monnet's negotiations were with the Regents, not with President Evans). Frank H. Randall, a professor of law at Monnet's alma mater, the University of Iowa, agreed to come. "Accept your offer," Randall telegraphed on September 3. "Will start [for Norman] probably Monday, possibly on Tuesday." Monnet had offered $2,000, and both Cruce and Lydick congratulated him on his selection. On September 11 Monnet presented his nominee to the full Board, the newly arrived Randall spoke a few words, and the Board apparently approved. Over their lunch break, however, some of the Regents had second thoughts about the salary. When they reconvened,

*Dean Julien Charles Monnet in 1910*

Regent Rowsey moved that Randall's salary be fixed at $1,500 and that if Randall (who had moved all of his worldly goods to Norman the week before) refused to accept the reduced salary Dean Monnet was authorized to "search further for an acceptable assistant."[68] Classes were to begin in four days. Rather than accept a 25 percent reduction in the salary he had been promised, a furious Randall returned to Iowa and started a law practice. The episode must have been extremely humiliating to Monnet.[69]

Next the new dean turned to a law professor at the University of Illinois, Thomas W. Hughes. Monnet hastily contacted him, and Hughes quickly replied in an astonishing letter:

> Permit me to thank you for your kind letter. I certainly would be glad to join your faculty since there are several reasons why I want to move to Oklahoma. However, I doubt if your Board of Regents would permit you to employ me in view of my unfortunate experience when I was interviewed by Mr. Ledbetter.[70] He was the cause of the bitterest disappointment I have ever had. I had my heart set on the job you now hold. I felt I had it cinched. Everything went well until my visit with him. He inquired what my political affiliations were. Unthoughtfully and in complete innocence, I told him that nominally I was a Republican. I then and there committed a blunder of the first magnitude.

68. Ibid., 165–69; Regents' "Minutes," September 11, 1909, 1–2. McKown gives the name as "Randall"; the "Minutes," however, give it as "Randell."

69. McKown (*The Dean,* 169) writes: "It is lucky for the Board of Regents that only Professor Randall left—instead of Randall and Monnet together." After a long correspondence, the Board agreed to compensate Randall $75 for his trouble.

70. This was W. A. Ledbetter of Ardmore, one of the three lawyers from the Oklahoma Bar Association that served on the search committee for the deanship of the law school.

Mr. Ledbetter's zeal for the Democratic party was such that he grossly misjudged me. He frankly and openly expressed the fear that if I were elected dean, Republican principles would be instilled into the minds of the students, and that newspapers of the state would be filled with speeches and articles I might give or write. He said that Democrats had built up the institutions of the State and that they were entitled to fill the important jobs. I was dumbfounded. With him, merely mentioning the world "Republican" was my undoing. . . . For these reasons, I don't believe it wise for me to accept your kind offer.[71]

No doubt by this time Julien Monnet (himself a Republican since college days but discreet about it) must have wondered what he had gotten himself into.

By a stroke of good luck, the fourth choice turned out better than anyone could reasonably have expected. Regent Cruce mentioned in a letter that a young attorney from Alva had made a good impression on the search committee when he interviewed for the dean's position. The committee felt he was not seasoned enough for the deanship, but perhaps Monnet might want to interview him for the position of assistant professor. By this time school had started, and Monnet was doing all of the teaching single-handedly. The desperate dean agreed to hire the Alva attorney, John Begg Cheadle, for $1,500. Cheadle was six years younger than Monnet. He had been born in Ohio, earned both his undergraduate and law degrees from the University of Kansas, lived for a while on a ranch in southwestern Kansas, and located in Alva in 1902. Like Monnet, John Cheadle quickly proved himself an able teacher and a good scholar and, like Monnet, won the respect and admiration of generations of law students on the Norman campus.[72] The two men labored side by side for more than three decades. Monnet served as dean and professor of law until his retirement in 1941 and remained in Norman until his death ten years later; Cheadle taught until 1951 and stayed in town until his death in 1960.

The University's new law school had one serious competitor. Once again it was Epworth, the Methodist school in Oklahoma City. But whereas during the next year the medical programs at the two institutions would be effectively merged, in law the outcome was different. Epworth simply sent its students to Norman and went quietly out of business at the end of Dean Monnet's first year. He was able to strike an amiable arrangement with Epworth's (unpaid) dean, who was eager to liquidate the operation anyway.[73] The two men agreed that Epworth's first-year students would join the second-year students in Norman, being given full credit for their work in Oklahoma City. The second-year Epworth students were asked to come to the University and find courses they could profitably take

---

71. Thomas W. Hughes to Monnet, September 13, 1909, quoted in McKown, *The Dean*, 170.

72. For a brief summary of Cheadle's life and career, see Richard L. Disney, "They Gave 234 Years of Service," *Sooner Magazine* 23 (June–July 1951): 12. McKown prints numerous fond and touching tributes to both Monnet and Cheadle from individual students and student organizations in *The Dean*.

73. The "dean" at Epworth's law school was C. B. Ames, an Oklahoma City attorney. He had been one of those serving on the search committee as a representative of the Bar Association.

*John Begg Cheadle in 1910*

(as there were still no third-year courses available). And Epworth's third-year students were simply given University of Oklahoma degrees at the 1910 commencement, despite the fact that they had never taken formal instruction there.[74]

Other problems lay ahead for Dean Monnet and the School of Law: ensuring high academic standards, hiring first-rate faculty and attracting first-rate students, getting the legislature to appropriate funds for a building that might serve as a proper home. But for the time being things seemed to be going fairly well. The University had found a highly competent, efficient, and principled dean and a dedicated and talented associate for him. The School of Law enrolled forty-five students in the fall of 1909, and more came for the second semester. By the time the first class graduated in 1912, the law school had been accorded membership in the Association of American Law Schools, the faculty had been increased, and an elegant new building was underway. The study of law at the University of Oklahoma was off to a promising start.

~

THE DISMISSAL OF ARTHUR GRANT EVANS was quick, decisive, and political. The simplest explanation is that Evans rose by the grace of his friend Charles Haskell and promptly fell once Haskell left the governorship. And again, as was the case with the removal of David Ross Boyd three years earlier, the story is characterized by petty ambitions and sordid motives, by inflated and wounded egos, hidden relationships, and entire indifference to any notion of the autonomy of institutions of higher education. One site of bitter conflict was Norman, both in the town and on the campus.

In Norman the aftermath of the 1908 shakeup plagued President Evans, even though he was not always to blame. Because they were not up to their jobs, Evans had asked for the resignation of Mortimer Gardner (the man Nathaniel Linebaugh had selected to replace Cole as head of the Psychology Department) and George Jones (the one Linebaugh had chosen to replace Jansky in engineering). But Gardner and Jones were not merely Southern Methodists: they were both ordained Southern Methodist ministers. To members of the Norman church it must surely have seemed like the same old story: a Presbyterian (and in this case a clergyman himself) dumping those who chose to worship

74. There were six such students; see Gittinger, *University of Oklahoma*, 64.

in their congregation. The division of the curriculum into colleges and the appointment of deans also caused disappointments as well as applause. The president's perhaps too enthusiastic endorsement of the Regents' moralistic dicta about card-playing, dancing, and smoking must surely have irritated those members of the faculty who were less committed to that definition of morality or who simply thought that such private behavior was none of a Regent's or a president's business. Evans's decision to strip authority from the general faculty and to lodge it in his new University Senate, a body dominated by administrative officials, must have raised democratic suspicions and ire among rank-and-file members of the teaching staff. Finally, David Ross Boyd still had numerous friends and admirers in town and on the campus, and no doubt some of them were simply never able to forgive Evans for the way he had come into his position.

But the main source of Evans's campus troubles stemmed from the creation of the School of Law and the arrival of Julien Monnet. We have seen how Evans had opposed the addition of a law school and how the Regents, at the urging of the Oklahoma bar, blithely ignored their president's views. We have also seen how the new dean demanded both absolute administrative independence and a salary equal to the president's. It would be hard to guess which of these exactions annoyed Evans more. In addition, the dean went about hiring his associates without consulting the president, and it must have appeared to Evans that Monnet was creating a little kingdom of his own in a corner of the campus. Evans probably hoped to conclude a friendly sharing arrangement with Epworth (as in medicine with Dean Bobo's approval and cooperation); but Monnet was uncompromising in his insistence that, as far as legal studies were concerned, Epworth cease its work and send its students to Norman. The law dean's official dealings, moreover, were almost entirely with the Regents and especially with Lee Cruce, who had headed the search committee that had fallen head-over-heels for him and who, as the election of 1910 approached, was being prominently mentioned as a strong possibility for governor.

It would have been high wisdom—or at least high diplomacy—for President Evans to have avoided forcing the governor and the legislature (which contained its normal contingent of lawyers) to choose between himself and Dean Monnet. Nevertheless, that is exactly what he did. The critical issue was the appropriation for a law building. Very probably, Monnet had included the matter of decent quarters in his initial bargaining session with the Regents. Beginning in the fall of 1910, Dean Monnet, his students, and many members of the Oklahoma bar began their assault on the legislature for the money to erect a suitable structure to house the School of Law. Evans had earlier submitted a building program of his own, but a law building was not at the head of his list. "It soon became clear," wrote Roy Gittinger, "that Monnet's plan would win in the Legislature. Evans, instead of making the best of the inevitable, fought against the appropriation for the law building, either on principle, as his friends said, or from stubbornness, as others said. By the end of the Legislative session Evans and Monnet were bitter antagonists."[75]

75. Gittinger, "Reorganizations of 1908 and 1911," 43–44. See also McKown, *The Dean*, chaps. 14 to 17.

Although these developments in town and on the campus were one source of Evans's difficulties, they were not the principal one. University presidents, after all, do not get fired by professors, deans, or townspeople; they get fired by Regents. The intrigues, animosities, and friendships of these powerful men are not easy to follow in all their devious complexity, but it was because of these machinations and rivalries that Evans and others were abruptly dismissed during the spring of 1911. This is a complicated story. It is also one of those stories in which almost nobody appears to very good advantage.

It will be recalled that back in the autumn of 1908 Governor Haskell gave Lee Cruce, then the president of the Board of Regents, the unenviable task of answering Lyman Abbott's ferocious onslaught in the pages of the *Outlook*. Cruce did his best, of course, to defend what the governor and the Regents had done to Boyd and the others (although he himself had not been in favor of much of it). And as part of his defense, he emphasized that the two Republicans on the Board had been in complete accord with the purge. He did this, obviously, to fortify his contention that partisan politics had not entered into the matter: "You state that Dr. Boyd was removed because of his politics," Cruce had written in his response to Abbott. "A sufficient answer to this is that *both* of the Republican members of the Board voted for his successor."[76] The two Republican Regents, C. J. Pratt and J. P. Hickam, were embarrassed and quickly responded that they did what they did because of heavy pressure from Governor Haskell.[77] Now it was the governor's turn to be embarrassed; incensed at their allegations, he went after the two hapless Republicans. As Gittinger puts it, "someone must have hired detectives to look into Pratt's private life. Either they discovered something, or the poor man was framed, and he soon found himself facing a morals charge."[78] Rumors at the time held that Haskell marched over to the office of the secretary of state, asked to see the list of his appointments to the University's Board of Regents, and scrawled across Pratt's name the words "Removed from Office." Former Regent Pratt promptly vanished from Oklahoma City, and no one seemed to know where he had gone. Hickam was handled with a little less dramatic flair, but he also was removed or requested to resign. One Regent (A. J. Rittenhouse of Chandler) resigned because of ill health, and one vacancy had never been filled. Haskell therefore had four openings to fill, and he filled them all with loyal Democrats.[79]

76. Lee Cruce, "Shall the People Rule—in Oklahoma?: Reply from the Board of Regents," *Outlook* 90 (October 3, 1908): 249. In several other places in his published letter Cruce noted the full accord of the two Republican Regents with the actions of the Democratic majority.

77. Gittinger ("Reorganizations of 1908 and 1911," 39) thought that the governor did pressure the two Republicans on behalf of Evans, but that "it is not clear" that he used his influence regarding the fired faculty members. As has been shown, these two, like the other Regents, had their own reasons for voting to fire certain faculty members and replace them with friends.

78. Gittinger, "Reorganizations of 1908 and 1911," 39. No doubt this development caused some quiet snickering in Norman; Pratt, after all, had been one of the three-man "smelling committee" that the Regents had sent to investigate allegations of faculty immorality in the spring of 1908.

79. Ibid., 39–40.

Haskell could not succeed himself in office, however, and in 1910 Lee Cruce, as expected, resigned from the Board of Regents to campaign for the governorship. On the basis of his considerable oratorical skill and his impassioned promise to keep the state government firmly in the hands of white men, he edged out Alfalfa Bill Murray in the Democratic primary and won a substantial victory over his Republican opponent.[80] The battle-scarred former Regent was now in charge; and in his very first message to the legislature he proposed a new plan for governing Oklahoma higher education. Cruce told the lawmakers that he wanted a centralized State Board of Education to supervise all of the colleges and universities in the state. This Board would replace the various Boards of Regents that had hitherto governed the separate institutions; it would consist of seven members, six of whom were to be nominated by the governor and approved by the state senate. It would be headed by the state superintendent of public instruction, an official elected by the people. The legislature acceded to the governor's wishes.[81]

In Norman this development was greeted with mixed feelings. On the one hand, the University would now be governed by men whose attentions would inevitably be distracted and whose limited resources would inevitably be claimed by the other institutions of higher education. It was likely, moreover, that the new Board of Education would be made up at least in part of champions of these smaller schools, men who would harbor suspicions of the University's ambitions and occasionally act to thwart them. On the other hand, those connected with the University in Norman were already deeply worried about the sheer number of colleges and universities the legislature had created. By 1911, in addition to the three original colleges of 1891 and the African American college at Langston, the legislature had lightheartedly established no fewer than six normal schools, a women's college at Chickasha, a school of mines in Wilburton, two "preparatory universities" at Claremore and Tonkawa, and other institutions for the blind and the "feeble minded." If there was any hope of closing down any of these places, that hope rested in an overarching board rather than in a dozen local ones, each fiercely defending its own little school.

Three weeks after the new State Board of Education was appointed, the *Norman Transcript* wrote one of its typical editorializing news stories: "The powers possessed by the state board of education and the well known opposition of some of the members to the multiplicity of state schools and duplication of courses of study has brought members of the legislature who have institutions in their districts to Oklahoma City until a view of

80. Smith, "Lee Cruce, 1911–1915," 52–53. Murray was as committed a racist as Cruce but had balked at placing Jim Crow provisions in the state constitution (in order to get it past the Republican administration in Washington), and Cruce made the most of that fact in the Democratic primary.

81. A "State Board of Education" already existed. It was the body that had tried to fire Boyd in the spring of 1908 but had been taken to the Supreme Court by the Regents in order to assert their own right to fire him. The board that Cruce proposed early in 1911 was vastly different. It would take over the governance duties of all the institutions of higher education except the agricultural schools (because their governance provisions were provided for in the Oklahoma constitution). The new board also assumed the duties of the State Textbook Commission. See Thoburn and Wright, *Oklahoma: A History of the State*, 2:650; and Litton, *History of Oklahoma*, 1:535.

the hotel lobbies gives the appearance of a legislative session." Nevertheless, the *Transcript* decided to be hopeful. "That the board will take steps that will result at least in the abolition of some of the small educational institutions is the opinion of many. It has been conceded generally of late by every one but the legislature that the state has too many such institutions, so many that the state can never build up a great university or a great central normal."[82]

Governor Cruce appointed the members of the new State Board of Education on April 8, 1911. Less than one week later they met for three days and required the heads of all the institutions they ruled to appear before them to give reports about conditions at their colleges.[83] No doubt the Board members were looking over these nervous men and quietly making their appraisals. Two weeks later they gathered again in Oklahoma City for a remarkable three-day meeting. On April 27 it was moved and seconded "that the Board proceed tomorrow with the election of the heads of the several institutions under its jurisdiction, beginning with the President of the University."[84] The next morning the Board agreed to vote on each president, phrasing the question: "Shall the present incumbent be retained?" There was a spirited discussion of whether the votes should be open or secret, and secret balloting was chosen by four to three. Then the names of the presidents came up one by one. Before the hour was over, members of the Board had voted to relieve eight of them of their duties. Evans, who was first in line, lost his job by a vote of five to two, but the vote (as in the cases of all eight) was quickly made unanimous.[85] The members of the Board had their reasons in the case of each fired president. Why did they decide to dismiss President Evans?

In order to get his reorganization plan for the governance of higher education approved, Governor Cruce had to make some deals. The chief obstacles were those both inside and outside the legislature who represented smaller schools in the state; they feared that the University would dominate the new Board and that their schools would suffer. The leader of those inclined to resist Cruce's scheme on that ground was the superintendent of public instruction, Robert H. Wilson. To placate Wilson, Cruce entered into an agreement with him: three of the new Board members would be chosen by the governor from a list submitted by Superintendent Wilson. This would of course give Wilson a majority of four votes on the Board, as he was to be a voting *ex officio* member and chair. In exchange, Cruce received from Wilson a pledge that the Board would not act out of narrow-minded favoritism. Only one member of the now defunct University's Board of Regents was named by Governor Cruce to the new State Board of Education: W. E. Rowsey. It had been Rowsey

82. *Norman Transcript*, April 20,1911, 1.

83. "Minutes of the State Board of Education," April 12–14, 1911, 1.

84. Ibid., April 27, 1911, 21.

85. Ibid., April 28, 1911, 23. The Board did not announce its decisions immediately, but naturally rumors began to filter out. The *Norman Transcript* reported the possibility of Evans being fired on May 4, 1911, 1.

who had voted with Cruce, in the minority, in the traumatic Regents' meeting in 1908 that fired Parrington, Cole, and the others and it was Rowsey who had accompanied David Ross Boyd in the extensive tour to study college architecture. He had voted to fire Boyd and hire Evans; but he was, at best, lukewarm toward the new president.

Superintendent Wilson's three men on the Board voted with him and gave him a majority of four to three. One of them, Robert Dunlop of Newkirk, had been elected state treasurer. The other two (Scott Glen of Shawnee and Otto Frank Hayes of Chandler) were school superintendents. Although one was a Republican and the other a Democrat, both were loyal to the smaller state schools and suspicious of the University. Both of them, but particularly Hayes, had been friends of President Boyd, who had been a school superintendent himself and had a wide acquaintanceship in that circle when he was in Oklahoma. Like Boyd, Hayes and especially Glen were said to have ties to the American Book Company. The other two members, who along with Rowsey were usually in the minority, were William Brandenburg, superintendent at Oklahoma City, and Angelo Scott, a Republican of Oklahoma City who had served during the territorial period as president of the A & M college at Stillwater.[86]

Robert Wilson, who controlled the State Board of Education, had not been elected superintendent of public instruction without a struggle. To attain his office he had to unseat the state's first superintendent, Evan Dhu Cameron, and this is exactly what he had set out to do in the 1910 Democratic primary. But Cameron (a Baptist preacher who had recently converted away from the Southern Methodist Church) was credited with helping to defeat the ambitions of the avid Southern Methodist Ernest Bynum to be Boyd's replacement in 1908. The primary, therefore, saw the friends of the University lined up behind Cameron's retention, while proponents of the smaller schools favored Wilson. And President Evans, in particular, was supposed to be especially involved in supporting Cameron; after all, it had been Cameron's defeat of Bynum and championing of Evans that had won the latter his present position.[87] But now Wilson had won, and maybe it was time to settle a few old scores. Thus Robert Wilson's defeat of Cameron, no less than the retirement of Governor Haskell, led inevitably to the abrupt dismissal of Evans.

The members of the Board probably had no one in mind to replace Evans on the day they fired him. On May 24, however, they started discussing the various deans at the University of Oklahoma with an eye to naming one of them as acting president.[88] In a decision that must certainly have caused Evans special pain, they decided upon Julien Monnet, who had been on the campus for only twenty-one months. Monnet made it perfectly clear that he would rather not take on the job; for one thing, he was scheduled to lecture at the

86. Gittinger, "Reorganizations of 1908 and 1911," 43–44.

87. Ibid., 44–45.

88. McKown (*The Dean*, 199) reports that "one by one they [the deans] were called in for an interview"; but the "Minutes" (May 24, 1911, 35) indicate that this was not the procedure; the deans were discussed without being interviewed.

University of Chicago that summer. He also made it clear that he had no interest whatsoever in taking on the responsibility permanently and that under no circumstances would he serve in the position for more than a year.[89] One member of the State Board, Robert Dunlop, happily asserted that the taxpayers had just been saved $4,000: Monnet would do two jobs, but get only one salary![90]

~

THE MEMBERS OF THE STATE BOARD OF EDUCATION were not content with removing only President Evans. They also had in mind replacing a few others at the University. According to Gittinger, "Monnet had expected to be consulted about any proposed changes in the faculty, but he was horrified to find that the four members of the majority faction [of the State Board] paid no attention to his wishes. Positions were filled as a result of trading among them."[91] In view of the sordid way in which the jobs were handed out, however, the University gained some surprisingly valuable additions.

W. W. Williams, who had been Linebaugh's choice for the position of treasurer of the University in 1908, was fired. He had gotten into a dispute with other state officials over the ordering of supplies for the University and was not popular in Oklahoma City. After a short term by a stopgap treasurer, Superintendent Wilson named twenty-nine-year-old Josiah L. Lindsey to the post. "This was a case," wrote Roy Gittinger, "of one good man succeeding another."[92] Lindsey quietly performed his duties until his retirement almost forty years later. In 1938 he was named to the new position of controller of the University. At his death in 1962, the president of the Board of Regents wrote that "many former students will always remember him with appreciation and affection for his kindliness and sympathetic help in their problems. His loyalty and efficiency in handling the financial affairs of the University cannot be measured but will always be recognized."[93] The street that for years marked the southern boundary of the campus was named for him in 1922.[94]

Two other Linebaugh appointments also left the University. Theodore Frelinghuysen Brewer, the elderly and genial Southern Methodist minister who was the uncle of the English professor and the patriarch of the family, was replaced as the high-school inspector by a professional educator; he was to reappear five years later as a member of the State Board

89. *University Umpire*, May 26, 1911, 1; McKown, *The Dean*, 199–200.

90. Gittinger, "Reorganizations of 1908 and 1911," 44.

91. Ibid.

92. Ibid., 45.

93. Leonard H. Savage to Mrs. J. L. Lindsey, January 4, 1962, in Josiah L. Lindsey's Personnel File, Office of the Provost.

94. See Lindsey's obituary, *Norman Transcript*, January 2, 1962; and "J. L. Lindsey Retires," *Sooner Magazine* 22 (August 1950): 16. Lindsey Street did not receive its name, however, because of Lindsey's connection to the University. Rather, he was one of the members of a corporation that developed Norman's Parsons Addition, which had that street as its southern boundary.

of Education, appointed by Cruce's successor in the governorship.[95] Similarly, the dean of the School of Medicine, Charles Bobo, who had come into office with the troubles of 1908 and supervised the merger with Epworth, was dismissed during the troubles of 1911. Bobo was "fully in sympathy with modern scientific medicine," but his own training was thirty years old and "was meager even for that time."[96] He retired to Norman and was a general practitioner in town until 1940.[97] He was replaced by Robert F. Williams, a Virginia physician, medical professor, and director of a sanitarium. His term as dean was short and stormy; it involved the summary demotion of fourteen clinical professors in Oklahoma City, the protest resignation of some of their colleagues, and their ultimate restoration by the next president of the University. By 1914 Williams was back in Virginia.[98]

As a result of the turbulence of 1911, however, the University of Oklahoma added two extremely valuable professors to the teaching staff. Both of them were hired on the basis of highly questionable—indeed, rather shameful—motives. But both of them were to render long and distinguished service to the institution. The State Board of Education, it seems, wanted to place one of its favorites as a teacher of German at the new Southwestern Normal in Weatherford. Unfortunately, an obstacle stood in the way; Southwestern already had a German teacher: Roy Temple House. In the academic year 1910–11 House was off teaching in Germany; but he was still a member of Southwestern's faculty and, as Gittinger sarcastically remarked, was "too good a man for even that board to drop."[99] How could this difficulty be overcome? The Board hit upon a solution: Henry Meier, who had been teaching German in Norman since 1907 and who had somehow weathered the massacre of 1908, was unceremoniously fired. His position was given to House, and the vacancy thereby created at Southwestern was filled by the Board's favorite. House had received his bachelor's degree from Miami University in Ohio in 1900 and was eventually to earn a Ph.D. from the University of Chicago (1917). For the next thirty-nine years, until his retirement in 1950, House taught German at the University. He is best remembered, however, for his founding and pioneering editorship of the international literary journal *Books Abroad* (called *World Literature Today* since 1977).[100]

A second case in which the disreputable motives of the Board of Education resulted in a valuable acquisition for the University involved John Alley. By the time he came to head the Government Department in Norman, he was thirty-six and already had an eventful and vaguely romantic career. Born in Nebraska, Alley came to Oklahoma with

95. Gittinger, "Reorganizations of 1908 and 1911," 45.

96. Ibid.

97. Everett, *Medical Education in Oklahoma*, 33.

98. Ibid., 79, 83–84. Gittinger ("Reorganizations of 1908 and 1911," 46) called Williams "a misfit."

99. Gittinger, "Reorganizations of 1908 and 1911," 46.

100. For an affectionate sketch of House, see W. A. Willibrand, "Roy Temple House: Septuagenarian Editor of *Books Abroad*," *Modern Language Journal* 32 (1948): 378–81. His career is summarized in an obituary article in the *Oklahoma Daily*, December 5, 1963. See also "Dr. House Is Honored," *Sooner Magazine* 20 (June 1948): 13; and William Riggan, "*World Literature Today* at 60," *Sooner Magazine* 7 (Spring 1987): 25–29.

*Roy Temple House*

his family in a covered wagon in 1890 when he was fifteen. He worked as a cowboy on a ranch near Wichita Falls for three years before returning to his family, now located in Perry. He joined the army for the Spanish-American War in the summer of 1898 (he was later to serve in the border skirmishes against the Mexicans in 1916 and with distinction in World War I: on campus he was known as "Major" Alley). He came home from Cuba, graduated from Kingfisher College, and taught high school for four years. Then he went to Harvard, where he earned another B.A. and played on the football team. He spent a year teaching at Stillwater. From 1909 until 1911 Alley was president of the Preparatory School at Tonkawa.[101] There he got into trouble.

It seems that the students and faculty at the school and many of the citizens of Tonkawa wanted the institution to become a college or at least a junior college. They even spoke of "the college" in town; President Alley, who was not in sympathy with their aspirations, asked them to refrain from that terminology and to call the place by its legal name. Robert Dunlop, one of the members of the State Board of Education, had nothing against the attractive and able Alley, but he was from Newkirk and wanted to please his Kay County neighbors in Tonkawa. At Dunlop's insistence, therefore, Alley was moved to Norman, where he taught until his death in 1944.[102] The maneuver, however, was not without its amusing side. Back in 1908 Regent Pratt had helped James H. Sawtell to gain a position teaching political science at the University. With Pratt now gone and apparently hiding out from the authorities who were pursuing him on the alleged morals charge, the members of the State Board felt free to fire Sawtell and replace him with John Alley. Astonishingly, Sawtell appeared before the Board to complain that he was being ousted because of politics! Gittinger reported that the members "ridiculed" him: "They told him that since he had got in by favoritism he should not complain if he was put out that way."[103]

---

101. For John Alley's career, see obituary articles in the *Norman Transcript* and the *Daily Oklahoman* on May 16, 1944, and in the *Oklahoma Daily*, May 17, 1944. For his leadership of the Government Department, see "Brought Best Men to O.U.," *Sooner Magazine* 16 (August 1944): 4.

102. For the circumstances of Alley's hiring, see Gittinger, "Reorganizations of 1908 and 1911," 46–47.

103. Ibid.

*John Alley*

~

NO DOUBT THE MOST BIZARRE of the Board's personnel actions in 1911 occurred in the Mathematics Department.[104] Of all the firings and replacements, this one seemed particularly blatant and partisan and therefore particularly revealing of the terrifying academic climate at the University of Oklahoma. It was true, of course, that the man being ousted, Edmund Pendleton Randolph Duval, was himself a political appointee; he had gotten his job in 1908 through Regent Linebaugh, partly on account of the prominence of his brothers-in-law in the Tulsa Southern Methodist church. But Duval had earned master's degrees from both the University of Texas and Harvard and at the time of his appointment had been teaching at the University of Wisconsin; he had, moreover, proved himself a fine instructor at Oklahoma and was highly regarded by others in the Mathematics Department. His replacement, Frederick Charles Kent, seemed on the face of it far less qualified; he had received a bachelor's degree from Michigan seventeen years before and had been teaching for years in the Oklahoma public school system. In 1910, however, Kent had worked tirelessly for the defeat of Superintendent Cameron and the election of Superintendent Wilson, who was now the president of the State Board of Education.

According to Gittinger, Kent "had contributed so much to Wilson's campaign that he was worse than bankrupt. At least he was always in financial straits afterwards. Wilson was eager to find a good position for Kent with a salary sufficient for him to live and have money to pay his debts." Professor Reaves, chair of the Mathematics Department, appealed to Wilson for Duval's retention; but Wilson (who probably thought he could quietly dump Duval, because Duval had come as part of the Linebaugh crowd) was adamant. Wilson accused Reaves of wanting Duval because of friendship and countered that he himself favored Kent for the very same reason and that "he was also entitled to have friends on the University faculty." The replacement of Duval by Kent caused considerable public outcry, because the motives were so patent. Indeed, the attention was so intense that Governor Cruce felt that he had no choice but to enter into the matter. "Cruce may not have liked other things that the board had done," Gittinger believed, "but it seemed clear to him that Wilson had broken his promise to avoid personal and political favoritism."[105]

104. My account of this episode closely follows Gittinger's, in ibid., 47–49.

105. Ibid., 48.

*Edmund P. Duval*

What followed was extraordinary even by University of Oklahoma standards. The governor called the entire State Board of Education together and asked them, one at a time, how they had voted on the matter of replacing Duval with Kent. The three in the minority (Rowsey, Brandenburg, and Scott) honestly replied that they had not voted for Kent. Three of the majority (Dunlop, Glen, and Wilson) claimed that they had voted for him but that their motives were pure: they had done so for the good of the University. The seventh member of the Board, Otto Frank Hayes (who, Gittinger thought, "must have feared removal"), said that he had *not* voted for Kent and that the minutes of that meeting were simply wrong in stating that he had. The governor left the room expecting that the Board would correct its minutes to show that Kent had not been chosen, and he reported all this to the press. He did not intend to remove those who had voted for Kent, he said, because he felt he must abide by his agreement with Wilson (which the papers referred to as a "bargain"). The story had been reported all over the country; and when the Board failed to "correct" its minutes and rehire Duval, Hayes became a laughingstock and Cruce was portrayed as a dupe and a weakling. But, as Gittinger put it, "the real sufferer was the reputation of the State and the prestige of the University."[106]

Kent remained at the University for three years, earning a reputation in town, Gittinger asserted, as a writer of bad checks. (In 1913 the treasurer of the Oklahoma Education Association, reporting on the financial condition of the organization, noted that its assets included a bad check from F. C. Kent of the University.)[107] By 1914 Superintendent Wilson's control of the Board had weakened, and a new president of the University was in place. He had to agree to the dismissal of his friend Kent and the rehiring of Duval. Kent left the state; and Duval taught mathematics at the University until his retirement in 1945.

The Duval-Kent episode, the firing of both Boyd and Evans, the numerous other political interferences had all sullied the reputation of the University in educational circles throughout the United States. Who in the world would choose to come to Norman, Oklahoma, to head an institution with so dubious a history? That was the question that the

106. Ibid., 48–49.
107. Ibid., 49.

State Board had to confront. Acting-president Monnet had made it plain that he would not stay beyond a year; and the Board's wild hirings and firings, undertaken without consulting his opinion, were not calculated to lead him to change his mind. Who could be found to take up the leadership of the battered University as it entered upon its twentieth year?

CHAPTER IX

# New Leader, New Programs, New Faces, 1912–1917

On the evening of April 25, 1912, more than five hundred elegantly attired Bostonians gathered at the Somerset hotel for a banquet. Most of the guests were Boston schoolteachers, but other local luminaries were also present. The master of ceremonies was A. Lawrence Lowell, the president of Harvard University. He was at his very best for this occasion: one observer at the dinner praised him for "such felicitous introductions, such tact, such keen and sublimated wit and such appropriateness of phrasing." Formal remarks were delivered by the president of Boston College, the president of the Boston Chamber of Commerce, the chair of the Massachusetts State Board of Education, and other dignitaries. The guest of honor was Boston's departing superintendent of schools. He was leaving the city and heading west. And the warmth of the tributes made it clear that there were many who were sorry to see him go.[1]

Stratton Duluth Brooks was forty-two years old when Boston tendered him this cordial farewell, and almost his entire adult life had been devoted to education.[2] He was born in Everett, Missouri, in September 1869, descended from a restless pioneering family that had moved west over the generations, from Connecticut to New York to Ohio to Michigan and then to Missouri. The pattern was broken after Stratton's father fell upon hard times and lost his farm. The little house where the boy had been born was moved into town by kindly neighbors. When he was two, the family returned to Michigan. Raised

---

1. "The Stratton D. Brooks Banquet: Farewell Reception and Dinner to the Retiring Superintendent of Boston Schools," *Journal of Education* (Boston) 75 (May 2, 1912): 497–98.

2. For short summaries of his career, see *Who Was Who in America* (Chicago: A. N. Marquis Co., 1950), 2:82; *The National Cyclopaedia of American Biography* (New York: James T. White and Co., 1922), 18:277; Joan Duff Kise, "Stratton D. Brooks," in John F. Ohles, ed., *The Biographical Dictionary of American Educators*, 1:180; and obituaries in the *New York Times*, January 20, 1949, 27; *School and Society* 69 (January 29, 1949): 73; and the *Daily Oklahoman*, January 18, 1949, 1, 8. For more substantial sketches, see Rex F. Harlow, "Oklahoma's Leading Educator," *Harlow's Weekly* 21 (December 23, 1922), 8ff.; and Harold Keith, "Pioneer Prexy," *Daily Oklahoman*, March 20, 1949, D10–11, large parts of which were taken from his *Oklahoma Kickoff*; Keith's article also appeared in *Sooner Magazine* 21 (February 1949): 7–11. Also of interest is Debra Levy, "A Daughter Remembers," *Sooner Magazine* 22 (Fall 2001): 31–32.

in the middle of a Michigan forest, the youngster lived a sort of Huckleberry Finn life, tramping through the woods, skilled in hunting and fishing, contemptuous of school. He actually failed in his first attempt at high school and left because, as he once remarked, he could not master the fourteenth chapter of Caesar's *Commentaries*.[3] His parents sent him to Ohio, where he spent his time hunting squirrels. When the youngster returned home, some friends introduced him to their new teacher, and the fourteen-year-old had his conversion experience.[4] He plunged into schoolwork and in two years was ready for college. His trek to the Michigan State Normal College in Ypsilanti (later Eastern Michigan University) was also a little unorthodox. The school was 140 miles from home. Since he would be walking there, and since his grandfather's farm was only about a hundred miles up the road, his father had him drive and deliver thirty cattle on his way to college.[5]

Brooks liked school and was good at it, despite the time he lost gaining a campus reputation for his performances on the baseball team. Unfortunately, his money ran out. He left Ypsilanti to become the principal of a small rural school in Millbrook at the age of eighteen. Returning to college, he finished his first degree in 1890 and immediately took the principalship of the high school in Danville, Illinois. He returned to Michigan after a couple of years and helped to organize the Mt. Pleasant Normal School, a privately run institution, serving as its vice president and business manager. Meanwhile, he was earning a bachelor of pedagogy degree from Ypsilanti (1892). He also won the hand of his college sweetheart, Marcia Stuart (the daughter of a Michigan lumberman), who had graduated from the Normal a year before him.[6] Brooks was now twenty-four, a family man, and conscious of the need to earn some money. He entered into the furniture business with his father just in time to be wiped out by the depression of 1893, incurring serious indebtedness that haunted him for years to come. No doubt the fling at the business world was chastening; and thereafter Stratton Brooks devoted himself strictly to what he knew best: education. He possessed considerable talents in that calling and rose with dazzling speed in the profession to which he was now fully committed.

After acquiring another bachelor's degree, this one from the University of Michigan (1896), Brooks was hired as a high-school principal in Adrian, Michigan. From there he moved to La Salle, Illinois, as a principal.[7] He was so successful in improving his school that he was invited to join the faculty of the University of Illinois as a professor of psychology and the high-school inspector. Within three years at Illinois, Brooks had earned an admirable reputation for his work in developing the state's high-school system. In 1902

---

3. Harlow, "Oklahoma's Leading Educator," 9.

4. Harlow reports (ibid.) that the teacher was Laurence A. McLouth, who became a lifelong friend and rose to chair the German Department at New York University.

5. Ibid.

6. For her obituary, see *New York Times,* January 19, 1941, 40.

7. The amusing story of Brooks's cunning campaign to win that job over two more experienced rivals is told in Harlow, "Oklahoma's Leading Educator," 10.

Boston advertised for an assistant superintendent of schools (one of whose duties would be as the school inspector), and Brooks got the job. He worked in this position for four years and, while doing so, crossed the river to earn a master's degree from Harvard (1904). In 1906, still only in his mid-thirties, Brooks was appointed the superintendent of Cleveland's public schools. But no sooner had he unpacked his bags, a short ten weeks in Ohio, than the Boston School Board asked him to return to the city as superintendent, because his predecessor had died. The Boston position was the first job he had ever held where his salary exceeded his living expenses, and at last he could begin repaying the debt that he and his father had incurred more than a decade before.[8]

The record of his accomplishments in Boston was impressive.[9] In the first place, he persuaded the School Board to confine itself to legislative and policy matters and to leave the direct administration of the system to the professionals. This crucial reform effectively divorced politics and patronage from day-to-day operations. Brooks regularized the appointment of Boston's teachers; henceforward they would be chosen and promoted strictly on the basis of merit and competitive exams. Teachers were now to have pensions and sabbaticals. He inaugurated a system for substitute teachers, insisting that they be trained and monitored. Brooks revised the curriculum, limiting the number of electives and reducing the number of elementary school grades from nine to eight. He tightened discipline, completely overhauled the schools' health-care system, established evening schools around the city, and reduced the number of students under each teacher's supervision. His most far-reaching reform, however, was the establishment of vocational education in the Boston schools. After spending six months studying vocational and industrial education in Europe, Brooks tried some experiments in Boston, which were widely copied and which mark him as an American pioneer of this form of schooling.[10] In short, by 1912, Boston had one of the country's most progressive urban school systems, and Stratton Brooks was one of the most highly regarded school superintendents anywhere in the United States. Each day he managed the city's 125,000 students, 3,000 teachers, and fourteen high schools with the "sure touch of a man who is master of such difficult tasks."[11]

While Brooks was off in Europe studying vocational education, the members of Governor Lee Cruce's new State Board of Education were trying to find someone to replace the University of Oklahoma's acting president, law dean Julien Monnet. They asked Columbia's president, Nicholas Murray Butler, if he might recommend someone. Butler asked a Bos-

---

8. Ibid.

9. For the general context, see Marvin Lazerson, *Origins of the Urban School: Public Education in Massachusetts, 1870–1915*; for innovations under Brooks, see *Brief History of the Boston Public Schools, 1635–1949*, 22–24.

10. For Brooks's views, see his "Industrial Education," *Journal of Education* (Boston) 70 (December 9 and 16, 1909): 597–99, 627–28; and his "Vocational Guidance," *School Review* 19 (January 1911): 42–50. In general, see Lazerson, *Origins of the Urban School*, chaps. 3 to 7; Bernice Fisher, *Industrial Education: American Ideals and Institutions*; and Sol Cohen, "The Industrial Education Movement, 1906–17," *American Quarterly* 20 (1968): 95–110.

11. Harlow, "Oklahoma's Leading Educator," 15.

ton friend of Brooks if the absent superintendent might be interested. His friend said no. When Brooks returned, the friend said: "I declined a state university presidency for you while you were gone." Brooks asked where; when he was told that it was the University of Oklahoma, he told his friend thanks and forgot the whole thing—until February 1912.[12] That month Brooks traveled to St. Louis for the National Education Association's annual meeting of school superintendents. Among the other delegates was William Brandenburg, the superintendent of the Oklahoma City school system and a member of the State Board. He had come to St. Louis with other Board members to interview possible candidates for the University's vacant presidency.[13]

In St. Louis Brandenburg tried to interest Brooks in the position, but the Boston superintendent insisted that he was not tempted by the suggestion. Brandenburg asked if he would at least agree to meet some other members of the Board, including Bob Wilson, its president. (It will be recalled that Wilson was the elected superintendent of public instruction, a crafty political manipulator who was currently in an uneasy truce with Governor Cruce. Wilson was the one who had shamelessly argued that his political supporter Frederick Kent, a man who had considerable difficulty balancing his own checkbook, should teach math at the University because Wilson was also entitled "to have friends on the University faculty"!)[14] Brooks shook hands all around and remarked pointedly that his train was leaving in less than half an hour. He then asked the Board members why they were interested in *him:* "Is it not unusual to consider a public school superintendent for the presidency of a state university?" Wilson tried to explain that the Board was under heavy pressure from Cruce and others, because their appointments to the presidencies of the state's normal schools seemed to be politically motivated. "We feel that it is desirable that we appoint a president at the university whom none of us has ever seen. Besides, you have a national reputation for freeing the Boston schools from political influence. This might be helpful in our situation."[15]

No doubt Brooks found Wilson's candor both amusing and refreshing. And before rushing off to catch his train, he offered the Oklahomans some gratuitous advice. He said that while he was not interested in the job himself, he knew to an absolute certainty that no future president would be able to cleanse the institution of politics or redeem its dubious national reputation until the Board agreed to two iron principles. "First, all appointments of faculty and other employees must be made only on recommendation of the president of the university. No member of the Board should recommend, directly or indirectly, any appointee. The Board should vote yes or no, but should not substitute for an appointee

12. Keith, "Pioneer Prexy," D10.

13. This account of the hiring of Brooks relies on Keith's article (ibid.) published in 1949, at Brooks's death. Since Keith's version of the events of 1912 is based on an interview with Brooks, apparently in 1944, thirty-two years after the incidents and conversations took place, the details should be regarded with caution.

14. Gittinger, "University Reorganizations of 1908 and 1911," 43–49.

15. The encounter in St. Louis is described in Keith, "Pioneer Prexy," D10.

they reject. Secondly, the Board should have nothing to do with the administration of the university." This was, of course, not the music that Bob Wilson was accustomed to hearing, and he made a disarmingly frank reply: "That's a big order," he said, "it leaves nothing for the Board to do." Brooks probably climbed aboard his train thinking that, as far as he was concerned, the matter was now closed.

There are two mysteries about the eventual hiring of Stratton Brooks as the University's third president. Why, given the abysmal reputation of the University, did the man agree to take the job? And why, given his insistence on the two principles he had enunciated in St. Louis, did the State Board of Education want him?

That Brooks was not *entirely* uninterested was clearly shown when he accepted Wilson's invitation to visit Norman. He later told Harold Keith that he was favorably impressed by the energy and friendliness of the people he met in Oklahoma. He also remembered a particular verbal exchange with Wilson that influenced his decision. He had mentioned to Wilson that he did harbor the ambition "to build a great university." Wilson pointed out that "this is the only state big enough to have one that hasn't already got one." "That argument fetched me," Brooks told Keith three decades later. "I didn't have any answer for it."[16] There is probably some truth in Brooks's reminiscence. But it is also likely that he was moved to accept the offer on other grounds as well. He had accomplished much in Boston and was the sort of man who was happier innovating than he was attending to the details of administration (although he was very good at that too). The presidency of a state university was undoubtedly more prestigious than a superintendency. And there was so much to do in Oklahoma, so much damage to be repaired, so many things to start and to fix and to build. He had succeeded in every aspect of American education from kindergarten teacher to high-school principal to college professor to superintendent of schools; only the administration of a university remained. In the end, Brooks probably agreed to come because he loved the challenge and considered that he was still young enough (in his early forties) to take it on with enthusiasm and vigor.[17]

The Board also had reasons to persist in courting him, despite his bold insistence that it would have to relinquish its accustomed prerogatives. There could be little doubt that the University was under a cloud in 1911 and 1912 or that the Board of Education was receiving harsh criticism for its political management and arbitrary manipulation of the state's system of higher education. It had been less than a year, after all, since the members sat around the table and blithely fired eight of the state's college and university presidents. The governor had called them on the carpet at least twice for their rank political behavior. Perhaps appointing someone so distant from Oklahoma, someone no one could accuse

16. Ibid. The sketch of Brooks in the following paragraphs derives from this source and from Harlow, "Oklahoma's Leading Educator."

17. Brooks did not take the job for the money. After one year in Norman, where he was earning $7,500, the Boston School Board offered him $10,000 to return, but he refused. Harlow, "Oklahoma's Leading Educator," 10.

*President Stratton Duluth Brooks*

the Board of supporting for personal reasons, would quiet some of the criticism. Moreover, even though no member of the State Board knew Brooks personally, three of the seven were school superintendents and probably knew about his sterling record in Boston; among professional educators, he had a national reputation.[18] In the end, however, it was surely Stratton Brooks's personal qualities that captivated the Board and caused its members to pursue him so strenuously.

Brooks was a small man, compact and fit, with a neat moustache and engaging brown eyes that became unusually expressive when he was making some point. He gave off an aura of health and tightly packed energy. Sometimes it was a little hard to tell if he was walking or trotting. When a subject engrossed him, he talked with his whole body. Brooks also impressed people with the lightning quickness of his mind, his enormous self-confidence, his talent for coming at problems directly and answering questions instantly and decisively. "He said yes or no in a flash," asserted Harold Keith. "When you went to his office to ask for something, you always knew when you walked out whether you had got what you went for." Football coach Bennie Owen once said of Brooks that "he made up his mind blam." He seemed entirely in control of any situation and, just as important, entirely in control of himself; and he had a gift for explaining things. As a string of Oklahoma governors and lawmakers were about to discover, Brooks also had great diplomatic skills and a remarkable ability to persuade. And he combined all of these qualities with a lively, bright-eyed, genial sense of humor. (Once, when Brooks was visiting Norman some years after leaving the presidency, someone pointed out to him the statue of himself that had been placed in the narrow niche at the main entrance to Evans Hall. "Looks like you're squeezed in there pretty tight," his guide remarked. "I've gotten out of tighter places than that," Brooks replied.)

Whatever the reasons—those of the State Board or those of his own—Brooks agreed to take up the duties of the presidency; and the Boston educational community was expressing its regret, good wishes, and gratitude at the Somerset banquet. One of the highlights of the evening was the reading of a sentimental poem written for the occasion by Frederic

18. Harlow reported (ibid., 9) that "in a national poll, among one thousand of the leading educators of America to select twenty-five of the most prominent educators in the nation, [Brooks] was selected as one of that group."

Allison Tupper, entitled "A New Ballad of East and West." Tupper's poem took as its theme the fact that the West had formed the man and sent him as a blessed gift to the East:

> The eastern land to the western land sent a message of import high:
> "From your prairies vast, from your rivers grand, from your mountains that seek the sky,
> From the freedom of your unreined winds that sweep untrammeled past,
> From the broad horizon of your sky so lofty and so vast,
> From the teeming wealth of your fertile farms, from your noble cities send
> A man who in himself all these harmoniously shall blend."
> And so he came to the eastern land, he brought the stir of the West
> The eager love of progress and the passion for the best,
> The soul that spares nor toil nor thought, if but the work is done,
> And the high ideal and the real are harmonized in one.

And now, alas, the West wanted him back: "I lent you my son, because my love for you can never die." But the time had come for this noble son to return to his own land. Said the West:

> "And now I have found him another task in this great, free land of ours,
> To mingle the best of East and West, where Oklahoma flowers
> In the glorious pride of sisterhood, in rivalry pure and high
> With Massachusetts, the old Bay state—he loves her and so do I."

But, the poet concluded, let there be no hard feelings:

> "Oh, East is East and West is West," but East and West are one
> In the proudest land and the greatest land that greets the glowing sun;
> Though great is he who wins the praise of either East or West,
> The man who wins the praise of both the greatest is and best.[19]

For reasons perhaps not difficult to understand, Frederic Tupper's production of 1912 never took its place among the masterpieces of American poetry. And one cannot help wondering how many of the Somerset guests were weeping, how many were quietly snickering, and how many were staring embarrassedly at the tablecloths in front of them. But if "A New Ballad of East and West" lacked a certain artistic authority, it undeniably expressed a genuine and deep feeling. Boston was losing an extraordinary individual, and Oklahoma was about to welcome him.

~

ONE OF THE FIRST THINGS BROOKS must have noticed as he took up his duties on May 1, 1912, was the lack of administrative help. He had come from managing a vast urban system: there were nearly four times as many *teachers* in Boston as there were col-

---

19. Frederic Allison Tupper, "A New Ballad of East and West: To Stratton D. Brooks," reprinted in the *Journal of Education* (Boston) 75 (May 2, 1912): 498.

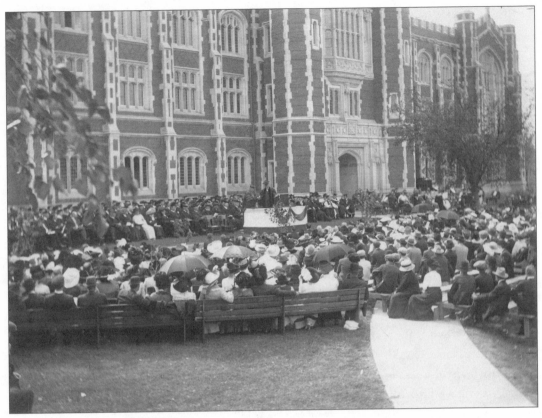

*The inauguration of President Brooks, in front of the new Administration Hall on October 21, 1912*

lege students in Norman, and the superintendent could assign duties to various lieuten-ants. But from the earliest days of David Ross Boyd, the multiplicity of details involved in running the University of Oklahoma fell on the shoulders of the president, assisted by a private secretary and a stenographer (often undergraduates or former undergraduates). Brooks had inherited an institution, however, that was larger than it had ever been before. He was expected to manage sixty-four employees in Norman, another thirty in Oklahoma City, and a student body numbering 870.[20] All the signs were auspicious, moreover, for continued growth; and Brooks himself had arrived with some big plans for expanding the University and its offerings. It was obvious that he would need additional administrative support.

The single assistant that Brooks found waiting for him in Norman was a twenty-six-year-old graduate of the University named Errett Rains Newby. During the summer of 1904, just before his arrival in Norman as a freshman, Newby enrolled at the Byrne Busi-ness College in Tyler, Texas, for courses in shorthand and typing. He brought these skills with him to the University; and when he was a senior, in 1908, President Boyd, who was

20. The official figures can be found in W. B. Richards, comp., *The Oklahoma Red Book*, 2:167–72.

*Errett Rains Newby*

on the verge of losing his own job, hired him to be his secretary at $25 a month. For the rest of his long life, Newby boasted of the cunning sleight-of-hand that he had performed in June 1908. Boyd had been fired and was preparing to leave town, but he had one last duty to perform: he had to sign the diplomas for his final commencement exercises. When Newby placed them on Boyd's desk, he slyly put his own at the bottom of the stack. Thus he could always say (and often did) that David Ross Boyd's last official act as president was to sign his diploma.[21]

Grant Evans asked Newby to stay on in the president's office, changed his title to "secretary of the University," and quadrupled his salary to $1,200 a year. In 1911 Evans had Newby assume the additional duties of University registrar. When Brooks came to Norman to look the place over and maybe agree to take the presidency, he asked Newby to go for a little walk with him. While strolling a couple of blocks down Main Street and back, Brooks said that he had been advised to bring his Boston private secretary with him to Norman but that people said that Newby "did not leak" and that he wanted him to stay. "Well," Newby recalled more than sixty years later, "I said, I'll be glad to stay and I'll be just as strong for you as I have been for anybody else. So I stayed." Unfortunately, Newby did not know what not "leaking" meant and went to ask Professor Buchanan. Uncle Buck told him that it meant "keeping your mouth shut on things that shouldn't be told."[22]

By the time Brooks arrived, Errett Newby was a very busy fellow; and the new president quickly added to his duties. Newby was handling all correspondence with prospective students, helping to judge the quality of the state's high schools for the purpose of admitting their students, supervising all of the University's publications (including the *Catalogue*), and performing all the work of the office of registrar. One good thing, he later admitted, came from his tremendous workload. A beautiful young woman from Blackwell started corresponding with him about entering the University; he was very careful *not* to answer all her questions so that she would have to write again. When she arrived in Norman, the registrar met her train personally and carried her suitcase to her rooming house; perhaps she thought all incoming students were accorded this treatment. The two married in 1914 and remained together for fifty-four years.[23] The job's unexpected benefits aside, it was clear that Newby needed some help.

In 1913 Newby hired a young man who was to play a central role at the University

21. In 1973 Newby gave a long interview to Robert Morrissey and then amplified it in a thirty-page "supplement." The interview is in the Herbert R. Hengst Oral History Collection. There is also much biographical material in the Errett Rains Newby MSS, Box 1.

22. Ibid., 10.

23. See Newby's touching "Tribute to a Lady: Lola North Newby, 'The Gentle One,'" typescript in the inventory to the Errett Rains Newby MSS.

of Oklahoma for the next five decades. Emil Rudolph Kraettli was not a University of Oklahoma graduate.[24] He had been born in Sterling, Nebraska, in May 1890. After high school in Clay Center, Kansas, he entered the Gem City Business College in Quincy, Illinois, and became proficient in typing and shorthand. His sister lived in Gotebo, and she helped him find a job with a Hobart hardware business. In 1913 he applied for the job as the overburdened Errett Newby's stenographer, moved to Norman with his wife, Eva, and went to work in Evans Hall. Three years later, when Kraettli was twenty-six, President Brooks took him on as his own secretary.

In 1919 two developments were to make Kraettli's career. First, Newby announced that at the end of the year he would leave the University for the oil business. His sister Merle, who had been an undergraduate with him and who went on to teach the violin at the University, had married the up-and-coming oil man Frank Buttram. Newby went to work for his brother-in-law, and Kraettli had to take on many of his Evans Hall duties. In addition, in 1919 the state legislature voted to abandon Lee Cruce's State Board of Education plan and to reestablish individual Boards of Regents. A new University of Oklahoma Board was promptly appointed and naturally found itself in need of a secretary to oversee its business. The Regents chose Emil Kraettli, who served as secretary to the Regents for the next forty-nine years, in addition to his heavy duties as secretary to the University.

He was the ideal person for these two jobs. A slight, energetic, blindingly efficient man, Kraettli gave his complete loyalty to the institution. He was intelligent, good-humored, witty, and diplomatic. And he was a stickler for the proprieties: he could work side-by-side with some professor or president or other University official for decades and still address that person as "Mr." or "Miss." (He went hunting and fishing with Stratton Brooks,[25] but would no more dream of calling him "Stratton" than he would dream of appearing at work wearing his bathrobe.) He had an uncanny sense of his place in the scheme of things and an uncanny instinct for never crossing beyond it. When he retired in 1969 (Roy Gittinger having died fifteen years before), he knew the history of the institution better than any living person. He carried on a prodigious correspondence with faculty members; they were forever complaining about salaries, asking about obscure University regulations, wanting reimbursement for travel expenses, or just away from Norman and hoping for the gossip. He exchanged daily memos with each of the five presidents under whom he served and conducted the institution's relations with outsiders on hundreds of pieces of business that touched every aspect of the University's life. By 1919 Brooks thought "it is scarcely possible to say anything too good about him."[26] Another president whom Kraettli served said:

24. For Kraettli's career, see "Always One Familiar Face," *Sooner Magazine* 35 (December 1962): 3–6, 22; press release from the University Regents, June 14, 1962, in Emil J. Kraettli Personnel File, Public Affairs; Don Emery, "Remarks of Don Emery at Regents' Dinner, October 27, 1962, Honoring Emil Kraettli," in ibid.; George Lynn Cross, "Remarks on Emil J. Kraettli Day, October 27, 1962," in ibid.; and an obituary, *Norman Transcript*, August 9, 1979, 1.

25. "Always One Familiar Face," 5.

26. Stratton Brooks to International Committee of the YMCA, January 21, 1919, in the Emil J. Kraettli Personnel File, Office of the Provost.

*Emil R. Kraettli*

"I suspect that I have been in contact with him more frequently than with any other employee of the University or any individual outside of my immediate family. . . . I consider this man to be one of the half-dozen finest men I have known during a lifetime."[27] Such was the affection in which he was held that it is likely Emil Kraettli was asked over the years to serve as a pallbearer or an honorary pallbearer for his colleagues more often than anyone else in the history of the University community.

In 1918 President Brooks made a personal donation of $200 to begin a student loan fund. Emil Kraettli administered that fund until the University was compelled to establish an office of financial aid many years later. In that capacity, he counseled and rescued the educations of hundreds of students, who remembered him with fondness and gratitude. He patiently tailored repayment plans to each recipient's abilities, constantly warned them not to borrow too much, listened sympathetically when they missed a payment ("We had a new baby, and I can't make the payment this month"), and always understood. "We didn't fuss with them. . . . I didn't want them to go down an alley to keep from meeting

27. Cross, "Remarks on Emil J. Kraettli Day," 1. See also the tributes from various Regents, in Emery, "Remarks of Don Emery"; and Regent K. D. Bailey to Mrs. Harold Gassaway, August 17, 1979, in Emil J. Kraettli Personnel File, Office of the Provost.

me." As a result, "his office is one of the first stops for alumni visiting the campus." Before long, of course, Regents were being appointed who themselves had grateful memories of having been helped and advised by Kraettli when they were undergraduates. They tended to continue to accept his advice, always modestly and tactfully rendered, and to regard him as a permanent fixture at the University.[28] Once in the 1940s the chair of the Board neglected to ask for the annual motion to reappoint Kraettli. He had simply assumed that "the Legislature of Oklahoma had by statutory enactment granted him life tenure as Secretary of the Regents."[29]

Even before Kraettli took over the student loan duties in 1918 and Newby announced that he would be leaving on January 1, 1920, it was clear that more staff help was needed. Before going, Newby arranged to hire one more person to help carry the load, and once again it was a lucky choice. George Ernest Wadsack was born in Prague, Oklahoma, in October 1895 and graduated from high school there. He spent the next few years teaching at his old high school during the school year and going to college in the summers. He was at Central State in Edmond during the summers of 1914 and 1915 and in Norman during the summers of 1916 and 1918. While in Norman, Wadsack took a class in business office management taught by Errett Newby, and he impressed the teacher. In September 1919 Wadsack became Newby's assistant registrar. He stayed at the University as registrar until his retirement in August 1964. Like his lifelong friend and co-worker Emil Kraettli, George Wadsack was highly competent, conscientious, and devoted entirely to the University and particularly to its students. Like Kraettli, he was diplomatic and self-effacing. One of his last requests was that no eulogy be spoken at his funeral. The request was honored, but a co-worker of thirty years recalled that "during his almost half century, he was friend, counselor, and refuge to anyone needing help—the failing, the lonesome and discouraged student, the Phi Beta Kappas, university presidents, faculty, administrators and the man on the street. . . . His home was open to any who needed a place to sleep or a meal. His purse was open to those who had this need and no questions asked. His counsel saved the education program of students, marriages, and guided many of the major directions of the University of Oklahoma."[30]

In August 1973 the eighty-eight-year-old Errett Newby reminisced: "I have often said that among things I have done to repay the University in part for the many benefits I have received from it, the best may have been when I brought Mr. Kraettli to Norman as a stenographer in 1913, and later when I persuaded Mr. George Wadsack to come there as Assistant Registrar."[31] The two young men he chose, joined by others over the years as the University became larger and more complex, were to provide the administrative backbone

28. "Always One Familiar Face," 6.

29. Emery, "Remarks of Don Emery," 2.

30. Boyce Timmons, "Wadsack Eulogy in Hearts," *Norman Transcript*, September 9, 1977.

31. Errett R. Newby to Whom It May Concern, August 15, 1973, copy in the Hengst interview.

*George E. Wadsack*

of the institution for nearly half a century. Their contribution to the stable and efficient functioning of the University equaled, in many respects, that of any of the presidents under whom they so loyally served. It was fitting that when the University opened student apartments south of the campus in October 1965 the housing project should be named for Emil Kraettli and the street running through it for George Wadsack.

~

NOBODY WHO KNEW STRATTON BROOKS'S BACKGROUND could have been surprised that he came to the University hoping to enhance the preparation of public-school teachers. The territorial legislators who had established the University twenty years before had stipulated that the training of teachers was to be one of its chief purposes. But it cannot be said that this function was pursued very diligently during the school's early years. In addition to the Central State Normal in Edmond, other schools had been created to perform the task. By 1912 normal schools were functioning at five compass points throughout the state.[32] These schools were not authorized to give degrees, however, and their graduates often finished their work in Norman.[33]

32. The schools were East Central at Ada (established in 1909); Northwestern at Alva (1897); Northeastern at Tahlequah (1897); Southeastern at Durant (1909); and Southwestern at Weatherford (1897). For brief histories and descriptions of their physical plants in 1912, see Richards, *Oklahoma Red Book*, 2:182–92.

33. By an act of the territorial legislature, anyone earning a degree from the University who met certain other

Formal instruction in education did not make its appearance at the University until 1904, when Lawrence Cole (whose principal field was psychology) introduced a two-course sequence. During the fall semester, students could study "The Principles of Education" and in the spring, "The History of Education."[34] The courses were offered in the College of Arts and Sciences. Five years later, Cole was gone; and the University had two men teaching courses in education. Walter Clifton Erwin had graduated from the University in 1906 and immediately began to teach as an associate professor. He also did graduate work toward a master's degree at the University of Chicago.[35] The second professor was none other than Monroe Floyd, the man who had been hired in the shake-up of 1908 largely because he was a friend and schoolmate of one of the Regents; he had replaced Gittinger as principal of the Preparatory Department.[36] By 1909 Erwin and Floyd were offering six courses in education. In addition to the original two courses, Erwin introduced a course on secondary education and another on public school administration. Floyd, meanwhile, taught two courses that examined classical and recent writings in educational theory.[37] In 1909, on the strength of these offerings (and, no doubt, with an eye on the legislature's creation of two new normal schools that year), the Regents created a School of Teaching in the College of Arts and Sciences. The new school was not to award degrees; its purpose was merely to help prepare graduates for successful pedagogical careers.

President Brooks, with his strong background in public-school education, moved quickly to strengthen the field he loved. The first thing he did was to change the title of the School of Teaching to the School of Education, still within Arts and Sciences. He also immediately hired Warren Waverly Phelan from Baylor University to direct the School. Phelan, a graduate of Columbia with a Ph.D. from George Washington University, supervised a virtual explosion in the School of Education's work.[38] By 1917 the operation had mushroomed; there were six professors teaching education, and they were offering forty courses, including seven at the graduate level. The School of Education gave instruction in everything from vocational education to principles of moral education, from rural education to educational measurement and foreign school systems.[39] By 1920, with ten pro-

requirements was authorized to teach in the state's public schools. The statute was quoted in the University's early *Catalogues*.

34. *University of Oklahoma General Information and Announcements for 1903 and 1904* (Norman: State Capital Co., May 1903), 55–56. See also Konrad K. Koch, Jr., "An Administrative History of the Academic Divisions of the University of Oklahoma," 34–38.

35. Gittinger, *University of Oklahoma*, 66. For a summary of Erwin's career, see "Former Alumni Chief Dies," *Sooner Magazine* 10 (December 1937): 22. Erwin left the University in 1912 to practice law with his brother. In 1911–12 he was president of the Alumni Association.

36. Gittinger, "University Reorganizations of 1908 and 1911," 25, 36.

37. *University Catalogue*, 1909, 74–75.

38. Gittinger, *University of Oklahoma*, 81–82. Phelan remained in Norman until 1926, when he assumed the presidency of Oklahoma Baptist University in Shawnee.

39. *University Catalogue*, 1916–1917, 124–33.

*Warren Waverly Phelan*

fessors and sixty courses in place, it seemed appropriate to free the School of Education from the College of Arts and Sciences and to make it an independent operation.[40]

Expanding the faculty and offerings of the School of Education did not exhaust President Brooks's ambitions for the field he knew so well. He persuaded the State Board of Education to return the high-school inspection function to Norman and hired Andrew Clarkson Parsons to perform the task. Parsons had done some undergraduate work in Norman but had graduated from the University of Nebraska. By audaciously lowering the standards for accreditation he deftly expanded the number of high schools that qualified. In 1913, Parsons's first year on the job, there were 86 accredited high schools; but by the end of 1914 the list had grown to 125. Parsons also deserves credit for much of the increased success in placing Oklahoma graduates in state high schools; hitherto, many local boards of education were accustomed to hiring out-of-state graduates.[41] Finally, in 1917 the University opened a laboratory school where prospective teachers could watch experienced teachers at work and where experiments in educational methods could be observed.[42]

~

IN ADDITION TO THE MARKED EXPANSION of the work of training young teachers, the University began giving serious attention during these years to two other fields that were to have great importance. Like education, these new fields began their organizational lives as "schools" within the College of Arts and Sciences. Both started their formal operations in September 1913, the beginning of President Brooks's second year.

As early as 1908 the faculty had planned to open a department of journalism. That

40. The School of Education became the College of Education in 1929.

41. Gittinger, *University of Oklahoma*, 82–83. The list of accredited high schools was printed in the catalogues during these years; for 1913, see *University Catalogue, 1912–1913*, 67–70. Some schools were only partially accredited. In 1919, with the state's return to individual Boards of Regents, the now-truncated State Board of Education assumed the high-school inspection function, removing it from Norman.

42. Koch, "Administrative History," 36–37.

high ambition, however, resulted only in a single two-hour course in the English Department.[43] It was taught by Theodore Hampton Brewer, newly arrived as Vernon Parrington's replacement, and the sociologist Jerome Dowd, both of whom had some practical experience working on newspapers. The course, according to the *Catalogue*, was "designed both for students of English who desire a wider range of work in composition and for those who intend to prepare for practical newspaper or magazine work."[44] Thus for five years the formal study of journalism at the University of Oklahoma consisted of taking a single course from the Department of English.

In 1913 the University separated the subject from the English Department and opened the School of Journalism in the College of Arts and Sciences. Students were to take the usual college requirements during their first two years and then move to a concentrated study of journalism in their last two, enrolling in at least sixteen hours of course work from the new School. Among the ten courses available to them were two each on newspaper writing, newspaper editing, and the principles of advertising. The School of Journalism also offered work on feature writing, editorial writing, and the history of journalism.[45] To teach these courses the University hired as an instructor a young Freeport, Illinois, newspaperman named Chester Wells. Unfortunately, Wells decided to have his tonsils removed before coming to Norman; and in a disastrous operating-room tragedy, he died during the surgery.

Wells had a boyhood friend who was also in the newspaper trade, however, and that young man wrote to President Brooks asking if the Oklahoma job was still going to be filled and offering his own services. He was Harold Harvey Herbert (students referred to him affectionately as "H to the third power").[46] Herbert had been born just outside of Freeport in December 1888. In 1912 he received his bachelor's degree from the University of Illinois; when he wrote to Brooks in the summer of 1913, the twenty-four-year-old was working on a newspaper in Peoria. He arrived in Norman in time for the start of school and stayed in the School of Journalism (which was named in his honor in 1961) for the next forty-six years. The field was a rather new one in higher education,[47] and Herbert was to play a part in making it a respectable academic field and in creating a place for

43. For the administrative history of journalism until 1950, see ibid., 15–18.

44. *University Catalogue, 1911–1912*, 95.

45. *University Catalogue, 1913–1914*, 111–13, 142–44.

46. For Herbert's career, see his Personnel File, Office of the Provost; "No Need to Worry for the Future," *Sooner Magazine* 23 (January 1951): 21–22; and Dick Ratliff, "Journalism's H. H. Herbert," *Sooner Magazine* 20 (February 1948): 10, 26. See also "Herbert Appointed Boyd Professor," *Sooner State Press*, May 29, 1948, 1; "Professor Is Given State Honor," *Daily Oklahoman*, April 21, 1959, 1, 7; "Herbert and Copeland Honored," *Sooner State Press*, March 25, 1961, 1–2; and the obituary in the *Norman Transcript*, October 2, 1980, 1.

47. When Herbert worked on a master's degree at the University of Wisconsin during the summers, he had to cobble together courses in political science, history, sociology, and English. As late as 1925, seventeen states still had no college-level journalism program. Although fifty universities offered an undergraduate major, only fourteen had separate Schools of Journalism like Oklahoma's. See Katherine H. Adams, *A History of Professional Writing Instruction in American Colleges: Years of Acceptance, Growth, and Doubt*, 99–122.

college-trained professionals. He became head of the School in 1917 and two years later divided the curriculum into two parts: one string of courses dealt with general editorial work and the other with the business aspects of journalism, including advertising. By 1938 at least 263 of H. H. Herbert's students were practicing the profession in one form or another all across the country. A survey taken at his retirement in 1959 revealed that twenty-five of Herbert's former students were at work in Washington, D.C., and that twenty-eight of his students were listed in *Who's Who in America*.[48]

*H. H. Herbert*

To a surprising degree, the development of "business" as a serious academic undertaking paralleled the development of journalism. The striking similarities between these two young fields occurred nationally as well as on the campus in Norman. Everywhere the two disciplines were evolving in response to the increasing complexity of the enterprises they were to serve. During the last years of the nineteenth century and the first of the twentieth, both newspapers and businesses became larger, more complicated, and departmentalized; in the process both increasingly required experts trained in particular specialties. Colleges and universities scrambled to meet the new needs. The founders of both fields assumed that some combination of a standard liberal education with specialized vocational training was the recipe for success. The new programs in journalism and business, moreover, were both given their births by respected traditional disciplines: journalism grew slowly out of English; business grew slowly out of economics. Finally, it must be said, the early graduates in both fields often faced suspicion, even ridicule, from the hard-bitten veterans who had risen without the dubious and newfangled benefits of college. If there were many who thought that you became a real newspaperman by starting as a copy boy and hanging around the police station with a notepad and pencil, there were also many who believed that the best training in any business was to rise from messenger-girl to stenographer to private secretary to head of a department. In both cases, therefore, the new programs had to prove their value to the skeptical.[49]

48. "Professor Is Given State Honor," 1. That article also gives a brief list of some of his most distinguished students.

49. The first university-connected business program was the famous Wharton School, founded in 1881 and attached to the University of Pennsylvania; but other leading universities did not attempt such a program until the end of the century. For the growth of college-level training in business, see Frank C. Pierson et al., *The Education of American Businessmen: A Study of University-College Programs in Business Administration*, 34–54; and Frances Ruml, "The Formative Period of Higher Commercial Education in American Universities," in Leon Carroll Marshall, ed., *The Collegiate School of Business*, 45–65.

During the days of David Ross Boyd, the University had offered several practical courses that were designed to help students find places in commercial life. These courses were introduced in 1900, probably to compete with the several little business schools springing up in Oklahoma; and they taught such subjects as bookkeeping, typing, and secretarial work. The classes were held in University Hall but did not carry college credit. As was also the case in music, the instructors were paid entirely out of student fees. The students worked at their own paces and upon the successful conclusion of the course were awarded certificates of completion. These vocational courses continued until 1906.[50]

It was through work in economics, however, that students chiefly prepared themselves for business careers. Starting in 1898, the University offered a course called "Money, Trade, and Industry." Another early (and curious) offering called "Taxation. Transportation" divided the semester in half, devoting equal time to both topics. The next year's *Catalogue* announced a "department of economics" under the direction of the historian James S. Buchanan. In 1904 it became the "department of economics and sociology," headed by a Wharton School graduate who organized an ambitious curriculum of ten courses in economics and two in sociology and promptly left town after one year.[51] Implementing the program became the task of a string of transient teachers starting with the versatile George Bucklin until the arrival in 1907 of the equally versatile Jerome Dowd; the sociologist who had introduced the first course in journalism became the chair of the Economics Department. During the next five years Dowd tinkered with the curriculum (adding eight courses and dropping five, for a total of thirteen).[52] The subjects listed in the *Catalogue* included two courses in business administration and others in insurance, labor problems, industrial combinations, and the economic histories of England and the United States. But staffing this curriculum between 1907 and 1913 was another matter. It was done, writes the historian of the college, by "borrowing faculty from other departments, cross-listing courses, employing recent graduates, frequent turnover of faculty, and intermittent offerings of courses."[53] This was the situation when President Brooks arrived in 1912.

The School of Commerce and Industry began simultaneously with the School of Journalism in the fall of 1913.[54] Both were subdivisions of the College of Arts and Sciences and were guided at the start by Jerome Dowd; and both curricula stipulated two years of

---

50. For a full discussion of fees, instructors, and numbers of students involved, see Daniel A. Wren, *Collegiate Education for Business Administration at the University of Oklahoma*, 8–10.

51. This teacher was Lewis Edward Coles. The courses are listed and described in Wren, *Collegiate Education for Business Administration*, 12–14.

52. Ibid., 14–18.

53. Ibid., 18.

54. The definitive study is Wren, *Collegiate Education for Business Administration*. See also Arthur B. Adams, "History of the College of Business Administration," *Sooner Magazine* 13 (August 1941): 26ff.; Charles J. Dellasega, "The Development and Present Status of Education for Business at the University of Oklahoma"; Findley Weaver, "History of the College," in *The Greater College of Business Administration: Issued in Commemoration of the Dedication of the New College of Business Administration Building, October 30 and 31, 1936* (no pagination); and Koch, "Administrative History," 28–33.

*Arthur Barto Adams*

general study, followed by professional courses in the last two years. To teach the business courses and relieve the chaotic problems of staffing, the University would need to find a person comparable to H. H. Herbert in journalism, someone who would bring order and continuity to the haphazard and makeshift arrangements that had characterized business education heretofore. To accomplish these purposes, the University hired a young economist from South Carolina for $1,200 a year.

Arthur Barto Adams was twenty-six when he first arrived on the campus. He had a bachelor's degree from the University of South Carolina (1910) and a master's from Columbia (1912); he had worked for a year at Central College in Missouri.[55] During his first two years at the University of Oklahoma, he taught every course offered in the School of Commerce and Industry.[56] He then took a year off to finish his doctorate at Columbia. Adams was an accomplished economist and a productive scholar; by the time he retired from the University, after forty-three years of service, he had published seven books and numerous articles. He held many professional offices, and his expertise was sometimes pressed into state or national service. In 1917 the School's name was changed to the School of Public and Private Business; Jerome Dowd stepped aside (to start what would eventually be the School of Social Work); and Adams was named the new director. In 1923 business education was separated from the College of Arts and Sciences, and Adams became a dean. He retained that position until 1948. It is not possible, in short, to measure or even to imagine the early history and enormous growth of business education at the University without acknowledging the determination and forcefulness of Arthur B. Adams.

There were many among his colleagues and students who admired him greatly. John Nichols, who was to become a prominent Oklahoma City businessman and civic leader, took four classes from Adams in the early 1930s: "He was not only a great instructor,"

---

55. The best account of Adams's career is Wren, *Collegiate Education for Business Administration*, chaps. 2–3. For shorter summaries, see *Who Was Who in America* (Chicago: Marquis–Who's Who, 1968), 4:12; and the obituary accounts in the *Daily Oklahoman*, August 11, 1959, 6, and the *Norman Transcript*, August 11, 1959, 1–2.

56. Adams, "History of the College of Business Administration," 26.

thought Nichols, "but also a great man who did a lot for the business school and the students."[57] But if Arthur Adams had admirers, he also had detractors. To many he appeared arrogant and imperious. He wrangled, often bitterly, with every president under whom he served.[58] The president pro tempore of the state senate told the governor that Adams should be removed from the deanship and returned to the classroom, lamenting that "nobody seems willing to put the halter or the blind bridle on the stampeding and prancing Dean."[59] One professor, whose hatred of Adams was extreme, wrote to the editor of the *Daily Oklahoman* that "Adams has fought every president of O.U. for the last eighteen years. . . . He brow beats those of his faculty that he can. And those whom he can not he tries to ostracize."[60] Another longtime colleague, who believed that "Adams and I on the whole got on pretty well," went on to acknowledge that "a large share of Adams' faculty hated his guts. . . . He was an enormously domineering figure. And well, grossly overbearing in many respects."[61]

In 1936, in connection with the dedication of the business school's new building, Jerome Dowd was given the delicate task of writing a few remarks about Dean Adams. Dowd described the dean's attributes very gingerly: "Arthur B. Adams is animated by self-reliance, intense energy, love of adventure and love of combat." Dowd insisted that it was "fortunate" to have a man "who has a large surplus energy, who loves to take a chance and who, if fighting is to be done, is rather glad to be in it." Dowd realized, of course, that Adams could not actually use his fists on his enemies ("the energy of such a man would be misspent if expended in physical combat"), but there was no reason his purposes could not be furthered by his "leading the assault with tongue, pen, or other appropriate weapon subjected to proper direction and control."[62] It was a diplomatic attempt to praise Adams while recognizing his quirks. For whether one admired or detested Adams, it was clear that he almost single-handedly laid the groundwork for the stunning expansion in business education that was about to take place: by 1917 the *Catalogue* boasted a range of courses (most of them from the Economics Department) designed to prepare students for

57. Cited in Wren, *Collegiate Education for Business Administration*, 86, as Lori H. Jackson, "Alumni Spotlight: John W. Nichols," *Price College Magazine* 2 (1998): 9–11. Adams's skill as a teacher was generally recognized by others.

58. The details of these quarrels can be pieced together from Adams's voluminous Personnel File, Office of the Provost.

59. Cited in Wren, *Collegiate Education for Business Administration*, 72, as Allen G. Nichols to Ernest Marland, July 3, 1937. A copy is in Adams's Personnel File. Adams's reply to Nichols, on July 7, is also quoted by Wren.

60. H. Grady Sloan to E. K. Gaylord, June 1, 1947, copy in Adams's Personnel File. Sloan, whose unrestrained animosity may make him a less-than-reliable witness, taught economics from 1929 to 1946.

61. An interview between Ronald B. Shuman and Daniel Wren, May and June 1978, excerpted in Wren, *Collegiate Education for Business Administration*, quotations at 66 and 76. Shuman taught management from 1934 to 1972 and became a George Lynn Cross Research Professor. Shuman also thought that "Adams hated [President William B.] Bizzell. He got on very grudgingly with some of the other powerful Deans. . . . And you name them and I tell you there were people who couldn't abide Adams."

62. Jerome Dowd, "Dean Arthur B. Adams," in *The Greater College of Business Administration: Issued in Commemoration of the Dedication of the New College of Business Administration Building, October 30 and 31, 1936* (no pagination).

"a variety of commercial and industrial vocations."[63] Even more dramatic developments lay ahead in the years to come.

~

MEDICAL EDUCATION WAS NOT ONE of Stratton Brooks's primary interests, but even he must have been dismayed by the disastrous news that came less than five weeks after his arrival in Norman. On June 3, 1912, the Council on Medical Education, which had been classifying the nation's medical schools since 1907, announced that it was demoting the University of Oklahoma's operation from its "A" rating to a "B" (roughly equivalent to being on probation). The University had enjoyed an "A" classification since its first inspection during the spring of 1907, even though Oklahoma's medical school (in common with only six other "A"-ranked schools across the country) was still only a two-year program.[64] The lower rating naturally caused considerable consternation. As one observer put it, the faculty and the dean "chafed under the humiliation of conducting a school of inferior rating."[65]

It was generally agreed that the problem was not in the two-year premedical program on the Norman campus. The work for the freshman and sophomore years—combining offerings in chemistry, anatomy, bacteriology, materia medica, histology, physiology, pathology, pharmacy, pharmacology, embryology, and hygiene—seemed entirely satisfactory.[66] The difficulty was in the clinical work of the junior and senior years, done in Oklahoma City. Even before the Council on Medical Education had delivered its blow, the new dean, Robert Findlater Williams, told the State Board: "I find that the work of the scientific years at Norman is acceptable, but that of the clinical years at Oklahoma City is not. . . . The immediately imperative needs lie in the clinical work in Oklahoma City."[67]

It is little wonder that the Oklahoma City operation was found wanting. There was no full-time teaching faculty. The facilities and equipment for training prospective doctors were completely inadequate. Rapid and debilitating changes in administrative leadership had occurred. After the firing of Charles Bobo in 1911, Williams had come from Virginia, but he lasted only a year. He was replaced by an acting dean, William James Jolly, an Oklahoma City physician who had been part of the Epworth faculty and was now a part of the University's teaching staff. He served for the academic year 1912–13 and for the first half of the next year, when he was replaced by another Epworth veteran, Curtis Richard Day.

---

63. *University Catalogue, 1916–1917*, 95–98. It should also be noted, however, that Adams was part of a nationwide trend that was greatly expanding the study of business in American higher education. See Leon Carroll Marshall, ed., *The Collegiate School of Business: Its Status at the Close of the First Quarter of the Twentieth Century*.

64. For the council and its classification system, see Everett, *Medical Education in Oklahoma*, 28–29.

65. Scott, "University of Oklahoma School of Medicine." See also the interesting work by John R. Sokatch, "Indians, Homesteaders and Molecular Biologists: A History of Biochemistry and the Department of Biochemistry and Molecular Biology of the University of Oklahoma Health Sciences Center," 25–28.

66. See *University Catalogue, 1912–1913*, 196–202, for the "synopsis of courses" for the first two years of medical study.

67. Quoted in Everett, *Medical Education in Oklahoma*, 83.

Like his predecessor, Day lasted for only a year and a half.[68] It was obvious that the medical school required some steady and permanent leadership, particularly in the Oklahoma City part of the undertaking.

The main reason for the demotion of 1912, however, was the lack of hospital facilities for training the students. The School of Medicine had entered into a questionable agreement with Joseph B. Rolater, an Oklahoma City doctor and teacher. Rolater owned a two-story home and a small private hospital, both located at N.E. Fourth and Stiles Streets. The University entered into a leasing understanding with him in 1911, promising to pay $6,000 a year for ten years.[69] The Rolater home became the School's administrative center, with offices, classrooms, and a small library (the old kitchen now was the clinical laboratory). The next-door hospital was to be enlarged to sixty beds, twenty-six of which would be for clinical purposes. But Rolater was to retain the use of a number of them for his private patients, and the small operating room was also reserved for Rolater's private use at specified times. Despite the confident assurances and boosterism of Dean Williams,[70] the arrangement was far from satisfactory. Even the twenty-five beds offered by the nearby Oklahoma City General Hospital and other offers from more distant hospitals were not adequate for the teaching purposes of the School of Medicine.

Three men combined their efforts to rectify the situation. Two of them were experienced physicians, longtime advocates of better medical education in the new state of Oklahoma, and old friends. Dr. Francis B. Fite from Muskogee had been a prominent doctor in Indian Territory and a president of the Indian Territory Medical Association. He was also a man with political connections, and in 1912 he found himself on Governor Cruce's new State Board of Education. LeRoy Long had come to Indian Territory in 1895 and practiced medicine in Atoka and Caddo before moving to McAlester in 1904. By the time of statehood, Long had earned a strong reputation as an able physician, a skilled surgeon, an accomplished speaker, and a man of high intelligence and principle. Fite and Long had known and admired one another for a long time; when both were appointed to the State Board of Medical Examiners, they became friendly co-conspirators for better medical training in the new state.[71] The third man who enlisted in the cause of improving the School of Medicine was the third governor of Oklahoma, Robert Lee Williams.[72]

68. Koch, "Administrative History," 85–86; Gittinger, *University of Oklahoma*, 93.

69. Everett (*Medical Education in Oklahoma*, 86) gives the figure of $6,000 per year; the figure of $8,000 is reported in Basil A. Hayes, *LeRoy Long, Teacher of Medicine*, 66. Hayes's detailed and admiring biography of Long was originally serialized in the *Chronicles of Oklahoma* 20 and 21 (1942 and 1943).

70. Published by the dean in the *Journal of the Oklahoma State Medical Association* 4 (1911–12) and helpfully excerpted by Everett, *Medical Education in Oklahoma*, 86–88.

71. Hayes, *LeRoy Long*, 59–60. For Long's early career, see the obituary tribute, L. A. Turley, "LeRoy Long, Doctor and Educator," *Sooner Magazine* 13 (December 1940): 18.

72. For a brief overview of his career and governorship, see Thomas Arthur Hazell, "Robert Lee Williams, Governor of Oklahoma, 1915–1919," in LeRoy H. Fischer, ed., *Oklahoma's Governors, 1907–1929: Turbulent Politics*, 66–86. For the governor's role in improving medical education, see Everett, *Medical Education in Oklahoma*, chap. 7.

The first step, clearly, was to get some permanent and able leadership for the medical school. That effort became a long campaign to persuade LeRoy Long to take over the deanship. The first suggestion to Long came at a 1913 meeting of surgeons in Chicago; the second occurred later the same year, when Fite urged him to accede. In 1914 Fite telephoned Long to say that the State Board of Education was going to choose him as dean whether he liked it or not; Long rushed to Oklahoma City to tell his friend that he could not accept the job. He was forty-six years old; he loved the daily practice of medicine (particularly surgery); and he felt he could not sacrifice the practice he had laboriously built in McAlester. He also told Fite that he did not want to be the dean of a class "B" medical school and that the effort to win back an "A" rating "would mean additional sacrifices, worry and expenditure of energy." But then, he recalled, "in May 1915, I was again requested to serve. . . . Great pressure was brought to bear. Appeal was made to my sense of duty to the medical profession. I hesitated and when I hesitated, I was lost." One day, in the midst of wrestling with the decision, he left his office and walked home for lunch to talk the matter over with his wife. When he got there, the phone rang. It was Governor Williams, calling from Oklahoma City, urging him to say yes and pledging his full support in the work that lay ahead. On May 27, 1915, the State Board of Education named Long dean, at $3,000 a year. The nomination was made by Francis Fite; and, finally, Long agreed.[73] He was to be the dean of the School of Medicine for the next seventeen years, and he performed the same pioneering role there that H. H. Herbert and Arthur Adams were simultaneously performing in journalism and business.

Long's appointment was not to start until September 1; but on June 14 he accompanied President Brooks and Governor Williams to a meeting of the State Board of Education, where the dean-elect explained what had to be done to get back an "A" rating. To begin with, the Rolater hospital (which was now being called University Hospital) was poorly equipped. The Board listened and immediately appropriated $4,000 to help repair the situation.[74] Simultaneously, the state agreed to rent the Oklahoma City General Hospital, just up the street from the University (Rolater) Hospital: for $1,200 a year, the School of Medicine gained another twenty-five beds and the chance to run the free outpatient clinic. Long was able to make other arrangements with St. Anthony Hospital and several maternity hospitals nearby. The old Rolater house was converted into a home for nurses being trained at the University. In September Long was given an assistant dean, Louis A. Turley, to help carry the administrative burden. But important as these changes were, the central problem remained. "We are in B grade," Dean Long observed, "and we believe we are kept there mainly for the reason that the work of our clinical years is conducted in rented property. We do not believe that the Council on Medical Education looks with

73. For the story of persuading Long, see Hayes, *LeRoy Long*, 61–63.

74. "Minutes of the State Board of Education, June 14, 1915," 6–7; Everett, *Medical Education in Oklahoma*, 117. Everett reports that this sum was "refunded" to the State Board by the 1916 legislature.

LeRoy Long

favor upon this temporary, unsettled situation of the school."[75] What the enterprise needed was a hospital of its own.

In the closing months of 1916 a full-scale campaign was launched for the creation of a hospital operated exclusively by the University for the training of students in the School of Medicine.[76] Williams promised to ask the legislature for a $200,000 appropriation when it gathered in January 1917. Both Dean Long and President Brooks sprang to the task of drumming up support for the University Hospital bill. The dean wrote to doctors around the state asking for their help with the legislature, and the Tulsa County Medical Society responded favorably during its meeting on December 18.[77] The very next day President Brooks devoted much of an Oklahoma City faculty meeting to urging the staff and students to get behind the effort to obtain the appropriation.[78] Brooks and Long had probably begun their relationship hesitantly. Long's biographer states that "Dr. Brooks was slightly hostile and felt that the appointment of the new dean had been forced upon him, which indeed it had been." (It will be remembered that from the start Brooks had insisted that appointments to the University had to come exclusively through the president.) But President Brooks was neither bullheaded nor a fool; he quickly recognized the exceptional merits of his new dean, and working together drew the two men into an effective partnership. "However Dr. Brooks may have felt, he soon adjusted himself to the situation and became a warm friend of Dr. Long."[79]

House Bill 366 was duly introduced in January 1917.[80] It proposed to set aside 15.6 acres of state-owned land southeast of the Capitol and to appropriate the funds to build a medical department of the University.[81] It also stipulated that any Oklahoma citizen could

75. Quoted by Everett, *Medical Education in Oklahoma*, 119.

76. The fullest account of the campaign is in ibid., 126–35. See also the reminiscences of two eyewitnesses: Fred S. Clinton, "University of Oklahoma Medical School Crisis Averted," *Chronicles of Oklahoma* 25 (1947–48): 342–57; and Scott, "University of Oklahoma School of Medicine," 8–9. See also Hayes, *LeRoy Long*, 67–69; and "The University Hospital," *Harlow's Weekly* 21 (March 3, 1922): 11–14.

77. Clinton, "University of Oklahoma Medical School Crisis Averted," 351–52. Clinton was involved in this effort.

78. Everett, *Medical Education in Oklahoma*, 127.

79. Hayes, *LeRoy Long*, 65.

80. *Journal of the Oklahoma House of Representatives*, 6th Sess. (January 2–March 2, 1917), 580. The bill's provisions are summarized section by section, in Everett, *Medical Education in Oklahoma*, 131–32; and in Clinton, "University of Oklahoma Medical School Crisis Averted," 345–47.

81. Subsequently the location would be given the address 800 N.E. 13th Street. Everett, *Medical Education in Oklahoma*, 144.

be treated in the new hospital and that poor and indigent patients would be served at no cost to themselves. The measure was vigorously opposed. Some Oklahoma physicians worked against it, apparently led by Dr. Rolater, who was worried about losing the payments for the use of his property. He suggested to Francis Fite that he would stop lobbying against the bill if only he could be sure that his lease would not be ended. He was suitably assured.[82] In any case, the Senate committee decided against the proposal and sent forward its "do not pass" recommendation. Dean Long and President Brooks requested a rehearing before the committee, and it also seems likely that Governor Williams added his muscle.[83] The request for a rehearing was granted.

The news that Dr. Long was to speak spread, and the event had to be moved from the committee room to the Senate chamber itself. Faculty and students came in large numbers; so did senators who were not on the committee as well as interested members of the general public. The proceedings began at noon, and Long delivered a passionate speech on "the odious stigma of 'B' grade" and the desperate need for a medical school that could provide Oklahomans with the physicians they needed and the services they deserved, physicians and services comparable to those of any other state in the union. He touched upon the needs of the suffering poor for a place where they could receive the best medical attention. Long was followed by other members of the faculty, who warmly reinforced his message. The Senate, persuaded by the eloquence (but also, no doubt, by the pressure from the governor and the cessation of negative lobbying by Rolater and his friends), passed the bill with a sizable majority shortly before the end of the session in March. The episode was surely one of the most significant and far-reaching in the history of medical education at the University of Oklahoma.

The construction of the new University Hospital, postponed by America's entry into World War I, was completed in August 1919 and formally dedicated on November 13. On March 11, 1920, the Council on Medical Education informed President Brooks that it was restoring an "A" rating to the University of Oklahoma's School of Medicine. The momentous announcement was marked on March 19 by a daylong celebration. The medical clinics in the morning were followed by a luncheon for the students and visiting doctors. The afternoon parade featured floats from each of the medical classes. And two hundred physicians came to the Skirvin Hotel that night for an elaborate banquet given by members of the senior class.[84] The *Journal of the Oklahoma State Medical Association* summarized things nicely:

---

82. Hayes, *LeRoy Long*, 68–69. Mark Everett aptly observes (*Medical Education in Oklahoma*, 133) that "Dr. J. B. Rolater was interested in financial and business affairs, with some concern for medical education. His reputed opposition to the bill . . . would seem to indicate that, in the balance, he was actually more interested in financial affairs than in medical education."

83. Hayes asserts (*LeRoy Long*, 69) that "the powerful influence of Governor Williams was on their side and even after the Senate had recommended that it not pass, the governor threatened to veto the college appropriation unless the bill was passed in three days."

84. Everett, *Medical Education in Oklahoma*, 149–53.

No happening affecting the Oklahoma doctors, since their organization for mutual bet-
terment, has been received with the very generous acclaim and enthusiasm as was the
news . . . that our school had been placed in Class A. . . . [T]he long fight to this end,
the unreasonable and selfish opposition met from many sources when legislative enactment . . . hung by a thread . . . the strange anomaly of opposition from a few members
of the medical profession, inspired by selfishness or pique.

The *Journal*, noting that "we are through with the first great fight," suggested that "after
this, it will be a matter of increasing pride to build, from the very effective nucleus and
organization existing, as great a school as our commercial wealth and resources warrant."
But then the writer of the *Journal* article, carried away by the euphoria of the triumph,
indulged in a bit of wistful utopian fantasy: "The question of lack of money should never
again be allowed to harrass [*sic*] the men [to whom] we entrust the great task of building."[85]
Not very likely.

~

ALONG WITH THE IMPRESSIVE ADDITIONS to the faculty in education, journalism, business, and medicine, the University was able to acquire other teachers between
1912 and 1917 who were to make notable contributions to the institution. Indeed, some
of the professors who joined the Oklahoma faculty during this five-year period were to
prove as important to the future of the University as were those pioneering professors
hired by Boyd at the turn of the century. Among the dozens of faculty members, most of
whom came and went quickly, were a handful who had lasting effects on the generations
of students who were to pass under their influence.

The School of Fine Arts was immeasurably strengthened by the addition of five young
men who were to teach side by side at the University of Oklahoma for decades. Two of
the newcomers were pianists. Lewis Spencer Salter had studied the instrument at the
University and earned his degree in 1912. But Dean Holmberg had enlisted him as an
instructor while he was still a senior; perhaps Holmberg took special notice of the young
man because of both his undeniable talent and the fact that he had previously studied at
Bethany College in Lindsborg, Kansas, Holmberg's own school. Salter eventually completed a second bachelor's degree, this one from the College of Arts and Sciences (1917),
and a master's degree from Columbia (1922). He was only twenty when he began; but he
taught for twenty-four years alongside Holmberg. When his mentor died in 1936, he took
over as dean of the College of Fine Arts, a position he held for eleven more years before
returning to teaching.[86] Lewis Salter was joined immediately by another piano instructor. Charles Francis Giard had grown up near Boston, graduated from the New England

85. The article ("Our Medical School into Class A," *Journal of the Oklahoma State Medical Association* 13 [1920]: 151) is
helpfully excerpted in Everett, *Medical Education in Oklahoma*, 150–51.

86. See Salter's obituary, *Norman Transcript*, July 24, 1965, 1; and Gittinger, *University of Oklahoma*, 80.

Conservatory (1905), taught for a few years at Epworth in Oklahoma City, and came to Norman in 1910 at age twenty-five to teach for a year. He then returned permanently in 1912 and taught both piano and composition (he was an active composer himself) until his suicide in May 1947.[87]

Two other significant additions to Fine Arts also came to teach music. When he was an undergraduate, Lewis Salter had roomed with William G. Schmidt, a German immigrant and a voice major. Like Salter, Schmidt finished his degree in 1912 and was hired by Holmberg in 1913. Before he died, at the age of forty-nine, Schmidt had trained more than two hundred vocalists, some of whom achieved considerable fame.[88] Another invaluable addition to the School of Music was eighteen-year-old Paul S. Carpenter, who began his long career at the University in February 1914; he was paid $750 to finish out the second semester. He had been a celebrated child violinist in Philadelphia and had just graduated from that city's Combs Conservatory. He joined Holmberg, Salter, Giard, and Schmidt both in the work of teaching aspiring young musicians and in encouraging the development of music throughout the state and region. For many years he conducted the University's symphony and also directed the work of smaller ensembles. A few years before his early death, Carpenter, who adeptly combined artistic talent with administrative skill and who was popular with his colleagues, became the director of the School of Music after Lewis Salter gave up the position in 1946.[89]

In 1915, a year after acquiring Paul Carpenter, Dean Holmberg hired one of the legendary figures in the University's history, Oscar Brousse Jacobson. Like Holmberg, Jacobson had been born in Sweden. He arrived in the United States at the age of seven in 1889. And like Holmberg (as well as Lewis Salter and football coach Bennie Owen), Jacobson was a product of Lindsborg, Kansas. He worked his way through high school there and then through a degree at Bethany (1908). For the next five years he taught at Minnesota College and at the State College of Washington and during the first part of 1915 was studying at the Louvre in Paris. He was hired, at $1,400, to be the director of the School of Art and the art museum ("There wasn't much to direct," he was fond of wryly reminiscing). After a year in Norman, Jacobson left to complete a bachelor's degree at Yale (1916). He returned to Oklahoma and remained at the University, rendering extraordinary service, for the next thirty-seven years.[90] Jacobson was a "man of commanding appearance" and

---

87. Gittinger, *University of Oklahoma*, 79–80; "Tribute to Giard," *Sooner Magazine* 13 (May 1941): 30.

88. Gittinger, *University of Oklahoma*, 88; see also Schmidt's obituary, *Norman Transcript*, April 8, 1936, 1; and "A Maestro Is Dead," *Sooner Magazine* 8 (May 1936): 192. Schmidt's most famous pupil was undoubtedly the opera singer Joseph Benton, who performed under the name Joseph Bentonelli.

89. For the details of Carpenter's life and career, see *Sooner Magazine* 19 (August 1947): 4; "Heart Ailment Fatal to Dean Carpenter," *Sooner Magazine* 21 (January 1949): 17; and his obituary in the *Norman Transcript*, January 5, 1949.

90. See Jacobson's obituaries in the *Norman Transcript*, September 19, 1966, and *Oklahoma Daily*, September 20, 1966; see also George Milburn, "Pioneering in Beauty: Professor Jacobson Is Internationally Famous as an Artist," *Sooner Magazine* 1 (February 1929): 149–51; and the catalogue for the *Oscar Brousse Jacobson Retrospective Exhibit, September 17–October 8, 1961*, 6. His career and his legacy are also explored in Carol Whitney, "A Place of Coming Together: The

"a gracious and magnetic personality."[91] Tall, distinguished, courtly and courteous, he was an accomplished painter, mostly of western landscapes. (Leonard Good of Drake University said that he painted "with Homeric simplicity the dignity and grandeur of the great west.")[92] Perhaps Jacobson's most famous work, however, was his discovery and sponsorship of "the Kiowa Five," Native American artists whose exceptional talent he recognized and nurtured at the University, starting in 1926.[93] Oscar Jacobson's name must loom large in any account of how Native American art came to be widely respected and valued by non-Indians in America and the world at large. On December 11, 1952, the University Regents named the art museum "Jacobson Hall" in recognition of his contributions; three weeks later, on January 1, 1953, he replied to the Regents with a very terse letter: "Gentlemen: THANKS! Sincerely, Oscar B. Jacobson."[94]

Although Fine Arts made perhaps the most spectacular additions in the flurry of hiring that occurred between 1912 and 1917, other divisions of the University also gained substantially. In 1914 and 1916 the Mathematics Department, for example, added two men who could not have been more different from one another but who were both to make valuable contributions to the institution. Edgar Meacham was born near Smithfield, Texas, in August 1887. He went to grammar school in Fort Worth and, when the family moved to the Cheyenne and Arapaho territory, to various Oklahoma country schools. His high school was the Preparatory School of the Southwestern State Teacher's College in Weatherford. He graduated at the advanced age of twenty-three in 1910, the same year he got married. Meacham came to Norman in 1911 and promptly discovered football. He soon was an outstanding guard on Bennie Owen's undefeated team of that year and, at 212 pounds, the biggest man on the squad. He remained in Norman until he graduated in 1914. He was not only a football star: he was a member of the track team, the president of his fraternity, and the editor of the *Sooner Yearbook*.[95]

Ed Meacham soon learned two important things about himself: that he was a gifted student, far superior to his classmates, and that mathematics, particularly geometry, held a special fascination for him. After graduation he stayed in Norman in a double capacity. He became an assistant to Coach Owen (put in charge of the freshman teams) and an instruc-

Historic Jacobson House," *Chronicles of Oklahoma* 78 (Winter 2000–2001): 444–67. The quoted remark is in the *Norman Transcript* obituary.

91. The quotations are from George Lynn Cross, "The President of O.U. Speaks: A Salute to Oscar B. Jacobson," in Jacobson's Personnel File, Office of the Provost. See also the affectionate letter, March 23, 1950, recommending him for a David Ross Boyd professorship, addressed to President Cross by eleven of his coworkers, also in his Personnel File: "He has brought meaning, honor, respect, prestige, and affection to the university for over thirty years. His integrity, his judgment and his courtesy remain irrefutable."

92. Quoted by Sam Olkinetzky, in *Oscar Brousse Jacobson Retrospective Exhibit*, 2.

93. Oscar B. Jacobson, *Kiowa Indian Art* (Nice, France: C. Szwedzicki, 1929); Enid Maxine Jones, "The Five: An Examination of the Indian Renaissance at the University of Oklahoma."

94. A copy of the letter is in Jacobson's Personnel File.

95. Keith, *Oklahoma Kickoff*, 216.

*Oscar Brousse Jacobson and the Kiowa Five, in 1929*

tor in the Mathematics Department. Although he coached until 1924, it was mathematics that eventually consumed his interest. Meacham went to Harvard for a master's degree (1917) and then to Chicago for a Ph.D. (1922). He was a popular teacher, especially of calculus. In 1926 Dean Samuel Reaves, a fellow-mathematician, asked him to become his assistant dean (without, of course, giving up his math teaching). After Reaves's retirement in 1940, Ed Meacham became dean of the College of Arts and Sciences, a position he held until his unexpected death in June 1952. He was good-humored, outgoing, unfailingly dignified, even-tempered, and courteous. He was also an extremely active member of the University community and of the Alumni Association.[96]

In 1916 Meacham was joined in the Mathematics Department by Nathan Altshiller.[97] While Meacham was big, athletic, Episcopalian, gregarious, and a product of rural Texas and rural Oklahoma, Altshiller was diminutive (five foot five and under 150 pounds), studiously intellectual and aesthetic, and a Russian Jew with a heavy accent, the first

96. Because of Meacham's prominence and because members of his large family (at least ten siblings) lived throughout the state, there are numerous obituaries. See *Oklahoma City Times*, *Enid News*, and *Clinton Daily News*, all on June 29, 1952, and *Daily Oklahoman*, June 30, 1952. See also the warm editorial tribute "Passing of an OU Great," *Norman Transcript*, June 30, 1952. A fuller account of his life and character is Eugenia Kaufman, "He Stood Tall," *Sooner Magazine*, 25 (September 1952): 9–11.

97. See Altshiller's obituary in the *Oklahoma Daily*, July 23, 1968, 1, 2; Billie Rhue Wiley, "Nathan Altshiller Court," *Sooner Magazine* 8 (December 1935): 63; and Arnold Court, "Nathan Altshiller Court, 1881–1968," in the Nathan A. Court MSS, Box 1A, Folder 1.

Jew to be hired at the University of Oklahoma. Ed Meacham's father was a farmer; Altshiller's was a shoe merchant. And if Meacham's academic talents lay principally in the classroom, Altshiller's did not. After he had been teaching math at the University of Oklahoma for almost thirty years, a University president once had to explain to him why his department had failed to recommend a raise for him that year: he "should establish better relationships with some of his students in order to merit an increase in salary," according to the department. The president, who was personally fond of the mathematician, elaborated: "I believe the Committee [of the department] feels that you too frequently use sarcasm as a part of your classroom procedure, and that students have complained of this during the past few years."[98]

But Nathan Altshiller was a first-class mathematician, one of the few faculty members at the University before World War II who gained a national and international reputation (one of his books was

*Edgar Meacham*

translated into Chinese, another into French). His primary and secondary education had been completed in Warsaw (then part of Russia). He earned a master's and a doctor's degree at the University of Ghent in Belgium (1907 and 1911) and then crossed the ocean to study at Columbia University for two years. After a year as an instructor at Columbia, Altshiller taught for two years at the University of Washington and for another at the University of Colorado. When he arrived in Norman he was already thirty-five years old. Altshiller, who bore a striking physical resemblance to Albert Einstein,[99] did pioneering work in geometry, publishing many papers and leading textbooks in that field.[100] In addition to his technical works on the geometry of the triangle and higher plane curves, Altshiller also wrote thoughtfully on such topics as "Mathematics and Esthetics" and "Mathematics in the History of

98. George Lynn Cross to Nathan Altshiller Court, December 5, 1945, in Court's Personnel File, Office of the Provost; six years earlier, Reaves's generally superb evaluation of Court contained the remark: "A good teacher for better students. Rather impatient with poor students."

99. Roy Temple House, "Oklahoma's Einstein Adds Two New College Subjects," *Daily Oklahoman*, March 29, 1936. His "resemblance to Einstein is so striking that it has been remarked all over the country. A short time ago he was walking through the Oklahoma City 'flats,' the river bank region where the homeless are allowed to camp . . . when a ragged little boy startled him by calling 'Daddy! Look—there goes Einstein.' "

100. A bibliography compiled by his son Arnold lists 146 publications; Nathan A. Court MSS, Box 1A, Folder 1.

Civilization."[101] He was brilliant, urbane, and cultured, a lover of art and music, occasionally a little on the cranky side. Until he retired in 1951, he tried hard (probably never once in thirty-five years missing a class because of illness) to interest students in the mysteries of mathematics.

While Nathan Altshiller was enlivening the campus with the unfamiliar influence of eastern European Jewry, Patricio Gimeno provided an unfamiliar taste of Spain and Latin America. He was born in Arequipa, Peru, probably on Christmas day, 1862.[102] His father was a Spanish actor-singer; his mother an Italian. Gimeno played his first role at six and gained a small reputation as a child performer. When his father died suddenly, his mother took him back to her own father's house in Spain. He studied art at the famous Valencia Academy and tried to make a living as an artist in Cuba, New York, Lima, San Francisco, and Chicago. Somehow he ended up teaching art and Spanish at Epworth College; and in 1911 he became the sole instructor in art and a teacher of Spanish at the University of Oklahoma. In 1916 he moved permanently to the Spanish Department,[103] where he taught until his death in 1940.[104] He was gentle, refined, and cosmopolitan; his students admired him greatly and praised him for introducing them first to the existence and then to the beauties of other cultures. One University president called him "one of the most versatilely gifted men that I have ever known."[105] Gimeno never abandoned his love of art, and both his original paintings and his copies still decorate the University's library.[106]

The scientific side of the University was enhanced by the arrival of two men during this period, one in the natural and the other in the physical sciences. Gayfree Ellison—like several others who were so important to the University—attended Bethany College in Lindsborg, Kansas, finishing his bachelor's degree there in 1898. He volunteered for the Spanish-American War and saw extensive combat in the Philippines. He received

---

101. His pioneering *College Geometry* was published in 1925 and went through several editions thereafter; Nathan A. Court, "Mathematics and Esthetics," *Sooner Magazine* 2 (November 1929): 58 (reprinted in *School Science and Mathematics* 30 [January 1930]), and "Mathematics in the History of Civilization," *Mathematics Teacher* 41 (March 1948): 104–11. See also his "Democratizing Mathematics," *Bulletin of the Kansas Association of Teachers of Mathematics* (1941): 55–57.

102. That date appears on a form completed by him in his Personnel File, Office of the Provost. As time passed, his birth year crept upward. The fountain erected in his memory near Adams Hall, whose construction was guided by his son Harold, gives the date 1864, as does Oscar B. Jacobson and Jeanne d'Ucel, "Art in Oklahoma," *Chronicles of Oklahoma* 32 (1954–55): 270–71; 1865 is given in other places, including Doris Ostrander Dawdy, *Artists of the American West: A Biographical Dictionary*, 2:106, and other sources.

103. Two years later, in April 1918, the State Board of Education ordered that the independent departments of French, Spanish, Italian, and German be combined into a new Department of Modern Languages, with the change to begin on September 1.

104. This account of Gimeno's life relies heavily on Jacobson and d'Ucel, "Art in Oklahoma"; and on William H. Witt, "Patricio Gimeno," *Sooner Magazine* 5 (April 1933): 198–99, 213. See also Gittinger, *University of Oklahoma*, 73; and the obituary notice in *Sooner Magazine* 13 (September 1940): 27.

105. William Bennett Bizzell to Mrs. Patricio Gimeno, August 31, 1940, Gimeno Personnel File.

106. Gimeno's work includes the two large copies of *Dante and Beatrice* and *Blind Milton Dictating "Paradise Lost" to His Daughters* at the south entrance to the library. He also painted portraits of Jesse Rader, Stratton Brooks, and William Bennett Bizzell that adorn other parts of the building. Some of his other copies hang near the Peggy V. Helmerich reading room.

*Patricio Gimeno*

his medical degree at Rush Institute five years later. Eventually Ellison opened a medical practice in Oklahoma City; but in 1912, after three years there, he came to Norman to teach bacteriology and epidemiology. He was thirty-seven when he arrived, and he stayed at this work until his death twenty-two years later. Ellison is best remembered, however, as the founder and director of the student health service. In July 1933, six months after his death, the Regents changed the name of Hygeia Hall to the Ellison Infirmary.[107] The principal acquisition in the physical sciences was undoubtedly Victor E. Monnett. Born in Missouri in December 1889, he came to Norman as an undergraduate and came under the tutelage of Charles Gould. After graduating in 1912, he attended the University of Michigan for a year and eventually received his doctorate from Cornell (1922). Monnett joined the Oklahoma faculty in 1916 and eight years later was appointed head of the Department of Geology and Geography. His specialty was structural geology, particularly as applied to the discovery of petroleum and natural gas; he also headed the Geological Engineering Department and no doubt trained as many prominent petroleum geologists as Gould himself. During World War II, Victor Monnett was to serve as the graduate dean.[108]

~

FINALLY, IN 1914 AND 1915 the University hired two men who were notable not merely for their unforgettably vivid personalities but also for their pioneering emphasis on the history of the American West, which was to influence the social sciences side of the University for generations. One of them taught history; the other English. Together, they and their successors did much to determine the intellectual direction and reputation of one part of the University of Oklahoma.

Few men arrived to teach at any American university with a more colorful past than Edward Everett Dale. He had been born in February 1879 in east Texas, where his pioneering family had moved a few years before. His family, he once said, had "restless feet itch-

---

107. See Ellison's obituary, *Norman Transcript*, December 22, 1932; and the full review of his career: John Alley, "Gayfree Ellison: Pioneer University Physician," *Sooner Magazine* 5 (April 1933): 193–95.

108. Monnett's obituary is in the *Norman Transcript*, September 19, 1972.

*Gayfree Ellison*

*Victor E. Monnett*

ing to scratch strange gravel."[109] "We were not exactly poor people," Dale once quipped, "we were just plain damn *pore.*"[110] His mother died when he was five. When he was ten, his father moved the family again, this time to Old Greer County, that disputed strip of land between the north and south forks of the Red River, which was thought to be part of Texas when the Dales got there but which was awarded to Oklahoma by the Supreme Court in 1896. During his first ten years, Ed Dale learned all he wanted to know about the backbreaking work of primitive farming on heavily timbered land; during the next twenty, he learned all there was to know about cattle ranching. Before long he knew intimately about horses and cattle and trail cooking and hunting out on the prairie.[111] He eventually went into the cattle business himself with his older brother, George. They went broke in 1900—defeated by limited pasture, a killing winter, an overstocked market, and low prices. Ed Dale went to work punching cattle for his neighbors, participating in drives, and picking cotton for fifty cents per hundred pounds.

In his autobiography Dale estimates that he had probably gone to school for less than a year, all told, during the first thirteen years of his life. Yet somehow he and his brother were always avid readers, a habit that set them apart from other boys in the neighborhood.

109. Dale's father was born in Kentucky, moved to Missouri, drove and walked an ox team to California searching for gold, returned to Missouri by boat to Panama and walked across the Isthmus, tried for gold again in Colorado, moved to Nebraska, and then headed south through Kansas and Indian Territory for a farm in the rugged Texas Cross Timbers.

110. Eighty years later, he wrote about his first ten years in *The Cross Timbers: Memories of a North Texas Boyhood.*

111. "Nobody who has ever listened to Dr. Dale's classroom lectures in which he discoursed expertly on the duties of a line rider, the equipment of the chuck wagon, or the techniques of trail driving," one of his finest students wrote, "will ever forget this stage of his career" (Angie Debo, "Edward Everett Dale: The Teacher," in Arrell M. Gibson, ed., *Frontier Historian: The Life and Work of Edward Everett Dale,* 23).

Their reading was largely the religious literature collected by their Primitive Hardshell Baptist father, but it kindled their imaginations and made them long for more. After a little more schooling Ed was hired to teach, for $35 a month, on the Kiowa-Comanche-Apache Reservation a few miles north of his home, an area that had just been opened to white settlement. By a curious coincidence, one of his pupils was the young, chubby-cheeked Ed Meacham, who was later to become Dale's dean. By 1906, at the age of twenty-seven, Dale was superintendent for a growing collection of schools in the region. After boldly trying out the teachers' college in Edmond—the biggest town he had ever seen to that point—he enrolled at Norman in 1909. His enrollment became the occasion for one of the favorite stories he liked to tell about himself. It seems that a cowboy friend back home in Greer County tried to talk him out of entering college at the age of thirty: "It'll take you three years before you get out of there with a bachelor's degree. By that time, for God's sake, you'll be thirty-three years old!" Dale (with that slow, easy, high-pitched twang of his) recalled the incident: "Well, I said to myself, in three years I'll be thirty-three years old *anyway*—with or without a bachelor's degree."[112]

He graduated in 1911, with a major in history. And then he went to Harvard. It was an extraordinary decision, and it tells much about his enormous courage, his frontier self-reliance and self-confidence. It is also the great mystery of his life. "Looking back over a period of more than half a century," he reminisced, "I am appalled by my colossal nerve in going to Harvard to work in the graduate school."[113] If he had been dazzled by Edmond, we can only imagine his thoughts upon getting off the train in Boston. He soon fell under the spell of Frederick Jackson Turner, the most famous historian of the American West who ever lived. Turner, eighteen years older than his new student, discovered in Ed Dale a real cowboy of the sort that he had written about, mostly theoretically. Dale occasionally showed off his cooking to Turner, inviting him over for sausages and biscuits, which he had prepared, he said, "à la camp!" The two probably taught much to each other. When Turner mentioned the lack of respect for the law on the frontier, Dale could tell his teacher that "even ministers of the Gospel living near Navajoe [his hometown] cut and hauled wood from the Indian reservation across the North Fork of the Red River, keeping an eagle eye out for the U.S. marshals or the Indian police." Turner's classroom discussion of "extra-legal associations" caused Dale to recall the livestock associations in Oklahoma that employed men to check brands and reduce theft. And when Turner remarked that "a man on the American frontier frequently worked at various vocations," Dale could point out that he himself had taken up half a dozen jobs.[114]

It would be pleasant to think that this rough, tall, lanky cowboy from Oklahoma could

112. Edward Everett Dale, *The West Wind Blows: The Autobiography of Edward Everett Dale*. For the decision to go to college despite his age, see xiv–xv.

113. Ibid., 123.

114. Ibid., 133.

teach the famous Turner a thing or two about the Southwest. But there can be no doubt that Turner transformed Dale. He did it by showing Dale that what he had lived for thirty years was actually American history and, in Turner's view, the most important and shaping part of American history, far more crucial to the development of the nation than the cultural or political importations from Europe. Turner's course on the American West, Dale remembered, "opened to me a new Heaven and a new earth in the field of American history. . . . It was a shock to realize that all of these things were a part of history." In short, Turner invested Dale's boyhood experiences with an importance he had never dreamed of when he was living them. It was a lesson Dale never forgot. For the next sixty years, he studied and taught about the American West; and before he was done, at the age of ninety-three, he had written twenty-four books and sixty articles on that subject.

Dale returned to Norman as an instructor of history, sharing the teaching duties with James Buchanan and Roy Gittinger. After five years, he returned to Harvard to work, again with Turner, on a Ph.D., which he completed in 1922. His return to the East was responsible for another curious and colorful episode. Dale arrived in Boston just as the famous police strike of 1919 broke out. Like other Harvard students, Dale volunteered to help enforce the law, patrol the streets, and help put down the lawlessness that was beginning to erupt around the city.[115] Unlike the other Harvard boys, however, Dale had brought along his own gun. The others were issued small pistols by the authorities. But Dale politely asked if he might not also use the bigger version that he had carried with him from Oklahoma. He buckled both of them on and went out on patrol. He never shot either pistol, but the newspapers picked up the story of the Oklahoma professor they called "two-gun Dale," and soon many newspapers across the country were telling his story and featuring his picture.

He returned to his teaching in Norman in 1922 and two years later began his eighteen-year term as chair of the History Department. He was known across the campus for his informality, his folksy good humor, his western hospitality, his modesty, and his ability to tell stories. He was also among the best-known historians of the West and among the most widely renowned professors at the University of Oklahoma.

Back in 1915 Dale was joined by another colorful character with a deep and affectionate passion for the American West. He had been born near the Flint Hills of Kansas in August 1887 and christened Walter Stanley Vestal.[116] When he was only a year old, his father died; and his schoolteacher mother moved in with her own mother at Fredonia, Kansas. She eventually married James R. Campbell, the up-and-coming school superintendent

---

115. See Stephen H. Norwood, *Strikebreaking and Intimidation: Mercenaries and Masculinity in Twentieth-Century America*, chap. 1.

116. The best source for Campbell's life is his diary, in the Walter Stanley Campbell MSS, Western History Collections, University of Oklahoma. See also Savoie Lottinville, "Walter Stanley Campbell," *American Oxonian* 45 (October 1958): 242–44; Donald Berthrong, "Walter Stanley Campbell: Plainsman," *Arizona and the West* 7 (Summer 1965): 91–104; and Julee Short, "Walter S. Campbell: Oklahoma Writer," *Chronicles of Oklahoma* 51 (1973–74): 473–86. For his career in Norman, see Len White, "The Triumph of Stanley Vestal," *Sooner Magazine* 30 (October 1957): 4–7, 31.

*Edward Everett Dale*

at Fredonia. The youngster took his stepfather's surname and was known thereafter as Walter Stanley Campbell, "W. S." to his friends. In 1898 the family moved to Guthrie, Oklahoma, where James Campbell had been hired as school superintendent. Five years later, Walter's father became the first president of the Southwestern State Normal in Weatherford, and his sixteen-year-old stepson enrolled there as an undergraduate.

Walter Campbell was absorbed by two intense interests. On the one hand, he imbibed the earnest intellectual habits of his two bookish parents. He grew up in a home filled with things to read, and he fell in love with Latin and Greek classics and with Shakespeare and English literature. Upon graduating from Southwestern in 1908, Campbell crossed the Atlantic Ocean as Oklahoma's first Rhodes Scholar, returning with a bachelor's degree in English language and literature. He was awarded a master's degree in absentia by Oxford in 1915. On the other hand, at the same time when he was steeping himself in the classics of Western literature, he was consumed by a fascination with the people of the Great Plains: Indians, traders, scouts, pioneers, mountain men. Weatherford was located in the former Cheyenne-Arapaho reservation, and Campbell made many friends among local Indians; before long, he had acquired a strong respect for the cultures and the peoples of the West. They reminded him of the ancient Greeks: "On those vast and perilous plains," he once wrote, "all men, rich and poor alike, had to meet the same conditions; the great man was great simply because he did what others did, and did it better—like Achilles, like Ulysses. Those Greek heroes would have felt perfectly at home with Sitting Bull or Buffalo Bill or 'Dad' Lemmon."[117]

Campbell got a job teaching high school in Louisville, Kentucky, but hated it: "I would

---

117. Cited by Short, "Walter S. Campbell," 478, as Stanley Vestal, *The Missouri: The Rivers of America* (New York: Farrar and Rinehart, 1945), 162.

rather eat from the same dish as a cow than teach these youngsters," he wrote his parents.[118] Rather than enduring it for another year, he quit in 1914, returned to Oklahoma, and began a serious study of the Plains Indians. When Stratton Brooks suggested that he come to Norman to teach English, Campbell accepted. Until his death on Christmas day, 1957, he remained an enthusiastic, popular, and sometimes controversial teacher of creative writing and the pioneering director of the University's famous professional writing program, at first in the English Department and then in the School of Journalism. And he wrote and wrote and wrote (after the mid-1920s, around a book a year). Thinking that there were too many authors named "Campbell," he decided to use a pseudonym; and his mother suggested that he revert to his original name, Stanley Vestal. By the time he died, "Stanley Vestal" had published twenty-four books, countless newspaper and magazine articles, poems, reviews, criticism, novels, short stories, and children's books.[119] Most of them were about the West: well-received biographies of Kit Carson, Sitting Bull, Jim Bridger, Big Foot Wallace, and Joe Meek, the mountain man; books about the Santa Fe trail, Dodge City, the Missouri River. He was a dogged and ingenious researcher, especially among the Indians, and there were apparently many Indians who loved and trusted him. He was officially adopted by the Sioux chief Joseph White Bull, the nephew of Sitting Bull (and, Campbell thought, the man who had killed Custer).[120]

Walter Campbell was a fiery man of strong beliefs and independent ways and great passions. He loved horses and camping and visiting Indian villages and talking to old-timers. He loved Oklahoma football. He probably drank too much and was sometimes boyishly oblivious to the niceties of formal occasions; once at a fancy alumni banquet in Oklahoma City, he took a few drinks and "chucked a piece of bread" to get the attention of an old fraternity brother sitting at another table.[121] As his health declined, he speculated on what should be done with his body. He did not want some undertaker "fleecing his children," and he suggested that his "carcass" be sold to the University hospital and the money be invested in a bronze equestrian statue. If that proved impractical, he favored a forty-dollar cremation with the ashes sprinkled by a friend "on some undertaker's head." The actual outcome was more dignified and symbolically apt. At his request, his body was placed in the cemetery of the Custer Battlefield National Monument; it rests among the Sioux warriors and their cavalry enemies about whom he had written so much.

To whatever extent the University has gained national celebrity over the years for its scholarly work on the American West, some of the credit must go to Edward Everett Dale and Walter S. Campbell. These two flamboyant, original, highly productive scholars, writers, and teachers—both of whom earned national reputations for their work—were

118. Cited by Berthrong, "Walter Stanley Campbell," 93, as a letter to Campbell's parents, March 1, 1914.

119. Dwight V. Swain, "Walter Stanley Campbell, 1887–1957," *Arizona and the West* 7 (Summer 1965): 87–90.

120. Stanley Vestal, "The Man Who Killed Custer," *American Heritage* 8 (February 1957): 4–9, 90–91.

121. David W. Levy, "The President and the Professor: With 'a Sense of Deep Regret,'" *Sooner Magazine* 14 (Summer 1994): 25–29.

present at the start. They helped to turn the institution in a promising and potentially important and useful new direction.

~

THE FACULTY MEMBERS WHO CAME to the University of Oklahoma between 1912 and 1917 were splendid additions to the institution. Warren Phelan and LeRoy Long; H. H. Herbert and Arthur Adams; Lewis Salter, Paul Carpenter, and Oscar Jacobson; Ed Meacham and Nathan Altshiller; Patricio Gimeno, Gayfree Ellison, and Victor Monnett; Ed Dale and Walter Campbell: these and perhaps half a dozen others who came during the first years of Stratton Brooks's presidency formed a particularly talented and loyal cohort. They stayed in Norman for a long time and, joining with the ablest teachers already on the scene, elevated the level of instruction at the University of Oklahoma to standards that it had never known before.

*Walter S. Campbell ("Stanley Vestal")*

The institution seemed at long last to be indubitably on the right track, headed in the right direction. It was being governed by a State Board that, for the time being at least, seemed willing to restrain itself. It was led by an able, incorruptible, and energetic president. Its various academic subdivisions were being efficiently supervised by competent if occasionally tyrannical deans. Behind the scenes, Emil Kraettli and George Wadsack were handling administrative affairs with an efficiency and discretion that had never been seen before. A number of fields—some of them brand new—were briskly growing: education and medicine, journalism, business, and the fine arts. The Preparatory Department was a thing of the past; and the University no longer had to function like a glorified high school. Student numbers were higher than ever and growing, and perforce the campus was adding new buildings. To all appearances, by 1917 the University of Oklahoma had recovered the ground that had been lost by the disastrous events of 1908 and 1911. What it lacked in reputation and library holdings and faculty salaries, it tried gamely to make up for with youthful energy and unbounded enthusiasm and football and bold optimism about what was coming. But the future is always dimly perceived and wildly unpredictable. The years ahead had many surprises in store—some of them pleasant and encouraging, some of them less so.

# Epilogue

By almost any standard, the University of Oklahoma had come a long way during its first quarter-century. There were still some people around in 1917 who could remember the primitive beginnings: that half-completed building standing alone on those barren forty acres southwest of the dusty little town; those fifty-seven students, shy and nervous and determined, climbing up the stairs of the old Rock Building on Main Street; the four teachers waiting on the second floor to get them registered and placed into the three empty classrooms behind them. Edwin DeBarr had been there on that first day; Del Larsh had been nearby. For twenty-five years they and a handful of other Norman citizens had been daily witnesses to the slow, transforming growth of the place. They had seen the fires and the firings and the never-ending fight against financial adversity; they had seen the new buildings going up and the new faculty arriving at the train station and the steadily enlarging student body. On those rare occasions when any of them bothered to reflect upon them, the changes must have seemed remarkable. To those who had been present at the start and left but came back at wide intervals on business or visits (French Amos and William Rice, who were both still living in Oklahoma; David Ross Boyd, who returned occasionally to see friends and tend to his real estate), the transformation must have seemed positively breathtaking.[1]

~

AT THE CLOSE OF THE 1916–17 ACADEMIC YEAR, the Norman campus occupied 120 acres, three times its original size. The twenty-acre addition donated by the city in 1902 was supplemented in 1914 by trading the section that Congress had given to the University in 1907 for sixty acres contiguous to the campus, thereby doubling the University's holdings. The bulk of the new land was situated south of the existing sixty acres, between what would one day be Brooks and Lindsey Streets. Another part of that trade of 1914, however, was with former president Boyd, who had been leasing his old home to the Uni-

---

1. The picture of the campus that follows is drawn from the *University Catalogues* of 1916–17 and 1917–18 and from the *Sooner* yearbooks of 1916 and 1917, both published by the University. See also Gittinger, *University of Oklahoma*, chap. 4.

*Boyd House, home of President Brooks, as it appeared in 1917*

versity since his departure. The University now owned the president's house (and a few lots to the west of it). Under the present occupant, Stratton Brooks, the president's home would turn its face away from University Boulevard and toward Boyd Street. Brooks had it remodeled in the neoclassical style and painted white; he added a portico and several porches and, at his own expense, four majestic ionic columns. It should be a home, Brooks thought, that could stand as a fitting symbol of the University's growing importance.[2] By 1917 a good part of the campus was enjoying the benefits of the pioneering tree-planting work of Boyd and others, and paths and flowerbeds had been added.

Whereas the students who had arrived back in 1892 found no building ready for their use, those coming for the 1916–17 academic year found an actual campus waiting to greet them. University Hall (not yet named in honor of former president Evans) had been the center of the Norman campus since it opened in 1912; it contained administrative offices and numerous classrooms. It was flanked by the two older buildings, Science Hall, with its laboratories and recitation rooms, and the Carnegie Library, housing books and the reading room and a big meeting space on the second floor.[3] Just north of the library stood

2. Carol J. Burr, "Back to Boyd House," *Sooner Magazine* 15 (Fall 1994): 3–7. See also "Old Aliases Remembered as Presidential Home Named Boyd House Again," *Sooner Magazine* 3 (Winter 1983): 3. The structure was officially named "Boyd House" by the Regents in December 1983.

3. Both buildings had some additional functions. Besides the recitation rooms for the sciences, Science Hall also housed education and philosophy. In addition to being the library, the Carnegie building also was home to the brand-new extension service and the Geological Survey, which the legislature had located at the University in 1908.

*DeBarr Hall*

the impressive law building opened in September 1913 and named Monnet Hall in honor of the law school dean. Across the oval from Monnet stood the newest addition to the campus. The chemistry building was opened for use that very September and immediately named DeBarr Hall in honor of the longest-serving member of the faculty. It was a stately stone and concrete edifice with four stories and a basement, exactly the same length (128 feet) as the law building that faced it but slightly wider (sixty-four feet to Monnet's fifty-five). The legislature had appropriated $115,000 for DeBarr Hall, and it contained everything the Chemistry Department needed for its work: labs for both students and faculty, classrooms, balance rooms and storerooms (including an underground area for inflammables and acids), and even an auditorium that could seat 220. The *Catalogue* of 1916–17 boasted: "In equipment and construction there is no more modern chemistry building in the United States."[4]

In addition to these five substantial and serviceable buildings, the University had constructed a number of less permanent structures over the years. A two-story engineering building had been put up in 1910 next to the heating and power plant (directly west of University Hall). The brick and stone edifice accommodated all the College of Engineer-

4. *University Catalogue, 1916–17*, 34. The third floor of DeBarr Hall was given to the Zoology Department for its museum, classrooms, and labs.

*Monnet Hall*

ing functions and was planned so that it could be converted exclusively into engineering shops after a permanent engineering building was in place. Meanwhile, the second floor housed the engineering library and classrooms; and the first floor, laboratories for mechanical and electrical engineering. Farthest west of University Hall, the string of temporary structures ended with a small anatomy building, although most of the medical work was done in Science Hall and DeBarr, with the advanced instruction taking place in the Oklahoma City facility at Second and Stiles Streets. Journalism also had obtained a small makeshift building; and the old gymnasium, built in 1903 east of University Hall, was still doing service. Finally there were storerooms, greenhouses, workshops, and the trusty heat and power plant that had been connected by tunnels to the other buildings since 1914. A small athletic field was set aside for women. The one for men (known as Boyd Field) was spacious: surrounded by a hedge, with two football fields, a running track, and two baseball diamonds. It boasted a grandstand that could seat three thousand.

If these structures were not sufficient evidence of how far the campus had come since 1892, word arrived fresh from the Sixth Legislature in 1917 that even greater bounty was in store. In addition to the $200,000 for the University's hospital in Oklahoma City, the lawmakers showered the Norman campus with $150,000 for an auditorium (later to become Holmberg Hall), $75,000 for one wing of a new library (later to be Jacobson Hall), and $100,000 for a brand-new geology building.[5] This beneficence may be taken as a

5. Ibid., 33; and Gittinger, *University of Oklahoma,* 104.

tribute both to the robust health of the state's economy and to the uncommon diplomatic skill of Stratton Brooks. The former state budget officer, Benjamin Harrison, asserted that "when Doctor Brooks and the state legislature met, Doctor Brooks found out how much money there was in the state treasury, then asked for all of it and usually got it."[6]

The University's library system owned around 25,000 volumes by the close of the 1915–16 academic year. Although the library's holdings were increasing at a healthy rate (there would be roughly 30,000 volumes by the close of the next academic year),[7] the University's collection was modest compared to those of other state institutions. Not even counting long-established libraries at state universities, such as the one at the University of Illinois (369,000 volumes) or Indiana University (109,000), the University of Oklahoma lagged far behind others in the region: the University of Texas owned about 130,000 books; and the University of Kansas, around 100,000.[8] The University of Oklahoma's limited holdings, moreover, were scattered among various departmental collections. Most of the books, of course, were in the Carnegie building, where students could consult them on weekdays from 7:45 A.M. until 6:00 P.M. and then after dinner from 7:00 to 10:00 P.M. On Saturdays the building was open from 9 A.M. to 5 P.M. The library had adopted the popular Dewey decimal system. Students could borrow the books and take them to their rooms; "persons not connected with the university, but known to the librarian, are invited to make use of the books in the reference room."[9] Small libraries devoted to medicine were to be found both in Science Hall and in the Oklahoma City facility. Students also had access to a law library in Monnet, a zoology library in DeBarr, a geology library in Science Hall, and an engineering library in the engineering building.

~

MEANWHILE, AS MIGHT HAVE BEEN EXPECTED, the University's faculty had been greatly enlarged. By the time students gathered for the opening of classes in the fall of 1917, the institution had a faculty of 107 on duty in Norman and another 47 in Oklahoma City.[10] As always, the faculty was almost exclusively male. Of the 131 individuals above the rank of instructor, only 7 were women, and they were to be found in fields where the prevalent gender stereotypes confined them: one taught French (Lucile Dora);

6. Quoted in Keith, *Oklahoma Kickoff*, 260. Keith went on: "Perhaps Brooks' outstanding achievement at Norman was his astute manipulation of the new state's legislatures. Although the president was quiet as a mouse about politics and never gave any outward indication that he participated in them, he was always thinking a couple of steps ahead of the embryo law-makers."

7. Figures from *University Catalogues* for 1915–16 and 1916–17.

8. *Report of the Commissioner of Education for the Year Ended June 30, 1917*, 2 vols. (Washington, D.C.: Government Printing Office, 1917), 2: table 17. Other state schools were also substantially ahead of Oklahoma: Colorado (90,600), Iowa (125,600), Iowa State (62,200), Missouri (200,000), Nebraska (123,000), and so forth.

9. *University Catalogue, 1916–1917*, 37.

10. Gittinger, *University of Oklahoma*, 102. Adding those on leave (including 18 in military service), the faculty numbered 176. Their names, ranks, earned degrees, and the year they came to teach are found in *University Catalogue, 1917–1918*, 5–24. The statistical breakdowns given here are derived from that listing.

one taught "domestic science"; one taught pediatrics in Oklahoma City; one was placed in charge of correspondence study and given the rank of assistant professor; the other three were in music. Among the forty-five instructors at the University, eleven were women; and, of these, four taught art or music. The University trailed behind national averages in employing women professors. (According to government statistics, in 1916 there were 28,472 male and 6,397 female professors in the United States, with women accounting for around 18.3 percent; women on the University of Oklahoma's staff accounted for only 5.3 percent.)[11]

Nineteen members of the Norman faculty had earned Ph.D. degrees, and numerous others were working on doctorates during the summers; forty-five of the professors in Oklahoma City held M.D.s and, we may assume, were dividing their time between teaching at the School of Medicine and their private practices. Only four members of the Norman faculty had been on the campus since the 1890s (DeBarr, Buchanan, Van Vleet, and Paxton); another nineteen had been employed before 1910; the rest were relative newcomers, forty-four of whom had been hired to teach during the last two years.

This faculty was dispersed into various colleges and schools. At the start of the 1917 school year, the University claimed two colleges: Arts and Sciences and Engineering. The College of Arts and Sciences, in addition to the traditional areas of study, had organized four specialized schools within itself (Business, Education, Journalism, and Social Service). The College of Engineering had under its auspices six subfields (Chemical, Civil, Electrical, Geological, Mechanical, and Manual Training). Alongside the two colleges were four free-standing schools: Fine Arts, Law, Medicine (including a new training school for nurses), and Pharmacy. There was also a Graduate School, but it had no separate faculty. Each of the colleges and schools had its own dean. And presiding over the administrative machinery and internal policy-making, subject only to the State Board of Education, was the highly undemocratic Administrative Council, consisting of President Brooks, Vice President DeBarr, and the deans.[12]

~

AT THE CLOSE OF THE 1916–17 SCHOOL YEAR, the University of Oklahoma claimed a grand total of 2,516 students. The figure represented a substantial and gratifying increase: during the preceding academic year, the student body had numbered only 2,090; and the year before that, only 1,682.[13] During 1916–17, students came to Norman from all seventy-seven Oklahoma counties, but 930 of them (37 percent) came from Cleveland

11. Department of Commerce, *Statistical Abstract of the United States, 1918* (Washington, D.C.: Government Printing Office, 1919), table 80. The figures were compiled from 574 institutions; some were women's colleges, where a high percentage of women faculty might be expected, but some were also schools of technology, where the faculty was predominately male.

12. *University Catalogue, 1916–17*, 28–29.

13. A full enrollment summary (including the names and home towns of each student) is included in the *University Catalogues* during these years; and these statistics are drawn from those helpful summaries.

and Oklahoma Counties. Some other counties made substantial contributions to the to-tal,[14] but most of the counties (forty-six) sent anywhere between ten and forty of their young people to the University. It was a measure of the institution's growing prestige that ninety-five students (almost 4 percent of the student body) came from other states. Texas contributed thirty-seven and Missouri, twenty-three; but fifteen other states also had representatives on the campus.

By this time, of course, the Preparatory Department had disappeared. More than two-thirds of the students (1,730) were studying in the College of Arts and Sciences. The School of Fine Arts enrolled 466 students, with Engineering (228), Law (175), Pharmacy (81), and Medicine and Nursing (116) trailing behind. The Graduate School claimed 111 students. The University was still enrolling a significantly larger percentage of women students than the national average. There were 1,458 men on the campus and 1,058 women (roughly 58 and 42 percent, respectively). National statistics indicate that around 63.2 percent of American college students were males; but if one subtracts the substantial numbers of women enrolled in all-women's colleges, the breakdown at typical coeducational institutions was probably closer to 75 percent men and only 25 percent women.[15] The distribution of women students at the University of Oklahoma revealed some of the usual patterns: they outnumbered men (385 to 81) in the School of Fine Arts and in the nursing program (31 to 0) but were almost invisible in engineering (227 to 1), law (171 to 4), medicine (81 to 4), and pharmacy (76 to 5). In the Graduate School men and women were evenly divided (56 to 55); and in Arts and Sciences, women were fairly well represented (981 to 749: 57 percent men to 43 percent women).

In the early days the small number of students made it not particularly difficult for individuals with good memories and well-honed social skills to get acquainted with almost every other student on campus. By 1917, obviously, that was no longer possible. The inevitable result was that students sought friendship and social life in smaller groupings. Living quarters were one place where such gathering might occur. The University had no dormitories in 1917, but some religious organizations provided living accommodations. The Episcopalians maintained a dorm for women; the Christian Church housed around thirty men in their building; both the YMCA and the YWCA boarded a limited number of students. There were also ten fraternities and six sororities on the campus, each of them typically accommodating twenty-five to thirty-five residents.[16] But most students lived in private rooming houses, paying around $5 a week for the privilege. The University had a

14. After Cleveland (621) and Oklahoma (309), the counties contributing the most students to the University were Pottawatomie (71), Kiowa (55), Kay (51), Muskogee (48), Tulsa (47), and Canadian (44). See the breakdown in *University Catalogue, 1916–1917,* 434.

15. This estimate is necessarily rough and is derived from *Report of the Commissioner of Education, 1917,* 290. In 1910–11 the commissioner stopped reporting separately the students enrolled in women's colleges and included them in the general college population figures; in the preceding year (1909–1910), however, there had been more than twenty thousand women in all-women's colleges in a total college population of 183,500.

16. The fraternities, in the order of their arrival on the campus, were Kappa Alpha (1905), Kappa Sigma (1906), Beta

firm rule against men and women living in the same house.[17]

Students could also seek friendship and a social life in dozens of organizations that catered to every imaginable interest and background. The *Sooner Yearbook* for 1916—with that charming innocence that comes from naiveté—listed these groups under the heading "Cliques." For those who came from places that had never sent many students to the University, there were eight "county clubs," designed to provide an unthreatening social base of familiar old high-school friends who had ventured onto the vast campus in Norman.[18] Many academic departments and schools had also organized clubs for their own students. Thus those studying German could join the Teutonia (which claimed more than forty members in 1916); those trying to master French, the Causerie (with a membership of almost ninety); and those learning Spanish, Las Dos Americas (which, in its very first year of existence, enlisted two hundred students).[19] Potential chemists, geologists, engineers of varying specialties, business students, mathematicians, teachers, politicians, and pharmacists all had opportunities to join in social activities with others like themselves.[20] Of special interest was a club for American Indian students called Oklushe Degataga. The group, started in 1914, tried to unite disparate tribes in a common organization (one of the words in its name was Choctaw, the other was Cherokee). The *Yearbook* blithely and patronizingly indicated that the club's purpose was "preserving the relics and traditions of the rapidly disappearing Redman." The club had more than forty members, representing six tribes, but the Cherokees, Chickasaws, and Choctaws accounted for thirty-eight, with the Osages, Comanches, and Sac-Fox each contributing one or two students to the total membership.[21]

During these years, the earliest attempts at student governance were becoming visible. Indeed, the *Yearbook* for 1917 claimed that student government "is constantly growing in favor among the students. The interest at each election constantly increases."[22] Every student was automatically a member of the Student Association, a body that had been in existence since the spring of 1912. Its executive arm was called the Student Council, and it consisted of thirteen representatives of various organizations, schools, and colleges and officers chosen at large. Even in these early days, student government was a gathering ground for those with political interests and ambitions. In 1916, for example, the presi-

---

Theta Pi (1907), Sigma Nu (1909), Sigma Alpha Epsilon (1909), Sigma Chi (1912), Phi Kappa Pi (1913), Phi Delta Chi (1913), the Masonic Club (1914), and Delta Theta (1915). The sororities were Kappa Alpha Theta (1909), Delta Delta Delta (1910), Pi Beta Phi (1910), Kappa Kappa Gamma (1914), Alpha Chi Omega (1916), and Phi Chi (1916). The *Sooner Yearbook* for 1917 features photographs of sundry fraternity and sorority houses.

17. *University Catalogue, 1916–1917*, 47.

18. In 1916 the "county clubs" had the following membership: Comanche (22), Cotton (12), Custer (26), Grant (14), Jackson (21), Lincoln (11), Noble (9), and Stephens (19). *Sooner Yearbook, 1916*, 235–38.

19. Ibid., 226–30.

20. *University Catalogue, 1916–1917* lists seventeen departmental clubs, 40–42.

21. Ibid., 41; *Sooner Yearbook, 1916*, 188–89.

22. *Sooner Yearbook, 1917*, 160.

dent of the student council was Leon Phillips, destined to become Oklahoma's governor in 1939.[23] Although women students were included in the Student Association and were represented on the Student Council, they nevertheless organized the Women's Council (also in 1912) to present the special problems and concerns of women students to the administration and faculty. Other student associations that had vague governance functions included the Oratorical Council (which superintended contests and meets), an Athletic Council (one alumnus, four faculty members, and four elected students), a Women's Athletic Association (for "fostering interest in outdoor athletics for women"),[24] and a Publications Board to oversee student publications.

Those students with intellectual interests or eager to enhance their public speaking or writing skills found awaiting them a large number of debating clubs, literary societies, and moot court groups: the *Catalogue* lists no fewer than eleven such organizations.[25] The Senate was limited to upperclassmen; its ranks were replenished by underclassmen who had served their apprenticeship in the House of Representatives. The Websterian, which had once been the literary outlet for the Preparatory Department, continued its work among freshman and sophomore men. That group was rivaled by the Athenaean, which specialized in debate. The main women's literary organization was still the Zetalethean. In 1912 the Zetas organized a subordinate branch, the Philologian, for freshman and sophomore women; but two years later the new group severed its ties and went into rivalry with its parent. Each year featured a contest between the two women's groups. Two newer women's literary societies, the Pierian (founded in 1915) and the Eudelphian (started a year earlier), also held an annual contest. By 1916–17 there was an intercollegiate women's debate team. Literary leanings were also nurtured by small groups of eager students gathered around the various University publications.[26] Probably more than three hundred students (12 percent of the student body) were involved in these intellectually oriented activities.[27] The University was also home to two prestigious honor societies (Pe-et for men and Owl and Triangle for women) and fourteen national professional honorary societies.[28]

Those who were devoted to the arts also found plenty of opportunities for social intercourse. Three organizations on the campus were devoted to social dancing. The one for fraternity men was called Tabasco; the one for sorority women was cleverly named the Enchiladas; a second men's dance club took the prosaic name Lotus, but what the group lacked in nomenclature, it compensated for with a snappy motto: "Watch Your Step."

23. Sara L. Bernson, "Leon Chase Phillips, Governor of Oklahoma, 1939–1943," in LeRoy H. Fischer, ed., *Oklahoma's Governors, 1929–1955: Depression to Prosperity*, 101–23.

24. *University Catalogue, 1916–1917*, 39.

25. Ibid., 40.

26. In 1916–17 the students published a daily and a weekly newspaper, a monthly magazine, and the annual yearbook.

27. Numbers in each group may be deduced from the *Sooner Yearbook*, but a substantial deduction has to be estimated for those students participating in more than one organization.

28. These are listed in *University Catalogue, 1916–1917*, 42–43.

Meanwhile, the energetic Dean Holmberg and his assistants maintained a full array of musical possibilities, including an orchestra (consisting in 1916 of forty-three members), a band (with twenty-four uniformed musicians), a women's glee club (of thirty-four voices), and two men's glee clubs (with a total membership of twenty-eight). The Drama Department presented three plays during the 1916–17 school year: one by Shakespeare, one by George Bernard Shaw, and one seductively entitled A *Pair of Stockings*.[29]

This impressive array of activities and organizations doubtless gave the University a good part of its flavor and attractiveness, at least as far as the students themselves were concerned. Their warmest memories and most lasting friendships surely sprang from these associations. If the banquet of social possibilities that was spread temptingly before the students distracted them from the more nutritious fare of serious academic study, one heard very few complaints about it (at least from them). Most of the organizations were admirably democratic and nonexclusive, and almost everybody partook. When the graduating seniors presented themselves to be photographed for the *Yearbook*, they were asked to list for posterity their extracurricular activities. Of the 163 who sat for their pictures in 1916, only about a dozen had nothing to list; of the 187 in the graduating class of 1917, only 17 had failed to join any organization while at the University; most of the students had belonged to three or four.[30]

~

MORE THAN ANY OTHER STUDENT ACTIVITY, athletics still held its obsessive and hypnotic sway over the student body. There were, of course, noble attempts to connect this obsession to high ideals and preparation for the struggles of life. No less a figure than Bennie Owen, in a public address during the 1916–17 school year, defined "a good sport" as "one whose strength is self-control, whose mastery is right thought and whose Faith, Courage and Confidence is an excellent model of God's most wonderful masterpiece, Man."[31] Sure. But one has the impression that the students were attracted to athletics for more mundane reasons: the pleasure and excitement that comes from watching skill, strength, and grace; the grandeur of the attendant pageantry; the thrill of competition; the satisfaction (and the right to brag) that comes from belonging to a victorious institution.

Intercollegiate oratorical and debate contests commanded an ever-declining following. The *Yearbook* for 1917 still dutifully listed each of the year's debate topics and the results of each competition,[32] but the handwriting was on the wall: not even the breathtaking oratory of a senior named Joshua Lee could revive the once-popular contests.[33] One ana-

29. *Sooner Yearbook, 1916*, 107–16, 302–17.

30. The names, pictures, and activities of the seniors of 1916 and 1917 are to be found in the *Sooner Yearbook, 1916*, 34–74, and *Sooner Yearbook, 1917*, 68–94.

31. Owen's talk, "A Good Sport," is reprinted in *Sooner Yearbook, 1917*, 372.

32. *Sooner Yearbook, 1917*, 178–80.

33. Josh Lee was hired to teach public speaking immediately upon his graduation in 1917; he stayed at the University

lyst of the flagging fate of debate and oratory complained that "it is discouraging to talk to empty seats after one has worked hard for six or seven months in the preparation of his subject." He advocated more interesting programs and more prizes, medals, and trophies; he also urged the administration and the fraternities and sororities to refrain from scheduling competing events on debate nights. But the day of the oratorical contest had passed, and much could be deduced from the fact that the *Yearbook* devoted seven of its pages to oratory and debate and eighteen to football. Each of the football players was photographed individually; his position, height, weight, and age were given; and a full page of description was provided for every game played during the previous fall.[34]

Coach Owen's teams were still performing their magic. Harold Keith did not exaggerate when he wrote that "football in 1915 was the great driving force of college life at Norman. Defeat in a football game was a college disaster." The student body was fiercely loyal to the team (around 80 percent of them paid the $5 for a season ticket) probably because, as Keith asserted, the team "represented, in a tangible way, the spirit and prowess of alma mater." The students always gathered at the train station to wish the departing heroes good luck and always met them there upon their return; even the practices were well attended. Cheerleading became an art form; and in 1915 a new organization of upperclassmen called the Ruf Neks was formed.[35]

Football fans had a good deal to be excited about. From 1911 through the end of the 1915 season, the football team won 84 percent of its games, scoring 1,612 points to its opponents' 289. During two of those years, the team never tasted defeat; and for eight consecutive years the University won every home game. The students dedicated the 1916 *Yearbook* to Bennie Owen, and the fans pitched in and bought him a Hudson Super-Six motorcar.[36] The 1916 season was somewhat less satisfying: despite squeaking past Southwest State (140 to 0), Shawnee Catholic (107 to 0), and Kingfisher College (96 to 0), the Sooners lost five important games: to Texas, Kendall (Tulsa), Missouri, Kansas, and Kansas State. It was a rebuilding year, the students concluded glumly; besides, losing to Texas was "the result of luck."[37] Not even a bad season could dampen the enthusiasm or reduce the loyalty. Football was still the principal sensation on the campus; and, as Mark Twain once remarked about the importance of money in the American psyche, nothing else was in second place.

Other sports had to content themselves with lesser manifestations of adulation. The basketball team, which was also coached by Owen, turned in a respectable performance in

---

until his legendary political career began in 1934: first in the U.S. House of Representatives and then in the Senate.

34. *Sooner Yearbook, 1917*, 335–52.

35. Keith, *Oklahoma Kickoff*, 295–97; "Ruf Neks' Origin Recalled," *Sooner Magazine* 10 (January 1938): 9–10.

36. Keith, *Oklahoma Kickoff*, 312–14.

37. Ibid., chap. 22; the remark about Texas luck was from a Dallas newspaper that the *Sooner Yearbook, 1917* reported with approval (345).

the 1916 season, winning twenty-one games and losing five. The team was disappointing in 1917, and one student summarized the record: "Winning thirteen and losing eight . . . does not bespeak a brilliant position in the caging world." Sometimes, he thought, the team outdid itself; but often the play was lackluster, and "the players might as well have been gathered around a table at the nearest confectionary, tuning up on 'Pity the Poor Sailor on a Night Like This.' "[38]

The baseball team, also coached by Bennie Owen, had a record of seventeen wins and four losses in 1916; but the less said about 1917 (six wins and ten losses) the better.[39] The track team (not coached by Owen) was more successful; but detracting from its creditable record of 1916 was the sad fact that John Jacobs, one of the greatest athletes ever produced by the University, was graduating. He would come back in September 1922 as the coach.[40] The school also fielded teams in tennis and gymnastics. The modest program in women's gymnastics involved fewer than three dozen young women.[41]

~

THE MOST DRAMATIC AND SIGNIFICANT new element in the life of the student body was the advent of a brand-new publication: the *Oklahoma Daily*. The old semiweekly *Umpire* had breathed its last in 1913. It was replaced by another semiweekly called the *University Oklahoman*. It sold for $1.25 a year (or $0.75 per semester) and announced in its opening issue in September 1913 that its purpose was "to give all the news all the time and to editorially champion the rights of the students."[42] The *Oklahoman*, under the influence of the new School of Journalism, adopted a newspaper format and abandoned the magazine-like appearance of the *Umpire*. But the campus had become so busy, so filled with news, activities, and gossip, that a semiweekly paper no longer sufficed. On September 18, 1916, the first issue of the *Oklahoma Daily* made its proud appearance. The first headline set the tone: "Oklahoma Gridsters Now Preparing for 1916 Schedule."

The new paper explained to the readership that a yearly subscription rate of $2.50 was still a bargain. It was more than the defunct *Oklahoman* had cost; but while that organ appeared only twice a week, there would be five issues of the *Daily*. The editors offered at least one important reason for the switch: "no more reading about a football game five days after it was played."[43] The pages were loaded with advertisements from local businesses:

38. Elbert E. Boylan, "1917 Basketball Season," in *Sooner Yearbook, 1917*, 356. For the 1916 season, see *Sooner Yearbook, 1916*, 156–58.

39. *Sooner Yearbook, 1916*, 160; and *Sooner Yearbook, 1917*, 358.

40. See the affectionate tribute to Jacobs by Harold Keith, "The Dean of Pneumonia Downs," *Sooner Magazine* 3 (Spring 1985): 10–16.

41. *Sooner Yearbook, 1916*, 178.

42. Quoted in Arnold, "A Descriptive Analysis," 96. The *Oklahoman* was a continuation of the *University Umpire* and merely continued its numbering of volumes (Arnold, "A Descriptive Analysis," 97). Arnold gives a full description of the various student publications in chap. 5 of his thesis.

43. *Oklahoma Daily*, September 18, 1916, 1.

clothing and shoe stores for men and women, pharmacies and restaurants and local hotels, doctors and dentists and optometrists, hardware stores and bakeries. A jitney service offered to drive students from the campus to anywhere in the city of Norman for a nickel.

To read the *Oklahoma Daily* for the first six months of its existence is to enter a self-contained world of youthful energy, bright enthusiasm, and unremitting activity. But it is also an isolated world, comfortably oblivious to events occurring off-campus. Were the peoples of Europe engaged in the most devastating war in human history? Were there problems on America's border with Mexico? Did the German government institute unrestricted submarine warfare? It would not be easy to tell if one relied solely on the *Oklahoma Daily*. Even the most dramatic national events were smuggled in surreptitiously, almost apologetically. Woodrow Wilson won reelection in the narrowest presidential victory in twenty-four years. The next day the main headline in the *Daily* was "1916 Oklahoma Football Season Will Soon Be Drawing to Its Close." Near the bottom of the front page the election story was treated with supercilious disdain. "The masses of the United States, including the university students have resumed work this morning as if nothing had happened. Beyond a few freak election bets four more years will elapse before another presidential election will invade the quietude of the campus."[44]

For six months the paper was devoted to the junior prom and the fraternity party and the changes in the Santa Fe schedule and the sillier doings of the faculty and the pious summaries of the talks of visiting ministers, prohibitionists, and lecturers. Who had been chosen by the Pe-et honorary; who had gotten engaged; who had spent the weekend in Dallas; who was starring in the new Drama School production. "Sooners Use 34 Miles of Shoestrings Yearly," said one front-page story in the week of Wilson's reelection.[45] It is hard not to envy them in their innocent and joyous delight, so secure in their happy and sheltered world, so earnestly preoccupied with their classwork and their dances and their sports and clubs.

It could not last. On April 6, 1917, the Congress in far-off Washington, D.C., responded to President Wilson's message: the United States was at war with the German Empire. On April 11 the *Daily* ran the following headlines: "Student Mass Meeting at 4:30 Today. To Launch Plans for Military Drill Work"; "30 Sooners Enlist after First Call"; "69 Sooner Women Offer Services to Red Cross." And the next day a blazing headline—the largest and boldest the paper had yet run in its half-year history—shouted: "SPIRIT OF WAR INVADES SOONERLAND."[46] The world had at last intruded, and things were about to change.

44. *Oklahoma Daily*, November 9, 1916, 1.

45. *Oklahoma Daily*, November 10, 1916, 1.

46. *Oklahoma Daily*, April 12, 1917, 1.

# Works Cited

## Unpublished Materials

### Manuscripts

"Minutes" of the State Board of Education, 1911–1919, Evans Hall, University of Oklahoma

"Minutes" of the University Regents, 1892–1911, Evans Hall, University of Oklahoma

Personnel Files, Office of the Provost, Evans Hall, University of Oklahoma
> Adams, Arthur B.
> Court, Nathan Altshiller.
> Dora, Lucile.
> Felgar, James H.
> Gimeno, Patricio.
> Gittinger, Roy.
> Herbert, H. H.
> Holmberg, Fredrik.
> Jacobson, Oscar Brousse.
> King, Grace A.
> Kraettli, Emil J.
> Lindsey, Josiah L.
> Reaves, Samuel W.
> Williams, Guy Y.

Personnel Files, Public Affairs, Whitehand Hall, University of Oklahoma
> Kraettli, Emil J.

State Archives, Oklahoma Department of Libraries, Oklahoma City
> Haskell, Charles N. MSS.

Western History Collections, Monnet Hall, University of Oklahoma
> Boyd, David Ross MSS.
> Buchanan, James Shannon MSS.
> Butcher, Nahum Ellsworth MSS.
> Campbell, Walter Stanley MSS.
> Court, Nathan Altshiller MSS.
> Dale, Edward Everett MSS.
> DeBarr, Edwin MSS.
> Gittinger, Roy MSS.
> Gould, Charles N. MSS.

Hadsell, Sardis Roy MSS.

Hengst, Herbert R., Sr. Oral History Collection.

Holmberg, Fredrik MSS.

Kraettli, Emil J. MSS.

Morris, John W. MSS.

Newby, Errett Rains MSS.

Newby, Errett Rains. Oral Interview. Herbert R. Hengst, Sr. Oral History Collection.

University Archives

    Boyd, David Ross. Presidential MSS.

    Cross, George Lynn. President Emeritus MSS.

    Evans, A. Grant. Presidential MSS.

    Evans, Arthur Grant, III. Scrapbook. Arthur Grant Evans MSS.

Vertical Files

    "Land Acquisition."

    "University of Ok. Essays."

    "University Statistics, circa 1892–93."

White, Lida MSS.

## Unpublished Papers, Reports, and Speeches

Love, Tom. "History of the University of Oklahoma College of Engineering." In possession of the author.

Personnel Files, Office of the Provost, Evans Hall, University of Oklahoma

Cross, George Lynn. "The President of O.U. Speaks: A Salute to Oscar B. Jacobson." Radio broadcast. Oscar Brousse Jacobson Personnel File.

Personnel Files, Public Affairs, Whitehand Hall, University of Oklahoma

    Cross, George Lynn. "Remarks on Emil J. Kraettli Day, October 27, 1962." Emil J. Kraettli Personnel File.

    Emery, Don. "Remarks of Don Emery at Regents' Dinner, October 27, 1962, Honoring Emil Kraettli." Typescript. Emil J. Kraettli Personnel File.

Sokatch, John R. "Indians, Homesteaders and Molecular Biologists: A History of Biochemistry and the Department of Biochemistry and Molecular Biology of the University of Oklahoma Health Sciences Center." Typescript, 2001. In possession of the author.

Western History Collections, Monnet Hall, University of Oklahoma

    Burke, J. J. "Why the University Is Located Where It Is: Address before Faculty Forum, March 27, 1929." Charles N. Gould MSS.

    Court, Arnold. "Nathan Altshiller Court, 1881–1968." Typescript, n.d. Nathan A. Court MSS.

    Gittinger, Roy. "Milestones." Radio broadcast, 1949. Roy Gittinger MSS.

    Hadsell, Sardis Roy. "Parrington in Oklahoma." Typescript, n.d. Sardis Roy Hadsell MSS.

    Henry, S. E. "Religious Development of David Ross Boyd." Typescript, n.d. David Ross Boyd MSS.

    Loftin, Dave. "The Geography of Cleveland County, 1873: A Reconstruction." Seminar paper, 1978. John W. Morris MSS.

    Newby, Errett Rains. "Tribute to a Lady: Lola North Newby, 'The Gentle One.'" Errett Rains Newby MSS.

    Parker, George B. "Commencement Address, 1936." David Ross Boyd MSS.

Studnicka, Frank E. "Some Aspects of the Norman Area Landscape, 1832–1889." Seminar paper, 1970. John W. Morris MSS.

University Archives

Gittinger, Roy. "The University Reorganizations of 1908 and 1911." Typescript, n.d. George Lynn Cross President Emeritus MSS.

Scott, A. C. "The University of Oklahoma School of Medicine." Typescript (prepared for the Oklahoma City Chamber of Commerce), 1943. George Lynn Cross President Emeritus MSS.

Vertical Files

Amos, French S. E. "Early Days in the University of Oklahoma." Typescript, n.d. "History of O.U. (1890–1908)."

Day, Judy. "University of Oklahoma Land Acquisition, 1891–1976." Seminar paper, 1977. "Land Acquisition."

Gumprecht, Blake. "Trees for a Prairie Town: Early Tree Planting in Norman Oklahoma." Seminar paper, 1997. "Tree Planting."

Hume, Carleton Ross. "The Beginning of Some Oklahoma University Traditions: A Story of Student Life in Oklahoma University in the Last Decade of the Nineteenth Century." Typescript, 1940. "Traditions of O.U."

Newby, Errett Rains. "Comments by Errett R. Newby. . . ." "History of OU (1890–1908)."

———. "Notes on Incidents at the University of Oklahoma." "History of O.U. (Newby)."

Parrington, Vernon L. Letter to Regents on the University's architectural future. Typescript, 1908. "Architecture of O.U."

## Theses and Dissertations

Arnold, Harold Donald. "A Descriptive Analysis of Selected Publications of the University of Oklahoma—Academic, Alumni, Student, and of Allied Organizations." Master's thesis, University of Oklahoma, 1951.

Bray, Alpheus C. "A Story of the Building of the Railroads in the State of Oklahoma." Master's thesis, University of Oklahoma, 1923.

Bray, William G. "The History of Pharmacy in Oklahoma." Master's thesis, University of Oklahoma, 1935.

Dellasega, Charles J. "The Development and Present Status of Education for Business at the University of Oklahoma." Ph.D. dissertation, University of Oklahoma, 1952.

Hatcher, Ollie Everett. "The Development of Legal Controls in Racial Segregation in the Public Schools of Oklahoma, 1865–1952." Ed.D. dissertation, University of Oklahoma, 1954.

Hubbell, John T. "Racial Desegregation at the University of Oklahoma, 1946–1950." Master's thesis, University of Oklahoma, 1961.

Jones, Enid Maxine. "The Five: An Examination of the Indian Renaissance at the University of Oklahoma. . . ." Master's thesis, University of Oklahoma, 1976.

Koch, Konrad K., Jr. "An Administrative History of the Academic Divisions of the University of Oklahoma." Master's thesis, University of Oklahoma, 1950.

Morrissey, Robert Stephen. "David Ross Boyd and the University of Oklahoma: An Analysis of the Educational Contributions of the First President." Ed.D. dissertation, University of Oklahoma, 1973.

Nunn, E. Sherman. "A History of Education in Oklahoma Territory." Ed.D. dissertation, University of Oklahoma, 1941.

Solomon, Lewis E. "The Personnel of the Oklahoma Constitutional Convention of 1906–1907." Master's thesis, University of Oklahoma, 1924.

Sorrels, Carolyn S. "Eight Early Buildings on the Norman Campus of the University of Oklahoma." Bachelor of Liberal Studies paper, University of Oklahoma, 1985.

Standley, Fred S. "The Oklahoma Historical Society, 1893–1943." Master's thesis, University of Oklahoma, 1986.

Storm, Clarence Dunn. "The Building Stones of the State of Oklahoma." B.A. thesis, University of Oklahoma, 1907.

Tompkins, R. R. "The Development of Secondary Education in Oklahoma." Master's thesis, University of Oklahoma, 1928.

Wardner, Dorothy Gittinger. "The Territorial University of Oklahoma." Master's thesis, University of Oklahoma, 1939.

Weidman, John M. "A History of the University of Oklahoma." Master's thesis, University of Oklahoma, 1939.

## Published Works

### Federal and State Government Publications

*Annual Report of the United States Commissioner of Education, 1892–1893*. Washington, D.C.: Government Printing Office, 1893.

*Congressional Record*. 53rd Congress, 2nd Sess. Washington, D.C.: Government Printing Office, 1894.

Fraker, Emil L. *Oklahoma Historical Society: Semi-Centennial of Oklahoma Issue*. Oklahoma City: Oklahoma Historical Society, 1957.

Gates, Paul Wallace. *History of Public Land Law Development*. Washington, D.C.: Government Printing Office, 1968.

George, Preston, and Sylvan R. Wood. "The Railroads of Oklahoma." In *Railroads of Oklahoma, June 6, 1870–July 1, 1974*, 7–25. Oklahoma City: State of Oklahoma Department of Highways, 1974.

Hornaday, William T. "The Extermination of the American Bison, with a Sketch of Its Discovery and Life History." In *Smithsonian Report, 1887*, 2:367–548. Washington, D.C.: Government Printing Office, 1889.

*Journal of the First Session of the Legislative Assembly of Oklahoma Territory*. Guthrie: State Capital Publishing Co., 1890.

*Journal of the House Proceedings of the Second Legislative Assembly of the Territory of Oklahoma*. Guthrie: State Capital Printing Co., 1893.

*Journal of the House Proceedings of the Sixth Legislative Assembly* . . . *(January 8, 1901–March 8, 1901)*. Guthrie: State Capitol Printing Co., 1901.

*Journal of the Oklahoma House of Representatives, 6th Sess. (January 2–March 2, 1917)*. Oklahoma City: New Publishing Co., 1917.

*Railroads of Oklahoma, June 6, 1870–July 1, 1974*. Oklahoma City: State of Oklahoma Department of Highways, 1974.

*Reports of Committees of the House of Representatives for the Second Session of the Fifty-third Congress, 1893–1894*. Washington, D.C.: Government Printing Office, 1894.

Richards, W. B., comp. *The Oklahoma Red Book*. 2 vols. Oklahoma City: State of Oklahoma, 1912.

Richardson, James D., ed. *The Messages and Papers of the Presidents, 1789–1897*. Vol. 9. Washington, D.C.: Government Printing Office, 1898.

*Statutes of Oklahoma, 1890*. Guthrie: State Capital Printing Co., 1893.

*Statutes of Oklahoma, 1893*. Guthrie: State Capital Printing Co., 1893.

U.S. Bureau of the Census. *Historical Statistics of the United States, from Colonial Times to 1970*. Washington, D.C.: Government Printing Office, 1975.

————. *Negro Population, 1790–1915*. Washington, D.C.: Government Printing Office, 1918.

————. *Religious Bodies: 1906*. Washington, D.C.: Government Printing Office, 1910.

*U.S. Statutes at Large, 1894*. Washington, D.C.: Government Printing Office, 1895.


## Newspapers

*Daily Oklahoman*, 1889–1917

*March Quarterly*, 1897

*Norman Transcript*, 1889–1917

*Oklahoma Daily*, 1916–17

*Umpire*, 1906–13

*University Umpire*, 1897–1907


## University Publications

*Greater College of Business Administration: Issued in Commemoration of the Dedication of the New College* . . . *Building, October 30 and 31, 1936*. Norman: University of Oklahoma, 1936.

*In Memory of Albert Heald Van Vleet*. Norman: University of Oklahoma, 1926.

*Mistletoe*, 1905–1908.

*Oscar Brousse Jacobson Retrospective Exhibit, September 17–October 8, 1961*. Norman: University of Oklahoma, 1961.

*Sooner Magazine*, 1928–2004.

*Sooner Yearbook*, 1909–17.

Tate, Leo Glenn. *Centennial: A History of the University of Oklahoma College of Pharmacy, 1893–1933*. Norman: University of Oklahoma, 1933.

*University Catalogues*, 1893–1917.

University of Oklahoma Center of Urban and Regional Studies. *The University of Oklahoma and Environs: The Physical Development Plan for the University of Oklahoma, 1965–1985.* Norman: n.p., 1966.

*University of Oklahoma Magazine*, 1920.


## Books

Adams, Katherine H. *A History of Professional Writing Instruction in American Colleges: Years of Acceptance, Growth, and Doubt.* Dallas: Southern Methodist University Press, 1993.

Alley, John. *City Beginnings in Oklahoma Territory.* Norman: University of Oklahoma Press, 1939.

Benedict, H. Y. *A Source Book Relating to the History of the University of Texas.* Austin: University of Texas, 1917.

Bizzell, William Bennett, et al. *An Appreciation of James Shannon Buchanan by William Bennett Bizzell and Others.* Norman: University of Oklahoma Press, 1930.

Bledstein, Burton J. *The Culture of Professionalism: The Middle Class and the Development of Higher Education in America.* New York: Norton, 1976.

*Brief History of the Boston Public Schools, 1635–1949.* Boston: School Committee of the City of Boston, 1949[?].

Brill, H. E., comp. *Story of the Methodist Episcopal Church in Oklahoma.* Oklahoma City: University Press, 1939.

Brown, Ira V. *Lyman Abbott, Christian Evolutionist: A Study in Religious Liberalism.* Cambridge, Mass.: Harvard University Press, 1953.

Brubacher, John S., and Willis Rudy. *Higher Education in Transition: A History of American Colleges and Universities.* New Brunswick and London: Transaction Publishers, 1997.

Catlin, George. *North American Indians, Being Letters and Notes on Their Manners, Customs, and Conditions, Written during Eight Years' Travel amongst the Wildest Tribes of Indians in North America.* 2 vols. Edinburgh: John Grant, 1926.

Clark, J. Brent. *Sooner Century: 100 Glorious Years of Oklahoma Football.* Kansas City: Richardson Printing Co., 1995.

Clegg, Leland, and William B. Oden. *Oklahoma Methodism in the Twentieth Century.* Nashville: Parthenon Press, 1968.

Clifton, Ronald L. *Memorial to Charles Newton Gould.* New York: Geological Society of America, 1950.

Cross, George Lynn. *Professors, Presidents, and Politicians: Civil Rights and the University of Oklahoma, 1890–1968.* Norman: University of Oklahoma Press, 1981.

Dale, Edward Everett. *The Cross Timbers: Memories of a North Texas Boyhood.* Austin: University of Texas Press, 1966.

———. *The West Wind Blows: The Autobiography of Edward Everett Dale.* Oklahoma City: Oklahoma Historical Society, 1984.

Dawdy, Doris Ostrander. *Artists of the American West: A Biographical Dictionary.* 3 vols. Chicago: Sage Books, 1981.

Dippie, Brian W. *The Vanishing American: White Attitudes and U.S. Indian Policy.* Middletown, Conn.: Wesleyan University Press, 1981.

Dowd, Jerome. *The Negro in American Life.* New York: Century Co., 1926.

———. *The Negro Races: A Sociological Study.* New York: Macmillan, 1907.

Droze, Wilmon H. *Trees, Prairies and People: A History of Tree Planting on the Great Plains.* Denton: Texas Woman's University, 1977.

Emmons, David M. *Garden in the Grasslands.* Lincoln: University of Nebraska Press, 1971.

Everett, Mark R. *Medical Education in Oklahoma: The University of Oklahoma School of Medicine and Medical Center, 1900–1931.* Norman: University of Oklahoma Press, 1972.

Fischer, LeRoy H., ed. *Oklahoma's Governors, 1907–1929: Turbulent Politics.* Oklahoma City: Oklahoma Historical Society, 1981.

———, ed. *Oklahoma's Governors, 1929–1955: Depression to Prosperity.* Oklahoma City: Oklahoma Historical Society, 1983.

———, ed. *Territorial Governors of Oklahoma.* Oklahoma City: Oklahoma Historical Society, 1975.

Fisher, Bernice. *Industrial Education: American Ideals and Institutions.* Madison: University of Wisconsin Press, 1967.

Foerster, Norman. *The American State University.* Chapel Hill: University of North Carolina Press, 1937.

Foreman, Grant. *The Five Civilized Tribes.* Norman: University of Oklahoma Press, 1934.

———. *Indian Removal: The Emigration of the Five Civilized Tribes of Indians.* Norman: University of Oklahoma Press, 1932.

Gara, Larry. *The Liberty Line: The Legend of the Underground Railroad.* Lexington: University of Kentucky Press, 1961.

Gibson, Arrell M., ed. *Frontier Historian: The Life and Work of Edward Everett Dale.* Norman: University of Oklahoma Press, 1975.

Gideon, D. C. *Indian Territory: Descriptive Biographical and Genealogical, Including the Landed Estates, County Seats, etc., etc., with a General History of the Territory.* New York and Chicago: Lewis Publishing Co., 1901.

Gittinger, Roy. *The Formation of the State of Oklahoma (1803–1906).* Berkeley: University of California Press, 1917.

———. *The University of Oklahoma: A History of Fifty Years, 1892–1942.* Norman: University of Oklahoma Press, 1942.

Goble, Danney. *Progressive Oklahoma: The Making of a New Kind of State.* Norman: University of Oklahoma Press, 1980.

Gordon, Lynn D. *Gender and Higher Education in the Progressive Era.* New Haven: Yale University Press, 1990.

Gould, Charles N. *Covered Wagon Geologist.* Norman: University of Oklahoma Press, 1949.

Griffin, Clifford S. *The University of Kansas: A History.* Lawrence: University Press of Kansas, 1974.

Hall, H. Lark. *V. L. Parrington: Through the Avenue of Art.* Kent, Ohio: Kent State University Press, 1994.

Hayes, Basil A. *LeRoy Long, Teacher of Medicine.* Oklahoma City: n.p., 1943.

Hoeveler, J. David, Jr. *James McCosh and the Scottish Intellectual Tradition: From Glasgow to Princeton*. Princeton: Princeton University Press, 1981.

Hoffman, Charles. *The Depression of the Nineties: An Economic History*. Westport, Conn.: Greenwood, 1970.

Hofsommer, Donovan L., ed. *Railroads in Oklahoma*. Oklahoma City: Oklahoma Historical Society, 1977.

Hofstadter, Richard. *The Progressive Historians: Turner, Beard, and Parrington*. New York: A. A. Knopf, 1968.

Hoig, Stan. *David L. Payne: The Oklahoma Boomer*. Oklahoma City: Western Heritage Books, 1980.

———. *The Oklahoma Land Rush of 1889*. Oklahoma City: Oklahoma Historical Society, 1984.

Horowitz, Helen Lefkowitz. *Campus Life: Undergraduate Culture from the End of the Eighteenth Century to the Present*. New York: A. A. Knopf, 1987.

Hughes, Dorothy. *Pueblo on the Mesa: The First Fifty Years at the University of New Mexico*. Albuquerque: University of New Mexico Press, 1939.

Irving, Washington. *A Tour on the Prairies*. Norman: University of Oklahoma Press, 1956.

Jones, Theodore. *Carnegie Libraries across America: A Public Legacy*. New York: Preservation Press, 1977.

Keith, Harold. *Oklahoma Kickoff: An Informal History of the First Twenty-five Years of Football at the University of Oklahoma and of the Amusing Hardships That Attended Its Pioneering*. Norman: University of Oklahoma Press, 1948.

Klauder, Charles Z., and Herbert C. Wise. *College Architecture in America*. New York: Charles Scribner's Sons, 1929.

Lackey, R. Vincent. *Our First Fifty Years: A Short History of the Kappa Alpha Order in Oklahoma*. Oklahoma City: n.p., 1955.

Lambert, Paul F. *Joseph B. Thoburn, Pioneer Historian and Archaeologist*. Oklahoma City: Western Heritage Association, 1980.

Lawson, Paul Clifford, with Susan M. Brown, eds. *The Spirit of H. H. Richardson on the Midland Prairies*. Minneapolis: University Art Museum, 1988.

Lazerson, Marvin. *Origins of the Urban School: Public Education in Massachusetts, 1870–1915*. Cambridge, Mass.: Harvard University Press, 1971.

Levine, David O. *The American College and the Culture of Aspiration, 1915–1940*. Ithaca: Cornell University Press, 1986.

Litton, Gaston. *History of Oklahoma at the Golden Anniversary of Statehood*. 4 vols. New York: Lewis Historical Publishing Co., 1957.

Logsdon, Guy W. *The University of Tulsa*. Norman: University of Oklahoma Press, 1977.

Long, Charles F., and Carolyn G. Hart. *The Sooner Story: Ninety Years at the University of Oklahoma, 1890–1980*. Norman: University of Oklahoma Foundation, 1980.

Marshall, Leon Carroll, ed. *The Collegiate School of Business: Its Status at the Close of the First Quarter of the Twentieth Century*. Chicago: University of Chicago Press, 1928.

McKown, Dave R. *The Dean: The Life of Julien C. Monnet*. Norman: University of Oklahoma Press, 1973.

McMurry, Linda O. *Recorder of the Black Experience: A Biography of Monroe Nathan Work.* Baton Rouge: Louisiana State University Press, 1985.

Milhouse, Paul W. *Oklahoma City University: A Miracle at 23rd and Blackwelder.* Oklahoma City: Oklahoma Heritage Association, 1984.

Morris, John W., ed. *Cities of Oklahoma.* Oklahoma City: Oklahoma Historical Society, 1979.

Morris, John W., Charles R. Goins, and Edwin C. McReynolds. *Historical Atlas of Oklahoma.* Norman: University of Oklahoma Press, 1986.

Nelson, David M. *The Anatomy of a Game: Football, the Rules and the Men Who Made the Game.* Newark: University of Delaware Press, 1994.

Nevins, Allan. *The State University and Democracy.* Urbana: University of Illinois Press, 1962.

Newcomer, Mabel. *A Century of Higher Education for American Women.* New York: Harper & Brothers, 1959.

Norman Development Co. *Norman, Oklahoma.* Norman: n.p., 1907[?].

Norwood, Stephen H. *Strikebreaking and Intimidation: Mercenaries and Masculinity in Twentieth-Century America.* Chapel Hill: University of North Carolina Press, 2002.

Oriard, Michael. *Reading Football: How the Popular Press Created an American Spectacle.* Chapel Hill: University of North Carolina Press, 1993.

Painter, Nell Irvin. *Exodusters: Black Migration to Kansas after Reconstruction.* New York: A. A. Knopf, 1976.

Patterson, Zella Black. *Langston University: A History.* Norman: University of Oklahoma Press, 1979.

Perrin, Tom. *Football: A College History.* Jefferson, N.C.: McFarland, 1987.

Pierson, Frank C., et al. *The Education of American Businessmen: A Study of University-College Programs in Business Administration.* New York: McGraw-Hill, 1959.

*Portrait and Biographical Record of Oklahoma, Commemorating the Achievements of Citizens Who Have Contributed to the Progress of Oklahoma and the Development of Its Resources.* Chicago: Chapman Publishing Co., 1901.

Rice, Elroy L., and George Lynn Cross. *A History of the Department of Botany and Microbiology at the University of Oklahoma: The First Hundred Years.* Norman: University of Oklahoma Foundation, 1990.

Rinehart, Mrs. Bennett. *Blaze Marks on the Border: The Story of Arkansas City, Kansas, Founded 1870–1871.* North Newton, Kans.: Mennonite Press, 1970.

Rister, Carl Coke. *Land Hunger: David L. Payne and the Oklahoma Boomers.* Norman: University of Oklahoma Press, 1942.

Roe, Frank Gilbert. *The North American Buffalo: A Critical Study of the Species in Its Wild State.* Toronto: University of Toronto Press, 1951.

Rudolph, Frederick. *Mark Hopkins and the Log: Williams College, 1836–1872.* New Haven: Yale University Press, 1956.

Rulon, Philip Reed. *Oklahoma State University, since 1890.* Stillwater: Oklahoma State University Press, 1975.

Runyon, Nadine, ed. *Pioneers of Cleveland County, 1889–1907.* Norman: Cleveland County Historical Society, 1971.

Shirk, George H. *Oklahoma Place Names*. Norman: University of Oklahoma Press, 1974.

Smith, Ronald A. *Sports and Freedom: The Rise of Big-Time College Athletics*. New York: Oxford University Press, 1988.

Sobel, Robert, ed. *Biographical Directory of the Governors of the United States, 1789–1978*. 4 vols. Westport, Conn.: Meckler Books, 1978.

Solomon, Barbara Miller. *In the Company of Educated Women: A History of Women and Higher Education in America*. New Haven: Yale University Press, 1985.

Speer, Bonnie. *Cleveland County: Pride of the Promised Land, an Illustrated History*. Norman: Traditional Publishers, 1988.

Strickland, Rennard. *The Indians in Oklahoma*. Norman: University of Oklahoma Press, 1980.

Szasz, Ferenc Morton. *The Divided Mind of Protestant America, 1880–1930*. University: University of Alabama Press, 1982.

Teague, Jane Frost, and Thomas G. Teague. *The Flood Family History*. Las Cruces, N.Mex.: n.p., 1999.

Thoburn, Joseph B., and Muriel H. Wright. *Oklahoma: A History of the State and Its People*. 4 vols. New York: Lewis Historical Publishing Co., 1929.

Thompson, John B. *First Presbyterian Church, Norman, Oklahoma: Golden Anniversary, Fifty Years of Service, March 22, 1891, to March 22, 1941*. Norman[?]: n.p., 1941[?].

Tolson, Arthur L. *The Black Oklahomans: A History, 1541–1972*. New Orleans: Edwards Printing Co., 1972.

Turner, Paul Venable. *Campus: An American Planning Tradition*. New York: Architectural History Foundation, 1984.

Wechsler, Harold. *The Qualified Student: A History of Selective College Admission in America*. New York: John Wiley and Sons, 1977.

Welsch, Roger. *Of Trees and Dreams: The Fiction, Fact and Folklore of Tree Planting on the Northern Plains*. Lincoln: Nebraska Forest Service, 1982.

Wendell, Barrett. *English Composition*. New York: Scribner's, 1891.

White, Gerald, T. *The United States and the Problem of Recovery after 1893*. University: University of Alabama Press, 1982.

Womack, John, ed. *The Annals of Cleveland County, Oklahoma, 1889–1959*. Norman: n.p., 1981.

———. *Norman: An Early History, 1820–1900*. Norman: Published by the author, 1976.

———. *The Wet Years in Cleveland County Oklahoma, 1889–1907: A Self-Imposed Investigation*. Noble, Okla.: Womack, 1980.

Work, Monroe N. *A Bibliography of the Negro in Africa and America*. New York: H. W. Wilson Co., 1928.

Wren, Daniel A. *Collegiate Education for Business Administration at the University of Oklahoma*. Norman: Michael F. Price College of Business, 2002.

Wright, Muriel. *A Guide to the Indian Tribes of Oklahoma*. Norman: University of Oklahoma Press, 1951.

# Articles

Adams, Arthur B. "History of the College of Business Administration." *Sooner Magazine* 13 (August 1941): 26–27, 32–34.

Alley, John. "Gayfree Ellison: Pioneer University Physician." *Sooner Magazine* 5 (April 1933): 193–95.

"Always One Familiar Face." *Sooner Magazine* 35 (December 1962): 3–6ff.

Bagby, Mary Emelyn Miller. "The History of the George W. Miller Family." In Nadine Runyon, ed., *Pioneers of Cleveland County, 1889–1907*, 130–34. Norman: Cleveland County Historical Society, 1971.

Balyeat, Frank A. "Arthur Grant Evans." *Chronicles of Oklahoma* 38 (1960–61): 245–52.

———. "Rural Schoolhouses in Early Oklahoma." *Chronicles of Oklahoma* 22 (1944): 315–23.

———. "Segregation in the Public Schools of Oklahoma Territory." *Chronicles of Oklahoma* 39 (1961): 180–92.

Belcher, Wyatt W. "Political Leadership of Robert L. Owen." *Chronicles of Oklahoma* 31 (1953–54): 361–71.

Bernson, Sara L. "Leon Chase Phillips, Governor of Oklahoma, 1939–1943." In LeRoy H. Fischer, ed., *Oklahoma's Governors, 1929–1955: Depression to Prosperity*, 101–23. Oklahoma City: Oklahoma Historical Society, 1983.

Berthrong, Donald. "Walter Stanley Campbell: Plainsman." *Arizona and the West* 7 (Summer 1965): 91–104.

Bizzell, William Bennett. "A Friendly Tribute." In *An Appreciation of James Shannon Buchanan by William Bennett Bizzell and Others*, 7–14. Norman: University of Oklahoma Press, 1930.

Boyd, David Ross. "Address of Dr. David Ross Boyd." In *In Memory of Albert Heald Van Vleet*, 11–19. Norman: University of Oklahoma, 1926.

———. "My Days as First University President: Told by Dr. David Ross Boyd to Dr. Roy Hadsell, '04, and Betty Kirk, '29." Five part series in *Sooner Magazine* 2 (October 1929–March 1930).

Boyd, Jennie Thompson. "'In the Lineup'—A Bit of History." *March Quarterly* (1897): 1–3.

Brewer, Theodore H. "'Uncle Buck' as I Knew Him." In *An Appreciation of James Shannon Buchanan by William Bennett Bizzell and Others*, 19–24. Norman: University of Oklahoma Press, 1930.

Brooks, Stratton D. "Industrial Education." *Journal of Education* (Boston) 70 (December 9 and 16, 1909): 597–99, 627–28.

———. "Vocational Guidance." *School Review* 19 (January 1911): 42–50.

"Brought Best Men to O.U." *Sooner Magazine* 16 (August 1944): 4.

Burr, Carol J. "Back to Boyd House." *Sooner Magazine* 15 (Fall 1994): 3–7.

Clinton, Fred S. "University of Oklahoma Medical School Crisis Averted." *Chronicles of Oklahoma* 25 (1947–48): 342–57.

Cohen, Sol. "The Industrial Education Movement, 1906–17." *American Quarterly* 20 (1968): 95–110.

Cotner, Howard. "Substantial Growth of O.U. Law School Outmatched Only by Its National Standing." *Sooner Magazine* 19 (January 1947): 12–13, 28.

Court, Nathan A. "Democratizing Mathematics." *Bulletin of the Kansas Association of Teachers of Mathematics* (1941): 55–57.

———. "Mathematics and Esthetics." *Sooner Magazine* 2 (November 1929): 58.

———. "Mathematics in the History of Civilization." *Mathematics Teacher* 41 (March 1948): 104–11.

Cross, George Lynn. "President Cross Salutes. . . ." *Sooner Magazine* 19 (May 1947): 21–22.

Cruce, Lee. "Shall the People Rule—in Oklahoma?: Reply from the Board of Regents." *Outlook* 90 (October 3, 1908): 249–51.

Dale, Edward Everett. "David Ross Boyd, 1853–1936." *Sooner Magazine* 9 (January 1937): 80, 92, 94.

———. "David Ross Boyd: Pioneer Educator." *Chronicles of Oklahoma* 42 (1964): 2–35.

———. "Wood and Water: Twin Problems of the Prairie Plains." *Nebraska History* 29 (1948): 87–104.

Debo, Angie. "Edward Everett Dale: The Teacher." In Arrell M. Gibson, ed., *Frontier Historian: The Life and Work of Edward Everett Dale*, 21–37. Norman: University of Oklahoma Press, 1975.

Dennis, Frank L. "The Professor Graduates." *Daily Oklahoman*, June 19, 1938, 1D.

Disney, Richard L. "They Gave 234 Years of Service." *Sooner Magazine* 23 (June–July 1951): 12.

Dowd, Jerome. "Dean Arthur B. Adams." In *The Greater College of Business Administration: Issued in Commemoration of the Dedication of the New College of Business Administration Building, October 30 and 31, 1936* (no pagination). Norman: University of Oklahoma, 1936.

"Dr. Charles Gould Dies." *Sooner Magazine* 21 (August 1949): 16.

"Dr. House Is Honored." *Sooner Magazine* 20 (June 1948): 13.

Felgar, J. H. "History of the College of Engineering." *Sooner Magazine* 12 (August 1940): 27–29, 34–36.

Finchum, Tanya D., and G. Allen Finchum. "Celebrating the Library Spirit: A Look at the Carnegie Libraries in Oklahoma." *Chronicles of Oklahoma* 79 (2002): 454–75.

"First Alumni President Dies." *Sooner Magazine* 18 (May 1946): 24.

Foreman, Grant. "Early Trails through Oklahoma." *Chronicles of Oklahoma* 3 (1925): 99–119.

———. "Survey of a Wagon Road from Fort Smith to the Colorado River." *Chronicles of Oklahoma* 12 (1934): 74–96.

"Former Alumni Chief Dies." *Sooner Magazine* 10 (December 1937): 22.

Gould, Charles N. "Beginning of the Geological Work in Oklahoma." *Chronicles of Oklahoma* 10 (1932): 196–203.

———. "Buchanan, the Man." In *An Appreciation of James Shannon Buchanan by William Bennett Bizzell and Others*, 15–18. Norman: University of Oklahoma Press, 1930.

Gumprecht, Blake. "Transforming the Prairie: Early Tree Planting in an Oklahoma Town." *Historical Geography* 29 (2001): 116–34.

Hadsell, Sardis Roy. "Dean of the Graduate School." In *In Memory of Albert Heald Van Vleet*, 23–26. Norman: University of Oklahoma, 1926.

————. "Kirby Prickett." *Sooner Magazine* 8 (November 1935): 36.

————. "Our Wedding." *University Umpire*, January 15, 1903, 13.

————. "Scholar and Teacher." *Sooner Magazine* 13 (November 1940): 28–29.

————. "The Umpire Story." In *Mistletoe, 1905*, 76–78. Norman: University of Oklahoma, 1905.

Hall, H. Lark. "V. L. Parrington's Oklahoma Years, 1897–1908: 'Few Highlights and Much Monotone'?" *Pacific Northwest Quarterly* 72 (1981): 22–28.

Harlow, Rex F. "Oklahoma's Leading Educator." *Harlow's Weekly* 21 (December 23, 1922): 8–10, 15–16.

"Haskellism in Oklahoma University." *Outlook* 90 (October 17, 1908): 325–26.

Hazell, Thomas Arthur. "George Washington Steele." In LeRoy Fischer, ed., *Territorial Governors of Oklahoma*, 9–22. Oklahoma City: Oklahoma Historical Society, 1975.

————. "Robert Lee Williams, Governor of Oklahoma, 1915–1919." In LeRoy H. Fischer, ed., *Oklahoma's Governors, 1907–1929: Turbulent Politics*, 66–86. Oklahoma City: Oklahoma Historical Society, 1981.

"Heart Ailment Fatal to Dean Carpenter." *Sooner Magazine* 21 (January 1949): 17.

Henslick, Harry E. "Abraham Jefferson Seay, Governor of Oklahoma Territory, 1892–1893." In LeRoy H. Fischer, ed., *Territorial Governors of Oklahoma*, 28–45. Oklahoma City: Oklahoma Historical Society, 1975.

"Herbert and Copeland Honored." *Sooner State Press*, March 25, 1961, 1–2.

"Herbert Appointed Boyd Professor." *Sooner State Press*, May 29, 1948, 1.

Hoig, Stan. "The Rail Line That Opened the Unassigned Lands." In Donovan L. Hofsommer, ed., *Railroads in Oklahoma*, 19–30. Oklahoma City: Oklahoma Historical Society, 1977.

Holland, Jean. "C. D. Adkins, 1868–1947." In Nadine Runyan, ed., *Pioneers of Cleveland County, 1889–1907*, 1–4. Norman: Cleveland County Historical Society, 1971.

House, Roy Temple. "New Oklahoma School Presidents." *Sturm's Oklahoma Magazine* 7 (December 1908): 38–41.

————. "Oklahoma's Einstein Adds Two New College Subjects." *Daily Oklahoman*, March 29, 1936, C13.

"How Norman Got the University: An Interview with Charles H. Bessent." *Sooner Magazine* 1 (February 1929): 157–58.

Ingler, Marilyn Davis. " 'Miss Grace' Put Life into O.U." *Sooner Magazine* 20 (February 1948): 9.

Jacobson, Oscar B., and Jeanne d'Ucel. "Art in Oklahoma." *Chronicles of Oklahoma* 32 (1954–55): 263–77.

James, Hunter. "Norman, Home of State University." *Sturm's Oklahoma Magazine* 7 (November 1908): 22–30.

"James Shannon Buchanan." *Chronicles of Oklahoma* 8 (1930): 353–54.

"J. L. Lindsey Retires." *Sooner Magazine* 22 (August 1950): 16.

Kaufman, Eugenia. "He Stood Tall." *Sooner Magazine* 25 (September 1952): 9–11.

Keith, Harold. "The Dean of Pneumonia Downs." *Sooner Magazine* 3 (Spring 1985): 10–16.

————. "Pioneer Prexy." *Daily Oklahoman*, March 20, 1949, D10–11.

————. "Soonerland's Undefeated Elevens." *Sooner Magazine* 1 (November 1928): 56–57.

Kimbrough, Mary. "Dean Holmberg." *Sooner Magazine* 7 (January 1935): 80–81.

Kinchen, Oscar A. "Oklahoma's First College, Old High Gate at Norman." *Chronicles of Oklahoma* 14 (1936): 312–23.

King, Grace A. " 'Hitch Your Wagon to a Star.' " *University Umpire*, March 1, 1898, 1.

———. "Unwritten Music." *University Umpire*, October 15, 1897, 2–3.

Kise, Joan Duff. "Stratton D. Brooks." In John F. Ohles, ed., *The Biographical Dictionary of American Educators*, 1:180. 3 vols. Westport, Conn.: Greenwood, 1978.

Kornfeld, Joseph. "Engineering History." *Sooner Magazine* 1 (1928–29): 176.

L.[earcy], E.[laine]. "Everyone's French Teacher." *Sooner Magazine* 17 (December 1944): 3–4.

Levy, David W. "Combating the Image of 'Godlessness' in 1909." *Sooner Magazine* 16 (Spring 1996): 28–30.

———. " 'I Had a Certain Pioneer Spirit So I Stayed': Fredrik Holmberg Comes to Oklahoma." *Sooner Magazine* 19 (1998): 25–29.

———. " 'An Imperishable Part of Our Traditions': Fredrik Holmberg Departs." *Sooner Magazine* 19 (1999): 25–29.

———. "The President and the Professor: With 'a Sense of Deep Regret.' " *Sooner Magazine* 14 (Summer 1994): 25–29.

———. "Why Did You Come to the University." *Sooner Magazine* 25 (Fall 2004): 15–19.

Levy, Debra. "A Daughter Remembers." *Sooner Magazine* 22 (Fall 2001): 31–32.

Long, Charles. "Gee Cly, Youse Guys." *Sooner Magazine* 36 (November 1963): 13–17.

Lottinville, Savoie. "Walter Stanley Campbell." *American Oxonian* 45 (October 1958): 242–44.

Lyle, Nellie Hefley. "The Hefleys: Early-Day Cleveland County Family." In Nadine Runyon, ed., *Pioneers of Cleveland County, 1889–1907*, 89–95. Norman: Cleveland County Historical Society, 1971.

"A Maestro Is Dead." *Sooner Magazine* 8 (May 1936): 192.

McClung, Paul. "The 'Y' Means Success at O.U." *Sooner Magazine* 20 (May 1948): 16.

Merten, W. H. "Oklahoma Territory's First Legislature." *Sturm's Oklahoma Magazine* 5 (January 1908): 36–41.

Milburn, George. "Pioneering in Beauty: Professor Jacobson Is Internationally Famous as an Artist." *Sooner Magazine* 1 (February 1929): 149–51.

———. "Planting a University: First Varsity President Recounts How He Did It." *Sooner Magazine* 1 (November 1928): 39–41.

Mills, Ed. "Genesis in Geology: Dr. C. N. Gould Tells of Establishing That Department Here." *Sooner Magazine* 1 (January 1929): 120–21, 124.

———. "Three Decades with the University: Adventure Called Doctor Hadsell, Learning Claimed Him." *Sooner Magazine* 1 (February 1929): 154–55, 175.

Mills, Luthera. "Second Varsity President Dies." *Sooner Magazine* 1 (January 1929): 107–108.

Montgomery, Ed. "Setting the Facts Straight on Abner Norman." *Norman Transcript*, July 28, 2003, 2.

Morgan, James F. "William Cary Renfrow, Governor of Oklahoma Territory, 1893–1897." In LeRoy H. Fischer, ed., *Territorial Governors of Oklahoma*, 46–65. Oklahoma City: Oklahoma Historical Society, 1975.

"New System of Enrollment." *University Umpire*, February 15, 1901, 14–15.

Nice, Margaret Morse. "A List of the Birds of the Campus of the University of Oklahoma." *Publications of the University of Oklahoma Biological Survey* 2 (1930): 195–96.

"No Need to Worry for the Future." *Sooner Magazine* 23 (January 1951): 21–22.

"No Other Like Him." *Sooner Magazine* 30 (October 1957): 18–19.

"Oklahoma's Territorial Governors." *Sturm's Oklahoma Magazine* 5 (January 1908): 61–66.

"Old Aliases Remembered as Presidential Home Named Boyd House Again." *Sooner Magazine* 3 (Winter 1983): 3.

"Our Medical School into Class A." *Journal of the Oklahoma State Medical Association* 13 (1920): 151.

Overstreet, May. "The Origin of the University Yell and Colors." In *Sooner Yearbook, 1916*, 326–27. Norman: University of Oklahoma, 1916.

Parker, Adelaide Loomis. "Vernon Louis Parrington: An Appreciation." *Sooner Magazine* 2 (October 1929): 20.

Parrington, Vernon L. "Albert Heald Van Vleet as I Knew Him." In *In Memory of Albert Heald Van Vleet*, 20–22. Norman: University of Oklahoma, 1926.

———. "Early Days." In *Mistletoe, 1905*, 82. Norman: University of Oklahoma, 1905.

Peery, Dan W. "The First Two Years." *Chronicles of Oklahoma* 7 (1929): 278–322, 419–57.

———. "The Struggle for the Removal of the Territorial Capital." *Chronicles of Oklahoma* 2 (1924): 319–24.

"Pioneer Sooner Dies." *Sooner Magazine* 16 (January 1944): 22.

"Possessed of a Grand Manner." *Sooner Magazine* 22 (July 1950): 7.

Ratliff, Dick. "Journalism's H. H. Herbert." *Sooner Magazine* 20 (February 1948): 10, 26.

Ray, Grace E. "Sooner Mishaps of Twenty Years Ago." *University of Oklahoma Magazine* (February 1920): 9–10.

Rice, William N. "The University in the Old Stone Building." In *Sooner Yearbook, 1911*, 15–17. Norman: University of Oklahoma, 1911.

Riggan, William, "*World Literature Today* at 60." *Sooner Magazine* 7 (Spring 1987): 25–29.

Rucker, Alan. "The Daddy of O.U." *Daily Oklahoman*, February 8, 1931, D1, 6.

Ruml, Frances. "The Formative Period of Higher Commercial Education in American Universities." In Leon Carroll Marshall, ed., *The Collegiate School of Business*, 45–65. Chicago: University of Chicago Press, 1928.

Schuyler, Montgomery. "The Romanesque Revival in America." *Architectural Record* 1 (October 1891): 151–98.

"A Serious Educational Blunder." *Outlook* 88 (April 11, 1908): 809–10.

"Shall the People Rule—in Oklahoma?" *Outlook* 90 (September 5, 1908): 15–18.

Short, Julee. "Walter S. Campbell: Oklahoma Writer." *Chronicles of Oklahoma* 51 (1973–74): 473–86.

Smith, Bobby Dean. "Lee Cruce, 1911–1915." In LeRoy H. Fischer, ed., *Oklahoma's Governors, 1907–1929: Turbulent Politics*, 47–65. Oklahoma City: Oklahoma Historical Society, 1981.

Starzer, Georgetta Larsh, and Nadine Runyan. "D. L. Larsh and Family." In Nadine Runyan, ed., *Pioneers of Cleveland County, 1889–1907*, 110–13. Norman: Cleveland County Historical Society, 1971.

"The Stratton D. Brooks Banquet: Farewell Reception and Dinner to the Retiring Superintendent of Boston Schools." *Journal of Education* (Boston) 75 (May 2, 1912): 497–98, 506.

Swain, Dwight V. "Walter Stanley Campbell, 1887–1957." *Arizona and the West* 7 (Summer 1965): 87–90.

Terry, John. "Coshocton County Native Was Founder of the University of Oklahoma." *Coshocton County (Ohio) Tribune*, October 15, 1972, 2.

Timmons, Boyce. "Wadsack Eulogy in Hearts." *Norman Transcript*, September 9, 1977, 17.

Todd, H. Coulter. "History of Medical Education in Oklahoma from 1904 to 1910." *University of Oklahoma Bulletin*, n.s. 402 (1928): 1–30.

"Tribute to Giard." *Sooner Magazine* 13 (May 1941): 30.

Turley, L. A. "LeRoy Long, Doctor and Educator." *Sooner Magazine* 13 (December 1940): 18.

"An Unforgettable Link." *Sooner Magazine* 24 (August–September 1951): 14.

"The University Hospital." *Harlow's Weekly* 21 (March 3, 1922): 11–14.

Vestal, Stanley [Walter S. Campbell]. "The Man Who Killed Custer." *American Heritage* 8 (February 1957): 4–9, 90–91.

Walker, Edith. "This Is College." *Sooner Magazine* 15 (October 1942): 16–17, 38.

Weaver, Findley. "History of the College." In *The Greater College of Business Administration: Issued in Commemoration of the Dedication of the New College of Business Administration Building, October 30 and 31, 1936* (no pagination). Norman: University of Oklahoma, 1936.

White, Len. "The Triumph of Stanley Vestal." *Sooner Magazine* 30 (October 1957): 4–7, 31.

Whitney, Carol. "A Place of Coming Together: The Historic Jacobson House." *Chronicles of Oklahoma* 78 (Winter 2000–2001): 444–67.

Wiley, Billie Rhue. "Nathan Altshiller Court." *Sooner Magazine* 8 (December 1935): 63.

Williams, Guy Y. "An Appreciation of Dr. Albert Heald Van Vleet." In *In Memory of Albert Heald Van Vleet*, 27–29. Norman: University of Oklahoma, 1926.

Willibrand, W. A. "Roy Temple House: Septuagenarian Editor of Books Abroad." *Modern Language Journal* 32 (1948): 378–81.

Witt, William H. "Patricio Gimeno." *Sooner Magazine* 5 (April 1933): 198–99, 214.

Womack, John. "Countdown to the Run." *Cleveland County Reporter*, April 17, 1980, 4.

Wood, J. Roberta. "The Oklahoma City Symphony Orchestra." *Harlow's Weekly* 23 (October 18, 1924): 9.

Wood, R. E. "History of Oklahoma's School Endowment." *Chronicles of Oklahoma* 13 (1935): 381–90.

Woods, Pendleton. "The Oklahoma City Metropolitan Area." In John W. Morris, ed., *Cities of Oklahoma*, 124–47. Oklahoma City: Oklahoma Historical Society, 1979.

Wright, Muriel H. "Pioneer Historian and Archeologist of the State of Oklahoma." *Chronicles of Oklahoma* 24 (1946–47): 396–414.

# Index

Abbott, Lyman, 162–63, 176, 179–14, 184–89, 224

Adams, Arthur B., 252–54, 256, 271

Adams Hall, 253, 264n102

Adkins, Pryor, 10–11, 22, 39

Administration Building. *See* Evans Hall

Admissions policy, 84

African Americans, 49, 52–53, 124, 225. *See also* Race

Agnes Hotel, 37, 44–45, 218

Agricultural & Mechanical College (Stillwater), 14, 43n56, 77, 79, 88, 122, 123n25, 133–36, 227, 230

Albert Teachers' Agency, 39–40, 54, 67

Alcohol, 104, 172

Alden, Arthur, 143

Alex, Okla., 48

Alexander, Frank, 183

Alley, John, 229–30

Alpha Phi Omega, 279n16

Altshiller, Nathan. *See* Court, Nathan Altshiller

Alumni Association, 68, 262

American Book Co., 178, 183, 227

American Indians, 5–8, 51–52, 171–72, 186–87, 197, 261, 269–70, 279. *See also* individual tribes

Ames, James Barr, 216

Amos, French S. E., 41–42, 45–46, 53–56, 102, 272

Anadarko, Okla., 100

Anatomy, 63, 89, 203, 254

Anderson, James, 55

Anthropology, 138

Architecture, campus, 25–27, 125, 127–30, 203–206, 209–11, 227

Architecture, study of, 122

*Arena* magazine (Boston), 153

Arkansas City, Kans., 9, 32–35, 39, 42, 50, 63, 66, 92, 94, 141

Arline Home, 120–21, 168

Art. *See* School of Fine Arts

Art museum, 260–61

Asp, Henry E., 36, 79, 122–23, 134, 152–53

Asp Avenue, 22, 83, 120, 219, 240n16

Association of American Law Schools, 222

Association of American Medical Colleges, 214, 231n44

Association of State University Presidents, 196

Astronomy, 44

Atchison, Topeka, and Santa Fe Railroad. *See* Santa Fe Railroad

Athenaean literary society, 280

Athletic Association, 60, 142, 176, 280

Athletics, 104–109, 147, 180. *See also* individual sports

Bacteriology, 254

Baker, Guy, 146

Ball, O. M., 48

Baptists, 137, 163–64, 168, 186, 227, 267. *See also* Southern Baptists

Barnard, Kate, 153

Barnes, Cassius M., 51

Barnes, W. H., 101

Baseball, 60, 106, 145, 275, 283

Basketball, 106, 145, 282–83

Beaver County, Okla., 21

Benton, Joseph ("Joseph Bentonelli"), 260n88

Best, Jesse, 146

Beta Theta Pi, 278n16

Bethany College (Lindsborg, Kans.), 132, 140–42, 259–60, 264

Biology, 88, 122, 214

Bixler, Mort L., 12–16, 95

Bizzell, William Bennett, 56, 137, 198–99, 253n61, 264

Blake, George, 10–11

Blake, Tyler, 10–11

Blakeny, John, 92

Board of Regents, University of Oklahoma, 15–16, 21–28, 34–35, 38–43, 51, 56, 58, 71, 74, 77–80, 83, 107, 114, 121–24, 128, 159–61, 165, 170, 178–85, 189, 190, 192–95, 198, 204, 206–207, 210, 212, 243

Bobo, Charles S., 192, 213, 215, 223, 229, 254

Boggle, Clyde, 108

*Books Abroad*, 221

Boole, Ella Alexander, 32

"Boomer, Sooner" (song), 143

Boone, Nathan, 6

Boory, Mr., 115

Boren, David L., 211n38

Borough Road College (London), 171

Boston, Mass., 234, 236–37, 239–40, 268

Boston School Board, 235–36

*Boston Transcript*, 7

Botany, 44, 63–65, 127, 180

Boyd, Alice, 32–33, 37, 42, 196–98

Boyd, David Ross, 50–54, 71–79, 82–85, 95, 97, 114, 116–23, 126–36, 139–40, 143, 146–56, 159, 176, 184–87, 189, 203, 206, 214, 224, 241, 251; arrival in Norman, 36–37; attitudes and character, 28–32, 36–38, 102–104, 198–99; early life, 28–34; firing of, 154, 162–73, 195; hiring as first president, 34–36; life after dismissal, 195–99; preparations for opening of the University, 38–47; recruiting early faculty, 39–42, 53–70; tree planting, 91–94

Boyd, James, 28–30

Boyd, Jennie Thompson, 32–33, 35, 37, 42, 63, 66, 145, 197

Boyd, Mary Ann Ross, 28–29

Boyd Field, 275

Boyd House, 37n38, 121n18, 158, 272–73

Boyd Street, 22, 98, 204n16, 210

Brandenburg, William, 227, 232, 237

Brewer, Bess, 190

Brewer, Theodore Frelinghuysen, 190, 193, 228–29

Brewer, Theodore Hampton, 190–91, 194, 249

Brewer, Virginia, 190, 193

Briggs, Frank, 115

Britt, Elma, 115

Britton, Okla., 48

Broadus, Dick, 122

Brooks, Marcia S., 235

Brooks, Stratton D., 197, 241–44, 246–49, 251, 254, 256–58, 271, 273, 277: character, 239; early life, 234–37; hired as president, 236–39

Brooks Street, 22, 272

Bryan, Williams Jennings, 62, 120, 166, 185n34

Buchanan, James S., 55–57, 61, 69, 73–74, 89, 92, 117, 126, 131, 139, 152, 160, 180, 183, 213–14, 242, 251, 277

Buchanan, John, 55–56

Bucklin, George, 60n52, 66–68, 73, 85, 111, 117, 119, 131, 251

Burke, J. J., 92

Business. *See* College of Business Administration

Butcher, Nahum E., 70–72, 111

Butler, Nicholas Murray, 236–37

Buttram, Frank, 243

Bynum, Ernest T., 163–68, 170, 173, 175, 176n4, 178, 183, 193, 227

Caddo Indians, 80

Cameron, Evan D., 176, 227, 231

Campbell, James R., 268–69

Campbell, Ralph ("Inky"), 166–67, 179

Campbell, Walter S. ("Stanley Vestal"), 268–71

Canadian County, Okla., 14, 21, 25

*Canadian County Courier*, 25

Canadian River, 4, 6, 8, 10–11, 22, 40, 100

Canfield, James Hulme, 36

Canon, John M., 21, 25, 35

Capshaw, Walter L., 192

Carey, Tom F., 148, 180, 192

Carnegie, Andrew, 128–29, 210

Carnegie building, 128–30, 157, 159–61, 173, 203, 273, 276. *See also* Library

Carpenter, Paul S., 260, 271

Catlin, George, 5–6

Causerie Club, 279

Centenary College (Tex.), 41

Central State Normal School (Edmond, Okla.), 56, 77, 79, 93, 122, 123n25, 142, 245–46, 267

Chandler, Okla., 224, 227

Chapel services, 83, 103, 118, 165, 173

Cheadle, John Begg, 221–22

Cheerleading, 283

Chemistry, 44, 83, 86–87, 122, 138–39, 122, 180, 203, 254, 274, 279

Cheney, Alfred, 148

Cherokee Indians, 171, 279

Cherokee Male Seminary (Tahlequah, Okla.), 171

Cherokee Outlet, 9, 33, 71, 79–80, 96,

Chickasaw Indians, 6, 8, 10, 22, 175, 279

Chickasha, Okla., 225

Chisholm, Jesse, 6

Choctaw Indians, 279

Christian Church (Disciples), 74, 103, 163, 168, 186

Claremore, Okla., 225

Clark, William J., 209n32

Cleveland, Grover, 12, 37, 74, 78–80, 170

Cleveland County, Okla., 6, 12, 14–19, 21, 24–26, 39, 53, 78, 277–78

Colcraft, C. H., 25

Cole, Lawrence W., 68–71, 73, 131, 148, 168, 176, 182–83, 191, 194, 222, 227, 247

College of Arts and Sciences, 52, 57, 84, 88, 90–91, 202, 213, 247–52, 259, 262, 277–78

College of Business Administration, 138, 250–54, 271, 277, 279

College of Engineering. *See* Engineering

College of Fine Arts. *See* School of Fine Arts

Colored Agricultural and Normal University. *See* Langston College (Okla.)

Columbia University, 247, 252, 259, 263

Comanche Indians, 5, 80, 279

Combs Conservatory, 260

Committee of Freshman Studies, 84

Constitutional convention (Okla.), 151–54

Copeland, Fayette, 36n36

Cornell University, 136–37, 265

Coshocton County, Ohio, 28, 29n13, 31

Costs of attending the University, 100–102, 278–79. *See also* Tuition

Council, Okla. *See* Senate, Okla.

Council on Medical Education, 214, 254, 256–58

Court, Nathan Altshiller, 262–64, 271

Crawford, Sam, 45

Creek Indians, 5

Cross, Bill, 189–90

Cross, George Lynn, 69–70, 137, 161n39, 243–44, 263

Cross Timbers, 4

Cruce, Lee, 54, 161, 173, 175–81, 185–89, 193, 209, 216, 218, 220, 223–32, 236–38, 243, 255

Cumberland University (Tenn.), 55

*Daily Oklahoman,* 167, 253

Dale, Edward Everett, 37, 79, 198, 265–69, 270–71

Daniels, A. N., 14

Darwin, Charles, 31, 162

Davidson, George, 164, 178, 180, 193, 196n61

Davis, Jefferson, 6

Day, Curtis R., 254–55

DeBarr, Edwin C., 39–42, 45, 50–51, 53–54, 63, 73–74, 83, 86–87, 89, 103, 105, 107, 117–18, 122, 131, 133, 139, 169, 180, 213, 272, 277

DeBarr, Hattie, 40–41

DeBarr, Helen, 40–41

DeBarr Hall, 274–76

Debo, Angie, 266n111

DeCou, Maude, 72

DeGolyer, Everette L., 177

Delta Delta Delta, 179n16

Delta Theta, 279n16

Democratic Party, 12–14, 21–23, 41, 50, 53–56, 62, 74–75, 78, 80, 137, 151–55, 160–61, 165–66, 169–70, 173, 175, 182, 184, 185n34, 220–21, 225, 227

Depression of 1890s, 51, 53, 78, 83

Dewey, Melvil, 72

Dibble, Charlie, 37

Dille, John I., 195n59

Donehew, Marion, 47n63

Dora, C. Lucile, 193–94, 207, 276

Dorrance, Lemuel, 86

Dowd, Jerome, 137–39, 164, 180, 249, 251–53

Drama School, 281, 284

Drummond, Henry, 32n23

Duffy Street, 9

Duke University, 137

Dunlop, Robert, 227–28, 230, 232

Duval, Edmund P. R., 192, 230–32

Dye, John M., 148

East Central State College (Ada, Okla.), 246n32

Economics, 68, 86, 122, 138, 180, 250–51

Edmond, Okla., 7, 14, 56. *See also* Central State Normal School (Edmond, Okla.)

Education, 176, 182, 213, 246–48, 271, 273n3, 277, 279

Edwards, L. J., 42

Elder, Frederick S., 63, 73, 87, 121, 133, 136–37

Ellison, Gayfree, 264–66, 271

Ellison infirmary, 265

Elm Street, 22, 94

El Reno, Okla., 14, 68–69

Embryology, 89, 254

Emerson, Ralph Waldo, 162

Emporia, College of, 58–60, 107

Emporia, Kans., 58, 181. *See also* Emporia, College of; Kansas State Normal School

Enabling Act (Okla.), 151, 153

Enchiladas Dancing Club, 280

Engineering, 87–88, 90, 122, 133–36, 180, 192, 202–203, 213, 265, 274–76, 277–79

English and literature, 44–45, 58–59, 61–62, 68, 84, 86, 179–81, 190–91, 194, 249–50, 270

Enrollment, 51–53, 83–84, 91, 149, 150, 202, 212n42, 241, 271, 277–78

Episcopalians, 74, 163, 182, 262

Epworth College, 90, 95, 107, 164, 166, 191, 214–17, 221–23, 229, 254, 260, 264

Erwin, Walter C., 247

Eta Beta Pi, 145

Eudelphian literary society, 280

Evans, A. Grant, 170–74, 179, 183–86, 191–95, 200–201, 207–16, 218, 220–28, 242

Evans, Katherine Robb, 171

Evans, William A., 89

Evans Hall, 209–11, 239, 243, 273–75

Everett, Mark R., 215

Ewing, Fred, 140, 142

Extension Service, 273n3

Faculty Senate, 213

Felgar, James H., 136–37, 139, 180, 213–14

Felgar Street, 204n16

Ferguson, Milton Jay, 72–73, 192

Ferguson, Thompson B., 135

Ferguson, Walter, 104, 145

Field, Walker, 117

Fire of 1903, 54n27, 117–22, 149, 160, 204

Fire of 1907, 157–61, 166–67, 204

First Baptist Church (Norman, Okla.), 120, 122

First Presbyterian Church (Norman, Okla.), 37, 53, 74

Fisher, Charley, 115

Fite, Francis B., 255–56, 258

Flexner Report, 214–15

Flood, F. W., 121, 180, 185, 192

Floyd, Monroe A., 179, 184, 192, 247

Flynn, Dennis, 96

Football, 60, 106–109, 132, 140–44, 149, 155, 261, 275, 282–84

Forum literary society, 110

Frantz, Frank, 154

French, 44, 59, 86–87, 163, 193–94, 279

Frisco, Okla., 21, 25

Gainesville, Tex., 7

Gamma Phi, 145

Gano, Bess, 189–90

Gardner, Mortimer S., 191, 222

Garfield, James A., 76

Geography, 65, 265

Geological Survey, 65, 273n3

Geology, 44, 63, 65–67, 86–87, 127, 180, 203, 213, 265, 275, 279

George Washington University, 216, 218–19, 247

German, 44, 86–87, 163, 229, 279

Giard, Charles F., 259–60

Gilbert and Sullivan, 115

Gilstrap, Harry, 135n64

Gimeno, Harold, 264n102

Gimeno, Patricio, 264, 271

Gittinger, Frances, 69, 115

Gittinger, Roy, 12, 43n56, 69–70, 73, 131, 139, 150, 154, 161–68, 172, 175–78, 181–84, 189–95, 207, 209, 223, 224n77, 228–33, 243, 247

Givens, Ruby, 168, 177

Glen, Scott, 227, 232

Glendale, Calif., 198

Good, Leonard, 261

Goodrich, Nellie, 168, 177

Gordon, J. Matt, 179, 184, 192

Gorton, Charles T., 10, 22, 83

Gould, Charles N., 65–68, 73, 87, 91, 115, 117–18, 127, 131, 133, 140, 180, 219, 265

Government. *See* Political Science

Grading system, 85

Graduate College, 213, 277–78

Grand Hotel (Norman, Okla.), 132

Gray, Elizabeth, 168–69

Greek, 44, 55, 86, 104, 122

Greek letter societies, 145–46, 149, 278–79, 284

Gregg, Josiah, 6

Griffin Memorial Hospital, 22, 97, 131

Guelich, Henry D., 168, 180

Guelich, Mary L., 180

Guthrie, Okla., 12–14, 20, 25, 35–36, 43, 50–51, 97–98, 106, 109, 135, 152–55, 160–61, 185, 269

Gymnasium, 83, 203

Gymnastics, 283

Hadley, H. M., 25

Hadsell, Sardis Roy, 66, 68, 73, 121, 131, 140, 143, 166–67, 179–80, 182, 190n45

Hall, D. C., 104, 196n61

Hardie, John, 162–63, 176, 178, 183

Hardie, Ralph, 176n5

Hargrove, R. K., 98

Harper, William Rainey, 51

Harrison, Benjamin (president), 8, 10, 12, 79

Harrison, Benjamin (state budget officer), 276

Harts, John A., 107, 140

Harvard University, 3, 55, 58, 61, 68–69, 148, 183, 192–93, 216, 218, 220, 230–31, 234, 236, 262, 267–68

Haskell, Charles N., 154–55, 161, 165–66, 170–73, 175, 179, 183, 185–86, 198, 207, 218, 224–27

Haskell Indians (football team), 142–43

Hayes, Otto F., 227, 232

Hayes, Walter, 96

Hefley, Jesse, 109

Hefley, Lem, 9–11

Hefley, Nellie, 9–11

Helmuth College, 193

Hennessey, Okla., 14

Henry, S. E., 29–32

Henry Kendall College. *See* University of Tulsa

Herbert, H. H., 249–50, 252, 256, 271

Hickam, J. P., 179, 183, 206, 224

Higher criticism, 31

High Gate College, 97–99, 102

Histology, 89, 254

History, 44, 69, 86, 122, 180, 183–84, 267–68

Hofstadter, Richard, 181

Holmberg, Fredrik Gustav, 131–33, 137, 139–40, 142, 168, 213–14

Holmberg Hall, 107, 275

Honorary degrees, 195

Hool, George A., 168, 180

Hopkins, Mark, 76–77

House, Roy Temple, 229

House of Representatives literary society, 280

House of Representatives (Okla.), 13, 15–16

Hughes, Thomas W., 220–21

Hume, C. Ross, 100, 109, 111

Humor, college, 112–14

Humphreys, W. R., 168

Hunton, Eppa, 96

Hygia Hall. *See* Ellison Infirmary

Hygiene, 254

Illinois Institute of Technology, 136

Indiana University, 135, 276

Indian Territory, 5, 7, 9, 48, 51–52, 81, 103, 151, 160, 171–72, 175, 186, 188–90, 255

Indian Territory Medical Association, 255

Ingle, Ed, 10, 17, 45–46, 93

Iowa State University, 202, 276n8

Irving, Washington, 4

Isaac D. Smead Co., 34–35

Jacobs, John, 283

Jacobson, Oscar B., 260–61, 271

Jacobson Hall, 261, 275

James, William, 69, 191

Jansky, Cyril M., 136, 168, 176, 180, 191–92, 222

Jenkins Ave, 83

Jews, 103, 262

Johns Hopkins University, 55, 63

Jolly, William J., 254

Jones, George C., 191–92, 222

Journalism. *See* School of Journalism

*Journal of the Oklahoma State Medical Association*, 258–59

Kane, Thomas F., 196

Kansas, 26, 50, 65, 74

*Kansas City Star*, 94

Kansas State Normal School, 177

Kansas State University, 282

Kappa Alpha, 145–47, 164, 278n16

Kappa Alpha Theta, 279n16

Kappa Kappa Gamma, 279n16

Kappa Sigma, 146, 279n16

Kay County, Okla., 230

Kearney, Stephen, 6

Keith, Harold, 107, 141, 237n13, 238–39, 276n6, 282

Kent, Frederick C., 231–32, 237

Kildare, Okla., 96

King, Grace Adaline, 57–59, 61, 74, 81, 90, 112, 115, 133

Kingfisher, Okla., 11, 13–14, 54

Kingfisher College, 230, 282

Kingfisher County, Okla., 21

Kingkade, Andrew, 9, 11

Kiowa Five, 261

Kiowa Indians, 5, 80

Kirk, Charles, 117, 120

Knott, John W., 35

Knowles, Frank E., 63, 168, 178, 180, 202n11

Kraettli, Emil R., 243–46, 271

Laboratory School, 248

Ladies Quartette, 145

Lamoreaux, S. W., 96

Lancaster, Joseph, 171

Land Ordinance of 1785, 78

Land Run (1889), 8–10, 21, 33, 41

Lane, Henry, 179

Langston College (Okla.), 50, 51n17, 93, 225

Larsh, Delbert L., 10–11, 13, 16n39, 17, 20–23, 39, 83, 159, 272

Las Dos Americas Club, 279

Latin, 44, 55, 84, 86, 104, 122, 180

Law building. *See* Monnet Hall

Law (study of). *See* School of Law

Leavenworth, Henry, 5– 6

Ledbetter, W. A., 220

Lee, Joshua ("Josh"), 281

Lexington, Okla., 19, 48

Library, 60, 71–73, 83, 118, 120n14, 128–30, 149, 159, 192–93, 203, 210, 264, 273, 275–76

Lincoln, Abraham, 12, 29, 37

Lindsborg, Kansas. *See* Bethany College (Lindsborg, Kans.)

Lindsey, Josiah L., 228

Lindsey Street, 6–7, 228, 272

Linebaugh, Nathaniel, 164–66, 168, 172, 175–83, 190–95, 206, 222, 228, 231

Literary societies, 110–11, 147, 280. *See also* individual literary societies

Logsdon, Guy, 171–72

Long, Beulah, 148

Long, LeRoy, 255–58, 271

Long, Stephen H., 6

Longfellow, Henry W., 143

Loomis, Adelaide, 62

Lotus Dancing Club, 280

Louisiana Purchase, 5

Lowe, T. J., 190

Lowell, A. Lawrence, 234

Lyceum literary society, 110

Lydick, J. D., 216, 220

Lysinger, J. L., 146–48

Maguire, Grace. *See* King, Grace A.

Maguire, James, 58

Main Street (Norman), 11, 21, 37, 39, 46, 97, 107, 117, 120, 202, 242, 272

Major, Charles C., 136

Masonic Club, 279n16

Materia medica, 89, 254

Mathematics, 44, 63, 84, 86–87, 122, 133–34, 136–37, 178, 192, 231–33, 261–64, 279

Matthews, W. D., 164–65

McAlester, Okla., 255–56

McBride, Katie, 104

McCarty's Saloon, 104, 145

McClain County, Okla., 198

McCosh, James, 31

McDaniel, Aaron, 95

McKinley, William, 170

McKown, Dave, 217n59

McLucas, John S., 192–93

McMahon, Mark, 140, 142

McMillan, Alonzo, 197

Meacham, Edgar, 261–64, 267, 271

Medicine, 64, 88–91, 122. *See also* School of Medicine

Meier, Henry, 229

Men's Glee Club, 281

Merkle, Fred, 108

Merkle, Joe, 108

Methodist Episcopal (Northern Methodist) Church, 74, 97–99, 102, 163–64

Michigan State Normal College (Ypsilanti), 235

Michigan State University, 40

Millar, John, 200

Miller, Clara, 180

Miller, George, 176n4

*Mistletoe Yearbook*, 111, 145

Monnet, Julien C., 217–24, 228, 233, 236

Monnett, Victor E., 265–66, 271

Monnet Hall, 223–24, 274, 276

Moore, Okla., 5, 22n62, 48

Moore, Seth, 19, 22, 26

Morgan, R. E. L., 168–69, 175, 177–78, 180, 182–83

Morgan letter, 168–69, 175, 177–78, 180, 182–83

Morrow, George, 88

Mountain View, Okla., 177

Mulhall, Okla., 14

Murray, William ("Alfalfa Bill"), 225

Museum of Natural History, 127, 159–60

Music, 90, 132–33, 145. *See also* School of Music

Muskogee, Okla., 166, 171–72, 179, 255

National Education Association, 237

Navajoe, Okla., 267

Navajo Indians, 197

Nelson, Flowers, 179

Newby, Errett R., 241–45

Newby, Lola N., 242

Newby, Merle, 243

New England Conservatory, 259–60

Newkirk, Okla., 72, 227, 230

*New York Times*, 8

Newkirk, Okla., 72, 227, 230

Nice, Margaret M., 92

Nichols, John, 252–53

Noble, Okla., 19

Non–sectarianism, 16–17

Normal University (Lebanon, Ohio), 30

Norman, Abner E., 6

Norman, Okla., 4, 6, 9–12, 17–24, 36–39, 42, 45, 52, 57, 81, 83, 94, 96, 99–100, 120, 124–25, 127, 146, 160, 167–69, 176, 182, 198, 200–202, 218, 222–25, 229, 284

*Norman Advance*, 12, 15

Norman Board of Trade, 18–20

Norman Business College, 95

Norman City Council, 167–68, 176n6

Norman Commercial Club, 200

Norman High School, 107, 176n5

Norman School Board, 69, 182

*Norman Transcript*, 17–19, 25–26, 45, 93–94, 100, 107, 121, 123–24, 126, 151, 159–61, 166, 169, 177, 179n14, 180, 183, 195, 206, 225–26

Northeastern State College (Tahlequah, Okla.), 246n32

Northwestern State College (Alva, Okla.), 246n32

Ohio Wesleyan University, 39

Oklahoma Bar Association, 216, 218

Oklahoma City, Okla., 7, 13–15, 21, 35, 41, 48

*Oklahoma City News*, 167

*Oklahoma City Daily Times*, 9, 15

Oklahoma City General Hospital, 255–56

Oklahoma City Symphony, 133

Oklahoma City University. *See* Epworth College

Oklahoma College for Young Ladies, 191–92

Oklahoma Constitutional Convention (1906), 57

Oklahoma County, Okla., 278

Oklahoma Daily, 283–84

Oklahoma Farmer, 134

Oklahoma Historical Society, 54

Oklahoma Pharmaceutical Association, 86

Oklahoma Press Association, 54

Oklahoma Sanitarium Co., 99

Oklahoma Teachers' Association, 106

Oklahoma Territory, 8–13, 17, 30, 33, 49, 52–53, 79, 92, 103, 134, 151, 186, 212

Oklushe Degataga Club, 279

Omega Psi, 145

One Study University (Ohio), 30

Oratorical Association, 120, 145, 147, 280

Oratorical contests, 108–109, 144, 281–82

Organic Act (1890), 11n29, 12–13

Osage Indians, 5, 279

*Outlook* magazine, 162, 184–89, 224

Overstreet, May, 109

Owen, Benjamin ("Bennie") G., 140–44, 147, 155, 180, 239, 261, 281–83

Owen, Robert L., 171

Owl and Triangle, 280

Parke–Davis Co., 86

Parker, George ("Deak"), 104, 145, 198–99

Parrington, Vernon L., 27, 58–62, 65, 68, 71, 73, 85, 107–108, 111, 115, 118, 122, 131, 140, 142, 168, 176, 179, 181–82, 190, 194, 196n61, 203–206, 209, 227, 249

Parsons, Andrew C., 248

Pathology, 89, 254

Pawnee Indians, 5

Paxton, Joseph F., 55, 57, 73–74, 85, 112, 118, 121, 131, 139, 168, 173, 180, 182–83, 277

Peery, Dan, 15

Pe-et, 280, 284

Pentecost, Andrew F., 26, 34–35

Perkins, Okla., 179

Perry, Fred, 107

Perry, Okla., 91, 135

Peters Avenue, 202

Pharmacology, 254

Pharmacy, 52, 86–87, 89–91, 122, 202–203, 213, 254, 277–79

Phelan, Warren W., 247, 271

Phi Chi, 279n16

Phi Delta Chi, 279n16

Phi Kappa Pi, 279n16

Phillips, Leon, 280

Philologian literary society, 280

Philomathean literary society, 110

Philosophy, 44, 86, 182, 273n3

Physical fitness, 104–105

Physics, 44, 86–87, 194

Physiology, 44, 63, 89, 254

Pi Beta Phi, 279n16

Pierian literary society, 110, 280

Pitman, Leander G., 21, 41

Pittsburgh University, 142

Platt, Orville, 79

*Plessy v. Ferguson*, 50

Political Science, 44, 86, 279

Ponca City, Okla., 7, 72, 96

Populist Party, 13–14, 62

Port, J. C., 148

Pratt, C. J., 175, 178–79, 183, 224, 230

Preparatory Department, 44–45, 52, 61, 63, 68–69, 72–73, 84, 91, 105, 125, 149, 176n5, 179, 184, 192, 202, 212, 247, 271, 278, 280

Presbyterian Board of Home Missions, 171, 196–97

Presbyterians, 28–30, 33, 37, 53, 58, 74, 99, 103, 163, 171–72, 176n4, 183, 186, 196–97, 223

Prickett, Kirby, 119, 180, 185, 192, 197

Princeton University, 30, 63, 87, 106

Professional writing program, 270

Psychology, 44, 69, 86, 176, 182–83, 191, 194, 222, 247

Publications Board, 280

Purcell, Okla., 5, 7–9, 11, 20, 48, 98, 153

*Purcell Register*, 10

Quarles, Bess, 115

Quarles, Frances, 115

Race, 17, 49, 52–53, 124, 225. *See also* African Americans; American Indians

Rader, Jesse Lee, 72–73, 120n15, 131, 140, 192–93

Railroads, 6. *See also* Santa Fe Railroad

Randall, Frank H., 220

Reaves, Samuel W., 137, 139, 164, 168, 178, 231, 262

Reed, Thomas Brackett, 120

Religious affiliations, 103

Renfrow, William C., 53, 56, 74, 78–80, 170

Rennie, Albert, 10–11

Republican Party, 12–14, 20–22, 25, 28–29, 41, 50, 53, 55, 58, 62, 65, 74, 78–80, 151–54, 160, 169–70, 175–76, 178, 185–86, 220–21, 224, 227

Rice, Bernice, 168, 177, 180

Rice, William N., 39–42, 46, 50–51, 53–55, 63, 70, 97, 272

Richardson, H. H., 25

Risinger, Bud, 107, 140

Rittenhouse, A. J., 179n14, 224

Roberts, C. C. ("Lum"), 108, 111

Roberts, Fred, 140

Robertson, Alice, 171

Rock Building, 39, 42, 46, 103, 110, 119–20, 272

Rolater, Joseph B., 255–57

Roman Catholics, 103

Roosevelt, Theodore, 151, 155, 162

Rowsey, William E., 179, 181, 195, 206, 209, 220, 227, 232

Rudolph, Frederick, 76

Ruf–Neks, 282

Rule, Maud, 72, 111, 114

Rutgers University, 106

Sac and Fox Indians, 279

Salter, Lewis S., 259–60, 271

Salt Lake City, Utah, 32

Samuels, Fantine, 121

Santa Barbara, Calif., 207

Santa Fe Railroad, 7–12, 21, 59, 71, 99–100, 115, 153, 284

Santa Fe Trail, 6

Sawtell, James H., 230

Schmidt, William G., 260

School colors, 109

School of Applied Science. *See* Engineering

School of Commerce and Industry. *See* College of Business Administration

School of Education. *See* Education

School of Fine Arts, 52, 90–91, 202, 213, 259–60, 271, 277–78

School of Journalism, 138, 191, 248–51, 270–71, 275, 277, 283

School of Law, 44, 216–23, 276–78

School of Medicine, 192, 213–14, 254–58, 271, 276, 277–78

School of Music, 57–58, 159, 277

School of Pharmacy. *See* Pharmacy

School of Public and Private Business. *See* College of Business Administration

School of Social Service, 277

School of Social Work, 138, 252

School of Teaching. *See* Education

School yell, 109, 119, 124, 126

Science Hall. *See* University Hall (first building)

Science Hall (1904), 127, 129–30, 157, 159–61, 203, 219, 273, 275–76

Scott, Angelo, 227, 232

Seay, Abraham, 26, 78, 91

Section 13 funds, 79–80

Seminole Indians, 5, 48

Senate, Okla., 15–16, 21

Senate literary society, 110, 280

Shakespeare, William, 281

Shaw, George Bernard, 281

Shawnee, Okla., 227

Shawnee Catholic School, 282

Shepley, Rutan, and Coolidge, 209–10

Shuman, Ronald B., 253n61

Sigma Alpha Epsilon, 146, 279n16

Sigma Chi, 279n16

Sigma Nu, 109, 279n16

Smith, George, 147

Smith, Hoke, 80, 96

Snow, Francis H., 34

Sociology, 68, 137–38

*Sooner Magazine*, 62

*Sooner Yearbook*, 261, 279, 281–82

Southeastern State College (Durant, Okla.), 246n32

Southern Baptists, 74–75, 137, 193. *See also* Baptists

Southern Methodists, 74–75, 97–99, 103, 162–65, 168–69, 176, 178–79, 183, 185–86, 190–92, 223, 227–28, 231

Southwestern College (Kans.). *See* Winfield, Kans.

Southwestern Normal College (Weatherford, Okla.), 93, 229, 246n32, 261, 269, 282

Spanish, 264, 279

Stanford University, 204

St. Anthony Hospital, 256

State Board of Education, 173, 184, 225–33, 238–39, 243, 248, 254–56, 271, 277

State Board of Medical Examiners, 255

Statehood (Okla.), 151–56, 187–88

Steele, George W., 12, 14–16

Stevenson, R. W., 34–35

Stillwater, Okla. *See* Agricultural and Mechanical College (Stillwater)

Stockwell, Dr., 168

Stone, William, 128n45

Stoops, Roy Philson, 89, 180, 192, 213n44, 214

Student Association, 279–80

Student Council, 280

Student government, 279–80

Sturgis, James W., 55, 104, 131, 139, 180

Summer school, 150, 183

Swensson, Carl, 132, 142

Tabasco Dancing Club, 280

Taft, William Howard, 185n34

Taylor, Archibald, 30

Taylor, John, 167

Tecumseh, Okla., 48

Tennis, 105, 145, 283

Territorial Board of Agriculture, 134

Territorial Educational Association, 79

Territorial Pharmaceutical Board, 87

Teutonia Club, 279

Thoburn, Joseph B., 134, 153

Thomas, W. E., 9

Timmons, Boyce, 245

Tonkawa, Okla., 225, 230

Toxicology, 89

Track and field, 65, 105–106, 145, 275

Tree planting, 26, 91–94, 127, 202–203, 273

Tribbey, Tom, 117

Tucker, Marshall A., 86

Tuition, 17, 45, 51, 146. *See also* Costs of attending the University

Tulsa, Okla., 171–72, 179, 192

Tulsa County Medical Society, 257

Tupper, Frederic A., 239–40

Turner, Frederick Jackson, 267–68

Tuttle, Barbara, 211n40

Twain, Mark, 282

Unassigned Lands, 6–7, 10

Underground Railroad, 29, 50

University Auditorium. *See* Holmberg Hall

University Band, 281

University Boulevard, 23, 37, 81, 94, 98, 106, 116, 204n16, 211, 273

University Hall (first building), 24–27, 117–19, 149, 251

University Hall (second building), 122–27, 157–61, 166, 203, 209

University Hospital, 256–58, 275

University of Arizona, 202

University of Arkansas, 123n25, 163, 167, 202

University of California, 69, 123n25, 136

University of Chicago, 51, 63, 68–69, 139–40, 191, 204, 209, 228–29, 247, 262

University of Colorado, 135, 183, 193, 263, 276n8

University of Ghent, 263

University of Idaho, 202

University of Illinois, 89, 123n25, 139, 220, 235, 249, 276

University of Iowa, 135, 202, 217–18, 220, 276n8

University of Kansas, 52, 85, 123n25, 135–36, 141, 143, 202, 221, 276, 282

University of Leipzig, 63

University of Michigan, 40, 42, 55, 86, 135–36, 141, 231, 235, 265

University of Missouri, 123n25, 128, 202, 276n8, 282

University of Montana, 202

University of Nebraska, 43n56, 66, 202, 248, 276n8

University of Nevada, 202

University of New Mexico, 197–98, 202

University of North Carolina, 80, 137, 143

University of Oklahoma: administrative structure, 212–14, 240–46; athletics, 104–108, 140–44, 281–83; buildings, 24–27, 122–30, 149, 160, 203, 206, 209–11, 273–76 (*see also* individual buildings); curriculum, 43–45, 86–90, 131–40, 214–16, 246–59; early competitors, 95–99, 214–15, 221–22, 225–27 (*see also* Epworth College); early policies and procedures, 84–86; faculty, 39–42, 53–70, 73–76, 131–40, 163–64; 168–69; 175–84, 189–94, 219–21, 228–32, 247–71, 276–77 (*see also* individual faculty members); finances, 77–81; land acquisition, 21–23, 83, 272–73; political and religious attacks upon, 162–70, 175–90, 222–33; purpose defined, 17; student body, 45–49, 51–53, 83–84, 99–102, 144–48, 155–57, 202, 277–81; setting and campus, 4–6, 81–83, 91–94, 202–203, 273 (*see also* Norman, Okla.); territorial legislature locates in Norman, 13–16, 18–21

University of Pennsylvania, 250n49

University of South Carolina, 252

University of Texas, 52, 108, 135, 143, 145, 191–92, 202, 231, 276, 282

University of Tulsa, 171–72, 282

University of Washington, 196

University of Wisconsin, 63, 137, 180, 192, 231, 249n47

University of Wyoming, 202

*University Oklahoman*, 283

University Senate, 213, 223

University Symphony, 277

*University Umpire*, 104, 107–109, 111–15, 117, 119, 121, 142–43, 145, 150, 155–56, 160, 173, 206n24, 219, 283

Upjohn, Lawrence N., 89–90, 214

Urinary analysis, 89

Vanderbilt University, 56, 190–91

Van Kirk, D. H., 124

Van Vleet, Albert H., 63–65, 67, 73–75, 83, 85, 88–89, 105, 115, 117–18, 127, 131, 139–40, 180, 213–14, 277

Van Wert, Ohio, 32–34, 196–97

Vestal, Stanley. *See* Campbell, Walter S. ("Stanley Vestal")

Vincent, John H., 97–99

Vinita, Okla., 54

Wadsack, George E., 245–46, 271

Waggoner, Thomas R., 10–16, 23, 26, 95

Wardner, Dorothy Gittinger, 43n56, 120n15

Washburn, Homer C., 213

Washburn College (Kans.), 141

Washington State University, 260

Washington University (St. Louis), 204, 205n23

Weatherford, Okla., 179. *See also* Southwestern Normal College (Weatherford, Okla.)

Weaver, Carlton, 152

Websterian literary society, 110, 280

Welch, P. L., 38

Wells, Chester, 249

Wendell, Barrett, 61

Wharton School, 250n49, 251

White, William Allen, 181

Whitehand Hall, 98

Wichita, Kans., 34, 36

Wichita Indians, 80

Wilburton, Okla., 225

Williams, Arthur J., 124

Williams, Ben F., Jr., 177

Williams Edward M., 168, 178, 180

Williams, Guy Y., 138–39, 142, 180

Williams, Robert F., 229, 254–55

Williams, Robert H., 226–28, 231–32

Williams, Robert L., 255–56, 258

Williams, W. W., 228

Williams College, 76

Willow Springs, Okla., 7

Wilson, Robert H., 237–38

Wilson, Woodrow, 284

Winfield, Kans., 32–33, 35–36, 39, 63, 66–68, 70–71, 91, 94, 107, 109, 148

Women's Athletic Association, 280

Women's Christian Temperance Union, 66

Women's Council, 280

Women's Glee Club, 281

Women students, 17, 48–49, 52, 90, 110–11, 130, 163–64, 193–94, 207, 275, 278, 280, 284

Woodruff, Wylie, 141

Wooster College (Ohio), 30–32, 35, 39, 195

Work, Edgar, 196

Work, Monroe N., 50

*World Literature Today*, 229

World War I, 258, 284

Wright, Frank Lloyd, 128, 211n39

Wright, Muriel H., 153


Yale University, 68–69, 143, 260

Yost, Fielding, 141

Young Men's Christian Association, 104, 145–46, 278

Young Women's Christian Association, 145–46, 278


Zetalethean literary society, 110, 280

Zeta Zeta Zeta, 145

Zoology 44, 63, 65, 127, 179, 276

# PHILADELPHIA
# MERCHANT

# PHILADELPHIA MERCHANT

## The Diary of
# THOMAS P. COPE
## 1800–1851

Edited and with an Introduction
and Appendices
by ELIZA COPE HARRISON

GATEWAY EDITIONS  South Bend, Indiana

## ILLUSTRATIONS

*following page 404*

Watercolor by Major André (*courtesy of Alan Emlen*)

Centre Square pumphouse (*Free Library of Philadelphia*)

Benjamin H. Latrobe (*Historical Society of Pennsylvania*)

Yellow fever epidemic of 1793 (*Bettmann Archive*)

Philadelphia waterfront (*Bettmann Archive*)

The *Monongahela* (*courtesy of Alan Emlen*)

Steerage ticket (*courtesy of Alan Emlen*)

First page of Cope's diary (*courtesy of Haverford College Library*)

Thomas P. Cope (*Mercantile Library of Philadelphia*)

"Procession of Victuallers" (*courtesy of Alan Emlen*)

Photograph of Thomas P. Cope (reproduced from *A History of Haverford College*. Philadelphia: 1892)

Friends Meeting House and Academy (*Free Library of Philadelphia*)

Sunday morning in front of Arch Street Meeting (*Free Library of Philadelphia*)

Election Day, 1815 (*Bettmann Archive*)

Mercantile Library, Philadelphia (*Free Library of Philadelphia*)

Merchants' Exchange (*Bettmann Archive*)

Charles Brockden Brown (*Bettmann Archive*)

Walnut Street Jail (*Bettmann Archive*)

Dorothea Dix (*Bettmann Archive*)

Blockley Alms House (*Free Library of Philadelphia*)

Lemon Hill (*Historical Society of Pennsylvania*)

Founders' Hall, Haverford College (reproduced from *A History of Haverford College*. Philadelphia: 1892)

*end papers*

"Bird's Eye View of Philadelphia," ca. 1840 (*courtesy Sessler's Bookshop*)

*title page*

"An East Perspective View of the City of Philadelphia" (*Bettmann Archive*)

*Book Design:* Carol Robak

Published by Gateway Editions, Ltd.
120 West LaSalle Street
South Bend, Indiana 46601

Manufactured in the United States of America, 10–78

Library of Congress Card Number: 78–60231

International Standard Book Number: 0–89526–689–X

# INTRODUCTION

*Eliza Cope Harrison*

"Without a dollar either of my own or of any other person," as he later wrote, young Thomas Pym Cope trudged to Philadelphia from inland Lancaster in the autumn of 1785. Although he became one of Philadelphia's wealthiest and most influential citizens, Cope started—in the best American tradition—as a lowly merchant's apprentice. In due course he made a fortune sending ships to Europe and the Orient, but it was into an amazing array of civic and charitable projects that he put most of his interest and energy. As a young man, he was a member of the Philadelphia City Council committee charged with introducing a public water supply to Philadelphia. In the 1840s, toward the end of his long life, he was one of the principal organizers of the Pennsylvania Railroad, and set the stage for the establishment of Fairmount Park by urging the city to purchase the estate known as Lemon Hill. In the intervening years he worked in many farsighted ways for the commercial welfare of Philadelphia and, sharing the common concerns of many fellow Quakers, devoted time and money to the poor and insane, the abolition of slavery, Haverford College, and even to the famine-struck Irish. His public accomplishments notwithstanding, it may well be, however, that Cope's most enduring contribution will be the diary he kept over a span of fifty years. In it, he not only described his own activities, but commented widely on contemporary life. He wrote vividly, even eloquently, so that, as we read, we become involved with Cope's life and are enticed by vignettes of prominent Philadelphia notables, thoughts on the value of simple Quaker garb, and spirited accounts of political caucus and boardroom.

Cope was born in 1768 in Lancaster, Pennsylvania, where his father, a plasterer and respected town burgess, had moved from the family farm in Chester County. The family were members of the Society of Friends, and Cope remained an active Quaker to the end of his life, although he sometimes had difficulty maintaining a balance between his Quaker principles and his delight in cosmopolitan friendships and fashionable living.

Young Thomas was ambitious. When he was a small boy, the influx into Lancaster of Revolutionary soldiers and prisoners of war, one of whom was the spy Major André, taught him—if he needed teaching—of the world beyond, and by the time he was seventeen, Lancaster seemed provincial to him. He was apprenticed to a dry goods merchant in Philadelphia, then the nation's capital. Arrangements were made for him to board with an uncle, and, before long, he was chatting with Franklin and welcomed into homes and offices of prominent Quakers.

By 1792 Cope was in business for himself, having disagreed with the uncle he had joined in partnership. Success came, but not without some difficulty. "I am but young in business and cannot afford to lay long out of money. . ." was Cope's constant refrain to those who had unpaid accounts at his store. Nevertheless, by 1800 he felt that he had enough money to support his growing family and he decided to retire from the market place. Thirty-two years old and married to Mary Drinker, the daughter of a prominent Quaker, he made plans—never realized—to travel abroad and threw himself into his work as a city councilman, and almost at once, into a quarrel with Benjamin Latrobe, the architect who designed the water system. This was only the first of the violent antipathies toward associates which Cope developed over the years, and since he clearly wanted to record his side of the story, and because he was well aware of the historic significance of a major city using steam power to provide running water, it is probably no accident that he started to keep his diary at this time.

Cope was always so vigorous and active that it is hard to believe he would have been satisfied for long with the life of committee work and gentlemanly leisure which he pictured for himself. But, as it turned out, he had no choice but to go back into business when he discovered that he had lost thousands of dollars because of an unfortunate choice of business partners in New York. In 1806, after an equally disastrous partnership with a brother-in-law who took money from the till, Cope branched out from dry goods to shipping. At the time, shipping was a risky business; with the Napoleonic wars in full swing, both the English and the French seized ships carrying goods to their respective enemies. But the potential profits were as great as the risks, and Cope, with his partner John K. Helmuth, were only two of many Americans who were enticed into the trade.

After 1807, when the Jefferson administration tried to force England and France to change their policies, first by restricting imports and then by prohibiting foreign trade entirely, shipping became very difficult. Nevertheless, Cope and Helmuth's firm survived through a jaunty combination of luck, good planning, and savoir faire—as the dairy recounts. The War of 1812 came and went, with Cope opposed both as a

Quaker and as a merchant, though before it was over he had the good fortune to see two ships arrive from the Orient. The profitable sale of their cargoes left him among the richest men in Philadelphia. But no partnership, regardless of its financial success, was ever satisfactory to Cope, and, after he had differed with the non-Quaker Helmuth, Cope kept to himself in business, taking only his sons as partners.

He did not, as so many others did, shift his money into manufacturing as a result of the decline of shipping during the War of 1812, but stayed with the sea. In 1821 he founded a line of packet ships sailing on a regular schedule between Philadelphia and Liverpool. As he also did when he invested, later on, in the Chesapeake and Delaware Canal and the Pennsylvania Railroad, Cope combined personal financial interest with a genuine concern for the improvement of Philadelphia's commerce, and he hoped that his line would help to prevent the city's business from being stolen away by New York's superior harbor. In subsequent years he again demonstrated his concern for Philadelphia's commercial future, as well as his own innovative approach to this end, by founding the Mercantile Library, for the use of young men in business, and the Board of Trade. The latter, with an influence which ultimately reached beyond Philadelphia, provided a mechanism through which all the diverse business elements in the city could speak with unity on matters of importance.

Although the Cope packet line was both fashionable and successful, Cope does not seem to have been overly interested in it, and by 1829 he had turned it over to two of his sons. What Cope apparently enjoyed most were his political and philanthropic activities. That he enjoyed knowing interesting and important people is clear from the procession of notables, from John Randolph and Charles Brockden Brown to Dorothea Dix, who appear at intervals throughout the diary. It is clear, however, that Cope was extremely effective as a public man. Although he may seem to us on occasion to have clung tenaciously to his own opinions, he was appreciated by contemporaries for his ability to reconcile opposing views. All his life, therefore, starting even before his 1807 election to the state legislature as the candidate who could speak to both sides in the rancorous feud between Federalists and Democrats, he was consistently asked to accept offices, sit on boards, and organize companies. Fortunately for us, he often took time after an active day to write about the events he had participated in. We hear Cope chatting with Dolly Madison, we wince with him as he foresees the possibility of civil war over slavery, cheer as he outwits roguish customs officials, and only wish that he had told us more about Nicholas Biddle and Stephen Girard.

So, when Cope died in 1854, Philadelphia lost—and soon forgot—a remarkable figure. He always assumed, as had the prominent Philadelphians he had admired in his youth, that it was his obligation, as well as his pleasure, to devote himself, and at least some of his wealth, to the well-being of his adopted city. Indeed, many things about Cope, from the interest in scientific matters, which won him membership in the American Philosophical Society, to his optimism about the possibility of making a better world, might lead one to think he was a typical eighteenth-century gentleman. He may have acted the part, but he was much more than that. Gay, vital, always independent and chary of fixed formulas, he was able to be effective not only in the eighteenth century, but also through half of the nineteenth, when waves of ill-absorbed immigrants and the spread of manufacturing had altered all of the old political and social rules of behavior. Evidence of the flexibility, compassion, and fundamental tolerance which enabled him to do this, in spite of the strong biases and prejudices of the class he belonged to, is found in page after page of his diary.

The preservation of Cope's diary seems to have been somewhat a matter of chance. It was found in the leaky shed of a family summer house in Maine in the 1930s. Its interest, and the personal nature of some of the comments, were immediately recognized and it was ultimately placed out of the way in the library of Haverford College. One way or another, quite a few people—members of the Cope family and others—had heard about the diary and felt that it should be published. On the other hand, there were those who disapproved of its being made public, and in addition it was not clear who, if anyone, owned the diary. But gradually a consensus has been reached among Cope's closest descendants that now, one hundred and twenty-five years after his death, it is appropriate to release his diary from its confinement and to allow the public to enjoy it.

As to the form of the diary, it consists of more than ten bound volumes. Having made the first entries in the summer of 1800, just before his thirty-second birthday, Cope made notes of his thoughts and activities at irregular intervals for the next twenty years. Sometimes writing daily, sometimes after a lapse of weeks or months, he filled more than five 8 by 5½ inch volumes with a total of over one thousand pages of fine, regular handwriting.

After his son Francis' death in 1816, Cope made relatively few entries and, without any explanation, stopped keeping the diary entirely in 1820. To date, nothing definite has come to light which explains why Cope recorded nothing during his most active years. Because his office letterbooks do still exist, we can piece together the outline of Cope's life during these years—Mary Drinker Cope's accidental death by poisoning, the founding of the Cope packet line, Cope's involvement in the national mania of canal and road building. Still, the gap in the diary is frustrating because it means that Cope's immediate reactions to such major events as the Hicksite schism in the Society of Friends or the failure of the Second Bank of the United States are not on record.

On March 19, 1843, noting that "years have elapsed since I ceased to keep a diary," Cope started once more to keep a fairly regular and copious record of his life. Picking up where he had left off, in the middle of a volume, he completed it and four and a half more (all roughly 8 by 6 inches and each containing approximately two hundred pages) during the next eight years. The last entry was made three years before he died.

Since a large percentage of the diary is published in the present volume, something of every subject Cope wrote about has been included. There is everything from comments about his family, his account of one of the first trips on the Erie Canal, and the details of his part in great charitable and civic projects, to his views on fashions, freaks, and the Mexican War. Every effort has been made to include the whole sense of Cope's ideas and remarks so that the reader can judge for himself what sort of a man he was. Entries which repeat a point already made, many routine entries of business or the weather, and parts of some which are very long have been omitted. A uniform method of dating entires, as well as some modern spelling and punctuation, have been adopted. Otherwise the diary is printed as Cope wrote it, with no changes except where an occasional personal pronoun or short word has been added for clarity. A typescript copy of the diary, along with the original, can be seen in the Quaker Collection, Haverford College Library.

Among the many people who have made it possible to publish Thomas Cope's diary, Eleanor Clark Emlen should be honored above all. Not only has she been unfailingly generous to all who have been interested in the diary, but it was she who spotted the diary's importance long ago and heroically typed a copy from the original microfilm. I would like to thank Katherine Evans Goddard and J. Morris Evans for their encouragement and help. Peter Parker, curator of manuscripts, has been generous of his time in helping me to use the treasures of the Historical Society of Pennsylvania; and my niece, Eliza M. Cope, has helped with the information found in the Appendix at the end of this volume. Dorothy Lobrano Guth, of New York, Helen Hill of Ann Arbor, Michigan, and Barbara Cary Curtis, of Haverford College Library, have given wise advice and steadied the faltering will, for which I am immensely grateful. Alan Emlen has made the project fun, and has helped greatly in finding suitable illustrations. Henry Regnery for many years has encouraged the publication of the diary and has, with Henry F. Regnery and Ben Barrett of Gateway Editions, had a vision of the high standards which Thomas Pym Cope deserves. Finally, I want most particularly to thank Richard D. Brown, professor of history at the University of Connecticut, and Lee Benson, professor of history at the University of Pennsylvania, for showing me, so graciously, the qualities which make Thomas Cope a much more significant figure than I had realized.

# PHILADELPHIA
# MERCHANT

# 1800

*August 9th.* It has frequently occurred to me to keep some note of passing circumstances, but my time hitherto has generally been so fully employed as to have rendered it impracticable. It may be useful to myself at least. When I may have little else to do, I may thus reduce my reflections into form & embody them into something that I can see & I hope understand. It may also serve as a companion in a solitary hour. When I feel but little disposed to society or other avocations, I can recur to my Commonplace Book. It will be like saluting an old acquaintance. He may be a sorry fellow & ill associate, but I trust he will at least prove to be a friend & perhaps a faithful monitor. Should I at any time be too much inclined to strut & crow with my own importance, a peep at myself in this mirror may lower my towering crescent & curb my folly.

It may likewise be beneficial to keep some account of transactions which would otherwise be forgotten. True, many of them may be trivial, that I don't doubt, but life itself is a compound of trifles & man a bundle of inconsistencies. Besides, I mean to write for my own amusement & should anyone choose to look over these sheets, to carp & find fault, let him remember, this Book is my property—he may therefore turn aside from the evil thing & depart in peace.

This is the 9th day of August, 1800. The day was ushered in by a fine shower. Grew sultry on clearing up. Succeeded by several plentiful falls of rain, a little a la mode de April. The City continues very healthy, no alarm of yellow fever. There is therefore additional cause of thankfulness & gratitude to Him who holds the destiny of nations in his hands.

Heard from our sons Henry & Francis, who are at School in Bradford near W. Chester. They are in health. This is good news. Many pleasant things befall me, yet I am not always content, but suffer myself to be discomposed by the merest trifles. How oft do we brave the greatest dangers, laugh at misery & become outrageous at the bite of a fly. We seek happiness where she is not to be found. We build our hopes on the wind, yet sometimes when we have rested our fondest expectations on what might be deemed a solid foundation, because rational, we are still deceived. It is good to have an anchor to windward & a home where the storms of this world do not prevail.

*August 10th.* "Be not provoked by injuries, to commit them," said a celebrated good man. It is good advice, but a hard lesson for a bad

scholar. When our sensibility is wounded & our pride mortified, we are too apt to retort evil for evil. Many difficulties would be removed & many thorns taken from the path of life, or rather, would lose their force, could we so far gain the mastery of ourselves as to blunt the keen edge of our material desires & root out the nice sensibility of our passions.

The more I contemplate myself, the more I am persuaded that I know but little of what I am. I have fancied myself capable of great things & a moment's reflection has brought me back to my reason & proclaimed aloud to my understanding, "Thou are but a worm."

I have learned to despise many of the grosser propensities of my nature, but my feelings will frequently rebel against my judgment & have their humour in spite of me. They swim in a high career of folly & count much on pleasure in prospect. Then comes the chilling blast of disappointment & gloom, dark as the midnight hour, enshrouds my habitation. Melancholy approaches & stalks around my abode. As yet I have not given her the hand of fellowship or invited her in, but I have known her to be so bold as scarce to wait for that ceremony. Who of my friends would conceive from my usual flow of spirits, that this had ever been the case?

Well, I am more than ever convinced that when we have no real grievances to complain of, we create imaginary ones. And I do not know whether the afflictions of the mind, even the offspring of spleen, are not frequently as intolerably insupportable as great physical evils. As the brightness of the sun transcends the glimmering of a taper, so do the enjoyments of the mind transcend the gratification of our appetites, but when the intellect is distempered, the whole system mourns & nature runs into decay.

The afternoon was spent in a trip to Springhead in company with Polly & our son William. The fields have been much refreshed by the late abundant showers & promise to be grateful receivers.

*August 11th.* Clear atmosphere, mild & pleasant. Part of the afternoon spent in examining the acc'ts at the water office. In the evening I presented my written report to the Committee for introducing water into the City, of the state of the works at Soho, whither I have lately been at their request. The Engineer B. H. Latrobe attended & expressed his displeasure at the report, in a manner hasty, intemperate & indecorous. It developed some truths which he could not well digest. Perhaps if I had been more governed by courtly policy & personal considerations, than an honest desire to discharge my duty, I should have given no offense, but I hope never to be so far the disciple of Lord Chesterfield, as to sacrifice my integrity to a false sense of what is sometimes called hypocrisy. Whatever can be done by a polish of the exterior, to smooth the rough manners of nature & to enable us to walk more harmoniously together, deserves our approbation; but I am no friend to that species of modish politeness which robs man of his sterling honesty and substitutes the foul grin of deceit and the accommodating spirit of falsehood in the place of his nobler properties. The heart, once accustomed to fraud & the tricks of courtly falsehood, seldom regains its original simplicity or that fascinating purity which gives dignity to our actions & forces esteem. An honest man is the noblest work of God.

If the Engineer had wished for the esteem & confidence of the Committee, or to have rendered himself respectable, he should have informed them truly as to the state of the works; by pursuing an opposite policy, he became suspected. I was dispatched to obtain accurate information. The result has been detection & exposure. In my report I studied to avoid personalities & have not gone as far as perhaps I ought in displaying the scene of deception practised on the Committee by their Engineer & others.

*August 12th.* Private accounts from Norfolk state that place to be afflicted with the yellow fever. There are also some rumours of a similar nature respecting N. York.

Rummaged a small trunk which I do not remember to have opened for years. It contains some collections of my boyish days. I cannot refrain from smiling as I look at them. A smooth stone, speckled shell, brass farthing & a brown thread netting to hold them, were once treasures of no inconsiderable value. Many a time have I fondled on them with as much delight as a miser feels in counting his precious guineas & hugging them to his bosom. Well, those were the rattles of infancy—I must now have larger playthings to amuse me, which bye & bye I may view with equal indifference. Our enjoyments are fitted to our years. I look back on those days with no frigid emotions; my heart feels an ecstatic throb as I contemplate the innocent, peaceful, pleasurable amusements which then beguiled time, but I have lost my relish for those enjoyments & however I may be inclined to be the eulogist of boyhood, I do not wish to be a boy.

In the afternoon the family was assembled at the late dwelling of my much honoured father-in-law, Jno. Drinker, to hear the reading of his

will. He died of a stroke of the palsy on the 27th last in the 68th year of his age. He was a man of uncommon worth & he lived the life of the righteous & his latter end was peace.

*August 13th.* The weather continues cool & pleasant. For a few days past we have experienced nothing like the sultry, relaxing air of August.

In reflecting on the conduct of the Com. for introducing water, I feel but little reason to be satisfied. They pressed me to visit Soho. I did not volunteer. I examined the works & made a report founded on a true state of facts. Yet they suffered the Engineer to brow beat & insult me. They knew that Latrobe had played a high game of deception towards them. As individuals they freely express their want of confidence in him, notwithstanding they have long permitted him to act in direct opposition to their resolves & in defiance of his written & positive agreement with them. They know that he has wasted the public money by employing villains in their service who have defrauded them & this in direct opposition to his engagements & to the advice of the members privately, yet a majority of them have ever been afraid to act worthy of the public trust reposed in them. They have dreaded either to adopt or to put in force suitable restrictive and prudential regulations for curbing his folly & extravagance. I have constantly warred against this pusillanimous policy & when H. D. Jr. was a member, I had indeed a powerful support, or rather I supported him. The present Com. have suffered their dignity to be trampled on, in permitting Latrobe to act towards me as he did. I was their member & in the act of discharging a duty imposed on me by their body. Others may, if they choose, be gulled & trampled on; for my part, I have made up my mind no longer to submit to the overbearing domineering spirit of a man who, being in the appointment of the Com. ought to be considered & treated as their servant & not be crouched to as a master & dictator.

The members present at reading my report are Jno. Miller Jr., Daniel Smith & Thos. Parker. Surely if my friend T. Paxson had attended he would not have deserted me. This affair may possibly lead to a discussion or controversy in the public prints. If so, I think Latrobe will repent the day—he has something to fear from me.

*August 14th.* This morning's paper in giving an account of much damage done by a mad dog in the western parts of the state of N. York mentions one circumstance respecting him that deserves the notice of the curious. "It is generally said that an animal labouring under the hydrophobia will on all occasions avoid water. With this dog it was otherwise, it is a fact that he would repeatedly go into the water to cool himself while on his ramble."

*August 15th*. Rain during part of the night & this morning. Headache & general languor, disqualifying me from business.

Robert Campbell, Bookseller, died this day at Frankford, some suppose of the yellow fever. He had lately been to Baltimore, & on returning from thence by water, got wet & neglected to change his clothes. A fever ensued, which in 5 days terminated his existence. The Board of Health have interdicted his interment in the City & ordered those who were lately about him not to come to Town.

*August 16th*. A sultry, muggy day, not well suited to my present state of health. What a variety of diseases is this poor tabernacle subject to. Man is indeed surrounded with infirmities. My neighbour A——y observed to me with a very significant, grave countenance that he can mostly tell when he is unwell by his feelings.

*August 17th*. Cloudy & warm with some rain, favoured with the company of our valued Friend, T. Paxson, who spent the day with us. Some of the poetical essays of my late father-in-law, J. D., were read as were also some passages from Cowper's *Task*.

*August 18th*. Brings a confirmation of the prevalence of yellow fever at Norfolk. Our Board of Health have restricted the intercourse. N. York & Baltimore are said to be healthy.

The French army of reserve in their late irruption into Italy, under their chief Consul Bonaparte, passed the Alps at St. Bernard, where the Cenobites have on the summit of one of the highest mountains fixed their abode amidst ice & snow & afford gratuitous shelter & refreshment to wandering travellers. The army dined on the snow attended by one of the society, who served them with wine & other refreshments. This must have been about the 20th of May, last. From this dreary spot the army descended into Italy over the most frightful precipices & along narrow paths where the horsemen had to alight & drive their horses one by one before them. They passed in sight of the rock which Hannibal, above two thousand years before, split, in order to make a passage for his troops, when marching against the Romans, at the commencement of the second Punic war. In this bold attempt Hannibal was successful & beat his opponents & the Corsican Hero seems to have poured from these heights on the Austrians with the velocity of a torrent, sweeping all before him. The Carthaginian was, however, defeated in turn. What

may be the event of the present expedition time alone can develop.

Wrote a letter of resignation to the Watering Committee, which by the advice of some of my friends I was prevented from presenting. Public considerations should have the precedence of private convenience & I hope never to be so self-willed as to reject the counsel of good men. I was even prevailed on to attent their meeting this afternoon. They ordered my report to be placed on their minutes & decided against Latrobe's protest being inserted. The Com. adjourned in time to allow of my walking to Schuylkill in company with the Mayor & some of the members, to view the progress of the works.

*August 19th.* Morning foggy, noon hot, evening cool. A gazette extra apprises us of the return of the Consul Bonaparte to Paris after reconquering Italy. It is extraordinary that so many years of carnage have not sufficed to satiate the brutal, inexorable spirit that presides over the present war in Europe. Millions of lives & hundreds of millions of treasure have already been sacrificed in this detestable strife. It moves my utmost indignation to perceive the appellations wantonly applied to the savage achievements of the contending butchers. Ten thousand men murdered is called "a brilliant affair." A town taken by storm after a siege in which many of its wretched inhabitants, men, women & children, have been starved to death by inches is a "grand exploit." A country ravaged with fire & sword—fathers, mothers & children involved in one universal ruin; old men perishing by the merciless hands of those they never injured; beauty & innocence violated & then put to the bayonet by the monsters whose lusts they had been forced to appease; children torn from their mother's breasts & put to cruel & tormenting deaths. Scenes like these, men are not ashamed to call "glorious." My very soul revolts at the idea when I remember that I am obliged to consider myself as belonging to the same species with these detested barbarians. This humiliating consideration is enough to drive a man of sensibility mad; to make him abandon all human society & fly into the uttermost corner of the dark, howling wilderness.

*August 20th.* Dispatched 14 copies of the address of the late convention of delegates from the different abolition societies to Burlington for signature of Genl. Jos. Bloomfield, their president.

The arrival of brother Jasper from Baltimore brings better news from that place than the rumour of the day, which states the existence of the yellow fever there. He discredits the report.

*August 21st.* Morning & evening quite cool—noon not unpleasant. The *Ganges*, sloop of war, captured 2 cargoes of slaves, which have been performing quarantine at the Lazaretto for some time past. The poor wretches were permitted to land with a view of promoting their health. They had not been long ashore when two of them belonging to different vessels recognized each other as man & wife. This unexpected meeting produced a powerful effect on the parties. The transports of joy in the woman were too great for her situation & a premature birth immediately ensued. The humanity of those who have the care of them induces a hope that the unhappy mother may recover. Would not a scene like this produce one sympathetic glow, one tender emotion of pity in the breast of a dealer in human flesh? No. Man has no bowels of mercy for man. It is sufficient that a fellow being is an African & black to justify the infliction of cruelty on him, such as a Mohawk might glory in when punishing his bitterest enemy. And do these monsters call themselves Christians? Yes, & under that sacred profession they do not hesitate to perpetrate the most daring crimes, in outrage of its best principles & in defiance of the majesty of heaven.

The Board of Health have this day restricted the intercourse with Baltimore.

*August 22d.* At the request of Bradford, Editor of the *True American*, wrote a short essay for his paper on the subject of the water works.

*August 25th.* Warm but not unpleasant. The largest boiler flue & some other parts of the engines have arrived in 5 waggons from Soho.

*August 26th.* Brother Jasper made his declaration of marriage with Rebecca Shoemaker at the monthly meeting for the northern district.

*August 27th.* The vanity, folly, & foppery of man in pursuit of that fantastic thing called fashion has often excited my admiration. We are all of us perhaps more or less the slaves or subjects of the whimsical jade. Many, conceiving themselves exempt from her sway, because they walk not with the common herd, but choose a different path, are nevertheless submissive idolizers of this empress. They have a fashion of their own, & it is surely no uncommon thing to see a straightlaced, prim, quaint unfashionably fashionable sectarian, valuing himself on the properties which he affects to despise in others. One man wears a powdered wig &, like Joseph of old, a coat of many colors. These gratify his pride. Another has every hair adjusted to a tittle, nicely curled, & plastered with perfumed tallow, a broad brim & drab suit; of all which he is childishly fond & ridiculously tenacious. Even the dead are not permitted to rest in peace, but must be decorated & set out agreeable to the approved taste.

A man from Northampton County was purchasing some very small padlocks of R. Wistar today, whose curiosity led him to ask the use for which he intended them. "To put on Coffins" said the countryman. "On Coffins?" "Yes, on Coffins, why that is all the fashion with us." The old adage is, that a man may as well be out of the world as out of the fashion, but it seems that death itself, whatever liberty it may give to the spirit, subjects the poor corpse to the rules of the prevailing custom, however absurd or inconvenient.

*August 28th.* The preceding night has been sultry. This morning is no better.

At length our literary friend C. B. Brown from N. York has made his appearance, & spent most of the day with us. Our little party was joined in the evening by Timothy, who has lately been much with us, as his Ruth is in the country. If the joram was not pushed about, conversation was—neither of the company being remarkably given to taciturnity.

Several smart showers have tempered the atmosphere.

*August 29th.* Great poverty of intellect & self condemnation. I am far from being as perfect as I ought to be & fall short of my known duties. How often have good resolutions been broken & my giddy head moved in opposition to my heart? Why do I so frequently suffer the ebullitions of the moment to run away with my reason? We sow briers & thorns with as much diligence & care as if it were a compulsory duty. We cultivate the evil growth & finally reap a wretched crop of sorrow & repentance. We do all this with our eyes open. We see the evil, put others on their guard, & being fully aware of the consequences, we next leap head-long into the gulf. So absurd, so perverse, so inconsistent, so stupid, so foolish is man.

Two traders from Kentucky, Keith & Caldwell, having under very suspicious circumstances attempted to pass counterfeit bank notes, I wrote to the Mayor, R. Wharton, requesting their apprehension. Saw one of the notes, it is of the Charleston branch, $20 & clumsily executed. It being late in the day & preparing for an excursion tomorrow, don't expect to hear the issue at present.

*August 30th.* Left home in company with Polly & son William in a

chair. A pleasant morning, soon overcast & sultry, halted & dined at
Baymont's, West Chester road. Made a disagreeable discovery, one
wheel of the chair in a shattered trim. Doubtful whether to proceed,
determined to try. Scarce left the tavern when it began to rain, continued without much interruption the rest of the day. Travelled cautiously
over this stony, hilly road & reached Uncle Nathan Cope's in good
season. There we had the satisfaction to see our sons Henry & Francis in
health. Uncle not well; rained smartly most of the night.

*August 31st.* Attended Bradford meeting on horseback. The quiet of
it disturbed by the ranting of Joshua Hoopes. That meeting has been
thus discomposed by this maniac for 19 years past. It is a good school for
the trial of patience & forbearance.

Afternoon spent in visits to relations. Most of the day blustering,
evening calm.

*September 4th.* Having broke my spectacles I have been deprived the
pleasure of reading & writing for several days & was under the necessity
of sending them to the City to be repaired. My time in the interim has
been variously spent. After getting my chair mended, I went to see the
County Poor House. It is about 6 miles west of West Chester & is an ill
constructed brick building, 2 stories, 100 by 40 feet. The 2 principal
doors 3 feet wide. Not a cloth press or closet in the whole building,
except one for the use of the directors. The lodging rooms, which are
next the roof, have not a fire place, & each but one small window,
except the largest, which extends the full length of the building, 100
feet. This the architect has thought worthy of three. The building is not
quite finished, but is intended to be in a state to receive the paupers this
fall, the whole of which it is supposed will amount to about 120. The
house is erected on a farm of 300 acres belonging to the establishment. It
is the design to make the poor cultivate some portion of the ground.
Both the act of incorporation & the bye laws of the directors will require
amendment—some glaring defects being observable in them. On the
whole, I could but be highly gratified in beholding this first practical
attempt at a scheme which I contended for the public prints several
years ago, & for ought I know was the first publicly to recommend. I still
believe it will under proper management prove highly beneficial. Hundreds of pounds have been yearly expended between the different
townships in the State in settling the residence of the poor. This plan
will also prevent that abominably inhuman custom of placing the
paupers with the person who would keep them for the least money. The

overseer called the township together, held an auction at which any person might bid, & whoever offered the lowest terms won the prize. Of course, as his intention was to make a profit, the consequences to the poor are easily to be conceived.

B. Cope in ploughing ground with high weeds uses a heavy chain about 8 feet long, one end of which is made fast to the false colter, the other secured to the outside end of the swingletree of the furrow horse. This chain levels the weeds, & the operation of the plough covers them completely.

*September 5th.* Leaving our son William to the care of cousin Rachel Cope, Polly & myself set forward this morning. Passed by Bradford & the Grove meeting, halted to bait at Hahn's Tavern on the Newport road & a little before sunset arrived at James Miller's, where the Newport & Strasburg roads intersect each other. Most of this day's ride has been over a rough chair road, & part of the country poor & badly cultivated, especially between the Grove meeting & Newport road. Day not unpleasant, evening cool enough for fire.

*September 7th.* What I have seen of Sadsbury (where we now are) is a rough country, very hilly, stony & gravelly, intermixed in places with clay & marl. Peaches & apples are plenty & some watermelons are produced here of a small size. This vegetable is uncommonly fine & abundant this year. In Philadelphia I have purchased them sufficiently large to satisfy 6 persons at 3 & 4 cents apiece & they have been offered of a good size at a Dollar a hundred.

The roads in this neighbourhood are almost inaccessible to a chair, in consequence of which Polly and myself had a painful ride to & from meeting.

*September 8th.* We again set our faces towards the westward, escorted by J. M. over a winding road about 3 miles to the Turnpike, which we entered between the 17 & 18 mile stones. The difference of soil was striking most of the way to Lancaster, bearing marks of that richness & fertility for which the lands in this neighbourhood are so remarkable. Reached Lancaster about 2 P.M. & found mother unwell, but hope on the mend.

*September 9th.* Forenoon occupied in business. Afternoon moved forward to Columbia & stopped at Wm. Wright's. Here again the pleasure of meeting was damped, by the indisposition of Susan. Thus briers & thorns grow where the choicest fruits are found, & the cup of pleasure is frequently mingled with gall.

This Town is 10 miles west of Lancaster & situated on a high bank of the Susquehanna, which is here about a mile & a quarter wide. The prospect is much enlivened by a number of small islands proudly mantled in vegetation. The land is rich & the place from its high bold shore healthy, tho' on the opposite side of the river the inhabitants are much incommoded with fever & ague. Columbia has many charms & were it planted with a colony of congenial spirits, I think I could contentedly fix my abode in its wild looking region. It has a navigation of between 3 & 4 hundred miles up the north branch of the river. The last spring about 25 thousand bushels of wheat, 3 thousand barrels of flour, & 2 million feet of boards, besides shingles & other lumber, were delivered in the Town. It is expected that the quantity will be considerably increased next year, as they are now employed in removing some obstructions to the navigation between this & Middletown.

About 2 miles above the Town on the same side of the river is Chicki's rock which, fronting the stream, is 230 feet high & as perpendicular as a wall.

*September 10th.* In the afternoon we crossed the Susquehanna & had an agreeable ride of about 11 miles to York Town. I seemed to have been drawn thither by inclination without any premeditated motive, & my feelings beat in unison with my reason in approving what I have done. It was a high gratification to receive & impart the testimony of affection & good will with persons nearly allied by kindred ties, but who from circumstances ever to be lamented, have been separated from me. The perversity of the human mind, & the deplorable infatuation which not infrequently bereaves man of all his wonted energies, & hurries him headlong into ruin, is such that it is no wonder we ascribe so many of the actions of this boasted child of reason to some demon that fixes on his destruction, & urges him to despair & madness. Surely the lessons of instruction, of warning, & of humility, which are to be derived from the contemplation of humanity thus degraded, are forcible indeed, & should rouse us to a careful examination of ourselves, that we may endeavour to avoid those rocks on which others have been wrecked. Our interview with sister P. C. & her 2 children, Lydia & Herman, was satisfactory & cordial.

*September 11th.* Before we left the Town we called on Jno. Fisher, a German mechanic of a curious & versatile genius. He is the maker of a number of time pieces of singular invention. He had but one going; this, in addition to what is usually represented on the dial of clocks, contains a chart of our hemisphere on which is exhibited the diurnal & annual

motion of the earth round the sun, defining by figures the time in every quarter of the globe & distinguishing night from day in each. The motion of the moon & its phases are also shown on the same plate.

Taking an affectionate leave of our connections we set our faces homeward, & towards evening recrossed the river to Wm. Wright's.

Doctor Houston informs me that, except a few cases of intermittents in the vicinity of the Town, the people in this part of the country are healthy.

This man is an eccentric character. Imbued with considerable skill in his profession, he scarcely possesses energy enough to be useful. His conversation is conducted with so much deliberation that one might suppose he was doubtful whether to sleep or talk. About 20 years ago, he resolved to visit Baltimore on business that required his personal attention & in which his interest was involved. For more than a dozen times, he accoutred himself for the journey & had his horse saddled & bridled ready to start. Once he actually mounted, moved a few rods, & turned back. The journey was never effected & his business remains to this day unaccomplished, tho' he occasionally talks of performing the jaunt, believing his property may suffer if he neglects it.

Before the Town of Columbia was laid out, a number of large cherry trees, some of which are still standing, used once a year to attract great collections of people to celebrate a festival which by common consent was called Cherryfair. Four & five hundred & even a thousand people have some seasons assembled on that occasion, to eat cherries & to make merry over the bottle, to sweat at a "hoop-si-saw," & riot on the green. This practice has lately been abolished by the townsmen & very wisely, as the morals of the people were greatly injured at those scenes of frolic.

I am not a little surprized at being informed by S. Wright that one of his neighbours had an acre of ground planted with Hops which it is believed will not yield less than 1700 lb. This at 3/6 per lb., the present price, gives near $800—an astonishing product.

*September 12th.* A little party was made up to visit the Roundtop, a mountain on the opposite margin of the river, and about 3 miles above the Town. At 10 we were equipped for the expedition. William Wright & his Deborah, Sarah Parish & my Polly in a carriage, Samuel Wright and myself on horseback. We passed the river in the usual time, 30 minutes, & proceeding along the York road between one & two miles, turned to the northward & by pulling down fences & winding about the woods, were enabled to take the carriage within a few hundred yards of the summit. We halted in several places to regale ourselves on peaches & I think I have seldom seen larger or better anywhere than we found beyond Moccasin Hill. Those high grounds seem peculiarly adapted to their growth. The trees were vigorous & did not appear to have been injured, or indeed touched by the worm. The fruit was finely flavoured, & hung on the branches nearly as thick as grapes in bunches. The ascent to the top was gradual & was effected without much fatigue even to our fair companions. We were richly repaid for our trouble when we gained it. The mountain is supposed by S. W. to be about 500 feet above the level of the river, & commands a very extensive prospect of parts of the counties of Lancaster & Dauphine, as far as to the Blue mountain, between 35 & 40 miles distant in a NE direction. Most of the lands within the free scope of the eye are rich & well cultivated, which gives them the appearance of gardens from this elevated spot. The river displays itself in all its grandeur for several miles up the stream. Anderson's Ferry is about ½ a mile off. A houseboat that crossed looked little larger than a duck afloat. Eastward the Town of Lancaster can be plainly discerned, tho' at present the view is interrupted by the growth of trees & bushes. On the York County side scarce anything but mountains covered with foliage is to be seen. Down the river you have a view of the Jochala islands, 8 or 10 miles off & a small distance above the blue rock, where the river begins to widen & presently becomes nearly 3 miles over. From this eminence it was easy to perceive that Howell has made a considerable blunder in defining the course of the river in this place. The bend is greater than a right angle, whereas he scarcely deviates from a right line. He has also placed the road on the western shore in a S. W. direction from Columbia & it should incline rather to the north of west. On the mountain we found a great many chink-a-pins, a small sweet nut that grows singly in a bur on a bush from 6 to 10 feet high—which in every respect has the semblance of a chestnut tree in miniature. At 3 o'clock we began to descend. When we reached level ground, we stopped at a spring house & had a most excellent repast of milk & biscuit, which our previous exercise gave us an appetite to relish. By 5. P.M. we found ourselves again at the hospitable mansion of W. Wright.

*September 13th.* The weather for several days past has been uniformly clear & moderately warm. This day it has become quite sultry. In the afternoon we made a trip to Chicki's rock, attended by W. Wright, his wife & C. Biddle. We approached it from the eastward. The ground is covered with trees & capable of tillage almost on to the precipice, the perpendicular height of which I have already mentioned to be 230 feet, notwithstanding which there is an evident descent for perhaps 40 rods before you arrive at the rock. The view up the river is much the same as from the round top, which is nearly opposite, but not so extensive. The rude appearance of the dismembered rocks thro' which the river finds its way, the rippling of the water & its perpetual murmur & the wild aspect of the scenery on all hands, renders this enchanting spot such as poets might love to sing & naturalists to admire. When the river is low as is the case at present, there is a space of a perch between the rock & the water. In order to view it from this position, you must either go a great way round or descend a deep declivity. As our time was short, we preferred the latter & Polly & myself, leaving the rest of the company, soon reached the bottom, but not before I was several times prostrated on my back. The prospect from below is grand & sublime. The rock at its base is connected, but towards the summit it is divided & ends in peaks, each having a form peculiar to itself. One recedes, another is directly upright & a third, on which we had been standing a few minutes before, is capped with a huge projectile mass. The surface is decorated with moss & here & there a tree or a shrub contrasts its green verdure with the sullen shade of the retiring mountain, or the leaden coloured aspect of the more prominent parts. The ground beneath is covered with large masses of stone, piled on each other in uncouth order & which have evidently been precipitated at different times from the ragged precipices above. It seems not improbable that at some very distant period this rock was united to the high grounds or mountains of the opposite shore & the country above for many miles round must have been a lake. Having remained as long at the foot of the rock as our time would admit, it being near sunset, we began to ascend. The day was excessively warm & by the time we regained our first position I had not many dry threads about me. C. Biddle had waited our return, but W. W. & his wife had gone towards the carriage, which had been left about 3/4 of a mile off. Night came on & as there was no moon, we had a dark passage of about an hour, over a bad road, before we got back. We had however a good appetite for a cup of tea &c. which the kindness of our friends had provided.

There is a tradition that the Indians who formerly inhabited this country used to punish their enemies by blindfolding them & leading them in that condition to the verge of Chicki's rock, whence the unhappy victims were plunged headlong into an awful eternity.

*September 15th.* Lancaster is one of the largest inland towns in the U. States & contains perhaps not less than six thousand inhabitants, a large majority of whom are of German extraction. All, however, ape the English & in doing it frequently commit ludicrous blunders. A person of the name of Gottlieb Nauman, a tavern keeper still alive, used when I was a boy to inform people of his vocation & that he provided for both man & horse by the following inscription which, for many years, remained on his sign, "Entertainment for man by Gott. Nauman horse."

The Poor House is very eligibly situated on the Connestogo on a bank 40 or 50 perches from the creek & 100 feet above its level. The building is 150 by 42 feet, constructed of stone on a plan much more liberal, tasty & commodious than that of Chester County. It is expected to cost about 6 thousand Pounds when complete. It is 2 stories, besides an airy light cellar partly above ground & the apartments in general are neat & commodious. It is not more than one quarter of a mile from the Stone bridge now erecting & nearly finished over the Connestogo on the turn pike. This bridge has nine arches, the largest of which is 35 feet span & the smaller better than 20. It is 475 feet from shore to shore & 586 including the abutments.

Left Lancaster in the afternoon & tarried all night at Amos Slaymaker's, who keeps a public house on the turnpike 13 miles from the Town. We were joined at supper by C. Biddle & T. Poultney. On this road travelling is cheap. We had good coffee, bread & butter, rusk, gammon, beef, cheese, fish & an excellent roasted turkey with vegetables. We were charged 25 cents a piece for the meal. Were lodged comfortably & 16th reached Pettits, 19 mile stone & were joined there at breakfast by brother Jasper who came from Lancaster in the stage. We left him there & kept company with C. B. & T. P. who were in a chair, till within a mile of Downingstown, when we took across the country by the Bradford meeting house & thence to Uncle Nathan Cope's & were favoured once more to see our 3 boys in the enjoyment of robust health.

This is the season for seeding & the farmers are busily employed in that necessary occupation.

*September 17th.* I have at different times seen a great diversity of soil & am persuaded if more attention was paid to adapt the culture to the quality of the ground, it would be rendered more productive. Scarce any spot, however barren, would be wholly useless if properly cultivated. Before we plant or sow, it should be ascertained that the tree or seed is congenial to the land. A mountain which disdains the plough would give nourishment to many valuable fruit trees & I doubt not, contribute as largely to enriching the owner as the lowlands. Peaches, for instance, grow luxuriantly on rocky, mountainous land. When dried, they usually bring three dollars a bushel in the Philadelphia market. An acre of poor ground would, in this way, yield a profit with scarcely any trouble beyond what more favoured spots do with much more care & hard labour. Besides, I believe that the land, however poor, might be made to sustain a crop of grass, provided you were to sow it with the proper kind.

*September 18th.* Clear & warm. I have been viewing a ram brought from the Cape of Good Hope about 6 months ago. He is losing the hairy coat of his native clime & exchanging it for wool. He retains his broad flat tail & thin flanks; properties which a better country cannot change. Like many other foreigners, who, in coming to America have forsaken barren heaths for fields of clover, he looks full fed & impudent & seems disposed to rule over the humble Pennsylvanian sheep that graze with him.

In a lime stone quarry on Uncle N. C.'s farm a substance is found of the consistence of wax & tallow & of nearly the same colour. It sometimes encrusts the stones & at others is discovered in crevices. It has a fat, oily feel, but will not burn. No use has ever been made of it by the family. Near the same quarry there is a species of soap stone almost as white as chalk & will mark nearly as well.

I was told of another quarry in the neighbourhood where a stone has been found, the fibres of which very much resemble cotton, it is called the cotton stone. I went in search of this stone & pretty soon obtained a number of pieces of it; one of which was as large as my hand. I am informed that they are procured of a much larger size. It has somewhat of the appearance of the inside of bark, of a dirty hue & the fibres have a coarse aspect. I have one piece of a cream colour. The parts on separation are very fine & do not bear the least resemblance of a stone. They are perfectly inconsumable & seem to be sufficiently tenacious to admit of being spun into a thread. The priests of Loretto, that hot bed of popish imposition, made a singular use of this species of asbestos. They had a cloth made of it which, if I have not forgotten, they pretended was wrapped round our Saviour after crucifixion, & as a proof of its sacred quality, they would throw it into the fire in place of washing it. This test carried conviction to the minds of the ignorant & induced many to make rich presents to the Holy fathers, who were entrusted with a relic of so much value & such high & sacred derivation.

*September 19th.* Dobbin was once more tacked to the chair & with a gentle jog under a hot sun & over a very dusty road, safely conveyed the same burden to the City he dragged into the country on the 30th last. During this period there has been no rain. The fields are of course much parched.

*September 20th.* Business demands my attention. Some prospect of rain, which the approaching equinox will probably hasten. A committee of Citizens are collecting money for the suffering poor of Baltimore, Norfolk & Providence, R.I., which places continue to be afflicted by a malignant epidemic. Philadelphia is healthy. One set of hypothesis makers had vauntingly prognosticated the disappearance of these awful visitations in the United States in the present season. When will men learn wisdom & instead of proudly erecting systems on airy & fantastic speculations, learn to know that He who "rides on the whirlwind & directs the storm" is not governed by theories of men & the visionary notions of philosophic demagogues?

*September 21st.* Two brothers of the name of McAllister, the youngest of whom is upwards of 60, have lately been convicted at Carlisle of the murder of a negro man. He was the slave of one of them & had committed an offence for which they thought he merited punishment. They put a rope about his neck & beat him with hickory withes until he could neither stand nor walk. They then dragged him by the rope on the ground. He survived their cruelty but a short time & expired about 2 hours after they began to beat him. Before that brutal affair those men are said to have sustained a good reputation. They did not probably design to commit murder but, having begun their work of revenge, their anger increased as they proceeded until their rage knew no bounds. This melancholy transaction should operate as a solemn warning to others not to suffer the passion of anger to lead them to such barbarous lengths. Man is little else than the creature of education. The infant is taught to revenge his fall by beating the stick that tripped him. He cries for something which he should not have & his passion is soothed by indulgence. He throws his top into the fire because he cannot spin it & tears his Book because he cannot read it. He receives an imaginary insult from his playmate & resents it by a blow with a hammer or a knife, for which he is either gently rebuked or praised. He is at liberty to beat his kitten or puppy without mercy & to do a thousand other things for which he should be instantly reprehended—but for which he receives no suitable reproof. He is thus fitted for deeds of savage ferocity when

arrived on the stage of manhood & freely indulges his brutal humour, until the halter stops his wicked career.

Rain all the preceding night & at intervals today. Wind SW.

*September 22d.* A conspiracy of the negroes has been detected at Richmond. Several of the unhappy wretches have been executed & others are expected to suffer the same fate. So long as seven thousand fellow beings are held in chains in these United States, their cruel & hardened oppressors may look for plots, conspiracies & insurrections. Nature revolts at the idea of bondage in any shape, but when that bondage is attended with other circumstances of barbarity such as tearing a fond husband from the arms of an affectionate wife & forcing the smiling babe from the breast of a tender hearted mother, of severing whole families & cutting asunder all the dearest ties of humanity, of dragging those innocent & hapless victims into a far distant country, never, never to return, but to endure every species of heart rending torture under the galling yoke of a never ending slavery, except by the welcome interposition of death; surely these forgers of fetters, these tyrants of their species, are not to expect from men, formed, like themselves, for the sweet enjoyments of liberty, a tame & unresisting submission to all their deeds of merciless injustice. I would not be a dealer in human flesh for all the riches of Indastan; nor a master of slaves for the fairest portion of my country. When I contemplate the nature of man, his restless spirit & daring efforts to regain that state of freedom of which he is wantonly deprived by his fellow man, I think I can see, in the sullen temper & discontented acts of the negroes in the southern states, a gathering storm, which may one day burst forth & overwhelm the oppressor & the oppressed in one general undistinguishable ruin.

*September 23d.* It is remarkable that this morning's paper announces the existence of an insurrection among the negroes near Charleston, S.C., which has already occasioned very serious alarm to the white people, several of whom have been killed by the insurgents. The blacks are embodied about 30 miles from the City in considerable force. I knew nothing of this insurrection when I penned my observations of yesterday. This is an age big with important events.

Much to do & little accomplished, yet it has been a busy day. It is a difficult matter always to command our best powers or to use them to the best advantage. System & calmness will do much; this I know. But I sometimes abandon both & heedlessly set to work without due consideration; at others, my faculties seem stupified & refuse to move one jot in my service.

*September 24th.* It is not improbable that my apprehensions with regard to the blacks may be realized at a period much earlier than I imagined. Today's paper contains intelligence from Boston that the police, fearful of some mischief from certain movements among the negroes, have ordered the banishment of about 300 free blacks.

Ten more executions at Richmond. Many more are expected to follow. Some Frenchmen are said to have incited the conspiracy there.

*September 25th.* The bones of a very large animal, supposed to be larger than any other quadruped yet known, have been lately discovered in Long Island. Its head is of the size of a puncheon or hogshead & other parts in proportion. Height of this beast is 20 feet.

Cloudy & rain daily since the 22d. Wind NE.

Accounts from Baltimore still unfavourable; from 20 to 30 fall daily victims to the fever. Business at a stand. The inhabitants from the City & point, in the latter of which the disorder prevails the most generally, removed. Brother Israel & some others have taken a house 4 miles out of the Town. Jasper remains with me.

*September 26th.* A contusion on my leg occasioned by a boy who ran his wheelbarrow with great violence against me in the street gives me a very hobbling gait. Should not wheelbarrows be excluded from the foot pavements? I once attempted this regulation in Council & have now an additional incentive to propose the measure anew. It suits me illy to be lame, as I have much out door business to do. A limping leg & a thick skull may make a bustle, but are poor appendages on a rainy day in the streets of Philadelphia. A man had need of a whole understanding both of mind & body to enable him to jostle & elbow thro' the crowd. True, some such there are who make their way most admirably thro' all the variegated walks of life & if at last they do but reach that country whither we are all journeying—whilst their broken shins will rest as quietly in the grave as the whole bones of more favoured travellers, their spirits may, for ought I know, enjoy an equal participation in the rich inheritance of the just. At all events the Scriptures teach that it is better to go to Heaven with a broken shin than to the other place with sound limbs.

*September 27th.* Heartily sick of Corporation business. If every member of the Council would take his share of the public burden, the duty of each would be light. But when one is called upon & pestered about every trifling matter it becomes irksome & "the willing horse may be rode to death." A public servant may be considered in the light of a public Jack ass, that everybody thinks himself authorized to mount, beat & drive at pleasure. Should the hapless scrub wince or stumble, he is forthwith trounced without mercy. Should he patiently jog on thro' thick & thin & bear his graceless rider harmless over every bog, it is a hundred chances to one if he does not receive a kick or a curse for his troubles.

The conspiracy of the negroes at Richmond had like to have proved successful. So near were they to the execution of their plot that, on the very night on which it was to have been accomplished, twelve hundred of them privately assembled in a large swamp in the neighbourhood of the town. Suddenly a heavy fall of rain raised the waters & prevented their passage. This providential circumstance alone in all probability saved the inhabitants. Some of the blacks, becoming dismayed from this bad omen, discovered the scheme & prevented the mischief. All the male whites were to have been massacred. The females were to have been spared & given up to their conquerors. A strange fact is also mentioned, the old black women were to be destroyed. They were considered as useless at best & might, by their tattling, discover secrets & ruin the cause.

Still cloudy with intervals of rain. Light NE wind.

*September 28th.* Doctors Woodhouse & Aspinwall of N. England have made extensive & successful experiments on the cow or kine pox. They have proven it to be void of contagion. It is only communicated by piercing the skin & inserting the matter. It occasions little or no sickness & is considered as a complete preventative of that vile disorder, the small pox.

Sancho Panza's blessing on the inventor of sleep was well enough, but now that the thing is common to most of us, I will give my blessing to any man who will invent an acceptable & certain mode to guard one from taking cold. I have hitherto failed to discover that secret. I once heard of a man who came within a hair's breadth of the invention but, like the horse that had nearly learned to live without eating, the poor fellow died just at the very time he found it out. Among other experiments made by this ill-fated genius there was one from which some instruction may be derived. He never shaved himself but on a clear dry day & then only on one side of his jaws at a time. The moment the hair was gone, the bare spot was carefully covered with a comfortable bit of flannel which remained for a few days till the other side underwent the operation, to which it was then removed. Great care was also taken always to sleep on the newly shaven cheek.

*September 29th.* Clear & pleasant. Met the Watering Committee as usual. Money is wanted. We have laboured under many difficulties in the prosecution of this important undertaking, arising principally from the want of funds. Three loads of machinery arrived today, others may be shortly expected. The large cylinder which has now been boring near five months is not yet quite finished. It was cast hollow and about 3/4 inch all around is all that was to be cut away at first. C. B. Brown spent the evening with us.

*September 30th.* Six or seven cases of the yellow fever are said to exist in Loxley's court near Spruce Street.

*October 1st.* My friend Zachariah Poulson has, by purchase of David C. Claypoole, become Editor of the *American Daily Advertizer* & this day his first paper has been issued. This gazette was the first daily newspaper published on the continent. It has passed thro' several hands & whilst I cannot but cordially wish success to its present proprietor, I have reason to believe it never was conducted by a more honest editor. My friend has assumed a very important duty. Newspapers are now so generally read & so extensively circulated that they have become very powerful political engines. They give a currency to opinions promotive of virtue, social order & moral harmony, or disseminating principles subversive to religion, morality & rational liberty. The worst doctrines are daily propagated by base & profligate wretches, with as much boldness as tho' they were sacred truths; & an ignorant multitude swallows them with all the greediness of starvation. So prevalent is the practice that, in spite of the barriers opposed by reason, justice & humanity, vice seems to flow like a mighty torrent down the streets, threatening the speedy introduction of anarchy, riot & confusion & the desolation of the choicest blessings of socity.

In conversing with the Mayor on the 29th last, he remarked of a citizen that he was "the most violent Jacobin" he ever knew, & kept his mind in a perpetual ferment, that he could not speak with another whose politics were dissimilar without flying into a passion, & he really believed the man would kill himself by the vehemence of his temper.

At this time, the person spoken of was walking about, tho' his health was impaired, as the Mayor believed, by his splenetic habits; today he is a corpse—a melancholy instance of the pernicious fruits of party malice & the ill effects of habitual ill nature. With pity that men having one common interest & being members of the same community should indulge antipathies & animosities so unreasonable, brutal, & mischievous. I differ from my neighbour on some speculative point; I think him decidedly wrong—but surely this is not enough to justify me in treating him with a ferociousness befitting a tyger or hyena. He is my fellow man, & as such worthy of my regard. Our education & habits of life, the disparity of our minds & sources of information prevent us from thinking alike. Perhaps I am wrong; or, if right, it may be owing to my poverty of intellect that I cannot convince him. I may be unable to reason with judgement or to exhibit truth naked & unfettered to his understanding. Notwithstanding this, we may both be good citizens, husbands & fathers, & exercising Christian charity towards each other, this very collision of opinion, if conducted with temper & moderation, may tend to the discovery of truth & the promotion of the general welfare.

*October 2d.* Is not the lust of power one of the most predominant passions in the human mind? If not, whence comes it to pass that we perceive such an everlasting struggle for dominion? "Better to rule in hell than to serve in heaven" was the consolatory ejaculation that Milton put into the mouth of his fallen angel. The motto is legibly inscribed in the Church, the Senate, the Town meeting, grog shop, market place & secret assembly. In town & in country, the rank offspring everywhere abounds & so pollutes the earth with its abominable stench that a man of common sensibility is disgusted at every step & compelled to hang his head, ashamed that he is a man.

I have heard so much talk about the approaching election among those who are candidates for office that I am faint & sick & mortified with the perpetual din. I pray God I may never be so much of a time server as to lie & fawn & cringe to obtain any post, however exalted. No, not tho' it were ruler of the first empire in the universe. Yet I have witnessed more than all this degradation in men from whom I expected better things. And for what? To procure a seat in a legislative body whose powers extend little further than to the cleansing of the streets, directing the sale of manure & the ordering of necessaries.

*October 3d.* The Board of Health have formally contradicted the rumour respecting the existence of the yellow fever in this City.

It appears from accounts from several of the southern states, that the inhabitants have removed from some of the frontier counties, apprehending a revolt of the negroes. It is to be hoped that means will be used to prevent a general rise of that unhappy people. I shudder at the idea of their gaining their liberty by force of arms. A day of retribution will come, I have no doubt, unless their masters can be persuaded to adopt suitable measures for ameliorating their condition & for their final emancipation.

*October 4th.* Gabriel, not the angel Gabriel, but Gabriel the ring leader of the conspiracy at Richmond, has been apprehended at Norfolk. It seems that the conspiracy had established an order of masonry that met at his house & concerted their plans. All were not entrusted with the whole secret. The novitiate knew nothing of the private debates of his superiors. Here then was a society of Illuminati. Shall not a slave practice what his master has taught him?

Wrote something for Poulson under the signature of Machine, which may excite a laugh if it does nothing more.

For several days the weather has been clear & ice was discovered this morning.

*October 5th.* Cool & overcast in the morning, followed by a violent storm of rain & wind from the NE. It is to be feared that much damage may be done to the shipping off the coast.

*October 6th.* I know of no stronger incitement to virtue than the hope of a future reward & the belief that life will not terminate with the present existence. It is the cordial balm that heals the wounds inflicted by disappointment & emboldens us to surmount difficulties which otherwise we should sink under. Indeed, I doubt whether virtue in its pure state is not wholly incompatible with a contrary doctrine. For if we reject the idea of a future state of being, each person must of course have no other standard of right & wrong than his own inclinations. Whatever interferes with his pleasures or gratifications must to him be evil. Whatever promotes these must be his chief good. He would live for himself merely & having no dread of after retribution, would have nothing to restrain him from the commission of any crime which he could perpetrate in secret & without the fear of detection. For it is this conviction, that all our actions however hidden from the scruntiny or observation of men, are nevertheless witnessed by an avenging & just God that stays the uplifted hand from being imbued in the blood of obscure innocence & checks the wild career of midnight murder. When men have no sufficient motive to restrain their sensual appetites, they naturally slide into licentious & ignoble habits, destructive of virtue & the sweet enjoyments of domestic tranquility. It is farcical to hear some of our modern philosophers talk of universal benevolence, when it is so evident that their domestic habits are so repugnant to the practice of virtue. It is vain that I attempt to mend the morals & promote the happiness of a community while I neglect my own family. The better plan of reformation is to begin at home & if each one will take care of himself & those who are immediately dependent on him, the whole will

of course be provided for. I do not mean to say our views of doing good should not go beyond our own threshold; far from it. But, on whom can it be so incumbent to take care of myself & family, as on myself? On no one.

My two little boys, Henry & Francis, have returned from the country. Surrounded by my little flock with their excellent mother at my side, my fire seems to burn more cheerfully; while the lisping accents of the one, the innocent prattling of another & the boisterous eloquence of a third, all anxious to be heard & intent on their own separate amusements, display a scene, sometimes noisy it is true, but of which even a Diogenes might be proud.

*October 7th.* Brother Jasper & some others on their way from Bethlehem yesterday were overset & considerably bruised. One young woman especially, whom they were obliged to leave at the house of a friend on the roadside. No bones broken or mortal injury received.

Joined by my son Henry in my morning's ramble to Schuylkill. It is gratifying to view the budding of the intellect & to lend a protecting hand to the tender shoot.

Morning air cool & bracing; evening in the language of a merchant, ditto.

*October 8th.* Much exercise has produced some weariness, even before noon. So various are our habits & avocations that what is hard labour to one man is recreation to another. Our capacity for usefulness in many respects depends so much on the proper exercise of the body. It is on the quantity & variety of its occupations that some men from this circumstance alone acquire a value & importance over others in the scale of being—almost incredible. Our hands are as susceptible of improvement as are the powers of the mind & it may be a question whether we are not as censurable for neglecting the one as the other.

A woman has this day been in my house who attained the age of 60 without having ever even pulled on her own shoes & stockings, or handled a needle. Yet her limbs are perfect & she appears to have been born with a good constitution, tho' unfortunately, perhaps, to a great estate which she now possesses. If she walks a few squares her legs swell & an attempt to perform the smallest household duty with her hands places her wrists in the like condition. She must constantly have a maid to attend her person, to dress & undress her, &c. She converses rationally & betrays no symptoms of a weak mind. Her health is also as good as that of most others at her age. Instances of this kind do not often occur in Pennsyla., but in the Southern states & in the W. I. they are not uncommon. What a contrast does this person form with an Irish kinsman of mine, of whom I have often heard some of my connections speak. He travelled over most of the countries of Europe on foot & even visited this continent, but how far his pedestrian excursions extended in America I don't recollect to have heard. When he arrived at a town or village penniless, which was not unfrequently the case, he endeavoured to ascertain the kind of handicraft most profitable in the place, and whatever that happened to be—silver smith, watchmaker, shoemaker, carpenter, mason &c. being alike his profession—he forthwith entered some shop in the capacity of a journeyman & worked until he grew weary of the place or procured sufficient to enable him to prosecute his journey. This man was alive not many years ago & is probably still living, as he possessed a remarkably hale constitution & strong frame of body.

Attended at the Water office between 4 & 5 P.M. & remained there til 9 in company with two others of the Com. examining acc'ts, &c. The moon being a little too late in her appearance to light us on our way, my blinky eyes & broken shin were found to be some inconvenience on my return.

*October 9th.* A warmer sun than we have been accustomed to for some days indicates the approach of the Indian summer.

By the official publication of the deaths at N. York, it appears that from 6 to 9 persons die weekly of the yellow fever, as many more of the bilious fever & others of doubtful cases. Total weekly deaths from 50 to 70, yet business seems to go on as usual.

*October 10th.* This day has been principally occupied in bringing to a close the examination of the Books, accounts & vouchers of expenditures, relating to the introduction of water into the City & in preparing a report of the result for the Committee & another for the Councils. The total am't expended is $148,806.57 & there is due for materials &c. an additional sum of $8,897.54. It is therefore probable that the disbursements will so far exceed the estimate that $200,000 will be requisite to complete this great undertaking. Latrobe's estimate was $127,000, but the Councils allowed him $150,000.

Somewhat discomposed with headache, occasioned probably by poring over papers, &c.

*October 11th.* A broker of N. York named Nathaniel Olcott has

contrived to swindle that Bank & certain individuals out of a large sum of money, supposed to be about $200,000. In order to impress a belief of his death, he sent a person to throw his suit of clothes on the margin of the river, while he himself eloped with his large booty. The trick was clumsily managed & as numbers are now in pursuit of him it is to be hoped that the villain will be defeated. The first teller of the Bank, who appears to have aided in the fraud, shot himself as soon as he heard of Olcott's elopement. This fellow did not lay his scheme so dexterously as did a Londoner, some years ago. Having got into his hands a large sum of money, he procured the dead body of a man of his own stature. This he conveyed into his chamber & having dressed it in the suit which he himself usually wore, he applied a brace of loaded pistols to the head of the corpse & discharged their contents in such a manner as entirely destroyed the countenance. The report occasioned a bustle in the family & neighbourhood, in the midst of which he effected his escape. Many years after he divulged the secret to a woman with whom he lived in Paris, who betrayed him. When apprehended, he denied the charge & professed perfect ignorance of the affair. He represented that however much he might have resembled the deceased it was cruel on that score to treat him as a culprit. He even brought his own relations into court to prove the circumstances of the suicide & funeral of the person they supposed him to be. His creditors could not establish the identity of the man & the court was considerably puzzled, until the woman was called on, whose testimony was so clear & positive that he was convicted.

Met the Watering Committee at 3 P.M. adjourned between 5 & 6 & at 7 met the Council. This is the last time the present Council will meet, as the election is to be held on the 14th.

*October 12th.* It was pleasant to hear the voice of Thomas Scattergood at this morning's meeting—after his long absence of near 7 years. What a striking difference there is between the humble, practical Christian & the selfimportant speculative sceptic.

*October 13th.* Rain with SW wind. For the last time, perhaps, met the Watering Committee. We had a doleful sitting. For weeks, aye for months past, we were amused with tales of the finishing of the large cylinder. Lately it has been frequently reported to be on its way hither. We have been looking out for it daily with all the eagerness that we feel when our last hope is at stake. Now there is reason to believe either that it never will arrive, or if it does, that it will not answer the purpose. This intelligence has almost palsied my patriotism. A plan was suggested for remedying this grievous disaster, which I could more rely on had not repeated disappointments impaired my confidence. The most vexatious deceptions have been practiced on the Committee, until I am wearied, chagrined, tormented, perplexed & soured almost into a misanthropist. At any rate I do most cordially detest & hate the whole tribe of sycophants, hypocrites & courtiers. Another cylinder is at last to be cast & bored here. So much is the public mind agitated on the subject of the water works that, altho' it has many friends, it would be dangerous to let this secret out. If this attempt should fail, some of us may as well pack up our alls and begone. Everything depends on the success of the proposed casting. Ah, me!

Plagues seldom come alone, say some folks—tho' here comes a waggon from (N. Carolina) between 5 & 6 hundred miles, to be loaded tomorrow, the day fixed on for brother Jasper's wedding. Well, driver, thou mayest tarry a little & rest thy weary bones for may I be whipt if after this affair of the cylinder, I feel in any humour to wait on thee in preference to going to a wedding.

This has been a day of gloom in several respects. The rain falls heavily & tomorrow it may be clear. In this world everything seems to be in motion, changes are ever occurring. Nothing is stable. We run an ever varying race. One day we pursue with fervour, what the next day we abandon as folly. One hour we bask in the sun & are all mirth & glee, the next we sit in darkness & despair & cover ourselves over with sackcloth & ashes. It is surely best amidst these vicissitudes to preserve a sound heart & steadfast eye towards the only certain source of consolation; a draught from that fountain can inspire health, hope & confidence.

*October 14th.* Brother Jasper married Rebecca Shoemaker. Mother & sister Hannah from Lancaster present.

The general election for the State was held today; altho' warmly contested, I have heard of no riotous acts in the City. A party of noisy boys marched thro' the streets after night with each a taper or candle in his hand, with drum beating & colours flying huzzaing for Israel Israel, the antifederal candidate for the Sheriff's office. Another company from the N. Liberties paraded a boat on fire about the City. They were of the same party; neither being opposed, no disturbances ensued. These exhibitions are usual on election nights.

*October 15th.* From the returns of the election it appears that the antifederal ticket has carried in the County of Philada. by a very large

majority. In the City, Wm. Jones, their candidate for Congress, is elected in opposition to Francis Gurney by a majority of 14. The total number of votes taken in the City is about 3,300 & so nearly are the parties divided, that the Federal tickets for the State Legislature & for numbers of the Select & Common Councils have on an average, but about 25 of a majority. Indeed, their opponents have trodden so close on their heels, that one of their candidates for the State Legislature & one for the Common Council have been elected in the struggle. Last year the Federalists had a majority in the City of about two for one. So fleeting is the public mind. It will probably always be thus in popular governments. The loaves & fishes are generally the object of contention in spite of the tales of patriotism & liberty of which we hear so great an outcry. "Ride & tie, you ride awhile, then I." If men were influenced by a sincere desire to promote the public good in their opposition to the present administration of the government, I should augur some advantage from a change, but I am afraid that noble virtue is not their stimulus to action.

*October 16th.* It is said that Olcott the swindler has been apprehended with about 3,000 dollars about him. Accounts from N. York state it as certain that his depredations amounted to between two & three hundred thousands.

Received an official notification from the judges of the election of my reelection to the office of a Common Councilman. I have already served three years on that capacity & the only inducement to my sacrificing another to the service arises from the conviction of its being the duty of those who began the great work of Watering the City of labour to accomplish the object; but if I were governed by mere personal considerations I should shrink from the task, as it is extremely unpleasant to encounter the abuse of the illiberal, the rancour of the malevolent & the perverse opposition of the ignorant. Some good men disapprove of the undertaking, others doubt, but many more oppose from interested & selfish motives. Perhaps the scheme is not the best that could have been adopted but it was thought so at the outset & I am not sure that a better could have been put in execution. It was not hastily agreed on; many others were proposed, but this under all circumstances was deemed the most eligible. Everybody seemed eager to have water brought from some extraneous source. The Councils were bored by petitions from all quarters of the City & the members were perpetually dinned with the cry of "Water, water; no matter as to expense, the citizens will support you, you are looked to as the fathers & guardians of the lives & property of your fellow citizens; the reputation & salvation of the City is at stake; you are therefore called on by the strongest ties of duty to gratify the wishes of your constituents." This language was resounded from all quarters. While the Com. appointed by Councils was engaged in examining plans & deliberating on the means of execution, the people were clamorous for a decision. How oft have I been told, "while you are considering what mode of introducing water is the most economical & productive of the City interest you will suffer the City itself to go to ruin." The petitions on this subject were signed by almost every man of property or respectability in the place. A plan was at length formally announced, preparations were made for carrying it into effect. No dissatisfaction was expressed except by the canal company, with whose interests it interfered. Contracts were formed, considerable progress in the works was made & everybody seemed pleased. But money was wanting. The Councils laid on a Tax & people began to discover that the plan was a bad one. Most of the opposition came from those very men who petitioned. Their pockets were touched & their patriotism took a different turn. They could not deny but they urged Councils to the measure. But one said, when he signed, he expected the canal water would be sought after, another supposed the water of Spring Mills would have been brought in, another meant to promote the introduction of the Wissahickon. Some wanted Frankford Creek, others Darby Creek brought across Schuylkill, or a number of springs, 6 or 7 miles on the west of that river to have been purchased, their waters united & conducted into Town. All perceived clearly that Councils mistook their meaning & therefore determined not to contribute to defray the expense of obtaining a thing they did not want. Compulsory means were resorted to & thenceforth the Councils were robbers, spendthrifts, tyrants, fools, madmen, pickpockets & public nuisances. The enforcing the payment of this tax is, in the eyes of the delinquents, a heinous crime in the Corporation, not to be forgiven. The whole blame is heaped on the Committee, or rather on a few of its most active members. Such meanness, selfishness & ingratitude spring from ignorance & avarice.

*October 17th.* Went to the Circuit Court of the United States at 10 A.M. & received a discharge from service as a grand juryman. That jury had little to occupy its attention. All for the better. At 11 attended the first meeting of the new council. The Mayor was present & qualified the

members. Received an appointment to my old station in the Com. for superintending the introduction of water into the City.

*October 18th.* The execution of the blacks concerned in the conspiracy at Richmond continues. Twelve, amongst whom is their General Gabriel, are to be hung in a few days.

Summoned as a juror to 2 district Courts now sitting. I was sent for by the Judges, but as no convenient mode of compelling my attendance in both places at once was adjudicated, it turned out that I turned in to neither.

Went to Schuylkill at 4 in the afternoon to witness the ceremony of laying the first stone of the Bridge proposed to be thrown over that River at the west end of High Street. The Mayor & several of the members of the councils & the president & directors of the incorporated company, who have the work in hand, attended. A cold collation was provided, of which about 70 persons partook in the old brick ferry house that now stands in the center of the street. About 2 hundred of the workmen & others had a table spread in the open air, over which they made very merry. It was lucky for them that the rain ceased a little before they sat down. It having poured very violently most of the day. More or less has fallen every day since the 14th. It was in the midst of such another storm that I, as the official agent of the City Corporation, went to this same spot last spring to make a formal delivery of the site, &c. to Judge Peters & others of the company.

Jn. Lewis, the stone mason, conducted me down into the pit, where the stone was prepared & waiting for the ceremony, to observe an inscription which he had cut on it. I had not sufficient sagacity to discover its import & was obliged to ask him to explain. The inscription is T.F.C.S.O.T.S.P.B.W.L. Oct XVIII-MDCCC. This stone, should it ever witness a resurrection from its present tomb, will doubtless afford rich food for the learned antiquaries of after times. Many a shrewd debate & wise hypothesis will ensue. T. being the initial of the word Tammany, will signify that saint; F. stands for feast all the world over; C. everyone will know to mean Council; S. will do in this place for Savages; O. cannot be interpreted into anything but Oneas, that is Wm. Penn; T. of course must be Tribes; S. it will be quite natural to suppose was intended for the river Schuylkill; P. will be Philada.; B. all will acknowledge to be the first letter used in spelling Bridge; & then it follows that there must be water, W. will therefore be water; & where great folks are, there will be Lords, L. must consequently be intended for

Lords. The interpretation of all this will be extremely simple & stand thus:

*Tammany,* the Columbian St., in his wisdom caused a great
*Feast* to be held one rainy day in the old of the moom & a
*Council* to be convened of divers white men and
*Savages* to which Feast & Council he invited his brother
*Oneas,* who loved mush & molasses & was withal prince of most of the
*Tribes* dwelling on the banks of the goodly stream, called
*Schuylkill,* whose waters flowed on the western side of
*Philadelphia* & then & there Tammany did erect this
*Bridge* with his own hands & place it across the
*Waters,* amidst the shouts & yells & whoops of the great
*Lords* of the province.

Few, of even the most sagacious of the brotherhood will imagine the true meaning of the inscriber, which is nothing more nor less than This First Corner Stone Of Schuylkill Permanent Bridge Was Laid Oct. 18th 1800.

*October 19th.* The great body of rain which has fallen for a few days past has caused a considerable fresh in the Delaware. Some of the wharves are overflowed today & the floating bridges on Schuylkill carried away. About noon the wind shifted from NE to NW & blew so violently as to tear up trees by the roots in several parts of the City. Some walls of unfinished buildings were also tumbled down, particularly of a large 3 story house in Chestnut Street, just prepared for roofing.

*October 20th.* A report that the basin at Schuylkill had been carried away by the fresh of last night occasioned me to go post-haste to the spot & I had the pleasure to find that no damage had been done.

I observed to Lewis the Mason that his inscription might be understood by himself & those to whom he explained it, but that when we were in our graves others might be at a loss to comprehend its meaning. "True" said he, "it may be so, but I expect that by the time this stone will be dug up again people will be more learned than you & I." This argument did not probably occur to the Superintendent of the road made thro' a part of Spain when governed by the Romans. The story, as I have heard it, is that a short time before the revolutionary war in France, a stone was found in Spain, bearing evident marks of antiquity, on which an inscription had been placed that time had rendered almost illegible. Four letters only were extant; these were V.I.A.R. The learned doctors were consulted on this singular discovery & all pronounced it to

be the precious monument of some martyr to the good faith. The pope was applied to & Viar was forthwith canonized. Not long after the usual ceremonies were performed to the Saint & pompous honours offered to his pious memory, a rude & incredulous fellow discovered a secret that at once put an end to further trouble on account of St. Viar. He made known that this stone was found on an old Roman road, that it was the custom in those days not only to have milestones on which distances were inscribed, but that it was usual to place the name of the prefect or superintendent also on the same stones. A nicer scrutiny than had been made by others enabled him to trace the words "Prefectus viarum"; tho' the name was lost, enough was left to prove the meaning of the inscription, "Prefect of the roads." Thus rose & fell St. Viar.

*October 21st.* This being the day fixed on by law for the election of a mayor, the two Councils assembled in the chamber of the Common Council at 11 A.M. The members present unanimously reelected Robt. Wharton, Esquire, who being informed thereof declined to serve. John Inskeep, Esquire, was then elected Mayor for the ensuing year by a unanimous vote; & Abijah Dawes, Andw. Bayard, Thos. P. Cope & James Milnor appointed a Committee to present him to the Governor to be qualified agreeably to law. On this occasion the members voted viva voce, that being the mode prescribed by the act of incorporation.

Clear & warm yesterday & today.

In April, May, June & July last there were imported into the island of Jamaica 6794 African slaves. Surely this infamous trade must have an end.

*October 22d.* The Board of Health passed a resolve restoring the intercourse with Baltimore & Norfolk.

*October 23d.* Preparations having been made yesterday, the Committee accompanied by the Mayor Elect left the City at 11 this morning for Lancaster, where Thomas McKean, Esquire, the present Governor, resides, at least during the sessions of the Legislature.

*October 24th.* Soon after alighting at Lancaster we wrote a polite note to the Governor announcing our arrival and requesting to be informed at what hour it would be convenient to receive us. To this he returned a prompt answer appointing the hour of 5 in the afternoon at the house of Timothy Matlack.

We had an hour & a half to dine & prepare for the interview—& at the appointed time, presented ourselves before him. We were ushered into a small apartment, up one pair of stairs, in which we found his Excellency attended by A. J. Dallas—the Secretary of State, a young man whom we afterwards understood to be the private Secy. of the Governor & Timothy Matlack, clerk of the Senate.

From the well known austerity & vindictive temper of the man & from the circumstances of our being opposed to him in political principles, we had calculated on a cold, if not a rude, reception. In this respect we were agreeably disappointed, for he received us with a smile, rose & took each of us by the hand & hoping we were well, invited us to take seats. Some commonplace conversations ensued for a few minutes, when he observed that "as we had come on business, he would attend to that first." He then administered the following oaths to the Mayor, who subscribed them in a Book of records: "You do swear that you will bear true allegiance to the Constitution & laws of the State of Pennsylvania, so help you God"; "You do swear that you will bear true allegiance to the Constitution & laws of the United States, so help you God"; "You do swear that you will well & faithfully execute the office of Mayor of the City of Philadelphia." During this ceremony, all present stood up. He then wished the Mayor "health, happiness & satisfaction" in discharging the duties of his office, after which we resumed our seats.

Addressing himself to Abijah Dawes, he said, "Wilmington"—where they formerly knew each other—"is now a considerable Town. I wonder that the ambition of the inhabitants has not induced them to call it a City." Abijah answered that "the old respectable inhabitants were dead & that the present race were Democrats."

Govr.: "Democrats, Mr. Dawes—we should all be Democrats. The Federal government is Democratic & the late elections in this State shew that a great change has taken place in the public mind in favour of Democracy."

Alexr. J. Dallas: "I really believe, Mr. Dawes, that you would have died of the gout"—Abijah is subject to that disorder—"had not the Federal ticket succeeded, or had you lost your election in the City."

A. D.: "I hope I may die before the Democrats rule."

Govr.: "Well, but you see that in the counties of Somerset, Allegheny &c. where last year the Federalists had a majority, there is this year a large majority against them."

"Yes," said Abijah, "I allow you to rule about 3 years & then, I think it will be over."

"But Mr. Dawes, you yet may become a Democrat," said Dallas.

"No," rejoined Abijah, "I don't like them. I like an energetic government."

"And, when I gave some examples of energy," exclaimed the Governor, "Your party were displeased." (This was most probably said in allusion to the recent circumstance of his displacing from office every Federalist in his power, without regard to merit or the sufferings which he thus occasioned to their families. Many of them were old men who had no other support for themselves, wives & children than the profits of their offices & were otherwise incapable of labour)—No direct or verbal notice was taken of this remark.

A. D.: "After your election we were disposed to forgive & forget, but your answer to the address from the N. Liberties spoiled all."

Govr. (his countenance much flustered): "You mean, I suppose, the observations made on the old Tories, aristocrats &c., but surely no part of that answer applies to you, Mr. Dawes." (In that publication the Governor, departing from the dignity of his station, treated his opponents in an illiberal, indecent & unjust manner, bestowing on them the epithets of "old Tories, aristocrats, refugees, British agents, expectants of office, and apostate Whigs &c."). "I knew your father, " continued he, "and he was a good Democrat."

"Yes," said Abijah, "my father used to think well of you & old Franklin, but none of his sons did, we never liked you."

It was fortunate that Dallas laughed heartily at what passed. It enabled us to give the same turn to it & the Governor seemed to be compelled to join in with us. An air of jocularity was, of course, given to the conversation & the whole was conducted in apparent good humour—but as we were not unacquainted with the irascible & domineering disposition of his Excellency, some of us judged it most advisable to put an end to the discussion & accordingly withdrew to our lodgings.

*October 27th.* Met the new Committee for introducing water. They had a meeting while I was at Lancaster & agreed to make an advance to Roosevelt, the Contractor for the Engines, which I regret. Latrobe is his surety for this advance & has pledged the remaining sum of his commissions, about $1300, to meet $2000, the am't agreed to be advanced to Roosevelt. The latter is now nearly paid off & the Engines are not erected. Latrobe has also by these means obtained all his commission, $6,350 & much yet remains to do. A little reflection would I think have induced the Com. to have withheld, more especially, as there is too much reason to fear that independent of a variety of other considerations, the pecuniary situation of these men is very desperate. R. was by contract bound to leave $12,000 in the hands of the Corporation until the Engines were in operation & found to answer. L. is not entitled by contract to any part of his commissions until the completion of the works. It was unfortunate that none of the old Committee explained the business to the new members, but the advance has been agreed on & it is too late to retract.

*October 28th.* Every day furnishes us with instances of the versatility of human affairs & the folly of inordinate ambition. Few men in our day possessed more general respectability or greater property than Robert Morris of this City. In the Revolutionary War when the credit of Congress was insufficient to obtain the necessary supply of specie for the prosecution of hostilities, he obtained a loan on his individual responsibility, which sustained their sinking reputation & gave a new energy to their cause. Since I have lived in the City his wealth was esteemed to be so great that there seemed to be no moral probability of his ever being any other than one of the richest men in the union. His popularity was unbounded, except by those limits which envy & malevolence prescribe to the greatest of men. But lo, the reverse. This once great man, now pines in the gaol of this City, loaded with the curses of thousands whom his overgrasping & inconsiderate speculations have reduced to poverty & wretchedness. This day a small part of his former immense possessions is offered for sale by the United States Marshall for Pennsyla. district. It consists of about six hundred & fifty thousand acres of land scattered mostly in small tracts or farms throughout the state & includes the iron works, houses, mills & plantations at Morrisville on the Delaware opposite Trenton.

Jno. Nicholson, who but a few years ago could count his millions, now languishes in the same prison. These two were intimately concerned in most of the schemes of trade & aggrandizement which have ended in the ruin of both. It is difficult to come at the am't of their debts. We can only conjecture, but I should suppose they could not owe less than twenty millions of Dollars. Some of Nicholson's property is also advertized for sale. It is, however, like Morris's a mere trifle of what he lately owned & consists of about eighteen hundred thousand acres of land in this state, a large interest in the Asylum Company &c., all in Pennsla. These men own lands in most of the states in the union & in some of them millions of acres. They were either the chief promoters or most extensive holders in almost every plan of a public nature that was great in design or expensive in execution throughout the state &

elsewhere. Had they confined their views to narrower limits they would in all probability have been among the foremost of our citizens in wealth, state & consequence, especially Robert Morris, whose talents as a statesman & financier are universally acknowledged & seldom exceeded. Nicholson never possessed any great political consequence tho' as Comptroller General of the state his talents as a clerk, however unfaithful he might have been to his trust, entitled him to considerable merit. He could dispatch more business in a given time than 3 or 4 active accomptants. I have frequently heard that he can write with one hand & copy with the other at the same time. From my own knowledge of him I don't doubt it. He possesses no literary acquirements tho' he is shrewd, accurate, agreeable & intelligent in conversation.

The great cylinder has at length arrived from Soho.

*October 29th.* The Commissioners of Health in Baltimore invite the return of their absent citizens.

Went to examine the cylinder. Jas. Smallman, who is the principal in erecting the Engines, has put it in its place. I entered it with a candle by the help of a ladder. It is somewhat defective; there is a small crack at the lower end & several flaws on the inner surface, all of which S. thinks he can remedy. In one place it is 3/8 of an inch less in its interior circumference than elsewhere. This is a disadvantage, as the piston cannot be made to work as it should.

*October 30th.* The politicians are busy in calculating & anxiously waiting the issue of the election for President.

Attended Council. The cry of fire occasioned an abrupt adjournment. It proved to be a carpenter's shop in 5th near Callowhill Street. The blaze was great & lasted about 2 hours, when the shop & an adjoining wooden building were consumed. There should be no wooden buildings in a populous city.

*November 2d.* From the 21st August to the 25th October there died in Baltimore of the yellow fever 978 adults & 219 children; total 1197. The total of deaths of the same disease in Philada. from the 1st of August to the last day of October in each year stands thus: in 1793, 3920 persons; in 1797, 1268 persons; in 1798, 3573 persons; in 1799, 1073 persons. In 1793 I remained in the City & had a severe attack of that violent disorder. In 1797 I was a volunteer overseer of the poor during the fever. I was of course much exposed yet preserved my usual state of health. In 1798 I left the City tho' not before I had taken the infection & had a slight attack in the country. In 1799 I also removed about the middle of Sept.

*November 3d.* The education of my children I have ever felt to be an important duty. There is a period in which children cannot comprehend the reason of many things which it is proper for them to do. Until then all that can be expected is to establish good habits & among the first is the habit of obedience. This prepares the way for future improvement. A good husbandman ploughs up the ground & puts the soil in condition to receive the seed, before he sows, or he may expect either no crop at all, or a crop of weeds.

A petition is now on foot to pray the State Legislature to enact that the electors of a President & Vice President of the United States shall be chosen by a joint vote of the two houses. The decision of this point will probably decide that of the Presidency. Adams & Pinckney are the Federal candidates & should Pennsyla. vote unanimously for Jefferson, there is little doubt of his success. At present there are 55 Democrats & 23 Federalists in the lower house, & 11 Democrats & 13 Federalists in the Senate. Of course, a joint vote will give a large majority to Jefferson, or to his partizan electors, which is the same thing. In two days the Legislature are by special call of the Governor to assemble at Lancaster to determine this matter, that is, the choice of Electors.

A short visit from my esteemed friend Jesse Kersey. The conversation of this man is always fraught with useful & experimental knowledge of the best kind.

*November 4th.* A curious account is given in some of the late papers of a wild boy found in the woods of Aveyron in France. He is supposed to be about 12 years old, has uttered no articulate sound, not even to express his wants, is docile but shews no symptom of civilization altho' several months had elapsed since he was taken. He takes no notice of the loudest noise, but the sudden opening of a door will make him start & endeavour to escape & he appears to hear the cracking of walnuts; except in these instances he is indifferent to all sounds. It is not known but he is deaf.

Clear & mild. Brother Jasper & his wife left this morning for Baltimore.

Jesse Kersey spent a few hours with us this evening. Some doctrinal points were discussed & elucidated much to my satisfaction. If the Christian religion will not bear the test of criticism & reason, let it fall. It is a cunningly devised fable & should be exploded, but it will bear examination & no system can better accord with sound morality or be more promotive of peace, harmony and happiness. It is not, however, by blindly adopting this or that mode of faith that a man becomes a disciple of Christ. Every man is possessed of certain faculties of perception & powers of judging. Let him therefore make a proper use of these & enquire for himself. That which he can believe, let him practice; that which on serious scrutiny he cannot believe, he will do right to reject. Let him however be honest to himself & before he discards any proposition as untrue, bring it to the touch stone of light, strip it of its superficial covering, examine its constituent properties & pronounce fairly on the issue. The precepts of religion are few & simple, but men have contrived to envelope them in a cloud of absurd, preposterous & extraneous observances.

*November 5th.* The beauty, order & harmony of the creation have ever afforded a subject of high admiration to all who have had leisure for contemplation, or a taste for the sublime & magnificent works of nature, and when or wheresoever we extend our researches we discover new sources of wonder & delight. The various grades of intelligence in the link that unites sensitive beings to inanimate substances is so exquisitely arranged, in the scale of visible objects, as to excite just conceptions of reverence for that supreme wisdom which called the whole into existence. The sensitive plant, the polypus, the passion flower, have each their share of consequential regard, but nothing as yet discovered has perhaps a more just claim to our admiration than a production lately found by an Englishman of the name of Briggs, in a cavern near Macoa. This singular plant bears a resemblance to the passion flower. "It grows out of the rock without leaves & the instant any object approaches within the distance of a foot, it suddenly contracts its blossoms & drawing itself into a sort of hollow stalk, something like the skin of a worm, it shrinks totally into the rock, with so quick a motion that it is not easy to take them, especially as they grow under water, which is more than knee deep." This curiosity has been called the *animal flower* & is supposed to possess animation.

*November 6th.* News of a convention between France & the United States having been formed at Paris, of the recapture of Malta by the English, of a new armistice granted by France to the Emperor of Germany, of preparations making for the speedy assemblage of a Congress to fix the basis of a general peace in Europe, are furnished by an arrival from London in a shorsage.

A countryman agreed to pay an oysterman on Market Street wharf half a Dollar for as many raw oysters as he could eat. The oysterman, believing he should have the advantage, exposed his store with alacrity, but he saw his mistake, for after opening three hundred, which the countryman greedily swallowed, he would have returned the money to get clear, but the fellow insisted on having more & was only dissuaded from it by the intercession of some standersby, who compassionated the poor oysterman. I give the report.

*November 7th.* Many riots have again taken place in London & other towns of England on account of the scarcity of bread. These tumultuous assemblages of the populace give rise to a variety of painful emotions. The poor wretches are generally deluded & the means they use counteracts the end in view, yet it is a deplorable picture to behold thousands of ragged, half naked & desperate men, women & children with haggard countenances demanding bread of those who perhaps have it not to give and threatening ruin to all who oppose them. To the inhuman ravages of war must his scarcity in a great measure be ascribed. It is the policy of the contending powers to burn & destroy whatever provisions of their opponents they cannot carry off or appropriate to their own use & when in addition to this we consider that millions of men under arms are to be supported, we need not wonder that temporary dearths frequently happen.

*November 8th.* It is a singular fact that thirty six days after the signing of the convention at Paris, between France & the United States, it was announced at Lancaster in this state. The intelligence came by the way of London & passed thro' this City.

Some difficulty having arisen for want of funds to pay the workmen employed by the Watering Committee, I mounted my horse, rode out to the buildings, and occasioned some pleasant countenances by advancing the requisite sum on loan, for which I am hereafter to be reimbursed. Other members have on different occasions made similar advances or the works must sometimes have stopped. In addition to this, several of us became responsible in our individual capacity for forty thousand Dollars obtained of the Bank of the United States in anticipation of the tax assessed & levied to carry on the scheme. We have also given up much of our time & attention to the business without pecuniary compensation, yet we are frequently abused as tho' we were public robbers & one writer has gone so far as to assert that we ought to be compelled to pay the whole expense out of our private estates. Such a thing is public gratitude for services rendered & such the justice that influences the human mind. But all are not such or our condition would be hard indeed. Yet after all, he who seeks the public favour from another motive than honestly to discharge his duty, in the promotion of the public good, will be & deserves to be, egregiously disappointed.

Dined with the Mayor, a select party of his friends were present, among the rest our late active & faithful Mayor R. Wharton. I am either intimately or well acquainted with every person who attended, but I have so bad a relish for formal entertainments that I cannot enjoy company as well in this way as on less set occasions. There is something of a primness & ceremony to be observed that damps the ardour of free enquiry & confidential confab. We sat down at 4 & left the table a little after 6.

*November 11th.* The plague is said to have lately prevailed in Cadiz & occasioned considerable mortality.

A fire has consumed most of the papers of the war office in the City of Washington, together with the building in which they were contained.

*November 12th.* In retiring from business I did not expect to be idle but my time hitherto has afforded but few sources of relaxation from what I before enjoyed. I hope it will not always be so. I contrive to walk to Schuylkill almost daily to examine the water works & frequently take time to make an excursion of a few miles on horseback.

Hazy all day, in the evening thunder & lightning & a smart shower.

*November 13th.* Attended Connelly's Auction & purchased Dobson's edition of the Encyclopedia &c. Amidst a great collection of garden seeds which were sold at the same time, I observed the barbary. It is a curious fact that in Pennsylvania that shrub is cultivated as a rarity while in the New England states laws have long existed to prevent its growth on account of its injurious properties in the propagation of wheat. Experience taught the farmer that when barbary grew in the neighbourhood of his wheat field & the wind blew from the former to the latter, the effluvia emitted by the barbary destroyed the wheat in the direction of the wind to a considerable distance. This is said to be more particularly the case at some seasons of the year than others.

*November 14th.* A neat & fashionably dressed young woman asked alms of me today. A pretty & modest countenance added to her other appearances drew more from one than I should probably have given to a beggar in rags. Was I right? It is reasonable to suppose that those who are miserably poor would not be clad in the vestments of opulence. True, but it is not those who look the poorest that most deserve our charity. Poverty in this country, that is extreme poverty, is generally occasioned by intemperate & idle habits. Yet it is sometimes otherwise & where neatness & elegancy is found in a poor person it seems with me to indicate more worth than is usual to bloated, filthy & tattered indigence. The public provision for the common poor is very abundant in Philada. & so good is the police at present that I do not recollect to have seen a common beggar in the streets for months.

Blustering & cool; some snow fell in the vicinity of the City.

*November 15th.* The situation of the funds rendered it necessary for me to advance an additional sum to pay the men employed in the Water Works. The advance of this day, added to that of the 8th, is near two thousand Dollars.

*November 16th.* Frequently visited by our friend C.B.B. of late. He purposes to reside in Philada. this winter. New subjects have occupied his pen & the public will probably soon be presented with some new ebullitions of his lively imagination, if this term lively be not improperly bestowed on an imagination fertile indeed, but generally devoted to the conception of gloomy representations. He would please one better if instead of employing himself in producing mere works of fancy he would apply the rare talents of which he is undoubtedly possessed to the promotion of science & the pursuit of useful & practical philosophy.

*November 17th.* The House of Representatives of this state passed a bill providing for the appointment of electors of a President & Vice President of the United States by a joint vote of the two branches of the Legislature. This the Senate has rejected & sent them down a substitute which ordains that the Senate shall appoint 7 & the House of Representatives 8 of the 15 electors to which Pennsylvania is entitled. The House rejected the Senate's substitute & committees of conference have been mutually chosen, but by the last accounts from Lancaster they have come to no agreement.

Visited by N. J. Roosevelt. He assures me that the steam engines will cost him forty thousand Dollars more than the price stipulated for in his contract with the City. If so, they will cost him seventy thousand Dollars. If, on a fair inspection of his accounts & vouchers, this should appear to be the case, I think the Corporation ought in justice to make him some allowance for this excess. I shall not, at a suitable season, hesitate to advocate the propriety of such a grant, for I think no individual ought to be ruined in a contract with an opulent City. But before he attempts an application, the engines must be put in operation & the citizens be satisfied of their utility. I don't doubt, indeed I am sure, that great want of economy has taken place on his part. Still, he ought not to suffer so severely if the cost be as stated.

*November 18th.* A short visit from my old friend Joseph Bringhurst, who has latterly resided in Wilmington. He is altered from what he once was & I hope for the better. Adversity may sometimes be considered as a blessing & since I first knew Joseph, he has passed some fiery ordeals. He seems at present to be happy in the possession of an intelligent, engaging wife, who is greatly attached to him. I walked with him to the water works, as he was desirous of seeing them. We conversed about some of our former friends with whom we had mutually exchanged offices of good will & spent many an agreeable & instructive hour, but who, years ago, sunk into untimely graves. I have lived but a short time & have seen great chasms in the circle of my intimates; Wilkins, Sayre, Price, Cooper, Smith; all men of worth whose minds were stored with the choicest fruits of learning, and whose hearts were the receptacles of the tenderest affections of humanity. How deeply do I deplore your early exit!! Scarcely had the liberal hand of nature decked you in all the pride of manhood, ere the chilling blast of death assailed you & ye fell beneath its withering influence, lamented, beloved & admired.

*November 19th.* The weather has for several days been warm for season & overcast. Yesterday it rained till noon, then cleared & a strong west wind prevailed. This morning there is ice in the streets.

The art of guiding the mental machine by an equal, steady & temperature principle is hard to acquire, at least I have found it so. Prone either by nature or habit to the indulgence of cheerfulness & to laugh when many would weep, my inconsiderate vivacity often gives umbrage to those whom I dearly love & am incapable of willfully injuring. Hence, I am sometimes compelled to lay the most severe restraint on myself in the society of those before whom I would unbosom my whole heart, lest an unguarded word should offend & when my soul would fain be playful, happy & gay, she finds herself enshrouded with the mantle of sadness, gloom & discontent.

Once I foolishly imagined that I could bear the ills of life in any shape or however vexatious with the fortitude worthy of a man, but there is no withstanding some things. I cannot bear to heap trouble on the head of any human being. When I perceive that I give pain where I meant to communicate pleasure, I regret that I have been mistaken & cannot prevent consequent dejection. I have no vices to charge myself with. Few men live a more regular & temperate life & as few have a better relish for the refined enjoyments of social existence. Strange, why am I then not at all times alike happy & why do I sometimes feel a pungency of heartfelt sickness in which I am ready to cry out, "I am the offspring of distress & every child of sorrow is my brother." Should these pages ever be examined by my friends, some of them will be puzzled to understand me. Others will easily comprehend my meaning & perhaps recollect the minute causes & effects of my occasional anxiety.

*November 23d.* A friend of mine who lately retired from business complains that time is heavy on his hands for want of employment. I am often surprized to hear similar sentiments from others. How can a man who has the least taste for knowledge, or the most moderate desire to do good, make this complaint? Were I to live to the age of Methuselah, I could employ every hour of my life. The field of knowledge is boundless, few of us have had more than a peep into it. Whole ages would not suffice to explore its regions & gather the rich fruits with which it abounds. Were I so lost to myself & society as to be possessed of no desire of improvement & to have no philanthropy or public spirit, rather than be idle, I would play pitch penny with my servant girl, and gallop the streets on a broomstick.

*November 24th.* The day has been thus employed. Rose at sunrise, took some recreation, read 2 morning papers & breakfasted after 8. Attended to some outdoor business, came home at 10; perused letters brought by the post, answered them & looked over & adjusted some accounts current. Waited on by Roosevelt, who is importunate to receive further aid from the corporation—I heard what he had to say on the subject & gave him my opinion with candour. I do not believe him entitled to a shilling when his accounts come to be settled. He suggests for the first time that his Engine for the Centre Square building is calculated of a power to raise the water 10 feet higher than the contract calls for. Latrobe has run the building that much higher & of course this difference of power will form a fair item of charge against the Corporation. I view all this as a mere scheme between him & Latrobe to get something more out of the public. At any rate, before the charge can be admitted, we must see that the Engine will raise the water. These men are in bad plight & are vastly indebted. At 12 a young man, who has owed me $700 for years, came to me in company with the Sheriff of Delaware county to request me to bail him in a suit brought against him for more than twice the am't of what he owes me. I know little of him & wish I knew less. Not deficient in brass to make this modest request. A denial was the consequence, yet he would not leave me till one. I dined & at 2 went to examine the works at Schuylkill &c. to judge of the propriety of stopping them on account of the weather. Wm. Young, also a member of Council with me, gave our directions & at 3 met a Com. appointed to examine Roosevelt's accounts at the water office. I continued there till five, returned home, ate a bowl of mush & milk & at 6 met with the Com. on Roosevelt's accounts. The Mayor incidentally was present. At half past 6 went to the Watering Committee & entered into a pretty lengthy discussion. I proposed some resolutions which were adopted. I came home at 9, read, wrote, ate supper & retired to bed between 10 & 11.

Each day brings with it its scenes of vocation. All are not alike throng, but from this sample of the nature & number of my employments, I suppose that to kill time I need not be driven to the expedient of mounting a broomstick.

*November 25th.* Several shocks of an earthquake were felt on the 20th in different parts of the Country. Particularly in the neighbourhood of Lancaster, where the inhabitants were considerably alarmed by the tremulous motion of the earth & the noise which is represented as having been similar to a rumbling clap of thunder. Some small articles of furniture were thrown down, but no material damage has been sustained. Perhaps no other of the long catalogue of calamities to which the inhabitants of this globe are subject occasions equal terror & dismay throughout animated nature with this awful & interesting phenomenon. I will defy even a stoic to read unmoved the account given of the dreadful earthquake at Calabria in 1638 as related by Father Kircher, who was a witness of that wonderful, melancholy & ruinous event.

*November 27th.* The love of independence is inherent in the human mind & the thraldom, mental & corporeal, in which women have been held for ages, is derogatory to justice & humanity. But before a woman indulges that practice of freedom so eloquently insisted on by Mary Wollstonecraft & by herself so proudly maintained, she should be certain that her charms will insure her the unalterable attachment of her husband, or she will find it a dangerous experiment. A woman in society must either be a mistress or a wife. A discreet woman will not long hesitate in making a choice, but she ought not to despise those winning & modest graces which are the peculiar ornament of her sex. She has a delicate part to act, fostering a becoming spirit of liberty & the right of thinking & judging for herself. She should nicely discriminate between capricious obstinacy & a proper respect for her own opinions. She should possess the art of convincing her companion & not of vauntingly despising his counsel & when she bursts asunder the shackles of implicit obedience to her husband, she should by a contented & studied line of conduct endeavour to make his home his chief delight & to hold his affections riveted to her person by an easy, cheerful, attentive & rational system of behaviour.

I had a daughter, peace to the memory of departed innocence. Had it pleased heaven to have spared the lovely babe, for the consolation of her father, I should have endeavoured to give her tender mind an early bias in favour of those principles of virtue, fortitude & self command, which would have given dignity to her character & which best entitle her sex to moral & political consideration; but I should have taught her the distinction between squeamish importance & true greatness of soul. Had she lived to have chosen the marriage state, I should have advised her, as she valued her own happiness & the peace & quietness of her family, never to have neglected the cultivation of those soothing & amiable qualities of the heart & that command of her temper which would have insured the affection, esteem & obedience of all its members. I should have told her that contentment does not so much depend on external circumstances, as on a well regulated mind, a judicious use of the good things in possession & a wise resolution to render our desires compatible with our means. Her household affairs should have been arranged with neatness, but without that disturbance & perpetual fretting about trifles which keeps the whole family in an uproar & saps the foundation of domestic comfort. Her husband should merit her purest & chief regard. If he were discontented she could not be happy & supposing him to be a reasonable man, she should strive to mould her inclinations by his taste. She should anticipate his wishes, administer to his best principles & even to his foibles, when not inconsistent with propriety. Had he been abroad, she should welcome his return not by a frigid & merely polite reception but by a warm & affectionate embrace. Had he suffered trouble, she should be the soother of his cares & sorrows. She should pour oil & wine into his wounds, and be the guardian angel of his repose. Thus, unless he were an ouran outang or something more savage, she should unalterably fix his love & her own happiness.

A man of feeling has his wishes thwarted by childish opposition. His home is rendered uncomfortable by the peevishness & cold manners of his spouse. Indifference ensues. His spirits are broken & if he does not seek to forget his chagrin by dissipation & unworthy indulgences abroad, melancholy follows & some fit of maniacal desperation finishes the tragedy; and all perhaps for want of a little common prudence in his wife.

*November 28th.* Eighteen years ago the British Army evacuated New York. That memorable epoch in the annals of the United States took place on the 25th of Nov. 1782.

The loss of sight is indeed a serious deprivation. It is however one with which I have been threatened. The use of glasses I find essential & have therefore good reason to set a high value on the invention. It is related of an Indian Chief who owned the territory of Rhode Island that he bartered that tract of land with a peddler for a pair of spectacles. The peddler displayed his little store to induce the chief to trade. The latter, who was an old man, was little inclined. His curiosity was at length attracted by the glasses. The European asked him to put them on. The Indian did so & was astonished & delighted with the effect. Negotiation commenced & the peddler affected unwillingness to part with so rich a treasure. The chief was determined to have them & finally made the offer of the Island & agreed to remove.

Last night an experiment was made on the Schuylkill steam engine. It operated well. The pump rod will shortly be fixed, when I hope to see water pumped into the tunnel.

*November 29th.* Whatever tends to lessen the evils of life is worthy of record. A friend of mind informs me that several persons have been cured of the gravel by using river water. Israel Bartram has lately had a mortification stopped by a poultice of charcoal, yeast, honey & flour. His leg from his ankle to his knee was black & emitted an offensive smell. The disease spread rapidly & his Physician advised an amputation. The poultice was applied & the part soon assumed a different appearance. The fetid smell left it immediately & in short a perfect cure was effected.

*November 30th.* Two thousand Dollars were remitted to Norfolk for the use of their poor, by the citizens of Philada. The Corporation of that place, with a disinterestedness rarely found, returned the money with an affecting address of thanks, in which they state their capacity to provide for their own wants. Wrote an essay for Poulson's *Advertizer,* in which I recommend the application of this money to the use of the Pennsyla. Hospital.

*December 1st.* Latrobe read a long report in pursuance of a resolution I submitted to the Watering Committee at their last meeting, respecting the adoption of regulations for the distribution of the water.

*December 2d.* The Committee for devising means for raising funds to carry on the water works met at my house this evening. I suggested a mode which was agreed to & is to be attempted at the next meeting of Councils.

The State Legislature have at length come to an appointment of electors; 7 by the Senate & 8 by the House of Representatives.

*December 3d.* My friend Poulson bores me for another essay. He says the first did much good. He brought with him a piece published in Bradford's paper of this morning containing some illiberal insinuations against the Hospital. It seemed to be right to combat this writer. I undertook it & P. went away well pleased with what I gave him.

In the evening the Com. for framing a bill for governing the distribution of the water assembled at my house. The business being novel, we made no other progress than to fix a few general principles. It was put on me to draft a bill to be submitted to them hereafter.

*December 4th.* Duty & inclination sometimes interfere. It was thus this evening I attended Council with reluctance. Had I remained at home I should have enjoyed the society of Timothy & Ruth at my fireside. The companionable qualities of this excellent woman are of no common kind. Possessed of an exuberant imagination, a cultivated taste, a correct judgment, she is brilliant in light conversation, pointed in serious debate, chaste in discrimination & pertinent in criticism. Fitted by nature with energies to shine in the first circles of the intellectual world, her domestic duties occupy her chief attention & are discharged with fidelity. Ardent & sincere in her attachments, her virtues, talents & accomplishments endear her to her friends. Such a woman, such a man as Timothy deserves. These are friends worth possessing.

*December 5th.* Intolerance of opinion in morals is not inferior to despotism in politics. A man is not content with the unrestrained indulgence of his own humour, however absurd, but must persecute his

neighbour for not conforming to the same standard. There are not only orthodox wigs, coats & hats, but even faces. History informs us that a long & sanguinary war was carried on by the Tartars against their neighbours, the Persians, because they perversely refused to cut their beards to the orthodox pattern.

*December 6th.* Yesterday Jno. Nicholson died in Prison. He has left a widow & 8 children miserably poor & destitute. Morris & he had for many years been at variance. One was Financier of the United States, the other of Pennsyla. A reconciliation was effected at a time when M. was in the zenith of his greatness. He had vast objects of speculation in view & knew N. had money. He therefore contrived to let him know that he would not be averse to acknowledge him as a friend. N.'s vanity was flattered by the proposal. He embraced the offer & came with his purse in aid of M.'s projects. I have been told that on one occasion N. advanced, in a single payment, three hundred thousand Dollars.

Nicholson's energy of character never forsook him. While in jail he published a daily paper under the title of *The Supporter or Daily Repast,* but not succeeding to his wishes the publication was declined for some months before his death.

At his request I paid him a visit in jail just before the paper was dropped. His countenance was cheerful, tho' it bore evident marks of inward grief. I could not avoid compassionating his condition. He thought I could befriend him by procuring him the adjustment of some complicated accounts, over which I had a partial control. I promised to do so & did not forget my word. Before I left him he said, "Mr. Cope, I remember your former accommodating & gentlemanly conduct towards me & am sorry I have it not in my power to make you a suitable return. The only thing I can do is to offer to publish any advertizements you may wish & you may give my old acc't credit for the am't." I thanked him for his good intentions & assured him that altho' in the immensity of his engagements he must have forgotten the circumstance, yet I was happy to inform him that he had long since discharged the debt. He expressed some pleasure & surprize at what I said & hoped I was not mistaken. I then reminded him of some facts which seemed to convince him.

Nicholson once owed me several thousand Dollars. I dunned him frequently, but always with temper & politeness. By these means I obtained a considerable portion of the debt when I found that many suits were instituted against him. I informed him that I should be obliged to follow the example. He made no objection, but, I thought, wished me to do so. We talked the matter over with pleasantry & parted in good humour. I procured a judgment against him & he paid me the balance—nearly three thousand Dollars. At this time he lived in his own house at the corner of Race & 7th Streets. If you wished to see him, you entered a small room adjoining the apartment in which he sat, attended by a single clerk. This antichamber was crowded from morning till night. One by one was admitted to his presence & each must wait his turn. Altho' most of his visitors were creditors & of course not likely to treat him very ceremoniously, he never suffered himself to get out of temper & went directly to the business they came on. In this way I saw him very often & never that I remember from his desk; he continued to write, which he did with amazing facility & correctness & conversed with me at the same time without confusion or perplexity.

*December 7th.* Some epicureans have lately discovered that the Susquehanna abounds with an animal of the testacious order, which from its taste & resemblance of the salt water tarapin they have called by the same name. A waggon charged with a thousand taken at Columbia (Wright's Ferry) arrived in Town last week. They are said to be more delicious than the common tarapin.

*December 9th.* Returns for President & Vice President are daily arriving from the different States. As yet there is no certainty as to the issue.

*December 10th.* A subscription has been set on foot for the relief of the widow & children of Jn. Nicholson. Three thousand Dollars were subscribed on the first day.

*December 14th.* This day completes a year since Washington died. He was the greatest man of his age, or perhaps of any other.

*December 15th.* This being the day assigned for putting the Schuylkill Engine in operation & being desirous of observing the first stroke, I rose an hour before day & got to Schuylkill before sunrise. At 8 the business commenced, but as all the parts were not sufficiently braced, little more was done than was necessary to exhibit the power of the machine. Some water was pumped into the tunnel & the experiment was satisfactory, for it is thus proved beyond a possibility of doubt that the Engine will perform its duty.

*December 16th.* All the votes for President & Vice President are not certainly known, but enough have been received to insure the success of

Thomas Jefferson to the Presidency. As soon as the information reached Philada. the public Stocks fell from 7 to 8 per ct.

*December 17th.* Barbarous punishments have been so generally exploded in the United States that it is with something like horror that I observe an account from Charleston of the execution of 2 negroes by being burned alive. This cruel exhibition might have given pleasure to a Mohawk, or a South Carolinian slave holder, but it is abhorrent to every principle of humanity & reflects but little credit on the State.

*December 20th.* An address of great violence from Govr. Jackson of the state of Georgia to the Legislature of that state, in their present sessions, has been published. It contains sentiments of high disrespect to the Federal Government & is evidently calculated to inflame their minds against it.

The federal government has had its constant & inveterate enemies to contend with from its first establishment. It is a government theoretically rational, founded on the best principles of civil & political liberty & the free choice of the people. Its administration has been consistent with its constitution; mild & virtuous, yet it has been as much vilified & complained of as tho' it had been in its origin a usurpation & in its practice a despotism. The party who have ever been opposed to it are evidently gaining the ascendency. It is not for me to predict the consequences. The subject is interesting to every reflective mind & is peculiarly so to an American & a friend to representative government. Some writers of no inferior merit have expressed their doubts whether a Republican government on an extensive scale can be long maintained. It certainly requires much temperate & dispassionate conduct both in the people & their representatives. There must be virtue in the State, or the commonwealth will not survive. When the laws are not duly respected, rottenness will seize upon the system and decay must ensue. Men cannot live without government & where there is not enough of prudence, moderation & disinterestedness to uphold the political fabric, it must be done by the iron hand of power. In a republic where every man has an equal voice in choosing his governors, all should be versed in the science of government & be acquainted with the best interests of the State, or very many improper votes will be given & improper selections made. In proportion as men are informed on these points, are they qualified to become citizens of a republic. But from the very nature of man in civilized society, it is next to impossible that he should be able, in a general way, to attend to the various pursuits of domestic economy, husbandry, manufactures &c. & yet have leisure to devote to the culture of political science. They in easy circumstances may, but they who have to toil daily for the daily sustenance of themselves & families cannot.

I believe I shall not be out of the way in supposing that the bulk, a considerable majority, are of this ignorant class. What is the consequence? Exactly what we see in the United States. Men approve or disapprove of the conduct of administration without understanding it & condemn laws & treaties without reading them. Thus under the reign, as it is usually termed, of Robespierre, in republican France, a person who with demoniacal fury was daily embruing his hands in the blood of the Federes—a party so called—on being asked the meaning of the term Federe, replied that "really he did not know, but somehow it sounded in his ears like a very great crime," & in America I have seen men equally disposed to punish Federalists, merely because they are Federalists, without knowing what Federalism means, tho' in their ears it doubtless sounds like a great crime. Men, thus ignorant & thus atrocious in their principles, being worked on by designing demagogues, are ever ready to perpetrate the most sanguinary crimes &—as factions will exist in popular governments & as licentiousness is apt to be mistaken for liberty—it is easy to perceive where a perpetual struggle for power, goaded by the cabalistical fury of the sovereign people, may land the republic.

Every citizen being politically eligible to office, the restless temper of man, the love of power inherent in the human breast & the dissatisfied spirit of ambition will naturally excite the efforts & rouse the energies of aspiring men to gain the summit by outrivaling all others in the chase for fame & dominion. Every faculty will be exerted, every nerve strung & every unworthy & diabolical passion called in aid of this primary object. Moderate & good men will be shuffled out of place. Modest worth will be either neglected, or hide its head from the fury of the storm. The lovers of peace will fly the contest; wisdom will be stifled, or retire in disgust; terror & dismay will at length pervade the greater part, who will be prepared by their sufferings & their thirst for repose to submit to anything—even the worst despotism: Some bold usurper, more successful than the rest, embracing the favourable moment, rises on the ruins of his country, proclaims a deadly truce & awes the multitude into obedience by the sceptre of victory, yet reeking with the blood of thousands & by the danger of chains which triumphant tyranny forges to manacle its hopeless victims.

*December 23d.* Went with some other members of the Corporation to the Centre Square to taste the first Schuylkill water brought in the tunnel.

*December 24th.* Brother Israel arrived from Baltimore.

*December 25th.* Had an interesting & affecting interview with the wife of J. C. Her husband came to this City last week & was immediately seized with the pleurisy. His symptoms are violent & his Physicians have this day given him up. When misfortunes assail us, the countenance & condolence of a friend is a balm to the soul. There are seasons of affliction which defy consolation, in which the mind, devoted to despair, loses its whole energy & sinks into impenetrable gloom. To be vehemently grasped by a lovely woman labouring under this load of misery, without the power of affording relief to her distracted soul, is a scene which I am not calculated to bear. It robbed me of the power of utterance & instead of saying what might have been proper on the occasion, I could but mingle my tears with hers. My fortitude abandoned me.

*December 27th.* The weather has been so remarkably temperate that there is still good pasture in the fields. Some people incline to think that there will be a fresh vegetation. The thermometer has latterly varied from 63 to 70.

Received a letter from N. J. Roosevelt expressing his desire that the Corporation would cancel their mortgage on his property at Soho. This I think they will not do.

*December 31st.* There is now in Philada. an old French nobleman of the name of Stuart, a descendant of the English kings of that name. In the early progress of the French Revolution he became an exile & with what he hastily collected, embarked with his two daughters for St. Domingo. There he purchased an estate & intended to spend the remainder of a life, already far advanced, but the troubles of that colony deprived him of this last hope. He made his escape after the burning of Port-au-prince by the negroes & the massacre of its inhabitants by that victorious & savage people, who had been goaded to madness by their former oppressions & who, under its immediate influence, were by the cruel & blind policy of the mother country let loose to satiate their fury on their former owners. The imagination can scarcely figure anything more horrible than the scenes which immediately ensued the proclamation of "liberty & equality" in the Island. The greatest enormities were committed, as might have been expected. Thousands of the planters made their retreat amidst the flames & the butchery of their nearest & most tender connections. Few were so fortunate as to save anything, but what they had on from the devouring desolation. As many as could get away fled to the United States. Many vessels crowded with these forlorn wretches arrived in our ports after enduring on their passage many & severe sufferings. Privateers frequently molested them & the poor pittance which had been snatched from the flames or the ruthless hands of triumphant ferociousness fell into the clutches of legalized robbers. Stuart & his daughters came penniless to our hospitable shores. Their property was confiscated & they have ever since been supported by charity. His sufferings have given a strong religious cast to his mind, bordering hard on superstition. After landing in America he made a solemn vow never to shave his beard until his property should be restored. He now appears in a long white beard & a few locks of hair of the same venerable color. His countenance is not unprepossessing & altho' misfortune has humbled his towering ambition, he has not forgotten his royal descent.

*December 31st.* C. B. B. has concluded to remain permanently in Philada. & talks of declining the publication of the *Monthly Magazine* at N. York. It has yielded him no profit.

# 1801

*January 1st.* The firing of muskets agreeably to vulgar usage & the cheering peal of the bells of Christ Church announced before dawn that another year had transpired. Now comes the paper carrier for his boon & the watchman for his New Year's gift. I love to make a cheerful heart. The awkward scrape of the leg, the smile of satisfaction & the thankee sir, thankee, are a rich regard for the trifle bestowed.

*January 5th.* By the returns of the votes for President & Vice President of the U.S. it appears that Thos. Jefferson & Aaron Burr have each 73, John Adams 65 & Chas. C. Pinckney 64. The total number of votes in all the states is 138.

*January 6th.* The multiplicity of my engagements in the public service, added to those which are occasioned by my ordinary pursuits, reduce me almost to the condition of a slave. I love employment, but too much confinement has already impaired my health. I stand in need of relaxation.

*January 11th.* It is fashionable in women to appear almost without clothing. Flannels are banished from the polite circles & it is quite vulgar to be seen with more than one skirt & that of some thin cotton fabric. This ridiculous practice has cost one of my neighbours, a young & beautiful woman, her life. A cold taken by indiscreet exposure terminated in the hives & sudden death. She possessed uncommon good health a few days before her decease & was gay & sprightly. Little complaining yesterday, today she is a corpse & left an infant at the breast. Poor Patty Dewees, may thy untimely death be a lesson of warning to others!

*January 14th.* It is singular that at the present moment considerable quantities of West India Molasses are exported from the U. States to G. Britain.

*January 27th.* The Centre Square Engine was put in motion at 12 today, in the presence of the Mayor & the members of the Councils. The first Schuylkill water is now afloat in the City, and the water runs freely.

*January 28th.* It is amusing to observe the crowd round the hydrant opposite to my door. Everyone must have a pull at the lever & even when the water flows, many seem as if they could not believe it.

Prepared several lengthy reports of Committee for the Councils & in the evening attended an extra meeting of the Watering Committee, convened to receive a report from the Engineer on the state of the works. Feel my spirits somewhat damped as the debts of the Com. am't to a sum of which I had no conception. The sum reported as necessary to a completion of the works is also vastly above my previous estimate. Latrobe is a cunning, witful, dissimulating fellow, possessing more ingenuity than honesty.

The office of the Secretary of the Treasury at Washington has been consumed by fire. This is the second public office which has been destroyed by the same element since the removal of the government to that place.

*January 30th.* There has been expended on the water works to the
26th in cash ................................. 166,445.85
The debts to the same period are .................. 20,715.29
And Latrobe's estimate, submitted on that day,
    for the completion of the works is ............. <u>24,299.36</u>
Making in the aggregate ......................... $211,460.50
    As this estimate provides for only $15,000 feet of pipe, in addition to what has already been laid, I have little doubt in my mind that the whole will ultimately cost $250,000.

*January 31st.* Another shock of an earthquake, said to have been more sensibly felt than the former was experienced at Lancaster on the 27th.

*February 2d.* This day the Ordinance regulating the sale of wood, hay, straw & lime, commences its operations. I prepared this ordinance 2 years ago & fought hard to get it thro' but owing partly to the intricacy of the subject & the novelty of the provisions & partly to other causes, the Select Council nonconcurred it several times. At last they agreed to pass it with alterations which, I have no doubt, on experiment will prove injurious, but they may easily be expunged & I hope the citizens will derive essential advantages from the ordinance.

*February 9th.* At 10 this morning I took the Stage for N. York, crossed the Delaware at Trenton about sunset. I had a cold disagreeable ride after night to Princeton, where a poor supper & bad lodgings, at Gifford's Tavern, but illy repaid the toils of the day. My bed was as hard as a matrass & was covered by an Indian blanket about 4 feet long & a thin bed spread of calico without lining. The season hitherto had been uncommonly moderate. Today the weather changed & the night was very cold. If I attempted to lie straight, either my feet were shoved out of bed, or my shoulders were uncovered. If I drew up my knees, the narrowness of my bed & coverings occasioned some part either "fore or aft" to become exposed to the nipping frost. Yet I slept some, but soon bounded to the welcome call of the driver, who about daylight announced by a rap at the door of my chamber that he was ready to proceed. For this bed I paid two shillings.

*February 11th.* It stormed all night & a considerable body of snow fell. After breakfast we set out & arrived at Paulus Hook at 11. As the wind was high & the snow continued to fall, the crossing of the Hudson was not very delightful, but we soon effected it, somewhat besprinkled by the waves, which ran high.

*February 12th.* Took a peep into the affairs of the late concern of C. W. & Co. I wish they appeared less extensive & more likely to insure more profit & a speedy issue. I fear trouble & delay.

*February 15th.* Dined with Mark, Roosevelt present. Says he & Latrobe have differed. These fellows are not easily seen thro'. They are always at points & yet are always as great as cronies. There is quite as much likelihood that they will hang together, as that they will kill one another.

The weather continues very cold. It scarcely thaws in situations exposed all day to the sun.

*February 16th.* Robert Bowne states the quantity of Pot & Pearl ashes inspected this year in N. York at 35,320 bbls. This at $25 a bbl. for the middle quality, which is the present price, gives $883,000. As pearl is more valuable & sells for more, he thinks it would not be wide of the truth to state the total value of the article this year at one million of Dollars.

*February 17th.* One of the convicts in the State Prison has discovered a method of tempering cut nails, so as to retain a sufficient degree of toughness to answer all the purposes of wrought nails. The inspectors have applied for a patent for the discovery, to secure the benefit to the State & promise the discoverer that when he shall be discharged, he shall be at liberty to dispose of it, securing the use to the state.

*February 18th.* Since I left N. York my feet have not been dry. My toes of course suffered by the cold tho' a change of apparel rendered me more comfortable.

In my ride of this day I was attended by 2 journeymen shoemakers & one journeyman currier. Both are young men in search of employment. From their conversation I inferred that they had little save what they had on, but they were as merry as birds & as happy. Such is man. They were seeking their fortunes & I don't know whether most people do not enjoy more solid content in the pursuit than in the absolute possession of wealth. At all events poverty & a cheerful heart are no strangers to each other.

*February 19th.* Entered the commercial stage at 5 P.M. Capt. Hays of Philada. & myself were the only passengers.

At night were overtaken at Brunswick by a French agent, his secretary, monkey, and parrot; this is travelling in stile. They are going post to Baltimore to embark for France, in the *Maryland Frigate,* now under sailing orders to carry the Senate's conditional ratification of the late convention with that nation. He had some misunderstanding with one of the stage proprietors. He thought himself imposed on & indeed it was the fact. He insisted on his right but without rudeness & was impertinently & boisterously told that others knew what was right as well as he did. "Sir," rejoined the Frenchman, in very good English, "it is your right to treat me very politely, as I treat you."

*February 20th.* At Trenton we heard of the election of Jefferson to the Presidency of the United States. On counting the votes of the electors, he & Aaron Burr were found to be highest on the list, each having 73 votes. The House of Representatives were to decide between them. They balloted by states. 35 ballots were taken with the same result; 8 states for Jefferson, 6 for Burr, & 2 divided. On examining the 36th ballot Jefferson was declared to have 10 & of course was elected.

*February 25th.* I have been visited by Latrobe several times since my return from N.Y. He is very courteous & would be familiar. What does this mean?

*February 26th.* While explaining some part of the works to several citizens, I slipped & should have gone to the bottom of the well in the Schuylkill engine house, but was prevented by laying hold of a cross timber & by the assistance of a friend. A slight fracture is the only injury I sustained. A very small matter saved me. I was aware that if I descended, death must have been the consequence. Why did I feel no trepidation, no misgiving of heart? So long as we can be useful, it is our duty to meet death with calmness & resignation. It is the common lot of all, nor is it for us to decide as to the time or manner of it. We may not be prepared for the call when it is made, but we may at no other times be better prepared. True, futurity is enveloped in clouds of uncertainty & the doubts which may prevail as to what state or form of existence the spirit may assume, when it departs from the body, should impress us with a proper degree of seriousness on the subject, but these considerations should not affect us with childish terrors on the verge of eternity. We should endeavour to die like men, resting our hopes on the justice & mercy of God.

*February 28th.* So! the secret is out. Two visits from Latrobe today & he wants two things: "an ordinance to regulate the distribution" & he would not refuse a fat berth as Engineer to the City. Yes, I will prepare an ordinance but it will not suit him. He is "hard run today & wants to borrow a little money." I have none to lend. Well now I suppose I shall not see him again very soon.

*March 4th.* This day Thos. Jefferson commences his administration. His partizans in this place have a procession & considering the kind of people who compose it, things seem to be conducted with decency and moderation.   ·

*March 5th.* Latrobe should be immediately discharged. It is now certain that he undertook more than he understood & has been making experiments at the expense of the City. He has talents—I wish I could add that he possesses equal economy, honesty & system. I foresee that we shall be burdened with an expence which makes me wish I had never promoted the work.

*March 6th.* Jefferson's inauguration speech has been published. It contains many excellent sentiments & professions & should he practice on the political creed which he there lays down, there will be little occasion to regret his election.

*March 7th.* Roosevelt's accounts against the City are now before me. Many of the items of charge are altogether inadmissable & several important points remain to be adjusted. That relative to the number of cubic inches of which the gallon is to consist is not one of the least. The wine measure is computed at 231 & the ale at 282. Of course, it is of considerable moment in the supply of water. The British engineers appear to have estimated the gallon of water at the rate of 282 cubic inches. R. insists on the wine measure as the standard for his engines & I fear the Com. will sacrifice the interest of the City & give in to his wishes. When I consider that he is to support the engines for 42 years, I cannot but think the Com. will, by yielding this point, be guilty of a dereliction of their duty & justly incur the censure of their fellow citizens.

*March 12th.* At length after much controversy my scheme for raising funds has succeeded by a unanimous vote in the Common Council & by the dissent of only one member (Saml. Fox) in the Select Council.

*March 30th.* Arrivals from Europe bring very important news. France & Austria have made peace. Russia, Sweden, Denmark & Prussia have united with France to force the English to acknowledge the principle that "free ships make free goods" whilst she is making the most formidable preparations to resist their united attack. The Imperial Parliament of G. Britain, Scotland & Ireland have been assembled for the first time. The King is dangerously ill. Pitt & his colleagues have resigned the ministry & provisions continue scarce & dear. It is fortunate for the United States that they are separated from Europe by an ocean three thousand miles wide.

*April 1st.* I have again met the Committee. Things do not work together for good. Latrobe has played the fool with the Committee & the Committee will play the fool with Councils & the public. Hitherto I have watched over the water works with the assiduity & affection of a parent for her child. I have been sorely galled to witness the little benefit which has been latterly derived from my experience & wishes to counteract improper measures & preserve the credit of the undertaking. I have almost persuaded myself to let things take their course, without further opposition.

*April 4th.* Sent for in haste to the Schuylkill engine house. Two of our hands have been suffocated in the boiler—one of them in attempting to save the life of the other. I wrote a paragraph in Poulson's paper giving a particular account of this unhappy accident. Wrote two essays for the same paper under the signatures of Cure & Correction.

*April 22d.* Engagements of various kinds have precluded me from keeping regular minutes for some days past & the weather has been unfavourable to the dispatch of outdoor business. There have been but few dry days this & the last month. The wind mostly eastwardly. Last night much snow fell. Had the ground & other circumstances been favourable to its reception, I believe it would have been nearly as deep as any that has fallen during the winter. This day has much of the appearance of the periodical equinox.

*April 26th*. My prospect with respect to pecuniary matters is much beclouded by the imprudent conduct of J. C. & E. W., my former partners in N. York. They have conducted the business with little judgement or discretion. I had contemplated a peaceful retirement from the battle of business, but this desirable & long wished for event may be wholly prevented by the imprudence of these men. Well, what I possess was acquired by my personal industry. Should it go I must again stand behind the counter & endeavour to acquire more.

*April 28th*. The snow which fell on the 22d. is said to be 12 inches deep in many parts of the country.

*April 30th*. The yearly meeting of Friends is just past. They resolved to recommend the raising of money by subscription among their members, for the relief of poor Friends now suffering in England for want of provisions. Several thousand Dollars have already been subscribed in this City.

*May 20th*. My sight has been uncommonly bad for a few days past. Cupping has produced little or no relief. It is the first time I tried the experiment.

*May 24th*. The Emperor Paul of Russia was lately found dead in bed. Report states that he went off in an apoplectic fit. There is some reason to believe that he may have been poisoned. His exit is not much regretted. He appears to have been a vain, weak, tyrannical monarch. His son, Alexander, has ascended the throne. The English Fleet, under Sir Hyde Parker & Lord Nelson, have attacked Copenhagen and defeated the Danes, with considerable slaughter on both sides.

*June 4th*. A fellow of the name of Rennie pawns himself on the public for a ventriloquist. Desirous of witnessing so extraordinary a property, my friend C. B. Brown & myself attended one of his exhibitions. He is an errant imposture. His attempts were futile, childish & disgusting. Our chagrin & disappointment were the greater on account of the confidence & effrontery with which he announced his powers in the form of a hand bill. He had a wooden doll with which he affected to hold a conversation, but the utmost force of our imagination could not for a moment beguile us into the belief that the voice at anytime came from the image. He also performed some slight of hand tricks, but even these were bungling and insignificant.

*June 10th.* Two days past have been employed in removing from Mulberry Street to No. 191 Walnut Street. I have sold my house in Mulberry Street to my friend James Milnor, Atty. at Law, for $5600, and am now placed under a Landlord. Altho' I have not yet found that "two removals are as bad as a fire," yet it is a troublesome business.

*June 11th.* We breathe a freer air than in our old habitation. The house stands on the Square on which Robert Morris had erected his very uncouth & expensive edifice, which is now erased.

*June 13th.* The voice of the woodpecker is a novelty in Philada. I never heard it in the City before today. We are not thickly surrounded with buildings. This circumstance has emboldened this solitary adventurer to take a peep at us.

*June 15th.* Altho' I am still tied to the City by a variety of cares, the recreation which I have latterly taken on horseback & in the chair in the neighbourhood has improved my health.

*June 16th.* The care of watering a newly made grass bed & of instructing my two oldest boys in spelling & reading has become a pleasing and daily avocation.

*June 18th.* Was it not that I have been & continue to be so run down with Corporation business I would, I think, endeavour to have some ordinance framed & passed for prohibiting boys from flying kites & driving hoops along the streets. The practice is attended with much danger & inconvenience to the citizens, especially to those who ride in carriages.

*June 22d.* Before the Revolutionary War in America, the trade of leather breeches making gave employment to two hundred families. At present it will not support three families. When we consider the increase of population since that period, it will give an idea of the little use of that article in the City. I believe that luxury & refinement have produced the same effects all over the United States. For winter wear the cotton manufactures of G. Britain are most generally substituted. They are made into cords to which various popular names are assigned;

such as Washington Cord, Federal Cord, Fancy Cord &c., which are nothing more than different forms of the old fashioned Corduroy respecting the first introduction of which into this country I have been told the following anecdote. Some pieces of it were consigned to a merchant in Philada. who could not persuade any person in the City to buy the article. He at length applied to Jas. Old, iron master in Lancaster County who is still living & very well known to me. James took a piece & clad his negroes in it, who were so much offended at the insult thus put on them by their master, as to threaten an insurrection. Their discontent compelled him to relinquish the idea of clothing them with the rest of the obnoxious article. It remained on the shelves of the consignee for years. At length a leader of fashions, a full blooded buck of those days, had a pair of breeches presented to him on the terms of his appearing in them in public. He accepted the conditions & Corduroy became the dress of every fashionable man & soon after of almost every class of citizens.

*June 24th*. A jaunt to N. York is proposed in company with Cha. B. Brown. Whether in a chair or in the stage remains for future decision.

*June 26th*. The quantity of flour shipped from the United States to G. Britain is beyond all former precedent. Within a few months past, several hundred thousand barrels have been sent from this port alone. 18/9 & 20 Sterling a barrel have been obtained for freight. Several of our merchants have made handsome fortunes by shipping that article. The present is not the only time of scarcity there. I have accidentally found a bill of lading for seventy-two barrels of flour & sixteen bbls. of gammons, shipped by my father-in-law, John Drinker, on board the Ship *Unity*, Captn. Enoch Story, dated 21st May 1768.

*June 28th*. The trade of the little village of Columbia on the Susquehanna has increased very rapidly. I have seen a Letter stating that my tenant Jos. Poole loaded 74 waggons with wheat in 3 days. All the store houses are full of wheat & flour brought down the river. Hundreds of barrels of the latter lie on the banks unsheltered for want of room.

*June 29th*. Wrote a Letter & an essay for Poulson, or rather a few hasty remarks exposing the folly of a set of citizens who have formed themselves into a company of rifleman & dress & arm in the Indian style with rifle, scalping knife & tomahawk. Is not this abominable? My friend C. B. Brown breakfasted with me & a little after 8 we set out together for N. York, in the stage. Lodged at Brunswick; hot enough.

*June 30th.* The day has been productive of no marvellous adventures or hair breadth escapes. We suffered something from heat, dust & fog & at 1 P.M. were safely deposited in N. York. Dined at the Paulus Hook ferry house & afterwards sought lodgings with the widow Avery on the battery, where I had been in the summer of last year. We were disappointed. Charles would, of course, lodge with his old friend Johnson & I with E. Whitehead. C. finds something to admire at every step; the air & the prospect from the battery (so far very well) & there is a certain indescribable something in the streets which gives them an appearance very beautiful & superior in taste & excellence to the streets of Philadelphia. I confess the observation never occurred to me. I always thought large, airy & straight streets preferable to narrow, crooked & confined ones. However, C. seems to be in his element & I am glad to see him enjoy himself. He flutters & hops about like a bird & I don't know whether I shall be able to catch him again without salt.

*July 1st.* Wrote to Uncle H. D. on business. It is curious to observe the complaints of some people to recommend themselves to the charitable notice of others. A hale looking huzzy asking alms of me this morning said that "the sweat run into her poor eyes & burned them like a fever."

It is a remark made by a modern writer that pickpockets & house breakers are generally possessed of genius & talents. This observation has been fully verified by others. It is found both in Philadelphia & New York to be extremely difficult to confine the criminals in the prisons so as to prevent their escape. Three fellows long since made their elopement from the State prison of the latter place, by an ingenious contrivance. They were lodged on the ground floor in one apartment & every evening, when locked in, underwent a search & an opening being left in the door, a sentinel looked in every hour or two during the night. One morning he hailed them to get up & as they made no answer he repeated the call several times. At last he procured the key and entered the room where he soon discovered that what he had taken to be three men snug asleep was nothing more than heaps of earth worked into the form of men, and covered except their heads with the shirts of the elopers. The parcels were finished at the ends in the form of men's heads with each a night cap & reclined on pillows. The fellows had, tho' watched, worked thro' very thick plank, removed a number of large spikes, dug down under the foundation of the building & gone safely off. To effect this they had removed 2 & 3 cart loads of earth.

*July 2d.* Several vessels laden with Irishmen have lately arrived in these parts. An order of the British Government has put a stop to further emigration. One cargo of these passengers forced their Capt. to sea & gave the vessel to him, only on condition of his pledging himself to land them in N. York. Another Ship load consisting of about 400 have been stated by a writer in this day's paper to be in the outskirts of the City destitute of almost every necessary & absolutely perishing for want of nourishment.

This City is improving very fast & its commerce is prodigious. The present population is 68,000, but as the City jurisdiction extends all over the island, so this enumeration includes the whole. Philadelphia including the suburbs contains 72,000.

*July 3d.* Visited some of the creditors of C. W. & Co. I believe to mutual satisfaction.

Notwithstanding the fine air of N. York, the grandeur of its streets & its inimitable prospects, my friend C. B. B. is this day confined to his chamber at Wm. Johnson's. Here I met Doc. Miller who was attending on him. The Doctor has suggested an idea entirely new to me. He gives it as the remark of a celebrated physician of England that the vaccine pox will not only prevent the small pox but even the venereal. He seems to think that, should it prove true, it will introduce a new & important era in morals, which may eventually destroy the bonds of civil society.

It rains very seasonably, but the storm is so violent that it seems as tho' it would shatter the house about our ears—it will doubtless temper the atmosphere, of which there is much need. The weather is very sultry; from sunrise till 10 in the morning, I find the air more oppressive than it usually is in Philada. After that hour, the sea breeze comes to the relief of the citizens—at least to such as have situations adjacent to the battery. It must blow a hurricane to reach the remote nooks & crooks of some of the twining, narrow & filthy avenues of this place. Some of the streets, such as Broadway, Broadstreet &c. are sufficiently commodious for most purposes, but the rest are generally so cramped that if two persons be walking together, the conversation is continually broken off by the necessity the parties are under of walking Indian file at every few paces, or be shoved from the foot way, which in many places will only admit one passenger at a time.

It is a bad regulation in N. York to permit the butchers to kill animals in the markets & especially at this hot season of the year. I am told it is frequently done. Their fish market may be called plentiful. It is supplied with about 60 different species, including shell fish. They may be purchased alive at most seasons.

*July 4th.* The ringing of bells & firing of guns awoke me & announced the 26th anniversary of American independence. After breakfast I wrote an epistle to my Mary. About eleven I walked to the battery. The enclosure was crowded with military & other citizens. Cannons were thundering, bells ringing in all quarters of the City, the shops generally shut, the streets alive with military parades & citizens driving to and fro. Societies & various clubs marched in regular order & the whole City wore the appearance of festivity. At noon called on Wm. Johnson & accompanied by him & Charles waited on Wm. Dunlap opposite to the park, where we dined. He is a valuable man & I cannot help regretting & feeling surprized to find him the manager of the N. York theatre. He does not, as his friends assure me, associate with the players—having a contempt for the loose profligate manners which prevail among them. He is contemplating a retirement from his present occupation. He is the author of several plays & the translator of a number by the pen of the celebrated German, Kotzebue. It is his relish for these amusements which has led him into his present employment. His wife is a charming woman & the very picture of courtesy & sweetness of temper. Our company formed no Bacchanalian club. We dined well, drank some one, some two glasses of wine & discoursed on various incidental & desultory topics. Might not this be called the "feast of reason & the flow of soul"?

There are no houses in N. York which answer to the Inns in Philada. for the accommodation of travellers, excepting the Tontine Coffee House may be ranked as of that class. There are however several very good boarding houses & for the convenience of tipplers, there are about twelve hundred licensed grog shops. This would appear to be exaggerated but my informant is respectable & has studied the subject.

*July 6th.* I remained all night at my friend's & in the morning about 5, in order to prevent him from sending me to Town in his carriage, returned on foot. I was joined by Jos. Grellett, a Frenchman who fled from the persecutions & political troubles of his country & was afterwards, with his brother Stephen, converted to Quakerism. Having rested a short time at E. Whitehead's, I proceeded to the lodgings of my friend C. B. B., roused him from bed & took him with me to the Millers with whom we had engaged to breakfast. These learned & agreeable men keep bachelor's hall & appear to live very comfortably together.

The Doctor in conjunction with Professor Mitchell conducts the *Medical Repository,* which is a work of much merit.

C. B. B. & myself have concluded to pay a visit to Albany & have this day actually engaged a passage in the sloop *Harriet* from Captn. Ripley, who expects to sail tomorrow afternoon.

*July 7th.* At 6 in the afternoon, C. B. B. & myself waited on Capt. Wm. Ripley. This was the hour fixed for his departure but as he was not prepared to sail, we returned to Wm. Johnson's & partook of a dish of coffee in company with Wm. Dunlap & Anthy. Bleecker. At 8 returned to the sloop & got under weigh from Coynties slip with a favourable breeze, which soon wafted us round the battery & out of sight of N. York. We passed Fort Washington in the night & in the morning of the 8th saw several objects which were rendered in nowise interesting to me than as they tended to revive the image of a man who was always dear to our family. His virtues made him so to others and perhaps no man ever met with a greater number of sympathizers. His hard & unfortunate sentence was lamented even by those whom the policy of war had created his enemies. Here, said my informant, Major André was taken. It was under that tree. There he was executed & in yonder house he & Arnold held their first conference. Altho' but a child when André lived in my father's family, he left me many interesting tokens of his urbanity. I have always been accustomed to regard him with the affection of a brother.

Peekskill may be considered as the Southern extremity of that large ridge of mountains through which the Hudson takes its course, known by the name of the Highlands. They form a link in that immense chain which runs in a NE & SW direction along the whole N. American continent & is variously denominated as the Blue Mountains, Allegheny, Appalachian &c. They skirt the river on both sides for about 12 miles & have a very dreary & impoverished aspect, being little more than a perfect wilderness covered with low cedars & some other shrubbery. Their surface is irregular & many of the promontories are lofty. One of them, called St. Anthony's Nose, is probably not less than 600 feet high. These wilds have been rendered memorable principally by the events of the Revolutionary War. The vestiges of Fort Montgomery may yet be traced in them, but the most considerable place in the whole distance is West Point, the fort & fortifications of which, together with barracks & outhouses, are now in good preservation & garrisoned by troops of the United States. This place is esteemed to be the Gibraltar of America in point of strength & inaccessibility to an enemy. It has a complete command of the navigation. The river makes two considerable & sudden bends within reach of its fire & is moreover not more than about 3/8 of a mile in width. These circumstances give the fort an incalculable advantage of the shipping of an enemy. We approached it under a favourable breeze, but were becalmed, so that we were obliged to ply our oars to move round the several points opposite the works. Our Captn. informed us that this frequently took place & the same wind that is fair to run to the fort is seldom favourable for passing it—so that no vessel could escape the fire from some of the fortifications.

*July 10th.* Were I to attempt a general description of the country we have passed on this river, I should say its shores are bold, rocky & romantic. The soil is gravelly, sandy & stony with a large proportion of clay & that sterility is stampt in legible characters on its extensive margins. This noble river is but little beholden to inferior streams for its importance & seems to move along self supported. We have scarce seen one rivulet, but two or three insignificant creeks come to offer their tribute to its full swelling tides. At night the shores resound with the solitary voice of whippoorwill. For two days past my friend has scarce been seized with one scribbling fit. The genius of the Hudson has at length inspired him & I perceive that he fills page after page.

I am now sitting at a table in the City of Troy, about 166 miles above N. York on the eastern shore of the Hudson & 6 above Albany. Soon after we passed the City of Hudson, what sailors would call a stiff southern breeze propelled us thro' the most fertile & best cultivated country between N. York and this place.

*July 12th.* From the insignificant village of Washington opposite to Troy we passed over a flat of rich soil to the City of Albany. We arrived at two o'clock & took up our lodgings at the Tontine Coffee House, which is kept by a person of the name of Gregory. It is a large convenient house, the most so of any we had stopped at. The rooms are spacious & the fare good. Travellers are better accommodated at this Inn than they usually are either in N. York or Philada. at any of the public houses of entertainment, especially in having chambers more capacious, less crowded & better bedding.

It may give some idea of the value of property in Albany to state that the house in which we now are rents for $1000. David Henshaw, who

resides in a back street & in an old ill fashioned Dutch house 2 stores high, pays $165 per annum. He says that rents & provisions are as high or nearly so in this place as in N. York.

*July 13th*.  At 6 this morning we recrossed the Hudson, five miles from which we breakfasted at a poor Tavern. We halted again at a small village of about 30 houses, called the Newstores, halfway to Lebanon. It is a pretty situation amidst hills & surrounded with rich vales.

It is common in these parts, as well as about Albany, to construct their waggons for the purposes of burthen as well as of pleasure. They have no covers & when used for the latter purpose, chairs are placed in them for seats. We met, in some of these vehicles, ladies apparently as well dressed & genteel as the better sort of that sex in the Cities of N. York & Philada.

A turnpike is forming thro' this country over parts of which we travelled. It is very differently made from the Lancaster turnpike. Stones are excluded from its composition & this renders it a very pleasant road. You have not that grating racket which on the Lancaster turnpike precludes ordinary conversation, nor that continual jarring which is so tiresome. It is about 18 feet wide & rounded in the common manner. It does not pretend to straight courses, nor to fill up valleys & slice off mountains. It winds round the steepest hills, cuts off the sharp & shaggy points of the smaller ones & fills up the worst hollows of the valleys. It is solid, smooth & tolerably direct. The nature of the soil over which it passes will always render it a good road with little expense & trouble. It has been undertaken by a company.

Having heard something of a sect of religionists who are settled in this neighbourhood, who differ much from the generality of other Christians, our curiosity prompted us to pay them a visit this afternoon. They are called Shakers & inhabit a secluded spot of a most delightful & fertile vale situated in the Township of New Canaan, three miles south of the springs of this place. We halted a few paces from the hamlet to converse with one of the Believers, so they call themselves. He was in a meadow & employed in attending on some grape vines. He knew or seemed to know little. We advanced & knocked at the door of a large house. A woman, oddly habited, a little in the stile of the Moravians & about 50 years of age presented herself. We asked for a drink of water & she in turn enquired whether we would not prefer beer. Our object was to view the interior of the building. We must therefore not be saucy &

gave water the preference. She soon returned with a pitcher & our wants were so far satisfied. We next asked whether we might be permitted to view their garden. Walk in, said she & sit down & I will enquire. We were ushered into a room in which 2 beds were placed, every part of which were of the best kind. The other furniture was simple & in no wise remarkable, except for its neatness & the order in which it was placed. The floor & every other part in sight had an uncommon indication of cleanliness & system. We were not many minutes alone. An old man appeared, to whom we expressed our desire. He observed that if we were strangers we should be gratified & led the way thro' the house into the garden. We employed our eyes as we passed thro' the hall, but the apartments were closed & we saw nothing. The garden occupies 6 acres of ground & is stored with common vegetables. Everything is cultivated for use, nothing for show. Harmony & the hand of industry prevailed throughout. Our guide told us that they sold annually one thousand Dollars worth of garden seeds, but instead of furnishing us with a solution to our questions, such however as would have satisfied us, he began to preach. He considered themselves the *true believers* & he not only *believed*, but he *knew* they were so & that all who would attentively examine the Scriptures must be of their way of thinking. We, however, obtained from him a knowledge of the following facts. Their whole family consists of 40 men and women, all advanced in life. They never cohabit as man & wife & from the stress laid on this article of their faith, it is evident that it is the foundation & fundamental of their religion. They employ themselves variously. The men are divided into farmers & mechanics. They have between 700 & 800 acres of land, and make hoes, nails & some other simple articles of iron & also carriages. Their women make the clothing for the family & all dress in clothes every part of which is made by themselves. There are four large dwellings & perhaps a dozen work shops. A meeting house, about 40 by 60 feet, is very neat & painted with white lead, as are also the 4 dwellings. The one we entered I judge to be 50 by 60 & is three stories high. They are all framed & weather boarded & have an air of neatness, taste & cleanliness seldom surpassed anywhere. This is singularly the case with the house of worship. Our conductor is certainly a wild fanatic. There was neither consistency, clearness, plausibility nor ingenuity in his preachment. In one part he so far mistook as to quote one text for another quite different. He perceived it, paused, apologized & ended by saying he could not remember what he intended to say. A bell rung & he excused himself from further attention to us by observing supper was ready & pointing to the way out of the yard, walked off. We saw tho' we did not converse with, several others of the sect. They are generally quite ancient men & women. Their apparel is simple, convenient & clean. The woman who gave us the water has a mild, benevolent & rather cheerful countenance. She had once possessed beauty, nor had age & seclusion deprived her of a claim to it. The man carries marks of labour, both of body & mind & if his outward concerns are as strangely confused as his intellectual ones, I would not give much for him as a farmer. His features in general bespeak goodness of heart & steadfastness in his principles, but his eyes have something in them which strongly mark the visionary aspect of his mind.

*July 14th.* Spent an hour at the quill & then, invited by the fragrance of the morn, swept the dew drops from the summits of the hills & afterwards made a pleasant pedestrian excursion into the state of Massachusetts & back again!

Lebanon is 3 miles from Albany in an eastern direction, 30 from Benninghove in Vermont & so near Massachusetts that the line between it & the State of N. York is within half a mile of the Springs.

Our table abounds with elegance & plenty. We have each a small chamber to ourselves in a house separate from the one in which we eat—& have also the luxury of clean beds & can mix with & retire from other company at pleasure. Some valetudinarians are here for the benefit of their healths & if even the waters do not relieve their complaints, the salubrity of the atmosphere may.

After breakfast the spirit of jingle came upon us & Charles, writing our names on the wall of his apartment, subjoined the following lines—

> They came at noon & chose to stay,
> The noon brought round another day,
> They rambled, loitered, mus'd & walk'd,
> They read & wrote & laugh'd & talk'd.
> Each neighbouring hill they scal'd & view'd,
> Each track below their steps pursued,
> They sipp'd each fountain head & scann'd
> What breezes blew, how turn'd the land.
> From all around that met their view
> Instruction & delight they drew
> And, parting, left these lines to say
> May all depart as pleased as they.

To which I added

> They visited the Shakers' Town
> And rounded their garden up & down,
> Snuff'd the rich fragrance of the gale
> That sweeps along that tranquil vale.
> And, near the margin of the road
> On which they pass'd to that abode,
> Inscrib'd with knife on bark of tree
> Their names—but not their pedigree—
> And fondly hope that some lov'd friend
> Whose devious steps that way may tend
> Will read & say, "Here Brown once stood,
> And there Cope letter'd in the wood."

This extraordinary effort of genius might well produce a necessity for the Bath. At any rate, I took one. The house is well contrived for the purpose. I cannot by any of my senses discover any essential difference between this & common spring water, except that it is rather warmer than is usual. It is quite palatable & perfectly lucid. We met here two daughters of Uriah Tracy of Litchfield, Connecticut—very agreeable young women—a gentleman & his 3 sisters from Charleston, S. Carolina & some others who are invalids & come from various parts. We leave the place with a zest for its beauties & enjoyments & of course with some reluctance.

We took our departure at 5 P.M. in the Albany Stage. Our course lay eastward over the Hancock Mountain, which bounds the Lebanon Valley in that direction.

*July 15th.* After a fatiguing ride of 33 miles on a turnpike over a rugged tract of land, we are now at Northampton, one mile west of Connecticut River. The part of Massachusetts which we journeyed thro' today is a perpetual hill & dale & exceedingly stony. Grass grows everywhere & scarce any other culture seems to be attended to. I don't remember to have noticed but one field of wheat, very few of rye & oats. They are not congenial to the soil. A mixture of herd grass & white clover is the most common coat of the fields. Foxtail & other kinds are also to be found. The first year after a piece of ground is cleared, I am informed, it will produce a good crop of rye, but will scarce ever do it a second season. The timber most general in the forests are pine, hemlock, maple, chestnut, beech & birch. There are but few streams of water & those small. The bridges over them are bad & even dangerous, being rarely anything but poor plank. Wherever we halted, water was brought to the houses by means of wooden trunks from high ground in the vicinity. The country is but thinly settled & the houses & barns mean, except in a few instances. We examined several that ranked among the better kind & found them to be of very slight construction. Not one of any description built of anything but wood. Almost every house that has a claim to elegance belongs to some lawyer, a circumstance not very flattering to the stranger, who must of course be inclined to believe, where gentlemen of the bar thrive better than others, that a litigious spirit must be prevalent to a reprehensible degree. So striking is this fact that when we saw a good or rather uncommonly good dwelling, we ceased to ask who lives there but "what lawyer lives there?" & were never mistaken.

The Taverns are bad & after the excellent fare we had been accustomed to at Caleb Hull's, whom we boarded with at Lebanon, we could scarcely swallow the miserable provisions we had served up to us, at Partridgefield where we breakfasted, & at Chesterfield where we dined. There seems to be a perfect rage for politics among them—every few houses were complimented with a newspaper by our driver—& at the Tavern where we dined, on opening the Book case, no other Books were to be seen than some volumes of the Laws of the U. States & several copies of a 4th of July oration delivered by Benjn. Parsons.

*July 16th.* The stage from Hanover which passes thro' N. Hampton for Hartford in Connecticut is arrived. We have engaged our passage & shall probably start in a few minutes.

The first thing that I noticed on taking my seat was the miserable appearance of our horses. They were so poor that every rib was to be seen. The backbone seemed as if it was going to start from a carcass which could no longer support it. The hip bones, possessed of the same humour, were not only attempting, but in one of these carrion horses, had actually made its escape thro' the skin, but had not energy to get any further.

Well, who would have thought of meeting Bonaparte in N. England? Strange as it may seem this actually took place today. We travelled several miles together. It is true his predilection for taciturnity precluded talk, but at any rate he can't converse in English. I did not like his looks, his airs, nor his gaits. Depend on it he is a worthless fellow & I would not give my grey horse for two of him.

*July 17th.* A South Carolinian got up from the breakfast table this morning at Hartford, walked out of the room into the hall & thence up several steps to call his negro from the third story to pick up a crust of toast which his little son had thrown down. Really, thought I, there is more gained by having a servant to wait on one than people generally imagine. This fact is literally true. The son is a promising hero about 4 years old. Soon after our arrival at the inn his father boasted to us of this fine child's uncommon prowess. Indeed, there was little necessity for making his goodly qualifications known, for in one minute after & in his father's presence, he volunteered in a quarrel with Charles & kicked him on the shins. Had his legs been long enough I should have trembled for my campanion's seat of honour. This affair doubtless tended to the comfort of this wise old man, who may yet live to have the supreme satisfaction of seeing his matchless boy knock out the brains of a few negroes, preparatory to still greater exploits.

*July 18th*. Notwithstanding the rapid rate with which one novel scene succeeds to another, I cannot keep my thoughts from continually straying to Philada. "Where the treasure is the heart is also" & surely I have treasure there of no small value. A line from Mary informing me that "all's well" would dispel a cloud which in spite of me hovers around my imagination & for two days past has not a little tormented me.

We allow ourselves so little time to breathe, at the places where we halt & so much of that time is devoted to rest, company & rambling, that I am compelled to scribble hastily & at snatched intervals.

The evening was spent at the house of R. Alsop, the Middletown Bard, who is absent from his family. The stage from Hartford has this moment arrived & is to proceed to New Haven in 5 minutes, so that there is an end to scribbling for the present.

We arrived at New Haven when the winds were untoward to a speedy passage up the sound to New York, & as we feel no particular predilection to being buffeted about to little purpose, we have made up our minds to tarry here until the next land stage shall pass, which will not happen until the day after tomorrow.

*July 19th*. This morning we attended at the delivery of a sermon, in the Chapel of the College, by Doctor Timothy Dwight, to two hundred students. He announced it as part of a series of theological discourses. The object was to prove the existence of angels pure & fallen & of their influence over & interference with the affairs of men. He did not treat the subject as being a metaphor, but substantially a matter of fact. On these nice metaphysical disquisitions I have seldom indulged much thought—they are beyond my capacity of comprehension.

The doctor appears to be about 45 & is of a full habit. He has a commanding presence, a good voice & a pleasing & distinct pronunciation. My friend calls him the "New England oracle."

*July 20th.* I have been amused with the language used by some of the drivers to their horses. He who drove his carrion steeds from Northampton seemed to have the most extensive knowledge of horse talk of any of them. It would be in vain to attempt an imitation. His tongue & whip were unceasingly going. Not an oath escaped from his mouth, but many a bang & twitch & thump & switch got Bonaparte that ruthless day. Nor did Nance or Domini, or even Sharon fare better. In vain they crouched beneath the last & by many a doleful wince & jilt proclaim their inability to jog on faster. It saved not their high boned ribs, their towering spines & slunken heads. The flagellation went on & loud & constant were the exclamations of "get along away there, phist, phist, phist, chirp, chirp, chirp, get along you rascal, Bonaparte, steady, phist, phist, mind what you're about there, now for it my hearties, come away Sharon, chirp, chirp, chirp, get away my lads, phist, phist, phist, take care of yourselves then, ho, ho, ho, Nance, get up with you, come my hearties, chirp, chirp, chirp, phist, phist, phist, so, so, so, you rogues."

*July 21st.* Thro' Massachusetts & Connecticut we met not one four wheeled pleasure carriage, very few chaises, except in the neighbourhood of Hartford & few travellers of any kind. Pumps are rarely seen. Those in use are the same as are worked on shipboard. We met with civility & attention where ever we went. Nor did we experience any of that impertinent inquisitiveness which I had always heard ascribed to the people of N. England.

*July 22d.* Having left my own & the business of H. D. in some state of progress & perceiving no essential advantage from a longer stay in N.Y., I have made up my mind to return today. This was unexpected to me yesterday & will prevent me from visiting several on whom I had intended to call. Took leave of C.B.B. & W.D. with whom I breakfasted. Wm. is preparing for the press a compendium of the laws of merchants adapted to the United States. Have no doubt that it will be a valuable work.

*July 23d.* The productions of N. Jersey are more various than those of Massachusetts & Connecticut in the route I took. Red clover & wheat were now seen, tho' not abundantly. In Pennsyla. barley, wheat, red clover &c. are more profusely scattered.

At 6 P.M. I was once more seated at my own table, enjoying the society of my family. My two oldest boys are out of town at school. Since I left home I have travelled six hundred miles.

*July 25th*. Attended the usual meeting of the Wat. Com. They are still in trouble with Latrobe & Roosevelt & have not energy enough to get rid of the leeches. L. makes a demand of an additional compensation for services. On this head the contract with him is positive & admits of no equivocation in his favour. Yet I expect he will obtain his object. The Com. are in the habit of being gulled & seem to court it.

*July 26th*. Visited Henry & Francis at Radnor School. They conducted me round their usual walks after blackberries & other fruit. Perhaps no fruit is more universal in N. America than these berries. I have eaten them this season in the states of Massachusetts, Connecticut, New York, New Jersey & Pennsylvania & have discovered no difference in their quality. It is evident that nature designed them for an important use. I am persuaded that they are a valuable medicine in their proper season. My boys amused me with their prattle & added to my happiness by being themselves happy. Their master, Josa. Maule, with whom they board, is a man of no great reading or capacity, but possesses as much knowledge as is requisite with sound principles and unpolluted manners to teach children to advantage. The school is kept in one end of the meeting house, 14 miles from the City on the old Lancaster Road. Went & returned on horseback & in spite of the sophisms of one sect of materialists I verily believe that the same horse & rider returned that went out. That our bodies undergo a perpetual change, so that the particles of which they consist at one period are not the same of which they consist at another period, every common observer of physics will acknowledge. But surely this is no conclusive evidence against personal identity. I might as well pretend to say that volition derives its original force from & is wholly dependent on the motions & actions of the body, the very reverse of which is true. That power in me which forces me to believe that I exist proves, by the same conscious & convincing operation, that I am the same identical person who felt this consciousness & who recollects that I felt it, two minutes before. To any other than a man whose reason & senses are entangled in a net of philosophism woven by himself or some other wise acre, it appears to be the height of absurdity to say that he is not one & the same person for a second of time. Yet such philosophers there were among the ancients & such also have modern times produced. Thus by this strange philosophy no man could drown himself. For as drowning is not a momentaneous act, the same person who began to drown would not be the same person who was actually drowned. I might drown another, but never myself, nor would the greatest folly or crime I could commit produce any lasting injury to myself, tho' it might bring another to the gallows. In this sense laws, whether human or divine, for the punishment of offenders, are nugatory & even abominably wicked, since the punished is not the criminal, but another who was in nowise accessory to the crime. Had the curious Tuscan, Gabriel Taliacotius, who imagined that he had invented a method by which noses & other members of the body might be engrafted on any part of it, contrived some effectual means for engrafting common sense on the sensorium of mad philosophers, he would have conferred a favour on mankind & perhaps on himself.

*August 4th.* Death hath snatched a son from me in a few minutes after his birth. This morning my Polly was delivered of a boy. Her labour was easy & the infant appeared to be perfect in all its parts, healthy, plump & large. Yet it sustained life only to weep & then quietly swooned away. To what its death is attributable is not certainly known. Doc. Griffiths, who was called in, conjectures that its internal organization was imperfect. It is most certain that immediately after parturition the child undergoes a very important change. Like a machine, it may arrive at apparent perfection. Fostered in the womb, it may be nourished & thrive until the important moment which ushers it into the world & confers real existence on it by putting its vital wheels in motion. Then indeed the essential spring may be found to be defective & altho' the functions of animation may for a time be performed as the wheels of a clock may be kept in action by the vibration of the pendulum, yet if this be not propelled by a superior & main principle, the vibrations become fainter & fainter, until at last the powers of life entirely cease to operate & the whole machine sinks into an everlasting rest.

In reflecting on the meteor like existence of this innocent babe, I cannot but be astonished at that vile doctrine propagated by St. Augustine, Mercator & other writers which condemns to endless torment the soul of an infant that dies without baptism & absurdly maintains that this washing of water is in itself sufficient to ensure salvation to the greatest criminal. Thousands, nay millions, of Christians have subscribed to this doctrine, but these men must have strange ideas of the justice & mercy of God. That a helpless infant has not been baptized is surely not chargeable to it as a crime. By this monstrous creed the most abandoned miscreant, who has been guilty of crimes of the greatest atrocity & grown grey in the continual practice of vice may nevertheless, without repentance, be instantly washed of his sins by a dash of water. It is in this way that men dispose of each other & are not ashamed & afraid to ascribe their own wicked notions to the Supreme Being.

*August 6th.* Mary is in a favourable way. She has a fair prospect of a speedy restoration to strength. Her escape from the ordinary risks of childbirth produce a tranquilizing influence on my mind.

*August 7th.* Brother Jasper has concluded to join me in an excursion into the country. Our mutual interest requires the measure. He is now in the City and proposes setting off in a week or 10 days.

Wrote to my friend C. B. B. whom I left in N. York. He lived there in fields of literary clover. His female associates I did not see. His male friends are all learned Doctors. All intimately acquainted with the whole anatomy of language. They have probed to the bottom of its most latent principles, dissected every letter of the alphabet & can tell, to a little, the number & species of every particle of which each is composed. Chas. is equal to any of them. He has analyzed the elements of thought. He has explored the innermost recesses of all articulate sounds. He can split the nerves of an idea & lay bare the sinews, bones & essential spirits of a conjecture. I don't know but Isaac Marshall would have found in him the man he so long sought after. He used to say he "would not give a farthing to talk with any man who would not talk about things before the world was, when all was water."

*August 9th.* Twelve months have revolved since the day on which I first began to scribble on these sheets! The task has helped to fill up some hours which might otherwise have been lost. So far at least the employment has been useful to myself.

*August 13th.* A person of the name of Turner who lives in Market Street was robbed last winter. The thief left a written memorandum behind him of the articles which he had stolen. Stated himself to be the father of a family & unfortunate & that hereafter he would return everything provided no bustle was made or attempts to discover him. He has lately been as good as his word & a number of trinkets & other things of value have been restored in neat order & all the money with interest. Nothing has been withheld & a pair of half worn gloves were replaced by a new pair, nicely folded in paper.

*August 15th.* Have occasion for the constant exercise of patience & forbearance. While on the one hand I have endeavoured to counteract the wild projects of Latrobe & have incurred the displeasure of his friends in the Com., on the other, I find myself frequently attacked with no small degree of asperity by my fellow citizens & charged with the very things which I have always warred against. I have often said & the proof is now in the teeth of every man, that the Engineer is ignorant of his business. Not a hydrant or other device of his contrivance answers the purpose. He has wasted enormous sums of money in making injudicious experiments. I have wished to have him effectually checked, to have him discharged. The Com., tho' sensible of the injury, have not virtue enough to get rid of him & I suffer the daily mortification of reproach, sarcasm & even reviling on account of his blunders & waste. Those who know me to be a member of the Com. very reasonably suppose me to have a hand in directing & authorizing his measures.

*August 19th.* This being the day fixed on for the departure of brother Jasper & myself on our projected jaunt up the Susquehanna, we mounted our nags at 6 in the afternoon & taking the ridge road arrived at the Wissahickon, where we halted for the night.

*August 20th.* Lodged as comfortable as a sultry night would permit at Peter Robinson's, where we breakfasted. My unruly steed chose to put her foot on mine before we started, so that lameness is added to debility.

We passed thro' a populous country & arrived at the pretty little village of Pottsgrove before sunset. At the entrance of the Town, a large stone house was erected by one of the Potts's on a high spot of ground, which never has been completed, as it was found impracticable to procure water on the hill. Altho' he must have expended some hundreds of Pounds, he was not more short sighted than the man who some years since built a mill in Dauphin County, intending to make it pump water to keep itself supplied & from which it was to derive its whole force. The land about Pottsgrove is fertile & well cultivated. It contains 150 houses, mostly stone or brick. Situated in a valley near Schuylkill, but not in sight of it, in the garden belonging to the landlord we measured a radish which was 22½ inches in circumference. Pottsgrove is 37 miles from Philada.

*August 21st.* Departed betimes, crossed the Mawnytawny, a small creek & breakfasted at the White Horse 4 miles on our way. Fared well. Soon after crossed the Monockas over a substantial stone bridge of six arches. We tarried an hour at Reading. It is an ill looking, considerable town, built in the German stile. Small, slovenly & inconvenient one story log houses filled in with brick, stone &c. A few modern dwellings clumsily ornamented have been erected. On one side is the Schuylkill, not in view. Hills obstruct the prospect in every other direction. Opposite to the Town the Tulpehocken empties into the Schuylkill. It was by means of this stream & the Quitipihilla, whose head waters approach very near together, that the Canal was to unite the waters of the Susquehanna with those of the Schuylkill. Reading is 16½ miles from Pottsgrove. Still pursuing the course of the river on its eastern side, we halted at Hamburg (Carter's Town or, as the Germans pronounce it, Kaarkers Shtettle). It is a small place of about 40 houses & seems to carry on a considerable trade in gambling & horse racing. It is 10 miles from Reading.

At Reading we met a Philadelphian who told us he could not, after repeated trials, hire a chaise or any sort of carriage in the Town. Reading is noted for its hatters. Large quantities of wool hats of good fabric are made here and sold to the Philada. hatters & thence dispersed in every direction. They manufacture them so cheap & their work is in such credit that no person in Philada. attempts the same business. Between that & Hamburg we crossed Maiden Creek, a smart stream, over a bridge supported by piers. There is good land about this creek, not so much on the reddish cast as has been general since we left the neighbourhood of the City.

We find the descendants of Germans everywhere. They are the principal settlers of the country. They are a rude, uncultivated people. Not prone to politeness nor very apt to render disinterested services either to strangers or to each other. They are a mean, selfish, thrifty, laborious race.

A mile from Hamburg we skirted the first range of mountains on a wild stoney road cut along their sides. The roughness of the road rendered travelling tiresome & occasioned us to be benighted—a circumstance, however, which we had little reason to regret. The air amid the mountains became very refreshing after a very hot day & the full moon rising majestically over their summits gave an appearance of sombre grandeur to the scenery around us, at once novel & interesting—the dark sides of the mountains forming a striking contrast to the silver illumination of the other parts of the landscape.

At length, we reached our contemplated resting place for the night & were received with significant bows & looks by a boorish looking

German, whom we discovered to be the landlord. Judging from appearances, we prepared ourselves for rough fare in this barren region. We asked what we could have to eat & were answered, "Anything you please." Jasper was for coffee, but I dissuaded him, expecting he would not relish it if made. We called for milk & had it produced in nice order & quality, with good butter & cheese in abundance. Jasper thought the addition of a pye would be grateful. "Well," said our host, "you can have it" & forthwith produced them of 2 kinds, both excellent. Such fare in a wilderness was unexpected & we did justice to the table by finishing near a quart of milk each. Our landlord's name is David Pensinger, his house is 9 miles from Hambg. He seems to be desirous of pleasing & amused us much by his awkward nods & singular remarks. As an instance, when oates were ordered for our horses, he stopped to point out to us the resemblance in sound between the English & German pronunciation of the word—in English oates, in German haaver.

*August 22d.* Several of us having been crowded together in a small, illy ventilated apartment & the weather being exceedingly warm, I slept little on my bed of chaff with one sheet—heard the clock strike every hour of the night & arose between 3 & 4 in the morning.

Jasper's horse is lame & mine is much galled. This is the more unpleasant as we have a rough, tiresome day's ride before us. We have now got among the mountains & expect to travel slowly. Pensinger, after examining Jasper's horse, gravely advised him of what he had no doubt would be a certain cure—"At the next house you stop at, look for a bag & steal the string. This tie round your horse's leg, but be sure that you do it without being seen by anybody." We were 3 hours in going to Reever's, a distance of between 9 & 10 miles—Jasper will scarce find it necessary to purloin a string, as his horse moves as usual. No improvements except a few log huts with small patches of ground cleared around them & every where the women are employed in the fields with the men. Their principal occupation is destroying the timber.

The air seems to be impregnated with a sweet fragrance from the wild flowers of the woods, of which I perceive a variety of kinds. The landlady appeared to exert herself to entertain us. Among other things, she gave us a large dish of fried onions swimming in fat. Here we were overtaken by 3 young men on foot from Philada. bound to Catawessy. They left Reading when we did—an active man on foot will, on a journey, keep pace with a horse.

*August 23d.* The effects of the land jobbing rage which was carried to such an extreme in the years '94 & '95, are yet very visible in the country. I have been told & don't doubt it, that all those immense mountains which we traversed are held by Philadelphians & others who were either speculators themselves, or became the dupes of the times. Many hundred thousand acres, which will probably never be worth a cent, have been sold from half a dollar to two dollars per acre. Englishmen & other Europeans were drawn into the vortex, and became heavy sufferers. About the same period the importations from G. Britain were enormous, credit was of little value & every City dasher could obtain goods & every fellow from the country who could muster enough to get himself a decent suit of clothes procured goods on trust from the citizens. The natural consequences of all this soon followed. Our merchants became insolvent & country traders, being no longer able to pay their debts in mountains, have been ever since groaning under grievous lawsuits. Today I have seen advertizements for the sale of the property of 31 poor shopkeepers, the whole to be sold between the 18th & 31st August, except in two instances.

*August 24th*. The previous rains having swelled the river, we preferred crossing in a boat & rowed to the ferry, a mile above Catawessy. We were set over at the mouth of Fishing Creek, whence we had an agreeable ride on the side of the river & over a level road, to us a rarity. We arrived at Abm. Miller's, 3 miles from the Town, early in the day. In the afternoon were escorted by him to my place on Fishing Creek. The mills, either for want of judgement in their creation, or for want of subsequent care, are going to ruin. They are but 3 years old, but must either be pulled down or will be carried off by the first freshet.

*August 25th*. Pursuing our route up the river, we passed thro' Berwick, 7 miles above Miller's. It is the very picture of poverty & ruin, consisting of about 25 log houses, all fast going to decay. The inhabitants are too poor or too lazy to afford themselves a well & therefore drink the river water. The land around it is level & of a good quality but little cultivated, owing in part, no doubt, to the unhappy dispute between the Connecticut claimants & the Pennsylvanians as to the right of soil. Six miles higher up we came to the residence of Nath. Beach, whose dubious conduct gave rise to our journey—a little observation strengthens our suspicions of his having abused the confidence we placed in him, to our considerable injury & his own aggrandizement.

We shall be compelled to spend a night in his house. Our interview is unpleasant. He has things in dirty trim about him & his wife is a finished slut—poor inducements to a long visit.

*August 26th.* Beach accompanied us this morning on a tour of inspection to some tracts of land on the east of the river, 3 miles from his house. Further conversation confirms our belief of his being an ungrateful knave. Having finished what business we could with him, we were on the eve of parting, but halted to be present at a wedding—15 persons, male & female, suddenly entered the room & seated themselves. The young men were in general without coates, but each had a scarlet coloured wild flower stuck in his hat. The bride & groom were distinguishable from the rest, he by large beaus in his shoes & she by a variegated ribbon carelessly tied round the waist. Beach, who is a Magistrate, performed the marriage ceremony.

At night, we were again at Abm. Miller's. We were treated with attention & hospitality by him & his young pretty wife.

*August 27th.* This morning we began our march homewards, accompanied by Abm. Miller & wife. We had heard of the appearance of an animal in the forest near the town of Northumberland, which occasioned much conversation among the inhabitants & as our route lay in his tract, were not without hopes of seeing him, but in this we were disappointed. He is described as being about five feet high, covered all over with black hair, with the face of an old negro & strongly formed in shape of a human being. Several people have seen him who agree in this description & that he always shows his teeth when they approach too near him, tho' he is not remarkably shy, but suffers them to come within a few yards of him. He is mostly seen erect & when pursued invariably runs in that position. We were told of a large party, mounted & on foot, who attempted his capture. They came so near that one of the horsemen struck him with a whip—taking to his hind legs, he outran them & hid in the woods.

As an animal of this kind is an entire novelty in the wilds of N. America, it naturally excites some curiosity to know whence this solitary creature came. He may be a negro lost in the woods in infancy, or a monkey escaped from some showman. This description of him does not materially differ from that given by naturalists of the ouran outang.

Having taken an expeditious view of Northumberland, we crossed the eastern branch opposite to the town & passed over an island, in our course, which is cultivated & contains 600 acres of prime land.

We have taken lodgings at Lorentz's Tavern. It is crowded, as the County Court is now in session. On looking over A. Kennedy's paper published in this Town, I observe several advertizements for the sale of

property & a Notice from the Sheriff that want of room in the paper
prevents him from inserting many more.

*August 28th.* Most of the day has been occupied in searching records
& in looking into the state of our business in the hands of others. All too
little satisfaction—there is a sad scene of roguery discoverable at every
step.

Near the Court House a crier has been striking off one piece of
property after another & scarce a man seems even to notice what he is
doing. He is mostly by himself, except that once in a while some Lawyer
or the Sheriff gives him a private nudge. I endeavoured to obtain from
him some account of the estates he was selling but had not a single
enquiry answered & the fellow affected to know no more of the matter
than I did myself. I could not help being disgusted at this mockery of
justice—no description of the estates was obtainable even from the Shff.
Seeing this crier afterwards at the Inn, I asked him for an explanation &
how it happened that no one could give the least account of the estates.
"Why Sir," answered the fellow, "the Lawyers understand it very well."
And so it seems they do, for we heard one of them (Cha. Hall), in the
course of his pleading, declare in open Court that he had bought an
estate worth eight thousand Dollars for between 60 & 70 Dollars—and
this was said with but a blush.

Here is a charming field open for corruption, peculation & knavery.
One of our fellow lodgers is a German of the name of Umberhacker,
from near Reading, who comes here to gamble. He is a simple looking
cool-headed sharper. We first met him at Hamburg & today he boasts to
us of having fleeced a young man, in whose company he then was, out of
about 70 Dollars. He prides himself on his tricks & is not backward in
telling us any of his management. He has a coadjutor—they mix in
company, pretend not to be acquainted. A game is proposed, they take
opposite sides & play into each other's hands. They have several race
horses with them & 2 lads as riders who are stationed in another part of
the Town. When a match is made, the boys are brought forward & it is of
no consequence on which side these swindlers bet. The boys understand
their duty & their masters are sure to win.

*September 1st.* This morning we entered Lancaster & tarried here the
day out in conversation with our parents & in the transaction of business. We are told that Lancaster contains upwards of two thousand
houses.

*September 6th.* Robert Morris is again at large. He has taken advantage of the bankrupt law. The am't of the debts proved under the commission awarded against him is no less than three millions of Dollars & yet this enormous sum does not include the whole. Many of his creditors will not incur the expense of proving their claims, from a belief that little will be gained by it.

*September 7th.* The Watering Com. continue to be embarrassed by Roosevelt & Latrobe. Was it not that the public suffer by it I should pity them. They richly merit to be tormented. A few weeks more & my time of service will expire, nor will a trifle tempt me to suffer myself to be re-elected. In four years of servitude in the Corporation, I have endeavoured conscientiously to discharge my duty. I have not been an inactive member of the Council, but latterly my seat has been exceedingly uncomfortable, having been compelled to witness a system of procedure which my judgement condemns & which I have not had it in my power to control.

*September 9th.* Jefferson's conduct is at war with the professions made by him at his inauguration. The Federalists are daily discharged from office, to make room for their political opponents. The Democratic party is gaining ground & the spirit of persecution & intolerance towards all who do not think with them is carried to a lamentable height. It is this unworthy & inhuman conduct which embitters the fairest faith of civil society & renders man a pest to his fellow man. The worst passions are thus roused into action. Malice rankles in the heart; envy, revenge & hatred exert their baneful influence on the mind & those energies which should be devoted to the common benefit are applied to the destruction of the species.

*September 11th.* Some of my friends seem inclined to censure me for my determined resolution to withdraw from Council, but surely it cannot be incumbent on me to remain. That I am supposed to understand the interests of the City is no sufficient argument. Others may acquire the same knowledge by the same application. This mode of reasoning will be strengthened every year. At the next election it will apply with more force than at the present & the longer I serve the longer I may serve. It is insinuated that if I refuse, another field of labour is open into which I must expect to enter.

*September 12th.* My friend the Mayor is desirous of knowing whether I will consent to serve in the State Legislature, expressing that several citizens who have held private meetings to fix on suitable characters have thought of me for that purpose. It required but little reflection to give him an unequivocal answer—no.

*September 14th.* The number of thinking & deliberative individuals in the community is extremely small compared to the aggregate mass. Yet in a popular government like ours, where every citizen has a voice in the councils of the state, a man might be led to expect a commensurate independence of opinion & speech. Probably the human mind is as unfettered in these respects in the U. States as in any portion of the globe. Yet one demagogue of bold front shall lead ten thousand of the common herd, like so many sheep, whither so ever he please, only taking care to supply his docile flock with an occasional & well timed lick of salt. Perhaps the body of mankind are incapable of thinking for themselves & there may therefore be a moral necessity for the active & best informed members of the community to step forward and place themselves at the van. This is however an important post & were it always assumed, as it should be, by virtue, merit & talents, it would be for the happiness of the republic. Unfortunately this is not always the case. Men of solid understanding & worth, aware of the magnitude & high responsibility of the undertaking, are rarely ambitious of possessing it, while others of less genius & honesty rush forward with alacrity & occupy stations which they are unqualified both by nature & education to fill with reputation to themselves or advantage to the public. A Town meeting affords a specious show of consulting the populace, but so far as I have observed, the sovereign people have nothing else to do at them than to approve of measures previously digested & arranged without their knowledge by a few who kindly assume the office of thinking and judging for the rest.

Brother Jasper & his Rebecca left us to return to their home at Baltimore.

*September 16th.* Would it not be the means of checking the increase of dogs to tax them? Would it not be rendering a service to the City? I will try the experiment.

The acc'ts of the Wat. Com. are to be made up. This burden will again rest on my friend Paxson & myself. I expect to find them correctly kept, for Jas. Todd is a good accomptant & he is clerk to the Com. but shall see many things which will only revive chagrin & vexation. One consolation is left, my time of service is nearly closed. Less than a month will rid me of the business & I hope for the first time since I arrived on the stage of manhood to spend one winter in the bosom of my family & in the sweet enjoyments of domestic repose.

*September 17th.* A ride to see our little sons in the country. Polly, her mother, Lydia Johnson & the last named, not the least important personage, our son William, formed the company. On our return took a peep into the Coffer Dam in Schuylkill, in which a great number of men are employed in erecting one of the strong stone piers of the permanent bridge. Poor Wm. lost this sight & was left to snore on a seat in the carriage, unconscious of what was passing.

*September 18th.* The social principle seems to have been implanted in us for the most wise & benevolent purposes. That man who is insensible of its numerous benefits & withdraws from its genial rays to mope out existence within his owns doors, without friends or associates, is his own persecutor & robs himself of the sweetest & best enjoyments of life. The mutual interchange of knowledge, the charms of conversation, the pledges of rational attachments, the exhilirating comfort drawn from the countenance of a friend while yet he speaks, the unutterable satisfaction derived from his approving voice, the generous & disinterested emotions reciprocally imparted & received; all conspire to endear the social intercourse between man & man & prove the possession of a friend to be one of the choicest gifts of heaven.

When from the head of my board I survey a circle of endeared friends whose smiling looks assure me of their happiness, and to the necessary & wholesome viands of the table are added instructive converse, guileness confidence & the unaffected & free interchange of feeling & opinion—I know mine is a situation not to be bartered for the temptations of popular & noisy applause. No, nor for the dazzling throne of an emperor, surrounded by his thousands of slaves.

*September 20th.* Still importuned to consent to serve in the State Legislature. I certainly feel obliged to my fellow citizens for their well meant intentions towards me and I have many & well founded objections to the proposal & hope the present federal members will continue, which will relieve me of those embarrassing importunities.

*September 24th.* The more I see of men in public life, of men who busy themselves on the theatre of politics, the more I am confirmed in my opinion that true happiness does not dwell in their society. Where tumultuous passions rage, there content cannot reside. Men differ on all subjects, but on none more than those which relate to government. Our disputes on that interesting science are frequently conducted with a degree of illiberality & asperity degrading to the understanding & the heart. Show me a zealous & inflamed partizan & I will show you a being racked & tormented by the lust of power & the thirst of revenge, a discontented, embittered & irritable mortal. The mind which is devoted to political intrigue & cabal must be tossed on a tempestuous sea & is in hourly danger of shipwreck.

*September 26th.* Virtue is said to be the basis of a republic. If so, I fear ours is approximating towards its grave. There appears to me to be less sterling honesty in the country than formerly prevailed. The principles inculcated by those sophists who were the pioneers of the French Revolution are certainly gaining ground among us & the moral virtues are giving place to gross depravity, licentiousness & corruption. The diffusion of useful knowledge is the only just corrective, but to this there are many powerful opposing obstacles. The disease is spread abroad, and those who ought to be physicians are themselves infected. I know that the world has ever run riot after something & when the frenzy of the times has a little abated, perhaps this spirit of universal commotion, revolution & disrespect for civil institutions, this leveling propensity, which has deluged the fairest portion of Europe with blood, may subside into a love of order & the promotion of peace & good will on earth. May heaven in mercy to mankind grant this happy issue to the present wanton & barbarous struggle for dominion & power.

*September 30th.* A town meeting has been held, not to deliberate and make a suitable choice of men to be put into office at the ensuing election, but to give their sanction to names privately agreed on by a knot of worthies who hold conclaves to apportion out the honours, duties and labours of public stations—tho' the business is so secretly managed by these kind directors of the public will that the common herd are ignorant of the matter. The conclave consists of some few respectable citizens, united to a larger number of boisterous & busy individuals who, in fact, govern the Federal cause in Philadelphia. To this man, say they, shall be assigned the post of Senator. That shall be a member of Congress, another a member of assembly & he shall be a Councilman. This shall be lord of the manor & that a hewer of wood & drawer of water. Mortifying as it is, this is literally the fact. Men are sought out to fill office not because of their possessing talents or merit, but because the junto will it. I have said that I felt obliged to some of my fellow citizens who wished to advance me in this way. Reflection

produces a contrary conviction. They have not thought of me to promote my interest, but their own. Should I therefore have accepted their invitation, the obligation would be on their side, not on mine.

*October 3d.* An agreeable visit last night at tea & this morning at breakfast from C.B.B. & his friends Bleeker & Doc. Irvin of N. York. Most of the day spent with them in visiting the Alms house, Penna. Hospital & Prison, those sad receptacles of human folly, misery, degradation & vice. My sensations on entering those abodes of the wretched are never unattended with pain. They are so many schools in which the man of flint is taught to pity, to feel; the moralist to reflect; the proud humility; the wicked repentence. All may receive lessons of instruction on the vicissitudes, frailties, sufferings, degeneracies & abasements to which humanity is subject & from which none have patents of exemption.

The Almshouse is less useful to the poor & less beneficial to the community than it might be under a more judicious system of laws. The change of managers is too frequent, nor have they sufficient power to control the conduct & employment of the paupers. Hence the establishment is expensive & ill conducted. The poor should be plentifully provided for, but they should be kept to labour & not suffered to escape from the house until in a capacity to provide for themselves elsewhere. To let loose a drunken abandoned wretch on the public to prowl about, a mere pest to society, when he might be usefully employed & acquiring habits of sobriety & industry, is neither humane nor politic. The frequent changes of managers give to none a fair opportunity of becoming acquainted with his business or of digesting, arranging & pursuing any regular plans of internal economy for the well ordering of the institution.

The Pennsyla. Hospital is a noble establishment & ably conducted. As an asylum for the diseased stranger & a place of security & kind treatment to the raving maniac, it is worthy of that public & private patronage to which it is indebted for its present splendour & usefulness.

The Prison is a glorious monument of the ascendency of reason & benevolence over prejudice & cruelty instead of that sanguinary and exterminating policy which hurled thousands of miserable criminals from the theatre of existence into the awful presence of omnipotence before they were prepared to die. The amelioration of the penal code has opened a bright prospect to the lovers of mercy & justice. Crimes do not go unpunished, but punishments are more equitable & salutary. The unhappy convict has time given for repentence, reflection & reformation, at the same time that society are in some measure remunerated for the injury done them.

There is yet a wide field open for bettering the condition of man. The harvest is great, but the labourers are few. Could men be persuaded to abandon the execrable pursuit of war & to apply their time & talents in the service of godlike humanity, what a heaven would they not make of this ball of earth!

*October 6th.* A trip to the little town of Woodbury in a chair with my late apprentice, Isaac Bryant, to prove my Book entries. It was in the vicinity of this place that my esteemed friend Wm. W. Wilkins was born & died. He was a young man of brilliant genius & had he survived, would doubtless have held a conspicuous rank in society. His ready wit & clearness of judgement, added to the flowery eloquence of his tongue, contributed to render his law knowledge a powerful weapon in his skilful hands. He was an entertaining, instructive companion & valuable friend.

*October 9th.* A considerable portion of my time occupied in examining & checking the acc'ts at the Water Office. They must soon be closed.

*October 12th.* Met the Watering Com. for the last time. A report which I had prepared on the state of the works was well received & ordered to be laid before Councils. This I did not expect, supposing the manner in which I had introduced Latrobe would have occasioned an alteration in the report. Quite the reverse, in fact, for it seems the *Aurora* contains some strictures on the Works, not very palatable to the members. Latrobe is complimented at their expense. They are vexed. Hitherto they have been cowed by this imposture, now they begin to fear the public. Not a man came forward as his champion & that weather cock, J. Parker, veering to the current of the moment, seemed inclined to slink out of the trap in which he has been caught by his own misconduct. Some men can dance to any tune. Councils met when the Com. adjourned. The report was read & followed by a concurrent vote of approbation & thanks. Five hundred copies are ordered to be printed for the use of the citizens. After which our Council adjourned *sine die.*

*October 14th.* Yesterday the general election was held & the Democratic ticket has prevailed in the City, the consequence of which will be

a change of all the police officers in the power of that party, at least this is probable.

*October 16th.* A man walking in our neighbourhood observed a child leaning out of a window in the third story of a house. At the moment he reached the spot, the child fell. He caught it in his arms unhurt, but he is considerably injured.

It is a circumstance of some moment that our new rulers should complete the plan of watering the City, of which there is some doubt. It is lamentable that the spirit of party should infuse itself so powerfully into every public undertaking. This, which in the hands of honest & discreet men might be rendered a great blessing to every description of citizens, will perhaps from sheer opposition united to ignorance & incapacity turn out a public grievance.

Things might have been better managed than they have been, but in the hands of unprincipled, inexperienced & rash men, they are not likely to be improved. A change of a few members of the late Committee would doubtless have been attended with good effects, but the total change of the former members of the Common Council & such a change too, cannot fail to produce mischief.

*October 22d.* Poulson has published the report of the Committee in his paper. The report has given umbrage to the Engineer & this morning's paper contains some very intemperate strictures on it, under his signature.

*October 23d.* So here are other observations published from Latrobe. They are particularly aimed at me & are extremely vindictive. He has taken exception to a note which I added to the report before it was published, simply stating the am't of his original estimate, without further observation. What a foolish man, thus to draw me into a paper controversy. It must greatly redound to his injury, but he has boasted to some of his friends of his talents at writing & imagines they will give him a superiority over me. He will find himself greatly mistaken. I am at least capable of detailing plain facts & such as will puzzle even this crafty, vain & sapient mortal to overturn.

Miller & Parker, I am informed, make themselves very busy against me. They also may have reason to wish they had acted with more justice & precaution. The former has written to Latrobe with intention to injure me & has published the Letter. Surely this proud Scotsman has not taken time to reflect on what he is about. I can & will make him ashamed of his conduct.

*November 4th.* No news from my sapient antagonist for some days past. He has retired to draw breath & is, I am told, gone to Susquehanna. It is a very convenient time to have business in the country.

*November 5th.* The genius of Susquehanna has inspired my talented adversary, but she must have been in doleful humour, for her hero seems to have made his dying speech & my friend Poulson has this morning given it to the world. It is a poor, lame performance & seems not to merit a reply.

*November 7th.* In mixing with the citizens, I cannot but be gratified with the marks of respect & applause which are bestowed on me. It indicates at least that I have not been in the wrong.

It is certainly a desirable thing to have the approbation of the public in a public concern. I know that a clear conscience needs not the support of popular encomium, but when to a self approving mind is added the disinterested commendations of the most respectable part of the community, it is an agreeable circumstance & such a one as no man possessed of common feelings can without the most ridiculous vanity affect to despise.

*November 12th.* This day brother Israel was married to Margaret Cooper at Friends meeting house, at the corner of Market & Second Streets.

*November 13th.* At twelve last night a smart shock of an earthquake was experienced in this City. It made a rumbling noise like the rattling of a carriage over the pavements, but did no injury as far as I can learn this morning.

*November 14th.* The Councils have appointed a new Committee to superintend the water works. One of its members, who was a member of the former committee, has called on me to ask information on several subjects which, had he been more attentive to his duty, he would have known something about. He ought to be ashamed of his ignorance.

*November 21st.* Brother Israel & wife left this day for Baltimore. In the afternoon there was a smart fall of snow, the first we have had this season.

The papers announce the important information of peace having been recently concluded between France & England.

*November 27th.* Granted a Letter of Attorney to Abraham Miller of Northumberland County to lease my lands in that county & the counties of Luzerne & Northampton. Gave him three patents to have recorded.

*November 30th.* My business at N.Y. requiring my presence, I set out this morning for that place accompanied by my friend C.B.B.

Took passage in the Swiftsure, a new line, which takes the Old York Road. Were disappointed, expected good roads & good inns & found both bad. From Ringo's to Summerset, 20 miles, passed after night, very dark, ran against a post & broke the tongue of the carriage. Detained till another was sent for & soon after were driven against a waggon in the road, which was not discoverable in the dark. No material injury sustained.

*December 1st.* Up & on our way before day. We travelled 25 miles to Springfield before breakfast. It was quite too far on a cold morning & the fare miserable. Crossed the North River & went to Little's Hotel in Broad Street before dark. Don't like the looks & airs of the Landlord. No doubt he is an avaricious churl.

*December 2d & 3d.* Spent in coming to terms with E. Whitehead. Have great reason to regret my connection with the late house of C.W. & Co. Shall suffer heavily. Reduced to a certainty that I shall lose some thousands of Dollars & can't see how to prevent future & perhaps heavier deprivations. It is a severe trial of my fortitude. I had calculated on ease & retirement for the improvement of health & understanding & may be compelled again to resort to the drudgery of business for a living. Have been most cruelly & grossly deceived & so far from ever having received any profits from the co-partnership, have never received one farthing, but in addition to the capital which I originally furnished, have been under the necessity of advancing large sums to pay their debts & may be forced to pay others of their contracting. Had I been informed by the house of the true situation of their affairs in time, I might have prevented some portion of the present evil.

*December 5th.* Hear much conversation on the subject of a duel lately fought in this place between a person of the name of Eckhardt & a son of General Hamilton, a youth of 19, in which the latter was killed.

Detestable, wicked & disastrous as is the practice of duelling, Eckhardt goes unpunished & struts the streets unblushingly.

Shame on the state of manners & religion which can tolerate & even encourage so foul a deed.

At Little's there is a person of the name of Miller from Boston who lately killed another in similar combat. By his own confession, he cannot deserve a better name than that of a deliberate murderer. The other had the first fire & missed his object. Miller then said, "If I shoot, I shall kill him." He then raised his pistol, coolly took aim & put a bullet through the heart of his adversary.

If two old women should happen to come to blows & one of them die soon after & tho' a physician should declare he saw no marks of violence on the body of the deceased which could have occasioned her death, yet the survivor shall be forthwith apprehended, tried & sentenced to death as a murderer. This fact has literally occurred at Baltimore, within a few weeks past.

Until this day paid no friendly visits. Today I paid several. Dined with Jn. Murry, Jr., where I saw Martha Rowth & her husband Richard. I received my introduction to them in the order in which I have placed them & it is that in which nature has placed them.

An elderly friend entered; he called to conduct a young woman to a packet about to sail up the North River to Poughkeepsie. I observed that the wind was untoward. That, he said, he did not regard—his sloop could sail against wind & tide & in fact if the wind blew very hard & right ahead, he would soon make his port. So as it blew hard, it seemed to make little difference to him from what quarter the wind came. His sloop must indeed by a very extraordinary sailor.

My opinion of Little has been fully verified. He is a rude, ignorant, selfish fellow whose object appears to be not the comfortable, easy accommodation of his guests, but to overreach them whenever he can. Have had but little intercourse with him & hope never to have any more.

Have contrived to spend more of my time with W. Johnson than with any other person with whom I had not business. His many good qualities entitle him to my respect & friendship.

*December 6th.* Breakfasted with John Keese, to whom I formally had an introductory line from my friend Inskeep. He lives in a sumptuous stile in his new & elegant house in Wall Street. He is a man of some distinction & a very affable & well bred gentleman.

Took tea with John Brown, printer & stationer.

My effort to cast off chagrin has succeeded so far that I begin to breathe & think with more freedom than I have for a few days past. It is folly to forestall evil, yet we have not always the command of ourselves & are, moreover, sometimes assailed with such apparent force as to defy resistance. But a man should never despair so long as the smallest glimpse of hope remains. In fact, despair under any cirumstances should never be indulged. It depresses us of our best energies & renders life a torment. Besides that, religion & true philosophy teach us never to repine at inevitable evils.

*December 7th.* Dined with Wm. Dunlap in company with Wm. Johnson & C.B. Brown & Richard Alsop, the Connecticut Bard. Richard is rather boorish in his appearance, awkward in his motions & unforbidding in his manner. His countenance is strongly marked & expressive rather of sober good sense than of the exquisite sensibility & fire of the poet. He was in the midst of his friends & gave way to hilarity & unaffected conversation, but I could not perceive any of that elegant sentiment & delicate refinement for which his high polished & charming verse is so remarkable.

He is of the middle size, nervous & well formed, dark visaged, round faced & has a heavy brow. His hair is black & abundant. His eye by no means indicates uncommon genius.

In the evening we adjourned to Doctor Miller's in Dey Street. His brother Samuel has lately been married to a daughter of the late Jona. Sergeant Esq. of Philadelphia.

One of my evenings was spent by invitation in the Literary Club at Wm. Johnson's. The members meet weekly & take each other's houses in rotation. The subjects of their deliberations & speculations are such as accident or choice may direct & are discussed without the order of regular debate. It is a mere conversation party, having for its object the cultivation of friendship & the mutual interchange of knowledge. The motives are laudable & the effects will be advantageous to the individuals & the community. Most of the members are now separately or jointly engaged in useful labours for the press. Doctors Miller & Mitchell are the authors of the *Medical Repository.* The Parson & W. Johnson are separately employed each in the compilation of an extensive work. W. Coleman is editor of the *New York Evening Post* which is very extensively patronized. And the *American Review* is conducted by the members at large.

C.B.B. has given birth to several works of the imagination & contributes very liberally to the *Review.* The same may be said of others.

A lady in N.Y. sent to Russia for a muff & has obtained one of fur at the immoderate price of fifteen hundred Dollars.

*December 8th.* Set out on my return, leaving C.B.B. in N. York. A blustering west wind rendered it disagreeable crossing. A young woman fainted through fright & had a succession of fits at landing. Roads are hard frozen & rough. Felt no inconvenience from cold, tho' the air was keen, having among other warm clothing provided myself with a pair of large cloth socks lined with wool, most comfortable appendages. Had my coach & four, most of the way to Brunswick, to myself, where I lodged comfortably.

*December 9th.* Breakfasted at Princeton. Just before entering the Town we met a stage going to N.Y. The driver halted & asked if we could take a passenger; being answered in the affirmative, a fashionably dressed, handsome young woman entered my coachee. She was evidently quite sick & having, according to the rage of the times, scarce any clothing on, at least nothing but thin muslin, she appeared to be almost perished with the cold. Humanity compelled me to lend her my cloak, which she readily accepted & retained for the remainder of the journey. She crossed the North River just before me, was taken sick & continuing to grow worse, when she reached Princeton, she had resolved on returning to N.Y.

She appeared destitute of friend, advisor or protector, was very handsome & genteel. She seemed scarcely to know the object of her journey at this inclement season & her whole deportment & conversation was studiously mysterious.

I fancied her to be an unfortunate, but the doubtfulness of her character forbid other attention to her than such as her forlorn condition from a man of feeling. I could not prevail on her to disclose her history. Her mind was in trouble & she continued quite ill the whole day.

We reached the City after dark & having procured a man to carry home her trunk, we parted.

*December 15th.* It is to be expected that in all parties men will be found who, guided by no principles of patriotism & justice, are ever ready to sacrifice their opponents under a pretext of patriotism, but in no instance have I before seen this abominable spirit of persecution

carried to such shameful lengths as at the present juncture of affairs in the U. States.

The party which has gained the ascendancy evince a degree of asperity towards the friends of the former administration of our country which if persisted in must provoke retaliation whenever the sufferers shall again come into power, which must one day take place.

No man who is a Federalist is allowed to hold an office. They are everywhere displaced, not merely such as hold offices under the General Government, but in the State Governments, wherever Democracy has gained the ascendancy over Republicanism & even in Municipal stations.

Every officer in the appointment of the new Mayor (Matthew Lawler) has been turned out to give place to the creatures of the reigning party. Merit, talent & long service avail nothing. Much irritation is the immediate effect & consequences highly detrimental to the public weal must ensue. Moreover, with this uncertain tenure of office, good men will scarcely be induced to abandon other pursuits to enter the public service, not knowing how soon a change of politics may disarrange all their plans & compel them to return to private life & the establishment of new habits of business.

*December 18th.* It has been told to me that Latrobe says he means to sue me for injuring his character. I rather think, however, that he is not quite so great a fool. Completely foiled in his paper controversy, his only resource must be in making a bustle in private circles. If his conduct comes to be scrutinized before a court of justice, it will not mend matters.

*December 19th.* Attended an interview between a committee of the Society of Friends & five Indian chiefs of the Miami & Potawatomi Nations. Some of the tribes of these nations, especially those who inhabit the countries of the Miamis on the Lakes, have as yet had scarce any intercourse with the white people. They own a large tract of about 150 by 250 miles & are said to be very numerous.

The Chiefs are on the their way to Congress, with whom they have business. The Little Turtle, who is the acknowledged chieftain of the whole & whom I have seen in this place on former occasions, spoke at some length. His principal object was to inform the Committee that certain articles or implements of husbandry which they had delivered to him were distributed among his people & that some of them had been used. He returned thanks for them in the name of his people & solicited the further aid & support of the Committee.

The Five Medals, so called from his wearing that number of silver pieces suspended from his nose, ears, &c. & who holds the 2nd rank in the confederacy, spoke next; he had little more to say than to echo the talk of his colleague, of whom he spoke in terms of high respect & mentioned him to be "by far the greatest man among them."

They spoke standing. Their motions were not those of a trained orator, but were energetic & very expressive. It was these people who gained such a decisive victory over the American Army commanded by General St. Clair. The Little Turtle headed the Indians on that memorable & sanguinary occasion. In a former interview he mentioned that his people prepared sugar from the juice of the maple. Being asked by one of the Com. how they obtained kettles for the purposes, he answered sarcastically that the unfortunate affair of Gen. St. Clair had furnished them with "a large supply of camp kettles, which answered very well."

Their interpreter is an illiterate man & I imagine does not do justice to the sentiments & expressions of his employers, tho' he appears to be expert at his business. The Chiefs seem desirous to have agriculture & the arts of civilization introduced into their country, but from the remoteness of some of the tribes & the wide range of hunting grounds which they possess, they expressed a well grounded fear that it would be very difficult to effect the object.

The Little Turtle once delivered a lengthy talk on this subject, at which I was present & which discovered a man of observation, reflection & acuteness. His person has nothing very striking in it. He is middle sized, has a penetrating eye, the countenance of a savage & the grave cast of a statesman.

The Five Medals is a much stouter man & has the air & aspect of a leader. His figure is prepossessing & his features are indicative of considerable powers of mind.

*December 24th.* It is said of the much celebrated Henry the 4th of France that a person of distinction once entered his apartment & found him in the attitude of a horse, galloping round the room with one of his sons on his back. The King stopped to ask his guest if he were a father & on being answered in the affirmative said, "Then I will continue my exercise & need make no apology." I was always prepossessed in favour of that monarch from the reading of this simple anecdote, because it

accorded so well with my humour. There is a solid pleasure in these innocent & child-like recreations, which the sternness of proud philosophy may condemn & into the spirit & humour of which the bachelor cannot enter but which, notwithstanding their apparent folly, I would not exchange for the pompous & splendid exhibitions with which politicians tickle their fancy & statesmen astound the gaping multitude on public occasions.

My little boys & I have many a sportive round, while the agile feat & side shaking laugh, the noisy exultation & newly tried prank add a singular zest to the frolic, unburdening the heavy heart of its cares, its anxieties & pains & infusing into it emotions which a father knows how to enjoy.

*December 26th.* Some women in the vicinity of Boston have made a cheese & presented it to President Jefferson as a token of respect & which on account of its uncommon size has been called the Mammoth Cheese. It is said to weigh twelve hundred & seventy five pounds.

# 1802

*January 6th.* The vaccine innoculation is gaining currency in Philadelphia & will no doubt in a very short time take precedence of the variolous, if it does not entirely banish that dreadful disease from among us. The happy effects of this discovery, which is ascribed to Doctor Jenner of England, are very considerable & extensive. Dr. Lettsom, in a late publication, mentions that thirty six thousand persons die annually in G. Britain & Ireland of the small pox. The new or Jennerian system will most probably prevent that mortality, it being asserted that not one, out of the hundreds of thousands to whom the infection has been communicated, has died of it. This may therefore be ranked among the greatest & most useful discoveries of the present times.

*January 13th.* One Lewis du Pre, a gardener in South Carolina, has announced his discovery of perpetual motion & made an application to Congress in which he says that "It has pleased Almighty God, for purposes most extensively benevolent, to discover to me the principles of the perfect motion, vulgarly called perpetual motion.

"I therefore trust that your justice & republican patriotism will induce you to take the subject in consideration & as speedily as possible obtain from the critical casket, where it remains deposited, the precious bounty where to effect which you hereby possess a promise of the cordial cooperation of your real friend & fellow citizen." Signed Lewis du Pre & dated 5th day of perpetual motion.

This singular production was presented to the House of Representatives on the 1st & referred to a committee.

*January 14th.* The measles are very prevalent in the City & its neighbourhood. My sons Henry, Francis & William have just had them.

*January 27th.* Moderate exercise in the open air occasions perspiration & fire in the parlour is oppressive. I sweat today from walking slowly in the streets without a surtout. There is no uncommon sickness in the City or country, except that some symptoms of jail fever have appeared in our prison, arising as is believed from the crowded state of the apartments alloted to vagrants & persons confined before trial.

*January 31st.* Perhaps no city of equal size ever had a Legislature so profoundly stupid & silly as that which at present composes the Common Council.

It seems as if extraordinary pains had been taken to select the most ignorant for the office. Their debates furnish high sport for the citizens, who flock in crowds to their meetings as to a farce or a pantomine & without exaggeration, had an equal number been collected to exhibit feats of buffoonery to the spectators, they could scarce have succeeded better than do these blockheads. Unless checked by the Select Council they must do mischief from sheer ignorance & folly. Whatever defects the members may possess, they are not chargeable with those of taciturnity & diffidence.

All are orators & so eager is each to be heard that 3 or 4 frequently rise at once to make motions & to speak to them.

Their president, who is a good specimen of the rest, seems to be in a perpetual daze & finds it hard work to preserve order among his Democratic brethren. As an instance of his ideas on the subject of order I might mention one which is of a piece with the rest.

A resolution came in from the Select Council for the appointment of a committee to do a certain piece of business on which he put the question, "Will the council agree to the resolution & then appoint the committee or will they agree to appoint the committee first & then adopt the resolution?" He could not himself decide this difficult affair & as his colleagues were equally unprepared to determine it, they wisely concluded on its postponement to gain time for reflection. One of these wise acres has published a scheme—the result of their joint reflections, or of several of them—for completing the water works by raising a tax on a part of the citizens to the exoneration of others. It is so fraught with absurdity & injustice as to scarcely merit notice, but as it may, if not resisted, be of serious import, I have attacked & exposed its principles by a stroke of ridicule in Poulson's paper, under the signature of "Another Schemer."

*April 28th.* A throng day. Henry & Francis were dispatched by 5 in the morning by the Lancaster Stage to Joshua Maule's. One servant goes by the West Chester Stage to Jn. Smedley's, where our William was sent last week. Another takes her departure by another route to the country & I have taken passage for myself & Polly in the Baltimore Stage tomorrow, whither we expect to be accompanied by several of our friends.

*April 29th.* Our company departed by 6 A.M. It commenced to rain while we breakfasted at Chester & continued during the whole day. A crazy & shattered vehicle in which we rode in the forenoon added little to the pleasure of the jaunt. Every few miles something gave way & we were in danger of being left on the road. By good luck we arrived safe at Newport where we were agreeably relieved by a new & convenient carriage, after having been well wet by the leakage of the other.

Dined at the Head of Elk, a place rendered memorable by the landing of the British troops prior to the Battle of Brandywine & the capture of Philadelphia.

When we reached Susquehanna opposite to Havre de Grace, night came on & the girls had a disagreeable tramp thro' rain & mud from the Tavern to the boat, whither we were left to grope our way without lamp or guide. A gentle breeze soon wafted us to the opposite shore where we found good accommodations for the remainder of the night.

The ground plot of this Town is extensive & it appears to possess advantages for commerce. It does not, however, enjoy much consequence at present, notwithstanding its vicinity to the Chesapeake which laves its eastern bounds. A few scattered houses, perhaps about one hundred, are the precursors of its future greatness.

*April 30th.* As the stage waggons do not pass the river, we were furnished with a carriage on this side. It was so small that, to procure seats, we were obliged to sit in each other's laps. It had but two seats, exclusive of the driver's, on each of which 3 persons could crowd. As we were eight in number, we could not think ourselves well used by the proprietors of the line, who should not engage more passengers than their carriages are calculated to accommodate.

In approaching Baltimore we were frequently gratified with extensive prospects of the bay & the high country adjacent to it. The falls on two branches of the Gun Powder, which we crossed, were picturesque & romantic. We arrived at the metropolis of Maryland at noon. Polly & myself are to make our home with brother Israel & his wife. Ann Shoemaker & Kitty Robinson, with brother Jasper & Rebecca.

*May 1st.* Delivered to the Baltimore Bank the money committed to my trust for that purpose by Jona. Smith, Cashier of the Bank of Penna. & Henry Drinker, Jr., Cashier of the Bank of N. America, to the latter of whom I have written on the subject. The whole sum conveyed by me is about one hundred thousand dollars.

Walked with brother Jasper to the observatory, which is on an eminence on the western side of the basin. It is an useful establishment for commercial purposes. Three masts designed to represent those of a ship, a schooner & a brig are planted in the ground, which reflect signals for

vessels in the bay. About 15 miles below, a telegraph is placed, which gives the first signal of the approach of a vessel. This signal is reflected by the observatory & that again by counter emblems fixed in the merchant's room in Bryden's Coffee House.

By these means it is frequently known to the consignee or owner that his vessel is in the bay 2 or 3 days before she comes to the point, where large vessels discharge, as there is not a sufficiency of water for any other than small craft in the basin.

*May 5th.* My old acquaintance Benj. Dearborn of Boston is now in Baltimore endeavouring to establish the sale & reputation of his "patent balance," a useful improvement for weighing with accuracy & expedition. In appearance his scale resembles the steelyard, but it possesses mathematical differences which give it the free & correct vibration of a well adjusted scale beam of the common kind, without being as expensive & cumbersome. He is on a tour thro' the principal towns in the U.S. & carries letters to the heads of departments in Washington, whither he means shortly to go. These letters recommend him in warm terms as a man of genius & good character & from what I have seen of him, he merits the distinction which has been conferred on him.

*May 6th.* The soil in the vicinity of Baltimore is generally sterile & naturally poor. That which is directly adjacent to the road leading to it from Philada. is, from what I have seen, the most so.

I am persuaded that there are but few good farmers & dairy maids in this neighbourhood. Slavery has been an evil to this as well as to other countries wherever it has existed. Men accustomed to lord it over their fellows & to exact of them, with rods steept in blood, the most brutish drudgery, were not likely to become practical farmers & husband-men—and wretches doomed to never-ending toil & stripes never would make economical cultivators or improve in any of the mechanical arts. A man who sees no end to servitude but in death, who receives no benefit of his own labours, has no inducement to make improvements. He who will not himself labour & who trusts to his Overseer to make his slaves do it for him cannot hope to have his land tilled to the best advantage.

Notwithstanding the sudden & deplorable decline of business in this place, rents continue extravagantly high, I think at least 5 per cent above those of Philada., yet building materials are considerably cheaper. Bricks are here 4½ to 5 Dollars a thousand—in Philada. 6½ to 7 Dollars.

Marketing is also in general dear. Good fresh butter from ⅜ to ½ Dollar per lb. Vegetables are abundant & very fine & tho' higher, do not seem to be scarcer than with us. Fish are also dearer & not more plentiful. Beef is of a good quality in common but the meat brought to market by country people is poor, badly managed & in some respects filthy. It is not sold by the pound but piece & miserable as it is, brings a round price. Their manner of exposing it for sale is disgusting—a dirty cloth is thrown on the pavement outside of the market house; on this, joints of veal & mutton are thrown in jumbled confusion & without much regard to cleanliness. The vendors of these articles are mostly either hirelings or slaves & therefore little better could be expected of them.

In Philada. the farmers, their wives & daughters stand in market with their provisions & no one thinks them disgraced by the office. It does one good to walk thro' the Jersey Market & to observe the spruce appearance of the blooming Quaker girls who came there to sell the various products of their industry. The nicely rigged, bucksome lass from Chester Co. with her butter wrapped in cloths as white as the driven snow & stored in a vessel as carefully scoured as if to serve at a wedding is a sight of which, however grateful, you would in Baltimore look in vain.

The butchers & a few others who are accommodated under shelter of the Market House, which is a commodious, well constructed building, make a decent appearance, at least much more so than the rest. Marketing must here be done by sunrise or the citizen will find his choice of some articles very scant.

Baltimore is a hot, dusty place, owing to the sandy light soil on which it stands & to the high banks which are in its rear. Most of the streets are roomy & paved, but a little more attention in laying them out at right angles would have been found convenient to the disposition of the buildings, some of which are necessarily cut into shapes that render them less useful & pleasant than if they were otherwise fixed.

The houses are mostly built of brick in the centre of the City & have a substantial, comfortable appearance. Hacks are stationed in the principal streets & you may have one of them at a beck & a moderate charge.

*May 10th.* A letter from the once celebrated beauty & poet, Nancy Emlen, now the plain & pious Ann Mifflin. On the afternoon preceding our departure from Phila. she came to pay us a friendly visit & in the course of conversation gave me some accounts of the extraordinary young woman who has lately arrived from England, on a volunteer errand, to teach a shanty school for the blacks in the city of Washington. While a school mistress in her own country, several years ago, she first conceived the idea & apprehended her duty to consist in carrying it into effect. Her relations, who were Methodists, disapproved of her schemes & for 12 months she suffered imprisonment from them as a lunatic.

Her zeal did not abate & when, as she supposed, the proper period for carrying it into effect had arrived, she embarked on board of a vessel & was landed at New York. Among other difficulties which she encountered before she left her native country, she dissolved an engagement which she had entered into with a captain of a vessel to become his wife. This was a severe trial to her. He appears to have been strongly attached to her & was much affected at the idea of a separation. He offered to abandon his profession & accompany her. This she would not permit.

He tendered her pecuniary assistance, knowing her to be poor, but she would accept nothing. She had travelled considerable distance to effect the interview. They had long been betrothed to each other & she loved him. But avowing no other motive for her conduct than an irresistible conviction of duty, she steadily persisted in her plans & bid him a final farewell.

The novelty of this undertaking had awakened my curiosity & from some expressions which fell from me, Ann has entertained an idea that I could be servicible to her friend, Dorothy Ripley, in furthering her views. She left this place a few days ago & is now at Washington.

There is something extremely novel & interesting in this affair. That a single female should abandon her country & her friends & travel 3000 miles to establish a school for the instruction of negroes & that, too, in a place where she can expect to meet with few congenial spirits—in short, in a place which is almost a wilderness, presented a spectacle rare & wonderful indeed.

In search of motives, I can discover none but such as are pure, Christian & heavenly. I hope her zeal has been tempered with wisdom, but as I have had no opportunity of conversing with her, I cannot pretend to form a correct judgement of the real utility & practicability of her scheme. Those who may be inclined to think it utopian must nevertheless admire the benevolence which gave rise to it & the perseverence with which it has been so far pursued.

Nothing could be more unexpected to me than a letter from Ann Mifflin; this excellent woman's injunction to me to burn her letter after perusal, must not be obeyed. The plea that it was written when she was half asleep won't do. If her sleeping moments produce sentiments so judicious & sensible, her waking hours must give birth to manifold excellencies.

I fear that in this instance she has mistaken her object. It is scarcely probable that I can be of any solid advantage to her friend, of whose talents, acquirements & opinions I have not sufficient knowledge to enable me properly to comprehend & appreciate her apparently romantic undertaking at a period when the slaves exhibit continual symptoms of insurrections & their masters view with so much scrutinizing jealousy the operations of all who, in any respect, interest themselves on behalf of the blacks.

Filled a sheet to my friend C.B.B.

*May 11th.* I find, on inquiry, that Dorothy Ripley has left Washington & returned either to Philada. or N.Y. I am told that in all her movements, even on trivial subjects, she professes to be directed by revelation from Heaven; truly then, she professes much.

When I first undertook to keep a journal, I promised myself some instruction from it, nor have I been disappointed. It makes some amends for a treacherous memory & furnishes me with some profitable opportunities of conversing with myself, of which I have frequent need. I can turn to my memorandum book as to a well tried confidential friend & speak out the unaffected language of my soul without fear or distrust, knowing my accuser & my judge. It is, to be sure, a very trifle. What of that? It is my own & I will love it as I would my brat, were he as ill-shaped as a monkey. I have laid down no regular plan & I follow none. My diary is like myself, a chequered maze out of which charity may extract a little good, but where the hawk eye of criticism & the penetrating glance of philosophy will discover much alloy, stubble & trash.

Well, as I turn over the pages, I present myself with a faithful mirror in which I perceive & may contemplate my own sad deficiencies to advantage. Many of them, it is true, are as with the hand of nature, deeply & indelibly impressed on my character & attached to my existence. For these, I trust, I am not accountable. Others, I am sensible, proceed from heedless neglect or headstrong folly. For these I often & deservedly endure the lash of self condemnation & regret. Turning from the dark shades of the portrait with blushing confusion, I resolve to become wiser & better & then straightway fall into the same errors & mischances as before.

We are like men groping their way in the dark, going they know not whither nor for what object.

Men who are accustomed to a circumscribed sphere of action & who study human nature in a closet are, almost of necessity, prone to bigotry & form very erroneous conceptions of man.

The observation applies to physics as well as morals. Travellers are not infrequently led into mistakes from this circumstance. The society of which I am a member is the best in the world, the hill in my neighbourhood affords the finest prospect in the world, the public inn in our Town is the best in the world, men are more robust & well proportioned & women more beautiful & accomplished, the horses are larger & stronger, the cows give better milk, the birds sing better, the water is better, it is not so hot, it is not so cold, the parson preaches better, the cocks get up sooner in the morning & crow louder & the hens lay more eggs & hatch more chickens in our country than in any other country in the universe. This, says my guide, is acknowledged by everybody far & near to be the largest, tallest, straightest tree that ever grew & perhaps I do not travel fifty miles before I see a larger, taller, straighter.

Philosophers of toadstool growth who regulate & adjust the laws of matter & motion with a pair of steelyards in the chimney corner can reason down the most stubborn facts & tell to a hair how long a grape vine can & will grow in any region of the globe.

*May 13th.* Rec'd a letter from my much valued friend T. Paxson. It contains very unflattering accounts of his Ruth, whose illness seems rather to have increased since we left home. I fear we shall lose this most excellent woman. My soul deeply & fervently sympathizes with her husband in the distress which her condition imposes on him. I feel for him. I feel for myself. I cannot bear the idea of parting with this dear friend whose existence is so near to my heart. The idea of losing for ever, her, from whose instructing & enchanting conversation I have so long been accustomed to draw rivers of delight, operates like a harrow on my feelings & in spite of my exertions, forces the tear of sorrow from my eye. Could my prayers save her from the opening tomb, long, long should she survive, a blessing & comfort to her friends.

Under trials like these, how heart consoling is the thought of meeting those whom we dearly love on earth in those regions of eternal felicity in the heavans, where foul disease shall no more disturb the full tide of exquisite enjoyment, nor the pitiless hand of death again tear us from each other. Could I but feel a certainty that this will be the happy lot of kindred spirits, it would have a tendency to reconcile my stubborn nature to many a bitter cup which the frailties of mortality & the freaks of fortune have forced me to drink.

That there is a world in which the souls of the just shall dwell with their father & their God, we have many convincing proofs. My mind revolts at the idea of an everlasting slumber in the grave. No, it cannot be—this essence which animates my frame & stimulates my thoughts cannot be doomed to perish with the body to all eternity. It must survive, but in what shape or on what conditions relatively to those whom it feels to be its sister spirits on earth, is hidden & doubtless wisely hidden from the keenest researchers of philosophy & human penetration.

*May 14th.* Wrote a letter of condolence to my suffering & anxious friend T.P. in reply to his affecting epistle. I know not whether it will do good or harm, for I have given a latitude to my feelings which I found it difficult to suppress. I meant to speak the balmy language of comfort to his sorrows & the free expressions of my own weakness may add to his dejection. I would do good if I knew how. I cannot speak without emotion on a subject in which my sensibility is so deeply interested & while I wish to steal upon him with a countenance brightened with hope, I fear that the gloomy presentiments which rankle in my heart will betray my own dreadful forebodings & the true state of my thoughts & apprehensions.

*May 17th.* Accompanied by Polly & sister Peggy, took passage at 6 for Washington. Elkridge Landing, an old place of inspection for tobacco, very much esteemed under the name of Maryland Kitefoot, is a poor looking spot of forty, fifty or more wooden buildings. It is on the Patapsco, over which we were ferried in a boat. We dined at Bladensburg, a small town of forty or fifty indifferent buildings on the eastern branch of the Potomac.

When we arrived at the City of Washington, we continued to pursue our route to Alexandria, where we arrived an hour before sunset.

The country, with the exception of a few farms, is very poor along the post road from Susquehanna to Alexandria. It is uneven, consisting mostly of sandy dales & gravelly hills & but thinly inhabited. There is little to be seen but scrub timber & shrubbery. The senses were nevertheless frequently regaled with the sweet odoriferous wild flowers with which the carpet of nature is so beautifully enamelled at this fine

season. Among others, the wild honeysuckle, the violet & blue lupin frequently appear.

They will furnish a much better & more plentiful table in Connecticut for 25 cents than is provided on this road for 75. After crossing the Potomac at Georgetown our olfactory nerves were greatly annoyed for the rest of the way by the smell of asafoetida, which had been given to the horses, as the driver said, to keep them from catching the distemper. It has been so cold & blustering all day as to render a surtout necessary.

*May 19th.* We have rambled over the major part of Alexandria & are much pleased with it. The site & plan give it much of the appearance of Philada. The streets are laid out at right angles, 2 of them are 50, two 100, all the rest are 66 feet wide. There is but one public square, about 350 by 250 feet, on one side of which a building is erected, the lower part serving as a market house & the upper, as a place for holding Court. It is 2 stories high. The rest is planted with trees.

The principal streets are paved & the modern buildings are mostly brick & neat. Those of the old Town (which lie on the north adjoining the present City) are wood, as well as many others. By the late census, Alexandria contains five thousand or so inhabitants, 500 less than it did in 1799, so says G.D., an assessor.

From the accidental circumstance of his having been seated at the table with his driver, Count Liancour (it ought to have been Lying Cur) has ascertained that in America, it is the practice for the driver of the public stage to eat with the passengers. Were I disposed to be equally shrewd, I might say that Alexandria is a cold, stormy, windy place, for ever since I came, I have found it convenient to follow the example of many of the inhabitants & wear my surtout, altho' the sun has shone almost all day. When in the house, we sit by a fire.

Rents are low in this place. A tolerable house & store in a good stand for business may be had at 200 or 250 Dollars.

The merchants of Alexandria have been grievous sufferers by French spoilations & trade here participates largely in the general languor to which American commerce has been latterly reduced. Flour is one of the principal articles of exportation & of this they have shipped from 80 to 90 thousand barrels in a year.

No curfew here, as in N. England, announces the hour of nightly retirement to the inhabitants, but the watchmen have a singular practice, before they disperse on duty for the night. They blow a number of horns together, in a steady, soft strain which strongly resembles the sweet melody of an aeolian harp, at a little distance from the Court House where they assemble.

Gadsby keeps a good inn & is a civil, obliging man. This is the country for bread, prepared of Indian corn & at the house we are furnished with an agreeable small cake made with that meal mixed with a suitable proportion of eggs & milk & beaten into a batter.

*May 20th.* This morning has been taken up with a visit to Mt. Vernon. We left our inn at 8 & arrived in about an hour & a half. The road, like all which we have seen in this country, is rough & badly attended, tho' a small part is pretended to be a turnpike & if large holes of mud & water in the centre & deep ruts & sidling banks be the true indications of a turnpike, then this deserves the name. A few negro huts & their ragged inhabitants, a small number of cultivated fields bearing miserable crops of wheat & rye & forests of crooked, knotty timber were the principal objects that saluted our eyes as we passed this dreary road, until we came in view of Mount Vernon, which suddenly bursts upon the sight at the distance of half a mile from the mansion as you emerge from a thick wood. The river is not seen after leaving the high grounds back of Alexandria till it is met with in front of the house, a space of between 8 & 9 miles of land.

The pleasure which we had anticipated in this visit was greatly diminished by the illness of Lady Washington. She is confined to her bed & from the account given of her by Doctor Craik, the family physician, has not many days to survive. This gentleman received us with attention, conversed sensibly & affably & politely conducted us round the premises. He evinced a disposition to render our visit as agreeable to us as circumstance would admit.

Doctor Craik is 74 years old & resides in Alexandria. He was sent for on the first indisposition of Lady Washington & has remained at Mount Vernon ever since, as she will not consent to his leaving her. She has been sick for a fortnight. He was the old friend & companion of her late illustrious husband & served with him in Braddock's army.

This venerable physician was with the General in his dying moments & supported him in his arms as he expired. He spoke of this circumstance with tender emotion & of the character of his departed friend with high veneration. His respect for the widow is little less enthusiastic. He tells me that she is advanced of 70 & has never left home since the death of the General.

Her time is spent principally in domestic cares. She is very industrious

& fond of reading & knitting. To visitants she is affable, hospitable & attentive. The death of her husband affected her very sensibly. She has not entered either his study or the apartment in which he died since the removal of his corpse, nor can any entreaty induce her to change the lodging room which she then selected for herself in the attic story immediately under the roof & which is a small, inconvenient, uncomfortable apartment. She now promises Doctor Craik that should she recover from the present attack, she will consent to lodge in some other part of the house more airy & commodious; of this there is little probability as her health has been wasting for the last twelve months & yesterday a chilly fit deprived her, during the paroxysm, of the power of speech. He thinks another must deprive her of life.

There is a grassy slope for several rods from the house, towards the river, terminated by a thicket of brush & small trees which was formerly occupied as a park. Just within the upper margin of this thicket the remains of the General are deposited in the family vault.

I approached this humble receptable of the once illustrious Chieftain with reverential respect. It was an awful involuntary sentiment inspired by the solemn recollection that it contains the mouldering corpse of the greatest man on earth; a loathsome carcass which, when animated with the ethereal force of Washington, was the love, the admiration, the dread of nations. Peace to the spirit of the mighty dead. May thy soul, Oh Washington, find in heaven a just & sure recompense for thy great services on earth & rest forever in the bosom of thy father & thy God.

The entrance to the vault is closed with a rude oaken, low door, raised perpendicularly on the side of the hill. A few bricks, crumbling into ruin, support the casement on which these lines are written with a pencil.

> Columbia groans beneath the dreadful wound
> And Europe echoes to the mournful sound.
> The sons of freedom shudder at the stroke
> And universal virtue feels the shock.

To these I added the following lines from Gray's inimitable Elegy:

> The pomp of heraldry, the boast of power
> And all that beauty, all that wealth e'er gave
> Await alike the inevitable hour.
> The paths of glory lead but to the grave.

The top of the vault is overgrown with low cedars & is not distinguishable from the rest of the bank into which it is inserted. Our small company remained for a considerable time as if riveted to this spot. One placed himself on the green turf & mused with his head resting on his arms. Another stood alone among the thicket with folded arms & downcast eyes. A third reclined against a tree & wept. For a time none ventured to break the deep silence of the place & when utterance came, it was in the form of a whisper. There was nothing artificial in this, nothing pre-meditated; all was the effect of nature & the offspring of the moment. After this involuntary pause we returned to the mansion.

We were conducted into several of the apartments, in all of which we discerned simplicity, neatness & taste. The building & stile of finishing is quite plain. There are a few architectural ornaments about it, considering that it is the produce of patch work & it preserves more uniformity than is common in like cases. It was an old family residence & the General had, from time to time, made such additions & improvements as occasion required. Yet on the whole, it is a slight building, neither is the furniture uncommonly rich or elegant. It has, rather, a comfortable, substantial appearance, not void of fashion or taste.

In the hall, a key of the Bastille is carefully preserved in a glass case. It is one solid piece of iron, with a handle of the barrel form, not larger than is usually found in front door locks.

The other apartments contain a number of engravings & paintings. The likeness of the General & his wife in younger life, of her children & of several persons of distinction were observed, but none of these rooms are as expensively furnished as the drawing-room & in general it may be said of the furniture, chairs, carpets, hangings &c. that they have seen their best days.

In the portico were several species of parrot, among the rest, a cockatoo who, on seeing Polly seated, left his cage with a quick pace & endeavoured to gain her favour by a familiarity which thwarted his design. Alarmed at the hurried motions & chattering of the poor fellow, she fled & left him as destitute as before. The Dr. observed to us that this bird was the favourite of Lady Washington, who fed & caressed him daily & being neglected since her sickness, he seemed quite lost & dejected.

I conversed with the steward or manager of the farm. The whole tract is said to consist of 8 or 10 thousand acres; of these, one thousand only are under tillage. The best parts are higher up the river & produce from 5 to 7 ½ bushels of wheat per acre; last year they sold 2700 bushels & this was considered as a good year's production.

General Washington was esteemed to be a good, practical farmer. It is

therefore probable that his lands are in as high a state of cultivation & improvement as any in the neighbourhood & yet this is a scanty crop for so extensive a farm.

It is the misfortune of this State, as well as some others, that the lands are held in too large tracts & that slavery, that pest to improvement, exists in full force among the inhabitants, for sterile as the soil naturally is, if it were divided into smaller farms & better attended, the country would soon feel the blessing in the increased products of her fields. Until the farmers of Virginia shall have but two or three hundred acres of land in a farm & all her sons shall enjoy the honest fruits of their labour, she will never reach that summit of wealth & true greatness to which she will then be entitled. There must be less clamour about liberty & equality & more rational security & justice, before she can attain legitimate respectability.

Although the untoward situation of the family cut us off from a large portion of our enjoyments, yet I experience something of a melancholy satisfaction in this trip which I should find it very difficult to describe. I would not divest myself of the conscious recollection that this had lately been the seat of the great Washington; that on these very grounds he had trod ten thousand times before me & that it still contains the cold remains of that matchless man.

We retraced the same dull road on our return, but with different feelings. The day was much in our favour, being bright, temperate & tranquil; the only one which had been so since we left Baltimore.

*May 21st.* This day we bid adieu to Alexandria which we think a handsome town & if we may credit the inhabitants, it is a healthy one. Perhaps the mineral properties of the water, though not palatable to a stranger, may tend to the promotion of health. I was told that no instance of yellow fever had ever occurred among them.

G. Drinker having politely offered to make one of our party to the Great Falls of the Potomac, we readily embraced the proposal & prepared to set out at 6 in the morning. Owing to the sulky fellow of whom I had hired a coachee, we were nearly disappointed. He did not appear at the appointed hour. I went to inquire the reason. He had made no preparation for going & would not budge till I agreed to allow him an additional compensation, of which he had said nothing before. Having complied with his demand, his negro & horses were in readiness to wait on us between 8 & 9. This fellow has the only two horse carriage that is to be procured for hire in Alexandria & he seems to have no scruples to embrace all advantages, right or wrong.

There are few who are so devoid of sense or sensibility as to feel no emotion of ecstasy or of enthusiasm when attracted by the sublime works of nature to their contemplation. This passion seeks for indulgence in placid admiration rather than in vocal expressions. Waterfalls have a peculiar tendency to tranquilize the soul & fix the roving imagination onto one delightful centre of quiet & refined enjoyment. That man who looks with stupid & heedless apathy on scenes like these must be possessed of a brutal heart, if not of a weak understanding.

The Potomac Falls have, indeed, very many charms. They made a forcible impression on my mind, but I should never succeed in an attempt to describe them.

We stole away from our rocky summit with regret & rambling down the stream, feasted our eyes on the rude masses of shattered rocks with which the shores are fettered. Nor were we inattentive to another object, equally novel to us all. It is at the place that the Potomac Nav. Co. have cut a canal & fixed locks for the safe & convenient passage of boats laden with produce from the upper country.

These locks are in complete operation & to those as unaccustomed to this species of water carriage as we were, a great curiosity. They are said to be excellent of their kind & I have no doubt they deserve the character. They have the essential property of effectually answering the purpose for which they were designed.

*May 22d.* We arrived at George Town an hour before sunset & put up at Barney's Inn. The day was too far advanced to admit of any new enterprize & we remained within doors to rest ourselves.

*May 23d.* The weather was unpromising, but as George Town has few charms for travelers cooped up in a tavern, we resolved to make the best use of our time & accordingly after breakfast rode to Washington. These two cities are separated only by Rock Creek & as the former falls within the ten miles square ceded to Congress & subject to their jurisdiction it will naturally lose its distinction & be considered in the course of years as a part of the former. We drove several miles to reach the Capitol, passing the President's house on the way. As Congress is not in session we experienced some delay before we gained admission. I was, however, recognized by the person who has the care of the building & who had seen me in Philada.

Little more than one fourth of this stupendous & magnificent edifice is erected, one wing only being completed. The foundation of the whole is marked out by solid stone walls, but all further labour on it is for the present & probably for many years suspended. It is built of white stone found in the neighbourhood & which in appearance is little inferior to marble & in point of durability & real utility quite as valuable. The Senate Chamber is on the ground floor & for symmetry, elegance & architectural magnificence, exceeds anything I ever saw. It forms a half eliptic, with the galleries supported on well proportioned arches sweep-ing in front of the President's chair. The white columns which ascend from the front or exterior line of the galleries have also a very noble effect. The tapestry is crimson moreen & contrasts very well with the clear white of the walls & ceiling. The rest of the furniture is rich & becoming, except the carpet, which is of the common quality of English manufacture. From the finished wing of this superb building there is a mean looking temporary covered passage of rough boards leading to where the other wing is to stand & on which a squat chamber is built for accommodation of the House of Representatives.

It rained smartly before we reached the Navy dock & continued to do so for the remainder of the day. This unwelcome incident prevented us from calling at the President's house on our return. The exterior is composed of the same stone with that of the Capitol & the stile of finishing is the same. It stands on a commanding position & makes a very respectable & noble appearance. It is two stories high & built on a liberal scale. A naked yard, in no part of which has vegetation as yet found a place, seems to say that the railing which marks out the ground is a mere mockery. I am informed that the interior is not more than half finished, a few apartments only being completed & these in a very common manner. The mammoth cheese lies undisturbed in one of the rooms, waiting, most probably, for some great occasion to call it out of being. Should it survive Thos. Jefferson's Presidency, the Federalists will have choice feasting, unless indeed the philosopher & his cheese should retire to Monticello together to spend the evening of their useful & glorious existence in happy retirement, solitude & rest.

The plan of Washington, except as to the diagonal streets of which I cannot perceive the propriety, is on an excellent, convenient & noble scale. Most of the streets are rectangular & for the comfort of building, all should have been so. The rectangular streets are from 90 to 110 feet wide. The transverse streets which run in the form of radii from the Capitol & President's are 160 feet. Ten feet are reserved on each side for foot pavements & 30 more for a gravel walk to be planted with trees, leaving 80 for a carriage way in the centre. Only one of these large avenues is improved. It is called by the name of Pennsyla. & runs by the President's to George Town. The whole distance is turnpiked in the middle & on one side has a broad foot way of flag.

In the evening I received a visit from John Hodskin, the unprincipled fellow from who I hired the coach to carry us to the falls. I had already paid him his full price per day for more time than I had used it. He had come to make an additional demand. I was unknown here & had engaged our passage to Baltimore by 5 the next morning. I could therefore do no otherwise than pay him. I confess I did not submit to this new imposition quite like a stoic, but felt chagrined that I was not in a place & under circumstances that would admit of my effectual resistance. I would much more cheerfully have given ten times the sum to an honest man in distress.

*May 24th*. Fair & charming day. Took stage at 5, breakfasted at Ross's, 12 miles from Town & halted an hour at Ridgley's Landing. It is really a sorry looking Town to have been once the rival of Baltimore. Arrived at the latter in time for dinner.

This last excursion has pleased me much. I have been agreeably disappointed. Heard so much said against Washington & so little in favour of Mount Vernon & scarce anything of the Potomac Falls that I had prepared myself to expect little entertaining, instructive or beautiful. Many are fault finders from their captiousness, others from an assumption of self importance & others from ignorance. Many run the common road, bawling out because others bawl & before they venture to praise, wait for the voice of fashion & fame as the true oracle of truth & the one thing necessary to be obeyed. Another source of deception is to be traced in the opposite extreme. Some give such exaggerated descriptions of everything they see that others, having their expectations wound up to a high pitch before they come to examine for themselves, meet with certain disappointment & thus disgusted, will not perceive beauty where it really exists.

Why has not my friend, T. Paxson, written to me? I requested him to do so, and said I should expect a letter on my return to Baltimore. His silence does not augur well. I fear he has no good news to communicate.

*May 25th*. The public paper announces the final exit of Martha Washington. She died on the 22d, two days after I was at Mount Vernon.

*May 29th.* There are two kinds of turnpikes in the viewing of Baltimore, one consisting of stones of all sizes & shapes from one to one hundred pounds weight & upwards thrown together with very little order & which form the roughest road I ever travelled & the other has neither a stone nor anything else in its composition that entitles it to the name of turnpike, except gates at which tolls are paid.

The country is most admirably adapted to the purposes of seats for wealthy citizens. The soil will yield plentifully with good manuring & is so highly diversified & divided into hill & dale that no one need be at a loss for a bold hill to build on. These seats are numerous & handsomely improved. Roses & honeysuckles are great favourites & liberally scattered round the houses in the gardens & even in the fields, giving a gay appearance to the whole. A rich man may enjoy himself here, but a poor man would be poor indeed.

Received a line from T.P. containing some encouraging information respecting his Ruth. Hope events will justify it.

*May 30th.* Have concluded to set our faces homewards tomorrow. Mean for the sake of variety to take a water passage part of the way. Will be joined by Nancy Shoemaker & sister Hannah. Shall leave Kitty Robinson in Baltimore. It rains very hard today. Have had much wet, cold, blustering weather since leaving Phila.

*May 31st.* At 9 took leave of our friends and embarked at Bowley's Wharf on board the Jefferson Packet for French Town, 70 miles from Baltimore. A clear fine morning with a light SW wind, but not enough to fill the sails. We moved very gently on the smooth surface of the basin & Patapsco Bay, past Fell's Point & the fort & did not reach North Point, 12 miles below the Town, till one. The Badkins were in view all the way. We had also a very distant prospect of Kent Island, a fruitful spot 32 miles long, but narrow. Scarcely entered the Chesapeake at North Point when perceived indications of a storm from S & SW. At 2 the storm came up and compelled us to take down all our sails, leaving only enough of the mainsail up to keep the vessel under steerage. The wind veered to the NW & blew with considerable violence. Being in our favour, suffered nothing except in sickness, with which some of the passengers were greatly incommoded. The rolling of the waves, the whistling of the winds, the darkness of the tempest, the beating of the rain, the flashing of the forked lightning & roaring of the thunder produced on our company no other emotions than those of admiration, wonder & delight—the prudent management of the mariners divesting us of all fear. We were now on one of the largest bays in the known world, the Chesapeake being 270 miles long & about 12 wide where the storm overtook us. The wind continued to increase till we entered Elk River, the mouth of which is divided from that of the Susquehanna by a bold gravelly & clay point called Turkey Hill. After passing this point we were enabled to hoist the mainsail & jib & had a fine run up to French Town, 22 miles above. This we reached after night amidst the bellowing of bull frogs, and the more pleasing cry of whippoorwills.

The shores of the Chesapeake do not appear to be highly cultivated where we coasted them. Saw few farm houses—the lands lie low. On the Elk, those on the right as we sailed along have the most fertile appearance. The Packet came to at a wharf half a mile below the Tavern, to which we were rowed in a boat, it being very dark. The house is a filthy hole. The first object that presented itself, on entering the bed chamber, was a full fed bug scampering lustily over the pillow. My female companions were put into this room, it being the best & I was left to shift as well as I could in another apartment, unprovided with a single article of furniture but beds huddled together wherever there was a vacancy to admit them. Seeing no place to put my clothes on if I pulled them off, concluded to keep them where they were. They served me as a coat of mail against many assailants & in spite also of the snoring of my fellow lodgers & the hard scrubbing and scratching which they kept during the night & in spite also of the racing of bugs over my hands & face, I stuck to my post like a good soldier till daylight, when the gladsome voice of the driver announced the hour of departure. The doleful long visages of my female companions soon informed me that they had fared no better than myself.

*June 1st.* A poor fellow who had accompanied us from Baltimore excited my curiosity & compassion. I was induced to draw from him the following short history of himself. He had lived with his father on the Monongahela & embarked with a load of flour down that river into the Ohio & thence on the Mississippi to New Orleans. There he was seized with a fever, from which he did not recover for 3 years. He then commenced his return & on his way married in February last a young woman in Tennessee whom he brought away with him & who is a bucksome lass in thriving condition. He has his fortune in a ragged dress of two stripe on his back. She has a chintz gown, a man's hat & a small handkerchief containing the rest of her wardrobe. When arrived at Frenchtown he had no more money left than would pay his wife's

passage to N. Castle & set out himself on foot. However, the rest of the passengers contrived to procure him a seat. When at the latter place, a subscription enabled them to obtain a breakfast & they went with cheerful faces into the Philada. Packet. They seemed scarce to know whither they were destined. The journey was undertaken with the view of returning to his father, but he was informed that the old man had sold off & gone to South Carolina, concluding that the son was dead, as he heard nothing respecting his fate after they separated. While the son was on his way home, the father passed within a few miles of him, both being unconscious of the circumstance. The father does not know even yet of the existence of his son, from whom he is now separated by little less than one thousand miles. Our young adventurer means to seek employment somewhere until he can either hear from his father or procure the means of going in pursuit of him. I think my friend C.C.B. could, with the aid of a little fiction, contrive a tolerable novel out of this story.

At New Castle, Polly & myself separated from the rest of the company, leaving Nancy & Hannah under the protection of a strapping Connecticut youth whose good manners had given rise to a prepossession in his favour. Wind, tide & sun all in their favour, they went on board about 9 & we pursued our journey by land to Wilmington, having obtained a two horse shackling vehicle for the purpose. We were now in a country which, compared with what we had been latterly accustomed to, was a paradise. In fact, so poor & so badly cultivated are most of the lands in the route which we had been thro' by Baltimore, Washington & Alexandria that a traveller might naturally wonder how the inhabitants were subsisted. It ought, however, to be remembered that the post road throughout that country lies on the most barren tracts belonging to the States. Westward of the road the soil in general is richer & better managed.

When I reflect on the immense surplus produce of the United States, particularly in the articles of flour, rice, tobacco & cotton, I am at a loss to conjecture in which quarter of the globe the enterprize of their merchants will find a market for it.

*June 2d.* Lodged at Wm. Poole's last night & this morning took passage for Philada., where we arrived after noon.

*June 3d & 4th.* Spent in company with our relations, not having as yet returned to housekeeping. On visiting my house today, I discovered that some person had violently forced out the hooks of the shutters belonging to one of the windows in the area. Expected I should find the rooms completely stripped, but on entering could not discover that anything was missing. What could induce anybody to open a passage into the house & yet not rob it? This is an enigma.

*June 9th.* The last four days have been taken up in visiting our children in the country. On the 6th, we attended Goshen meeting in the forenoon. In the afternoon Jno. Smedley (at whose house William is) & myself rode to a schoolhouse in the neighbourhood where some blacks were to preach. We found the building crowded on our arrival. About 300 persons were assembled, of different ages & colours, among whom were the sons & daughters of the most respectable farmers in the neighbourhood. The principal speaker was lately the servant of my next door neighbour in Philada. He had never in his life read a page in any book, yet he was at no loss to expound the Scriptures like a true doctor in his own way. He had all the action of the negro & seemed to be at no loss for words. He spoke with great vehemence & apparent confidence, occasionally wiping the sweat from him face with a white handkerchief, which he held in his hand. After returning to John Smedley's, I took down some parts of this curious sermon which, before I would venture to copy, I read over to him to see that nothing was misrepresented & he pronounced the following to be correct.

"Memba dat now, memba dat my friends. We muss all be bawn ob again. An if you no blieb dat you may go Pildelpi an see.

"I pose you wonda dat bracka man peak. Dere tis now, dere tis. You look a for great ting, but I speck you disappoint.

"Well lotta us hea what John Bapatis say, why he tella you Chrise maka Balam ass peak. Yes, an he maka bracka man peak too.

"De Cripta tella you oua Saibyou wa tempt tirty year by de debil who follow him all bout de wildaness an offa him de whole wold. For de debil wa President of de wold den, but oua Saibyou wa greata dan he, an say get dee hind me Satan.

"Now I'me juss going for say someting. Juss going for say someting my dea friends. You memba Nicodemus? Ah! now I touch de great folk. Well, you memba Nicodemus, oua Saibyou come to Nicodemus, pooa, low, humble, in a mainja, not proud as I, an dee, an dou.

"He cure an work a miracle, an say to de deaf take up die bed an walk. You know for what people muss take up dere bed an walk? I tella you, cause dey so tiff an wicked.

"An he for true. You no can run way from oua Saibyou. If you go

Heaben he pulla you down, if you go to place torment he pulla you up, an if you go in de sea he bite you.

"Well I pose, indeed I speck dere some in dis audense hea my voice, no blieb in God. Juss like wicked man I was wid yesaday afanoon in oua yard. He tella me de Cripta lia an Chrise lia. Ah, but he hab bottle rum in he han. Dere tis now, dere tis my friends.

"Now my dea tenda sistas, now I peak to you, an I wa tinken bout de Jews, de wicked Jews. I hope dere no tiff Jews mong you my dea, tenda, freemale sistas.

"Ah, some you may laugh, but tis solemn ting. An you an I hab to ansa for it. I hat to ansa for preach to you, an you hab to ansa for listen to me."

During the delivery of this sermon the blacks who were inside the building, being rather more than half of the congregation, preserved a profound silence & were very attentive, tho' an occasional smile was perceptible on some of their countenances. The house was too small to contain all who attended & several crowded the doors & windows. My companion, on observing some blacks who stood outside, inattentive to what was passing, invited them to walk in & endeavoured to make way for them. Some obeyed, others excused themselves; one said he thought the preacher "would look better with a hod on his shoulder" & another, carelessly throwing himself on the grass, yawned out, "I'de rada go an see a good hoss draw."

This is the season for the swarming of bees & the clattering of the well-beaten frying pan may be heard at almost every farm house. Whether this old custom is really serviceable in keeping back the flight of the adventurers when determined on seeking a distant residence, I have not been able to discover. There is something very wonderful in the temper & conduct of these little insects. From all that I have seen & heard there can be no doubt that a beehive is a regular establishment of civil polity in which every member of the community performs his separate & conjoint duty. Those who come home laden, it is observed, merely deposit their charge with others whose business it is to form the cell & stow away the honey, while the outdoor labourers, thus relieved, return for a fresh cargo. At the entrance of the hive, I have constantly noticed several to be stationed who seem to have no other employment than fluttering their wings, which they do with so rapid a motion as nearly to elude the sight of the spectator. During this time their heads are held down & their tails raised as high as they can elevate them. These I am told are guards who give the first alarm on the approach of an enemy & commence the attack. They are occasionally relieved by others & when off duty march into the hive. To deprive them of their chief is to destroy the government. Everything runs immediately into disorder & ends in the total desertion of the hive. Different hives often wage a most furious, vindictive & sometimes ruinous war against each other. These political disturbances, like those which sometimes rage among men, frequently terminate in the loss of many lives & much treasure on both sides, without any particular advantage to either of the parties. At others they end in the total destruction of the weaker government & the entire loss of all their goods, for the wax & honey of the vanquished fall a rich booty to the conquerors. I have heard it suggested that they take each other captive. Corroborative of this is an incident which my kinsman Benjn. Cope related to me. His house is about ½ mile from my Uncle Saml. Cope's. At each place it was perceived that one of their hives was at war with some other. Many were hourly slain at each place for days together. Benjn. sprinkled flour over the antagonists at his house & on going afterwards to Uncle Samuel's discovered some of the combatants there to have flour on their backs. This led to a mutual detection of the parties. Various means were resorted to to appease their wrath & put an end to hostilities, but all in vain; the battle continued until the hive at Uncle Samuel's went off in a body & entered that at Benjamin's. In what capacity they remained there he could not tell but supposed they mixed promiscuously with his hive which was previously much the most numerous & powerful. After this, labour which was toally suspended during the war was gradually renewed & everything went on as before.

I have found two rules for myself in travelling; one is to keep my watch regulated by that which, by common consent of the place in which I sojurn, is admitted to be the true standard of time. This saves myself and others a deal of trouble. It is not material that I am right & they wrong, for by an obstinate adherence to my own timekeepers, indeed I am sure, where all others differ from me, to lead myself continually into error & disappointment. The second rule is that, when I meet with a quagmire or other dangerous pass on the road, to always give a preference to the path which is most used. The beaten track in all doubtful cases is safest; where others have trodden safely, I may reasonably expect to find safety also. By striking out some new way I might probably succeed better, but I might also, when too late, discover it to end in ruin. The analogical application of these rules to the moral system will not be difficult to the candid & judicious.

*June 10th.* Introduced to Stuart, the celebrated portrait painter. His countenance bespeaks a nervous, versatile mind. Like many other men of preeminent genius, he is his worst foe. His passions are impetuous, nor does he appear very regardful to control them. His conversation was lively, vehement & free. We were at the house of Any. Simmons, who was carelessly lolling in a chair. This induced Stuart to observe that the Americans were remarkable for not knowing how to sit. "You would think," said he, "very strange if I were to offer you a chair with only two legs, yet you throw yourself back in such a manner that more than two of the four legs are useless. Why," continued he, "this is a very awkward & mischievous practice. A friend lately brought a gentleman to my house whom he introduced as Dr. Martin. To the doctor I offered my best mahogany chair, but no sooner had he seated himself than he kicked up his legs & smash went my chair. Sir, said I, advancing close to him, I could have invited you to dine with me & given you a bottle of wine into the bargain & it would not have cost me more than 3 dollars, but I cannot afford to treat you to a mahogany chair, which costs me ten dollars every time you come to see me."

Stuart's portrait of Washington, the best perhaps ever taken, will insure him a lasting & conspicuous position on the records of fame. He was related to the late Joseph Anthony, of whose handsome daughter he painted a striking likeness, but agreeable to his usual custom, could not be persuaded to finish it. The parents frequently importuned him & one day beset him with uncommon earnestness, on which the painter snatched up a brush & with one daub across the face of the likeness destroyed a piece on which he had bestowed much attention & thus put an end to further parley.

*June 11th.* A meeting of the stockholders of the Bank of Penna. was held in the large back room of the new building today, at which I acted as Secy. The object was to authorize the President & Directors to accede to the proposition of the State to discharge a debt of one hundred thousand Dollars due to the Bank in 6 per ct. stock of the U.S., Dollar for Dollar, which was agreed to.

*June 14th.* Anxious to see our beloved Ruth, we again left the City this day for Solebury, where we found her better than we expected, at the house of B. Paxson.

We took our passage in the Swiftsure & were crowded with raftsmen who reside in the State of N. York, 300 miles from Phila. & having disposed of their boards were now on their return home. These are in general a very unpolished race, but civility & good manners will mostly meet with a return in kind, even from a savage.

Nature seems to be in one of her most charming plights—cattle grazing on hills covered with luxuriant clover, extensive fields waving with the richest harvest & trees bending beneath their burdens of ripening fruit are among the blessings & beauties of the season in this highly cultivated & prolific country. Here the senses have each their subjects of gratification. The eye dwells with placid content on the woodlands, fields & lawns. The ear attends with ecstatic emotion to the voice of melody as it issues from the gay songsters of the shady grove. The smell receives the rich presents of fragrant effluvia from the blackberry & grape blossoms & above all from the odoriferous magnolia. Feeling may find a thousand gratifications in the wide range of sensitive objects & the taste fares luxuriantly on the delicious fruits of the garden & the field.

The lands in Solebury are very similar in quality, improvement & production of those of the great valley in Chester County. Limestone lands are famous for springs & Solebury produces one which in its course to the Delaware, a distance of 2½ miles, turns 11 water wheels, giving force to 7 distinct mills.

*June 16th.* The disease with which my friend is afflicted is distressing & alarming. Its seat is supposed to be the heart, but altho' Physicians have given it a name, the disease itself appears to be very imperfectly understood. It comes on by paroxysms with scarcely any previous notice & is a violent gasping, resembling what occurs in the agonies of death. The fit is preceded by a short, hacking cough & is generally induced by fatigue. It continues for perhaps a quarter of an hour & sometimes longer & then leaves her very much exhausted with severe stricture in the breast & a painful sensation in the arms.

Previous to her leaving the City these fits were periodical & recurred daily. Since being in the country, they are irregular, nor has she sustained but one for three weeks. In other respects she enjoys good health & indulges freely in that vein of gaiety & social glee for which she is so admirably constituted.

Her case differs in many respects from those of angina pectoris which are noticed in the Encyclopedia & in a late work entitled *Annals of Medicine,* in so much that I am induced to hope that hers may not be a genuine case of that fatal disease. If the coronary arteries were affected with ossification or an internal crustation, her aptitude to the paroxysms

would be more positive—her intervals of ease more of less duration & her general health more interrupted by spasmodic affections. In the true angina pectoris, the fits are brought on by running too rapidly upstairs & by facing a strong current of wind when walking. In the first instance, the patient found immediate ease by stopping & in the last by facing about. Not so with her. She has had no fit under either of those circumstances. Hers have always happened when she has been sitting or lying down & when they have begun, no alteration of position nor any application, internal or external, has insured relief, tho' when sensible of their approach, they have been effectually diverted by a dose of ether & the immersion of the feet in warm water. These have produced a free circulation & restored the pulse to its usual tone. Except from these or the application of a warm brick to the feet, she has found no means of keeping off an approaching fit.

In her first attack she was, by order of Dr. Griffiths, freely bled in small quantities at a time & blistered on the forepart of her arms above the elbows, but it is doubtful whether too frequent venesection, by weakening her system, did not dispose it to more frequent attacks of her dreadful disease.

*June 18th*. Our time is chiefly spent in reading & in conversation with our friend to which an occasional & delightful little stroll is added—the pleasant scenery of the neighbourhood giving a zest to our mental enjoyments. How charmingly do the hours pass as I move thro' the grove locked arm & arm with my Mary on one side & our Ruth on the other of their happy gallant. We sat down together on the oak crowned hill, the thick foliage sheltering us from the noon time ray of the sun. We surveyed the fertile, chequered & far retiring valley, watered by the powerful & clear current of the great spring. We contemplated the beauteous works of the all creating, all cherishing hand. Our thoughts rose on the pinions of meditation. We reasoned with each other on life, death & immortality. Memory rapidly retraced the actions of the past, friendship bound us to the present & hope pointed the way to a more glorious inheritance.

*June 19th*. Left Polly at Solebury & returned to the City on business.

*June 22d*. Received a Letter put into my hands by Jn. Thomas, written by Doc. C. to the overseers of the southern District complaining of the conduct of Elizabeth West, his wife's sister, & calling on them to disown her from the Society of Friends. He says she has charged him falsely with first kicking her out of his house; second that he & his mother, by their improper conduct, were the cause that his wife became crazy; third that when he went out of an evening he locked his wife in her chamber to keep her from young company; & fourth that he had communicated the venereal disease to his wife.

How true or how false these aspersions are I don't know, but he is a block head to give them so much publicity & perpetuity. It seems that the overseers after a hearing of the parties have not thought proper to disown E. West.

*June 23d.* A duel was fought a day or two since by Capt. Izard, commanding officer of Fort Mifflin & a Frenchman. The former is an American. The story is that when in France he dishonoured the Frenchman's sister under the promise of marriage. Three brothers resolved to devote their lives to revenge. This one crossed the Atlantic to Charleston, S.C. in search of Izard & not finding him there, pursued him to Phila. The alternative of marriage or a duel was proposed, the latter was preferred. The parties met on the Island opposite the City & Izard is wounded in the breast & it is said the ball cannot be extracted. His antagonist waits his recovery & should that take place, another battle must ensue until one pays the forfeit of life.

*June 26th.* Retraced my steps to Solebury in company with Timothy. On our arrival his aunt, aged 83, mounted a ladder & picked us a plate full of cherries.

*June 28th.* Polly has promised her two eldest boys that they should spend two weeks with her in the City during the school vacancy. She must fulfill her promise. Was it not for that, I believe I would keep her a while longer from the cares of housekeeping.

Promises should be sacred, children should be early impressed with this important truth. Punctuality & good faith must be supported inviolate or society, law & order cannot exist. All habits are inveterate—the force of example in some cases irresistible.

If I expect my sons to keep their word with me, I must keep mine with them. It will be in vain to attempt by precept to inspire them with a love of truth, if I do not practically evince my reverence of it. We must therefore return to the City & open house if it be only to receive our sons.

It is said of Lord Holland, the father of the famous Charles Fox, that when the latter was a boy, the father promised him that he should see

the rebuilding of a certain wall, but at a time when Charles was absent, the wall was undertaken & completed. He reminded his father of his promise & so much importance did that nobleman attach to his plighted word that he ordered the wall to be pulled down & rebuilt in the presence of his son.

*June 29th.* Returned to the City in company with Polly & Timothy & once more resumed the cares & pleasures of housekeeping.

*July 1st.* The hand of adversity is laid heavily on me. I am harassed day & night with present evils & with gloomy apprehensions & presentiments. I feel my frame sinking under them & pray God in mercy to afford me patience in these my severe trials. I ardently wish to be resigned to whatever may be my lot & to improve under the chastening rod. I have doubtless in many respects been an unfaithful steward & if I am found to be unworthy to rule over much, may I be content with a little. May I be favoured to use that little wisely and gratefully to acknowledge the Donor.

Since the period of my declining business, my pecuniary prospects have sustained a most sad reverse. My N.Y. concerns have been singularly destructive & unpropitious. Thousands have already been swallowed up in the vortex of ruin & thousands more must perhaps follow to pay debts which I never contracted for & for which I never received any value. It is not the mere loss of property which preys on my spirit, but to be vexatiously dunned after all the advances which I have made to E.W. to enable him to meet his engagements is indeed a trial, to the mortifying effects of which I am not callous.

*July 3d.* Have written to E.W. thrice without being answered. This seems to forebode no good. While yet there is any chance of my exertions being useful, it is my duty not to sleep. My friend C.B.B. being now in N.Y., I have written to him to make some inquiries for my satisfaction.

I enjoin it on my sons to be very guarded in forming partnerships. They are sometimes attended with advantages, but often with great vexation & difficulty. I speak from experience. I formed several & wish I never had formed any. In that which now occasions me so much anxiety, I have been grossly imposed on. The real situation & character of J.C. & E.W. were hidden from me. They maintained the character of honest men, but from the commencement of the connection until the death of the former, I was never truly informed of their means, capacity

& conduct. His private estate, instead of being properous, as I was taught to believe, was much embarrassed when he solicited & obtained my consent to the copartnership. It remained so without my knowledge & will fall very far short of paying his debts, altho' property of the company was used by him in discharge of some of them.

With respect to the business of the house, the same deception was practiced. I was told by him, a few weeks before his decease, of large profits being made. I thought them prosperous & was led on in this way into most grievous disappointment & loss, but I will not dwell on these perplexities, without it is to place them as a beacon of warning to myself should my eye be directed to these pages in better days. Perhaps they may be otherwise useful.

*July 8th.* Rec'd the answer of C.B.B. It affords but a glimmering of hope & scarcely that.

*July 17th.* The Board of Health have this morning publicly announced the existence of a malignant fever & confine it to the neighbourhood of Vine Street. They state that 9 persons have died since the 4th, mostly on the 3rd or 4th day after the attack. Twelve remain sick, 4 of whom are dangerous & that in these cases no instance of contagion has been ascertained.

*July 19th.* It is quite probable that the climate of Pennsyl. may under certain circumstances generate yellow fever. Surely those partizan Physicians who deny that it can be imported or contained in the hold & among the timbers of a ship evince much prejudice & folly. A pertinacious adherence to a favourite system, formed on theoretic dogmas, often renders its staunch advocates very ridiculous in the eyes of impartial, plain thinking, but well informed men who have neither theory nor hypothesis to support.

*July 22nd.* The Board of Health have this day informed their fellow citizens that the fever has entirely subsided.

*July 25th.* Wrote a long epistle to Ruth. It is well if it does not lull her into a doze, but even then, it may save her the price of a dose of laudanum. Felt little qualified for lively communications. Have suffered a wound which is not healed. It has been dressed, but proves obstinate. Dullness presides over my intellect & my heart is oppressed with care. How few are happy, how many are otherwise. Shall I call myself

miserable? No, I have many comforts left & tho' my path has some thorns it has also its rose, and the wild honeysuckle grows there.

My prospect is at present involved in mist, impenetrable obscurity, but the sun will again arise and gild my way.

These midnight glooms shall be chased from before me & day open again to my view. I feel a confidence that this will be the case. It upholds me & will not permit me to be overwhelmed.

Few men appear as they really are. We know little of each other. We walk about enshrouded. The whole world is a masquerade. Could we see each other as we actually are, it might have a tendency to reconcile each to his separate allotment. Our pains & our pleasures, our anxieties & our hopes, our enjoyments & our deprivations are more equally distributed than superficial observers imagine. Of this, my short pilgrimage has furnished many convincing evidences.

The smile of content is frequently accompanied with a heart racked with care & the sombre visage may be worn by the possessor of secret joy, as a ragged garment may cover a healthful body.

I am often complimented on account of my having retired, as it is supposed, full handed, from business to the enjoyment of ease, by those who know not my concealed misfortune. Many seem to envy me who, if they knew all, would be unwilling to barter conditions. But this state of perplexing solicitude cannot long continue—I will arouse from the apathy into which I have been seduced. All is not yet lost. Who knows what yet may be saved by diligence from the wreck? Nay, I am determined that I will not be unhappy—reflection shall come to my aid & I will ride triumphantly over the grovelling evils which beset me. Misfortune is the softener of the heart & he who has not tasted of her bitter potion will scarce now how to dash with sweets the noisome cup which adversity may administer to another & I could not have a heart callous to the sufferings of a fellow being, for all the pompous equipage of the great & the fulsome adoration which venality pays to gluttoned wealth.

Thus a proper use of my disasters may be highly advantageous & what I conceived to be an absolute loss, prove eventually a positive gain.

I affect not to despise wealth. It is a great & valuable possession, when wisely applied, but it requires a dignified soul to enjoy it rationally. It should not be a selfish, but a diffusive substance, or it loses its best properties & becomes a scourge instead of a blessing to the wretch who crawls beneath its load. Yet I hold the commonplace declamations against riches to proceed generally from narrowness of conception, envy & other base passions & frequently observe that the most intemperate railer is he who is the most servile in his devoirs to the dubious & unstable good.

*August 5th.* Left the City in a chaise attended by sons H. & F., whom I left at Jos. Maule's & proceeded to Euchland. Arrived there at 11 & sat monthly meeting, which lasted till 4. Went home with Isaac Bonsell, met there with Jesse Millhouse & we lodged together.

*August 6th.* After breakfast Isaac conducted me about 7 miles SW to a plantation to view which was the principle object of my journey. It is about 2 miles NW of the manor meeting house & 9 from Downingtown. It is a cold, sterile soil & the buildings on it scarcely tenantable. Here we parted & I drove to Downingtown to dine. Made some inquiries for a retreat, in case we should be obliged to leave the City. Spent an hour at the house of my much respected friend, Jesse Kersey & proceeded to Caleb Baldwin's to lodge.

*August 7th.* Having breakfasted with my hospitable relations, I returned by Radnor. Spent a few hours with my sons & arrived at home before sunset. The road was crowded with people, flying with their families & furniture—the Board of Health having in my absence declared that a malignant, contagious fever prevailed in the City to an alarming degree & advised the healthy to take refuge in the country.

It is affecting to see the tumultuous flight.

*August 13th.* Many idle stories are, as usual on these occasions, propagated respecting the state of the City. Persons are reported to be dead & buried who are soon after seen in sound health & spirits. The credulous are ever on the alarm & continually the subjects & vehicles of gross impositions, but the majority of the alarmists have fled & I can now walk the streets with calm tranquility. It is like a Sabbath of rest.

In one of the former seasons of yellow fever, a man related to a wondering crowd that one of his neighbours who died of the yellow fever had actually vomited 3 black crows. "Three black crows," exclaimed a standerby "who told you so?" Such a man, was the answer. This man, being called on, declared "he had not said 3 crows, he said only two." "But who told you the patient vomited 2 crows?" He named his informant, who was then questioned as to what he knew about the crows, but denied that he had seen asserted to two crows; he had named only one & the attending physician was given as his author. This seemed to be coming nearer the point & the doctor was resorted to, who, on hearing the story, burst into laughter & thus addressed the informer. "Friend, I

did not tell you my patient vomited a black crow, but that he vomited matter as black as a crow."

So goes the story.

*August 20th.* The practice of duelling, so inconsistent with Christianity & common sense, has become very prevalent in the U.S. Sober argument seems to be lost on its advocates. I have this day attacked it with the weapon of ridicule under the signature of Nero Crocodile.

I cannot but feel surprised how, under present circumstance, I can bring my mind to indulge in sportive effusions. I am a bundle of inconsistencies.

*August 27th.* The fever does not sensibly increase. The season continues to be marked with thunder, lightning & storms of heavy rain.

*August 29th.* To soothe the asperities of party cannot be wrong. Our papers teem with violence. If the evil cannot be cured, it may be softened. Men who are not lost to reason, morality & decency will not refuse an ear to a temperate discussion of the subject. I have attempted it in Poulson's paper under the signature of "An Old Pennsylvanian," which I find is read with satisfaction & seems likely to produce a good effect. I hear many conjectures as to the supposed author. He is believed to be an aged, discreet & experienced Friend. So much the better, the advice will go further. It is a trifling deception I have played on the public in feigning a character calculated to attract their attention.

*September 8th.* At a late meeting of the Federalists they have thought proper to nominate me as one of their candidates at the approaching election to represent them in the State Legislature. If the other candidates felt as little pleasure in this contemplated promotion as I do, they would not take much pains to advance their election.

*October 10th.* The fever has not entirely declined, but the reports are rather more favourable than they have been.

*October 13th.* The general election was held yesterday. It has resulted unfavourably to the Federalists—the Democratic party having a majority of more than 200 votes in the City. Larger majorities will doubtless be given in the counties. This cannot long continue; those who are at present in office have raised themselves by the most vindictive, unjust & foul aspersions of the former administrations. They will be able to keep their seats by similar misrepresentations & falsehoods, but truth must eventually prevail.

Washington has been called a murderer, he & Adams have been charged with the most villainous attempts to enslave their country. All those who were associated with them or held offices under them & who favoured their measures have been branded as traitors, peculators or hypocrites. The *Aurora* & other public prints in the guidance of the popular faction continue to give daily utterance to almost every species of calumny & falsehood & such is the frenzy of the times that men seem to lend a willing aid to hoodwink themselves & help on the ambitious, profligate & wicked usurpers of power & to promote measures tending to destroy the virtue, liberty & happiness of their country.

The popular party invite the disaffected & turbulent of all nations to their banners & men who have very lately been compelled by their crimes to fly their native shores are among the most noisy & forward on the election ground. Several of the judges & inspectors were of this class & such is the mortifying condition to which we are reduced that some of our old, native & most respectable citizens, in the attempt to offer their votes, have been indecently & grossly insulted & even had their votes refused by domineering wretches of infamous characters who have but recently been admitted to the rights of citizenship.

The wholesome restrictions on those rights which were enacted during the administrations of Washington & Adams have, since the elevation of Jefferson to the Presidency, been annulled & in this City alone, between 400 & 500 factious Irishmen were naturalized a few days prior to the election. Besides this, an expedient was adopted which gave to others, who were not legally entitled to a vote, that important privilege.

The tickets which were authorized by Law to be printed were, by the Democratic party, stamped with a peculiar mark, by which the inspector knew, when a ticket was offered, whether it was for or against the popular faction & he acted accordingly. Although it answers the present purpose of party zeal thus to invite the interference of foreigners in our public concerns, yet the practice is evidently fraught with mischief & will doubtless eventually produce a very dangerous influence on the peace & sober habits of the community.

*October 21st.* This morning has made an accession to my family by giving me a daughter. The still deserted state of the City occasioned some difficulty in procuring the necessary assistance for the mother & infant. I cannot help feeling many emotions of pleasure at this event & ardently pray that the future days of my child may be gilded with

happiness & that she may be blessed with a life of virtue, wisdom & usefulness.

*November 6th.* An affair happened this morning which must excite the sympathy of the humane & may possibly produce, in the flinty heart of slave holders, a sense of shame & remorse. A Frenchman resident in Trenton conveyed to this City a negro man, wife & child, who were his slaves. They were to be sent to the West Indies. Their conductor stopped at Howel's Tavern in 2nd above Arch Streets. While there, the woman contrived to elope & carry off her child. The husband, finding they were about to drag him away to a vessel, drew a pruning knife from his pocket as he passed out of the Tavern door & cut his throat in so shocking a manner that he expired a few minutes after in the street.

Surely, there is another world in which a God of righteous retribution will reward both the oppressor & the oppressed.

*November 7th.* It forms no inconsiderable part of my present anxieties to determine on the most eligible means for procuring a subsistence for my family. This is to me an important era. It will not do to be an idle spectator of the wreck of my property; yet all that appears to be in my power is to urge for an arrangement which may possibly, at some distant period, bring back a very small part of it. In the interim, I must endeavour to better my condition by an industrious application to business. Could I but command a mere trifle of the large sums which have escaped from my hands, I should not long hesitate what to do.

Offers of a copartnership are made to me by a respectable family connection. I have something of a dread in the idea of forming any new engagements of this kind, so much have I suffered from them, but at this juncture of my affairs, I may be induced to do what, differently circumstanced, I would not listen to.

*November 18th.* About dusk this evening a young man entered my house & requested a private interview with me. The hurry & agitation with which he accosted me prepared my mind for some sad recital & filled me with melancholy forebodings. I conducted him into a separate apartment. He faltered as he proceeded to inform me that he had arrived from Lancaster & that last night my father's house was consumed by fire.

Misfortunes are rapidly accumulating on me & come in various shapes & from various quarters. From the southward, where I have much at stake, I have information that my affairs have assumed an unpropitious appearance. I have sustained large losses in debts in the country, which I had esteemed secure & at sea, the same train of destructive events has pursued my shattered fortune. And now, as if the measure of my afflictions had not been enough, this melancholy piece of intelligence is added.

*November 21st.* Yesterday I brought my sons Henry & Francis from Joshua Maule's & placed them today under the tuition of Elisha Pickering.

*November 28th.* Suspense still hangs over me like a portentious weight suspended by the slightest thread which ever & anon is threatening to give way. Sometimes a glimmering of hope beams through the dark tempest & opens a faint prospect to fairer climes.

Sometimes this prospect becomes vivid & strange, then suddenly disappears, leaving scarce a ray to aid the midnight traveller in his mazy path of thorns.

On examining myself I not infrequently feel surprized that I do not endure these tormenting & chilling vicissitudes with more equanimity. Is there not something of vanity & pride at the bottom? I cannot doubt it, for the idea of a failure to a merchant of feeling is extremely grating. While exertion promises to be useful, it is my duty to exert myself to avert the worst.

When I shall be convinced that labour is vain & the game shall be up, then indeed I shall despise myself if I any longer indulge in painful & corroding, but useless regrets. In the solemn contemplation of what we are & whither we tend, few things that can befall us in this state of ephemeral existence should be suffered materially to disturb the tranquility of the soul on this journey to another & better country.

*December 10th.* My thoughts are so continually occupied day & night with my situation that I can scarce think of anything else. I endeavour to be tranquil, but it is hard work.

*December 15th.* Preparations for entering into a new commercial copartnership & attempts to bring two others to an issue are engagements of no small magnitude. They are as great as my jaded faculties can well support. May a just & all wise God give me grace to profit by the reverses which I have experienced & indulge me once more with a peaceful mind & that measure of prosperity which may be promotive of my best interest.

*December 24th.* Partly by way of relaxation I have written several

small essays for the paper of my friend Poulson, which I hope will do no harm. Have ocular demonstration that good has arisen out of two of them published under the signatures of John Quam & Solomon Horrib-legolf.

*December 31st.* Visited by my kinsman Pim Nevins of Leeds, G.B., attended by his son John Jowet Nevins. P. has been brought to this country by the misconduct of his resident partner here, L. Gatliff, who, it seems, has in his private speculations absorbed so much of the funds of the House as to have compelled his partner to stop the manufactury at home & discharge several hundred workmen who were dependent on them for bread. Pim has the character & appearance of a worthy & intelligent man. I am not alone in misfortune on account of the misconduct or untoward speculations of distant partnerships.

# 1803

*January 1st*. This day finds me once more personally engaged on the theatre of the busy & illusory world. It may be good for me to be a drudge & to be exposed to temptation for the trial & perfection of my virtue, but there are such scenes of iniquity & deception practiced in trade, so much selfishness & narrowness of soul displayed in bargain & contract among dealers that I cannot but fear that I should be unequal to the preservation of what I hold dearer than life—a fair reputation among men & a conscience void of offence towards God.

I have heard it said that no man can follow the business of a merchant & be strictly an honest man. What a slippery path must I then tread! May Heaven preserve me in rectitude of principles.

I have commenced business at my old stand in 2nd Street in company with my brother-in-law, Jn. Thomas, under the firm name of Cope & Thomas. I wish I felt less depression of spirits now, in the first onset of this new & important undertaking.

*January 9th*. Attended the opening of the Convention of the delegates from the different Abolition Societies in the United States as one of the representatives from Penna. Four societies only were represented—N. York, N. Jersey, Penna. & Delaware.

*January 13th*. The Convention adjourned this day. No delegation nor any communication was received from any societies other than those represented at the opening of the Convention. Our brethren to the southward labour under so many difficulties in the presentation of the noble & great work of protecting the unhappy African from the merciless grip of avarice, fraud & violence that it has cast a damp on their proceedings & in some instances, been the means of disbanding their associations.

But while eight hundred thousand of our fellow men are held in a state of abject & cruel bondage in our country, while two hundred vessels in violation of every principle of humanity & in defiance of the Laws are employed in the villainous & impious traffic of human flesh in the U. States alone (that is, owned in the U.S. & engaged in the slave trade to Africa), while perhaps not a day passes but free blacks are stolen by force or decoyed by the most wicked artifices from the Northern & Middle States & sold for slaves in the Southern—there is surely a large field of action open to every man who has bowels of mercy & compassion for this persecuted race & altho' the times may be unpropitious to the cause & disheartening to many of its advocates, the period I trust will arrive when a just sense of this enormous evil will so powerfully affect the minds of the citizens at large as to induce a change favourable to humanity & that the captive shall be proclaimed free.

It is astonishing to me that no plan has been adopted in the Southern States for the gradual emancipation of the negroes. It appears to me to be essential to the happiness & prosperity of the country & is, no doubt, the only proper & rational ground on which the measure ought to be accomplished.

This is the eighth convention & the first that has been regularly organized by the adoption of a constitution. In the election of officers I was chosen Treasurer.

Previously to their adjournment, a com. was appointed to procure a suitable person to compose a history of slavery in the United States, from materials we have been for some time collecting, by the Convention. The com. consists of myself & two others who are to approve the work before it can be published.

If undertaken by a man of talents & executed in a manner commensurate to the magnitude of the subject, it will be rendered an interesting & popular work.

*February 2d.* The crisis of my affairs seems to approach & altho' it will probably be very disastrous, yet that it is the crisis brings with it some comfort. I have been most singularly duped & led along step by step into my present labyrinth in a manner which, on retrospecting the course, seems scarce credible to myself. Have taken some measures to engage my friend W. Johnson Esq. of N.Y. in my service. Hope he will not refuse. I calculate much on his integrity, talents & legal knowledge. As E.W. will probably fail in the course of a few days, I shall need a trusty agent to manage the affairs to the best advantage—have full confidence in the one now in view.

As my thoughts are constantly engaged on subjects connected with my situation, I have often been led into a train of reflection hitherto very seldom the companion of my mind. I have seen some things in a new point of view & not only things but men. Money is the touchstone of character. You shall be intimately acquainted with a man for many years, he shall be placid, generous & feeling—touch his purse & he shall suddenly become an unprincipled savage, a being wholly different from what you previously knew him.

*February 19th.* Having lately, in the name of myself & colleagues, given C.B.B. the offer of writing the History of Slavery, he has this day accepted of it & is to proceed with all dispatch in that interesting undertaking.

*March 10th.* Robbed by man, in whose fidelity I had unwittingly confided, taken advantage of also by some others into whose power I have fallen by my unwary, unsuspicious temper & who owe me obligations of no trivial magnitude, harassed by cankering care which pursues unceasingly my wearied soul in my occupations by day & in my nightly visions, in constant pain from an old & inveterate pectoral affection—much to regret in retrospecting the past & little to hope from the future but a life of turmoil & drudgery to gain bread for my family, my spirits oppressed & my feelings frequently harrowed by hands which ought rather to soothe my sorrows & bind up the wounds inflicted by the rudeness & injustice of others. What have I to render this state of existence desirable?

It is now near 12 at night, the family are at rest. I am alone in my parlour, except that my little daughter, sweet babe, slumbers in the cradle beside me. The time is favourable. Silence prevails all around me. Yet, I pause—shall I do this thing? Shall I rush into the presence of my God, uncalled, and leave a wife & helpless family of innocents to struggle with poverty in a selfish, unkind & treacherous world? My hand trembles at the thought—

Tears come to my relief—no, this is a crime of so deep a die that, as I contemplate its near approach, I cannot but turn from it with horror. I will not commit this abominable act. I will pray God to give me patience & fortitude to endure the allotments of his Providence.

I am deeply beset, it is true. To others I complain not, but if it be criminal to feel & sometimes to stagger & faint under the weight that oppresses me, I shall have much to answer for.

My mind is more tranquil than when I took up my pen. I will embrace the auspicious moment, carry my lovely infant to her mother & seek to compose & drown my cares in sleep.

*March 15th.* Amidst the many perplexing subjects with which my mind has latterly been engrossed, I have conducted a very interesting & embarrassing correspondence with my brothers I. & J. of Baltimore respecting the terms on which I might be permitted to withdraw from the mercantile connection which has subsisted between us. We have at length come to an agreement which dissolves the House of Cope &

Brothers. The conditions to which I have submitted are far from being favourable in a pecuniary point of view. I have never received a cent from the profits of the business. If I have my capital returned to me some years hence without diminution, it is all that I expect. I am nevertheless much gratified in being now rid of every mercantile connection not under my direct inspection.

*April 20th.* Vaccination is making rapid progress both in Europe & America & promises to banish the variolous disease from all civilized communities, perhaps from the face of the earth.

The new method is so simple in practice & mild in its effects as scarcely to merit the name of disease. We have just had our little daughter Caroline vaccinated & have scarcely been sensible of her being incommoded by it.

*April 25th.* Invited to become a manager in the projected canal between the Delaware & Chesapeake. It is an important work & very interesting to the commerce of Phila. Yet my present avocations oblige me to decline the offer. I would willingly be useful where I can, but at present I have other duties to discharge. The respectable citizens who wish me to serve merit my thanks for the handsome manner in which they have treated me on the occasion. Was it not for the reverses of fortune which have pursued me with so much asperity, the proposition which is made would meet my concurrance & I should doubtless derive some satisfaction to myself in being useful to others.

*April 30th.* The war which continues to be waged between the French & the negroes of S. Domingo is one of the most wicked & barbarous that ever disgraced men who profess to be civilized.

In order more effectually to harass & torment the unfortunate blacks, the French have deigned to import well trained blood hounds into the Island & to accustom them to human gore & to be adroit at mangling their prey. The negroes who have fallen into their hands suffer death by being torn to pieces by these voracious & active animals. The horrid & diabolical policy adopted by France of exterminating the whole race of the present inhabitants of S. Domingo & repeopling it with new importations from Africa accords well with the abominable philosophy which presided over the late revolution & to which so many hundreds of thousands, nay, millions of men have been cruelly sacrificed.

*May 15th.* Left home on a visit of business to Baltimore. Took passage in the Mail.

*May 16th.* At 6 this morning I reached Baltimore, having travelled all night & been about 22 hours in performing the ride. The effects of the late cold weather are very striking. The leaves on the forest trees were killed in many places, so that the woods in parts have more of the appearance of Fall than Spring.

*May 21st.* Set my face homewards. During my stay in Baltimore, I had several interviews with the Mayor at his request on the subject of watering the City. One plan in contemplation is to derive a supply from several unconnected small springs, yielding in the whole about 140 thousand gallons of water in 24 hours. Another is to introduce the waters of either Givins or Jones Falls.

Having surveyed the grounds in company with Edw. J. Coale, the present Register of the City, I did not hesitate to give a decided preference to the latter scheme. The springs cannot yield a sufficiency. The waters of Jones Falls are abundant & may be conveyed by a natural fall into the highest parts of the Town, but then it must be by the destruction of several valuable mills. The same may be said of Givins Falls. On the whole I advised as the least expensive & most eligible mode to pump the waters of Jones Falls below the mills, by means of a steam engine & to raise them sufficiently high to be distributed over the City.

*June 8th.* Have just had a most affecting interview with my brother John, whose irregular conduct has for years estranged him from his family. Heretofore I twice procured his discharge from the army: on the latter occasion, when sickness & exposure had reduced him almost to a state of insanity. Now his condition is, if possible, worse, disease has robbed him so effectually of the powers of both body & mind that he is scarce capable of the least effort of either.

For several months I had known nothing of him & only this morning heard of where & how he was. I found him at a public house in a state of neglect & human degradation, enough to melt a heart of stone. Means must be immediately used to have him removed.

*June 9th.* With some difficulty have removed Jn. in a carriage from a tavern at the corner of Filbert & 8th St. to the widow Rudys in Fifth Street, where he will be constantly attended by experienced nurses & a physician, but it is not probable that anything can be done to restore his lost health. Life is almost extinct, nor can it be reasonably expected that this unfortunate man will ever leave the chamber in which he is now placed, until carried to the grave.

My feelings have been harrowed & my senses so offended in discharge of the duties of the day that my spirits are oppressed & my very soul sickened.

*June 13th.* This morning between 10 & 11 my brother John expired. His principal disease was an infection of the liver, attended with symptoms of dropsy & yellow jaundice. Altho' he evidently suffered much pain he would not complain & died in apparent tranquility.

In the contemplation of what he actually was, contrasted with what he probably would have been, had the early bent of his genius and inclination been properly cultivated, I cannot refrain from the indulgence of some melancholy, though perhaps useless regrets & reflections.

During the Revolutionary War in America, when the highly celebrated & deeply lamented Major André was a captive, he resided in my father's house, on the most intimate & familiar footing. His very engaging & amiable manners, added to the goodness of his heart & the brilliant accomplishments of his mind, induced in all our family a fervent affection for this person & a high interest in his fortunes.

My brother John, the eldest of five sons, was at that time a youth of very promising talents. His mind was uncultivated by education & experience, but his heart was affectionate & pure, his person attractive & his genius versatile, active & powerful. His thirst for knowledge greatly exceeded his means of acquiring it. A similarity of taste & character ripened into a mutual & ardent attachment between him & André. They formed the resolution to spend the residue of their days together. London, as affording the best hope to rising genius, was designed as the place of their permanent abode. André made known their intentions to my father & craved his approbation. John also pressed the suit, but he pressed in vain; neither argument, solicitation nor tears availed. Father was inflexible. He would not part with his favourite child & André, when exchanged, was compelled to leave his friend behind him.

Whether by a private understanding between them, or whether it was the offspring of his own motion alone, I cannot remember, but John soon attempted to follow his friend to New York. His escape was private, but would not long be concealed from his father, who went in search of him & having overtaken him before he reached the British lines, John suffered the mortification of being brought back & the bitter anguish of seeing his schemes of future greatness & happiness blighted by what he deemed a cruel interposition of parental authority.

This formed a memorable epoch in his life, for from that moment his character & pursuits assumed a new direction. The palette & pencil were thrown aside, he no longer had his friend & prompter at this side. No André to take him by the hand & lead him up the path of science. Home & study became equally irksome.

His talents for conversation & conviviality, the uncommon placidness of his temper—for it was uncommon, his ready wit & accommodating manners, rendered him a desirable companion to the gay, the voluptuous & the devotees of frolic of every description, with which Lancaster, his native Town, overflowed.

It was the hotbed of dissipation, rendered more rank & offensive by the prevalence of the war & the pestiferous vices which grew out of it. He was courted & cajoled into the society of men who were proud of his acquaintance, but whose unrefined souls, immoral practices & evil examples rendered them dangerous associates & wholly unworthy of his familiarity.

In this company he imbibed early and inveterate habits of dissipation & as his father kept him wholly unemployed at that dangerous season of life, rendered doubly so to him by the chagrin of disappointed hope, he had a full opportunity of indulging his appetites & passions. His native good sense oft warned him of the vortex into which he was gliding. He pressed his father to apprentice him & he was at length, tho' too late, placed with a clock & watch maker in Yorktown, Penna.

He served his short apprenticeship faithfully & gained the friendship & esteem of his employer & of all who knew him, for he was of a temper & had the means to communicate pleasure wherever he went. But the poison had been imbibed. His habits were polluted & he could never after refrain from occasional indulgences in practices which ruined his constitution & destroyed the best energies of his mind.

During all this degeneracy he maintained an honest pride which preserved him from doing a willful injury to the character, person or property of others.

> No farther seek his Virtues to disclose
> Or draw his frailties from their dread abode
> There they alike in trembling hope repose
> The bosom of his Father & his God.

*June 14th.* How forcibly do these solemn lines impress me. I was about to resume my melancholy subject on my return from the funeral, which took place at 9 this morning, but my Mary, having intermediately taken

hold of my book & penned this appropriate appeal, I shall pursue the task no further. Yet, I can scarce refrain from my first purpose, for I intended this short & humble biography for my own instruction.

Had John's inclination to follow the fortunes of André been gratified, what might not have been the present condition of both? How opposite from what it is? André was richly qualified by nature to shine a splendid luminary in the fair regions of science & he entertained a high respect for the talents & genius of his youthful friend. So firm & ardent was his attachment that he offered to abandon the army on condition of my father's consent to their plans. He went further; he offered wholly to defray John's expenses until they should both be settled in some honourable & lucrative employment, which he did not doubt they would easily accomplish.

Painting was their principal object. The disappointment sustained in hopes & schemes thus formed stamped the character of the after man.

> 'Tis education, forms the human mind
> Just as the twig is bent, the tree's inclined.

*June 30th.* Things have at length come to a crisis with Elisha Whitehead. This morning's mail brings me a letter from him announcing his intention to convene his creditors. I am invited to attend. This it may be prudent to avoid. I have therefore written to W. Johnson to request him to attend on my behalf. I shall doubtless soon be informed of the extent of my responsibility. This seems cold comfort, yet it will be some satisfaction to see the bottom of the pit and know the depth I am to fall.

*July 1st.* Every man finds his own affairs of moment to himself. Kingdoms may moulder into ruin and Empires be hurled from their foundations, and—provided they do not involve his peace or fortune in their fall—they pass before his view and are regarded with more apathy than the deprivation of one night's repose or the loss of a single Dollar to himself. Thus my tranquility is disturbed, and my feelings most grievously assailed by circumstances which I deem of importance and which are really so to me, but which in comparison of what is now acting on the theatre of the world, are as a grain of sand to a mountain, or as a drop of water to the ocean.

This day brings a confirmation of the renewed hostilities between England and France, an affair in which the lives & property of millions are involved. It is also stated that our late mission to France has been successful and that Louisiana is ceded to the United States.

*July 6th.* The annexation of Louisiana and the Island of New Orleans to the territory of the United States has been officially announced by the government. France could not maintain this newly acquired possession. Her government was reduced to the alternative of permitting the English to wrest it from them, or of surrendering it to the United States for an equivalent in money. The vast schemes of aggrandizement and colonization which the first consul Bonaparte had intended in the new world have thus been abandoned, and the people of America left to themselves without suffering the fraternal embrace of the grand nation. By this simple cession we are put in possession of a country equal in extent to the whole of the United States. The free navigation of the Mississippi, which has so frequently been denied to us by the Spaniards, is now effectually secured. The price of purchase is estimated at fifteen millions of Dollars.

*July 20th.* Frequent letters pass between W. Johnson and myself. From the usual indecision of E.W., he has as yet done nothing with his creditors at large. He still keeps me in a state of anxious suspense.

*August 4th.* Loss of property has in some respects opened a new era to me. I am no longer in a condition to give, without sensible inconvenience, to the various calls of charity those sums which once I could. "Here comes Mr. Cope, we shall obtain something from him," said two young men in the street who presented me with a book of subscriptions for a benevolent object. I disappointed them. They gazed at each other & at me. I did not explain to them my situation. They doubtless believed me to be rich & most probably felt contempt for my supposed selfishness. May this be a profitable lesson to myself, whenever I may hereafter attempt to condemn others for what I may call a want of humanity, but which may in reality be nothing less than the dictates of prudence arising from poverty.

*August 6th.* Tranquility of mind is so desirable that when it can be purchased, the opportunity should not be lost. Let those who place their happiness in the possession of gold, no matter how acquired, take it and all its consequences. If any reasonable surrender on my part can satisfy the cravings of their maw, they shall be gratified. Their pretensions are various and when left to themselves will be resisted by each other. I will throw them the tempting bone & while they squabble for their respective shares, will endeavour to make my escape.

*August 16th.* A monied association stiled "The Philada. Bank" has just been created. I am invited to the cashiership with a salary not to be despised, but must decline its acceptance. Under some circumstances this would have been an eligible post for me, but I can neither suddenly abandon my present occupation, nor consent to render myself dependent on an institution which does not come forward under very promising appearances, and may be quashed by the Legislature.

*September 20th.* The fever has not made any considerable progress. At any time prior to the year 1793, the same degree of mortality would scarcely have excited alarm—now business is at a stand & everybody is anxious & fearful.

In the fever of 1797, of the twenty persons whose duty it was by Law to take charge of the poor in the City, not one remained at his post except it could be said of two and sometimes three who came from their country retreats & attended irregularly at the Almshouse, without affording any assistance to the out door paupers & as it is a standing rule of the house to admit no patients when a disease suspected to be contagious prevails in the City, much suffering was of course experienced by the middle & lower classes of the inhabitants. The trades & occupations by which thousands usually supported themselves, from day to day, were in many instances nearly & in most, totally suspended. A large & respectable committee of citizens distributed relief from the State house on fixed days of the week—to whom however many could not, from mere inability, and many would not, from motives of delicacy & modest pride, make their wants known. These partook not of the public bounty which others, less helpless & less deserving, boldly demanded & as freely & regularly obtained. The mass of misery thus sustained by persons who were respectable housekeepers was very considerable & enough to melt an heart of iron. I saw & felt it, my spirits were borne down by it, the subject haunted me by day & by night.

I had previously served as a guardian of the poor. Some, who had known me in that station, applied to me to administer to their wants. They also sought relief for their suffering fellow citizens. After a solemn consideration as to the propriety of exposing my personal safety and that of my family, I came to the resolution that if I could prevail on some humane & active citizen to unite with me, I would undertake to act as a volunteer overseer of the poor until the fever should subside. Wm. Young, painter & bookseller, had been one of my former colleagues; to him I turned my attention. I had not seen him lately, but sought him at his usual abode. The City was at this time much deserted. William, however, had not fled. He received me with no common cordiality and, immediately after my being seated, began the following discourse:

"Mr. Cope, I wanted to see you. I have had my thoughts very much turned towards you for some days past & had concluded to pay you a visit. The poor are in a suffering condition & abandoned by those who ought to provide for them. Many must perish with hunger and despondency if not speedily relieved. You & I have already served harmoniously together & I had it in my mind to propose that we should undertake the care of them. I am free to acknowledge that I have been confirmed in the resolution by a dream in which I thought that we had separately determined to propose this measure to each other, that we had met & were comparing sentiments, when we received a message from our friend Hilary Baker (then Mayor of the City, and who afterwards fell a victim to the disease while in the discharge of the duties of his office), desiring to see us on the same subject. We obeyed the call & after making suitable arrangements with him cheerfully entered on our employment."

This unexpected address made a forcible impression on my mind & my friend was no less surprized & affected when I informed him of the object of my visit. If there was a singular coincidence between his dream & what had then actually passed, it is equally remarkable that, soon after we held this conversation, we received a communication from the Mayor, expressive of his concern for the suffering poor, his anxiety to procure them relief & his hope that we would call on him to consult on what was proper to be done. We readily obeyed & made a voluntary offer of our services. Being furnished with power to draw on certain funds for whatever sums we might find it necessary to disburse on the objects of our care, we divided the City into two districts & immediately engaged in our arduous task. William superintended south of Market St. & I north of that line, and notwithstanding the apparent risk & magnitude of the undertaking we escaped the disease & found the business less burdensome & difficult than we had apprehended.

In this field of labour, I had an opportunity of proving how much good might be done with a little money well economized. It was my practice to have a quantity of bread constantly provided to bestow on such as chose to call for it. This mode of distributing relief I greatly preferred to the indiscriminate application of pecuniary aid—if the money be not used by the pauper in the purchase of ardent spirits, he may otherwise use it to very little good purpose, for economy is not always the companion of poverty. I also frequently gave a small pittance to pur-

chase flesh in the market & on the return of the individual with the meat in his hand to convince me of the certainty of the purchase, he received his ration of bread as a reward for his fidelity. When I went abroad, I usually carried some loaves in a handkerchief to distribute where I found occasion & often have I thus supplied persons who, I had reason to believe, had none in the house for days, except what they thus received.

*October 12th.* This Book might be filled with anecdotes, interesting to the feelings of humanity, which have occurred during times of yellow fever. The precipitate interments which take place & which have been deemed necessary from the nature of the disease have given rise to some peculiarly calculated to awaken the tender heart to sympathy & the sober mind to reflection. One of these, as related to me by a particular friend, it cannot be improper to preserve on record. In 1798 a woman was ill of the fever in the Hospital. Her brother came from the country to see her. She informed him that if she had an orange she believed she should get well. He lost no time in endeavouring to procure one. The Hospital is nearly two miles from the seat of business in the City. After obtaining his object he hastened to the apartment in which he had left her, but her place was vacant. He eagerly enquired for her & was informed that "the woman with whom he had been conversing was dead & buried." He exclaimed "it is impossible," but was assured that her body was actually carried out & interred with the corpse of another who died at the same time. He ran to the burial ground & by presents induced the grave diggers to raise the body. It was the undermost of two buried in one grave. He forced open the coffin & bore the body into a neighbouring house, where by proper attention his sister was in a few minutes restored to life & lived afterwards to be the mother of several children. She was married & respected.

*October 17th.* For three days past the physicians have reported no new case of maglignant fever to the Board of Health & the disease is considered as nearly or quite at an end, for this season. Yet we have had no black frosts, except one or two slight touches last month.

*November 4th.* Have been engaged for four days past in removing my family & furniture from Walnut Street to No. 36 North 4th. Three removals are as bad as a fire, said Ben Franklin. This is my third, but much loss of property has not been sustained. It is however a fatiguing, harassing affair, little to be coveted.

*December 9th*. Last evening our kinsman Pim Nevins took a final leave of us preparatory to his embarking for his native country, which he expects to do in a few days from N. York. His amiable manners & correct conduct while among us have much endeared him to myself & family.

*December 15th*. My mind is still kept in a state of anxious suspense as to the issue of my pending negotiations in N. York. No decisive arrangement has been made with the creditors of C.W. & Co. The most troublesome among them is Jas. Robinson of this place, whose demand is founded in fraud.

*December 20th*. The long projected invasion of England by the French Consul Bonaparte is a subject of much speculative & interesting conversation. The preparations on both sides are vast. On the part of France it is said that an army of 300,000 are assembled for the purpose of invasion & on the part of England there are about half a million of volunteers armed & equipped for effective resistance, besides the militia & regulars. On the whole it is supposed that the English will be capable of resisting their enemy with an army of one million of men on land, exclusive of an immense naval force.

# 1804

*January 13th.* This day the Convention of delegates from the several abolition Societies in the U. States adjourned. They had been in session for near a week, during which they were engaged in some very interesting deliberations. I never met any former convention or any other public body with more satisfaction than this. So much harmony prevailed among the delegates, who were for the most part very respectable for their talents and information. A memorial to Congress requesting that in the organization of the Government of Louisiana they will prohibit the importation of slaves was, among other things, resolved on.

*February 14th.* Were I disposed to ascribe omenous effects to dreams, I have often thought of one from which I might draw no inconsiderable portion of courage under the pressure of adversity. From infancy I have occasionally been accustomed to dream of falling from precipices, from the tops of houses & other elevations & of being pursued by men resolved on my death & by ravenous wild beasts. Yet it has uniformly happened to me in all those visions that, when I have been in the most imminent danger, I have found myself suddenly empowered with the means of flight & I have escaped unhurt. I have often in this manner soared high above cities & countries & laughed at evils which threatened me below. When I have found myself falling I have taken to my wings as a bird & after amusing myself by gently skimming through the atmosphere, I have alighted when & where I pleased. When a robber, a mad bull, or a roaring lion has pursued me & the power of running has failed me, when escape appeared no longer practicable & destruction inevitable, I have unexpectedly eluded my pursuer & mocked at his folly by forsaking the earth & wafting myself far above his reach, leaving him to spend his rage in tearing up the ground & in empty threats. In days of Grecian or Roman superstition these visions might have been the means of insuring me no trivial degree of popular *éclat,* and perhaps have inspired me with courage to attempts which, by their successful issue, might have ranked me among the Alexanders & Caesars of antiquity. Purely my dreams might presage as much as the accidental flight of a few crows, the discovery of a bituminous or oily spring to an army on their march, or the healthy appearance of the liver & entrails of a sacrificed bullock. From such wondrous forebodings as these were those renowned scourges of mankind emboldened to undertake and accomplish the most astonishing enterprizes. And by appearances equally natural & simple were the hearts of those great warriors equally appalled. The fighting of crows, a defect in the lobe of a liver, the circumstance of a she ass kicking a lion to death filled Alexander with horror & astonishment, completely unnerved him & most probably contributed to his death, immediately after his having conquered the greatest part of the known & habitable globe. Of such materials is man in all his glory composed.

Dreams have in all ages been esteemed omenous & altho' I am satisfied that they usually proceed either from physical causes operating on the brain during sleep or from some previous affection of the mind, yet far be it from me to say that the Divinity may not disclose his will to man in the visions of the night. There may be invisible spirits or genii sent as guardian angels from God & messengers of his decrees to man, to warn, defend & arm us against danger & to encourage & urge us to good works.

Whether my dreams are to be understood as the friendly but allegorical premonitions of my guardian angel or have an origin merely physical & which habit has perpetuated, certain it is that I have been preserved from sinking under trials with which, both in my boyish & more mature days, my peace & happiness have been not unfrequently assailed. Yet after all I have little expectation of living to realize a prediction which was early made in my favour, by a person then unknown to me & whose name, if I ever knew it, I have forgotten.

When I was a boy, some travelling Friends paid a religious visit to my father. As they were departing, one of them, who was an elderly woman & a preacher, holding me firmly by the hand & looking steadfastly in my face, after giving me some good advice, bid me be careful of myself, "for," said she, "I perceive that thou wast born to become a great man." I don't know whether it was noticed by the rest of the family. There was, however, something so remarkable in her countenance, so grave & fixed, as she spoke, that I never could forget the circumstance.

*March 5th.* At length, after many meetings, the referees have awarded me to pay Jas. Robinson three hundred & twenty-five dollars for his demand on C.W. & Co. Altho' I feel it an act of injustice to pay even that sum, I mean to comply with the award. It was incontestably proven that his demand was founded in a fraud committed by him on Cox & Whitehead & on that acc't it was reduced from near twelve hundred dollars, the am't claimed, including interest.

*March 27th.* The mail of this day has at length brought me from my friend Wm. Johnson the ratified articles of discharge from the creditors of C. W. & Co. They have not realized the expectations originally held out to me as the equivalent for the total surrender of my claim on E. W. but, independent of that surrender, I have been left to pay some of them separately, who would not act in concert with the rest. This termination, tho' not in unison with my wishes nor in conformity to the original stipulation, is however a most agreeable circumstance.

> When things are done & past recalling
> 'Tis folly or to fret or cry.
> Prop up a rotten house that's falling
> But when it's down e'en let it be

For years I have not seen the postboy enter my door without some palpitation of heart, nor opened a letter, bearing the New York post-mark, but with a trembling hand & anxious mind. To be relieved from this state, even in part, is a subject of consolation & for which I hope to be grateful to the all wise disposer of human events. I have said in part, because there are some creditors in N. York who hold securities for their claims & have not joined in the discharge to me & who, should the securities become insufficient, may eventually resort to me.

No part of this unpleasant affair has been attended with so many disagreeable circumstances as the settlement with Jas. Robinson. This man was once & but for a few months my partner, during which his character was so developed by himself & others that it became necessary for me to dissolve the connection, in doing which I placed him on terms of his own choice & by which he assumed the risk of no outstanding debts & remained responsible for none contracted by the House. He was at first very reluctant to dissolve the connection but, finding me inflexible, he gave vent to threats which he has ever since very industriously carried into execution, nor spared any pains to injure me whenever it has been in his power. It is his maxim—& he makes a boast of it—to revenge to the last day of his existence & at the expense of his last shilling any person who has become the object of his displeasure. All his life accustomed to disputes & arbitrations, he excels any man I ever saw in the dexterous management of them. His plain appearance, his confident manner, his positive & unequivocal assertions, added to a hundred little arts & meannesses which he practices in private inter-views with the arbitrators, their families & friends, give him great advantages in this kind of controversy. He affects to be under the guidance of religious impressions; to wish nothing but what is right, the consequence of which is that, unless they to whom he addresses himself believe him to be a hardened & base villain, they must give some credit to his story. Such is my deliberate & candid opinion of this man & of the effects, the most powerful influence, produced by such conduct, on the minds of good men who do not know him. If he were to rob me of my watch in the street & a dozen men of unimpeached integrity were ready to prove the fact, rather than refer the matter to a tribunal composed of friends it would be better to give him the watch & rest content, for I should expect they would not only suffer him to retain the booty but, being persuaded by him that the allegations against him were all false & merely created & supported by interested men all of whom were his enemies, they would award him damages in the bargain for the injury done to his reputation. This may seem an extravagant position to persons who have not seen & known as much of this man & the wonderful effects produced on others by his contrivances & misrepresentations as I have. I have witnessed decisions in his favour equally incredible & which, if fairly stated, would be equally extravagant.

It is a fact which cannot be denied that Friends, from the nature of their principles & professions, are very susceptible to the grossest impositions. If a person in membership with the Society asserts himself to be under the influence of duty & conviction, he is likely to be believed, tho' he is doing secret violence to both. It is however in this way that J.R., as well as some others, have effected very unrighteous purposes to which others have given a sanction in consequence of their being imposed on by these powerful & specious appearances & pretensions. It is amiable to err on the side of mercy, to extenuate rather than to aggravate faults, to heal rather than to wound. These aphorisms are in unison with the best principles of Christianity, but it is not safe to trust to appearances of sanctity, lest we do homage to a whited sepulchre, nor to blindfold ourselves & take things on trust when, by opening our eyes, the truth may be fairly discovered—neither to salve over known, long-repeated & wanton misconduct, where contrition & reformation have not taken place, for these things must tend to the encouragement of corrupt practices, to the growth of hyprocrisy & to the injury of that high profession which we make. I have also been apprehensive that, even in some of our good friends, human pride may sometimes take precedence of duty & that, where a man is in exterior a Quaker, constant in his attendance of meetings & well practiced in the cant of language & sectarian phraseology, that they will for which is called the

honour & reputation of society stand by him & each other & expose a formidable row of whetted tusks to keep off assailants, when in fact the protected deserves to be worried for his mischievous practices & should be given up to punishment, not only to deter him from the commission of further depradations, but to operate as a warning to others.

*March 30th.* J. Robinson has lately had a reference with some of his neighbours on a subject which, had it been investigated before a court of justice, would in all probability have terminated very injuriously to his reputation & property. The arbitrators have, as might have been expected, decided in his favour, to the very great surprize, mortification & loss of several honest men opposed to him. On subjects of general information & in what is usually termed genius or talents, J.R. is deficient, but in arbitrations he takes the precedence of any man I ever saw or heard of. He would not succeed so well before a tribunal composed of any persons but Friends. He knows how to manage them to a hair & some of them by the aid which they have given him in his unjust pursuits, have done but little credit to themselves or their society. However they may choose or decide, they cannot blind everybody & some who feel the effects of his rapacity cannot be very favourably impressed towards the Society who harbour & cherish men who, if dragged before the public tribunals, must suffer severely for their villainy. "All flesh is grass."

I revere the principles on which Quakerism is founded, but I feel for the honour of Society & fear that such partial & palpable conduct will make us a reproach to our neighbours. The name of a Quaker was once equivalent to the title of an honest man. I pray it may never become synonymous to that of cheat or knave.

*April 1st.* For some days past the citizens of all ranks, ages, sexes, colours & conditions have been flocking in crowds from early dawn till sunset to deposit, each grown person ¼ of a dollar & each youngling an eighth, in the hands of a man who has stationed himself at the door of a shabby board building by the bridge leading to the Kensington causeway & so very zealous are they that I have heard it said from good authority that about ten thousand dollars have been collected in these dribs. What is the stimulus to this voluntary & universal taxation? Is it to give alms to the poor, to raise a fund to build a public edifice to be dedicated to the service of religion or humanity, a contribution for the relief of sufferers by fire, by shipwreck, or by earthquakes? Is it to redeem our captive brethren in Tripoli or to purchase another & better condition for the thousands who pine in slavery in our country? No, not one of these is the object. It is questionable whether the whole of them together would possess sufficient inducements to this unprecedented press to get rid of money. It is not the citizens of Philada. who thus rush forward alone to part with their silver; crowds on foot, on horseback & in carriages come flocking from the neighbouring villages of Germantown, Frankford &c, & from the surrounding counties, all fired with equal zeal to lay down their mite, and for what? Why, to gape at a huge lump of flesh & bones thirty eight feet long & eighteen in circumference & which lump of flesh & bones is called a whale. Who, being lately on a voyage of discovery, came as far as Reedy Island to gratify his curiosity, where running foul of dry ground, to which it is said he was driven by ice, he was attacked & captured by the natives & thence towed to Philada. to gratify the curiosity of others. He now lies stretched on his belly, deprived of his tongue & entrails & his mouth extended by means of a tackle. The lower jaw is, in front, of the form & appearance of one end of a batteau, into which the owner of the carcass has introduced a large armed chair, where visitors seat themselves, while the upper jaw serves them as a canopy, and where no doubt they are quite as comfortable & as well satisfied as Jonah was, tho' it is said that when he entered a whale, he explored the regions of the monster's belly.

*April 13th* Rose rather earlier than usual to write to my old friend, Ewd. J. Coale, now Register of Baltimore. Have lately received two letters from him on the subject of introducing water into their city. He wishes information. The scheme is to erect a company with certain privileges to effect the object. This is wrong; it should be done by the public. No city should be dependent for that essential article on any company or private association, however constituted, or respectably supported.

*April 20th.* I have had frequent occasion to remark that ruminations of an unpleasant nature are accompanied with more gloom & despondency when the head is reclined on the pillow than at other times. This may be owing to a partial & incomplete operation of the powers of mind & body induced by the state of relaxation into which the system is thrown at that season. I am more inclined to this opinion, as I have also found that, when my thoughts have been directed to pleasant contemplations, they have run into the opposite extreme & erected airy edifices which, when tested by the vertical sun, have presently mouldered out of view. When we go to bed we should sleep & when we awake in the

morning we should rise. Night is the season alloted by universal nature for the repose & relaxation of her children, but rest & sleep are not always practicable. True, but if neither body nor mind be diseased, most people find little difficulty in sleeping when in a comfortable bed. If they cannot sleep or procure rest it is because something is disordered & when we set our mental machine to work, we had need to have all the faculties unimpaired & capable of action if we mean them to perform their several duties, to work to any good purpose & to come to any accurate conclusion. I am convinced that our chamber lucubrations are generally deserving of no better name than waking dreams. This may not always be the case, but we know that even dreams have not unfrequently a degree of consistency which might well mark them for realities. The mind sometimes takes a range, during sleep, in which it appears to rid itself of the fetters of mortality, as if on purpose to convince us of its heavenly birth. Altho' this be true, we are also certain that while it dwells in its house of day, it must be affected by the condition of its habitation & be more or less influenced in all its operations by the good & ill, the spring & lassitude of the corporal powers. The mind may also, during the course of the day, especially when eagerly & deeply engaged in any interesting pursuit, receive such an impetus as shall last through the hours of sleep & go on with its varied operations with considerable facility & clearness. An instance of this occurred in myself when a schoolboy. A person of my age & myself entered on our arithmetical studies at the same time & under the tuition of the same master. My colleague was the favourite of the tutor, who took uncommon pains to urge, or rather to make him skip over the different rules, by working most of the sums for him. I was ambitious not to be left behind, nay was resolved to lead. My weak & partial tutor frowned on my attempts & would not deign to instruct me. I was therefore forced to use the most indefatigable industry. I laboured both in & out of school & so fully was my mind absorbed in pursuit of my object that, in my sleep, I have worked a complicated rule, which I did not previously understand & on waking had nothing more to do than to place the figures on my slate in the order in which, while asleep, I had carefully arranged them. My antagonist was out-stripped & our master disappointed & the consequence of this conduct was that I understood what I performed, while my colleague was little the better of the silly pains bestowed on him. My place became very unpleasant to me & I was soon after obliged to leave the school. Had I continued many years under this tutorship it is probable that I should have made a figure in figures & perhaps have excelled in some other branches of science of which I never gained a knowledge & all from a persevering determination to excel my colleague and from sheer opposition to my unjust & weak tutor, if tutor he might be called. That affair called genius which enables one man to outstrip all his fellows in the pursuit of a particular object has its origin not unfrequently, perhaps almost universally, in some apparently trivial accident which has nevertheless given a bias to the taste & a direction to the faculties of the mind, which has confined the exertions of the individual to a single channel, abstracted from all others, until the goal has been reached.

*May 15th.* Occupations of business allow me but little leisure for reading. I have, notwithstanding, at snatched intervals, read Hayley's *Life of Cowper.* The letters of the latter, written in the most unaffected & familiar style, are singularly calculated to inspire the reader with affection & esteem for their learned, meek and pious author. Some of the poetical productions introduced into this work are also of a nature to excite considerable emotion & do equal credit to the genius & heart of the amiable poet. Of this number is "The Cast Away" & the address "To Mary." The short epistle "To the Reverend Mr. Newton on his return to Ramsgate" is no less pathetic & affecting to the sympathetic mind. I am out of humour with Cowper's biographer who, whatever may be his general merit as a writer or a man, has not I think been judicious in his style, not satisfactory in his manner. Some of the most interesting periods in the life of Cowper are barely glanced at, or hurried over in a manner which cannot but displease all who are desirous of a more perfect knowledge of him. I am particularly dissatisfied with Hayley when, in speaking of his departed friend, he says "a disappointment of the heart arising from the cruelty of fortune threw a cloud on his juvenile spirit. Thwarted in love, the native fire of his temperament turned impetuously into the kindred channel of devotion. The smothered flames of desire mixing with the vapours of constitutional melancholy & the fervency of religious zeal produced altogether that irregularity of corporal sensation & of mental health which gave such extraordinary vicissitudes of splendour & of darkness to his mortal career." Why are we not informed of the particulars of Cowper's disappointment in love? It was one of the most important & eventful circumstances in his life. I cannot forgive Hayley for this strange omission. He should have spoken in the plain terms of a sober & correct biographer or, if he must appear learned & profound, he might have

presented his readers with an anatomical & metaphysical dissection of Cowper, couched in scientific terms & words of definite meaning.

Few poets in comparison of the whole number have sustained moral characters void of reproach. This may in part be owing to the ardency of their temperament, heightened by a lively imagination & inflamed by the contemplation of subjects calculated to wind up the nervous system to its utmost pitch of irritability. Doubtless, it may in part be ascribed to the effects of that adulation and deference which men are universally disposed to pay genius & talents. Cowper was an exception to the general rule. Few men appear to have received the palm of praise more deservedly. Few were ever more pure in their motives, more chaste in their affections or more actively alive to a nice sense of the rights of others & a scrupulous discharge of their own duty. His extreme shyness & modesty, his extraordinary colloquial powers, the uncommon urbanity of his disposition, added to those most depressive seasons of gloom into which his gentle spirits occasionally declined, rendered him an object of the most disinterested & ardent affection to all who possessed his immediate friendship—& of deep sympathy, respect & veneration to many others who know him only by his works & the report of his associates & correspondents. His character in many respects forms a striking contrast to that of the celebrated Scottish bard who in Doctor Currie has found such an accomplished & faithful biographer. Burns possessed many extraordinary accomplishments of the understanding & the heart. He had great talents & great failings. I am enamoured of Burns & sigh for the enjoyment of his society. I reverence Cowper, & long to place myself under his guardianship & tutorage.

*July 20th.* My Mary has been absent from me for some weeks. This day had been fixed for her return. A letter informed me of my disappointment. Some interesting circumstances have occurred to me in her absence. I could have wished for the benefit of her opinion. Have interchanged some letters with her on the subject. Many things may be explained & understood in a few minutes conversation which months of correspondence on paper cannot satisfactorily elucidate. This is not always the case. On abstract subjects of science the pen is perhaps the best vehicle for the conveyance of our thoughts, but where the heart, the affections & feelings are engaged, this otherwise faithful slave cannot perform for us as we can for ourselves. We must see the countenance, mark the expression of the eye & catch the language of the soul before it can gain utterance from the lips. I hoped to have enjoyed this delightful interchange, now, at the very moment, when the quill alone can be used.

*August 5th.* Took an airing on horseback. Breakfasted & dined at Nathan Spencer's. Sat meeting at Germantown. After dinner rode across the country to H.D.'s, returned in the evening—a little jolted & a little rubbed. Had scarce been astride of a horse for two years before. It is sorrowful to observe how scarce birds are in the vicinity of the City. Our sportsmen wage perpetual war on them. The wren alone has escaped their rapacity. His diminutiveness is his protection. Even that may not serve him when his fellow songsters shall be completely exterminated & the voice of music no longer resound in our groves.

*August 9th.* Before a man can become a hermit he must abandon many of the best sentiments & instinctive propensities of nature. To have no companion to commune with, no one to share his pleasures & his pains, is to be a wretch indeed. Much as my experience has taught me of the insincerity of the human heart, I had rather become extinct than be an exile from society. The mind, when tempest tossed, seeks for some haven of repose & next to heaven the best port of rest is the bosom of an affectionate & sympathizing friend. To be deprived of this support would be to rob me of more than half the stay & staff of life. A man may have many resources within himself, founded on reading, experience, observation & reflection, but then these he cannot but half enjoy without the zest of a companion. And if that companion be possessed of congenial habits, views & feelings, one on whom his soul dwells with rapture, who can reciprocate the indescribable sensibilities of nature, the sympathetic impulses of the understanding & the heart—then, & then alone, may he be said to enjoy life. All else is but endurance.

*August 10th.* One of the most important events of the day is the crowning of Napoleon Bonaparte, Emperor of the French. Thus has terminated a revolution which removed the Bourbons from the throne to make room for a new dynasty with powers not less despotic than the first. It is however lamentable to reflect that while the democratic frenzy lasted, not less perhaps than three millions of people lost their lives in assassinations, proscriptions & wars. It is also mentioned as an extraordinary fact that the actual duration of the Republic of France has been exactly equal to the duration of the Commonwealth of England, which was eleven years & four months to a day, if the commencement of both be dated from the death of the King.

Another event, highly interesting to the friends of humanity, is the abolition of the slave trade by the British Parliament (or rather House of Commons).

*August 12th.* Mary has returned with our little daughter, having placed son Wm. at Jas. Embree's boarding school.

*August 30th.* A family visit to the elegant seat of William Hamilton near Gray's on the west bank of Schuylkill. It is a place of much public resort, owing to his having that rare curiosity—an Aloe in bloom. It is the Agave or common South American Aloe, of which the vulgar opinion is that it does not flower until a century old. The one now in flower has a stem about fifteen to eighteen feet high, from the top of which the flowers put forth in separate clusters & are of a yellowish green. They occupy about a fourth part of the whole height of the stem & have a pleasant aspect. It will be in flower from 2 to 3 months, after which the seed is formed & the plant dies. The Agave thrives best in a warm climate, where it flowers at a much earlier period than in higher latitudes, so that the common opinion as to the age which the plant must attain before the stem shoots up is a very erroneous one.

Hamilton's garden is the best furnished of any in the vicinity of Philada., with rare plants both domestic & exotic. Among the variety are a number from Botany Bay, which at present have a drooping winterlike appearance, and the gardener observes of them that they have not yet become naturalized to our climate but, as the seasons of their native country are opposite to ours, these plants continue to vegetate & flower in winter & to decay in the summer. It is expected that time will familiarize them to our hemisphere & induce them, while in America, to act like Americans & to put forth at the customary season & not to mourn when all others rejoice.

*September 3d.* It may be wrong for me to find fault with any of the institutions of Friends, considering how excellent the major part of them are, yet they are not perfect & might in some instances be much improved. If, for example, a person unacquainted with their principles were to contemplate the conduct of J.R. & the knowledge which the Society have of that conduct & yet perceive that he retains his right of membership & has even accompanied public friends on tours of religious duty, he must think Quakerism consists in wearing a plain coat, in using the plain language & in going frequently to Meeting & that, conforming to these, he may lie, cheat &c. as if by potent right & still be a good member of the Society.

*September 7th.* Have recently been discharged from a heavy suretiship. Two others & myself were bound in the sum of sixty thousand Dollars for T.M., Cashier of the Savannah Branch Bank. He has at length procured three substitutes. Ought to have been done more than a year sooner agreeably to promise. 'Tis well 'tis done now. Entered at first into the measure with reluctance. He could not have procured the appointment had I not done so. He had long been unpleasantly circumstanced in his pecuniary matters, had tried many schemes for amassing property but had not steadiness enough to pursue any long at a time. This appeared to promise a permanency—his heart was fixed on it. He thought he had some claims on me on the score of consanguinity. I much desired his welfare but, believing the risk to be considerable, hesitated, refused. Was again & again appealed to—and finally consented.

Suretiships, and more especially when the sum is great, should be entered into with much caution, as total ruin may be the consequence. It is nevertheless certain that, without these acts of friendship & confidence, many would suffer. My feelings have often been wrought on, so as to induce me to enter into those risks—have sustained some losses in consequence & if I have any advice to leave my children on this subject, it is never to become bound in large sums for any person, unless in some very extraordinary case of great urgency & where the claim is cogent.

If we are sincerely disposed to do good, let us first take the beam out of our eye & place matters to rights at home, so that we may go stronger handed & clearer sighted abroad to do good to others. Our benevolence will then be like a stone cast into tranquil water, circle will extend beyond circle until the whole surface is embraced. A Godwinite would commence his building in all parts at once, any where & everywhere. He would begin at the top & proceed downwards, whereas if he would have a good superstructure, or build to any useful purpose, he should begin at the foundation & by carefully adding brick to brick go on gradually to the completion of the edifice, making solid work of the whole.

The true method of reforming mankind is to begin with yourself & the right way of evincing your bounty is to provide first for those whom nature & the laws have cast on you by the most powerful claims to your justice, your sympathy & your generosity & for whom, therefore, it is your indispensable duty to make competent provision. If you neglect them, whose duty can it be to take care of them? If you are not bound to

do it, who is? He surely is a vile pretender to philanthropy who spends his substances abroad & leaves his wife & children to be supported by others or to starve.

*September 11th.* Every man owes something to Society. The social compact enjoins it. The Christian creed enforces it. To contribute to the accommodation & happiness of each other is therefore not only our moral but our religious duty. The discharge of this duty is frequently neither consistent with our ease nor our inclination. These in themselves do not form a sufficient apology for remissness. There is something peculiar to every case in which we may be called on to act & which may either render it proper & just to join in promptly with the call, or may justify our absolute refusal. The settling of differences in the form of arbitrations is, generally speaking, much preferable to a resort to law & yet it may not always be our duty to serve as arbitrators when solicited to do so. There are some cases again in which it may be difficult to discern the path of duty. That is my present situation. Party has wormed itself into all our public bodies & into all our public proceedings. Even our Board of Health underwent its revolution & men of the new school—that is, of the Democratic faction—took place of their Federal predecessors. Jas. E. Smith was Steward of the Lazaretto. He was found in the office when the Democrats came in & being a Federalist was obnoxious to them. They lately displaced him. On this subject both parties have appealed to the public & each accuses the other of gross misconduct. Doctor Reynolds, an Irish patriot who fled from his native country to escape the vengeance of the laws, is Secy. to the Board & is represented as being one of the most violent of its members in the proceedings against Smith. Matters of account are involved in the dispute. The Board refuse to pay Smith's demand of salary, alleging that he has embezzled the public property. This charge he resists with indignation. They have each agreed to leave the matter to the decision of two disinterested men & Smith has named me as one.

*September 25th.* All my hours are not devoted to painful subjects, tho' my muscles have been so much accustomed to the rigid modifications of a troubled mind that they can scarce accommodate themselves to the supple variations of a laugh, yet I have many enjoyments left. I often survey my family with placid delight & while I interchange opinions & sentiments in sober conversation with the mother, occasionally unbend the stern bow of business & lighten the heavy brow of care in innocent gambols with the children—& if I have sustained privations in social intercourse with persons with whom I have been accustomed to spend much of my time, the near residence of my brother Israel's family gives us frequent & daily opportunities of enjoying the society of him & his amiable wife. In casting my eye over the pages of my Diary, it is apparent that they exhibit more of my painful than of my pleasurable experience. Whence does this arise? I have for some years past suffered much it is true, but I have also enjoyed much. Perhaps we naturally feel more inclined to complain under the pressure of evil than openly to exult in the enjoyment of good. Beside that, I have been gaining a knowledge of men, new to me until acquired by experience & which of course made deep impressions on my mind. It is well if I do not in the end become a morose & gloomy misanthropist.

*September 27th.* Accounts from the interior & western parts of the state are of an unpleasant nature. Bilious complaints very generally prevail & many fall victims to them. The mortality in some parts, particularly in York Town is said to exceed that of the year 1793 or 1798 in Philada. The farmers in some of the counties have been unable to get in their last crop of hay or to put their winter grain in the ground. The western counties of Virginia are reported to be in the same condition.

*September 28th.* Notwithstanding the war, the commerce of G. Britain is extensive to a very surprizing degree. In one of the late papers the arrival of several fleets is announced as having taken place within a few days of each other. They were from China, Newfoundland, Jamaica, the Leeward Islands, Lisbon & the Baltic. Their cargoes together are valued at upwards of seventeen millions Sterling or about 80 millions of Dollars. The duties on them to the Government are estimated at four millions, or about 16 to 17 millions of Dollars. It is a question whether any other country has ever witnessed such an extensive influx of wealth in so short a space of time.

*October 6th.* Life is an ever varying scene. Property is fleeting, opinion unstable, attachments inconstant. These are not speculative assertions, but experimental truths. I have purchased them & paid for them. All have their problems, some in one way & some in another. The furnace of affliction may not be equally heated for all, for all are not equally obdurate & insensible, but perhaps all who are pure have been made so by passing thro' fire.

The farmer complains that his harvest is light. His horses die of the distemper, vermin destroy the little that the fields have yielded & his year's labour is lost. The merchant is tried by the sudden & unexpected fall in price or change of fashion in goods, after he has just been induced, under the most flattering prospects of gain, to purchase the amount of ten times his fortune & often, after he has acquired an independency, the failure of persons in whom he had confided, loss of property by capture or by shipwreck, plunges him in a moment from affluence to a condition below poverty, one in which he finds himself bereaved of the means of subsistence, and thousands in debt without the shadow of a hope that he shall ever be able to pay his numerous & suffering creditors. Not so disastrous has been a recent affair, but it shows how miserably short sighted are our best calculations. I suffer but the common fare of others in business & tho' much disappointed shall endeavour not to complain.

Purchased, about five weeks since, a parcel of German goods amounting to upwards of sixty thousand Dollars. They had been a long time & much in demand. Few packages except our own were to be found, nor could we learn that many were expected. In Baltimore, a greater scarcity prevailed. The probability of large profits were therefore great. A vessel was advertized for Baltimore to sail about the 6th last. The wind was favourable. We shipped sixteen thousand Dollars worth by the Captn. who, notwithstanding promises, did not sail for 4 days after he engaged to do it, nor was it until this day that we heard of his arrival. He put into Cape May, spent a day or two there & afterwards into Norfolk, where he remained for a week. Before he reached Baltimore, a number of cargoes of German goods arrived & stocked the market, so that what had promised large gain may end in considerable loss. Our sales at home have been tolerably good, but a large amount is unsold & we learn today that several vessels may be hourly looked for, laden with the same articles. Beside these unpleasant circumstances, our minds have been uneasy until we heard of the arrival of our goods at Baltimore. The Capt., whose name is Dickinson, might, had he done his duty & been favoured with wind & weather, have accomplished his voyage in 7 or 8 days, instead of which a month has elapsed since our articles were shipped by him. Many vessels from this port have arrived in England in less time. My mind has been so much accustomed to cross occurrences & disappointments that these, tho' certainly not trivial, have affected me but little & I feel gratitude to God that my peace & happiness are not disturbed by them. I am convinced that whatever befalls us may be turned to good account & that an honest man who does as well as he knows how need not suffer any apprehension, that happen what will, he will have as much of the good things of life as will contribute to his best interest and enjoyment. I know that I am far, very far, from being as good as I ought to be & that my precepts are better than my practice. If improvement would but keep pace with probing experience, I might hope to be better.

*October 8th*. An evening visit from my old friend C.B.B.—has not, except once, been to see me for several months. His time has been principally devoted to a female to whom it is understood he has for some years been betrothed. She has lately left the City for N. York where she resides, so that, unless some new freak takes him, may expect to see him oftener.

*October 24th*. Accounts from the eastern states mention that during the gale of the 9th & 10th, snow fell to the depth of 12 & 15 inches & afforded good sleighing.

A present of apples & nuts from our son William. This memento of our child accompanied by a letter dictated by himself & written by another could not but be acceptable. His brother Henry has written an answer, to which I perceive their affectionate mother is making a large addition. A temporary separation between the nearest connections, if it does not always produce pleasurable feelings, certainly tends to strengthen the affections, by calling them frequently into activity. Disappointed in some whom I had long esteemed as friends & with whom at present I have scarce the semblance of intercourse, deceived in many of my dreams of happiness & smarting under the lash of fortune, my mind naturally seeks repose in the bosom of my family. The feelings & sympathies of the heart return with double force to those whom the ties of blood had already rendered dear to me.

*November 7th*. The instances of mania which have lately occurred are said to be unprecedented. Within a few weeks past, several have taken place within the circle of my acquaintance. I could perhaps enumerate a dozen or more. Among them are two men who have heretofore held conspicious stations in our Society. One is in the hospital, the other —who married a second time a few months ago—is confined to his own house & so raving as to require constant attention & the application of a mad shirt.

This is a sad state of human degradation. To behold the active & godlike spirit of man, his exalted genius & exquisite talents suddenly prostrated to the earth, to crawl with the meanest reptile, furnishes

indeed a very striking & awful picture to the reflecting mind. Let the vain boaster of his own mental energies but cast an eye on this wreck of intellect, of all that is dignified or great in man & remember that the next moment may reduce him to the same condition & if he does not feel humbled, he must be a hardened & thoughtless wretch.

The texture & organization of the mind may be very ingeniously, very logically & very metaphysically discussed, but it is nevertheless true that learning & philosophy have fallen short in their attempts to explain the nature & secret operations of that most wonderful machine. At one moment it appears a desolate waste, powerless & useless; at the next it shall be luxuriously fruitful & almost omnipotent. A cause shall be sufficient to produce its total derangement in one man, which in another shall produce no effect at all or, if any, to inspire it with new vigour.

Fear, which includes anxiety, is perhaps one of the most powerful annoyers of its fabric & under one or other of the various forms in which it assails the human intellect, may be considered in the light of an unwearied & vigilant adversary, a disturber of the peace & destroyer of the best faculties of man. The fear of coming to want, the fear of death & of misery after it, are so many powerful engines which have worked the destruction of some & of many of the most shining mental qualities, properties & powers.

*November 12th.* The present Mayor, Mr. Lawler, who is a considerable ignoramus & irritable, lately sent for one of our citizens in a violent passion & charged him with propagating a story that he, the Mayor, had kicked a man & broke his leg. The citizen denied the charge but acknowledged saying that a mare had at the drawbridge kicked a person & broke his leg.

*November 17th.* For some years past Republics were in vogue & in France no oath was more common than that of eternal hatred to kings. Fashion has in this instance exhibited her usual fickleness, for now we hear of his Imperial Majesty Bonaparte Emperor of the French & his Imperial Majesty Jacques 1st Emperor of Hayti, the latter title being assumed by the present chief of S. Domingo, Dessalines, a negro.

*November 20th.* In business so many disagreeable things happen from the clashings of interest & the perversity of human nature that no man who values tranquility of mind above the mere accummulation of wealth can enjoy much satisfaction in it. There are so many disposed to take advantages whenever opportunity favours them, that an honest man finds himself, like a sentinel in time of war, under the necessity of unwinking vigilance to prevent surprize & ruin. Nor is it, I believe, possible, with the most upright views, to preserve harmony & a good understanding with all with whom he traffics. To resist an unjust demand involves him in direct hostilities, to crouch beneath it or to conciliate by sacrifies invites insult & further injury.

I have often remarked that a man in trade is like a horse in a team. He *must* draw & also take good heed to his steppings, or his leaders will pull him down, or his followers tramp him down.

*November 28d.* Have this day paid $900, the last sum, as I hope, of the claims made on me by the creditors of C. W. & Co. This ought to give me pleasure & in some respects it does but nevertheless revives very painful reflections. In recurring to my books of account, I perceive the many dilapidations which my fortune has sustained by those men & I have not sufficient command of my feelings to bear the consequent cogitations with composure. For some years after I entered the stage of manhood I accustomed myself to the contemplation of the pleasant side of the events which occurred, casting gloom behind me. Latterly I feel like a hunted hare, my ears are ever open to catch the sound of the enemy & even when I feel myself secure, my heart pants from the remembrance of the past. It is next to impossible to disengage my mind even for a few hours at a time from anxious thoughts. Such is the condition of a man whom many would esteem happy & who in effect, notwithstanding the many trials & conflicts which he endures, possesses many things for which he ought to be more thankful than, I have sometimes had a jealousy, he is. Yet from amidst these probationary seasons & darksome hours of affliction I have frequent glimpses of enjoyment ahead & which it is my consolation to believe I shall live to overtake. I have vexations of a nature which I dare not trust myself to pen, for possibly these sheets, tho' intended for my own improvement & use, may hereafter fall into the hands of persons who might, were they to perceive how much my peace is disturbed by their conduct, feel a pang of self reproach which it is not my wish to occasion them. I am much aggrieved by circumstances which I have not detailed & by a particular person whom I believe I have not named in this volume & to whom, notwithstanding, I should be sorry to give pain. If it should so happen that any who may have been mentioned by me in the course of these records should feel hurt on account of the manner in which I have

spoken of them, I beg their forgiveness, for I really intended them no wrong—altho' my feelings may sometimes have hurried me into expressions which they may deem severe & which might perhaps as well have been avoided & which in some instances would undoubtedly have been avoided, had I considered myself as writing for the examination of others rather than for my own amusement & instruction. The troubled mind derives a secret, almost indescribable satisfaction from thus conversing with itself. It is true that we are much more keen in searching out the defects & in animadverting on the faults of others than in discovering & endeavouring to amend our own. It would perhaps be more profitable & more charitable were we to hold up the mirror of our own errors, follies & vices to ourselves, rather than to scan & expose those of others, or even to dwell on them in our retired contemplations—tho' we should design nothing more than a development & fair understanding of the truth & to place the evil like a way mark before our eyes, to serve us as a memento of quicksands to be shunned in our future excursions.

*November 25th.* Some writer has said that conscientious & learned men are seldom fat—supposing no doubt that much thought & deep study are productive of leanness. Of the truth of this adage I have little doubt; like every other general rule, it has also its exceptions. Laborious thinking, especially on painful subjects, does, as my lank figure can well attest, leave but a scanty supply for the body. Well, some day my poor bones may find a more comfortable covering of flesh, but never I sincerely hope if it is to depend on the loss of my conscience. As to learning, it is not likely to run away with any portion of my corporal substance, either now or hereafter. I may therefore make myself easy on that score & rest satisfied that whenever a light heart shall dispose me to laugh & be fat, that learning will not interpose to prevent it.

*November 30th.* The education of his children is to every sober & thoughtful parent an interesting, pleasing, painful, arduous, and important undertaking requiring much diligence, circumspection & deliberation. One rash, incautious step towards them may give a direction to their temper & habits which may prove injurious to them throughout life. In our endeavours to curb the early propensities of evil we should be careful to govern rather than to tyrannize, to mend but not to lacerate, to prune but not to hack—& when it becomes necessary to root out an ill weed, to do it with patient skill, lest we wound or tear up the good also.

Youth is & ought to be the season of activity & pleasure & while we endeavour to regulate the conduct of our offspring in that eventful &

momentous period of their existence, so as to prevent their effervescent passions from hurrying them into licentious practices, we should be guarded not to mar the regular & well ordered course of nature, nor to rob innocent infancy of that portion of happiness which belongs to it & which it may never after be in our power to restore.

Children often form reflections & draw inferences which they are incapable of expressing. The mind can very early in life distinguish between justice & oppression & when a fault is committed, if the punishment be disproportioned to the offence, mischief instead of good will be the result. In infancy as in manhood, force may restrain the body when the will is free & reason revolts at the imposition. Hence the temper may be soured & a sullen spirit of revenge rankle in the bosom, which may ultimately involve both the punisher & the punished in one common scene of misery & ruin.

*December 1st.* My time is thus occupied. I rise with the sun or a little after. Read or write until breakfast time, then I go to the store & attend to the calls of business until one. I then dine & at two return to the store where I remain until twilight calls me home to tea. This beverage being disposed of I resume either my reading or writing, enjoy myself in conversation with my family, attend to arbitrations or such other business for other people as I cannot conveniently dispatch in the daytime, or accompany my wife on a visit to some of our friends. I rarely visit unless in her company. Thus I jog on in what many would esteem a dull & slavish round & so far as mere business is concerned, it is dull enough truly. They who know me know that I am not inattentive to business or slothful, for I hold it to be my indispensible duty to provide for my family & am therefore diligent at business, not from pleasure, but necessity. Yet if my circumstances would admit of it, I should quickly abandon the crooked paths of trade & all my intercourse with the sordid lovers of gain & seek for other employments & for other associates than I am compelled now to endure. This is not meant as a reflection on merchants. I believe there is to be found among them men of great integrity & moral worth.

I know that true philosophy would teach us to bear with our lot wherever cast & to reconcile ourselves to whatever befalls us. But who obeys her dictates? Is not the life of man one continued scene of solicitude & variation? It is an uphill trudge, in search of some imaginary good which he never overtakes. In youth, he sets out vigourously in the determined chase, fancying he shall certainly & speedily succeed. The

phantom eludes him & mounts higher, whence she smiles him full in the face & invites his approach, making a deceitful display of her fascinating charms. He presses forward with new hopes, expecting to arrive at some resting place where he may repose his wearied limbs & undisturbed enjoy the darling object of his pursuit. The demon disappointment, armed with bludgeons & whips of scorpions, follows close in his train to beat him from every foothold & place of shelter, while driving rains & withering blasts contribute to wear away the powers of nature & render existence a burden. As old age creeps on, his labours become more arduous & painful & scarce the bended frame can sustain the illusory pursuit. At last the summit is attained. What then? Why then, hopeless with the dreariness of the surrounding prospect & unable to return, he sinks into the expanded jaws of a volcano, down, down we know not whither and is heard from no more. His exit serves but to make way for the myriads who throng in his rear, each allured by the same infatuation, each destined to the same pains & disappointments & to the same final end.

*December 3d.* On the 6th October I noted some circumstances respecting a shipment of German goods to Baltimore to which I might add that, a few weeks after their arrival there, a letter informed us that the cellar in which they were deposited was broken open & a number of them stolen. The thieves were detected but the goods could not be recovered. The market there was glutted by numerous & unexpected importations. We therefore ordered a part back, as few of the articles remained in the warehouse in Philada. & we had an immediate demand for them. The parcel thus ordered were accordingly sent to us but came too late for the persons who wanted them & on the very same day that we received them, a European vessel arrived with a large supply of the same articles. In the meantime, the demand in Baltimore revived & I this day wrote to my brother, resident there, preparatory to sending the same goods back again. I had just closed the letter & was in the act of sealing it when a person called in & bought them. Many of the more important schemes of life are planned with the same wondrous sagacity & forethought, executed in the same style of wisdom & terminate in equal conformity to our sage calculations.

*December 15th.* Some author has said that no conceit, however absurd or ridiculous, can enter the mind of man but has been reduced to practice. Whether this be actually true or not, still it cannot be doubted that we continaully meet with caprices & humours which level the boasted reason of man with the instinct of the meanest reptile. Our affections for some objects and our antipathies to others, are frequently not to be accounted for upon any principle of rationality. In the circle of my family connections there is a man between 50 & 60 years of age, of a benevolent turn & affectionate heart, sound in his morality & religion according to common acceptance & one of whose discretion and judgment many think highly. This man has taken a strong dislike to one of his nieces, a child about two years old, which certainly commenced within a month after her birth, if not before. He often visits in the family & evinces considerable attachment to the parents & the rest of the children, not one of whom has more attractive powers or is more promising than the little object of his dislike. He will not even look at her & to all her many prattlings and gambols around him appears wholly insensible. Well now, could anybody guess the cause of this rooted antipathy? It is this—he came to visit the mother in her lying in & when she was much indisposed & the nurse affronted him by not inviting him into the sick chamber!

*December 16th.* Am informed by one of the creditors of C.W. & Co. that he expects the effects of E.W. will not produce as much as will amount to a dividend. How strange! Should it prove true, then in the course of about four years he & Cox contrived to waste $40,000, on a moderate computation, at the same time that they uniformly flattered me that they were making money. Hard as my bargain with the creditors appeared to myself, if the information now given to me is to be relied on, I was lucky in effecting the compromise.

*December 31st.* After some days of vacation from the employment of making these occasional notes, I feel considerable reluctance to resume it. Can scarce assign the cause. Perhaps it arises from an innate sense of their trifling nature or perhaps also from sheer indolence & barrenness of thought.

# 1805

*January 20th.* On the 14th the Convention of delegates from the
different abolition societies in the U.S. commenced their annual sessions. On returning in the evening of the 15th from their meeting, my
fortitude was reduced to a trial of the keenest anguish. My Mary, my
beloved & excellent Mary, had been attacked with rheumatism or gout
in the stomach. Her pains were excruciating, her pulse gone & a
death-like cold, clammy sweat had seized her whole frame. Her physician gave me no hopes of her recovery. That night the disease would not
yield to medicine. The next day the symptoms were more favourable.
Her pulse was partially recovered & the coldness had passed off. The
pain began gradually to abate & on the 17th the paroxysm subsided.
Yesterday, however, she was again seized with spasm in the stomach,
nausea & vomiting & so great was the irritability of the principal seat of
the disease that for several hours the stomach rejected everything
thrown into it & it was with great difficulty & constant attention that at
last this propensity gave way to medicine & nursing. Towards midnight,
relief was procured & this morning the regularity of her pulse & freeness
from pain give me new hopes that a life so dear to me & so valuable to
her children may be preserved. Last night I sat up with her & administered the doses ordered for her relief, persuaded that in a case so critical
much depended on a careful & proper attention to passing symptoms, so
as to seize every favourable moment for procuring ease. In no instance
have I more powerfully perceived the benefits of this kind of attention
than in her case. I have found that in both these attacks, a rigid & literal
adherence to the directions of the physician was ineligible. Symptoms
would occur in his absence against which no provision had been made &
it required great caution to adapt the applications to these unforeseen &
varying circumstances. This, in the height of the paroxysms, I was not
willing to trust to other hands than my own & I have consolation in
believing that she has derived great advantage from the caution. In
disorders which do not affect the stomach, I am persuaded that much
care is necessary not to overcharge it with either medicine or food & in
diseases which seize on that delicate portion of the system, the caution
is the more essential. The patient anxious for relief is ready to receive
what is offered & nurses are too apt, from a desire to be doing, to do more
than is proper & frequently aggravate the symptoms & prolong the
disease by premature attempts to restore strength to the patient. "He is

weak & miserable & should have something nourishing," is the common language of attendants on the sick. Whereas but lop off the excrescence, that which is the cause of the malady & nature will very shortly rectify herself.

My children, tho' much attached to their mother, are yet too young to be sensible of the irreparable loss they would sustain in being deprived of her. In order to the well bringing up of children it is essential that the parents agree as to their mode of treatment. No two perhaps have in general harmonized more perfectly than we on this very interesting subject. We have enjoyed much satisfaction in the reflection & also in the persuasion that the coincidence has been very beneficial to our offspring. Hand in hand with her, I have been thus twelve years engaged in endeavouring to discharge my duty as a father. Alone, how could I pursue the task? The thought is too painful to be endured.

"A house divided against itself cannot stand" is a saying tested by the wisdom of ages & of the truth of which daily experience furnishes us with many examples. For one parent to indulge their children in practices which the other disapproves is at once striking at the foundation of domestic peace & must produce consequences injurious to the children themselves. If the father forbids his son from resorting to places of public amusement & the mother encourages him secretly to disobedience of the injunction, she undermines the authority of the father & destroys perhaps the filial affection of the son. One act of disobedience leads to another until at length the boy, losing all respect for the father, considering him in the light of a tyrant, first clandestinely & then openly disregards all his admonitions & perhaps finally deserts the parental roof to procure a less restrained indulgence of his appetites & passions. The mother, being an accessory & accomplice, is soon viewed with less regard than formerly & having sown the seeds of filial disrespect in her hopeful boy, must expect to gather the bitter fruits of her folly, when repentance is too late & to find herself treated with disaffection by the child of her womb & probably reproached by him as the cause of all his errors & sufferings, when experience shall have taught him that he has chosen misery for his portion.

I am no friend to the discipline of the rod, but there are cases in which it not only is useful but necessary. If after I have exhausted my powers of reason & persuasion to no purpose, either to prevent my son from the commission of evil or to reclaim him from the practice of it, he prove obdurate, it becomes my duty to restrain him by coercion. A weak mother frequently interferes & by taking part with the undutiful son,

hardens him in iniquity & changes the wholesome medicine of correction into a baneful poison. If even she secretly disapproves what I have done, it is extremely ill-judged openly to avow it & to tell my son she thinks I have treated him with unmerited harshness. Children educated under such discordant authority may nevertheless become respectable members of society, but there is more than an equal probability that they will turn out mere vagabonds, a burden to themselves & pests to the community. An inordinate attachment to the reading of novels is in a variety of respects injurious to the mind, especially if not defended by judgment to discriminate the good from the bad contained in them. Life as it is usually displayed in them must, in order to be attractive to the common mass of readers, contain incidents, principles & practices not usually found in real scenes of business & pleasure & as rarely proper for imitation. The parent, therefore, who spends much of her time in the perusal of these works of the imagination is not likely to become a good example to her offspring, nor to quality herself for the proper discharge of the important duties of her station. If, besides misspending time herself in greedily devouring the contents of novel after novel, she indulge her children in the same species of reading, in preference to the study of works of more practical utility, it is scarcely to be expected that either parent or offspring will have much relish for the ordinary & to them dull & uninteresting vocations of common life. Surely this is a state much to be regretted & from which great danger to the usefulness & happiness of both is to be apprehended. I therefore trace many of the evil dispositions and conduct of children to the pernicious practice of inordinate novel reading in their parents & the improper habit of it in themselves. To say that all novels have an injurious tendency would be rash & ill founded. It is the common herd that I condemn & but few even of the best are wholly unobjectionable. Few of the heroes & heroines can be copied safely by persons in the ordinary walks of society. None of these are so bad but what contain some good, but this is no more a sufficient recommendation to their perusal than it would be to pattern after a bad man because he had some valuable properties; for none are so wicked but that some good may be found in them.

A complete novel enamorata may almost be known by her theatric deportment & conversation, continually reminding the beholder, by these circumstances of the ages of chivalry & romance, when every waiting maid was a lady & every lady a goddess whose principal occupation was to sit in state to receive the adorations of her knight & to award his destiny. No wonder that such a woman should imagine her children to be something superior to the common mass of mankind & requiring extraordinary indulgences & the homage of their neighbours of more vulgar origin. They are not to be thwarted like brats of coarser materials. They cannot bear it. They must not be contradicted by their playmates & whether they choose to go to school, to go apprentice to some honest & respectable trade of profession, is entirely at their own choice. For even their parents must not force the inclinations of the young heroes, lest the latter, in the high effervescence of their wounded spirits, should commit some dreadful & tragical act. I have known such language to be held by a mother to her son, over whom the father was occasionally disposed to exercise his parental authority, to compel the young knight to his duty. Nay, she had gone further; she has reduced her theory to practice. The boy has been permitted to desert his place at school & his master's compting house; & after the father had beaten him for repeated & daring disobedience of orders, she has encouraged him to resent the affront by leaving home, telling him, or at least saying in his presence, she thought his father had used him so ill he could no longer live under his roof or be dependent on him—all this to a boy in his teens.

*January 23d.* Just returned from a town meeting convened to devise means for the extra relief of the poor, who suffer much from the unusual severity of the winter. Delaware has been frozen over for some weeks & the weather continues very cold. Wood has been high. Oak is $12 per cord but large quantities are now brought over the ice & it may be purchased at $7½. A letter from N. York states the price there at the enormous rate of $48 & that the Lombardy poplars in the streets have been cut down for fuel. The Indians, who are very accurate observers of the operations of nature, say that the waters in the lakes rise seven years & then fall seven & that last year they began to rise. When the waters rise, they add, the winters will be long & cold. When they fall, the weather will moderate accordingly. There may be some exaggeration in the quotation of the prices of wood in N.Y., but a respectable merchant told me that his correspondent in that place, a man on whom he could rely, had stated that to be the price.

*January 27th.* The present sufferings of the poor have given rise to various schemes, or rather projects, for their more permanent relief, especially in the article of fuel, among which the most prominent is a plan for raising by voluntary subscription a considerable capital, the amount of which is to be applied to the purchase of wood in the summer & to sell it in the winter at the cost. How far this benevolent design will

be productive of benefit, if carried into execution, is a subject well worth the consideration of the public. Some doubts have arisen in my mind as to the expediency of the measure. No city perhaps abounds in so many charitable institutions as Philada. Independent of the public provisions for the relief of the poor, there are a considerable number of private associations, both male & female, who dispense very largely of their bounty to suffering humanity.

It is a fact well known to all who are conversant on the subject, that in those countries in which the poor are the most abundantly provided for, they are found the most to abound. Like vegetables, they shoot up wherever nourishment is the most copious. Idleness & want of forethought & economy prevail very generally among this unhappy class & to these causes may be traced not only the origin of poverty in the aggregate mass, but the continuance of it. Laying the axe therefore to the root of the evil, we should rather endeavour to reform their bad habits & teach them the arts necessary to the comfortable support of themselves, than to keep them in a situation of dependence on others for subsistence. I have had some experience on this subject & have observed that generally when a poor person has once thrown himself on public bounty, he considers himself ever after as having a lien on the public purse & neglects to make the necessary exertions for his own support. Thus his idle habits become more powerfully fixed than ever & as idleness is the parent of crimes, he at length becomes a public nuisance, encouraging by his example many others to pursue the same track of laziness & infamy.

I have a feeling for the sufferings of my fellow men, but our feelings should not be permitted to run away with our judgment & it is always better to use means for preventing disease than to rely on methods of cure, however efficacious & skillfully applied. If fuel is to be supplied for nothing, there never will be a lack of applicants & if it is at any time to be furnished at considerably less than the market rate, I take it for granted that no quantity within the means of any association to purchase will remain long uncalled for. Many depending on this supply will neglect to provide it for themselves in the summer but, acting consistently with the character of man, will wait until the article is wanted & cannot be done without & then call for it. It is to be feared that when this period arrives, they will generally be very illy if at all supplied with the means of payment. The money which in the summer or autumn ought & might have been applied to the purchase of fuel for the winter will perhaps have been spent in absolute debauchery or on some useless object. Colquehoun mentions it as a fact that in London, when the season for oysters arrives, the poor are found to be the first purchasers of them—people of the higher & middle class refusing to buy until the price moderates. In Philada. it is no uncommon circumstance to see the poor carrying from the market many of the most expensive articles of provision, such as geese, turkies, &c.

It is not merely our reasonable but our indispensable duty to provide for those who cannot provide for themselves & I have not a doubt that many deserving objects might be benefited by the proposed plan. My fears arise from an apprehension that the charity will be so much abused as to counter balance more than all the good which can arise out of it & that while those for whom it is intended will, from motives of honest tho' perhaps mistaken pride, be prevented from making application, a throng of forward & selfish creatures, little meriting the bounty, will be found to be the principal partakers.

I had rather, therefore, when any pressing emergency like the present shall render it necessary to provide more amply for the poor than on ordinary occasions that temporary but efficient sums should be raised for supplying their necessities than to see any plan adopted which shall increase the number of our permanent charities & which may have the effect of increasing the number and sufferings of the indigent, by teaching them to rely on the aid of others rather than on their own provident & industrious exertions.

*January 29th*. The lucubrations on the preceding topic have given rise to a conviction in my mind of the propriety of furnishing the public with some remarks, in which I have treated the subject rather more copiously & given the essay to Poulson for publication.

*February 6th*. The weather continues severely cold. The ice on the Delaware is from 14 to 20 inches thick. In some of the eastern states the thermometer is stated to have been 10, 15 & sometimes 18 degrees below 0. In N. York, there was lately a fall of snow which continued, with one hour's intermission, for 48 hours. The same storm continued with us about the same length of time & fell very fast. An article in the *Gazette* mentions that in Plymouth NE its duration was 75 hours & that it was the 39th snow storm which they had experienced in about 6 weeks. In Connecticut, they have had a storm of thunder & lightning in the midst of all this severity & when the ground was deeply covered with snow & ice. Almost every paper contains accounts of shipwrecks. Many lives have been lost & many who survived have lost their limbs by frost. The mass of suffering is great both by land & sea. In most of the large towns, the poor are provided for by voluntary subscriptions. The scarcity of fuel in N. York has occasioned their corporation to petition the Legislature for permission to cut up the wooden batteries. Scenes like these proclaim the uncertainty of human possessions & enjoyments & the incapacity of man to protect himself against adversity. It is during these seasons of suffering that the voice of omnipotence is heard & confessed. In the plenitude of power, in the enjoyment of prosperity, in the fruition of health, we are frequently deaf to the calls of wisdom. Trials are therefore necessary to reclaim us to a sense of our duty & to remind us of our frailties. In the high career of pleasure we are sometimes suddenly arrested & forced to reflect on the ultimate tendency of our course. It is done in mercy & if the monition, thus given, be attended to, we may be saved from many future evils. We are too often disobedient to the holy vision and make it necessary that we should be visited with some new calamity to bring us back to the path which leads to peace. Have I been bereaved of a darling child, have I been deprived of a fortune, has a near & dear friend forsaken me, am I harassed with daily cares & perplexities, do not these severe & heart rending reflections on my varied imperfections & faults teach me to seek comfort from the father of the afflicted & the only sure fountain of consolation?

Yet on not even these probations, sorely as I have been tested by them, have sufficed for my purification, for not a day passes without witnessing in me the commission of some act which my better reason disapproves, the utterance of some expressions which should have been withheld or the indulgence of feelings which should be repressed.

*February 23d.* Have been amused in remarking the effects of a publication under the signature or Simon Slow, intended in a good humoured way to excite more punctuality among tradesmen. Had left my watch with a person more than 3 months to have a very trifling repair. I tired of his tardiness & frequent breach of promise & resolved on an expedient which has succeeded. I knew he was a subscriber to "The Evening Fireside," the editors of which had been boring me to write for them. The number containing Simon Slow came out about noon. The cap was seized by my watchmaker. The first job he undertook after dinner was my watch, which he brought me repaired before night. He laughed, yet his confused manner & more confused countenance bespoke his suspicions of the author of the piece & its immediate object—tho' not the most distant allusion was made in it which could have led any other person to suspect that he was aimed at. Simon appears in the character of a shoemaker & may be of use to others as well as my watchmaker.

*February 26th.* Understanding that the Com. lately appointed by the citizens to distribute donations to the poor have had several meetings to devise means of reforming the laws & perceiving that the subject has been brought before the Legislature by the guardians of the poor, I deemed it not amiss to bring my plan before the view of the public & accordingly published it in the *American Daily Advertizer.* Today I have been called on by the editor to say that several respectable citizens belonging to the Com. of Distribution waited on him with a request to know the author, that they might invite him to attend their deliberations. Poulson did not feel himself at liberty without consulting me. My answer was, if the public good be the object, I have no objection to being introduced to the Com. but I do not wish my name to be given up merely to gratify curiosity.

*February 27th.* Called on this evening by two members of the Distributing Committee & at their earnest request went with them to the house of E. Hazard where I met their colleagues. They unanimously agreed to my plan respecting the poor & referred to E. Hazard, T. Paxson & myself to prepare something for the adoption of the citizens, preparatory to a memorial to the Legislature.

*March 10th.* The Democrats gained their ascendency in this City in a great measure by the outcry they raised against the water works. In their first council, frequent attempts were made to put an end to further improvement & to destroy what had already been done. The advocates of the violent measures did not hesitate to openly avow, in debate, that they owed their seats to the expectations that they had given to those who deputed them, that they would destroy the water works. The works had, however, received their impetus & as a majority of the two Councils could not be persuaded to realize the hopes of their Jacobin constituents by voting with their ignorant and intemperate colleagues, the works moved on by the means previously provided & under the immediate management of persons employed by the former Councils. Notwithstanding the hostility evinced by the Democrats towards the Federalists & their measures, some of the members of the old Councils, throwing aside party considerations, took early measures for manifesting a disposition to give all necessary & useful information in their power to their new rulers. These friendly overtures were not met, nor the information communicated or attended to. The consequence of this is, as might have been expected, that the City interest has materially suffered and much of the care exercised by the old members of Council has been lost labour. Finding themselves entangled by their ignorant & perverse measures & not having the ability or information necessary to their extrication, they have at length appealed in a formal manner to some of us to help them out & I have this day been invited by a com. appointed for this purpose, to attend one of their meetings. I shall not go. I gave myself some trouble on some other occasions to communicate a knowledge of facts on certain points, yet they acted in direct opposition to what they knew to be right. One of them afterwards said to me in explanation, "We make it an invariable rule, first to find what had been done by the Councils in Federal times on any subject that comes before us & then to do the very reverse."

Roosevelt, on completing the engines in all their parts, which he never did, was to receive from the corporation a lease of the extra power of the Schuylkill engine & certain adjacent lots of ground. Previous to which, however, it was stipulated in the articles of agreement he was bound to give good & sufficient security to pay the annual rent, to keep the engines in order, to supply them with fuel & to pump water for the City. Roosevelt, knowing the kind of men he had to deal with, has taken possession of the lower engine house & erected a slitting & rolling mill & other works there, without obtaining a lease or complying with the terms prescribed in the articles to entitle him to one. Some pains were taken to make our new rules comprehend the contract with Roosevelt & to induce them not to suffer him to erect his works until the corporation should come to a settlement of acc't with him. They should compel him to complete the engines agreeable to contract & receive from him the security provided for. The caution availed nothing. R. has lately threatened them that if they do not pay him a large sum which he demands, he will stop the supply of water. So far from his being entitled to what he thus demands, he must be thousands of Dollars indebted to the corporation. I should not be surprized if he frightened them into his views, for I find that Latrobe, pursuing his object steadily, has lately scared them out of a handsome sum to which he had no manner of claim in law, justice or equity & which his written contract with the City expressly forbids him to demand.

*March 14th.* At length the detail of the plan relative to the poor has been completed. A subcommittee of seven have this night reported it to the Ward Committees & Committees of Distribution, the first appointed to collect & the last to distribute the late donations of the citizens to the poor. They were convened at the City Hall for the special purpose of receiving the report, which was read to them & unanimously adopted. It is highly gratifying to me to find that a plan which I had long since matured in my own mind should have received the approbation of so large a number of respectable citizens.

*April 1st.* A set of thieves of the most dastardly kind infest the City. Confining their depredations principally to defenseless women, shopkeepers and children, from the former they pilfer various articles of merchandize & from the latter lockets & any trinket of which they may be possessed. Today my little daughter, about 2½ years old, was missing for a few minutes. Search being made, she was found in the neighbourhood, deprived of her gold chain & locket.

Have this day had in my hands the original charter of Pennsylva. It is contained on several sheets of parchment in good preservation & written very neatly & correctly in the old secretary hand. The margins are decorated with various engravings of an emblematic import among which is the half length likeness of the Royal granter & the arms of England, Iceland, Scotland & France, all executed in a masterful style. The grant is from Charles the 2nd to William Penn for a tract of country commencing twelve miles north of the Town of New Castle & thence along the river Delaware, for the eastern boundary, to the forty-third degree of North latitude & thence westwardly five degrees, thence on a line parallel to the river Delaware to the latitude of 12 miles north of New Castle, and thence on a direct line to the place of beginning. The reasons assigned for the grant are that the realms of the King may be extended & the "commodities" of his empire increased by enabling the said Wm. Penn to transport an ample colony to the country & by just & mild "manners" to teach the "savage natives the love of civil society & the Christian religion." It is also in grateful remembrance of the services rendered by Admiral Sir Wm. Penn, father of the grantee, to James Duke of York, in the defeat of the Dutch fleet commanded by the "Heer van Obdam in the year 1665."

The instrument was executed "on the 4th of March in the thirty-third year of the King's reign & by writ of the privy seal."

1682                    signed "Pigott"
John Thale, Chev.

*April 2d.* A merchant should be as particular in the choice of a partner as in the choice of this wife. There should be an entire coincidence in principles, view, habits & practice; otherwise their business cannot be conducted to mutual benefit & satisfaction. Of these truths I am at this moment a practical experimental example. Perhaps I may be fastidious & attach more importance to correctness in keeping books of account and to punctuality in engagements than some men of business may think essential, but to omit to charge goods when sold on credit & to neglect to give credit in the books when debtors make payment must be acknowledged by everybody to lead to very pernicious if not ruinous consequences. Nor can it be justifiable on any principle for one partner to put in & draw out from the common stock, at his pleasure and unknown to his colleague, sums of money. When transactions of that nature occur to the amount of thousand of Dollars & are persevered in for a course of years, notwithstanding the repeated entreaties & remonstrances of the other, it evinces something on the part of the offender, however honest his intentions, which must be extremely embarrassing & dissatisfactory to the injured party. When business is thus conducted it must be next to impossible, in case of the death of the partner who is in this practice, for the other to fairly settle the concerns of the house & ascertain the balance due to each. On the other hand, should the opposite party die first, his heirs must entirely depend on the integrity & justice or will of the survivor to render them their due, since the partnership books contain no certain criterion as their guide. Worse than even these must be the consequences, should both die in such an unsettled & perplexed state of their affairs. There would then remain no possible means of adjusting matters between their respective heirs on any sure data. How it is possible for any man of sense thus to trifle with the peace & property of his partner & to expose their joint interest to such confusion is difficult to conceive.

*April 6th.* Have received no visit from C.B.B. in all the last winter. He has "married a wife & cannot come." Am fearful he is making small progress in the history of slavery. With T.P.'s family I have latterly had no intercourse. He & I often meet on our ancient friendly terms. For years, a night scarcely past without some intercourse between these my old friends & myself. Deeply regret the change. Once I fondly believed it impossible. We are doubtless each in error. Perhaps a more discerning judgement & suitable opportunities of explanation might induce me to think differently of the cold returns made me for former proofs given them of my attachment. Surely I have been & continue to be sufficiently tried & have trouble enough without this fruitful source of painful reflections. The heart, once engaged, reluctantly yields up its object & it is probable that, whatever may be the conduct of these persons towards me, I shall not be able to alienate all my affection from them. Yet, had they not turned away from me in the midst of some of the severest afflictions of my life, I could perhaps have borne the conflict with more serenity. It is no doubt a wise ordination of providence to place the enjoyments of this life on a precarious footing, to wean us from the world & to induce us to place our dependence on Heaven. It really appears, as I advance in years, that the sources of my vexation become more numerous. Happy will it be for me if wisdom should increase with experience, so as to enable me to bear the burden with fortitude proportioned to its accumulated weight. Had we less asperity & more charity in our composition than have fallen to the share of some of us, we should certainly avoid much of the corroding feelings which otherwise torment us. Properly to appreciate the merits of others & to make just estimates & allowances for their errors & defects; to bear with philosophic temper their caprices, follies & vices—is to acquire more self command & to exercise more Christian mercy & forbearance than is commonly practiced & yet, even self-love might dictate it, as the surest mode of self-enjoyment & that peace of mind which surpasseth all understanding.

*April 16th.* The yearly meeting of Friends commenced yesterday. The new meeting house in Arch Street, having been recently finished, has been opened for the first time for the accommodation of the women & nearly two thousand assembled there yesterday.

*April 23d.* Lydia, the daughter of my late unfortunate brother John, has arrived on a visit from Yorktown. Have not seen her before for six years. She was then a child & is now a young woman. Her appearance has revived a train of serious reflection. This orphan is dear to me.

*May 10th.* Amidst the various avocations of business in the day & my frequent engagements on arbitrations &c. in the evening, I spend but a small portion of time in social intercourse. I have nevertheless lately had at my house & elsewhere several very pleasant & instructive interviews & conversations with some agreeable friends—some of whom I accompanied to the Penna. Hospital & to Bartram's garden, our principal object being the gratification of my newly arrived niece & the accomplished Elizabeth Laurence from Flushing on Long Island.

*May 12th.* Have frequent occasion to feel my ignorance & to regret my want of knowledge—doubtless I have not made the best use of my time. Had I received a more liberal education I might have derived a vast fund of improvement & enjoyment in ranging the wide spread fields of science which my limited acquirements now bar me from entering & been more useful in the varied walks of life among my fellow citizens. Am also conscious that the few talents which I do possess are far from being devoted to the wisest & best purposes.

*June 20th.* Have had a most agreeable visit from my friend Wm. Johnson, who has spent some days in our City. Several afternoons have been devoted to excursions in the neighbourhood of the City in company with this excellent man, C.B. Brown & T. Eddy. No plan had such powerful attractions for him as the Woodlands, the elegant seat of Wm. Hamilton. His garden is unquestionably the richest in the variety & value of its plants & in the taste displayed in their arrangement of any in this state or perhaps in the United States. The gardener informed us that the collection consists of eight thousand species; of some of these, there are several varieties & in many instances, several plants of the same kind—so that, on the whole, the number is very considerable.

*July 3d.* Have placed my sons Henry & Francis at Weston School. Conducted them thither on the 30th last & returned today.

*August 18th.* Amid a thousand cares & avocations, one subject has lately engrossed a considerable portion of my thoughts: I have a nephew, the son of my late unhappy brother John. He lives in York, Pennsyla. with his mother & has arrived at an age which renders it proper he should be apprenticed to some business by which he may hereafter support himself. Have not seen him since he was a child & know but little of his qualifications or natural disposition. He has claims on me which I feel powerfull & I am anxious to see him well placed. His sister is yet under my roof; should he possess a disposition as amiable, I shall have hopes of his making amends for the defects of his father who, notwithstanding, had many excellent traits of character & under different circumstances might have been the best ornament of the family.

*August 20th.* It is an extraordinary fact that the very men who so lately vilified the Federalists & used every unfair means to drive them from public employment & to rob them of public confidence are now soliciting them to become their representatives in the City as well as State Legislature. A large schism has been made in the councils of the

Democrats—the more violent part of them urging their disorganizing schemes to an extreme at which their more thinking & moderate partizans have become alarmed. The latter now form a third party in the State, known by the name of Tertium Quids. These have now marshalled themselves against their late friends. I have been urged to serve them as a member of the House of Representatives of this State. One great object of their present views is to prevent the overthrow of the Constitution of Pennsyla., with which the anarchists, or—as they falsely call themselves—Republicans, threaten the community.

Many of my friends press me to accept of the office & urge some powerful reasons to induce my assent, but I must refuse them. Nor can I believe it incumbent on me to make so large a sacrifice of feeling & interest as they call for at my hands. A considerable portion of my life has been employed in one way or another in public service—nor have I ever received or sought for a cent in return for my labours. I am now engaged in mercantile pursuits which, if not diligently attended to, may involve myself & others in ruin.

*September 2d.* Attended as a juror in the Supreme Court & signed a remonstrance to the Judges to request them to adjourn their sittings. The paper was drawn up by Edwd. Tilghman & intended to be signed by the bar as well as the jury. It stated that malignant fever *rages* in the district of Southwark, that it has spread into *many* parts of the City & *increases rapidly every day.* With his permission & that of several others who had signed it, I varied the expressions so as to render them nearer what I apprehend to be the fact. In place of *rages* I introduced *prevails,* instead of *many, some* & struck out *increases rapidly every day.* After which several others signed it, but the Court came to no conclusion.

*September 5th.* Such is the temper of the world that, if a man humbly solicit a favour, it will be granted with a reluctant grudging hand, or not at all, but if he wants not its favours, they will be pressed on him. Had I been desirous of a seat in the State Legislature & sought it with assiduity, it is quite probable it might have been refused. Now that I have so repeatedly declined the offer, it would seem as if my fellow citizens were resolved to force it on me. I have had no less than four separate deputations on the subject this day. To each I have given an unequivocal refusal. As these deputations were composed of men of the first respectability & selected from different parties, I might feel my vanity flattered by the deference shown to me, was I not too conscious of my own demerits & did I not know myself to be the sport of conflicting passions, which I have not sufficient strength of mind to control.

*September 16th.* Have been absent for a week on a visit to our children. Went in company with Mary & have returned with my mind more tranquilized than when I left home. Could I suppose myself worthy of the minute regard of Providence, I might be induced to think that the varied mental conflicts to which I have been subject for some time past were designed for my more effectual purification. Certain is it that my unruly passions are very far from being reduced to a proper state of order & subordination. My life is a daily contest, under which my spirits are often greatly depressed. Altho' my partner perceives it & is sensible of the cause & altho' he professes a friendship for me & has frequently acknowledged the impropriety of his proceedings, yet he does not change his practice. His account with the house remains unadjusted & he perseveres in taking money so irregularly that I cannot preserve my faithful record of the amount. Neither does he interest himself in planning or arranging matters of business, particularly relative to making sales & providing in time for the payment of our contracts. Oft when we have thousands & tens of thousands of Dollars to pay at Bank, he appears quite unconcerned, leaving it to me to concert the means. If in my absence letters are received requiring prompt answers, they are left till I return & when I am at home, he will not be prevailed upon to write at all. Well, if I can only be favoured of Heaven to make a right use of these probations, I may come out a better man & live to see more happy days. I am sometimes surprized at myself to think that these things should so torment me & yet, that the mind should meet with daily & hourly frustrations of its plans & have constant cares corroding its peace which it knows not how to escape from, is enough to wear away its energy & shroud all around it in gloom. I bear all these vexations rather than resort to the only alternative—an immediate separation—because I fear that by whatever means I might bring it about, the strange humours of J.T. would lead to a breach of our family harmony, involving others as well as ourselves.

*September 23d.* The third party have announced their ticket. The Federalists are not content with it. Since the publication I have had several of the leading men among the latter to call on me, who yet insist on my serving them. A deputation of two came to me today, when the following conversation ensued.

"We are requested to express the hope of your Federal friends that you may be prevailed on to suffer your name to be run."

Answer. "It gives me pain to repeat to so respectable a part of my fellow citizens the denial I have so repeatedly given. I have reasons of a private nature for wishing to be excused & did not refuse capriciously but after much reflection. Had I consented, had my business permitted it, I greatly fear my friends would have been much disappointed in the expectations they have formed of me. Others of greater experience & better talents may be had who are willing to go. Why not select from among them? I have invariably declined when pressed by the third party & by the Federalists who came to me on their behalf. They finally made choice of another & that other has been formally offered to the public. How can I now consent? Moreover, if you now form a new ticket, or alter the one proposed, your influence will be lost. The Federalists are not sufficiently powerful to carry a ticket of themselves. You will cause dissension among the friends to the Constitution. Its preservation is the great object & altho' some of the candidates agreed on may be obnoxious, they are all presumed to be friends of the Constitution. I therefore entreat you to make a magnanimous offering of your private feelings on the public weal & to vote the ticket which has been published. Every vote taken from it will throw one into the counter scale & as the third party have pledged themselves to support it, you can scarce expect them to forego that pledge in favour of other candidates, however respectable. You had best vote the ticket as it is, or all may be lost."

Rejoinder. "We cannot give you up. Your name & the name of Jos. Hemphill—in the place of Israel & Samuel Carver, for whom we cannot vote—will reconcile us to the rest of the ticket. Several others have been mentioned in your stead, but none in whom all are so united. If the third party perceive that we will not adopt their ticket unless they consent to our modification of it, they must concur. They cannot succeed without our aid & if the alteration we contemplate is not made, we will not go to the election ground. We therefore entreat you to reflect well on the consequences of your persisting in your refusal. The sacrifice of compliance to you may be great, but remember the stakes & that your country demands your service."

The conversation was prolonged much to the same effect & we parted without any definite result.

Some of the Federalists are for remaining neuter & suffering the other two parties to maintain the struggle. Democracy, say they, is a mighty torrent which is not to be arrested. It must & will finish its course—when it has spent its force, the people will have felt. They will be taught wisdom by experience & not by precept; you must therefore suffer them to go on in their own way. Any opposition made to their mad career will

only serve to increase their fury. You may cast rocks in the stream, but in recoiling, it will surmount them & sweep over all obstacles.

This picture, however gloomy, may be fairly drawn; but if we stand listlessly by until the torrent shall have swept off everything dear to us as men & citizens, what shall we then have to contend for? We have had no demonstration that it cannot be resisted. It is therefore our duty to oppose its destructive progress, while means are left us & there is a chance of success. Democracy, in our form of government, instead of being a mountain torrent which, after having spent its force, may emanate in vapour, is rather a permanent current, rising & falling with the ebbings & flowings of popular opinion. It has its source in the vital fountains of our general & state constitutions & when properly bounded, runs a lively current, disseminating health & vigour, throughout its various channels, to the whole body politic. Its wild inundations are principally to be dreaded; they should be carefully & vigilantly guarded, lest the stream—bounding over the wholesome mounds of the law—spread terror in its headlong course & involve, in one general deluge, the destruction of all the fairest & best fruits of society. It behooves, therefore, every guardian of the public weal—& every good citizen is one—perseveringly to watch the ebullitions of this wanton stream, to oppose timely barriers to its licentious overflowings & speedily to restore the breaches which, in the mad career of its occasional ravings, it may tear from its salutary embankments.

*September 26th.* A visit from H. Drinker, Jr., delegated by a number of Federalists who have had a meeting this morning. They wish to unite with the third party in support of the constitution but resolve not to vote the ticket in its present form. My positive refusal to serve them, if they formed a separate ticket, has occasioned most of them to abandon the project. They will no longer press me but wish that I would act as a mediator between them & the third party. They ask for no alteration in the ticket for Governor or for Councilman but insist on substituting Jos. Hemphill in the place of Israel Israel. They also wish another person to take place of Carver, but the latter change I am not to make a *sine qua non.* The assembly ticket thus modified, they will vote the residue, otherwise not attend the election.

I will cheerfully obey this call & if, in my character of ambassador of peace, I can succeed, it will afford me a very pleasing gratification. There are difficulties of no trifling magnitude to be surmounted. Promptness is also requisite, for the day of election is nearly at hand.

*September 27th.* Mortality still increases in Southwark. Cases more frequent in the City, principally confined to servant girls, apprentice lads & wandering poor. Few instances among respectable heads of families.

*October 5th.* The Federalists still adhere to their candidate. Israel Israel does not decline. This unpleasant situation may occasion both to fail, for a coincidence of action is indispensable. Hemphill is much the most preferable man & 'tis only to be regretted that he has been brought forward so late & under such embarrassing circumstances.

*October 9th.* Yesterday the election took place. Have returned from it somewhat fatigued, having acted as one of the Judges & been diligently employed from 10 yesterday morning until late this day, without sleep or other rest, save when taking necessary refreshment. The Constitutionalists—that is, the Federalists joined by the third party—have succeeded in their election in the City by a considerable majority. Hemphill is elected.

*October 15th.* 'Tis gratifying to perceive that the change of affairs in the City has again brought some of my old friends into public notice. T. Paxson has been chosen President of the Common Council & Jno. Inskeep, Mayor, tho' it is understood that the latter will not consent to serve long.

*October 16th.* The fever has nearly subsided.

*October 18th.* Another deficiency occurring today in our cash account, I made a formal proposal to J.T. to dissolve the firm. He received it with better temper than I expected, yet did not actually assent. I represented that, from whatever quarter these depredations came—as I had found it impossible to prevent them—I deemed it but a common act of prudence in which I hoped the concurrence of his judgment to bring our business to a close, as early as the nature of it would admit.

*November 12th.* The resignation of Jas. Gamble, a State Senator, renders it necessary to enter on an election to supply the vacancy. Have been called on to know if I will serve. The same reasons which induced me to decline serving in the House of Representatives still exist & of course decided me in giving a prompt negative to the present application.

*November 14th.* Attending a meeting of a few Federalists to consider

of measures proper to be pursued relative to the choice of a Senator, was appointed one of a com. of five to nominate a suitable character, with liberty to confer with the third party.

*November 18th.* After meeting twice, the Com. made choice of Jno. Hallowell for Senator & reported this evening to a meeting of citizens by whom he was unanimously adopted & a com. of 10 appointed to favour his election.

*November 29th.* The election for Senator was held yesterday. Took my station as judge; it was orderly, but altho' a majority have decided for Hallowell in the City & it is likely he will also have a majority in Delaware, yet the county of Philada. will give so great a majority for Jno. Dorsey, the Democratic candidate, that the latter will most probably succeed.

*November 30th.* Dorsey is the Senator by a small majority.

*December 28th.* General Eaton, who has lately acquired so much celebrity in the war with Tripoli, particularly by his fatiguing & hazardous march over the desert of Libya & subsequent conquest of Derne, Capt. Decatur, who has also greatly signalized himself as a naval commander in the same war & Capn. Stewart, who was engaged in the same service, were invited to the Conversation Society & spent this evening with us. They spoke without much reserve in condemnation of the treaty concluded by Consul Lear, by which the latter stipulated to pay $60,000 to the Bashaw for the ransom of Cap. Bainbridge & crew, at the moment when the Tripolitans were seized with terror by the news of the capture of Derne & at the formidable appearance of our fleets come to renew their attack on Tripoli itself. General Eaton had surmounted very great difficulties in Egypt. There, however, by the aid of the Ex-Bashaw, he collected an army of undisciplined barbarians which he marched across the Libyan desert, accompanied by a handful of his countrymen, who after being three days without water amid burning sands, carried the City of Derne by storm & were preparing to attack Tripoli, when the peace was concluded. In the course of conversation it was mentioned that Decatur had offered to land the men from the fleet, about two thousand & bring away the Bashaw in open day. He had previously destroyed a 44 gun ship under the walls of Tripoli & with three gun boats attacked the whole Tripolitan line of seventeen, moored under their batteries—driving them into port with the loss of three, which he captured.

They spoke with contempt of Doc. Cowdery, one of the prisoners with Capt. Bainbridge, whose journal has been published in our newspapers & doubted his capacity to write, attributing the composition to some other hand.

General Eaton appears to be under 40 years of age, about 5 feet 8 or 9 inches high, well made, rather robust than corpulent, light complexion & possessing a small, penetrating eye. He is lively, communicative & facetious. Decatur is nearly of the same size, between 20 & 30 years old, has a long aquiline nose, large mouth, black eye, dark visage & appears more like a Frenchman than an American. He is not so flippant in conversation as the General, nor does his mind appear to have been so highly cultivated, yet he was unreserved & appeared much at his ease among us.

# 1806

*January 16th.* The abolition convention adjourned today for three years, having been in session but four days & resolved on no very important measure, save addressing Congress to pass a law more effectually to prevent the carrying on the slave trade in Rhode Island. I was a member.

*January 20th.* Wrote a letter to Wm. Milnor, now one of our representatives at Lancaster, from the county of Bucks. He was one of the companions of my youth & has talents & integrity. The object of my address is to enlist him in the cause of our Poor Law.

*January 26th.* On the 20th received a note from C.B.B. enclosing a communication for the Abolition Convention relative to the causes which have operated to delay the completion of the history of slavery which, some years ago, he undertook to write. 'Tis in character with the man; geniuses should not be governed by common rules & maxims. His note comes 4 days after the adjournment of the Convention, yet T. Paxson had informed him of the time of meeting a few days before it took place. I did the same the last year & told him a communication would be expected. He promised to make one but forgot it until some weeks after the adjournment.

My friend C.B.B. possesses a humane heart, a very lively imagination highly cultivated by reading & observation & is, to a lover of knowledge, a most agreeable & valuable companion. His colloquial powers are exceeded by few & his command of language by none—at least, of whom I have any knowledge, but—having at an early period become contaminated by Godwin's Political Justice & works of a like tendency—he has not that delicate respect for his plighted word which would give dignity to his other accomplishments & is indispensible to the finished character.

*January 28th.* It is understood that a chasm which appears in one period of Marshall's life of Washington was occasioned by the loss of some of the General's notes. Tobias Lear, who was his private secretary & is now Consul at Algiers, it is shrewdly conjectured, could give some account of the missing papers & that the disclosure would not reflect much credit on President Jefferson.

*February 3d.* Wrote a letter to S.L.M., Senator from N. York, introducing J. Waln, who is the bearer of the memorial from the late convention to Congress.

*February 6th.* Our political horizon is lowering. With the Spaniards we have for months been considered as on the eve of a war. They refuse to make restitution for spoilations committed on our commerce or to acknowledge the boundary lines claimed by us for Lousiana. The French privateers in the W.I. rob our merchant vessels wherever they meet them. The English, under pretext of principles unacknowledged by us & not found in the law of nations, have captured very many of our richest shipping & daily continue their aggressions. Remonstrances from our merchants have reached Congress at the same time that the Minister from France has made our government a very intemperate representation relative to our trade with the revolted blacks in St. Domingo. A bill is now before Congress interdicting this trade. Resolutions are also before them for suspending all commercial intercourse with G. Britain & her dependencies.

Monroe is our Minister at London. He had been previously so at Paris. When at the latter, he intermeddled in the jealousies & quarrels of the two countries, evincing himself on all occasions the avowed enemy of G. Britain. Was he a fit person to send to that court? Was it not an insult offered them? Can they confide in him? Will they not rather consider him a spy & withhold from him every kind of information & knowledge, the development of which might, by his means, become injurious to them in their struggles with France?

*February 7th.* The plan for amending the laws respecting the poor is not likely to succeed with the Legislature. The country members are opposed to it, yet it does not contemplate any interference with them & is calculated solely for the City & districts. It is difficult to accomplish an abstract good where so many are to be consulted, numbers of whom will not take the trouble to become acquainted with the subject & if they did would probably not have the sense to understand it or sufficient patriotism to promote any measure from which they expected to derive no personal advantage.

*February 10th.* War in Europe continues. Lord Nelson lately defeated the combined fleets of France & Spain. He destroyed & captured 19. Lost his life in the battle. On the other hand, Bonaparte has taken Vienna. Russia &, 'tis said, Prussia have joined the coalition against France. Some battles of great carnage have been fought. The issue still doubtful.

Congress have come to no decision respecting our disputes with the belligerents. Marquis Yrujo, the Spanish Minister, has been requested by our Executive to leave Washington.

Much conjecture afloat respecting an armed ship called the *Leander*, lately sailed from N. York. It carries with her a considerable quantity of military apparatus; destination unknown. General Miranda, a native Mexican & implacable enemy of Spain is commander of the expedition. Report says he has drawn bills on the President of the East Indian Company of England for the outfits. Several young men of the first families in N. York have embarked as volunteers. Two printing presses & several journeymen printers are on board. Miranda is well known as an intrepid commander in the French service in their last war with Holland. I understood that the ministers of France & Spain have remonstrated to our government on the sailing of this ship & that the latter deny any knowledge of its outfits or object. Conjectured that other vessels similarly equipped have left other ports in the U.S. to join this mysterious expedition.

*February 12th.* My partner J.T. has bought & dispatched a small sloop on a trading voyage to Cape François. His son A.T. & my other nephew, H.W.D., have gone in her. Do not approve this purchase. The owner has not the requisite qualifications for a shipping merchant. For want of discretion & suitable management this vessel has cost him nearly twice her actual value.

*February 15th.* The first bridge across the Delaware has been completed within a few days past at Trenton.

*February 20th.* Yesterday & today so warm that moderate walking produces perspiration. Wood is lower than the usual summer price. Hickory is $6 a cord. The common summer price is $7 to $8.

Almost ever since the present Mayor came into office, the violent party have made him an object of calumny. Wrote a short paragraph for Poulson condemning the assailants. May give rise to some answer. If so I shall probably treat the subject more copiously.

*March 5th.* Formerly a cashiership in a Bank was offered to me. I declined it, but used my influence in favour of a person of whose integrity & capacity I had the highest opinion. This man lately died & left a widow & helpless family. I applied to some of the directors to endeavour to procure some gratuity for them. Preparatory to the grant they appointed a com. to settle the cashier's accounts. My surprize &

regret were great on being informed by one of that Com. that the result of their investigation proves the cashier to have applied some thousand Dolls. of the money of the Bank to his private use. This is another melancholy instance of the force of temptation on a man in needy circumstances whose household economy was not sufficiently circumscribed by his means.

*March 18th.* Returned from placing son William at school with James Embree, whither I was accompanied by my kinsman Henry S. Drinker & his charming little daughter Esther, 7 years old, whom he designs to place in the same family. The weather was cold & has been considerably more so during the present than the last month.

*March 20th.* Poulson has resigned the office of Librarian to the City Library. I have used some influence to procure the station for my old literary friend C.B.B. & with prospect of success. P. held the station twenty-one years.

*March 26th.* Late arrivals from Europe have brought important political intelligence. Bonaparte in the short space of two months has completely overrun Germany, capturing, destroying & driving before him the combined armies of Austria & Russia. A peace between France & Austria, greatly to the loss of the latter in territory, is the consequence. New kingdoms have been created, such as Bavaria, Wirtemberg, &c. Pitt, the celebrated prime Minister of England, is dead & notwithstanding the high stations which he has held, he died so much in debt that Parliament have voted 40,000 Pounds for the payment of what he owed & have ordered his burial at the expense of the nation. In three months the English have lost their first naval commander, Lord Nelson, their first military General, Lord Cornwallis, & their first minister, Wm. Pitt.

*April 12th.* For two days past the weather has been so cold that the gutters in the streets freeze, even in the daytime in a bright sun. No part of February has been so severe. Thus we perceive the singular spectacle of fruit trees in blossom contrasted with the rigour of winter.

C.B.B. has not succeeded in his application for Librarian. There were 23 candidates. He was, however, very ably supported. The votes on several trials between him & the successful candidate were equal. To relieve the Directors from their embarrassment, he withdrew his name. The other had powerful claims on their feelings, being a young man having no employment & having an aged father who has a numerous family to support & destitute of either the capacity or means.

*April 14th.* Yesterday my 4th son was born. The use of a name is to distinguish the person & this purpose is but illy answered by the common & long established custom of naming after family connections. I have departed from the general practice in this respect. Neither should a name be such as to excite preposterous or ridiculous emotions. It is an ill service rendered to your child & may in its consequences, immediate or remote, commit his happiness & respectability. It should not be too long, it is inconvenient to the possessor & to others. I have called this son Alfred.

*April 18th.* Have this afternoon had my feelings much excited by an occurrence in the neighbourhood of the store. T. Marshall made an attempt on his life by cutting his throat with a razor. The wound is ghastly. I saw him after the act & remained with him until other suitable assistance was procured. I left him alive, but there is scarce any probability that he will recover. For this rash act no sufficient cause is assigned. He is a single man of large fortune & in very prosperous business. Symptoms of melancholy had appeared on him for a few days past. While held to the floor by myself & others, weltering in his blood & apparently dying, he suddenly broke from us & thrust his hands into the gaping incision, endeavouring with frantic rage to rend it wider. Nor was it without considerable exertion that they were forced from his throat. The trachea is entirely separated, except by a slight membrane, but the carotids are not cut. Hence, he may linger for hours, a most miserable & melancholy spectacle.

*April 19th.* Marshall died today, in about 48 hours after he gave himself the wound. A physician tells me it is the third instance of suicide which occurred in the City on the same day.

So deep has the impression been in my imagination that I have scarce been able for a moment, day or night, to drive the horrible image & its attendant circumstances from my mind.

*April 30th.* Served with a notification from the Secretary informing me of my being elected a member of the Philada. Chamber of Commerce.

Two British Frigates, the *Leander* and *Cambrian* & the *Driver,* sloop of war, are now stationed off the harbour of N. York & bring to all vessels that attempt to pass. Some they discharge, others are sent to Halifax. A shot from one of them lately killed a man of the name of Pearce on board a Brandywine coaster bound to that port. This wanton act of aggression within our jurisdiction has produced great popular indignation in N. York, whither the body was conveyed & attended by an immense concourse of citizens to the grave. About 12 months ago these same Frigates occupied the same station & gave great umbrage by their conduct.

*May 10th.* A most destructive fire broke out last night on the north side of Dock Street between Third Street & Goforth Alley, which ended in the destruction of much property—upwards of thirty buildings being either totally destroyed or materially injured. It commenced early in the evening & was not conquered until very late at night. The wind blew strongly from the westward & conveyed the flakes of fire in such abundance that it required great exertions to prevent the whole mass of buildings between Third Street & the river from being consumed. Numbers caught fire & one house on Front Street was nearly burnt down. In aiding to extinguish that house, I suffered in common with others by the beating down of the smoke & ashes which we were compelled to inhale for hours. Some of the shipping took fire, but timely exertions prevented their being much injured.

It is a remarkable fact that the flakes fell so thickly on the Jersey shore as to render it necessary for the inhabitants to extinguish them with buckets of water on their houses & barns. I am informed by my brother Israel, who has been over the river since the fire with Isc. Cooper, that some of the flakes were discovered on the plantation of the latter, two miles from the Delaware.

This has been the greatest fire that ever happened in Philada. & it is no less singular than true that the next most destructive occurred on the same spot on the 9th of May 1791, exactly 15 years before. I was present at that fire & at one other in the same place, so that this is the third time within my memory of destruction by that element in the same spot of ground.

*May 12th.* Attended a meeting of the citizens convened to take measures for the relief of the sufferers by the late fire. I acted as Secretary. Committees of collection & distribution were appointed. I am to serve on the latter.

*May 13th.* My friend Wm. Young, who resides on the Brandywine in the vicinity of Wilmington, informs me that the late conflagration in our City was very distinctly seen several miles round him. He computes his paper mill to be 500 feet lower than the bank of the creek on the east of it, yet the blaze was powerfully visible from the mill.

The manufacture of paper has become extensive in this country. Prior to the American revolution, the article was imported from G. Britain. As it arrived in very uncertain quantities, printers were often put to inconvenience for want of it. The celebrated Benjn. Franklin was at that time a printer in Philada. Being in want of paper, he stopped a cart in which he saw some to enquire whence it came & was surprized to be answered that it was for sale. The carter was the owner & maker & had a mill on the Wissahickon. It was the only mill for the manufacture of paper on the continent. Franklin made a contract for a regular supply of paper with the maker, whose name was Chloss, whom he pursuaded to take apprentices & carry on the business more extensively.

It is extraordinary that the English, who are so celebrated as a nation of manufacturers, should be indebted to France for the paper on which their best copperplate printing is wrought. The war now carried on between them has put a stop to all direct commerce & the consequence is that importations of that article have lately been made into this City and thence exported to England.

*May 14th.* Several persons have died lately of a disease which I am informed Doctor Rush has pronounced malignant fever. Should this be true what are we to expect as the season advances?

*May 22d.* A man in membership with our Society whose wife has been dead for some years, a man of some education & a physician, the father of a lovely girl thirteen years of age, has, if our information be not grossly incorrect, been training up his child to sell her chastity. The innocent creature has been wrested from him & is at this moment under my roof. The aunt of this child, who is married to a person now exercising the office of an overseer, has declared in a fit of folly & pride, that rather than have her family exposed, as it necessarily must in consequence of the arrest of her niece, she would have seen her lodged in a brothel. Hitherto I have known nothing of this family, but it is difficult to repress the emotions of horror & indignation which I feel towards the miscreant father, or to find any palliation for the indiscreet & censurable conduct of the aunt. I pray God I may never suffer a diminution of my Christian charity, but I am often disgusted with the base hypocrisy which I have met with in some of the members of our religious community. The crime in Quakers is more detestable than in other sects, because no others profess so highly.

*May 29th.* This day took possession of the ship *Rebecca*, which I purchased of Saml. Coates in company with my friend J.K. Helmuth & Capn. Barry, who is to command her. This is an essay towards changing my business. That which I now follow is too confining for the delicate state of my health, more especially fettered as I am with a partner who does not divide the toil with me nor can be persuaded, by all my entreaties, to settle his accounts with the house.

*June 6th.* On the night of the 4th, there was a smart frost in Bucks county & its neighbourhood which remained on the ground till after sunrise the next morning.

*June 16th.* Capn. Barry of the *Rebecca* was this day dispatched for Liverpool. The day was rendered remarkable by an eclipse of the sun, almost total in this City. The sky was clear & afforded a fair opporuntity of observing this grand phenomenon. About eleven digits of the sun's disk was obscured. It commenced at half past nine in the morning & ended between 12 & one—the greatest darkness being at eleven, at which time the heavens assumed the pale sombre appearance which accompanies the approach of a heavy thunderstorm. Some stars were visible to the naked eye. A very singular & beautiful effect was produced by the shadow of the trees—each leaf marking the exact state & progress of the eclipse in the form of a crescent on the ground. The light was rather more brilliant than bright moonlight. The temperature of the air underwent some change, the thermometer having fallen 4 degrees.

*September 1st.* The day after the eclipse I discovered that my sight had sustained so much injury that I was compelled to relinquish my usual avocations. I ascribe it principally to an indiscreet use of my eyes in viewing that sublime spectacle. Many others suffered in the same way, yet I spent but little time in looking at it & attempted it but once without the aid of a smoked glass or quadrant. This was at the point of its greatest obscurity & but for a moment. My sight has been bad for years & the spectacles which I am forced constantly to wear contributed no doubt on this occasion to my greater injury. My sight will probably never be wholly restored, but I can now attend, with care, to my common concerns.

*September 3d.* The electioneering campaign commenced some weeks ago. Having had much trouble & little satisfaction in the part I took in it last year, have determined to keep clear of it this. Have, however, been pressed to suffer my name to be used on the Constitutional ticket as a

candidate for Congress. My present pursuits forbid it. I have of course declined the proposition.

*September 19th.* For some week past I have been urged by the Federalists & persons of the third party to serve in Congress. A memorandum of the attendant circumstances may be useful. Ward committees, selected so as to give two of each of the parties in a ward, were appointed; these, united, formed a Com. of Conference for the City. On the part of the Federalists, Hemphill was put in nomination for Congress. The third party named Sergeant; neither would yield. In this situation my name was brought into view. I was called on by individuals & at length by formal deputations. Still I declined. The third party, relying no doubt that I would in any event continue to do so, became more pressing & I was told that unless I would yield my private views & agree to serve, all hope of conciliating the parties must be abandoned & I would alone be blamed for the schism. Unwilling to incur the popular odium, I very reluctantly consented to suffer them to use my name, in case no other means of preserving a union of the parties could be devised. I declared at the same time that I would not take a seat in Congress as the advocate of any set of men or measures. If the present administration should in my opinion act for the public good I would support them; if, however, I should believe their motives to be insidious & their conduct injurious to the country, I would oppose them. These declarations were admitted by the Federalists to be orthodox, but the third party wished me to avow a determination to support Jefferson's administration, right or wrong. As an honest man, I could not pledge myself to uphold any administration. I was much less disposed to sacrifice the independency of my character to one which I cannot but condemn from my conscience. In saying this, I do not mean to pass an indiscriminate & therefore uncharitable censure on their measures. Some of them may have originated in pure motives, others bear the stamp of unwarrantable partiality, hypocrisy & selfishness. My political creed not suiting the turbulent & ambitious views of the leaders of the third party, they would not concur in my nomination & the parties have separated without fixing on any person for Congress. The fact is, they had resolved to support Sergeant at all hazards, for my political sentiments were well known in the City & had been frequently avowed before & during the time they appeared so anxious to call me to a Congressional seat. I had been so much worried to serve them, that I feel as if relieved from an immense load & most cordially hope I may be permitted to walk the path of obscurity in private life without being called into public notice on the present or any other occasion.

*September 20th.* This day was launched from the yard of Franklin Eyre the ship *Susquehanna,* built for Jno. K. Helmuth, Capt. Gamble & myself. A nearer acquaintance with the latter induces both H. & myself to wish we were rid of him. He is an ignorant, conceited, suspicious man & we fear will be a burden to us rather than prove useful. We had intended to send the ship to Europe, but the prospect of peace between France & England having checked the spirit of enterprize to that quarter, we have offered her for Calcutta. Some of the shippers object to Gamble as master & H. & myself find no small difficulty to induce him to yield his place to another, yet to another he must yield it.

*October 16th.* The election, as might have been foreseen, has terminated unfavourably to the Federalists & Quids in respect of a Congressman; each having adhered to their separate choice, the Popular party prevailed.

*October 20th.* Jno. Blakiston is chosen to the command of our new ship. She goes to Calcutta. My cousin H. S. Drinker & Thos. Firth supercargoes.

*November 30th.* Yesterday there was an election for a member of Congress in place of Leib. Have now served as one of the Judges at 4 successive elections. It is an unpleasant station & rendered more so on account of the little respect which is paid to the sacredness of an oath—many seem willing to swear to anything which will entitle them to vote.

*December 8th.* Was this day elected one of the Directors of the Delaware Insurance Company. Was not consulted on the occasion but, as the stockholders have thought proper to place me there, must I suppose consent to serve, rather than give them the trouble of making another choice.

*December 9th.* On the 15th last the act prohibiting the introduction of certain articles of English manufacture into the U.S. came into operation. The President has by a special message to Congress recommended its suspension. Should it be rigourously enforced it must prove ruinous to some of our citizens—the penalty being a forfeiture of the goods & three times their value. Our ship *Rebecca* having on freight

about 1.00.000 Pounds Sterling, mostly of the interdicted articles, left Liverpool 19th August & after suffering by storms was compelled to put into Cork, where she was by the last advices. Should the law be in force when she arrives, the consequences must be very serious to some of the consignees.

*December 10th.* Great events are daily taking place. Attempts were lately made between G. Britain & France to effect a peace. It has however failed & the news of the day is that Prussia, having been driven into a war with France by the injustice of the latter, has in the space of a few days after the commencement of hostilitites been beaten & her immense armies annihilated. Thus has France become master of Austria, all of Ialy, Venice & Venetian Dalmatia, Switzerland, Holland & Prussia. Whatever Continental powers remain unconquered owe their independence, Russia perhaps excepted, to the favour of Bonaparte. Perhaps the whole European continent may yet bend to his yoke. England however maintains her maritime superiority. She had recaptured the Cape of Good Hope & taken Buenos Ayres in S. America. So completely do her navies scour the ocean that France, with all her vast resources, cannot maintain a single fleet at sea.

On our side of the Atlantic, important events have occurred. Miranda landed at Coro on the Spanish Main & is endeavouring to wrest that portion of the world from Spain. We are ourselves at partial war with the troops of the latter in some of our newly acquired territory in Louisiana. It is said & believed that Aaron Burr, lately V. Pres. of the U.S., has been organizing a force to conquer Mexico & with Louisiana to form a new Empire to which also is to be added such portions of the U.S. as can be severed from the Union. President Jefferson has issued a proclamation against the abettors of Burr's scheme.

While these great events are going on in the political world, very extraordinary things come to light in the walks of private life. At least one affair has been recently developed to me of which I could scarce have formed a conception. A man whose character for integrity, sobriety, discretion, acuteness, fidelity & calm reflection is not excelled by any in the City; who appears to live on the best terms with his wife; who is the head of a numerous family of children; who is as much respected as any man in Philada.; who is now past the meridian of life; whose conversation is always chaste & whose whole study appears to be the pursuit of useful & practical knowledge; who seems to have no relish for the frivolities of the gay, or the low bred indulgences of the sensual world—this man has for many months been assiduously engaged in the monstrous act of seducing a girl of 14! The fact is unquestionable. I know him well & have long esteemed & loved him. When the circumstances were communicated to me I could not venture on any other mode of warning him of his guilt & folly than writing him an anonymous letter through the Post Office & which I hope will recall him to his senses & save him the ignominy of exposure. With such maniacal rashness has he conducted his intrigue that it may be impossible to prevent its publicity. It may be difficult to assign the true cause of this dereliction of principle in a man whose general habits have been so remarkably correct. I doubt not however, that it may in no inconsiderable degree be attributed to the pestiferous influence of novel reading. His wife has been long in the habit of taking this trash from the circulating libraries. He at first looked them carelessly over for mere relaxation but has gradually imbibed a relish for their poison.

# 1807

*April 9th.* Months have elapsed since I last took up my diary. It has been a round of dull uninteresting events. Little has happened to myself varying the usual scene. Trials of temper I have at all times; it would be happy for me, had I so far profited by my own experience as to have been substantially instructed in lessons of patience & forbearance. I have had enough to have rendered me a better man.

*April 30th.* An extraordinary affair has happened in the vicinity of this City. Between Germantown & Norristown stands the Barrenhill Church. A son of Saml. Wheeler & another person of this place attended a funeral there about two months ago. They remained on the ground after the company had retired. One of them observed to the other, "Is it not very extraordinary; that skull is in motion," pointing to a skull which had been thrown up in digging the new grave. "I perceive it," was the answer. On examination they found a toad had entangled himself in some of the interior bones. His efforts to escape had caused the irregular movements which occasioned them so much surprize. Another discovery ensued; they found a nail firmly fixed in the skull. It had evidently been driven there by design. They asked the grave digger, who was still engaged in covering over the recently interred body, if he had any recollection of the person who had been buried in the same spot before. "Yes, he remembered him well. He was a journeyman carpenter who died suddenly in a fit about 13 years ago & lived at such a house in the neighbourhood." Without making their discovery known to this man, they went in search of the house & soon found it. They enquired for the journeyman carpenter by name & were answered that he had lived there but died of a fit many years before. From the moment the subject was introduced, the visitors were forcibly struck by the appearance of an old man who was seated in the chimney corner, listening very attentively to what passed & who seemed to be much agitated. They suddenly produced the skull & asked who drove that nail in it? The old man instantly fainted. On recovering, he confessed that he had done it, to come at the possession of about $120 which the journeyman had acquired. The interposition of the law to punish the murderer was unnecessary. He died two days afterwards. This event furnishes matter for contemplation & reflection.

*May 1st.* Am by no means pleased with my situation as one of the

Directors of the Delaware Insur. office. Too much cunning practised on the unwary. Too much selfishness. Too much disingenuousness. Too little frankness. Too little honour & integrity. Too much hawking & sharping. Too much insolence assumed towards claimants. Too mixed a set of Directors. Too little harmony among them. Do not meet them very frequently.

*May 20th.* Moving in the humble sphere in which I do, it cannot be expected that incidents should occur to me of a nature deeply to interest others. But there is frequently much satisfaction derived from thus chatting with one's self. Business nevertheless frequently throws me in the crowd of active life & enables me to make observations on conduct & character which, if rightly estimated, would turn out to my improvement. Man is indeed but a fallible being & we had need to exercise much charity & forbearance towards others, that we may the more reasonably claim allowances for our own errors & misconduct.

Have just returned from a visit to my sons at school in the country & have cause to be thankful to God that I found them so well in health & so much advanced in knowledge. They are blessed with good natural capacities, good constitutions & I hope have already imbibed good principles. They are so near that in half a day's ride we can pay them a visit. We correspond by letter & that is advantageous to them. They snuff a purer air than our crowded city furnishes & can, moreover, freely indulge themselves in exercise abroad without that risk to their morals which rambling our streets would expose them to. There is however, in this life, scarce any good which has not some evil tacked to the end of it & accordingly I am not wholly satisfied with the school at Weston.

*May 28th.* There has lately arrived here from England a man of the name of Richard Penn, one of the descendants of Wm. Penn & prior to the Revolution a Provisional Governor of Pennsla. He is old & poor, was lately confined for debt in London & has come hither, as it is understood, to make an effort to reclaim some of the wreck of the former fortune of his once illustrious family. How mortifying must be his condition, when he looks around him at the vast improvement & wealth of the country & reflects on what he might have been & on what he is actually. "Fallen, fallen, fallen!" Such are the wonderful changes to which we are subject in this tempestuous sea of existence.

*May 29th.* It is useful, under the pressure of sufferings & privations, real or fanciful, to contrast our situation with that of others more afflicted than we are or who have manifestly more substantial reasons for being so. This comparison of our lot with the lot of others would furnish us with this species of solace that, however much we suffer, others equally if not more deserving suffer much more. We should also see that thousands around us who labour under infinitely greater trials complain not & would think themselves happy indeed to barter their situations for ours. Other advantages would also result from this research; we should perceive with what apparently inadequate means, with means so vastly inferior to our own, works of labour & of skill of which we supposed ourselves incapable are without murmur readily performed.

The celebrated philosopher Doct. Noyes, who delivered public lectures in this City twenty years ago, informed me that he became totally blind when 18 months old by the smallpox & ever after remained so. He had himself made an eight day clock. He had acquired much learning & a sensibility of touch truly extraordinary, enabling him not only to distinguish colours with facility but to detect inequalities on surfaces of which I could with difficulty be rendered conscious, with all my senses about me. When I was boy, a man lived at Lancaster who followed the business of cleaning & repairing watches. He was stone blind & frequently pursued his business in a darkroom at night, when other people were asleep, in order to avoid the troublesome curiosity of visitants.

But I have this day visited a person whose performances appear to me to exceed those of both the philosopher & the mechanic. She was born in the state of N. York without hands or even arms, having, in the place of them, two diminutive stumps projecting but a few inches from the shoulders. She has but one leg, which is also diminutive & ill formed & on that leg she has a stump similar to those which are substituted for arms. Would not a person so deformed be a hideous object of contemplation? Not so; she cannot stand, but sits erect with perfect grace & ease.

Her features are regular & even handsome; her complexion fair & blooming. Her countenance animated & captivating. Her limbs excepted, she is well formed & of the usual size of persons at her age, which is sixteen years. She conversed very freely & cheerfully & performed her work at the same time without any apparent labour or perplexity. She cut me a very neat watch-paper in a few minutes, holding the paper between two of her toes, moving the scissors with her lips & steadying the motion with what should have been an arm.

I also saw her work with the needle & purchased of her a piece of her work, which for the rich variety & beauty of the flowers & the elegancy of the design is not frequently surpassed by young girls who possess all their limbs & have had much pains bestowed in their instruction. This young woman is said to be self taught. She embroiders with her toes & lips, the former officiating below & the latter above the frame. She threads her own needle, knots her thread & designs her own pieces. She writes tolerably well by holding the pen in her mouth. Marking & common needlework she executes correctly.

I knew not whether most to admire her ingenuity & taste, or the cheerful resignation with which this interesting phenomenon submitted to privations which many others would doubtless consider as intolerable. It is really very extraordinary that a girl without hands or feet should be able not only to provide by her industry & talents for her immediate subsistence, but to collect, as in all probability she will, a sufficiency to be independent, so far however as the possession of money can contribute to that end.

Surely if a person thus circumstanced can be happy & succeed so well in temporal concerns, others who are blessed with perfect limbs & a capacity to use them need never fear being able to procure a living; & instead of repining, as we are too apt when trifling ills befall us, should have hearts filled with gratitude to God for the blessings bestowed. Instances like this should put our folly to the blush & stimulate us to persevere in habits of industry under the conviction that labour & ingenuity will be rewarded. The name of this singular person is Martha Ann Rogers.

*June 1st.* The citizens have become so fond of the Schuylkill water. It is found to be so much more pure than the water from the pumps, so necessary to the proper cleansing of the gutters & streets & so important in times of fire that to deprive them of it now would occasion abundantly more clamour than was raised against its introduction.

Many also objected to the circular form given to the Centre Square & to the erection of the House in the middle of it who are now highly pleased with both. The shady walks already afford a refreshing retreat. Few of those who railed against the measure ever understood all the reasons that induced its adoption, one of the most powerful of which was this: It was known to myself & a few others that, notwithstanding no doubt could exist as to the intention of Wm. Penn to make the City a gift of the public squares, no title whatever could be traced for them. It was a matter of no doubt also to those who were acquainted with the temper of the State Legislature that, should this secret reach them, they did not want the disposition to wrest that property from the City as they had done in another case of very recent date.

At the time that it became necessary to fix on some place for the engine house, several committees were appointed by the Watering Comm., as they were styled, to seek out & purchase some convenient lot in the vicinity of the Centre Square, but all these attempts were abortive. At length S.N. Fox & myself received authority finally to report the spot which, under all circumstances, should be deemed the most eligible. Both of us inclined to report the Centre Square, but my colleague entertained some doubt as to the right of the Corporation to impede the straight course of High & Broad Streets. This fear was strengthened by the opinion of a celebrated counsellor-at-law, taken, however, as I was convinced, from my knowledge of the subject, on a partial & limited view of the City rights. He was not in possession of all the documents necessary to a correct judgment. He afterwards confessed to me that had he been apprized of the existence of certain documents which I mentioned to him, his opinion might have been different.

I had some difficulty at first to persuade S.N. Fox to come to my views, but at length we reported in favour of the Centre Square. The Watering Committee hesitated & H.S. Drinker openly opposed the measure. He was induced, however, on my taking him aside, to agree that the report should be on the table. Before the next meeting of the Committee, I so fully developed my views to him that he promptly stood forth an able & zealous advocate of the report. This change was so extraordinary that it gave rise to some pleasantry among the members, it being said by one of them that "Cope was the only person who had ever occasioned Drinker to change his mind." Be this as it may, the Com. were soon unanimous.

But all obstacles were not yet removed. They did not choose to take the responsibility of the decision on themselves. The approbation of the Select & Common Councils was therefore to be obtained.

When this application was made a violent & almost unanimous opposition arose in both Councils. The advocates of the measure were, however, prepared to meet their opponents.

To avoid the animosity which sometimes proceeds from public discussions, it was proposed & carried in the Common Council to adjourn for half an hour, to give the members an opportunity of free conversation. We had procured Holmes's plan of the City, in which the draftsman had placed a public building on the confluence of the street in the very spot contemplated for the Engine House. By this & other means, every difficulty was made to vanish & the Council, with the exception of a single individual, adopted the report of their Committee.

The Select Council was next appealed to & their vote soon after confirmed the measure.

During these discussions not a hint was given, except to a few of our most confidential friends, of the main reason that influenced us to have the building fixed where it is. Great caution was necessary to prevent a public knowledge of the tenure on which the City held that & the other public squares & to this day few of even our public officers know anything of the matter but are under the mistaken impression that the Corporation are possessed of legal conveyances for their public grounds.

Another circumstance in this preference operated powerfully on my mind. It had come to my knowledge that the Centre Square, as originally located, had actually been sold as vacant town lots, the confiscated property of the Penn family & that John Nicholson, controller of the state—having been directed by the Assembly to make out a plot of the City lots for its use—discovering the error, placed the Square on the next unappropriated ground west of the old site, without disclosing what he had done to correct it—no part of this ground being then enclosed, nor even the lines of the cross streets market out. This anecdote Nicholson himself privately communicated to me & I did not feel at liberty to mention it to anybody except H. Drinker, whom I knew I could trust. It would have been dangerous to make it public.

*June 8th*. T. Clarkson of London, author of the *Portraiture of Quakerism*, is now writing a History of Slavery. Have been applied to by one of his friends to furnish some materials for the work. Am doubtful whether I can with propriety. C. B. Brown has the papers of the Convention. They are at best but scanty documents for so great an undertaking. Should the latter ever publish, it would be rather ungracious, thus to anticipate him. Moreover, these documents are the property of the Convention. I have their safe keeping, in capacity of their Treasurer. I have also the command of them as one of a Committee to direct & superintend the publication & altho' I have my fears that my friend C.B.B. will ever perform what he has undertaken, I do not know that I am at liberty to yield these papers to another.

The preceding pages of my Commonplace Book were penned for myself & are fit only for my own perusal. A retrospection of their sheets gives rise to very mixed sensations. Some of the events recorded in them cannot be recalled without pain—others, it is true, revive pleasure. If I were to act wisely, would I not destroy them & cease to write more? Yet is

it useful to commune with my own heart & to retrace the pages of my past experiences.

Besides, they afford a delineation of my own character & if I have canvassed the character of others with freedom, I have designed no injury to anybody, nor have I willfully misrepresented anything. My private opinions are, moreover, my private property. But should they fall into the hands of others, an event not unlikely to happen when the head which dictates & the hand that pens them shall be laid in the grave, will they not prove me to have been a foolish man & that I lived to little good purpose? Let then the reader, warned by my example, learn to do better & he shall be both wiser & happier. Such as they are, they are the unstudied & unbiased effusions of a man who means well, however ill or erroneously he may act.

*June 9th.* The period is approaching which will terminate my present copartnership. On the 1st Jany. next, it expires by its own limitation. Look forward to the event as to a period of emancipation. Have had conversation with J.T. on the subject. He does not wish to separate, yet separate we must. To do so & keep on terms will require great caution. I am resolved to make almost any surrender of property rather than incur the risk of disputation. Have a new line of business in view that holds out some temptation of profit & some of leisure. Thus it is; we are perpetually on the wing in the hope of at last finding some snug roosting place.

Steering our bark for some point ahead which, when attained, affords us perhaps a less secure anchorage than the port of departure. But whatever safety or emolument may grow out of my new undertaking, shall at least have the satisfaction of knowing my situation—a pleasure which the unaccountable conduct of my present partner will not allow me.

It is an excellent rule of the Society of Friends which imposes on its members the necessity of inspecting their affairs at least once a year. The infringement of this rule is chargeable with moral turpitude. Yet in the period in which I have been connected with J.T., nearly five years, I have not been able to prevail upon him to come to any settlement that would enable me to have our books balanced. Before our copartnership commenced, it was my invariable practice to balance once in twelve months. All correct merchants, Quakers & others, deem this an indispensable act of prudence & propriety. Strange indeed that a man who possesses many amiable properties should be so difficult to manage &

that one who is in many respects neat & correct should in this instance be so culpably deficient.

Never had a partnership which in a pecuniary point of view did not result to my disadvantage. Had I remained unconnected with any other & left master of my own business, I should long since have retired or at least have had a sufficiency to warrant my retiring from the thorny path of business.

*June 28th.* Commodore Barron, commanding the U.S. Frigate *Chesapeake,* sailed lately from Hampton Roads for the Mediterranean. As he passed the Capes there lay at anchor a British squadron of three two deckers & a frigate. One of the two deckers, the *Leopard,* Capt. Humphreys, put off & went to sea before the *Chesapeake.* About three leagues from land, Capt. Humphreys hailed the *Chesapeake* & demanded three men whom he stated to be deserters from the British Navy. Com. Barron refused to give them up, alleging them to be American citizens, whereupon the *Leopard* commenced a heavy fire on the *Chesapeake,* killed three & wounded about 20 or more of the crew. Barron, who was among the wounded,—not being in a condition to resist, having most of his guns below & not apprehending any hostile attack—struck, but the British refused to take possession of his ship. She returned to port in a shattered condition. The *Leopard* also returned within the Capes & joined the squadron at anchor.

This affair has excited great public sensibility. We now stand on precarious ground. The treaty which was negotiated last winter in London between our ministers & the English was refused ratification by our Administration & was not long since returned. The Non-importation Act was suspended by Congress until the present month, authority had been vested in the Pres. further to suspend it until December next. This he did by Proclamation; in the mean time the Fox administration, as it was termed in England, has been superseded by another, supposed to be less friendly to us.

*June 29th.* Almost worn out with arbitrations. 'Tis a pleasure to be a healer of differences & a negotiator of peace but, as in all disputes, each party apprehends himself in the right. He against whom a decision goes is apt to censure & sometimes with acrimony the arbitrators; besides, 'tis very unpleasant to sit for hours & hear people abuse each other & to travel over musty titles & unravel old complicated & perplexed books & accounts.

*June 30th.* Rumoured on the report of a pilot that the British squadron has landed a party of marines within 10 miles of Norfolk & forcibly carried off 40 horned cattle. Parties have been sent from the town to prevent further depredations.

*July 2d.* An immense assemblage of the citizens in Town meeting yesterday. A large party headed by Judge Woelpert from the N. Liberties, colours flying, drums beating & a band of music joined together in the State House yard. Resolutions expressive of high resentment at the conduct of the British & determinations to support the Government in seeking redress adopted. All parties joined in these proceedings.

Similar measures are taking in other cities. In all, they have agreed until the sense of Government be declared to interdict all supplies to British shipping. Notwithstanding these hostile appearances & the public ferment, I cannot believe we shall have war.

The attack on the *Chesapeake* was most probably the act of a rash commander & will be disavowed by the English ministry. With half of Europe already their enemies & contending for their existence as a nation, they cannot be so insensible to their own interest as wantonly to add America to the number of their enemies.

Few ports in Europe remain open to the introduction of their manufactures, the U.S. afford them an immense & increasing vent. Their navy is their boasted bulwark; the downfall of their commerce must sap the foundation of their navy & cut the sinews of their greatness.

On the other hand, the U.S. have little to expect in a maritime contest with England & altho' her privateers might swarm the ocean & pick up many of the merchantmen of her enemy, her trade, the source of her revenues, would in a great measure be annihilated. With so much at hazard on both sides, nothing but mad ambition can precipitate the two countries into a war. Yet many believe we are on the verge of that greatest of all evils. The insurance offices will scarce insure any but risks that promise a speedy termination. Commercial enterprize is at a stand & foreboding & alarm pervade the coffee house politicians.

*July 3d.* One of Pres. Jefferson's intimate friends breakfasted with me. He informs me he had it from the Pres. that the reason of the treaty being returned was this; in a note attached to it, the English declare they cannot formally abandon the right of impressing their subjects from our vessels, but that they were disposed to wave it in favour of America on condition that the latter would take certain measures towards France in relation to Bonaparte's blockading decree & which measures, if taken, must in the opinion of the Pres. have led to an immediate rupture between the U.S. & France.

*July 6th.* The Fourth passed without any act of violence or outrage. It being the anniversary of American Independence, fears were entertained that when the fumes of liquour were added to the effervescence already induced by recent transactions, mischief would be the consequence.

*July 22nd.* The subject of peace or war was discussed before the Directors of the Delaware Ins. Co. when J. Sperry, one of the Board, assured his brethren with great gravity that "he had made calculations, the result of which was that the English would declare against us on the 20th October next." He did not develop the basis of the calculations which could produce such wonderful accuracy. He had perhaps consulted the stars.

*July 25th.* At no period within my recollection has my property been so much exposed to injury from war as at the present. It may induce me to incline, without sufficient reason, to the belief that it will not take place. Should my expectations be baffled & the total loss of all I possess ensue, I shall not be more severely chastened that I merit. Such is the unbiased opinion I entertain of my own unworthiness.

*August 13th.* A disease called the Influenza has made its appearance among us. In N. York it has prevailed to a great extent. A person just from thence assures me that 5000 are supposed to have been seized with it. It is rarely fatal, resembling in its symptoms & effects what is usually termed a bad cold.

*August 31st.* The electioneers are again in motion. Clay, our present representative in Congress, it is expected will resign his seat. On this ground I have had a Quid deputation to know if I will stand a candidate. My answer is in the negative.

*September 15th.* Have returned from visiting my children at Weston & J. Embree's. I extended my ride to Lancaster & Columbia.

*September 20th.* Clay does not resign. I am now asked to serve in the State Legislature. This I have also declined.

*September 30th.* Our differences with England have not yet terminated. It is however understood that they disavow the attack on the *Chesapeake* & promise reparation.

*October 14th.* Yesterday the general election was held & terminated in favour of the Constitutionalists. Clay did not resign & of course there was no election for Congress.

*October 25th.* S. Carver, a Quid & obnoxious to the Federalists & who was recently elected to the House of Representatives of this State, died very suddenly. A vacancy is created, I am pestered to stand as a candidate. My friends have on this occasion much worried me with their importunities & seem disposed to accept no denial. A visit on the subject from my friend Charles W. Hare, a member elect, has not a little perplexed me.

*November 1st.* A comet for some weeks has been visible to the naked eye. It is seen in the westward soon after sunset & continues in view until 10 or 11 o'clock at night.

It is of a faint light with a very long nucleus or tail & is supposed by astronomers to be a stranger in our system.

Comets were once considered as portentious of evil. This opinion has, however, given place to a much more probable supposition that they are intended by the all wise Creator to correct the atmosphere of other orbits round which they revolve & therefore indispensable to the health of the latter.

*November 20th.* Attended a meeting of the Chamber of Commerce at which a memorial to Congress requesting a repeal of the Nonimportation Act was adopted.

*November 21st.* The memorial was read & agreed to at a general meeting of the merchants held this evening at the Coffee House. The Quids do not concur in it. This Act, so embarrassing to the American merchants & so inefficient & irritating to the British, is to take effect on the 14th of next month. Should it go into operation, it will probably be the cause of war. If so, the memorialists will have the satisfaction of having borne their testimony against it.

*November 28th.* The disturbed state of Europe has greatly embarrassed our commerce. If a neutral ship enter a British port, either voluntarily or otherwise, the Emperor of France does not permit her an entrance into his dominions. Scarce a vessel bound for the continent escapes the vigilance of the English cruisers. They are as uniformly sent to an English port & altho' generally released afterwards, the voyage is of course frustrated. 'Tis expected many will have to return hither with their cargoes.

*December 5th.* A visit from E.Y., one of the overseers of the Society of Friends. His object was to caution me against suffering myself to stand as a candidate at the approaching election. The Society disapprove of their members serving in public stations & of course many of them cannot feel easy to vote for me.

It is right to pay a becoming deference to the scruples of well meaning individuals, notwithstanding their inconsistency, but if I feel, under all circumstances, that my duty as a good citizen demands the surrender, I shall not refuse. As yet, however, I have not consented to serve.

They who conscientiously feel themselves concerned not to participate in the labours of the Republic would do well to withdraw from it. But neither Friends nor any other set of people have as yet been able to live without civil institutions. If all were pure as Angels, there might be no necessity for government or law, but so long as men continue to be mortal there will be a necessity for laws to constrain & punish the wicked & to protect the peaceable & the virtuous in the enjoyment of life, liberty & property.

If the principles of Quakerism rest in the immutable basis of truth & justice, as I trust they do, why not disseminate them? Why not carry them into the public councils of the country? Did Wm. Penn & his adherents & associates withdraw from Civil government? But Friends of the present day will vote into office men who are not of their profession. And is there then any difference between doing that by agents which they refuse to do of themselves? While they can peaceably exercise their civil rights under a government of laws, is it not their duty to exercise them? Or are some of them wearied of the enjoyment of those rights & desirous to invite persecution? Does it become them no longer to remain content in their habitations, quietly enjoying their privileges, but must they run about the streets with naked backs, crying out for some one to come & beat them?

If they decline to exercise their rights guaranteed them by the Constitution at elections, if they permit bad men to usurp the offices of Government, when by a simple vote they can confer them on good men, can they with propriety complain either of the Laws or the Administration?

On the one hand, I am much urged to serve, while on the other, if I give my consent, I shall not be supported by some Friends who express great respect for me.

Another visit. Dr. M. called to pay me his compliments—he hoped I would agree to serve in the Legislature. He had several objects of public

utility to effect. He did not expect he could impress them so forcibly on another as he felt them himself & on that account had paid me this visit today that, altho' he would rather I should be the candidate, yet if I was not willing to serve, he would consent to do it himself. I named him but he would not go down.

*December 12th.* The gazettes contain the formal annunciation of the Constitutionalists to support me at the special election to be held on the 22d for a representative in assembly in place of Saml. Carver, deceased. Thus there appears no alternative but submission. I have resisted the call as long & as strenuously as I could consistently with my duty as a good citizen.

Several efforts & attempts have been made in different meetings to substitute some other in my place. An open rupture had like to have been the consequence, the majority being bent on having me. Had I wished the appointment, their determination might have been otherwise. Finding that Quids & Feds. can concur on no other terms, I am compelled from motives of public duty to an extorted consent.

*December 14th.* The crisis is important. Late arrivals bring intelligence that Bonaparte will no longer permit us to remain neutral. We must declare either for or against him. While on the other hand, the Nonimportation Act against G. Britain went into operation yesterday.

*December 20th.* Rumours of an embargo. Arrival of Monroe at Norfolk. Rose, the English envoy extraordinary, expected daily.

*December 23d.* Yesterday was the election. At 12 at night I was roused by a loud rapping at my door. About 50 came to present me with credentials of my election & to congratulate me. My majority over Sharswood, my antagonist—a Democrat—is 801. Unprecedented for many years & is the cause of great triumph to the Federalists. I can scarce walk the streets today, I meet so many with their gratulations, services & compliments. A vis. from C.L., a Lancaster representative, tells me I must be there by the 28th. Don't know how that will be. I expect to begin to load a Brig for Havana tomorrow. Must be very expeditious. Many work day and night to complete their loading, expecting an embargo by every mail.

*December 24th.* Up betimes & got all ready for loading the Brig. Had just commenced when official intelligence was received of an embargo. Much anxiety & alarm at the Coffee House. Vessels laden & cleared are not exempt. Those even as far down as Reedy Island will be compelled to return.

Many offers of assistance from my friends in my absence. Loans of some thousands are presented. It is flattering, but I hope not to stand in need.

*December 26th.* My wits are in an uproar. I shall be obliged to proceed to Lancaster in two days. I have many things to digest & arrange first. Am called on every minute & much interrupted by persons who have petitions & other public business. All narrate their stories & expect, no doubt, that I should remember them. I have also many private engagements. 'Tis well if they do not turn my brain. Rose early, planned a coasting voyage for the *Eliza*. Visited many persons throughout the City to obtain freight. Went to Custom House to procure a coasting license. At noon met a committee of the German Lutheran Congregation. I paid & received visits from divers persons. Had an interview by request with three of the Elders of the Society of Friends. They gave me good advice. I attended in the evening the committee of the citizens on the Poor Laws & the guardians of the poor at the County Court House. I afterwards met & supped with the Conversation Club. Returned home & arranged some private business, selected & packed up clothing for an absence of three months & retired to bed a little past ten.

*December 27th.* I left home at 12 in a coach & four in company with Hare, Sergeant, Biddle & Clawges, who with myself compose the City representation, accompanied by Smith, a representative from Lancaster & George Emlen, Jr. We dined at the Buck & arrived at Downing's after night, where we supped & lodged. Left Downing's after breakfast. Dined at Slaymaker's. Arrived at Lancaster at four, just as the House assembled, was qualified & took my seat.

A few unimportant matters transacted. The House adjourned at five. I proceeded to my father's & lodged.

*December 30th.* Principal business for the House for the last two days is the receiving & disposing of petitions on local subjects. Hare moved today to fix Monday 4 Jany. for considering Leib's resolution for altering the Constitution of the U.S. so as to have the judges appointed for a term of years & removable by two thirds of the House & Senate. Leib manifested considerable displeasure. He wished, no doubt, to call them up when the absence of some of his opponents would give him the opportunity of taking the rest by surprize. The motion agreed to.

Feel myself at considerable loss from being elected so long after the opening of the sessions. It requires more attention to the comprehension of passing events.

I discover that most pecuniary grants are given by lotteries. Have as yet uniformly voted against them. Their moral tendency cannot be doubted, nor am I convinced of their political expediency.

# 1808

*January 5th.* Received letters from home mentioning the arrival of the *Susquehanna* in the river. I am under some anxiety lest she should have articles in the cargo which are prohibited, in which case vessel & cargo & double the amount are forfeited. Apprehensions arise from knowing there is twine on board & all manufactures of which hemp & flax are the materials of chief value are prohibited. This is no very pleasant situation to be in. I ought immediately to go to the City. Here is a conflict between public & private duty. I will however remain at my post.

Leib's resolution has been under discussion yesterday & today in Committee of the Whole. It is not yet decided.

*January 7th.* A letter from H. Baker, a lad in my service, relieves me from anxiety on account of the *Susquehanna*. She has been permitted to enter at the Court House. The super cargoes produced certificates proving that Calcutta twine is made of an article different from either hemp or flax.

*January 9th.* Leib's resolution received its quietus today. In Com. of the Whole & afterwards in the House, the votes were equal, 43 to 43, the whole number of which the House consists. Resolution consists of three parts: 1st, judges to hold their office for a term of years; 2nd, to be removable by the President on address of the two branches of the Legislature; & 3rd, for high crimes & misdemeanors, a majority of Senate to be competent to convict.

In committee a separate question was taken on each when reported to the House. The Friends of the Constitution called for a decision. Leib & his friends, to prevent it, called for an adjournment. House equally divided. An adjournment was called for & attempted to be frustrated by another motion of adjournment. The same thing occurred a third time. Finding they could not prevent a decision, the favourers of the resolution attempted, by a substitute & then by amendments, to divide their antagonists. Finding these attempts vain, they at length submitted to the final question which was taken on the three parts as in Committee. The result being the same, the resolution was of course not carried. Nine times the yeas & nays were taken. The House sat from 10 till past 4. During the whole discussion, which lasted an entire week, Leib manifested great intemperance & party rancour & in the course of the debate dropped these remarkable expressions, after vilifying the judges of the U.S. & indulging in bitter reproaches against the framers of the Constitution & the Constitution itself, which he said was "formed in dark divan."

"We are asked if we obtain this alteration—if we mean to stop here. I answer no. If I meant to repair my house I would not stop at one chamber, I would repair the whole. If I could not do that, I would do as much as I could. I would put on a single shingle."

*January 12th.* Both Houses met this morning in the chamber of the House of Representatives for the choice of a State Treasurer. Wm. Findlay was reelected. I voted for him. He is a Democrat, but I hope I may never be so far influenced by party motives as to vote out a good officer merely because he differs with me in politics.

Received a letter from J.K. Helmuth announcing the unwelcome intelligence that the Court House officers have taken possession of the ship *Susquehanna,* under the pretext that the twine on board is made of hemp—notwithstanding the documents accompanying it prove it otherwise. Eager as they may be to create so serious a forfeiture to us, I trust they will not succeed. 'Tis however very unpleasant news.

*January 13th.* More agreeable information. The ship is released & that principally through the instrumentality of Wm. Duane. Strange that we should owe our safety to such a man. He has at least done one good act & I feel under obligations to him for it.

*January 14th.* This day a flaming address to the general government which had previously passed the Sentate was adopted in the House of Representatives by the desertion of some of the Quids from our ranks. The insolence & vindictiveness of Leib & some of his party was conspicuous. They were permitted a wide range of declamation & falsehood. Great Britain is the only nation complained of. On a motion to amend by striking out Great Britain & thus rendering our expressions of foreign aggressions more general, I rose to correct some of the many misrepresentations which had fallen from Leib & Co. I had, however, done little more than to usher in the argument by a short notice of what had been before stated when the speaker (Snyder), perceiving no doubt that I was disposed to make a considerable opposition to the address, abruptly interposed & would not permit me to proceed.

This act of partiality was the more flagrant as Leib immediately resumed the subject & was suffered to run his own course without any species of restraint. He vilified Great Britain & sang praises to France & Spain.

*January 16th*. Dined with W. Hamilton in company with a number of the members & some of the heads of departments.

A great change has been wrought among the latter. They indulge in very free expressions against some of the measures of Jefferson & his adherents. Ellicott said he knew Wilkinson was in Spanish pay. He had seen positive proof of it when engaged in running the boundary line between us & the Spaniards.

*January 17th*. A Boston wit, in noticing my election, observes that the "Constitutionalists will now be able to Cope with the Democrats."

*January 18th*. Engles, a Democratic representative from the county of Philada., left us yesterday in consequence of an arrangement between us which leaves me at liberty also to return home. I took the stage & arrived in Phila. & found all well.

*January 19th*. The ship *Susquehanna* began to discharge. News arrived that England has declared all ports from which she is excluded to be blockaded. Rose, their envoy extraordinary, has arrived at Washington. He is understood to state—notwithstanding the French decree which interdicts all commerce with them & confiscates all English manufactures found in the dominions of France or her allies—the am't of exports from England to those very countries was greater the last quarter by two millions Sterling than in former quarters.

*January 21st*. Attended a number of citizens who met this evening at my request in the chamber of the Phila. Insurance Co. to canvass for a suitable character to fill the office of Governor at the ensuing election. Present were S. W. Fisher, H. Drinker, Jr., G. Latimer, T. Paxson, W. Jackson, Horace Binney, R. Waln, D. Smith & Wm. Rawle.

The persons named were Jas. Ross, Wm. Tilghman, the present chief justice & Chas. Biddle. The conversation was free & confidential; the choice rested between the two first named candidates & resulted in their giving me a carte blanche to be filled with either of their names when the Constitutional members of the Legislature shall meet to name a candidate. Weight of opinion inclined in favour of W. Tilghman.

*January 22d*. Several daring robberies have lately been committed in the streets. Nightly patrols are established. I am almost overwhelmed with business, principally public. I can scarce find time to eat.

*January 23d.* I am weary running after my own affairs & in attending to the various calls of persons who have business with the Legislature. Took supper with the Conversation Club.

*January 24th.* Returned in the stage to Lancaster.

*January 25th.* Laid report from the managers of the Penna. Hospital & report from the managers of the Lancaster & Phila. Turnpike, both placed under my charge, on table, Lower House. Gave duplicates to John Dorsey, Senator.

*January 26th.* Presented petition from President & Directors of the Marine & Fire Insurance Co. It was referred to com.

*January 27th.* Presented petition from the U.S. Insurance Company, referred it to the same committee. Reported a bill for appointing Wardens, Pilots &c. for Phila. In evening I met Constitutionalists at Slough's to fix on persons as directors for Banks of Penna. & Phila.—to be voted for tomorrow. Meeting appointed Committee of Six, of whom three were Quids, three Feds., to make selection; Sergeant, Spearmen, Ingham, Biddle, Smith & self.

*January 28th.* This day was fixed on for the election of bank directors. The Demos. made several motions to postpone it & to adjourn; finding they could not succeed, they surlily submitted. The election took place & we put in our men, same as agreed on at Slough's. Here Duane was also one of their candidates & rejected. Considerable vexation & disappointment were very visible among the party & threats used against us for taking advantage of their absence.

*January 29th.* Agreeably to appointment, the meeting of the Constitutional members of both houses took place at Slough's this evening. I prevailed on my friends to permit the Quids to take the lead, that when we should discover their course, we might shape ours accordingly. Jas. Brady of the Senate in the chair. Some time was spent in silence, each party waiting the motions of the other. At length they proposed to proceed to a nomination & Sherman, a member from York Co., named Judge Spayd of Reading. He stated that they had been promised a German governor when McKean's time should expire. He was followed by several of his party, not Germans, all of whom acknowledged the pledge & thought we were bound by it. I named Wm. Tilghman & Wm. Trimble of Del. named Jas. Ross. Sergeant then offered two resolutions—one to fix a day certain when we would make our choice, the other to pledge ourselves to support the candidate who should have a majority of votes. This last was precisely what I expected. We avoided the trap, gave the resolution the go bye & fixed on 22nd Feby. to meet & consult further on the subject.

These Quids, educated in the school of Democracy, are high intriguers. To acknowledge before the German members of Berks, Northampton &c. that they conceived a pledge given to support a German was calculated to prevent free discussion & to enlist at once all the German interest against us. The Federalists acknowledge no such pledge. Peter Muhlenburg, who had a longing eye to the office for himself, wrote a letter to influence the Germans to vote for McKean in which he threw out a hint that the next candidate would probably be a German.

This Spayd is a man heard of but yesterday—a country lawyer of talents scarely rising to mediocrity & who derives all his present consequence from his alliance with the Hiesters. Jos. Hiester, his father in law, had it seems a sufficient influence to procure for Spayd the office which he now holds. His pretension to the governorship is founded on the simple circumstance of his being a German. Yet the Quids will support him—not a man of them but acknowledges that for fitness & capability he is almost immeasurably inferior to either of our candidates, who certainly are two of the first men, not only of the State, but of the U. States.

If we must have a Dutchman of incompetent talents & of no political importance, better to have Snyder than Spayd, for the latter the Federalists will not vote & of course will not be bound to uphold his administration. It will be imbecile & ruin itself—our principles will grow stronger with its decay. If we vote for Spayd, we must support him & may prepare ourselves to become the hewers of wood & drawers of water to an illiterate, stubborn set of Dutchmen operated upon by crafty, timeserving politicians.

The meeting was exclusively intended for the members of the Legislature & to be kept secret, but Elisha Gordon, a Quid, from the City & not a member, contrived to enter among us & was busy to promote Spayd's interest.

Before we separated, Ingham of Bucks, a Quid, said to me, "You Philadelphians (meaning the Federalists, no doubt) are the worst politicians in the world."

*February 2d.* Am uneasy about home. I left my son Alfred unwell. I

have written twice to Mary since my return to Lancaster & received no answer. What means this silence?

*February 3d.* Offered a resolution to appoint a com. to enquire whether any & what alterations are necessary in the Poor Laws so far as they relate to Phila. & districts.

*February 5th.* Amused, while waiting in the House after adjournment, with some of the members catechizing each other in spelling—a knot of them in dispute about spelling Jail. At last one of them hit it, by calling out J-O-A-L, to which his colleagues, who listened with gaping mouths, assented.

One of them had prepared a lottery bill for building a church, which he spelled gurggh. Another corrected him by saying, "Vool, you dunno how zu sppel. I never sppel church mit more as two gg's in all my life."

*February 10th.* Today the Democrats stole a march on us. By an arrangement with their friends in Senate, where they have a large majority, a resolution similar to the one which had previously been rejected in our house for an alteration of the judiciary of the U. States was sent down to us & as several of our friends were absent on leave, they hurried it immediately through, without deigning to say one word in its favour. It was declared merely by Leib that they would make hay while the sun shone.

*February 23d.* The number of letters which I receive is so great I cannot answer them. Some write on public, some on private & some on no business at all.

I lately introduced a resolution for taking account of births in the City & districts, to be recorded by the Board of Health & published annually. I scarce never originate any business but perceive some symptoms of jealousy in Sergeant. If he can't lead, he is apt to take the stud—neither is he backward in availing himself of matter not his own to gain *éclat.* He is, however, a man of good talents.

*February 25th.* Very unpleasant news from the City. Several great failures occurred. I shall doubtless suffer by some of them. I ought to immediately return home. I am expected, yet I cannot leave my post.

*February 29th.* At night, made a bargain with Sheetz of the County to take a stage for Phila. in the morning. We are to return together and, should either choose to remain at home a day or two after the other, no advantage is to be taken of it.

*March 1st.* Arrived in the City. Gloomy appearances as new failures are contemplated. Had an interview with T. A. of House B. & A. at my Comptg. House in presence of brother Israel.

*March 3d.* It turns out that the security which was promised was never executed. About four years back, B. & A. were in difficulty. They were then indebted to J. & A. for about $17000 & to me $6000. A security was voluntarily offered. J. & A. being the largest Crs. were to have the instrument perfected. A solemn promise was given by B. & A. to apply certain funds to the extinguishment of our indorsement in equal proportions to our respective claims. I had great reliance on the honour & honesty of both Houses. How am I rewarded? T. & A. are entirely paid off without my having known it. Instead of procuring & holding the joint security, they surrendered to B. & A., who gave them judgment bonds to my exclusion & which bonds have been since paid. Oh! the ingratitude & faithlessness of some men.

*March 4th.* Met a com. of citizens at G. Latimer's, who determined on calling a general meeting of the Federalists & to announce Ross for Governor. If Tilghman is not persuaded to decline, this measure may produce a compromise with the Quids. Some of them will not vote for Ross, who will vote for Tilghman, but if the intention be to support R. to the exlusion of all others, I fear the consequences. There is not perhaps a more fit person in the State but, as many entertain the most violent prejudices against him & as on such an occasion even prejudices ought to be consulted, we should not rashly pursue measures which may place Tilghman out of view. The latter is unquestionably the most popular.

*March 5th.* Cannot succeed in procuring security from B. & A.

*March 7th.* This afternoon Federalists met at City Hall & announced Ross for Governor & appointed Com. of Correspondence. Hope it may end well.

*March 8th.* Returned to Lan. Duane was part of the company. Conversed on general subjects & found entertainment as well as instruction.

*March 9th.* Sheetz returned two days before me & kept his word by entering the House & voting on every subject. A small alteration in favour of Berks by separating it from Dauphin in senatorial district induced them to vote for the bill, against the wishes of the Con-

stitutionalists. 'Tis the same narrow policy that governs them in supporting Spayd—he lives in their country & is a German.

C.W.H. has a letter from W. Tilghman declining to stand a candidate
for Governor. I advised him not to bring it into view at the caucus to be
held tomorrow evening. Some of the Quids say they will support T. but
will not vote for Ross. I would not, by withdrawing T.'s name, shut this
door to conciliation.

*March 10th.* Met the caucus. Sergeant's resolution was so amended as
to render it necessary that ¾ of the whole of the Constitutional members must concur in a candidate. A ballot was then taken; 53 were
present of which Spayd had 34 & Ross 13 & Tilghman 6. Hare withdrew
T.'s name on the second ballot & Spayd got 36 & Ross 17. We were
alarmed for our situation. H. brought forward a resolution for calling a
convention to fix on a candidate, which was negatived. Quids called for
another ballot which we declined & at 11 at night adjourned from
Slough's to meet in Senate chamber evening of the 15th.

*March 11th.* All with whom I converse express discontent at the
withdrawing of Tilghman's name from our list of candidates. Had it
remained, this good effect—if no other—would have resulted from it. We
might have tested the sincerity with which Feds. & Quids both in & out
of the Legislature aver they would have voted for him, but who now
support Spayd.

*March 12th.* The period for adjournment is fixed by both Houses for
the 28th. Sincerely hope they will not rescind the resolution. Am
cordially sick of the business. I feel little disposition to interest myself
deeply in their proceedings; besides, we have already more speaking
than is useful. The session is nearly at a close & we have not passed more
than 74 of the bills on our files. Less said & more done would best serve
the public weal.

*March 19th.* Often have occasion to remark the strong partiality of
Snyder, the speaker, in favour of his political friends. The leaders of the
party are Leib, Boileau, Lacock and Ogle. First, well known as a villain.
He has nevertheless great declamatory talents & speaks more than any
other man in the House. Boileau is a sly, deceitful fellow, possessed of
more solid powers of mind than Leib, whom he so cordially hates that
they never speak to one another. Lacock is an illiterate man who has
great application & is inferior to neither of his coadjutors in natural

understanding. Ogle, though an unprincipled man, has more generous feelings, but is more ignorant & vulgar than the rest.

*March 21st.* Among other Bills reported by me to the House is the Port Wardens, very interesting to the trade of Phila. It was reported early in Feby. & numbered 80. Snyder contrived to place it out of view. As the session advanced it become an order by common consent to take up bills of the lowest numbers first, yet he called from his list at least 100 bills of higher number than mine. Tonight he could no longer avoid bringing it into view. I had so often called for it that his conduct became too glaring. No sooner was the bill called up than some of his friends moved for an adjournment which immediately took place. House now sits twice a day & two evenings in the week. Among others S. named last night from his list, Bills 238 & 239 & the House considered them.

*March 22d.* Impressed by a sense of duty, when the Bill making appropriations for the civil department was this day under considera-tion, I moved a section granting $5000 for the relief of our seamen deprived of employment by the existing Embargo. Leib & Lacock opposed it & it was finally lost. About 260 of these distressed mariners have during the winter been supported by voluntary subscription by the merchants of the City, but the fund is exhausted, the merchants are themselves greatly distressed & these poor fellows with their wives & children have now neither employment nor support. The conduct of Sergeant on this occasion was of a piece with that selfish ambition which has hitherto induced him not to support any City measure not original with himself. Have reason to believe that, altho' he silently voted in the affirmative, he underhandedly used his influence with the Quids to vote against me. Miner of Luzerne had early in the session moved a resolution to give some assistance to the sailors. Sergeant voted against that resolution. In former times our Legislature bestowed large sums on persons suddenly reduced to poverty. To the French refugees from S. Domingo, $5000; to the sufferers by fire at Savannah, $15,000; besides other liberal donations—yet no persons, surely, could have a fairer claim on their bounty than their own suffering Tars. My colleague C. W. Hare supported me manfully.

This Embargo if continued a few months will create a revolution in politics. The people complain loudly. Wheat in Lancaster county is at 76 cents the bushel.

*March 30th.* On the 28th both branches of the Legislature adjourned. I left Lancaster the same evening after candle light. Lodged at Slaymaker's & arrived in Phila. on the 29th in an extra stage occupied by the City representatives & others.

*May 15th.* The Federalists are gaining ground in various parts of the Union. Many of the former supporters of Jefferson's Administration have abandoned him.

*May 20th.* The continuance of the Embargo has become very oppressive. The farmers generally condemn it. No prospect of its speedy removal. The Russians, backed by France & her allies, are endeavouring to destroy Sweden, the last remaining ally of G. Britain on the European continent. Numerous French armies have entered Spain. The old King has been compelled to abdicate the throne in favour of his eldest son who, it is supposed, must shortly give place to Bonaparte, who has entered the kingdom & gives his orders as to a conquered nation. Much American property is under seizure in France & it is generally understood Bonaparte means to force us into a war for or against him.

*May 25th.* Money is abundant. The suppression of commerce has thrown large sums out of employment—yet in the country they feel a scarcity, as the farmer cannot sell his produce unless at great sacrifices.

Our Embargo has given enterprize to many of our neighbours. Cotton & rice are shipping in large quantities from S. America to England. The W. Indians are turning their attention to the culture of new articles of subsistence & an unusual degree of activity is given to the traders of the British settlements in Canada & Nova Scotia. Will not these things lessen our future traffic?

*July 14th.* Returned from a speculating trip to Baltimore, whither I went on the 4th with my friend J. K. Helmuth. We purchased near 400 packages Calcutta & German piece goods.

*August 10th.* Published lately some essays on Embargo &c. Hope they will do no harm.

The young King of Spain has been compelled by Bonaparte to restore the crown to his father Charles the 4th, who has in turn been forced to confer it on Bonaparte. Murat, dubbed Grand Duke of Berg, governs in Madrid in character of Lt. Governor of Spain, while both kings have been snugly secured & carried as prisoners to France.

*August 17th.* Left home in company with my Mary in our own chaise—an excursion of pleasure & recreation undertaken principally with the view of visiting her friend Edith, wife of Joseph Laurie of N.J. Cold wind from the NE but no rain. It is very dusty & uncomfortable. Dined at McElroy's Inn, Bristol. Crossed the Delaware Bridge at Trenton. It is an elegant structure of 5 arches from which the floor is suspended by iron chains. Owing to the mode of bracing the arches it does not look well, viewed obliquely. Arrived at J. Laurie's, 5 miles from Trenton, in the afternoon.

*August 18th.* Spent the day principally in fishing. There was frost in several parts of the neighbourhood last night—appears however to have produced little effect on vegetation. Slept comfortably under two blankets, sheet & coverlet.

*August 19th.* Extended our visit. Accompanied by E.L. & her son Wm., a lad of 14, we dined at Any. Bullock's—wife, a lady; himself a brute. They have a large fine farm. 'Tis the lamb & hog yoked together in a clover field.

Went to Jona. Curtis's to lodge. He & his wife a sensible, agreeable couple—rendered happy by an only child. A boy now in arms—born in their old age to a plentiful inheritance.

*August 20th.* Lodged at J. Curtis's & dined with them. A shrewd fellow in liquour, called Dr. DeCou, forced his company upon me & behaved rudely. He is a Democrat but, on my affecting to be one, condemned several of the measures of his party. Called on the widow Sykes this afternoon & returned to J.L.'s at night.

*August 21st.* At J.L.'s. Went to Croswix meeting. 'Tis a pity some of our preachers fall into the practice of singing their sermons so dolefully.

*August 22d.* Left my horse & chair at J.L.'s & set out in a Jersey waggon for the spring on Schooley's Mountain, accompanied by E. Laurie & her son Wm. Trenton is 5 mi., Pennytown 9 mi., Ringo's 9., & Quakertown is 11 mi. Most of the road is over a red slate stratum, badly calculated to sustain drought & accordingly many of the rivulets & creeks are entirely dry. Halted for the night with our hospitable & worthy kinsman Hy. Clifton at whose house we met some of our friends on a visit from Phila.

*September 1st.* Rode to Trenton with J.L., who is director of their Bank. They sit twice a week to discount. Today they discounted $9000; before the Embargo they discounted from $30,000 to $50,000 a day.

With most persons with whom I have conversed in this state, the

Embargo is considered a most mischievous & futile measure. Many will be ruined by it.

*September 2d.* Our friend has 1000 acres in this tract, 600 of which are incultivation & 400 in wood. He has also a large grist & saw mill. His wheat this year yielded 30 bushels an acre. This is a very large product for Jersey soil. Their best usually do not exceed 15 to 20. In many parts they do not attempt to grow it, as rye & Indian corn are better adapted to the soil. Ten to fifteen bushels of the former & twenty to twenty-five of the latter is esteemed a large crop. 'Tis surprizing to see how well these sandy lands bear the drought. They appear to suffer less than the loamy & clay soils of our own State.

*September 3d.* The good eccentric Jas. Simpson & wife arrived late yesterday afternoon & spent the night with us. I was charmed with the conversation of this unlettered advocate of the Christian faith. The simplicity of his manners, the liberality of his opinions, the contemplative turn of his thoughts & the native beauty & appropriate similes with which he illustrates his communications bespeak him a man singularly qualified to make a favourable impression on his hearers.

This morning we took an affectionate farewell of our friends. Passed through Bordentown four miles away. 'Tis evidently on the decline. Whitehill Landing takes the lead of it now. Vessels cannot at all tides come to the wharves of this town. The latter place is a mile below it. Arrived at Burlington, 10 miles & put up at the house of our kinsman Josa. Smith.

*September 4th.* Attended meeting in the morning. Dined with our cousin H. S. Drinker & set out in the afternoon for home, and put back, on the appearance of a storm, which ended in a slight shower. After a long course of dry weather the earth, by being deprived of its accustomed degree of moisture, ceases to prevent an efficient body of attraction to the passing vapour, which is of course dispersed in an arid, thirsty atmosphere & the usual indications of rain often fail to bring that blessing to the parched lands. When on the contrary the earth has been abundantly moistened, the clouds promptly yield to the attractive influence. Arrested in their progress, they presently draw other clouds around them until, by compressure & condensation, the surrounding atmosphere becomes supercharged with water & it falls in the form of rain. Hence we frequently perceive shower after shower pursuing the same course & visiting the same regions, while other places, scorched by a burning sun, remain unrefreshed.

It is now as common to place potatoes on the dinner table as bread & yet I am assured that within the memory of some of the present inhabitants, the farmers in this vicinity thought their families amply supplied with 2 or 3 bushels a year.

*September 5th,* Left Burlington & crossed at Dunk's Ferry 3½ miles down the road. Taking the river road, we arrived at home by noon.

*September 7th.* Waited on by a com. of the citizens & have declined serving in the State Legislature. For this, some of them censure me, but I surely must be at liberty to think for myself.

*September 12th.* The drought continues. The second crop of hay must be scanty, and in most parts there will be none. Fields of buckwheat have perished & the Indian corn, potatoes &c. are greatly injured. We are in general healthy & our cities are free from that dreadful scourge, the yellow fever.

I am pressed to suffer my name to be used for Congress. A com. of citizens appointed at a late Town meeting have the election of a candidate. I have the offer of their suffrage, but various reasons concur to induce me to decline it.

*September 18th.* Often called on by my old friend Isaac Briggs, who is very intimate with Pres. Jefferson & a warm admirer of his character. With all his zeal, he cannot form a satisfactory apology for certain charges brought against his patron. The attempt made by Jefferson on the chastity of Walker's wife is ascribed to the folly of youth. The encouragement which he gave to Callender to asperse the character of Washington is attributed to a mistaken zeal for the welfare of our country.

*September 22d.* A heavy storm of rain yesterday. There has been little since the 31st of July. It has such an effect on the atmosphere that the thermometer has fallen 35 degrees in 24 hours.

The Embargo, the election & the successes of the Spaniards & Portuguese against the invading French are almost the exclusive topics of conversation among the politicians. Joseph, King of Naples, has been created by his brother, Napoleon, King of the Spaniards. He has entered Spain & proceeded to Madrid, but it is expected he must quickly retire.

*October 8th.* At the late Ward elections, the Democrats contrived to introduce a number of persons from the districts to vote in the City. Several of these & some of the judges have been bound over to answer for the fraud.

*October 12th.* Yesterday the general election was held throughout the state. The poll in the City was 5613, about 1200 more than on any former occasion. The Democratic ticket has prevailed. Snyder's majority over Ross is 160. This is contrary to all expectation. About 400 Frenchman & 300 Irishmen, recently naturalized, have joined with the Democrats against the Federalists to enable this triumph. This freedom of suffrage, which places the most unprincipled foreigners on a level with our best citizens, will one day prove the destruction of the Commonwealth.

*October 20th.* Accounts from various quarters of the state render it certain that Simon Snyder will be our Governor. Penna., whose politics are directed by foreigners, may now be considered as the most Democratic state in the Union. The devotion of that party to France is not decreased, altho' Bonaparte makes an indiscriminate capture & condemnation of every American vessel he can lay hands on. One of their editors in this City, a foreigner of the name of Binns, has gone so far as to declare himself of the French party in this country.

*October 21st.* The mail from Baltimore brings accounts that the Democrats of the City had in open day, tarred & feathered & conducted thro' the streets mounted on a cart, a man whose crime was finding fault with the Embargo!

*November 7th.* Congress assembles this day at the City of Washington. It will probably be one of the most important sessions held since the Revolution.

*November 12th.* 'Tis now understood that Congress will not raise the Embargo. A total nonintercourse with the Belligerents is contemplated & such is the confidence that these measures will take place that merchandize is daily advancing in price & large fortunes making by speculations. A sample of this spirit. T. & S. sold 4 bales muslins at $2.55 per ps. to J. & T.—bot them back again at $3; sold to J. & L. at $3.25 who sold them to the same J. & T. at $3.60 who again sold them to T. & S. at an advance & the latter have lately sold them at $4.25.

This is on a small scale—many have embarked not only to the am't of thousands, but hundreds of thousands.

*November 24th.* A com. of the House of Representatives in Congress, to whom were referred sundry addresses & resolutions relative to our present situation, have concluded a lengthy report by recommending the continuance of the Embargo under more rigorous restrictions of a total interdiction to the waters of the U.S. of all vessels belonging to either of the belligerents & all articles, the growth, produce, or manufacture of either of them or their dependencies. This has operated as another spur to speculation & many of our traders are realizing immense fortunes by their purchases & sales. I am not an idle spectator of the passing scene but endeavour to come in for a slice of the loaf & to make hay while the sun shines.

*November 30th.* Merchandize continues to rise & our capitalists are making extensive investments. Calcutta muslins, which sold in the summer at 80 cents the Rupee, are now current at $1.20 & $1.50. The House of Representatives have passed the resolution interdicting foreign commerce.

# 1809

*January 1st.* Rode to Germantown on horseback, it being as moderate as a May day in the morning, but as night approached it became blustering.

*January 6th.* Speculations have subsided. Most of the articles which were the objects of it have passed from the original holders.

*January 12th.* The American Convention for abolishing slavery has just had its triennial meeting. Among the delegates from N. York is a young man about 23 named Aron H. Palmer, who is understood to be master of nearly as many languages as he is years old. He was born in the city that he represents & owes his extensive acquirements to his own exertions. He lately acted as an interpreter to a Chinese who had business with our Government. He is considered as a second Sir Wm. Jones.

Before the Convention adjourned a motion was made by a Democratic delegate from Wilmington, Delaware, to present a complimentary address to Thos. Jefferson, Pres. of the U. States. The resolution offered by him ended in these words, "that he, Thos. Jefferson, be requested on retiring from public life to use his influence among his fellow citizens to promote a gradual abolition of slavery." To which I moved the following addition, "and that he set them a laudable example by manumitting his own slaves." This brought on a warm discussion, but the amendment was carried; after which the friends of the resolution voted against it & it was lost. At their request the whole of the proceedings were struck from the minutes.

*January 13th.* Congress have passed another law enforcing the Embargo. It gives the collectors of the revenue authority to seize any goods which they may suspect are on their way to be sent out of the U.S. & in case of resistance to call on the military to aid them.

Vessels laden, in whole or in part, must discharge in 10 days after notification or the owners enter into security for 6 times the value of vessel & cargo not to sail without permission. Several of the Eastern states have already manifested strong symptoms of opposition to the present measures of government. The promulgation of this law will doubtless increase the ferment. Many begin to be apprehensive of a Civil War. The present majority in Congress, while they fear to meet the real enemies of the nation with open force, appear disposed to rule their fellow citizens with a rod of iron.

*January 20th*. The Collector & Deputy Collector of Boston have resigned rather than act under the new Embargo law. Town meetings have been held in various parts of the Eastern states, disapproving in strong terms the present measures of the general Government. In some of them the inhabitants have appointed committees of safety to watch over their rights & warned the military not to intefere with the citizens.

In one instance a vessel was arrested by the U.S. sloop of war, the *Wasp* & carried into an Eastern port for attempting to evade the Embargo. A number of men, disguised as Indians, boarded the *Wasp* & turned her officers & crew on shore, stating themselves to be "the descendants of the aborigines who burnt the tea in the year 1774." They liberated the prize & sent her to sea.

In the town of Bath, a vessel was loaded & sailed in defiance of the officers of the Customs. She beat off the revenue cutter. The fort fired on her as she passed, but on a second command to fire, the soldiers refused to obey, declaring "they would not fire on their fellow citizens." The vessel gave three cheers to the Fort & went to sea.

*February 10th*. The Legislature of Mass., now in session in Boston, have passed a resolve declaring the enforcing law of Congress unconstitutional. They disclaim any intention to dismember the union but are taking active & energetic steps to protect their citizens from military coercion. Either Congress must abandon their present system or, if the people of Mass. persist in theirs, a civil war seems inevitable.

*February 11th*. Have lately employed my pen & much of my time in endeavouring to thwart a scheme of the Baltimoreans of robbing us of much of our interior trade, by forming a turnpike road from the Conewago falls on the river Susquehanna to Yorktown, from whence a turnpike is already in forwardness to Baltimore. When one of the representatives from the City last winter, I contributed to frustrate the measure for that time, but fear the ignorance of our present representatives will suffer it to go into operation.

So little, in fact, do our citizens in general understand the subject, so engaged in pursuit of their individual concerns & in the more important political scenes passing before them that it has been difficult to arouse them to a sense of the threatened mischief & now that they have, by dint of perseverance, been induced to sign a memorial which I prepared & circulated, I fear it may be too late.

*February 14th*. Have set on foot a scheme for erecting a bridge over

the river Susquehanna at Columbia. It will require the united & zealous cooperation of many to carry it through, but it is nevertheless very practicable.

*February 22d.* By direction of the late Convention, I sent one copy of Clarkson's History of Slavery to T. Jefferson, Pres. of the U.S.; one copy to G. Clinton, V.P.; one copy to Jas. Madison, Secretary of State & one to Jas. B. Varnum, Speaker of the House of Reps. for the use of the National Library at Washington & addressed a short letter to each.

Today I received a very polite reply from the Speaker, enclosing a resolve of the House acknowledging the receipt & acceptance of the copy presented to them.

*March 6th.* The Nonintercourse-Embargo Repealing Act has passed & received the signature of the President. Its continuance is limited to the end of the next congress & as they are to meet on the 20th of May, this new experiment may not prove very long lived. It is at best a puerile expedient but can scarce be worse than the Embargo which has occasioned great distress to our own country without having affected any one of the objects for which it was professedly laid. Such an embargo is unprecedented in the annals of history. It took effect on the 22nd Dec. 1807 & is to end, except as to France & England, on the 15th; with respect to those nations & their dependencies it is still to be in force.

*March 7th.* On the 4th, Madison became President of the U.S. Should he harbour the same inveteracy to G. Britain & the same devotedness to France with his immediate predecessor, the country will not derive much benefit from his administration.

From my brother Jasper, now in this City from Baltimore, I have the following anecdote.

Turreau, the French minister, has a daugher under the tutorage of Nancy Smith, an accomplished & amiable young woman in Lexington, Virginia. She lately sent a draft for $40 to my brother, on Turreau. This draft my brother transmitted to Edgar Patterson at Washington to be presented to the minister, who is known to be very violent in his temper & very remiss in the payments of his debts. As this was a demand for the support & education of his daughter, it was expected he would pay it. He rudely & peremptorily declined. Patterson, being an independent & spirited man, threatened to expose the draft for sale. To his no small surprize Jas. Madison called on him & "requested he would not push the matter any further," as it would offend the minister & through him perhaps the Emperor Napoleon, his master. This was while Madison was Secy. of State. It does not augur well. The draft remains unpaid.

*March 14th.* After a mild spell which dispersed the snow, we had yesterday a severe storm & this morning the earth is covered from 12 to 14 inches on a level. It is the deepest fall we have had this winter.

*March 15th.* Tomorrow vessels will be permitted to clear for foreign ports not interdicted. It was not until the 13th that orders arrived from headquarters authorizing their being laden. There is some little bustle, but such are still the restrictions under which our commerce still labours from acts of Congress that prudent merchants are not very eager to embrace the partial opening. No specie is permitted to be shipped out of the country. We may sail to China, Batavia, &c. (not to Calcutta & Madras) but, as specie has been heretofore the chief article sent thither for the purchase of return cargoes, few vessels without an evasion of the laws can go direct to any of those eastern ports. There is no restriction on the merchant to sell his ship abroad, but if he makes sales in the U.S. he is liable for all the penalties which may be incurred by the breach of the laws in the purchaser.

No vessel can load without special permission from the Custom House nor until the owner presents a complete manifest of every article to be shipped. On clearing he must give bonds with approved surity in double the value of vessel & cargo that he will not infringe the laws. (Specie has since been permitted to be shipped.)

*March 16th.* By the last accounts from Europe, Bonaparte is carrying the war against the Spaniards with great vigour. He is now in the heart of that devoted country, having recaptured Madrid. The Spaniards make a spirited resistance. The contest is bloody & doubtful. Such is the strange perversity & inconsistency of our Democrats that every success of Bonaparte in this attempt to conquer Spain is to them a subject of rejoicing.

*April 22d.* The President (Madison) has announced by Proclamation that, in consequence of an amicable agreement with G. Britain, the commerce with that nation will be restored to its ancient footing & that vessels may depart for their ports after the 10th of June next, on which Erskine, the British Envoy, has pledged his government to re-move their order in council, so far as respects the U. States. It is a subject of great rejoicing among the Federalists, but is loudly con-demned by our Democrats, who perceive in the measure an end to their

wicked hopes of involving the two countries in war.

This unexpected event has caused a great depression in the value of foreign commodities & it is not improbable that fortunes will be lost with the same facility & to the same extent with which they were so recently made. I cannot calculate on wholly escaping its effects.

*May 25th.* Rumours that Austria & France are at war. Our differences with the latter remain unadjusted. Congress are now holding an extra session at Washington.

*June 1st.* A letter from father announces to me the afflicting intelligence of the death of my mother, in the 71st year of her age. Set out immediately in company with brother Israel to attend her funeral at Lancaster. Travelled with heavy hearts thro' storms of rain & arrived in my one horse chaise at Pettit's after night, where we lodged.

*June 2d.* By 10 A.M. we arrived at Lancaster. We found our father & two sisters very disconsolate, nor was our grief abated by the circumstance that the remains of our dear mother had been consigned to the earth the preceeding afternoon. The letter containing the unwelcome information of her decease was delivered to me a day later than was expected.

*June 3d.* Spent at Lancaster.

*June 6th.* Returned to Phila. by early stages. Left Lancaster on the afternoon of the 4th, having visited several of our kinsmen on our way home.

Father enjoys sound health & a vigorous constitution in the 73rd year of his age. All the brothers & sisters he ever had are still alive & tho' most of them are occasionally afflicted with rheumatism, which appears to be a family disorder, they are all in the full enjoyment of their faculties. I have not been able to ascertain the day on which two of them were born. Their ages stand thus:

| | | |
|---|---|---|
| Hannah | born | June 25, 1724 |
| Samuel | " | August 10, 1726 |
| Mary | " | February, 1729 |
| John | " | Jany., 1735 |
| Nathan | " | July 7, 1733 |
| Joshua Caleb (my father) } twins, | " | Nov. 4, 1736 |
| Joseph | " | Aug. 1, 1740 |

Eight in all, whose ages together make 620 years, which I think a remarkable instance of longevity in one family.

Europeans entertain the opinion that this country is unfavourable to long life, yet these people were all born & brought up in Chester County, within about 25 miles of this City, where 5 of them, Hannah, Samuel, Mary, Nathan & Joseph, still live. Joshua, who is my father's twin brother, resides near Winchester, Virginia & my father at Lancaster. All the men except my father are farmers & attend daily to the business of their farms. All but Mary, who remains single, have been married & have numerous flocks of children.

John, whose offspring is the most numerous, had thirteen sons & one daughter when, 20 years ago, he removed to Red Stone, Penna. Hannah is a widow & all the men have survived their wives.

*June 27th.* Aaron Burr, who took refuge in England, has by order of the Government been lately sent out of the country. This man, whose talents & accomplishments are preeminent, who was so lately the idol of the people of the U.S. & who held the 2nd place in the nation, is now a poor wanderer, without friends or support. General Hamilton stood in the way of his ambition & has become a fugitive & outcast from society.

The young man who addresses my niece is a stranger to me. He is a bookseller & said to be largely in debt for his stock. Tho' young, he has already buried a wife. He possesses some amiable traits of character, but fears are entertained that his habits are not sufficiently stable. I have written her a letter in which I have delicately hinted what has come to my knowledge respecting him & advised her to postpone the connection for another year.

It is the custom for girls to deny even to their friends & connections the suits in which they are involved & the vows of constancy which they have exchanged with their lovers, until the moment of consummation. The natural & timid delicacy of the female character would forbid an ostentatious display of their intentions to enter the circle of matrons, but they too frequently make shipwreck of their peace by the deadly secrecy with which they screen from their friends what is passing in their hearts.

I know not when society will be properly modelled, perhaps never. But in most countries men are culpable for the artificial manners which they are nevertheless apt enough censoriously & therefore most ungenerously & yet, generally, with truth to charge to the fair sex.

We rivet on them their frailties & expect them to act like angels. We

worship & abuse them. But while I thus freely condemn my own sex, I do not think our fair companions wholly exempt from a portion of blame.

A woman should be guileless, dignified, modest. She should forever discard all affectation & act in her native character & neither pretend, on the one hand, to a platonic purity which is void of all passions nor, on the other, make a display which may catch the libertine & invite aggression & insult but which seldom fails to displease men of refined understandings. Their charms should neither be mantled in the impenetrable garb of cloistered obscurity nor yet be vauntingly set open like apartments, to be occupied by any one who will pay the rent. Give me the girl of nature, unsophisticated by the maxims of the prude & untarnished by the manners of the licentious.

My niece is a most amiable & charming girl, gentle, timid, lively, affectionate & neither so beautiful as to be vain, nor so homely as to be shunned. She is handsome enough to gratify even the fastidious.

Her opportunities of education have been very limited, but her understanding, unless love has blunted its edge, is penetrating & solid. She cannot fail to make a good man happy. She is the daugher of my unfortunate & deceased brother John. Hence she has a variety of claims to the interest I take in her. She is now with her mother at York, Pa.

*July 4th.* The continent of Europe continues to be the theatre of the most bloody wars. Austria & France have commenced hostilities & several severe battles have been already fought between Bonaparte & the Arch Duke Charles.

*August 3d.* Part of last evening was spent in company with Dr. Rush at my friend S. Coates's. He is the great champion for the domestic origin of yellow fever. In the course of conversation on this subject he was asked if it could be imported. To which he answered with great emphasis, "It is impossible, it is contrary to the laws of nature & I would believe it as possible to restore a dead man to life."

Left home in company with son Henry in a chaise for Burlington on business. On the way we were thrown out by the falling of our horse. I received some contusions on my head. By the help of a traveller who stopped to assist us, we got up our nag & proceeded. We crossed the river at Dunk's Ferry but the high wind drove us ¾ mi. above the landing. We arrived at Burlington & lodged with Jas. Smith. He lives like a prince, as he is wealthy and equally hospitable. When I was an apprentice, this man was poor & unable to pay his debts. A fortunate train of business succeeded & he satisfied his old creditors & it is probable that he is now worth half a million of Dollars. In the evening his partner arrived from Philada. & brought intelligence of the return of the *Mentor,* a dispatch ship sent by our Governor to France. Napoleon from his headquarters at Vienna has at length so far relaxed as to have appointed a minister to hear our complaints in Paris. It appears that he has suffered a loss of between 30,000 & 50,000 men in a late engagement with the Arch Duke Charles of Austria.

Procured a sample of clay taken from the banks of the river above the village, white as fine paper, free of grit, heavy as metal & very fine. May it not someday become the medium of a great china manufactury? All the samples are not equally white.

*August 28th.* Attended to business in the morning. Having now only to wait the motions of the sapient Judge, rode out this afternoon to Dutchman's Neck on the bank of the Delaware & visited the clay & sand pits, 5 miles above Burlington. The clay, of which I have already spoken, is said to be the best as yet discovered in America for pots to melt glass in & we here found a vessel loading the sand to carry to the glass works at Albany, as it is said to be of a superior quality for the purpose. The clay & sand are found in the same bank. Would not this be the spot to carry out the manfactury of glass?

Dutchman's Neck is a flat, sandy point, poor & badly improved.

*August 29th.* Judge A. has not yet prepared the deed. He boasted to me that he could write 60 sheets in a day, but from the specimen he gives me of his talents, it would puzzle him to write two. Having no business, crossed over the river & after visiting the bath, hired a horse of one man & a chaise of another & taking them together rode with H.S.D. to his former farm at Pennsbury Manor, the ancient residence of our great founder Wm. Penn. The old mansion is till standing & in tolerable preservation. The woodwork of the house has much carving on it & must, when erected, have awed both natives & settlers by its grandeur. In one of the apartments in which Gov. Penn gave audience to the Indians, he had erected a rude throne of wood, ascended by a flight of steps which he occupied on public occasions. He knew well how to conciliate & awe. He was plain but preserved the dignity of his station. H.S.D. has still in being an arm chair which belonged to Wm. Penn. The frame is of English Oak, carved, arms walnut, back & seat cane lattice. It is in good preservation.

It would wound the spirit of our great & good Founder, were he now to witness the sad declension of his descendents, one of whom, the son of Richard, not long since arrived in this country. He has lately married a girl who was a common prostitute & with whom he lives near the falls of Schuylkill.

*August 30th.* While waiting the return of the steamboat this morning from Trenton, a boat put off from her & landed several of her passengers, who reported some of her works to be in disorder; among them was the celebrated Gen. Moreau, who now resides with his family at Morrisville. Rec'd an introduction to him. He was dressed in a round blk. hat, short coatee of drab cotton cassimere, white vest & nankeen pantaloons. He appears to be abt. 5 ft. 9—well set, but not corpulent, dark complexion, blk. hair, a firm, penetrating hazel eye & aquiline nose. As he was on his way to Phila. we hired a stage waggon & proceeded together. Had understood he was reserved but found him the very reverse. He spoke English correctly & with passable fluency. We spent between 5 & 6 hours together & finding he had no objections to conversation, I plied him so well that ours was the opposite of a silent meeting. He surprized me with the freedom of his remarks on the varied topics connected with France, her Emperor & other great men, their policy, conduct & character.

C. "It seems to be generally believed that Napoleon is of a morose, selfish disposition & seldom relaxes in even the company of his friends. Has he any social or colloquial powers?"

M. "Perhaps no man knows the Emperor better than myself or has been treated by him with more familiarity. He is a man of liberal education, possesses a large fund of knowledge & when he chooses can be witty, amusing & agreeable, but this has generally been when we were alone. On the appearance of others he became reserved, nor indulged himself or permitted the indulgence of levity in his presence, preserving in mixed companies a stately distance."

C. "Does the Empress exercise any influence over him & how is she respected by the French people, since it is pretty well known that, prior to her connection with Bonaparte, she bore among the Parisians the character of 'une femme gallante'?"

M. "The Empress is a good tempered, elegant woman, fond of parade & show. She does not give herself any trouble about public concerns & if she did the Emperor would not permit it & so long as she studies to gratify the taste of the people for amusements, they will give themselves but little trouble about her former gallantries."

We conversed on a variety of other subjects relating to Europe & America, on all of which I found the General communicative & apparently well informed. Since his arrival in this country he has travelled through most of the Atlantic states & passed from Pittsburgh down the Ohio to N. Orleans. He gave me some account of these excursions. He does not consider the American climate so favourable to health as the European. Speaking of our municipal & more general polity, he thought we entertained too much jealousy of power & thus deprived ourselves of some important advantages, particularly in our City regulations, which would result from arming our functionaries with more effectual means of promoting the public weal. "And," continued he, "your elections are too frequent, the public are thrown into a state of ferment once a year, on the approach of your elections. Your representatives, being thus continually dependent on popular favour, become time serving politicians, nor do you permit them to remain long enough in office to acquire a sufficient knowledge of their duties."

*September 4th.* The new English minister, Jackson, has arrived at Norfolk.

*September 6th.* The electioneerers are again in motion. A deputation from the conferees appointed by the different Wards, called on me. They press me to serve either in Congress or the State Legislature & have received my negative.

Considering that I have been uniform, year after year, in refusing to serve in public stations & that I do not possess the necessary qualifications of a statesman, it is surprizing that I am so continually called on. I can look around me & see men in abundance who, in my opinion, would serve the public with more ability & who would willingly make the trial & who could do it without the same sacrifice of feeling & interest; but these are passed over, a fickle people will not have these men to rule over them, while I am literally pestered with applications. To be absent at Washington six months of the year would be equivalent to an abandonment of my business. I could not reconcile it to my sense of duty & propriety to be an idle member of the House & when once I became active, my time would be so much occupied with public events that on my return, I should be unfit for the resumption of common avocations. Added to which, I should not relish the exchange of my domestic enjoyments for the bustle & acrimony of public debate. My health, moreover, at all times delicate, would doubtless be injured by it.

To these considerations another might be added, which, although it would not deter me from serving, cannot be agreeable to any & certainly is entitled to the reprehension of all good citizens. No sooner is a candidate announced for any important public station than his character is assailed by the most vindictive & dirty aspersions. He at once becomes a target for the sharpshooters & every whelp in the kennel of obscenity is let loose to hunt down his fair name. He is fair game for all who choose to bespatter & annoy him.

*October 10th.* In a late eastern paper it is stated that in the state of Massachusetts, they have had frost in every month this year except July.

*October 20th.* Until within a few days, the weather has been hotter during the present month than it was in August by 8 or 10 degrees.

*November 12th.* In addition to the restrictions thrown on our commerce by England & France (against whom our nonintercourse is still in force) we are now advised of the closing of the Spanish Ports in the island of Cuba & on the Main to vessels of all nations.

*November 14th.* In the course of correspondence between our Excutive & the English minister, Jackson, the latter has been charged with so much indecorum that the Pres. has refused to receive any further communications from him.

*November 18th.* A most affecting circumstance occurred to me yesterday. I was sent for in the morning by the wife of a much valued friend on account of her husband having attempted his life by a dose of laudanum. I hastened to the spot & found him quite delirious under the influence of the poison. Medical assistance was immediately procured. Ten potions of emetics immediately administered, the feathered end of a quill thrust down his throat, he vomited copiously & was given vinegar & water to drink. A vein was also opened from which near a quart of blood was taken. After the operation of the emetic, 10 grains of calomel were given to him, to which was added copious draughts of strong Senna Tea, into which a little brandy was occasionally introduced. In the after part of the day he also drank brandy & water. I remained with him all night, nor left him until he was past danger, exacting from him, during the night, a solemn promise that he would never repeat the attempt.

Language cannot describe what I have suffered on this occasion. This man is my bosom friend. His accomplishments & talents are great, his powers of conversation rarely exceeded, his manners free & interesting, his integrity unsullied, his feelings, warm, generous & disinterested to a very unusual degree. His fortune is independent. His wife & children devoted to him. His constitution is sound. He possesses not only the qualifications, but the means of enjoying life. What could have induced such a man, under such circumstances, to commit such an act? He has been dealt with deceptively by a near connection in whom he once placed a great confidence which, for want of employment, he has dwelt on until his delicate sensibility has wrought on him a fit of distraction & temporary derangement. It is a striking & painful instance of great imbecility mixed with great mental powers. No one among the circle of my friends could I less have suspected of so much weakness. Without the superintending providence of God, we are indeed but frail creatures.

*November 30th.* On the morning of the 25th, the river Schuylkill was frozen over. It has been preceded by a heavy fall of snow which fell from one to two feet in different parts of the country & appears to have extended far north & south. It is now more mild & the ice has vanished.

*December 16th.* After another hard fought battle, the French & Austrians came to a line truce, which has been followed by a peace, by which the latter make further considerable cessions of territory. Bonaparte left Vienna for Spain, which it is suspected must now fall beneath his weight.

*December 17th.* A periodical work is published in Paris, the political department of which is superintended by one of the Senators. In this work it is declared on the 4th of November that Jackson, the English minister, had been rejected by the American administration. This was before the rejection was made known to the American people. It is a fact equally curious that our late very extraordinary Embargo was announced in France antecedent to the passing of that act by the American Congress. What must the English ministry think of all this?

*December 21st.* The first meeting of the Directors of "the Pennsyl. Compy. for assurances on lives & granting annuities & reversions" took place in the Coffee House.

I took my seat among them. An act of incorporation is forthwith to be solicited from the Legislature. If this is not obtained, 'tis questionable whether the plan will go into operation.

Another company for the same purposes has just been formed. These are the first of the kind attempted in America.

*December 23d.* The system of arbitration which is now, as Thos. Jefferson would say, in the full tide of experiment, is found to be very burdensome to some of us, who are in perpetual requisition & often called on to decide cases involving the nicest cases of law. One of the great objects of its framers was to get rid of the Lawyers, but so far from its answering that purpose, it has doubled their employment. Any man can compel his adversary to an arbitration. Lawyers plead before the arbitrators, appeals are admitted & the gentlemen of the bar are again called on to argue the case before the courts of Justice.

*December 25th.* Took my station for the first time, as a manager of the Pennsyl. Hospital.

*December 28th.* Ever since the dismissal of Jackson, the British Envoy, public rumour has been busy in placing us on the eve of war. Congress menace & the Democratic party, in & out, cry aloud for it, yet I cannot believe the country will prove so mad.

# 1810

*January 31st.* Until the 18th of this month was mild when of a sudden, when there was no frost in the ground, no ice in the Delaware, the wind, unattended with snow, shifted to the NW & blew a heavy gale accompanied with such intense cold that the thermometer in the space of a few hours fell near 40 degrees & in two nights the river was completely frozen over & hundreds crossed on the ice. It appears that the change was extensive & more in the extreme in the Eastern states. From Portsmouth they write, from the 18th to the 19th the mercury fell 54 degrees, being, on the latter, 15 degrees below 0. Its lowest declension here was six above 0. On the 20th vessels were frozen in at Reedy Island. A brig of mine, outward bound, was caught there & so firm was the ice that 3 of her hands deserted on that day & footed it to the shore whence they effected their escape. We caught them afterwards in Phila. & sent them back.

*February 3d.* A most tempestuous day. A gale from the NE & a heavy fall of snow. It occasions serious apprehensions for the vessels & crews in the Bay. On the 28th last a fleet of about 20 sail left Reedy Island. They were soon met by a large body of ice & most of them either driven ashore or left entangled among the cakes. Information has already been received of the destruction of several near Morris Liston's & it is not known that they are quite safe. By the last accounts, my brig (*Eliza*, Capt. Moody) was aground near Cohanzey. Hopes are entertained that she may have entered that creek, otherwise the storm of this day will probably destroy her. Fear more for the lives of those on board than for the vessel & cargo. A valuable young man (Hilary Baker) from my Counting House went in her as supercargo.

*February 4th.* Have employed my pen lately in writing several essays relating principally to municipal affairs. Published one in Poulson of this morning, signed Giles Homespun, in which I have endeavoured to expose & hold up to ridicule a preposterous plan for selling the present Almshouse & building one in the country. Other essays signed Civis, in the style of serious argument, on the same subject were written by me.

*February 7th.* Have information of the safety of the brig *Eliza* in Cohanzey Creek.

*February 15th.* My friend C.B.B. whose literary talents have pro-

cured him considerable celebrity is, I fear, in the last stage of consumption. Visited him today. It was an affecting interview. He spoke with difficulty but great composure. After disclosing some interesting affairs in relation to himself & family, he pressed me with his cold hand & bid me, I fear, a last adieu. Poor fellow! If learning, genius & a mind capable of grasping the whole store of knowledge, or if an amiable heart & almost unequalled candor in weighing the conduct & opinions of others could arrest the awful stroke of death, thou wouldst live, to enliven, instruct & console one whom thou hast, in thy last moments, honoured with the title of thy best friend. This amiable man has not been free from error. He was educated for a lawyer but, possessing no relish for the profession, he abandoned the study without applying to be admitted to practice in the courts & for several years after he attained the age of 25, his time was spent not absolutely in listless idleness but without that regular application to business which is necessary to the acquirement of steady habits & to the formation of a settled character. His hours were spent in seclusion from the world & were principally devoted to reading & the society of a few select friends. He was poor, nor had his parents the means of conferring on him anything beyond a bare subsistence in their family. They pressed him continually to the practice of the law & his friends, who believed him to possess the necessary qualifications for becoming a shining character in that leading profession, urged their suit, but they urged in vain. He had too much good nature to deny them flatly; he gave expectations of compliance but, without sufficiently explaining his objections, he secretly fostered a determination adverse to their wishes & was fully resolved never to appear at the bar. In this very embarrassing situation he became unhappy & often, to shake off importunities with which he thought he could not comply & yet wanted fortitude openly to resist, he wandered from home & gave himself up to gloomy reflections. While in this state of mental perplexity he became acquainted with the poisonous writings of the celebrated Godwin. He read them with avidity, imbibed many of the visionary & pernicious notions contained in them & even opened a correspondence with their author. Full of these speculative ideas, ingenuous & eloquent in their elucidation & at all times fond of canvassing opinions, he soon entered the lists with this friends, few of whom concurred with him. The doctrines of Godwin & others of the same school frequently occasioned long & animated discussions between us. I was not a match for him in these discussions. I sometimes lost my patience so far as to treat him with considerable personal asperity, yet he never resorted to abuse or lost his temper, even when loaded with invective. I had the vanity to believe that the weight of argument was usually on my side, but then his ingenuity suggested so many refined subtleties & these were urged with such force of eloquence—for no man could exceed him in the force & ready command of language—that I found great difficulty in detecting & exposing his errors. He possessed other advantages. He had been liberally educated, he had a much more extensive knowledge of books & had, moreover, leisure to prepare himself for these controversial interviews, while I, deeply immersed in business, had but little time to devote to literary acquirements. Amid all these warm disputes we never lost our friendship for each other & his visits were continued as usual. Soon after this period he commenced author & published *William Ormond* &c., which could not fail to be admired as the works of genius, but which were strongly tinctured with the new philosophy & of course met not my entire approbation. His ready desire to please his friends induced him to submit to some alterations in the manuscripts, but the works came out very much as they were originally composed. I have reason to believe that, had he deferred their publication for a few years, they would have undergone considerable amendments & been more acceptable to good men. Be that as it may, they soon obtained for him the notice of the learned & he has been enabled ever since to acquire by his pen a very sufficient competency. He has amassed nothing, but has lived in abundance. He married the daughter of a clergyman of the name of Lynn in N. York & has living four small children by her. Their whole subsistence is his pen. He receives $1500 per annum for editing a periodical work & what seemed most to press on his mind in my last interview was to engage my friendship in soliciting from the proprietor a continuance of the editorship to his widow. It had been my uniform advice to him so to economize as to lay by one third of his income. This was not done & I greatly fear he will leave his family very destitute, for altho' the proprietor of the magazine may possibly be induced from motives of humanity to continue the editorship to the widow (for even now I cannot but so style her) it cannot be expected that the subscribers will long remain satisfied with a work which will have lost its life spring & vigour. He spoke to me calmly on the interesting topic of his too probable speedy departure & wept not until he pressed my hand, called me his best friend & took leave. We were not more than half an hour together. He had taken care that we should be alone. I propped him in bed, but he found it necessary frequently to shift his position before he concluded what he wished to say. An instance of his accuracy of language occurred as he wept & I was about to leave the room. I begged him to be tranquil & remarked that much depended on it. He answered with a feeble voice & in broken accents, "I know it is my duty to labour for rest both of body & mind" & then added, with a smile, "if it be not an absurdity to say labour for rest."

*February 17th* A heavy rain accompanied with a southerly wind has unbound the Delaware & put the ice in motion.

*February 24th.* Have just returned from the funeral of C. B. Brown. He died on the 21st in a happy frame of mind & obtained in his last moments that satisfactory evidence of the truth of religion of which he had so often & so long doubted & which he always appeared anxious to acquire; for he frequently said to me that there was no condition in life which he so much envied or more ardently craved than a firm belief in the divinity & doctrines of Christianity & in his worst state of scepticism I never heard him irreverently speak either of pious professors or of their principles.

But he was in the habit of admitting nothing on trust. His reason was his touchstone & whatever was brought to that standard & stood not the test was rejected. He trusted nothing to faith or revelation.

His incredulity did not lead him into libertine excesses or to the immoral indulgence of his appetites & passions. Few were more exemplary in these respects & if he did advocate the wild & mischievous doctrines of Godwin, his goodness of heart was ever a bar to his putting them into practice. He composed with more facility than any other person I ever knew & appeared to be at no loss to express himself on any subject, however incidentally or unexpectedly it became the topic of conversation. His genius was of the first order; his capacity for the acquirement of knowledge, preeminent; his education, liberal & greatly improved by study & research; his attachments ardent, disinterested & sincere.

His untimely exit deprives me of one of my most instructive companions & I do most deeply feel & mourn his departure. I live in the fond hope that our spirits will be reunited in a more glorious & happy state of existence, where disease shall cease its desolations & even death itself be forever disarmed of its terrors. "Where the wicked shall cease from troubling & the weary be at rest." Adieu! a long adieu! my much loved companion & friend.

*February 25th.* A visit from the two brothers of the deceased to request me to compose an obituary for publication. I complied with their wishes. Poulson is to publish it tomorrow. Whether it will please, I know not. I have endeavoured to produce a faithful sketch of the character of the deceased & if they expect a fullsome strain of uninterrupted panegyric, they will be disappointed.

I have spoken warmly in his praise, but I have spoken what I believe to be true & while on the one hand I have bestowed warm encomiums where they were due, I deemed it right, on the other, to make some apology to the public for the juvenile & early errors of my departed friend.

*February 27th.* Such is the vicissitude of our climate that yesterday & today we experience the warmth of summer—Fahrenheit's thermometer being up to 65.

*March 6th.* In a squall of wind last night, the venerable & large Elm tree at Kensington, under which it is said Wm. Penn held his first treaty with the Aborigines, was blown down. It has been on the decline for some years, previously to which it was a princely tree, its branches extending sixty feet from the trunk on every side, forming a shade impenetrable to the sun. In the summer of 1806 I built, in company with others, the ship *Susquehanna* within the precincts of its shade.

The proper regulation of the temper, so as to smother or destroy the first ebullitions of spleen & ill humour, is found by many to be a very difficult task, assailed as we often are by the petulance, injustice or indiscretions of others. I find it so & yet more is in our power than we are willing to acknowledge.

The wrongs or errors of others form—in the correct estimation of reason—but a flimsy apology for our own, but we are too apt to seize with avidity any excuse to save our pride from mortification. Thus, after the indulgence of an ill natured expression or splenetic retort to which we should not have given utterance had we been sufficiently on our guard or attentive to our own comfort or the happiness of others, instead of making a prompt & manly acknowledgement to the injured party for the fault which we had committed, we seek either to justify it openly by the provocation we had received or—knowing we had in fact received no sufficient provocation—we sullenly harbour our fretful feelings as a consuming fever which preys on our vitals & deprives us, as a just punishment for our perseverance in error, of that peace & serenity which never fail to reward virtue & magnanimity.

*March 25th.* A very alarming disorder prevails in Worcester, Mass. & neighbourhood. Those who are seized frequently die in 24 hours. It is called the Spotted fever. Its origin has been ascribed to the use of bad provisions. The grain harvest last season was not well got in, much of it was green & flour made from grain in that state has long been esteemed unwholesome. Horses & other animals have been killed by eating green Indian corn.

*March 28th.* The edicts of France against our commerce, the English orders in Council & our nonintercourse law are still in force. By the former we are prevented from trading with England & her dependencies—by the orders in Council, from trading to France & her dependencies & by our nonintercourse from trading to either.

France, by her Berlin & Milan decrees, declares the whole of her enemies' possessions in a state of blockade & her cruisers capture, burn & sink American vessels trading in contravention of those decrees or for having been spoken by an English vessel at sea. England contents herself with turning off our vessels attempting to enter French ports.

*April 25th.* Congress have suffered the nonintercourse laws to expire, but as they have not come to terms with either England or France, our commerce is still greatly restricted.

*May 15th.* Bonaparte, having repudiated his Empress Josephine, has married the Arch Duchess of Austria, daughter of the present Francis.

*June 1st.* All American property in France & the countries under its immediate influence to the amount, as is conjectured, of twenty-five million dollars, has by order of Bonaparte been seized & sequestered & the proceeds are placed in this private treasury. Our Government takes no measures of resistance.

*June 10th.* It seems probable that Spanish America will become independent of the Mother Country. Some of the provinces on the Main have taken the reins of government into their own hands.

*June 25th.* An unexpected event, in the sudden death of Thos. Annesley, may throw me into a new branch of business. For six weeks past, my Countg. House & his have been under the same roof on Walnt. St. Wharf. He went to bed in apparently good health & spirits on the night of the 23d. & died before daylight. It has been to me a great shock. Have taken the stores myself & shall probably continue his business —the purchase and sale of tobacco.

*June 26th.* Commiserating the widow & children, none of whom are capable of carrying on the business. I have made her, unasked, a gratuitous offer to share the profits of whatever may be made on consignments of tobacco for 12 months. It is to be considered as a voluntary gift from me, not as a partnership, for she will furnish neither money nor service of any kind. By the failure of B. & A. I lost a considerable sum, but I ever considered the deceased as less culpable than his partner. He could have made but little since that period; whatever it may be, I will try to secure it to the widow.

*September 1st.* The aggrandizement of France at the expense of her neighbours goes on swimmingly. Last spring Bonaparte married the daughter of the Emperor of Austria & the latter power stipulate to furnish 150,000 troops for his use. His brother Louis has abdicated the throne of Holland, publicly announcing that he could no longer satisfy the ambition of Napoleon & discharge his duty to his own subjects. Holland has in consequence been annexed to the French Empire. Thus ends a nation who for many centuries made a very important figure in the annals of Europe. What will be the end of this tremendous concentration of power in the hands of one man?

*September 15th.* A fast trotting horse was sold at the Merchants Coffee House for $500. He lately trotted on the point-to-point road in a sulky, for a wager, at the rate of two minutes & 48 seconds in a mile. That is, a mile in 2 minutes & 48 seconds.

*November 6th.* The President's Proclamation dated 2d of this month announces that he has official information from France of the repeal of the Berlin & Milan decrees, to take effect on the 1st. & declaring that unless G. B. shall in three months thereafter rescind her orders in Council, the Nonintercourse Act will again be put in force against her.

The turpitude & devious policy of our rulers in their temporizing schemes of embargo & nonintercourse has uniformly operated more injury to the American citizens than to the belligerents. The present expedient is of a piece with the rest.

Some weeks before the issuing of this Proclamation & when no one expected it, J.K. Helmuth & myself dispatched our ship *Susquehanna,* laden principally on our own account, to Liverpool & ordered our funds to be invested in goods to return in the ship, which cannot be expected back until after the period fixed for the commencement of the nonintercourse. We are therefore placed in this situation: Either we must suffer

our property to remain in an enemy's country or bring it home under the certain expectation of seizure by our own government & incur the additional penalty of double the value of vessel & cargo.

People in after times will scarce believe it possible that any government could act with so much folly & wickedness.

*December 20th.* Much popular interest is excited on the subject of the renewal of the charter of the Bank of the U.S. It will expire in March of next year.

# 1811

*January 24th.* The subject of the U.S. Bank charter engages the public attention to the exclusion of almost all others. The fear that it will not be renewed has destroyed confidence so far that scarce any business can be done & failures to a great extent, especially in N. York, are daily taking place.

Numerous memorials have been presented to Congress praying a renewal, but the latter seem to laugh at the wide spread ruin which they are heaping on their fellow citizens. The merchants & traders have resolved on another memorial to Congress.

*January 26th.* T. W. Francis, J. Sperry, W. Newbold & myself have been appointed to proceed to Washington with the memorial & to use our influence with the government to procure a renewal of the charter.

*January 28th.* Com. left the city in the stage via Lancaster, where we halted for half an hour. Saw Brady of the Senate who thinks, notwithstanding the resolution to instruct our Senators & representatives in Congress to vote against the Bank, there is a large majority in the state in favour of it. He believes that no new Bk. will be chartered in the present session by the state. If the U.S. Bk. is continued by Congress, there will be no occasion for other; if put down, then an improper time to create new banks.

Wm. Wright is here pressing for charter Mechanics Bank who engage, in lieu of douceur to the state, to build a bridge over Susquehanna at Columbia. Richard Cooke, member of Congress from Wiscasset, & wife, also a gentleman named Fowler, form part of our company.

Lodged at Kline's Ferry House on the western shore—a dirty hole. On examining beds, Francis & Sperry decided to sit up all night. My rule being to take the world as I find it & make the best of a bad bargain, I went upstairs & perceiving that my covering was a muslin sheet, blanket & thin muslin bedspread, robbed a neighbouring bed of a stout coverlet & went snugly to roost. Fowler soon followed suit & snatching the blanket from the disrobed bed, placed it on his own. Our night walkers, changing their mind, entered our chamber. F. took possession of the only bed which retained a cover & S., finding nothing but sheets left for him, made a great outcry which brought the Landlord, who is no less a man than a militia general, into our chamber. On understanding the cause of the uproar, he brandished a lighted taper which he held in his hand & casting an eye around, exclaimed with military vehemence, "Shentilmen, dere iss some of you is quite too bolt. You makes too tarn free in taken dem clodes. I winch i only knowt once who hat 'em, I am tamt I soon pull 'em off." This gasconade was affected. It was evident enough who were the perpetrators of this deadly crime, the robbers & the spoils were in full view. He did not think proper to disturb either. I was ready to burst with laughter as I lay, apparently asleep, listening to the vengeful threats of the enraged host.

*January 29th.* Up by 5 & reached Spangler's at York Town at an early hour, where we breakfasted & afterwards took the route of the new turnpike to Baltimore, 48 mi. This road is cut through great hills & is an expensive affair. Including its continuance to Conewago, it is said to have cost $500,000, the whole of which except about $6,000 has been furnished by Baltimore capital. About 9 at night, when within 3 miles of Baltimore, the strap which secured the baggage was cut by some villain & my trunk, containing my wardrobe, introductory letters &c. was stolen. The driver rode back in search of it but the thief had escaped with his booty. On arrival at Baltimore I proposed to tarry till I could procure a supply of clothing. My colleagues objected & offering me a participation in theirs I concluded to continue my course with them in the morning, placing myself a pensioner on their bounty. I had now nothing left but what was on my back. I had, it is true, preserved my umbrella, but in handing it from the stage, it also made its escape & could not afterwards be found. Put up at Gadsby's.

*January 30th.* Having hired a light coach & 4 we proceeded by ourselves & arrived at Washington, some 42 miles. We put up at Coolidge's, Penna Avenue near Capitol.

*January 31st.* Called at Long's Hotel to pay our respects to the Com. from Mechanics, who arrived the day preceding us: Lieper, Grice, Vodges, Foering & Ord. Senate assembled at 11. President took the chair at 12. Leib presented our memorial—referred to the Com. previously appointed on the Bk. question, viz. Crawford, Lloyd, Anderson, Pope & Leib. House of Representatives having before our arrival passed a resolution of indefinite postponement, they cannot again act on the subject in the present session unless sent from the Senate.

Soon after our arrival, the right wing of the Capitol in which the House of Representatives meet was discovered to be on fire. Helped to extinguish the flames. There was not much damage done.

*February 1st.* The delegation waited on Secy. Gallatin. He informed us that he had yesterday made a report to the com. of Senate, favourable to the continuation of the Bank. Why did he not do so at an earlier period? It would doubtless have prevented many from committing themselves, on whom this report cannot be expected to produce a change. He also informed that, although he had recommended a renewal of the Charter, he had little expectation of its being done & that the gentleman who retired as we entered was Clay of the Senate, who was willing to allow the Bank time to wind up but came to consult on the best means of shutting the door to all hope of an extension beyond that period. The Secy. appeared to be fully apprized of the destructive consequences which would result from a stoppage of the Bank. He spoke of the resolutions of the State Legislatures instructing their Senators & Reps. in Congress to vote against the Bank as decisive—for although some would not, yet many would feel themselves bound to abide those instructions. He was satisfied of the inefficiency of the state Bks. to afford to the Government the same facility & security in their fiscal arrangements which were derived from the Bk. U.S. & doubted not that, when it should be defunct, Congress would establish a National Bk. in its place.

On being asked how they would escape the charge of inconsistency, he replied that, altho' a majority of the present Congress might think the incorporation of a Bank by the general government unconstitutional, their decision could have no binding effect on a succeeding Congress, as the latter will possess equal right to judge & determine for themselves. He remarked to us further that the immediate representatives from all our great commercial Cities, except Boston, opposed a continuation of the Charter. He was well informed of the state of the Mother Bank & all its branches & of the situation of the state Bks. & their incapacity to afford relief to the debtors of the Bk. U.S.

G. is a man of sallow complexion, thin visage, aquiline nose, black hair & eyes. He possesses considerable talents & with the air & step of a clodhopper has the keen & scrutinizing qualities of a Frenchman adept at intrigue.

After leaving the Secy., I went to the Capitol & was by Seybert introduced to Newton, chairman of the Com. of Commerce & Manufactures. I was invited into their com. room where they read to me a Bill they proposed to introduce to the House this day, one of the provisions of which is to interdict the exportation of American produce in American bottoms to countries into which they are not permitted on paying the same duties as if carried in vessels of such countries. My opinion was asked & I did not hesitate to declare "that I should consider the measure as giving the finishing blow to our already distressed commerce. It is directly in opposition to the British Navigation Act, which they have maintained against the united forces of all Europe & from which you will in vain attempt to drive them. You have already tried your skill in a war of commerce with that nation & you have not failed to suffer by it. Tomorrow your nonintercourse with them commences anew & will prove, as it did before, more injurious to your own citizens than to the subjects of G. Britain."

Newton said but little & it appeared evident that he had not well digested his subject. He said "I will report the Bill & suffer it to take its course." Seybert replied, "You may do so, but on reflection, mind, I do not promise it my support." As we passed into the lobby, Seybert introduced me to the celebrated John Randolph. He looked sickly & appeared to totter as he walked. After the interchange of a few words, he turned towards S. & said, "I came here today to stir you up but, finding I have no chance & feeling very unwell, I will return to my lodgings."

I am resolved to keep near the Capitol, that I may be present at this stirring match. He spoke in a voice resembling that of a girl, with a smile on his countenance. He has much of the appearance of a quick grown stripling. He is about 6 feet high, slender, a little knock-kneed, light hair & eyes, & nearly beardless. His dress bespoke a mind above the frippery of fashion, but was sufficiently neat. His flaxen hair was carelessly tied with a simple string & spread over his back and was without powder. He must be near 40.

Having rejoined my colleagues, we paid a short visit to Pres. Madison, who received us with great courtesy. We stated the object of our mission to Washington & communicated some facts relating to it. He made a few enquiries but expressed no opinion either for or against the Bank. The subject of the recent dispatches was introduced. Here again, he expressed himself with great caution but nevertheless intimated his apprehensions that "the Emperor of France was dealing doubly with this nation."

*February 2d.* The com. of the Senate gave us an audience this morning in a small apartment above the Senate chamber. The deputation from our Mechanics had been previously examined. We commenced by stating that we did not appear as the agents of the Bank, nor at the instance of the Directors, but as the representatives of the merchants & traders of Philada. We came to make an unvarnished statement of facts & to express the apprehensions of our constituents that, unless the Bank Charter should be renewed, great individual & public distress must ensue. The evil had already commenced & unless confidence were speedily restored, we apprehended little less than a general state of Bankruptcy. Already, the mistrust of the Banks had occasioned an unprecedented demand for their specie, as people are anxious to secure themselves from loss & bring in Bank Notes from all parts of the country, demanding gold or silver. The com. listened to us with respect—even Leib, who was expected to break out, behaved respectfully & kept silent.

This business over, I went to the House Reps. & found Randolph had just commenced a speech which I would not have lost the opportunity of hearing for the loss of my baggage. He is the most impressive & accomplished Parliamentary debater I ever heard. On mentioning this opinion afterwards in the presence of several Senators & members of the lower house, they concurred with me & one of them added that he had heard Pitt, Fox, Sheridan & others of the most celebrated men of the English Parliament & thought none of them in this respect equal to Randolph. Even his youthful & effeminate appearance & voice which, in a man of weak or mean talents would be disadvantageous, are in Randolph's favour. His feebleness excites sympathy & his voice, which is clear & sonorous, becomes more masculine as his subject rises. His expression is deliberate & solemn & I could scarcely help fancying, as I saw the meagre sprite before me, like a being tottering to the grave, that I heard the voice of an angel sent down from Heaven to warn the deluded from their errors. In the zeal with which he inspired me, I could gladly have leaped from the gallery to clasp him in my arms. When he spoke, every ear was attentive & every eye fixed on him. Everybody appeared riveted to the spot & afraid to move or breathe.

He had moved a resolution to instruct a com. to bring in a Bill to repeal the nonintercourse with England which goes into operation this day & if reason or argument, if satire or persuasion could have moved the ministerial party in the House, he must have succeeded. He spoke on a great national subject & did ample justice to his cause. He told the Nation & that House some awful & momentous truths & his opponents in vain attempted their refutation.

Notwithstanding my praise of Randolph, I do not consider him qualified to shine as the leader of a great party. He shines most in opposition & has too much asperity of temper & perhaps too great a spirit of independence to be shackled by those rules of discipline & that spirit of the corps, so essential to a well organized partizan. He darts upon his audience like a blazing irregular comet of the first magnitude, emitting in his wayward course a light so dazzling as to astonish & awe but which moves not in any path by which the political astronomer can predict its future motions or reappearance.

*February 3d.* This said City of Washington is a sad theatre of intrigue & the Bank question affords a fine scene. The curtains are up & the players in action. Smith, Secy. of State & his brother the Senator, are said to be at the head of a party who are endeavouring to work the destruction of Gallatin. If the Bank falls, there will be embarrassment in the finances. The scheme is therefore to put it down at all events; the consequent distress & confusion—after it shall have effected the downfall of Gallatin & Pres. Madison & placed Robert in the Presidential chair—will justify them in the erection of another bank with enlarged capital & powers & which shall be placed in the control of the Government, the Mother Bk. to be at Washington & thus secure their family influence. Whether there will be enough of integrity & good sense in a majority of Congress to save the present Bk. & thus to thwart the ambition of their men, time will discover. Perhaps they may also, like Sampson, holding in his grasp the pillars of the edifice, crush the thousands who sit beneath & involve themselves in the general ruin. This latter consideration may indeed deter them.

Regret the loss of my Letters for, although I find no difficulty in gaining an easy access to any of the members, I was mentioned by my kind friends in Philada. in terms which would have led me into a more rapid acquaintance.

The loss of my trunk has not escaped public notice & the newspapers have it the whole of the baggage of the delegation, including the memorial, was stolen. Luckily, I am the only loser, the polite attention of my colleagues enables me to wear clean linen & having procured a suit here, I am almost as fine on partly borrowed plumes as the rest.

The delegation from the Mechanics, discontented with their accommodations at Long's, have come this day to join us. They are all Democrats, or were, when they left Philada., but express an entire disapprobation of the dominant measures. The once celebrated Luther Martin who has greatly degraded himself by his habits of intoxication, is one of our inmates. He is a living chronicle & deals out his stock ungrudgingly. His memory appears unimpaired & his legal opinions have still great weight at the bar, where he is often seen so drunk as not to be able to stand without a prop, pleading with correctness the most important causes. He is rarely entirely sober, as he constantly offers his libations to Bacchus before his morning's meal. He rises early. This morning he was up two hours before daybreak, drinking & studying. When at home (Baltimore) he is frequently seen reeling through the streets pouring over a newspaper, the contents of which he will afterwards repeat verbatim. So much are his talents respected that, notwithstanding his habits, he is constantly engaged in the most important trials. He has received much money in the course of his practice but is poor, owing principally to his generosity in relieving the wants of others.

*February 4th.* Went to the office of the Treasury, Secy. of State, Patent office & then to the President's House to pay our respects to his Lady. I knew her formerly when she moved in a more humble sphere. She was always considered a good tempered, elegant woman, nor do I know that she has forfeited either. Few of her sex at 45 look so well. We thought her cheek rouged but might have been mistaken. Our confab was common place. In half an hour we retired.

*February 5th.* We have also another agent of the Smith interests, a shrewd Jew named Sol Etting, who began this evening to make calculations & statements tending to mislead. Francis entered the lists with him, Sperry attempted to elucidate & brought F. on his back. They were each a little mellowed with something a little stronger than water & a loud, angry, stubborn dispute ensued. N. & myself retired to our chamber. S. soon ran up in a violent heat & all out of breath to make his appeal to me but was too full of his subject to listen patiently to explanation but, gathering that I concurred in one of his positions, he flew back to the combat. The battle raged—& the roar of words resounded thro' the House.

The door opened again & F. entered, swollen with indignant fury. He had the better cause. I endeavored to calm him, but he had not as yet expended his ammunition & rejoined his antagonist. Louder & more loud rang the din of tongues & the war at length reached my peaceful chamber & violated my neutral rights. I now interposed in good earnest. Sperry swore he knew as much of banking as Mr. Francis & would not give up his opinion to any man. (He had told us before that he knew more of the German trade than any man in America.)

A parley now ensued & peace, smiling peace inclined to revisit our chamber. "If," said S. in a tone of negotiation, "what you assert is right, then I agree in your conclusions." This was the first point of concession & was hailed as a good augury by me (for N., the only remaining neutral, had prudently made a safe retreat from this ocean of contention & lay self-embargoed in bed).

Not so with the warrior F. He spurned the condition & damned the if. It was now 12 & our Heroes at length prepared for rest, yet each, to evince that he was not beaten, gave an occasional crow & flap of the wing, as he retreated pecking from the pit. Even from their roosts the vaunting chuck & answering clarion were ever & anon interchanged, until sleep, that blessing for which Sancho Panza had so high a veneration, shook her magic wand over the belligerents & lulled them to repose.

*February 6th.* In the evening we attended the levee. Met here Secy. Gallatin & expressed my hope that his report to the com. of the Senate would produce a favourable effect. He replied, "Don't deceive yourself, Mr. Cope, it will have no effect whatever. The Bank will not receive a Charter. I think the Bill introduced by the Com. all lost time."

Morier, English Chargé d'Affaires & about 100 persons of both sexes attended. Dolly looked remarkably well. The President intermixed with the throng & conversed affably. He is a slender man of 5 feet 6 or 7 & bears the furrows of age—has the countenance of a person who is laden with care. S.M., who is not likely ever to be charged with an over postion of modesty, thrust himself unasked into our carriage & was the first to get near the President, whom he engaged in conversation for half an hour.

The court dress for the men appears to be a black or blue coat with vest, black breeches & black stockings. The ladies were not remarkable for anything so much as for the exposure of their swelling breasts & bare backs. It was a stormy night & the attendance was considered small. Coffee, wine, cakes & ice creams were occasionally carried round & the company either stood or sat as they pleased. We entered at 7 & retired at 9.

I appear in Washington in true style for a humble petitioner, without a second shirt that I can call my own & have had some jesting with the members on the propriety of their bringing in a Bill for my relief.

*February 7th.* In one of the side rooms of the House, I saw Zera Colburn, accompanied by his father, Abia Colburn of Cabot, Vermont, a poor labouring man. Zera was 6 years old in Sept. & has never been at school but 6 or 7 weeks & that to a woman who taught nothing but reading & spelling. He does not know figures & was never in a situation to hear arithmetical calculations nor can he read, yet he will give answers to many & most questions in arithmetic almost as instantaneously as demanded, provided the result does not exceed his knowledge of terms to express it.

For instance, being asked how many times will 9 goes into 690? How many are 35 times 14? How many does 6 times 24 — 7 times 39 — 11 times 27 make in all? His answer to each was correct & in the most complicated, was given in less than half a minute.

Again, I am now 42 years of age, how many months, weeks, days & hours old am I? The reply to months, weeks & days was immediate, but when he came to the hours he said, "I can't tell." The question was repeated, he moved his lips rapidly &—hopping off—said "I can't, no, I can't tell that." His mind is continually bent on play & engaged in making impressions with sealing wax & never once looked me in the face but gave his answers with as much apparent ease & indifference as he would pronounce the monosyllables yes & no.

In the morning I had an hour's conversation with Clay of the Senate, who is averse to the Bank except to allow time to wind up. He says the Bill before them will not pass. If not immediately crushed on a third reading, it will be debated for a week or more. I suspect there has been some caucussing among them, in which the fate of the institution has been decided.

There seems to be little further use in our stay at Washington. Having told our tale, we had best perhaps retire & leave these mad men to their own reflections. Already, it has been insinuated that we are in the pay of the Bank & some of the members affect to be alarmed at the possibility of our bribing them.

*February 9th.* We have concluded to return via Lancaster to sound the members of our State Legislature on the subject of their granting a charter to the bank in the event Congress refuses it. As the regular stage will not leave this until the 10th, we have engaged a hack & 4 to convey us via York to the river for 30 Dolls. tomorrow.

Wrote to F. Fitzsimmons, Pres. of the Chamber of Commerce, giving him some account of our mission.

The Society of Friends in Balt. have interdicted the use of ardent spirits & subject to disownment those who violate the injunction. It is

unorthodox to have them in the house. They have also forbidden their members to hand a glass of wine to a visitant.

Jn. McKim, brother to the Congressmen, a high Democrat, & religious disciplinarian, prides himself in saying he treats his friends with three kinds of liquour—river water, pump water & rain water. May not the cord be strained till it break?

Let the mind be correct, establish good principles & the conduct will be pure. I confess I am no friend to monkish austerity or puritanical excesses.

*February 10th.* Commenced our journey at 5 this morning. We halted at Weiss's, 24 mi. He is an obliging fellow & gave us a tolerable meal, but his women are dirty huzzies. Our next stage was Doudle's, 36 miles. Arrived at York, 48 miles, at sundown. The turnpike hence to the Conewago is now forming.

They tell me that wild deer are abundant at a short distance from York & that they have lately been shot within 6 miles of it. Wild turkies are also still abundant on the mountains in the vicinity of the river.

Saw sister P.C. & had the satisfaction to find her well. Lodged comfortably at Spangler's.

*February 11th.* On our arrival at Lancaster I went into the H. of Reps., where I saw some of my old friends. They were in com. of the whole on a bill to grant aid to the canal from Susquehanna to Schuylkill & which they seemed little disposed effectually to do.

It is almost as fruitless to convince some of these people that the country is benefitted by the prosperity of the City as that they have an interest in the interior trade of Africa.

*February 12th.* Arrived at home through a heavy snow storm. In several places the U.S. Bk. Notes were viewed very shyly & in one instance a landord refused one from us. Can this be wondered at when, in addition to the general distrust, we were assured at Washington that the members who receive their pay by checks on the branch almost to a man carried off specie instead of notes, which they formerly preferred?

*February 23d.* The fate of the Bk. is decided. Letters this day mention that on the 20th the question of striking out the 1st section of the Bill was taken in Senate, 17 to 17. The Pres. gave the casting vote for striking out & thus the Bank falls. Strange infatuation."

Our papers continue to furnish instances of Privateers fitted in our own ports which sail under the French flag & capture our own vessels off our own coasts & harbours & afterwards come into those very ports to refit & provision.

The captured vessels are either burnt or, if valuable, carried wherever convenient & appropriated to the use of the captors. Will after historians believe this? Will they also believe that, at the same time, we actually forbid even American vessels to enter our ports with merchandize from England, tho' that merchandize belong to our own citizens? England who, with a Navy which rides triumphant in every sea & who could at a blow annihilate our whole commerce but who, notwithstanding, affords protection to our vessels by annoying them! Numbers of our vessels are at this moment under seizure in our different ports, whose crime is, they have returned with goods bot in England with American capital!

*March 10th.* Congress would grant no Charter to the Bk. U.S. It is therefore most fortunate for the community that the Stockholders had previously resolved not to separate for 15 months & that those who manage the concerns of the Institution are prudently determined to grant all the indulgence in their power to their debtors. I am not in their debt, not ever having had a discount or asking one from them—neither have I ever owned any of their Stock. I have therefore no interest in its favour but what is common to our best citizens.

*March 20th.* The papers continue to teem with acc'ts of the burning & sinking of our vessels by French cruisers.

*March 25th.* It is a strange war which is carried on between France & England. We are also strange neutrals. England transports to her enemy clothes &c. for the supply of the armies; so far good—she clothes the naked. France sends, in turn, vast supplies of grain to England. She therefore feeds the hungry. England protects our commerce in her ports & we interdict her vessels & merchandize from ours. France seizes all property in her reach & destroys what she cannot secure. We permit a free commerce with her & even permit her privateers to enter & refit in our harbours, whence they cruise for our vessels. If she slap us on one cheek, we turn the other. Is not the millenium approaching?

The conduct of our government in the present nonintercourse is similar to that of a blustering brag who sallies into the street swearing that he will be insulted by nobody. He receives a kick from one & a cuff from another, then goes home & vents his rage on his helpless wife & children.

*April 5th.* We have information that the ship *Susquehanna* had cleared for sea in Liverpool on 29th Jany. and was completely full but could not get out of dock owing to neap tides. Her cargo will not, it is probable, be short of a million of Dollars, yet if the law be rigidly enforced the whole must be forfeited, the penalty of treble in addition. Several of our ships are on the coast, fearful to come in & yet not knowing whither to go.

*July 20th.* French Privateers continue to plunder our vessels on the ocean & then enter our ports with the booty, to refit. One of this description, named the *Diligent,* commanded by Capt. Grassin & owned by a Frenchman by the name of Guyon in N. York, lately arrived here after robbing many American vessels & among them, some belonging to this port. Here he underwent a thorough repair & by his conduct gave rise to such strong suspicions of a design to follow the ship *Lancaster* (owned by J. K. Helmuth & myself) down the river, that it became necessary to call on the civil authority to interfere. We used the plea of the Brig having made an illegal armament & which was fully proven & thereupon had Grassin arrested. He refused to give bail & was therefore sent to prison, where he now is. Our ship has sailed & will soon be out of his reach. She is bound to Canton. As this is her first voyage she has on board a considerable sum in specie. Ship & cargo are worth nearly three hundred thousand dollars. This is no trifling temptation to a pirate & yet, altho' his intentions to pursue her were a common town talk, not a step was taken to prevent it by the officers of Governt. until pressed by us & furnished with such proof as they could not resist. Soon after the arrival of this French Brig in our port, Simon Snyder, Governor of the State, apprehending that perhaps indignation for the piracies which she had perpetrated on our defenseless countrymen at sea might induce the injured to avenge themselves by personal efforts, issued a proclamation offering a large reward for the apprehension of anyone who should molest the pirate or any of her people.

*August 29th.* Principal part of the month occupied in a tour among my family connections in Chester County, accompanied by Mary. 'Tis a fine, healthy, productive country, which the industry of its inhabitants & the late improvements in agriculture have greatly contributed to enrich. When my grandfather, Jno. Cope, took up the land on which several of his sons now live near West Chester, his friends observed of him that he might have the satisfaction to know "that nobody would ever settle beyond him." This was in the early part of the 18th century.

They were surrounded by the native Indians, with whom they lived in the greatest harmony & in the interchange of reciprocal good offices. The cabins of the natives were in the meadow just before the door of my grandfather. The men hunted & fished. The Squaws made baskets for the new comers, which they bartered with the whites for as much flour as the baskets would hold, that being the established price. As the country became better cultivated & game grew scarce, the Aborigines retired westward. As an instance of the honest simplicity which prevailed in the early settlement of the country, the following anecdote, related by Uncle Saml. Cope, now 85, may be mentioned. Wheat for many years was about 2/6 per bushel. On some very extraordinary occasion it rose to 9/-. This great price induced so many to sell that Grandfather became apprehensive the poor must suffer. One of his neighbours, knowing that grandfather had a quantity which he dealt out to the poor at the old price, made sale of all his own stock at the advanced rate & then applied to Grandfather for a new supply. The latter declined to sell to them. "Why Jn.," said the applicant, "I will give thee 3/-, which is 6d. more than thee asks." "Nay," said the old gentleman, "but I will not sell it to thee nor any other at that price. If, notwithstanding thy greedy conduct, thy families be suffering for bread, I will spare thee some to supply thy needs." "John" said he, "it will spare thee a deal of trouble & I will pay thee cash, whereas thou art now selling out in dribs to poor people who have no money and cannot pay thee." "For that very reason I will sell it to them—because they are poor & have no money. I shall someday want their labour & they will work it out & if not, it is better to give to the needy than to let thee have it, for in that case they might starve." Uncle added that these poor people did afterwards work it out, "for the people were not so tricky then."

It was not until within a few years that Friends were reconciled to the general use of pleasure carriages, either two or four wheeled. They are now common in the country. Formerly they were deemed an article of such extravagant luxury as to excite the constant reprobation of the ministers & elders.

In those days, when a young woman was about to be married, she rode behind her brother to meeting on horseback & returned behind her new husband—the practice of two riding on one horse being then almost universal. In many parts of New England the custom still prevails, where they call it "riding twice."

# 1812

*January 30th.* My time is so much occupied in the dull pursuits of business & there is so much of a sameness in the rounds of each day that I have necessarily neglected my diary.

About the commencement of Sept. a comet was perceived. For some weeks it appeared to approach us & discovered itself to be one of the largest magnitude. It first was seen about NW, afterwards its nightly motions brought it nearer to the zenith. Now it sets early in the evening, nearly SW & is almost invisible, even in a clear atmosphere. It has a long spreading tail which some of our astronomers say is eighty millions of miles in extent. This comet has been observed & commented upon in Asia, Africa & Europe & is considered a stranger.

*February 12th.* Jn. Rush, son of the celebrated Doctor, is a maniac in the Penna. Hospital. He was bred a physician under his father but abandoned the profession for a lieutenancy in the Navy. While in the latter station a quarrel took place at N. Orleans between him & an intimate friend in the same service. What the world terms honour enjoined a duel, in which Rush killed his antagonist.

Soon after this event, he became melancholy & finally mad & was conveyed to our cells. He will rarely speak or notice even his father, but occasionally he is heard incoherently raving on the unhappy occurrence at N. Orleans.

*February 18th.* It is a period of great events. The sanguinary war in Europe, which has now raged for upwards of 20 years & which in its headlong course has swept from the chart of the globe many of the ancient kingdoms of the earth & given existence to others unknown to former times; the paralyzed state of the commerce of our own country & of the world generally; the recent appearance of a strange comet of the first magnitude in the solar system & still more recently, of another announced by the astronomers of Europe; the frequency & great extent of the late earthquakes, for they have been felt from Florida to Canada—are very interesting & very important events. And now, we are informed of the sudden breaking out of a volcano of considerable extent & violence in the western parts of N. Carolina.

I know not if it be true but, as the account is contradicted, a little time will ascertain its truth or falsity—but if the report be groundless or otherwise, it cannot be doubted, from the flames which have in various places during the recent earthquakes issued from rents made in the earth, that a great internal fire must exist in the bowels of this continent & to which may be ascribed the very numerous concussions which our papers still continue to inform us have been felt in various places & particularly in the latitude of the Carolinas.

*April 2d.* The whole City is in a bustle. An express arrived yesterday from Washington mentioning that an immediate Embargo was contemplated. Vessels were loading all last night. The intelligence arrived about 2 P.M. Vessels chartered after that hour have been loaded & dispatched early this morning. War with England has been long called for by the party in power. An Army has been voted with the avowed object of attacking Canada & a loan authorized to defray the expense.

The intention is to compel G. Britain, by menace, to relinquish her maritime pretensions. The nonimportation act against her is most rigorously enforced, yet she evinces no desire to yield.

*April 6th.* The Embargo is laid. It reached us this day by express. Its continuance is limited to 90 days. The same mail brings intelligence that the U.S. troops have taken possession of Amelia Island, part of East Florida belonging to the Spaniards. It is an attack upon the sovereignty of an independent nation now struggling for its existence. Can honest Americans justify this outrage?

*April 7th.* A meeting of the merchts. who have property in England. Com. of five, of which I am one, appointed to draft a memorial to Congress.

*April 10th.* Susan Horn, a public friend from near London, attended by Thos. Scattergood of this place, took dinner with me today. She had previously paid my family a religious visit. She appears to be a well informed, cheerful woman. In the course of conversation, Thomas mentioned his visit to the King (George III) & thought there was a disposition in him to turn Quaker. Upon which Susan replied that "if ever he gave such indications, it must have been when he was cracked."

*April 11th.* During Tom Paine's last illness, he was several times visited by Willet Hicks, a public friend of N. York. P. was desirous to have his body interred in Friends burial ground, but when he found he was not likely to be gratified, he said he once thought if there was any religion in the world it was among the Quakers, but he now found they were as bigoted & superstitious as others. "As to myself," he continued,

"I care very little where my body be laid. I have no doubt my soul will survive & go either to a very good or a very bad place. I believe very few will exist in a future state, not one in ten, none but such as have done much good or much harm. I know not where mine will go but I have done all the good in my power. I have opposed successfully two of the greatest evils among mankind—kingcraft & priestcraft—& given them a wound from which I think they will never recover."

*April 15th.* A negro man, at service with a Chester county Friend, has been noted for being a good fellow for work, but once every few weeks he will have a complete drunken frolic. The Friend admonished him to be more circumspect & not to squander his money, but to lay it up. "Suppose I do," said the negro "then bye & bye I shall die & then people who will get it will say, "What a fool that fellow was, he didn't know how to spend his money."

*April 16th.* My letters from Washington, written by J.M., one of our representatives, speak of war as almost beyond doubt & it would not be surprizing if the infuriated zeal of the dominant party should bring on the measure. The country is without navy or army. The Govt. has destroyed the Bank of U.S., which was a powerful aid to their fiscal arrangement. They absolutely refuse to permit their citizens to bring home their property, now in England & her dependencies & which is supposed to amount to not less than 50 millions of Dollars, thus depriving the country of the means of sustaining a war & placing those means in the hands of the selected enemy. At the same time that the Secy. of the Treasury has issued proposals for borrowing 11 millions to meet the demands of the current year & yet they threaten a war of aggression with a nation which possesses upwards of one thousand ships of war, ready at a brush to sweep the last remnant of our commerce from the ocean!

*April 21st.* As an evidence of the perplexing circumstances of the times, I may notice some cases of my own. The *Lancaster,* owned by J.K.H. & myself, is now on a voyage to Canton. She was insured to that port, but not home. The constant cry for war in Congress has so alarmed the insurance offices that most of them decline to take risks at any premium & such as will, have so much to lose in case war does take place, as to afford little or no security. Congress, moreover, threaten to double the import duties immediately & the market is, for want of a foreign vent, much overstocked with Canton goods.

The *Susquehanna*, owned in like manner, is on a voyage to Liverpool. She has orders to take in a cargo & proceed off this port & in case the nonimportation exists on her arrival (& Congress have not evinced any disposition as yet to remove it) off the coast, she was to go to Havana, but fears are now entertained that the late seizure of East Florida by the U.S., together with the Embargo, may provoke the Spaniards to retaliate on American property & especially should we commence hostilities against G.B., her ally. But if even the Spaniards do not thus resent our conduct, there can be little chance of our ship escaping capture by the British in the event of war.

It would be boasting more philosophy than I profess to possess, more indifference to the support of a beloved family than I hope ever to feel, not to be moved by this train of apparent evils. But I am thankful to God in that he has blessed me with a disposition to be contented with his allotments & that the equanimity of my mind is but little interrupted by this unpropitious current of events.

I began the world with nothing. He has crowned my labours with more success than I have merited & if it shall please him, for the trial of my faith & patience, to recall the loan, I shall have no right to complain but, on the contrary, ought to be grateful for what benefits I have already enjoyed.

*May 7th.* We are kept in a state of anxious alarm & suspense, threatened by the dominant party in the Government with immediate war. Their attempt to raise by loan 11 millions has not succeeded—not half the sum being subscribed. Men will not enlist. Recent popular elections are adverse to them & petitions against their measures are presented in abundance. They are chagrined & disappointed—afraid to move forward & too proud & stubborn to recede. In this state of distraction, many attempts at a recess have been made, but a majority still approve the measure & declare they will have war before they separate.

*May 11th.* Have consented to act as Secty. to the Board of Managers of the Penna. Hospital, which my friend Saml. Coates has filled with great ability for upwards of twenty years.

*May 13th.* Accounts from England state the existence of riots in several of the interior Towns on account of the scarcity of provisions. The people can only be kept down by the military. Flour was at $22 per barrel. What must be the situation of that country when they hear of our

Embargo? What the condition of their large armies in Spain & Portugal, the supplies for which have been hitherto drawn from us? To what dreadful extremities & sufferings are people driven by the ambition & misuse of their governors? How horrible are the effects of war! At no period have we in America ever had so large a quantity of wheat & flour as at present. We can indeed consume but a very small part of it, while the inhabitants of England are, without having heard of our Embargo, threatened with famine.

*May 15th.* The speaker of the House of Reps. of the U.S. is directed by a resolution of that House to command the attendance of the absent members forthwith when, it is said, a declaration of war against England will issue. It seems impossible for a deliberate, dispassionate mind, viewing all the circumstances of our situation, to admit the possibility of such a measure & yet party rancour & disappointed rage may force on that dreadful alternative. The leaders of the dominant party are violent men, void of sober discretion. D. M. Williams, member from S.C., lately said in debate that "if he could command the red artillery of Heaven, he would soon drive the fast anchored Isle (England) from its moorings." Clay, speaker of the House, another deadly foe to Britain, is—as many of his colleagues—a noted gambler & spends a considerable part of almost every night in that disgraceful practice.

A friend of mine lately returned from Washington says that Clay, in one of those orgies, lately played a game of cards with another member of Congress for the stake of fifty thousand Dollars. Their friends interposed in vain. The combatants were infuriated with wine & madly went on until, at length, a bystander swept the cards from the table & thus broke up the game. The loss of such a sum could not have been sustained by either of the parties. Men who act so rashly in their private stations cannot be expected to conduct with more prudence in their public character.

*June 10th.* All other topics seem merged in the interesting question of war. The Post Office is daily surrounded by crowds waiting the arrival of the mail from Washington. The news of the day is that war will be declared.

*June 14th.* A dark, impenetrable covering still envelopes the recent transactions & intentions of the Government. The secret sittings continue, but nothing certain has transpired. Strong resolutions & remonstrances from various parts of the Union against the projected war are daily presented to Congress. It is evident that a large majority of the people are against the measure. This may cause our rulers to pause, yet they have so long kept up the cry that to preserve consistency & to maintain their party, they may shut their ears to the public voice.

By entering on hostilities, they may calculate on commanding the physical force of the Nation in their hands & by proscription & persecution, bear down all opposition. If war be proclaimed, they may—by charging their political opponents with treasonable designs—crush every man who does not fly to their standard. Indeed, from the spirit of intolerance already manifested by these war hawks, both in & out of Congress, it would be no matter of surprize to see such a system very speedily commenced. The *Democratic Press*, the Government vehicle in this City, has already announced that it is high time to put a stop to tattling against the Administration & that, unless it be checked, the editor (who is an Englishman who fled his country for crimes committed against its peace) will publish the names & residences of the disaffected & this, no doubt, with the view of correcting the refractory by mob law.

I employed two days in going round with a memorial against the projected war & had the satisfaction to receive the signatures of most on whom I called. I conscientiously believe that nine tenths of the citizens of Philada. are averse to war.

*June 20th.* Doubt & uncertainty are at an end. Congress have hazarded the bold measure of war against England. I can scarce credit my senses, yet the fact is certain. This day brought it to us officially. It was passed on the 18th in despite of petitions & remonstrances pouring in daily from all parts of the Union.

Six passengers arrived from Ship *Susuquehanna,* owned by J.K.H. & self & report the ship to have been left by them cruising off the Capes for orders. She has cargo of prohibited wares on board, intended for Havana in the event of the nonimportation being still in force. That Act is still unrepealed, but as we have certain information of the British Frigate *Belvedere* being on the coast & as we cannot expect to proceed to Havana without an almost certainty of capture, we have resolved on ordering the ship up & throwing ourselves on the justice of our own country.

*June 22d.* Having had information filed with J. Steele, our Collector, J.K.H. & self went to Wilmington & procured my friend Thos. Lea of Brandywine to file information with Allan McLane, Collector of the

District of Delaware. This is done with the view of securing to ourselves half the forfeiture in the event of condemnation.

*June 26th.* The ship, having come to New Castle, is there under seizure of McLane. He had previously told T. Lea that he would not do so but, after placing an officer on board, suffer her to proceed to Philada., that being her port of destination. Took an early stage & breakfasted at Wilmington at 6 o'clock. I proceeded thence to N. Castle & engaged as our attorney there young Read, son of the Dist. Atty. Called several times on the latter before he was up. At 10 his son called with us & roused him from bed. Received us very politely. Don't like his coxcomical air & fawning grin. Depend on it, he is deceitful. It seems he & McLane had taken a sail down the river yesterday in the Revenue Cutter to make sure of their game. Returned immediately to Wilmington & saw McLane. He received us rather coolly, at first, but a little pleasant conversation induced a favourable exchange.

It seems he has also a son, an Atty., now absent. He expected him home in a day or two. Engaged him in our service by leaving the father a fee for him. Parted in much mutual good humour. The district Judge, Fisher, resides at Dover. He is to be sent after, to hold a court for the special hearing of our case.

Not knowing when the court will be held & nothing more remaining for us to do at present, on the 27th returned home.

*June 30th.* Proceeded again for Wilmington. An interview with L. McLane—his appearance & deportment please me. The Collector, his father, considers the ship as entered from the day of seizure. It will save us from the double duties threatened by Congress.

*July 1st.* Went to N. Castle. The more we see of G. Read, the District Attorney, the more we are persuaded of his want of principle. It is understood to be his practice to extort money by filing or threatening to file, capriciously, a great many libels against a cargo, each of which, if prosecuted to judgement, will cost about $200.

In our case, all the cargo is shipped to one House & consigned to us as sole owners. The Captn. has, however, three crates amounting to 10 Pounds Sterling against which young Read says his father will file a separate libel unless we consent to pay $17, the amount of his fee on it. We have agreed to this & in order further to appease this cormorant, we made the sum $50. This being paid, his son tells us all matters are settled, that we shall have but 2 libels, one for the Ship & one for the

Cargo. We will have them restored to us on the valuation of three men & give bond with sureties in Philada. for the am't to await the issue of a trial.

*July 2d.* It is said that, our agreement yesterday notwithstanding, R. means to file 10 libels. His son affects to be ignorant of it but promises to interfere. The father is, however, invisible. The pretence is that he is abed & unwell. The court did not meet in the forenoon, but 3 men, Riddle & Janvier of N. Castle & McKinney of Wilmington, are named by consent of parties to value ship & cargo. Fisher, the district Judge, came this morning to our lodgings at Bennett's. He appears to be a good tempered, intelligent man. As if to put us on our guard he voluntarily stated that, should the question come before him, he would not authorize more than one libel against a cargo unless where different consignees should not choose to be implicated with each other & request separate libels.

The Judge dined at our table in company with the Marshall of the district, a morose catchpole. At 3 P.M. the court met. Read came in as frisky as a wren, holding in his hands 10 or a dozen libels. He had been so poorly all the morning that we could not be permitted to see him. Don't believe he will dare to file these libels. His object is to compel us to give him more money. The villain has us in his power. At six the valuers reported under oath. The cargo which cost three thousand, three hundred Pounds Sterling, these conscientious men value at thirty nine thousand Dollars! We have prevailed on them to reconsider their report & to permit us to a hearing. Read proposed thro' McLane, our Atty., that if we could give him one thousand Dollars, he would consent to the appointment of another set of values & file but two libels. I was called out from the resitting of the first to listen to this delicate overture, which I indignantly rejected. Called out again. Read will consent to file but 2 libels & permit another valuation on condition that we pay him his legal fees on only ten libels, viz. $170, deducting the $50 already paid. Otherwise he will oppose us with all his power & compel us to give security in N. Castle instead of Philada., as was first agreed. They shall be such men as he approves & he will oblige them to swear in open court that they are .worth the sum for which they shall be bound.

Having no alternative, we consented to his terms. We have gone over the Cargo item by item with the valuers. Shame & compunction have produced some effect—between 9 & 10 at night they signed their new report, valuing the Cargo at nearly 20 thousand Dollars less than before!

Can it be that we are before a court of justice in our own country? Are we not rather in Algiers? Read seems well qualified to be the Dey.

*July 3d.* Court met at 10, until within a few minutes of which none of the Lawyers were out of bed. The last valuation presented & confirmed. Our sureties offered & approved in court. The Judge directs that the consent of the Collector & District Atty. shall be filed in writing with the clerk, to which Read agrees. This done, our Ship's Papers were restored with which we proceeded to Wilmington to make our entries. McLane, Collector, has gone to Philada. to celebrate the 4th of July. His deputy refuses to enter the goods, acting in this respect, as he says, by the instructions of his superior. What is the meaning of this? Are we to be saddled with the double duties? It is understood that the law has passed, to take effect from the 1st, but the office have no official knowledge of it. We entered the Ship & tendered the entry of her Cargo & then proceeded home to have our bonds signed.

*July 6th.* The Collector was at home & gave us a favourable reception; he signed his approval of our sureties & permitted us to entries on the old duties. We are now at liberty to discharge the Cargo, which must be done here & the goods sent up in Shallops. The Ship is at anchor in the Christianna, opposite the Town.

*July 16th.* Read has signed his approval & no further interruption is expected. We sold the Cargo this day at public auction at a very large profit. Salt at $1.59 a bushel. The queensware generally from 6 to 9 hundred advance on the Sterling. Calicoes that cost from 5 to 7½ went for 45 to 56 cts. per yard.

*July 22d.* The Ship *Lancaster* has not yet arrived. She is now fairly due. *Pekin,* also from Canton, sailed a month before the *Lancaster* & is still out. Should these two ships fall into the hands of the British, it will prove a heavy loss to the City & to myself individually. The duty which these two ships would pay to the Government would amount to between four & five hundred thousand Dollars.

*August 3d.* Yesterday afternoon an express brought me tidings that a Ship believed to be the *Lancaster* from Canton was below New Castle. At 11 at night the intelligence was rendered certain by the arrival of the supercargoes at my house. This is an event of considerable pecuniary importance to me & a joyful one to the City at large. The *Pekin* is lost in the straits of Sunda.

*August 13th*. Information is received from several sources that the English Ministry have removed the orders in Council about the same time our government declared war & that American vessels are loading with goods for the U. States with licenses to protect them from British capture, but unless the President issues his Proclamation removing the Nonimportation Act, these vessels & cargoes will be liable to confiscation on arrival.

*August 24th*. The President has not as yet issued his Proclamation. Meanwhile, it is known that three vessels which left England fully laden since the removal of the orders in Council have been captured by American privateers. Another Privateer is fitting out in this port for the avowed purpose of capturing other vessels daily expected. Thus the enemy spares the property of our citizens, while our own government & privateers prey on it. Strange! To what state of wickedness & folly have we arrived.

*August 31st*. Our war commences badly. Gen. Hull, with an army of 2500, entered upper Canada. He was compelled to retreat & has been captured at Fort Detroit. His whole army have capitulated to the British.

*December 15th*. Bonaparte has entered the ancient city of Moscow with an immense army through scenes of immense carnage. Sixty thousand at least are supposed to have fallen in a conflict just before the entry. The Russians set fire to the city & consumed ¾ of it. One thousand palaces & fifteen hundred churches are said to be destroyed.

*December 20th*. The public, vulgar, & learned, are highly agitated on the subject of a machine lately invented by Charles Redhoffer of Chestnut Hill, Germantown & called perpetual motion. The inventor exhibits at one Dollar apiece to visitants & such is the excitement of public curiosity that the proprietor takes from $50 to $100 a day. No person has as yet been able to discover a deception in the machine & of those who have examined it, much the greater part have become converts & among them, many of our first artists & mechanics.

*December 31st*. An ingenious mechanic named Lukins has made & exhibited a very neat machine, apparently on Redhoffer's plan. Myers Fisher, esteemed a man of learning & talents, formerly an eminent lawyer, is so completely enthusiastic on the subject that he has composed an elaborate essay in vindication of the principle of self motion.

This he read with much parade to a number of us who were collected by an invitation from Lukins to examine his model. The learned lecturer, who indulged in a profusion of new coined & hard terms, taking it for granted that the model contained no deception, read & expatiated, affirmed & exemplified, as an experimental philosopher with his apparatus before him, to demonstrate by experiment the correctness of his theory. In a few days afterwards, Lukins confessed the cheat. He had introduced a secret spring into his model to give it motion. The disclosure has much staggered the disciples of Redhoffer, yet as the latter stoutly denies that any deception exists in his machine, many remain true to the faith. I have examined both machines & altho' much inclined to believe that Redhoffer is an imposter, it is obvious that the cheat, whatever it may be, is not the same in his machine as in the model made by Lukins.

M.F. in his essay makes frequent use of the term Conatus, to understand which it becomes necessary to give some idea of the construction of Redhoffer's machine. It contains two small wheeled carriages, laden with weights & suspended from two levers transversely affixed to the extreme ends of a bar which passes horizontally thro' an upright spindle moving in a frame on two finely pointed gugeons. These carriages rest on two inclined planes which have a bearing on a horizontal cog wheel that moves round the spindle without being attached to it. This wheel is suspended by four chains descending from a small circular projection firmly secured to the spindle, near its top. The chains are not plumb, but contrive to hang back or awry. The theory is this: the weights pressing on the carriages are supposed to excite in them a conatus, or tendency to descend on the inclined planes but, being resisted by the levers connected with the upright shaft, the conatus takes a horizontal direction & communicates a circular motion to the wheel & by means of the levers &c., drives the shaft round with equal measure.

The horizontal wheel in Redhoffer's machine is about 4 feet in diameter & revolves 37 times in a minute.

# 1813

*January 15th.* Confined to the house by a storm, I composed & sent to Poulson's for publication the following:

Perpetual Motion
The Testament probendi
Of motion non mutendi
According to St. Windi
Three tail'd Basha Effendi
A sturdy stick upendi Circumbendibus
  rotundi
Four pendant chains quite bendi
Two carriages suspendi
On inclined planes down tendi
With leverets addendi
  Begat
Centrifugal, petal gendi
  Which begat
Conatus descendendi
  Which begat
Conatus revolvendi
  Which begat
Whirl-a-gig never endi.

*January 31st.* The preceding has received a very angry answer in Latin from the pen of M.F. It has nevertheless been very widely circulated through the evanescent publications of the day. The author remains unknown & has been not a little amused with the conjectures of the knowing ones as to who he is.

*February 7th.* The committee of the Legislature have pronounced Redhoffer's machine a deception & himself an imposter. He has rebutted their report by a publication in which he still asserts that his machine is perpetual motion & contains no deception.

*February 15th.* Great commercial speculations are carrying on & doubtless the fortunate adventurers will realize immense wealth. Now this may all be well enough for men who have a talent for it, but I have always preferred regular business. The honest Dutchman was quite right in saying "if he could only see so well pefore as pehint, he would soon pe rich."

*February 20th.* We have suffered the loss of another army near the rapids of the Miami. The English having attacked & totally defeated General Winchester's army of about 1100, all of whom except about 30 are killed or taken prisoners.

*February 28th.* The French have been compelled to retreat from Moscow & have suffered immense loss in retracing their steps. They acknowledge the loss of 30,000 horses as having perished with the cold within a few days. It is believed that of their army few if any can escape the vengeance of their enraged adversaries.

*March 3d.* It is certainly a singular fact that while our armies have been so unsuccessful in their attempt on Canada, another English frigate should have been captured by one of ours. The *Guerrier, Macedonian* & now the *Java* have been made prizes by our frigates. The English papers are full of regret & lamentation on account of their losses. They cannot endure the mortification of suffering defeat on what they esteem their native element. It has been the policy of the Democrats in this country to cry down the Navy. Since they came into power they have not built a single ship of war but, on the contrary, sold several built & in use during the administrations of Washington & Adams & yet this impolitic war has produced nothing but loss & disgrace except on the ocean & that under federal commanders.

*March 22d.* Some military bustle in the City. Volunteer militia have marched to man the Fort & aid in guarding the shores of the River & Bay. Reports in circulation that Russian Minister, Dashkoff, offers to mediate between U. States & G. Britain.

*March 26th.* The U.S. sloop of war *Hornet*, mounting 20 guns, engaged & sunk after an engagement of 15 minutes the English sloop of war *Peacock*. Many were killed on board the latter & a considerable number sunk with her—while on board the *Hornet*, scarce any injury was suffered. Three of the crew, however, were lost in attempting to save the lives of their sinking enemy. The vessels are said to be of about equal force.

*March 31st.* A typhus fever of a very malignant cast prevails in many parts of the Union. It made its appearance in the northern sections of the Union some years back & has gradually found its way into this City & neighbourhood, extending into Delaware & Maryland. The patients if not timely & properly treated are usually swept off in a few days, but it is found to yield to medicine in its early stages. Very many have however been victims to this disease.

Symptoms of insurrection have appeared among Virginia slaves.

*April 24th.* Our distinguished fellow citizen, Dr. Benjamin Rush who has been for nearly 30 years one of the physicians of the Penna. Hospital, died of the prevailing typhus fever on the 19th, a victim, as it is said, to his favourite system of depletion. Blood letting has been found to be very destructive in this disease while high stimulants—wine, brandy, opium &c.—prove very efficacious. The Doctor had himself bled. Physicians being called in perceived this error &strongly urged the use of brandy, which however he declined taking.

*May 2d.* A ride in the neighbourhood with H.S.D. This unhappy man has formed a strange scheme in relation to himself & family & which he seems determined speedily to execute. They remain ignorant of it. A few years back he was possessed of active funds to the amount of between 20 & 30 thousand Dollars. He could not bend his mind to business & has been living in a style of expense which has now reduced his means to about half that sum. He has ten children, the eldest a promising lad of 17, the youngest an infant at the breast. A more charming little flock I never beheld. All these & his wife, a sweet tempered, handsome woman, he is resolved to abandon. All entreaty on my part is unavailing.

He possesses by nature a strong & active mind, highly polished by education. His habits are temperate. His conversation refined. His perceptive powers are acute. His conversation chaste. His frame robust & his health good. His family are devoted to him. His friends are numerous & respectable, but he is headstrong & perverse. A more striking instance of the perversion of great talents & of the wilfull rejection of great blessings I have never witnessed. I am grieved to the soul. I am sick at heart & sad on his account, but to no purpose. I had received former intimations of his intentions. He now asserts his mind to be conclusively fixed & spurns all advice. Once, he appeared to possess uncommon sensibility, now his heart seems insensible to the sympathies of love & friendship & his ear deaf to the voice of reason.

H.S.D. in his intercourse with others has been fastidiously delicate except where he has entertained deep rooted antipathies from real or supposed injuries. He has been equally scrupulous in the honest discharge of pecuniary engagements. He is not attached to drinking, gambling, or any other species of dissipation & until very recently appeared to relish very highly the society of his family & friends. How strange then is the infatuation which is hurling him to destruction. Alas for poor human nature, of what a bundle of inconsistencies art thou made up. How great, yet how little. How magnanimous yet how mean. How powerful yet how frail.

*May 15th.* The Russians, after having almost totally destroyed the invading French army, have pursued their successes across Poland & Prussia into Germany. The desolating sword is again unsheathed on the confines of Canada. Our troops have taken York, the capital of Upper Canada.

*May 16th.* In the numerous instances in which I have been engaged as an Arbitrator, I have often had occasion to mark the very great advantage which a plain, honest, unsophisticated & even illiterate & ignorant man has over cunning & knavery, tho' aided by learning & talents. The one tells a consistent unvarnished tale & his guileless narrative unfolds the naked truth, whether by technical form & matter it makes for or against his cause, while the more wary adversary, prompt to seize every advantage, shifts his ground as occasion may present, cavils, perplexes & falsifies—frequently contradicting himself & disclosing nothing but what he supposes will subserve his own interest. He is thus often caught in the very snare which he had been industriously contriving for the entanglement & destruction of his opponent.

If I have a legacy of advice to bequeath my dear children, it is to be studiously honest in all their dealings. In a religious point of view, it is the one thing needful & as it regards our intercourse with our fellow men, it gives that propriety & dignity of character which will ensure effectually the confidence & esteem of the good & wise—nay, of even the sons of folly & wickedness.

*June 14th.* On the morning of the 9th as B. R. Morgan, Esq., was proceeding with five others, in a small sailboat, to his seat on the Delaware a few miles above the City, the boat suddenly sunk, by which distressing occurrence my beloved relative Lydia Johnson, one other female & a negro man were instantly plunged into eternity. The boat had been injudiciously laden & the day was stormy. B.R.M. & two other men were saved by some fishermen who pushed off to their relief. The accident happened about five miles from Town.

Several days were spent by B.R.M. & myself in searching for the drowned bodies. On the 10th the negro & young woman were found by grappling, but the body of L.J. was not discovered until the evening of the 13th. when it floated. This morning we had it interred in Friends burial ground at the corner of Mulberry & Fourth Streets. The funeral procession moved from my house & was attended by a respectable number of sympathizing relatives & others. It was a season of deep probation to some of us & especially to myself. The deceased was in her 59th year & had greatly endeared herself to my family by her unaffected kindness & correct conduct.

A decent respect to the remains of the dead is a sentiment implanted in our nature, doubtless for wise purposes; it tenders the heart & solemnizes the soul, whilst an opposite feeling tends to brutalize the disposition. I have derived some comfort under this afflictive dispensation, in having had it in my power to bestow on the body of this beloved friend, disfigured as it was, the accustomed rites of sepulture.

Scarcely had I returned home after the performance of this solemn office, when H.S.D. called to take leave of me. My feelings had previously been greatly tried, now they sunk. Poor infatuated man, how I mourn over thy strange condition. Unless God preserve thy infant & deserted family I know not what is to become of them. His current expenses for the last year have been between 4 & 5 thousand. He has now about 14 thousand left. By papers which he left me, it appears that he has made over to his oldest son William, a lad under 17 who has been brought up to no business, 4 thousand Dollars. And to myself & three other persons about ten thousand in trust for the support of the rest of the family, consisting of his wife & 8 small children. On this parting interview I addressed his feelings & his judgement in such language as seemed befitting the occasion. His stubborn mind gave way & we mutually melted in tears. He condemned much of his recent conduct but persisted in his determination, as the only step in his mind, proper to keep his family from beggary. He alleged that if he should remain much longer with them, as he could not reduce his expenses or stile of living, inevitable want must overtake them all & he will not admit himself capable of any kind of business, tho' all who know him, know the contrary.

He professes a full determination to throw himself on Divine Protection & to do nothing adverse to heavenly approbation; even in the measures now adopted, he affects to be persuaded that he is governed by conscious duty.

*June 28th.* I have today for the first time put on a coat without a cape. In some respects this would seem a very small matter, but as proceeding from a religious concern of mind & as an open evidence to the world of a life of more guarded circumspection & a more strict unity with the Society of Friends, it becomes an affair of serious import. From my boyhood, I have been unaccustomed to a plain habit. I have not run the extravagant rounds of fashion, having ever deemed it beneath the dignity of a rational being to be employed with such vain conceits, but altho' I have been thus bounded, I am conscious that I have sustained loss in better things from the stile of my dress, which has been such as might be termed moderately gay.

It had the effect to draw me into a description of company, not vicious, for I always abhorred it, but not of the most profitable class & of course more out of that society of religious characters that would doubtless have proved beneficial to me in the promotion of piety.

In addition to these considerations, I have latterly believed it my duty to set an example to my sons now growing up around me. While I continued my gay dress, I could with the less force or justice urge on them the use & propriety of abstinence. Every man of sense must acknowledge that dress can not be a substitute for principle, that a person may be as good in a gay, as a plain coat & that abstractedly considered, it is of no consequence in what form or colour of cloth we cover these perishable bodies. Hence the gross absurdity, the incomprehensible folly of a being destined to a glorious immortality, suffering his mind, during the short space of his pilgrimage here on earth, to be occupied in studying & pursuing the puerile, empty baubles of the fashionable world.

But altho' no external covering can purify the heart, the sober mind is naturally led into simplicity of dress. It has moreover this advantage: It holds up to our fellow men a signal that the wearer has enlisted under banners which do not permit liberties that wound the cause of truth & betray the mind into forgetfulness of sacred things & hence he may escape invitations & importunities to unbecoming levity & sinful practices.

A wantonly clad woman is more exposed to the assaults of libertine men & more liable to attempts on her virtue than a modestly, chastely dressed virgin whose appearance will awe a rake into respectful reserve. A plain garb may even operate as a curb to licentious inclinations & passions, as the honest mind must feel desirous & even constrained to do nothing inconsistent with its avowed principles & professions.

These are among the considerations which have induced me to make an alteration in my dress & I pray I may be preserved to walk consistently with the change.

*August 27th.* Left home accompanied by my Mary & arrived at Burlington, N.J., where we lodged at the house of our kinsman D. Drinker & met with my wife's mother, Rachel Drinker, on a visit.

*September 1st.* Spent the afternoon with John Cox & family. Met them here with our estimable friend Richard Jordan. How valuable is the society of these excellent men, these servants of the living God. "How bountiful are thy cedars, Oh Lebanon!"

The following anecdote was related by J.C. in the course of conversation. He introduced it by remarking that in times past, practices were not uncommon in our monthly meetings which would not now be tolerated.

In a meeting of business, Israel Pemberton rose & discoursed at some length on the inutility & danger of worldly possessions & advising the poor to be moderate in their desires & contented with their allotment. After he sat down, Anthony Benezet remarked that the advice of the Friend brought to his mind the recollection of a story of certain rats who were feasting on a cheese on the top shelf of a pantry, when a number of little mice, attracted by the good fare, were struggling hard to scramble up from a lower shelf to get their share & who kept scratching & scratching & jumping & jumping but could not get a bit. The rats, looking down on these poor starving little creatures, bid them to be quiet & contented & not make such a disturbance.

Israel hung down his head & made no reply.

*September 4th.* Moved forward thro' Newton to New Hope where a bridge on stone piers is erecting over the Delaware. My friend Hulm accompanied us to this place where we dined at the house of Benj. Perry, at whose mill I saw for the first time a blower for forcing up the meal, as a substitute for Evans' elevator. He has also some small horizontal water wheels, on a new construction, the principal benefit of which appears to be in the smallness of the space they occupy.

*September 5th.* Lodged with our friend P. Attended Solebury Meeting & dined with Hugh Ely. Afternoon proceeded on our way to Kingwood, N.J., having crossed the D. at Mitchell's, five miles above N. Hope where a bridge over the river is also erecting. Arrived in the evening at the house of our kinsman H. Clifton.

Remained here employed in conversation, reading & making small excursions in the neighbourhood. In a visit to Flemington six miles away, we went to see their celebrated cheese dairy. It is an old saying that sluts make the best cooks. If a dirty mother, a house full of dirty children & filthy apartments are recommendations to good cheese making, then this dairy is fairly entitled to preeminence.

George C. Maxwell lives in Flemington. He is a Democratic member of Congress. He voted for the present war, soon after which he became melancholy & deranged in which state he still continues, confined to his house.

*September 17th.* Dined with T. Newbold. He like his colleague Maxwell was a staunch supporter of Madison's administration, but when he perceived the rage of the party for war, he made a firm stand against them & is now an advocate for peace.

The following curious circumstance, as related by him, happened at his brother Bara Newbold's lately. Some of the children having reported that a snake was coming out of the grass before the door, some of the elder branches of the family came out & to their surprize beheld a most beautifully variegated appearance of between two or three feet long moving leisurely over the pavement of the piazza & which on closer inspection, altho' it had the regular form & motion of a snake, they could not believe to be that animal. They threw hot water on its head, when it instantly separated & was found to have consisted of a number of small worms of about an inch in length which scampered off in different directions & were soon invisible.

Altho' I have never seen anything of the kind, I am informed that similar appearances have taken place elsewhere & it has been conjectured that these worms give themselves this form, when changing their quarters, to deceive their enemies the birds who tho' they would greedily seize a diminutive worm would have little inclination to attack a snake.

*September 19th.* Attended Burlington meeting & in the afternoon arrived at home.

*September 25th.* Last night we had the first illumination of the City since the commencement of the war. It took place by persmission of the Mayor (Barker), who is an advocate for the war & passed off without much injury. A few Friends had their windows broken, my house however escaped, as did several others which were not lighted.

*October 10th.* The Creek Indians have attacked Fort Nimms on the Alabama River & committed an indiscriminate massacre of all within it, consisting of nearly 400 persons, including women & children. Twenty or thirty persons only are supposed to have escaped & they principally wounded. How horrible are the fruits of war! How thoughtless or depraved must be the heart of that man be who can be instrumental in bringing so great a calamity on his country.

*October 15th.* I have been favoured this evening with the company of three of the greatest men belonging to the Society of Friends. This I say without meaning to disparage others, for I have no doubt they have their equals: John Cox, Jesse Kersey & Richard Jordan. There is a placidity & meekness, a cheerful & unaffected frankness & dignified decorum in the conversation & manners of these good & truly enlightened men for which, however well they may be trained in the arts of politeness, we look in vain among the jejeune foplings of the fashionable world.

*October 22d.* Last night the City was again illuminated & so far as I have heard little damage has been done to those houses which were not lighted. This may be ascribed to two causes, the measure itself was not generally approved even among the dominant party & the lights were extinguished at 10 o'clock. It was occasioned by the capture of the English army under Gen. Proctor of 700 & by Gen. Harrison of 10,000. Proctor escaped.

*October 25th.* The pressure of the war has been as yet but little felt by people in general. Those who had foreign goods on hand have mostly sold them at a great profit, while the domestic manufactures obtain large profits on what they make. The stoppage of foreign commerce has in various ways thrown the redundant capital of the cities into the country. The farmers obtain good prices for their produce, which finds its way out of the country in neutral & licensed vessels. The Government subsists on loans—the internal taxes not having as yet been brought into operation.

*December 18th.* A rage for speculation has seized our traders which, unless the war proves very protracted, will in all probability end in the ruin of many. Fortunes are making very rapidly. Coffee, which a few months ago sold for 15 cents a pound, now sells for 35. Sugar has risen to 36 dollars a hundred. W.I. molasses $1.70 per gal. The English have

declared our whole coast in a state of blockade from N. Orleans to the eastern extremity of Long Island Sound.

*December 21st.* Today our river packets of every description have been stopped by an order from the Executive, in consequence, as it is said, of an embargo law having been enacted by Congress. So rigorous was the execution of the mandate that not a boat of any kind was permitted to proceed up or down the river.

*December 23d.* The new embargo law has arrived & the little trade which was permitted by the enemy or eluded their cruisers is wholly cut up by this measure.

The Patriots of the N. Liberties have had a meeting & have resolved not to use sugar, tea, &c., until the prices are reduced. Poor simpletons, they begin to whine at the consequences of their own folly, but all their resolutions will not prevent their suffering a portion of the evils brought on the country by this wicked war.

The Resolvers bind themselves not to use coffee until reduced to 25 cents a pound, nor sugar until at 20 cents. Tea, they interdict altogether. They at the same time give pretty broad hints that the holders of these articles may have their stores & warehouses gutted.

*December 28th.* The U.S. Army, under Gen. McClure, have burned the flourishing little town of Newark on the river Niagara in Canada & the miserable inhabitants have thus been deprived of all their property & even a shelter during this tempestuous season. It is a most disgraceful & barbarous transaction & will doubtless be revenged in kind. The village consisted of about 130 houses.

*December 31st.* It appears that the British have commenced a system of retaliation for the burning of Newark by laying waste several of our frontier villages. Alas for my country, to what a pitch of folly, madness & suffering, art thou driven by the wicked men who rule thee.

# 1814

*January 2d.* A British sloop of war called the *Bramble* has arrived at Annapolis as a flag of truce. It is said her dispatches are of a pacific character.

*January 5th.* How unstable are human calculations. Today coffee has been sold at about 25 cents a pound & sugar from $18 to $24 per C. Hyson skin tea, which last week sold at $2.75 is now $1.50 & cotton has fallen from 40 to 25 cents.

*January 7th.* My ear is pained—
My soul is sick with every day's report
Of wrong & outrage with which earth is filled.

We have from the continent of Europe the most afflicting intelligence of carnage & from our own frontiers, every day's mail brings us some account of scenes of burning & bloodshed committed by the English in revenge for the burning of Newark.

*January 10th.* The dispatches by the *Bramble* reject the mediation of Russia & propose on the part of the Prince Regent of England to treat with our government on the subject of peace, either at London or Gottenburg. Our President has notified Congress of his acceptance of this proposal & it is expected that our Commissioners now at St. Petersburg will be directed to proceed to Gottenburg to meet Commissioners to be appointed by the Prince Regent. Thus we have a glimmering hope of peace.

*January 18th.* H.S.D. returned to his family at Burlington late in the fall. He has been several times with me. His mind is far from tranquil & yet I have some faint expectation he may yet do well. He possesses still a feeling heart & lively sensibility. These are symptoms of good promise.

*January 22d.* The President by & with the consent of the Senate has appointed H. Clay, speaker of the House of Representatives of the U.S. & Jonathan Russell, together with Adams & Bayard, to meet commissioners on the part of G.B. to treat of peace at Gottenburg. As the late appointment is composed of men—Clay & Russell—known to be very hostile to England & in some measure pledged to a course of conduct adverse to her known claims, it augurs an unfavourable issue to the negotiations. Clay & his party moreover say the U.S. must possess

Canada at all events & with this in view Congress have voted a large additional army.

The principal subject of dispute is drawn to this point. The American Government alleges that a subject of G.B. may expatriate himself & that after becoming a citizen of the U.S., by our laws of naturalization, he is free to navigate our ships & that to impress him from thence is on the part of G.B. a violation of our neutral rights & an infringement of our Sovereignty.

While G.B. maintains the doctrine that no man can abandon his natural allegiance to his King & that, whenever his services are required by his Monarch, the latter has a right to them & therefore, so long as we continue to entice their seamen from them & suffer them to enter our merchant service, they will continue to take them from us whenever they catch them, on the ocean.

Now, whether the principle contended for by G.B. be abstractedly right or wrong, it is agreeable to the long established maxims of public law & it is therefore worse than folly in us to attempt, with our means, to force them to abandon it—especially as the English Govt. allege that their safety & even their existence as a nation depends on their enforcement of the doctrine. Thus circumstanced, it does not require the gift of prophecy to predict a long continuance of the war or an abandonment of the ground which we have assumed.

*April 1st.* H.S.D., whose family remains at Burlington, is frequently with me. He has at last determined with his son William on entering into the improvement of his late father's estate. They are to proceed into the woods, with a view to form settlements on a large tract of land in Susquehanna Co. Should he give up his mind to this object it will be advantageous to himself & the estate, but I have my fears.

He has cancelled his former assignment & made a new one in which he constitutes me his sole trustee, leaving me, thus, the very important charge of his family. Nothing but a high sense of duty could induce my acceptance of so interesting, singular & perilous a trust. Was there sufficiency for their comfortable maintenance, my task would be less painful & arduous.

*April 5th.* An armistice is spoken of, probably a piece of the political juggle so often played by our administration in favour of the new loan. Congress have, in order further to replenish their exhausted Treasury, done away the Embargo & Nonimportation Acts. This last measure was most unexpected & sudden. These violent & unlooked for changes produce corresponding fluctuations in the value of merchandize & accordingly, we have several heavy failures.

*April 15th.* Such have been the reverses of Bonaparte that the Allies —viz. the Russians, Austrians & Prussians—at the head of powerful armies are now dictating terms to him near the gates of Paris.

*April 25th.* The Legislature of this state have authorized the erection of upwards of 40 new banks which are actually going into operation. It does not require the gift of prophecy to predict that this mania will one day prove a great public evil. Just before the war, they refused a charter to the Bank of the U.S. tho' tendered a bonus of $500,000. No bonus now.

*May 8th.* Hitherto the English have contented themselves with declaring in a state of blockade the line of coast from N. Orleans to Montauk Point. They have now extended it to the whole coast of the U. States. Unless peace shall relieve us, the country must soon suffer beyond anything it has yet endured in this war.

*June 7th.* The French Senate has dethroned Bonaparte. He has made his formal resignation & is to retire on a pension to the little island of Elbe in the Mediterranean. Louis XVIII, brother of their murdered Monarch, is called to the throne & a general peace in Europe has taken place.

Ferdinand, 7th king of Spain, who has been so long in French custody, has been restored to his country. Holland had been previously wrested from the usurper & placed in the government of its former sovereign, Wm., Prince of Orange. How astonishing & unexpected are these changes. What an important era of the world is this.

If men would be taught by the experience of others, what lessons of instruction might they derive from these interesting & momentous occurrences. Well may Napoleon exclaim in the language put into the mouth of Cardinal Wolsey:

> Farewell, a long farewell to all my greatness—
> This is the state of man. Today he puts forth
> The tender buds of hope, tomorrow, blossoms
> And bears his blushing honours thick upon him.
> The third day comes a frost, a nipping frost
> And while he thinks, good easy man, full surely
> His greatness is a-ripening, nips his shoot
> And then he falls, as I do.

No event of equal magnitude with this has occurred since I entered on the stage of manhood. It appears that the Emperor Alexander of Russia, the Emperor Francis of Austria, whose daughter married Bonaparte, after he had repudiated his first wife, Josephine, the King of Prussia, the Crown Prince of Sweden & Lord Castlereagh, Prime Minister of the King of England, negotiated with the French Senate within the walls of Paris. Bonaparte, who was at Fontainebleau, signed a formal resignation & Louis XVIII, who has for some time resided at Hartwell in England, soon after made his public entry into London, where he was received in great stile, as King of France, by the Prince Regent, who exercises the office of Sovereign in the name of his father, George III, who has for some years been in a state of insanity.

England & the United States are now left alone to maintain the tug of war & unless a speedy peace between them shall take place, we must be grievous sufferers by this unequal contest into which we have been plunged in subserviency to Bonaparte, by the madness & wickedness of the dominant party in this country.

*June 14th.* The English shipping are very active in capturing our coasting vessels. The papers teem with these disasters & so closely are our ports blockaded that our foreign commerce may be said to be annihilated.

On our southern border a most sanguinary system of extermination has been carried on against the Creek Indians, who possess a tract of the finest land of any in North America & under the most delightful climate. Unprincipled men have long envied them these enjoyments & they have not found it difficult to persuade a venal government to lend its aid in wresting so fine a country from the Aborigines of the soil.

*June 20th.* The well ordering & proper governmt. of our families is among the most important of our duties. It is in families as in the body politic: There may be too much as well as too little Legislation, & I have often thought that we were more prone to run into the former than the latter error. Better a few rules easily comprehended than cart loads of complicated laws; and better a little charity & good nature than a perpetual ding dong of directions & fault finding. Love & affection must preside in our domestic commonwealth, or passion will sap the basis of our happiness.

There must be grades of authority: Sovereign & subject, a head & a foot. Where differences—even in matters of opinion—occur between husband & wife, it is the duty of the latter, if she cannot think with, at least to succumb to the wishes of the former, unless conscience forbid. In doing this she will act wisely & set a good example to her children & menials. If he be right, she acts in aid of truth; if wrong, the responsibility is removed from her shoulders & fixed on him. A wife is never degraded by a dutiful submission to her husband.

*June 24th.* Today I met for the first time the Overseers of Friends Incorporated Public Schools, of which I have been chosen a member.

*June 28th.* We already experience great inconvenience from the flood of Bank Paper thrown into circulation by the newly created banking institutions. The old banks in the City, from a principle of self preservation—that is, to guard against being entirely drained of their specie —refuse to receive on deposit the notes of other banks. Distrust is the necessary consequence. In fact, the precious metals are vanishing very fast from among us.

*July 12th.* Rumours of the landing of the British at French Town, head of Elk. Elkton said to be burnt. Enemy marching towards Wilmington or New Castle. They were first stated as 800. During a few minutes I spent on Change, they had increased to 1500, then to 8000 & then to 10,000. People are much agitated & talk of calling out the militia. Americans talk much.

*July 13th.* It does not appear that the English landed at Elkton. They captured some vessels in Elk River, among them a Packet for Baltimore. Two hundred thousand Dollars in specie left that river a few hours before their arrival & got safe to Baltimore. Their force is inconsiderable—a 74, a frigate & some tenders.

Ninety three thousand & five hundred militia are ordered out by the President. The states called on for their respective quota, to be in readiness at a moment's notice.

My father & sister Hannah left us today to take their abode in Burlington, N.J., having removed from Lancaster where he resided for more than 53 years. Not one Friend remains in Lancaster.

*July 15th.* The fleet which occasioned so much alarm at Elkton appear to have dropped down the Chesapeake. They were probably in search of provisions & water. No force has been stationed this season in the Delaware, owing perhaps to the danger of the navigation. Fort Erie taken by the Americans under Gen. Brown.

*July 16th.* It is a curious circumstance that one of the greatest lenders

of money to the government to carry on the existing war is Jacob Barker of N. York, *a member of the Religious Society of Friends.* A report having been circulated that he had not regularly paid up the installments of his last loan, of five millions, he published a notice dated "7 Month 14th" in which he asserts that he has not only paid up but anticipated installments not yet due. Friends of N. York assign as a reason for still retaining him in membership that their discipline does not reach his case. If so, it is high time to amend it, or to give up their testimony against war.

"Davy," said the late Gov. Mifflin to David Evans (who was repairing the Governor's House), "how are you coming on?" "Pretty well, I'm obliged to thee, but the saw says, dry, dry, dry." "Very well, Davy, what would you like?" "A little spirit & water if thou please, Governor." "You shall have it, Davy, but mind, the next time you ask for Grog don't say thee & thou."

*July 18th.* A respectable board merchant informs me that there are more good buildings, principally dwellings, erecting in the City this summer than at any period within his recollection. Real Estate in Town & Country has in general considerably advanced since the war. Lands are at least ⅓ higher & many plantations have sold for double what they would have brought three years ago. The most probable cause of this state of things, so contrary to what many might have apprehended from the war, is this: Our commerce being destroyed, the Capital which had been employed in it has been diverted into other channels & objects of investment. Many capitalists & others have turned their attention to the raising of sheep.

*July 27th.* I have paid this season, commencing with the spring, upwards of thirty thousand Dollars for freight on the article of tobacco alone. This is part of the war tax which must come out of the consumer.

*August 3d.* This morning there was exhibited, at the Bank of Pennsylvania, a French Crown bearing the impression of Louis XVIII, brought by a young man just arrived from Bordeaux. Quick work.

*August 10th.* Congress are to meet, by special call of the President, in the latter end of next month. People in the interior, who have suffered little by this war & who in general are very ignorant of its causes or effects, still cling to the policy in which it originated.

*August 12th.* It appears that the Allied forces lately acting against France amounted to upwards of one million of men.

*August 20th.* An English Fleet of 46 Sail, great & small, are standing up the Chesapeake. The inhabitants of Baltimore are flying & the Militia are under arms. Much alarm also prevails at Washington.

*August 25th.* The Town is full of vague & contradictory rumours respecting the movements of the enemy & his force. It seems agreed, however, that he is rapidly advancing on the Capitol. The public offices are removing. Notice is given that no further mails are expected to issue from Washington. Confusion & dismay prevail here. The next mail from the southward is expected to bring intelligence of the British being in possession of that City.

*August 26th.* By the stage arrived last evening from Baltimore we have information of a battle having been fought on the evening of the 24th. at Bladensburg, 8 miles from Washington, in which our troops under Gen. Winder were defeated with considerable loss. They retired to the Capitol, pursued by the enemy. The State House bell is ringing, the trumpets & drums are sounding, the citizens are assembling (10 A.M.) to devise measures of defense.

One o'clock P.M., the Baltimore mail has arrived. Washington has fallen into the hands of the British. They entered it on the evening of the 24th. It is said they have destroyed the shipping, Capitol, Navy yard, President's House & other public buildings & that a proclamation has been issued in the name of Lord Hill stating that private property should be respected. The inhabitants of Baltimore are greatly alarmed, expecting to be visited by the enemy & many people here are predicting that Philada. will go next. A large frigate, called the *Guerier,* recently launched & a 74 on the Stocks, it is supposed may tempt the avidity of our active adversary. If they do come it is probable I shall be a heavy sufferer; the *Lancaster* & *Susquehanna,* two valuable ships owned by myself & Jno. K. Helmuth, being now in this port.

*August 27th.* Yesterday some of our Militia marched for the seat of war. Others are departing today. A Committee of Safety was appointed at the Town Meeting of yesterday. They are a mixture of low violent men & some respectable citizens.

*August 28th.* It is believed the enemy have retired from Washington to their shipping, to prosecute their work of destruction elsewhere. The banks have removed from Baltimore & the editors of newspapers give notice that they shall suspend their regular publications. It is confirmed that the Navy Yard, public shipping, Capitol, President's House, six other public buildings & a few private houses from which people fired on the invaders have been destroyed. Gales, editor of the *National Intelligencer*—the government gazette—had his office destroyed, otherwise private property was respected. The English forces are said to have consisted of about 6000, commanded by Gen. Ross & attended by Adml. Cockburn. Lord Hill has not yet arrived, tho' is momentarily expected. Among the demolished private buildings is Albert Gallatin's, late Secy. of State & one of the Commissioners now absent to treat of peace. Some person fired from it & shot Gen. Ross's horse from under him, on which the general ordered its demolition.

Thus while we have been endeavouring to carry fire & sword into Canada, our wickedness has recoiled on our own heads & the seat of government itself has been laid waste by 6000 foreign troops. It was the great naval depot of the country. The stores were considerable & all have been destroyed, or fallen into the hands of the enemy. The government had provided no military force to protect the place, even now that they have entered the third year of a war declared by themselves but trusted to militia hastily collected & who, as might have been expected, were found incompetent to face veteran troops.

People here are much agitated & it is apparent that those among our citizens who were most eager for the war are the most alarmed. This is natural. They have been guilty of great crimes & now that the day of retribution is at hand, they tremble for the consequences. Our young men are flying to arms & such as now turn out are generally of the party who were adverse to the war. It sickens my heart to see so many of our respectable youths marching to meet an exasperated foe, before whom they must be expected to fall, should their arms come in contact. It was said by an ancient philosopher that the difference between peace & war consisted in this, that "in time of peace the sons bury their fathers, but in times of war the fathers bury their sons."

I am told that the Government have provided no suitable accommodations for the volunteers now assembling, either in camp equipage or provisions, but that they are left very much to shift for themselves & lie on the bare ground at night for want of tents & blankets to protect them. What a wretched pack are the men now in power, how is the country suffering under their imbecility & wickedness!

*August 30th.* The banks in this city have unitedly resolved on the desperate expedient of paying out no more specie. So long as they were obliged to pay specie for their notes, the public had some security that they would confine their emissions within prudent & reasonable bounds, but there will now be no constraint on their issuing Notes to any extent & thus carrying on a scene of the most extensive gambling at the public risk. The clouds thicken apace. Simon Snyder, our Governor, has ordered the Militia of 9 of the eastern counties of the State to hold themselves in readiness to march at a moment's warning.

The merchants are transporting their ships up the Delaware.

*September 1st.* The enemy is said to be employed in carrying from Alexandria a very heavy contribution, levied on the inhabitants, of flour, tobacco &c.

*September 2d.* It appears that Alexandria capitulated. The terms are hard indeed, all the shipping, flour, tobacco & merchandize of every description to be surrendered to the enemy, including even whatever had been removed thence from the 19th.

Hearing a noise on my wharf I looked out of my Counting House just over it & perceived 10 or a dozen men endeavouring to persuade another, whom they surrounded & held fast, to step into a boat. He refused to go & was at length carried off by violence. In the bustle I could distinctly hear him declare that he did not belong to the vessel, that he had not signed the roll & never would & much more to the same effect. They did not deny his assertions but hurried him off & rowed expeditiously down the river, the man resisting & raving with rage. I ran down to make inquiry, but they were soon out of hearing. I was however informed that the gang belonged to a Privateer prepared to sail & waiting somewhere below the City for hands. I called on one of my neighbours, who has been for several years a Democratic member of assembly & who has often indulged in bitter invectives against the British practice of impressment. I wished to interest his feelings, but he treated the subject with great levity & some others, among whom was a person that I afterwards found was one of the officers of the Privateer, gathering round me & justifying what had been done, I soon found myself in a situation which, in such times, compelled me from motives of prudence to withdraw from their presence. The motto & watchword of the dominant party is "Free trade & sailors' rights," for the accomplishment of which they hypocritically pretend the present war is waged & yet in broad day, in a crowded city & in the face of authority has this most violent outrage been committed on the liberty of a citizen, for even the officer himself did not pretend to tell me that the person thus seized was one of their crew or that they had any claim on him.

The banks in this City have commenced the removal of their specie into the interior of the country & some people are removing their merchandize. The banks of N. York have published their determination to pay away no more specie.

The enemy is retiring from Alexandria with his plunder.

The President is much railed at by many of the Democrats. Poor wretches, they wish a scape goat for their follies & evil doings. He is the mere creature of their making & the organ of their will & is therefore probably not more culpable than themselves.

*September 3d.* The banks so pertinaciously refuse to part with specie, even in small sums for family purposes, and country people are so unwilling to part with silver in change that with more than ten thousand Dollars which I have idle in the Bank of Penna. I have this morning been driven to the necessity of borrowing a few Dollars in silver from a person in my service to go to market.

*September 4th.* Democracy ever has & ever will prove the ruin of any country in which it predominates, because it is void of principle & takes the government from the guidance of the most moderate, virtuous & enlightened men in the community, to place it in the hands of the most violent demagogues & a vicious and ignorant rabble. And I cannot doubt that—unless some effective stop can be given to the present unlimited freedom of suffrage in our country—our Republican institutions will decline & perhaps settle in despotism. It is certainly most unwise & unjust to suffer the most stupid beggarly & criminal wretch, just escaped from the hands of justice, or vomited from the jails of Europe, with not a rag to cover his nakedness but what he has either stolen or received in charity, to possess the same political consequence at our elections with a native citizen of the first rate, probity & talents, the largest landholder & most wealthy of any in the commonwealth—& yet such is the fact. Moral, political, physical & religious worth are entitled to no more consideration or weight than low vice, infamy & ignorance.

*September 5th.* Pres. Madison has got back to Washington & issued a Proclamation in which he abuses the enemy very roundly & soundly, & calls on all the good people of the U. States manfully to resent the affront put on the Capitol of their country. Poor man—it is too late now for proclamations. But the Pres. has in this instrument forgotten what is due to the dignity of his office & asserted several barefaced falsehoods degrading to the character of the Nation. As, for example, "The British Commander has avowed it to be his purpose to destroy & lay waste the Towns & districts which are assailable on the coast, adding to this declaration the insulting pretext that it is in retaliation for a wanton destruction committed by the U.S. in upper Canada, *when it is notorious that no destruction has been committed*"&c. &c. Oh shame, where is thy blush! Alas, to what an unhappy pass have the morals of the country arrived when the Chief Magistrate of the Nation thus deliberately proclaims an untruth which any school boy might expose!

Entrenchments are forming on the eastern banks of Schuylkill.

My niece writes me from Baltimore that during a week past the citizens have been busily employed in removing their furniture, shop goods & tobacco; that not more than 3 or 4 stores of dry goods remain open; & that they are in as much terror from the violence of their mobmen as of the enemy, as some of that class have been heard to say that, rather than the British should gain possession of the Town, they would themselves destroy it by fire & render it—like Moscow—a heap of ruins.

*September 7th.* The present unhappy condition of the country has been brought on by such a train of folly as probably has not a parallel. The bank of the U. States which, had it not been put down, could have afforded great facility to the fiscal concerns of the nation, was wantonly annihilated. Two pretexts were urged for that measure: to charter a bank was said to be unconstitutional, and Englishmen were stockholders. As to the first objection, the wisest & best men of the nation established that bank, men every way as well qualified to judge of the Constitution as their factious successors; and as to the 2d, no person but a citizen could vote for or be a director. If we were purposely to study in what way we would contrive to fix in England a number of vigilant agents to watch that their ministry should not jeopardize the peace of the two nations, none more effectual could be devised than to procure persons to invest their funds in our country. "Where the Treasure is, there is the heart also." Besides, we were enriched by the use of their capital. We must have an embargo; that measure impoverished our citizens & did little or no harm to anybody else. We tried nonimportation. We would not suffer a cent of the many millions which our own people had in England to be introduced into the U. States. It would relieve the English manufacturers & moreover, if we should permit bona fide American property to be imported, why then Englishmen would contrive to send us some of

theirs. But at the same time that we resolved to suffer nothing to return to our merchants, we let them send out the most immense quantities of flour, rice &c. ever exported, the proceeds of which were remitted from Spain & Portugal to England & there invested in English goods, giving ample employment to their work shops. Well, after we had thus drained the country & deprived ourselves of almost all revenue, for we had scarce any but that which arose from commerce, then we entered on the climax by declaring war. With an empty treasury—six frigates & no army—we declared war against a nation having every means of an-noyance & possessing the greatest naval force ever known at any period of the world—a nation having more than one thousand ships of war & whose pecuniary resources have extended to four hundred millions of Dollars in a single year. Altho' these things have passed before my eyes & I have felt & handled of them, yet even at this moment, while I am smarting under their deleterious effects, I can scarce persuade myself that they are real.

*September 23d.* Our bay is again clear of the enemy. The force recently before Baltimore has gone down to near the mouth of the Patuxent. Congress are assembled at Washington. The Pres. message is as usual full of low, bitter invective against the enemy, and of gross misrepresentations. It holds out no hope of a speedy termination of the war.

*September 28th.* Very heavy failures in N. York—one house, it is said, to the extent of about two millions. Many are involved in their ruin.

Little business doing in Philada. & much military bustle. 'Tis said that in a few weeks 20,000 men in arms will be assembled in the neighbour-hood. Grass is growing profusely in some of the streets, where formerly some of our most active scenes of traffic were witnessed.

*October 30th.* Our national concerns are becoming more serious. Heavy additional taxes are to be laid forthwith. Notwithstanding the outcry which was raised by the party in power against the late Bank of the U. States, on the ground of its being unconstitutional to have a national bank, that very party are now employed in Congress in the creation of a National Bank, with very extensive powers & a capital of fifty millions. The New England States are about to hold a convention, the object of which has not yet been made public, unless in general terms, to consult on measures relative to their common interest. They talk of having a new constitution which is to exclude the slave representation. To this it is presumed the Southern States will not consent & hence a separation of the present union may ensue.

*December 15th.* This is the day assigned for the meetings of the New England Convention at Hartford, Connecticut. Should Congress pass the conscription law now before them & it appears to be a favourite measure of the majority, I shall view it as the signal of a civil war. It is the Napoleon system of classing the people & forcing them into the army & I have no doubt will be opposed by all the Eastern states & perhaps by some of the others.

*December 20th.* It is said that there are now published in the United States 294 weekly newspapers, 39 twice a week, 13 three times a week & 28 daily, making a total of 374. They issue annually upwards of twenty three million papers. Did the editors labour honestly in their vocation to disseminate the truth, what a vehicle of useful information would the press afford, but too many of them prostitute their papers to the propagation of falsehoods which poison the public mind & hence are the source of so much error & misrule.

*December 25th.* So troublesome & destructive have been the American Privateers on the English Coast that insurance across the Channel is at 20 per ct.

*December 28th.* Congress have at length abandoned the system of conscription. It is a most happy event.

It is expected that the English will make a descent on N. Orleans.

# 1815

*January 1st.* The New Year commences with a gloomy prospect for the country. Congress have resorted to a widely extended system of taxation in support of the war. If we may judge from the forces continually arriving from England, there will be much bloodshed before the contest is ended.

*January 5th.* The Hartford Convention has adjourned and published its proceedings, which are temperate but firm. They deprecate the idea of a dismemberment of the Union & propose to the Legislatures of their respective states the adoption of certain amendments to the Constitution of the U. States tending to give to New England its fair & equal influence in the Councils of the Nation; the most prominent is to do away the slave representation. It is not improbable that the threatening attitude of New England, followed by the murmuring of some of the other states, may have driven Congress from their recent attempt to force a conscription on the country, the effect of which would have been to place the liberty of the citizens completely in the hands of the Military. It was one of the favourite measures of Bonaparte & tended more than any other to enslave the French people.

*January 10th.* Reports of formidable preparations for an attack on N. Orleans continue. There is much property there owned in this section of the Union. It is supposed that of cotton alone there are in that City & vicinity about 140,000 bales.

*January 20th.* As one of a Com. for the purpose, I attended this day to the discharge of a very interesting duty—the distribution of clothing to the free scholars taught in the schools under the care of the school corporation. About 70 girls & half the number of boys were comfortably clad on this occasion. It did my heart good to observe the joy which beamed in the countenances of these poor children as they received their allotted portions. Some of them were the children of persons in membership with Friends & others of persons of other religious persuasions. The previous week the Board handed out money to aged & infirm persons not in membership, but the personal attendance of these was not given or expected.

*January 21st.* Information is received of the arrival of a large English

Fleet off N. Orleans & great fears are entertained for the safety of the place.

*February 3d.* The Delaware is alive with skaters—several hundred persons moving on its smooth surface in all directions. Men, women & children are perambulating the ice & sleds & wheel carriages cross as on dry ground. The sky is clear, the air tranquil & cold, the ice firm & smooth.

*February 8th.* It appears that the English have suffered a severe defeat in an attack on the American lines before N. Orleans in which their commander, Sir. Ed. Packenham, lost his life. Our people had entrenched themselves behind bales of cotton so piled that, while they effectually resisted the balls of the assailants, they left small openings through which the assailed could take deliberate aim. The result is that in killed, wounded & prisoners, the English lost about 1500, while our people had in killed & wounded not more than about 20 persons. All accounts concur in this statement.

*February 12th.* First day of the week. Whilst sitting quietly at my fireside, my ear was saluted with the merry chiming of the bells, which satisfied me that something new & important had taken place. I felt most easy to make no inquiry on the subject, for I feared it might prove a rejoicing on account of some recent victory. I could take no pleasure in hearing of the destruction of my fellow men. I went to afternoon meeting as usual & on my return, was greeted by the heartily cheering intelligence that the preliminaries of peace had been signed by the Congress at Ghent. The messenger bearing the joyful intelligence arrived yesterday at N. York in the English sloop of war *Favourite* & passed through Philada. today on his way to Washington. Peace, oh delightful guest—sent by a merciful God to stop the further effusion of blood & to save this nation. I cannot but believe that a continuation of the war must have ended in our political dissolution.

*February 13th.* The town is in a great bustle, joy sparkles in almost every countenance. Nevertheless, many of the Democrats are displeased to have peace with England on any terms. But even they have some cause of exultation, for information is received of the retiring of the British from before N. Orleans.

*February 16th.* There was a general illumination of the City last night. No accident, fracas or violence occurred that I have heard of. It

seemed as if everybody capable of going out had by common consent agreed to perambulate the streets, peaceably to enjoy the spectacle. About 10 the lights were extinguished & all remained quiet. Friends who do not from principle join in these external & superficial marks of joy were not disturbed on account of their noncompliance.

*February 17th.* No official intelligence of the ratification of the treaty by the Pres. & Senate has been rec'd here, but it is announced by the proper authorities that hostilities have ceased between Great Britain & the United States. The public manifestations of joy are almost unbounded.

*February 20th.* The treaty is announced by Proclamation of the President, having by advice and consent of the Senate ratified it on the 18th. Every object for which the war was commenced on the part of the U. States, at least every ostensible object, has been abandoned on their part.

*February 27th.* The ground still remains thickly covered with snow. Loaded sleds are still crossing the Delaware on the ice opposite the City. Oak wood sells at $15 per cord, pine at $10 & hickory at $18. It is a severe time on the poor; but exclusive of the usual provision for that class of people & liberal contributions among Friends for the poor at large, public measures have been taken for voluntary subscriptions for their relief. It hath thus pleased the Lord to open the hearts of the wealthy & to incline them to contribute to the assistance of their afflicted fellow creatures.

*March 2d.* Yesterday the wood sleds were very busy on the river. A few are crossing today, but they proceed with caution as the ice begins to soften.

I have been for a long time sensible that I have sustained loss, pecuniary & otherwise, from a connection which has for several years subsisted in shipping between myself & a man not in religious membership with the Society of Friends. I am convinced that Friends would do well, in general, to avoid such connections. Transactions may take place on principles adverse to the cause of truth & especially to our peaceable principles. On this subject I have frequently had my best feelings much tried & wounded. The person concerned with me had as much right to order as myself. Arms were in consequence sometimes put on board by him under the plea of protecting the property from pirates & my remonstrances treated either with levity or disregard. Now I have thought that the safest way for me to prevent these embarrassing circumstances & to keep out of temptation was to separate our interests & leave each at liberty to act as most easy to his own mind. We owned two ships, the *Lancaster* & the *Susquehanna*. I have this day arranged with my friend to take the former ship & to leave him in possession of the latter.

I have had some trouble to effect this object & am filled with gratitude to the Father of mercies for preserving me throughout in a temper of mind to brook affronts & to bear injuries & pray that I may now enjoy that peace of mind without which all other enjoyments are as but shadows & have his blessing on my endeavours. I am fully persuaded that without his blessing no effort of mine can prosper.

*March 6th.* Yesterday the ice in the Delaware gave way & today vessels are in motion on its tranquil waters. It had been closed about five weeks. It is said that seamen's wages in New York are from 50 to 60 Dollars per month. Here they are about 40. These extravagant wages are owing to the suddenness of the demand, but must very soon decline.

*March 20th.* Many people are greatly disappointed in their expectations of the effects of peace & no class more than our farmers, who have held back their wheat on the calculation that peace must create a demand for exportation & of course enhance the price. They forgot to take into account that when we had peace before, almost the whole mercantile world were at war. We were therefore their carriers & obtained great profits on our business. Now those nations supply each other & are our competitors. The fact is that flour has fallen to $7¼ a barrel & sells very slowly at that.

*April 27th.* A most extraordinary event is announced today, the restoration of Bonaparte to the throne of France. The schooner *Sine-Qua-Non* has arrived in N. York in 29 days from Bordeaux with Paris papers to the 23d March, from which it appears that Bonaparte landed at a small port on the Mediterranean called Frejus with 600 men & was joined by Berthier with 25,000. He marched direct for Paris, which he entered on the 20th of March. The Royal Family fled the preceding evening. He immediately issued a proclamation announcing his restoration & ordering the confiscation of all English property.

While the Congress at Vienna, consisting of the Emperors, Kings & other great potentates of Europe, were employed in parcelling out states & squabbling for power & by way of pastime have been ever & anon

spending millions in routs, feasts, sham fights & dances—Bonaparte has entered Paris like a whirlwind & blasted their schemes of folly, ambition, aggrandizement & revelling.

This man must have been reserved by Providence for the accomplishment of some of his great & just purposes, among which doubtless is the further chastizement of the nations of Europe who, it would seem, have not suffered enough to induce them to act wisely or righteously.

The torch of war will most probably once more emblazon Europe & light millions of unhappy wretches to their graves.

# 1816

*August 20th.* Owing partly to the engagements of business, partly to disinclination, but principally to the state of my sight, I have for a long time been negligent of my Diary & should probably have continued so still longer, but for the melancholy & heart appalling event which I am about to record.

It has pleased God, in the wisdom of his providence, to visit me with a very heavy affliction.

My son Francis, while bathing with his brother William at Cape May, was overwhelmed by a wave of the sea & drowned.

He was born on the 27th of the 10th month of 1795 & between the age of 16 & 17 was put apprentice to Johnson & Warner, Booksellers. He served the term of his apprenticeship but, not inclining to pursue the business for himself, tho' it had been one of his own free choice, I invited him to a place in my Counting House. I intended to take him & his elder brother into partnership with the ulterior view of withdrawing from business & leaving it with them. Owing to a weakness in one of his knees occasioned when a boy by an apparently slight contusion a little below the cap, he had been but little engaged with us, having for several months been much confined to the house, where he spent his time principally in reading & with his pen.

Having been ineffectually treated by the most eminent of our physicians they at length advised, as matter of experiment, sea bathing & his brother William accordingly accompanied him to Cape May. They had been there about 2 weeks when Francis, finding no relief, became anxious to return to the family & on the evening of the 9th they paid off their bill & engaged their passage in the packet for Phila. to sail the following morning. Few others presented themselves as passengers & since many who were at the Cape wished the captain to take them on a fishing excursion, which it was his practice to do, the few yielded to the many & the packet boat accordingly put off to sea with as many as chose to go in her. William invited his brother to be of the party but, Francis declining it, they went about 11 o'clock by themselves to bathe in the surf. They were about mid deep when William mentioned his apprehensions that they were too far out. "Well," said Francis, "let us go further in." William approached & took him by the hand. At that instant a sea broke over them & separated them. When William recovered, he perceived that the same wave that had driven him towards the shore had forced his brother out & before any assistance could be procured, my endeared son Francis sunk forever!

The distressing intelligence reached us on the morning of the 12th. It came like a blasting tempest on my house, prostrating & withering all before it. But blessed be God who chasteneth but in mercy & afflicteth not willingly. He hath, after a season of deep humility & baptism, before his dread presence, been graciously pleased to raise us up & to pour oil & wine into our wounds & enabled me to say, "Have I not received good at the hand of the Lord & shall I not receive evil?"

*September 3d.* Oh how strange are the ties of nature, how powerful the cement of love & affection!

While I strive to suppress unprofitable & intrusive recollections & to reconcile myself to my irrecoverable bereavement, memory—that restless principle of my mind—is continually calling up some image to lacerate my wounded heart & to remind me of the void in my family.

The first perturbations & excess of grief being past, the soul derives an indescribable satisfaction in the indulgence of placid sorrow & does not willingly abandon that state nor suffer itself to be awakened into active life but with pain. It is in these seasons of abstraction from the world, its indulgences, privations & concerns, that the immortal spirit aspires to a communion with God & is disposed to rest on him for comfort & support.

*September 5th.* The body of my son has not yet been found, tho' diligent search has been made for it for a considerable distance along the coast. It is in itself a matter of no importance & yet, if the remains should be found, of which I have no expectation, I should choose them to be decently interred & measures to that effect were early adopted. Whether our bones bleach on the sand, moulder in the earth, or decay in the water is of no consequence. The one, only, & all essential point is that the soul rest in peace with God.

*September 7th.* To forgive injuries & to return good for evil are among the most sublime of our moral precepts & hold a conspicuous place in the doctrines of Christianity.

Is it in human nature to act up to these precepts on all occasions? I believe that, unassisted by that divine intelligence which first gave them forth, it is impossible. I judge so not only from what I see in the world, but from what passes within myself. Let us not deceive ourselves. We may not resent an affront by open violence & yet, something may rankle at the heart, very different from Christian forgiveness. I am myself often very, very often self condemned on this subject & sometimes suffer great conflicts of mind in reflecting on my frequent transgressions.

Well, if this be so, how careful should we be, how guarded in our expressions, in our actions & even in our very looks, not to excite in others those feelings which we find it so impracticable—of our own efforts—to repress in ourselves.

*September 10th.* We usually find early impressions difficult to eradicate, hence the importance of instilling good principles into our children & preventing their imbibing bad habits. "Train up a child in the way he should go & when he is old he will not depart from it."

A German physiologist mentions a striking instance of these truths. The Kalmucks are said in general to be thieves. A young Kalmuck was brought to Petersburg & employed in attending at the altar. He grew melancholy & pined. On being strictly interrogated by the Priest, he avowed he no longer stole, but he longed to steal even though his religion forbid it. The priest, perceiving the boy to be pining away, gave him permission to indulge his disposition, provided he would speedily restore what he stole. In the evening the boy came back full of gratitude & joy & brought the confessor his watch which he had stolen from him while he was elevating the Host.

*September 30th.* Our commerce has taken a novel course. We import beef, pork, butter, ham & potatoes from Ireland, molasses, rum & sugar from England, Indian corn from the Island of Hayti, formerly called S. Domingo & some of our vessels are now actually engaged in carrying back to England dry goods, the manufactures of that country.

The articles from Ireland have afforded a considerable profit to the importers & while Indian corn sells in this port at one Dollar & one half per bushel, that brought from Hayti is said to have cost no more than from 50 to 75 cents. It is but a very short time since the rulers of this nation in the plenitude of their wisdom & power, sought by embargoes, nonintercourse laws &c. to starve the very people who are feeding us.

*November 15th.* My mind has been kept in a state of great anxiety for some days past on account of my son Henry, who was seized with a fever which, from its obstinacy, excited fearful apprehensions as to the issue. His life appeared to be in much danger, but the disease has at last yielded to medicine & we have strong hopes of his recovery. Had he been taken

from me so soon after the loss of his beloved brother, I fear my feeble frame must have fallen beneath the stroke.

May my merciful Redeemer bestow on me a grateful heart & strengthen me to improve under these conflicts.

*November 20th.* Henry seems fast recovering. He has ever been a dutiful child & his correct conduct is an example to the whole family. I have reason to rejoice that he is still preserved to me. Indeed, I have great reason to be thankful that all my children appear inclined to walk in the path of virtue & live in the fear & admonition of God.

*December 13th.* Crimes appear to be multiplying among us. Robberies occur almost daily & the stores, houses & stables of the citizens are set on fire so frequently as to cause great alarm. We have had as many as 5 & 6 alarms in one day.

# 1817

*February 17th.* I caused the ice on the Delaware to be bored this morning opposite my Counting House & found it to be 14 inches thick in the channel.

The River exhibits a lively scene of pleasure & business. Sleighs & sleds ply it very briskly & in great numbers. A stage runs from this City to Woodbury, N. Jersey, on the ice & others might run to Fort Penn, the ice being strong enough even there to admit of it. At least so others say, for I have no personal knowledge of the fact.

A resident of Cape May, now in my Counting House, tells me that thousands of codfish have been so benumbed with the cold that they were driven ashore by the waves & lay strewn along the beach & that vast numbers of wild fowl, particularly ducks, have perished for want of their accustomed food & by the inclemency of the season which has so frozen the rivers & swamps as to prevent their access to the mussels, roots & other articles which they ordinarily subsist on. He mentions that he never before knew these circumstances to happen.

*February 18th.* Committees of the citizens have been appointed at a public meeting to collect money for the relief of the suffering poor. Notwithstanding the want of labourers to till the soil, the cheapness of lands & the generous reward which is bestowed on every species of industry, the poor increase very rapidly among us. No wonder—they may be cultivated until they swarm like locusts in the land. We have our public agents & our public taxes for their support. We have numberless private associations, of male & female composition, so that every nook is hunted up & every corner ferreted, that none who will receive may escape. The poor are thus taught to depend on the bounty of others, rather than on their own exertions. Many who at first receive assistance with downcast modesty & by persuasion soon learn to ask & then to demand boldly & as a matter of right.

The whole system is radically wrong. Supply them with labour & not with the means of idleness & corruption & you will be rendering both them & the community an essential service. While I am disposed to think well of the motives, I cannot but condemn the practice of many of our philanthropists. There is merit in relieving distress but when measures are pursued which, instead of diminishing, increase the number of paupers, no matter what the motive, the consequences must be con-

demned by all reflecting minds. That must surely be a mistaken zeal which adds to the mass of human misery by augmenting the number of its victims.

*May 2d.* By the arrival of the ship *Galen* at Boston, we have the unpleasant intelligence that the ship *Lancaster* has been run down by a British West Indiaman, off Holyhead, or that she had run down the W. Indiaman.

The surviving ship is reported to have arrived in Ireland with the crew of the other. This will doubtless be attended with a very heavy pecuniary loss to me. If the *Lancaster* has been sunk, I shall have lost not only the ship, but a considerable amount in merchandize on board & if she has survived, I shall be at the expense of repairs &c. & should it be proven that her Captain wantonly or carelessly ran down the other vessel, I may in addition be compelled to pay for her.

*May 7th.* Information is received from Captain Jackson of the *Lancaster* that while crossing the Irish channel from Liverpool, the ship *Isabella* of Glasgow, on an opposite tack & probably by mismanagement on both sides, was brought into such violent contact with the *Lancaster* as to carry away the cut water, head, bowsprit & one anchor of the latter ship & also to spring her foremast & stove in her starboard bow.

The *Isabella* was so greatly injured that she sank in a few minutes. Her passengers & crew were providentially saved by getting on board the *Lancaster,* after which Captain Jackson bore away for Campbell Town on the Clyde to repair his damages. Intimations were given that the owners of the *Isabella* intended to detain the *Lancaster.*

*May 24th.* I am still in a state of suspense respecting the *Lancaster.* If I am to form an opinion from letters received from Captain Jackson & the consignees of the ship in Liverpool, I need entertain no fears of a claim from the owners of the *Isabella.* Still, however, there are rumours in Town that the *Lancaster* has been detained.

*May 27th.* The *Lancaster* has arrived & if I may credit the representations of those on board, the *Isabella* was so much in fault that no claim could be established on her behalf & it would seem that her owners must be of the same opinion as they did not think proper to molest the *Lancaster* when so completely in their power.

The repairs at Campbell Town have cost me some thousand Dollars, but it is a small consideration in comparison of the loss which at one time threatened me.

*July 10th*. Having for some time contemplated visiting some of my wild lands in Penna., I with that view left home this afternoon in a light carriage & pair of horses, accompanied by my son William & arrived at Plymouth, 14 mi. away, where I had the satisfaction to find my two youngest children, Alfred & Elenor, in good health.

*July 11th*. Lodged last night at Josiah Albertson's. Had calculated on his joining us. He decided several times for & against it this morning & I thought designed to go with us, until after our horses were geared, when he finally declined. He is an old bachelor & will remain so unless he assumes a more decisive character.

*July 13th*. Breakfasted at Myerstown, 7 mi.—dirty house, kept by Andrew Stouch, son of Conrad. Travelers should not be dainty.

*July 14th*. Wm. turned up his nose this morning, at breakfast, at the very common German dish of fried onions which the landlady presented to us in her best stile, swimming in fat.

John Bickel, Esq., of this Town, from whom I obtained a tract of between 1200 & 1300 acres of land in the upper part of Dauphin County, agreed to attend us thither & we accordingly put forward in his company. Passed Stump Town, 3 mi., crossed the Blue Mountain & dined at Barr's, 9 mi. Then crossed the Broad Mountain, on which we saw coal apparently in great abundance & arrived at Abraham Hoffa's, about 30 mi. from Jones Town, where we halted for the night—B. leaving us & Abraham consenting to go with us to the land in the morning. On returning, we found good, clean feather beds, furnished with but one sheet each & Hoffa seemed somewhat surprized at our calling for more but speedily supplied our wants.

*July 15th*. Leaving our carriage at Hoffa's, we went with him on horse back to view the lands & returned at night, after riding about 30 mi., going & coming.

*July 16th*. Left Hoffa's & passed over a poor country, stony & gravelly. Houses erected of rough logs, rarely filled in except very partially, so that we could see quite through them & discover their scanty furniture. One of them was entirely open at one end & we could see the contents as plainly as if they were in the road. This hovel was, however, like the rest, well stocked with ruddy children clad in Tow cloth. The women have, when young, a healthy, contented appearance. They soon look weather beaten & the old ones shriveled. They are of all ages seen

engaged in the common labours of the field & wear men's hats universally.

Dined at the Brick Tavern, kept by a widow named Boter. She has 4 daughters, neither she nor they speak English. My little knowledge of the German I have found useful on this, as well as on other occasions. Her third daughter, a pretty girl of 13, was ploughing & came home to her dinner astride of one of the horses with his gears on. I entered into conversation with her & found her a modest, well behaved girl.

When about 5 mi. from Sunbury, we met with the first English spoken to us this day—all else were Germans. It is the principal language of this part of Penna. nearly the whole distance from Phila. Germans, with us, do not migrate to the new settlements like other people.

A German does not readily part with his Patrimony & he will strain every nerve to acquire the means of adding another acre to his land, in which he is powerfully aided by the labour & economy of his wife. We have been told, however, that the facility with which some of them obtained loans from the country Banks sharpened their avidity for increasing the number of their farms until, at last, lands were worked up to most extravagant prices—pay day came, many sellers were seen but few buyers found. Great losses ensued & many who had been esteemed rich are now reduced to poverty.

*July 17th.* We had taken lodgings in Sunbury at Peter Jones's, to whose house we had been especially recommended by some of our friends in Philada. We had no reason to complain of the eating, but oh, the number & unmerciful rapacity of that man's bugs. I arose but little refreshed and, altho' the Town was covered by a thick fog, we were off before breakfast.

*July 18th.* We are now in Penn's Valley, rendered such by high mountains on the right & left, otherwise it would itself be deemed a hilly country, at least so much of it as we have seen. It commenced on leaving the narrows.

Cultivated lands command $20 to $40 per acre. Twenty five & thirty bushels of wheat an acre is a good crop. Some times forty are gathered.

Felt some surprize at being awakened by the song of chimney sweeps uttered in precisely the same strain as in Philada. & on enquiry we discovered that they came from the City & were, like other gentlemen, travelling to spend the summer months in the country.

Continuing our route along Penn's Valley, we halted for dinner at Early Town, 13 miles along. It consists of about half a dozen poor houses.

Wm. Longwill, at whose inn we stopped, could not spare enough water to satisfy the thirst of our horses. The little he had was brought on a sled from the mountain. He says that one may ride 10 or 12 miles on the valley without meeting with water. Our ride this morning was partly over a well cultivated, rich, limestone soil. I never saw more beautiful wheat. We met scarcely a dwelling. We saw some, very distant under the mountain, doubtless placed there for the benefit of water. The springs from the mountain very commonly sink in the valley.

Frequently questioned as to who will be governor at the approaching election. Findlay & Hiester are the candidates. The first supported by the zealous Democrats, the latter, by the more moderate of that party & the Federalists. I am not a little amused to perceive how much the people speak of the result according to their respective wishes. None appear to take a deeper interest in the contest than the day labourers & hostlers.

In our country, every man feels authorized to dabble in politics & to take care of the Republic whatever may become of his own affairs—even if he know nothing whatever of the candidates for office & can neither read nor write.

Having dined, we proceeded. Left Penn's Valley & bearing to the north, crossed Nittany Mountain. The western side is very rough, which continued nearly the whole way to Bellefonte, 19 miles, where we arrived before sun down. We increased the distance 2 miles by going past a furnace. There are many iron works in this country.

Met here with Doc. Dewees, a devotee to trout fishing. He lives at Phillipsburg, 2 miles westward across the Allegheny Mountain & had come here to indulge in his favourite sport. He presented us with a mess for supper.

Nittany Mountain, like some others we had passed, was clothed with a variety of wild flowers, among which the two kinds of laurel & wild rose were very conspicuous. However jading to a traveller in a carriage, yet these mountains are very refreshing to the senses. There is much of grandeur in'their gigantic & rude forms & the dark solitudes with which they abound excite to meditation, while the limpid streams, which tumble & foam down their craggy sides, add not a little to the general effect. The contemplative mind becomes harmonized & is naturally & almost irresistibly led to adore that Almighty Being who created not only the fathomless caverns of the great deep but also these stupendous monarchs of the wilderness.

About 2 miles from Bellefonte, passing one of those places very

appropriately called narrows, with a rattling creek down a precipice on our left & a steep mountain on our right & a carriage way just sufficient with care to enable a single vehicle to pass safely, we met a waggon drawn by two horses. It proved to be empty & being of light construction the person who had it in charge thought by our aid he might contrive to force it up the side of the mountain & prop it there until we could drive by. All our efforts were however fruitless when, to add to our perplexity, another waggon came in sight. We were now at a complete stand. The second waggon was stopped at some distance from us & the driver approached us on foot. After surveying the ground he selected a spot on which by his assistance the light waggon & horses were forced up & propped until our carriage passed. The principal difficulty remained, but this man was not only ready at expedients but prompt to execute. He drove his team of four horses among the trees & bushes next the precipice, availing himself very dexterously of their support for his heavily laden waggon & having thus yielded us one half of the road, contrived to get our carriage by. We felt under obligations to both these men & particularly to the last, for their kindness, for had they been disposed to give us trouble, we must have suffered, but instead of putting us to hazard they took that on themselves.

Bellefonte is the Court Town of Centre County. It stands on the side of a hill surrounded by mountains. In fact it seems planted in a hole & the idea that first occurred to me on viewing it was to enquire what could have possessed any person to fix a Town in such a place. It was founded by one Jno. Dunlop, who owned the ground. His brother, a lawyer, on seeing it, broke out into the following soliloquy. "Well, I was always told that my brother John possessed more genius than myself, but I never believed it till now, for surely no man but a fool or a man of genius would have thought of putting a Town in such a place as this." We are told that every chimney in Town smokes in the winter, owing to the eddy of wind produced by the height around, which also occasions it to be very hot in summer. We took lodgings at Miles's & soon after our arrival were waited on by Wm. Potter, Esqr., whom I had constituted agent of my lands in this quarter.

*July 20th*. This being the 1st day of the week was spent principally within doors. There is no place of worship in the Town. Wrote a letter to my Mary, the second since leaving home.

This day we journeyed towards the lands attended by W. W. Potter as our guide. He tells us that he has known the daughter of one of their judges to drive her father's horses, pitch hay, grub & make fences.

Repassed the Nittany Mountain. Wild tulip, saffron, sun flowers & yellow lilies were in profusion. We were particularly pleased with a species of wild raspberry. They had a large purple flower of five petals which would cover a Dollar, with a leaf as large as my two hands. Altho' in full bloom we here & there could pluck a ripe berry—it is larger than the garden raspberry & finely flavoured. They call it here the English raspberry, tho' it is a native of these wilds. We were met by Judge Potter, father of Wm., at an inn where we dined. He conducted us to his house where we were most hospitably received by himself & family.

*July 22d.* Were confined to the house by rain. We had previously noticed the very flat sleek appearance of the cattle running on the mountains & today we dined on a piece of beef which Judge P. says had no other feeding. We found it excellent, juicy, tender & well flavoured. The Judge says the neighbouring mountains are inhabited by deer, bear, wild turkies & occasionally wolves & an abundance of foxes, which destroyed all their poultry until they kept hounds, who now keep them at a distance. Judge lives in a handsome two story brick house, well furnished & has a grist mill, saw mill, store & distillery. The store managed by his son, James. He has large possessions of valuable lands. People consider him very keen & close to his interest. We found him very kind & frank.

*July 23d.* The day being fair, we went in search of the lands. W. W. P. had previously surveyed them. About five miles from Judge P.'s we entered on them. They lie SE of his house & of Bellefonte in Centre County, principally. We called on several persons who had illegally settled on them. We were civilly treated. They are all Germans & some have pretty good plantations. We passed within the northern line of survey several miles on. One of the settlers, named Peter Homan, appeared disposed to render us his best services. We had some bread, milk & butter from him & having provided ourselves with other fare we had a truly rural repast by the side of a cool stream of excellent water, which rises a short distance from his house. A large stone served us for a table & smaller ones for seats. The heavens were our canopy & our appetites for sauce. The bread was of wheat & white & light as our best City bread. Homan conversed in the German only, as indeed did all the rest. He appeared a good humoured funny fellow. I offered him some compensation for what he furnished, but he declined it. "Nevertheless," said he, "if you think proper to give me something, *for good will*, I will accept it." I gave him a trifle & his sparkling eye evinced the joy he felt. The Germans are superstitious & attach great consequence to certain events which among others would pass without exciting any particular attention. A cent for *good will* is ominous of good fortune. I was a stranger. I had never been at his house before & was, moreover, proprietor of the land on which he lived. A good will offering from me was therefore highly desirable & to have charged such a one for the first meal's victuals furnished to him might have brought an evil spell over Peter's house, his family, cattle & land. We parted in good friendship.

I had seen enough to satisfy me that, altho' I had heretofore considered this property as worthless, it was of some value & must ultimately be much more so. Much of it is stony, mountainous & rough. The worst will serve bye & bye as timber land for the valleys & there is abundance of good water. There are several streams large enough for mills. We had this day an evidence of that kind of imposition which is too successfully practiced on distant landholders by what are called improvement rights. One fellow, to give himself a claim to a few hundred acres, had cut down a few of the native trees & planted a peach tree & an apple tree & put a small fence round them. Another had served himself to a slice of the tract by putting 6 or 8 logs together in the form of a house without door or roof & to give greater security to his possessions had, as Homan informed us, brought his wife & slept with her there one night. Another fellow, quite as confident as the rest, had actually made a house of three logs on each side & thus secured, as he supposes, a plantation for himself. Another great evil is the frequent burning of the woods, which destroys the young timber as fast as it grows.

*July 24th.* Breakfasted with Jas. Potter who lives near his father's & having taken leave of our hospitable friends, we set our faces homeward.

*July 26th.* We had comfortable quarters last night & an agreeable landlord & handsome landlady. Both were very attentive & parents of grown up children. On the road we have been on, going & returning, we have met with flocks of emigrants to the westward. Most of them consisted of very poor people scantily provided for. We are told here that it is no uncommon thing to see families passing with a single horse cart for their accommodation who had owned good farms in Lancaster County which were sold by the sheriff in consequence of the wild speculations in land, which seemed to set even the plodding Germans mad. The landlady says it has often made her heart ache to see these dejected people pass along. So much for the evils of country banks.

At Carlisle we stopped at the inn kept by Thos. Carothers. It had been recommended to us by Judge P. or we should have passed on to some place of better promise. The weather-beaten sign & tottering signpost, added to the worn out appearance of the buildings, made us pause & think we had mistaken the place. It was otherwise; we alighted & were accosted by a gloomy bloated fellow whom we find to be barkeeper. He did not deign a welcome look. We walked in & could seat ourselves if we pleased. None else but tap was there & he left us quite at liberty to stand & that, too, either in or out of doors as we fancied, it seemed no concern of his. The tattered, greasy paper on the walls & scanty broken furniture were of a piece with all we had yet seen. The landlord came—he spoke to us when we spoke to him, but it did not appear his business to further notice us. After having our horses taken care of, we sallied out to view the Town & on our return had a good dish of coffee. A young woman, of stately manners, waited on us & the table was constantly shifting its guests. We sat down with the landlord & some others. I had scarce begun when he departed the board. Another & another succeeded & retired until I suppose we had the whole family, wife, children, tap & all. None spoke but when they seemingly could not avoid it & all crammed & hurried off, as if to set us an example. We deliberately ate our meal & sat them all out, ending as we commenced with the company of the girl who poured out the coffee.

Among the small vexations of travelling, at present, may be reckoned the number & variety of small paper notes which infest the country —bank notes, bridges, turnpikes & notes of individuals, from 6¼ cents to 50 cents. The innkeepers endeavour to force these on you by various contrivances & assurances, but we have generally found their sphere of credit so circumscribed as to render it difficult to get rid of what we receive. Silver change, tho' abundant in the City, is excluded circulation in the country by this trash.

*July 27th.* Halted to bait ourselves & horses at Hinney's. William is wonderfully tickled at a phrase used here & at some other houses for that meal which is usually denominated a snack & which they here call a check, with equal propriety, tho' neither of us had heard this use of the word before. There are some very good houses & barns in this neighbourhood & the soil looks well. It is limestone which continues to the Susquehanna, 8 miles away & still preserves the same fertile level appearance. The forests are thickly studded with beautiful young timber among which hickory is very conspicuous. A mile from Hinney's we passed Mechanicsburg, a village of twenty houses. The great western turnpike takes this route & is now forming between the river & Carlisle. Crossed the Susquehanna to Harrisburg on a bridge of stone piers & wooden superstructure, called a mile in length, including a small island over which it passes. Put up at Buffington's where we met with several Philadelphians. They have good quarters & extensive accommodations for lodgers. Isaac Morris, wife & three children who had been travelling for their health, arrived soon after us & formed an agreeable addition to out company. Harrisburg, now the seat of government, has become a considerable Town.

*July 28th.* After the transaction of some business at the public offices, we left Harrisburg in company with I. Morris & family. Stopped at Greenawalt's at Hummel's Town & while dinner was preparing Wm. & I with their children paid a visit to the cave, which is one mile from the Town on the eastern banks of the Sweetara. I believe all the visitors of the cave were gratified. It is a considerable natural curiosity. To me it was no novelty, having paid it my respects more than twenty years back. It has been much disfigured during that period by the frequency of burning straw, which is always used to light the apartments when entered by strangers. A stream of water which was considerable & which passed through it then, has disappeared & thus robbed it of one other of its wizard charms. After dinner we passed Palmyra, a neat village of twenty houses in a delightful country. Next to it is Miller's Town, consisting of about eighty houses five miles further on. Then we came to Lebanon, five miles further on, where we halted for the night. Our whole course today has been thro' a limestone country. It is highly cultivated in general & gently undulating. It is limestone throughout. When we left home we were apprehensive that we should suffer by the use of limestone water & accordingly prepared ourselves with ingredients to ward off the effects, but we drink it with entire impunity.

Lebanon is now a county Town & contains about 250 houses. It is doubtless the richest county for its size, Philadelphia excepted, of any in the State. They are now erecting a large court house of very ill looking brick. We are at the house of Linaweaver & have a clever good tempered landlord & good accommodations.

The Germans evince an itch for music with but little taste or skill in the performance. Most of their inns at which we have been have been supplied with instruments of some kind & we have sometimes, tho' poor judges, had enough to set us to gaping & yawning & laughing also. At Jonestown, young Bickel called his daughter to play to us & the good natured girl very obligingly thrummed & thrummed thro' all her stock of tunes until I began to fear that her music had no end. Today, Linaweaver's son of two years of age—whether by directions of his father or otherwise, I know not—abruptly entered our apartment & played on his fiddle with as much gravity & seeming state as tho' he was performing a funeral dirge. I hailed the young urchin but could not extort a smile from him. When done, he departed.

Another circumstance, producing feelings of a very different cast, was frequently noticed by us—the abominable & destructive practice of morning tippling. The actors in this scene, conscious of the meanness of their vice, were often seen sneaking in & out of the bar, ashamed that others should witness their degradation. The immoderate use of ardent spirits is perhaps the greatest evil in the United States, but I have more hopes of any other class of drunkards than the morning tipplers.

*July 29th.* A circumstance occurred this morning which awakened in my mind very painful recollections. Sarah Morris put into my hands a book containing an account of a very pious & highly gifted young man, named Spencer, who had officiated as a clergyman in Liverpool, England. I had proceeded but a few pages when a call to breakfast interrupted my reading. She took the book & packing it in her trunk, we all took our seats at the table. My feelings had become interested. I perceive, said I, that there was something extraordinary in the life of that young man & that his death must have been sudden & signal. How did it happen? She replied, "He went into the water to bathe & was swept off by the flood." I was taken by surprize. The feelings of nature could not be repressed & I was compelled to retire to recover a sufficient degree of composure to enable me to appear in the company of others. I struggled to be cheerful, that I might not interrupt the enjoyment of the rest, but my heart was sad & during the remainder of the day, even when the idea was not present to me, I felt a weight at my heart which new subjects of observation & conversation could not remove.

Here we parted reluctantly with our new travelling companions. They proceeded homewards by the way of Womelsdorf & Reading & we pursued our course towards Lancaster. I wished to give Wm. the opportunity of viewing parts which he had not seen.

Halted at Barruff's, Manheim, 15 miles. It is a rich limestone country.

Five miles from Lebanon, we entered on a mountainous uncultivated district which continued about three miles when we descended into a variegated tract of slate & limestone, some poor spots, some handsome farms on a fruitful soil, becoming more uniformly valuable as we neared Manheim.

After refreshing ourselves & horses we continued towards Lancaster; when within about 5 miles of that place (it is 10 miles from Manheim) the steeple & some buildings of the Town came in view, together with an extensive range, as far as the eye can reach, of one of the most charming countries we had yet beheld. I suspect that, combining all circumstances of soil & climate, there are few if any better countries than this in the U.S.—but it is not inhabited by the most enlightened people in the world.

*July 30th.* The night was to us sultry & altho' we had good beds in a large well ventilated apartment, we slept but little. Besides the heat, we were greatly disturbed by the incessant barking & howling of numerous dogs. The streets were constantly crowded with them & from the violence & constancy of their uproar, one might have suspected the Town was attacked by an army of beggars. We had also the Town clock close to our chamber, to remind us hour after hour that neither it nor we slept. We had been all along sensible, after descending the Blue Mountain, of the difference of the air we were to breathe but, until last night, had not been much inconvenienced by it.

Last evening after tea we perambulated the Town. Here I was born & here the remains of the dear woman who bore me moulder in the earth. At almost every step, I met with some object to remind me of my boyish days & altho' I never had much attachment to Lancaster, I could not tread this ground with feelings of indifference.

After breakfast we went to Strasburg (8 miles) where we refreshed ourselves at Sample's. I supplied myself with some articles as presents to sister S. & daughters. We had here an evidence of the little reliance which is sometimes to be placed on vague testimony. I asked Sample, who had the manners & conversation of an intelligent man, how many houses there are in Strasburg. The idea might never have occurred to him. He answered between 700 & 800. I put the same question to a resident watchmaker & he answered 300. It was repeated to a saddler on whom we called to do a small job & he said 130. This last number I believe to be correct.

*July 31st.* We arrived early yesterday afternoon at sister's & tarried with the family until after breakfast. It was a seasonable visit & I am glad I yielded to my inclination to pass this way on my route. Towards midday we reached the house of my uncle Nathan Cope, or perhaps with more propriety the house of his son Benj., who has lately brought home his second wife named Rest. It may now be truly said that after all our journeyings, we have at length safely arrived at the Mansion of Rest.

*August 3d.* Having spent some days very agreeably among our kinspeople in Chester County, we this day took our final departure for home.

*August 16th.* Met a number of Friends of the several monthly meetings, convened in consequence of the arrival of about 250 persons, men, women & children in the Russian ship *Vaterlandsliebe* from Antwerp & who have letters from Friends in London recommending them to the notice of Friends in Philada. It appears that they are from the Kingdom of Wirtemberg, where they suffered severe persecution on account of their religious principles, having separated themselves from the established worship of the country & assumed the denomination of Separatists. A Committee of 15 were nominated to afford them such aid & advice as their situation may demand.

*August 18th.* Met the Com. They appointed three of their number to attend to the provisioning of the newly arrived & six others, viz. Jno. Cooke, Thomas Stewardson, Ellis Yarnall, Saml. Bettle, Isaac W. Morris & Thos. P. Cope to be the organs of communication between them & Friends & to afford them such counsel & advice & especially relative to their future settlement, as their case may require. In the afternoon the Com. of advice proceeded to the Hospital & mentioning their views held a conference with three of the principal men, viz. John Godfrey Banzhoff, Michael Baeumler & Caspar Fetter. Jno. Cooke & myself acted as interpreters, for these people only speak German. The conference lasted nearly two hours & ended, I believe, to the comfort & satisfaction of the parties.

*August 20th.* The Com. met again this morning. Steps were taken to procure temporary employment for about 150 of the Separatists (for so the newly arrived style themselves), who do not think of joining the proposed settlement until some accommodations can be made for the whole body. It was also agreed to invite proposals from landholders, so as to make a judicious selection of a tract for their use. It is likewise determined to submit the choice to themselves & with that view to induce their personal inspection of whatever spot the Com. may think it eligible to recommend to their examination. One of their number, a man of 30, died suddenly yesterday from drinking too profusely of cold water after heating himself at labour on a neighbouring farm. It is an affecting circumstance. He was a single man & had two sisters with him.

A short time before they decided on coming to America, they had become acquainted with the existence of such people as Friends & had obtained a copy of Barclay's *Apology* printed in their own language at Germantown by directions of Friends in this City. One of their number, viz. J.G. Banzhoff, had visited Friends in London. They had believed themselves for some years the only people in the world who hold the doctrines professed by Friends.

*August 22d.* Met the Com. It seems that the Separatists deny themselves the use of swine flesh, alleging him to be an unclean beast. It has been said that they also prohibited their members from marrying & enjoin celibacy on all. But this, they inform us, is an error & that they deem the marriage state highly honourable.

*August 23d.* It appears that this Society owes its origin to a pious person in Switzerland, about 25 or 26 years ago. One of their principal tenets is a testimony against war. Their appearance among us has excited considerable interest, not only among Friends, but among people of other persuasions, with whom they are generally esteemed to be of our Society. We do not identify them with our body, leaving them to be judged by their fruits. Nevertheless, from the good character they have brought with them, from the recommendation of Friends in London, from their decent orderly appearance & modest sober deportment, Friends have sympathy with them & as strangers claiming the advice & assistance of the Society, feel constrained to afford them countenance & protection.

*August 26th.* The Com. met again this morning & received some further propositions respecting lands. No selection has as yet been made.

*August 29th.* Yesterday in an interview with Banzhoff, Fetter & Baeumler, they informed us that it was their settled conclusion to fix themselves in Penna. if, on examination, land can be found to answer.

*September 27th.* Jno. Cooke returned & met the Com. on the 26th. He & his companions visited but one of the tracts of land they had in view before leaving the City. They did not approve it & returned without seeing the rest or at all entering Susquehanna County. Since then Baeumler & his companions have concluded to remove the entire body of their people to Ohio or Indiana without further delay.

*September 30th.* I have concluded to pursue my long intended prospect of a visit to my lands in Susquehanna County.

*October 2d.* Agreeably to previous arrangement, left home with my Mary & daughter C. on a visit to the beech woods. Brother Israel, wife & their daughter M.A. in company. Dined at Widow Rex's at Willow Grove & halted for the night at Doylestown. Harvey, who keeps the inn, has no wood this evening to replenish our fire. He is *just out.*

*October 3d.* Stopped to refresh at Burson's, 44 miles from Philada. & arrived at Bethlehem. In this day's ride our attention was particularly arrested with the number of substantial stone bridges which we passed. The strangers here complain that the table is so scantily provided that they often have not sufficient food to satisfy their appetites. It is a scandal to the place that any such complaint should exist. It is a plentiful country & they charge largely at the inn for everything, but these people admit of no rivalry, not permitting any person to settle among them who is not of their sect. Travellers have no alternative. There is but this one inn & it is kept for the benefit of the Society—the landlord receiving a salary. Nor do visitors ever receive invitations to break bread in private houses, which appears rather selfish, especially as these people have no objection to be entertained by their friends when from home or to participate with them at the public inn.

*October 4th.* Dined at Nazareth, 10 miles from Bethlehem. On the door case of the parlor door into which we were ushered are the following lines, which, if not very elegant poetry, may serve as an advertizement.

> I, John Hoffenockel, live here.
> I sell good brandy, gin & beer,
> And if this board was a little wider
> I let you know I sells good cider.

*October 6th.* H.W.D. took his seat with us this morning & we journeyed forward over a mountainous country, 17½ miles to Wilkesbarre. The land is almost wholly in a state of nature. Five or six small settlements—that is, 5 or 6 log houses with each a small cleared spot of

land. When we arrived within two or three miles of the Town, a most delightful prospect opened to our view. We alighted partly to enjoy it the better from a pile of rocks by the wayside & partly on account of the steepness of the descent. Wyoming Valley lay spread before us, about twenty miles in length & three or four in breadth, thro' the center of which the Susquehanna runs with a smooth and gentle current. Wilkesbarre is close on the eastern shore & the village of Kingston on the western about a mile from the river. The valley at this distance has a gardenlike appearance, the farm houses here & there resembling little specks of white amid the variegated autumnal hues of the distant fields & forests. This valley is bounded by immense mountains & on casting the eye over this interesting scene, the mind is led back to a period when, in all probability, these mountains were the boundaries of a lake the bed of which was this very valley.

*October 7th.* "Every man," said H.W.D. this morning, "has a right to his own humour & to be as singular as he pleases." And so say I, with certain limitations & restrictions. A man's whims & humours are as much his own property as is his house. He may use them as he pleases, provided he does not interfere with the whims & humours of others.

*October 8th.* My kinsman has been disposed to give me a practical lesson on the rights of humour. We were to have been off early this morning but his humour was to lay abed so late that it was ten before we were ready. He & I then crossed the river on our way to the woods, leaving the rest of the company to wait our return.

We crossed the river opposite to the Town in a flat—& passing through Kingston went northwardly along the western course of the river near to the spot on which the fatal Battle of Wyoming was fought & which still excites great interest in this country. No traces of the old fort are visible, but some few moulding tombstones give notice that the bodies of the slain were there deposited. These were but a few who could be recognized among the mangled & scalped corpses that had strewn the bloody field. The story is this:

During the Revolutionary War—the people of the village & vicinity having gained information of the approach of 900 Indians & a number of English troops to break up their settlement—the men to the number of 360 who were capable of bearing arms retired to the fort, about 3 miles above the Town, to which the women & children fled for safety. The command was given to Col. Butler, father of the present Lord Butler. A counsel of war was called & he advised their remaining in the fort to await the attack of the enemy. His counsel was overruled & those 360 marched forth & meeting the foe 8 mi. up the river, the conflict began. The unequal contest could not be long sustained. The Indians & their friends prevailed & a dreadful slaughter ensued. Three hundred of these rash men were slain & tomahawked. The survivors made good their way to the fort to communicate the sad news to the women & children. Butler was among the survivors. He immediately retreated with the wretched company & such effects they could hastily carry off, leaving the rest a prey to the savages. Several who were in that battle are yet alive & still reside in Wilkesbarre.

As we coasted the river at the termination of the valley, 9 or 10 miles on our way, our attention was arrested by the appearance of the opposite mountain. An immense mass of it has sunk from the rest, quite across the whole ridge. It is as if gouged out with some sharp instrument, the side from which the part has sunk presenting a surface of stone very much resembling a stone wall & rising, as nearly as we could judge, 80 or 100 feet above its fallen member. It retains a position at its base as nearly allied as one step is to another in carpentry. We were not near enough to form any tolerable estimate of the size of the lower step, but it contains several acres & together with the mother mass, is thickly covered with trees in full foliage. It is so considerable that it might in itself be called a mountain. This may have been the effect of an earthquake or of the undermining of water. We halted at Ayres, a poor looking place, but we ate heartily of a coarse dinner. After four or five miles, we recrossed the river at Smith's Ferry. The river here is, I suppose, not less than 1300 feet over & 10 to 12 feet deep. There is here a small, good tract of land & we found some small tracts equally good, but generally both sides of the river are mountainous down to the water's edge & incapable of tillage. The river nevertheless winds its silvery course among them with an almost unruffled current. We now entered the narrows. They consist of three distinct points of mountains, terminating with the river— the road being cut on their steep sides just wide enough for a single carriage & in parts, we conjectured, certainly not less than 200 feet above the water, being almost perpendicular. The united length of these passes is three miles. The first is the most steep and dangerous. In one of the most elevated parts H., who kept an attentive lookout, thought our carriage passed within an inch of the precipice. Had we slipped off our carriage, horses & riders must have been irrecoverably lost. People accustomed to these narrows pass them unheeded. The road should certainly be cut wider. Except its being so very narrow, it is not otherwise

bad, as pains have been taken to remove the stones & rocks pretty generally out of the way. The turnpike now forming from Wilkesbarre to Montrose on the western side of the river will avoid these very unpleasant narrows.

We had now another difficulty to encounter. The rains in the early part of the summer had carried off almost all the bridges & among the rest that of the Tunkhannoe, a large & rapid stream at which we had arrived. The rain of the preceding day & night had swollen it into a torrent & H. would not risk his life in an attempt to ford it. To increase our troubles, night had set in & there was no place at which we could procure accommodations but by venturing over or returning thro' the narrows for four miles to the nearest inn. I considered the latter a more hazardous expedient than encountering the wild & to us unknown current. There was no boat. The place had been supplied with one, but it was in use elsewhere. The only vehicle of passage left was a tottering canoe, in which a person came to us from the opposite shore. This person was willing to convey us & our baggage over in his frail machine &—another man having been procured who said he was well acquainted with the stream & would venture to drive over the carriage if we were willing to run the risk of the horses—the affair was arranged accordingly & all arrived in safety to the opposite shore. After bailing the water from the carriage & returning our baggage into it, we proceeded. It has become so intolerably dark that I could not see the road & permitted the horses to pick their way as well as they could. Luckily we had but half a mile to go, when we arrived at Slocum's Inn. Altho' I did not upbraid my companion, I could not avoid thinking of how much benefit it would have been to us had it suited his *humour* to have risen an hour sooner this morning.

*October 9th.* My companion's humour inducing him to lay abed again this morning between two & three hours after I had risen, I thought I might reasonably so far indulge mine as to call him up. We had each had but one sheet & kept ourselves warm by throwing our coats over us—"The sheets they were short & the blankets were thin." We set down to a breakfast of tea, as they were *just out* of coffee & had bread baked of grown wheat. At 10 we were fairly under way for the woods. My carriage & one horse were left at Slocum's, the other we took to carry our baggage. We are told that the Tunkhannoe cannot be forded this morning & that the Susquehanna has risen three feet since last evening. We soon entered a wilderness in which hemlock formed the principal timber. As we proceeded, we met with maple & ash & passed what is called a sugar camp. The beech next made its appearance & presently became the predominant tree. Some tolerable land is found in this wild & in time, the major part will doubtless be inhabited, especially as the turnpike is to pass this way. We saw men at work on it. We crossed the eastern & principal branch of the Meshoppen, six miles from Tunkhannoe & had now entered good land under tillage. It is a fat, black mud & so slimy that, in picking my way, I fell several times. This soil continued the rest of the road to Jerh. Spencer's, 10 miles from Tunkhannoe. We halted and expected to meet with W.D., Jr., but felt disappointed at being informed of his absence & that he may not return for some days. H. & myself concluded, with permission of the family, to tarry some time here in the hope of meeting W. & to employ our time in short excursions into the neighbourhood. We commenced exploring around us but had not been absent two hours when W. came to join us. Our party was now complete & the rest of the day was occupied in examining some of the cultivated grounds of the vicinity. The soil is uniformly rich, the grass most abundant & all the crops look well. Springs are numerous, the country undulating & there are no flats or swamps. White clover & blue grass grow spontaneously & form in places the thickest coat or mat of grass I have ever yet seen, my friend Lawrence Seckel's famous meadows at Schuylkill Point not excepted. Some spots had been sown with timothy. I measured some of the blades now standing—they are generally as high as my breast & some reach to my lips, standing erect.

*October 10th.* The fields are covered with a heavy white frost this morning. Spencer's house is a frame building, 40 by 20 feet, covered externally with thin boards, but not lined or plastered within & the wind has free access thro' every part of it. Sheets are suspended against the sides opposite to our beds to keep the wind from blowing directly on us. The house is two stories & has twenty windows—two of which are entirely glazed. This is a very kind, respectable family. Our eatables are well dressed & everything is clean. They grow millet here, forty bushels to the acre. It is a small grain & greatly resembles Indian corn in taste. It is excellent for fattening poultry & swine. Spencer has ⅛ of an acre in turnips. We have concluded on examination that they will turn out 100 bushels. The quality is excellent. Rails made of wild cherry, which is plentiful in this country, are common & esteemed very durable. We have satisfied ourselves in this & yesterday's enquiry & examination

 *October 1817*

that, however valuable these New England men may be in clearing lands, they are but poor farmers. Ezra Tuttle, for instance, whose place adjoins this, has lately removed his barn to avoid the manure which had accumulated around it. Spencer's barn yard is in such a state, from the same cause, that it is very unpleasant. Whether he means to move his barn out of its way we have not asked him.

At 10 this morning the triumvirate set out on an exploring expedition, on foot traversing the woods & improved farms for some distance along the eastern limits of my tract without entering on it. We returned by four in the afternoon to Captn. Spencer's. We dined at Isaac Bebee Terril's, who lives in a log house of one apartment which serves his family for parlour, kitchen & hall. We were sumptuously entertained, altho' we were unexpected guests. When we left our quarters, we did not contemplate calling on him. I mention this circumstance because of the surprize we felt at meeting with such a reception & that gratis, too, in this wooden country. We had fresh boiled beef, mutton steaks, turnips, potatoes, beets, cucumber pickles, preserved peaches, Indian pudding, rye bread, light sweet wheaten cakes, butter, cheese & honey. All were good & well served up with a dish of green tea sweetened with maple sugar. Our fare was probably more profuse in consequence of the presence of Isaac's mother, who was on a visit to the family.

I am well pleased with the conduct & appearance of the settlers & particularly with their women, whose cleanly habits, cheerful & healthy countenances & unaffected kindness, added to their social manners, are calculated to gratify strangers.

*October 11th.* Entered my lands on horseback near Chester Adams's farm & passed thro' them in a SW direction about three miles, when we halted at Geo. Haverly's, who lives on the tract. He gave us a good dinner & while it was preparing, conducted us to a deerlick a half a mile SE of his house. Deer appeared to have been there this morning, from the fresh print of their feet, and numerous paths lead to it in all directions. We tasted the water; it is different from that of common springs, but we could not certainly detect a saline taste in it. Afterwards, however, on putting our fingers to our mouths, the salt was very perceptible. Geo. lives on a county road. A short time before we reached his house, we met several men, one of whom had the fresh scalp of a wolf which he had just shot. For this he is entitled to the public bounty of $8. It was one of six which had visited the adjoining farm, belonging to his father, last night & killed two sheep. Their throats were cut & the blood drank, but the carcasses were not otherwise mangled. As we had mutton for dinner I have no doubt we dined on one of them. This suspicion excited such qualms in the stomach of my companions that they were nearly deprived of the benefit of their meal. As I could not perceive but a four legged butcher could do his office as well as a two legged one, I felt in no humour to forego my repast on that account.

*October 12th.* Everywhere there is abundance of water & we saw many fine springs in this day's excursion. The southern & largest branch of the Wyalusing has its origin in two fine small lakes, occupying together perhaps 100 or 120 acres, where we now are. We crossed it frequently in coming hither. The number of fallen trees which we encountered today—added to the same kind of roads & even worse than any we had before travelled—obliged us frequently to alight to jump our horses over them or, where that was found impracticable, to lead them round. I believe none of us escaped without wounds & bruises & altho' my colleagues are professed woodmen & young hearty men, it is no small comfort to find that I fared no worse than they. A project is in contemplation to form a turnpike from near the forks of the Wyalusing, directly thro' the main body of my tract, to come out a few miles from the Tunkhannoe. This would cut off a large angle now taken by Montrose in coming from Owego to Wilkesbarre. In the distance of between 40 & 50 miles, people here tell me it would save 15.

At Asa Lathrop's, where we now are, we are given a very cordial reception, the female part of the family appear equally disposed to make us comfortable, so we are quite at ease. On our arrival Asa, giving me a hearty shake of the hand, said, "Sir, I am happy to see you at my house & hope for a better acquaintance." His wife informed us that their son James & wife had been to see them that day at her special invitation. Altho' it was the Sabbath & she did not approve of neighbours visiting on the Sabbath, she thought it might be excused as they had not seen each other for a long time. I suppose she deemed this explanation necessary to her good character, as we had witnessed the departure of her guests upon entering the premises. She probably did not think so ill of our visit, as we were strangers & travellers. The sun soon set after our arrival, when one of the daughters fell to darning stockings. Another began to reel yarn & the son to chop wood. Such are these people's notions of Sabbath keeping. They would think it sinful to work after sun rising & before sun setting. Others seem more disposed, in order to evince to the world that they are free from a superstitious regard for that

day above any other, to turn these scruples into ridicule & plow & harrow on the road side, that the whole world may witness how much more enlightened they are than their neighbours. Now while on the one hand it would be to me a subject of deep regret to see a due respect for the Sabbath laid aside, there appears, on the other, reason to fear that we are sometimes in danger of falling into a bigoted reverence of the day, not called for by reason or revelation. Some time should be set apart for the observance of religious duties for the rest of both man & beast for example's sake or we shall be in no small danger of suffering our selfish & avaricious pursuits, so to absorb our time that we should live as without God in the world, wholly forgetful of his superintending providence, his mercy & his goodness. But I see no reason why a man should not visit his father or his friend on the Sabbath, if it be otherwise convenient & proper, any more than I perceive the necessity of saying special grace every time I put a piece of bread into my mouth, or sit down to a meal's victuals. My viands are of God's bounty & I ought to be equally thankful for my clothing, my comfortable bed, my cheerful fireside & for the daily rising of the sun. Indeed this latter is the greatest of all terrestrial blessings, for without it we could have no other. And the wild Arab who regularly performs his morning orisons to that great luminary is no more chargeable with superstition than is the pertinacious observer of meats & drinks & of set times & seasons.

*October 13th.* We had tea for breakfast, sweetened as usual with dark maple sugar. We have not had coffee offered us since we crossed the Tunkhannoe. For our breakfast we had also boiled turnips & potatoes, both very nice, the latter little if any inferior to the Irish. These two articles have been served up constantly at all our meals.

After our morning's repast we departed for Montrose, which we reached in a ride of 7 miles, nearly north.

As we pass along, the boys & girls invariably salute us, in the manner of the children of New England. We meet with no drunkards. All are civil & courteous. Both men & women have received good common school learning & school houses are numerous. I have not heard an oath or obscene word in the county, even the men who are employed with their oxen at the laborious work of logging use no foul language. We hear them urging their cattle with, "Go along there Buck, go away now, Brown," but no violent rage is expressed nor do they beat their beasts in the manner I have seen practiced among people considered otherwise humane.

*October 14th.* It was my intention to cross over that part of the tract which is situated between Avery's & Billing's but, finding it cannot be accomplished so as to return in a day & that if I did attempt it I should have to sleep in the woods & since my companions have no other inducement to expose themselves to this additional fatigue than to oblige me, I have this morning abandoned the thought. My nephew H. W. D. expresses a wish to return to Stoddartsville & it was concluded to take our departure. We accordingly took leave of W. D., Jr. & the kind family where he has his present residence & commenced our retrograde march. I mounted my horse, having first made H. the offer, but he declined for fundamental reasons & preferred walking. It is in fact necessary one of us should ride, to keep our luggage from falling off.

I observe that the people of this quarter always precede an answer to any question by the word "well," which seems to be a convenience as affording them a little time to collect their thoughts. As for instance, I accosted a man going our way on foot with, "How far is it from hence to the mouth of the Tunkhannoe?" The answer was "Well, I guess about two miles." "Is not Doc. Rose a manager of this turnpike?" "Well, I rather guess likely he is." They are all Yankees & since leaving Wilkes-barre we have seen none other, the two Haverlys excepted.

At Slocum's we regained our carriage. He has a fine farm of 270 acres which he offers for $15,000. It is said some person has nearly come up to his price.

We returned by the route we came & were no better pleased with the narrows than before. We could not feel quite at ease until we repassed them, for I cannot see how we should have managed had we met a carriage. A woman on horseback could barely pass us & would not attempt it but by alighting & leading her horse.

*October 15th.* We lodged last night at the widow Scholfield's, 9 miles from Wilkesbarre, and this morning rejoined our company at the latter place, where we found them comfortably accommodated at the Widow Jackson's. In the afternoon some of us paid a visit to Solomon's Gap about four miles below the Town.

A road passes through this gap & were it continued in a direct course, it would form much the nearest & best route to Philada., cutting off a great angle made by Stoddartsville & Bethlehem.

The unexpected sound of the village bell this evening startled me, for everything else was silent as the midnight hour. I thought of fire. It was, however, the kerfew. Nine o'clock had arrived & these good people, in

imitation of their forefathers, keep up this ancient English custom. Had we no other evidence of the stock from whence they spring, this would suffice, for so far as I know none other of the people of the United States, but those in New England, are in this practice. I cannot tell how others are effected, but to me there is a certain something in the observance of these ancient customs which leads to contemplation & to solemn feelings mixed with pleasure. They seem to carry us back to the ages of antiquity & to bring us into something like an intercourse with the dead.

*October 16th.* We continued our perambulations. We visited a coal bed—the quantity in this vicinity is immense & will probably never be exhausted. The quality is esteemed superior to most. In burning it emits but little smoke & leaves scarce any residuum & gives a powerful heat. The inhabitants use it generally & I am much better reconciled to a coal fire than I have been. It is sold for about 6 cents the bushel at the quarry & delivered in the Town at 12. It lies on the very surface of the ground in strata piled on each other of 12 to 20 inches in depth & is split off with wedges in large blocks. I observe different kinds in the same quarry. Parts appear scarcely at all impregnated with sulphur while others show it very plainly. Some veins are a dull black, some copper coloured & some exhibit the colours of the rainbow.

*October 17th.* Departed from Wilkesbarre, on our way home. We were two hours in ascending the mountain, a distance of five miles by the course of the road. As we approached the summit, it began to snow & continued to do so & to rain until we arrived at Stoddartsville.

*October 18th.* We took leave of Stoddartsville & of our interesting nephew, who is a character of no ordinary stamp. He possesses, by nature, strong intellectual powers, is considerably cultivated &—having met with some buffetings from a rude world—he entertains rather a contemptuous opinion of men in general. He has the most exalted love of independence & says of himself that he will not be second to any man. It was doubtless in obedience to these elevated conceptions & as a public proclamation of his rights that he occasionally set the women to scampering from the doors at which he & I stopped by the performance, in their presence, of a certain office which other men do aside in private.

Doc. Johnson says that the Isle of Muck gave subsistence to 160 persons on less than 500 acres, who paid a rent to their landlord besides.

No part of the country seen this day, I may venture to predict, will ever equal Muck.

We stopped at Buck's, 11 miles from Stoddartsville, with intention to bait but, as they were *just out* of oates, we continued to our old quarters, S. Heller's, at the foot of the Blue Mountain. As some hours of daylight were yet unspent, I set out with the girls to ascend the summit, the rest preferring to enjoy themselves round a comfortable fire.

*October 19th.* Passing thro' Nazareth, we continued on to Easton, 7 miles beyond.

*October 22d.* Arrived at home. After a tour of three weeks during which we have been much favoured by the weather, for which & the many blessings we enjoy, may we possess thankful hearts.

*October 24th.* About half of the Germans have gone. Banzhoff & Fetter called to take their leave of me today. Baeumler is to go in a day or two & Fredk. Pfersich, who has lived for some years in my family goes with him. I find that the Com. have had some trouble in my absence. These people appear to have dealt rather disingenuously with us & B. in particular is thought to be an artful man. He exercises great authority & influence over them & his views in hurrying them off into the western wilderness are considered to be selfish. Some of the Com. think him a second Rapp. It now further appears that, besides their disuse of pork, they have the same objections to certain fish & not only disapprove of marriage but it is made a matter of dismemberment from their fraternity for any of their people to engage in it.

They abstain from flesh on sixth days. Baeumler came to take his leave today. I had but little conversation with him. His eyes were moistened when he thanked me for my attentions to him. I should have noticed the same thing of Banzhoff & Fetter. These men were much affected when they bid me farewell.

*October 27th.* "Man that is born of a woman is of few days & full of trouble. He cometh up like a flower & is cut down. He fleeth like a shadow & continueth not."

I rose this morning as usual & was employed in writing by myself, when I was suddenly seized with strange & indescribable sensations. That they had any connection with what followed, I do not say, but simply state the fact. I was alarmed at myself & knew not why. I laid down my pen & walked the floor with some agitation. A call summoned me to breakfast. The family took no notice of my state, nor did I mention it. While taking my first cup of coffee, the servant announced a person at the door who wished to see me. I went forth to meet him. It was Thos. Firth. Grief was on his countenance. He came to inform us that sister Margaret had attempted her life by strangulation. I hastened to the house. Two physicians had been there before me. It was too late. They strove to recall life, but they strove in vain. The vital spark had fled beyond their reach. It had fled forever & she lay a lifeless corpse before me. A coroner's inquest was called. The law requires it. The jury pronounced the act to be the effect of insanity. The day was spent in mourning & anguish. The family were in a state bordering on delirium. The evening came. The body had been laid out & they put on me the painful task to conduct my distracted brother & his wretched children to take their last adieu. The scene was awful & afflicting. I was compelled to force my brother from the dead body. At seven, the remains were conveyed in a hearse to the burial ground, attended by a few relatives. The streets were silent, an uncommon, profound darkness prevailed. Not a lamp gleamed, save the one which glimmered at the head of the grave, to light the sexton to the performance of his solemn office. The rain descended & the tempest howled. Nature seemed also in unison with the passing scene. Horror thrilled through my veins & I retired to my pillow, exhausted, bewildered & overpowered by my feelings.

*October 29th.* This & the preceding were spent with my brother Israel & his family.

*October 31st.* Altho' not in a situation of mind to attend to business, I was constrained to meet the Overseers of Friends Public Schools in the afternoon. The Com. to assist & advise the Separatists met in the evening. A letter to Wm. Allen of London was agreed on, giving him some account of these people. As it was by letters from him that they were introduced to Friends here, I thought this a proper step. It may have the effect to prevent them (Friends in London) from too easily imposing again so heavy a burden on us. I am to sign this letter on behalf of the Committee.

*November 1st.* As the enjoyments of the mind transcend those of the appetites, as much as the roar of thunder exceeds a whisper, so do imaginary evils surpass those of mere corporal sufferance. The latter admit of cure, the former scarce of palliation. This has its meets & boundaries; that is void of limit. This has something on which medicine may act; that is an untangible will-o-wisp, which can be neither reached nor compassed. Wealth, so far from securing us from the ills of life, is frequently the parent of our unhappiness. When the mind has full occupation in providing for the wants of the body, it is less subject to disease than when bereft of that powerful stimulous to action. How often is it found that a man, after having spent his best days in pursuit of a fortune which he has at length acquired, finds himself incapable of enjoying it from mere want of occupation. What he pursued with pleasure, when caught, has instead of adding to his stock of enjoyments only insured his misery. Nor is he who is left a rich patrimony more secure. He knows not the worth of what he has. How should he, when he has given no value for it? The labouring man, on the contrary, who acquires his possessions by active industry, knows what they cost & their worth. His exercises give him an appetite for his food. He is fatigued & sleeps sound. He rises refreshed & vigorous, to renew his occupations. Not so the rich voluptuary. Want of exercise creates indigestion. He fancies himself sick & the dainties with which he pampers his stomach make him so. He cannot sleep. He dozes & is alarmed with frightful dreams. He rises & is languid. His body is beset with pains & his mind racked with apprehensions. All things are given us rationally & richly to enjoy & it is our duty to enjoy them with cheerfulness & gratitude. But we subvert the order & laws of nature. We frustrate the beneficent ordinations & dispensations of Providence. We reject the blessings conferred on us & pervert the good gifts, material & intellectual, with which we are endowed. Consequently, in place of the happy beings for which we were so evidently constituted, we become miserable by our errors, our follies & our vices.

*December 21st.* After 10 or 12 days of mild weather, it became again cold last evening. There was then no ice in the Delaware, but this morning the navigation is so completely obstructed that vessels cannot pass up or down.

# 1818

*February 1st.* The weather has not been so cold during the preceding month as to close the river. Vessels continued to navigate it, with occasional interruptions from floating ice, most of the time.

*March 23d.* On the 20th, between 9 & 10 A.M., the powder works (5 miles from Wilmington) on the Brandywine blew up with such a tremendous explosion as to cause the sensation of an earthquake not only in this City, Burlington & Lancaster but even in N. York. Between thirty & forty persons lost their lives by this sad catastrophe.

*July 15th.* There is in the atmosphere a very striking haze, as if a great fire prevailed at no great distance.

*August 9th.* The haziness observed in Philada. on the 15th appears to have been general along the Atlantic states & has excited some speculation as to the cause.

*August 10th.* About a year back, a question of considerable interest was agitated in the Pennsyla. Abolition Society. About 100 slaves had been bequeathed to them in N. Carolina, with the humane intent to ensure their manumission. If the Society should accept the bequest, the slaves were to be conveyed to Philada. & placed at service in the county for a term proportioned to their respective ages & other circumstances, otherwise these poor creatures would continue in bondage. My judgement & feelings were deeply enlisted in their cause & I strenuously advocated the acceptance of the bequest. I was opposed by R. V., an active intelligent member. He was fertile in expedients, but all his efforts failed. He was greatly disappointed & betrayed so much temper & indiscretion & took moreover such unwarrantable liberties with some others, much his superiors in years & experience, as to call forth from me some very cutting remarks, He could not endure the lash, but ran about in a paroxysm of rage. He stammered, stormed, threatened, and raved & finally became incapable of utterance, exhibiting a most melancholy instance of the debasing effects of unsubdued passion.

From that time he passed me in the street without speaking. It was an affair of his choice, since I had no disposition to preserve any coolness between us & was therefore prepared to accost him as usual. I perceived in him a studied avoidance of my company & we therefore continued to pass each other as strangers until today, when he stopped me. His eyes were full. He could no longer sustain the reproaches of his own convictions. He tendered a very feeling apology. I assured him that I entertained no hardness towards him & cheerfully stretched out my hand to meet his. He was greatly agitated & wept so profusely that I was compelled to break away to hide my own emotions.

*September 28th.* Left home this morning in company with my wife, son Wm. & daughter Caroline for Susquehanna County. Understanding that a safe carriage road would be found by pursuing the course of the Hudson River to Newberg & thence westwardly to the Great Bend, we determined to visit N. York in our way & accordingly set out in that direction. We halted at Nathan Spencer's & dined at Jno. Newbold's above Bristol. We passed, on the road, Jos. Bonaparte, ex-King of Spain, who assumes the title of Count Surveillante. He lives very retired near Bordentown, N.J. He affects no state, is friendly & sociable with his neighbours & courteous to visitors. He was in a plain carriage drawn by two horses & accompanied by his secretary. His unassuming manners have gained him the good opinion of the neighbourhood. He arrived in this country shortly after the final overthrow of his brother Napoleon & purchased the estate in which he now resides & which he has considerably improved & extended. His wife has not yet joined him, but he says she will do so in a few months.

*September 29th.* Last night we lodged at Jno. Anderson's inn. Our servant gave offense to a coloured man, who is our only attendant at table, by cleaning our shoes—this fellow alleging it to be an encroachment on his rights, it being his privilege to clean gentlemen's shoes & to hand the baggage & for which services he expects compensation. As we were taking our departure, the sudden appearance & courtesies of the chambermaid reminded us that she also had her claims. We are thus sliding into the English custom of bribing servants to the performance of their duty.

*September 30th.* Arrived at Paulus Hook, by 11, twenty miles from Bridge Town & crossed the Hudson in a steam boat. No improvement of modern times can excel this. Formerly, besides long detentions, the risk in crossing this ferry was often so considerable that many lives were lost & few attempted to take their carriages to N. York. We now crossed with as much ease & safety as we could drive along the streets.

*October 5th.* Our time for the last four days has been spent in looking

round the City, in a visit to Flushing on Long Island & in a short excursion on York Island.

Paid a short visit to the Almshouse, a very extensive range of buildings on the East River. It was meal time. The paupers were flocking into the kitchen with bowls, mugs, plates &c., with which they crowded around the cooks to receive each his portion, which they carried away & ate in any part of the buildings at their convenience. Some carried away soup, some meat & potatoes, & some mush. The disorder struck me unpleasantly. The floors & other parts of the buildings were, of course, greased & bedaubed in an unseemly manner. We were particularly pleased, however, to notice the healthy appearance of the children, of whom there were between 3 & 4 hundred—all too young, perhaps, to be apprenticed. We were ushered into one apartment where a large table was spread, the furniture of which gave indications that persons of more consequence than the poor were to dine there. A feast was preparing for the City Corporation & the display of dishes, glasses &c. evinced that Corporation men on this, as well as on the other side of the Atlantic, love good eating & drinking. This feasting & carousing in the very midst of pauperism is reprehensible—it cannot fail to be attended by bad consequences.

Our intention had been, on leaving N. York, to recross the Hudson to Hoboken but, owing to a mistake, we were landed at Paulus Hook. We travelled thro' sands three miles to Hoboken, where we took our leave of the river & taking a northwardly direction we arrived in the little town of Hackensack, where we baited. It is situated on the river of the same name & insignificant as it is, is the County Town of Bergen. We stopped for the night at John Hopper's. Two of the same name live within a stone cast of each other. We had previous information as to the best house & were not disappointed. He is the elder of the two, has a mill & no sign up, probably to enable him to select his company. They are nice people—Low Dutch. This is 21 miles from Hackensack. Hopper's son-in-law is here on a visit. He lives at Kingston, N.Y. He says, "There are some Friends in that place who have a woman for a Minister who performs all their church service." He adds that "they are a very respectable people & increase quite fast. They marry their young people to young people of other congregations & then take them all into their Society."

*October 6th.* Left Hopper's after a comfortable night. A mile from his house we entered the Newberg Turnpike & in about 8 miles more, that immense chain of mountains which traverse from SW to NE the whole continent of North America.

Within a few miles of our day's journey, we perceived that we had exchanged the Dutchmen for Yankees. The woman at one of the turnpike gates, on being asked the rate of toll, replied, "Well, I guess a shilling."

*October 7th.* Newberg is said to contain between four & five hundred houses & the buildings are substantial. The Town has the semblance of a thriving place. The U.S. have it in contemplation to establish a Navy Yard here which will probably add to its consequence.

Fishkill is on the eastern shore of the Hudson opposite to Newberg. Jno. Quincy Adams, Secretary of State, is there at present, having crossed from Newberg the day before our arrival.

*October 8th.* We had designed to dine at Forbes's, six miles on the Penna. side of the Delaware & to lodge at Mount Pleasant, 81 miles from Newberg. At 4 A.M., when we reached Forbes's, we found ourselves & horses too much jaded to proceed all night, altho' our prospects of accommodations are not very brilliant.

*October 9th.* Our landlady says that between 40 & 50 persons lodged here last night. We might think ourselves well off to be in the possession of two entire beds in our small room. Father & son occupying one & mother & daughter the other. The stage from Newberg came in soon after we retired & that from the westward, sometime after. Both departed during the night, but if we did not see we most assuredly did hear the passengers. Our little cubby was divided from their lodging apartment by a thin board partition, open at the ceiling.

Wild lands sell here at $6 per acre on the turnpike & $5 back.

Soon after leaving Forbes's, we parted with the hemlock to enter the beech woods.

Wm. lost the key of the carriage box at old Hopper's & we have not been able to get at our shaving apparatus or clean clothing since. Now it is discovered that Mary has lost the key of the trunk in which she & Caroline have their goods & chattels. It will be well if we are not, bye & bye, taken up for vagrants. We may perhaps persuade folks that we have clean clothes in our trunks, tho' we may not on our backs.

*October 10th.* We arrived at the G. Bend early in the afternoon & were kindly received by our cousins Wm. Drinker, Jr. & wife.

*October 11th.* Spent in doors with our relations. It is the first day of the week. Tomorrow I purpose to visit my lands.

*October 12th.* This morning W.D., Jr., my son & self left the G. Bend on horseback. We stopped to dine at Montrose, having passed thro' a tract of pretty well improved land, called Lawsville, from Saml. Andw. Law, who sold the land to the settlers. They have as yet no house for worship, but are building a dwelling for a clergyman. There is no village, but an agreeable assemblage of farms. From Montrose we went to Jerh. Spencer's to spend the night. His son Daniel entertained us most of the evening with anecdotes of his adventures in hunting, at which he appears to be an adept. With one pound of powder he killed 60 deer, 9 bears, 1 wolf & 3 foxes. He mentions an instance of the contrivance of a panther to elude his pursuit, which he thinks common to the species. He got in pursuit of the animal early in the morning & continued, by the help of a dog, to follow him till near the close of the day before he got an opportunity to shoot him. During part of the time, Daniel found himself much perplexed by coming to the end of the animal's track. At length, on a cautious inspection, it was discovered that he had retraced his steps so exactly in the snow, for the ground was covered, that the original impression only remained. This he had performed for a considerable space & then sprung aside into a thicket, whence he was again roused by the dog. Daniel says that notwithstanding the amazing agility & strength of the panther, he is soon exhausted in the chase & any active man may run one of them down. The one here spoken of, he says, measured 12 feet from the nose to the end of the tail. He was finally shot on a tree, on to which he leaped not less than 20 feet from the ground by a single spring & this after he had been much worried by his pursuers.

*October 13th.* Visited W.D., Jr.'s new clearing. His tenant has some fine wheat in the ground. If it succeeds according to present appearances, he expects to have about 40 bushels per acre. Wm. intends to have a large grazing & dairy farm.

Having entered my tract, we proceeded in a SW direction & called to take dinner with George Haverly. This industrious German has a small nursery of fruit trees which we encouraged him to increase, as likely to be profitable to himself & useful to the country. His nice wife prepared us a comfortable repast & had at the same time to attend a cross child only eight weeks old. George & his wife settled here a few years ago when they were very young. Everything was in a wilderness state. They went out together to make maple sugar. The ground was covered with snow &

night overtook them. They lost their way & did not reach their hut till daylight came to their assistance. They were nearly perished with the cold. Geo. stripped himself of his coat to keep his wife warm & kept himself from being greatly injured by constant exercise, but they were nevertheless both frostbitten. The poor fellow frequently labours by moonlight. They appear a cheerful happy couple. It does one's heart good to see people so contented with such scanty means. We had tea according to custom. It was served to us in a large canopy tin coffee pot & water was given us to drink in a tin pudding basin. One humble apartment serves these people for parlour, best chamber & kitchen. The ceiling is at present ornamented with garlands of pumpkins cut into slips & hung up to dry for future use.

From Haverly's we went to Asa Lathrop's at the Lakes. At supper we had beans baked with pieces of fat pork. W.D. thought them excellent.

*October 14th.* At breakfast we had venison steaks, boiled potatoes & onions, stewed apples, preserved peaches, plums & tea.

From Lathrop's we proceeded on the state road westwardly, thro' my lands & continued over course to where it intersects the road from the forks of the Wyalusing to Montrose, five miles from L.'s & 10 to Montrose. Then, keeping the eastern branch of that creek at first on our right & then on our left, we arrived at Montrose by noon.

It commenced raining about 10 A.M. & did not cease until we arrived at N. Milford, whence we took the turnpike to the G. Bend & rejoined our friends.

*October 17th.* In the afternoon we all paid a visit to Judge (Wm.) Thompson & family, whose farm occupies most of the point on the opposite side of the river. We had the best bread we have eaten since we came into the neighbourhood. It was made of spring wheat grown by himself. In general we have had bread of what they here term the lake flour. It is such as would be considered inferior to Philada. condemned.

Judge T., speaking of the depredations committed on the property of absent proprietors & of the light in which it is generally viewed, stated that he had frequent arguments with one of his associates on the bench to convince him that stealing a tree worth $5 is equally criminal with stealing the same value in hay or oates. His colleague does not see it so & thinks there is little harm in it.

Judge T. is favourably inclined toward a road to be run from the G.B. to intersect the Wilkesbarre & Easton Turnpike. Such a road would

doubtless be highly advantageous to the trade of Philada. & from all I can learn can be accomplished over good ground.

*October 18th.* This morning, taking leave of our friend, we began to retrace our steps homeward.

Halted at St. John's, Mount Pleasant, for the night. While engaged in the important act of eating our evening meal, a smart young woman, coming up to me & looking me full in the face, was understood by us all to ask, "Who, Sir, would you chuse for a bed fellow?" I felt somewhat disconcerted & my little party burst into a general laugh. An explanation ensued. It turned out that the girl intended to ask whether I chose she should give supper to my black fellow.

Just before our arrival at this place we were near being run down by a heavy waggon which, descending the same hill we were toiling up, abruptly changing its course ran direct against us. It was guided by a little boy whose confusion & sorrow was so artlessly expressed that we could not believe he designed us any injury. We thought ourselves well off to have suffered nothing more than a bruise of our carriage.

*October 19th.* The sun rose this morning in a bright sky & discovered to our astonished view, at a great distance to the south, a large lake beyond which a considerable tract of wood crowned country appeared. Still further in the background, a mighty river rolled, beyond which again the more distant mountains bounded the azure horizon. So magnificent a prospect had seldom greeted our delighted eyes & we were utterly at a loss to account for the circumstance of its having escaped our attention when here before. We called our landlord to enquire the name of the lake & of the river. He answered that the lake was the fog hovering over the Elk ponds, about 12 miles off & what we took for a river was the fog of the Delaware. There was no denying his testimony & yet the optical delusion was so complete that it required some exertion of faith to believe him. It must be recollected that Mount P. is a high point of land, from which the eye can discern objects said to be 60 miles distant.

Met several waggons returning from Newberg with merchandize—two horses each, loaded with abt. ½ a ton. Only one had a cover. We also overtook several of the same description carrying the produce of the country to market. I examined the contents of one of them—a cask of whiskey, three barrels of flour & three or four kegs of butter made up his load.

Took dinner with Forbes. This man, by way of recommending himself

& giving a salutary caution to travellers, has painted on his sign in conspicuous characters:

> Little on this side
> Nothing on the other
> Nothing in the house
> Nor barn either.

This is no great exaggeration, if we confine the limits to 10 or 12 miles on each side of him.

*October 21st.* We are now at Goshen, having travelled about 35 miles yesterday & the same the day before.

Most people preserve some decent respect for the remains of the dead. The clay which was once animated by genius & virtue in a near connection or endeared friend cannot be altogether indifferent to feeling survivors. In some instances, it is true, this sentiment is carried to a superstitious extent at which reason & true piety revolt. These Goshenites appear not to have erred in this respect. Their grave yard is an open common over which dogs may prowl and hogs root at leisure. Perhaps it is thought sufficient to have placed tomb stones on the graves. The broken fragments now strew the ground.

After fruitless enquiry as to the distance & best road to Patterson, we left Goshen & bent our course towards Algers on the Newberg Turnpike.

*October 22d.* We continued to retrace our former route till we reached Hopper's, where we bore towards the west & in 7 miles arrived at Godwin's Tavern in Patterson.

*October 23d.* We have heard the distance between Patterson & Morris Town computed at 22 miles. From the time occupied in compassing it, we judge it to be several miles more.

Having arrived at Morris Town & put up at Bull's Tavern, we sent for Joshua Edwards, formerly of Philada., with whom we spent the evening very agreeably. Our friend E. is a man of reading & observation and, having leisure—being also a man of fortune—he indulges his propensity for both. Our friend says that those things with which we are at first particularly pleased are soonest apt to cloy & such as are most disagreeable at first we become more lastingly & inveterately attached to. In proof of the first he evidences our experience of turtle soup & other rich dishes & of the latter, the use of tobacco, ardent spirits &c. He applies this maxim on morals, "I tell my daughters," said he, "to beware of

young men with whom at first sight they are particularly pleased, not merely because on further acquaintance they will prove less agreeable but, being particularly pleased, they are the less capable of exercising a dispassionate judgement in the case."

Joshua does not appear entirely content with his present situation & wishes to change it. "Should I make a change," said he, "I will not go to a place in which the majority of my neighbours will be either Presbyterians or Democrats. The former do very well when mixed with others who can be a check on them but, when left to themselves, they inculcate the high toned doctrines of election & reprobation & are therefore bad moralists & where the majority are Democrats, there is little chance of justice, since the law is made to bend at all times to passion and prejudice." If this opinion be correct, no marvel he should incline to shift his residence, since here he is subject to both these evils. Another of his opinions is that mountaineers are more naturally attached to liberty than lowlanders & possess more energy of character. Bonaparte well understood this & selected his best troops, whom he stiled voltigeurs, from high countries. "People who from infancy are accustomed to see straight lines, in surrounding objects, are more correct, systematic & straight forward in their conduct than where they are brought up among crooked avenues & sharp angled paths. The Philadelphians, from their infancy accustomed to straight & regular streets, are a people of steady habits in morals & business, while the N. Yorkers, where the streets are crooked, their corners more diversified & the terminations more abrupt, are more adventurous, less chaste in their principles & more perverse. The Bostonians, where the streets are still more various & the angles more acute, are more enterprizing, crafty & subtle than either." These notions of our friend may not be substantial & yet, man is so much the creature of habit & education that the moralist will not be disposed to reject them without examination.

*October 24th.* From Morris Town we went to Vealtown, a poor little place of half a dozen buildings. The soil & improvements so far are good. Thence on to Lamberton, a still more poverty stricken place. The soil is a thin red shell. The farm houses are mean. We halted at the White House Tavern, kept by Kramer, on the turnpike leading from Easton to New Brunswick. It is well kept, the hostess a nice, well behaved woman.

*October 25th.* This is the first day of the week & we attended divine worship, it being the only opportunity of attending a Friends meeting since leaving N. York.

*October 27th.* We lodged unintentionally with our kind friends Hugh Ely & wife & reached home towards evening. We have travelled on this journey between 6 & 7 hundred miles.

# 1819

*July 29th.* The state of my health requiring, in the judgement of my physician & friends, some absence from the City, I left home this morning accompanied by my son Wm. Passing thro' Lancaster & Columbia we arrived at York, 85 miles from Philada. From York to Berlin & thence to York Springs. Tarried a week, drinking the waters freely. I derived benefit from their use. From these springs we travelled westwardly.

Spent 2 days at Greensburg. Lodged at Deniston's—good house. Our kinsman Frederick Cope & mother live here. There is coal by the Town; quality not very good, too slaty. From Greenbg. to Gibson's, 12 mi. Widow Rippy's at Wilkinsburg, 12 mi.—lodged. Pittsburg, 7 mi.

Pittsburg contains about 10,000 inhabitants & a number of extensive factories of Iron, Cotton, Glass & Wool &c., now principally idle. It lies on a level spot surrounded by hills, having the Allegheny on its northern & the Monongahela on its southern limits, both with elevated banks.

The whole appearance of the City is of a sombre cast—the dust & smoke of the coal resting on all the buildings. It is a dirty place & a body can scarce touch an article in or out of doors without sullying the hand. I never saw so many smutty faced children in all my life as we meet in the streets.

We have our lodgings at the widow McCullough's. It is said to be one of the best houses there, but it does not want bugs. It is surprizing that people are so neglectful of the Christian duty of cleanliness as to have these filthy vermin, to their own shame & the great annoyance of travellers. It would be considered quite out of character to be put to sleep in the same chamber with your horses, and yet, I should prefer it to being sent to a bed decorated perhaps with some useless finery but swarming with bugs.

We entered a coal pit on the western banks of the Monongahela near the summit of a hill perhaps 500 feet high. The shaft is horizontal. We coursed it 1000 or 1200 feet, the height of the passage being but 5 feet, the thickness of the vein of coal. It is about the same breadth & damp, so that we had no very agreeable tramp. We were conducted by a guide with lights. The passage is just wide enough to admit a hand cart, which a single man drags or shoves & in this way delivers 100 bushels a day, which he procures by a pick axe. The tunnel branches off in various directions & hence a person, without a guide, might be a long time entangled in these labyrinths.

*September 6th.* Today we forded the Potomac on our route to Bath in Berkley Co., Virginia. The water is about to the hubs on our carriage wheels. The river is as broad as the Schuylkill at the permanent bridge at Philada. at high water. Bath is 6 miles from Hancock & has a distressed, ruinous appearance. The best looking house in it belongs to a company of gamblers. When in session, they place two sentries, one up & one down stairs to prevent the entrance of informers or the officers of justice. Who will enter must give the countersign. Strange that dupes can be found to enter this den of thieves. Last year was esteemed profitable & the Compy. cleared, as we are told, upwards of $20,000. The present season has been less productive, as only $7000 having been gleaned by them. A quarrel lately broke out among them in which some others engaging houses were stoned, windows broken &c. but their own escaped. There are not in the place a sufficient number of respectable inhabitants to keep the rabble in awe. The town contains about 50 dwellings, one of which is stone & one of brick & the residue wooden. Nearly all have a ruinous appearance. One third of them are deserted, among the latter is the former residence of Lord Fairfax, a humble one story frame mansion & the summer residence of Gen. Washington, equally humble.

*September 13th.* Left Bath & breakfasted at Sheckle's halfway house. It was pretty good. The road passes over uncultivated barren hills & crosses Sleepy Creek. The lands are more cultivated. The first half a dozen miles from the halfway house are poor & slaty but are succeeded by a rich limestone soil. This is much better farmed. The lands, we understand, in this vicinity are tilled either by whitemen wholly or by whites who work with their slaves. An elderly farmer of Lancaster County, Penna.—having been asked the reason that one of his sons succeeded so much better than another—answered, "When my oldest son wants work done he says, Come, let us go do so & so" & sets to labour with his men. When my other son wants anything done he tells his labourers to go & do it, while he himself remains in the house.

Dined at Graham's in Martinsburg, 26 miles from Bath. It is the seat of justice for Berkley. At night we were at Minghinie's Sulphur Spring, now kept by one Brown. They are 8 miles from Martinsburg & within a few rods of Opeck on Creek, which divides Berkley from Jefferson Co. There are several other sulphur springs in the neighbourhood. We find

ourselves the only visitors & Brown tells us he shall remove with his family in a few days.

*September 15th.* We had a wedding last night. Brown's sister married a young man in the neighbourhood. The ceremony was performed in our presence, there being but one convenient sitting room. It was conducted with gravity & good order. There was no dancing or music, no improper drinking, no noisy talk or boisterous mirth. There were about 20 guests of both sexes, all respectable in their appearance & conduct. There was a very appropriate preparatory address to the young couple from the officiating clergyman & the ceremony was performed by him & the parties with becoming dignity. At midnight the cry of fire resounded thro' the house. A great bustle ensued. The lonely situation of the place, far removed from any other habitations & the combustible materials of the house being altogether composed of wood & that principally pine, added much to the general anxiety & confusion. Luckily the flames were soon extinguished & it was found that some clothing & a table were the only articles injured. The fire had been communicated to them by a spark from a candle.

Minghinie was an Italian & valet to the late Gen. Lee.

*September 16th.* Left Brown's & passing through a dirty little village called Bunker's Hill, attended Hopewell meeting, 12 miles distant & about 8 miles from Winchester. We returned back 4 miles with Thos. Wright. There was a wedding at meeting & it would have been gratifying had it been conducted with the same decorum & solemnity as that we had so recently witnessed at the springs. It is not unlikely that Friends may find it necessary to change their mode of marriage. There is at present too much public parade & too much levity—many attending these meetings out of mere idle curiosity & who are therefore apt to be restive & to disturb others.

*September 17th.* We left Thos. Wright & his kind wife this morning, he having very politely accompanied us some miles on our way. Our next stage was Harper's Ferry, 20 miles onward. On the route passing thro' Charleston, a handsome town of 150 dwellings, which is the seat of justice for Jefferson & a lively looking place. We had limestone to within a mile of Harper's & we saw many fine farms, but still it is a slave country. The marks of this evil are everywhere visible. Oh, this is a foul blot on our nation.

I wish Tom Jefferson had not said so much in praise of Harper's Ferry.

When descriptions exceed the just limits, the usual consequence is disappointment. Much as I find here to admire, I should not think it worth a voyage across the Atlantic to look at.

We have visited the arsenal & work shops. We coursed the canal to its entrance from the Potomac, mounted the hill up to Jefferson's rock. We stood on the table & surveyed the surrounding scenery & have therefore nearly accomplished all we expected.

*September 19th.* The slaves are seen today disposing of their small wares to the inhabitants. It is the only day allowed them to labour for themselves & to sell their scanty earnings. We purchased some peaches of one of these poor fellows at a cheap rate & he appeared very grateful for our custom, offering more for our money than we took.

The quarry of variegated marble whence the columns of Congress Hall in Washington were obtained is 12 miles distant from Frederick on the Potomac.

*September 20th.* We had scarcely entered our native state when the extensive barns which met our eyes announced that we were in Pennsyl. How striking also in other respects the difference between a slave cultivation & the labour of freemen. At F. we were informed that free negroes could not find employment among them & whenever a free negro makes his appearance, they rid themselves of him as soon as possible. They are fearful that their slaves might be injured by his presence. May not this fear, this desire to keep their slaves in ignorance, have prompted some of these slaveholders to become members of the Colonization Society? Not with any view to the freedom of the blacks, but to render slavery more secure.

*September 27th.* On this day we reached home. My health is much improved. I have the inexpressable comfort to find my dear wife & children well. For this & many other unmerited blessings, I hope I may be strengthened to never forget the Bountiful Giver.

Passing thro' east Bradford in Chester Co. on our return we saw, at the house of our kinsman Saml. Cope, a root of wheat from a single grain on which there are one hundred & twenty two stalks with well filled heads, one of which, being counted, was found to contain 61 grains. It was one of the largest but it was supposed the heads would average fifty grains. If so the increase is upwards of six thousand fold.

*October 13th.* From a passing cloud there was today a sprinkle of snow in Philada.

I have made a mistake. There are but 102 instead of 122 stalks of wheat as stated above.

*October 15th.* Europe remains in a state of tranquility, but war rages in the Spanish provinces in South America. Ferdinand is a weak prince & little inclined to ameliorate his government at home or abroad. It is quite probable all those possessions will be lost to the Mother Country. Bonaparte is still a prisoner in the Isle of St. Helena & Geo. III of England continues in a state of mental derangement.

# 1820

*March 1st.* There have been between 20 & 30 falls of snow the past winter. The ground has remained pretty generally covered. The cold has been regular but not severe.

*March 15th.* The public mind has for some weeks been much agitated by the debates in Congress on the question of prohibiting slavery in the new State of Missouri & at length that body, by small majorities in both Houses, have determined not to impose the restriction. Shame on these babblers for liberty. The Southern States consider this a great triumph over the Northern & non-slaveholding States.

*April 3d.* The City has been kept in constant alarm by frequent attempts to set it on fire. The incendiaries have succeeded in burning several buildings but in most instances the combustibles thrown into them have been discovered in time to prevent much damage. Last night these villains were successful in a second attempt on the Theatre in Chestnut Street, which was entirely consumed. The light was so great that the inhabitants of Darby & Frankfort could see to read by it. The night was cloudy & the ground & roofs of the houses were covered by several inches of snow, which commenced falling in the morning & continued during the fire.

*June 11th.* I have just returned from an excursion to Luzerne County, where I have been in company with brother Jasper to explore some wild lands of which we have been long possessed without knowing their quality. Having accomplished our object, we passed over to the Lehigh & came to Mauch Chunk on its western banks where White, Hazard & Co., who are engaged in the arduous task of improving the navigation of that wild stream, have their headquarters & whence they expect to transport coal in large flat bottomed boats (which they are now preparing) to Philada.

*July 12th.* I have long had a desire to visit the falls of Niagara, Montreal & Quebec & finding myself at leisure to gratify my inclination, I have taken my son Alfred, as a companion. Left home this day for the accomplishment of my purpose.

We took passage at 12 in the steamboat *Philadelphia* & after a pleasant run arrived at Trenton by 4 where we entered the stage coach for N. Brunswick. The day was warm, the roads dusty & the wind followed us.

*July 13th.* We continued our route in the same coach to Perth Amboy & arriving by half past 7 A.M., entered the steamboat *Olive Branch* for N. York. A singular & to travellers, inconvenient dispute exists between the states of N. York & N. Jersey, by which each prevents the steamboats of the other from navigating their waters. Hence we were conveyed over the sound from Amboy to Staten Island in batteaux, landed & then in other boats & by other ferrymen, brought back half way & put on board the *Olive Branch*. As we left the Jersey shore we were served with a process forbidding us at our peril to proceed. Surely the laws of the U.S. must guarantee to its citizens free ingress & egress to & from the several states.

*July 14th.* We lodged at Harriet Robbin's boarding house on Pearl Street & being joined this morning by Wm. Bowne, a merchant of this City, took passage in the S.B. *Paragon* for Albany. The views on the river Hudson have become so familiar & their description so hackneyed that I shall not do more than preserve memorandums of distances. Twenty-five miles from the City we entered Tappan Bay which extends 8 miles to Croton River at Teller's Point. Here Haverstraw Bay commences & extends to Stony Point, 38 miles from N. York. Peekskill is 42, then comes the Horse Race & then Buttermilk Falls, 40 miles & West Point, 51, New Windsor 58, & Newberg 60. The highlands commence at Stony Point & extend to near N. Windsor. We passed Poughkeepsie, 75 miles from N.Y., in the night, also Red Hook 97 and Catskill 111.

*July 15th.* The *Paragon* is crowded with passengers and during the night made frequent halts to discharge some & receive others. The noise from this cause, from the machinery & the trampling overhead were illy calculated to insure sleep. We were on deck by sunrise. The city of Hudson is in full view. 'Tis a large handsome Town on the east bank of the river. At half past 9 A.M. we were at Albany, 143 miles from N. York.

This Town has heretofore derived much of its consequence from supplying the distant interior traders with imported merchandize. The establishment of steamboats will in a great measure put an end to that branch of their commerce. Formerly it occupied many days & often weeks to make a trip to N. York. Now a country trader can jump into a steamboat & in 24 hours or less, without fatigue, arrive at the Metropolis. After dinner our little party engaged a hack & visited the Cohoe Falls, where the river Mohawk is precipitated 70 feet over a ledge of rocks. I had seen this cataract in company with my deceased literary

friend, Chas. B. Brown, in the year 1800. We next passed thro'
Waterford & Lansingburg & arrived at Troy on the east side of the
Hudson 6 miles above Albany. We have engaged lodgings for the night
at Titus's inn.

*July 16th.* Troy stands on an elevated bank of this great river & is laid
out with regularity, the streets are spacious & many of the dwellings are
large, brick is common. It is a place of business—some persons trading to
the extent of $150,000 annually. As the place is new, it makes a nice &
respectable appearance.

*July 17th.* Took our departure for Saratoga Springs, 30 miles distant,
in a two horse hack for which we paid $10 & found afterwards that
another party hired one with four horses to go from Albany, 6 miles
further, for $6. I note this as something to be rememberd in the future.

Two persons breakfasted with us whom we found very conversable &
intelligent, but did not know till afterwards that one of them was
Governor DeWitt Clinton & the other Gen. Stephen Van Rensselaer,
Patroon of Albany.

*July 18th.* A poor labouring man in this place has two pet ground hogs
called, throughout this country, woodchucks, which he suffers to run at
large. They have already laid waste his whole garden of vegetables,
sufficient to have supplied his family during the winter. It is another
instance of the same folly & mismanagement that so greatly enlarge the
pauper lists elsewhere.

It is too early in the season for this place to be much crowded & yet we
conjecture that 400 persons drank of the waters this morning. There are
five springs, some of them tonics, but that called Congress is strongly
cathartic & the most active I ever drank. Five or six tumblers full
produce a powerful effect. It is apparent that a large portion of the
visitors come to spend time, to feast & carouse, rather than for health or
because of disease.

Saratoga village contains from 50 to 60 houses & boarding can be had
from one to ten Dollars per week. As the springs are public property &
accessible to everybody, the poor & rich both can enjoy the benefit of
the waters.

Governor Clinton & Gen. Van Rensselaer arrived here today & I was
regularly introduced to them. Clinton is a stout, florid, handsome man
in the prime of life & a man of fine talents. His companion is slim made,
of mild gentle manners, much inferior in mental energy, past the wane

of years, but a most amiable excellent man of whom everybody speaks well. His humanity & charity are proverbial. He is very rich, possessing the major part of the county of Albany. His liberality induces him frequently to forgive years of rent to a poor deserving tenant. They are both very friendly & communicative & their information will doubtless prove serviceable in the further prosecution of our tour. They have as public commissioners been to visit the Northern canal, whence they are now returning.

*July 19th.* "How many glasses have you drunk today, Mr. Cope?" said Gov. Clinton, by 5 this morning. Six was the reply. "Why, Sir, I have drunk 12." Well, I should expect a governor to drink more than a common citizen.

N. Silsby, member of Congress from Salem, Mass., is among our company. He relates to me some anecdotes of my friend John Randolph which confirm the opinion I have for some time entertained respecting the diseased mind of that most singular & conspicuous statesman. Last spring, after the adjournment of Congress, he took passage in the steamboat from Baltimore to Norfolk. Observing a Frenchman in the cabin, he called his servant Jube & asked if he had not seen that man at the French Minister's at Washington? On being answered in the affirmative, he called to the Frenchman in a loud & angry tone & asked him how he dared to be there among gentlemen, telling him that if he did not instantly get on deck he would shoot him, pointing at him with a loaded gun which he had ordered Jube to hand him. The affrighted man withdrew, but after the company had dined, he quietly returned to the cabin & was eating at the table when Randolph, perceiving him, seized his gun & furiously ordered him to be gone or he would blow his brains out. Again the man obeyed. When arrived at Norfolk, however, he left the boat but Randolph, seating himself on the deck with his gun resting on his lap, was heard talking to himself thus, "He'll be here again & I'll then shoot him. Yes, he'll come bye & bye & I'll blow his brains out." The man however kept away & the affair ended.

Several other circumstances, equally indicative of a deranged mind, were mentioned of this extraordinary man, who still retains a seat in Congress where, last winter, he conducted in such manner as to alarm his friends & disgust all others. Can this be the effect of strong & indulged passions, rankling & cankering on disappointed ambition? Or are these the ripening growth, the natural product of some inherent effect or predisposition to mania? His poor interesting nephew, Jno. St.

George Randolph, was long under my care as a madman & even the Uncle himself may one day become the tenant of a hospital. What a melancholy instance of fallen greatness would such an example prove!

*July 20th*. Left Saratoga for Ballston & took lodging at Sans Souci. Ballston is 7 miles from Saratoga & may contain 50 or 60 dwellings.

*July 21st*. Were I to say that there have been at this place today from fifteen to twenty thousand visitors, it would appear extraordinary & yet of the fact there is little doubt. The occasion is to us a very melancholy one. A man named Bennet, in the prime & vigour of manhood has this day expiated his crimes, so far as respects this world, on the gallows. He had been convicted of murder & appears to be a most hardened, abandoned culprit, evincing nothing like contrition or repentance even under the jibbet. Till the hour of his execution he has been visited by any person who chose it & his time since condemnation appears to have been spent in obscene conversation, in drinking & abuse of courts, juries &c. Can this be the best mode of managing such cases? If society will persist in the infliction of death for crime, why thus suffer the criminal to be exposed to idle, vicious company? Why not, rather, by seclusion from the world, afford him the opportunity of reflection & repentance? There is something in my mind very affecting in the circumstance of forcing such a man into the awful presence of the Divinity. The legitimate end of punishment must be mainly the reformation of the criminal, but is this the way to reform him, or even to deter others from the commission of crime? More than half who attended this melancholy exhibition are women.

Hanging does not prevent crime. In England, where men are strung up by the dozen, it is notorious that robberies are perpetrated under the gallows. It is generally a rich harvest for the light fingered gentry. Reason & mercy weep together at this mockery of justice, this wanton shedding of human blood, this sport of mortal life. Pursue men with savage ferocity & you convert them into brutes. Treat them with kindness & they will improve, may even be grateful under the chastening rod. The defect in our penitentiary systems is not that they are too mild, but that the power of pardoning is too liberally exercised & that our jails are too crowded. Let punishment without the hope of pardon always follow crime. Let the convicts be strictly confined in separate solitary cells & these systems will have been more fairly tested than they ever yet have been.

*July 22d.* The Mayor of Albany, Phillip Van Rensselaer, brother of the Genl., is here. An honest knickerbocker, chatty & intelligent. I am quite pleased with him. He was acquainted with the celebrated Indian Chief called Col. Brant, of whom he related the following anecdote. The Col., it is known, had been liberally educated in England & was accustomed to what the world calls the best company. He was moreover a shrewd man. One of the Van Rensselaers' neighbours had taken a fancy to a very fine tract of land owned by Brant & in order to negotiate for it invited the Col. to a supper. The glass was briskly plied. The land jobber observed that his guest applied it to his lips without drinking, on which he said, "You are not fond of wine, Col. Brant?" "Oh yes," said the Col., "I like wine very well." "Why then do you not drink? I can assure you it is the best Madeira." "It is tolerable *Sherry*," said the Chief & quickly retired.

*July 28th.* At 9 this morning we went on board the passenger boat *Montezuma*, Captn. Brown, on the great canal finished from Utica to Montezuma, a distance of 96 mi. This boat is 75 feet in length, 12 beam & draws 20 inches water. Captn. B. has $18 per mo. & says that for weeks he has not had 3 hours regular sleep at one time. This is hard duty for such wages. The Boy who drives the horses has $10 per mo. Today he is to drive 50 mi. & must return tomorrow.

Our boat is towed by two horses attached to a line 110 feet long. Chains are not permitted, on account of their tearing away the banks. There is but one tow path & when two boats meet, the one going to market stops &, dropping her line, the other passes over it. Passenger boats pay 5 cts. a mile, country produce one cent pr. 100 pds., & dry goods 2 cts. The bridges over the canal, of which we are told there are 70 between Utica & Montezuma, are so contracted as to leave barely room for our boat, the abutments projecting too far into the canal.

Captn. B. is sick with the fever & ague & says all the lads in their employ on the canal—the one who now drives our horses excepted —have the same disorder. It is an unpleasant omen.

One of our company has amused himself with hooking bullfrogs, which are numerous & display themselves in great stile on the banks. We have had a mess of them for dinner & deem the flesh not inferior to that of a chicken. The banks of the canal are falling in some places, owing to their having been made too steep. This error, however, they appear to have corrected.

*July 29th.* We made no stop at Manlius, which we passed late at

night, just previous to which the Boy, getting asleep, fell from the horse
& luckily was not much injured, but it was so dark that the accident was
perceived only from the fright of the horses. There had been a heavy
storm of wind & rain, accompanied by thunder. The *Oneida Chief*,
another passage boat, bound to Utica, passed us some hours afterwards
& reported that she was near being destroyed by the falling trees—
indeed, the danger was considerable. About daylight this morning,
we arrived at the first locks, 3 in number; they descend together 27 ft. to
the west. Halted for half an hour at Syracuse, 61 mi. from Utica—a
village of 20 houses on the north side of the Canal.

We were much too crowded last night. Captn. B. says he can accommodate 10 or 12 passengers with comfort & does not wish more, whereas
there are 21 of us. The women occupied all the berths & the men spread
themselves on settees & on the floor & were said to have fared better
than their fair companions, who complain of having been annoyed by
vermin. Alfred, who slept on the floor, got up with one arm much
swollen & inflamed, apparently from the bite of some insect.

We reached Montezuma before twilight, 96 mi. from Utica & have
been 33 hours in coming that distance & therefore travelled at a rate less
than 3 mi. an hour. We had 4 meals on board & for these & passage paid
$4 each. It has been a listless, dull voyage—the novelty alone rendering
it tolerable. None of our company probably regret having taken it, but
none, I believe, would be willing to renew the trip.

*July 31st.* We stopped a short time at Batavia, 11 mi. further on our
way. It is a handsome Town of about 200 houses. Thence to Buffalo, 28.
All these towns are of recent growth & have arisen almost as by magic.
Ten years back, nearly all the country over which we have been coursing
these 2 days was a wilderness, the range of wild beasts & savage men. It
is capable of a dense population & New York is destined to become one
of the greatest trading communities in the world. With her vast territory, her inland navigation, her fertile soil & her superb seaport, she can
have but few rivals. From the Genessee westward, the produce has been
heretofore carried principally down the St. Lawrence to Montreal. But
that trade will be greatly checked, if not entirely counteracted, by the
Grand Western canal, now in a train of completion & the Northern
canal, nearly finished, to connect Lake Champlain & the Hudson. By
means of these & her more southern latitude & above all her free
government, she must cripple—if she does not annihilate—the trade of
the upper country from Montreal & Quebec, from the latter of which

places to sea, 400 mi. of a tedious & dangerous navigation is to be encountered, even when the fetters of winter are broken up in the St. Lawrence. She will doubtless, therefore, command the Lake trade & with it, the wealthy products of the immense—nay, almost boundless —regions watered by the numerous streams which bear them tribute. The mind is absolutely lost in the immensity of the object. Even Pennsylvania, yes, the riches of Pennsylvania, will be subject to her control & come in aid of her grandeur, power & influence.

*August 1st.* There are several small buildings in Buffalo over which are written in very large letters the words *Market*. They are substitutes for shambles & contain butcher's meat. At one of them we saw an elderly squaw driving a light bargain for six cents worth of Beef. She is the wife of the great Red Jacket & well smeared with grease and dirt. After making her purchase, she placed the meat in a basket containing other things & which was suspended over her shoulders by a leather strap passing round the forehead. In this way, it is said, these squaws will frequently carry home a stout deer, it having been shot by their husbands in the woods. She had a staff in her hand & was accompanied by a dog & two little girls. It was amusing to see the simple artifices practiced by this old woman to make the most of her money, putting the meat to her nose & then spurning it as if putrid & excessively offensive, it being at the same time perfectly sweet & fresh. Of the girls, one was her daughter & the other a white child. On pressing her to know how she became possessed of the latter, she made us understand that the child having been deprived of her mother when an infant, she had adopted & nurtured her as her own. We presented each of the girls with a small piece of silver. The Indian received hers with a fixed countenance & without the least expression of joy or gratitude, while the other gave vent to her pleasure in antic gambols & smiles of satisfaction. These characteristic traits were equally striking in the whole demeanor of the two girls. The one was shy & sullen & apparently unmoved by anything passing around. The other was sportive, animated, cheerful & observant. Neither can speak English & both wear Indian garbs.

*August 2d.* It commenced raining this morning & a storm raged on Lake Erie, the sombre wave & white cap blending together in alternate & every varying grandeur but, the wind shifting to N.W., the clouds dispersed & the day proved fine. After breakfast we took our departure from Buffalo & crossing the Niagara at Black Rock, 2 miles below the Town, entered the dominions of his Britannic Majesty.

The entire fall of the river from Lake Erie to Lake Ontario, a distance of 3.4 miles, is estimated at 375 feet including the Great Falls. The portage is about 8 miles. Doubtless there will be at some period a canal & lock navigation at this place. Darby, who has visited this country & who was employed for some years as a surveyor in Louisiana, estimates this great river to be three fourths of a mile wide and 50 feet deep on an average & that it discharges one half more water than the Mississippi. The Niagara, above the falls, is generally much wider. He says also that the Lakes contain more fresh water than is found on all the earth besides. However this may be, it serves in some measure to show how great must be the body of water precipitated over this unequalled cataract. Goat Island divides the sheet; on the U.S. side of this Island the perpendicular fall is 165 & on the Canada side, where much the largest body of water is projected, it is 150 feet.

*August 4th.* It has been said that a New Castle grindstone & a rat may be found in every portion of the known globe. To these may in time be added a Connecticut Tinman. One of these indefatigable travellers passed by this morning. He tells me he pays $40 a year in permission to carry his wares into all parts of the Canadas & 10 per cent duty on their value & that on payment of the like duty he can introduce any American fabric. From his own account he is not subjected to a very rigorous inspection.

Oxen are much in use in these parts & teams of three & four pair frequently pass our door.

This morning we have taken another & perhaps a farewell view of the falls from Table Rock. This rock approaches within a few feet of them & part of it, apparently about two feet thick, projects forward from the main mass by 12 or 15 feet & from which there is an uninterrupted view of the entire sheet and of the fearful abyss directly under the feet of the beholder. It is a hard slate stone & of such easy access that altho' sensible of a tremulous motion occasioned by the cataract, I felt perfectly secure standing on the very brink of the overhanging precipice & he who can stand here & witness the sublime spectacle before him, without a glow of fervid devotion towards that Almighty being by whom it was called into existence, must indeed be destitute of feeling.

*August 6th.* While at the falls I was much gratified to meet with Adam Hodgson, of the very respectable House of Rathbone, Hodgson & Co., Liverpool, & our correspondents at that place. He is a very intelligent, affable man & by his candour & liberal views reflects credit

on his country. He has put into my hands a small original memorandum book of the great Howard, written by himself. Howard was as remarkable for his piety as for his humility. As he was in the constant habit of abbreviating his words & even sentences, much of this little volume is unintelligible to me. The last leaf contains sentiments truly characteristic. They are believed to have been penned by him at Cherson, a few hours before he expired. The faithful servant of Howard died in the poor house at Liverpool some years after his master. He had retained this book in his possession & from him my friend Hodgson obtained it. The book concludes thus, "I hope the business I am engaged in is God's cause & is the promoting of his interest in the world. Then the more God does for me the more let me be zealous in his cause & my heart warmed with the love of God."

*August 7th.* Last night we entered the mouth of Genessee River, 85 miles from Fort Niagara by water. The Genessee at the landing place is about 300 feet broad & 20 deep. It moves sluggishly & is turbid. The land between it & the lake is marshy & unhealthy. To prevent the labour & expense of dragging heavy burdens up & down the steep bank they have constructed at the landing a railed way of heavy timber 369 feet in length & at the angle of 30 degrees. Two trucks or low carriages of four wheels each are employed: the descending one, being laden for the purpose, draws the other up. Large warehouses are erected at either extremity of the railed way for the reception of merchandize & are at present pretty well filled with flour, salt, potashes &c. in barrels. Alfred & myself were drawn up in one of these trucks, the descending one being heavily charged with salt & as it was probably purposely overloaded, we were drawn up with a velocity not quite agreeable to ourselves, but to the great amusement of the men employed. Our little carriage struck with such force against the upper warehouse that we were in no small danger of being thrown out. A short time after our flight, another company were precipitated from one of these carriages. One person had several limbs broken, another was badly bruised & a third killed on the spot. This melancholy event may put an end to these most unwarrantable tricks played on unwary visitors.

*August 9th.* This morning we find ourselves at Ogdensburg on the right bank of the Oswegatchie at its entrance in to the St. Lawrence. Judge Ford, who made some noise in the late war in consequence of his quarrel with Genl. Wilkinson, has his residence just without the Town in a fine looking house fronting the St. Lawrence. The Town itself contains from 80 to 100 houses. A large quantity of military stores were lodged here without being properly protected & were carried off by the British. There is a building in the place which serves for a court house, jail, school house & church. A criminal court is held but once a year & as none was held at the last regular term, one man now in confinement & believed innocent must await the coming round of another term before he can receive his trial. There is no yard to this building. The case of this man is therefore pitiable. It is an instance of oppression not I presume often met with in our country.

*August 10th.* The river shores are generally bold & exhibit few or no appearances of alluvial land & no mountains are in view until we arrive in the neighbourhood of Montreal. On our passage we saw numerous batteaux rowed by the Canadian voyageurs, a hardy race of men who never failed to exchange some coarse joke with our crew, in the French language. From the boisterous manner of these salutations, I sometimes apprehended a quarrel, but they always ended in good humoured vapouring. The rowers rise from their seats at every stroke, the weight of their body giving additional effect to the well directed oar. They never are seen with hats, but go either bare headed, or wear woolen caps in which red seems a favourite colour. Their song is proverbial. The oar beats to the tune & their boats are driven with a regularity & rapidity both pleasing & surprizing. I presume there are no better boatmen in the world. These songs are never sprightly, but amid the roaring & foaming of the wild rapids & the answering strokes of the quick moving oars, they have in them something most singularly romantic and touching. They are in French. One of them translated reads thus:

> Faintly as tolls the evening chime,
> Our voice keeps tune & our oar keeps time,
> Soon as the woods on shore look dim
> We'll sing our lonely parting hymn.
> Row, brothers, row, the stream runs fast,
> The rapids are near & the daylight past.
>
> Why should we yet our sail unfurl?
> There is not a breath the blue wave to curl.
> But when the wind slows off the shore
> Oh sweetly we'll rest our weary oar.
> Blow breezes blow, the stream runs fast
> The rapids are near & the daylight past.

Montreal was not lighted, but it was easy to perceive a Town totally differing from any of our own. The somber grey of the stone houses & of massy walls connected with them, the folding windows universally thrown open so as to display the economy of the interior, rude heavy furniture & French faces met the eye in all directions. We entered by the Recollet Suburbs & the streets presently became so narrow & gloomy that it had the semblance of our skulking by some back alley to our lodgings which, when at last we reached them, were found to be spacious & in high stile. We had arrived at the hotel called Mansion House.

*August 12th.* During yesterday & today we have visited most of the public buildings & have been in almost every street & lane in Montreal. In this tour we have been constantly attended by our eccentric friend Gibb, who appears to be familiar with almost everybody & everything worthy of notice in the place. He is one of the most wealthy benevolent & public spirited citizens, ever ready to succour distress & to patronize a good work. This excellent man nevertheless has high failings, but who is without them? His good properties entitle him to my esteem. I will therefore cast the mantle of charity over his errors. With his oddities I have a right to be merry. He introduces me to half the people we meet & the manner is peculiar to himself. "Mr. Gates, here is Mr. Cope from the States, a rich Yankee, come to look at we poor Canada Devils." "Mr. Morilson, this is my good friend Cope, come all the way from Philadelphia to see your pretty face."

There are no monasteries of monks or Friars in Montreal, but several Institutions which are superintended by about 120 nuns of different orders. They are the Hotel Dieu, Convent of Grey Sisters, Recollet convent & General Hospital. The black nuns have the care of sick & disabled poor. Their building was undergoing repairs and we did not go generally thro' it, tho' the rooms we saw are neatly kept & the patients seemed comfortably provided for. The Grey Nuns have charge of about 20 foundlings, four years old & under, as many very old women, mostly worn out persons of the class falsely called Ladies of Pleasure & 6 or 8 lunatics. The four apartments of the two former do credit to their keepers, but I was pained to see how miserably the latter are neglected. Their dank & contracted cells have neither light nor ventilation, save what enters through a small hole perhaps six inches square, cut in the door of each. The stench from these abodes of filth & wretchedness is extreme. The inmates appear, from the account we received, never to be taken out either for air or exercise, but are suffered to wear away their hopeless existence confined like wild beasts, in their gloomy dens. There is among them an interesting pretty girl of fifteen whose situation demanded & received our warmest sympathy. I do not wish, even in thought, to stand as the accuser of these high professing Nuns but cannot avoid the suspicion that they are more intent on counting over their beads at their senseless Ave Marias & in keeping clean the outside of the cup & platter (the apartments usually permitted to visitors) than in visiting these dungeons of the insane & administering relief to the forlorn indwellers. They are left to the care of an ignorant, dirty, one legged old veteran who appears to be stoically indifferent to the suffering of his prisoners & who, on my remonstrating with him on the cruelty of their treatment, shrugged his shoulders & gave us a look which seemed to say it was none of my business. He was otherwise civil enough, but too stupid to comprehend my recommendations for ameliorating, by either moral or physical means, the hard conditions of these poor outcasts from society & social intercourse.

There are in Montreal no wheel barrow porters, as with us, but boys are seen going about with dogs harnessed to small carts & dragging burdens of astonishing magnitude. Ashes for the soap boilers are exclusively collected by them. The dogs are not larger than those common in our streets. We could not help pitying them, as they crept along gasping & sweating under their heavy burdens.

The house of our friend Gibb, which is on the model of Philada. dwellings & two or three more, are the only brick buildings in the Town. In several of her other edifices, public & private, Montreal is assuming a more modern stile of architecture & they form a striking contrast with their antiquated neighbours. Stone is the universal material used in building, with the exceptions mentioned. The principal covering is tin, sheet iron is not uncommon, but I have not seen a wood or shingle roof in the place.

*August 13th.* The Host is carried in Montreal—as in Catholic Europe—& when a Priest visits the sick, four men carry a Calico Canopy over his head. In one corner of Notre Dame, we observed two of the Grey Sisters very busy with their needles in one of these miraculous canopies. These Priests are a calculating, shrewd set. The Bells of the Cathedral are ringing from early dawn all night, with little intermission—for vespers, high mass, some person sick or just expired, for funerals, births, christenings & prayers, for those that are in Purgatory waiting the aid of these kind Doctors to get out. For the ringing, on

most of these occasions, a charge is made & made, too, in such manner as to be a heavy tax on the vanity or piety of their parishoners. A single bell is charged moderately, 2 much more than double, but when the whole 4, of which number the peal consists, are rung, then one hundred Dollars must be paid to them.

We find also that they are not retail, but wholesale traders. Having been invited to a funeral, we attended at the appointed hour at Notre Dame. A number of large, wax candles were burning round the altar, before which the officiating & two other Priests were seen, in white robes, while a dozen boys in the same attire, each with a taper or crucifix in hand, danced around it, as to a minuet. High mass being said, the actors advanced to three coffins, previously placed in the great aisle. They were covered with black velvet & embroidery. Incense was strewn over & about them. They were elevated on the shoulders of men &, preceded by the Priests & boys, carrying their crucifixes & candles, the procession moved out of the Cathedral & were joined in the street by a crowd of other people who followed to the place of interment. Being struck with the apparent ease with which the coffins were carried, we were informed that they were empty, the bodies of the deceased having been previously laid in the earth, so that all this mummery was performed in vacant shew.

*August 14th.* Accompanied by our friend Gibb, Edward Clarke & some others, we set out on a visit to the Indian village of Canghnewago, which means, as explained by the interpreter, the people of the rapids. The village is laid out with some order, the houses are principally stone & two stores. There are between 150 & 200 of these dwellings. The windows are glazed & the interior arrangements comfortable. The men, two old chiefs excepted, were absent. The women & children are cheerful, healthy & well clad. One of these chiefs, called Capn. Thomas, invited us into his house. He was inquisitive to know where I came from & on being told, said he had once been in Philada. when a great sickness prevailed & that he saw the dead thrown into a common grave. This was probably in the year 1793. He remembered the name of Penn & spoke of our great founder in language honourable of his memory. As these people are of the Mohawk nation, they had no possessions in Pennsyla. It is probable therefore that Wm. Penn's reputation for justice & good faith extended to nations of savages far beyond the limits of those with whom he had direct intercourse. Thro' the carelessness of one of their people, who slept in the woods & kindled a fire to defend himself from wild beasts, a fire was communicated to the trees, which has been burning for some weeks & is now raging with great fury, threatening in its progress their entire settlement. Today it has approached so near that it is devouring their corn, hay & growing vegetables & is within less than a mile of the village.

Some of the men are engaged in attempts to arrest the fire, but we fear, from the great extent, their efforts will prove fruitless. One woman appears greatly distressed, but the rest view the threatening calamity with perfect sang froid. All wear leggins, generally a blue shoud & throw a blanket or piece of cloth over their shoulders. The girls are generally bare headed, but when they go abroad are sometimes covered with white fur hats decorated with bands of silver or gold lace. Ear rings & breast plates are rarely dispensed with. One quite pretty girl of 18 is amusing herself in the river, swimming about & shaking her long black locks like another mermaid. She is apparently not at all discomposed by our presence but throws her fine limbs about with much agility. Her body is partially covered with a calico robe. These Indians possess a tract two leagues on the river & three in depth, a very small part of which is under tillage. They possess cows, horses, hogs & poultry & live very well. Altho' they have made some progress in civilization, they have yet much to learn. The use of that bane of their species, ardent spirits, is I fear too common among them. The squaws are not unfrequently seen in the market at Montreal with poultry, eggs, vegetables & moccasins wrought by themselves for sale. I observed some of them take out their snuff box & whip a pinch into their nose with as much grace & comfort as could be expected of their fairer sisters. Having finished our visit we recrossed the St. Lawrence as we came & returned to Montreal on the turnpike thro' the tanneries—our eyes dazzled with a bright sun beating on the tin roofs & church spires.

*August 15th.* Earl Dalhousie, Gov. General of the Canadas, arrived here yesterday, on his way to the upper Province, where he is going to inspect the public works on the Ottowa.

The Ottawa, or Grande Riviere, has its source in Lake Huron, & running in an eastwardly direction, empties into the St. Lawrence by several outlets, forming the Islands of Jesus & Montreal. A fine tract of country intervenes which it is the policy of this Government to colonize as rapidly as possible. The lands designated for settlement are previously surveyed into lots, in every seven of which one is reserved to the use of the Government & another for the Episcopal Clergy & this rule, we are informed, is extended to all the recent settlements in the Canadas—the Church lands being free from all taxation, even for making or repairing roads. The Government has doubtless its policy in this measure—perhaps to give to the Episcopalians an ultimate preponderating influence over the Catholics—but, whatever the policy may be, the thing itself cannot fail to produce discontent. This favoured Sect, thus unequally enriched, must excite the envy & jealousy of others—& this country seems destined to become the fruitful theatre of much internal contention.

*August 17th.* About 9 last night we went on board the steamboat *Malstrum* commanded by Capt. McLane for Quebec.

We procured an accession to our passengers at Three Rivers, among them is a son of Bouchet the topographer, who possesses all the vivacity of a true born Frenchman, with gab enough to make himself ridiculous & ignorance enough to make himself pitied. He was curious to know where I came from & on being informed, he replied, "Aye, aye, Pennsylvania. I know very well—Pennsylva. County joins on Lake Ontario." This knowing youth of 25 is, we are told, assistant surveyor to his father.

Perceiving a disconsolate German on board, I entered into conversation with him. He seemed delighted to meet with a person who could speak to him in his own language & mentioned himself to be one of a number of his own countrymen who had been sent out by the British Government to form a settlement in a wilderness SE of Quebec.

*August 19th.* The river water at Quebec is fresh & is drawn up in carts for the use of the inhabitants. Salt water is not perceived until about 30 miles below the City, whence to the gulf there is still a distance of 370 miles.

Everything here, as at Montreal, gives us the idea of a Catholic country & so common is the French language that even in the English families which we visit, the parents, children & domestics use it familiarly towards each other. I had visited the market place before breakfast. It is held in an open space half the size of one of our squares, a small building being erected on one side of it for the butchers, in which there was some poor beef & veal, better mutton & the entire carcass of a large hog, tho' the weather is very warm. The open space was occupied by carts, with avenues between them to pass thro'.

*August 20th.* In the course of our morning's perambulation, we unwittingly attempted to pass a guard house into forbidden ground. A sentinel stepping from his companions ordered us, in broken English, to return, unless we could produce a passport. Perceiving them to be Germans, I accosted them in that language. Their eyes sparkled with joy, they looked at me & at each other as if doubting their senses. All difficulty was removed & we might have passed where we pleased.

*August 21st.* The principal part of this day has been taken up in perambulating the environs & places in the City not previously examined.

It was my original intention to pursue a southern course across the country, from Quebec to Boston, but I find on enquiry that the only road in that direction is the path cut by Gen. Arnold when, during the Revolutionary War, he effected his march through the wilderness to fall on this City by surprize. This path can be travelled only by horseback and doubts are expressed whether it would prove practicable even in that manner. I therefore abandoned my purpose & determined to return to Montreal.

*August 24th.* We this day took our departure from Montreal. At 10 in the morning, accompanied by B. Gibb & Ed. Clarke, we repaired on board the steamboat *Montreal* for LaPrairie—their kindness having induced them to see us thus far on our return. We did not arrive at that village till near 2 altho' the distance is but 9 miles & the engine is a 30 horse power. Most of the way we ran against the current & in one place among the rocks we contended nearly half an hour against the violence of the stream without gaining an inch. Sometimes we advanced & were again forced back & so doubtful was the strife that some of the passengers apprehended we should either be wrecked or forced back to Montreal. At this spot an anchor & buoy were permanently fixed with a long line swimming from them. This line was the length seized by the crew but, by some unexplained accident, it became entangled with one of the wheels & the boat was driven so rapidly towards the rocks that several gave themselves up for lost. Much confusion prevailed when the Captain, by great presence of mind, seized an axe & in a single dexterous blow cut the rope. The boat, at that time within two yards of the breakers, swung round & we escaped. Scarcely had we recovered from this alarm, when it was announced that Lord Dalhousie was descending rapidly towards us. An elegant bark canoe, manned by 16 oars & bearing his flag, approached. All rushed forward to see his Lordship. Preparations were hastily made to salute him & for that purpose the powder canister, containing 6 or 8 pounds, was brought out to load the swivel. The passengers, unconscious of this intention, had surrounded the gun in a cluster. The crowd was considerable. The man who brought the canister ran in among us, elbowing his way & tearing off the lid, peeped into the vessel, with a lighted pipe in his mouth. The Captain stood aghast, the colour forsook his cheeks & for a moment he seemed utterly appalled. With one arm he seized the canister & with the other the collar of the thoughtless man & he separated them & thus probably prevented the destruction of the whole company. In the midst of the uproar & confusion the canoe passed swiftly by, but the Governor was not on board, having landed with his suite at Lachine to avoid the danger of these rapids. To have been twice preserved from death within so short a space of time warmed my heart with gratitude to the Preserver of Men.

We have found house flies more abundant in Canada than we have ever known them in Pennsylvania, notwithstanding their tyrants the spiders, especially at our inn, are also very numerous, but we cannot say of them as Churchill did of their kindred tribes in Scotland, "Here cobwebs spread of more than common size, and half starved spiders preyed on half starved flies." For both appear full fed & riot in luxury.

*August 25th.* We were gratified on rising this morning to meet with our friends Jacob Harvey of Ireland and Jn. Beaumont of England. They arrived late in the night & we are to have the pleasure of their company on Lake Champlain. At 8 we went on board the steamboat *Congress*, Capt. Sherman.

When the boat was about departing from St. John's, a woman with an infant of 6 or 8 months old came on board as if to take passage. Alleging that she had forgotten something of importance, she suddenly placed the child in the arms of an Irish girl, newly arrived in the country & to whom she was an entire stranger & saying she would immediately return ran into the Town. She did not however reappear, the boat put off & the poor girl was left in possession of the legacy. It is a sportive little innocent & while its smiles & gambols cannot but amuse its foster mother, the girl—who is about 19—is occasionally much distressed & weeps bitterly as not knowing what to do with her charge. If the mother designed this as a trick, she must be an abandoned wretch, if not, she must be greatly distressed. I could not part with the babe without concern for its future destiny; we made a present of money to the infant's foster mother.

It is often amusing & sometimes disgusting to see the airs which are assumed at public houses. The lordly petulant cry of waiter do this & waiter bring me that, so vociferously & captiously repeated by certain consequential personages, serves to remind us of the facetious Baltimorian, on a like occasion. A company of these fastidious and effeminate gentry had worn out his patience by their constant cries of waiter here & waiter there when, jumping up, he roared out lustily, "Waiter, bring me a cool chair."

Two stages are to leave this morning for Boston at 3 tomorrow morning; one by the way of Montpelier, the present seat of Government, the other via Middlebury, which we are advised is the pleasantest route.

*August 27th.* It is painful to perceive, by the N. York papers found at our inn, that the fever has become more alarming in Philada. Among others we perceived that our neighbour Abm. Barker has died of it. These circumstances cause us to be very desirous to hear more direct from home, which we do not expect to do until we reach Boston. This being the first day of the week, we are not permitted to travel. To gratify these puritans, we must therefore remain cooped up in an uncomfortable tavern whose landlord is the gaoler of the place, tho' residing at a distance from that building & not be at liberty peaceably to pursue our journey to the annoyance of no one. A tavern must afford to a traveller more opportunities for vicious indulgence than are to be found in the public highway but, no matter, we must

> Keep up appearances, there lies the test
> The world will give us credit for the rest.

Middlebury is a pleasant village in a fruitful country. It lies on both sides of the Otter & may contain about 200 houses. The ground is agreeably hilly. The Green Mountains are within 4 miles in full view on the NE. There are two colleges here, a cotton factory & a mill for sawing marble, in which they carry on a considerable inland trade.

*August 28th.* Today being at liberty to move on, we engaged the same carriage in which we arrived to carry us to Rutland.

*September 1st.* Since leaving Rutland, we have paid our stage hire about every 17 miles—these good folks adopting the old maxim that short reckonings make long friends. The practice is for every driver to furnish his own team & carriage & to receive pay for the distance he

drives. They are universally well informed, respectable men & therefore fit companions for their passengers, to whom they are ever civil, preserving at the same time a proper degree of self respect. They are altogether different from the vulgar, ignorant, drunken, swearing set we meet with in the middle & southern states.

We passed thro' Concord & Lexington, both celebrated in the annals of the American Revolution. The stone houses & barracks, in the former, where the munitions of the war were deposited—respecting which one of the earliest squabbles took place—have been substituted by a row of respectable dwellings. At Lexington a monument has been erected to commemorate the first shedding of blood between the conflicting parties. As we passed by it, a person was engaged in giving it some repairs.

Massachusetts has made very liberal appropriations for the education of her children, rich & poor. There are no fewer than thirty six hundred public schools in the Commonwealth. Every taxable inhabitant must contribute to their support & can save nothing by not sending his children to them, for whether he send or keep his children at home, he must equally pay. The advantage of this system has been tested by experience & is evinced by the superior intelligence & good moral habits of her Citizens.

In the course of our ride today, we noticed several plantations of sunflowers, regularly set out in hills, in the manner of Indian corn. The oil extracted from the seed has become an article of commerce & is said to be nothing inferior to the best oil of Olives. If this be the fact, the cultivation being very simple, it may prove profitable & should be encouraged.

Having crossed the upper bridge over the river Charles, we found ourselves in the great Gotham, the ancient city of Boston itself & were presently among its towering spires, its substantial & well arranged warehouses, its well stored shops & its crooked, winding, busy streets. We took lodgings at Stone's boarding house in School Street, opposite Stone Cathedral.

*September 2d.* We have already met with many polite & friendly attentions, especially from Edmund Dwight & his amiable wife, who formed part of our company from Ogdensburg to Montreal & from his kinsman & partner Wm. Dwight. The latter conducted us to the several parts of the city which are more immediately worthy of the notice of strangers. The reading room of the merchants is the best arranged of anything of the kind we have yet seen. Newspapers from all parts of the continent are arranged in files at desks, each having its appropriate place whence it must not be removed, so that one hundred persons may read without interfering with each other. Arrivals & clearances from all parts of the commercial world & particularly in America, are recorded. The whole forms a mass of daily intelligence highly useful to the man of business.

*September 3d.* By a letter from son Henry, as well as by the public prints, it appears that altho' the fever has somewhat abated, there still exists cause of alarm in Philada.

After breakfast we visited the Asylum for the Insane recently erected in Charleston near Bunker Hill. The situation is in every respect eligible, for air, prospect & accommodation & it is not a little gratifying to perceive the attention which the benevolent inhabitants of Boston have thus evinced to the personal convenience of the patients. About 26 acres belong to the institution.

Next to the State house is a respectable stone mansion which, during the Revolution, was the residence of the celebrated John Hancock, Pres. of Congress. The Mall—or Common, as it is also called—is surrounded with splendid private houses & there is more appearance of opulence and Princely stile in Boston than in any other City on the North American continent. The inequality of the ground on which the City stands, the various twinings of the streets, the different materials used and opposite taste displayed in the formation of their buildings, present to the eye of a stranger a continued novelty. They have in use a species of light coloured granite which, for closeness of texture & beauty of appearance, can scarcely be excelled by any of the species.

The propensity to erect large magnificent dwellings in Boston has been carried to an excess, not very well according with the general frugality & prudence of this calculating, cautious people. Most of the great dwellings, erected in former years, are now occupied as boarding houses—the children of the original Proprietors having, in most cases, been unable to hold them. But this folly of building costly houses is not exclusively confined to Boston. We have seen too many instances of the like indiscretion among ourselves. Children are often ruined by it. In the United States, where property is so evanescent, it generally happens that the parent cannot leave all his offspring the means of supporting the luxury & extravagance consequent on these costly establishments. The education of the children, moreover, very generally unfits them for

business. The consequences must be ruinous, not only to their Estates but, frequently, and almost certainly, to their morals. The Sheriff and the mad house often close the scenes of the drama.

I should probably give offense were I publicly to utter the sentiment, & yet I have no doubt of the truth of the assertion that the merchants of Boston are better educated, possess more knowledge & cultivate a better taste for science & letters than the men of business in Philadelphia. They are also, as a necessary consequence, men of polished manner—& we spend our time agreeably & instructively among them.

*September 4th.* This morning we rode over to Lynn, probably the greatest shoe shop in the world. It being the 1st of the week, the people were not at work. Our main object was to attend Friends meeting.

From Lynn we went to Salem, where we dined. There are about 60 families of Friends in this commercial entrepot. Some of the private houses are very superb & many others, very mean. The ground plot is flat & like neighbouring country, hilly. The harbour is spacious & secure, the principal wharf projects upwards of 2000 feet into it & contains many wooden, but not one fireproof store. It nevertheless carries on an extensive trade, particularly beyond the Cape of Good Hope & Cape Horne. The present population is between 10 & 12 thousand. In the sanguinary reign of the wizards & witches, Salem took the lead & many curious specimens of the Blue Laws of those days are preserved among its archives.

*September 5th.* The weather continuing to favour our views, we this day made another excursion into the neighbourhood, passing thro' Cambridge, Water Town, Waltham, Newton, Brighton & Brookline & returning thro' Dorchester & Roxbury to Boston.

The great cattle shows are held in Brighton & occur next month. Besides these annual exhibitions, fairs are held here weekly. Today there is one & accordingly several hundred head of cattle, some sheep & some hogs are exposed for sale & the village is thronged with butchers, drovers, graziers & farmers.

*September 6th.* When we were at Walpole waiting for the stage, amid the rattle of drums & din of a noisy multitude, a man entered our apartment whose appearance attracted my attention. His arms were folded, his countenance fixed & melancholy, his step wavering, his attitude a little inclined & his manner timid & distant. He bowed respectfully as he entered & then walked the floor, seemingly absorbed in his own reflections. There was nothing wild or extravagant in his motions, but discontent lay heavily on his brow. After some minutes, I made an essay to draw the stranger into conversation. He looked as if surprized that I should notice him & answered my enquiries with modest intelligence. At length I appeared to gain his confidence. He asked which way we were travelling & on being informed said, "I will go with you to Boston." We had not been long seated together in the stage when he began to give me some account of the state of his mind. I spoke to him the language of consolation, for by this time my feelings were more warmly excited towards him. He listened with attention & finally expressed his fixed determination to consider the present as a new era in his life & henceforth to cast off repining & to indulge brighter hopes. I commended this awakened mind, the necessity of a constant depen- dence on that Almighty Power without whose approbation & blessings our best resolutions & efforts are in vain. From this time he became more cheerful & I found him an agreeable companion. I took lodgings in Boston at his request in the same house with him, tho' my intentions had been otherwise. On enquiry I soon learned that I had not been mistaken in the character of the man. He is much respected as an upright pious citizen, a good husband & parent & a steadfast friend. His name is Aron Dean. He has a wife & three daughters whom he loves, in Charleston, N.H. on the Connecticut, a few miles above Walpole, where he resides in the possession of a considerable estate. He has been our constant companion, ever since we arrived in Boston & appears uneasy whenever I am absent from him, tho' it be for a few minutes. He tells me that he left home after several attempts, as often abandoned, at the pressing solicitations of his wife, who urged him to travel & that my notice of him at Walpole had determined him to accompany us to Boston. His friends here remark with satisfaction the improved state of his spirits & the equanimity of his mind.

My friend Dean proposing another excursion into the country, I readily consented. We crossed over to South Boston, whose locality is sufficiently indicated by its name. An inlet divides it from the City. Over this inlet there is a bridge of 1000 feet in length. This place has been the theatre of much unprofitable speculation. A company of schemers purchased the ground & endeavored to make it the site of a trading community but, the plan not succeeding, the parties suffered heavily by the attempt. We next visited Dorchester Heights, on which Genl. Washington was so long encamped, in the early stages of the

Revolution, & passing the village of Dorchester, proceeded to the plains & pond of Jamaica.

We traversed several excellent turnpikes which lead from the Metropolis to different parts of the State. One of them passes over a pond & was formed by filling in with gravel; after having been used for several days, it suddenly sunk & disappeared with 12 feet of water covering the spot. This took place in the night & no further injury was sustained. A wag in the neighbourhood advertized that the road had absconded & offered a reward to any person who would apprehend and bring it back.

In the course of this ride, D. gave me voluntarily the history of his life, which has not been void of interesting incident. He unburdened his heart fully & freely & concluded by saying, "You now know more of me than any other man living." He told me I was the first member of our Society with whom he had ever exchanged five words.

*September 7th.* This morning early, we were seated in the stage for New Bedford. Our friend Dean had kept us up very late last night and then, with tears in his eyes, took an affectionate & I supposed final farewell. When I arose at 4 this morning I found him up to see us off. He held me long by the hand & then exclaimed with much emotion, amid sobs & tears, "Oh, Mr. Cope, I shall never see you again, I shall never see you again, but I shall never forget you." It was not possible to remain unmoved in a scene like this. The stage was waiting for me at the door. I hurried into it. The dim light of the opening day prevented my perturbation from being observed by the passengers. We were soon out of Boston & I had parted with poor Dean forever.

*September 11th.* A Frenchman who took his residence in Burlington, N.J., made a practice of accosting every man he met with, "How do you do, Mr. Smith?" thinking that in 9 times out of 10 he would be right. Were he to visit Nantucket he might apply his rule to the Coffins. A captain of that name accompanied us to Sciasconset. He tells the following story,—that, having been brought to by a British frigate, the boarding officer enquired his name & received for answer, "My name is Nehemiah Coffin." "And what's yours?" said the officer to his mate, "Eleazar Coffin." "And yours?" to one of the men, "Amasa Coffin." "You are a death-like set," said the Englishman, "and you may as well proceed, for I want nothing more to do with you." The first names of these people are generally Scriptural, or such as are uncommon with us. Another of their captains, whom I very well knew, being on a trading voyage, entered a Spanish port. The officer of the customs, putting the

Bible into his hands to swear him, demanded his name. "Mayhew Folger," was the reply. "What *Saint's* that?" "I don't know," said the Capt., "some *Devilish* Saint or other."

An anonymous poet has described the leading families in the following terms & the description is said to be correct.

> The Rays & Russells, Coopers are,
> The knowing Folgers, *lazy*.
> The *learned* Colemans, very rare,
> And *scarce* an honest Hussey.
> The Coffins shifty, fractious, loud,
> The silent Gardners, plotting,
> The Mitchells good, the Barkers proud,
> And Maceys eat the pudding.

There is no militia in Nantucket and consequently no training or muster days, so destructive of the morals of our youth & oppressive to men who are conscientiously scrupulous of bearing arms. The Island constitues one of the counties of Massachusetts, whose mild & judicious laws permit this indulgence. The inhabitants, on account of their peculiar and exposed situation, were permitted to remain neutral during the Revolutionary War & were afterwards admitted into the Union.

*September 13th.* In the evening we took tea with Gilbert Coffin. These Nantucket men understand their interest too well to spend their efforts in unprofitable attempts to cultivate a barren soil, or in forcing manufactures. They know it to comport with the best economy to purchase what they want & to confine themselves to the more certain & lucrative pursuit of the whale. Some of our indiscreet advocates for prematurely forcing manufactures on the country might derive some useful hints from their example.

*September 14th.* The fury of the equinoxial gale being spent, we had allotted this day for our return to N. Bedford. The wind proving adverse, we are necessarily delayed & yet our time passes so agreeably among these very hospitable Islanders that we scarcely regret the disappointment.

*September 15th.* A summons at 5 this morning from Captain Burdett apprized us of a favourable wind. We took a hasty & affectionate leave of our kind friends Mattw. & Eliz. Barnett & their two amiable daughters, Lydia & Abigail, from whom we had received the most hospitable reception.

The inhabitants of Nantucket possess strong local attachments, notwithstanding the sterility & dreary aspect of the "Little Isle" and live in great harmony with each other. About 25 years ago this good understanding was greatly interrupted by the robbery of one of their banks of all its specie, just as it was commencing operations. Twenty one thousand Dollars were carried away in the night, under circumstances which induced a strong suspicion that some of the principal inhabitants were concerned in the plot. Altho' the accused were on trial acquitted, we find that many respectable people do not believe in their innocency.

A fleet of 20 sail came out with us & as the wind was light, they were for some hours in view, tho' all bound to different quarters & dispersing themselves in various directions. Three ran aground on Bran Bar, off the mouth of the harbour & would have to await the swelling of another tide to get off. In this small fleet were 2 schooners fitted out to catch the Humpback whale in the neighbouring seas.

Having run down Martha's Vineyard, a lofty sail was espied on our larbord quarter, coming round Gay Head. It was but a mere speck on the distant horizon. The glass being resorted to, this speck was pronounced to be a Ship & as all these people take a lively interest in such an event, the Captain & his two men were presently in close confab about her & various were the conjectures as to her character. The most perfect freedom & interchange of opinion prevailed among them & except that occasionally we heard the title of Captain given to one of them we might have been puzzled to know which was in command.

We sailed thro' the narrow and rocky passage of Wood's Hole, at a rate of which Captain B. said was 20 knots an hour, having a stiff breeze in our favour & a furious current. As the wind had been light the fine part of the day, night came on before we arrived at N. Bedford. We were again received under the hospitable roof of our friend, Saml. Rodman.

*September 17th.* Having hired a neat Coachee to carry us to Howland's Ferry, a distance of 18 miles, we took our departure at 12 this morning, expecting to meet at that place the stage from Taunton to Newport.

An arm of the sea about 1800 feet wide divides Howland's from Rhode Island proper. Over this arm, there is a most uncommon bridge. The water is 60 feet deep. Into this, large stones are thrown, which spread 150 feet at the base & pile up until they terminate at the surface in a carriage way 30 feet broad. That part which is above the water is formed of regular masonry. An opening is left in the center for vessels to pass through. The bridge cost $100,000. The hurricane & swell of Sept. 1815, which for its unparalleled fury & the vast destruction of property which it occasioned, will long be remembered & deplored all along this seaboard; it washed round the Rhode Island abutment & overthrew some of the wall. The damage has been so effectually repaired that people now think the bridge may henceforth defy the winds & the waves. When Gen. Sullivan made his perilous retreat from the British during the Revolutionary War, he crossed with his army at this place. No bridge, however, was there at that period.

We arrived at Newport before sun set, 13 miles from Howland's, which is the greatest length of the Island, N & South. It is 4 miles broad & highly esteemed for the salubrity of its air, having long been the summer retreat of valetudinarians. Took lodgings at the Widow Duprey's near the State House.

*September 18th.* Newport has for some time been on the decline. The census just taken is 900 less than that of 1810, which in the United States is a very unusual circumstance. Previously to the Revolution, Newport owned more shipping than N. York. The disturbances of those times drove away her capitalists. Commerce, a coy, unstable dame, sought & obtained new channels for the exercise of her empire & disdained ever to return. The men of wealth, having acquired their fortunes under the mild sway of the Mother Country, were inimical to a contest, which to them appeared to portend utter ruin to the revolters. They miscalculated, but their ancient attachments rendered them objects of jealousy & persecution to a new race who sprang up around them. Men of little character & less property, however, like the scum of a boiling vessel, soon rose to the top while the more solid materials sunk to the bottom. The rich inhabitants, the merchants of wealth, were compelled to fly & the intolerance of the party in power, blinded by their passions, even after the storm had subsided, outlawed these & barred their return. Newport soon dwindled under this unwise policy and most probably will never revive unless the present scheme of colonizing it with the German Jews, on whose behalf Grand Island in the Niagara River had been asked, should succeed. The present inhabitants amount to about 8000.

*September 19th.* We had engaged our passages in a neat little packet, to sail at 9 this morning for Providence, but the Captn. called at 9 to say that wind & tide being ahead, we should have a tedious passage & be all night on board. Supposing that would not be our wish, he thought it his duty to apprize us in time to engage a seat in the stage. This man's name is Sangley. We have not often met with an instance of more disinterested kindness. To add to the weight of obligation, he went to the stage office for us & sent the carriage to our door. It may however be remarked that the custom, in the Eastern states, is not only to call for passengers but, on entering a Town, to deliver them at their respective lodgings. At 10 we were seated & retracing our steps to within 2 miles of Howland's, crossed the same stream in a boat & arrived to dinner at Bristol, 15 miles from Newport.

Four miles further on in a still northwardly direction, we passed thro' the pleasant village of Warren. It contains about ⅔ the number of inhabitants of Bristol. It is also a Seaport. We arrived at Providence an hour before sun set & took lodgings in the upper part of the City, as the fever prevailed to a slight degree on the water side. Providence is 30 miles from Newport & at the head of navigation on the beautiful Narragansett Bay. This we had on our left all day & generally in view. We passed a fruitful, handsome country most of the distance.

*September 20th.* At Chapotin's, where we lodged, we met our townsman David Brown, who accompanied us this morning on a visit to the cotton factories on Pawtucket at north Providence. This creek divides the two States of Massachusetts & Rhode Island. There are in all the factories about 10,000 spindles now in use. One of these factories has been 30 years in operation & is the oldest in the United States. None of them will compare with the Waltham establishment. Great attention is paid to economy & the wares are cheap & good.

Our temporary abode is at Wilkinson's Inn, a respectable house. Here we dined & supped with one bishop, two pastors, two lawyers, one deacon & one colonel, assembled as an arbitration between an Episcopal clergyman & his congregation of this village.

The disputants are also assisted by a limb of the Law. The Clergyman has already been displaced & they are now trying him on a charge of defamation for that he, the said Divine, not having the fear of God before him, but instigated by the Devil, did falsely, maliciously & with malice prepense circulate an evil report of a certain Doctr. Black & a certain Lady, not a black, in manner & form following—that is to say, that on a certain occasion, at a wedding, when the Gentlemen present kissed the Ladies present, it was observed that when it came, in course, for the said Doctr. Black then & there to kiss the said maiden Lady, he did not kiss her, as of ancient rite & usage he was bound to do, on her lips but merely smacked—or seemed to smack—a buss on her cheek. This grave Court had been employed all day on this & other serious charges & left us after supper to continue their sittings.

*September 21st.* The court did not close until three this morning. They have agreed, but as yet do not promulgate their decision. The accused, from what has leaked out, had best make a precipitate retreat, or besides suffering the anathema of this solemn tribunal, he may have to bear the scorn and front the brunt of more than a single defamed belle. We breakfasted with Saml. Slater, an Englishman by birth, who has accumulated a large Estate as a manufacturer of Cotton—being the first who commenced it in this country. His cook & Coachman ate at the same table with us. Samuel's wife, thinking perhaps that an apology might be due, stated it to be the custom of the place for servants to eat with their employers. She added that she should be glad to have a negro boy to wait on table, as their white menials would consider it a degradation to perform that office, or not to be invited to the same table with themselves. We rode to Pawtucket in a Hack, but Saml. was so kind as to send us back to Providence in his own Coachee, driven by the same man who had sat at our table.

*September 22d.* We took our departure this morning at 11, in the stage for Norwich, Connecticut & arrived there after night under the favour of a bright moon. That portion of the country which lies within the State of R. Island is hilly, stony, sandy, gravelly & poor. After entering Connecticut, the soil became much better, though equally hilly & stony. The three staple commodities of Connecticut are said to be onions, girls & geese & to this triumvirate might be added, stones. I remember when in 1800 travelling over a part of the State with my literary friend, C.B. Brown, that an inhabitant pleasantly said, "Look here, at the fruitfulness of our soil, where even the stones produce," pointing to a tree which had taken root in a fissure of a rock. "Why aye," said another, "they have nothing else to grow out of."

*September 25th.* Having made good speed last night, we find ourselves by peep o'day abreast N. York. It is agreeable enough to be 85 miles nearer home than we were last evening at N. Haven. I regret, notwithstanding, to have lost a view of the scenery on that part of the sound.

That inscrutable disease, the influenza, prevails in N. York & from

what we learn, in various other places. From Philada. the accounts are more favourable, as the fever has nearly disappeared.

*September 27th.* By 12 at noon we were in the steamboat *Olive Branch* for N. Brunswick. Having had a pleasant run to Amboy, the Captn. persuaded the passengers that the stages designed to carry them from Brunswick had come to Amboy & that the boat could proceed no further. Great haste was made to turn all on shore. That effected, the *Olive Branch* put forthwith about & was presently out of hail. Not a carriage had been provided for the 100 passengers. The fellow had taken care to get paid the entire fare to Philada. & we were left, with our baggage, to get on as well as we could. I had seldom met with a more impudent or provoking trick, but complaint could do no good. We therefore picked up our trunks & bore them to the nearest inn, prepared to take comfort from the reflection that better men had sometimes fared worse. About 50 persons procured country waggons & escaped from the Town. We employed ourselves in rambling about, having dispatched a lad to procure a carriage from N. Brunswick. We were *cast ashore* about 3 & at 7 called for a cup of tea in company with 4 others. Unluckily the landlord was *just out* of milk & *just out* of bread too & to mend the matter, added that the Baker was drunk & no bread could therefore be obtained. It was night before our carriage arrived. We halted a short time at N. Brunswick &, continuing on, reached Trenton, between 1 & 2 in the morning of the 28th.

*September 28th.* We were called up at 4 to proceed. At Bristol we left the stage & crossing over to Burlington, were in season to breakfast with our relatives P.B. & wife. Here we learned that my Mary was to be this day in Trenton, having during my absence placed our daughter E. at school. Leaving Alfred at Burlington, I mounted a nag & by one had the satisfaction to meet wife & daughter & son William at I. Newbold's in Trenton.

*October 2d.* Having spent some days among our friends in N. Jersey, we this day returned to Philada. in the steamboat from Burlington. Wirt, Atty. Genl. of the U.S. & author of several popular works, was in this boat. I found him chatty, witty, unostentatious & frank. While at Clayton Newbold's, I ate of an apple sweet on one side & sour on the other. It was plucked from a tree full of the same kind of fruit, now growing on his premises. On the same branch, with a space of 6 or 8 inches, may be seen the sour fruit, the sweet, & the sweet & sour united. Each as distinctly marked as if produced by separate trees. To effect this whimsical result, the halves of two buds of opposite qualities are united, or placed in close contact in the act of inoculations. It is nevertheless very inexplicable to me by what admirably delicate process of nature the juices should so distinctly flow from this germ as to preserve the separate & several results.

We arrived at home after an absence of nearly three months, during which we had travelled upwards of twenty five hundred miles. If we were to include our minor excursions from places where we occasionally had temporary sojourns, the distance would not fall short of three thousand.

It is a great satisfaction to find, on our arrival, that the City enjoys its accustomed good health & that the Board of Health have publicly proclaimed it to the absent citizens, inviting their return. In all about 140 persons have died of the fever & our physicians are busily employed in their old disputes as to the origin of the disease: whether from foreign or domestic causes, whether imported or endemic.

On my temporary sojourns in N. York, I am continually reminded of the advantages which Philada. enjoys, over that thriving City, in the article of water. The water supplied by the Manhattan Company is very deficient in quantity & inferior in quality. The City authorities should themselves undertake to furnish it from some more abundant source. They have it in their power. Several considerable streams discharge into the Hudson, north of the City. It is true these streams are far off & the expense will be great but the benefits are incalculable. It should be the work of the City, as so important an article should not be entrusted to any private company, however respectable.

When our City Councils entered upon that measure, my favourite scheme was to introduce the waters of Spring Mills, 12 miles north of the City, for I could not be easily reconciled to the use of water taken from an open river into which every unclean thing, man & beast, had free access & which I therefore feared would always be charged with impurities. That was for want of better knowledge. I went with some of my colleagues to Spring Mills & caused the waters of the Spring & also of the Wissahickon to be gauged to ascertain whether either would be sufficient. We returned satisfied with the former but apprehended that the latter in dry seasons would not do to rely on. While some of us were thus engaged, others had their attention drawn to Schuylkill. Anxious to avoid mistakes in an affair of so much importance to the City & to posterity, we caused chemical tests to be applied to each & we likewise experimented on various other sources of supply. To my no small surprize, the Schuylkill water proved to be the most pure of all. I at once yielded to this conviction & it was well I did, for the waters of Spring Mills, however tempting the crystal fount, were strongly impregnated with lime & therefore objectionable to our house wives for washing & culinary purposes & perhaps to many others as an article of drink. That point settled, the next was to fix on the most eligible mode of obtaining it. Various projects were suggested, but the most approved was to raise it by machinery on to Morris Hill, now Fairmount & thence to distribute it over the City. While this matter was under consideration, Benj. R. Morgan met me in the street & asked whether we had not that project in view & on my answering in the affirmative, replied, "We will prevent you." He was a director in the Delaware & Schuylkill Canal Co. & shewed me their charter, by which it appeared that the Company possessed the exclusive right to water the City from that quarter. This discovery caused the Watering Com. no little perplexity & eventually gave rise to a tedious & abortive negotiation to buy out the Company. This negotiation was carried on between a Com. of the City Councils, of which Com. I was a member, and a Com. on the part of the Compy. After finally disagreeing, I was proceeding from the City Hall (where we met) in company with Thos. Harrison, one of the Com. from the Canal Co., when he accused me of causing the rupture. I repelled what I considered an unjust accusation by reminding him that their own Counsel, William Rawle & William Lewis, Esqrs., had furnished their company with a written opinion that the Company could not make the City a title. "Poh! Poh!" rejoined Thomas—"don't talk to me about Lawyers, a Lawyer is like an old Horse, give him plenty of Oates & he'll carry you wherever you please. Stop his Oates & he'll stop." The fact was that the Compy., after the expenditure of several hundred thousand Dollars, had become bankrupt & were ultimately compelled to abandon the work. They however joined the Company for Cutting a Canal from Schuylkill to the Susquehanna & the two companies, thus united, formed what has since gone by the title of the Union Canal Co.

As we could not avail ourselves of Morris Hill, we resorted to the only feasible alternative, the adoption of Latrobe's plan. This was not hastily done, much time & thought were spent before we came to this conclusion. The citizens had however become clamourous & we were incessantly urged to action. Many had persuaded themselves that the immediate introduction of a copious supply of pure water could alone save the City from the scourge of yellow fever from which they had suffered so much & from the effects of which the City had not recovered.

"While you are deliberating," said they, "the City may be ruined." No wonder that we hesitated. Not one of us had any experience. The subject was new not only to ourselves but to all. No City in the United States & few over in Europe could furnish us with a model. If they could, we had no time to go in search of it. The power of steam was just beginning to develop itself in England. Here it had no location & was treated as an *ignis fatuus*. No sooner did we call for money to carry on the work than these same clamourers turned round upon us in hostile attitude. We offered proposals for a loan; few subscribed. We resorted to taxation & they refused to pay the taxes & seizures of furniture, horses & carriages ensued as a necessary consequence. While thus beset on the one hand with complaints, opposition & vituperation, we were mortified, vexed & embarrassed by the assumptions, extravagance & lack of skill, too manifest, on the other, of our crafty Engineer. But amid all, the work went on as some of us were determined it should—if perseverence & a steady eye to the end in view could avail anything. As to myself, I had come to the conclusion that if this attempt to supply Philada. with water failed, I should be compelled to leave the City, greatly as I was attached to it by interest & affection & settle elsewhere. I saw no alternative. Several of my friends declined all intercourse with me & many shunned me in the streets, crossing or dodging to avoid speaking with me. A near family connection, addressing me on the subject, told me to my face that he considered me no better than a thief, or a highway robber. Our difficulties were greatly aggravated by the want of funds & not unfrequently, when I could illy spare it, I had to take of my scanty means to pay off the workmen. Jn. Davis, clerk of the works & by the way one of the most useful & faithful men in our service, not unusually broke suddenly upon me at my Counting House saying, "The men refuse to work until their wages are paid. I have no money, but have prevailed on them to remain until I could see you." What could I do? I forthwith raked up my small resources, hurried on horseback to the discontented labourers, satisfied their wants & kept them at work. I waited to be reimbursed from these inconvenient advances, on my part, by the tardy collections from taxes. Besides these temporary loans, several of us borrowed on our individual credit from the old Bank of the United States—sums without which the works could not have been carried on & I became, in this way, bound to an amount exceeding all I was worth. Some of my colleagues were more prudent & would neither lend nor become personally bound for anything.

When finally the Schuylkill engine was in readiness to operate, two

other members of the Watering Committee & myself, by an arrangement with the workmen, proceeded by break of day to witness the first
stroke of the machine. It was an anxious moment & when the signal was
given to put the engine in motion, my heart beat so furiously against my
side I could scarce keep my feet. When I beheld the elevated fountain
gush forth, tears of joy came to my relief. A worthy citizen, named Jacob
Lex, who had been violently opposed to us, being an early riser,
followed us at a distance to Schuylkill & took his station just within the
door of the Engine House to watch our proceedings, expecting something extraordinary was going on. I shall never forget the face of that
man when he saw the flood flow into the tunnel. Had he seen the sun
rise in the west, he could not have looked more utterly astounded. This
man had for months declined speaking to me but his countenance soon
relaxed & his ancient friendship returned. He attached himself to me
more closely than ever. From that day, I met smiling faces where I had
long been accustomed to contumely & scorn.

These works having given place to the present more efficient &
economical plan, it will not be amiss to preserve some record of their
general character & how they came to be abandoned.

The Delaware & Schuylkill Canal Co. having become extinct, they
were succeeded by the Schuylkill Navigation Co., by which means the
City Corporation were enabled to make arrangements for carrying into
effect their favourite project of introducing the Schuylkill water from
Morris's Hill—& the old works were consequently useless. Their general
features were these. Two engine houses were erected; one of them, a
large square stone building, north side of Chestnut, about 5 feet from
Schuylkill. A well, 10 feet in diameter & 54 feet deep, was excavated
within that house. The water of the river below low water mark was
introduced, thro' a sluice gate into an open canal & partly thro' a
covered tunnel, into the well. Here it was pumped up by the engine into
a brick tunnel, 6 feet in diameter, extending about 3150 feet to the
Centre Square Engine House, a circular marble edifice, standing at a
point exactly where High & Broad Streets intersect. A circular railing
extended round the House, leaving room for carriages & foot passengers
outside of the railing. The four small corners of the square thus cut off
being designed for public fountains, baths, &c., & the grounds were laid
out in gravel walks & planted with ornamental trees, shrubbery, &c.

The engine of the Centre House elevated the water from the tunnel
to a reservoir within the building containing about 16,000 gallons,

whence it descended into the distributing chest constructed of iron outside of the building & thence was let into the conduit pipes for distribution thro' the City.

# 1843

*March 19th.* Years have elapsed since I ceased to keep a Diary. Many events deeply interesting to my feelings have occurred during the interval. Whether I shall again resume the task, I am unable to determine. One event has recently happened which I propose to record—the recent appearance of a magnificent comet in a southwesterly direction. The nucleus is not very distinct nor visible to the naked eye. The tail is long, very beautiful & well defined. It is visible in the evening soon after sunset & disappears in 2 or 3 hours.

*April 15th.* The comet is no longer visible. It was seen at the high school observatory, I believe for the last time on the 11th.

*May 30th.* The centennial meeting of the Philosophical Society, of which I have become a member, closed this day after a session of several days. It was well attended by the members & several distinguished savants from other States. Much knowledge & science were displayed & the body broke up in much harmony.

*June 3d.* A person from Pottsville tells me that ice of an inch thickness was formed there on the night of the 1st.

*June 5th.* I was induced to enter the Select Council in the fall election of 1841 for three years. Besides the public service, I wished to accomplish three special objects of no inconsiderable interest to myself. First, a final settlement of the account of the Executors of Stephen Girard, second, the obtaining of the amount long awarded to the owners of wharf property between Chestnut & Walnut Streets taken by the City for the Delaware Avenue, and third, to procure an extension of the piers so as to afford better accommodation to our shipping. The first two have been accomplished, the third is in progress. I have neither taste nor desire for public life. The path of the politician is strewn with thorns.

*June 6th.* The late comet has been observed in various parts of Europe & given rise to much speculation among the Quidnuncs—one of whom predicts most awful consequences from the supposed coincidences between the Zodiacal & Cometical systems, whence he deduces the end of the world in the year 1850. In our own country a clergyman of the name of Miller has for some time past made calculations on the prophecies, shewing that this event would happen in the present year 1843 in the month just passed. He has many followers. Several of his disciples have committed suicide to avoid the dreaded event, but as yet the world moves on in its usual course.

*June 10th.* President Tyler, attended by some of the heads of departments, arrived here yesterday on his way to Boston to be present at the celebration of the Bunker Hill Monument, erected by private subscription & recently completed. It will be a great gala day. Twelve thousand troops under arms are to form a part of the company. A military escort paraded the President thro' our streets to the United States Hotel, Chestnut Street, where he received the calls of the citizens.

John Tyler was elected Vice President when the lamented Harrison was called to the Presidency by the Whig party. The sudden demise of the public favourite, before he had well entered on the duties of his high station, placed Tyler at the head of the administration. He turned traitor to the party that elevated him & soon gave proof of a vascillating policy which destroyed all confidence in his measures.

He abandoned his friends & the principles which they had ever advocated, by turns advocating & rejecting those deemed fundamental to the preservation of the Union—his ambition to secure another term of the Presidency appearing to be his predominant passion. Silly man, not to perceive the impossibility of success. His appointments to office have that object steadily in view. Freedom of opinion is not permitted & all are expected to give active proof of political devotion to him.

While I write this at 4 P.M., the thundering of cannon gives notice of his departure for the eastward.

*June 11th.* A visit to Haverford School as one of the Com. of Instruction. The new steward & matron, Johnathan & Margaret Richards, are in favour. At first there were three instructors of equal grade, neither exercising a controlling power & some laxity of government was the consequence. We have now one head, Daniel B. Smith, who is likewise teacher of moral philosophy &c., aided by one teacher of mathematics & one of languages.

The Steward is provider, keeper of the accounts &c. His wife looks to the household. This arrangement seems to work better than that for which it has been substituted. There is now a responsible head in D. B. Smith. This school was established by private subscription & is exclusively for the children of Friends. There are more than 200 acres of land & the grounds are beginning to assume a pleasant appearance. The situation, 8 miles west of the City, is high & healthy. It has already cost

$100,000. May it prove a lasting benefit to the Society & the blessing of the Almighty rest upon it.

Daniel O'Connell, in his movements to effect the repeal of the Union between England & Ireland, is driving on his country to the confines of rebellion. Great exertions are made in our own country to aid in the cause. Large meetings are held in our Cities by Irishmen & others to encourage the malcontents. At one of these assemblages held in N. York while Pres. Tyler was there on his way to Bunker Hill & which was attended by his son Robert, who made a speech in favour of repeal, several very inflammatory resolutions were passed & among them the following—"Resolved, that the government of G. Britain has ever evinced, both in her foreign & domestic policy, a rapacious & cruel disregard of the rights & interest of the People; that it is a political monster useful only to a class of comparatively insignificant numbers, covered with the plunder & stained with the blood of unoffending nations & that, however great our indignation, we feel no surprize at its threatened course towards Ireland." The last expressions have no doubt regard to the recent declaration of Sir Robert Peel that the British Ministry would at all hazards crush the rebels.

Now, whatever just cause Ireland may have of complaint against the rule of her more powerful neighbour, we have no right to interfere & it is most surprizing that the President of the U. States should lend his countenance to measures so well calculated to involve us in war & that too, immediately following the Treaty which, by settling the long vexed question of the boundary between Maine & the British Provinces in N. America, had given us hopes of lasting peace.

The meeting in N. York, it is said, was attended by 4000 persons. The Catholics, who are grasping at power everywhere, are doubtless the real agitators.

*June 22d.* Afternoon rode round the country & called on Dr. Spencer in Moore's Town, a retired physician & a man of wealth. Dr. Stokes, who dwells near the village, is a constant visitor. Dr. Spencer has a dog, a bull terrier, who ever manifested a very surly temper towards his friend Stokes. The latter dreaded his attacks & tried vainly to soothe him. The dog met with an accident by which his thigh bone was broken. Stokes happened to call immediately after the accident & by the aid of Dr. Spencer, set the bone & secured it by splinters. The dog bore the operation with perfect submission & from that moment evinced his gratitude by the kindliest attentions to his benefactor. He is an intelligent animal with a fierce visage. I should not fancy to encounter his hatred.

Some years ago this same Dr. Stokes, who is cousin to my wife, spent the evening with his kinsman, N. N. Stokes, at whose house we now are. When about to go home, he found his horse had escaped with his gig. It was late & the night tempestuous. He went home on foot, about three miles & there, to his joy, found the horse had preceded him, but with the loss of his cloak, cushion &c. The gig was uninjured. The following morning the Dr. retraced his steps, enquiring as he went for the lost articles. He at length discovered them in custody of a small white dog who ran to meet him playfully. The Dr. took possession of his property, returned home & the dog, following, remained at this new home the remainder of his days, where I have frequently seen him.

Now, what is remarkable in this case, is this. Dr. S. had never before seen that dog & never could learn whence he came—no person in the vicinity knowing him & previous to the Dr.'s appearance, he furiously resisted every attempt of others to come near to the guarded articles. These are certainly curious specimens of canine character.

*June 26th.* Dr. Stokes, now about 35 years old, is in extensive country practice. I asked him if he had ever thought of how many miles he had coursed in visiting his patients. He answered yes & that the distance would extend five times round the world. No trifling ride, that.

*June 27th.* Paid an official visit to the Girard Farms in the Neck, accompanied by my colleagues, the Commissioners of the Girard Estates, over which I preside.

*June 29th.* A short visit to son Alfred & son-in-law Ewd. Yarnall, Germantown. Evening met the Commissioners of the Girard Estates.

*June 30th.* At 3 P.M. attended the meeting of the Overseers of Friends Public Schools, at 8 the Com. on Legacies & Trusts (Councils), at 9 Philosophical Society. Still hot & dry. The quarrels of the fire companies occasion much disorder. The whole system requires remodeling. Councils hold but a feeble restraint on them.

These associations, instead of being voluntary, should be appointed by Councils & the members paid for their services.

*July 1st.* A letter from our niece, E. W. Stokes, gives me a painful & discouraging account of my dear wife's health. I shall proceed forthwith to N. J.

Left home at 3 P.M. for N. N. Stokes. Jersey sand is deep & the day very hot. The little wind stirring kept the dust round the carriage & horses. A most uncomfortable ride. I found my dear wife too unwell to leave her chamber, but well attended by kind relatives.

*July 3d.* All nature teems with freshness. Returned to my solitary home, leaving my E. in charge of our estimable friends & attended by her cousin, Dr. Stokes.

*July 4th.* The early roar of cannon announces the usual celebrations. At 4 P.M. met the Managers of the House of Refuge. Important alterations in the discipline of the House are in contemplation. The use of the rod is too common. It is easier to apply that than to correct by reason & patient labour & it is more frequently indulged to gratify the ill humour of the inflicter than the reformation & substantial good of the offender.

At 8 P.M. met the Cleansing Com. of Councils. The City is now cleansed by contract at $9500 per annum. This is about ⅓ of what it once cost. The time will no doubt come when it will be accomplished for nothing. After that, people will pay for the privilege & remunerate themselves by the sales of the dirt for manure.

At a meeting of the Irish Repealers in this City on the third, Robert Tyler, son of the Pres., addressed the assembled & among other things, applauded Danl. O'Connell in the most exalted terms. Nine cheers were given him & the same number for the President. What mischief to our country may not these movements entail upon us.

*July 6th.* Money has become so abundant & so little of it is demanded by our diminished commerce that loans have been made at an interest of from 3 to 5 per ct. per an. I have known more than these rates to have been paid for it per month.

At 12 noon, met the Managers of the Bible Society. A communication sent to us from the Indiana auxiliary, asking for Bibles. Some time back, Bibles were sent to them & returned because the edges of the front leaves were marbled. Others were then sent to supply their place. Such ridiculous scruples, instead of advancing, injure the cause of religion. These people owe the Society at this time $500, which they cannot or do not pay. So much for their consistency & assumed piety.

In the evening attended Select Councils. Among other things the two bodies passed an ordinance for extending the wharves & that unanimously. The wardens & districts must concur before this ordinance can go into operation. It will meet some selfish opposition from some of them.

*July 8th.* Last evening went to N. J. & this morning brought home my poor sick wife. The influenza has exerted a very baneful influence on her weak frame.

*July 12th.* The steamer *Columbia* which left Boston on the 1st for Liverpool via Halifax, full of passengers, has been wrecked near Seal Island, N. S. No lives were lost—the vessel a total loss. Not many months ago the steamer *President* from N. Y. to Liverpool was lost at sea & all on board, including more than 60 passengers, perished. Swift messengers but dangerous sea boats.

Robert Fulton, who was the first man that applied steam successfully to the propelling of boats, was my school fellow in the town of Lancaster, Pa., where I was born. He was the son of a poor widow & Caleb Johnston was our schoolmaster. At that time my brother John had, without instruction, employed himself in painting, both in oil & water colours. The latter he placed in mussel shells & when much used & cast off, I often took them with me to school. Bob looked so longing for a part of my treasure that I freely admitted him to a participation. He soon outshone me so much in the use of these shells as to induce me to give up my share & make him, from time to time, sole proprietor of all I obtained.

Fulton possessed a versatile genius & like men of that stamp, never acquired wealth. While in England, he turned his attention to canaling & with the view of gaining knowledge on the subject, visited Holland. After publishing a pamphlet commending the use of this mode of internal conveyance, a copy of which was sent to me, he returned to the United States with the intention of pursuing that branch of engineering. He met with Chancellor Livingston, who had long been essaying unsuccessfully to impel a boat by steam. They speedily formed a connection which, by the aid of the Chancellor's money & the ingenuity of Fulton, was soon achieved—to the lasting fame of the latter & the incalculable benefit of mankind.

*July 15th.* I have taken my Elizabeth a short ride this morning. She bore it well. 'Tis the first time she left her chamber since I brought her to the City a week ago.

The influenza still remains in the City & we hear of it from the far west, from the south & as far north as the Canadas. It is said also to have

seized on & destroyed several valuable horses. Whence cometh it & what can it be?

*July 17th.* Met the Board of Trade, over which I have presided since its establishment. It was a thin meeting, so many being absent from the City. This Board has evinced much activity & has been very useful to the community.

*July 19th.* Last evening met the Com. on Legacies & Trusts. Much business transacted, principally on account of the Fire Department & Will's Hospital. Today the Com. of the Girard Trusts, or Councils, should have met but both have taken a recess for summer recreation.

Had S. Girard lived some years longer he would doubtless have greatly diminished his vast estate of 6 or 7 millions. He was not in the habit of acting on the advice of others but was self moved & a greater affront could scarcely be offered to him than an attempt to pry into his concerns.

Acting exclusively on his own generally sagacious judgement, had he been more communicative, I think he would have made a different will.

His mercantile operations, which were generally successful, were planned & executed when all Europe was belligerant. After the general peace & foreigners became competitors in the commerce of the world, his judgement failed, for he could not adapt his movements to this new state of things. In about one year's time, he encountered losses to the extent of more than twelve hundred thousand Dollars. His Ships were not calculated for the change, they carried too little & drew too much water in proportion to their tonnage. The large Ship he was building when he died possessed these defects.

His houses were built with more judgement, being of the best materials, as indeed were his Ships & calculated for posterity, differing in these respects from those of our late wealthy townsman Jacob Ridgway, who built for present income. A characteristic anecdote is related of these two men.

They had some personal altercation about property. When Ridgway exclaimed petulantly, "I could buy & sell you," Stephen coolly replied, "I could buy you, Mr. Ridgway, but I do not think that I could sell you again."

Some years before S. Girard's death, a careless carter ran against him & severed a large piece of flesh from one of his cheeks. When he had partially recovered, I called to see him & found him sitting up, but confined to his chamber. His head was muffled with poultices, his only eye peeping thro' the bandages—the other had been lost long before. He conversed cheerfully about his business & on my saying that he could not then attend to his banking concerns, replied briskly, "To be sure I do—I attend to everything. I make Roberts (his cashier) bring me all the offerings & I see to all the discounts myself. Certainly I cannot look after my buildings & I know that the rascals cheat me."

All this was said with animation, in his own peculiar French accent.

As an evidence of his minute attention to business, I may record that, having purchased from a person in my employment a load of stable manure, he sent his clerk to me with his Receipt Book & one Dollar 75 cents, the price of the load, after deducting 25 cents for deficiency in quality. I gave him a rec't in conformity.

It may be said of Stephen Girard that he was a compound of meanness with occasional liberality, unfeeling harshness with disinterested be-nevolence. His mother in law was for years a pensioner on my bounty. I strove to induce him to relieve her wants, but in vain. I represented to him the unreasonableness of his permitting her to be a burden to others & that he could board her in the country for $1.50 a week. He turned upon me with the emphatic declaration, "Mr. Cope, I will not be told what I am to do with my money." I felt angry & left him. She was a poor, distressed, intemperate cripple & did not long survive to be troublesome to either of us. And yet this man, in the Yellow Fever of 1793, was a voluntary nurse, at Bush Hill Hospital, performing with alacrity by day & by night the most menial & offensive services for the sick—& when called on for a contribution in aid of the poor, in the fever of 1798, he freely gave to the committee $800, saying to them, "When more is wanted, call on me, gentlemen, for you must not let the poor suffer."

*July 22d.* Last night I met the Philosophical Society. It was election night for new members. Among others, Julien of Paris was in nomina-tion. Doc. Chapman raised objections. Julien had been private secy. to Robespierre & guilty, like master, of the horrid barbarities, among other things, of having seduced a girl of 15 & getting tired of her, he caused her accusation before the revolutionary tribunal & had her guillotined. Duponceau, Pres. of the Society & very hard of hearing, being informed of the objection, rose & said that the candidate was not the person supposed but a man of unblemished reputation—the author of several learned works & the best Chinese Scholar now in Europe. On this testimony Julien was elected.

*July 23d.* Walking this morning in one of our public squares, I met &

spoke to J. B. He was once a noted drunkard, but for many years has been a sober man. On one occasion I saw him surrounded by a crowd in Market Street, a stout countryman grasping his collar with one hand, while with the other, he was trying to wrest from him a pair of fowles which he accused him of having stolen from his waggon. I pressed near to them & assured the accuser that he was mistaken, that J. B., tho' intemperate, was an honest man, quite independent in his circumstances & of a respectable family. He then let him go & the accused staggered home, greatly mortified & agitated. I saw him not again in public for years. He became a sober man from that time.

I knew another citizen who was a common drunkard & who was cured of the vice by the following circumstance. Reeling in the street & sensible that he must fall, he threw himself between two cellar doors. While prostrate there, beastly drunk, a large dog passing by applied his nose to him & then, lifting a leg, applied a copious sprinkling to his breast & face. Stupid as was the man, he was greatly annoyed by this canine freedom & most severely felt the degradation to which he was reduced. He got to his feet as soon as he could, resolved never more to encounter the hazard of a similar greeting. He was forthwith a reformed man & lived long, a much esteemed citizen.

*July 26th.* "Watch & pray, lest ye enter into temptation." I am often made sensible of the need of this gospel injunction, so admirably adapted to the frailty of man, for without Divine aid, freedom from errors & misdoings I believe to be impossible. Even the best are sensible of the necessity of its daily observance—how much more such erring men as myself. I am constantly making mistakes from a naturally hasty temper. Repent & mistake again. May God grant me grace to overcome this weakness.

*July 30th.* Dr. Pusey of the Oxford Tracts has created no trifling hubbub among the Episcopalians. The controversy has reached this country & is well pleasing to the Romanists. One thing is sufficiently obvious: The Doctr. & his coadjutors the Clergy are not far removed from the disciples of the Pope & it would be honourable in them at once to throw off their cobweb coverings & acknowledge him as their head. It is equally obvious that all are ambitious to accumulate power in their own hands. The eucharist & baptism, say the Episcopalians, are essential to salvation, but none can lawfully administer either except a Bishop & he derives his authority in regular descent by the laying on of hands from the Apostles—a tremendous power indeed over eternal life.

This assumption of power is not confined to the Episcopal Church. Priestcraft claims it everywhere.

Even in our own favoured Society, these claims are not wanting. It has been said the Quakers are as completely Priest ridden as is the flock of any other Christian denomination. The road to promotion here is simple enough. Use the plain language, dress plain, hang down the head, go to meetings & above all, take care always to jump in judgement with the ruling powers, praise when they praise & blame when they blame. Should the aspirant ever become a preacher, his temporal reward will be sure. He may travel, certificate in hand, leave the drudgery of bodily labour to others & his family to shift as they may. His children get their education as they can, himself being entertained everywhere as a Prince in the House of Israel, taking care all the while to assure his hearers how much he suffers for their sakes. By way of pastime he may amuse himself in feasting on the fruits of the earth, in traducing the character of a brother & in idle gossip—then, returning home, to render an account of his labours, he may have the satisfaction of receiving the benedictions of the Church for having "given up" to this hard service.

But all are not such, there are preserved to the Society, thro' the mercy of God, men as the salt of the earth who, thro' the influence of the Holy Spirit, are lovers of truth, of charity & of piety, men who are too deeply imbued with the benign spirit of the Gospel to attempt Lordship over the consciences of their brethren, equal heirs with themselves to life eternal in the Heavens.

*August 1st.* Met Managers H. Refuge—suffered myself to be too much excited in debate. The Matron leaves tomorrow—taken a house near the Refuge, her husband remaining in charge of one of the workshops. Most injudicious arrangement, giving them the opportunity of intermeddling in the concerns of the Institution. She is known to be vindictive. Her husband is a weak man & is governed by her counsels—in fact, he dare not disobey her. Hence my warmth, which I regret.

*August 10th.* Met the Commissioners of the Girard Estates. A suit is now pending before the U.S. Supreme Court, by the heirs, to recover his Estate from the City under the plea that the Corporation is incompetent to carry out his will. Besides other counsel, it appears that the heirs have engaged the services of John C. Calhoun, Senator of the U.S. & Daniel Webster, late Secy. of State. This City will be advocated by Horace Binney, John Sergeant & Wm. M. Meredith, members of the Philadelphia Bar.

*August 12th.* The Com. of Instruction of Haverford School met. Teachers are not yet engaged. We shall doubtless have to resort to a person not a member to instruct the pupils in the classics. No competent person belonging to Friends can be discovered—we have never been well suited in that department.

*August 14th.* Attended a meeting of the Managers of the Mercantile Library & afterwards their Com. on Lectures. Some discussion as to the propriety of a course the next winter. These lectures have heretofore exercised a salutary influence over our young people in diverting them from attendance in the theatres & other scenes of folly & vice. Yet it may be well to suspend them for a season so that they may not pall on the public taste.

Received & answered a letter from son Henry at Cape May, where he & other members of his family are enjoying the benefit of sea bathing. It was there that my dear son Francis lost his life soon after he had attained his majority. The sea swept him away while bathing in company with his younger brother, William, who providentially escaped. It was one of the most painful events of my life. He was a highly gifted young man & his awful exit caused me an affliction of which I cannot think without a bleeding heart.

The two brothers, hand in hand, had ventured far from the shore when William proposed their return. Francis had scarcely given his assent, when a thundering billow broke over & washed them asunder. Another succeeded which drove them still further apart, wafting W. towards the land & his poor brother further to sea. Francis was lame from an injury of the knee. Incapable of contending with the mighty wave, he cast a parting smile on his distracted companion & sunk to rise no more. The sad tidings came fearfully & darkly on our peaceful family circle & its withering influence had but little abated when, if possible, I was visited with a still more overpowering affliction, by the sudden & heartrending demise of my endeared bosom companion, in a way well calculated to appall my very soul.

A careless domestic had given her arsenic instead of magnesia. Speedy medical aid proved unavailing, she closed her mortal career peacefully, but in great suffering.

Awful & enduring have been these visitations to Divine wisdom. My prayer is that I may submit in all humility to the chastening rod. Many comforts & blessings are left to me. Oh that I may be grateful to these unmerited mercies & may I be favoured so to live as to have an assurance in the end that my spirit be found worthy to join the pure spirits of these, my much beloved & tender connections, where sorrow cometh not, but where harmony & love dwell forever.

*August 19th.* Visited the monument erected to the memory of General Anthony Wayne, called Mad Anthony—a small marble pyramid surrounded by a low, mean stone wall on the ground where his small force was attacked in the dead of night, dispersed & a number of them slain by a party of the British Army soon after the Battle of Brandywine. Wayne was that night absent from the encampment & lodged in a neighbouring farmhouse. His own farm & residence was in the same vicinity. His son Isaac is now resident there & altho' wealthy, labours under the melancholy delusion that he will come to want.

Many persons, male & female, on horseback & in carriages, passed us today on their way to Harvest Home, held in the barn of one Jacobs in the Valley, 25 miles from Philada.

*August 20th.* On a ramble this afternoon in a neighbouring forest, came unexpectedly on an assemblage listening to an animated preacher with stentorian voice. We were informed it was a congregation of Baptists. It was a pleasant scene.

*August 21st.* Our host is Genl. Evans, a good tempered man of the Locofoco school, formerly a member of Congress. His son, who now plays the landlord, is of the same school & likewise dubbed General. He relates an anecdote of Washington which he says is well attested, but which is so contrary to the mild & humane character of that great man as to defy belief. He says that when Gen. W. lay with his army at Valley Forge, he issued orders to his troops to shoot every person going towards Philada. with marketing & that several farmers were accordingly shot while on their way to the City, then in possession of the British under General Howe.

*August 22d.* Our son-in-law J. R. T. & wife left us today. Departed for Jabez Jenkins's in the Valley & reached there in the afternoon.

*August 23d.* Attended meeting at Downingtown. My E. too weak to accompany me. Fifteen males & about as many females present. Afternoon paid a short visit to our kinsmen over the South Hill & took tea with Saml. Cope. Witnessed the operation of a machine for making shingles of Chestnut wood. They are sold at $10.

*August 24th.* Called on the bereaved widow of my old friend George

Ashbridge, interred a few days ago. His end was thought to be hastened by the recent losses on stocks amounting, I have heard, to $80,000. What wretchedness has been inflicted on the community by such men as Gen. Andrew Jackson & Nicholas Biddle.

*August 26th.* This is my birthday. I have now accomplished my 75th year & would that I had lived a life more worthy of the Divine favour. According to the record of my father, I was born in the town of Lancaster, Pa., August 26th, 1768 & this is the 26th of August of 1843.

*August 28th.* Left the Valley with my dear wife for the residence of our kinsman Benjamin Sharpless, whose first wife, Abigail Cope, was daughter of Uncle Nathan Cope, my father's brother. She was my playmate when very young, an agreeable child & lovely woman. His present wife well supplies her place. Benjamin has made my house his home for more than 40 years when attending yearly meeting. He is a man of sound & liberal principles with a good understanding & generous heart. On the way to his house we were overtaken by a violent rain, accompanied by thunder & lightning. We reluctantly sought shelter under some trees, compelled by the driving rain, which even our light carriage could not resist. My E.'s garments did not wholly escape a wetting, but she appeared to have received no injury. I am indeed very thankful to perceive some improvement in her health.

*August 29th.* On my way to monthly meeting at West Chester, I passed R. Strode's mill pond, where Fanny Butler, late F. Kemble, was with others fishing with rods & lines. She was dressed in a light frock coat, pantaloons, boots & man's hat, having every outward appearance of a male. Altho' an actress & accustomed to exposure of the person, it seemed wonderful that she should thus outrage the accustomed laws of female decorum among so plain a people. She drives her own carriage & pair round the neighbourhood, with her own hands to the amusement of the sober natives. She boards close by with a family of Hicksites.

*August 31st.* Attended by B. Sharpless, I spent yesterday & today in calls. Among others we visited John James, Joseph Cope, Benjamin Cope, Girard Cope, Amy Hoopes, Jasper Hoopes & Ann Hoopes, his mother. The two last named are Separatists (Hicksites) but I have not as yet felt it my duty to shun social intercourse with others, merely because of a difference of faith.

*September 2d.* Accompanied as before, rode over to Westtown Boarding School. About 150 children of both sexes are in attendance. Took some fruit to my wife's nephews, Henry & Francis Stokes, now there. It is painful to think that in a seminary under the sole charge of Friends & consisting of the children of Friends, there should prevail such a laxity of morals. These lads have had presents of fruit from their parents of which other boys have robbed them with impunity. They did not complain to me, I know it from other quarters. They are both generous, kind hearted lads & ever ready to divide what they have with others.

*September 3d.* First Day—attended meeting at Birmingham. The House is divided between the Friends & Hicksites, a board partition separating them. Thermometer stands at 92.

In the cemetery here was interred the body of Earl Percy, of the English Army, who fell in the Battle of Brandywine, fought near these grounds. The story as related by my kinsman, the late John Forsyth, who was present tho' not engaged in the contest—a man of strict veracity, is this. When the two armies approached each other Percy said, "Here I shall lose my life. I saw this place in a dream before I left my native land & that I should on this spot fall by the enemy. I know the place well." He then took the watch from his fob & giving it, with other trinkets, into the hands of his servant to be delivered to certain persons whom he named, moved on with the troops & fell. This story has not, I believe, gained a place in history but has been so well & so familiarly spoken of as to have become traditional. Forsyth often related the whole affair & could point out the precise spot in which the remains of Percy were interred.

I was a small boy at the time, having with my brother Israel been placed at school in the neighbourhood. We were within hearing of the battle, even to the small arms. Our teacher was sadly alarmed & the scholars but little at ease. The morning following there was a skirmish, still near to us, at the Turk's Head, now West Chester—a cannon ball cutting down the limbs of trees in our sight & the cattle running with their tails in the air as fast as their legs could carry them from the scene of action.

We were then with others on our way to school & perplexed to know which course to fly from danger, but at length went on our way without injury or further alarm. In the night after the battle, the family where we were—our uncle Nathan Cope's—were aroused out of their sleep by a small party of Americans who demanded shelter & something to eat. Having eaten some pye & milk, they hastily withdrew. When gone, I

told Uncle I knew one of them, Col. Ross, of the Lancaster Militia. He was a handsome man, but in a sad plight, being destitute of hat & coat & his hands & face besmeared with gunpowder.

The story went that the Lancaster Militia were encamped in a forest when they were so affrighted in the night by a large herd of swine grunting & racing towards them, having broken away from an English scouting party, that they took to their heels & were never collected again during the war.

*September 4th.* Dined at James Forsyth's, son of John above mentioned. His mother, my cousin Hannah, now near 90, related to us some interesting scenes of the Revolutionary War. She has a sound memory, can read her Bible, hears well, but is afflicted with rheumatism in her limbs & moves about the house by the aid of a staff. She shewed us her wedding gown, still in a good state of preservation. It is a changeable worsted, quite handsome & was spun by herself at the age of 16. She wore a pretty check apron she had spun at the age of 18. She conversed cheerfully of by-gone days & bears evidence of a well spent life. My aunt, her mother, lived to be 93 & upwards. Her facilities failed her some years before her decease. She was an exemplary Christian. What more can be said? The day was very warm—the thermometer rising above 92.

*September 6th.* Indications of a change of weather having taken place last evening, we determined to retrace our way home & accordingly left our friends after breakfast & by half past 12 were once more under our own roof. The wind was eastwardly, the sky overcast, but we had no rain. We had many of our friends at our usual evening repast. My E. bore the ride pretty well.

There are recently arrived, from England via N. York, 3 ministering Friends—John Pease, gone to Canada, Rachel Priestman & Isabel Casson, now with us in the City. I hope they may be received with more Christian charity & brotherly kindness than were extended towards others from the same country who lately travelled among us.

*September 15th.* My son Henry left home today as a companion of Wm. Evans on a religious visit to Indiana Yearly Meeting. There has lately been a split in the Society there, the abolitionists having withdrawn & set up a Y. Meeting for themselves. When will men learn that more is gained by moderation, charity & persuasion than by acrimony, intemperate zeal & splenetic personal abuse. A man is not readily convinced by the calling of harsh names. Our friend E. has yet something to learn in the exercise of his ministerial duties on these several subjects. Discretion is a diadem.

*September 17th.* First Day & if ever I heard the Gospel preached, I heard it this forenoon from the lips of Elizabeth Evans, wife of Wm. She rose with these words, "Draw nigh to God & he will draw nigh unto thee. Forsake the Devil & he will flee from thee. Cease to do evil & learn to do well." These three great points of Christian doctrine she enforced with dignity, eloquence, feeling & effect, occupying more than an hour.

*September 19th.* The thermometer yesterday reached 90. At 10 A.M. visited the House of Refuge. The recently appointed Matron finds the duties too arduous for her advanced age. I feared it would be so. At 12, met the Directors of the Ins. Co. of N.A.

*September 21st.* A visit to son Alfred's at Germantown. In the evening met the Com., Girard Estate. The weather continues oppressively warm.

*September 22d.* Visited the annual exhibition of the Penna. Horticultural Society & beheld a splendid display of flowers & fruit, among them a curious fungus called Tuckahoe, belonging to the family of truffles, from the State of Delaware. It is found from 3 to 5 feet below the surface, having neither root nor branch, having much the colour & appearance of an elongated penny roll of bread, weighing between 1 & 2 pounds. The internal contents seem like starch. In Europe, where the truffle is much esteemed by Gourmands, they are discovered by dogs, trained for the purpose & disinterred by men who pursue it for a livelihood. I am not aware by what means the Tuckahoe is detected in its hiding place so far underground. It is evidently an eatable commodity.

*September 28th.* The last stated meeting of City Councils was held this evening—the general election being close at hand, when four members of the Select & the whole of the Common Council are to be voted for. Having served 2 of the 3 years for which I was elected, I had intended to resign but am induced—from a desire not to injure the City interest—to serve out my time. The districts which have hitherto been supplied with water from the City Works are making efforts to do it for themselves by drawing supplies from the dam above Fairmount. This is believed to be a violation of the rights of the City & will probably give rise to a legal controversy. I wish we had at the head of our Watering Com. a man of more accommodating disposition then J. P. Wetherill, who has earned for himself such a character for obstinancy as to mar even his good intentions. The City has offered to supply them on the same terms charged to our own citizens, but that doesn't suit the political wire workers of the districts. Their object is not so much the study of economy as to create offices & places. So wags the world.

*September 29th.* Afternoon met the Overseers of Friends Public Schools—in the evening, the Philosophical Society. Peter Stephen Duponceau present. He is almost blind & so deaf as to render conversation with him difficult. His mind is bright & his knowledge very extensive. He sustains the reputation of being the most accomplished linguist in America. He still possesses a clear & happy mode of expression, tho' now in his 80th year. He wears glasses & stoops very much.

Invited to become a member of the Wistar Club, consisting of the elite of the City. It is a high compliment, but I have declined. This club was established by the late accomplished, hospitable & learned Caspar Wistar, M.D., of Philada. After the lamented death of the Doctor, his friends & others got up the present association & meet alternately once a week at each other's Houses—no person being admitted to membership but by a unanimous vote. Some Friends disapprove of these assemblages & I do not wish to give offense by becoming a member.

*September 30th.* The Farming Com., of which I am chairman, paid a visit of inspection to the Girard Farms in the Neck. Nothing seemed to demand more than the accustomed attention. We were accompanied by our agent & dined at Point Breeze on the Schuylkill.

*October 3d.* Met the N.A. Ins. Co. at 12 noon. No very special business. The Managers of the H. of Refuge met at 4 P.M. Elected another Matron & accepted the resignation of Martha Dugan, whose age renders her unfit for the station.

*October 4th.* The following anecdote of Franklin was related to me this evening. He was in the company of the French & English ambassadors when the Frenchman gave as a toast, "France, like the silver light of the moon, she sheds a soft lustre on everything on which her beams are cast." The Englishman gave, "England, the sun which enlightens the moon, that reflects only a borrowed light." Franklin being called on gave, "America, the Joshua of the world, who commanded the sun & the moon to stand still & they obeyed him."

*This drawing is by Major John Andre of the British Army. when a prisoner. & living in my Fathers family in Lancaster, during the war of the Revolution. I was at that time a small boy. but well remember Andre's bland manners. sporting with us children as if one of us. To my brother John he was more especially attached from a nearer approach of age. & a congeniality of genius & taste I often played marbles & other boyish games with the Major*

*I cannot remember what he said the drawing represented, but think it the place of the authors birth, or some place at which he had resided. but I have carefully. preserved the relic, in memory of the Artist & of my affection for that gifted & deceived. that noble minded, generous man,*

*Thos P Cope*
*Phila 1851*

Watercolor by Major John André, kept by Thomas Cope as a momento of André's internment—"on the most intimate & familiar footing"—with the Cope family in Lancaster after his capture in 1775.

The Centre Square pumphouse of Philadelphia's original waterworks, located at the intersection of present-day Market and Broad Streets.

Benjamin H. Latrobe (left), America's first architect of international reputation, designed Philadelphia's waterworks; Cope distrusted him and believed he made "experiments at the expense of the City."

Woodcut shows Stephen Girard, a friend and rival of Cope's, helping a victim of the yellow fever epidemic of 1793.

"Preparation for War to defend Commerce." Engraving of Philadelphia waterfront, ca. 1800.

The *Monongahela*, with the black cross of the Cope Packet Line on her foresail.

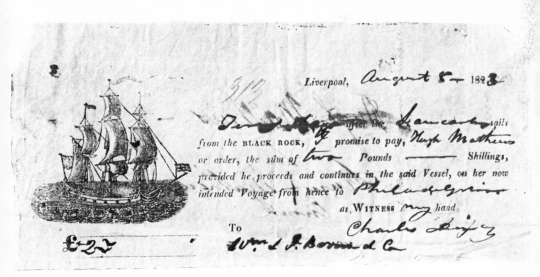

Steerage ticket between Liverpool and Philadelphia on the Cope Packet ship the *Lancaster*.

It has frequently occurred to me to keep some note of passing circumstances – but my time hitherto has generally been so fully employed as to have rendered it impracticable. – It may be useful to myself at least. When I may have little else to do I may thus reduce my reflections into form, & embody them into something that I can see & therefore understand. – It may also serve as a companion in a solitary hour. – When I feel but little disposed to society, or other avocations, I can recur to my Commonplace Book – It will be like saluting an old acquaintance. – He may be a sorry fellow & ill associate – but I trust he will at least prove to be a friend, & perhaps a faithful monitor. – Should I at any time be too much inclined to strut & crow with my own importance, a peep at myself in this mirror may lower my towering crest, & curb my folly.

It may likewise be beneficial to keep some account of transactions which would otherwise be forgotten. – True, many of them may be trivial – that I don't doubt – but life itself is a compound of trifles, & man a bundle of inconsistencies. Besides, I mean to write for my own amusement, & should any one choose to look over these sheets, to carp & find fault, let him remember this Book is my property – he may therefore turn aside from the evil thing & depart in peace –

This is the 9th day of August 1800 – The day was ushered in by a fine shower – grew sultry on clearing up – succeeded by several plentiful falls of rain, a little a la mode de April. The city continues very healthy – no alarm of yellow fever – there is therefore additional cause of thankfulness & gratitude to Him who holds the destiny of nations in his hands –

Heard from our Sons Henry & Francis who are at School in Bradford near W. Chester. They are in health. – This is good news – many pleasant things befal me – yet I am not always content – but suffer myself to be discomposed by the meerest trifles – How do we brave the

Left: First page of Thomas Cope's diary: August 9, 1800.
Below: Thomas P. Cope by John Neagle. The 1847 portrait, which hangs in the Mercantile Library of Philadelphia, captured Cope's strength and charm but almost certainly made him appear younger than his nearly eighty years.

"The Procession of Victuallers." Aquatint after J. L. Krimmel's painting records Philadelphia butchers "conveying the meat of the stock of exhibition Cattle to Market" in 1821.

Photograph of Thomas P. Cope,
ca. 1850.

Friends Meeting House and Academy. Lithograph by Kennedy and Lucas, ca. 1829.

Sunday Morning in front of Arch Street Meeting House, ca. 1812. Pavel Petrovich Svinin, in America as secretary to the Russian consul, caught the contrasts of Philadelphia by showing two fashionably dressed ladies and a severe Quaker couple.

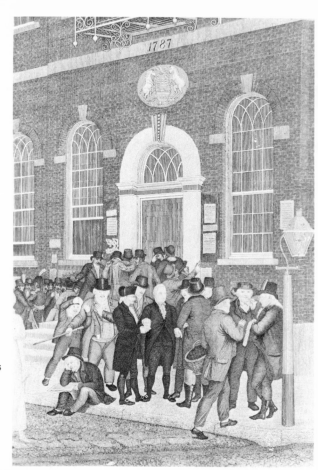

Right: Election Day 1815 in Philadelphia. Engraving after a painting by John Lewis Krimmel.

Below: The Mercantile Library was founded for the encouragement and education of young men in business. Cope, a founder in the 1820s, was president nearly until his death.

Merchants' Exchange, built in 1831 by William Strickland.

The novelist Charles Brockden Brown.

Jail on Walnut Street in Philadelphia, ca. 1799. The "penitentiary" was built by Quakers in 1790 for the purpose of reforming rather than simply punishing prisoners, as was the common practice of the day.

Dorothea Dix, whose singleminded
drive sometimes bothered Cope,
won him over; he contributed to a
much-needed institution for
Pennsylvania's insane poor.

The Blockley Alms House, Philadelphia, ca. 1838. Cope devoted much time and
energy throughout his long life to better the lives of people less fortunate than
himself.

Founders' Hall, Haverford College.

Lemon Hill; David J. Kennedy's watercolor shows the estate in the 1840s, much as it must have looked when Cope suggested the city buy it.

Before the year 1790, when I was an apprentice to a dry goods merchant, I boarded with my Uncle Thos. Mendenhall, who visited Doc. Franklin of evenings to discuss the subject of electricity. My Uncle was at that time more conversant with the subject perhaps than any other man in America, the Doc. excepted. I sometimes accompanied my Uncle & had thus the opportunity of seeing & conversing with that celebrated man. He was polite, talked freely & always instructively. Tho' but an ignorant boy, he did not permit me to escape notice, but addressed me in the language of kindness, accompanied with good advice. Finding that I slept in a large open apartment, into which fire was not permitted, he asked if I did not often suffer from cold feet. It was then winter. "Yes, indeed I do, Doctor, to the interruption of my rest." "Well, Tommy, I'll tell you how to prevent that. Before getting into bed, strip yourself of your shirt & walk about the room until you feel yourself growing too cold, then jump into bed, cover yourself with your blankets & you will have no occasion to complain of cold feet."

I followed the Doctor's advice & found the cold was soon succeeded by a delightful glow, which lulled me to sleep, from which I seldom awoke until it was time to rise in the morning.

During the troubles preceding the Revolutionary War, Franklin was in England as agent of some of the provinces—among others, the province of Pennsylvania. He was examined before a Committee of the House of Commons, who proposed to recommend the removal of the obnoxious Stamp Act, provided the Americans would defray the expenses incurred by its enactment. Franklin told the Com. it reminded him of an affair which occurred when he was in Paris. A Frenchman ran into the street with a red hot poker in his hand & meeting an English sailor, proposed running it up his back side. Jack would not consent. The Frenchman insisted vehemently & at length asked permission to run it up, "wan leetel bit." The sailor, with an oath, said he would not have it run up at all. "Well, then," rejoined Monsieur, "you pay me for heat de poker."

*October 10th.* This day the general election is held & I have just returned from casting my vote. I have ever felt it my duty, as a member of the Commonwealth, to exercise my right of suffrage. He who will not take even that trouble complains of bad laws with a bad grace, he has in fact no right to complain. If he be scrupulous about voting, then let him be scrupulous about finding fault. Rather let him go to the polls & publicly demonstrate by throwing in the ticket of his choice, that he

prefers for his lawmakers, men just & wise to fools & knaves. By staying away he in effect promotes the latter to office. "He who is not for me is against me."

On my way to the City Hall to attend one of the committees of Councils, I passed the assembled multitude at the Polls. Of the thousands thro' which I passed, I heard not an oath or even a loud angry word. It is a most gratifying circumstance, owing doubtless in a great measure to the temperance cause. This was after night fall.

*October 15th.* Memory is a wareroom or lumber garret in which we stow away the gleanings & savings of our mental toils & spoils. These, whether golden treasures or valueless gew-gaws, are sometimes so secreted or hidden by rubbish as not to be found when most needed, while anon & uncalled they come before us with all the brilliancy of new born thoughts, we know not how or why or wherefore. This has happened to me on the present occasion & here is the result.

When Charles Maurice de Talleyrand-Perigord was in Phila., an exile from France, between the years 1792 & 1796, he resided in a small two storied house in Goddard's Court, two above Sassafras Street & was in the habit of calling on me at my store, No. 19, Second Street, on which occasions he was attended by a French gentleman named Bonnette, on whose arm he leaned when walking, being himself lame. They had been introduced to me by my friend Wm. Young, Bookseller. Their object was social & to spend an idle hour, for they appeared to have no employment. T. was then a slender man of ordinary height, dark hair & complexion, piercing eye & grave intellectual physiognomy, generally taciturn, not speaking our language fluently. Bonnette, a laughing, joking, jolly fellow. They appeared to be poor. They came & went as suited them, seemingly having no object but to while away time.

While I had leisure to attend to them, we held conversation on the various topics of the day. I was then a good deal engaged in some of our City concerns & they were fond of gaining information respecting our public men & City institutions. Bonnette generally led on the conversation, Talleyrand listening attentively. When I was occupied in my business, they amused themselves in looking over the newspapers. These were morning calls. I had a partner, but he was never present, his duties as a clerk in the Bank of N.A. inducing his absence.

On one of these occasions, Talleyrand produced a number of gold watches & wished me to sell them for him. I declined, telling him I was no judge of their value & might do him injustice. To satisfy him, however, I placed them with a neighbouring watchmaker, with directions to account with T. for the proceeds. Had I then been aware of the after destinies of this celebrated man & the important part he occupied in the political arena of Europe, I should doubtless have paid more attention to him, for I certainly observed little ceremony towards him & his facetious companion.

While resident in Goddard's Court, he became familiar with the daughter of a poor woman whose dwelling was next to his—both houses being the property of Goddard, who lived at the corner, a respectable mechanic, well known to me. The girl gave birth to a child & it is at least one feature of good feeling on the party of Talleyrand that, after his return to France, he sent frequent presents to mother & child who were thus comfortably provided for. Of these presents, I was from time to time informed by Goddard. After his death, I heard nothing more of either the girl or her babe. G. always spoke of her as a decent, comely young woman.

Talleyrand bore the general reputation of an artful, insincere man & yet the great Duke of Wellington bore this testimony to his worth in the British House of Lords. "In all the transactions in which I have ever been engaged with Prince Talleyrand, no man could have conducted himself with more fairness & ability in regard to his own country or with more uprightness & honour in all his communications with the ministers of other countries than Prince Talleyrand; no man's public & private character has ever been so much abused & belied as those of that illustrious individual."

It would appear that at one time Talleyrand seriously contemplated becoming a citizen of the United States. I had in my possession his autographed application to the proper authorities to that effect. In compliance with the requisites of our laws, he declares in his own hand writing that he renounces allegiance to all foreign powers & potentates, but here the matter appears to have ended. He never applied, I believe, for a certificate of naturalization, the altered state of affairs in Europe, soon after, deciding him to return to France. The Pope absolved him from his vows to the Church & he absolved himself from his pledge to our Government.

At this same period we had among us a certain John de Marsellac, who made the appearance & used the language of a Friend. He had never been formally admitted to membership, but he attended our meetings and preached to us from the upper seat in the gallery. He at first spoke in French & sometimes Samuel Emlen, Saml. Powell Griffiths or

some other Friend who was familiar with the language, standing up beside him, rendered into English what he had said.

My excellent & clear headed & pure hearted father-in-law, John Drinker, never approved of Marsellac's appearances in the ministry, but others were pleased with him & he continued to preach among us. For my part, I did not pretend to set up my judgement in the case. As M. became better acquainted with English, he discarded his interpreters & amused young folks with his blunders. Quoting Scriptures on one of these occasions, I remember, he exclaimed, "I am de sheppare & you are de muttong." Few of the large audience preserved their gravity.

After a stay of some years, Marsellac returned to France, having excited some suspicion among politicians as to his real character. Some weeks subsequent to his embarkation, my Uncle, Henry Drinker, a most respectable & influential citizen & Friend, invited me to a walk. Among other places at which we called was that of the office of the Secretary of State—the Secretary, Timothy Pickering, being an old friend & acquaintance of my Uncle. After some common place chit-chat, Secy. Pickering said, "Oh, Mr. Drinker, I have been very desirous to see you." Then, rising from his seat, he drew from his desk a bundle of papers, which he placed in Uncle's hands—who read with much emotion, the colour frequently flushing his cheeks. They contained the evidence of Marsellac's having acted, while among us, as a spy of the French Government, at the development of which Uncle D. expressed his deep mortification. Congress then sat in Phila.

About the same time, we had among us another distinguished personage, whose identity was known but to few, as he was incognito & a recluse. Once a day he generally passed, with solemn firm step, my place of business & soon moved back on the same path. We saw him no more that day. At length he disappeared altogether. This man was the Pretender, the last of the royal race of Stuarts. He died some years afterwards at Rome, entitled the Duke of York.

Yet another & a greater, among the exiles of the day, was Louis Philippe, the present King of the French & the best King France ever had—a slim, tall young man of unpretending appearance. He was the guest of David Hayfield Cunningham, of the firm of Cunningham, Nesbit & Co. in Front St. below Walnut. I occasionally met him in the street, but never in society. He had but little intercourse with our Citizens in general.

Phila. then abounded with French exiles, not only from the Mother Country, but from the Island of Hayti. After the burning of Cape

François & the massacre of the whites, the wretches & despoiled survivors fled by hundreds & by thousands to our shores & Phila. became their favourite retreat. Generally, they escaped with little more than what they carried about their persons, in the confusion & hurry of the flights from the flames & their infuriated assailants. Yet, stripped as they were, I never knew an instance of their asking alms. From the highest to the lowest, all sought honourable employment rather than beg. Many, who had been liberally educated & accustomed to indulge in the luxuries & splendours of a voluptuous life, did not hesitate to engage in humble occupations in preference to eating the bread of idleness.

I myself gave employment to many females, in making coffee bags, from a very coarse German article called Hessians. They took the cloth to their rooms—the husbands aiding their wives, by cutting out the bags & even by using the needle themselves. The fabric was harsh & husky, skinning the soft fingers of these delicate, worthy women & causing the blood to stain the cloth. Low as the wages were, it furnished them with bread. They complained not, but turned their voices to melody as they plied their hands to their labour. It did my heart good to witness the cheerful resignation with which these people submitted to their hard lot.

There arrived with these exiles from Hayti, some of the prettiest girls I ever beheld. They were very slightly tinged with African blood, their skins smooth, cheeks ruddy, eyes soft & sparkling, teeth without blemish & white as ivory, their countenances ever decked with smiles & good nature. Their hair was long & glossy black, their forms unexceptionally graceful, not inferior to the most elegant Grecian beauties & highly captivating.

They were always dressed richly & gracefully & moved as sylphs on the wings of the wind, their light feet seeming scarcely to touch terra firma. They mixed not with the other islanders but were a class by themselves & seen mostly in clusters.

By what means they lived was best known to themselves. The story went that some of them were rich & brought with them considerable sums of money. When affairs became more settled in their Island, they suddenly disappeared like splendid birds of passage & we saw them no more.

The Irish & German emigrants to our Cities contrast very disadvantageously with the French. Trained in the sinks of vicious & hardened mendicity in their own countries, they at once set to begging on their arrival here & often become a heavy charge on our charity, filling our

streets with their clamourous appeals & our alms houses with unproductive, haggard pauperism.

A Frenchman rarely meddles with our Institutions, an Irishman interferes at once. One of the number, before he stepped from on board ship—being asked by a countryman who had been here before him whether he was a Federalist or a Democrat—said, "I don't know about them there, but anyhow, I'm against the Government." And Pat said truly, for he must have a bubbery wherever he goes &—ignorant as he may be—he is unwilling to believe that anybody knows more than himself.

*October 18th.* The large bequest of Stephen Girard is placed, by Ordinance, in the management of the Commissioners of the Girard Estates, over which I at present preside.

It has been greatly lessened by the failure of the Bank of U. States, thro' the mismanagement of its late President, who has thus inflicted a deeper injury on Philada. & the country at large than any man living, involving ruin to thousands on this as well as the other side of the Atlantic & impairing greatly the means of our other City Banks, to whom the Bank of the U.S. was indebted five millions of Dollars. The fund is likewise crippled by the non payment of interest due it by the State.

*October 19th.* After going thro' our business this evening, I called the attention of the Girard Estate Commissioners to the importance of Council's purchasing the Lemon Hill property (about fifty acres), now for sale, to prevent its falling into hands that may render it a nuisance to the City. It can now be had on fair terms. I regret my inability to persuade them to my views.

*October 24th.* My late worthy father-in-law, John Drinker, used to speak to me of a certain Daniel Trotter, a minister in the Society of Friends. He was a man of few words & often engaged in these expressions—"There is nothing but trouble this side the grave." At a funeral in Friends grounds, the corner of Mulberry & Fourth Streets, few attending, a sailor passing by—seeing a number of persons standing round a grave in perfect silence—advanced to examine into the cause. Just as he arrived & was peering about, Daniel uttered his accustomed exclamation, "There is nothing but trouble this side the grave." "Well, Daddy," said Jack, "come this side, there's none here."

Next door to my father-in-law lived a certain Dr. Abm. Chovet, of no inconsiderable celebrity. He was once overtaken by a shower in the neighbourhood of Samuel R. Fisher's & asked Saml. to lend him an umbrella. "I have none to lend but will lend thee my great coat & as I know thou art in the practice of using bad language, I must enjoin thee not to indulge in it whilst thou hast my coat on." Now Dr. C. was a sort of licensed character & took great liberties with his tongue & Saml. was known to be a little tricky in trade, tho' a Friend. The coat was returned in good time. "Well, I hope thou didst not forget my charge." "No, I did not," rejoined the Dr. "I did not swear a single oath all the time I had your coat on, but in all my life I never felt such a propensity to lie."

Attended in the evening the Com. for Cleansing the City. As usual little to do.

*October 26th.* Councils met this evening when I offered the following preamble & resolution in Select Council.

"Whereas the City of Philada. has been at great expense & incurred a heavy debt by the introduction of a copious supply of pure water from the river Schuylkill into the City & whereas it is essential to the health & comfort of the citizens & the prosperity of the City that the water used for culinary & other domestic purposes should be free from all impurities & whereas the possession by the City of the Lemon Hill Estate may prove the means of more effectually protecting the basin at Fairmount from the introduction of substances more or less prejudicial to the community & whereas it is the bounden duty of Councils as the Guardians of the City interests to pursue all proper means to protect the health & comfort of the inhabitants, be it therefore—

"Resolved that a joint committee to consist of five members from each Council be appointed with authority to purchase on behalf of the City at either public or private sale & on the best terms they can obtain, the property on the river Schuylkill above the water works, known as the Lemon Hill Estate, provided it can be obtained on such terms as they may deem equitable & just."

The resolution & preamble passed in Select Council. There were eight ayes and 2 nays. In Common Council, after some attempts to evade it, they also passed. The joint com. of which I am Chairman will meet in a few days. I regret the publicity of the proceedings, to which I have been driven by the intrigues & contrivances of others.

*October 30th.* Spent some hours with the other referees in valuing the estate of Cad. Evans, deceased. Made considerable progress.

The firemen still continue to disturb the peace of the City by their brutal fights.

*November 2d.* Have come to an understanding with the trustees of the Bank of the U.S. so far as to name a price, on their part, for Lemon Hill & neither they nor myself are to name it to others at present for very obvious reasons. They have consented to take $75000 from the City. They tell me that on a former occasion, J. P. Wetherill offered them $180,000, but as their price then was $250,000, the negotiations were broken off. How can you then account for his present opposition? Because, replied the agent, the motion to purchase at this time did not originate with him.

*November 7th.* Called on by my nephew, Herman Cope, agent of the trustees of the Bank to say that the price, $75000, for Lemon Hill had got out notwithstanding the pledge of secrecy & that a company was forming to buy it on speculation. Some of the trustees must have divulged the secret, for I have not named it to a single individual.

*November 8th.* Sleep last night disturbed. The Lemon Hill affair engages my thoughts by day & by night.

*November 10th.* When Councils adjourned, the Com. on Lemon Hill resumed their sitting, which proved long & tumultuous, made so by Wetherill, Gilpin, Barton & Hagert, Secy. After much opposition the following was adopted by yeas & nays & we adjourned in very bad humour. "Resolved that the sub-committee be authorized to purchase the Lemon Hill property from the Trustees of the Bank of the U.S., provided it can be had not exceeding $75,000." There were six yeas & four nays. Attempts were made by these four men to deprive me of a vote because I occupied the chair. The sub-committee remained a few minutes after the departure of the rest & instructed me to proceed in the negotiation for the Estate. It is the first time I have been clothed with authority. I hope it may not come too late.

*November 13th.* A communication from the trustees of the Bank of the U.S. received at 12:30 P.M., requiring an answer before 1 P.M. whether we will purchase the Lemon Hill Estate, yea or nay. I hurried to the Banking House, found the trustees in session & a person in waiting for my answer. I could not hesitate, the prosperity of our beautiful City, the health & comfort of its inhabitants, all seemed imperiously to demand my unqualified assent. I have given it & in doing so, think I have rendered the City one of the most important services of my life.

The consideration is, as previously stated, seventy five thousand Dollars, a price in my opinion greatly below its value. There are about 52 acres in the whole, about 7½ of which are flooded by the City dam at Fairmount, never paid for by the City & which, had the property fallen into other hands, would have involved a claim on the City Corporation of more than twenty thousand Dollars. I am almost surprized at the success with which I have been able to conduct this negotiation to such a happy issue, so blindly & willfully as I have been opposed by the very men who ought to have given me their support. It has caused no little thought to me by day & by night. I know not what yet may be in store for me when the Com. meets this evening.

The Com. met at 7 P.M. All present. The campaign opened by an attack on the minutes by Snowden. The secy. had made a minute to refer a certain matter to Councils, when no such reference had been ordered. The minute was stricken out. Other corrections were made & then commenced the battle. The members who had voted for the purchase at the last meeting of the Com. did not think it worth while to dispute the omission of the vote for the purchase, but called for the question on the resolution anew. I requested the secy. to call the yeas & nays as they had been previously ordered; instead of doing that, he began to dispute about it. I said at last, "Will the secretary proceed with the call or shall I?" He hesitated, but finally proceeded.

Several names were called when Barton commenced a speech. I called him to order & said that after we had commenced the call of the members no other business could be entertained until the names of all the members were taken down & the result announced from the chair. He remained on his feet until I intimated that he must take his seat & from that seat he requested that he might be excused from voting. I put the question—four yeas & four nays. I decided that he should vote but added that I would reverse the decision if, when his name should be called by the secy., he still wished to be excused. The secy. proceeded. Barton was called, he wavered for a minute & then answered in the affirmative. On the final passage of the resolution the yeas were seven, the nays three. When the decision was announced from the chair, Gilpin moved that before the completion of the purchase, the Com. should report the price, $75000, to the Councils & await their decision. The yeas & nays were taken on this motion & were three yeas & seven nays. The Com. then adjourned, Wetherill & Gilpin uttering threats as

they departed. The sub. com. remained & instructed me to purchase the Estate forthwith.

*November 14th.* This morning addressed a note, of which the following is a copy, to the Trustees.

"In consequence of the renewed instructions from the Joint Com. of the City Councils authorizing the purchase of Lemon Hill Estate, passed last evening, the 13th of November 1843, I hereby accept the offer made to me by the Trustees of the Bank of the U.S. to sell to the City of Philada. the Lemon Hill Estate, containing about fifty two acres of land for the sum of seventy five thousand Dollars." Signed by myself as chairman & directed to James Dundas & other Trustees. I who laboured so hard & spent so much time in bringing the Schuylkill water originally into Philada. cannot but rejoice at the consummation of this purchase.

London is supplied with water from several sources. The New River supplies 13,000,000 gallons a day. The East London water works supply 6,000,000. The Grand Junction Canal supplies 2,800,000. The West Middlesex Company supplies 2,250,000. These together furnish the city of London with 24,000,000 gallons daily. Besides these, the inhabitants receive from the Thames, running thro' London, 4,000,000 daily. This latter is doubtless filthy, as some of the common sewers enter the river near the source of supply. It is, however, but a seventh part of the entire quantity, 28,000,000 gallons. We are not yet & I trust never will be, driven to the necessity of drinking impure water.

*November 15th.* Met the Directors of the Mercantile Library. A proposition from the Historical Society to join them in getting up a course of lectures the coming winter. The board declined, it being too late to engage Lecturers & to make other arrangements.

*November 16th.* In the evening met the Com. of the Girard Estates. Gilpin present & civil. Wetherill absent—but sent us a present of a dozen of very fine wine!

*November 17th.* Today was spent at Haverford in a dense fog. The board met there & resolved on some interesting matters. Townsend Sharpless, one of our number, read a very good address to the scholars. The school is in fine order. The new teachers succeed well, but the pupils are few.

*November 18th.* In passing thro' Washington Square, I thought I perceived something like a butterfly & on saying so to the Keeper, he said that he saw one yesterday. Everywhere I meet citizens who express their satisfaction with the purchase of Lemon Hill for the City. It is considered a very cheap purchase & so, undoubtedly, it is.

*November 21st.* At half past 3 P.M., read my essay of a report on the purchase of Lemon Hill to the five other friends of the measure on the joint com., who approved. Barton was not invited. He may perhaps give it his signature.

*November 23d.* Spent the principal part of the morning in preparation for the evening. An interview with Edw. Olmstead, City Solicitor, on the modeling of an ordinance providing for the payment of Lemon Hill to accompany my report. Have just returned from Council. My report was read & the bill making an appropriation for payment was, to my surprize, read & agreed to by every member of Select Council but Wetherill & unanimously adopted in Common Council. It would, after the purchase, have been disgraceful to do otherwise & many of the members voted for the measure because of its popularity, afraid to meet public opinion if they did not, but it would not surprize me if an early effort were made to divest the City in some way of this very valuable possession.

Such men as Wetherill & Gilpin are unaccustomed to be so signally defeated & will seek their revenge. Before Councils met, reports reached me from various sources that W. would make most deadly attacks on me this evening, not in the fashion of olden time, with 39 lashes of the cat-o-nine tails on my poor, naked, sinful back, but with the Russian knout, until all life should be beaten out of me! He contented himself with one assault, not on me, but on Lemon Hill & by recording his solitary vote. Now that I am still alive & kicking, he may wish me banished to Siberia or sent to a warmer place to which he seems fond of sending refractory offenders. This remarkable being is in stature below the common size, dark complexion, sharp visaged, keen black unsettled eye, black bushy hair & beard. He shaves once a week & has a savage aspect. He is a great sloven, often so dirty as to be offensive, dressing with one or two of his garments coarse & mean & another fine & dashing & very costly. He prides himself on these eccentricities & in his actions is governed by impulse & passion. A great egotist, continually boasting of his great achievements & possessing indomitable obstinacy. When he seizes on his prey he is like a small terrier on a rat; he'll shake & shake & shake & will not be driven off by sops or kicks.

When at Harrisburg, with myself, as delegates to the Harrison elec-

toral college in 1840, he amused some of us one evening with his usual rodomontade & among other things said that his father was one of City Council & member of the Watering Com. that originally introduced the Schuylkill water into Philada. & that he wrote all the reports of the Com. to Councils at that interesting & anxious period. Now the fact is this, the water was introduced by the party then known as Federalists, of which I was one & Saml. Wetherill, his father, was of the Democratic party & came into power by their opposition to the water works & that, with the exception of one report written by my brother-in-law, Henry Drinker, Jr., I myself wrote all the reports of the Watering Com. to Councils at that eventful epoch.

*November 24th.* Rain last night. Met the Overseers of Friends Public Schools at 3 P.M. Some rules for teachers & pupils adopted. Wm. Evans objected that where the Scriptures are required to be read daily & especially the New Testament, a distinction was drawn as if the Old Testament were of inferior authority.

*December 15th.* In the evening attended one of Dr. Lardner's lectures on Astronomy. His planetarium & dioramas are splendid & his explanations were clear & very interesting. At the close he treated us with an exhibition of the Drummond Light, the most brilliant light I ever beheld.

Instructive as are his lectures, I could not but feel some qualms on the propriety of giving him countenance by my presence. He is an Englishman & tho' a clergyman, has abandoned his own & attached himself to another man's wife, with whom he cohabits. Her legitimate husband's name is Heavyside. He prosecuted the Doctor & recovered, it is said, damages to the extent of 8000 Pounds Sterling or $40,000. Lardner's audience tonight, notwithstanding, was very large & very respectable, drawn together by his science & powers of definition. It is not, however, probably that I shall attend another of his lectures.

It was said that when John Turner, of Turner's Lane, was married, he asked the clergyman who tied the knot how much was to be paid. "I charge nothing," was the reply, "I think you have a hard bargain enough without." Dr. L. has probably discovered by this time that he has paid enough for his bargain.

When my nephew Dick Drinker was a lad, he called on the late Davenport Marott, a good natured tradesman in Coomb's Alley & importuned M. to turn him a top, a service he was wont to render gratis when at leisure. Dick was urgent & when at last the top was finished, asked M. what he charged, "Why, I charge thee never to enter my shop again," was the quick retort.

*December 18th.* Information is given me by Elliott & Co. Scriveners, that the title to Lemon Hill is imperfect. I had apprehended from the long delay that something of the kind, either real or imaginary, would be got up. If the title be not perfect, the purchase must be waived. We must see further before a final decision. A brief must be made out & submitted to able counsel or I shall not be satisfied, knowing that these Scriveners & our City Solicitor are not free from prejudice & certain influences on the subject of this purchase.

*December 19th.* Our firemen do not improve in their morals. Riots take place on almost every alarm of fire. On the night of the 17th, a board yard was consumed in Kensington. The Weccacoe Hose Co. from Southwark attended & was attacked by the Fairmount Engine Co. of the Northern Liberties & the carriage totally destroyed. This volunteer system, once so efficient in the hands of respectable citizens, is found no longer to answer.

*December 26th.* A separation has recently taken place in the Indiana Yearly Meeting of Friends—a part having formed a Y.M. consisting of persons favourable to the schemes of the anti-slavery Societies, which associations are—by Friends in general—considered as influenced by more zeal than discretion. Some Friends here talk as familiarly of a separation among ourselves & Y.M.'s to the east of us as tho' it were an every day common concern. Not on the anti-slavery question but questions of doctrine. What a lamentable & marvellous state of affairs. It would really seem as if Satan were let loose among us—already are the bonds of social intercourse broken & confidence impaired to a degree in which it has become necessary, in speaking, to do so as if surrounded by spies & informers, even among family connections.

Most of our members have attained considerable perfection in splitting hairs & in distorting & perverting the meaning of words. Gossiping & eavesdropping occupy no inconsiderable portion of the time of both sexes, not excluding our Preachers, in fact they are the most active in the unholy warfare of undermining the reputation of others, whether travelling in the ministry or in the domestic circle. There is as much scuffling for office & place as among politicians, but conducted with more secrecy & private caballing. This is a disgusting picture of our once favoured Society, but alas too true. "Whom God means to destroy, he first makes mad."

*December 28th.* An interview with Jas. Dundas, Esq., Pres. of the Board of Trustees of the Bk. U. States & also of the Commercial Bk. He informs me that several objections to the title of Lemon Hill have been made. When one is removed, another is urged, that removed, then another. He considers them all frivolous & put forward to defeat the sale. He told me that at the Trustees' late public sale, J. P. Wetherill made open objections to their title to coal lands in Schuylkill Co. to deter other bidders & then purchased the tract himself.

Muggy weather still. *Muggy* is too expressive a word to be discarded merely from the learned calling it vulgar. So say they of *gawk*, but that is too good to be lost to the English vocabulary. The vulgar must have words in which to utter their meaning of things, as well as the book-worms.

At the monthly meeting yesterday, my son Henry was appointed an elder. My prayer to God is that he may, in this important station, be favoured to serve Him with a perfect heart & willing mind. So may he be qualified, without favour or partiality, to be useful to the Church, to his fellow members & to the Society at large.

*December 31st.* This is the first day of the week, the last of the month & the last of the year, circumstances calculated to excite reflection. The sun rose without a cloud & having run his appointed course, went down gloriously & now night has come. In her solemn march & silver robe, the moon shines in all her brilliancy.

When to me, the end of all things in this transitory scene shall be proclaimed & the awful cry shall be, "Time to thee shall be no longer," may the Father of Mercies grant that my setting sun shall also descend brightly & serenely & my spirit awake in that celestial abode where sorrowing & sighing are unknown—in that blissful City which has "no need of the sun, neither of the moon, to shine on it for God doth lighten it & the Lamb is the light thereof." But should I ever be thus blessed, it will be from no merit of my own, but from the mercy of my Saviour & Redeemer.

# 1844

*January 1st*. The termination of one year & the commencement of another—whether we look back on past transactions or forward to events yet to happen—it is an epoch in our lives, a point at which we may stop to breathe & take refreshment, it being so much of an advancement in our journey to that bourne whence no traveller returns. Usually a season of mirth, it is also a time for solemn thought on the past, the present & the future. May it prove to myself a season of amendment & good resolves.

The first day of a new year has, from time immemorial, been observed as an interesting era in the history of man. The Jews esteemed it as the day on which God held & passed judgement on his creatures. They considered the day to be the anniversary of the creation of Adam. The Romans sacrificed to Janus—a King while living & worshipped as a God after death. On this day also the Roman Senate repaired in a body to the Capitol & offered sacrifices to Jupiter. Some of their Emperors received involuntary presents on this festive occasion from the people, to many of whom it was very oppressive. Some of the monarchs of England, among them the famed Elizabeth, copying this example, extorted no small presents from their subjects. Many of the fineries were thus obtained by the Queen as appeared on her demise. Her 3000 dresses were believed to have mainly been obtained by these impositions.

The long accustomed practice among us of firing away the old & saluting the new year was not forgotten today & guns & pistols were in requisition, tho' I think there is some diminution of this absurd fervour.

While at dinner, a note was handed to me from Ed. Olmstead, Esq., City Solicitor, stating that the title to Lemon Hill is so defective that the City is not bound to take the Estate. I sent a copy of this note forthwith to Jas. Dundas, Esq., Chairman of the Trustees of the Bk. U. States. I have looked for some such result, altho' this same Ed. Olmstead, City Solicitor, informed myself & others some weeks back that after an examination of the title papers, he was satisfied that the title was good. So we go.

*January 4th*. Received a note from Jas. Dundas, Esq., Chairman of the Trustees of the Bank of the U.S. acknowledging the receipt of mine enclosing to him the communication from the City Solicitor, asking to have the deficiencies complained of in the title to Lemon Hill to be

specified, expressing confidence in its sufficiency & intimating that if the City should not comply with the contract, the Estate may be sold publicly & the City sued for the loss, as loss may be expected under an alleged defect of title.

*January 5th.* Had the sub-committee on Lemon Hill together & submitted to them my reply to the Solicitor in which I desire him to furnish specifically & at large, the reasons on which he founds his objections to the title, to see whether the Trustees can remove them. The letter being approved, I sent it by a person into whose hands it was given by the City Treasurer at my request.

In the evening an arbitration between two members of our religious Society met at my house. We had but little trouble in the case—the claim of one, viz. Wm. C., on the other, J.C., being to our minds very clear. The arbitrators were Isaiah Hacker, Uriah Hunt & myself. How much better to settle differences in this peaceable way than by litigation. The sum in dispute is about $2200.

*January 10th.* This morning the sleigh bells jingle merrily thro' the streets.

Ezra Comfort was at our weekday meeting this morning & disburdened his mind in his usual invectives against learning, accompanied with some just remarks on the poor in spirit. He quoted the scripture, "Thou hast hid these things from the prudent & the wise of this world & revealed them to babes & sucklings." After which Eliz. Evans rose in approbation of his discourse & among other things said, "If it were the last words I should ever utter, I must say there are persons present & I wish I could say they are few who, in the pursuit of wealth & the honours & distinctions of the world, are the leprosy of this meeting." Indulging for some time in other severe remarks, she again repeated the same words & concluded with awful imprecations on such of our members as "live in palaces." For whom these severities & denunciations were intended, I know not. My conscience acquits me, but I must consider them as unjust, illiberal & unsanctified.

The gathering was, as usual on weekdays, quite small, which made the address the more pointed. As to myself, I can truly aver that I never was greedy of wealth & as to political distinction, I never did covet that. I have given many thousands of my own earnings to the use of our religious society & have for more than 40 years had almost yearly importunities to become a member of assembly, a Senator or a Representative in Congress & these I have constantly resisted, tho' I have not felt myself bound to decline all usefulness to my fellow citizens in works of charity, in public improvements & other social & public duties. I am reminded on this occasion most forcibly of Emmor Kimber—taken from the dregs of society, he became exalted to the station of a minister in this same meeting & a more insolent preacher never entered our gallery. He spoke much & long, travelled, like some others, far & wide thro' our country & none more active in meetings of business or more censorious & invective. Well, he ran his course—tho' for a long time praised as an eloquent minister & a great favourite among Friends, he fell, was disowned & disgraced. "Set a beggar on horseback, etc."

Now Wm. & Elizabeth Evans lived for some years in a cooped up place, on Front Street, where Wm. still has his drug & paint shop. As their means increased, they removed their family to Pine Street & when their father, Jonathan Evans, died, they went into his dwelling on Union Street. They remodeled the house, put up fashionable folding doors between the parlours, fashionable marble mantels, made the front door more modern, took away the old fashioned window sashes, put up new & much larger panes, disposed of the old furniture & substituted fashionable mahogany, sofas, tables &c., &c. A member of our meeting remarked to me on this subject, "While Wm. & his wife occupied their confined accommodation on Front Street, that was the pattern for others & when they got into their house on Pine Street, that became the pattern. Now again they have removed into their new model dwelling on Union Street, & that became the standard which none might exceed." Well, mark what happened—a little busy, meddling body named Wills from N. Jersey paid a visit to this abode & found fault with the fashionable alterations, deeming them unbecoming the occupants. Elizabeth happened not to be at home, but when told of the remarks of her visitant said, "She is very impertinent."

It has long been remarked how much more easy it is to preach than to practice & how much more severe is a lewd woman than a chaste one on the weak sisterhood. Now, I am not disposed to find fault with the changes in Elizabeth's stile of living, nor with the rich dresses in which she always appears, nor with the shining hat & shoes & fine coat of her husband, when coarser clothing would answer as well, but I want them to exercise a little more Christian forbearance & charity towards others. They are both eminent ministers, but I much doubt if either of them have ever made one convert.

*January 11th*. When the Blockley Almshouse was building, I was

Pres. of the Board of Guardians & John Moss was one of the Building Com. On occasion of inspecting the progress of the work, a cold collation was provided. Moss helped me to a slice of ham & ate heartily of it himself. I asked him how he, being a Jew, could indulge in such food. "Oh, Mr. Cope," was the reply, "Moses never tasted a Burlington ham or he never would have made such a Law as he did."

*January 12th*. Roses, a late writer says, were first sent from Italy to England in 1522 & consecrated as presents from the Pope. In 1526, they were placed over confessionals as symbols of secrecy. Hence originated the phrase "under the rose," implying secrecy.

It is a gratifying circumstance to notice the increased employment of young females in our shops. In France this practice has long been in use. There, they are also engaged as clerks in counting houses & banks & are found to be more steady than young men, dispatching their duties with cheerfulness & correctness. The government, it is added, contemplates their employment in the public offices. While I should be glad to see the sex thus engaged in our own country, I feel an abhorrence to their ever being employed as scavengers, as is the case in Paris.

*January 13th*. Yesterday afternoon it commenced raining & continued all night with the wind veering to south.

I stated on the 10th that I had constantly resisted importunities to serve in Legislative bodies. I should have made one exception. I was elected in 1808 to the House of Representatives of Penna. It was a special election. The House consisted of 43 Democrats & 42 Conservatives. One vacancy, by the sudden death of Samuel Carver of the latter party, from the City. If the Democrats should succeed, much mischief was apprehended. If the Federalists, much might be prevented. My friends assailed me in such way that I consented & was elected. It is true that I served in the late Convention for revising the Constitution of Penna. & on the Harrison Electoral College, both of a temporary character. I sought neither, nor do I regret serving. I never in my life sought or courted office, for two reasons—first, from a consciousness of want of qualifications & secondly because I had neither pleasure, desire, nor taste for political distinction. Had I been ambitious of the honours or emoluments of public life, I might have been gratified to the extent of my wishes, unworthy as I am.

But time was when the government of Penna. was almost exclusively in the hands of Friends. Wm. Penn was himself the Governor. The

Assembly was composed of Friends & the Magistracy, high & low, including the Judges, were members of the Society.

And as to large dwellings, we have nothing now amongst us to be compared to many within my memory. There were Samuel Rhoads, John Pemberton, Jas. Pemberton, Henry Drinker, Samuel Emlen, Edward Pennington & others—particularly the two last named—& Israel Pemberton, whose gardens occupied each nearly a fourth of one of our squares & were filled with trees, both fruit & forest & a splendid variety of strawberry shrubbery & flowers. Were these men inferior to the Friends of the present time? By no means. They were, on the contrary, a galaxy not only in the firmament of our Society but in the community at large & it is my firm opinion that had they been coeval with the day of Elias Hicks, Hicksism would not have prevailed, nor would the Society be, as it now is, rent from one end of the continent to the other. Several of the houses specified & several others belonging to & occupied by Friends had four rooms on a floor, wide halls & back buildings. The house still standing at the NW corner of Front & Walnut Streets, late the dwelling of Samuel Coates & built for his Uncle John Rennel, both Friends, is a pretty good example of the size & stile of those to which I have referred.

*January 15th.* Ice, between 3 & 4 inches taken from the ponds, is now being placed in our ice houses. There is but little floating in the Delaware & the Schuylkill is only partially frozen.

Met the Board of Managers of the Mercantile Library & was again elected President. It is a most useful Institution. The number of young men who spend their evenings in the library room reading & acquiring useful knowledge, instead of resorting to the corrupting influences of theatres, does not diminish & if we succeed in our present scheme of procuring better accommodations, great additional benefit to the youth of our City will doubtless be the consequence. The subscriptions for the erection of the proposed edifice seems, so far, to work well. When the mind acquires taste for literature, it will have less relish for indulgences of a debasing character.

*January 18th.* I have often occasion to think that Lawyers & especially young Lawyers do not make the best Legislators. Accustomed in their vocation to advocate but one side of a question, it becomes a habit from which it is difficult to depart & the juniors of the profession are too apt to convert the Legislative hall into a school for debate & the

exercise of skill in defeating an antagonist or of sustaining some measure of their own, as they would that of their client, right or wrong.

*January 22d.* That wit & punster, Tom Dibdin, had a horse he called Graphy. He said, "When I made up my mind to own a horse, I said I would buy a Graphy (biography). When I mounted him I was atop o' Graphy (topography). When I want him to canter, I say, Gee O Graphy (geography) & when I want him to stand still & he won't I say, But you ought to, Graphy (autography)."

Some years ago there was a Tavern in High Street west of Broad with a swinging sign of Shakespeare bedizened with gold lace & other gaudy trappings—the name appended in large letters from this. Two Germans, passing by, stopped to admire the splendid painting. One of them, conning over the name, exclaimed, "Oh, I knows dat fellor." "You know him?" said the other, "Yes," rejoined his acute companion, "I knows Shake Sperry very well," meaning Jacob Sperry, a German merchant, then residing in Philada. but now deceased.

*January 23d.* The ice men are busy hauling fine ice, 4 inches thick.

Murders & suicides have become more in favour than duels. Within a week, two cases of self destruction have occurred in the City, each of a peculiar character, both young men on the eve of marriage, with fair prospects of competence & happiness.

When Congress met in Philada., a delegate named Jackson from Georgia challenged a Representative from R.I., whose name I have forgotten. He refused to fight, on which Jackson, who was a passionate man, called the other, in the course of debate, a coward. His antagonist arose with these words, "The gentleman calls me a coward. Well, I acknowledge that I am a coward & he knows it or he would not have challenged me." The House was in a roar of laughter & the matter passed off.

*January 29th.* Have just received by mail from J.M. Porter, Secy. of War, his annual report for 1843-1844 of the Department on Indian Affairs, including the report from T.H. Crawford, Commissioner of Indian Affairs, to the Secy. Among the many wrongs inflicted by the whites on the red brethren, it is some consolation to perceive that progress in the arts of civilization is making its way into their new abode west of the Mississippi.

The Cherokees & Choctaws have written constitutions & laws, courts of justice, juries, sheriffs, &c. The latter tribe have 10 or 12 cotton gins. The Creeks, too, the most powerful of all the tribes, cultivate large tracts of land, have a printing press & a regular government. All these & other tribes have schools which are said to be well attended. Now, if our people would admit them into the Union, that is, permit them to form a state & be represented in our Congress, as other states are, it would be but a simple act of justice & would prove their political as well as their physical preservation. Without that, I fear there will be a termination of their whole race.

*February 2d.* From an official account it appears that within the last twenty-five years, no less than 45,000 new houses, forming 750 streets & squares have been erected in London. Great as has been the growth of the City, the increase of buildings & inhabitants in several of our Cities in America has been, within the same period, in even a greater ratio.

New York, Philada., Pittsburg, Cincinnati, Baltimore may be taken as examples. Since I engaged in mercantile business, the ground on Sixth Street west of Independence Square was in grass & surrounded by post & rail fences. Between 1793 & 1800, when I was in business, corner of Jones Alley & Second Street, Samuel Emlen lived in & owned the dwelling, south side of Mulberry below Sixth Street, his lot being then bounded westward by Sixth Street. That part was planted with fruit trees, surrounded by a post & rail fence & an occasional building only was seen between his premises & Schuylkill.

Samuel not infrequently addressed me thus, "Tom, I want thee to buy my house. It may suit such a young chap as thee, but I am tired of living so far away & wish to live nearer in Town." Samuel was an eminent minister & a learned man, a good classical scholar & an instructive, agreeable companion. He often quoted Latin in his public discourses. He was short-sighted & when a person accosted him frequently had to ask who it was. On one occasion he met a young man named Reynolds. "Who is it?" said Samuel. "Why, Tom Reynolds." Tom was a great gallant—wore a double breasted blue cloth coat with gilt buttons & was always gaily attired. The parties were well known to each other.

"Tom, why dost thou not wear a plain coat, in place of that gaudy one?" "Why should I do that, Mr. Emlen?" "To mortify thyself," was the reply. "Well, Mr. Emlen, if you'll wear my coat, I'll wear yours & then, I think, we shall both be mortified."

*February 3d.* The day has been fine & soft, with a blue October sky. The Mercantile Library Board met in the bright moonlit evening &

transacted their usual business. The building subscriptions are still on the increase.

*February 6th*. It seems there was another battle among the fire companies on the evening of the 3d. A young man, a spectator, received a blow from a club that knocked out eight of his teeth. The authorities of the districts quail before the rioters, having submissively in Board voted the annual appropriations last night of $300 to each of the very companies engaged in the last & previous fights. When the vote was announced the firemen, in & out of Commissioners Hall, gave loud & repeated cheers.

*February 19th*. Attended, on behalf of the City, a meeting of the stockholders of the Philada. Insurance Company, which is about closing its concerns. I lately attended a meeting of another insurance company, the Penna., for the same purpose. There remain still enough of such institutions to satisfy our diminished commerce. New York & Boston are going greatly ahead of us.

Met the Board of Trade in the evening. Several memorials resolved on—one for the repeal of certain provisions in the Act preventing imprisonment for debt, so as to guard against its abuse, it being found that persons arriving from other States & indebted to our citizens escape being arrested & made to pay their debts tho' their pockets may be full of money. Nor can their property be attached when they are present. Thus a man may purchase goods for cash, get possession of them & go with them to Pittsburg & the defrauded creditor can neither arrest the rogue nor yet attach the goods. This ought not to be.

*February 22d*. A Western paper thus discourses, "There is a town out west which appears to have been overlooked by Dickens & other English travellers of his class & which is all sorts of a stirring place. In one day recently, they had two street fights, hung a man, rode three out of town on a rail, got up a quarter race, a turkey shooting, a gander pulling, a match dog-fight, then a race for drinks all round & as if this were not enough, the judge of the court, after losing a year's salary at single handed poker & whipping a person who said he didn't understand the game, went out & helped to lynch a man for hog stealing." A stirring place truly.

*February 24th*. The question of the annexation of Texas to these U. States is again agitating the Councils of our country & Senator R.J.

Walker, of Miss., has sent me a copy of his letter to citizens of Kentucky containing his views on the subject.

*February 25th.* It is First Day & our two English Friends gave us some close doctrine this morning, with encouraging advice.

Dugan & Aseneth Clark (his wife, daughter of Nathan Hunt) of N. Carolina, on their way to England, appeared at our afternoon meeting & spoke. They were also at the evening meeting at Mulberry Street & again addressed us. Her farewell appeal to the audience was affecting & drew tears from my eyes & probably from many others. She appeared also in supplication. They have engaged passage in my son's Ship, the *Thomas P. Cope*, for Liverpool, to sail tomorrow morning.

*February 26th.* The two Clarks took their departure this morning. The Ship towed out by the City Ice-Boat. May God prosper the errand whereunto they are commissioned. They are poor as to the mammon of this world but, I trust, rich in faith & good works.

In relation to Texas, I am not aware that its southern boundary, if ours, would insure us from annoyance any better than its northern. Supposing us to have acquired that country, we would be placed in direct contact with Mexico. That great region acquired, we should next have to contend for Guatemala &c. & next in turn for all the state of South America to Cape Horn. A pretty large tract for one Republic.

The Pope of Rome has just given to the United States a metropolitan Bishop & five Arch-Bishops. This ambitious community is making great strides towards power in the United States. The Jesuits, the most intriguing of all people, are becoming numerous in our country. Priests by dozens are sent among us & scattered over the country. Cathedrals, nunneries & schools under Catholic supervision & Catholic teachers are becoming numerous. One of our near neighbours, a widow Keating, has within a few weeks left her family of children & grandchildren to enter the nunnery at Georgetown, D.C. & a female distantly connected with our family, who lately joined the Catholics, married & the mother of several children, has hinted to us something like her intention to follow the example & thus shut herself out from the world.

Successful efforts have been made in N.Y. & are attempting here, by the Catholics, to exclude the Bible from our public schools. No boundary line, not even the annexation of Texas, can bar out this overflow of Catholicism from this country.

The Directors of the Public Schools in Moyamensing have discontinued the reading of the Bible in their schools. The attempt to do the same

thing in other parts of the country is resisted by the Protestants. There is a good deal of excitement on the subject.

*February 28th.* Nicholas Biddle, late Pres. of the Bank of the U.S., died yesterday morning at his farm on the Delaware, above Frankford, in the 59th year of his age. My sincere wish is that his spirit may rest in peace, but his reputation has suffered irretrievably by his management of that Institution. Gen. Jackson excepted, no man known to me has inflicted so deep a wound on the credit & character of the country.

I have no doubt that he entered the Bank with good intentions, tho' there are persons who think that his morality, especially in his gallantries, was modeled too much after the French school.

I saw nothing, for some time, to lessen my confidence in his integrity & served in the Direction for several years. His views were, however, at all times too extensive & speculative for prudent banking & his ambition was unbounded. These circumstances were the cause of anxiety & no little trouble to me & I left the Bank in 1831. It was then in a prosperous condition. My situation as Chairman of the Com. on the Branches & also on the Com. of Exchange gave me the opportunity of being well acquainted with its financial concerns. It then possessed, besides its capital of $35,000,000, a clear surplus of not less than $5,000,000 & after the termination of the Charter from the U.S. & after the Government withdrew its $7,000,000 of the capital, it received also its portion of the profits at the rate of $15.69 per ct. above the par value. Hence there remained for the Stockholders more than $32,000,000—of which immense sum the whole has been squandered & scattered to the winds!

After the expiration of the old Charter, another was obtained from the State of Penna., it is believed by bribery & other contemptible means. N. Biddle retired from the Bank & managed to place his kinsman Thos. Dunlap in the presidency. The Bank failed soon after, pulling down with it all our other City banks & involving in ruin thousands & tens of thousands of individuals on both sides of the Atlantic, inflicting also a mortal blow on the prosperity of the country —from which it is but slowly recovering. Our own poor City & State—I do not ascribe it all to the Bank—remain still in a sickly condition, tho' I hope convalescent.

Dunlap gave place to Col. Wm. Drayton. I was much urged to take the station, but had wisdom enough to decline & calling one day at the Bank to pay my respects to him, he asked me if I had any idea of the amount of the funds of the Bank which N. Biddle had used at different times without the knowledge of the Board. On my answering in the negative, he said, "Sixteen millions of Dollars—there is the statement." I did not understand him to say that N.B. had appropriated that sum to his own coffers, but that he had used that amount in various speculations in Cotton &c. without consulting with the Board & without its privity.

*February 29th.* Information is received that the United States Supreme Court has decided the case of the heirs of Stephen Girard vs. the City in favour of the latter. This decision is of great importance to our citizens at large. I feel it so to myself, for altho' the executors have settled their accounts & received a discharge, yet—had the decision been in favour of the heirs—that settlement & discharge might not have been respected. The decision reached us last night.

*March 6th.* Several of our newspapers contain eulogies on the character of N. Biddle. I am sorry for it & wish they would permit his ashes to slumber in peace. The effect will probably be to stir up spirits which also had best be permitted to slumber. His conduct as Pres. of the Bank U.S. cannot be justified, but has inflicted a heavy, perhaps irretrievable calamity on our once prosperous City & extending in its consequences over the whole United States.

The Bank was one of the best Institutions of a monetary system that was ever created in this or in any other country. Its credit & usefulness were unbounded. Its paper, whether in the form of Bank Notes or Bills of Exchange, passed freely & without question, not only in all America, but in Europe & Asia. Being located in our City, its good reputation gave strength & credit to our especial community. Philada. was the center of exchange, foreign & domestic. When the Bank failed, our commerce & good name took forthwith a downward course—to rise, I fear, no more. The time will come when the wants of our traders, the people at large & the Government itself will demand another National Bank. But whenever that day shall arrive, we cannot expect our fallen City to become the seat or focus of its operations.

*March 8th.* A Boston paper contains a solution of the common phrase "mind your P's & Q's." In the old English ale houses, it was the custom to chalk down on the side of the wall the number of pints & quarts drunk by each toper, whose attention was called to his ability to pay the reckoning by "mind your P's & Q's." It was probably at one of

these Houses that the landlord called to his wife, "My dear, did you chalk down that pint to the gentleman?" "Yes, sir." "Well then, chalk it again, for fear you forget it."

A short interview with Hor. Binney. Found him still engaged in writing out his speech. Nothing conclusive yet about the title to Lemon Hill. Discover that he has been called on by J.P.W. Had a little conversation respecting Millerism & said I was informed that Doctr. T., a popular Episcopal preacher, was tinged with the doctrine. "Mr. Cope," said H., "whenever you witness unusual zeal in religion, as in politics, you may rely on it that ambition & the love of power are at the bottom of it. I care not who is the person." H. belongs to the same profession as Doc. T., but I believe is not of his immediate congregation.

Ambition & a thirst for distinction, no doubt, often sway the intemperate zealot, even in my own highly professing religious Society. In stating that H. is of the same profession with Doc. T., I mean not that he is a clergyman, but that he is an Episcopalian.

To some of our D.D.'s & others who teach without that scholastic distinction, the definition of an M.D. might be applicable—"A man who puts drugs, of which he knows nothing, into stomachs of which he knows less."

*March 10th.* First Day. My dear wife & her niece M.S., who lives with us, have gone to meeting & left me to my own reflections. I believe that social worship is a duty, but God is to be met with everywhere & may be worshipped as acceptably in our closet as well as in the congregations of the people. Being under the influence of a cold, I feel as if I might be excused for remaining at home. If we are in a right frame of mind, we may improve when listening to a discourse with which we cannot unite & the spirit & temper of which we feel to be wrong. It is a trial of patience & should excite us to an examination of ourselves, to try of what spirit we are. The Church, however, suffers. When persons in high stations become ambitious & fond of power & indulge these propensities to the injury of their fellow professors, by either overt or covert attacks, to which the offended, whatever they may feel, have not the opportunity to reply, it cannot be otherwise than injurious to the harmony of the body.

My observation teaches me to believe that there is often covered under a broad brim & demure face as much of the spirit of intrigue, desire for distinction & thirst for power & place as swells the bosom of the political stump orator & the declaimer at our party Town Meetings.

Jesuits are to be found elsewhere than in the Papal order. Lord preserve me from becoming an accuser of the brethren, but I cannot deny that which mine eyes have seen, mine ears heard, my understanding knows & my heart feels.

*March 11th.* This, according to old stile, would be the first day of the month & my mother-in-law, Rachel Drinker, would not acknowledge that March began until the 11th, new stile. It was a saying of hers that we "might alter names as we pleased, but that the weather would not change for us." Well, be it so. This day, lovely as it is, is not more so than was the first.

A morning call from a Yankee with a considerable notion under his arm, a model in tin of a Canal Boat, a contrivance to carry merchandize & passengers by detached sections to be shifted from boat to carriage & vice versa, propelled in either case by steam. His name is Gilman Converse. He wants aid to put his machinery in motion, for money can make a boat or car go, as well as a mare. I gave him a trifle.

Also, a call from a coloured man, with a very different notion: An asylum for coloured inebriates. Gave him something, for my notion is that, if well managed, it will be useful. So long as our benevolent Institutions are conducted with skill & honesty, which is usually the case at their commencement, those who set them agoing being fraught with zeal, they may do well. But when they fall into the hands of the lukewarm & men who labour for ambition, these same Institutions may be productive of evil.

These intemperates should not eat the bread of idleness. A potent curative is to be found in laudable industry & as early after admission as prudence would justify, they should be placed out in the country with conscientious people, removed from evil example. We much need a House of Refuge for coloured juvenile offenders.

*March 13th.* I revere a tender conscience & would recommend all to obey its dictates without hesitation or scruple, but let it be a conscience, not a whim. Few would, I suppose, think the little girl right who, in her love of the plain stile, made it her practice, when reading, always to substitute the word thee for you, no matter whether it made sense or nonsense. Of the same family of scruples was that of a female in a neighbouring monthly meeting. In olden times, accounts were kept in Pounds, Shillings & Pence. After a new denomination of coin had been established by Congress, the treasurer submitted her account in Dollars

& Cents. A member forthwith expressed her strong disapprobation, saying it was "the first time she had ever witnessed the like" & she "hoped it would be the last."

*March 16th.* A note from H. Binney informing me that he has received the decree of the Supreme Court in the case of S. Girard's will.

*March 26th.* The Texan question continues to agitate Congress & the country. The national debt of that new Republic is given at $10,000,000 & the scrip sells for ten cents in the Dollar. Some of our public men are said to have possessed themselves of large amounts at that depreciated rate & hence their zeal for annexation, altho' it should involve us in war with Mexico. This same class of politicians are stirring up strife with England about Oregon, a subject which is in negotiation between the U.S. & G. Britain. This peaceful operation is too tardy for their ardent spirits.

*March 29th.* A report from the Com. on Legacies & Trusts, of which I am one, recommending the Councils to authorize that Com. to withhold from the refractory Fire & Hose Companies the annual appropriation of $300 each unless they submit to the ordinance of Councils in all next month. Nineteen out of the twenty-nine companies have given in their adhesion. Ten hold out.

Ever since the passing of that ordinance there have been no such disgraceful quarrels among them in the City as before, but four out of the five districts—after having by their committees united with the City —refuse to adopt the regulations. Spring Garden has voted to their rioting companies their usual compensation. Wm. Penn was a wise man, but he made a mistake in limiting the bounds of the City. It will ever be difficult for many distinct corporations fully to cooperate. They should form but one municipality. The recommendation of the Com. was unanimously adopted.

*March 31st.* Received information today of the decease of Rest Cope, wife of Benjamin, to be interred at W. Chester tomorrow at 10 A.M. Attended evening meeting, the last for this season. That dear, tender spirited friend Isabel Casson appeared in testimony & in supplication. Wm. Evans also in testimony.

*April 1st.* Have been engaged in reading Phelp's *Botany for Beginners* & *Child's Class Book of Nature,* by J. Frost, with a view to their use in the schools of the Overseers of Friends Public Schools & think them well adapted. An instructive & impressive air of piety breathes thro' them.

Received a note from Chas. S. Folwell, stiling himself agent of Jas. Dundas, Trustees, saying that their Solicitor was instructed to ascertain, if practicable, what the alleged difficulties are in regard to the conveyance of the Lemon Hill Estate.

Peter Stephen Duponceau, Pres. of the Am. Philosophical Soc., died about 1 this morning at the age of 84. He was one of our most learned men, his knowledge, embracing the wide cyclopedia of literature, directed more especially to languages. He was born a Catholic & educated for the Priesthood, but deserting that faith he became a Huguenot, a term applied contemptuously in France to Protestants. He came to this country in the Revolutionary War & after the peace studied law. He practiced successfully in this City, where he settled, but withdrew from the bar several years ago, devoting his time to the cultivation of literature. He was an instructive, pleasant companion. I loved & respected him. He not only could read, but speak most of the modern languages of Europe & what are termed the dead languages. He was familiar with the Chinese & the Indian tribes of our own country.

A remarkable instance of his knowledge of the latter occurred some years ago. A person calling himself Dr. John Dunn Hunter made his appearance among us, bringing with him letters from the west to some of our citizens & among the rest, one to me. He represented himself to have been captured when an infant by a party of Osage Indians, by whom he was adopted & with whom he lived as one of their nation, in all their habits of hunting & fishing, war, &c. until considerably advanced in manhood. He made his escape & returned to civilized life, studied medicine & came here to increase his knowledge of the science, for which purpose also he visited England. He was introduced to some members of the Royal Family & became quite the Lion of the day. On his return to Philada. he called on Peter Duponceau who, after some conversation, abruptly said "Sir, you are an imposter, you know not the Osage language in which you pretend to have been instructed." This detection drove Hunter from the City & he soon sunk into insignificance & oblivion. I scarcely ever heard of him afterwards & know not now whether he is living or dead.

At a meeting of the Managers of the House of Refuge, elected Ladies Com. & a newly established com. called the Com. of Supervision. This consists of three members of the Board. In the evening the Managers N.A. Ins. Co.—nothing very particular.

*April 10th.* The Com. on Lemon Hill met at 4 P.M. Gilpin as a matter of course indulged in severe invective against the sub-committee & myself in particular. A resolution passed to require from the City Solicitor a statement of facts in relation to the title & another instructing me to ask a continuance of the joint com. Another offered by G., requiring the Trustees of the Bank to furnish a similar statement, was not agreed to, altho' I voted for it—those in the negative considering it as having already been done in effect by the sub-committee. I voted for it to prevent clamour.

In the evening a special meeting of the Com. on Legacies & Trusts. A deputation of three from the firemen to present their new regulations. These contemplate no head, but each company to be governed by its own Engineer, irrespective of the rest—like an Army without a Commander-in-Chief.

*April 12th.* Councils met last evening. I made my report—quietly laid on the table. I expected an attack from Gilpin or Wetherill, who came in late. They had probably been in consultation & concluded to forbear. Notwithstanding their cunning & unreasonable oppositon to a measure of such vital importance to the City, in securing the purity of the water we have to drink & use in all our ordinary operations, I hope to succeed at last.

Visited Matilda Hodgson School. It is in good order & the children improving.

A new party has sprung up. They are called the "Native Americans." They have succeeded in the charter election in N. York. The ambitious strides of foreign Roman Catholics among us & especially in their efforts to exclude the Bible from our schools is the occasion of this association. The American spirit resists the dictation of a Pope & yet Puseyism, which is so nearly allied to Catholicism, is gaining ground & rending the Episcopalians in our country as in England. Besides this political fraternity, the Protestants—among whom the Presbyterians appear to take the lead—have combined to counteract the Papal influence & it will be well if, amid this strife of tongues, the contest for preeminence should terminate without the shedding of blood.

A story is somewhere recorded that a certain monarch in the East asked a Jew which of the three religions, the Mohammedan, the Jewish or the Christian, was the true religion. The Israelite, aware that the answer might cost him his life, replied by relating an anecdote. He said that a powerful Prince was in possession of a ring which had descended to him & had been the property of his ancestors' family for countless generations, conferring on the fortunate possessor wealth, prosperity & merit.

This Prince had three sons & not wishing to give a preference to either, caused two other rings to be made just like the original. After his death, a dispute arose among the sons as to which of them had in reality the genuine magic gem. Astrologers could not decide. At length, however, it was agreed that each should wear his ring & whichever of the three was found to live the most virtuous, moral & pious life was to be deemed as having the precious inheritance.

Received this morning a letter from my kind friend John Elliott, admonishing me to withdraw myself from public concerns. So far as regards our Councils, I have long determined to do so.

*April 15th.* The Yearly Meeting of Friends commenced its session.

*April 16th.* Forenoon, the state of Society to the 6th Query was considered & some salutary advice given. Several of the reports state that young persons, members of their body, had attended places of worship where "hirelings" performed the service. This drew forth strong expressions of disapprobation. Ezra Comfort, among other things, said it was no wonder, when older members called these "hirelings" ministers of the Gospel. He did not approve of Friends attending the burial of persons who belonged to other societies. Christopher Healy held the same opinions. These sentiments are harsh & uncharitable & will probably produce, on the minds of our intelligent & educated youth, effects the very opposite of what the speakers intended.

*April 17th.* The reports from the several Quarters on the use of spiritous liquors drew forth some discussion. About sixty persons, members of the Y.M., still use it themselves or give it to their workmen. Although it is to be regretted that even 60 of our members can be found to make moderate use of the pernicious article, it should be remembered that not many years since, it was more or less in use as a common drink in our families & placed on our tables & sideboards free to all.

When I was a small boy I remember that my Uncle Thos. Pim, after whom I was called, was in the constant practice of giving with his own hand, to all his labourers, before they went to work in the morning, a glass of rum to each & he was not only a very estimable exemplary man, but a worthy elder in the Church. It was also a practice among Friends of Chester Co. to appoint committees in their Monthly Meetings to see

that poor Friends were provided with rum to enable them to get in the harvest & I have seen, in years past, members stagger into Y.M. under the influence of liquor. The use of ardent spirits in any form, except as medicine, is banished from every respectable family.

*April 24th.* At length the papers announce the presentation to the Senate, by the Pres. of the U.S., of the Treaty for the annexation of Texas. The Democrats of the country are said to favour it on party grounds. They join the South to promote the re-election of Martin Van Buren to the Presidency. The Senate were in secret session on this subject.

*April 25th.* The voice of the busy wren, heard the first time this spring in my garden. The country is in considerable commotion on the subject of annexation.

Councils met in the evening & among other things passed an ordinance forbidding the use of the fire plugs in the City to the Hose & Fire Companies of the districts. This became necessary in consequence of district companies having recently, at a fire, taken possession of such plugs & debarring the City Companies of their use. Law & order have been in disrepute ever since Gen. Jackson became Pres. of the U.S. His despotism has ever found advocates among the Democracy of the country. The example of that man has had & still exercises a pernicious influence on the morals of the country.

*April 26th.* Forenoon devoted principally to the Lemon Hill concern & the interests of the Mercantile Library Co.

Afternoon met the Overseers of Friends Public Schools. Little more was transacted than the ordinary business.

*April 27th.* Today the annual dinner given by the Watering Com. at the works on Schuylkill takes place. Tho' invited, I shall not go. If I had no other objection, I cannot be reconciled to be the guest of a com. at the head of which J.P. Wetherill is placed.

It is a serious evil to the City to have such an irritable, intriguing, unfair man at the head of that important com. It would be a strong temptation indeed that could induce me to leave a comfortable home, amid such a storm as prevails today, to eat dinner two miles off.

*April 29th.* The Treaty is published, but the Senate has not as yet ratified it. Henry Clay, in a letter to the Editors of the *National Intelligencer*, comes out against annexation. He says, "I consider the annexation of Texas at this time, without the assent of Mexico, as a measure compromising the national character, involving us certainly in war with Mexico, probably with other foreign powers, dangerous to the integrity of the Union, inexpedient in the present financial condition of the country & not called for by any general expression of public opinion."

I find also that that cunning, twining politician, Martin Van Buren, has thought it expedient to dissent from the annexation, so that Pres. Tyler will have fearful odds against him in this game.

*May 4th.* In the evening met the Directors of the Mercantile Library Co. Martial music in the street & crowds of excited people, marching to the State House to hear Daniel Webster, so interrupted us that we adjourned. D.W., whose political course has for some time been equivocal, is now fairly enlisted in the Whig cause. He addressed the multitude in Baltimore altogether in favour of Clay's election & is at this moment most probably haranguing the vast assemblage before the State House in the same strain. I passed thro' the throng on my way home.

While writing, there is a cry of fire & the engines are out, doubtless with a view to interrupt the meeting.

*May 7th.* Several riots between the Native Americans & the Irish Catholics took place yesterday in Kensington & were continued up to one o'clock last night. Fire arms, brick bats & other missiles were freely used. Numbers were badly wounded & several lost their lives. The Natives held a meeting in the afternoon & were attacked by the foreigners, who appear to have been much the most numerous. The disturbances of the public peace are greatly to be deplored. The Catholics have become numerous among us & seem disposed for mischief. Several new chapels have lately been erected in the City & districts & in fact generally over the U. States.

The indigent poor & discontented of Europe are constantly arriving among us & exercise no small influence at our ballot boxes. In the Kensington riots, the Irish women are said to have been particularly active, gathering brick bats & stones in their aprons to supply their husbands. No inconsiderable part of our poor rates are expended on these people—the men deserting their numerous families in the winter, under the pretence of searching for work & leaving their wives & children to be provided for as they may & sturdy beggars they prove. What may be the issue, time will develop.

*May 8th.* Rode out between 4 & 5 P.M. & pursuing a north course up

Seventh Street before turning into Camac's Lane, witnessed, at a distance on my right, a large building on fire. Fear it is the Catholic Chapel, east Kensington. Went as far as Laurel Hill & returned on the Ridge Turnpike, the flame & smoke issuing from the same spot where we first saw them. No noise or bustle near us but a wounded man was carried by on a litter. He proved to be a militia officer who had put a ball into his own leg by the careless handling of a pistol.

A great crowd is collected about St. Augustine Chapel—the Sheriff addressing them. Fear further mischief. Returning home, find a busy multitude moving like disturbed bees in a hive. It augurs nothing good. The military are posted on the battle ground, near Master St., cannon pointed so as to rake the streets, but 'tis said they will not use their arms, having no right to do so until authorized by the Gov., to whom messengers have been dispatched.

10 o'clock—Cry of fire—engines out—State House bell ringing. A powerful light in the direction of St. Augustine, no doubt 'tis on fire. The flame ascends higher & the whole City is lighted up. The large buttonwood trees at the Penna. Hospital, close by me, exhibit a splendid but awful spectacle. Thick darkness shrouds the trunks, for there is no moon, but cloudy—while the fresh leaves reflect a silvery brilliancy.

A quarter past ten—there is no longer any doubt as to the object on fire. The flame has reached the cupola & that structure, in full blaze, is plainly in view. ½ past—the cupola has fallen & the sparks are ascending rapidly aloft. A message from my son Henry, whose dwelling is in Fourth Street, nearly opposite Willing's Alley, in which St. Joseph's is situated & within a few doors of St. Mary's—both Catholic chapels.

He announces that dense crowds are collecting & threaten the demolition of both. His mother-in-law, an aged, very infirm person, incapable of walking, is greatly alarmed & unless speedily removed, may fall a victim to the burning element, should it reach their dwelling. Arrangements made forthwith to remove her to my house. At 11 she arrived, accompanied by Henry & wife & their little daughter, Anna & her cousin, Julia Reeve. Henry & myself carried his mother-in-law in our arms from the carriage to her chamber & then he returned to his home, leaving the others with us.

Half past eleven—the State House bell still gives note of flames & destruction, reminding us of the awful tocsin of Revolutionary France. After 12, all being quiet in our immediate vicinity, retired to bed, the sky still reddened with the embers of St. Augustine.

*May 9th.* Our apprehensions of yesterday have been more than realized. Murder & riot prevailed throughout the day. St. Michael's Chapel in Kensington, Priest Donahue's dwelling in which a loaded musket was found, the Catholic Seminary, corner of Phoenix & Second Street, were all consumed by fire during the day together with an additional number of dwellings from which Irishmen fired on the mob & also several groceries kept by Irishmen from which it was alleged their countrymen were supplied with powder. The contents of the dwellings & stores were scattered to the winds. This destruction effected, during which lives were lost, as night came the rioters advanced into the City & spread themselves in dense masses before St. Augustine. Mayor Scott arrived & addressed the crowd. He was listened to with patience. When he ended he was asked if he had anything more to say. Answering in the negative, he was advised to retreat, lest he should be hurt, for they were determined to destroy the building.

Firemen were there with their engines, but the mob would not permit them to play on the chapel & their engines were applied to saving the surrounding property. Meanwhile, armed men took possession of St. Mary's & no injury was done there or at St. Joseph's. A mob, however, collected before St. John's. St. Gen. Cadwalader had cannon placed so as to rake the street & gave notice that, unless they dispersed in five minutes, he would fire on them. They quickly withdrew. We naturally enquired why the same energy was not applied to save St. Michael's & St. Augustine. The General is personally well known to me, he is an amiable, courageous young man. I mean therefore to cast no reflections on him. He had probably received fresh authority from headquarters. The same course might have prevented the demolition of other buildings. The military were present at the burning of St. Michael's & the mob quickly accomplished their incendiary work.

At the meeting of the citizens this morning, at the call of the Mayor, strong measures were adopted to preserve the peace of the City —eminent counsel (H. Binney & John Sergeant) having given it as their opinion that the military will be legally sustained in firing on the mob. The mere knowledge of this fact will restore order. Men in pursuit of incendiarism or other atrocities are always cowards & will not easily be induced to hazard certain loss of life.

Gov. Porter has arrived in the City & three companies of volunteer infantry, ordered from Harrisburg, are expected tonight.

Councils met in the evening. I told W.M. Meredith, Pres. of S.

Council, that I had caught the spirit of the day. I had become quite belligerent & never felt a stronger disposition to do anything than to put his eye out. "Why, Mr. Cope, what do you mean? How have I offended you?" I answered that a paper had been sent to me for my signature, placing the Girard Banking House at the disposal of the City police for the accommodation of the citizens on patrol, to which he had written, "I approve of the above," when he should have said we, as my signature was to follow his. I had therefore no alternative, as I thought, but either to put out his I or to put another there to make a better face & added, "So do I2" & signed my name.

Armed men & extra police officers are met every few steps. Troops are stationed with cannon at the City Arsenal & at the several Catholic Chapels with strict orders to permit no person except those whose habitations are within the lines to pass certain limits after sunset—a speck of martial law.

it appears that a boy about 16 entered St. Augustine Chapel thro' one of the windows, cut the gas pipe & applying a match, put the whole interior into an almost instant blaze. How happened it that those who were previously in charge of the building did not shut off the gas as a measure of precaution?

*May 11th.* Yesterday passed quietly. The rioters, at least for the present, are subdued. The City presents the appearance of a garrisoned Town. We meet armed men everywhere. Several companies arrived from the country yesterday & it is said that we are now guarded by four thousand soldiers under arms, besides the new policemen & patrols.

Blame attaches to both parties for what happened—but I hold the Irish Catholics the most culpable as the original aggressors. Bishop Hughes of N.Y. stirred up the flame in that City by preventing the use of the Bible in the public schools & his indiscreet interference with the popular elections. A Roman Catholic Priest in the interior of that State had a number of Bibles publicly burnt, for which outrage a very awkward & evasive explanation was rendered by the Bishop, confirming in effect this violence on Protestant feelings.

Next came the efforts here, partially successful, to banish the Bible from our public schools. If the Catholics were unwilling to conform to the rules of the Directors & made a matter of conscience of it, why did they not remove their children to schools of their own & thus avoid offence to their Protestant neighbours? The Society of Friends, on other grounds, educate their own children & at the same time, contribute their quota to the maintenance of the public schools.

*May 22d.* Catholicism, as practised under the discipline of the Church of Rome, is not consistent with our free Institutions. With the Pope at its head, issuing his mandates to all his various subordinates—his Cardinals, Archbishops, Bishops & Priests—the rank & file can scarcely be said to have a will of their own.

To whom, then, does a Roman Catholic feel bound to render obedience? To the Government or to the Pope? If he is a sincere Catholic, to the Pope, of course, who holds—according to his ignorant conception —the keys of Heaven, into which no soul enters unless this potent key-holder unlocks the gate. I would not insinuate that all Catholics are bad citizens—far from it. I know many worthy men among them. It is the system to which I object.

*July 18th.* Dined with son Alfred & his little flock at Germantown. After dinner went with him to the factory on Cresheim Creek to witness the operation of a newly invented machine for expelling burs from wool, of which that from S. America is greatly charged. It consists of parallel toothed cylinders in close contact, occupying a small space, but so efficient that the operator informed us it performs the labour of 500 men every 24 hours. It is the invention of a Yankee & cost $500, tho' it could be made for $100—the patentee meaning no doubt to be paid for his ingenuity, skill & labour. If it really accomplishes all the workmen ascribed to it, the price is low enough.

*July 20th.* Made several attempts to see the City Solicitor in consequence of a suggestion he made to me yesterday that the City could not hold real estate in the district of Spring Garden. Strange indeed—what, then, is to become of our Water Works, for Fairmount is in the same district & was obtained, as Lemon Hill, by purchase. The Solicitor has at no time favoured the purchase of the latter.

Several additional companies of military have been sent home. 'Tis well, for the weather is very oppressive. Arrests continue & among them, the man who set fire to the Penna. Hall some years ago. The fellow boasted of the feat to another, who betrayed him.

*July 24th.* After several more fruitless efforts I have at last succeeded to obtain an interview with the Solicitor. He has not yet discovered the Law which is the new bug-bear! Well, this procrastination will come to

an end some time. Elliott & Robinson, Scriveners, tell me that they will complete the deed of conveyance in perhaps a week more! We might have had a conveyance of Texas & taken possession of the country too, in less than one fourth of the time spent in acquiring Lemon Hill, right under our nose.

A good looking young negro presented himself to me this morning. He had escaped from slavery near Havre de Grace. He was fatigued & hungry & anxious to reach Canada. Gave him some money & his breakfast. He was then conducted to a place of safety & is this night to proceed with six other runaways on his journey.

Men condemned to interminable slavery have a right to escape from it & I feel no scruple to help them on their way. There are more of these cases than the public are aware of, but I greatly wish they could get to a warmer climate. Canada winters are too severe for the African race.

*July 25th.* The military have mostly departed & as a measure of precaution the rioters have been removed from the County Prison, Moyamensing, to the eastern Penitentiary, more secure from assault.

*August 19th.* The deed for Lemon Hill has been executed & the consideration money, $75,000, paid. Have ordered a call of the Com. for 12 o'clock tomorrow.

When Edmund Burke was slandered he said, "Loose libels ought always to be passed by in silence. If I cannot live down those contempt-ible calumnies, I shall never deign to contradict them in any other manner."

*August 20th.* We had a thunderstorm & heavy rain last evening. Some trees blown down & two vessels struck by lightning.

The Com. on Lemon Hill met & instructed me to report the comple-tion of the title to Councils, the payment of the consideration money & an ordinance to defray the expenses, viz. $100 to H. Binney, $100 to G. Mallery & $335 to Elliott & Robinson, Conveyancers. The latter seems to be extravagant enough. They were not of my selection, but appointed by the Solicitor.

A member of the "Native American Association" informs me that as I would not consent to serve as Mayor of the City, a party had put Elhanan Keyser in nomination. Keyser is a respectable citizen. Had I no other objection to serve, the administering of oaths would be sufficient, but I have many others & important ones, too. Mayor Scott, a sound lawyer & pure minded man, will not serve beyond his present term.

The Native American Association is professedly composed of persons selected for their patriotism & free from the trammels of party discipline, but excluding foreigners from office. Time will develop how far this new party may prove more worthy of confidence than either the Whigs or Locofocos, the two great political divisions into which the people of these United States are at present separated.

As to myself, I have but little faith in the pretensions & professions of a thorough going politician, whatever appellation he may assume.

*September 3d.* An interview with Jos. R. Chandler, who is deputed to persuade me to serve again in Councils. He & others of the Whig party well know of my determination to retire & should not have placed me in nomination. I think his eloquence will fail.

*September 5th.* Perplexed & worried by the members of the Whig conference. They represent that if, now that my nomination has been published, I withdraw, it will endanger the success of their ticket, that if the City be lost the State will probably follow & thus the election of H. Clay to the Presidency will be endangered. These men place a value on my name far beyond my merits & seem determined to admit of no substitute. Three several tickets are in circulation—Whig, Native American & Locofoco—issue doubtful. My friends of the Conference say, as a further inducement, that I received the unanimous vote of the delegates & am the only person who did.

There is somewhere a sentiment to this effect: He who seeketh Glory pursueth a shadow that fleeth before him, while he that seeketh it not, shall find it following close upon him. It is a beautiful & true saying, to which may be added a kindred axiom, that he who seeketh office shall find the community unwilling to gratify him, but to him that desireth it not, it shall be pressed upon him.

Met the Commissioners of the Girard Estates at 8 P.M. Little business —later in the evening the Building Com., Mer. Library.

*September 13th.* Last evening presented a report to Council, of which I preserve the following copy:

The Committee on Lemon Hill have at length the satisfaction to report:

"That the Deed of Conveyance to the City for that valuable Estate has been duly executed, the Consideration Money paid & the Deed, together with the other title papers, placed in custody of the City Surveyor as provided for by Ordinance.

"Doubts having been expressed as to the validity of the title to this Estate, the Committee felt it to be their duty to consult able & experienced counsel on the subject & they accordingly applied to Horace Binney & Garrick Mallery, Esqrs., for their opinion, who, after a laborious investigation, met & removed every item of objection & the Com. can therefore with great confidence assure Councils that the title to Lemon Hill is unexceptionable. The opinion of those distinguished Lawyers is deposited with the other papers relating to the Estate.

"The Committee present herewith the essay of an Ordinance to defray the expenses incurred by them, viz. $100 to H. Binney, $100 to G. Mallery & $335 to Elliott & Robinson, Conveyancers."

The Ordinance passed has caused me no little time & anxiety but which secures to the City a very important benefit. No opposition was made either to the report or to the Ordinance, tho' J.P. Wetherill muttered something in his seat.

*September 14th.* "We have no cats at our house," said a small lad to me. "Then you have mice." "No, I catch them. When I see one I whistle to him. He will stop & listen. I approach him gently, whistling any tune all the while. He seems entranced & will suffer me to take him in my hand. No mouse escapes me." I know this lad to be veracious.

When I was a boy, Lancaster, Pa., where I first drew breath, might have been called a frontier town. Joseph Simons, a Jew resident there, carried on trade with the Indians & made an annual tour on horseback all the way to Shamokin on the Susquehanna, below where Harrisburg now is, but where neither Harrisburg nor any other burg then was. This visit was a stirring event in Lancaster, his departure & safe arrival back from so much hazard thro' the wilderness agitated the townspeople about as much as would a voyage to the poles of Arctic or Antarctic, in the present day. There were Mechanics in the Town who employed themselves in making metal breastplates, rings for noses & fingers & bracelets for the arms & legs & brooches for the breasts of the savages of both sexes, besides tomahawks, hatchets & rifles &c. for the red men. Furs were received in return & it was said, but I do not vouch for the truth of it, that in weighing them, when received from the untutored inhabitants of the forest, S. placed the skins on one side of the scales & his own arm or foot on the other, having discovered, by repeated experiments, the exact weight of those convenient & useful members of his body.

It was at this period of my boyish days that I witnessed a scene calculated to make a durable impression on my mind. Sporting with other boys in the square in the centre of which stood the Lancaster County court house, our hilarity was interrupted by the sudden bursting of a crowd from that building, increased by the rush of others to the scene, occasioned by the appearance of a stout negro beating with a cart whip the back of a white man very genteelly dressed. The crowd were indignant & were about to interfere when a stentorian voice, issuing from a person in military dress, commanded a circle & with pistol in hand & an elevated position on the steps, exclaimed that the negro was acting under his orders & that he would blow out the brains of any man who should interrupt him. The application of the whip was long & severe. The person on whom the lash fell bore the infliction for some time by merely struggling vainly with his antagonist, but at length broke out in loud cries, when the military man ordered a cessation, taking the coloured actor away with him, while the fainting creature who was so miserably beaten was led from the ground.

The man in uniform turned out to be Col. White of Revolutionary & partizan memory, then quartered with companies of his dragoons in the Town. The sufferer was no less a person than Jonathan Sergeant, Esq., father of one of our estimable citizens, John Sergeant & his brother, one of the judges of the Supreme Court of Penna. Their father was a celebrated Lawyer who indulged in the habit—too common, especially at that time—of assailing the character of opposing witnesses to rob them of the force of their testimony. Col. White, aware of this considerable practice & knowing that he was to give testimony in a case in which S. was engaged, called on him & said that if he, S., took any liberties with his character he would punish him. Well, the trial came on, the Col. delivered his customary testimony, Sergeant resorted to his customary abuse & the remedy of the cart whip was the consequence. I understood that S. ceased to visit Lancaster after that memorable day.

Col. White was an intrepid soldier, but an honourable man. My father, being a Friend, could take no part in military affairs & like most of his sect was attached to the British Government, under which they had enjoyed protection & liberty of conscience. Hence he soon was considered by the rabble & bitter revolutionists to be a Tory & treated accordingly by the ignorant multitude, while he continued to retain the esteem & good will of his more enlightened & liberal minded neighbours of the Whig party. He nevertheless suffered persecution, in which the family of course participated.

Our dwelling was on an elevated spot on the eastern borders of the

Town. In front was a fruit orchard to the west, on the north & east our garden & on the south an open green lawn, afterwards built up. On that lawn refractory soldiers were often ordered for punishment, the cries of the sufferers greatly annoying the family.

The occasion, of course, drew together many low people who amused themselves at intervals in pelting our house with stones. It was a substantial brick edifice & well barricaded with shutters, yet at one of these scenes of riot, we were so furiously assailed as to endanger our lives & the safety of the building. In the midst of the uproar, a voice was heard commanding the mob instantly to disperse. It was that of Col. White, who called the assailants a set of cowardly rascals, thus to attack an unarmed, peaceful citizen & swore with uplifted hand, in which he exhibited a pistol, that if they did not forthwith desist & move from the ground, he would order his dragoons among them to cut them to pieces. They knew the determined character of the man & scampered off in all directions.

The Colonel soon after paid father a friendly visit. To shew his respect for my father & his contempt of his assailants, he used to order his band to assemble & play before our door, very much against my father's will.

*September 21st.* Among the improvements & discoveries of modern times, none seems to promise more important results than the electro-magnetic Telegraph. The astounding facility of communication between distant parts almost passes human comprehension.

*October 1st.* An immense procession of the Whigs is parading our streets today. It took them two hours to pass by. It is to be followed by a mass meeting. Assemblages in mass, as it is termed, are frequent in all our political parties, distinguished orators addressing the crowds. Thirteen thousand persons within the City & districts have been naturalized by our courts within a few days to prepare themselves for voting at the approaching elections. This influx of foreigners & their speedy admission to the rights of citizenship inflicts a serious injury on our country. A great preponderance are Irish Catholics. It is believed that thirty thousand of the latter class are imported into the United States annually.

*October 4th.* The Commissioners of the Girard Estates held their last meeting under the present Councils. Made a report to them on behalf of the Com. on Farms. Previous to adjournment, the Commissioners passed a resolution highly complimentary to me as their presiding officer. The streets were so crowded by a noisy rabble, mostly boys, moving with torchlights & lanterns, as made it difficult to worm my way thro' them. They were hurrahing at the utmost pitch of their voices for Polk, Dallas & Shunk, the Locofoco candidates for Pres. & Vice Pres. of the U. States & Gov. of Penna. Night assemblages of such people are of present bad tendency & evil foreboding. A spark thrown among such an excited body might quickly be followed by riot, bloodshed & treason. It is a bad training of boys, who are rendered impudent, headstrong, conceited & vicious. Many things, moreover, can be perpetrated in the dark & go without discovery of the perpetrator & which he would be ashamed or afraid to commit in broad day-light.

*October 8th.* The day of our general election. Clear & bracing but not chilly. The polling commences in quietude. There are five parties on the ground striving for ascendency, the Whigs, the Locofocos, the Native Americans, the Anti-slavery & Firemen—the latter consisting of men unwilling to submit to the City Ordinances.

*October 9th.* The City & County election passed over in surprizing quietude. While on the ground to hand in my vote, I heard not an angry or unbecoming expression. The average votes were, for the Whigs 6384, Native Americans 4891, Locofocos 5345.

*October 11th.* Councils met at 11 P.M. to receive the election returns. I appear to have received the highest number of votes of any on the list of Councilmen. Altho' I have never sought popularity, it is some satisfaction to perceive that I am respected, however unworthy, by my fellow citizens. Wm. M. Meredith was again elected Pres. of Select Council. Common Council re-elected Sam Norris.

*October 12th.* It appears that the Democratic (Locofoco) party, have succeeded in electing their candidate, Francis R. Shunk, to the office of Gov. of Penna, by a small majority.

*October 17th.* Commenced a new tour of duty as President of the Commissioners of the Girard Estates. A full Board—the new Mayor, Peter McCall, attended. The Mayor & two presidents of the City Councils are *ex officio* members of the Trust. Gilpin has become very polite to me. John Price Wetherill is no longer a member.

*October 24th.* Councils met in the evening, when I submitted the two following resolutions which passed Select Council *nem con* but were postponed in Common Council.

"Resolved that the Committee on City Property ascertain at what price the ground between the City Water Works & Lemon Hill, being about 500 feet front on the river Schuylkill, can be purchased & if the terms be reasonable, whether it would not be of material benefit to the City to make the purchase.

"Resolved that the Committee on Police be instructed to inquire & make report on the expediency of modeling the Fire Dept. of the City so as to embrace the following principles, viz.

1st. The Dept. to consist of 20 Fire & Hose Companies, in suitable porportions of each.

2d. That each Company consist of 20 or 25 able bodied men in the prime of life & of good moral character, to be annually elected by Councils, subject to be dismissed at any time on failure of duty.

3d. That the members of the Companies, so to be formed, be paid a reasonable compensation for their services, that they be constituted Policeman & Conservators of the Public Peace; thus forming an efficient police establishment of from 400 to 500 men, to be called out at any time, day or night, as occasion may require, into which body the watch & police department might be merged, not merely for economy, but for unity of action.

4th. That, in addition, to one person to be designated by each of the companies respectively & approved by Councils to act as Engineer, Councils shall elect an Engineer-in-Chief, with suitable aids, to have command of the whole.

5th. That to give effect to this arrangement, Councils do purchase from the Fire & Hose Companies of the City the requisite number of fire engines & hose carriages, together with apparatus, provided that they can be obtained at reasonable prices & if not, that measures be taken otherwise to supply the number needed.

6th. That the Fire Department thus to be created be placed under the control of the Mayor of the City, who shall be authorized to command the services of the members under such regulations & restrictions as may be by Ordinance enjoined."

*October 25th.* At the stated meeting of the Managers of Haverford School, an interesting communication from the Principal, Daniel B. Smith, was read & committed.

Afterwards the Committee on Instruction held their meeting. Afternoon, visited the Institution for the Blind, in company with Aaron Griffith & wife, an interesting couple from Virginia. The Institution is flourishing, the pupils well taught & employed, the boys in making brushes, baskets, matting &c. & the girls with their needlework & toy baskets, &c. All are taught music, of which they are very fond & it appears, adds to their few enjoyments.

In the evening attended a meeting of the Board of Trade. On passing thro' the streets this morning, I was accosted by several persons to say they approved of my plan for reforming the Fire Dept. — urged me to forward its accomplishment. One of the number, addressing me, said, "I am a member of a Fire Co. & have been so for 40 years & it is my belief that the evils of the present system can be cured only by the plan proposed by you." Judge Parsons of the Criminal Court, with whom I have had no previous acquaintance, spoke of it to me with much approbation. There is some satisfaction in these voluntary commendations.

*October 29th.* There has been abundance of rain lately. It fell all day yesterday & was heavy during the night.

The arguments of Binney & Sergeant—together with the judgement of the Supreme Court of the U.S. in the case *Vidal et al.* vs. *the Mayor &c.,* including the will of Stephen Girard—having been printed in pamphlet form by order of the Commissioners of the Girard Estates, I have been engaged in directing the distribution of copies among our Institutions & private citizens of distinction.

The learning & research of our two Advocates cannot fail to prove interesting to thousands not directly implicated, if the decision of the court settles the law on charitable uses throughout the U.S. Had that decision been adverse to the defendants, the consequences to Penna. would have been most disastrous, nor would the mischief have ended there. The whole country would have suffered. There is not a charitable use nor an object of charity in Penna. that is not affected by this decision.

The millions at stake in the suit itself were of a magnitude exceeding anything in amount ever before adjudicated in an American court of law. But these millions were far exceeded by the millions of millions involved in the consequences. I greatly rejoice, therefore, at the issue & do not at all regret the time & attention I have given to the subject, however humble & subordinate have been my services.

*November 8th.* Our cities abound with foreign rogues. Robberies, burglaries, pocket picking are daily occurrences. A few days ago, a clerk of the Bank of the N. Liberties was stopped in Sixth Street near

Mulberry & robbed of between $8000 & $9000. A gang of fellows stopped him & while one of them throttled him, the others eased him of the money. It was raining at the time & they had umbrellas raised & altho' the daring crime was perpetrated within business hours, the villains escaped with their booty. Nothing so daring as this has occurred in Philada. within my recollection.

*November 9th.* N. York has declared for Polk & Dallas & the question respecting the future Pres. is deemed to be settled.

*November 19th.* Now that it is reduced to a certainty that Jas. K. Polk is the Pres. elect, a great decline in stocks has taken place. Penna.'s five per ct. loans which, before the election, were up to 74 have fallen to 66 with a downward tendency. The uncertainty of his policy regarding the tariff has produced quaking among our manufacturers. In the northern states his friends asserted him to be in favour of protecting duties, while his advocates in the south claim him as opposed to that system. This state of suspense has a paralitic influence on the commerce, the manufactures & the agriculture of the country.

In the evening the Com. on Property of Haverford School met at my house. Various subjects were discussed—planting fruit trees, building ice house, a pig pen, a gardener & an assistant in place of Carvill, &c., also increase of salaries, for the steward & matron, are considered.

The first ice of the season was made last night in our street gutters. This day has been clear & cold.

*November 20th.* An interview with Jonathan Richards, steward of Haverford School, on the several matters discussed by the Com. yesterday & other subjects connected with the institution. It was satisfactory.

The Com. on Legacies & Trusts met. Measures were taken for the distribution of wood the coming winter. My old district of Schuylkill 6th to Delaware 10th, from Chestnut to Cedar, allotted me.

An interview with Mayor McCall, by invitation. One of his most efficient officers, a High Constable, has been guilty of an atrocious breach of the peace. He went over to Camden, got in liquor, met a man against whom he had an old grudge & advancing upon him said, "Now I have you in Jersey, I'll have my revenge." He beat him severely, altho' the individual had given no new ground of offence. The Mayor's feelings are appealed to by the offender, who has a wife & children. I join with him, however, in the justice & propriety of forthwith discharging the culprit from office.

We conversed on my plan for a Fire Dept., which he commends. We talked also on the subject of an amalgamation of the City & districts, on which our thoughts appear to have run in the same channels. My fears are that the City will not be met on fair & liberal terms. It would otherwise be desirable. Called on the City Solicitor, who has prepared a plan of the new wharf line to be presented to the Court of Quarter Sessions for record.

*November 21st.* Councils met & received a communication from the "Cadwalader Greys," one of the voluntary companies who are to protect the City. They complain of grievances at the hands of the others. These military defenders will, I fear, cause no little trouble & expense to the City. The Councils had better adopt my peaceable system of police & shake off these military squabblers as quickly as possible.

*November 27th.* The ponds about the City have a mantle of ice, on which the juveniles are sporting with fair prospects of wet feet. There are several indications of a severe winter. The Indian saying is that winter does not begin till the ponds are filled. That point is probably attained, as there has been much rain. Our farmers allege that a plentiful fruit season is followed by a hard winter. No reason is given. 'Tis probably a goose-bone theory, but M. Arego, a distinguished French savant, has predicted a severe winter, whether confined to Europe or to extend to other quarters of the globe, is not stated.

*November 30th.* The tongue is an unruly member & hard to govern. I often verify this truth & wish to have a better command of its issues. A friend once said in my hearing, "I never knew a man who would beat his wife, if she would only hold her tongue." "Keep thy tongue from evil & thy lips from speaking guile," said the royal psalmist & he knew what he said. It makes enemies & it is unwise to make an enemy, for whether he be of high or low degree, if you have done him an injury, or he thinks that you have, he may never forget or forgive. If in power, he may oppress, if in poverty, he may undermine. "The fly hath her spear & the emmet is not without her choler."

A hasty expression may so wound the pride of the person to whom it is addressed as to cause him on any favourable occasion, however remote, to avenge the wrong. A wound inflicted, whether designed or otherwise, may never heal, but some day fester into madness & produce frenzied action.

> Watch the hour
> There never yet was human power
> Which could evade, if unforgiven
> The patient search & vigil long
> Of him who treasures up a wrong.

*December 4th.* Should Texas be annexed to the U. States, our wise anti-slavery men may be as much puzzled to find their true position as was the addle-headed carter;

> As sleeping in his cart, he lay
> Some wicked pilferer stole his team away
> Giles waked & cried aloud, "Odds, dickens what
> How now, why, am I Giles or am I not?
> If Giles, I've lost my horses, to my smart
> If not, odds bodkins, I've found a cart."

We have several land tortoises in our garden who retire underground in the 10th month & make their appearance again in the 6th month following. One of them, well known from the others, was missing last summer. It happened that our gardener removed some earth in the spring, piling it in a heap in a corner. This pile he removed last month & the missing tortoise was discovered underneath the mass—the coverlet under which he had been sleeping for more than a year having proved too cumbersome for him to remove.

*December 5th.* Stated meeting of Councils. It seems that one or more of the military companies under Gen. Cadwalader decline changing their present dress to conform to a uniform prescribed by him & Common Council approved his course. In Select Council the subject was referred to the Com. on Police to enquire & report. I, of course, do not participate in these matters, but deeply regret that Councils have placed the preservation of the public peace in warlike hands, instead of a civil police.

*December 8th.* It appears by a late publication that in the British W. Indies, there are 32 coloured editors, 26 magistrates, 75 legislators & that the Chief Justice, Attorney General & Judge of the Court of Appeals are all coloured men.

At a recent public execution at Nottingham, England, when the drop fell, a boisterous movement among the immense, rude crowd that attended the execution ensued, in which 16 persons were killed & a great many more badly wounded. This is a sad comment on this barbarous custom of taking the life of a criminal.

*December 10th.* An Anti-Slavery Convention has just been held at Albany at which they passed resolutions condemnatory of the other political parties without distinction, couched in a very bitter spirit. A little more moderation would better promote their cause.

*December 12th.* People begin to be seriously alarmed at the prospect of war. McDuffie, Senator of the U.S. from S. Carolina, has introduced into the Senate a joint resolution for the annexation of Texas. If it pass that body, it will soon pass the House of Representatives & war can hardly be avoided. Mexico can annoy us but little, by land or by sea, but she can commission Privateers to prey on our commerce & the rich bait will be too tempting not to call out unprincipled marauders from Europe, from the W. Indies, from S. America & even from our own ports to share in the booty.

Were it a settled principle that the promoters & advocates of war should be placed in the front ranks of every battle, wars would be less frequent, for then the miseries of these conflicts would light more immediately on the heads of the guilty, who would thus be made to bear but a just portion of the suffering of their own misdeeds.

At the meeting of the Commissioners of the Girard Estates this evening, directions were given to have insurances made on many of the buildings belonging to it. A new feature has been lately introduced by some of the offices into their policies, to include loss by mobs as a matter insured against.

*December 13th.* In the evening attended a meeting of the Penna. Seamen's Friends Society, I being one of the Vice Presidents, of which there are a number. Most of them are clergymen, it being the design to enlist the members of the several religious societies in the City & districts in this benevolent work by a V.P. from each. I am aware that some persons object to this mixture, but I do not perceive why I should not join others in the promotion of Christian charity, altho' I may not subscribe to their peculiar tenets. So far as we can agree, let us do so, for one Lord is our Master & all we are brethren.

> For forms of faith, let zealous bigots fight
> He can't be wrong, whose life is in the right.

*December 19th.* Councils met. A long communication from Mayor

McCall, pointing out the inefficiency of our present system of police & asking for an increase of force. This was referred to the Com. on Police. He says nothing about a remedy for our disorderly firemen. My resolution sleeps in Council—one of the members assigns as a reason that the firemen are now more orderly. No doubt, for they are alarmed at the threatened change, but it must take place, eventually. The voluntary system did very well in former days of simplicity, when the inhabitants were comparatively few, but now a different class of persons have taken possession of the engines. The men are young & full of their own consequence & little disposed to be ruled by law & order.

*December 21st.* Among the wonders of the day is the application of electricity & galvanism as a manure. It is said that there is a constant current of these subtle fluids from east to west over the whole earth. Upright poles 4 or more feet high are planted exactly north & south, between which a wire is suspended, the ends being inserted in the ground. Potatoes growing there are much larger than others—barley producing a heavier crop, the head large & the grain fuller. Grass assumes a deeper green & is more luxuriant. Other experiments will doubtless be made & that powerful agent, lightning, the cause of so much destruction of life & property, be made subsidiary to the wealth & comfort of man. Truly marvelous are the goodness & power & works of the Almighty towards his dependent, ungrateful children.

*December 27th.* Excused myself from presiding at a public meeting to be held to take into consideration the moral condition of the poor & to get up an association for their improvement.

I had some days ago consented, but on mature reflection felt myself at liberty to decline, thinking I had engagements enough on hand & understanding, moreover, that the several clergy were expected to be present. I feared I might be annoyed by some of their embarrassing ceremonies. The object is commendable & if well got up & honestly carried out, is worthy of patronage & I may then aid the concern in some other way.

# 1845

*January 1st.* The cycle of another year has closed & certainly many interesting matters have occurred in that period. It is so mild that at noon the mer. indicated 61, the sky clear.

We have, according to our annual custom, had such of our children and grandchildren as are in the City to dine with us today—William & his little flock being absent, which we regret. These family assemblages are very gratifying.

*January 3d.* A visit from D.L. Dix—the Elizabeth Fry of America. Has just accomplished her tour of inspection of the Poor Houses of Penna. & gives a better acc't of them than I expected. She wishes my opinion on the propriety of petitioning our Legislature anew to provide Hospitals for the Insane Poor of the State. A work of mercy—but attended at present with but little hope of attainment & I can therefore give her but little encouragement. With a public debt of more than forty millions hanging over us, it is unlikely that our public men will incur the responsibility of an increase. She proceeds on a tour to N.J. & may afterwards make a report to our Legislature respecting our State Institutions.

*January 6th.* A busy day & little done. This is the epitome of my life, constantly occupied & doing but little to good purpose.

There are now before Congress 5 or 6 distinct resolutions for annexing Texas. So far, the Whigs take no part, leaving the whole ground to their political opponents.

*January 7th.* It is a painful fact that Bishop B.T. Onderdonk of N.Y. has been suspended from his official duties on the same charges that occasioned the suspension of his brother of this diocese—"unchaste conduct & intemperance." The canons, it seems, do not authorize the absolute dismissal or discharge of an Episcopalian Bishop, no matter what the offense. Once a Bishop, always a Bishop.

The cause of religion is deeply wounded by these cases of licentiousness, this spiritual wickedness in high places. What poor, frail creatures we are was the soliloquy of Joe Smith, when I found him beastly drunk one dark night behind a cellar door over which he had fallen. We are indeed but poor, frail creatures & had need to be ever on the watch to be preserved from temptation.

Those Onderdonks are a disgrace to their profession. It might have been to such a priest that the poor fellow addressed himself when the priest said, "I'll pray for your soul." "Oh, then, I am ruined," exclaimed the man, "for I never knew anybody to thrive when you prayed for him."

*January 8th.* Attended the annual meeting of the contributors of the House of Refuge. The Com. on Cleansing & the Comissioners of the Girard Estates also met—nothing very special at either.

*January 12th.* The weather for more than a week has been of the May temperature. Neither in the Delaware or Schuylkill is there any ice & wharf building is going on.

Elizabeth Evans preached one of her eloquent, scorching sermons in our morning sitting. How fond some people are of snatching the sceptre from the Almighty to wield it on the heads of their fellow mortals. That was a wise choice of David when he said, "Let me fall into the hands of the Lord, rather than the hands of men."

*January 16th.* The weather continues mild & the dealers in ice are alarmed lest they should lose their harvest. Our navigation is as free as in mid-summer, while dates from England to the 12th Dec. state the cold there & on the continent to be very severe.

There is a singular mortality among the fish. Our coast is strewn with millions cast up by the sea. No account of the cause is given. May not some internal commotion of the earth have sent forth a poisonous gas & infected the water? Volcanic eruptions in the ocean have not beeen infrequent.

> To some hath God his words addressed
> Mid symbols of his ire
> And made his presence manifest
> In whirlwind, storm & fire
> Tracing with burning lines of flame
> On trembling hearts, his Holy name.

Councils met & appropriated $225,000 towards the building of the Girard College. The Building Com., of which I am not one, seem confident they can complete the whole for a little over $400,000 if the assets can be made available for that purpose. I hope they may not deceive themselves & Councils too.

The South Portico is finished & the one north is designed to be so the present year. S.G. could have entertained no idea of the disasters which have happened to the splendid means he provided for the College.

Many extravagant demands were made on his Executors, most of which were successfully resisted.

Among others, came a certain Chas. Panosi & demanded payment for 600 boxes of vermicelli, due for several years. I asked him why he had not been paid. "Oh, I hava tink de cash more safe in Stephen Girar Bank dan me." "But what could Stephen Girard want with 600 boxes of vermicelli?" "Oh, tis for one jentilman." "Then I suppose Stephen gave an order for them?" "Oh, dere is happen to me one grand a misfortune, de ordare is in me pantaloo, de pantaloo is wash & de ordare is wash." "Well, my friend, the claim is wash too." He left a bill but I saw no more of him.

*January 20th.* In the evening the newly elected Boards of Trade & the Mer. Library Co. held their separate meetings & organized by the appointment of officers, committees, &c. My grandson Francis R. Cope has been elected a member of the first named Board & attended for the first time. I continue in the Presidency of both Boards.

*January 23d.* Bricklayers are employed as in summer & plasterers at work, with open windows & doors, carrying in the tempered mortar from the streets.

Our old, long napping tortoise is dead. It is his last hibernation. We know not his age, but some of the species have outlived a hundred years. Bishop Laud, well known in history, had one in his garden at Lambeth, placed there in 1633 & died in 1753, not so much from old age as from neglect. He was then of course 120 years old at least. Was his life insured?

I was a member of our Legislature when our present Life Ins. Co. was created. The nature of such an Institution was then (1808) but little understood in Penna. & the charter met with warm opposition. Thos. McKean was then Governor. He was chosen by the Democracy, but turned against his party. Spangler of York, a thorough going Demo, was outrageous. He said if the charter was granted, McKean might insure his life & we should never get rid of him.

*January 26th.* Moses Thomas tells me that when about 10 years old he met with an accident by which his hip was dislocated. The celebrated Dr. Wistar attempted to replace it, but the pain attending the operation & the screaming of the boy caused him to desist. Moses soon went again to school & one day fell from a desk onto which he had scrambled. The fall restored the joint & he ever after remained well.

A still more memorable affair happened to Captain Serrell of the ship *Tuscarora* when owned by me. He was on his return voyage from Liverpool when the ship was suddenly involved in a tremendous hurricane, accompanied by hail & rain, thunder & lightning. The Ship, labouring heavily, fell into a trough of the sea, that is, between two mountainous waves, one of which broke over the deck & washed overboard six of the seamen. This was immediately succeeded by the opposite wave, which wonderfully & most Providentially cast them all back, the men seizing the rigging & whatever else they could grasp. They were bruised but none of them seriously injured. In the midst of the uproar & confusion the Ship was struck with lightning & terror & dismay appalled the crew.

The storm speedily passing away, it was found—to the inexpressible joy & gratitude of all—the Ship was not on fire, tho' a sheet of blaze had seemingly at one time hid everything else from their vision. When the men were dashed overboard & back again, Capt. S. (who was the older of the two Captains of the same name) thought there were eight feet of water on the deck. The lightning had stunned some of the men, but they recovered & the *Tuscarora* proceeded on her course, the crew, seamen like, as merry hearted and as thoughtless as if nothing had happened.

*January 27th.* A Bill for the annexation of Texas has passed the House of Representatives. Mexico is distracted by Civil War. Secy. Calhoun's letter to our minister, King, justifying slavery & impuning the motives of England in suppressing it, has given umbrage to the English people.

*February 1st.* Winter is upon us in earnest. My thermometer at 7 A.M. stands at 12.

*February 7th.* A Yankee called Omasa Whitney had petitioned Congress to patronize a R. Road projected by him from Michigan to the Pacific at Columbia River, a distance of more than 2000 miles. Other R. Roads are formed or forming to Michigan, making the entire distance from ocean to ocean 3000 miles. He offers to complete his part, Congress conceding to him 60 miles of unappropriated lands on each side of the road throughout the whole line. He demands no other compensation & estimates the cost at seventy five millions of Dollars. China would thus be reached in about 9000 miles, securing to the U.S. that rich trade, preventing the tedious & hazardous routes by Capes

Horn & Good Hope & making it the interest of Europe to visit China by means of his Rail Road.

This is certainly a most magnificent project. The subject has been referred to a committee. Whitney is a travelled man & bears a good reputation.

*February 8th.* Have just subscribed to a fund to relieve Henry Clay from pecuniary embarrassments brought on by his sons. They amount to about $25,000—which will doubtless be soon subscribed by his friends, of whom I consider myself one. I have known him for more than 40 years. I believe him an honest, honourable man of distinguished abilities, but so much of his time has been devoted to the service of his country that his private affairs have suffered & his sons have become spendthrifts.

*February 15th.* Thick fog & the mercury is at 38. The snow is melting fast & sleighs are very busy.

President Polk has arrived at Washington. Another revolution in Mexico. Santa Anna overthrown. Congress busy in conning measures to annex Texas & to take possession of Oregon. Memorials presented to them to annex the northern & eastern British provinces, from whom, know not, but mysteriously signed. Better while our hands are in, keep the ball in motion & go at once for all between the Arctic Pole & Cape Horn—'twould form a republic on a grand scale. We might be abused for our grasping propensities, but have we not a right? Only look at the natural boundaries, the sea all round. "Garrick is my dog," said Johnson "& no one shall abuse him but myself."

*February 22d.* Bells ringing—military parading, &c., it being Washington's birthday. The City Square that bears his name was once the Potters Field. I well remember when it was thus used, surrounded by a common post & rail fence. The victims of the yellow fever of 1793 were lain there. A large excavation was made on the west side, into which the dead were promiscuously cast & a little earth strewn on them as they arrived by men stationed on the ground for that purpose. The driver of the hearse was the only other attendant. When the fever subsided, the entire trench was covered over. There were many graves of persons who died at other times & little vacant space remained when the Square was abandoned as a cemetery. Headboards were not uncommon, marble being too expensive. On some of these were inscriptions, simple

enough, most of which I have forgotten, but one of them I distinctly remember. It ran thus:

> Here lie Dinah, Sambo wife
> Sambo lub her like he life
> Dine get sick & den she die
> And poor Sambo he do cry.

*February 28th.* Have had an interview with the female philan-thropist, Dorothy Dix. She is now engaged in urging the Legislatures of Penna. & N. Jersey to establish hospitals for the insane poor. She had previously sent me copies of her Memorials to each, containing her personal inspection of the prisons, &c., in these states. Written with spirit & feeling & disclosing sad scenes of wretchedness.

*March 1st.* John Pease & Isabel Casson are now paying family visits to the members of the western M. Meeting.

This morning brings the important intelligence from Washington that the two Houses have passed a joint resolution for the annexation of Texas. It is an important era for weal or woe in the history of our country.

*March 3d.* Fine spring weather for several days past. Last evening it rained & the wind was southerly. Today, 7 A.M., the mercury stands at 60. Wild geese are wending their way to their summer abode, northerly.

The roaring cannon is announcing the joy felt by a certain class of politicians by the annexation of Texas. They had better clothe them-selves with sack cloth & ashes & sit with their heads down on a dung heap. Besides the augmentation of slavery which this measure is de-signed by its southern advocates to extend & perpetuate, another monstrous evil has been committed in the mode by which it is effected, the violation of the Constitution of the United States.

*March 8th.* Shad were yesterday caught in the Delaware & exposed in our market.

*March 11th.* The storm continued thro' the night & daylight is this morning ushered in with a brisk fall of snow, melting as fast as it descends.

The Keeper of the N. York City Prison states the commitments for one week ending the first to be 90 males & 65 females. Of the males 55 were Irishmen & of the women, 54 were Irish. The rest consist of Swedes, Germans, English, Scots & Americans. These foreigners are a heavy tax on our sympathies as well as our purses.

*March 14th.* Now that Congress has adjourned & the excitement of party legislation is stilled, people are left to their own reflections on the past & forebodings as to the future & we have a portentious murmuring of coming evil to grow out of annexation & the dispute about Oregon. There is little use in making ourselves unhappy with these things. We are in the hands of a merciful & all wise God who orders all things well. Let us adopt the motto, never give up.

> Never give up if adversity presses
> Providence wisely has mingled the cup
> And the best counsel in all our distresses
> Is the stout watchword of, Never give up!

*March 19th.* The brick building in Chester in which, under Wm. Penn, the first assembly of the then province of Penna. met is being now torn down together with the stone addition in front, which tradition says was used by our forefathers as a place of worship. It may be superstitious, but I confess the demolition of these ancient fabrics produces a very unpleasant effect on my feelings. Our fathers, where are they? And the prophets, do they live forever?

The Com. on Legacies & Trusts met. 'Tis gratifying to witness the improved conduct of the firemen. No fights for months except among those of the districts. Weather all day tempestuous. Alterations of snow freaks, high winds & peeps of sunbeams.

*March 26th.* A Letter from D.L. Dix at Harrisburg, where she is attending the Legislature to urge the passage of a Bill for an Hospital for the Insane & asking me to give the assurance that I will subscribe $10,000. Not seeing my way very clearly to authorize such an exaction, I have replied that, if the proposed building is to be for the Insane Poor of the State, then let the State provide means for its erection & maintenance without calling on individuals to do it or to enter into partnership with them in the accomplishment of the object, & that—besides the Hospital for the Insane Poor, connected with the Almshouse—we have 2 others, to both of which I am a contributor, &c. She can prefer no just claim on me to meet her "modest" tax on my means, for considering the heavy indebtedness of the State, I could not encourage her application at this time & if even the scheme were now practicable, I should hesitate, for my experience teaches me that the Institution in its incipient state & after management would be placed in the hands of partizans selected, not for their competency, but as rewards for political sycophancy, with whom I wish to have no connection nor to become in

anywise responsible for their doings. When on a former occasion, thro' the exertions of myself & others, a Law was obtained for a similar purpose, it was frustrated by committing the carrying it out to party men, more intent on making jobs for themselves & political friends than anything else.

A lot was contracted for at an extravagant price & another agreement made with an unprincipled demagogue who afterwards ran away to escape the punishment awarded to his crimes & who was to furnish the requisite materials for the building. The consequence was, as might have been expected, that neither contract was consummated & the whole thing was abandoned.

*March 28th.* Met the Directors of Haverford School. Advanced the salary of the mathematical teacher to $1000—a forced push.

The late Nicholas Waln, a minister in high standing, had a friend to dine with him who scrupled to use a silver spoon, on which Nicholas sent to his kitchen for an iron spoon. None forthcoming but a large one used in basting, Nicholas handed that to his guest saying, "Here, take it, choke at a gnat & swallow a camel." I suppose Nicholas knew his man.

I respect a conscientious scruple, but a mere whim proceeding from ignorance, conceit or pretended sanctity, I reprobate, come from whom it may.

*March 31st.* Another note from D.L. Dix, informing me that the Bill for creating an Asylum for the Insane Poor has passed the House of Reps. two to one. She is a persevering woman.

*April 1st.* Passing a crowd in Independence Square, I enquired the meaning and am answered, a strike of the Journeymen Carpenters. They have, as usual, selected the time when their services are most needed & are enabled to stand out by aid of their common fund provided by stated contributions. This fund is ostensibly raised by the Craft to help their disabled members, and would, if so applied, be commendable, but applied in support of idleness & disorder, it is of bad example & ultimately injurious to themselves.

*April 9th.* The *Allegemeine Zeitung* states that Prof. Geisling at Brunenburg, after a series of experiments continued for 14 years, has succeeded in creating an egg by galvanism & in its subsequent hatching, producing a fine, lively bird of a perfectly unknown species & without feathers. The editor of the *Allegemeine* says that he has seen that bird hopping about & feeding upon the seeds given it. He adds that the

Professor has been compelled to close his laboratory by order of the Church.

*April 10th.* A call from a clergyman named Baldwin from Brunswick, N.J., self introduced, who has an extensive scheme for improving the moral, literary & religious education of people of colour in these U. States & Africa, which he states to comprehend ninety millions of the human race. In the paper which he read to me, he uses the phrase, "to preserve them from perishing by enlightening their understandings." I suggested that it was a strong expression, asking if he had not better substitute one less liable to criticism, as I could not suppose they would meet condemnation merely because of their want of knowledge. He replied that he would think of it. His plan, among other things, embraces the establishment in our country of a college in which the coloured people may receive a finished classical education—a measure of doubtful expediency at this time of excitement & prejudice against them. A mob would probably soon level the fabric to the earth, while the slave-holders of the South might deem it designed in many ways to be inimical to their safety.

If slavery is ever to be extinguished in these United States, it must be by the cooperation of men who hold others in bondage. The slave states must themselves move in the matter, they must set the ball in motion. A commencement has been made by Cassius M. Clay, a slave holder in Kentucky & if our fierce, rash, anti-slavery men will keep hands off, this germ will grow & ripen into wholesome fruit.

There is an abundance of schools among us in which coloured people of both sexes receive a good English education & in some of which they are taught the languages. These less ambitious trainings better become the condition of the pupils than pompous colleges.

*April 13th.* First Day. Distressing accounts from Pittsburg. A fire is said to have destroyed ⅓ of the Town. Tomorrow's mail will give the details.

*April 18th.* Received a notice of my appointment to go round & collect for the Pittsburg sufferers. I shall decline. Men young enough to be my children & grandchildren have done me this *honour* while they remain at home, having done their share by attending the public meetings & placing G.M. Dallas in the chair before the hour for assembling, as I am told they did, for I was not there. Shall not refuse to contribute my full share tho' I may not incline, now in my 77th year, to be a pack horse to politicians.

*April 23d.* The Com. on Indian Affairs made a report. Three schools, two of them taught by natives, within the reservation. Husbandry is increasing, the use of ardent spirits decreasing, new substantial dwellings erected, women improved in housewifery, use of the needle, &c. Certain white men lately commenced a survey & division of their lands, causing great alarm to the natives, but were persuaded to desist. Report directed to be printed.

*April 29th.* The Mexican Government has suspended diplomatic intercourse with the United States & Wilson Shannon, our Minister Plenipo, is supposed to be on his way home. Several armed vessels have sailed for Vera Cruz to join the U.S. Squadron already there, but as yet there has been no declaration of war on either side.

Mexico has appealed to foreign powers. From G. Britain we learn that a debate on the Oregon question had occurred in Parliament in which Peel, the Prime Minister, had been drawn out to say that if negotiation failed, his government was prepared to vindicate its rights by force. Thus one rash step more may involve us in two wars at once. A threat & a blow is no new thing with John Bull. He don't menace in fun.

*May 2d.* The Managers, Haverford School, met & had a long discussion whether to admit the grandsons of members of the school, father not being a member. No positive decision. The debt is again on the increase. Unless means are used to increase the number of scholars, the Institution will go down & the end for which it was established—the classical education of our youth free from the corrupting influences of our public colleges—will fail, of course. It seems as tho' a blighting spell was coming over our Society.

*May 13th.* Just returned from the funeral of Abbe Ann, wife of my nephew Caleb Cope & daughter of Brother Jasper, interred in Laurel Hill Cemetery, by the side of her only child. My niece was a woman of a meek & pure spirit & died in her 40th year of stricture of the intestines of long standing. She was wedded to her first cousin, a kind, affectionate man. They were a happy couple, abounding in all the conveniences that plenty could supply, another affecting instance of how little wealth can do in securing health & length of days.

*May 16th.* I was not aware until reading in Vol. 5 of the present mo. of the *Am. Review* some sketches of the life of John Quincy Adams that he was the author of a series of essays published in 1791 under the signature of Publicola, his father John Adams having been considered as the writer. Those essays attacked the doctrines & principles of the French Revolution, which at that period & until the murder of the King & Queen, were hailed by acclamation & approval by the friends of liberty the world over & especially by the people of the United States.

I had the temerity & folly to attack those essays as they were issued from the press, under the signature of Agricola, in the *Am. Daily Advertiser*, published by Dunlap & Claypoole. Jefferson was supposed to be the writer & for anything I know, has to this day the unenviable credit of that paternity. With the exception of my friend Peter Thomson, lately deceased, who was kind enough to correct my manuscript, none other than the editors knew Agricola. Had the public known him, it is likely his essays would not have been read. Nothing but the reputation of the supposed author could have gained for them the singular popularity which they then bore: I should now be ashamed to own them. The subject was also then popular & any advocacy of it might pass. Strange, however, that the public should mistake my puerilities for Thomas Jefferson's practiced pen.

*May 17th*. A hippopotamus, not said whether dead or alive, is now exhibiting in N. York, the first ever brought to this country. It was captured by an American crew at the mouth of a river in Africa. We shall doubtless have as a show here this novel visitant & pay, for a peep at him, more than the old Scotsman offered Boswell for a sight of Dr. Johnson. The Doctor hated the Scots & when on a tour to the Hebrides, halted at Edinburgh. An old Scot went to his lodgings & meeting Boswell at the door, asked to see the Dr. B. pointed to him. The man gazed for a while & turning to go away, said to B., "Here's your sixpence." "What do you mean by that?" queried B. "Why, sure you canna show sic a Beast for nothing."

*May 20th*. The whole country abounds with incendiaries & other criminals from abroad & our laws are but a scanty protection to our lives & property. So much is yielded to partizan influence & demagogism. At no period of my life have I heard of so many destructive fires, extending from Louisiana to Maine.

*May 28th*. A call from Dorothea Dix, to head a subscription for the purchase of a site for the Insane Poor of Penna., which I have done cheerfully in a moderate sum, tho' I cannot avoid fears on the subject. Honestly & judiciously administered, it cannot fail to do good, but in the hands of greedy politicians it will fail of its purpose. Men will

probably be appointed as physicians, &c. to have charge of it, who will have an eye to their own gain, rather than the comfort & cure of the patients. But we may as well hope for the best.

*May 31st.* Another short interview with Dorothea Dix. She is making but slow progress with subscriptions, yet resolved to succeed. I admire her zeal, but wish her movements had been directed to the object of her present concern when the State was less indebted & our citizens less exhausted by other numerous calls on their liberality. She is not, however, very easily deterred or diverted from her purpose. Discretion is said to be the better part of valour. Constant excitement in the pursuit of even a praiseworthy object may warp the judgement & impair the intellect.

*June 2d.* Afternoon went to Burlington, N.J., to attend the funeral of John Gummere, a worthy man, lately Principal & Mathematical teacher at Haverford. The attendance was large, the deceased having been highly & justly respected. The day was warm & clear, the sun scorching & we remained a long time in silence at the grave & were ready to depart when Granville Woolman of Rancocas addressed the company in a long, dull, inappropriate speech to the no small annoyance of all. When I left the ground, I expressed my regret to an Elder at this interruption to the prevailing solemnity. "Oh," was the reply, "I don't know what can be done with him, labour seems lost on him." I heard this Friend on a similar occasion last summer, in a protracted, equally ill-timed & wearying speech. I suppose him to be an honest, well meaning man, but every honest, well meaning man is not necessarily qualified to preach. It is a great point gained to see ourselves as others see us.

*June 3d.* A fire in N. York which has consumed one hundred dwellings & left homeless & deprived of all their means, four hundred families. Twenty five to thirty carcasses of horses were left smouldering in the ruins.

Boston has also recently been afflicted with destructive fires, supposed to have been designed & the Mayor has offered a reward of $2000 for the apprehension of the incendiaries. Much of this mischief may be attributed to the unrestrained use of Lucifer matches which are hawked about the streets & sold so cheap that any boy can procure the means of purchasing them.

*June 6th.* City Councils met this evening. Some bills of little consequence passed. The Natives applied for the use of Independence Hall, 4th July, to hold a convention in. This was referred to a com. who will report adversely. No party meetings should be held there, especially on that day.

*June 8th.* First Day & the mercury has risen to 93 in the shade. Attended meeting as usual. I fear I am not much the better. I feel as if I could quarrel with anybody that stood in my way. I have, at the same time, a very humble opinion of myself. Lord have mercy on me.

*June 9th.* Yesterday a fight took place between the Goodwill Fire Engine Co. & the Fairmount Fire Co., both of the County, in which the engine of the latter Co. was destroyed & several persons seriously injured. Some months ago the Fairmount Co. destroyed the Goodwill Engine, which has thus been retaliated.

Mayor McCall informed of a duel this morning between two of our young citizens, one the brother of Wm. M.M., Pres. of S. Council, who is badly wounded. The parties fought in the State of Delaware. 'Tis the second instance (between two other young fools) within a few days, of like folly, fought same place, neither killed but both wounded.

*June 11th.* If common sense cannot prevent duelling, Legislation might. Suppose a law were enacted depriving principals, seconds, aiders & abettors forever thereafter holding an office of trust, honour or profit in the State, whether the offense should be committed in the State or out of its limits, by any of its citizens & putting it out of the power of the Governor to pardon, unless by the advice & consent of ¾ of the Senate. Would such a law not put an end to the practice—at all events, greatly damp the energies of the parties? Faithfully enforced, it would & if all the States cooperated by similar enactments, the evil would in all likelihood cease entirely. If such a law were passed by Penna. only, it would scarcely fail to have a salutary effect.

*June 14th.* Besides a number of considerable fires in other Towns, the morning papers notice one in N. York which has turned one hundred miserable families loose upon the world.

There is a rumour today of the death of Gen. Jackson of famous memory.

*June 16th.* The decease of Gen. Jackson is confirmed. He died at his home on the 8th in his 78th year.

Another attempt to set the fire to the Academy of Fine Arts was made

last night, but timely discovered & extinguished. There could be little doubt of this renewed piece of villainy. Flames were issuing from two places when first seen. The Directors have offered $500 for the apprehension of the incendiary. There were also several fires yesterday. All were soon extinguished & little injury suffered.

The papers, as usual of late, contain notices of incendiary fires in various places. One of them adds, "It is computed that there has been consumed by fire in the U.S., during the last two months, property to the value of $12,000,000."

*June 20th.* Councils held their stated meeting last night & having attended to their municipal concerns, passed resolutions directing their chambers to be hung in black & their members to wear crape on their arms for 30 days. The State House bell to be tolled on the 26th & Penn Square to be used by General Patterson on that day, from whence to fire minute guns, that being the day set apart for funeral solemnities in honour of the memory of the deceased Gen. Jackson.

In these doings, I could not of course participate. Jackson is now lauded by men who despised & condemned him when living. Such is the manner of men. I say, peace to the memory of the dead but it is due to impartial history, while we render praise to good actions, not to offer incense to vice, however cloaked by worthy blandishment.

Editors seem striving to surpass each other in fulsome panegyrics on the departed hero, while politicians assemble in Town meeting to pass resolutions of gratitude, lamentation & applause & yet no American President ever played the Tyrant as did Andrew Jackson, nor trampled the Constitution & laws of this country so recklessly under his feet.

It was well said by one of the most accomplished writers of the English Press that "he who undertakes to record the actions of Princes & to paint their characters is not at liberty to cast a veil over undeniable imperfections or suffer himself, like the giddy vulgar, to be so dazzled by vulgar glory that his eyes are blind to crime."

*June 25th.* Yesterday the coloured masons had a grand parade thro' our streets accompanied with all the decorations of their order. Well, they have as much right to play the fool as their white faced brethren. How far it is prudent in them, while so much prejudice exists against them, is another matter. Very fortunately, however, I believe they were not assailed, as before, by the populace. Tomorrow the white devotees are to make their display in funeral ceremonies in honour of Andrew

Jackson. The Democracy are busy in converting these follies into political capital & their opponents are unwittingly joining in the general mock jubilee.

*June 26th.* The morning dawns with the firing of minute guns & the City in a bustle. On going early to market, find the streets thronged with military volunteers. A commander of one of the corps stepped up to me & offering his hand, accosted me as General. This piece of witticism has its origin in the visit to Ohio which I made some years ago in company with General Cadwalader. We drove a coach & four with attendants, for C. was fond of shew & of course attracted no little attention on our route & it being quickly buzzed wherever we halted that a General was one of our company, curiosity induced our quarters to be thronged with visitors & odd enough, I was usually addressed as that great personage, probably from my plain coat being taken as a military undress. It caused us many merry jokes as we passed on our way & still serves as a means for pleasantries.

*July 3d.* Yesterday we retired to Calcon Hook, the former residence of my dear E., to while away in quietude a portion of the summer, instead of our accustomed visits to our old friends, returning their annual respects to us.

We are induced to this course mainly by the present unhappy state of our religious Society. Cordiality & confidence are giving place to jealousies, distrusts & evil surmisings & we are spies & informers of each other's private actions & familiar conversations, all brought about to gratify the stubborn self-will & ambition of a few, under cover of high pretensions of purity & zeal for the cause of truth.

*July 7th.* Rode with my E. to the City. It is dusty & hot, the mercury having reached 96. Son H. & wife & others came to see us. A cry of fire proved to be three frame stables kindled by a small boy with a match. Another melancholy scene at Quebec. On the 28th a second fire broke out which consumed 1300 houses & turned more than six thousand people out of house & home. Thus in the short space of about 30 days, ⅔ of that City has been laid in ashes. Marvellous that Quebec & Pittsburg should each have suffered by two such awful calamities so nearly together. The Judgements of the Almighty seem upon us. May we improve under his chastening.

News is received that the Congress of Texas have, by unanimous votes of the Senate & House of Reps., agreed to annexation with the U.

States—so that, whether for good or for evil, the thing is done & we must make the best of it.

Next comes California & then—what then!

*July 8th.* This morning we returned to Calcon Hook. This is a fine farm, pleasantly situated, two miles from the Delaware, of which it commands an extensive view. In the hands of a managing, intelligent farmer, with ample means, it might be rendered very productive.

*July 19th.* Dreams are often the vagrant offspring of our waking thoughts & actions & inconsistent & incoherent. They are often the consequence also of uneasy feelings produced by an unsound & disturbed condition of the stomach, by fatigue of the body or an excited state of the mind. That they may contain spiritual intimations of duty or interest, few who believe in the Sacred Text would deny. From boyhood I have had but little confidence in dreams, but still I have had some from which I have derived consolation in the hour of trouble & others which I was induced to believe were pointings, to say the least of them, not to be disregarded. Of the latter, there was one which deeply engaged my feelings & paved the way to my present happy matrimonial connection & which, at the time, I reduced to writing. It occurred on the night of March 1st, 1827.

I dreamed that I was taking a solitary ramble in a dense forest, deeply engaged in thought, when at the outer margin, I perceived the figure of a female which, on a nearer approach, I discovered to be that of Elizabeth Waln, with whom I had previously had but a slight acquaintance. She was alone, met me with a smile & seemed as if waiting for me. She directed my attention to a smooth path on which she was standing & invited me to a walk, seeming to be at home. The path led thro' a cultivated country surrounded by delightful scenery. Indeed, my imagination could conceive of nothing more beautiful & interesting. At this moment her husband, Joseph Waln, with whom I had been long acquainted but never had much intercourse—& I may add, still less with his wife—made his appearance, advancing with a quick step towards us. I was not a little surprized at seeing him & could not realize his presence until he spoke & offered me his hand, having been under the impression that he had been in his grave for years. He gave me a cordial introduction to his wife & placing her arm in mine, bid us move forward, he stepping on her opposite side. I had never seen him look so well—indeed, he possessed the freshness & vivacity of youth. He pointed to the beauty of the surrounding country & the fair prospects ahead. I turned my face towards him to express my pleasure & satisfaction, but he had disappeared. I awoke with impressions not easily effaced & the more especially from a circumstance which it recalled to my recollection but which, when it happened, I little thought of but as one of those caprices which sometimes seize the wayward mind.

Ten or twelve years at least before my Mary was so suddenly & distressingly snatched from me, seemingly to the loss of all my earthly comforts, I was conducting her & our cousin Abigail Barker to West Town, when we stopped on our way at Joseph Waln's, where I am at this moment writing. While waiting in the hall, Elizabeth entered it from an adjoining apartment. I had never seen her before & was struck with her manners & appearance. I said mentally, "What a lovely woman," to which there was instanter, a mental reply, "She will one day be thy wife." Nothing more unlikely, then, could have suggested itself to the mind of man. We were then both not only married, but happy in our respective connections. The strange thought passed as rapidly from my memory & as effectually, as it entered—until the dream revived the remembrance. Two years after that dream Elizabeth became mine, but it was not until months after that happy event that I told her either my waking or my sleeping dream, for I had not the slightest wish to embarrass her mind by any such means, pending my visits & now that I find myself under her roof, it is not unnatural that it should call up these Providential interpositions & events to my long grateful heart. Oh, that I may prove worthy of the mercies & blessings & favours conferred on me, my life long, by my gracious Saviour.

I ought perhaps to add that in 1827 my E. had been a widow for some years, that she is now in that Hall in which I first saw her, while I am writing in the apartment from which she entered. She knows not what I am penning. Her delicate health causes me much anxiety.

*July 27th.* U.S. troops are rapidly on the march for Texas. A convention of that people have unanimously, one delegate excepted, sanctioned annexation. Mexico has not yet declared war, but grumbles loudly. Our people are pouring into Oregon. One caravan of seven thousand are on the route, having with them 500 waggons & 10,000 head of cattle. When on the move the whole body forms a line of three miles. Indians follow on their wake & on their flank, to steal what they can catch, but the emigrants are too numerous & well provided to admit of a successful attack. There is something not a little exciting & very interesting & romantic in such a scene, its encampments, its order of march over prairies, uncultivated paths for thousands of miles to establish new abodes in a wilderness, far removed from the lands of their birth, their friends & associates. In this party there are men & women of education accustomed to good society. I feel as if I could be almost wild enough to join such a fleeting company.

Poor Audubon, the ornithologist, has met with a severe loss by the fire in N. York. The plates of his large work, valued at $15,000 & uninsured, were destroyed. He & his son, an interesting couple, were with me lately & I subscribed for his work on Quadrupeds, a splendid work now in progress. I had previously possessed his smaller work on birds.

*August 2d.* My dear E. had suffering, sleepless night—worn out with fatigue & disordered stomach, her elder & experienced domestics being left in charge of our City abode, the two young girls we have with us, however willing & obedient, having no knowledge of nursing—while from the rude, unfeeling females of this household we neither receive nor look for sympathy, much less for help, notwithstanding they are under unrequited obligations to her generosity & kindness. She wantonly gives offence to nobody & whoever cannot live with her without a quarrel should be consigned to the pigs, provided always, nevertheless, to use the language of the law, the pigs would consent to live with them.

When she let this Estate, which was before our marriage, she reserved the privilege of occupying certain apartments. This was in 1829. She availed herself of it, once in the lifetime of the Father & now but this once, during that of the son. It is manifest that he is more intent on working the farm for his own emolument than with any regard to the preservation of the buildings or fences. We have accordingly been obliged to repair both since our arrival, to prevent absolute ruin.

*August 5th.* The French in Algeria under command of Col. Pellisier attacked a company of Arabs who, being hard pressed, retreated into a cavern into which the French threw combustibles, burning & suffocating the whole of the unhappy inmates, men, women & children, in all 500 persons. As these people could not escape but by the entrance to the cave, they must in a short time have surrendered at discretion, but that would not suit their impetuous Christian enemies, so to save time, they resorted to a more summary expedient, acting in the same savage spirit that governed the Spaniards in the conquest of Mexico & Peru. The Catholics are ever cruel.

> The auld will speak, the young maun hear
> Be canty, but be good & leal
> Your ain ills hae a heart to bear
> An' ithers hae a heart to feel.

The French Catholics took a somewhat different method, tho' not less brutal, to gain a little territory than that, recently mentioned by Lord Howick in the course of debate in the House of Lords. He stated that a chief in New Zealand claimed title to land because he had slain & eaten its former possessor.

*August 6th.* Son Henry & wife, accompanied by their daughter Anna & niece Juliana Reeve, dined & spent the day with us at Calcon Hook. They are still located at White Hall, Haverford.

*August 9th.* The mammoth steamer *Great Britain* arrived at N. York on the 10th. She moves by a screw propeller & is furnished with iron life boats which, it is said, cannot be sunk even when filled with water. The largest of these will hold 140 persons & there are three others of smaller size, each of which will contain from 50 to 60 without sinking. She is considered in all respects the most perfect specimen of naval architecture ever accomplished. Her cost is admitted to exceed $1,200,000.

> What man is rich? Not he who doth abound
> What man is poor? Not he who has no store
> But he is rich who makes content his ground
> And he is poor who covets more & more.

*August 14th.* I took my departure from C. Hook this morning, leaving my dear E. to follow me tomorrow. This visit has produced but little satisfaction to either of us—the female part of D.R.'s family seeming little inclined & perhaps as incapable, from their vulgar habits, to promote her comfort while with them & we have been daily mortified to witness the injuries he has most ungratefully inflicted on the farm, brought to light during our short residence. He proves not only to be a slovenly farmer, but a destructive, deceitful, unfaithful tenant.

*August 15th.* My E. has returned to the City also. We are once more settled at home.

*August 21st.* Met the Commissioners of the Girard Estates, probably for the last time. Chandler took me aside to urge me not to withdraw from Council at what he termed this critical moment. I replied that I

had been induced by the solicitation of my friends, himself especially, to suffer my name to be again placed on the list last year but that he knew I then said I would withdraw at this time.

*August 23d.* The largest & most perfect skeleton of a mastodon yet discovered has lately been excavated 6 miles west of Newberg, N.Y. It is said to be complete & was found erect, as if mired. The contents of the stomach, consisting principally of forest leaves, were distinctly visible. The tusks are 9 feet long, the enamel of the teeth preserved, the skull weighs 700 lbs. & it measures 7 ft. across the hip bones.

Dichearchus, an ancient learned writer, asserts, I know not on what authority, that whole nations have been destroyed by wild beasts & no wonder, if the earth was then inhabited by ferocious beasts of the magnitude of this mastodon.

*August 29th.* Met the Managers of Haverford School at the Farm. My worst fears are realized. In ten days, vacation occurs—39 pupils are now in the house, 17 are going away & but one known as a new applicant. If 39 bring us in debt, how can the school be sustained with 23? A free discussion arose on this state of things—D.B. Smith attending part of the time. He offers to resign & no wonder. His abilities are unquestioned & so is his honesty, but the school must go down or at least be suspended—the latter I should prefer. No decision was had & the Board adjourned to meet in the City on the 3d. Sept. The grounds were never before in such fine order & the idea of abandoning this noble enterprize after so many years of toil & expense is too painful to be indulged. What will not our poor, disjointed, distracted Society suffer, should this attempt to give a liberal education to our children prove a failure? Alas for our folly. We have expended among us $100,000 on this property. If put under the hammer, it would probably not bring above $30,000.

*September 8th.* U.S. troops, horse & foot, continue to pour into Texas but Mexico has not yet declared war.

*September 10th.* Soon after reaching home last evening, Geo. Howland, a wealthy, benevolent Friend from N. Bedford arrived at my domicile. Having heard of the proposed suspension of Haverford School he hastened hither to endeavour to prevent it. We had much conversation on the subject in consequence of which he proceeded early this morning, accompanied by Wm. E. Hacker, to the school to consult with D.B. Smith. Fear his efforts will not avail.

*September 12th.* Last evening Councils held their stated meeting. Before going to business, I was surrounded by the members & pressed not to resign. Pres. Meredith said, "Mr. Cope, I have consented to serve again under the impression that you would not retire." To which I could only answer that it was unauthorized by me & that, however flattering these importunities, I could not consent. I must retire sometime & this, it appeared to me, was the proper time.

*September 13th.* Meeting Capt. Mann, I said to him—pointing at the same time at his white cotton stockings & wide nankeen shortees, tied at the knees with ribbons—that I perceived he preserved the old stile of dress. He answered, "Mr. Cope, I have not altered the stile of my coat, my jacket, my breeches or my stockings for 60 years." He is now 83 & of course looks antiquated, every inch of him.

There is one other of our citizens who mounts a similar costume with the addition of a Pigtail, made up of a few scanty white hairs. Each have been buckish in their day & proud of sporting a handsome leg. The latter I presume to be older than Capt. Mann. He moves with short unsteady step, but is still fond of displaying his ambling beauties to gazing eyes. I can remember him for nearly half a century, always the same well trimmed beau with his snow white hose & his bunches of knee ribbons dangling gaily.

*September 14th.* I think my retirement from the Council was seasonable, having no ambition to gratify & having accomplished the main objects I had in view—the final settlement of the accounts of the Executors of S. Girard, the extension of the Delaware piers, etc. The acquisition of Lemon Hill for the City was an after affair & would not have taken place but for my exertions.

Another matter of mine is not finally concluded but favourably under way—the introduction of the Schuylkill water on the Delaware Avenue for the protection of the immense interests there from the ravages of fire & the supply of shipping, with that water.

*September 15th.* Reports have reached us that war has been declared. I am, however, still incredulous.

If anything could have induced me to remain longer in Council, it would be to effect if possible a thorough reformation of the Fire Dept. It seems the recent fight at Arch Street was not of the District but City Companies. Some day our Corporation will be compelled to assume the management of the system & rid the City of these disgraceful scenes.

The fear of incurring the enmity of the Firemen is a paltry consideration, unworthy of a statesman. Let Councils do their duty & leave the
event—the public would bear them out. If they will not act let them give
place to men of more nerve.

*September 18th.* My old friend Miner spent the evening with us. I had
called at his lodgings without meeting him & then sent him the
following note—

> Twice have I called at Charley's house
>     And found him not at home
> I wanted him at my house
>     To munch a marrow bone.
> If Charley cannot go a bone
>     Will Charley come to me?
> My wife will give to both of us
>     A dish of good black tea.
> The time for sipping, at my house
>     This eve at seven will be.
> Then do not fail, my Charley dear,
>     To visit T.P.C.

My friend came at the appointed hour, bringing with him the following
lines—

> When genius writes & so invites
>     With pride we haste to meet
> And one & all, at friendship's call
>     Prepare our friends to greet.
> I long to view your palace new
>     So elegant & rare
> And let me say, respects to pay
>     To your good Lady, fair
> If nothing ail, I will not fail
>     To meet your kindly wish
> And of your tea, whate'er it be,
>     To take a cheerful dish.

This facetious, imaginative, sportive friend of mine was at one period
engaged with Thos. Stiles in conducting a daily newspaper in Philadelphia. Stiles was profligate & involved Miner in debt. He escaped with
his skin & fled to W. Chester, where he established the *Village Record*,
which he conducted for many years with unmitigated ability, as a
Federalist advocating that cause with unflinching ability & integrity,

and so that his constituents sent him as their Representative to Congress, where he distinguished himself, among other things, as the advocate of prison reform in their district. I had previously served with him in our State Legislature when Thos. McKean was Governor & Simon Snyder, afterwards Governor, was Speaker of the House of Reps. His manly course & unflinching integrity on that occasion gave rise to an attachment between us which, while life lasts, I trust will never be severed.

*September 25th*. Many of our respectable citizens accost me in the streets in commendation of my proposition for improving the Fire & Police Depts. Mayor McCall expresses his strong favour of it. It seems to be approved by all lovers of good order.

Had a confab in the street with an old acquaintance, Saml. D. Ingham, now of Bucks Co. & Gen. Jackson's first Secy. of the Treasury. As neither of them lacked temper or obstinancy, Ingham wore his honours but a few months. The principal cause of quarrel was a female who, after being the mistress, became the wife of Gen. Eaton, one of Jackson's particular friends, who persisted, despite public opinion, in forcing her into society. The wives of the Democracy therefore admitted her into their houses, with one exception. Ingham's wife would not —and he consequently was dismissed forthwith.

*September 30th*. Among other expedients to raise money to rebuild the Academy of Fine Arts, a bazaar is to be held, under the supervision of females. Their dextrous digits will furnish articles which others are to purchase & a post office is another creation of theirs. Into that department fictitious letters are to be thrown, to be called for by Gentlemen who pay postage at a rate charged by their fair friends. I am asked to supply a letter directed to anybody & on any subject. After some reluctance & puzzlement I have concluded on the following:

To Nobody

Address to nobody—how will that do?
Who is nobody? Echo answers, who?
A lurking, knavish, tricky, wily sprite,
That skulketh ever out of mortal sight.
Who broke my parlour windows, yes, thou did
And when I thought to catch thee, thou wert hid.
Torment of housewives & all woman kind
A good for nothing scrub, time out of mind.

Could I but find where dwells thy ugly Daddy
I'll tell thee what, my mischief making Laddy,
I'd have him give thee, spite of groans & yelping,
A proper, stinging, good old fashioned skelping.
Thou spoiled my Books, turned over chair & table
And set my horses scampering from their stable,
Let loose my gaspipe, as I snored in bed
So when I waked, 'twas well I was not dead.
Thou smashed my looking-glass, upset the lamp,
Broke tumblers, dishes, plates, thou errant scamp,
China bowls, tea cups, coffee pots & wine glasses,
Spilt on my floor tar, grease, oil & molasses.
Tantalizing, brutalizing, scandalizing Imp,
Eavesdropping, evil sopping, love betraying pimp.
When caught at ill, thou whiningly say'st Lo,
Somebody did it long, long time ago.
If thou'lt be good & shun thy naughty ways
I'll stuff thy empty craw with golden praise
But if to teach thee manners be in vain
Quick, get thee off, nor venture back again.

*October 5th.* I pray God so to enlighten my understanding & to soften my heart that I may not become entangled in the unhappy controversy which is now tearing Friends asunder, nor involved in its bitterness. It is so absorbing as to occupy almost all conversation in our social intercourse—to the ruin of our better feelings & religious improvement, nay, to our advancement in useful knowledge. How much better might we be employed. There is a vast field of labour open to us in the exercise of benevolence, in the study & contemplation of the works of the great Creator & Preserver of all things—how infinitely more rational & useful to ourselves & fellow beings. We can neither visit nor receive visits as once we could—a mark is put upon us & suspicion attends our steps. Men, once sociable, pass each other with a scowl or as not knowing one another. Little circles engaged in private chat, when interrupted by a newcomer, are mute until they ascertain on which side he ranks, or know him to be of their party. Why should this be? Let the master spirits & wireworkers answer. My soul, come not thou into their counsel.

*October 14th.* Our general election today. I voted early. Good humour appears to prevail. Had some conversation with Capt. Mann & also with my other drab breeched friend, Robert Andrews. He is very tottering, but converses well & learnedly. He was educated for the pulpit & was assistant teacher under his namesake in the U. of Penna. when Domini Davidson was one of the professors & spoke with bitter recollection of the disorder which then prevailed among the pupils who, he said, used to put tar in Domini's wig. On asking him his age he replied, "Oh, I have forgotten that, but people say I am almost 90." I think, from his appearance, that is about the truth. His exposed stockings are as white as ever & the bows of ribbons at his knees nothing diminished.

A sad event has just come to light. Thos. Winn, a young Englishman & member of Mulberry Meeting of Friends, who keeps a dry goods store in Second below High Street & is respectably connected, has been detected in extensive forgeries. Tully's test of an honest man is this: "He is one that you may venture to play with at even & odd in the dark." Poor Winn was not of that school of morality, but has heretofore sustained a good reputation.

> How rude soe'er the exterior form we find
> How e'er opinion tinge the varied mind
> To all alike, by kind impartial Heaven
> The seeds of truth & happiness are given.

*October 29th.* Last night I presided at a meeting of citizens held at the Board of Trade room, the Phila. Exchange, convened to consider the propriety of constructing a Rail Road from Harrisburg to Pittsburg. There was a good deal of debate, especially between Charles Gibbons & Wm. Crabb, two of our State Senators, the former advocating & the latter disapproving of the extension of the Baltimore & Ohio R. Road from its terminus at Cumberland to Pittsburg, 169 mi. thro' Penna. with a connecting branch from Wills Creek to Chambersburg. The western terminus of the Harrisburg & Cumberland Valley R.R. is estimated to be from 90 to 100 miles.

But the project which gained the most favour was a line from Harrisburg by the Juniata to the Portage over the Allegheny, using for the present the public inclined plains over that mountain but contemplating their ultimate avoidance—the whole distance by that route being 336 from Philada. & the cost for a single track $7,500,000. And that from Chambersburg to Wills Creek, to join the Balto. Road, $4,000,000 over a rough country & a grade of 60 feet in the mile, while the other would in no instance exceed 45 feet & all in our own State.

There was no final action on the subject, but a Com. of 15 was ordered to be selected by the chair at his leisure, with authority to call a Town meeting should they think it advisable or to petition the Legislature to carry out the measure by the incorporation of a company. We adjourned about 11 P.M.

*October 28th.* Samuel Bettle, a minister of the middle district, attended our meeting today, it being monthly meeting & before the separation of the sexes delivered a sound discourse in his usual deliberate manner, not forgetting his rambling practice of interludes. He is a small person, was formerly a tailor & then for many years a successful importer of London cloths. Having by shrewd management & attention to business become rich, he is now a retired gentleman & an active member of our Society, travelling but little.

After he was seated, Elizabeth Evans stood up & poured out, in a strain of eloquent vituperation, a vial of wrath, as customary, on some of our poor heads. If this ambitious woman had the power, she would make some of us a head shorter in quick time or cause the *auto-da-fé* to send our bodies off in vapour & smoke. Masculine in body & mind she exercises uncontrolled sway in our assemblies & knows well how to wheedle submissive necks to her purposes. Raised, like Emmor Kimber, from the dregs of society to a giddy eminence, she may, like him, become intoxicated with power & experience some day a mortifying fall.

*October 30th.* As an evidence of the besetting mania in England, it is stated in one of their R. Road Journals that the advertizements of one week relating to R. Roads amounted to a sum equal to the annual salary of the Pres. of the U.S., viz. $25,000 in that single Journal. This frenzy surpasses the Tulip Lunacy & falls little short of the South Sea bubble. The roads may, however, & doubtless will have value to the public, whatever may happen to the adventurers.

The immorality of the lower classes in the City of N. York is evidenced by a communication made a few days ago by the Matron of the Belleview Almshouse to the Grand Jury. She stated that the births in that House averaged more than two a day, that she had been present at over six thousand births & that a very large proportion of them were cases of bastardy & in some, a repetition.

*October 31st.* I have occasionally noticed Elizabeth & Wm. Evans, but never in malice—nor penned any remarks on them which I cannot conscientiously abide by. Well, if so, it might be asked, Why do they not receive the censure of the Church? They have not escaped admonition from its officers. They are too whole to be improved & if any individual incurs their displeasure, he may expect they—& she especially—will attack him publicly from the gallery, not by name, but in a manner sufficiently pointed to mark him to the audience. He cannot, of course, reply.

The Poet has put into the mouth of Cardinal Wolsey, words like these:

> This is the lot of man—
> Today he buds, tomorrow blossoms
> And bears his blushing honours thick upon him
> And while he thinks—good natured, easy man—
> His greatness is fast ripening
> The next day comes a frost, a chilling frost
> And nips his root & then he falls, as I do.

*November 1st.* Met the Directors of Mercantile Library Co. The Hall is well attended. The members rapidly increasing & the Institution flourishing. With the blessing of Heaven it must do good. It is pleasant to see the tables occupied by so many promising youths, all quietly intent on their books.

*November 2d.* The discoveries which modern science is constantly making in geology & astronomy may alarm the ignorant & superstitious as being inconsistent with Scripture record, while the enlightened believer may find in them confirmation of his faith of the truths of sacred history.

It would be presumptuous in me, who am so deficient in knowledge & education, to attempt by reasoning to reconcile science & the lights of the Bible so as to satisfy even the honest inquirer after truth, but I may hazard the suggestion that the Christian believer is in no danger from the developments of these researches into nature. All the works of the Almighty must be consistent with revelation & to doubt it shews a want of reflection.

*November 3d.* An acceptable letter from Miner with a present of a copy of his *History of Wyoming*, published in the form of letters to his son, Wm. Penn Miner.

Our Quarterly Meeting—nothing of special interest. Several ministers spoke & among them Saml. Bettle. His communications are persuasive, never censorious, but considering his opportunities he is very ungrammatical. He also uses the W in place of the V in his pronunciation. Wm. Hodgson of England says, "It sounds very hodd to 'ear Sammy Bettle say 'winegar'."

*November 4th.* The Managers of the House of Refuge held their stated meeting at 4 P.M. The Com. to consider of providing for more leisure & exercise for the boys & a shed to cover them from the weather reported favourably & the Board directed them to erect a shed, a ball alley & certain simple gymnastics.

Our worthy Pres. Alexander Henry has seldom, of late, been able to attend us, in consequence of ill health, so that I as V.P. usually occupy the Chair. Alexander, who in his early manhood was not remarkable for rigid morality, has for many years devoted himself to religion & the good of his fellow men. Being both wealthy & liberal, he bestows labour & money freely in works of charity & public utility. True, his infirmities have for years confined him very much to his house, but that does not prevent him from the exercise of an extensive benevolence.

He is a strict Presbyterian but values men for their worth & not for their creed. Such men are the salt of the earth. I can cheerfully extend the right hand of fellowship to a good man of any sect, I care not for denomination. And while I prefer my own as founded on the immediate principles of truth, I am neither so blind nor so bigoted as not to know that it may be made a covering for ambition & hypocrisy. The course now pursuing may in the end so purify us, however, as to create a Church such as Chalmers speaks of. He said he knew a family in Scotland consisting of a man, his wife & his sister who claimed to be the only true Church. The sister dying, this man & wife became the only true Church in Christendom. Now who can say that the same may not happen to Wm. Evans & his wife? Would not that be the Millenium?

*November 6th.* A number of persons convened at my house at 4 P.M. to hear Ammi West, now of Maine but formerly a Lottery Broker in this City, who proposed to develop some villainous practices of the craft by which they not only evaded the laws, but defrauded the dupes who purchased tickets. There were present, besides myself, Wm. Meredith, Job. R. Tyson, Townsend Sharpless, Thos. Earp, Isaac Collins, Robert Earp, Doctr. Shippen, John Farnum & Edward Yarnall.

I was called to the Chair & Ed. Yarnall acted as Secy. The statements made by West, interesting & curious, but too complicated to be understood fully—only by a patient, laborious examination into the force of figures. He shewed that the managers of Lotteries so arranged their schemes, the numbers of tickets, the denominations of prizes that, in drawing, not more prizes could by possibility be drawn than the adventurers paid for the tickets, while the managers were themselves protected in any event from loss & in certain cases were as sure to realize immense gain.

They knew, for instance, that in one of the schemes in which they would sell 794 tickets, the purchaser might select any of the numbers below 60 & the drawing would invariably produce the same result, well known to themselves beforehand, but of which the purchaser would be ignorant. A person present said he tried the experiment, selected tickets at random & in several trials the final issue was the same.

West communicated a number of other facts tending to prove the extent of Lottery transactions, here & in N. York, laws to the contrary notwithstanding. As it was deemed important, before any further action on the subject, to have tables of figures tested by some able mathematician, J.R. Tyson & I. Collins were appointed a com. to have that done & the meeting adjourned.

*November 10th.* Papers in the influence of the Administration still urge war. Oregon, the entire Oregon, no arbitration—California also. This rashness may bring on a contest which can end in no good but may prove ruinous to the prosperity & happiness of our country. Suppose Oregon & California ours, is it likely that these acquisitions would tend to the preservation of the Republic? Would not a separation sooner or later become inevitable? Our affairs with Mexico are not yet settled & may not this insatiable grasping propensity for territory excite the jealousy of European powers & incite them to curb our ambition before we become so powerful as to prescribe laws to them?

An adjourned meeting for suppressing lotteries & exposing the frauds of the managers assembled at my house at 4 P.M. to receive the report of the Committee. This being read, another committee was appointed to raise a fund to carry out the purposes of the meeting. Seras E. Walker & E.O. Kendall, two of our most prominent mathematicians, had Ammi West before them & examined his calculations & lottery schemes & certified their correctness under their respective signatures, thus confirming the statements as to the deceptions practiced by lottery managers on the unwary by the use of combination numbers which are equivalent to marked cards & false dies among gamblers.

It seems to be a new discovery of the force of figures, which they deem sufficiently important to claim the attention of some of our learned bodies.

Before separating, a subscription was started to reward West & to defray the expense of printing three thousand copies of Job. R. Tyson's *Essay on Lotteries*, to which new edition note will be appended of the present development in order to arouse public indignation & put the purchasers of tickets on their guard.

*November 21st.* At 3½ P.M., presided at a meeting of citizens at Carpenter's, convened at the instance of a com. appointed by the Philada. Prison Society to consider the practicability of establishing a House of Refuge for coloured children. After a rather desultory debate, it was finally resolved to send the subject to a com. to take the matter into consideration & having authorized me to name that com., I appointed John Swift, Mayor of the City, Richard Vaux, Recorder, Townsend Sharpless, Frederick Packard, Thos. Earp & Chas. B. Trego. There were present some ultra-slaveryites who urged their doctrine of non-distinction of colour & that one establishment should exist for both, while the majority inclined to the necessity of separate buildings. This diversity will endanger the scheme at present in view. Some years ago the managers of the House of Refuge made an essay towards the erection of a building within their enclosure, corner of Coates Street & Ridge Road, preserving a stone wall of division between the two races, but even that approximation met not the public approbation & very significant hints were given us that, should we carry out the measure, we might expect to see a mob to level the entire structure. The sovereign people would teach us better. I feel the necessity of having something done to improve the morals of our coloured youthful population, but between the overzealous, heated imaginations of some of their friends & the prejudices of others, there is great difficulty of effecting any radical improvement. Chremes said, "I am a man & accordingly ought to be concerned in whatever relates to the welfare of any other man."

The steamer just arrived at Boston brings intelligence that the R.R. bubble in England has burst & as might have been expected, to the utter ruin of thousands, while the knowing ones have realized immense fortunes. An association of female speculators are alleged to have made 500,000 Pounds Sterling by their operations in this rage. I fear the news may produce an unfavourable effect on our schemes.

The German physiologists affirm that of 20 deaths of men from 18 to 20 years old, throughout this country, 10 have their origin in smoking tobacco. It is an awful warning to our own youth. Lads many years younger are constantly met in our streets with cigars in their mouths.

Some years ago it was the practice of females, called Ladies of pleasure, to visit Havana in the autumn, spend the winter there & return to the U.S. at the approach of warm weather. They were the cause of so much jealousy & bickering between the Spanish Grandees & their wives as to induce the interference of the public authorities who, by ordinance, prohibited the landing of single women in their City. Married women were not excluded.

The forbidden class found the means of evading the prohibition. They possessed themselves of children & thus gained admission. In the selection, female infants were preferred, as they could be inducted into the same infamous course of their foster mothers. When I presided over the Board of the Guardians of the Poor, before the removal of the Almshouse to Blockley, there was ushered into the presence of the Board a young woman. An elegant young woman, dressed very richly in full mourning, she represented herself to be a widow. She had lost her only babe & was extremely anxious to procure an orphan child to be brought up as her own, to console her in her sad bereavement.

Having doubts as to her true character, strengthened by her answers to my several questions, I desired her to retire into another apartment, when the Board would deliberate on her application for a female infant. On her retirement, several members of the Board expressed their assent to her, I however told them of the Havana affair & that I strongly suspected her story & as she informed us that she boarded in the neighbourhood, I prevailed on the Board to send a com. to make inquiry, while we would detain her in the House. It being my duty to appoint, I named three of the members who were most favourably disposed towards her. They were not long absent & John Keefe, of their number, reported that they found the dwelling she had pointed out, that it was superbly furnished. The Lady who kept it was very polite. She spoke in highest commendation of the applicant, but the Com. made certain discoveries which induced them to form an unfavourable opinion of the establishment—that on departing from the place, they perceived a well dressed matron on the opposite of the street, whom they accosted & asked the character of the place they had left. "Why do you ask me?" replied the Dame. "You impudent fellows, didn't I see you come out of the house? I should like to know who you are." Keefe, who is a ready Irishman, addressing this matron, said "This is Wm. Binder, who lives in the N. Liberties & is Pres. of the Board of Health. This is Jas. S. Spencer, Esq., a Magistrate of Spring Garden & I am myself, Madam." "Well," answered the good Dame, "you are three impudent

fellows, call yourselves what you may & you had better be off." Keefe concluded this detail by adding that they were now satisfied & would recommend that the applicant be refused the child. The Board agreed & he was required to give the answer to the elegant Lady in deep mourning who had been all this time waiting in the adjoining apartment & who manifested little of her true character on receiving the intelligence.

*November 27th.* A late writer says that in the 17th century, 40,000 witches were put to death in England alone. In Scotland & Ireland the executions were doubtless in proportion. A wretch named Matthew Hopkins followed the profession of witch finder & even that great man, Sir Matthew Hale, condemned two women to death as witches in 1684. Posterity may discover that we, in the practice of war & the death punishment & in the slavery of our fellow men, are not much wiser or humane.

Yesterday was held our monthly meeting. The principal business—as usual, the disowning of our members. These meetings have but little interest for me, a spirit of intolerance being too prevalent & the person who may bespeak a charitable judging of offenders will hardly escape a tart rebuke—if not forthwith, he will be lucky if he escapes when the next sermon is preached from the gallery.

*November 29th.* The *Wyoming* came down from Kensington to my wharf, Walnut St.—the largest Ship for commerce ever built in this Port & I have no doubt never surpassed in workmanship & accommodations.

*November 30th.* Dr. Hare's Wistar party last evening. The Dr. is Professor of Chemistry in the U. of Penna. & well merits the distinction. He is also a member of the Am. Philosophical Society. He is a hale, stout man of 70. His brother Chas. W. Hare, long since in his grave, was a distinguished member of the Philada. Bar & one of my earliest associates on the stage of manhood. He was a slim, tall man, careless in his habits but, in halcyon days, of vigourous intellect. I served with him in Com. Council 45 years ago & in the Legislature of the State in 1807.

Some years after the latter period he exhibited proofs of insanity & was confined in the Penna. Hospital, of which I was then a Manager. He had been a most ardent politician in the Federal ranks & was mainly instrumental in getting up the Washington Association, whose hall in 3rd, above Spruce St., is still standing, tho' appropriated to a different purpose, the association having dissolved many years ago. I was not a member. They were too ultra & uncompromising to gain my affections.

There were a large number of the elite at the party, mostly professional, the few others ranked generally as Whigs, for the Doc. has little sympathy with the Democrats. Good humour prevailed throughout the evening, blended with instructive conversation. Indeed, these meetings have a tendency to soften the asperities of party & to improve both the heart & the understanding.

*December 8th.* Another letter, to which the initials J.L.S. are affixed, comes to me thro' the P.O. The writer says he is a Presbyterian minister & modestly requests me to send him $300 thro' the same channel. I had another of the same stamp a few days ago, written by another hand. How these anonymous applicants can expect answers shews great ignorance, if they are nothing worse. If they are in distress & deserving, they should resort to other means for relief. A prudent man would be cautious of giving either his name or money to such applicants. The snow, in the afternoon, has been converted into a warm rain, which occasions very splashing trudgery.

*December 9th.* It rained nearly all last night. This day is spring like. Our Grandams used to say that when the cold had come down out of the sky we had fine weather, but could not have it before.

*December 10th.* Last evening Richard H. Dana, Jr., of Mass. & author of *Two Years Before the Mast* delivered the lecture before the Mercantile Library Co. & considering the bad walking, a numerous audience. His subject was "American Loyalty." He is a small man, about 5 ft. 6—florid complexion, benevolent, manly, youthful countenance & appears to be under 30 years of age. He considered the people of England to be the most loyal of any in Europe & that we ought not to dishonour our Mother Country. France he deemed unloyal, defining loyalty to be love of country even in a state of anarchy & independent of the sovereignty. He paid a compliment to Maryland, as setting us the first example of religious toleration & to Pennsylvania, as standing alone in the history of the world as an immense sovereignty acquired from uncivilized owners without aid of intimidation or injustice. Mass. he said has been sanctified by the privations of its Pilgrim founders. On these & other topics he was affectingly eloquent & pious in expression, being greatly applauded by the audience.

Between day & candlelight, a well dressed, slim man entered my

house & asked me if I had not received letters thro' the P.O. signed J.L.S. I answered in the affirmative. "Well, I am that man." I then said he was an entire stranger to me, it would be well for him to refer me to some who knew him & if he was what he represented himself to be, I was willing to join others in aiding him. After a pause he said he wished not to do so & on my declining to supply his wants, he quietly took his departure. I could not well see his countenance.

*December 11th.* The meeting of citizens last night at the Chinese Saloon on the proposed R. Road to Pittsburg was numerously attended & quite enthusiastic. I was called to the Chair on motion of Geo. W. Toland, late member of Congress from this District. On taking my station, I made a short address to the immense crowd, pointing out briefly the necessity of immediate & effective action. Every man in the community, from the day labourer to the man of wealth, the dealer in stocks, the mortgage holder, the owner of Real Estate, are all interested in the success of this great undertaking. Boston by means of R. Roads had reached the great West & was now obtaining large supplies of produce from that quarter. New York, besides her magnificent canal, was engaged in constructing a R.R. to contend for the prize—while on the south we have Balto. & Ohio R.R. Co. seeking the same object, having completed their road to Cumberland, 189 miles & desiring to pass thence thro' Penna. to Pittsburg, 157 miles, offering us, as boon for the privilege, a connection with their road. Much as I wished success to that spirited Company, I could not wish it at the expense of my own State. I objected to the connection, in the first place, because in reaching that point we must pass over a mountainous district with grades of 60 feet to the mile at an expense of more than $4,000,000 & after all, as the road would be in the hands of rivals—who would consult their own interests, without regard to ours—the road might prove of little value to us, as they could run their trains so as to baffle us.

W. Chester has, by charter, the right to connect with the Columbia R.R. There is no unkind feeling towards the Company on the part of the State authorities & yet the latter, consulting what they apprehend to be the interests of the State, so run their trains that those of the Company, after reaching the point of junction, are often detained one hour, two hours, three hours & even four hours before they can proceed.

A route under the authority of our State has been surveyed thro' the heart & centre of the State with a grade of 45 feet, making the whole distance from Philada. to Pittsburg via the Columbia R.R. &c. to

Harrisburg, 336 mi.—10 mi. less than the R.R. from Balto. to Pittsburg. This R.R., if completed, far from injuring the public works, would double, perhaps quadruple the business on them, for when people from the West could have a certainty of passage at all seasons, ten would travel to us where we now have but one, bringing with them their money & produce & taking back our merchandize. After some other remarks, I concluded with these words, "Nature has done much for us, let us now see what we can do for ourselves."

*December 13th.* This day opens cold, bright & calm. John K. Kane, Attorney General of the U.S. for this District, being in the confidence of Pres. Polk, I endeavoured last night to obtain his opinion as to the probability of war, but he affected ignorance on the subject. From him I obtained the knowledge of a circumstance connected with our last war, which has remained secret till now & is most probably but little known anywhere. Near the close of that war, a flotilla was quietly got up in N.Y., under command of Commodore Porter, designed to visit the English channel, make a sudden landing & lay waste some of their Towns & be off before alarm or effective resistance could be made. This was to avenge the destruction of Washington by the British.

Porter was a daring commander, was well provided with engines for mischief & had a trained body of desperadoes under him who were, however, kept in ignorance of his destination. Peace prevented the departure of the flotilla, just as it was prepared to sail. The English probably never heard of it, so Kane thinks.

*December 14th.* Yesterday 6½ A.M. the mer. on top of the Exchange stood at 11 & was the same at Frankford, where my son Alfred resides. It commenced snowing last night, this morning it was succeeded by rain, which continued to fall with little intermission all day. The street lamps were lighted at ½ past 4 P.M. in consequence of the darkness.

Last night, in a party of citizens, I was addressed separately by 3 of our Supreme Court Judges—Gibson, Chief Magistrate, Rogers & Burnside, associates—on the subject of the contemplated R. Road. The former advocated the Balto. & Ohio R.R. to Pittsburg & on my stating my preference to one direct thro' the centre of our own State & my objections to a connection with the former, he said I was prejudiced & I thought I might well have returned the compliment. Rogers was more reasonable & listened to argument, but evidently favoured the connection. Burnside entertained more of a Penna. view, reprobating the connection as injurious to our State. He appears to have full knowledge

of our interior & gave me interesting information on the subject & useful advice as to our best mode of procedure—promising to aid us all in his power, adding that his son James, an influential member of the last & present H. of Reps., would cooperate in sustaining our project.

James Burnside was the means of defeating the intrigues of the B. & O. Co. in our Legislature last winter. Judge Gibson is perhaps 6 ft. 4 & stout in proportion, a sound Lawyer, but savouring strongly of external & political influences. Rogers is a small man of good understanding, labours diligently in his vocation & is more popular. He formerly was connected with James Buchanan, the present Secy. of State of the U.S. in the practice of Law in Lancaster, my native Town. They were then piping hot Federalists, but changed their creed for Jacksonism. Burnside, who was once an ardent politican of the Jefferson School, obtained a judgeship in a county district, from which he was removed to the Supreme Bench. There is more of what is called character in him. He is of middle size, grey headed & hard featured—a shrewd, far seeing, calculating man, well instructed in the game of Legislative shuffle board, the machinery of party tactics & the arcana of demagoguism & withal a well meaning, honest, sagacious judge.

One of his eye lashes, unless when animated in conversation, is apt to close over a scrutinizing orb within, giving to his rough countenance an air of rough cunning & cockering. He looks more like a clown than a gentleman learned in the Law, but I believe he stands well with the Bar & being withdrawn from the political arena, will doubtless render good service in his present elevation.

*December 18th.* Thomas Jefferson was not very scrupulous of means, when he wished to attain an end. I never considered him a good teacher of ethics. During the Revolutionary War, Congress had a sum of money in the hands of their Banker in Paris. It was all drawn for, but it happened that by capture or loss at sea, drafts for $3000 of the am't never made their appearance. Thomas never abounded in money, the $3000 were tempting & he contrived to possess & pocket the amount. Jefferson was not a Jesuit, but sustained the charge of being Jesuitical. Witness his double dealing with Washington, in which case he acted with profound duplicity.

*December 19th.* A Canton paper states that the Commander of the Chinese Army reports that he lost 16,000 soldiers who died from the effects of opium.

J.L.S. has addressed two other separate notes to me. What am I to think of such a man? Is he a fool or a knave? An utter stranger, declining to give me his name or reference for character & yet importuning for money & no pittance either. Our country never so abounded with thieves & imposters.

*December 21st.* I never was ambitious of office in Church or State & never sought it. When I entered Select Council, I did so at the solicitation of the citizens, prompted also by a desire to effect a settlement of the accounts of the executors of S. Girard, in which I happily succeeded. And if, in meeting the wishes of others, I have consented to serve the Mer. Library as their Pres., the Board of Trade in the same capacity & various other of our benevolent & useful institutions, I have incurred the reproach of certain envious & narrowminded Friends—I am sorry for it, nor will their abuse deter me, for so long as God shall bless me with health & the means of doing good to my fellow men without regard to country or colour, I trust I shall not decline the service & think I shall thus be more honourably & worthily employed than by writing insurrectionary & defamatory epistles for secret circulation or in engaging in private cabals & associations to scalp the unwary, to injure the good name & fame of absentees, to riot in secret or open scandal, under the hypocritical plea of promoting the cause of truth. Religion is never benefitted, but sadly frustrated by such unhallowed doings. Let their authors profess or pretend what they may.

If, while I was a member of Council, I had accomplished no other service than obtaining for Philada. the acquisition of Lemon Hill, I should feel amply rewarded & have conferred on the City a more lasting benefit than those selfish revilers have ever rendered to their country.

Thick ice covers the face of the Delaware & merry skaters wind their devious courses over the smooth bosom of Schuylkill, which is frozen tight below the bridges.

*December 25th.* A Senator from Florida has submitted a resolution to that body for the purchase of the Island of Cuba. Why did he not include Ireland & Madagascar?

A few sleighs whirled by this morning, but a thaw ensued & in place of snow there is mud.

*December 30th.* Flying clouds & winds from the SW.

Some time spent today in traversing sloppy streets to visit a few of our representatives in our State Legislature to engage their services in procuring a supplement to the Bill incorporating Haverford School, so

as to admit pupils professing with Friends or whose parents are desirous of having them educated in the school & willing their sons should conform to our rules.

Chas. Yarnall accompanied me. We were well received & assurances given of cordial support. Our memorial will be placed with Chas. Gibbons of the Senate & Chas. B. Trego of the House Representatives. I embraced the occasion to urge the claims of our Central R. Road to Pittsburg. Gibbons, I fear, will embarrass us, for altho' he promises us support, he advocates the Baltimore route & is the well known author of a series of essays now publishing in the *U.S. Gazette* in favour of that company.

I am in favour of a road thro' our own State & under our own control, in preference to one passing to a rival City & under the management of persons having no Pennsylvania interest. After providing for ourselves, it will be time enought to be generous to others & not put a staff in an enemy's hand to break our own head.

# 1846

*January 3d.* The warm weather & rain have caused the ice on the Delaware at Burlington to give way & the broken mass is floating by our wharves.

In the evening the Directors Merc. Library Co. held their stated meeting. A closing report was made from the Building Com. The rental amounts to $3075, reserving the Library apartment & a small room for the Directors. The essay of the annual report to the stockholders was read & approved, in which we shall read them a homily in morals, induced principally by a proposition submitted to them at a late meeting by that busy body, John B. English, one of their number, to open an apartment in the building to contain a chess board for the use of the members & to which I can never give my assent.

That game may be played innocently & so may other games & if it be allowed, cards & dice may follow & the Library be converted into a gambling shop. I said, if the measure should be sanctioned by a vote, I would resign. I trust, however, that this mischievous, silly scheme will not succeed.

*February 10th.* My slumbers much disturbed last night. Senator Choate of Boston was to deliver the lecture this evening before the Mer. Library Co. On learning that he would not attend, Jos. Grubb & Wm. Shaffer of the Lecturing Com. engaged Wm. B. Reed to fill the vacancy. Late yesterday I was shown the title of Wm. B. Reed's lecture, viz. "The Life & Time of Thos. Paine."

The annunciation has caused me much anxiety. Paine was a drunkard & a notorious infidel. His *Age of Reason* has branded his name with infamy & I know not language in which to express my contempt of that man. To make a wretch like him the subject of a lecture before a Christian community is an outrage on decency & good manners. I object likewise to the Lecturer. He does not lack talents, but his morality is not free from suspicion. He is suspected of participating in the bribes so freely dispensed by N. Biddle in obtaining the Charter of the Bank from the State of Penna.—W.B.R. being at the time a member of the legislature. He cannot deny having received large sums from the Bank but alleges them to have been for professional services. His father was Treas. of the U. of Penna. & defrauded that Institution of some thousands. His grandfather, sometimes called Gov. Reed, was con-

spicuous in the American Revolution & strongly suspected of trimming between the contending parties, ready to join either that would pay him his price. Gen. Washington, a discriminating Patriot, had no confidence in his integrity.

The grandson seeks constant occasions to glorify the grandfather, to wipe away the deep stain on his reputation & in selecting the infamous Paine for the subject of his discourse has doubtless in view to whitewash his Grandsire's reputation, with but little concern for that of his impure subject.

My uneasiness induced me this morning to call on Jos. Patterson & Chas. Wood to express my discontent & unhappy feelings. The former is of the Com. on Lectures, the latter a member of the Board, both unite with me in sentiment. P. expresses a wish that I would speak to the Lecturer, which I declined, saying it would be treating our colleagues who had selected him with the same disrespect which they had, in this instance, shewn for me.

Paine was a lank, slovenly looking man of about the usual height, hard features, thoughtful countenance, large purple nose & awkward gait. I often saw him, during my apprenticeship, walking back & forth in the Market House, between Second & Third Sts. with stooping shoulder & downcast eye, staggering with folded arms, under the influence of liquor & as in deep meditation, his clothes & general appearance indicating carelessness & poverty. At that time the Jail was at the SW corner of Third & High St. The old Court House connected with the Market House at the west of Second St.—the whipping post, pillory & stocks on the east of Second St., opposite the Court House, & the Friends Meeting House at the SW corner of High & Second, close by the Court House, a cart way between.

The last time I witnessed the use of the pillory was in the case of Luke Cating, a gallant, handsome fellow who had been guilty of forgery. The last time I witnessed the punishment of the cat & nine was on the back of a pretty girl, apparently 17 or 18 years of age. She was bare to the waist & the cat was applied by a stout ruffian with such force as to cover her back with much blood, the lash occasionally cutting round & causing blood to flow from her breasts. I felt at the moment as if I could willingly have blown the fellow's brains out with a pistol.

I went not designedly to witness these relics of barbarity, but the store in which I served was in Second, a few doors above High St. & I consequently frequently passed the spot on which they were exhibited. The poor girl had committed a petty theft. Thank Heaven, these savage spectacles have long ceased to disgrace our Commonwealth. When a person was pilloried, the universal practice was for boys to pelt him with rotten eggs, grown persons cheering them on & huzzaing as each missile took effect.

There is surely some improvement in our penitentiary system. While writing, I am favoured with a note from Jos. Patterson stating that he entirely coincides with me in my views of the lecture. He has been unsuccessful in his efforts to see Wm. B. Reed, but will make a further attempt. The hour for the lecture is near at hand, but I cannot sanction it by my presence. As Pres. of the Board I usually occupy a seat on the platform near the Lecturer.

*February 16th.* Yielding to the besetment of some of my fellow citizens, I have given my reluctant consent to visit Harrisburg to further the construction by a company, of the projected R. Road from Harrisburg to Pittsburg. It might seem strange that objections should be urged against the passage of a Bill for so worthy an object, but the Balto. & Ohio R. Road Co. have great influence & will resort to almost any means to prevent our success & on our northern borders, N. York has enlisted the interest & feelings of the inhabitants in favour of their scheme for pushing their R.R. thro' those counties to Erie & the friends of that measure unite their strength with counties on our southern line in array against us & hope, by mutual pledges of support, to defeat us & carry out their several designs. We have therefore to contend with forces both without & within our camp.

Some years ago, a stockholder in the Balto. & Ohio R.R. Co. assailed me on their projected right of way thro' Penna. & on my replying that they ought not to suppose we could consent to make such a sacrifice to a rival, he slapt his hand on his breeches pocket, exclaiming, "Mr. Cope, we can do anything with your Legislature."

*February 18th.* Pursuant to arrangements, left home for Harrisburg in company with Geo. W. Toland, Geo. N. Baker & Jas. Bayard, representing the City interest in favour of a R. Road from Harrisburg to Pittsburg & to oppose the scheme of the B. & O. R.R. Co. in their attempt to rob us, on our own soil, of the western trade.

Arrived at H. by 4 P.M., where we learned that a vote had yesterday been taken in our Senate denying the Co. the right of way by a single vote. A reconsideration will doubtless be moved on so close a vote.

*February 19th.* The Com. paid Gov. Shunk a visit of ceremony in

which no allusion was of course had to our errand. He received us very kindly, but we were struck with his worn, haggard appearance & stiff gait. We next paid our respects to Treas. Snowden, an energetic officer. He was courteous & familiar. He is of middle stature & generous aspect. Both he & Gov. S. invited us to call again. Our business was with the members of the Legislature, with many of whom we conversed on the objects of our visit & trust we made a favourable impression on some of them.

While we were in the Senate Chamber, the H. Reps. were occupied in an alleged case of bribery. It seems that a man named McCook of Ohio, having some interest in the renewal of a charter to the Northampton Bank, had several interviews with Victor E. Piolett, Representative from Bradford Co., in the course of which he put $400 in P.'s hands, with the promise of $100 more, to forward the enactment of a charter & that P. received the money, handed it over to a public officer & then informed the House. A com. of investigation was thereupon appointed to report to a future sitting.

A Senator informs me that Piolett does not maintain a good character & thinks, had the sum been $4000 instead of $400, the House would not have been troubled with the case.

McCook is a good looking man of well formed person, rather above middle height, hair blanched, pleasant countenance, mild dark eye. From appearance should never suspect him of being a rogue. Thaddeus Stevens is his Counsel, who, seeing me in the lobby, came to offer his hand. He is a shrewd, hard mouthed fellow & should he have the chance, will, whatever else happens, serve up Piolett in high stile. He was a member of the Convention of 1837 for reforming the State Constitution & then, a political demagogue. He took an active part in its proceedings, had a constant eye to party & none was more expert at such tactics. Luckily, he ranked among the Conservatives, or he might have perpetrated much mischief & altho' dreaded by his Locofoco antagonists, was dubiously respected by his friends. Wm. M. Meredith & he had a trial of strength in a rough & tumble debate in which Thaddeus, with all his skill, came off second best.

Pierce Butler, a puerile fellow who married Fanny Kemble, the celebrated actress, was fool enough to strike a wordy blow at him but was never again heard in that Convention. T., in reply, said there were some insects so insignificant that if you tramp on them, they would escape under the hollow of your foot. S. told some of the members who were present, when he accosted me, of an occurrence in Convention at which, I remember, he laughed heartily & which, it seems, he has not forgotten.

We had in that Convention two men in particular who wore us out with their interminable, dull harangues—Geo. Chambers, a Lawyer & worthy citizen, and Ephriam Banks, a third rate country practitioner. As each was in the habit not only of long speechifying, but of making long pauses, I proposed a Resolution that when either came to a pause the other should fill up the gap and, thus alternating, there would be a saving of time & other members would be preserved from going to sleep, by the novelty of the amusement. The Resolution, tho' penned, was not offered officially.

*February 21st.* Yesterday the Senate agreed by a vote of 19 to 10 to reconsider the vote on the right of way, but no further action on the subject was taken. This is no test vote & only a courtesy. We see much done here for political effect. John Jay said that "From Absolom downward, there never was an honest demagogue."

*February 23d.* Some time was spent this morning in considering, on second reading, our Bill, to which several burdensome incumbrances were offered, principally by Geo. Darsy from Pittsburg, one of which he was seen to place in the hands of Jas. M. Gillis of Warren, who ignorantly took up another on a different subject & handed to the Chair but—the blunder being detected—the original was substituted, when the Senate adjourned to the Chamber of the H. Reps. to hear Washington's Farewell Address read & I to my chamber, having little inclination to press thro' a crowd of both sexes to listen to a document familiar to us all & which anyone may read at leisure.

This reading being ended, the discussion was resumed & the same game of trifling & opposition carried on, but the Bill passed a second reading, notwithstanding.

*February 24th.* The Bill was finally disposed of in Senate, having passed by a vote of 26 ayes to 5 noes & as it is uncertain when it will be called up in the House & the weather is lowering, Toland, Baker & myself have concluded to return to the City by this afternoon's train.

*February 25th.* We reached home last evening at 9½ & this morning perceive the ground covered with snow. We were not mistaken in our apprehensions of the weather, which remains cold & blustering.

*March 2d.* On the 26th Feby., I was favoured with a call of friendship from Bishop Potter & in conversation found him take a lively interest in favour of our Central R. Road & against the pretensions of Baltimore, and today have a visit from another distinguished personage, expressly on the same subject, viz. Richard Rush, at one time our Envoy to the English Government & at another, Secy. of the Treas. of the U.S. He is an accomplished writer & on this occasion takes statesmanlike view of Penna. interests. He thinks that strenuous efforts should be used by Philada. in particular & by the State to prevent the success of the Baltimore scheme & to promote the Central R. Road.

*March 4th.* A citizen has called to show me a letter from one of our representatives in the House of R. of a desponding character. He thinks that by fair means or foul the Baltimoreans will carry their Bill.

This afternoon, I met for the first time as a Manager of the Board of the Deaf & Dumb Asylum. I have no expectation of becoming an active member, owing to the press of other engagements. Why did they elect me?

*March 6th.* A note from Samuel Breck, one of our spirited citizens, now perhaps 84, formerly of Boston, in which he informs me that he is preparing for publication an account of the charities, donations & trusts of Philada. I shall willingly aid him if I can.

Later in the evening, a note from R. Rush accompanied by a communication for the press on the all absorbing topic of the right of way & Central Railroad. It is too late for the press of tomorrow.

*March 7th.* Called on the editors of the *North American*, who engage to insert R. Rush's essay in their paper of the 9th, as tomorrow is the first of the week. It is—as might have been expected from the author—a pungent, liberal, statesmanlike production.

*March 9th.* My time much occupied about the right of way, &c. Rush appears in the *N. American*. Have directed at my own expense one copy to each member of the Legislature, 133 in all & one to each of our Reps. in Congress, 26 in number, one to G.M. Dallas, V. P. & another to Secy. Buchanan. The issue is yet doubtful.

*March 12th.* John Duncan, a military Englishman, visited Dahomey in Africa in 1845 & says that the King caused an army of six thousand females to be received before him whose arms, accoutrements & performances were truly surprizing. What a shameful departure from delicacy, decency, humanity & propriety—even in a brutal African.

*March 13th.* An interesting, thrilling statement of premature interments—or, rather, of their fortuitous prevention—is given in the *Constitutional*, in a period of about 10 years in France, amounting to the number of 94. Of these, 35 persons awoke of themselves from their lethargy at the moment their interment was commencing, 13 recovered from the affectionate care of their families, 7 in consequence of the falling of their coffins, 8 or 9 were recovered by the providential infliction of wounds made in sewing up their winding sheets, 5 from the sensation of suffocation on closing their coffins, 19 from their interments being delayed by accidental circumstances & 6 from doubts having been entertained of their actual death. These cases present very serious subjects for caution & reflection.

A short visit from Wm. Brown, son of C.B.B., deceased. He aided John Randall to fleece the Ch. & Del. Canal Co. out of a large sum. R. then turned on him & is pursuing him to ruin. I pity him, he is in bad hands. Some would say he richly deserves it. He laboured hard for a villain & he has his reward.

*March 14th.* The Managers of the Mer. Library Co. held an adjourned meeting this evening, at which was discussed the propriety of setting apart one or two entire days of the week for the exclusive admission of females. On the final vote the scheme obtained the affirmative of but one member, Isaac Barton—the majority considering the project as inconsistent with the original design of the Institution & liable to prove of evil tendency by the introduction of dissolute girls within our walls. It was agreed to open the Library from 3 to 10 o'clock daily, on common days. There is nothing to prevent females from attending if they incline to do so on such days, as in the Philada. Library.

*March 17th.* Opposition to chartered companies has become talismanic with the Democracy of the country & our present Gov. seems disposed to extend the doctrine to its utmost limits. I understand him to have recently vetoed a Bill for chartering a company under the silly plea of charters being aristocratic. He may drive capital from among us & send it to enrich our wiser neighbours. A single individual, however otherwise qualified, may not be of ability to carry on to any extent or to any profit to himself or benefit to the public, a certain manufacture. He applies to some of his wealthy neighbours who are willing to furnish means, to a given extent, willing to risk that portion of their effects in the concerns, but not disposed to hazard their all in case of failure. A charter secures them. The united capital need & indeed cannot be kept a secret, for the act itself proclaims the amount. No man who credits the company is forced to do so, but he can have no just claim beyond the capital & effects of the company, if it becomes bankrupt.

How, therefore, is the public harmed by such associations? So of Banks. Break up our Banks & send their capital to seek employment in other States, as has partially already happened & it will be worse than idle to think of competing for wealth, for success, for prosperity or for competency with our more wise & powerful rivals & yet we appear willing to hazard the attempt. Banks, like every creation of man, are liable to abuse. The vetoing & pardoning power lodged with the Gov. are liable to abuse. Water & fire are inestimable blessings, but each may cause desolation to the best hopes of man.

In the present instance, Gov. Shunk turns Legislator & will not sign a Bill unless prepared by himself & that, too, on a subject which he does not understand.

*March 24th.* Among the several rude attacks which are made on me for my advocacy of a R. Road from Harrisburg to Pittsburg & disapproval of the Baltimore right of way is a pamphlet under the signature of Jas. S. Craft, hailing from Pittsburg & which, so far as I can discover, is little else than a puerile attempt to injure myself & associates in public estimation. I pity the author for his ignorance & impudence.

*March 27th.* Stated meeting Managers Hav. School. No quorum. Men are apt to absent themselves when Institutions are not prosperous. Money was needed to meet demands & of the few present, some of us had to advance means to meet them.

*April 16th.* The Central R. Road Bill, the title changed to Penna. R. Road, having passed both Houses & rec'd the Governor's signature, is now a Law.

*April 29th.* The penny post has brought me an anonymous note without date or place written in a feigned hand, making heavy charges against me, designed probably to extort money. In England such expedients for raising the wind are said to be common. The writer will, in the present case, be disappointed.

*May 2d.* The Board of Mer. Library Co. held their stated meeting. The opening of the Hall in the afternoon as well as evening has occasioned a small additional attendance. A female is sometimes seen but not often. That extravagant, good natured lawyer David Paul Brown, who occupies one of the offices, was ordered out, not paying his rent. As evidence of his folly, it is said that he purchased a copy of Shakespeare for $600 & some hundred yards of linen for shirts for himself at $3 a yard. His furniture & library are not unfrequently seized & sold for rent & a sheriff's officer is often a lodger of weeks in his family, which is numerous. He is a pleasant companion, a powerful pleader & given to no grovelling vice. He has industry in his profession but is vain & wasteful as a spoiled, untutored child.

He is in the prime of life, vigorous in body & mind, but what is to befall him & his family when old age overtakes him presents but a gloomy prospect. He has, however, seasons of seriousness in one of which he not long since resolved to study divinity & yield himself to the service of the Church, but the fit did not last. He rarely passes me without a smile & a pleasant word.

*May 3d.* First Day. An eloquent discourse from Eliza. Evans, not in her stile of anathema, but persuasive & charitable—rather an unusual circumstance.

*May 8th.* From N. Orleans we learn that something like war has actually occurred on the Texan borders. Two officers of the Am. Army & three privates are slain by scouts of the Mexicans. Porter, son of the late Commodore Porter & 3 men are known to have been killed. The other officer, it is hoped, has been carried away prisoner. The American Gen. Taylor has ordered the blockade of the Rio Grande to prevent supplies from reaching the Mexican forces at Matamoras. This news creates some sensation. No declaration of war has been proclaimed on either side.

*May 10th.* In our morning meeting (First Day) E. Evans favoured us with another eloquent discourse. She is probably the most finished female orator belonging to the Society in this country, but she would be none the worse for indulging a little less vanity & ambition & a little more charity & less self-importance. She seems so whole & such a standard of perfection as renders her but little inclined to see anything but beams in others' eyes, having not a mote in her own. May God preserve me from harsh judgements, but I have lived long enough & seen enough to know that all is not gold that glistens & that it is much easier to preach than to practice. We have rain again today.

*May 11th.* If the intelligence of the 8th from our Army on the frontier was calculated to create a sensation, that of today will not diminish the interest. The Mexicans have crossed the river & surrounded Gen. Taylor's encampment, cutting off, at the same time, his sources of supply & he has but two weeks' provision for his 2500 men. The Mexicans before his camp are said to number 8000. Great exertions are making in Texas, N. Orleans, &c. to reinforce Taylor, but they may not reach him in time & must necessarily be detached in separate divisions. The enemy may therefore cut them up piecemeal, little by little, as they arrive. These are strange doings.

*May 23d.* Horace Binney is opposed to the Penna. R. Road. I never knew him to contribute towards any public improvement. He is wealthy, but proverbially selfish—hence that saying of a wag, "Binney's grace is, for me & my wife, my son Horace & his wife, we four & no more." This son is now a member of Common Council & of course, adverse to the Council's taking any stock in the Company. My opinion is that, if they do not, they will at the next election be all turned out of office. If all our citizens had been Binneys, Philada. would now be but a village & if this project fail & the Balto. & Ohio R. Road unites with Pittsburg, our City will be reduced to the condition of a village & we shall lament in vain over our short sighted policy, when too late.

*May 25th.* More intelligence from the seat of war. Gen. T. has had two battles with the Mexicans—taken 8 pieces of cannon—killed or taken 1200 men. Paredes in person with a large army marching to the scene of action, while reinforcements are arriving to the aid of Gen. T.

*June 1st.* Presided at the annual meeting of the Ches. & Del. Canal Co., held at their office on Walnut above Third St. A small attendance, indicative that the affairs of the Co. have been prosperous the past year. This neglect is censurable. When stockholders fail of their duty, the officers may be tempted to become unfaithful. This Co. was for years the object of my labour & anxiety, my fears & pecuniary solicitude & heavy personal expenditures. I hope at last to be repaid.

After midnight last night, the Matron of the Magdalen Asylum was awakened by the wailings of a distressed infant nearby. Calling others to her aid, they proceeded to a vacant lot, directed by the cries. There they found a well-dressed male child, about 7 months old, extended on the bare surface with no one near. They conveyed him to the Asylum but, not possessing convenient means for his support, sent him this morning to the Almshouse. He is a pretty boy & has evidently been well cared for before. No explanation of the mystery has as yet elapsed. The ground being damp & the night bleak, the child might have perished but for the providential & timely aid of the matron.

*June 5th.* Com. Council passed a Resolution last evening to refer the R.R. subject to the Com. of Finance, it being well ascertained that that Com. is inimical—12 voting for & 8 against. Sent in to S. Council & miscarried by a tie vote—6 & 6. Strange lack of public spirit. These selfsame Councilmen, when the subject was pending before the Legislature, passed a Resolution unanimously recommending the passage of a Bill creating this very line of Railroad. Our opponents then accused us of insincerity. What will they say now? Fie on such doings. I am unwilling to bear this reproach, personally having signed a paper written & headed by myself, agreeing, when the Books of subscription shall be opened, to take 400 shares of the stock, amounting to $20,000. How many will follow this example remains to be seen.

Another anonymous application for money by note thro' the P.O. signed "English Engineer." The writer says he thinks it not necessary to give his name. That might indeed indulge a secret. Besides there being resident a British Consul whose duty it is to protect his countrymen, the St. George's Society is expressly formed to assist & advise Englishmen in distress.

*June 6th.* The Managers of the Mer. Library Co. met in the evening. That silly man, David Paul Brown, has suffered the furniture of his office to be seized the third time for rent. The Sheriff has also made a seizure for some other claim. Brown has been warned out but "don't choose to go." Did D.P.B. possess a little more common sense, he might rank among the most talented & respected of our citizens.

*June 10th.* Attended a meeting of a few citizens at the Exchange to promote the R.R. After free discussion, resolved to call on persons in the several wards to procure signatures to a remonstrance to Councils, urging on them a subscription. The apathy of some people on a matter so deeply interesting is most surprizing. Had all our citizens been Horace Binneys, we should now have no Schuylkill water running in our streets, no gas to light us, no turnpike, canal or railroad. It tries my temper to have to do with such men & I am in constant danger of using harsh language in speaking of them & thus doing harm to the cause I would advocate.

> Patience, quiet toil, denial
> These, though hard, are good for man
> And the martyr'd spirit's trial
> Gains it more than passion can.

*June 11th.* The Senate are occupied with debating a message from the Pres. stating the terms offered by the British Ministry for settling the Oregon controversy. It is understood that he declines acting on those terms, unless they are previously sanctioned by a vote of ⅔ of the Senate, of which vote there is some doubt. We have indeed arrived at a very important crisis of our public affairs.

*June 15th.* A day of rejoicing & joy, physically & politically. The morning dressed in sack cloth & threw away its unseemly garb & put on the vestment of gilded splendour by noon, at which time the southern Telegraph brought us the glad tidings that the Treaty with G. Britain had been officially consummated & simultaneously the eastern Telegraph announced the arrival of the *Great Western* in 15 days from Liverpool. Three events of great interest.

*June 22d.* Attended in my place as Chairman of the Commissioners for receiving subscriptions to the Penna. Railroad.

The Books were opened at the Merchants Exchange, 9 A.M. & closed 3 P.M., when it appeared that 6,180 shares were subscribed—a pretty good beginning.

*June 23d.* Subscriptions to the R.R. are much smaller today. Many who would be most benefitted are willing others should make it for them. They talk big & if that would make the road, they would make it.

*June 26th.* Received a letter thro' the P.O. signed Anna Willson —probably a feigned name—in which the writer tells me she has often wished an opportunity to speak a few words with me. She adds, "I have now made bold to write, trusting you will receive it as coming from a person who is worthy of your notice. I have been situated in a pretty little business but, having been unfortunate, I am now depending on my needle, which is a very laborious task. I would be glad if you would meet me for a few minutes tomorrow evening or the following one, in Thirteenth St. between Spruce & Locust Sts., west side, at 8 o'clock or a little after. Please excuse me for appointing this place but I would rather not give my place of residence until I know how these few lines will meet with your attention."

If the writer waits at Thirteenth St. between Spruce & Locust until I meet her there, she will be apt to wait long. She addresses me "Mr. Thos. P. Cope, Esq." & if a woman, must contrive better.

*June 27th.* The subscriptions drag on, there are now about 12,000 shares taken. In the evening met the Board of Mer. Library Co. Nothing particular before us. The Institution continues to prosper. Rode out in the afternoon to Alfred's new purchase near Logan's Mill, Willow Grove Turnpike. Workmen are busy repairing. He is absent.

Have some suspicion that the person who addressed me under the signature Anna Willson may be a male. The determined place of assignation on Thirteenth is occupied by unfinished houses running from Spruce St. open in the rear & would afford a ready shelter for a villain who might suddenly rush up on an unguarded person, level him by a blow, then rob his victim & in the twilight, retire unobserved. The handwriting does not seem that of a female, but male or female, the scheme—whatever the design—has proved abortive.

*June 29th.* The subscriptions proceed with a slow but steady pace. They have now reached beyond 14,000 & the measure is growing fast into public favour.

The introduction of the Schuylkill water was much more violently opposed, so was the formation of the Lancaster Turnpike, the German-town Turnpike—in which the late Dr. George Logan rendered himself very conspicuous—& the Ches. & Del. Canal. Squeamers & croakers & selfish men abound at all times & are always ready to show themselves in opposition to enterprize & novelty, however useful or praiseworthy.

*June 30th.* Subscriptions flat. Rain set in at 3 P.M. & continues falling briskly at 9½ P.M. At 9 a brilliant light in a SW direction from my dwelling, 272 Spruce St. A great fire somewhere lighting my premises as if close at hand & suddenly ending in total darkness. What can it be? None I ask can tell, perhaps the railroad bridge at Grey's Ferry. State House bell is sounding the alarm & engines & masses of people are running furiously towards the emanation. Instanter all come to a dead halt & then move back. Morning will elicit the cause.

*July 1st.* The fire proved to be in a stable, the work of an incendiary. The subscriptions progressed better today. The Com. of Councils who applied to John Sergeant, Judge Pettit & T.J. Wharton, Esqrs., for their opinion as to the power of the Corporation to subscribe, have rec'd a full answer in the affirmative. H. Binney, Jr., a member of C. Council, has denied that right & his father is looked to as his back—but the latter would not openly hazard his reputation on that side. It would be in direct contradiction to his clearly expressed argument in the Girard Will case & the opinion of the Supreme Court of the U.S. in rendering judgement on that case.

*July 3d.* Councils met last evening. The Joint Com. submitted the following Resolution, appended to a luminous report accompanied by documents, among the latter the opinion of the 3 members of the Bar decidedly in favour of the power of Councils to subscribe—1000 copies of Report & Documents to be ordered to be printed. John Price Wetherill & Hor. Binney, Jr. submitted a minority report.

> Resolved that the Mayor be & is hereby authorized & directed to subscribe in the name of the Mayor, Aldermen & Citizens of Philada. for 10,000 shares in the Capital Stock of the Penna. R. Road Co., whenever 50,000 shares shall have been subscribed in conformity with the provisions of the Charter of said R.R. Co. & that the said Mayor be authorized & directed to subscribe an additional 10,000 shares when 100 miles of said Railroad shall have been finished & in use & that the said Mayor be authorized & directed to make a further & final subscription of 10,000 shares when 200 miles of said Road be finished & in use.

This Resolution does not come up to the requirements of the petitioners. It is evidently the contrivance of some crafty limb of the Law, but the publication of the Report & Documents can scarcely fail to produce a favourable effect & if the present Councils will not come up to the mark, other men must be chosen who will. The number of petitioners in favour of Councils' subscribing is 5,797 & the remonstrants 133—a pretty fair symptom of public feeling on this interesting subject. Our Councilmen are inclined to practice on the Gibbons principle of disregarding the instructions of their Constituents. We ask bread & they give us a stone, Fish & they give us a Scorpion.

*July 4th.* It rained again last night & this morning is ushered in by the firing of guns, the rattling of crackers, the jingle of bells & the noise & pelting of a heavy shower with some symptoms of a clear up.

*July 7th.* The subscriptions move slowly. My confinement to this & some other pressing duties begins to be felt & I must be permitted to retreat & indulge awhile in the country.

*July 8th.* Afternoon left town with my E. to spend some time at

Calcon Hook. I previously put forward an arrangement to the effect that 25 persons should voluntarily engage each to procure signers to 1000 shares of stock in the Railroad. A few have entered on the service & hopes are entertained for recruits for the balance. The Commissioners then adjourned for a week.

A writer under the signature of a "Voter" who has indulged heretofore in strains of unmerited asperity against us & has been refuted, again & again, is out today on new ground & maugre the opinion of John Sergeant &c. denies the right of the Corporation to subscribe & cautions the public against receiving City Bonds, if issued for this stock, as they will be illegal & consequently be null & void.

It will be easy to refute his assumptions, but it seems like wasted time to encounter such an antagonist. "He who washes an ass's head," sayeth the Spanish saw, "will lose his soap."

*July 11th.* I have always abhorred idleness, but it is difficult to find employment in the time when the fervidness of a sun reaching to 98 deg. is glaring on us. Action outdoors is oppressive even to the husbandman & labourer & has few charms for the mere saunterer. To read becomes laborious if, with the admission of light, painful & infested with flies; & to search or ponder over a volume with closed shutters, uncomfortable & tiresome. To sleep away time is listless & unprofitable. What then? Why, meditate on the goodness of God & resolve under his guidance to be serviceable to men, thankful for the blessings of seed time & harvest, for health & prosperity & the thousands of other unmerited favours with which ourselves, our families & our country abound.

*July 12th.* Attended Upper Darby Meeting, it being First Day & an exercising time we had, the starved musketos permitting us no rest. With my handkerchief constantly in motion I could not protect even my face from their poisonous assaults, but one Friend remarked that, annoying as they were, they could not deprive some present of a nap.

*July 13th.* A trip to the City. Met the Directors of N.A. Ins. Co. They consented, after some skirmishing, to take 100 shares in the Railroad. This was the principal object of my visit.

*July 17th.* Another visit to the City. The subscription to the Railroad was lost in the Com. Council by a tie vote, but the coming general election will correct the evil.

*July 21st.* Much excitement prevails both in & out of Congress on the

subject of the Tariff. Pres. Polk obtained the vote of Penna. in consequence of a pledge to sustain that policy & that vote gave him the
Presidency. He is now using all his efforts to destroy American protection as provided for by the Act of 1842. Gen. Cameron, Senator from
Penna., was asked on the floor of the House whether it was not from the
assertion, often & constantly reiterated, that Polk would sustain the
Tariff that he succeeded in obtaining the vote of the State. The Gen.
—who, by the way, is of the Polk party—answered unhesitatingly that
the flag borne at the election contained the words "Polk, Shunk, Dallas
& the Tariff" & that, without the last, the three first could not have
obtained the State.

*July 24th.* Another visit of business to the City. The Tariff is still
before the Senate & great anxiety is expressed for the result. A compromise between the contending parties is on the tapis.

*July 25th.* Train up a child in the way he should go (or in the way he
should not go) & when he is old he will not depart from it.

One of the greatest nuisances, in the ordinary course of domestic
affairs, is the annoyances we suffer when confined under the same roof
with spoiled children & selfish parents. Their weakness & partiality for
their offspring occasion them to expect all others to yield their own
convenience to these little pests & their silly papas & mamas. One of
the first lessons to be taught a child is that of implicit obedience to the
commands of his parents who should take care that these commands be
reasonable & of which they are to be the sole undisputed judges. Then,
as the intellectual powers of the boy develop themselves, he will from
duty & habit be prepared to act well his part before he enters on the stage
of manhood & be qualified to discharge his more important duties to
God & his country when no longer under parental surveillance.

A rude, undisciplined child makes no friends. Others feel under no
obligation to indulge his impertinence. He rewards the care of his silly
parents with ingratitude, perhaps with cruelty. He becomes the slave of
evil passions & ends in being the tenant of an Almshouse or Prison or
perhaps terminates his miserable existence on the gallows.

We need not marvel that our country people who take citizens as
summer boarders object so much to children. I dearly love little children, their prattle & antics & even their boisterous mirth & could spend
days & years in their innocent, artless, unsophisticated society. Much
do I love to chat & gambol with them, to watch the budding idea, the
unfledged thought & half expressed, blushing sentiment; but at no time

a rude, impudent, wilfull, immodest churl, a young, untamed savage, a fretful, peevish, dallying little pest.

*July 29th.* This morning the *Susquehanna* from Liverpool is passing up in full view, deeply laden. When the Line was first established we had a ✚, strongly marked in black, painted on the foresail of each Ship. It was not, as has been supposed, to designate the Catholicism of the owner but a sign, easily seen at a distance, to denote the vessel distinctly from all others—few emblems in any shape displaying more visibly. The private signal at the head of the mainmast bears likewise a black cross on a red ground. These emblems are separate from the Holyhead signals which disclose each Ship of the Line apart from the rest of her consorts.

*July 31st.* I continue to receive left handed compliments, alias abuse, from some of the country papers, opponents of the Railroad. To elucidate small things for great, this was the invariable policy of the French pending the revolution & afterwards under Bonaparte. Whenever they perpetrated or meditated aggression on a neighbouring power, they boldly accused the innocent party with actual or designed wrong. To become conspicuous is to invite envy, malice, injustice from little minds & enemies, open or secret. If great men & even Nations suffer this injustice, why should I complain? Well, I have not, but treat this injustice with silent contempt—without however in any wise claiming for myself exemption from error. He who has a clear conscience may sleep quietly & soundly.

Midges and musketoes sufficiently active & ticks abound in the wood & are lively enough. To make amends, Annesley Newlin & Elizabeth, his wife, are very kind & attentive to our accommodation. They are the present tenants of the farm. We eat at their table & have as companions, Edward Yarnall & his flock.

*August 1st.* The Tariff question has been finally disposed of by the final casting vote of Geo. M. Dallas, V.P., who has cast that vote contrary to the expressed will of Penna., his native state & against his own declared opinion before the election that placed Polk & himself in power.

*August 2d.* The deluded Mormons, after having been driven by force from Missouri, have at length been compelled to abandon their new abode in Illinois & their temple in Nauvoo by their no less superstitious neighbours of the latter State. About 12,000 of them are now slowly wending their way over the vast deserts to California, 3000 to 4000

more, being the balance of their community, are scattered in various parts. The same injustice which has driven them from their homes will probably rob them of the property left behind them—among which is their costly temple on which, it is said, they have expended half a million of Dollars.

They are charged with many crimes & gross superstitions, but are their persecutors much better? Have many of them a better claim to consideration in these respects in the eye of reason, philosophy & religion? Witness the reverence paid by the Catholics to images & relics, to feigned Sepulchral garments & old musty bones of pretended Saints. Do not some of their wise accusers believe in witch craft & nail horse shoes on their stable doors to protect their cattle from Sorcerers & witches?

*August 7th.* My son-in-law E.Y. informs me that a certain Daniel Griscom of Chester Co. has been spreading a report that I have resigned my right of membership in the Society of Friends. Another of those idle inventions but too common among us. Some of our members gad about the country busying themselves in traducing others as if it were a part of their religious duty & that, too, under the plea of preaching the Gospel.

*August 8th.* The last information from Washington left the Senate in secret session on a supposed proposition from Mexico to suspend hostilities & to offer terms of peace. Would that it prove true & that war may terminate. It would make some amends for the mischiefs which Congress & the present Executive have entailed on the country by recent Acts.

Some of the papers attack Dallas in no measured terms for his treachery to his native State & he has been repeatedly burned in effigy by his political friends. Efforts will therefore be made by the party officers and dependents to sustain him. He is a handsome man with very white hair, a pleasant companion, a conspicuous member of our bar —but sadly deficient in sound morals, very extravagant in his living & very poor. At one time he was said to owe his Baker $1500. Great as his treachery has been & unscrupulous his morality, I hope no Whig will disgrace himself & party by joining in these burning operations or in personal insults to this man of accommodating principles. He is Vice President of the United States & his office demands respect, whatever may be thought of the man.

*August 9th.* A hot, dusty ride to Meeting which was silent & thinly attended. A thunder gust visited us after noon & rain fell copiously. "Och! Och!" exclaimed a domestic of foreign birth as she ran into the parlour, agitated, with a pan of milk in her hand. "Och! Och! What sort of a baste is this? Is it a snake or what is it?" On looking into the vessel held at arm's length by the terrified girl, a small tree frog was perceived floating about, as if enjoying himself in the delicious fluid. He was, no doubt, a roving ambitious member of his fraternity on a voyage of experiment & discovery &—having fallen into this luscious sea—had little desire hastily to resume his abode on a dry stick, where he never enjoyed the luxury of such a feast. Cows, as far as he knew, had not been in the habit of grazing on the territory allotted to his race. We, however, sent him packing to his native residence, there to proclaim aloud the fruits of this adventure to his credulous associates of more staid propensities, none of whom—brought up in ignorance of the world as they have been—may have heard of the like before.

*August 14th.* Returned to Calcon Hook from a short visit with my E. to our home. Sons H. & A. dined with us in the City. Weather very warm. The thermometer in our closed up apartment was 77, while in the yard it was fairly 98.

A chimney bird, in frolicsome mood, has darted on the sharp point of our lightning rod, where he remains transfixed as a monument of heedless daring or carelessness equal to many committed by unfeathered bipeds.

*August 15th.* I cannot readily forgive the injury inflicted on our country by the anti-slavery mania. The Association would not vote for H. Clay because he holds slaves but cast their votes for one of their own number, thus giving a majority for Polk, another slave holder & increasing the spread of that evil over a vast country by the annexation of Texas, which has already added two members to our Senate. We are therefore subjected to slave influence perhaps for all time. They cannot plead ignorance—they were forewarned & acted with their eyes open. Some of them, now that the mischief is accomplished, regret their folly & say they would not do so again, but what does that signify? They seem not aware that, in their frenzy, they were the dupes of a political faction.

In these remarks I hope I may not have violated charity, yet I cannot help being provoked at the extent of evil which these frantic men have brought upon us. I have spent time & money in the cause of suffering Africa & am willing to do so again. I am & have been, for half a century, a member of the Penna. Abolition Society, but must condemn that conduct which defeats its own professed object.

*August 20th.* The remains of the dashing chimney bird adhere to the lightning rod. Whether birds, like men, will pass on regardless, in their way, without improving by the mistakes of others is to be seen. The rest chirp & frolic as usual now.

*August 26th.* This day completes the 78th year of my pilgrimage on earth. How many more are allotted to my unprofitable existence in this state of being is not for me to know. To regret past errors is vain, however many I may have committed. To live better for the future is my most ardent desire. May God bless my efforts, be my remaining days many or few—many they cannot be. May I endeavour to be prepared for my final departure, whenever He, who gave it, shall be pleased to cut short the thread of my existence. Amen.

Calculations on the duration of life are thus made. Deduct the age from 86 & add half the amount to the age. It is not applied to persons under 27. By this table my course will terminate in 4 years, that is, when I shall have attained 82.

*August 31st.* Took tea today with our neighbours Ephraim Inskeep & wife, a couple of querities. She condemns all modern improvements on the dwellings of our forefathers. The house in which her daddy dwelt should never be altered, it is disrespectful to his memory. Her kinsman, Jno. Jackson, whose father, Holladay, was a farmer & lived in a small house inherited by said John. He keeps a boarding school for girls & has made accommodations—by additions & alterations in the old house—for 40 to 50 pupils. It is all wrong. She does not object to his keeping school, but he had no business to make any change in the dwelling. Her husband has his notions. He put up a fence & commenced, as of right he should, in the old of the moon, but other duties called him off when the fence was half done & he could not go at it again until a new moon happened. He then finished the other half. The ground was the same on the whole line, the posts & rails the same, no difference & the same care bestowed on all. The posts planted in the old of the moon remained firm in their places to the last; every one of the rest sank down in the earth & soon required resetting.

One of E.'s neighbors cut himself badly. Doctors were sent for & came but all their art would not stop the blood, so a message was dispatched for a *blood stopper* who lived seven miles off. "I can stop the blood," said the blood stopper, "but it will make me very sick." The messenger required the blood to be stopped—& the blood stopper fell sick & said, "It is done." The messenger, having a watch, noted the exact time & returned. The blood had ceased to flow at the precise moment the blood stopper became sick. These be marvellous things, making it very clear that we can do better without Doctors than without the moon—& that we can better spare blood suckers than blood stoppers.

*September 1st.* We attended Darby Monthly Meeting. Small as usual. Ester Levis present, who read among her sisters the accustomed lecture, to encourage the *burden bearers* of whom she is, of course, one—& a heavy burden some such must needs bear if they carry on their shoulders but a portion of the immense mischief they have wrought by their constant efforts to break up the Society. The consequential airs these burden bearers assume might excite our ridicule, were it not for the lamentable consequences which follow in the train of their doings. Some—& indeed most of the burden bearers—have such a generous portion of suffering brought on themselves that it has put not a little fat in their heavy sides. One of them, our great City burden bearer, has grown as fat as a pig & struts the streets as though she were sole mistress of our destinies & so, I believe, she would be if she could. Luckily we have neither Pope, nor Queen Mary to consume us with fire.

*September 2d.* Left C.H. for the season & reached home by 10½ A.M. Pleasant but warm. Went forthwith to see daughter Elenor, who with her husband were of the number overturned on the Long Island Railway, by running against a cow. She is badly bruised—not otherwise seriously injured. Dr. Mütter is in attendance on her & assures me that she is doing well. There should be some Legislative enactments as to these accidents.

*September 18th.* Santa Anna has reached the City of Mexico & accuses Paredes of designing to establish Monarchy & whom he has cast into prison.

*September 22d.* Among the interesting occurrences of the day, not the least extraordinary is the war now actively waging between the Mormons at Nauvoo & their no less deluded neighbours. Cannon are used on both sides. Several battles have been fought. Lives have been lost yet the public authorities do not, to their disgrace, interfere. The Gov. of Illinois says, "Let them fight it out." Nauvoo is besieged & has

several times repelled the invaders but must ultimately surrender to their white savage enemies.

*September 25th.* Three P.M. I met the Overseers of Friends Public Schools. A great number of applicants, all of whom selected, eleven, for admission. They prefer our schools to the less select common schools of the public, not only on account of the indiscriminate immoral mixtures in the latter & consequent danger of corruption, but also perhaps from a spice of vanity, no obvious distinctions of classes as to poor & rich being visible with us, whereas children of common schools are apt to be treated in the light of paupers in the conception of others.

*October 4th.* On the last voyage of the *Wyoming* from Liverpool, an Irishman who had taken & paid for his passage was observed to bring with his baggage a rough looking box that attracted the notice of the Captn. as something unusual. He therefore caused it to be opened & discovered it to contain a woman still alive but so far gone as to be incapable of motion or speech—the box containing no opening to admit air but closely secured by nails. The body was removed on shore —together with the man, who claimed the inmate as his wife—& placed in custody of the proper authorities. The ship departing forth-with, the Capn. had no opportunity of knowing if the body was restored. Whether this curious affair is to be treated as a piece of Irish ingenuity to escape the payment of a passage, or whether the fellow designed at some favourable moment, when at sea, to cast the box & contents overboard could not be ascertained. When Capn. Mierken put the man ashore he returned the passage money to him. Whatever the intention of the parties to this contrivance, all will agree that the fair one could be little better than an idiot to suffer herself to be the subject of such a prank.

*October 7th.* My dear wife passed a comfortless night, her racking cough exhausting her delicate frame. The air this morning is balmy, but she is too weak to ride out. My tenderest sympathies are excited for her, but I confess with little hope of her permanent restoration to health.

*October 10th.* The Ticket favourable to the R.R. has made its appear-ance in the morning's papers. The address recommending it to public attention contains the signatures of more than 1000 citizens.

*October 12th.* Have cast my vote for the Railroad Council Ticket— voting the regular nominations of the Whigs in all other cases. The election is going on very quietly, amid a storm of easterly wind & rain. How Friends will act on this occasion is unknown to me, but I think with Wm. Penn that no man should neglect the peaceable exercise of this Civil duty. If we will not take this trouble, we have no right to complain of bad Laws.

*October 15th.* The result of the City election is published this morning—the R. Road Ticket has not been successful. The politicians of the successful party, proclaiming that theirs was a Railroad ticket, produced its effect. Their sincerity is questionable. We shall soon see it put to the test.

*October 25th.* For several days past, my dear wife has been confined to her bed in a state of great suffering from pain & want of rest. Last night she was refreshed by some hours of natural sleep & this morning, to my no small comfort, her physician, Doc. Shallcross, pronounces her better. I feel grateful to our Heavenly Father for this mercy. She attained her 66th year on the 22d.

*October 26th.* Our daughter-in-law Susan Cope, who with her daughters Clementine & Caroline are on a visit to us, have received letters from their home in Susquehanna Co. which state that they then had snow up to four inches in depth on the ground. These letters are dated on the 18th but don't express when the snow fell. The weather here still continues dry & clear with some symptoms of a change.

The bells of St. Peter's are ringing a merry peal for the arrival of the Ship *Thos. P. Cope* from Liverpool. It is the invariable practice there to compliment that Ship. She brought their bells from England.

*October 28th.* I have seldom spoken in Orange St. Meeting of business, feeling my opinions to be but slightly esteemed by certain members of that body, whose course in many respects I cannot approve. I sometimes have qualms as to whether I am right in withholding, yet I have ever felt reluctant to make myself conspicuous & especially where I am conscious of not being welcome. If I have thus erred, I pray to be forgiven of my Heavenly Father.

*October 29th.* A new planet has been discovered in our system by Le Verrier, a French astronomer & bearing his name. It is far beyond Uranus & makes its circuit once in two hundred years.

*November 1st.* Our Grandson Francis R. Cope, who dined with me

today, informs me of his engagement to marry Anna, daughter of Jeremiah Brown. My dear E. is still confined to her chamber.

*November 5th.* At length the sun shines out & the air is more bracing. During the five days of rain just past, the warmth was oppressive. Tonight Councils hold their stated meeting—big with the fate of the Railroad.

At 10 P.M. my son-in-law, J.R. Tyson, Esq. came with the gratifying intelligence that C. Council, had passed the Railroad Ordinance. S. Council, of which he is a member, had not time to act on it. They will no doubt respond favourably.

*November 6th.* In the evening attended the Philosophical Society. Some interesting discussions, the principal of which was on the newly discovered planet of Le Verrier, in which Professors Patterson, Henry of Princeton College, Frazer of the High School & Doc. Bache were the speakers. It was admitted by all that, long before, other astronomers were convinced from certain analogies & mathematical demonstrations that such a planet did exist. Did we of N. America, with our lucid atmosphere, so superior to that of England or Ireland, possess Lord Rosse's mammoth Telescope, might we not trace the path of another planet in the Heavens millions & millions of miles beyond the limits of *Le Verrier*?

I wish astronomers would bestow on this stranger a name more becoming its dignity.

*November 13th.* After a hard fought battle, the Bill authorizing the subscription to the Penna. Railroad was carried in Select Council last night by a vote of 8 to 4, all being in their places—Meredith, President Wetherill, Trucks & Gilpin voting in the negative. Fie on them & especially on Meredith. From the other three, little better could be expected.

*November 14th.* The old Indian saying is that there will be no winter till the ponds are filled. It is likely we shall not fail of winter this season for the lack of water—the rain still descending copiously.

Another name is proposed for Le Verrier's planet, which may take if no better is found. It is Atlas. Instead of miles, a Paris Journal places this planet to be distant from the sun twelve million five hundred thousand Leagues—rather too far off to be soon visited by any of our aspiring Baloon navigators.

*November 27th.* Met the Committees of the Pennsyla. Railroad. Subscriptions are small. Will have to beat up the wards by calls. The address to the public composed by J. R. Tyson & signed by me as Chairman of the Coms. published on the 25th is well received.

*December 10th.* The mail brings me a Pittsbg. paper containing embittered reflections & threats on our efforts to get subscribers to the Railroad. Why this vulgar uncalled for vituperation?

*December 16th.* The Comrs. of Spring Garden have agreed to subscribe 2000 shares to the Penna. Railroad. Some of the other Districts have the subject under consideration. Jno. M. Read, Atty. General of the State & a violent opponent of the Road, has resigned & Gov. Shunk has appointed a successor.

I copy the following from a document in possession of Caleb S. Cope, grandson of my late Uncle Nathan Cope.

"Oliver Cope came from England in the year 1681 & settled at Naaman's Creek, New Castle County. (He was a farmer.)

"John Cope, son of Oliver, was born at Naaman's Creek in 1691. Settled in Bradford Township, Chester County, Pennsyla. & died in 1773." John had Issue:

| | | | | | |
|---|---|---|---|---|---|
| Hannah Cope | born 1724 | deceased 10 mo. | 10, | 1817 |
| Samuel | born 1726 | deceased 9 mo. | 20, | 1817 |
| Mary | born 1728 | deceased | | 1812 |
| John | born 1730 | deceased | | 1812 |
| Nathan | born 1733 | deceased 12 mo. | 3, | 1820 |
| Caleb ⎫ twins | born 1736 | deceased 5 mo. | 30, | 1824 |
| Joshua ⎭ | born 1736 | deceased | | 1813 |
| Joseph | born 1739 | deceased 12 mo. | 11, | 1820 |

*December 18th.* The sun shines calmly today & the snow yields to his rays. The gale of yesterday was severe on the Delaware, preventing steamers from running. No material damage has as yet been reported. A metal roof was riven from a stone house on Front St. The land mails pro & con interrupted. Influenza among children prevalent. Volunteers for the Army moving from most of the States to join the U.S. forces in Mexico. The Gov. of Virginia, in his annual message to the Legislature, recommends them to banish from the State all the free people of colour, numbering about 50,000. Humane man—in many of their veins flow the blood of their oppressors, even perhaps of the precious Gov. himself. That such a proposition should be entertained by any man in the 19th

Century or by any professing Christian, at any time, is marvellous indeed. What a commentary is this on our boasted devotion to liberty & the rights of man.

Among the volunteers lately departed from Philada. are two companies of youths, long a pest to the neighbourhood, known by their own assumed titles of "Bouncers" & "Killers." They went about at night, armed with knives, dirks &c., attacking & maiming unoffending citizens & especially of the coloured race, some of whom rec'd ghastly wounds & crowd our Hospital, even now. The principal abode of these young ruffians has been Moyamensing & Southwark. Such has been the imbecility of the Police in the two Districts that no efficient measures were taken by either to arrest the offenders. We are happily rid of the gang, who have gone where they can find employment suited to their habits & tastes. On their way to Pittsburg, a Letter writer says they committed robberies & other violences on the inhabitants & after reaching that City they caused a disturbance there in which several persons were badly wounded.

*December 21st.* Am importuned to preside at a public meeting to further the views of Asa Whitney in his splendid scheme of a Railroad to the Pacific. Have excused myself.

While abroad I met the Comrs. of the Railroad. The subscriptions are progressing slowly, but I trust surely. 'Tis the first of my going out for 10 days, having been prevented by the effects of a cold. Selfish interests are still at work adversely & we have as yet no subscriptions from the interior.

*December 22d.* A little ice is floating on the Delaware but not sufficient to obstruct the navigation. Today is calm & balmy.

The Foreign Journals state the quantity of coal produced annually by the English mines is at 23,500,000 tons; Belgium 4,500,000; France 3,783,000; & all Germany 3,000,000 tons.

After penning the above I visited the Philada. Exchange to attend the Railroad Commissioners. Being about to retire, Martin, keeper of the House, called me back to communicate the painful intelligence that the Ship *Thos. P. Cope*, three days out from this port for Liverpool, was struck with lightning & both ship & cargo totally consumed by fire. The Capt., crew & passengers all saved. The lightning struck the mainmast & descended into the body of the ship, setting the rigging on fire in its course. The mast was cut away by the crew & thrown overboard, but fire had been communicated to the cargo, part of which consisted of tallow

& hemp. The suffocating smoke soon drove passengers & crew on deck, 82 in all, where they remained on scanty allowance for 6 days & seven nights, the flames within gaining strength all the while & baffling all efforts to extinguish them—the sea being in a ferment at the same time. Some of the crew attempted their escape in one of the boats, but it was no sooner overboard than it was swamped.

They then lashed the long boat to the stern of the Ship, to be used in the last extremity. The wind & waves, however, soon carried it away. A raft was next prepared when, providentially, the British ship *Vigilant* hove in sight & took off a number of the sufferers—being prevented by the violence of the storm from relieving the residue that night but keeping as near to the distressed Ship as practicable. The whole number were removed in the course of the succeeding morning, with the exception of a child belonging to a steerage passenger who, in the hurry of escape to the upper deck, had been left behind & doubtless soon after suffocated. As the last were taken from the Ship, the main hatch was removed, whence the flames issued to a great height. In a short time afterwards an explosion was heard & the goodly Ship *Thos. P. Cope* was seen no more.

The *Emigrant* was spoken by the Packet Ship *Washington Irving*, Commander Caldwell, & the passengers & crew of the lost Ship taken on board & conveyed to Boston. Capt. Henry Mierken of the *T. P. C.* has written to his owners from thence. Much as the destruction of this valuable Ship is to be regretted & serious as is the loss to her owners, it is no small satisfaction that but a single life & that of an infant, fell a victim to the raging elements. It is of God's mercy, for which may all concerned have grateful, thankful hearts.

In the afternoon I had another visit from Asa Whitney, the projector of the great project of a Railroad to the Pacific, inviting me to preside at the meeting tomorrow evening in furtherance of that splendid scheme. I could with propriety plead the present state of my health in excuse, but I had other reasons. I felt the scheme too magnificent for the grasp of my intellect & little inclined to assume the responsibility to sponsor so great an undertaking.

Besides, as I am now engaged with the Central Railroad, to which Road there is much unmanly opposition, I should at once be attacked as the wild patron of every immatured contrivance & thus strengthen the hands of prejudice, ignorance & selfishness against more humble efforts.

*December 23d.* Received a visit from R. Rush, at one time Secy. of

State & at another our Minister at the Court of St. James. He came to offer condolence on the loss of the Ship, after which we conversed on various other matters. He is a courteous, well informed gentleman, son of our distinguished fellow citizen, Benj. Rush, M.D., who ranked high in his profession & with whom as one of the Physicians of the Penna. Hospital, while I was a manager, I formerly had pleasant intercourse & frequent arguments.

The Bells of St. Peter's, which so long & joyfully welcomed the arrivals of the *Thos P. Cope* by their merry peal, are this day employed in the mournful office of tolling a requiem for her loss. It comes dolefully & painfully on the becalmed atmosphere as weeping for the dead. It is stated in the newspapers as a singular coincidence that the abandonment of a Brig bearing the same name & owned in New Brunswick took place at sea simultaneously with the destruction of the Ship. I know not the truth of the story nor by whom the Brig was named.

These vessels, the last that will bear my name in all probability, will soon be heard of no more but pass as the mere echo of the day. The original cannot long survive.

Having written as above, my eye caught a paragraph in one of our papers as follows, "A letter was received in Portland on Saturday from Halifax announcing the arrival there of the crew of the Brig *Thos. P. Cope Merryman* of Brunswick, from Portland for Baltimore. The Brig was knocked down by a squall, lost rudder, masts, &c. The crew remained on the wreck six days when they were taken off by a vessel bound for Halifax."

Six days! the precise number the crew of the Ship *T. P. C.* remained on her deck after being struck when they were taken off by the Ship *Emigrant*. How wonderful the concurrence of this event & of the preservation of life in both instances. When the final wreck of my mortal frame shall take effect, may my spiritual existence be alike preserved to praise & magnify the God of my salvation. Amen & Amen.

*December 25th.* The manner in which I throughout life have been favoured, even in my pecuniary concerns, demands my gratitude to Heaven. I commenced business with my Uncle Thomas Mendenhall literally without one cent of Capital. Soon after we associated, there sprung up a wild scheme of speculation in scrip of the first Bank of the U.S. Thomas was a speculative man & urged me from day to day to embark in the game, for which I had no relish or tact—he continually pointing out the fortunes which others were accumulating. Still I resisted, not being willing to hazard my own character & the property of others who had trusted us in such a lottery.

At length he privately entered the lists, when I providentially discovered that he used the name of the firm in carrying on his speculations, on which I strongly remonstrated, saying that if he persisted he would drive me to publish a dissolution of the firm. Finding I could not prevail, I called on John Field & John Drinker—the latter afterwards becoming my father-in-law—& they, as Overseers of the Meeting of which Uncle & myself were members, effected an arrangement by which I was left in possession of the business of the House.

The responsibility was great in my unprotected situation. I felt it severely, fearful I might not succeed. My health was delicate & as I spent time by daylight & candlelight in poring over our Books & Papers my eyesight gave way & from that time forward I have been compelled to the use of spectacles, but I was favoured to survive my troubles & to carry on business with reputation & success.

In a few years afterwards I became acquainted with Mary, daughter of this same John Drinker, a female endowed with many attractive qualities of body & mind & who became the happy mother of my children.

John Field was, at the period referred to, a highly respected citizen, an influential member of the Society of Friends, largely engaged in Mercantile pursuits, a portly, pleasant, goodlooking man, esteemed very wealthy. An Overseer of the Monthly Meeting of Friends at Philada. & clerk of that Meeting.

After I had become acquainted with him in the manner mentioned, he often called to see & chat with me. These calls were long, repeated & flattering to me, as a person of little means & little known. He at length spoke of his business, of its growing extent & the need he had of some young man to relieve him of some portion of the burden, inquiring if I could recommend some such person to him—to which I pled my want of knowledge of our citizens, &c. At last he became more pointed & aimed at myself. It was a powerful temptation to my ambition & most young men situated like me would probably have found the overture irresistible. But I suffered to pass it off. I reflected that John Field was much my Senior in age & experience, that he controlled & had long managed his concerns alone, that I would be a cypher in his hands & subject to his will—equally responsible for mishaps, but not equally influential in guarding against them. I concluded, therefore, to remain in my humble

situation rather than embark on a voyage of discovery in seas of which I was inexperienced & with a Captain over whom I feared I could have no command, whatever storms & breakers might betide me.

It proved to be a wise conclusion, a Providential escape from shipwreck. John Field—then esteemed rich & prosperous in business—failed not many years afterwards, losing his high character as a merchant & citizen.

Not very distant from this period, George Pennock—one of my personal friends with whom I had transacted business, confidential & profitable, & who was withal a respectable citizen & member of our religious Society—came to me one day saying, "I have just chartered the Ship *Amiable* of 3000 bbls. at 15/Stg. per barrel to be loaded with flour on our joint account. Have purchased the cargo at $14½ a bbl. & am on my way to engage the remainder." I replied that I was sorry he had been so hasty, as I would not be concerned in the shipment. He then put a letter into my hands from Foxes of Falmouth, quoting sales of flour at Havre at 26 Crowns the bbl.—on which I remarked that the letter was a circular & might be in the hands of hundreds & he could not tell the extent to which shipments might be made. France was in a wild revolutionary state & that if flour should maintain the price quoted, the famished mob in Havre might seize & feed on it, the robbed having no remedy when law & order were disregarded.

George went his way, leaving me to my reflections. He soon returned saying he had purchased the balance from $14¾ to $15 per bbl. On my still declining he again left me but, quickly coming back, told me Gideon Hill Wells had agreed to be ⅓ interested & now another ⅓ was for me, but time did not change my views & he again went & returned, saying George Bickham had assumed a third & as he wished me to make some money by the shipment, I might take ½ of the ⅓ allotted him. Thanking him for his kind intentions, I replied in sailor phrase that I would not own a timber head in the concern, so adverse was I to the shipment.

The *Amiable* was speedily loaded & sailed. The result of the voyage was that the flour sold for less than the freight & the parties were drawn upon for the loss. It proved to them a most unfortunate adventure indeed. Bickham was of the House of Bickham & Reese, importers of dry goods; the loss afflicted him to the injury of his intellect & the unhappy man did not long survive.

Wells failed. My friend George Pennock bore his loss as became a Christian, but it produced a serious drawback on his means & he left but little property to his family. These diminutions of the fortunes of the adventurers were not sufficient of themselves to ruin the parties, but it injured their credit, depressed their spirits & gave an impetus to their downward course. I claim no pretension for superior sagacity in these matters. It was of the Providence of God that I was saved from the evils when my means were very circumscribed, tho' my credit was good.

*December 31st.* A short visit this morning to the House of Refuge to be present with the members of the Legislature. Could not tarry. Then employed in obtaining subscriptions to the Railroad. Not a few who ought to subscribe liberally, act, when called on, as if you were soliciting a favour. Fell in with several such patriots today. We nevertheless made some progress, even with persons lately inimical. Two hundred thousand Dollars, in addition to what we now have, will secure the City subscription & the Charter. I am satisfied that this deficiency—& even more—would have been made up before this time, but for the mistake of our colleagues in heading the Books. Man is not only an imitative, but generally a vain being. Set him an example in morals or in physics & he will be prone to follow it.

Some of our collectors began with 10, 5 & even 1 share & seldom got beyond. All see it now when too late. The Book on which I subscribed at the head, four hundred shares, contains in succession a dozen or more of the same amount. Had I commenced with 100, probably not an individual would have subscribed more. I admire a firm, but not an obstinate man. I have been rather unpleasantly associated in this concern—some of the most public spirited & active of the Commissioners having yielded their places to less popular & efficient men. Beyond Philada. we have no subscriptions, as yet, worth recording. Not a single share, west of the Susquehanna River. Several of our Banks & insurance offices have subscribed & others will doubtless follow. It is vain to attempt opposition to public opinion—& that is daily becoming more impressed with the necessity of this important thoroughfare.

# 1847

*January 1st.* This day gives birth to a new year. What may befall its youth & its old age is hidden in the womb of time. The infancy is brilliant & spring like. The sky is clear & the mercury at 7½ A.M. stands at 49. Wind from the SW.

As usual, we had such of our children as are in the City to dine & spend the day with us. Henry & Rachel Cope & their children, Mary D., Francis R., Thomas P., Jr. & Ruth Anna Cope. Alfred & his 3 children, Edward, Elizabeth W. & Mary Anna. Edward & Caroline R. Yarnall & their children, Francis C., Mary H., Caroline C., Amy E. & Lucy. Job R. & Elenor Tyson & son William's daughter Clementine, at present a member of my family, going to school. 25 sat at our table. Meteorologists say we have not had so warm a New Year's Day since 1825.

*January 7th.* John Price Wetherill, who occasioned me no little trouble pending my negotiations for Lemon Hill & whose ill temper induced him to break with me, so that we ceased to speak to each other from that time, has expressed to my son-in-law his regret for past misbehaviour & desire for a reconciliation. Now, altho' I cannot think well of the man, I have no desire to harbour ill will towards him & take no blame to myself for what took place between us, yet I do not wish to be on bad terms with him or anybody else. I can freely forgive, if I cannot forget.

Gov. Shunk, in his message to the Legislature, says, "Some apprehensions have been expressed that the construction of the great Central Railroad between Philada. & Pittsburg may be the means of diminishing the income from the improvements of the State. In this I do not concur. On the contrary, I entertain the opinion that the increased commerce which it will invite between our great eastern & western Emporiums & the regions which connect with them will not only add to the revenues of the Columbia Railways, but will greatly increase the productiveness of all our public works. Such I believe has been the experience of N. York & such, I doubt not, will in a very few years, be that of our own Commonwealth."

The Gov. takes the right view of the subject. The completion of this Road will add greatly to the travel & commerce of the State & consequently to its income. Attention to the concerns of the Road, to the cause of the Irish sufferers &c. prevented me from visiting the schools assigned to Dr. B.H. Coates & myself. The Dr. called late in the day to apologize for his own non attendance, so that I was not the only delinquent.

I dreamed last night that Maria Bispham, wife of Samuel & cousin of my wife, came to me in the street unexpectedly, took hold of my arm & walked with me for some distance. Today the thing actually occurred. It is singular, as I had neither seen nor thought of her lately. Now, altho' I am conscious of the dream, I cannot divine the interpretation & doubt if Maria can, but when I told her of it we joined in a laugh unbecoming the gravity of Necromancers or Astrologers.

When my kinsman Wm. Harvey Pim was lately with us, I gave him in charge for his father, Thos. Pim, a cane made from wood taken from the building recently demolished at Chester, in which Wm. Penn held his first Legislative Assembly. That cane William placed in custody of Capt. H. Mierken of the Ship *Thos. P. Cope*. Today the cane has been returned to me, being, as Capt. M. says, *the only article saved from the Ship*, with the exception of his chronometer & sextant. The heat & stifling gas had driven crew & passengers into the upper deck, the mate descended into the Captain's stateroom to save what he could. He seized these three articles & hastily retreated. He knew not what the stuff was, it being wrapped in paper, but finding it with the others, he supposed it valuable and therefore bore it away.

*January 13th.* Spent a little time today with the Comrs. (we are now within $75,000 of securing the Charter) & also to Irish Friend concerns.

*January 16th.* A bitter & unqualified enmity against our R.R. continues to be manifested by Gibbons & Darsie of the Senate. One might suspect that the alleged quarrel between the B. & O. Railroad Co. & the Pittsburgers was a mere sham to beguile us. Take it as we may, gross deception prevails somewhere. I sometimes fear I shall never attain that self-possession & equanimity which philosophy & religion demand. I cannot avoid marvelling at covert duplicity. A person, being asked if he had not been ill or complaining, is said to have given this reply, "I have been unwell but I never complain." Now I complain when I have not been unwell & that by the mere force of feeling. It is a weakness I allow. I have a notion that duty may sometimes demand complaint, at public grievances & wrongs.

*January 20th.* Somewhat of a new era seems at hand. The nonslaving States appear resolved to prevent the extension of the slave influence by refusing to sustain appropriations for carrying on the war of conquest, without some declaratory act of Congress to prohibit slavery in all territory which may be acquired by the present war. Southern members threaten a dissolution of the Union & are answered "go off as soon as you please." I am gratified by the spirit now manifested by the Free States & trust they will not yield to the Slave States.

*January 23d.* Among other remittances today I have one from a person, without date or place, containing a Bank note of which he says it is "of as good a Bank as any in the country" & concluding in these words, after having expressed sympathy for the suffering poor of Ireland, "I could say much more if I knew how to begin & how to finish to my satisfaction." He uses the plain stile & is certainly a very *plain* correspondent, as an Englishman would say. For he asks me to reply to his Letter.

*January 27th.* The most interesting donation I have yet rec'd reached me today from the Girls of Woodberry School, called by them "Pin money" for the suffering poor of Ireland.

*January 30th.* Letters from our Friends in England state that the contributions there for the Irish poor amount to 22,000 Pounds Sterling. Saml. & Jas. Gurney gave each 500 Pounds. These are noble examples of Christian charity.

*January 31st.* The *Spectator*, a London Journal, holds this language in relation to the present state of Ireland: "The arming of the people goes on so fast that the gun maker's trade is briskest in the Island. The people who declare they are starving have food to buy guns withal. Not only so, but they have money to spend in powder & shot, for wantonly firing about the country even in volleys." If this be true, it evinces how imprudent it is to place money in their hands.

There is no question as to the present suffering. Six or eight persons are sometimes found huddled together on the ground of their miserable huts with no rag of covering besides & dying from lack of food—the living being too much emaciated to carry the dead away to their graves. This is not a class to purchase or bear arms. The Catholics are generally—that is, the mass—an ignorant, bigoted, idle race. Their case is hopeless, for it seems to admit of no remedy save that of a total overthrow of the uncompromising arbitrary system.

*February 1st.* Small sums continue to be remitted from distant meetings of Friends, all requiring answers & of course entries. I am not very likely to rust from want of employment.

> Rest, thou must not seek for rest,
> Until thy task be done;
> Thou must not lay thy burthen down
> Till setting of the Sun.

In sober fact, I rested not last night, that is, I was not conscious of having slept. I was not ill but my mind, early after retiring to bed, became so occupied with perplexing thoughts as to drive sleep from my eyes & slumber from my eyelids. Sleep is difficult of courtship; she is best wooed by not attempting to coax her. We enjoy her when we think not of her, coquet as she is, of kin to the Irishman—the more you urge him, the more he won't.

*February 2d.* A dull, giving day. There is again a check to ice forming. Called a while on the Commissioners, then rode out with my wife in our closed carriage, as has been my practice daily for benefit of her health, weather permitting. Rec'd & answered Letters relating principally to Irish concerns. Called on the Editors of the *North American*. Left them, for publication, copy of a Letter dated 3 Jany. from Jon. Pim of Dublin to Jacob Harvey, N.Y. & sent by his name. It gives a heart rending acc't of the deaths from starvation. The *Garrick* at N.Y. from Liverpool brot out numbers of those poor people, flying for their lives —emaciated & illy provided. 12 died on the passage. One young girl, utterly destitute, strolling from the ship, was picked up in the street & attempt made to convey her to the Almshouse, but she died on the way. No doubt all who can will come upon us in swarms & add heavily to our poor rates. Let them come, poor creatures, we must not flint our hearts against them, nor see them perish. They will be expensive & troublesome, but their offspring may make good citizens & we have in our extensive West room enough for all.

*February 10th.* Rumour that Santa Anna has been shot by his own soldiers is doubtful.

*February 20th.* A Telegraphic dispatch from Harrisbg. announces the passage of the supplement to the Pa. Railroad, by a vote of 47 to 37 & that it is believed it will pass the Senate. The Bill authorizes & confirms the City subscription, the Districts & other municipal corpo-

rations & that the loans or bonds issued by them may be received by the Commissioners & the Compy. as cash. It is important the Bill should become a law.

*February 22d.* A snow storm—for one week past we have had cloudy weather. Among other sums rec'd today for the Irish sufferers is one from Dalton, Wayne County, Indiana, signed by Miles Mendenhall, Secy., & Jas. Davis, Treas., of a meeting at which committees of collection were appointed & the sum total, viz. $10, was remitted to me. They add, "If the demand is pressing, it may be we can do something more."

The first payment of the City loan has been consummated & Mayor Swift has in consequence subscribed, on the part of the City, the thirty thousand shares of stock (authorized by ordinance) to the Penna. Railroad Co. It is to me a glorious event & a proud day for the prosperity of Philada. & the State at large. The ten proposers for the loan advertized by the City convened again this morning amid a snow storm & so modified their offering as to make it more palatable to the majority of the Finance Committee. Gilpin was not expected to be conciliated & he accordingly made fight to the last. Our next step is to secure the Charter, for which we are now prepared.

*March 4th.* The British Government has agreed to pay the freight on all food shipped from America for the Irish poor. It is a noble & no less judicious resolve. It has not as yet been officially announced in this country but comes under the authority of Letters without contradiction. I am in consequence shipping, from funds gratuitously contributed, 700 barrels corn meal to Limerick, consigned to Friends in Dublin.

*March 7th.* First Day. The stereotype declamation from E.E. against wealth & worldly distinction. Have often wished some Friends had been more successful in their love of worldly possessions that they need not be so envious of others.

*March 12th.* Councils met last night & the enemies of the Railroad abated nothing of their violence. If in their power, they would defeat the measure even now. The same reckless hostility is persisted in by Gibbons in the Senate, who would, if he could, rouse Heaven & Earth against us.

*March 15th.* In a note received this morning from Jacob Harvey, New York, he says, "The Irish emigrant remittances for Jan. & Feb. in small bills—to their families & connections from Boston, New York, Philada.

& Baltimore—is $623,000. There is no mistake about it. I have taken pains to come at the truth & I am under the mark."

Now whatever errors or faults may justly be charged to the illiterate, ignorant, & low bred Irish, want of kindly feeling & generous sympathy is not one. An Irishman must be hard pressed & poor indeed who would not share his potato even with a known adversary in distress.

*March 20th.* Gibbons, to create a prejudice against the Railroad, compared it to the late Bank of the United States as calculated to swindle the public, being patronized by the same influence. In this remark he was supposed to have allusion to me, but it is singular enough that of the 15 persons who remonstrated adversely to the Road, 4 of them were my associates in the Direction, viz. Horace Binney, Richard Willing, John A. Brown & Charles Chauncey.

I left the Bank in 1831, just after the commencement of the war with Andrew Jackson & from intimations given me then, by a high functionary of the Government, that if I would consent to become Pres. of the Bank in place of Nicholas Biddle, he, Andrew Jackson, would sign a Bill for the renewal of its charter. That arrangement, even if I had assented to it, I knew to be impossible. The Gen., with all his influence & power, could not carry out the measure, Nicholas Biddle having taken care to possess himself of Proxies more than enough to control the election, putting in & out of the Direction whom he pleased.

When I left it, the assets of the Bank, clear of all claims, were not less than forty millions, seven of which belonged to the Government & was returned with a premium of about 15 per ct. The present market value of the stock is $4½ for $100. To account for this immense deficiency is a problem of not very easy accomplishment. It might, indeed, add one more to the old seven wonders of the world—but this I know, that directly or indirectly, I never borrowed from it & that in no shape or form was I ever indebted to it a cent & yet I was an active Director of the Institution from 9 to 10 years of my life & had I chosen, might have obtained hundreds of thousands.

*March 25th.* The Railroad Com. met at 10 A.M. Twelve constitute a quorum. Adjourned at 11 for want of enough to do business. Our merchants remain at home behind their counters & in their Counting Houses, expecting others to labour for them. If they, for whose benefit this Road is, are thus selfish or indifferent, why should I wear myself out to serve them?

*March 27th.* Chambers *Edinburgh Journal*, a publication of no small merit, contains the following singular announcement: "Apart from the papers of professed female writers, considerably more articles suitable for our purpose are contributed by Ladies in Ireland than in England, while but a few of any kind are sent by Ladies in Scotland. It may add interest to this announcement to state that the greater number of Irish Ladies who furnish acceptable contributions are either the wives or daughters of clergymen of the established Church. It is at any rate a strange fact that a number of these pages are filled with material from beyond the Shannon."

*April 1st.* There is confirmation, but not official, of a destructive battle between Gen. Taylor & Santa Anna. About 60 officers of the American Army, among them Henry Clay's son Henry, were killed. The Mexicans fared much worse. People here rejoice at what they call our victory, so dearly purchased. It will be poor consolation to the families of the slain. A writer in the *American Review* says, "We regard this war as the great political & moral crime of the period & for which the Administration of the day is to be held responsible before God & man. We must hold the guilty authors of it to their just responsibility."

*April 2d.* The Directors of the Railroad held their adjourned meeting last night & discoursed on the subject of appointments. Offers were read & recorded. A com. of three are charged with procuring suitable accommodations for our future meetings. The Pres. read a prospectus for an Engineer Corps.—ordered to be printed for the use of the members & then adjourned to the evening of the 5th. Deliberation in the outset is preferable to repentance for rashness.

*April 3d.* A portion of this fine Spring day devoted as usual to Irish concerns. Another to confabs at home & abroad relative to the Railroad, then a short ride with my sickly wife. In the evening met the Mer. Library Co. As to my Irish affairs I rec'd a Letter from a member of the Society of Friends in North Carolina enclosing $100 to be remitted to the Dublin Com. for the use of a person named. The writer tells me the donor was "formerly a native of Ireland." What birth had the writer?

*April 4th.* Our afternoon meeting, First Day, commenced to be holden at 4 P.M., previously to which I attempted a nap, but as common with me in daylight, didn't succeed. I am apt rather to employ the time in thinking than sleeping.

That very extraordinary man, Napoleon, that master of the world, could set himself to sleep during an hour or two for the purpose of recruiting his strength & wake at a fixed time. This he could do at any hour of the day or night he pleased. Eyewitnesses have declared that, even on the days of battle, he would designedly set himself to sleep to be the better prepared for the coming conflict. A giant indeed, who waked up to carry out schemes of ambition which, like an earthquake, shook to pieces the kingdoms & empires of the earth.

*April 6th.* The Directors of the Railroad held another & last meeting in the Board of Trade Room. We elected Geo. W. Toland Treas. by a unanimous vote—salary $1500 & $500 in addition for a clerk. After many ballots, Oliver Fuller was elected Secy.—salary $1000. There followed a long debate on the organization of the Engineer Department. Coming to no result on the subject, we adjourned. It will behoove the Board to move cautiously to be not imposed on or misled by private & selfish interests in their appointments, location of the Road & in the formation of contracts.

*April 9th.* Paid an official visit to the schools of Matilda Hodgson & Esther Ellis, both in their usual good order. At 4 P.M. the Directors of the R.R. assembled at the Hall of the Franklin Institute. The election followed. John Edgar Thomson, now in S. Carolina, was elected Engineer in Chief, Ed. Miller & Wm. B. Foster, assistants—the first at $4,000, the other two at $3,000 each per annum. All natives of Pa. & highly recommended. We think they will form a strong corps.

If we have first rate men, we must pay them. It is poor economy to employ inferior persons to conduct a work of such magnitude.

*April 16th.* My son A. has in his employment a well instructed handy young man from Ireland, very capable of earning a living in agriculture & gardening. A brother arrived in one of the late Ships with nothing but what he had on, having not changed a garment for lack of clothes on the passage. A. has employed him also. Both were educated in an agricultural school & can render themselves very useful—but these are rare instances.

*April 24th.* Have just seen in the hands of a Friend a Letter stating that, while the millions are suffering death & pestilence from starvation, some of the nobility keep their hunting horses & packs of hounds, consuming food which should supply the poor. These they have to place guards over to prevent the famished multitude from destroying. This violation of decency & the common rights of humanity may provoke an outbreak involving the brutes & their more brutal masters in one general massacre—& who could pity them, the unfeeling monsters. None dare openly complain for fear of being secretly shot. There is land enough in Ireland to sustain its inhabitants but—while the great mass have not the means of subsistance—these ignoble nobles keep their thousands on thousands of acres uncultivated & have them as preserves for game, in the pursuit of which they may fill up their idle time.

*April 25th.* At afternoon meeting, Samuel Leeds took the head seat of the gallery & preached a well connected sermon, being an approved minister. He had been an insane tenant of Friends Asylum near Frankford for some years, returned two years ago to his family & for several months gave little evidence of returning reason, but lately resumed his former habits, among which is that of a pretty constant preacher.

For 17 consecutive years he was a moping maniac, paying no attention to business of any sort, being seldom found but in a sitting posture, his chin reclining on his breast & his eyes closed or cast down, nor could he be induced to enter into conversation beyond the simple yes or no in answer. Nor is his restoration to reason the consequence of medical treatment of any kind. I wish it may be permanent—that is, I wish his restoration to be so.

*April 26th.* Adjourned meeting of Board of Trade. J.R. Thompson moved a memorial to City Councils to prohibit the landing of peaches & oysters within the City limits. A strange proposition, debated & rejected. He is afflicted with paralysis which has twisted his external man awry & I fear his internal man too. As if conscious of his affliction, he exerts his energies as if to convince others that his mental powers had not relaxed. He does an extensive business as a grocer & evinces no inconsiderable shrewdness & tact in buying & selling. His obliquity of thought renders him troublesome.

*April 27th.* Among the novel & interesting occurrences of the times, not the least extraordinary & gratifying is the circumstance of the Choctaw Indians having held a meeting at their agency for the relief of the starving poor of Ireland at which $710 were contributed—the Agent, the missionaries & the Indians subscribing.

*May 1st.* The developments of science & the arts for the comfort & benefit of man are continually on the increase. The inhaling of sulphurous ether, by which the patient is thrown into total insensibility during the most painful operations of surgery, is not among the least. The discovery was made by Dr. Jackson of Boston & is in extensive use in Europe & America.

In the hands of a skillful practitioner it is attended with so little danger that one person out of ten thousand cannot suffer injury from its application. Next comes the use of chalk as a fuel. This is of incalculable consequence to the poor where that mineral is abundant & other fuel scarce. The chalk is surrounded by a small quantity of coal & in that form gives out a brilliant, powerful heat.

*May 3d.* At 10½ A.M., attended the annual meeting of the Lehigh C. & Nav. Co., where I occupied the Chair. The Pres., James Cox, submitted the report of the directors. The most satisfactory for several years—the company is again prosperous. The election ensued & I then attended the stated meeting of the directors of N.A. Ins. Co. Very little else was done than the ordinary routine of business. Among the losses reported was that of a citizen who has done frequent business at the office, almost invariably ending in sea disasters & to whom the company has paid $10 for $1 received from him. The Pres. considers him a respectable man, but a director said he would not insure for such a person as was habitually unlucky, born, he probably thought, under an evil star.

*May 6th.* Yesterday I suffered myself to be put out of temper with one of my neighbours, a most unreasonable man, which I regret. He indulged in a vehement vituperation, often repeated by himself, against the Directors of the Lehigh Coal & Nav. Co. I endeavoured to explain & to shew him the injustice & ingratitude towards a set of honourable men who served without emoluments & by whose faithfulness & skill the wreck had been restored to usefulness & profit to all concerned, himself of the number. It was in vain for, instead of acknowledging the obligation we were under to men who thus devoted themselves to our services without pay, he cast reflections indelicately on my own son, who is a member of the Board. That provoked to anger & I rebuked him with keen severity. Besides my son Henry, my nephew Caleb Cope is on the Board, both having from a sense of duty & persuasion been induced to serve.

My neighbour was most unreasonable but I ought to have borne him with more temper—for my own comfort, if from no better motive. The Lehigh Company's property involves a capital of 7 millions of Dollars. The flood of 1841 so injured the works as to require $600,000 to put them

in their present condition. The company was millions in debt at the time—men of less nerve & intelligence might have abandoned them. Not so the spirited Directors. They braced themselves up to the task. Stockholders came to the rescue—not all, for some, like my neighbour, contented with grumbling, gave no pecuniary or other aid whatever. The money was obtained & hundreds of widows & orphans preserved from ruin. They who contributed nothing, either in labour or money, are now among the first to complain & condemn. I am not & never was in the direction but I hesitated not in the hour of need to lend a helping hand.

*May 18th.* Have been to see that astonishing Lad known under the title of Genl. Tom Thumb, whose family name is Strattan. He was born in Connecticut & has lately returned from a visit to Europe, where he saw most of the crowned heads & was exhibited, it is said, to millions of people. He is 16 years of age, weighs 15 pounds & 27 inches high— light complexion, ruddy cheek, flaxen hair, lively, moving, smiling face & facetious. Well proportioned & has a sweet voice, infant like. Sings well & moves gracefully & actively, has a healthy appearance & said never to have been sick. He is not restrained in his diet. He seems to be a universal favourite, especially among the Ladies, who delight to kiss him, which he evidently enjoys & says he is engaged to 8 of the sex & thinks that enough for one person. Queen Victoria appears to have been highly pleased with him & made him several costly presents—a gold watch, a handsome tiny coach & pair of grey Shetlands the size of Newfoundland dogs. The vehicle, elegantly finished, cost 100 Pounds Sterling. He has a casket of Jewels, presented by the great in Europe —which he displays to longing eyes. When I saw him, there were by computation 1000 visitors present & he gives audience about 1½ hours thrice a day & receives probably $500 free of expenses every day. He returned from Europe, people say, with two hundred thousand Guineas. After visiting some of our principal Cities, he proposes to retire to enjoy his fortune. He is the most diminutive specimen of humanity of which history tells. His family say he is now no larger than at 7 months of his age, when he ceased to grow. During the exhibition, he showed himself off in various characters & costumes in which he performed gracefully & dexterously, such as Napoleon, Highland Chief, Fred. the Great, a Grecian, Roman &c, suiting the dress to the character. During the entire exhibition he appeared not to tire. The exercise of his faculties &

body contribute no doubt to the preservation of his health & improvement of his mind. Besides his vernacular he speaks French.

*May 25th.* The war in Mexico has assumed a savage character. Santa Anna's Army is much broke up. A Guerilla war is to be substituted. Genl. Carnales has issued orders to kill every American found on the Mexican soil, armed or unarmed & without regard to sex or condition & all Mexicans, not excepting the Clergy, are commanded to take up arms or to be shot.

*May 27th.* Peter Wilson, an Iroquois Chief & a man who has received a collegiate education, has again called on me, to make known the condition of some of his people.

I did not hesitate to pen in a small book, prepared for subscription, the leading circumstances of those poor deceived & distressed Indians. I gave into the hands of Wilson a donation which I hope may be followed by others who possess the means & the hearts to aid & feel as Christians should feel for suffering humanity. I could not send this interesting Chief away empty handed—let others do as they may.

*May 28th.* I obtained some subscriptions for Peter while some dance & others pay the fiddler. There are men & members of our religious Society who commiserate the poor Indian by fine speeches—they cost nothing, but, tho' able, decline shewing their good will by pecuniary aid—which costs something. Cheap kindness that. "If a brother or sister be naked & destitute of daily food & one of you say unto him, Depart in peace, be ye warmed & filled; notwithstanding ye give them not those things which are needful to the body, what doth it profit?"

*June 7th.* Peter Wilson left us unexpectedly yesterday to proceed to the relief of his suffering people in the west, having heard of other deaths among them & their great anxiety to escape from the pestiferous land to which they have been decoyed.

*June 12th.* It is understood that certain leading opponents of the Central, or Penna. R. Road, have been in caucus, to devise measures to thwart the company, perhaps to procure an injunction on the compy., or more probably to try to induce Councils not to pay the interest coming due 1st July—or perhaps to contest the payment of taxes levied to pay interest on the loan authorized by Councils to meet their subscriptions. Be the measure what it may, it comes forth at this time with a bad grace, is unpatriotic, malicious & unworthy. There is nothing new in this insurrectionary species of opposition to a great public work. At the introduction of the Schuylkill water, many of our opulent, influential citizens would not pay their taxes, but the City Councils were then composed of men true, firm & enlightened—and seized furniture, horses & carriages to carry on the great scheme, sparing no man, however distinguished. The water was thus made to flow in our streets & in our dwellings, in spite of traitors, malcontents & selfish, ignorant obstinacy.

*June 14th.* Stated Meetg. Board of Trade in the eveng. A Com. of 7 appointed by the Chair to attend a convention from the States at Chicago 6th July to promote internal improvements—to which the Board chose to add their Pres., he informing same time of his inability to do so.

*June 17th.* New Indian corn for the table has been in the City for several days, brought from the South.

The Board of Trade forced me, *nolens volens*, on the delegation to attend the Chicago Convention, placing me at the head. I would willingly undertake the service but, sensible of the indications of advanced life as I am, they should have excused me & saved me from excusing myself.

*June 19th.* Met some citizens by invitation at the Exchange relative to a public meeting on the subject of the Chicago Convention. Decided in the affirmative to take effect on the 23d. Declined presiding at it & also to being one of the delegation. While I approve of the object, I wish not my name to be so continually before the public. Boston, N. York & Albany have each appointed large delegations of their distinguished citizens.

*June 21st.* Men who cannot claim a descent from blood of the Emerald Isle may nevertheless claim to qualifications of like distinction. A connoisseur of the tribe, in Paris, asked Dumas, a west Indian by birth & celebrated writer, if he was not a Mustee? Yes—what was your father? My father was a Mulatto—what was your grandfather? He was a negro —and his father? His father was an Ape. My pedigree, said Dumas, began where yours ends.

Come, come, said one man to another, Get up, the morning is breaking. Let it break, replied the lounger—it don't owe me anything.

*July 12th.* A Chinese Junk, the *Keying*, 10 months from Canton, manned by 20 Chinese & 20 Europeans, has arrived at N. York—being the first of the "Celestial Empire" that has visited our waters. She is in ballast, but many Chinese curiosities on board. She is built entirely of teak, her anchor included, which is slung by ropes & drawn up or let into the water as occasion may require.

*July 29th.* Returned to Calcon Hook in the P.M.

As we passed into the City we met crowds of rowdies, in open waggons, in carts & on foot—learned they were wending their way to Hog Island, well suited for the purpose, in name at least, to witness a pugilistic combat between a butcher & a blacksmith thinking, doubtless, to escape the lash of the law. In a civilized community, these savage exhibitions should be promptly & effectually arrested.

*August 12th.* While in the City, I attended a stated meeting of the R.R. Board. Much business transacted—2 hour session—the Engineer in Chief present. Govr. Shunk has issued his proclamation that agreeably to the terms of the Charter, one million has been paid by subscribers & fifteen miles at each terminus of the Railroad placed under contract. This puts an end to the Balt. & O. right of way.

*August 16th.* Paid a short visit to the woolen factory of Jabez Jenkins, at the Blue Bell. He is an active intelligent young man & I hope he may succeed. His machinery is of modern construction & operates well. He should, however, provide himself with a discreet wife—yet he may think of Sir Thos. More's saying. He would compare the multitude of women which are to be chosen for wives "unto a bag full of snakes having among them a single eel. Now if a man should put his hand into the bag, he may chance to light on the eel, but it is a hundred to one he shall be stung by a snake."

*August 23d.* Last night I slept comfortabley at Calcon Hook. The previous nights, I scarcely slept at all, especially that of the 20th, for while paying a friendly visit to the agreeable family of Abraham L. Pennock, our grandson F.R.C. came with the painful intelligence that our daughter, E. Tyson, was very ill of dysentery at the Paoli Inn where she & her husband, J.R.T., are boarding. It being too late in the day to proceed thither, we hurried back to our lodgings & spent a wearisome night. Next morning I proceeded to the Paoli, a distance of 17 to 18 miles over a fine country, but with a heavy heart, uncertain that I should find my dear child alive. I found her living, but extremely low.

She had been ill for a week without our knowledge, but I had the inexpressible satisfaction to learn there was a manifest abatement of her disease & hopes of her recovery, for which may I be sufficiently thankful to our Merciful Father. I tarried at the Paoli all night &—being assured that the dear sufferer was still better & in good hands—I returned to relieve the mind of my wife, between whom & the sick, I am glad to record, exists an affectionate attachment.

Among the Letters that awaited my returned is one from R. T. Walsh & W.L. Shaffer, a com. of the directors of the Mercantile Library Co., requesting me in very flattering terms to sit for a portrait to be assigned a permanent place in the Library room. They have made the necessary arrangement with John Neagle, a distinguished artist. Undeserving & unambitious of such a compliment, I do not see how I can decline a request tendered in pressing terms by persons with whom I have been long associated pleasantly & I hope, usefully, in the promotion of a great public good.

I have, on reflection, come to the conclusion that if, by my assent, I can contribute to the pleasure of my respectable companions & others, I ought not to indulge in what many would pronounce overweening fastidiousness. I cannot in truth say that I have any conscientious scruples on the subject & therefore make them the following reply:

My dear Friends,

Your letter of the 18th came into my possession yesterday at this my quiet retreat & I can truly say that I am deeply affected by the flattering kindness of its contents.

Unambitious & undeserving of the distinction you propose to assign me, if the possession of my portrait can confer pleasure on gentlemen with whom I have been so long & so agreeably associated, I should in my own estimation incur the odium of ingratitude were I, from any fastidious notion of my own, to refuse compliance with your request. I expect soon to return with my family to the City, when I will cheerfully submit myself to your disposal.

Your Friend,
Thos. P. Cope

*August 25th.* Went to see my suffering daughter E. at Paoli. Found her painfully low & exhausted but, before my departure, there was an evident improvement & I left her under charge of Doc. Biddle, who lodges in the House & attends her closely. My other daughter, Caroline, spends much time with her, much attention is likewise bestowed on her by her attached husband.

*August 26th.* My birthday, it having pleased the Almighty to pro-long my existence to the completion of my 79th year, blessing me, unworthy as I am, in basket & in store. May I never cease to praise the bountiful Giver.

Somebody says that men, like books, have at each end a blank leaf—childhood & old age. The first I have passed over safely, by favour of the Author. The second state, which cannot be very distant, will finish the Book. I pray it may pass unsullied from my hands by the same unmerited favour.

*August 27th.* Afternoon, we returned to our home in the City, cov-ered with dust. Our sojourn at Calcon Hook was pleasant & altogether widely different from what it was when D. Richards was tenant—the present occupant, Annesley Newlin & his family, being agreeable people & disposed to make us comfortable as their boarders.

Some author informs us of a very striking case of how early & how injuriously young minds may be affected by passing scenes. The circum-stance occurred in Paris, a short time prior to the French Revolution. A boy 5 years old hanged his brother, 2½ years of age & when reproved, replied, "I did not hurt him, for he did not cry. I only did what I saw Punch do two or three times." It appeared that he had been accustomed to visit the exhibitions of Punch.

*August 29th.* Every time my front bell has been rung today, it has felt as the knell of my poor Elenor & startled me. Son Henry caused one of these. He brought us the latest intelligence, having left the Paoli yesterday P.M., when she was thought rather better. It being by all deemed desirable to cause her removal to the City as early as prudent, we came to the conclusion to instruct Dr. Morton to fix the time & mode of removal, thus throwing the responsibility on his judgement & a note was written & forwarded to J. R. T. to that effect.

The latest intelligence is by our grandson, T. C. Yarnall, at 10 at night. He left the Paoli after the receipt of our note & reports that Dr. M. will, if practicable, remove the dear sufferer to the City tomorrow. However great her pains, she complains not, in which respect she resembles her worthy mother, who bore with Christian meekness the most agonizing bodily torments. Her family, the Drinkers, were noted for their firmness of character.

*August 30th.* My sick daughter has been brought home on a truck bed-stead in a Railroad car to the depot at High St. & thence to her dwelling on the truck, borne on the shoulders of four men.

The confined chamber at the Paoli was but a few feet from the Railroad. The noisy revolving wheels & loud screaming whistle were a great annoyance, continued by night & by day, permitting no rest to the invalid & rendering recovery almost hopeless. She was, moreover, anxious to be again under her own roof.

I paid today 110 cts. a cwt. for hay, about twice the price of last year.

*August 31st.* I found my daughter much exhausted this morning but more free from pain. She, however, improved as the day advanced. She cannot turn herself in bed, nor lisp but in a whisper—her fine eye is dim & when I gaze on her, mine becomes so too.

*September 1st.* Did not retire to bed until late last night, fearing I might be summoned at any moment to the chamber of our dear Elenor to witness her dissolution, so low was she when I left her abode after 9 P.M. under afflicting feelings. Most of the morning spent at the house of mourning. My dear daughter is no better. My heart is full. I kissed her, I fear, for the last time. Her mind is unclouded but her utterance so impaired & low as scarce to be understood or articulate with the ear close to her lip. Her Physicians give small hope.

While dining, a messenger arrived to say my dear child was fast sinking. I hurried to her chamber & found the report too true. She lingered till between 8 & 9 P.M. & expired. Oh, the trial of this bereavement.

*September 2d.* Most of the day spent with others of the family at the dwelling of J.R.T., who seems almost distracted. Alfred arrived at this scene of desolation & mourning & we could fix the day of interment —the 4th at 5 P.M. He had been, for the benefit of his health, on a journey to the east. The day is sultry with rain & thunder. Before A. arrived, we had among us some painful discussion on the spot of earth in which the mortal remains of the deceased should be deposited. His absence relieved him from participating. My surviving daughter wished them to rest in the Woodland Cemetery, which was pleasant to Job, both of them believing that was the choice of the departed. They wished for a spot on which should be inscribed some memorial to which to resort as the resting spot, so that, as Caroline said, she could point the place to her children & tell them at all times where the remains were interred. Henry utterly refused his sanction & I alarmed Job by stating that there, the body would be subject to be disinterred by men obtaining a living by such doings & who might, by bribery, procure the cooperation of that unprincipled man, Wm. Carvell, who has charge of the ground & whose wife, like himself, is a drunkard. We finally agreed to prefer Friends ground on Mulberry St. & Fourth St., where lie the bones of my Mary, mother of my children.

*September 3d.* On first visiting my son-in-law this morning, I found him greatly excited, saying he had not slept from distressing thoughts that ice had been applied to the body of his dear wife when life might not have been extinct. I assured him of the contrary & that, according to the testimony of those who laid her out, there were indubitable evidences that the work of dissolution was come 10 or 12 hours before the ice had been applied, referring him to all who had been employed in this solemn service & to Dr. Morton, to all of whom he resorted for confirmation of my statement.

I assured him also that mortification had commenced hours before the final close. His feelings were at length more composed & when, late in the evening, I went home, he assumed more rationality, for I feared his imagination & anguish would end in absolute derangement of intellect. Dr. M. prescribed for him medically & I trust it may please his heavenly Father to award him a night's rest & strength to bear the remaining offices to the dead.

Wrote to my son William on the 2d informing of our bereavement. It will be sad intelligence. Except the demise of her dear mother, no potion has been so bitter & racking to my feelings as this event. Nay, let me correct myself, it pleased the Almighty to have visited me with one other, the tragical death of my beloved, talented son Francis. God in mercy has thus visited me with afflictions grievous to bear. May I kiss the rod with which I have been afflicted & endeavour to improve under these several chastizements & of which I am conscious there is no small need.

*September 4th.* Visited J.R.T. after breakfasting & was gratified on finding him more settled but complaining of exhaustion. Admonishing him to get some rest, he reclined on a couch & I retired, closing the door after me. I had done so but a few minutes when his mother & sister entered & inquired for him. I stated that he was endeavouring to repose & asked them to permit it for a short time, but they immediately passed in, the mother assuming an air, as much as to say, I am now Mistress of this House.

Why should these two choose thus to break in upon his repose & add torture to his worn out frame & spirits? Could they not have sat down

quietly for a few minutes without disturbance? The mother said the daughter was not well & must see him, but she was well enough to come many squares & to sit in quiet a short time would not have injured her.

*September 5th.* The last melancholy office to the dear departed has been performed. Last evening about dusk the funeral was ended. Herman said it was large. I saw not, but know it was solemn. The remains were deposited in the eastern division of the lot, Mulberry St. & 4th, no one spoke at the grave.

*September 10th.* The yellow fever is prevailing to an alarming extent in N. Orleans. Hitherto, this season, it was mostly confined to the intemperate labouring classes & emigrants. It is spreading into the upper circles by last reports.

*September 18th.* A simple circumstance in my own experience has taught me of how much importance are early impressions. When a small boy, I was told that to see the new moon over the right shoulder portended good luck, while to see it over the left shoulder predicted ill. Now altho' I very soon perceived the folly of that superstition, I think I hardly ever witness the appearance of a new moon without a secret wish to have it over my right side, knowing at the same time the nonsense of the predilection.

*October 3d.* A lad on a visit to my family, complaining of headache, I advised him to try my remedy. I told him I took my head off every morning & washed it right well with cold water. Looking doubtfully at me, he asked how I put it on again. I said, Very easily—that on retiring to rest at night, I put it on my pillow & in the morning, took it off.

*October 5th.* Met Managers of H. Refuge, my mind thro' mercy feeling more at liberty to attend to my accustomed duties. Some exchange of grounds with adjacent proprietors sanctioned for mutual benefit—decided also to proceed with the building for coloured delinquents with our own means & credit, should even the public subscriptions fall short of the stipulated sum. The Managers were pledged to appropriate $25,000 towards the purchase of a lot & erection of buildings, on condition that an equal am't should be raised by public contributions, but there have been as yet less than $14,000 subscribed, owing to the ultra anti-slavery advocates refusing their aid unless the coloured & the whites are associated indiscriminately in all respects—which public opinion will not at present sanction.

My creed is that if we cannot obtain all the good we wish, it is no reason why we should not achieve all in our power. Moreover, it is my belief that under existing prejudices, both will fare better than if mixed—the coloured will feel under less restraint, as it would, if mixed together, be very difficult if not impossible to guard them from being insulted & abused by the whites.

*October 6th.* Attended the meeting for the western district, at Twelfth St., to witness the marriage ceremony between Geo. Randolph & brother Jasper's daughter Rebecca. Tho' I occupied a seat with the wedding guests, I did not dine or sup with them, not for want of invitation or inclination but because my sad heart is not in condition to participate in mirth & having no wish to mar the festive joy of others, I retired to my home.

*October 29th.* The Meetg. of sufferings have done something better than breeding quarrels. They have put on foot a subscription for collecting statistical information of the condition of the negro population in the City & Districts. With a knowledge of the evils that abound among them we may hope with Divine aid to be the better enabled to apply a remedy.

Many of those blacks are known to be deeply sunk in ignorance, vice & poverty. The attempt was made to do the same thing some years ago, but it fell into hands of persons who were suspected to have been more anxious to give a flattering account of the race than to expose their unvarnished condition, their morals, their destitution and evil associations, their habitual idleness & lack of economy. Many are industrious & of good example to the rest, while others are idle, filthy, intemperate & dishonest.

I have contributed on the present, as well as on the former occasion—we need the unvarnished truth. We need correct information as regards the House of Refuge, now in progress, if for no other purpose. But the knowledge is of interest to the public at large & especially for the friends of humanity & the afflicted, down-trodden children of Africa.

*November 1st.* Qy. Meeting. Very fully attended, and passed off harmoniously. Saml. Bettle, Sr., appeared acceptably in the ministry. I seem to have almost neither lot nor part in our meetings of business, especially in our own M.M. It may be owing to my want of faithfulness—but I cannot unite with the destroying spirit among us, nor can I reconcile to my feelings the painful issue of appearing publicly in

opposition to my dear son Henry, who is so deeply involved in the dividing movement. I know him to be honest & sincere & think, when the Society shall be broken into shreds & patches, he will regret the countenance he has given to the destroyers. Let a separation take place & it will not be long before another & another will succeed, until but the skeleton of our former greatness will remain to proclaim our folly.

A call after night from R. Walsh & associates of the Mer. Library Co. to inquire when it would be convenient to receive a visit from Neagle, Portrait Painter. My answer, any time that suits him.

*November 6th.* At 7½ P.M. attended the Board of Mer. Library Co. Ten or twelve new stockholders were admitted. The room was well attended.

*November 8th.* In the evening Neagle, Portrait Painter, introduced by Wm. L. Schaffer of the Mer. Library Co., called—& agreed to sit to him on the 11th at his studio at 9 Sansoms Row, Walnut St.

*November 10th.* The operations of some of the English private Bankers are extensive to a degree of which we here, in general, have but little conception. I have been told that, in one year, Overend Gurney & Co.'s transactions amounted to eight millions of Pounds—$100,000,000—& expressing my surprize to another, he said it had exceeded even that enormous sum.

The country, bad as is the present state of commerce, must be in better condition than it was in the panic of 1825, when the query was not "Who goes?" but "Who stands?" When the opinion expressed by William Huskisson was that "in 48 hours all dealing would be stopped between man & man except by way of barter" & at which period it was said that the Bankers who were compelled to sell stock to raise cash paid at the rate of seventy two per ct. for the money.

*November 11th.* Had my first sitting this morning to Neagle. He took but a sketch.

*November 15th.* A singular account is published in the papers of an old pair who lately died in Scotland, 100 years old. They were born on the same day, married when 19, died on the same day, in the same bed & were buried in the same grave, each being exactly one hundred years old. They of course lived together in wedlock 81 years, a very extraordinary case indeed.

*November 17th.* The Mayor of Montreal is dead of the Ship Fever, contracted in discharge of his official duties. The number of deaths among the Irish immigrants, at Grosse Isle, below Quebec, was lately stated at nine thousand. No small apprehensions are still felt for the poor of Ireland in the coming winter. They are a miserable, incorrigible set, for whom it is difficult to provide.

*November 20th* At 9½ A.M. Com. of Finance, Pa. R. Road—none but Pres. M. & self attending. Made arrangements for the payments of the month. Met the Board at 4 P.M. The Pres. submitted the draft of a report to the stockholders, who meet early next month. It is well drawn up but contained one sheet that I thought was objectionable & it was stricken out. It referred to our controversy about the City subscription, recommending an application to Legislature to confirm that Act. This appeared too much like rousing the Lyon from his den. The Co. can ask, and I trust will, for power to authorize the Districts & Counties to subscribe, and in the Bill use language to cover the whole ground. To indicate, at this time, any doubt would be to invite the enemies of the Compy. to renewed opposition. Things at present are working well. The Compy. is growing more into popular favour. The Pittsburgers even are opening their eyes to their true interest & have ceased courting & coquetting with the Baltimoreans. My intention is, however, to carry out my original design of withdrawing from the Co. when completely under weigh, to use the mariner's term, which is now attained. But I have consented not to do so until after the election, now near at hand. I think myself entitled to some rest.

*November 25th.* Thanksgiving day to be observed throughout most of the States—& truly, we have much to be thankful for, so as to call for the gratitude of all, not merely at set times but at all times. Friends of course do not comply with these set & external observances, but I am far from censuring others who do. The Almighty looks to the heart & not to the outward form.

*November 28th.* I often feel humbled under my own unworthiness & troubled in mind from a sense of my shortcomings. Matters which in the vigour of manhood I could cast behind me as trifles not to be regarded, now afflict me & disturb my repose.

*December 4th.* A project is on foot for throwing a wire bridge over the Niagara, between the falls & whirlpool at an elevation of 230 feet above the water. The plan, it is said, has been agreed on & the money subscribed. What would Geo. Buck have said to that? George was an

Englishman & lived west of the Schuylkill. He would never trust himself on the Permanent Bridge & being asked by Jno. Stokes why he would not, he replied, "John, does thee know there's no appointed time for that Bridge to fall?"

Am called on by the Assessor for a schedule of my taxable property. This has always been to me a perplexing subject. The Law, not the practice under it, define with accuracy every item that is or is not taxable. Years ago I tendered a list to the Assessor for the time being, who declined receiving it. I said it enumerated some things nor previously returned, but he gave me the paper back, saying, "Mr. Cope, you already pay more than any other man in the ward." From that time I have made no enumeration, for while I am willing to bear my full proportion of the public burdens, I have not felt it incumbent on me to do more. Added to which we all know that the Legislature, composed principally of country members, contrive so to frame the Laws, and I may add, the administration of them, as to throw on the City burdens which they themselves escape.

*December 31st.* At noon met the Managers, Haverford School. Several offers of teachers & some prospects of a Superintendent. So the School may be reopened next spring. I hope party views may not govern the choice, but that we may be favoured to obtain a Friend befitting the station.

# 1848

*January 1st.* We had our annual family assemblage. About thirty sat down to the table, including a new addition to the flock in the lovely person of Anna, wife of F.R.C. Delightful as are these jubilees to my best feelings, there was on this occasion a drawback on the pleasure. One dear object was not & her place was vacant.

*January 8th.* I called by invitation on Pres. Merrick at the office of the Penna. R.R. Compy. He read to me the private correspondence between himself & Jno. Edgar Thomson, Engineer in Chief, from which it appears that jealousies exist as to their relative prerogatives, powers & rights. He attributes to three members of the Board—Toland, Wright & McGee—a design to supplant him & place Toland at the head of the Compy. This I believe to be unfounded & endeavoured, with what success I cannot tell, to convince him of it. He charges Thomson with disrespecting his orders & especially with not forwarding contracts to guide the Board in its expenditures & other arrangements, and with entering into contracts of his own mere motion, without consulting him or the Board. I advised him not to do anything that should lead to any serious misunderstanding with either of the parties, to press on the Engineer, in good humour, the propriety of a compliance with the request of which he spoke, but to use no harsh language of complaint, as he must perceive that an open rupture which might end in the resignation of either of them would prove most disastrous to the Company.

The love of power manifests itself in every state of Society, whether of civilized or Savage life—in civil communities everywhere, Church & state, in our great political circles, our social intercourse & domestic retirement.

*January 23d.* The influenza, considered by many as the precursor of cholera, is very prevalent in some parts of Asia & Europe & consequently excites no little alarm. It rages in London, carrying off many. Liverpool, Marseilles & other populous Cities are suffering from the epidemic. The most grievous lamentations come from Scotland. Whole schools & colleges have been suspended & places of worship closed. At Glasgow, 70 out of 480 policemen were rendered unfit for duty. In Russia it is very fatal; in other parts, if timely remedies are applied, it mostly yields to treatment. Isolated cases have appeared on this side of the Atlantic, but not amounting to an epidemic. In troublesome times

the maladies to which we are incident become the most deadly; it is a great preventative to keep the mind tranquil.

*January 29th.* Sat again to Neagle. The portrait has assumed a shape which gives me an advantage over the Irish maid who, riding past the House, wished she was at the window that she might see how she looked riding in a carriage. Neagle is an accomplished artist & seems ambitious to exercise his best skill on this portrait. I think he will succeed.

*February 5th.* In the eveng. the Directors of the Mercantile Lib. Compy. held their stated meeting. It appears that at the late annual meeting of the stockholders, a Resolution was adopted to require of the Board an apartment for conversational purposes, intended doubtless to accomplish the purposes formerly declined by the Board as a room in which to play chess. Now chess may be an innocent exercise of the mind, perhaps even salutary, but I fear the consequences to our inexperienced youth. If chess, why not cards, and if cards, why not any other game. When a lad, my associates were card players & to gratify that propensity met at Taverns & occasionally, nay I believe generally, played for drink, for the landlord must be compensated. I was much urged to join in, but apprehending the ulterior result, I would not even learn the use of cards & it was, under Providence, my preservation. I cannot now call to mind a single person among those, my juvenile companions, who became a truly respectable citizen. They generally turned out to be gamblers & drunkards.

These remarks apply to Lancaster, where I was born & which I left about my 18th year. The Board took no action on the proposition—there is at present no vacant apartmt. in the Liby. building.

*February 8th.* Several mad dogs are said to have been killed in the City within a few days. Dogs are prohibited from going at large, unless muzzled. Ice was formed the last two nights & the sky is clear.

*February 12th.* Friends are making a collection for the blacks of Moyamensing. These miserable beings are generally tenants of Irishmen who exact enormous rents from them. They are huddled together in small rooms & are ragged, filthy & covered with vermin. Too many of these sufferers are lazy, idle & vicious—but we must not permit them to starve. The whites of the District, or a majority of them, are not remarkable for morality & correct citizenship. It appears that, while penning the preceding, Moyamensing was the scene of most disgraceful riots, confined principally to boys & young men. The District has for a long time been headquarters for associate rowdies of the young.

*February 15th*. This morng. at 11 the Ship *Tuscarora*, the largest merchantman ever built in this port, was safely launched from Vaughan's yard, Kensington—built for H. & A. Cope & Co. for their Line of Liverpool Packets. She is the 2d of the same name, the first having been sold years ago to persons in N. Bedford for a whaler. 10,000 people were computed to attend the launch.

*February 16th*. Attended at the office of the Pa. R.R. Co. at the appointed hour—it being the stated day by the rules. None were there but the Secy & myself. I told him he might make an entry in his Journal similar to one I minuted myself when an attempted meeting failed in a body of which I was a member, viz. "At a stated meeting of the Philada. Board of Trade—present Thos. P. Cope who, not being a quorum, adjourned.

*February 23d*. Monthly Meeting, forenoon. Little business except disowning members. Were it not for the natural increase, we could not long keep us a Society.

*February 24th*. John Quincy Adams died yesterday. Pres. Polk communicated to the Senate the treaty with Mexico, not yet made public. It is said to be unsatisfactory & may not receive the sanction of that body. Whatever the stipulations may be, it will doubtless be found that we shall in this war have paid dearly for our whistle. The death of J.Q. Adams will probably procrastinate the action for some days, unless the corpse should be conveyed to Massachusetts for interment. In that case Congress will soon assume business again. It has been said that the deceased kept a regular Diary & as he occupied, in a long life, so many public stations, that document, when published, will disclose matter interesting to the American reader, statesmen & the civilized world at large. Some allowance will have to be made for party prejudices, for he was a man of keen observation, ardent feelings & strange biases. He possessed at the same time vast knowledge and a highly cultivated mind. It is said that every night he recorded in his Diary the material occurrences of the day & that he never destroyed even notes of invitation or ceremony, but filed them with other papers carefully away—preserving thus, within himself, the means of reviving his memory as to facts & dates. On one occasion in an interesting debate in the House, the parties—differing in their statements as to the precise time in which a certain circumstance had occurred—appealed to Adams, who said he would inform them in a few days. He then wrote home for a certain volume of his Diary & gave the exact date.

While writing I hear the tramp of horses, carriages & men. The sound of voices & martial music. It proceeds from an immense crowd conducting Henry Clay from the depot of the Balt. Railroad to Mayor Swift's dwelling on North Tenth St. The Mayor, alongside of the City's guest, in a Barouche & four white horses. H.C. visits the City on the invitation of a com. of Whigs—the Councils opening Independence Hall to his reception.

*February 26th*. George Washington Smith, one of our distinguished literati, has brought & introduced to me Oliver Dyer from N. England, who is now delivering lectures in this City on *Phonography*, commonly called short hand writing. Oliver says that he can take down one hundred words of a speech in one minute. He is a red headed Yankee.

*March 2d*. We are apt to think the cultivator of the soil is more exempt from mental anxieties than the Citizen. The annual Report of the Pennsylva. Hospital, recently published, makes the following exhibit. In a table of 663 male patients, 95 are farmers, 49 labourers, 19 physicians, 40 clerks, 28 carpenters, 21 shoemakers, 18 seamen & watermen, 15 teachers, &c. Of 513 females, 54 were domestics, 53 seamstresses, 48 wives of farmers, 30 wives of labourers, 29 wives of merchants, 26 daughters of merchants, 23 daughters of farmers. Not one merchant is named in this list of the insane & yet the life of a merchant is a life of constant care & anxiety. Can it be that imaginary evils are more injurious to the mind than actual misfortunes?

*March 3d*. It appears that the funeral of J. Q. Adams at Washington was but ceremonial & that the body is to be conveyed to Quincy, its final resting place, accompanied by a committee consisting of one member of Congress from each State in the Union.

*March 4th*. Henry Clay still keeps in the City, visiting & being visited, greeted everywhere with *éclat*. I suspect this to be a tour of electioneering & am sorry for it, being convinced that much & deservedly as he is admired, he cannot be elected to the Presidency. Yesterday he visited the Girard College, shaking hands with all the boys—one of the urchins making him a set speech, to which he replied. The day before, he met 6,000 Ladies in the Great Hall of the museum, young & old eager to catch his hand & e'en his lip. No Sovereign could desire greater adulation. Hours were spent by these ardent females, coming & going from the audience chambers & cart loads of bouquets showered on the Statesman. All these doings seem rather out of place, at a time when the country is clothed with sackcloth & the unburied corpse of his old friend & public fellow labourer, John Quincy Adams, is by order of Congress moving to its last resting place. I cannot avoid indulging the thought that Henry Clay would have gained quite as much of the affections of his countrymen had he gone to Washington & been seen in the House of Mourning, rather than the Saloons of rejoicing & this I say without approving the entire political course of the deceased great man. H. Clay has, as a politician, pursued a course more to my liking.

*March 5th.* It has often surprized me how honourable members of the Bar can lend themselves to assist a villain in cheating & robbing others.

Many years ago, when I was at N. York & Alexr. Hamilton was living, I was at the time informed by my friends there that a wealthy citizen called on that great Statesman & Lawyer, with a fee of $500, to engage his services to gain a large Estate. H. took time to examine the justice of the claim & when his would be client called again, he returned the papers & fee, saying to the applicant, "Your claim is unjust." The reply was, I do not ask your opinion as to its legality, but I want your services to obtain possession. H. said the property of right belonged to a poor widow, who probably had no means to pay an Advocate, but, added he, "if you persist in your claim, I'll volunteer my services in her cause & defeat you, if in my power"—& this noble minded Advocate was as good as his word. He sought out the widow, entered without fee into her cause, defeated the unjust claimant & had the woman placed in possession of the Estate. I may have recorded this anecdote before; no matter—noble deeds such as this cannot suffer from repetition. They should be fastened in our memory as encouragement to others & in justice to that accomplished, upright & generous Individual, a favourite of Genl. Washington & of whose friends none were more variously gifted or more deserving.

*March 8th.* Clear, calm spring atmosphere. The mercury 7 A.M., 39—noon, 50.

The body of J.Q. Adams left the City at 8 this morning for N. York, attended by the committee from Congress. It rested last night in Independence Hall, which was hung in deep mourning. After entering the

City yesterday & until deposited in the Hall, minute guns were fired, bells muffled, &c. Many houses & shops closed. The occurrence recalls to my recollection the period when I was one of the City Councils in 1797. I accompanied my colleagues in a congratulatory visit to John Adams, father of the deceased, on his election to the Presidency. We met him at his dwelling, corner of 6th & High Streets.

Acting in the same capacity, I joined the same body to hear a eulogium on Washington at the Lutheran Church, at Fourth above Mulberry, delivered by Richard Henry Lee, member of Congress from Washington. A procession was formed at the State House & moved to Fourth, members of Congress & distinguished strangers in front; City Councils, Mayor & Aldermen at their head, next in order; citizens bringing up the rear. Washington had closed his mortal career some days before. The discourse was esteemed worthy of the orator & of the great departed hero & statesman.

It was on that occasion that Lee used the expression which long afterwards formed the texts for political harangues & which was not doomed to be soon forgotten, "First in war, first in peace & first in the hearts of his countrymen."

*March 13th.* An informal meeting of members of the Railroad Compy. at my house. Our supplement drags heavily thro' the Legislature & it is hinted that a majority could easily be obtained, by the rise of a little money among the members, which several present said was not unusual. It is painful to reflect on the possibility of such corruption, but I fear the scandal is not without foundation.

*March 20th.* Many of the details of the revolution in Paris have arrived. A provisional government has been created & the royal family have retired from the City. Louis Philippe may have the opportunity of testing his saying to the English ambassador, "I am the only King qualified to govern in Europe"—the Plenipo looking as if surprized at the presumption.

"Yes," continued Louis, "I am the only monarch in Europe who has cleaned his own boots & I can do it again." He may indeed clean his own boots again, but King of the French again, he never can be.

*March 31st.* John Jacob Astor of N. York, aged 85, died this day, the richest man in the U.S. Estate variously estimated from twenty to forty millions of Dollars. His brother was a beef butcher in N.Y. & I have heard my Aunt Pastorius say that John used to bring meat to them from his brother in a wooden tray. Aunt lived with her brother Thos. Mendenhall in that City when the English Army were in possession of it during the Revolutionary War. John Jacob was born in Germany & made most of his immense wealth in the fur trade & in early investments in landed estates, since forming a portion of N. York City.

*April 2d.* After centuries of persecution, the Jews seem likely to be admitted to common rights of man. In England, they can now sit in Parliament & on the continent of Europe, the powers have greatly ameliorated their condition. All this is but just; if we ever expect to Christianize them, it must be by treating them in a Christian spirit. How many of these people there are in the world it would be difficult to say. A writer in Prussia has lately given their population throughout Europe, the sum total of which is about two millions five hundred thousand.

Altho' there is still much destitution in unhappy Ireland, it is cause of thankfulness that the prospect of a plenteous harvest both in Europe & in our own country is very encouraging, so that I hope even the poorest will have bread without resorting to the expedient recommended by that droll wit, James Benezet, brother of Anthony, who had visited the English metropolis. "If you wish to live cheap," said he to a person who was going abroad, "go to London & when you get there, go to Black Friar's Bridge & there, in a snug corner, you'll see a little old woman with viands to sell. She will supply you with a pen'oth of coffee & a pen'oth of bread & if you wish it, with a hapeth of sausage & after you have eaten them, they'll make you so sick that you'll not want to eat anything more for three days. 'Tis the cheapest living I know of."

It was said by Dr. Johnson that no man was ever written down but by himself, an aphorism that would apply very pointedly, among others, to Frederick the Great. He had an ambition to be a poet & wrote, if we may believe history, till he wrote himself out. But if he could not write better than his friend Voltaire, he could beat him in taking snuff. One of the King's biographers says that Frederick's valet made money by washing the snuff from his master's pocket handkerchiefs & drying the precious commodity. Fred. was, however, a shrewd economist in his household & especially with persons who were in his service. One of his Generals wishing to retire on a pension, the King granted him permission to resign but refused him a pension, saying he kept no hens that would not lay eggs.

The editors of some of our daily journals are not in a little danger of

writing themselves down. Those of the *N. Am. & U.S. Gazette,* for instance, with their long editorials which few take the trouble to read. Short, pungent, pertinent paragraphs, on the contrary, are read with avidity because not wearisome, if for no other reason. A long, level, straight road over a flat country is more fatiguing to man & beast than a path diversified by hill & dale, mountain scenery & gently winding courses, presenting new objects for observation & feasting the senses with beauty & variety.

Cases of hydrophobia continue over the country. We hear of them almost daily.

*April 3d.* I have this day signed my will & in disposing of my estate have endeavoured to do justice to each of my children & pray my Heavenly Father who gave it me to bless it to them. For my dear wife I have made such provision as I trust will enable her to live comfortably & plentifully.

*April 25th.* Europe is in a state of unprecedented excitement—not a government is exempt. Everywhere the populace are aroused, demanding their enfranchisement & potentates are compelled to yield submission. Even G. Britain is not free from alarm. The Chartists advertize a meeting & parade thro' the streets of London, counting their numbers at 500,000. Government has interfered & forbidden the movement & if the parade is attempted, blood must flow. Ireland, as might be expected, is in ferment, pikes & other weapons are clandestinely preparing. People are secretly training & English troops arriving to meet threatened rebellion. A deputation of Irish leaders presented themselves before the Provisional Government of France, soliciting aid, but Lamartine, on the part of his colleagues, said they would not interfere. The Poles have made a similar application & have met with the same denial, but whether the wild spirits of the French democracy will long submit to this forbearance remains to be seen.

A com. consisting of Wm. Evans, Thos. Wood, son Henry & Jos. Scattergood met at my house last evening on the subject of Friends Schools for coloured children. The new school house back of Locust St. is adapted to 160, 80 of each sex but, for want of sufficient funds to pay teachers & assistants, is greatly short of that number. Present means between 8 & 9 hundred Dollars—$300 more needed to the effectual use of the school. The Com. agreed to recommend the sum to be contributed by the 4 Monthly Meetings, $75 each—they being equally-interested in maintaining this useful, humane Institution, founded originally thro' Anthony Benezet of pious memory, its first teacher.

The present occupant of that station, John Reeve, being in the habit of using the cowskin, I called the attention of the com. to the barbarous practice—the punishment being in general the offspring of passion & its gratification on the part of the teacher rather than the reformation of the pupil, which it rarely effects, but excites in him a spirit of revenge. He may be conquered but not reformed by this savage usage. I hope the instrument will henceforth be discarded—better turn a refractory boy from the school than continue to use brute violence on his person. An orderly lad named Samuel Guilliams, well brought up & son of a very orderly woman, well known in my family, was recently so severely whipped by Reeve with that barbarous weapon that he could not sit upright & that, too, for a childish offense requiring nothing but reasonable admonition. His coloured friends were prevented from prosecuting R. at law by the interference of my family. Had that not been done, it might have occasioned severe reflections on the whole body of Friends. In no other school, public or private, so far as I am aware, is the use of the cowskin permitted.

*April 26th.* Have sent in my resignation to the Board of Directors, Penna. R.R. Co. Declined doing it until the passage of the supplement & its adoption by the stockholders. Now that both have been happily accomplished, I have deemed my retirement seasonable.

*May 13th.* The American Traveller Jno. S. Maxwell says there are in Russia forty million of serfs, alias Slaves. The standing army consists of 600,000—the daily pay of a soldier being one cent. The serf cannot accuse his master, who can compel him to do anything but marry against his will. If he dies within three days after a flogging the master is fined, if after that time he is not liable. They are bought & sold with the soil. He was at the great Annual Fair of Novgorod, which was attended by 200,000 people from all parts of Asia & Europe. At that fair there were exposed for sale 60 cassimer shawls valued at ninety thousand Dollars. Twenty two were sold. The official published accounts of the value of all the merchandize sold at this fair from Europe & America amounted to three millions of Dollars, those of Asia to seven & a half millions & those of home growth to the enormous sum of twenty one millions of Dollars.

Another case of hydrophobia is reported as having recurred in the

northern part of the City in the instance of a little girl & my next door neighbour Levy thought it necessary to kill one of his three dogs this morning from the animal exhibiting symptoms of rabidness. To what cause this general prevalence of canine madness is to be attributed it is difficult to conjecture. It is certainly unusual & alarming.

A case is published in which a girl of 15, by singular intermarriage, became a grandmother—more strange than that my son Henry should actually be my Elder & yet, so it is. The girl was grandmother at 15.

*May 17th.* Visited the Academy of Fine Arts. That witty man, D.N. Chapman, accompanied us thro' the apartments, pointing out the perfections & imperfections of the various paintings. His own likeness presented by & taken at the request of the Medical students & my own by Neagle at the request & expense of the Mercantile Library Co. are exhibited there for the first time. I said I thought his too tame for a person of such lively spirits when he remarked that "all portraits should have something of the Devil in them, but in a subdued state."

*May 18th.* That thrilling exciting revolutionary song, *The Marseillaise,* composed by Rouget de l'Isle, a sub-Lieutenant in the French artillery, again resounds from the lips of devotees of change & has probably produced greater effects than the writings & speeches of prosaic politicians all put together.

*May 19th.* While I am writing, drums are beating, cannon firing, the military horse & foot parading & the multitude huzzaing to welcome Genl. George Cadwalader on his return from the campaign in Mexico. He is not the greatest hero who saves the most lives of his fellow man, but who scientifically destroys the greatest number. Strange perversion of reason, knowledge & worth among professing Christians. Certainly the day is not yet when men beat their spears into pruning hooks & their swords into plowshares.

*May 20th.* Two mad dogs were killed yesterday in different parts of the City.

The Haytians have caught the insurrectionary spirit & are again trying their hands at massacre. By recent accounts the blacks were endeavouring to destroy all the mixed colours, some of whom had escaped to Jamaica.

For some days past the weather has been very warm for the season. The shad have been unusually scarce in the Delaware this spring & have made their appearance in the Ohio, a river to which they have not hitherto resorted. Fish are seized as well as men with the spirit of revolution, mayhap not for the better, but let 'em try.

*May 26th.* 3 P.M. Stated meeting, Overseers of Friends Schools, amid a heavy rain of which we have lately had abundance. It is usual about this time of year & occasions the *Strawberry freshet.* Scanty attendance & only 3 admissions.

Among the impositions recently practised on me is that of a young woman of genteel appearance & good address possessing the manners of a well educated Lady. She asked assistance for a school of 400 coloured children, the offspring of coloured seamen, situated near the Sailors Snug Home. She represented herself to be one of three sisters, the daughters of the late Capt. Benners, who formerly sailed in my service. She also spoke of her brother, Geo. Benners, well known to me. The three sisters devoted themselves voluntarily to teaching those children. I have since discovered the whole story to be untrue & that my fair visitor is an errant imposter. She, however, had succeeded in obtaining a contribution from me.

*May 29th.* The intercourse with Europe by means of steam affords us weekly opportunities of information. We have another arrival with important intelligence. Pope Pius 9th has been forced by the Roman populace to declare war against Austria with threats if he would not they would deprive him of secular power. Austria being the stronghold of Catholicism, Pius was reluctant, but compelled to submit. Great events are in progress & the downfall of Papish tyranny seems rapidly hastening to a termination, with its superstitious intolerance & darkness.

Sweden has come to the aid of Denmark against Prussia & the Poles have taken up arms against the latter powers—there has been hard fighting there. France is forming an Army in three divisions consisting in all of 180,000 men on the Austrian frontiers. They are prepared for events & are fortifying the coasts. England is quiet & Ireland blustering.

A visit from another gaily dressed female asking for charity & very importunate, telling me a dismal tale of woe. This time I packed up courage enough to adhere to my resolution not to give but to those I know. She said she had lately arrived from Ireland, with two sons that she expected to have employed on our Railroads & some smaller children; had taken board, but possessed no means of paying for it. She left me dissatisfied—had a written recommendation drawn up by herself but vouched by nobody, tho' she had several names of $5 each on her subscription paper. I strongly suspect her to be an imposter. She calls

herself Mrs. Boyd & is probably 45 years old—slim make & theatrical air. I have not so soon forgotten *Capt. Benner's daughter.*

*May 30th.* A Letter by the last steamer from Liverpool written on the eve of her departure says that a Telegraph dispatch has just been rec'd stating that Pius, having recalled his declaration of war against Austria, has been cast into prison by his people. I should regret if this were true & yet it seems probable that the spell bound power of Catholic darkness is drawing to an end—& that would be an event at which to rejoice.

*June 1st.* The times are pregnant with memorials & important events in which the destinies of man are deeply involved. Europe is convulsed & the blood of her people flows freely. The unfettered mind, like the colt broken suddenly loose from its trammels, is in no small danger to life & limb from freaks committed for want of knowledge & experience. There is also, it is to be feared, a melancholy lack of true Christian feeling.

Pius was not imprisoned, but his subjects are resolved on war with Austria, notwithstanding he pleads conscientious scruples to declaring it.

*June 3d.* The intelligence from Charleston, S.C., is rec'd that the Steamer *Edith* has arrived at N. Orleans from Vera Cruz, bringing tidings of the ratification of the treaty of peace with Mexico. May it prove true.

*June 4th.* Called at the office Pa. Railroad—the Pres. is absent at Pittsburg, forwarding a subscription by Allegheny County which, he telegraphs, has been made for $1,000,000 with a stipulation that a depot be made in their City. The Board has not yet accepted my resignation. The Secy. informs me that jealousies & bickerings have crept into their counsels—Toland & Magee adverse to Pres. Merrick. He says that, if I were among them, I might prevent it & therefore the members are unwilling I should retire. They must, however, sanction it—my health demands relaxation.

*June 7th.* The Whig Convention to nominate a candidate for the Presidency assembles in Philada. today.

At 4 P.M. met the Board of Directors of the Pa. Institution for the Deaf & Dumb. Tho' a Director & long one of the Company, I have rarely met them, other engagements prevailing. 'Tis however a noble, useful Institution.

*June 9th.* The Convention has selected Zachary Taylor as Whig candidate for the Presidency. They could not have done better. Henry Clay as a non-combatant would have been my choice, but he could not carry the Whig vote.

*June 16th.* One of the most extraordinary events of these spasmodic times, almost defying belief, yet too well authenticated, is the savage conduct of the King of Naples. Finding himself beset by the Lazzaroni, to pacify them he gave the City up to pillage, when those abandoned wretches laid waste to hundreds of buildings, carrying off their valuables & murdering ten thousand of the inhabitants.

*June 17th.* In the published account of the sitting of one of the female clubs, it is said the debates were very tempestuous. The question discussed was the exciting one of divorce. On separating, the members met loud cheers from the crowd, the men opening a passage for them in the streets. It is not said what result these persons arrived at before adjournment, but assuredly these Parisian Feminines are not over-charged with bashfulness.

*June 26th.* Meetings have been held in Philada & N. York & other places in favour of the Irish malcontents & encouraging opposition to England. It is all wrong; we have no right thus to intermeddle with the policy of other Nations. Besides, if the Irish were wise they would, instead of rebellion, use their best efforts more fully to amalgamate with the British as Scotland & Wales have done & thus put an end to border wars & separate interests.

*June 29th.* I cannot avoid a consciousness of failure in both body & mind. I am certainly more susceptible of imposition, for one thing. Today I have again suffered myself to be gulled, by a female who gave her name as Miss Carty & living in my neighbourhood. She professed to be collecting money to furnish an apartment in the Sailors Home for the Sick. I knew such a measure was in view & gave her some money. Having some qualms, I then went in search of information & found I had suffered myself to be again cheated. Will I be more guarded hereafter?

*June 30th.* The Com. of Instruction & the Board of Managers met at Haverford School—the first at 10 & the Board at 11 A.M. All terminated satisfactorily. The Principal, Matron, teachers & pupils eat dinner, according to rule, at one common table. It is delightful to witness the good feeling & confidence which subsists between the lads & the Matron.

*July 1st.* At 5 P.M. attended to laying the cornerstone of the House of Refuge for Coloured Delinquents into which, as Pres. of the Board of Managers, I placed a tin box containing as follows: A copper plate with the inscription, viz.

> House of Refuge for coloured Juvenile Delinquents, laid July 1, A.D. 1848 in the 72d year of the Independence of the United States of N. America, James Polk being President thereof & Francis R. Shunk, Governor of the Commonwealth of Pennsylvania.

*July 2d.* The immigrants into N. York alone last month am't to 25,047, nearly ½ of them from Ireland.

*July 4th.* Frightened but not hurt—between 1 & 2 last night my whole family were aroused from their beds by loud thumping on the doors of the back buildings facing the yard. Men were there with torches, whose light induced a fear that our premises were on fire. They called out to us to get up. They proved to be 2 watchmen who, going their rounds & trying the gates on Elizabeth St., discovered ours to be unfastened. Explanations ensued—no injury had occurred & we retired to our chambers to be saluted soon after by the roar of cannon announcing that the fete of the 4 July had commenced—and a more brilliant moon never shone on Philada.

*July 7th.* The Pres. has officially communicated to Congress a copy of the Treaty of Peace with Mexico. He says the territory acquired is an indemnity for the past & our victories an indemnity for the future. Where is the indemnity for the thousands slain & sufferings of their surviving connections?

Exciting debates are still carrying on in Congress respecting the prohibiting of slavery in the newly acquired territory—the slaveholding States advocating the extension & the free States the prevention of that cruel inhuman evil practice.

*July 13th.* An outbreak in Paris, attended with great loss of life. An insurrection of the ultra-Republicans to destroy the new Government, for which purpose the 200 clubs had formed secret preparations. Interior communications had been opened from house to house by breaking openings in the partition walls for long distances. Streets were barricaded, forts established at convenient stations, supplied with competent forces of men & munitions.

Affairs in Germany are little more pacific, mobs attempting

everywhere to prostrate law & order. In these excesses the students manifest an evil example. One of the maxims of the disaffected is that he who possesses private property is a thief. Ireland continues to be greatly disturbed, men are openly arming & training. But the Government is not idle.

*July 27th.* The accounts from Paris are very unsatisfactory. Another revolt is attempted.

*July 28th.* Congress has for some days been occupied with that vexed subject, the slave question, arising in the Bill to provide for the government of Oregon, California & New Mexico, called the Compromise Bill, the object being to refer to the decision of the Supreme Court of the United States to declare whether the Congress can constitutionally prevent the introduction of slavery into the newly acquired Territories.

The Bill, after protracted & warm debate, has passed the Senate by a vote of 33 to 22 & has now to await the action of the House of Repres., where its fate is deemed doubtful.

*July 29th.* First Day. Attended Darby Meeting—lifeless as usual.

*July 30th.* The House of Reps. by a vote of 104 to 70 has laid on the table, equivalent to a rejection, the Compromise Bill from the Senate. It may be best for them to have done so, if the effect of that Bill would have been to create new Slave States, thus yielding an advantage to the cause of slavery unbecoming a free people, to the great injury of the Free States—each state, free or slave, being entitled to two Senators & every person owning 5 slaves being in effect entitled to 3 votes, while the citizens of a Free State has but one. This surrender the Free State ought never to yield. It is a mortifying reflection that, while we boast of our free Institutions, we cleave to the practice of slavery with a pertinacity wholly at variance with our professions.

It is 2 weeks today since, with my dear wife, I have been at Calcon Hook. During this time she has been principally confined to her chamber, rarely being well enough to ride abroad to enjoy the beauties of nature & the benefit of the open air—the country exhibits all the while a delightful freshness & vigour of production. No season has probably at any time been blessed with a more plentiful harvest. May we be sufficiently grateful to the God of Harvest for this abundant supply.

*August 5th.* I have for several days been debarred the use of my

travelling desk from loss of the key, which has today somewhat mysteriously been recovered.

*August 6th.* First Day—attended Springfield Meeting with Eliz. Newlin. A sermon from Thomas Evans. He invited me to dine, but I excused myself, saying that I had that morning gone off with another man's wife & wished to restore her for fear of consequences. On our way home, passed the two story stone dwelling in which Benj. West, the celebrated Portrait Painter, was born. It is near to Isaac Newlin's & Sketchly Morton's, two eminent farmers. My dear thought herself not well enough to bear the ride & sit meeting, having been confined to her chamber most of the time since our stay at Calcon Hook. We have for fellow lodgers Jos. Jones of Philada. & family, among them a son of the same name, 7 years old, who, when one year of age, was seized with paralysis & now moves about on his hands & knees, with a hunch back, being unable to use his legs below his knees, which dandle after him. He is a lively, intelligent boy, well calculated our deep sympathy to excite, conversing cheerfully & fond of instruction. His parents are agreeable associates.

*August 8th.* Congress is still agitated with the slave question, which is growing into an angry dispute.

*August 13th.* First Day. Went to Springfield Meeting & took my fellow boarder, Jos. Jones, with me. We spoke to not one body. Formerly, on visits to a country meeting, invitations from residents to dine with them accompanied by friendly salutations were numerous. Now, we may come & go without a friendly notice of any kind. This may be owing to citizens making a convenience of people for whom they may have no other regard, besides transient visitors being more numerous. After all, however, it must be acknowledged that, since the unhappy divisions in the Society, men are more shy of each other & good fellowship much laid waste.

*August 14th.* Annesley Newlin goes twice a week to the Philada. market. He relates to me the following anecdote. A female, richly dressed, robust & well formed has been in the practice of buying butter from him. On one occasion she invited him to her house, "to spend a short time with her, her husband being elsewhere & would not return till late in the day or evening." Her motive was sufficiently explained; he however declined the invitation. A. is in the vigour of manhood, well formed & comely, about 6 feet high & well proportioned. He would anywhere be called a handsome man, his manners are also engaging. This woman is a constant visitor of the market & from her genteel appearance & good looks attracts no little attention. She is always well supplied with money.

*August 15th.* We should feel the privation of salt a very serious affliction, it being esteemed a healthy & necessary preservative substance & yet it may sometimes prove otherwise. In the year 1630, eight men of the English Whaling Ship *Salutation* spent the winter on Spitzbergen whose preservation from that fell disease, the scurvy, was ascribed from their having had no salt to use—while even Dutch sailors who were persuaded to remain during the winter of 1834 & were provided with food, medicine & clothing perished, the mortality being ascribed to the use of salt in preparing their food. These facts are worthy of a record.

Have heard the number of Lawyers at the Philada. Bar computed at more than 300. When Peter the Great visited Westminster Hall, seeing so many persons in wigs & gowns, he inquired who they were & being told they were Lawyers, he said, "Why, I have only two in my Dominions & I intend to hang one of them when I get back."

*August 20th.* First Day. Went to Darby Meeting accompanied by my dear E.—the only time she has attempted since our arrival at Calcon Hook. I am thankful for her being well enough. That neither was much benefitted was perhaps our own fault, but there is such a want of harmony & good fellowship among the little flock composing the Assembly as to be painfully felt & deplored. That a society so blessed with the true faith & spiritual knowledge of vital Christianity should ever have become so wonderfully estranged from its first love & fallen from its high elevation in the Christian community might seem to indicate that, having sown the good seed, it had abandoned the field, leaving to others the care of the crop & reaping of the harvest.

We are not merely at variance with English Friends, but Meeting is at variance with Meeting & even members of the same Meeting at variance with each other. And we are told that a house divided against itself cannot stand. But I trust the good seed will not be lost & that it will be cared for by the Lord of the Harvest & provide even more abundantly. Certain it is that several of the important testimonies of Friends, such as temperance, abhorrence of slavery & war &c. have been adopted by other Christian professors & are continuing to spread over the civilized world.

*August 21st.* A visit to our home in the City. Domestic matters are in usual good order.

Executed as Pres. of the Board at J. J. Barclay, Secretary's office, Atheneum, several contracts for workmen at the new building, H. Refuge. B. informs me that some of the contractors ask for an increase. 'Tis a usual practice & should be discountenanced for men to enter into contracts on low terms to secure jobs & then claim allowances in the midst of the work, to skim the best part & then threaten to throw up without an increase of terms.

*August 26th.* My birthday, causing me to be an octogenarian. That neither my body nor my mind possess their former vigour are sufficiently made manifest by these puerile records, yet I have much to be grateful & thankful for in many ways. Tho' conscious of failing nature, I suffer but little physical pain. Am blessed with a family of dutiful, pious children, a wife better than I merit & plenty to live on. May the Lord in mercy prepare me for that awful event that happeneth to all & which cannot be very distant from myself.

*August 30th.* The Asiatic cholera has entered the eastern parts of Europe & is gradually moving westward. It is pronounced an atmospheric influence, depriving the air of a large portion of its electricity, as ascertained by actual experiment.

In the evening Wm. Hy. Brown came in to tell us that his kinsman Moses Brown & our son Alfred had arrived in safety at Boston after a stormy passage by sea for the benefit of their health. It is gratifying intelligence. The announcement is by Telegraph.

*September 7th.* Spent with my E. most of this day at son Alfred's, 6 miles on the Willow Grove turnpike. Henry, his wife & daughter Mary joined us after dinner. They stayed at Germantown. The fields have a parched appearance, fruit drying & falling from the trees, the dust intolerable. Annoyed by rowdies driving like crazy men from the Race ground. Their violent driving no small nuisance.

A mile in 2 minutes not unusual. Genl. Cadwalader has a horse it is said can do it in 1¾ minutes—but I have never seen him in the scuffle & should think he would not lower his dignity by making the attempt.

*September 8th.* The Com. on Property of Haverford School met at my house relative to the greenhouse, cooking range, &c. Orders given to reduce the size of the former & to provide a more economical & useful range than the present worn & inefficient one. Complaints made that the gardener indulges too freely in strong drink. I fear we shall have to discharge him.

*September 12th.* A call by Wm. J. Mullen, Pres. of the Philada. Society for the Employment & Instruction of the Poor, inviting me to lay the cornerstone of their proposed new building at Catherine above 7th St. While I cannot but approve the object, I have no desire to make such a display. Neither do I feel well enough were I otherwise inclined.

*October 4th.* The storm is over & sunshine brightens all without, yet it's deemed prudent to keep the house, being annoyed by headache & a tickling cough, obliging me prudentially to keep from Meeting where, owing to the coldness of the apartment, I increased my ailments a week since. The Keeper has a hard time of it, so many temperaments & whims are to be accommodated for. While the apartment may be too warm to suit one person, it may be too cold to suit another. Friends are as difficult to please as other people & perhaps a little more so. That at least has been my experience.

It seems difficult to realize the fact, but figures shew it that the exports from Cincinnati for 1847 exceed by several millions those from N. York for the same year. The exports from N. York, including five millions of specie, which in this comparison should be excluded, are stated at $52,879,274, while those from Cincinnati are $55,735,252—a City founded in the wilderness since I have been on the stage of manhood. If this be trade of Cincinnati in the milk, what will it be in the gristle? And what the commerce of the Great West in another century? And what the population of the United States when another hundred years shall have rolled round? That is, in 1948.

But will the Republican form of government so long continue? Very doubtful, truly.

*October 5th.* A pleasant trip to Haverford with my grandson T.P.C., Jr., & Francis Stokes, son of John, who is entered as a pupil.

Tho' unwell, I enjoyed the day & trust I am no worse for the excursion. The curtailed greenhouse is nearly finished, looks very well. The grounds are improving & as the trees grow on the lawn even the present beauty & attractions of this delightful seat at Haverford will be further inviting.

*October 9th.* It hath pleased the Almighty to call from this transitory state of being, Lucy, the youngest daughter of Ed. & Caroline Yarnall. She died this morning in the 4th year of her age of Scarlet Fever, the

only case of that disease, Physicians say, in the City. Little innocent, she has experienced but few of the evils of this Life & none of its vices. Who, then, can doubt the present happy state of her Being? "Suffer little children to come unto me, for of such is the Kingdom of Heaven."

*October 10th.* This day is held the General State Election. I went early to the Polls & cast my vote, as I have ever felt it my duty. We are not compelled to engage in party strife, but if we will not take so much trouble as to give a vote for the preservation of good order, we have little right to complain of oppressive Laws. First put thy shoulder to the wheel & then, if thou wilt, call on Hercules, he will help thee. I spent scarce a minute at the window, the citizens kindly making way for me. The day is fine but I returned speedily in compliance with medical advice. Order & good humour prevailed on the election ground.

*October 12th.* The notorious Honora Shepherd was tried & condemned in N.Y. for passing counterfeit money after having been recently discharged from prison for another offense & applied to Wm. Price, a Lawyer of note, to defend her. His answer is published & is so remarkable that I copy it. He says:

> It is no use to defend you. Concurrent testimony alone would be sufficient to convict you. Your father died in the Philada. prison, your mother is at Sing Sing. You have one brother in Moyamensing Prison, Philada., another in the Mass. State Prison & two others in Sing Sing. I was District Atty. when your mother was sentenced & also when your two brothers were. I can be of no service to you.

Honora's husband also served out his time in the State prison & afterwards died. What a family! Such another, it is to be hoped exists not in the United States. Honora Shepherd is said to be a handsome woman & possessed of strong mental powers.

*October 17th.* There is some uncertainty as to the issue of the election, the Whigs claiming Johnston to be the Gov. elect, while their opponents lay claim to Longstreth. In an election so close there is danger of fraud & we know that party now called Locofoco, under whatever name, have never been very scrupulous in these matters.

*October 18th.* Several worrying things press upon me. The Managers of the H. of Refuge need $30,000 to complete the new building & altho' they offer ample security, their efforts to procure it have been unsuccessful. I have tendered $3,000 if they can procure the balance—having already lent them my note for $5,000.

The Schuylkill Nav. Co. need $150,000 to relieve them from pressing demands & I have consented to advance nearly $4,000 provided others will make up the balance.

I have became a greatgrand sire by the birth this day of a daughter to my grandson Francis R. Cope.

*October 23d.* First Day. Two sermons, first from a new female minister, the other from W.E., both clad in terms of severity on offenders in dress, causing considerable offense. My opinion has ever been that more is gained by persuasion than abuse, by kindness than severity. Flies are caught with honey but not with vinegar.

The public have long abandoned the pillory, cropping, stocks & whipping posts—those relics of barbarity. Gaiety in dress is frequently more the offspring of thoughtlessness in our youth of both sexes than of vicious inclinations. I know it from my own experience. Cruel punishments are not, however, wholly abandoned among Friends, a fact of truth & dependence. J.S., now under my roof, a Westtown scholar, has reluctantly, on being questioned, explained an occurrence which took place at that seminary last summer. 20 boys of whom he was not one—being an uncommonly good boy—went into the woods on the 4th July & gave three huzzas. Being heard by Davis Reece, their Governor, he called them up & flogged them each with a rattan—one of them, the ringleader, so severely that gashes were cut on his back, our informant said, the size of his finger.

Supposing even some exaggeration, this flogging must have been such as should not have been tolerated in any school, especially in a school belonging to our Society, as being inconsistent with humanity & the mild spirit of the Gospel.

This savage castigation might have satisfied & gratified a spirit of morbid revenge, but was illy calculated to reform the offenders & accordingly they did not hesitate to bestow on their cruel flagellators the title of "strait coated butchers." If, instead of the harsh treatment, the lads had been mildly addressed on the impropriety of their conduct, they might have been benefitted by the advice, instead of which they were probably enraged & rendered more lastingly obdurate. Advice, like snow, the softer it falls, the longer it dwells & the deeper it sinks.

# 1849

*January 1st.* Yesterday terminated one of the most eventful years of modern times: The overturning of the ancient order of political powers & privileges on the continent of Europe; the flight of Pius 9th from Rome; the election of Louis Napoleon Bonaparte to the Presidency of the French Republic; the resignation of the Emperor of Austria; the acquisition of N. Mexico & California to the U. States; the threats of Calhoun & others to separate from the U.S., &c. &c.

In the morning attended the annual meeting of the Girard College. Two hundred & more pupils & not less than one thousand visitors present. J. R. Tyson delivered a discourse of great merit, in which he did justice to Girard & the forthcoming benefits to be derived from the magnificent bequest of the donor.

*January 8th.* I am confined to my house with sore throat & other symptoms of cold, brought on solely by my own imprudence. Corns in the prominent joints of my great toes had so inflamed them that I was prompted to substitute my shoes, while at home, with light slippers. Very comfortable to toes but pernicious to my health. In this act of imprudence I have done an act which may be attended—at my time of life—with serious consequences, tho' Shallcross, my Physician, seems disposed to think of it lightly. May the will of Heaven be done, for whatever that is, religion & wisdom demand my humble submission, unworthy as I am.

The weather is still freezing cold & I am deprived of attending the meetings of bodies over which, by the partiality of my friends, I have long presided.

*January 9th.* The Wyoming, lying in the dock above Walnut St. with her bow-sprit toward the stores as usual, was driven last night with such force by a field of ice applied to her stern that her bow-sprit drove thro' the door of the fourth story. Aid being procured, the bow-sprit was extricated without further damage. This field of ice was jammed between the wharves & the island, where it remains firmly fixed, affording fine skating for the multitudes today.

Had the bow-sprit been driven against the wall, it is believed that the wall, instead of the door, must have been forced in. The door is badly broken.

*January 10th.* Our powerful ice-boat has been set to work & having cut her way thro' the ice, it is again in motion & the navigation renewed.

A very exciting affair occurred yesterday afternoon on the Schuylkill. Crowds of persons had assembled to amuse themselves on the ice above Fairmount dam, when a portion of it on which 150 persons—men, women & children—were enjoying themselves suddenly separated from the mass & with its burden of living mortals floated away towards the precipice.

The parties were horror-struck—confounded. Wild shrieks of despair were heard where all, a few minutes before, had been joy & merriment. Many jumped into the water; some escaped by aid from the shore. Luckily, the float was on the weaker side of the dam where the water was shallow. But the sheet moved on. A girl of 15, a smaller one & a full grown female went over the dam on the float. The whole were, however, picked up by boats & altho' nearly perishing with cold, were restored. All were saved notwithstanding the imminent peril. The sheet of ice had been detached from the main body by the ice cutters.

*January 12th.* Congress is doing but little. The slave question is the all-absorbing subject. Calhoun is expected soon to be out with his manifesto, to be spread before the committee of fifteen where it may possibly be shorn of some of its points. With our over-zealous free soilers on the one hand & the heated advocates for slavery on the other, the Union is in more danger than at any former period. In a few days, we shall have more light on the subject. May we be preserved from Civil War!

Some Catholics have held a meeting in N.Y. to invite Pope Pius 9th to take refuge in the U.S. He will not be likely to accept—as Pope he had better tarry in Europe. Wherever he may pitch his tent, he will find himself shorn of his former High Supremacy.

*January 13th.* The accounts from Europe brought up to the 1st Jany. speak of Louis Napoleon having been duly installed Pres. of the French Republic & his ministry formed & it is further apparent that the cause of Democracy is waning on the Continent, mainly owing to the intemperate zeal of its advocates. These Red Republicans in France have already organized in opposition to the new government.

The cholera prevails in Scotland & is making its way in London. We hear no more of it in N.Y. & from N. Orleans the reports are more favourable.

I perceive by this morning's paper that on the 26th at a meeting of the Mercantile Library Co., they have had before them & caused to be published the correspondence—consisting of a single Letter from the com. of the Board & my brief reply from Calcon Hook—respecting my portrait & that they passed on me a highly flattering resolution. However unmerited, it cannot be otherwise than gratifying to have met the approbation of this respectable portion of my fellow citizens, being as it is the spontaneous production of their own free will.

*January 17th.* While the cholera is abating in N. Orleans & the waters of the Miss., the California fever abates nowhere. An enumeration is published of the adventurers from Boston, N.Y. & Philada., amounting to nearly 2300. Some go by the route of Chagres & Panama & across the Isthmus, the greater number sail round Cape Horn—among them are miners, carpenters, bricklayers, jewelers & various other mechanics & clerks. From Valparaiso & other S. American ports & the Polynesian Isles, all are hurrying on, expecting to realize fortunes.

*January 23d.* Commodore Jones, of the U.S. Navy, writes officially from California to our Government confirming in extenso the published accounts of the Gold Region, adding that lumps of gold weighing 1, 2 & 3 lbs. each have been found & he was informed of two pieces, one of them weighing 16 lbs., the other 25 lbs. No wonder people are crazed on the subject & that vessel after vessel is daily departing with hearts to gather the rich harvest.

*March 27th.* Having inadvertantly skipt a leaf, I have concluded to fill up the pages thus made vacant, by copying a memorandum made years ago on a loose sheet & thus occasion its more sure preservation. I may have done it before—no matter, a repetition can do no harm & may insure the record from oblivion & prove interesting to others who succeed me. The facts are derived from authentic sources.

Oliver Cope was born in the village of Auburne, Wiltshire & emigrated to Penna. about the year 1682. Being a farmer, he purchased land on Naaman's Creek, New Castle County, Delaware, then the lower counties governed by Wm. Penn. How long Oliver dwelt there the writer cannot tell. His son John, my grandfather, was born there in 1691. He had a brother Wm. who went to Virginia & from whom from that time little appears to have been known to the family, but several of the name of Cope appear to have been proprietors of land in that province.

Smith mentions them among the Proprietors of the Colony. John removed to Bradford Township, Chester County, where a number of his descendants still reside & where he died in 1773, having offspring viz:

| | | | | |
|---|---|---|---|---|
| Hannah | born 1724 | deceased 10 mo. | 10, | 1817 |
| Samuel | born 1726 | deceased 9 mo. | 20, | 1817 |
| Mary | born 1728 | deceased 2 mo. | 3, | 1813 |
| John | born 1730 | deceased 7 mo. | | 1812 |
| Nathan | born 1733 | deceased 12 mo. | 3, | 1820 |
| Caleb ⎫ twins | born 1736 | deceased 5 mo. | 30, | 1824 |
| Joshua ⎭ | born 1736 | deceased | | 1813 |
| Joseph | born 1739 | deceased 10 mo. | 11, | 1820 |

John, my grandfather, appears to have been thrice married. He was first married in his 19th year. His wife died in childbed & her infant also. Of her name & parentage no record appears to have been preserved.

In 1721, he married Charity Evans, a widow, the daughter of Robert Jeffries, by whom he had 9 children. The first born was a female who died between 3 & 4 years of age. The remaining offspring are the 8 enumerated in the statement herein made. When Charity died, I can find no record, but in 1740, John married Elizabeth Fisher, a widow by whom he left no offspring. The certificates of these two last marriages are now in my possession.

When I arrived at the age of manhood, my Uncles spelled their name with 2 o's—Coope—as did also my father for many years. But on recovery of some property in Philada., the title to which the family derived direct from Wm. Penn, I discovered that great grand father Oliver used but one o—Cope. The only explanation I had of the change came from Uncle John Cope, who said that when Grandfather & his brother William were school boys, their teacher instructed them to use two o's—Coope.

The eight children of Grandfather Cope with the exception of Mary were all married & left offspring. She remained single. Uncle John used facetiously to·say that he had 13 sons & every one of them had two sisters. He first resided near the borders of Chester & Lancaster Counties in this State, but removed with his numerous family to Redstone Fayette Co. where he settled his several sons on good farms & there several of the flock still live, others of them having fleeted into the State of Ohio.

The German Copes of Philada. are not of our family—their German name being Gaab, which they converted into Cope, which one of their

number, surnamed Godfrey, told me was the English of it. That family has become numerous in the City.

*March 10th*. March has fairly set in now, with a pleasant mood too, a brilliant sky & roaring Nor'wester.

Notwithstanding the unanimous vote of the Kentucky House of Reps. not to discard slavery, a Letter is published from that distinguished statesman Henry Clay, dated New Orleans, Feby. 17, 1849, where he had gone on a visit, recommending its abolition in unmistaken terms. He disapproves of the system in the abstract & shews clearly that it is injurious to the State. He does not wish a sudden, but a gradual emancipation. Without admitting or denying the inferiority of the African race, he says that "if it be inferior, that don't justify our reducing them to slavery, for admitting it to be true, we then might exercise the same power over any inferior race of whites."

His plan is to fix on a day certain, after which all that are born should be free at a specified age, all born before it remain slaves for life, the free to be sent to Africa; in order to defray the expense of transportation, to be bound out to service for a term not exceeding three years. The fund thus provided for each individual would, besides paying his passage, be sufficient to maintain him in his new abode for six months, after which he could support himself by labour or handicraft. Will Kentucky be wise enough to adopt some such scheme?

This profound statesman has been elected by the Kentucky Legislature, a Senator for six years, commencing the 4th March, where he has heretofore served his country with ability & great popularity. What effect this Letter will have on the citizens of his State is to be yet witnessed. The existing Constitution of Kentucky does not authorize the extinction of slavery—the present object is so to modify it at their approaching Convention as to authorize the measure.

Slavery would long since have ceased in that State had it not been for the folly of our anti-slavery people, who passed such resolutions that the citizens became alarmed & thought those zealots designed to set the slaves to cutting the throats of their masters.

*March 13th*. A suit is now on trial before Judge Burnside of the Supreme Court in which Morgan Hinchman, a member of our Society, is plaintiff & all the Managers, Stewards & Physicians of the Friends Asylum near Frankford are defendants. Morgan was committed to that Asylum on the plea of insanity & he sues for damages, claiming to have been sane but persecuted. His friends should, if practicable, have prevented this exposure, for the best apology that could be made for his brutal conduct toward his wife would be mental derangement. He is either a bad man or a mad man—perhaps a mixture of both.

*March 17th.* We had a family gathering to tea this evening, not in honour of Saint Patrick, but to welcome under our roof John Haines, of Germantown, who is engaged to Mary, daughter of son Henry. There were in attendance the Guest & his betrothed, son H. & wife, his sons F. & T., the wife of the former & the betrothed of the latter & son Wm. Also N.N. Stokes & David Roberts & wife of N.J.—the 3 latter coming accidentally on a visit, spending the night with us. Son A. was necessarily absent. We were pleased with the Guest, with whom we had previously a slight acquaintance. He sustains an unexceptionable character, is in prosperous circumstances & his connections are respectable. The time passed pleasantly—the entertainment closed with Ice Cream, now so common & so refreshing & the company separated seasonably without a particle of Irish merry making.

The New Yorkers have a saying that St. Patrick usually comes down the Hudson River on floating ice, whereas, not having his steam up, the Emerald Saint remains firmly anchored in his winter quarters, while Pius 9th has too much business on hand at Gaeta to come to his relief. The Fates are against both. The fact is that Popes & Saints are not exactly in fashion & as to the Fates, they have been out of service "long time ago."

*March 26th.* Received a Letter dated 24th from my old friend Meredith, Secy. of the Treasy., asking me to name some half dozen Friends from whom may be selected a Commissioner to proceed forthwith to Green Bay to make distribution of $40,000 among half breed Indians "in a manner designated by law." In a P.S. he adds, "If your health & convenience will permit you to go, I do not wish any other name." Very kind indeed to me, my waggish friend, Treasurer of the United States.

Have replied to my friend Meredith & have seen T. Wistar & Josiah Tatum of Friends Indian Committee who will meet & perhaps name some persons to me. Meanwhile, as M. in his appeal to me, says he wants just such a man as Joshua Redgauntlet, one of the heroes of Sir Walter Scott's fictions, I have in reply said to him, "Thankee for the preference tendered me, but I have no ambition to run the gauntlet with half breeds, red, black or white."

*April 2d.* Secy. W. M. Meredith has a Commission to me naming Thos. P. Cope, George Cadwalader, J. Pemberton, Hutchinson, Henry D. Gilpin of Philada. or any two of them.

*April 4th.* A splendid day. Went with my nephew Caleb Cope on a visit to his seat near Homesburg. Were accompanied by sons Wm. & Alfred & after spending some hours in the inspection of greenhouses, conservatories &c. and their rich contents, principally of exotics of every hue & form, together with ripe strawberries, peaches the size of hazel nuts, pease, beans & cucumbers fit for the table &c. &c. We returned to C.'s house in the City & dined.

One of the guests was asked by me how a certain measure of a public nature, in which he was concerned, has fared before the Legislature now in session. He replied, "Finding firm information not to be misunderstood that we should not succeed without money, we sent $1000 to Harrisburg & soon got our Bill passed."

So we are on the high road of bribery & corruption in this fair Republic of ours with which we charge the corrupt monarchies & aristocracies of Europe. Shame on our boastings & pretensions of superiority & purity. If such rogues in the gristle, what will be in the bone? I fear this declension of morals is not confined to our State, for corruption is said to have walked abroad in Washington, pending the last Presidency, to an alarming extent. I do not doubt it.

*April 7th.* The Czar of Russia has recalled his Ambassador to France, while the latter has recalled theirs to Russia & as the Russians have a large force on the borders of Poland, France is moving an army of observation on her frontiers. While Pius 9th is calling on the Catholic Powers to restore him to Rome & his temporal possessions, the Romans themselves resolve to resist by force & have created an army of 40,000 men.

*April 9th.* T. Wistar Jr. called on me & I gave him the Commission. Secy. Meredith being on a short visit to the City, I introduced T. to him. The Secy., on his return to Washington, is to send me a copy of the Menomonee Treaty for T.W.'s information. A little joking about my letter on running the Gauntlet & we parted with mutual good wishes. Few are more fond of a joke than M.

The case of Morgan Hinchman was this morning sent to the jury by Judge Burnside. It has occupied about 4 weeks & excited the community greatly. In the course of the argument, David Paul Brown & his coadjutor handled Friends without gloves & were insolent, Brown especially, using language referring to mind & soul, strongly bordering on impiety, which so pleased the crowded audience that, on the close of his argument, they caused the Court-room to ring with cheers for Brown, contrary to usage & propriety.

Brown said, "The Pope was a fool compared to a Quaker Overseer." His irreverent language when referring to the Deity, I do not attempt to quote. He is fluent, verbose, scurrilous, but not esteemed a well read lawyer. His extravagant habits have occasioned him to have been frequently sold out by the Sheriff. He gave $600 for a copy of Shakespeare & $3 a yard for linen to make his shirts. His father, Paul Brown, was a slop-shop Taylor & an honest man.

I have sold him many a piece of plains (7/8 wide stout cloth) for sailor's jackets. He lived on the east side of Front St. above High St. There was no yard to his house. His death was singular. He frequented the Wharf for purposes of nature. While in the act one night, he fell overboard & was drowned.

*April 10th.* Rec'd a very complimentary & friendly note from Benj. Rush, Esq., grandson of the celebrated Physician & son of Richard, our minister in Paris, on his having seen a sketch of my life—drawn up by Jas. R. Chandler, our Representative in the present Congress & published in *Hunt's Merchant Magazine*, accompanied by a likeness of my person, presumably taken from my portrait in the Mercantile Library.

*April 14th.* The jury in Hinchman's case have at last found a verdict in favour of Hinchman—damages $10,000. The defendants will of course appeal. 'Tis a shameful verdict evincing gross ignorance or gross prejudice, perhaps both. But Friends are not at present in good public odour.

*April 17th.* On arriving at my dwelling yesterday, our family Physician, Dr. Shallcross, was sent for & he placed me in bed, from whence I was not permitted to depart till 9 this morning, feeling myself much recruited by medicine & kind nursing.

*April 23d.* Among the interesting events of the day is the departure from N. York for Calfornia of 2 vessels—the first, the *Crescent City,* having on board a number of Ladies for California; the second, the Ship *Angeline,* with Ladies bound direct for San Francisco, under the direction of a female named Farnham.

The Narrator exclaims, "We look upon this feminine migration to our brilliant & promising State of California as one of the most gratifying (to say nothing of pretty features) in the gold excitement. Their influence on the already savage-tending miners must be as beneficial as delightful."

They are unmarried young women of respectable families & of irreproachable characters, yet it is certainly a very extraordinary adventure, occupying months of sea life & a passage round Cape Horn of 3500 miles. May the Almighty be their Guide & Protector at sea & on land.

*April 28th.* Riot in Montreal. The Parliament House burnt by the mob, together with public Records—originated probably in jealousies between the French & English population.

*May 2d.* A grand parade yesterday of Firemen. I heard, but did not see it. This morning's paper states that one Company, on passing thro' Moyamensing, was attacked by an armed band of rowdies formerly called "Killers," now "Stingers"—wounds & bruises the consequences, but no lives lost. The night previous, lamps, gas pipes &c. were destroyed by those ruffians. The Civil Authorities of the District are culpably remiss in duty.

*May 3d.* A large meeting of citizens was held last night at the Chinese Museum, Jos. R. Ingersoll in the chair, to forward additional subscriptions to the Pa. R. Road. A good spirit is said to have prevailed. Ward Coms. were appointed & no doubt the necessary funds will be supplied.

Previous to this meeting, I added 80 shares to my subscription, thus constituting me a holder of 500 shares. A much less addition from others will prove sufficient to finish the work. There is in the Act of incorporation a provision authorizing—in time of war—the transportation of military stores on the Road at half price. As the Act was not published when the subscriptions were first taken, this provision was known but to a few & has been the cause of uneasiness to Friends who had subscribed. But should the privilege ever be claimed, Friends can then withdraw & leave the Road to others, should it be found impracticable to have the Law altered.

*May 4th.* Anonymous Letters, purporting to proceed from a friendly source, were two days ago addressed thro' the Post Office to the Authorities of Frankford, Germantown, Richmond & Kensington, stating that attempts would be made to burn Friends Asylum for the

Insane, on a certain night, in consequence of which the Sheriff called out an armed posse & proceeded to the premises. No attempt was made & doubts may reasonably be entertained whether the affair may not be a hoax, got up by Morgan Hinchman or his coadjutors, merely to worry Friends.

*May 7th.* France has dispatched a force to Civita Vecchia to reinstate Pius 9th on his throne at Rome. How they will dispose of the liberal Government there is not made manifest, but liberalism seems on the wane in Europe.

Tom Paine said, among many bad things, some truths. He said we could not unlearn what we had learned. The people of Rome have a taste of liberty & will not forget it, tho' it may be smothered for a time. Can the frippery, puerility, bigotry & false claims to purity & infallibility be ever restored in fullness to Popery?

*May 10th.* A German named Houftaling near Binghamton, while ploughing, was so overcome with liquor that he fell into a furrow. His son, about eight years old, perceiving what had happened, took an axe & chopped off his head—assigning as a reason that his father had whipped him the evening before.

*May 11th.* Rec'd a gold piece for one Dollar, coined at the mint, Philada., from California gold—the first emission. 'Tis a beautiful coinage, very liable to be counterfeited & from its small size, to be lost.

The first Congress of Roman Catholic Bishops, held in these United States, is now in session in Baltimore.

*June 8th.* A Letter from Jas. Hubbard hailing from Raysville County, Indiana, having removed from Richmond. Seems inclined to fix himself on me as a regular pensioner. He is building & lacks money to finish his House. I suppose I must assist him. He also lacks delicacy, can I cure him of that? 'Twould be difficult, I trow.

*August 26th.* Eighty-first birthday today. Root unsound—trunk shattered, branches withering, the tree cannot much longer last. The great Husbandman may spare it a little longer until saying, "Why covereth it the ground? Cut it down as useless." When He shall be pleased to issue the mandate, may I be prepared cheerfully to obey the call.

*September 11th.* Weather is fine—& has been so for several days. Mercury about 50 at sunrise. Sun bright, pleasantly warm as the day advances. Many blessings does our Heavenly Father confer upon us His favoured children. While afflicted Europe has been drenched with blood & contest, we are in the enjoyment of peace & prosperity—no potent Tyrant to place yokes of iron on our necks & fetters on our feet, every man enjoying in peace the fruits of his labour & none to make him afraid. Even that dread pest, the Cholera, has dealt mercifully with us.

Ever since our return to the City, except for domestics, I & dear wife have been living alone—our sons H. & A. & others of the family occasionally taking a meal with us & sometimes a bed. We cannot ride out as has been our custom, one of our two horses being lame & in charge of the Farrier. Nevertheless, we get along comfortably for old people.

*September 13th.* For weeks, perhaps months, there has been reason to suspect that men have been enlisting & training secretly in the U.S. for an attack on the Island of Cuba, having in view the annexation of that Island to our Republic. Orders to frustrate the movement have been issued by our Pres. & several vessels on the eve of sailing have been seized & are in custody. The Cubans themselves have originated the scheme.

*September 14th.* The House of Refuge for Coloured Delinquents still dragging for want of means. I am induced, in addition to a former gift, to make them an advance of a considerable sum to enable them to complete the building & I now hope it may be opened the approaching winter for the reception of inmates. The advance is secured by a mortgage on the premises.

Sally, daughter of the late Judge Peters, dropt in & dined with us. Her gift of tongue has not failed, neither hath her familiarity with the renowned of this great world of fashion, in this great City, great Commonwealth & still greater Union. She had a fancy for a walk in our garden & a bouquet, so I plucked her one made up of tamarisk, peryanthus in full berry, cutting off some of the thorns, roses, &c. &c. After this gleaning, she bid good-bye to favour some others with her presence. She, a lone maiden, was once a great belle but, having weathered over three score winters, her beauty is rather on the wane, but I do not undertake to say she thinks so.

Then came in that nondescript Elliott Cresson, who is troubled that the Board should have elected a Pres. of the Pa. R. Road without consulting him. He had moreover a paper for me to sign—a recommendation couched in glowing terms in favour of some friend of his, to Gen. Taylor, for any foreign Embassy to fill of which the Pres. might stand in need. But as I had never before known the individual, I declined the honour of setting my signature—at which he marvelled, as he knew him well. This folly of certifying to characters & facts of another of whom you are personally unknown is quite too common & tends not a little to discredit testimony. In truth, utterly wrong & discreditable.

*September 21st.* J.J. Barclay, Thos. Earp & myself called on Gov. Johnston at the U.S. Hotel to invite him to visit the House of Refuge, old & new. He agreed to accompany us on the morning of the 24th. He was surrounded with company & rec'd us courteously. He is about six feet high, stout in proportion & florid complexion. I told him I could say to him, as I did to his predecessor, Gov. Shunk, that I ask not office for myself or any friend, but asked of him the favour "not to set all the rogues loose upon us"—at which he smiled assent & the company present laughed heartily.

*September 22d.* A deputation of four citizens waited on me & urged me to become a candidate for Select Council, which of course I declined. They wished to place me on what they call an Independent Ticket, but I will not serve on any. There will be a split among the Whigs in the City. Swift, the Mayor, has become unpopular. Chas. Gilpin, who aspires to be his successor, is as little liked as himself. There however will be other candidates.

*September 24th.* Gov. Johnston visited by invitation—accompanied by J.J. Barclay, Thos. Earp & myself—the two Houses of Refuge. In the old House he made short but pertinent addresses, first to the boys & then to the girls. Partaking of a cold collation, he then visited the unfinished buildings now nearly completed for the coloured race, with all of which he expressed his satisfaction.

Gov. Johnston is a pleasant man—manners popular, assuming no false dignity. A lawyer by profession.

*September 25th.* Our grandson T.P. Cope, Jr., son of Henry, passed meeting today at the Northern District Meeting House with Eliz. W., daughter of John Stokes, with the full approbation of all their connections & friends. They are well fitted to make each other happy. May God's blessing rest upon them. The extraordinary man Saml. Leeds was present & spoke acceptably in both sittings. His quotations from Scriptures are correct & pertinent—he deals not in harsh epithets or fault-finding, but generally in the language of encouragement.

*September 27th.* T. Wistar & Alfred left yesterday for Washington to render an account of their Indian doings. T. has a Letter from Secy. Meredith asking if he will go to the Choctaws—if not, to consult me on the selection of some other person.

*October 1st.* After a considerable drought, rain commenced yesterday, continuing thro' the night & all this day.

A visit from Jos. Jones & his nephew J.R. Baker who wish to make interest for a friend of theirs to be U.S. Agent for the removal of a remnant of the Chickasaw Indians from Tennessee, where they have no land & wander as vagabonds, to join their brethren west of the Miss., saying that they are informed that Gen. Taylor will appoint the person I may recommend.

There must be some mistake, as I possess no such information & have no disposition to volunteer my services. Moreover, there are no Chickasaws to remove—the whole tribe being already seated west of the Miss. on lands which they cultivate, growing cotton &c. as do the whites by the help of slaves, having due to them, in public U.S. Loans, a million & a half Dollars.

There are, however, a scattered body of Choctaws answering the given description, which the Government is desirous to send to their brethren in the Indian Territory.

*October 2d.* Judge Parsons, in his charge to the Grand Jury, recommends that the City & Districts should be united in one Corporation & in respect of the Fire Department, advocates the same plan I proposed to Councils—to take the department entirely into their hands, appointing the Firemen & constituting them Police officers. By these measures he thinks an end would be put to the riots so disgraceful to the community. Will politicians permit these improvements, so essential to our peace, to our reputation & the security of property?

A note from Jos. Jones in commendation of his friend Henry M. Scott, the person who offers his agency for the removal of the Choctaw Indians. I have nothing direct from Govt. on the subject & it is probable, shall not.

*October 5th.* Worried with the Politicians. Two separate visits this morning urging services. Am resolved not to be again dragged into public life nor into the scuffle of party. I long for repose.

*October 8th.* Tomorrow will be held the general election for Penna. Am puzzled to know what ticket to vote for Mayor & City Councils.

*October 9th.* I have this day practiced one of the Christian virtues by returning good for evil. I have voted for Chas. Gilpin who, when I was in Select Council, made it a rule to oppose every liberal measure of mine. The feverish pleasure he indulged in thwarting others may lead to a rigorous execution of the Laws against rogues & violations of the City Ordinances.

*October 10th.* A fire commenced about 9 last evening & the alarm bell is still ringing now at 9 this morning. It commenced in St. Mary St. near Cedar St. by an attack of the "Killers" on a Beer House, 6th & St. Mary's, which they destroyed. The flames spread to contiguous buildings & when Engines arrived, they were not permitted to play, but were shot at & one man was shot down from one of them.

Many shots took place during the night which we distinctly heard from our chamber. The blaze so lighted our back premises & the sparks so flew in the air near us as to alarm my family.

*October 11th.* Chas. Gilpin has been defeated by a small majority & Joel Jones is Mayor Elect. I am glad of the result. It is a well merited rebuke. His fellow townsman of Wilmington, D., Chas. Gibbons, lately representing the City in the State Senate, could not protect him. They are of a kidney. This last Chas. grossly misrepresented us while in power, refusing compliance with instruction from his constituents, especially in opposing the Bill incorporating our Great Pa. R. Road.

The military who had possession of the Riot district withdrew a short time yesterday, when the "Killers" reappeared & fired off several guns, as if in defiance. The military are again on the ground & find none to oppose them. The "Killers," no doubt, have spies.

*October 12th.* As I passed to visit the Schools on Pine St., I saw several black men in a cluster, Pine & 6th. On the corner opposite was an armed guard of soldiers. I admonished these blacks to retire quietly to their homes & not thus to invite aggression, for it seems the demolished House, 6th & St. Mary's, was kept by a negro, but they little regarded my friendly hint & still kept their station.

Several of the rioters were examined yesterday before Mayor Swift & committed for trial, among them George Hosey, coloured & well known as a bad character. Proof was made that he was seen deliberately taking aim at individuals, among whom was Cornelius Spell from the Engine, while playing on the fire & fell dead. Were Hosey a white man he might escape; as it is, he will probably expiate his career of crime on the Gallows.

*October 14th.* Gov. Morehead of N. Carolina called to see me. He is one of a commission to examine the various Asylums for the Insane preparatory to the erection of one in their State.

Dr. Kirkbride of the Penna. Hospital had an attempt on his life a few days ago by a lunatic named Wiley Williams. The weapon used in the attempt was a large Duck gun, so heavily charged that, in firing, the lock burst. The Doctor a short time previously received a letter from Williams dated Richmond, Va., in which this man said he was coming to shoot him for saying he was crazy & which he could effect with impunity under the plea of being insane. It appears that he, unperceived, scaled the wall with a rope & fixed himself on a tree where Dr. K., seeing him, asked what he was going to do & the maniac answered, "to shoot you." Dr. K. turned away & was advancing towards the building when he received on the head a large Duck ball, penetrating the bone but not entering the brain. It was extracted & the wound is not deemed dangerous.

*October 17th.* Elizabeth, wife of Thomas Smith, School House Lane, Germantown, dined with us. A lively, zealous, kind-hearted body—a Catholic devotee. He, if anything, a quiet Episcopalian. She wants a subscription for the new Catholic Establishment, the St. Joseph Hospital, at Green Hill. It professes to be for the free admission of patients of every denomination, but is attended solely by a Catholic Sisterhood, with the Catholic Bishop of the diocese, for the time being, at the head. Under this cardinal arrangement, I did not feel it my duty to contribute, deeming the Institution a school for proselytism. The Catholics are aiming at the ascendence among us, their chapels & seminaries springing up in every direction over our country. Aside to her bigoted devotion to her sect & its superstitions, Elizabeth is a pleasant companion —subject to occasional constitutional deep depressions of spirits from which she awakens full of mirth & glee. While dining, a person at the table spoke of a contemplated match between a man & a female, the male old enough to be her father, an affair that the narrator vehemently condemned. "Nonsense," exclaimed E. briskly, "I think nothing of that, I had rather be an old man's darling than a young man's slave."

*October 21st.* Feel forcibly the necessity of daily help from above to protect me from error. Conscious of my inability to do so myself, my Heavenly Father has dealt mercifully with me my whole life. May He be pleased to vouchsafe His protection & guidance the few remaining days allotted to my pilgrimage.

*October 25th.* The accounts from Ireland are distressing. The potato rot is extensive, threatening misery to the poor, while the taxes render the middle class less able to assist them. Many of the latter are escaping from the country to the U. States.

*October 31st.* T. Wistar Jr. spent last evening with us, conversing on Indian matters. He is undecided to accept an agency from the Government to the Chickasaws. He & Alfred go this morning to Washington, principally in relation to their late embassy to the half-breed Menomonees.

*November 2d.* Our grand-daughter Clementine from Susquehanna Co. came last evening to continue her education. Edward, son of Alfred, is also at Friends Select School—takes dinner with us & returns to his father's to lodge.

The Kentucky Convention has decided on the continuance of slavery in the State, although slaveholders are only about ¼ of the inhabitants. This is probably caused by the intemperate zeal of the non-slave holders of the Free States. Well, a day of retribution will come. Slavery, by consent or by force, must end in these United States, but power over right is at present in fashion. From the cradle to the grave, the unregenerated man is a Tyrant & loves to Lord it over his fellows.

Applications for money to redeem slaves are almost of daily occurrence & are well calculated to excite our sympathy. But doubts sometimes arise whether slaveholders may not find it convenient thus to dispose of their slaves. The plea for the slaves, by the applicant for money, is frequently that the slave had absconded, was caught by his owner & unless redeemed—& mostly at a high price—would be forever separated from his wife & family & sold into a distant state.

I have now before me an appeal of which the statement is that a man & his wife, in an attempt to run away, were caught & unless $1300 were paid for their redemption, they would be separated—the husband sold into one state, the wife into another. This may be true but it may also be a deception, on the part of the master, to make sale of a worthless slave; but in no event is it possible for citizens of the free state to purchase & emancipate all the slaves in the Union. The thing is impossible. By the census of 1840, there were then three millions of slaves in our country & some hundreds of thousands have since been added. Valuing them at $200 a head—a price the holders would deem too low—the total would amount to seven hundred millions of Dollars! A sum it would be rather difficult to command.

*November 6th.* At a stated meeting of the Board today, we appointed the following officers for the House of Refuge for the coloured children. Thos. W. Summers, Superintendent; Jas. H. McBride, Doorkeeper; George Birmingham, watchman; E. H. Toland, Matron; Anna M. McPhail, assistant Matron; Mary Howard, second assistant; Maria Smith, nurse; & Physician Ellerslee Wallace. There were for Superintendent 70 applications, for the other offices not so numerous. All were sifted by a large committee & reported to the Board, who approved their report unanimously. The Refuge is to open first of next year. Of the successful candidates I know not one, so that I cannot be charged with partiality.

*November 10th.* The Grand Jury, just discharged, have recommended the same plan that I urged on our City Councils to assume the Fire Department & to constitute the Firemen Police officers & also recommended the scheme of connecting the City & Districts into one body for Police purposes.

*November 13th.* My grandson, of my name, was married this day at Friends Meeting House, North District, to E.W., daughter of John Stokes. Their residence will be 272 Pine St., so that it happens singularly enough that Thos. P. Cope & Elizabeth Waln Cope live at 272 Pine St. & Thos. P. Cope & Elizabeth Waln Cope live at 272 Spruce St. Mistakes will doubtless arise. May the blessing of God rest on the young couple & their days be as bright as the day they were happily united, which was brilliant indeed—not a cloud was visible & the temperature most exhilarating. The wedding guests, about 70 in number, were well selected—conversation was cheerfully maintained, nothing occurred to mar enjoyment & the party separated about 10 P.M.

The Overseers, George G. Williams & wife, John Lippincott & Rachel Cresson, joined cheerfully in the festivities on this occasion so that I am in hopes they will not report the wedding to have been disorderly accomplished, because the company indulged in Ice Cream as was the case at a similar occasion in Moorestown, N.J., reported to the Meeting by E.R., one of the Overseers—he never having seen the like before & George Fox, when he was married, had no Ice Cream served to the guests.

*November 16th.* The Ministry of Louis Bonaparte have all resigned They were not sufficiently submissive to his will. He'll win the horse or lose the saddle.

*November 17th.* The Ship *Tuscarora*, the largest & best of the line of Packets, went ashore in the night on the beach a few miles south of Cape Henlopen. Steamers have been sent to her assistance. She has 450 passengers & a cargo of merchandize from Liverpool. The weather being favourable, she may be got off. If lost, it will be a heavy disappointment & injury to H. & A. Cope & Co., to whom she belongs. She lies near where the *Swatara* of this port was wrecked last year.

*November 19th.* The Telegraph account published this morning says the *Tuscarora* is bilged with 16 feet of water in her hold, so she will prove a total loss.

I hope my sons may bear this heavy destruction of property with Christian fortitude. I confess, it preys on my spirit this dull day. They will have many sympathizers. This costly Ship had not her equal in our Port & probably not in the Union.

The same paper announces a most melancholy steam boat explosion at N. Orleans. The *Louisiana*, Capt. Kennon, for St. Louis, was just pulling out from the levee as the steamers *Storm* & *Boston* were coming in, the decks of all three crowded with passengers, boats side by side, when an explosion took place on board the *Louisiana* & 200 persons were instantly destroyed & many others badly wounded. The scene is described as horrible—scattered limbs & bodies mangled being strewed over the ground & on the water, the screeches of the wounded being heart rending. The Capt. of the *Louisiana* was arrested & held to $8000 in bail, the explosion being attributed to carelessness.

Great as will be the loss of my sons, it is less to be deplored than this loss of life & the misery entailed on survivors. The loss of this Ship will, however, make a serious inroad on the means of H. & A. Cope & Co., but H. tells me that they have been so successful, they can bear it—certainly it cannot now be avoided. It has been permitted, doubtless, for wise purposes & may teach the House a lesson not to be forgotten.

It is the 3d Ship they have lost. On the *Algonquin*, they had no insurance at all. On the *T. P. Cope*, partial insurance & on the *Tuscarora*, valued at $80,000, which is much under her cost, they had insured but $40,000. Men are prone to envy & harsh reasoning & H. & A. Cope & Co. may gain the reputation of odd, imprudent Traders. It is however, to me, a consolation that they can pay all demands on them & continue their business which, with the exceptions above, have by the blessing of Providence been very successful & it is to me a great happiness to know

that they sustain, and deservedly, a good reputation among men, and what is infinitely more important, walk in the fear of God.

*November 20th.* The wreck of the *Tuscarora* will fall more heavily on F. & T.P.C., Jr., just setting out in the world, than on their Father or Uncle, who have acquired property, but they possess talents & worth.

> When things are done & past recalling
> 'Tis folly or to fret or cry
> Prop up a rotten house that's falling
> But when it's down, e'en let it lie.

*November 21st.* The passengers by the Ship were all safely landed, 470 in number. Most of them saved their baggage & such as have not may hope to do so, the Ship still remaining entire. They were brought to the City by steamboat, a few of them behaving unruly. The dry goods are loading into schooners & are partially damaged. Iron & hardware will be got out & removed, of course damaged. Salt, washed away. The wreckers hope to float the Ship again—my fears are against hope—much difficulty occurred in landing the passengers, boat after boat being staved in the attempt. At length an empty barrel, with rope attached, was floated ashore by means of which all were got on shore, but wet to their middle. Not a child, of which many were on board, was lost or injured. Praises to the Almighty.

*November 23d.* A fright & disaster. Previously to dining with the new bride & groom at son Henry's, my E. & self rode out. While jogging on in Broad St. opposite the Rising Sun, one of our horses, a fractious animal, by running & kicking broke both of his traces & injured the front of the carriage. By the skill of our coachman aided by others who promptly seized the animal, we made our escape from the carriage. Broad St. being a great thoroughfare, my E. found a passage home with one of our neighbours & while I was trudging on foot, a countryman in a waggon, well stowed with marketing bound to the City, overhauled & called to me by name, offering me a seat amidst his truck, of which kindness I accepted till we reached Callowhill Market, whence I coursed the rest of the way, partly by an omnibus, with thankful heart towards the Preserver of men for our deliverance from threatened destruction.

*December 3d.* At 10 P.M. met the stockholders of the Pa. R.R. at their annual meeting. Just on the eve of my going, I was served with notice to attend Court as an Executor of S. Girard, stated to be at the suit of Henry Simpson, administrator of George Simpson. 'Tis the first notice of such suit, tho' the notice has the caption "July term 1849." I could not obey on such a short notice. It looks like a trick—no time being given to consult counsel or my fellow Executors.

*December 13th.* Intelligence from the Ship discouraging. Two steam pumps cannot free her. A vessel with empty oil casks has reached her from N. York but the casks cannot be forced under the lower deck on account of the water. They are designed to float on its surface, the air within them keeping the fluid from rising. The next effort is to force a sheet under the Ship to stay the further entrance of the water. That would be easily done were she afloat, but—grounded as she is—to work the sheet under her is a job passing my comprehension. Her weight, increased by the weight of the water, must render the success extremely doubtful.

*December 14th.* My grandson F.R. Cope explains in what way the cotton canvas is expected to operate on the *Tuscarora.* This sheet instead of 180 is to be 380 feet long, so as to reach quite round the Ship, her length being 180 feet. The lower edge of the sheet is to be in bag form & that filled with sand to sink the sheet to the bottom. Then the pumps are to commence operations. As the water in the hold is thus passed it will occasion a suction which it is hoped will press the canvas against the break in the Ship's bottom, the empty casks meanwhile floating in the water within. Should this process terminate successfully, appliances will be made to move the Ship from her bed in the sand onto her element, the ocean. I hope this plan may answer & that the Ship may be restored to her station in the Liverpool Line of Packets.

*December 22d.* A storm accompanied by rain—wind NE. The swell may assist in getting off the Ship & may injure her afterwards.

An agent from California is at Washington with the Constitution from that State, asking its ratification by Congress. A deputation from the Mormons, who have cut out from the vast wilderness west of the Rocky Mountains a State for themselves, is also knocking at the door for admission. Slavery will not, by consent of the applicants, be permitted in either State & the South threatens that if expressly excluded, the Union will be dissolved. Yet these vast regions are not adapted to slavery. They do not compare with India, where in effect the mass are but slaves, but are to be peopled by the race of Saxons, fitted to the soil & climate.

Notwithstanding the population of India, there abound in that country great tracts uninhabited by man. A British officer on a hunting excursion states the extent of the forest he visited as a strip of low, level land lying along the provinces of Oude & Bakar, nearly seven hundred miles in length & varying from 10 to 15 miles in breadth. The pine, the oak, rattan & bamboo, all of enormous size, abound—the elephant, rhinoceros, Tygers &c. having exclusive possession.

*December 26th.* Yesterday was a cold Christmas. At 4 A.M. the thermometer was 20 & at night 16.

*December 27th.* The weather moderated, mercury 8 A.M. 30, noon 43—clear & calm. Ship not off yet.

*December 28th.* Attachment to the union of the states should be habitually fostered in every American heart. For more than half a century during which Kingdoms & Empires have fallen, this Union has stood unshaken. The patriots who formed it have long since descended to the grave, yet still it remains a proud monument to their memories & a proud object of affection & admiration with every one worthy to bear the American name. In my judgement, its dissolution would be the greatest of calamities & to avert that should be the study of every American. Upon its preservation must depend our own happiness & that of countless generations to come. Whatever dangers may threaten it, I shall maintain it in its integrity to the full extent of the obligations imposed & the power conferred upon me by the Constitution.

*December 31st.* The Board having on the 29th resolved to open the house for coloured delinquents, House of Refuge, this day a meeting of citizens took place at 11 P.M. at the building, when Judge Kelly of the criminal court addressed the audience in an eloquent, appropriate speech occupying more than an hour. The apartment was well filled—6 or 8 coloured men attended. The day was pleasant. The ground is covered 3 to 4 inches with snow & sleighs move briskly. 'Tis an era in the history of the coloured race that may prove a blessing to their offspring in Philada. Judge K. spoke without notes.

The *Tuscarora* is still unmoved. It being full moon & consequently the swell greatest, it was hoped she would have been got off last night. It was discovered that the steam pumps would not do service & the attempt was not made. It is but another instance of mismanagement. Nothing further can be done until other pumps can be sent from N. York.

# 1850

*January 4th.* Met the Managers of the Deaf & Dumb Asylum.

*January 5th.* At the House of Refuge the annual report was read & approved. Cost of the Asylum for the coloured race is $68,000 which is $18,000 over the estimate. $11,000 are still needed to pay the balance. The Directors of the Mercantile Library Co. met & the annual report read & adopted. The Institution flourishing—new catalogue in hands of the printer. The election soon follows & 'tis understood an opposition ticket will be got up.

*January 7th.* Managers of Ridge Turnpike & then at Bank of N. A. to act as one of the judges of the election, in which capacity I have served for many years. The Bank is flourishing, having this day declared a semi-annual dividend of 5 per cent & 2 per cent extra, with a surplus of $200,000.

*January 12th.* Accounts from the Ship lead to the hope that the next swelling tide will set her once more afloat. The attempt will be made this evening if the tide prove high enough to warrant the trial. At 4 P.M. met the newly elected Managers of the House of Refuge. The members are the same as before. Returns of the election were read, committees re-appointed & report ordered to be printed. Memorial to the Legislature adopted & $16,000 to defray arrears &c. to be sanctioned. This is expected to be obtained from the Philada. Saving Fund.

*January 16th.* At a meeting at 12 o'clock, the Directors of N. A. Ins. Co. reelected Arthur G. Coffin, Pres.,—salary as before, $2,000 a year. Declined dining with them & to sup with Wm. E. Bowen, both from disinclination for such enjoyments while my Elizabeth is confined to her chamber by sickness—other causes also operating. My own health & advanced age may likewise be pleaded, conscious as I am of frailties both of body & mind, of which these sheets may be evidence enough.

A Telegraph after night states that the Ship has been moved some feet nearer deep water & requesting that the steamer *Goliath* of N.Y. should be sent to assist in moving her off & taking her to that City. Should the weather be propitious, we may now hope the *Tuscarora* will be saved.

*January 18th.* Have a letter from a family connection stating that on a late visit to Ohio, he had visited my cousin Sarah Johns, now 97 years old, eldest daughter of Uncle Nathan Cope. The writer says she is middling active on her feet & in possession of all her faculties & goes to meeting a distance of three miles, whenever the weather is favourable. So now I have two female cousins, Sarah Johns & Hannah Forsyth, each 97.

*January 28th.* The *Tuscarora* moves but slowly from off the strand. If ultimately saved it will be at an expense nearly equivalent to the cost of a new Ship.

*February 2d.* Congress continues to be agitated with the slave question to the injury of the public service. Two months have now been wasted on sectional & angry disputation.

*February 17th.* Jos. Patterson, Treas. of the House of Refuge, has returned to me several cancelled notes that I had issued from time to time for carrying on the new building for coloured delinquents, amounting together to $20,000. Besides this am't, I made the Institution a gift of $1600 & made it a loan of $13,000. I trust that when my colleagues erect a new building for the whites, they will not commence without previously providing the means. It is dull sailing, against wind & tide.

*February 18th.* Met the Board of Trade. 'Tis an active body, composed of active business men.

*March 27th.* At our monthly meeting, Orange St. today, John S. Haines of Germantown & my granddaughter Mary D. Cope declared their intention of marriage with each other. John's parents are deceased.

We contemplated spending a portion of the summer at Calcon Hook but Alfred wishes us to resume our station with him, which undoubtedly presents very strong inducements—his agreeable family—Henry's summer abode at Germantown close by—the healthfulness of the surrounding country—the various pleasant rides & the facility of access to & from the City.

A call from Captains Magruder & Turner of the United States Navy. They desire my opinion on the propriety of dispensing with corporal punishment on board Ships of war & request me to furnish them with my written opinion on the subject. This is a compliment, truly, to a man opposed to war & violence from principle in every shape & form & quite ignorant of the discipline usually enforced in the Navy.

To enlighten me, Captain Magruder placed in my hand a manuscript sheet written by himself. This is rather a delicate subject for me to meddle with.

When I established the first line of Packets between Philada. & Liverpool, I expressed to the Captains a wish to dispense with the practice of giving ardent spirits to their crews, being persuaded from experience that benefit would arise from the discontinuance. The Captains pled in answer that seamen accustomed to drink when ashore would not be content or do their duty at sea if deprived of their usual allowance of grog. At length the Captains agreed to try the experiment on my proposing to increase the wages of the men. The essay proved successful. But after some years the Captains stated that the men were often exposed to cold & wet without the opportunity of getting their clothes dry for weeks together & became weak & disheartened & unfit for duty, especially those accustomed to whiskey on shore, thus endangering Ship & Cargo together, with the lives of all on board, when a moderate dram would revive them & restore their activity. To which I answered, *It was not the use, but the abuse of liquor to which the prohibition* was intended to apply & they would, on such occasions, use their own best discretion in dealing out spiritous liquors medicinally, not as rations.

Thus matters were settled & remain, so far as I know. My son Henry, who is head of the House since I resigned, cooperated in these measures. The temperance has also come in aid of these reforms. If, in the Navy, they would carry out the same reform, the punishment of the cat & rope's end would soon grow out of fashion, altho' the application should by the Commander be deemed indispensable to the backs of thieves, burglars, highwaymen & such like rogues who are sometimes placed on board their Ships by public authority. Common sailors, these Captains say, they can easily manage—they do not require rigorous treatment—but some vagabonds such as here specified cannot be kept in order without flogging. To confine them is to exempt them from labour & put double duty on better men.

*March 28th.* An association is forming to be called "The Female Tailor Association," the object being to establish a ware room with materials for the employment of women who now work for tailors on such terms as scarcely afford them a decent living. It is a good, benevolent design & I shall cheerfully lend my aid. Females who work for the tailors receive from one fourth to one third of the price charged by their employers to their customers—an unjust system.

*July 1st.* The *Tuscarora*, with her old Captain, Turley, took her departure yesterday from New York to Liverpool, staunch & sound as when

launched from the stocks, having been repaired & fitted at the expense of $5,000.

*July 5th.* This morning my E. & self left home to tarry some weeks with Alfred, taking with us Rebecca Sorin, one of our domestics. We have just arrived in season to escape a thunder gust which came up five minutes after our arrival. The weather is sultry & not much relieved by the storm.

*July 6th.* At 6 o'clock this morning the mercury in Alfred's entry stood at 79.

After breakfast took a small neighbouring excursion. My E. is very weak, but I trust the country air will improve her health. At 2 P.M. the mercury in the open air reached 93.

*July 7th.* Attended meeting. The room pretty well filled; no inconsiderable part by citizens of Philadelphia, to whom Germantown has become very attractive from its healthiness & easy access. After meeting stopped a few minutes at son Henry's, where we met with his son Francis & wife & little daughter Elizabeth, who with T.P.C., Jr. & wife (now absent on a visit in N. Jersey) all have their summer residences under the same roof with Martha Pleasants, sister of Henry's wife.

Housebreaking has become so common that for the first time before leaving the City, I left my most valuable papers at the Bank of North America, to be placed in their vaults, altho' I have a fire proof in my dwelling, erected originally with the house.

*July 9th.* The office of the Gas Company, 7th below High Street, was entered at night & a circular hole as large as a hat crown was cut into the iron door of the fire proof & the money thence extracted. Bars & bolts seem to be of little avail against the night marauders. Some new contrivance must be adopted.

Pres. Taylor is so ill that fears for his recovery are entertained. His death would, at this time, prove a serious evil indeed.

Congress is still battling the Compromise Bill & the combatants are in no better humour with each other.

We took a ride to Germantown this morning & paid a short visit to Henry's family & to the farm of John S. Haines in the neighbourhood, on which he is erecting a convenient, neat dwelling, from which there is a distant view of the City & vicinity.

The heat of the weather has abated, but flies all day & some musketoes at night are no small annoyance.

*July 10th.* Sad tidings this morning, the death of Zachary Taylor & a most disastrous fire in Philada. Three hundred houses & twenty persons destroyed.

Pres. Taylor died yesterday at the seat of government after a short illness, brought on by eating freely of cherries. He departed in peace & expressed entire resignation, adding that he had doubtless committed many mistakes in the course of his life but that his intentions had always been honest. The demise of this great man at the present crisis is a calamity the extent of which it is difficult to estimate.

The cause of so many lives being lost in the fire was the explosion of salt petre stowed in a building in which the fire originated. Besides the killed, many others were so dreadfully mangled that their recovery is doubtful. The total loss of property is estimated at a million of Dollars. A considerable portion of the buildings were old & of comparatively little worth. Others were more modern & costly.

The fire commenced about 4½ P.M. & continued till towards midnight when, by the Divine favour, it was finally subdued.

It commenced in a store in Water Street above Sassafras, sweeping the blocks between Vine Street & Delaware Avenue to Second Street. We had a view of the blaze which rose high in the air & seemed not abated at 10 o'clock when we retired to rest. At eight this morning thick volumes of smoke are moving rapidly westward, the wind blowing from the east, as at the commencement.

Here will be room for the exercise of charity & sympathy. The papers state that in the midst of the confusion a gang of ruffians from Moyamensing were employed in pilfering the goods of the sufferers. Some of them were apprehended. They should receive exemplary punishment.

*July 11th.* The number of persons discovered to have been killed at the fire is 30 and wounded 100. Several others are missing. City Councils have appropriated $10,000 for the needy sufferers. Generally, those who were burnt out are able to bear their loss. A large amount was covered by insurance. The ground on which many of the old buildings stood is worth as much as it was before the fire & will be hereafter occupied by better buildings.

Gen. Taylor's cabinet have all resigned & Vice Pres. Millard Fillmore has been installed as Pres. of the United States.

*July 12th.* Among the many thrilling incidents that occurred at this fire, few if any can have occurred of a more exciting & affecting character than one which is related by Alexander Derbyshire, flour merchant, whose place of business is in Water above Mulberry St. & dwelling on the west side of Front below Vine St. When the explosion took place he ran to his home & found at the door the mangled & burnt bodies of 4 person over which he stumbled, one of which was the corpse of a child so charred that the arm dropt off when handled. On entering his yard to render aid in the removal of his furniture, he discovered a man in flames, stretched on the ground begging for water, while his sisters were employed in throwing buckets of water over him to extinguish the blaze from his clothing. There was no accounting for the man being there otherwise than that he must have been hurled into the air by the explosion of the salt petre & thrown over the house. His spine was fractured & his legs broken. Alexander placed the man in the custody of some others, to be conveyed to the Hospital, but it was not known that he reached that Asylum & if he did, he could not long have survived.

*July 13th.* In our morning's ride, we called on the family of the late Jacob S. Waln, School House Lane & found them very pleasantly situated—the widow had a more healthy appearance than any of the daughters. The wife of Jos. Ryers & his son by his former wife, sister of his present spouse, who has a sickly appearance, were present. Richard Vaux, who married one of the daughters of J.S.W., has taken a diminutive hut close by with the view, as it is understood, of becoming a candidate, in the approaching election, for Congress. A good natured Loco who will never set the world on fire.

We also called on Thos. & Elizabeth Smith, on the same Lane, both out of health. She again reminded me that her Bishop Kendrick tells her that the Quakers in their spiritual worship & faith, ceremonies excepted, are more like the Roman Catholics than any other religious denomination. Elizabeth can therefore, she tells me, extend the right hand of fellowship to Quakers, but to no other Christian denomination. Apropos, there is a split among the Catholics in Philada. The dissenters, mostly German, to the number of 1500, met in the City a few evenings ago & have published their faith to the world. They disclaim the supremacy of the Pope, deny auricular confession, claim the use of the Bible & allow Priests to marry.

Doubts have been expressed whether salt petre will explode as gunpowder. Several distinguished chemists have published that when wet with water & confined, a gas is generated which will cause explosion.

*July 19th.* A storm of wind & rain commenced here 6 A.M. yesterday, increasing in violence thro' the night. The gale abated this morning but the storm had not ceased up to 6 this morning—the rain gauge exhibits 4 inches & 2/10 of water, while rain is still falling. Trees have been blown over in some cases, limbs torn off in others, Indian corn & oates laid flat—doubtless damage on the seaboard & to our canals will be reported.

*July 20th.* In the midst of the gale, the ship *Wyoming*, Captain John Miercken, arrived safely from Liverpool, one of my sons' line of Packets.

*July 21st.* The house fly is here a pest. They make so free with the frontispiece that I have difficulty in the use of my pen. I should think that for one fly at my dwelling in the City, there are one hundred at Germantown & vicinity. They may be of service in keeping people from Meeting, but most certainly do not assist me in writing, rendering me service neither in my eyes, nose, cheeks or ears, with all of which they are more free than welcome. I shall dispense with further writing, there being neither profit nor honour in a war with flies, as experience to my cost. I yield the field therefore to my active, persevering foe, content to make my retreat before all my ammunition of patience & temper are wholly spent. Here, then, I ground my pen.

*July 26th.* Yesterday the mercury at Alfred's reached 96. Last night rain tempered the atmosphere. In our morning's tour passed in view of the two splendid expensive edifices now in progress of erection by Chas. Henry Fisher on Green Lane & Joshua Francis Fisher near Abington, several miles apart. These are not Fishers of small fry, but are Whalers.

*July 27th.* Wrote to my kinsman Jonathan Pim of Dublin in reply to a letter from him giving a statement of his expenditure of money sent to him in which, among other things, I give him some account of what we have suffered by fire & flood. He is a benevolent man & one that I can cheerfully acknowledge as a blood relation.

*July 28th.* Strollers on the Highway, mostly in rags & intemperate, frequently call at Alfred's. One of them knocked him up at 3 this morning soliciting a dram. From his description the same vagabond had been at the house on the same errand the previous afternoon.

I am today visited with a renewed attack of vertigo. Luckily Dr. S., our family Physician, had a few days before given Alfred a prescription for the affection, same as before. This remedy will, I hope, prove again effective. A call from my Granddaughter M. Haines & her newly acquired relation, Ann Haines, an elderly, intelligent maiden of Germantown. She administers consolation by telling me she is subject to such attacks which she ascribes to a disordered stomach. This is doubtless a main cause.

The mercury yesterday at Alfred's attained 94 in the shade. Today it is 92. There was yesterday afternoon a shower producing little change. This weather suits the mosquitos better than it does me. Edward has returned from a visit to his Uncle Ed. Comley loaded with trophies —Indian darts, Indian stone hatchet & the skin of a large snake, skinned by himself, fine additions to his museum.

*August 3d.* Daylight has not yet shed its rays over Congress—we know not in what the gloom may end. From Texas, almost daily intelligence is received of menaces against the U.S. authorities should Congress prevent or attempt to prevent Texas from exercising authority over New Mexico. She will not consent to submit her claim to the Supreme Court of the U.S.; however preposterous or unjust her pretensions, she is resolved to maintain them at the point of the bayonet. The amount of her debt, which is in the form of certificates of loan sold in all our States at very reduced rates, has of course gained for her many advocates among the loan holders. It is a high game her leaders are playing. Her total indebtedness is nowhere published, but is variously stated at ten to twenty millions of Dollars.

Her politicians entertain expectations that they will eventually possess themselves of all Mexico—the Empire of Montezuma. Should that event not happen, my opinion is that the Saxon race is destined at some period to spread over all North America. Their conquests may not stop even here, but may spread over the Empire of the Incas. Could that event be accomplished without bloodshed, it might prove in the ordering of Providence beneficial to the entire continent, now involved in the dark superstitions of Rome, now endeavouring to spread its influence over our country—chapel after chapel rising up all around us.

*August 4th.* At Germantown Meeting—attendance of Philadelphians large. The Town has attractions for our citizens. Thirty minutes take them to the Village Depot. This place is healthy. One great mistake, in some measure irremediable, in the plotting has been committed. Avenues are too narrow. They should be 60 feet broad at least, instead of the narrow lane strips in which a carriage can scarcely turn, when they might as well have been broad enough to admit convenient foot paths & rows of trees which would have added so greatly to the beauty & convenience of passengers & residents.

While I am writing, a red-headed wood pecker is rattling his pipes close by me. He has become a rare bird in our vicinity. The constant irrational war waged on the feathered tribes deprives us not only of much innocent enjoyment but inflicts on us serious injury by the increase of destructive insects & other vermin.

*August 5th.* Guilty of rudeness & inhospitality, the reflection depriving me of my nap after dinner. Two travellers asked permission to eat some apples, which I abruptly denied them by a simple negative. Others had claimed the like privilege just before & others yesterday. Both parties loaded baskets &c. greedily, so that I was not in good humour. The fruit, it is true, was not mine to give, yet I might without hesitating on the rights of another (Alfred being absent) have indulged a civil act propounded by strangers. It seemed uncourteous & the denial scarcely escaped me, when I felt condemned for the part I acted. I had rather have given one hundred times the value than to have denied the men the small favour asked. I will try not to act so inhospitably again. I was, however, punished by the loss of my siesta. May I not, as naughty boys were wont to do, promise not to do so any more & straightway recommit the fault.

*August 8th.* The slave advocates in Congress have adopted the mean artifice of preventing legislation by speaking against time. Yulee, of Florida, after occupying the floor for two days in succession, still, by last advice, keeps the floor. Will the friends of order long suffer this imposition? There surely are means of putting an end to the evil. 'Tis a game of desperation these political madmen are playing.

Gold dust continues to arrive in large parcels from California—2 vessels just arrived at N.Y. have together brought three millions in value.

*August 10th.* The Senate has passed the Texas Bill. It is a great concession to that State, but preferable to civil war, for which their people, aided by malcontents of the Southern States, seem rife.

*August 11th.* First Day. Owing to so many absentees from the City, Thos. Elkington, whose summer retreat is at Germantown & son Henry, both Elders of the S. District Meeting, alternately go to the City to attend Orange St. Meeting. Henry's turn came today. Passenger cars traverse the road on First Day.

*August 12th.* The famed Ship *Tuscarora*, Turley, is at Liverpool from N.Y. I dare predict Turley will not again run her ashore.

*August 15th.* A small attendance at Germantown Meeting today. Several of the members absent at Cape May.

Eleven members, slave holders, of the Senate have offered a written protest & asked to have it placed on the Journal against the admission of California, New Mexico &c. without providing for the introduction of slavery into either of them. No protest has at any time gained admission into the Senate's Journal, nor is it likely this will. It is high time the Free States should make a stand adverse to the further extension of slavery on American soil. The U.S. is now, I believe, the only Christian Community in which slavery is tolerated &—should the Slave States withdraw from the Confederacy—they will experience the fate of Hayti. The great bulwark of their safety is in their connection with the Free States.

*August 20th.* From the news of the day it is apparent the House of Reps. are disposed to procrastinate action on the Bills from the Senate for the admission of the new States.

Outrages, robberies & murders continue to disgrace our once orderly City. Fire arms & bowie knives are of nightly use, tho' the carrying of deadly weapons is forbidden by Law & the Police officers carry neither pistol nor gun.

The storm has not ceased with the day, but still has abated. We dined comfortably by a fire, the mercury at 6 A.M. 57. The family profess to breakfast at 6—the hour not strictly observed, except when the calls of business demand it. Today, I aroused the flock at 7. As Alfred partakes not of that meal, but uniformly presides at the table, it is a matter of indifference to him, except when business requires dispatch. His uniform practice, after the meal is finished, is to read some portion of the Scriptures before rising from the table—'tis a good example.

*August 22d.* Marvelous—A. Derbyshire says that the man found in his yard pending the great fire is alive & hopes are entertained that he may recover. His only recollection of the event is that when the explosion took place, he was on the roof of an adjoining building, but of what happened after that time, he is totally unconscious. He is still capable of conversation, giving answers with difficulty to simple questions. Alexander adds that Ed. Paxson, whose dwelling was on the west side of Front St., was in the upper part of his house preparing to remove his furniture when the explosion occurred & a large beam in full blaze fell on his roof end foremost & dashing through, set his house so completely on fire that the family escaped with difficulty, saving nothing but their lives. The streets in every direction were overspread with fiery missiles.

*August 25th.* First Day. A violent storm of rain & high wind deterred us from going out.

Late in the day the rain was stayed & a bright sun & a brisk norwester succeeded. The insects again making merry, but the birds, sweet songsters, are silent. Many of them, having accomplished their summer's destination of rearing a progeny, have winged their way to distances in furtherance of the Laws of Nature, while others may have secreted themselves in dark forest shades to complete their moulting.

I attempted a siesta after dinner but the flies would not give assent, neither would the romp & loud laughter of certain urchins, so I took to my pen for amusement.

*August 26th.* The anniversary of my birth, ending my 82d year. Half a century ago I had no expectation that my life would be so long extended. May my remaining days be better spent than have been the past. May I be favoured to do justly, to love mercy & to walk humbly with my God, conscious as I am of having been but an unprofitable servant.

The morning paper states the fire of the 23d, at night, to have been the burning of the large barn filled with hay situated near the Schuylkill, below the Marine Hospital. It is the work of an incendiary, so common in our City & suburbs.

Having dined, we rode over to the pleasant seat of that enterprizing, intelligent woman, Harriet Rowland, whose aged mother, Sarah Anderson, daughter of Amos Wickersham, lives with her & is entirely blind, while her memory & other intellectual faculties are quite bright & I held with her a long & pleasant conversation in which subjects of bygone days were canvassed. Her father kept a grocery store in 2d St., corner of Coombs Alley, when I kept a dry goods store, 2d St. corner of Jones, otherwise Pewter Platter Alley, within ½ a square of Coombs Alley. At that period, 2d between High & Mulberry contained several families of Friends altho', at present, not a single family of members live there.

*August 29th.* Mornings & evenings have become cool, giving evidence that a return to our home in the City would not be unseasonable.

*September 3d.* The day being propitious, we returned to our home. The damage caused by the storm to the Schuylkill & Lehigh Nav. is very serious. The Reading R.R. has also suffered, no business is going on by

either. The Public Works have not escaped. Some say 6 in. water fell.

Alfred & his companion T. Wistar have gone to Washington this morning where 9 Chiefs of the Menomonees, accompanied by Bruce, Indian Agent, have arrived. These greatly injured people have gone to implore a postponement of their removal, especially now so near winter, to the place assigned to them on the Crow River. They have visited the land, found it sterile & scarce of game. They wish to have land assigned to them in a climate less rigorous & furnishing better means of subsistence. A. & T. have gone to aid them in their appeal to Pres. Fillmore, taking with them a Letter of introduction from Wm. M. Meredith. The Menomonees are very much addicted to intemperance, hence the more liable to imposition. Could not some pious people be induced to make efforts to reclaim them? They are entitled to the sympathy of Christians of every denomination.

*September 9th.* Midnight of the 5th while in bed, I was suddenly seized & awakened with violent pain in my stomach, followed on getting up by copious discharges from the bowels. Camphor water, a teaspoon at a time, was administered by my attentive wife every half hour unavailingly, to which I wished to apply 12 drops of laudanum, but I could not persuade her to do so, as she deemed it dangerous. Dr. Shallcross being sent for, he came early next day & at once prescribed that mixture, which was repeated throughout the day, producing relief before nightfall. He visited me thrice thro' the day & the day following. Last night I rested comfortably & am this morning free from pain & enabled again to use my pen.

*October 7th.* This is general election day & I have just been to cast my vote for the Whig ticket, including Chas. Gilpin for Mayor. I took him as I take Physic, not because I like it but because it is that or more nauseous dose. Among other votes called for at this election, there is one, to assent or dissent to a proposition to make the Judges of our Courts elective. I voted against that measure but headed a circular showing how it might prostrate the ends of justice to have our Judges dependent on popular favour for their seats, to hold power from the mob, to be chosen to favour partial interests & party purposes. One of the brightest gems in English liberty is the stern independence of their Judges.

Formerly our Judges were appointed during good behaviour. They were then appointed for a term of years—now they are to be still further degraded & subjected to be mere tools of the populace. The paper was signed: Thos. P. Cope—Richard Rush—Horace Binney—Wm. J. Duane—Jos. R. Ingersoll—John Keating—Chas. J. Ingersoll—Wm. M. Meredith & about 50 others. I wished not to head the list, but my associates in the cause placed me there.

*October 9th.* Chas. Gilpin is Mayor. The lack of energy of Joel Jones—who, on trial, has been found wanting—has caused this result, for Gilpin is not popular even in his own party. I have no fear of his want of energy. He will, if I am not mistaken, prove tart enough to satisfy the most severe advocate of high handed rule. And so far as appearances justify, our Judges are to be appointed by ballot at the public polls. We may have to sing the nurse song of the late John Edge—the bigger the fool, the better the nurse (substitute Judge for nurse). Andrew Miller may be elected, having already proved his competency. He is now head, Commissioners of Moyamensing & a favourite of the rabble, encouraging mob law & assassinations by saying they are good schools for training soldiers. The experiment is in a fair way of consummation, for if Philada. gives a vote in favour, what can we expect but confirmation from the interior of the State?

Wm. M. Mullen & Thos. Mitchell call to say I was selected to preside at a meeting of anti-slavers & inviting my attendance, which I promptly declined, having no inclination to become involved in the existing exciting controversy. Besides that, I possess little confidence in the prudence of its advocates, that is, such advocates of anti-slavery as Lucretia Mott & others of the same school, who are to attend.

*October 12th.* Met the Board of N.A. Ins. Co. at 12—losses are considerable but the Co. prosperous. Application to take a risk against floods on Schuylkill declined, as was also a proposition to subscribe stock to a sea steamer. The withdrawal of agencies from N. Orleans, St. Louis, further confirmed.

Have felt unpleasant at the course pursued by some of the Drinker family, on whom I have conferred voluntary & disinterested favours. My brother Israel has truly said that family has ever been a trouble to me. Some of them are certainly most ungrateful recipients of favours. H.W.D., to whom I advanced money to prevent his being, by his creditors, banished from his Native Land many years ago, told me to my face that gratitude was not a virtue, but that he who conferred a favour was amply repaid by the pleasure derived from the act. He makes good his system of morals by remaining largely in my debt, tho' possessing the means of remuneration.

I consider the inordinate love of novel reading as having in no small degree destroyed their sense of correct thinking & acting. The present race have sadly degenerated from their noble predecessors, John, Henry & Daniel Drinker. I am not aware that a male bearing the name is now a member of the religious Society of Friends.

A jubilee in the evening at brother Jasper's. He & his wife, Rebecca, whose maiden name was Shoemaker, having lived in married connection for fifty years, thought fit to celebrate the event by a friendly greeting of their relatives over a generous cup of tea, after partaking of which their marriage certificate was produced, endorsed afresh & signed by those present, numbering about thirty, among them by myself as the oldest survivor of the family (my dear E. being too unwell to attend —Henry, Wm. & Alfred being in the country). Next came brother Israel & Sarah, his 2d wife, his son Marmaduke & Sarah, his wife (daughter of Thos. Wistar), Wm. Collins & his wife, Eliza, daughter of Israel, Mary & Lydia, his two unmarried daughters. Caleb Cope, my nephew John Cope, son of nephew Herman, who is absent from the City. Chas. Yarnall & wife, daughter of brother Jasper. Geo. Randolph & wife, also daughter of Jasper. Susan, wife of son Wm., now on a visit to us. Mary Stokes, niece of my wife & resident with us also.

Time spent agreeably. All were happy & at 10 P.M. the company separated under a brilliant moonlight & temperate atmosphere.

*October 19th.* A negro claimed as a slave was brought before Judges Grier & Kane of the U.S. Court. The claimant, failing to produce testimony, wished the Court to postpone the case to allow time for obtaining it. The Judges said the party should have been prepared to prove his right before he came before them & he forthwith discharged the negro. Great excitement prevailed among a crowd of blacks & others, pending the examination. Order was, however, preserved by a large Police force.

*October 21st.* The proceedings as published of the party that attempted the opening of the Pa. R.R. to Hollidaysburg, occasions me no cause of regret for my absence. One great object appears to have been the fulsome whitewashing of Gen. Patterson, brother of the Pres. of the Road & incidentally others of the same political faith. About 300 persons attended, at an expense to the company of $2500, as estimated by a person who is well informed.

A call from a man producing the recommendation of Wm. Lloyd Garrison & Jas. Mott, two madcaps of the anti-slavery school. This

man, it would seem, had been engaged in running away with slaves—
has been detected & mulct of a large sum. His object is to collect by
subscription an amount to replace that sum. I declined to contribute. If
men will hazard these violations of the Laws of their country, they must
be left to suffer the consequences of their folly. Such acts irritate the
slaveholders & render the condition of the slaves more stringent &
oppressive.

*October 22d.* A congress of medical men from all parts of Europe is
advertized to be held to test the value of a new cure for insanity & the
bite of poisonous serpents by means of cedrone seed. Auguste Guillemin
& Hippolyte Furnier, two savants, have offered themselves as subjects
on which the experiment is to be made. What cedrone is, I know not.
Should the issue prove favourable it will be marvelous indeed. I confess
my lack of faith.

*October 23d.* Our Monthly Meeting—a paper received & read from
the M.M. to which the young woman, married at ours, removed with
her husband in N. England, saying their discipline requested, when a
person appearing among them as a member remained there a given time
without producing a certificate of removal, that inquiry should be made
of the Meeting whence he or she came, into the cause of the non
production. The same debate ensued as on a former occasion & principally by the same parties but with more civility, yet with like result. The
paper was not noticed on our minutes & the subject passed by.

It strikes me that we cannot consent to grant a certificate to this
female. We ought not to have received one for the man to whom she was
married. On this occasion I as usual held my peace—had I spoken, it
would have been in disagreement with my son Henry—a painful circumstance.

*October 24th.* At 2 P.M. my grandchildren Clementine & Edgar
Cope arrived to go to school. She to Select School in the City & he to
Westtown.

*October 26th.* The New Albion, Indiana, *Bulletin* carries the following, "William Gross, the young man who was lately convicted of
murder, in the confession of his guilt, which was given in evidence in his
trial, stated that he had no motive in the perpetration of the inhuman
act except the desire to gratify a fiendish thirst for blood & a demoniacal
satisfaction in seeing the death struggles of his fellow beings, which
feelings he had imbibed during the Mexican Campaign."

We here in Philada. are now reaping some of the bitter fruits of the Mexican War in the corruption of our young men, the "Killers" "Schuylkill Rangers" &c. &c. It is expected that a check will be given to these rowdies by the new Police just going around.

# 1851

*March 15th.* For several days the sun has shone brightly, the air bland & the welcome songs of the feathered tribe heard in the early morn. Today the sky is mantled in mourning, giving notice to pedestrians to call their umbrellas into requisition. I can remember a time when it was not consistent with manly dignity to take shelter under an umbrella from pelting storms of rain, hail or snow & when our grandmammas called them not into use—about seventy years ago. Now, the porter on his dray mounts his umbrella. Men then covered their beaver hats & women their paduasoy bonnets with silk oil cloth; the male his back, with double-milled drab cloth cloak, the female with worsted camblet; sagathy for men's tight-bodied coats & buckskin for breeches; grogrums, peneascoes & poplins for women's gowns. Elderly female Friends wore bee hive bonnets of black silk in the City &—in some instances—of undressed straw in the country.

My aunt Pim, of Chester County, wife of Thomas Pim, after whom —at his request—I was called, wore a bonnet of straw made of rolls more than one inch in diameter—just such rolls were then used for real bee hives & for making bread. Such baskets were, when I was a boy, in use by all our housewives. Coloured aprons, dark blue & green, were also worn by our matrons on the upper seats of the gallery.

Four wheeled pleasure carriages were a rarity. Some few dashing blades drove phaetons. Two wheeled vehicles, called chairs, were in use, often conveying small parties to shady, secluded neighbouring seats to sip a cup of tea in places over which the dense population of the City has now spread.

On these occasions, we carried with us in our rural, temporary seclusion, our tea pots, cups & saucers, tea kettle & viands, our seats being the virgin, green grass. Thus I enjoyed many a happy hour in innocency with my youthful companions. These were the true feasts of reason & flow of souls—the halcyon days of youth.

Afternoon a special meeting of the Overseers of Friends Public Schools. A man proposing to discharge a ground rent owing to the Board took counsel of E.H. Price, Atty., who has given an opinion adverse to our power to convey—a right never before questioned since the first charter from Wm. Penn, 1697.

After discussion, referred to a committee. Another case—one of our tenants has placed an under tenant in the house, the under tenant

refusing to give possession. He is suspected of an intention to open a place for the sale of lager bier—a German invention, now in fashion, of an intoxicating nature. Also referred.

*March 17th.* Pat may venerate & commemorate his saint within doors, but has a poor chance of frolic without—rain besprinkled with hail covering our foot paths plentifully. But Pat, spite of the weather, will have a bit of fun on Saint Patrick's Day. Our present very efficient Police will I trust, rain or shine, preserve the peace.

# APPENDIX A

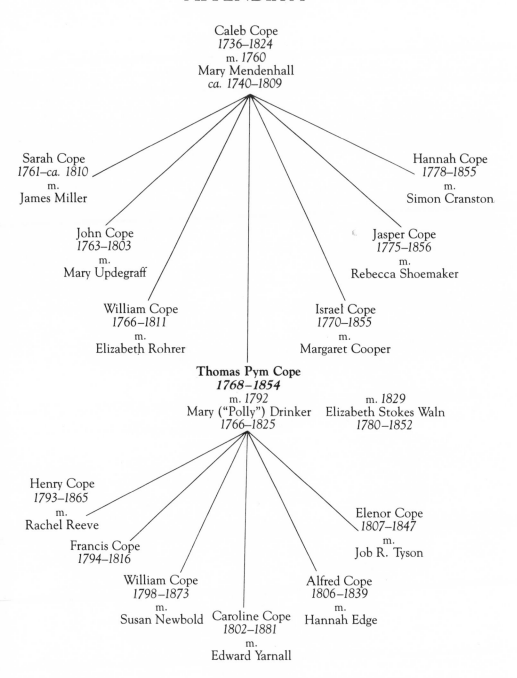

Caleb Cope
*1736–1824*
m. *1760*
Mary Mendenhall
*ca. 1740–1809*

Sarah Cope
*1761–ca. 1810*
m.
James Miller

Hannah Cope
*1778–1855*
m.
Simon Cranston

John Cope
*1763–1803*
m.
Mary Updegraff

Jasper Cope
*1775–1856*
m.
Rebecca Shoemaker

William Cope
*1766–1811*
m.
Elizabeth Rohrer

Israel Cope
*1770–1855*
m.
Margaret Cooper

**Thomas Pym Cope**
***1768–1854***
m. *1792*
Mary ("Polly") Drinker
*1766–1825*

m. *1829*
Elizabeth Stokes Waln
*1780–1852*

Henry Cope
*1793–1865*
m.
Rachel Reeve

Elenor Cope
*1807–1847*
m.
Job R. Tyson

Francis Cope
*1794–1816*

William Cope
*1798–1873*
m.
Susan Newbold

Caroline Cope
*1802–1881*
m.
Edward Yarnall

Alfred Cope
*1806–1839*
m.
Hannah Edge

# APPENDIX B

*Toward an Orientation Regarding the Names in the Diary*

*Alsop, Richard* (1761–1815). A turn-of-the-(19th)-century American satirist and poet from Connecticut.

*André, John* (1750–1780). Highly popular British major captured during the War of the American Revolution; was held in the home of T.P.C.'s father in Lancaster, Pennsylvania; upon his exchange in 1776, was appointed to negotiate with Benedict Arnold, whose wife André knew, for betrayal of West Point to the British but was caught while wearing civilian clothes and executed as a spy, on the orders of a reluctant George Washington.

*Barker, Jacob* (1779–1871). Prosperous Quaker shipping merchant; aided government in financing the War of 1812.

*Bayard, Andrew* (1761–1832). Philadelphia insurance broker; served as president of the city's Commercial Bank.

*Benezet, Anthony* (1731–1784). American educator and leading Quaker advocate of the antislavery cause.

*Bettle, Samuel* (1774–1861). Minister of the Society of Friends; one of the founders of Haverford College.

*Biddle, Nicholas* (1786–1844). American financier and man of letters; as president of the Second Bank of the United States (1822–1836), he made it the first effective central bank in U.S. history.

*Binney, Horace* (1780–1875). American lawyer and legal writer; argued on behalf of the city of Philadelphia against the heirs of Stephen Girard when they attempted to overturn Girard's bequest to the city.

*Bloomfield, Joseph* (1772–1860). A military man, fought in the American Revolution; served as governor of New Jersey; advocated a gradual emancipation of the slaves.

*Brown, Charles Brockden* (1771–1810). A gifted writer who pioneered in the Gothic manner, he was the first United States novelist to gain international reputation; was a close friend and traveling companion of T.P.C.

*Butler, Fanny Kemble* (1809–1893). Famous English actress with an autobiographical bent; wrote *Journal of a Residence on a Georgian Plantation*, a record of her marriage to the U.S. plantation owner.

*Cadwalader, John* (1805–1879). Lawyer, congressman, judge; raised and commanded a company of militiamen to help quell the Philadelphia riots of 1844.

*Chandler, Joseph R.* (1792–1880). Whig congressman from Philadelphia; was editor of the *Gazette of the United States*.

*Clay, Henry* (1777–1852). American lawyer and strong political leader in both the U.S. Senate and the House of Representatives; was three times a candidate for the presidency; his advocacy of internal improvements and his skills as a compromiser on the slavery issue made him one of T.P.C.'s most admired political figures.

*Clinton, DeWitt* (1769–1828). Lawyer and statesman; was a governor of New York and the major proponent of the construction of the Erie Canal.

*Coates, Samuel* (1748–1830). Well-known Philadelphia merchant, active in city affairs.

*Comfort, Ezra* (1777–1847). Minister of the Society of Friends; strongly opposed to the doctrines of the Liberal Quakers, or Hicksites.

*Constitutionalists.* Federalists and moderate Democrats who united to defend the Pennsylvania state constitution against alteration by radical Democrats in 1807–08.

*Cox, John* (1754–1847). Minister and prominent member of the Society of Friends in New Jersey.

*Craik, James* (1730–1814). Chief physician of the Continental army during the American War of Independence.

*Dallas, Alexander J.* (1759–1817). American administrator and lawyer in Philadelphia; was U.S. secretary of the treasury at critical period of government finance (1814–16).

*Dallas, George M.* (1792–1864). Lawyer and staunch Pennsylvania Democrat, was the son of Alexander J. Dallas; served as U.S. senator, minister to Russia and to Great Britain, vice president under James K. Polk.

*Democrats.* Members in the early 1800s of the political party—originally led by Thomas Jefferson—which favored, at least in theory, a central government which performed only minimum, necessary functions while leaving wide powers to the states; were more sympathetic, in general, to the French Revolution and to Napoleon than were the Federalists, and favored a policy of closeness to France while mistrusting Great Britain; also known as Democratic-Republicans and anti-Federalists.

*Dix, Dorothea* (1802–1887). American philanthropist, reformer, and writer of children's books; was a pioneer in the development of more humane treatment for the mentally ill.

*Drinker, Henry, Jr.* (1757–1822). T.P.C.'s brother-in-law; active in Philadelphia politics during the early 19th century.

*Drinker, John* (1733–1800). Prominent Philadelphia Quaker in the late 1700s; father of Thomas Cope's first wife, Mary, nicknamed Polly.

*Duane, William* (1760–1835). Outspoken editor of the *Aurora*, the leading Democratic newspaper in early 19th-century Pennsylvania.

*Dundas, James* (1788–1865). Chairman of the trustees charged with winding up the affairs of the Second Bank of the United States; also president of Philadelphia's Commercial Bank.

*Dunlap, William* (1766–1839). American painter, historian, and the country's first playwright; as manager of the Old American Company, he did much to shape the tastes of American theatergoers.

*Duponceau, Peter Stephen* (1760–1844). Lawyer and respected philologist, whose writings include original studies of various North American Indian languages; was also president of the American Philosophical Society in Philadelphia.

*Eddy, Thomas* (1758–1827). New York Quaker, noted particularly for his concern with the question of prison reform.

*Evans, Elizabeth Barton* (1794–1861). Minister in the Society of Friends in Philadelphia.

*Evans, William* (1787–1867). Druggist in Philadelphia and, like his wife, Elizabeth, a minister in the Society of Friends.

*Federalists.* Members of the political party led originally by John Adams and Alexander Hamilton during Washington's administration who favored a strong central government, commercial and industrial development of the country, and close ties with Great Britain; at times accused of favoring aristocratic, even monarchical ways by the anti-Federalists, or Democrats, to whom they were violently opposed.

*Findlay, William* (1768–1846). Pennsylvania statesman; served in the state legislature; was state treasurer, governor, U.S. senator, and director of the United States Mint.

*Fisher, John* (1771–1846). Lawyer, Quaker, ardent Democrat; was U.S. district judge for Delaware.

*Fitzsimmons, Thomas* (?–1811). A prominent representative of the Philadelphia business community; was a signer (for the state of Pennsylvania) of the Constitution; in 1801 initiated the founding and served as first president of the Philadelphia Chamber of Commerce (to which T.P.C. was elected in 1806). Also spelled his name Fitz Simins or FitzSimons.

*Francis, Thomas Willing* (1767–1815). Philadelphia businessman.

*Fulton, Robert* (1765–1815). American engineer and inventor, best known for his development of the steamboat; was also a portrait painter in Philadelphia, and a classmate of T.P.C.

*Gallatin, Abraham Alfonso Albert* (1761–1849). U.S. secretary of the treasury under Jefferson and Madison, minister to France and Great Britain, president of the National (later Gallatin) Bank, born in Geneva, Switzerland; was a great shaping force in the foreign and financial policies of the United States.

*Gilpin, Charles* (1809–1868). U.S. district attorney in Philadelphia and one-time mayor of the city.

*Girard, Stephen* (1750–1831). Philadelphia shipping magnate, financier, philanthropist, born in Bordeaux, France; a large part of his fortune was bequeathed to the city of Philadelphia for municipal improvements and for a school or college to train "poor, white, male orphans" in the arts and trades.

*Godwin, William* (1756–1836). English philosopher and writer of strongly rationalistic views; a thoroughgoing intellectual, he denied feeling, habit, or tradition as forces motivating human conduct, truth, and justice and the goal of a "benevolent anarchism" being for him the sole ideals for society.

*Gurney, Francis* (1738–1815). Staunch patriot of the Revolution, merchant in Philadelphia and highly respected political figure in the city.

*Hemphill, Joseph* (1770–1842). Lawyer; served in Pennsylvania state legislature and in Congress.

*Hicks, Elias* (1748–1830). American Quaker minister, identified with liberal thought; was responsible for separation of Quaker communities into conservative or "orthodox" Friends and "Hicksites" or "Separatists."

*Hiester, Joseph* (1752–1832). From the time of the American Revolution, was a leading political figure from Pennsylvania; served as governor, and in both state and federal legislatures.

*Howland, George* (1781–1852). Wealthy Quaker from Massachusetts.

*Hughes, John* (1797–1864). Foremost Catholic prelate of the United States; vastly expanded Catholic churches and institutions; publicly defended his faith against attacks of Protestants.

*Ingersoll, Charles Jared* (1782–1862). Lawyer; represented Pennsylvania in Congress; was also U.S. district attorney for the state (1815–29).

*Inskeep, John* (1757–1834). Philadelphia merchant, fought in the Revolution; served as mayor; was president of the Insurance Company of North America.

*Jones, William* (1760–1831). American importer and banker in Philadelphia; served in Congress; was later secretary of the Navy under Madison; first president of the Second Bank of the United States.

*Jordan, Richard* (1756–1826). A Quaker minister of little formal schooling but great power; lived in New Jersey in later life.

*Kane, John Kintzing* (1795–1858). Lawyer, active in Philadelphia affairs; attorney general of the state under Governor Shunk, later judge of the district court for eastern Pennsylvania.

*Kersey, Jesse* (1768–1845). American minister in the Society of Friends, became a follower of the liberal teachings of Elias Hicks.

*Lacock, Abner* (1770–1837). Radical Pennsylvania Democrat, was involved in the attempt to impeach Governor McKean in 1807–08; later a U.S. representative in Congress.

*Latrobe, Benjamin Henry* (1764–1820). Born in England, he was the first American architect of international stature; helped to popularize the Greek revival style; designed Bank of Pennsylvania building in Philadelphia; proposed, designed, and built Philadelphia city water-supply system; built steamboats in partnership with Robert Fulton and others; rebuilt the Capitol after its destruction by the British in 1814.

*Little Turtle* (1752–1812). American Indian chief of the Miami tribe, one of the most important Indian leaders in the Northwest Territory; led a crushing attack against federal troops under General Arthur St. Clair in 1791, later became a strong advocate of peace.

*Locofocos.* Originally a dissident group within the Democratic party which sought equality and freedom from privilege, especially in economic matters; opposed to monopolies, corporations, and paper currency, they influenced Democratic policies during the 1840s.

*McKean, Thomas* (1734–1817). American statesman; member (1774–83) and president (1781) of the Continental Congress; signer of the Declaration of Independence; served as chief justice and as governor of Pennsylvania.

*McLane, Allan* (1746–1829). American Revolutionary officer; commanded troops in the Philadelphia area; later became a customs collector at Wilmington, Delaware.

*McLane, Louis* (1786–1857). The son of Allan McLane, he was a U.S. congressman, diplomat, cabinet officer, and business executive; served as U.S. secretary of the treasury and secretary of state; in 1837 became president, for ten years, of the Baltimore and Ohio Railroad Company.

*Madison, Dolly* (1768–1857). Famous and much admired hostess in Washington while her husband, James Madison, was secretary of state and president.

*Martin, Luther* (1748?–1826). American lawyer and Revolutionary leader; member of Continental Congress and federal Constitutional Convention; opposed plan of strong central government and adoption of Constitution; defended Aaron Burr in treason trial in 1807.

*Meredith, William* (1799–1873). Prominent Philadelphia lawyer; U.S. secretary of the treasury and attorney general of Pennsylvania; during the 1840s, president of the Select Council in Philadelphia.

*Merrick, Samuel Vaughan* (1801–1870). Well-known Pennsylvania iron manufacturer, and a founder of the Franklin Institute; first president of the Pennsylvania Railroad Company.

*Miner, Charles* (1780–1865). Philadelphia politician, newspaper editor, and inventor; experimented with the use of coal and silkworms; wrote a history of Wyoming county in Pennsylvania; a lifelong friend of T.P.C.

*Milnor, James* (1773–1844). Lawyer in Philadelphia; later, an Episcopal minister; served in Congress from 1811–13.

*Moreau, Jean Victor Marie* (1763–1813). French general of the Revolutionary and Napoleonic armies; exiled on the suspicion of his having plotted against Napoleon.

*Morris, Robert* (1734–1806). American financier and statesman; member of Continental Congress and signer of Declaration of Independence; arranged financing purchase of supplies for Washington's armies; founded Bank of North America; financially ruined by speculation in western lands.

*Native Americans.* Members of political party formed in response to the increasing numbers of immigrants to America in 1840s; they advocated that the waiting period for immigrants seeking citizenship should be extended, and that new immigrants should not be allowed to hold public office.

*Neagle, John* (1796–1865). American portrait painter, whose studio was in Philadelphia. His *Washington* hangs in Philadelphia's Independence Hall; his portrait of T.P.C. is in the city's Mercantile Library.

*Nicholson, John* (?–1800). Having been powerful as the comptroller-general of Pennsylvania (1782–94), he became a partner of Robert Morris; together, they bought, among other things, 7000 lots in Washington, D.C., and 2,000,000 acres in Georgia.

*Paxton, Timothy* (1764–1839). A Philadelphia Quaker, active in civic affairs.

*Peters, Richard* (1744–1828). American jurist; served as secretary of Continental Board of War, member of Continental Congress, and as judge on the U.S. district court of Pennsylvania.

*Porter, David* (1788–1867). Two-term governor of Pennsylvania, popular for having preserved the state's credit after the financial crisis in the late 1830s.

*Poulson, Zachariah* (1761–1844). American newspaper editor and publisher, whose *American Daily Advertiser* in Philadelphia was successor to the first viable American daily, the *Pennsylvania Packet and Daily Advertiser,* which became a daily in 1784; frequently printed articles by T.P.C. in the pages of his newspaper.

*Quids.* Nickname for group of modern Democrats; they opposed extremist attempts (1807–08) to limit Governor McKean's power in Pennsylvania; occasionally, they united with Federalists, thus dividing the strength of the Democrats.

*Randolph of Roanoke, John* (1773–1833). Flamboyant member of Congress and plantation owner in Virginia, he was one of the most brilliant of American public men; a passionate partisan of state sovereignty; opposed interference with institution of slavery (though he freed his own slaves in his will); at times, in state of mental derangement.

*Randolph, John St. George* (1792?–1860). Nephew of John Randolph of Roanoke; was a patient in the Pennsylvania Hospital at the time T.P.C. was a member of the hospital's board of managers.

*Rapp, George* (1757–1847). Leader of a religious communistic society called Harmonites, or Economites, in Indiana and Pennsylvania in early 1800s; rule of celibacy led to extinction of the society in 1903.

*Read, George* (1765–1836). U.S. district attorney for Delaware for nearly thirty years, he was the son of the signer of the Declaration of Independence and the Constitution of the same name.

*Roosevelt, Nicholas* (1767–1854). American inventor; granted patent for invention of vertical steamboat paddle wheels; worked with Robert Fulton on project for introducing steamboats on western rivers; married architect Benjamin Latrobe's daughter.

*Rush, Benjamin* (1745–1813). American physician, medical educator (professor of chemistry at U. of Pennsylvania), and political leader, he was a member of the Continental Congress and a signer of the Declaration of Independence; a fierce proponent of the abolition of slavery; served under John Adams as treasurer of U.S. Mint.

*Sergeant, John* (1779–1852). Lawyer and congressman from Pennsylvania; was Republican candidate for vice president in 1832.

*Seybert, Adam* (1773–1825). Philadelphia chemist, member of the American Philosophical Society; served as representative in Congress (1809–19).

*Shunk, Francis R.* (1788–1848). Pennsylvania politician (Democrat); elected governor in 1844 and 1847.

*Slater, Samuel* (1768–1835). English-born industrialist; inventor of cotton-spinning machinery; regarded as founder of American cotton industry.

*Smith, Daniel B.* (1792–1883). Quaker pharmacist, active in Philadelphia's scientific and community affairs; held the chair of moral philosophy, English literature, and chemistry at Haverford College (1834–46).

*Snyder, Simon* (1759–1819). Having served as speaker of the Pennsylvania House of Representatives, he was elected governor in 1808; was the first Pennsylvania governor who was not from the relatively well-off upper class and the first born outside one of the original Quaker countries.

*Stevens, Thaddeus* (1792–1868). American lawyer and legislator from Pennsylvania; vigorously opposed slavery; was one of the most influential Republicans in Congress during the mid-1800s.

*Stuart, Gilbert* (1755–1828). Celebrated American portraitist, his unfinished head of George Washington being the most famous of his nearly 1000 portraits.

*Talleyrand-Périgord, Charles Maurice de* (1754–1838). French statesman and diplomat; was educated for the priesthood, became a bishop, but was excommunicated by the pope in 1791 for his unprincipled behavior; held high office during the French Revolution, under Napoleon, and under Louis Philippe.

*Van Rensselaer, Stephen* (1764–1839). Wealthy American army officer and politician; lieutenant governor of New York, major general of state militia in War of 1812, later served in Congress; advocated canal to connect Hudson River with Great Lakes (Erie Canal).

*Waln, Nicholas* (1742–1813). Pennsylvania Quaker; one of the most impressive preachers in the latter 1700s, was noted for his wit.

*Wetherill, John Price* (1794–1853). American chemical industrialist; important member of Philadelphia's city councils in 1840s.

*Wharton, Robert* (1757–1834). Philadelphia merchant and political figure; fifteen times mayor of the city.

*Whigs.* Members of American political party formed in mid-1830s in opposition to Jacksonian Democrats; associated mainly with manufacturing, commercial, and financial interests; succeeded about 1854 by the Republican party.

*Wollstonecraft, Mary* (1759–1797). English writer, passionate advocate of women's right to place in society equal to that of men; her book *A Vindication of the Rights of Women* (1792) urged equal educational opportunities for women and suggested that intellectual companionship was important to a happy marriage.

# INDEX

Abolition Society, 8, 137-38, 150, 172, 192, 234, 335, 338, 402, 511
Adams, Chester, 330
Adams, John, 39, 56, 133, 280, 289, 464, 552
Adams, John Quincy, 341, 464, 549-51
Adams, Judge, 241
Albertson, Josiah, 313
Alexander I, emperor of Russia, 150-51, 292
Allen, William, 336
Almshouse, 90, 146, 340, 421, 461, 485, 502, 527
Alsop, Richard, 75, 96
Anderson, John, 339
Anderson, Sarah, 599
André, Major, 68, 142-44
Andrews, Robert, 475, 478-79
Annesley, Thomas, 252
Anthony, Joseph, 124
Anti-Federalists, 29
Arego, M., 451
Arnold, Gen. Benedict, 68, 369
Ashbridge, George, 399-400
Aspinwall, Doctor, 22
Astor, John Jacob, 552-53
Audubon, 472
Augustine, Saint, 78

Bache, Doctor, 516
Baeumler, Michael, 323-25, 335
Bainbridge, Captain, 190-91
Baker, George N., 495, 497
Baker, Hilary, Jr., 217, 247
Baker, Hilary, Sr., 147
Baker, J.R., 580
Baldwin, Caleb, 131, 463
Banks, Ephraim, 497
Banzhoff, John Godfrey, 323-24, 335
Barclay, J.J., 564, 579
Barclay, Robert, Scottish Quaker, 324
Barker, Abigail, 471
Barker, Abraham, 371
Barker, Jacob, 294
Barnett, Abigail, 377
Barnett, Elizabeth, 377
Barnett, Lydia, 377

Barnett, Matthew, 377
Barron, Commodore, 211
Barry, Captain, 199
Barton, Isaac, 412-13, 415, 499
Bartram, Israel, 48
Bayard, Andrew, 34
Bayard, James, 495
Beach, Nathan, 83-84
Beaumont, John, 370
Benezet, Anthony, 285, 553, 555
Benezet, James, 553
Benners, Captain, 557
Benners, George, 557
Bennet, murderer, 357
Berthier, Louis Alexandre, 305
Bettle, Samuel, 323, 480-82, 543
Bickel, John, 313, 321
Bickham, George, 522
Biddle, Charles, 15-16, 217, 221-22
Biddle, Doctor, 538
Biddle, Nicholas, 400, 428-29, 493, 529
Binder, William, 485
Binney, Horace, 221, 397, 430, 432, 439, 442-44, 449, 502-3, 529, 601
Binney, Horace, Jr., 505
Binns, John, 232
Birmingham, George, 584
Bispham, Maria, 525
Bispham, Samuel, 525
Black, Doctor, 380
Blakiston, John, 201
Bleecker, Anthony, 68, 90
Board of Health, 9, 24, 34, 129, 131, 148, 162, 224, 383
Board of Managers of the Mercantile Library, 398, 414, 423, 425, 436-37, 457, 481, 490, 493, 499-501, 503-5, 538, 544, 548, 556, 570, 589
Board of the Guardians of the Poor, 485-86
Board of Trade, 394, 426, 449, 457, 479, 490, 530, 532, 536, 590
Bonaparte, Empress Josephine, 242, 252, 292
Bonaparte, Joseph (Count Surveil-lante), 339
Bonaparte, Louis, 253, 584
Bonaparte, Napoleon, 7, 145, 149, 159,

Bonaparte (cont), 166, 193, 195, 202, 212, 216, 228, 231-32, 237, 241-43, 245, 252-53, 277, 291-92, 305-6, 339, 346, 352, 509, 530, 534, 568
Bonsell, Isaac, 131
Boileau, Nathaniel, 226
Boswell, James, 465
Boter, Widow, 314
Bouchet, topographer, 368
Bowen, William E., 589
Bowne, Robert, 58
Bowne, William 354
Boyd, Mrs., 558
Braddock, British general, 111
Bradford, editor, 9, 49
Brady, James, 222
Brant, Col., Mohawk Indian chief, 358
Breck, Samuel, 498
Briggs, Isaac, 231
Bringhurst, Joseph, 44
Brown, Anna, 516
Brown, Charles Brockden (C.B.B.), 10, 23, 43, 55, 62-76, 79, 90, 94, 96-97, 107, 120, 128-29, 139, 165, 182, 184, 192, 195, 209, 247-50, 355, 381, 499
Brown, Captain, 358-59
Brown, David, 380
Brown, David Paul, 501, 503, 575
Brown, General, 293
Brown, Jeremiah, 516
Brown, John, printer, 96
Brown, John A., 529
Brown, Moses, 564
Brown, Paul, 575
Brown, sulphur spring keeper, 349-50
Brown, William, 499
Brown, William Henry, 564
Bruce, Indian agent, 600
Bryant, Isaac, 91
Bryden, coffee house proprietor, 104
Buchanan, James, 490, 498
Buck, George, 545
Bullock, Anthony, 229
Burdett, Captain, 377-78
Burke, Edmund, 442
Burns, Robert, 158
Burnside, Judge James, 489-90, 572-74
Burr, Aaron, 56, 59, 202, 239
Butler, Colonel, 326
Butler, Fanny, 400
Butler, Lord, 326
Butler, Pierce, 496

Cadwalader, Gen. George, 556, 564, 574
Cadwalader, Gen. John, 439, 451-52, 469
Caesar, 150
Caldwell, Commander, 519
Caldwell, Kentucky trader, 10
Calhoun, John C., 397, 458, 568
Cameron, General, 508
Campbell, Robert, 7
Carnales, Mexican general, 535
Carothers, Thomas, 319
Carty, Miss, 559
Carvell, William, 541
Carver, Israel, 187
Carver, Samuel, 187, 214, 216, 423
Casson, Isabel, 402, 432, 460
Castlereagh, Lord, 292
Cating, Luke, 494
Cenobites, 7
Chalmers, Thomas, 482
Chamber of Commerce, 196, 214, 255-63
Chambers, George, 497
Chandler, James R., 575
Chandler, Joseph R., 443, 473
Chapman, Doctor, 395
Chapman, D.N., 556
Charles IV, king of Spain, 228
Charles, arch duke of Austria, 240-41
Chauncey, Charles, 529
Chesterfield, Lord, 5
Chloss, paper manufacturer, 198
Choate, Senator, 493
Chovet, Abraham, 410-11
Clark, Asenath, 427
Clark, Dugan, 427
Clarke, Edward, 366, 369
Clarkson, T., abolitionist, 209, 236
Clay, Cassius M., 463
Clay, Henry, 213-14, 257, 263, 272, 289, 436-37, 443, 459, 511, 530, 550-51, 559, 572
Claypoole, David C., 23, 464
Clifton, Henry, 229, 285
Clinton, George, 236
Clinton, DeWitt, 355-56
Coale, Edward J., 141, 155
Coates, Dr. B.H., 525
Coates, Samuel, 199, 240, 271, 423
Cockburn, Admiral, 296
Colburn, Abia, 262
Colburn, Zera, 262-63
Coleman, W., editor, 96
Comley, Ed., 596

Commissioners of the Girard Estates, 391, 394, 397, 403, 410, 414, 443, 446, 449, 453, 456, 473, 475, 490

Committee for Introducing Water into the City of Philadelphia, 4-6, 8, 23, 27-32, 36-38, 41, 43, 49, 60-61, 77, 80, 86-87, 91, 179-80, 207-9, 383-87, 403-4, 416, 436, 441

Committee on Lemon Hill, 410-20, 429, 433-36, 441-44, 475, 491, 524

Coffin, Amasa, 376

Coffin, Arthur G., 589

Coffin, Eleazar, 376

Coffin, Gilbert, 377

Coffin, Nehemiah, 376

Collins, Isaac, 482-83

Collins, William, 602

Colquhoun, Scottish writer, 177

Comfort, Ezra, 420, 435

Conservatives, 422

Constitutionalists, 189, 199, 214, 221-22, 226

Converse, Gilman, 431

Cooke, John, 323-24

Cooke, Richard, 255

Coope (spelling of Cope used by T. P.C.'s uncles), 571

Cooper, Isaac, 197

Cooper, Margaret, 93

Cope, Abbe Ann, 464

Cope, Abigail, 400

Cope, Alfred (T.P.C.'s son), 196, 223, 313, 353, 382, 391, 441, 489, 505, 511, 524, 531, 540, 564, 573-74, 578, 580, 583, 590, 592, 595-97, 599, 602

Cope, Anna, 438, 473

Cope, Benjamin, 12, 123, 323, 400, 432

Cope, Caleb (father of T.P.C.), 142-43, 217, 238-39, 293, 400, 445, 517, 571

Cope, Caleb (nephew of T.P.C.), 464, 517, 533, 574, 602

Cope, Caroline (T.P.C.'s daughter), 140, 160, 325, 339, 341, 538, 540

Cope, Caroline (granddaughter of T.P.C.), 515

Cope, Charity Evans (second wife of T.P.C.'s grandfather), 571

Cope, Clementine (granddaughter of T.P.C.), 515, 524, 583, 603

Cope, Edgar (grandson of T.P.C.), 603

Cope, Edward (grandson of T.P.C.), 524, 583, 596

Cope, Elenor (T.P.C.'s daughter), 313, 382, 513, 524, 537-42

Cope, Elizabeth Fisher (third wife of T. P.C.'s grandfather), 571

Cope, Elizabeth Stokes Waln (T.P.C.'s second wife), 391, 393, 399, 402, 429, 469-73, 506, 511, 514-15, 525, 563, 586, 589, 592, 602

Cope, Elizabeth Waln (wife of T.P.C.'s grandson Thomas P. Cope, Jr.), 584

Cope, Francis (T.P.C.'s son), 3, 26, 77, 101-2, 131, 135, 184, 307-8, 398, 540

Cope, Francis R. (grandson of T.P.C.), 457, 516, 524, 537, 547, 567, 587,

Cope, Frederick, 348

Cope, Girard, 400

Cope, Hannah (T.P.C.'s aunt), 238-39, 517, 571

Cope, Hannah (T.P.C.'s sister), 29, 118, 293

Cope, Henry (T.P.C.'s son), 3, 26, 77, 101-2, 131, 135, 165, 184, 240, 309, 398, 402, 418, 438, 469, 473, 511, 524, 533, 538, 544, 554-55, 564, 573, 578, 586, 590-92, 602-3

Cope, Herman (nephew of T.P.C.), 184, 412, 602

Cope, Israel (T.P.C.'s brother), 21, 54, 93, 103, 139, 225, 325, 336, 601-2

Cope, Jasper (T.P.C.'s brother), 8-9, 21, 26, 29, 39, 79-87, 103, 139, 236, 353, 464, 543, 602

Cope, John (T.P.C.'s brother), 141-44, 183-84, 393

Cope, John (grandfather of T.P.C.), 266-67, 517, 570-71

Cope, John (uncle of T.P.C.), 238-39, 517, 571

Cope, Joseph (uncle of T.P.C.), 238-39, 517, 571

Cope, Joshua (uncle of T.P.C.), 238-39, 517, 571

Cope, Lydia (T.P.C.'s niece), 183

Cope, Marmaduke, 602

Cope, Mary (T.P.C.'s aunt), 238, 517,

Cope, Mary Anna, 524

Cope, Mary D., 524, 590

Cope, Mary Mendenhall (mother of T.P.C.), 238

Cope, Mary "Peggy" Updegraff (wife of T.P.C.'s brother John), 13, 109, 184, 264

Cope, Mary "Polly" Drinker (first wife of T.P.C.), 4, 10, 12, 14, 16, 67, 75 78-79, 88, 103, 120, 126-28 143-44, 158, 160, 172-73, 186, 224, 228-29, 266, 285, 316, 325, 339, 341, 382, 398, 471, 521, 541

Cope, Nathan (T.P.C.'s uncle), 11, 18, 238, 323, 400-402, 517, 571, 589

Cope, Oliver, 517, 570

Cope, Rachel (T.P.C.'s daughter-in-law), 524

Cope, Rachel (T.P.C.'s cousin), 12

Cope, Rebecca (wife of T.P.C.'s brother Jasper), 87, 103, 602

Cope, Rest, 323, 432

Cope, Ruth Anna, 524

Cope, Samuel, 319, 399

Cope, Samuel (T.P.C.'s uncle), 123, 238-39, 267, 517, 571

Cope, Sarah (sister of T.P.C.), 322

Cope, Susan (daughter-in-law of T.P.C.), 515

Cope, Thomas P., Jr., 524, 565, 579, 584, 592

Cope, William (brother of T.P.C.'s grandfather), 570, 574, 602

Cope, William (T.P.C.'s son), 4, 10, 12, 88, 101, 121, 160, 165, 195, 307-8, 319-20, 339, 348, 398, 455, 524, 540

Cornwallis, Lord, 195

Cowdery, Doctor, 191

Cowper, English poet, 157-58

Cox, James, president of Lehigh Coal & Nav. Co., 533

Cox, James (T.P.C.'s partner in N.Y.), 58, 62, 66, 128, 151, 171, 553

Cox, John, 283, 287

Crabb, William, 479

Craft, James S., 500

Craik, Dr. James, 111-13

Crawford, Senator, 256

Cresson, Elliott, 578

Cresson, Rachel, 584

Cunningham, David Hayfield, 408

Currie, Doctor, 158

Curtis, Jona., 229


Dalhousie, Lord, 367, 369

Dallas, Alexander J., 35-36

Dallas, George Mifflin, 447, 450, 463, 498, 508-10

Dana, Richard H., Jr., 487

Darsie, Senator, 525

Darsy, George, 497

Davidson, Domini, 479

Davis, James, 528

Davis, John, 385

Dawes, Abijah, 34-36

Deaf and Dumb Asylum, 498, 558, 589

Dean, Aron, 374-76

Dearborn, Benjamin, 104

Decatur, Captain, 190-91

DeCou, Doctor, 229

de l'Isle, Rouget, 556

Derbyshire, Alexander, 594, 598

de Marsellac, John, 407-8

Democrats, 35-36, 39, 86, 91, 98, 102, 132, 162, 179-80, 185-90, 216, 220-24, 229, 232, 237, 246, 297-98, 303, 315, 346, 410, 416, 422, 435, 447, 469, 487, 499

Dewees, Doctor, 315

Dewees, Patty, 56

Dibdin, Tom, 424

Dichearchus, Greek philosopher, 474

Dickens, 426

Dickinson, Captain, 164

Distribution Committee, 179-81

Dix, Dorothy, 455, 460-61, 465-66

Donahue, priest, 439

Dorsey, John, 190, 222

Drayton, William, 428

Drinker, Daniel, 602

Drinker, Esther, 195

Drinker, G., 114

Drinker, Henry, 602

Drinker, Henry, Jr., 6, 103, 188, 209, 221, 416

Drinker, Henry Sandwith, 195, 201, 208, 230, 241, 281-83, 289-90

Drinker, Henry, Sr., 65, 76, 408

Drinker, Henry W. (T.P.C.'s nephew), 194, 325-28, 333, 601

Drinker, John (father of T.P.C.'s first wife), 5-7, 64, 408, 410, 423, 521, 602

Drinker, Rachel, 285, 431

Drinker, Richard (T.P.C.'s nephew), 416

Drinker, William, Jr., 290, 329, 333, 341-43

Duane, William, 220, 222, 225

Duane, William J., 601

Dugan, Martha, 404

Duke of Wellington, 407

Dumas, French general, 536
Duncan, John, 498
Dundas, James, 414, 418-20, 433
Dunlap, John, printer, 465
Dunlap, Thomas, 428
Dunlap, William, 67-68, 76, 96
Dunlop, John, 316
Duponceau, Peter Stephen, 395, 404, 433
du Pre, Lewis, 101
Duprey, Widow, 379
Dwight, Dr. Timothy, 75-76
Dwight, Edmund, 372
Dwight, William, 372
Dyer, Oliver, 550

Eaton, General, 190-91
Earp, Robert, 482
Earp, Thomas, 482, 484, 579
Eckhardt, dueler, 94-95
Eddy, Thomas, 184
Edge, John, 601
Edwards, Joshua, 345-46
Elizabeth, queen of England, 419
Elkington, Henry, 597
Elkington, Thomas, 597
Elliott, John, 435
Ellis, Esther, 531
Ely, Hugh, 285, 347
Embree, James, 160, 195, 213
Emlen, George, Jr., 217
Emlen, Nancy, 105
Emlen, Samuel, 407, 423-24
English, John B., 493
Erskine, British diplomat, 237
Etting, Sol, 261
Evans, Cad., 411
Evans, Charity (second wife of T.P.C.'s grandfather), 571
Evans, David, 294
Evans, Elizabeth, 403, 420-21, 456, 480-82, 501, 528
Evans, General, 399
Evans, Jonathan, 421
Evans, Thomas, 562
Evans, William, 402-3, 406, 421, 432, 480-82, 554, 567

Fairfax, Lord, 349
Fairmount dam, 384, 403, 411, 413, 441, 568
Farnum, John, 482

Federalists, 35, 39, 53, 86, 89, 98, 116, 132, 162, 179-90, 200-201, 214, 216, 222-28, 232, 237, 315, 410, 416, 422,
Ferdinand, king of Spain, 291
Fetter, Caspar, 323-24, 335
Field, John, 521-22
Fillmore, Millard, 593, 600
Findlay, William, 220, 315
Firth, Thomas, 201, 336
Firth, Margaret, 336
Fisher, Elizabeth (third wife of T.P.C.'s grandfather), 571
Fisher, John, 13
Fisher, Judge, 274-76
Fisher, Charles Henry, 595
Fisher, Myers, 277-79
Fisher, Samuel R., 411
Fisher, S.W., 221
Fitzsimmons, Thomas, Chamber of Commerce president, 263
Five Medals, Indian chief, 99
Folwell, Charles S., 433
Folger, Mayhew, 377
Forbes, innkeeper, 344
Ford, Judge, 362
Forsyth, Hannah, 402, 590
Forsyth, James, 402
Forsyth, John, 401
Foster, William B., 531
Fowler (traveling companion of T.P.C.), 255
Fox, Charles, 127-28, 259
Fox, Samuel N., 61, 208
Francis, emperor of Austria, 292
Francis, Thomas Willing, 255, 261-62
Franklin, Benjamin, 36, 148, 198, 404-5
Frazer, Professor, 516
Frederick the Great, 534, 553
Friends Indian Committee, 464, 573
Fry, Elizabeth, 455
Frost, J., writer, 432
Fuller, Oliver, 531
Fulton, Robert, 393
Furnier, Hippolyte, 603

Gaab, Godfrey, 571-72
Gabriel, General, 25, 32
Gales, Joseph, editor, 296
Gallatin, Albert, 257, 260, 262, 296
Gamble, James, senator, 189
Gamble, Captain, 201

Garrison, William Lloyd, 602
Gatliff, L., 136
Geisling, Professor, 462-63
George III, king of England, 352
Gibb, B., 364-66
Gibbons, Charles, 479-492, 525, 528
Gibbons, D. Charles, 581
Gibson, Judge John Bannister, 489-90
Gifford, innkeeper, 57
Gillis, James M., 497
Gilpin, Charles, 412-15, 434, 447, 516, 581, 600-601
Gilpin, Henry D., 574
Girard, Stephen, 394-95, 410, 429, 449, 456-57
Goddard, landlord, 407
Godwin, English philosopher, 192, 248, 250
Gordon, Elisha, 223
Gray, English poet, 112, 160
Gregory, coffee house proprietor, 69
Grellett, Joseph, 67
Grellett, Stephen, 67
Grief, Judge, 602
Griffith, Aaron, 448
Griffiths, Doctor, 78, 126
Griffiths, Samuel Powell, 407
Griscom, Daniel, 510
Gross, William, murderer, 603
Grubb, Joseph, 493
Guillemin, Auguste, 603
Guilliams, Samuel, 555
Gummere, John, 466
Gurney, Francis, 30
Gurney, James, 526
Gurney, Samuel, 526

Hacker, Isaiah, 420
Hacker, William E., 474
Hagert (member of Lemon Hill Committee), 412
Haines, Ann, 595
Haines, John, 573
Haines, John S., 590
Haines, M. (granddaughter of T.P.C.), 595
Hall, Charles, 85
Hallowell, John, 190
Hamilton, Gen. Alexander, 94, 239, 551
Hamilton, William, 160, 184, 221
Hancock, John, 373

Hannibal, 7
Hare, Charles W., 214, 217, 226-27, 486
Hare, Robert, 486-87
Harrison, Thomas, 384
Harrison, William H., 287, 389
Harvey, Jacob, 370, 527
Haverly, George, 330, 342-43
Haverford School Board, 389, 398, 448, 450, 462, 464, 474, 491-92, 500, 546
Hayley, English poet, 157-58
Hays, Captain, 59
Hazard, E., 179
Healy, Christopher, 435
Heller, S., 335
Helmuth, J.K. (shipping partner of T.P.C.), 199, 201, 220, 228, 253, 266, 270, 273, 295
Hemphill, Joseph, 187-89, 200
Henry, Alexander, 482
Henry, Professor, 516
Henry IV, king of France, 99
Henshaw, David, 69-70
Hicks, Elias, 423
Hicksism, 400-401, 423
Hiester, Joseph, 223, 315
Hill, Lord, 296
Hinchman, Morgan, 572-77
Historical Society, 414
Hodgson, Adam, 361-62
Hodgson, Matilda, 531
Hodgson, William, 482
Hodskin, John, 117
Hoffa, Abraham, 313
Hoffenockel, John, 325
Holland, Lord, 127
Holmes, city planner, 208
Homan, Peter, 317-18
Hoopes, Amy, 400
Hoopes, Ann, 400
Hoopes, Jasper, 400
Hoopes, Joshua, 11
Hopkins, Matthew, 486
Houston, Doctor, 14
Howard, Mary, 584
Howick, Lord, 473
Howland, George, 474
Hopper, John, 340, 345
Horn, Susan, 269
Hosey, George, 581
Hospital for the Indian Poor, 461
Howe, British general, 399
Hubbard, James, 577

Hughes, Bishop, 440
Hull, Caleb, 74
Humphreys, Captain, 211
Hunt, Nathan, 427
Hunt, Uriah, 420
Hunter, Dr. John Dunn, 433
Huskisson, William, 544

Ingersoll, Charles J., 601
Ingersoll, Joseph R., 576, 601
Inskeep, Ephraim, 512
Inskeep, John, 34, 42, 56, 86, 95, 189, 194
Irvin, Doctor, 90
Israel, Israel, 188-89
Izard, Captain, 127

Jackson, Andrew, 400, 428, 436, 467-69, 529
Jackson, British diplomat, 243-46
Jackson, Captain, 312
Jackson, Doctor, 533, 553
Jackson, Holladay, 512
Jackson, John, 512
Jackson, W., 221
Jacques, Emperor, 166
James, Duke, 181
James, John, 400
Janvier, ship valuer, 275
Jay, John, 497
Jefferson, Thomas, 39, 52, 56, 59-60, 100, 116, 133, 192, 200-202, 211-13, 221, 231, 234, 236, 350, 465, 490
Jeffries, Robert, 571
Jenkins, Jabez, 399, 537
Jenner, English physician, 101
John the Baptist, 121
Johns, Sarah, 589-90
Johnson, Doctor, 334
Johnson, Dr. Samuel, 465
Johnson, Lydia, 88, 282-83
Johnson, William, 65-68, 95-96, 138, 144, 152, 184
Johnston, Caleb, 393
Jones, Commodore, 570-71
Jones, Joel, 581, 601
Jones, Joseph, 562, 580
Jones, Peter, 314
Jones, Sir William, 234
Jones, William, 30

Jordan, Richard, 283, 287
Joseph, king of Naples, 231
Julien, Noël, 395

Kane, John K., 489
Keating, John, 601
Keating, Widow, 427
Keefe, John, 485
Keese, John, 95
Keith, Kentucky trader, 10
Kelly, Judge, 588
Kemble, Fanny, 400, 496
Kendall, E.O., 483
Kendrick, Bishop, 594
Kennedy, A., 84
Kennon, Captain, 585
Kersey, Jesse, 39, 131, 287
Keyser, Elhanan, 442
Kimber, Emmor, 421, 480
Kircher, Father, 46
Kirkbride, Doctor, 582
Kotzebue, German dramatist, 67

Lacock, Abner, 226-27
Lamartine, 554
Land, Bishop, 457
Lardner, Doctor, 416
Lathrop, Asa, 331, 343
Lathrop, James, 331
Latimer, G., 221, 225
Latrobe, Benjamin H., 4-8, 36, 49, 57-61, 77, 80, 86, 91-93, 98, 180, 384-95
Laurence, Elizabeth, 183
Laurie, Edith, 229
Laurie, Joseph, 229
Laurie, William, 229
Law, Samuel Andrew, 342
Lawler, Matthew, 98, 166
Lea, Thomas, 273-74
Lear, Tobias, 190, 192
Lee, General, 350
Lee, Richard Henry, 552
Leeds, Samuel, 532, 579
Lehigh Coal & Navigation Co., 533
Leib, Michael, 201, 217-27, 256, 259
Lettsom, Doctor, 101
Le Verrier, French astronomer, 515-16
Levis, Ester, 513
Lewis, John, 32-33
Lewis, William, 384

Linaweaver, innkeeper, 320-21
Lippincott, John, 584
Liston, Morris, 247
Little, innkeeper, 95
Little Turtle, Miami Indian chief, 98
Livingston, Robert R., 393
Locofocos, 443, 447, 566
Logan, Dr. George, 505
Longwill, William, 315
Louis XVIII, king of France, 291-92, 294
Louis Philippe, king of France, 408-9
Lukins, mechanic, 277, 278
Lynn, clergyman, 249

McAllister brothers, murderers, 19
McBride, James H., 584
McCall, Peter, 447, 450-54, 467
McClure, General, 288
McCollough, Widow, 348
McCook, bribery suspect, 496
McDuffie, Senator, 453
McKean, Thomas, 34-35, 222-23, 457
McKim, John, 264
McLane, Allan, 273-76
McLane, Captain, 368-70
McLane, Louis, 274
McPhail, Anna M., 584
Madison, Dolly, 261-62
Madison, James, 236-37, 244, 258, 261-62, 298-99
Magruder, Captain, 590-91
Mallery, Garrick, 442-44
Managers of the House of Refuge, 392, 397, 404, 431, 433, 456, 482, 483-84, 542-43, 560, 566-67, 578, 588-90
Mann, Captain, 475, 478
Mark, Jacob, 58
Marshall, Isaac, 79
Marshall, Christopher, 192
Marshall, T., 196
Martin, Doctor, 124
Matlack, Timothy, 34-35
Maule, Joshua, 77, 102, 131, 135
Marott, Davenport, 416-17
Martin, Luther, 260-61
Maxwll, George C., 286
Maxwell, John S., 555
Mendenhall, Miles, 528
Mendenhall, Thomas (uncle of T.P.C.), 405, 520, 553
Mercator, Renaissance geographer, 78

Merchants Exchange, 504
Meredith, William M., 397, 439-40, 447, 467, 475, 482, 496, 516, 573-74, 580, 600-601
Merrick, Samuel Vaughan, 547, 558
Miercken, Capt. John, 595
Mierken, Capt. Henry, 514, 519, 525
Mifflin, Ann, 105-106
Miller, Abraham, 83-84, 94
Miller, Andrew, 601
Miller, Doctor, 66-68, 96
Miller, dueler, 95
Miller, Ed., 531
Miller, John, Jr., 6, 92
Miller, Samuel, 67, 96
Millhouse, Jesse, 131
Milnor, James, 34, 63
Milnor, William, 192
Miner, Charles, 227, 476, 481
Miner, William Penn, 481
Miranda, General, 194, 202
Mitchell, Professor, 68, 96
Mitchell, Thomas, 601
Monroe, James, 193, 216
Montezuma, Aztec ruler, 596
Moody, Captain, 247
More, Sir Thomas, 537
Moreau, French general, 242
Morehead, Governor, 582
Morgan, Benjamin R., 282-83, 384
Morier, British diplomat, 262
Mormons, 509-10, 513-14, 587
Morris, Isaac W., 320, 323
Morris, Robert, 37-38, 50, 63, 86
Morris, Sarah, 321
Morton, Doctor, 539-40
Morton, Sketchly, 562
Moss, John, 422
Mott, James, 603
Muhlenburg, Peter, 223
Mullen, William J., 565
Mullen, William M., 601
Murat, grand duke of Berg, 228
Murry, John, Jr., 95

"Native Americans," 434, 437, 443, 447, 467
Nauman, Gottlieb, 17
Neagle, John, portrait painter, 538, 544, 548, 556
Nelson, Lord, 62, 193, 195

Nevins, John Jowet, 136
Nevins, Pim, 136, 149
Newbold, Clayton, 382
Newbold, I., 382
Newbold, John, 339
Newbold, William, 255, 261-62
Newlin, Annesley, 509, 539, 562
Newlin, Elizabeth, 509, 562
Newlin, Isaac, 562
Newton, Thomas, 257-58, 286
Nicholson, John (Jno.), 37, 50-51, 209
Nicodemus, 121
Nonimportation Act, 214, 216, 269, 277, 290
Nonintercourse Act, 232, 236, 252-53
Norris, Sam, 447
Noyes, Doctor, 206

Obdam, Heer van, 181
O'Connell, Daniel, 390, 392
Ogle, Alexander, 226-27
Olcott, Nathaniel, 27-28, 30
Old, James, 64
Olmstead, Edward, 415, 419
Onderdonk, B. T., bishop, 455-56
Oneas, Prince, 32-33
Overseers of Friends Public Schools, 391, 404, 416, 432, 436, 514, 554, 557,

Packard, Frederick, 484
Packenham, Sir Ed., 303
Paine, Tom, 269-70, 493-94, 577
Palmer, Aron H., 234
Panosi, Charles, 457
Panza, Sancho, 22, 262
Paredes, Mexican general, 513
Parker, J., 91
Parker, Sir Hyde, 62
Parker, Thomas, 6, 92
Parrish, Sarah, 14
Parsons, Benjamin, 74
Parsons, Judge, 449, 580
Patterson, Edgar, 236
Patterson, General, 468, 602
Patterson, Joseph, 494-95, 590
Patterson, Professor, 516
Paul, emperor of Russia, 62
Paxson, B., 124
Paxson, Ed., 598
Paxson, Ruth, 10, 49, 108-9, 118, 124-26, 129

Paxson, Timothy, 6-7, 10, 49, 87, 108-109, 117-18, 127-28, 179, 182, 189, 192, 221
Pease, John, 402, 460
Peel, Sir Robert, 390, 464
Pemberton, Israel, 285, 423
Pemberton, James, 423
Pemberton, John, 423, 574
Penn, Richard, 205, 242
Penn, William, 32, 181, 207-9, 215, 241, 251, 366, 422, 432, 461, 515, 570, 605
Pennington, Edward, 423
Pennock, Abraham L., 537
Pennock, George, 522
Pennsylvania Hospital, 90, 183, 222, 246, 271, 281, 438, 486, 550
Pennsylvania Railroad (Central R.R.), 458, 479-509, 514-19, 523-31, 535, 537-45, 555, 558, 576, 580
Pensinger, David, 82
Percy, Earl, 401
Perry, Benjamin, 285
Peter the Great, 563
Peters, Judge, 32, 578
Peters, Sally, 578
Pettit, Judge, 505
Pfersich, Frederick, 335
Philadelphia Prison Society, 484
Philosophical Society, 388, 391, 395, 404, 433, 516
Pickering, Elisha, 135
Pickering, Timothy, 408
Pim, Jonathan, 527, 595
Pim, Thomas (T.P.C.'s uncle), 525, 605
Pim, William Harvey, 525
Pinckney, Charles C., 39, 56
Piolett, Victor E., 496
Pitt, William, 61, 195, 259
Pius IX, 557-58, 568-69, 574, 577
Pleasants, Martha (sister of T.P.C.'s son Henry's wife), 592
Polk, James K., 447, 450, 459, 489, 508-11, 549, 560
Poole, James, 64
Poole, William, innkeeper, 120
Porter, Commodore, 489, 501
Porter, J.M., 424
Potter, Bishop, 498
Potter, James, 317-18
Potter, Judge, 317, 319
Potter, William, 316

Poulson, Zachariah, 23, 25, 49, 61, 64,
  92-93, 102, 132, 136, 177-79, 194-95,
  247, 251, 279
Poultney, T., 17
Price, E.H., attorney, 605
Price, William, 566
Priestman, Rachel, 402
Proctor, General, 287
Pusey, Edward B., 396, 434

Randall, John, 499
Randolph, George, 543, 602
Randolph, John St. George, 356-57
Randolph, Rebecca, 543
Randolph of Roanoke, John, 258-59,
  356-57
Rapp, religious leader, 335
Rawle, William, 221, 384
Read, George, 274-76
Read, George III, 274
Read, John M., 517
Red Jacket, Seneca Indian chief, 360
Redgauntlet, Joshua, hero of Sir Walter
  Scott's fictions, 573
Redhoffer, Charles, 277-79
Reece, Davis, 567
Reed, Joseph, 493-94
Reed, William B., 493-95
Reeve, John, 555
Reeve, Juliana, 438, 473
Reeve, R., 473
Rennel, John, 423
Rennie, ventriloquist, 62-63
Republicans, 185, 298
Rex, Widow, 325
Reynolds, Doctor, 162
Reynolds, Tom, 425
Rhoads, Samuel, 423
Richards, D., 539
Richards, Jonathan, 389
Richards, Margaret, 389
Riddle, ship valuer, 275
Ridgway, Jacob, 394
Ripley, Capt. William, 68
Ripley, Dorothy, 106-7
Rippy, Widow, 348
Robbins, Harriet, 354
Roberts, David, 573
Robespierre, 53, 395
Robinson, James (T.P.C.'s partner),
  149-54, 160
Robinson, Kitty, 103, 118

Robinson, Peter, 80
Rodman, Samuel, 378
Rogers, Judge, 489-90
Rogers, Martha Ann, 206-7
Roosevelt, Nicholas J., 36, 43, 45-46,
  54, 58, 60, 77, 86, 180
Rose, Doctor, 333
Rose, English diplomat, 216, 221
Ross, General, 296
Ross, James, 221-22, 224, 226, 232
Rosse, Lord, English astronomer, 516
Rowland, Harriet, 599
Rowth, Martha, 95
Rowth, Richard, 95
Rush, Benjamin, 198, 241, 268, 281
Rush, Benjamin (grandson of the cele-
  brated physician), 575
Rush, John, 268
Rush, Richard, 498, 520, 601
Ryers, Joseph, 594

St. Clair, Gen. Arthur, 99
Sample, innkeeper, 322
Sangley, Captain, 380
Santa Anna, Mexican general, 513,
  527, 530, 535
Scattergood, Joseph, 554
Scattergood, Thomas, 28, 269
Scott, Henry M., 580
Scott, Mayor, 439, 442
Scott, Sir Walter, 573
Sergeant, John (Jona.), 96, 200, 217,
  222, 224, 226-27, 439, 445, 449,
  505, 507
Sergeant, Jonathan, 445
Serrell, Captain, 458
Seybert, Adam, 257-58
Shaffer, William C., 493, 544
Shaffer, W. L., 538
Shakers, 70-72
Shakespeare, 424, 501, 575
Shallcross, Doctor, 515, 568, 575, 595,
  600
Sharpless, Benjamin, 400
Sharpless, Townsend, 414, 482, 484
Sharswood, James, 216
Sheetz, Christian, 224-25
Shepherd, Honora, 566
Sheridan, Richard, 259
Sherman, Captain, 370
Shippen, Doctor, 482
Shoemaker, Ann, 103

Shoemaker, Nancy, 118
Shoemaker, Rebecca, 9, 29, 602
Shunk, Francis R., 447, 496, 500, 508, 517, 524, 537, 560, 579
Silsby, N., 356
Simmons, Anthony (Any.), 124
Simons, Joseph, 444
Simpson, George, 587
Simpson, Henry, 587
Simpson, James, 230
Slater, Samuel, 381
Slavery, 9, 19-21, 104, 137-40, 150, 182, 192, 209, 234, 339, 351-53, 442, 453, 463, 484, 526, 562, 569, 572, 583, 597-98, 602-603
Slaymaker, Amos, 17
Smallman, James, 38
Smedley, John (Jno.), 102, 121
Smith, Daniel, 6, 221
Smith, Daniel B., 389, 448, 474
Smith, Elizabeth, 582, 594
Smith, Georg Washington, 550
Smith, James, 240
Smith, James E., 162
Smith, Joe, 455
Smith, John, banker, 103
Smith, Joshua (Josa.), 230
Smith, Maria, 584
Smith, Nancy, 236
Smith, Robert, statesman, 260
Smith, Thomas, 582, 594
Snowden (Lemon Hill Committee member), 413, 496
Snyder, Simon, 220, 223, 227, 232, 266, 297
Society of Friends (Quakers), 98, 105, 108, 126, 153-54, 160, 165, 183, 198, 209-10, 215-17, 263, 267-69, 284, 287, 294, 304-5, 323, 336-40, 376, 397, 401-2, 407-8, 417, 420, 423, 435-36, 440-41, 469, 475, 478, 486, 491, 501, 510, 514, 521, 543-44, 562, 567, 572-73, 594, 605
Sorin, Rebecca, 592
Spayd, John, 222-23, 226
Spell, Cornelius, 581
Spencer, Captain, 330
Spencer, Daniel, 342
Spencer, Doctor, 390
Spencer, English clergyman, 321
Spencer, James S., 485
Spencer, Jeremiah, 329-30, 342

Spencer, Nathan, 159, 339
Sperry, Jacob, 213, 255, 261, 425
Stevens, Thaddeus, 496
Stewardson, Thomas, 323
Stewart, Captain, 190
Stiles, Thomas, 476
Stokes, Doctor, 390-92
Stokes, E. W. (niece of T.P.C.), 391
Stokes, Francis, 401, 566
Stokes, Henry, 401
Stokes, John, 546, 565, 579, 584
Stokes, N.N., 391-92, 573
Story, Capt. Enoch, 64
Stouch, Andrew, 313
Stouch, Conrad, 313
Strode, R., 400
Stuart, Charles Edward, 408
Stuart, French nobleman, 54
Stuart, Gilbert, 124
Sullivan, General, 379
Summers, Thomas W., 584
Swift, John, 484, 528, 550, 581
Sykes, Widow, 229

Taliacotius, Gabriel, 78
Talleyrand, 406-7
Tammany, Saint, 32-33
Tatum, Josiah, 573
Taylor, Zachary, 502-3, 530, 559, 580, 592-93
Terril, Isaac Bebee, 330
Tertium Quids, 185-90, 200-201, 213-16, 220-27
Thale, John, 181
Thomas, A., 194
Thomas, John (T.P.C.'s partner), 126, 137, 186, 189, 194, 210
Thomas, Moses, 457
Thompson, Judge William, 343
Thomson, John Edgar, 531, 547
Thomson, Peter, 465
Tilghman, Edward, 185
Tilghman, William, 221-22, 225-26
Todd, James, 87
Toland, E. H., 584
Toland, George W., 488, 495, 497, 531, 547, 558
Tom Thumb, 534
Tracy, Uriah, 73
Trego, Charles B., 484, 492
Trimble, William, 222
Trotter, Daniel, 410

Trucks, John, 516
Tully, William, 479
Turley, Captain, 591, 597
Turner, John, 416
Turner, Captain, 590-91
Turreau, Louis Marie, 236
Tyler, John, 389-92, 437
Tyler, Robert, 390-92
Tyson, Elenor, 524, 537-42
Tyson, Job R. (husband of T.P.C.'s daughter Elenor), 399, 482-84, 516-17, 524, 540-42, 568

Umberhacker, gambler, 85

Van Buren, Martin, 436-37

Van Rensselaer, Gen. Stephen, 355, 358
Van Rensselaer, Philip, 358
Varnum, James B., 236
Vaux, Richard, 484, 594
Vaux, Roberts (R.V.), 338
Victoria, Queen, 534
Voltaire, 553

Walker, R. J., 426-27
Walker, Seras E., 483
Wallace, Ellerslee, 584
Waln, Elizabeth, 470-72, 579, 584
Waln, Jacob S., 594
Waln, Joseph, 470-71
Waln, Nicholas, 462
Waln, R., 221
Walsh, R. T., 538
Washington, George, 51, 111-14, 124, 133, 192, 231, 280, 349, 375, 399, 497, 551-52
Washington, Martha, 111-13, 117
Wayne, Gen. "Mad Anthony," 399
Webster, Daniel, 397, 437
Wells, Gideon Hill, 522
West, Ammi, 482-84
West, Benjamin, 562
West, Elizabeth, 126-27
Wetherill, John Price, 404, 412-18, 429, 434, 436, 444, 447, 506, 516, 524
Wharton, Robert, 10, 23, 31-32, 34, 42
Wharton, T. J., 505
Wheeler, Samuel, 204
Whigs, 36, 389, 437, 443-47, 487, 514, 550, 558-59, 566, 600
White, Colonel, 445-46

Whitehead, Elisha (T.P.C.'s partner in N.Y.), 58, 62, 65-67, 94, 128, 138, 144-45, 151-52, 171
Whitney, Omasa, 458-59, 517, 519
Wickersham, Amos, 599
Wayne, Isaac, 399
Wilkinson, General, 362
William, Prince of Orange, 291
Williams, D. M., 272
Williams, George G., 584
Williams, Wiley, 582
Willing, Richard, 529

Wilson, Anna, 504-5
Wilson, Peter, Iroquois chief, 535
Winder, General, 295
Winn, Thomas, 479
Wirt, William, 382
Wistar, Dr. Caspar, 404, 457
Wistar, R., 10
Wistar, Thomas, 573, 580, 599
Wistar, Thomas, Jr., 574, 583
Woelpert, Judge, 212
Wollstonecraft, Mary, 46
Wolsey, Cardinal, 291, 481
Wood, Charles, 494
Wood, Thomas, 554
Woodhouse, Doctor, 22
Woolman, Granville, 466
Wright, Deborah, 14
Wright, Samuel, 14-15
Wright, Susan, 12, 14
Wright, Thomas, 350
Wright, William, 12-16, 255, 547

Yarnall, Amy E., 524
Yarnall, Caroline C., 524
Yarnall, Caroline R., 524
Yarnall, Charles, 492, 602
Yarnall, Edward, 391, 482, 509-10, 524, 565
Yarnall, Ellis, 215, 323
Yarnall, Francis C., 524
Yarnall, Lucy, 524, 565
Yarnall, Mary H., 524
Yarnall, T. C., 539
Yellow fever, 7-8, 24, 27, 38, 129-32, 148, 189, 231, 371, 383, 395, 459, 542
Young, William, 46, 146-47, 197, 406
Yrujo, Marquis, 194
Yule, filibusterer in Congress, 597